# Handbook on the Politics of Regulation

T0319336

*Edited by*

David Levi-Faur

*The Hebrew University of Jerusalem, Israel*
*The Free University of Berlin, Germany*

**Edward Elgar**
Cheltenham, UK • Northampton, MA, USA

Published by
Edward Elgar Publishing Limited
The Lypiatts
15 Lansdown Road
Cheltenham
Glos GL50 2JA
UK

Edward Elgar Publishing, Inc.
William Pratt House
9 Dewey Court
Northampton
Massachusetts 01060
USA

Paperback edition 2013
Paperback edition reprinted 2016

A catalogue record for this book
is available from the British Library

Library of Congress Control Number: 2011925767

ISBN   978 1 84844 005 0 (cased)
       978 0 85793 759 9 (paperback)

Typeset by Servis Filmsetting Ltd, Stockport, Cheshire

Printed on FSC approved paper
Printed and bound by CPI Group (UK) Ltd, Croydon, CR0 4YY

# Contents

# Figures

# Tables

# Contributors

**Steven J. Balla** is Associate Professor of Political Science, Public Policy and Public Administration, and International Affairs at the George Washington University, USA, where he is also a Research Affiliate at the George Washington Institute of Public Policy and a Senior Scholar at the Regulatory Studies Center.

**Ian Bartle** is a Research Associate at the Department of Politics, University of Sheffield, UK. He is currently working on governance and sustainable transport policy.

**Tim Bartley** is an Associate Professor of Sociology at Indiana University-Bloomington, USA. He was previously a Visiting Scholar at Princeton University, the Max Planck Institute for the Study of Societies, and Sun Yat-sen University in Guangzhou.

**Meike Bokhorst** is a Researcher at Tilburg University and at the Scientific Council for Government Policy in the Netherlands. Her research focuses on issues of legitimacy of regulation.

**Andreas Busch** is Chair of Comparative Political Economy and Head of the Department of Political Science at the University of Göttingen, Germany.

**Paul James Cardwell** is a Senior Lecturer in Law at the University of Sheffield and the Deputy Director of the Sheffield Centre for International and European Law (SCIEL), UK.

**Jørgen Grønnegård Christensen** is Professor of Public Administration at the Department of Political Science, Aarhus University, Denmark.

**Tom Christensen** is Professor at the Department of Political Science, University of Oslo and also Senior Researcher at the Stein Rokkan Centre for Social Studies, University of Bergen, Norway.

**John W. Cioffi** is Associate Professor and Director of Graduate Studies in the Department of Political Science at the University of California, Riverside, USA. He is the author of *Public Law and Private Power: Corporate Governance Reform in the Age of Finance Capitalism* (Cornell University Press, 2010).

**Margit Cohn** is a Senior Lecturer in the Faculty of Law and the Federmann School of Public Law and Government at the Hebrew University of Jerusalem, Israel; she teaches and researches comparative public law and regulation.

**Neil Collins** is Professor of Government and Dean of Commerce, National University of Ireland, Cork.

**Salo Coslovsky** is Assistant Professor of International Development at the Robert F. Wagner School of Public Service, New York University, USA.

**Steven P. Croley** is a Professor of Law at the University of Michigan Law School, USA.

**Michael W. Dowdle** is Assistant Professor of Law at the National University of Singapore. He was previously Chair in Globalization and Governance at Sciences Po, a Fellow in Public Law at RegNet at the Australian National University, and Himalayas Distinguished Visiting Professor of Comparative Law at Tsinghua University School of Law.

**Sandra Eckert** is Assistant Professor in European Studies at the University Osnabrück, Germany.

**Marc Allen Eisner** is the Henry Merritt Wriston Chair of Public Policy and Professor of Government at Wesleyan University, USA.

**Yuval Feldman** is an Associate Professor at the Faculty of Law, Bar-Ilan University, Israel. He received his Ph.D. from the University of California, Berkeley in 2004.

**Matthias Finger** is Co-Editor-Chief of the journal *Competition and Regulation in Network Industries*. He is a Professor at Ecole Polytechnique Fédérale, Lausanne, Switzerland and part-time Professor at the Florence School of Regulation, European University Institute, Florence, Italy.

**Nuno Garoupa** is Professor of Law, the H. Ross and Helen Workman Research Scholar and Co-Director of the Illinois Program on Law, Behavior and Social Science, University of Illinois College of Law, USA.

**Sharon Gilad** is a Senior Lecturer at the Department of Political Science and the Federmann School of Public Policy and Government at the Hebrew University of Jerusalem, Israel.

**Fabrizio Gilardi** is Associate Professor of Public Policy at the Department of Political Science and at the Center for Comparative and International Studies, University of Zurich, Switzerland.

**Avshalom Ginosar** is a Senior Lecturer at the Department of Communication, Academic College of Emek Yezreel, Israel. He is also a Ph.D. candidate in Public Policy, School of Political Science, University of Haifa, Israel.

**Jörn-Carsten Gottwald** is Chair in East Asian Politics, Ruhr-University Bochum, Germany.

**Martijn Groenleer** is an Assistant Professor of Public Administration in the Faculty of Technology, Policy and Management at Delft University of Technology, The Netherlands.

**James K. Hammitt** is Professor of Economics and Decision Sciences at Harvard University (Center for Risk Analysis), USA and at the Toulouse School of Economics (LERNA-INRA), France.

**Sangyong Han** is a Ph.D. student at the College of Communications at the Pennsylvania State University, USA, where he is a Research Fellow at the Institute for Information Policy. His primary academic interests lie in analyzing the impact of technological change on telecommunications industries, policy makers and society, focusing on public interest issues and participatory democracy.

**Jacint Jordana** is a Professor in the Department of Political and Social Science at the Universitat Pompeu Fabra (Barcelona) and at the Institut Barcelona d'Estudis Internacionals (IBEI), Spain. His research interests are in the field of public policy analysis, with a special emphasis on regulatory governance and institutional development.

**Sylvia I. Karlsson-Vinkhuyzen** is assistant professor in the Public Administration and Policy Group at the University of Wageningen, the Netherlands and a Research Fellow of the Academy of Finland based at the University of Turku, Finland.

**Sukkoo Kim** is an Associate Professor of Economics at Washington University, St. Louis, USA. He is also a Research Associate of the National Bureau of Economic Research in Cambridge, Massachusetts.

**Per Lægreid** is Professor at the Department of Administration and Organization Theory, University of Bergen and Senior Researcher at the Stein Rokkan Centre for Social Studies, Bergen, Norway.

**Marc T. Law** is an Associate Professor in the Department of Economics at the University of Vermont, USA. His research interests are in the fields of regulation, political economy, and economic history.

**David Levi-Faur** is a Founding Editor of the journal *Regulation & Governance*. He is based at the Department of Political Science and the Federmann School of Public Policy and Government at the Hebrew University of Jerusalem, Israel. He is currently a Senior Fellow at the Kolleg-Forschergruppe "The Transformative Power of Europe" at the Free University of Berlin, Germany.

**Deborah Mabbett** is Reader in Public Policy in the Department of Politics, Birkbeck, University of London, UK. Her chapter was written during fellowships at the Hanse-Wissenschaftskolleg, Bremen, and Wissenschaftszentrum Berlin.

**Martino Maggetti** is Lecturer at the University of Zurich, Switzerland. He participates in the project "Internationalization, mediatization, and the accountability of regulatory agencies" funded by the Swiss National Science Foundation, and teaches Comparative Regulatory Governance and Comparative Methodology.

**Giandomenico Majone** is Professor of Public Policy, Emeritus, European University Institute, Italy. His latest book is *Europe as the Would-Be World Power* (Cambridge University Press).

**Axel Marx** is Research Manager of the Leuven Centre for Global Governance Studies, University of Leuven, Belgium.

**Peter J. May** is the Donald R. Matthews Distinguished Professor of American Politics at the University of Washington, USA.

**Barry M. Mitnick** is Professor of Business Administration and of Public and International Affairs at the University of Pittsburgh, USA.

**Cor van Montfort** is Professor at Tilburg University, The Netherlands and Head of the Public–Private Sector Department at the Netherlands Court of Audit. He is also Senior Research Fellow at the Centre for Governance of the Private Public Sector Enterprise in Tilburg. His work is on public governance, hybrid organizations and public–private partnerships.

**Andrew D. Murray** is Professor in Law at the London School of Economics, UK. He is a Fellow of Gray's Inn and is Legal Project Lead of Creative Commons England and Wales. He specializes in cyber-regulation and governance, and new media and communications regulation.

**Mirjan Oude Vrielink** is Senior Researcher at the University of Twente, The Netherlands. Her research focuses on issues of innovation in governance and regulation.

**Oren Perez** is a Professor at the Faculty of Law, University of Bar Ilan, Israel. He received his Ph.D. from the London School of Economics and Political Science (2001).

**Dieter Pesendorfer** is Senior Lecturer in Regulation at the School of Law at Queen's University Belfast, UK.

**Roberto Pires** is a Researcher at the Department of State, Institutions, and Democracy Studies, Institute for Applied Economic Research in Brasilia, Brazil.

**Matthew Potoski** is Professor of Corporate Environmental Management at the Bren School of Environmental Science and Management, University of California-Santa Barbara, USA.

**Aseem Prakash** is Professor of Political Science and the Walker Family Professor for the College of Arts and Sciences at the University of Washington, Seattle, USA. He is the founding General Editor of the Cambridge University Press Series on Business and Public Policy and the Co-Editor of the *Journal of Policy Analysis and Management*.

**Lisa A. Robinson** is an Independent Consultant who specializes in the economic analysis of environmental, health, and safety regulations.

**Susan Rose-Ackerman** is the Henry R. Luce Professor of Law and Political Science, Yale University, USA. Her recent research concerns corruption, democratic accountability, and comparative administrative law. Her most recent book is *Comparative Administrative Law* (co-edited with Peter L. Lindseth, 2011).

**Amit M. Schejter** (Ph.D., Rutgers) is Associate Professor of Communications and Co-Director of the Institute for Information Policy at the College of Communications at the Pennsylvania State University, USA. He is the Founding Editor of the *Journal of Information Policy*, author of more than 40 journal articles and parts of books, and author, co-author and editor of three books, among them . . . *And Communications For All: A Policy Agenda for a New Administration* (Lexington Books, 2009).

**Colin Scott** is Professor of EU Governance and Regulation at University College Dublin, Ireland.

**Stuart Shapiro** is an Associate Professor and Director of the Public Policy Program at Rutgers University, USA. He has written extensively on regulation and cost–benefit analysis. Before coming to Rutgers, he worked at the Office of Information and Regulatory Affairs in Washington, DC for five years.

**Susan S. Silbey** is Leon and Anne Goldberg Professor of Sociology and Anthropology at the Massachusetts Institute of Technology, USA.

**Annette Elisabeth Töller** is Professor of Public Policy at the University of Hagen, Germany and was previously a Visiting Scholar at the Center for European Studies, Harvard University. She works, among other things, on national and transnational kinds of voluntary approaches to public policy.

**Brigitte Unger** is Professor of Public Sector Economics at Utrecht University School of Economics, The Netherlands. She has published three books with Edward Elgar on money laundering and edited a special issue about money laundering in the *Review of Law and Economics*.

**Frans van Waarden** is Professor of Policy and Organization Studies at Utrecht University and Fellow at its honors college, University College Utrecht, The Netherlands. Being a sociologist, he is particularly interested in issues at the interface of economics, politics, and law.

**Kai Wegrich** is Professor of Public Administration and Public Policy at the Hertie School of Governance in Berlin, Germany.

**Michelle Welsh** is a Senior Lecturer and the Deputy Director of the Workplace and Corporate Law Research Group at Monash University in Melbourne, Australia.

**Bruce Yandle** is Alumni Distinguished Professor of Economics Emeritus and Dean Emeritus, College of Business and Behavioral Science, Clemson University, USA. He is a Senior Fellow with PERC, and Adjunct Distinguished Professor of Economics, Mercatus Center at George Mason University.

# Preface

The study of regulation is the study of the politics, policies, institutions and effectiveness of formal and informal controls. Such controls may take many forms: some are hierarchical with clear sanctions attached, while others are softer; some are in the domain of one actor, while others are highly divided among actors, arenas and institutions; some are exerted by governmental organizations and some by private organizations; some emphasize participation, while others emphasize compliance; some reflect well-designed systems of delegation, monitoring and enforcement, and others are at best patchworks. They are all however the products of politics, and they all have redistributive effects, even if these effects are often blurred and not transparent. Politics is intertwined with regulation, and the efforts to depoliticize the topic makes it all the more interesting.

The study of regulation is also the study of the limits of control and the overt and covert resistance of rulers and their rules. In the age of governance, regulation is also the study of regulatory regimes in shifting levels, arenas and spaces of control. As a mode of control, regulation represents an alternative to taxing and spending on the one hand and nationalization and public ownership on the other. As a hybrid mode of control, regulation is not only control by government but also the control over government, control without government and shared forms of control. It is also a multidisciplinary field that in the last decade has rapidly developed a common language and shared understanding of the problems and challenges. The increased invasion of regulation into everyday life and the growing attention paid to it by both citizens and scholars is well attested to by the creation of the European Consortium for Political Research's scholarly network on regulatory governance (with currently 1600 subscribers), by the establishment of the journal *Regulation & Governance* (2005) and by the growing body of scholarly work published in the area. There is definitely a distinct "hype" around the study of regulation at the moment. The extent to which this will have a long-term impact on the social sciences and law is still unclear, but there is no doubt that the relevant literature is coming of age.

The present handbook seeks to contribute to the study of regulation and to its consolidation as a multidisciplinary field. The diversity of material and comprehensive manner in which its various aspects are covered in the handbook is evidence of this. The scholars currently active in the field come from diverse academic backgrounds, and I deeply hope that readers will recognize not only the substantial contribution but also the freshness of their outlook, and the creativity and originality they bring to this volume. To the best of my knowledge, this is the largest collection of essays ever published on the subject/topic of regulation, as well as being the most interdisciplinary. Our field is rapidly expanding, and it is my hope that this handbook presages a promising future.

# Acknowledgements

The invitation to edit the Handbook on the Politics of Regulation came from Edward Elgar and his team. Following some hesitation, I humbly undertook it in order to ensure and consolidate the work done by my colleagues and me in the ECPR Standing Group on Regulatory Governance and with the interdisciplinary journal *Regulation & Governance*. I also trusted the professionalism of the publisher and his contribution to the social sciences. I was not disappointed. This is the second edited collection that I have published with Elgar (the first being *The Politics of Regulation: Institutions and Regulatory Reforms for the Age of Governance,* co-edited with Jacint Jordana, 2004). The contribution of Edward Elgar's team to the development of the field is evident to anyone familiar with their catalogue on regulatory governance.

My interest in the study of regulation was first ignited by a public seminar on "Governmental Regulation in the Global Economy" chaired by Robert Kagan and David Vogel at the Center of Law and Society at UC Berkeley in 1995/96. It took, however, some time before I placed regulation on my research agenda. Its relevance became all the more clear when I studied the so-called deregulation of the Israeli, European and global telecommunications regime and even more so when I developed a strong interest in EU public policy. Regulation, EU public policy, and international and comparative political economy all came together during a research fellowship with Jeremy Richardson at Nuffield College between the years 2000 and 2003. After this, I had the opportunity to develop my interests and extend my perspective first, briefly, at the Centre on Regulation and Competition at the University of Manchester and then for a longer period with RegNet at the Australian National University, mainly with John Braithwaite, Peter Drahos and Peter Grabosky. During this period I cooperated with Jacint Jordana, who became not only a partner in my scholarly explorations but also a friend.

I started to work on this handbook in 2008 shortly after moving from the University of Haifa to the Hebrew University of Jerusalem. It took three years of work, with the final stages being done during a research leave in Berlin. This is an opportunity to thank my colleagues and friends at the Hebrew University of Jerusalem who warmly facilitated my integration into the Department of Political Science and the Federmann School of Public Policy. I am also grateful to my hosts in Berlin: Tanja Börzel and Thomas Risse at the Free University and Dieter Plehwe and Arndt Sorge at the Wissenschaftszentrum Berlin für Sozialforschung (WZB). The excellent research assistance provided by Hannan Haber and Michal Alef is deeply appreciated. Finally, it is a pleasure to note and acknowledge my gratitude to the 57 contributors of the various chapters for their cooperation and dedication to the project and to the field of regulatory governance. Their work in this handbook, and beyond, extends the scope of research in this field and lays strong foundations for a better understanding of the politics of regulation. I do hope that what we present here allows us to be optimistic about further, ever better and more exciting research than we can currently envisage.

*Berlin, January 2011*

# PART I

# INTRODUCTION

# 1 Regulation and regulatory governance

*David Levi-Faur*

[O]ur life plans are so often impeded by rules, large and small, that the very idea of a life plan independent of rules is scarcely imaginable. (Schauer 1992: 1)

Like many other political concepts, regulation is hard to define, not least because it means different things to different people. The term is employed for a myriad of discursive, theoretical, and analytical purposes that cry out for clarification (Baldwin et al. 1998; Black 2002; Parker and Braithwaite 2003). The notion of regulation is also highly contested. For the Far Right, regulation is a dirty word representing the heavy hand of authoritarian governments and the creeping body of rules that constrain human or national liberties. For the Old Left it is part of the superstructure that serves the interests of the dominant class and frames power relations in seemingly civilized forms. For Progressive Democrats, it is a public good, a tool to control profit-hungry capitalists and to govern social and ecological risks. For some, regulation is something that is done exclusively by government, a matter of the state and legal enforcement, while for others regulation is mostly the work of social actors who monitor other actors, including governments.

State-centered conceptions of regulation define it with reference to state-made laws (Laffont 1994), while society-centered analysts and scholars of globalization tend to point to the proliferation of regulatory institutions beyond the state (e.g. civil-to-civil, civil-to-government, civil-to-business, business-to-business, and business-to-government regulation). For legal scholars, regulation is often a legal instrument, while for sociologists and criminologists it is yet another form of social control; thus they emphasize regulatory instruments such as shaming and issues of restorative justice and responsive regulation (Braithwaite 1989; Ayres and Braithwaite 1992; Braithwaite 2002). For some it is the amalgamation of all types of laws – primary, secondary, and tertiary legislation – while for others it is confined to secondary legislation. For economists it is usually a strategic tool used by private and special interests to exploit the majority (e.g. Stigler 1971; Jarrell 1978; Priest 1993). Not all economists are alike: for institutional economists regulation might be a constitutive element of the market and is often understood as the mechanism that constitutes property rights (North 1990) or even as a source of competitiveness (Porter 1991; Jänicke 2008). The French Regulation School seems to have developed a similar institutional perspective but with a more critical tone and without the normative preferences that dominate Anglo-Saxon economists (Aglietta 1979; Lipietz 1987; Boyer 1990).

While scholars of public administration seem to perceive it with direct and intimate reference to the scope of state authority, formal regulatory organizations, and the "art of government" (Bernstein 1955; Mitnick 1980; Coen and Thatcher 2005; Gilardi 2005, 2008), scholars of global governance tend to focus on standards and soft norms (Mattli and Büthe 2003; Scott 2004; Jacobsson 2004; Trubek and Trubek 2005; Dejlic and

Sahlin-Andersson 2006). While some seem to think of the rise of regulation as yet another indication of the advance of neoliberalism and the retreat of the welfare state (Majone 1994), others tend to see it as a neo-mercantilist instrument for market expansion (Levi-Faur 1998), high modernism (Moran 2003), and social engineering (Zedner 2006). In the European parlance, and for most of the 20th century, regulation was synonymous with government intervention and, indeed, with all the efforts of the state, by whatever means, to control and guide the economy and society. This rather broad meaning of the term seems to have faded, and scholars now make efforts to distinguish rule making from other tools of governance, and indeed from other types of policy instruments, such as taxation, subsidies, redistribution, and public ownership.

Regulation not only is a distinct type of policy but also entails identifiable forms and patterns of political conflict that differ from the patterns that are regularly associated with policies of distribution and redistribution (Lowi 1964; Wilson 1980; Majone 1997). In addition, while other types of policy are about relatively visible transfers and direct allocation of resources, regulation only indirectly shapes the distribution of costs in society. Government budgets include relatively visible[1] and clear estimations of the overall costs of distribution and redistribution but hardly any of the cost of regulation.[2] One of the most important features of regulation is therefore that its costs (and some suggests also its politics) are opaque. The most significant costs of regulation are compliance costs, which are borne not by the government budget but mostly by the regulated parties. The wide distribution of these costs and their embeddedness in the regulatees' budgets make their impact, effects, and net benefits less visible and therefore less transparent to the attentive public. Some efforts to assess the costs and benefits of regulation are made in some countries and over some issues via the institutionalization of regulatory impact analysis assessments (Sunstein 2002; Radaelli and De Francesco 2007). Yet the transparency of these impact assessments and their theoretical and empirical foundations are contested (Sinden et al. 2009). At the same time the scope of their application at least for the moment is narrow.

For some, regulation is a risky business that is prone to failure and costs that exceed the benefits, but for others the business of regulation is the business of risk minimization (Hood et al. 2001; Hutter 2001; Fischer 2007). Some contend that regulation comprises mostly rule making while others extend it to include rule monitoring and rule enforcement (Hood et al. 2001). For some, regulations are about the rules and functions of the administrative agency after the act of delegation; for others, as already observed, regulation includes every kind of rule, including primary legislation and even social and professional norms. Multiple definitions of regulation are evident in the Law as well. The American Administrative Procedure Act defines the term "rule" but not the term "regulation," and what it defines as rule is confined to the scope of the Act itself (Kerwin 1994).[3] Other laws may include, and indeed apply, other terms, definitions, and terminologies in a somewhat chaotic manner. This is how Ira Sharkansky described the situation in the legal system of the US:

> In dealing with laws and rules that govern the behavior of administrators, we must enter a language thicket where terminology is crucial but generally haphazard. In most places, a decision is an agency's determination of how it will act in a particular case. In the Treasury Department however a decision is a general rule. According to the US Administrative Procedures Act, an order is a judicial-type decision issued by an administrative body. Often, however, an order is a

general regulation. A directive likewise can be a general regulation, or rule, or particular decision. (Sharkansky 1982: 323–4)

To add another layer of "comparative" complexity, the European Union's legal system "regulation" has a different meaning altogether and denotes one of five forms of law: regulation, directive, decision, recommendation, and opinion. "Regulation" means a rule that is directly applicable and obligatory in all member states. Thus Law cannot save us from the recognition that there are many ways in which regulation enters the public and academic discourse.

Instead of forcing unity, we should recognize the many meanings of regulation and devote our efforts to understanding each others' terms. This pluralist aptitude was also adopted by Julia Black, who has distinguished between functionalist, essentialist, and conventionalist definitions of regulation (Black 2002). A functionalist definition is based on the function that "regulation" performs in society, or what it does (e.g. risk minimization and economic controls). An essentialist definition asserts that "Regulation is. . ." It identifies elements that have an analytical relationship to the concept in an attempt to specify an invariant set of necessary and sufficient conditions. For example, "Regulation is a form of institutionalized norm enforcement." A conventionalist definition focuses on the way or ways that the term is used in practice; for example, "For [such and such a party] regulation means [such and such] but for [another party] regulation means [something else]." It is unproductive, Black suggests, forcing a definition on a diverse community of scholars and public policymakers with different interests in regulation. It is however important to clarify different meanings, and to point to the way that definition characterizes the practice, the conceptions, and the paradoxes that are involved in the study and practice of regulation. At the same time it is important to draw up definitions of regulation that allow us to examine and understand rule making in light of social, political, and economy theories, developments in national and global governance, and regulatory trends that are identified in this chapter, namely the consolidation of regulatory regimes, the autonomization of regulatory agencies, the emergence of new forms of civil and business-to-business regulation, and the hybrid architecture of regulatory capitalism.

One important aspect of any discussion of the different connotations and characteristics of regulation is the intimate relations between regulation and the existence of an administrative agency. Rule making and rule-making agencies are closely connected. An emphasis on the workings, characteristics, failures, and merits of regulation by administrative agencies is prevalent in the literature on regulation. Indeed, these aspects are expressed in one of the most widely cited definitions of regulation, namely as "sustained and focused control exercised by a public agency over activities that are valued by the community" (Selznick 1985: 363). Not only does this definition include an explicit reference to public agency, but it also stresses the sustained and focused nature of regulation. Regulation involves a continuous action of monitoring, assessment, and refinement of rules rather than ad hoc operation. Implicit in this definition is also the expectation that *ex ante* rules will be the dominant form of regulatory control. The definition is apt also in the sense that it recognizes that many, perhaps the most important, regulations are exercised not by "regulatory agencies" but by a wide variety of executive organs. This definition is less successful, however, in other respects. It recognizes regulation only as public activity by "public agency" and thus excludes business-to-business regulation as well as civil regulation. It also does not clarify which kinds of focused control the public agency applies (is it rule making only or also other forms of control such as arbitrary commands?), and the definition unnecessarily limits regulation to those actions that are valued by the community.

The focus on the administrative elements in the study of regulation might be less useful for scholars who emphasize the limits of "hard law" and who are aware of the importance of social norms and other forms of "soft law" in the governance of societies and economies. A wider definition of regulation that captures regulation as soft law would suggest that regulation encompasses "all mechanisms of social control" including unintentional and non-state processes. Indeed, it extends "to mechanisms which are not the products of state activity, nor part of any institutional arrangement, such as the development of social norms and the effects of markets in modifying behavior" (Baldwin et al. 1998: 4). Thus a notion of intentionality about the development of norms has been dropped from this definition of regulation, and anything producing effects on behavior may be considered regulatory. In addition, a wide range of activities which may involve legal or quasi-legal norms, but without mechanisms for monitoring and enforcement, might also come within the definition. Thus Scott defines regulation as "any process or set of processes by which norms are established, the behavior of those subject to the norms monitored or fed back into the regime, and for which there are mechanisms for holding the behavior of regulated actors within the acceptable limits of the regime" (Scott 2001: 283). This approach connects widely with the research agenda on governance, "the new governance" (Lobel 2004; Trubek and Trubek 2005), and the "new regulatory state" (Braithwaite 2000), where elements of steering and plural forms of regulation are emphasized in the effort to capture the plurality of interests and sources of control around issues, problems, and institutions. This rather wide definition of regulation also allows us to "de-center" regulation from the state and even from well-recognized forms of self-regulation (Black 2002). Decentered approaches to regulation emphasize complexity, fragmentation, interdependencies, and government failures, and suggest the limits of the distinctions between the public and the private and between the global and the national (Black 2001; Scott 2004; Gunningham 2009).

While recognizing pluralism and its strengths, it is also important to clarify my own preference. I define regulation as the *ex-ante* bureaucratic legalization of prescriptive rules and the monitoring and enforcement of these rules by social, business, and political actors on other social, business, and political actors. These rules will be considered as regulation as long as they are *not* formulated directly by the legislature (primary law) or the courts (verdict, judgment, ruling, and adjudication). In other words, regulation is about bureaucratic and administrative rule making and not about legislative or judicial rule making. This does not mean that for other scholarly purposes they shouldn't be included. Nor does it mean that legislatures or courts are not important engines for regulatory expansion, and of course it does not mean that they cannot be critical actors in the regulatory space. The definition emphasizes the role of diverse sets of actors in this process in order to point to the importance of hybrid elements in the systems that govern our "life plans." It does not, however, suggest what the functions of regulation are; specifically, it is neutral on the question whether regulation aims to reduce social and ecological risks, to control costs, to promote competitive markets, or to promote private interests.

## 1.1 REGULATING AND THE REGULOCRATS: WHO, WHAT AND HOW?

To better understand regulation we need to pay close attention to the questions: Who are the regulators? What is being regulated? How is regulation carried out? Each of these issues is critical for a more thorough understanding of what regulatory governance and regulatory capitalism are all about (on regulatory capitalism see this volume, Levi-Faur, 2011). Let us start with the *who* question. Different approaches to regulation would identify different regulators. For criminologists, policemen are the regulators; for public administration scholars regulators are employees of regulatory agencies; for socio-legal scholars we are all regulators. If we adopt this broad approach to regulation, it follows that, while only a few of us are acting as professional regulators, most, if not all, of us act as regulators in some capacity. We frequently monitor our government, corporations, and NGOs. We often act, consciously or not, like gatekeepers of the social order and raise "fire alarms" in cases of corruption, violence, or other forms of deviant behavior. This of course saves on "police patrols"[4] and helps us to understand that regulatory networks are embedded in the social system and do not represent a distinct, stand-alone part of it.

Nonetheless, while we are all regulators in some capacity, it is possible to identify a distinct class of regulators. The agencification of regulatory functions and the increasing autonomy that they enjoy suggest the transformation of the bureaucracy of the modern administrative state and indeed private bureaucracy as well to a regulocracy (Gilardi et al. 2007). To live in an age where regulation is expanding means that we expect our colleagues, and even ourselves, to invest more of our resources in regulation. In other words, we are all immersed in the regulatory game. Yet the scope of this phenomenon is still an open question. Also open is the question to what extent new forms of governance offer new opportunities to the weak to deploy new strategies of regulation to their own advantage. While some suggest that this is the case (Braithwaite 2004) and that indeed even a female sex worker can regulate police brutality (Biradavolu et al. 2009), others suggest that the new networks of regulators are constrained by entrenched structures of power (Shamir 2008; Sørensen and Torfing 2008).

Regulatory games of demands for accountability and transparency, on the one hand, and political and bureaucratic responses towards blame shifting, on the other, are becoming central to our organizational, social, and political behavior (Hood 2010). Organizations such as the mass media are developing monitoring and regulatory capacities via ranking and grading techniques. Similarly social movements find that public education campaigns, demonstrations, and lobbying are not enough and therefore develop monitoring capacities. To exemplify this process, it might be useful to focus for a moment on the role of three different types of non-governmental organizations (NGOs) that may develop important regulatory capacities: MaNGO, CiNGO, and GoNGO. MaNGOs are market-oriented NGOs that are controlled (owned or otherwise dominated) by market actors and works, whether explicitly or not, to develop their own regulatory capacities (cf. Shamir 2005: 240; Barkay 2009). MaNGOs blur the distinction between civil society and the economy and do not conform to the traditional image of NGOs as independent from both business and the state. CiNGOs are NGOs that are controlled (owned or otherwise dominated) by civil society actors and works, whether

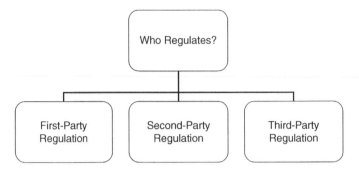

*Figure 1.1    Who regulates?*

consciously or not, to develop their own regulatory capacities. CiNGOs do conform with our image of the independent civil sphere, but, unlike the traditional NGOs which focus on service provisions or advocacy, CiNGOs are mainly regulatory organizations that function as alternatives and complementary to the regulatory state. Finally GoNGOs are NGOs that are controlled (owned or otherwise dominated) by state actors and work, whether explicitly or not, to develop their own regulatory capacities. This distinction between different types of NGOs which act as regulators will allow us to develop a clearer understanding of hybrid designs of regulatory institutions.

It is sometimes useful to distinguish between three major strategies of regulation: first-party regulation, second-party regulation, and third-party regulation (see Figure 1.1). These strategies deal with how to regulate, but the *how* is intimately connected to the question of *who* regulates. In first-party regulation the major form of regulatory control is self-regulation. The regulator is also the regulatee. In second-party regulation, there is a social, political, economic, and administrative division of labor between the actors, and the regulator is independent and distinct from the regulatee. While we often identify second-party regulation with state regulation of business, this is not always the case. Business regulation of business is a case in point. Here the growth of regulation is driven by the ability of some businesses (most often big businesses) to set standards for other businesses (most often smaller). One relevant example is the ability of big supermarket chains to set contractual standards of food manufacturing, processing, and marketing all over the world (Levi-Faur 2008). In third-party regulation, the relations between the regulator and the regulatee are mediated by a third party that acts as independent or semi-independent regulatory-auditor.[5] Processes and procedures of accreditation by third parties are a central enforcement strategy and "contractual relationship between firm and the party auditing the facility in place of relying solely on the regulatory agency as enforcer" (Kunreuther et al. 2002: 309).[6] One of the most popular forms of third-party regulation is "auditing." Indeed, the notion of audit is now used in a variety of contexts to refer to growing pressures for verification requirements (Power 1997). Third-party regulation is a prevalent feature of modern life and it opens the door for a more comprehensive understanding of regulation as a hybrid of the interaction between state regulation, market actor regulation (MaNGOs and other business organizations), and CiNGOs (civil society regulators). Table 1.1 presents the various options for regulatory hybridizations when three different types of third parties are enlisted by three different types of regula-

*Table 1.1   Types of third-party regulatory designs*

| Type of third party enlisted | State actors as regulators (e.g. regulatory agencies, GoNGOs) | | | Market actors as regulators (e.g. MaNGOs) | | | Civil actors as regulators (e.g. CiNGOs) | | |
|---|---|---|---|---|---|---|---|---|---|
| | S | M | C | S | M | C | S | M | C |
| State actors as regulatees | **SSS** | SMS | SCS | MSS | MMS | MCS | CSS | CMS | CCS |
| Market actors as regulatees | SSM | SMM | SCM | MSM | **MMM** | MCM | CSM | CMM | CCM |
| Civil actors as regulatees | SSC | SMC | SCC | MSC | MMC | MCC | CSC | CMC | **CCC** |

*Note:*   First letter means the regulator; second represents the enlisted third party; third letter means the regulatee. S=state; M=market; C=civil.

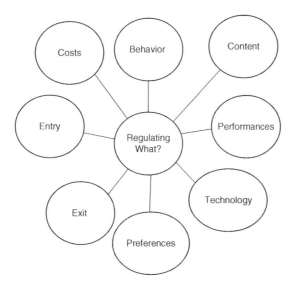

*Figure 1.2   What is being regulated?*

tors to regulate three types of regulatees. The intersection between the regulator (state, market, civil), the third party (state, market, civil), and the regulatees (state, market, civil) creates 27 different forms of third-party regulation. Only three forms of third-party regulation (SSS, MMM, and CCC) are pure forms of self-governance. All the others involve different types of actors and thus blur the distinctions between state, society, and markets.

Moving to the question of *what* is being regulated, we suggest that regulation can be exerted on at least eight aspects of any governance systems: entry, exit, behavior, costs, content, preferences, technology, and performances (see Figure 1.2). Entry regulation determines who is eligible to offer service, supply a product and offer advice and information. Regulation can be exerted on exit from a business, for example when

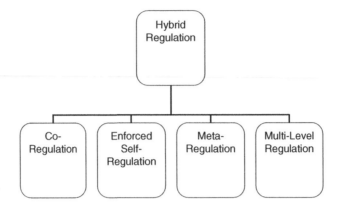

*Figure 1.3    Hybrid forms of regulation*

a license is revoked. Regulation on behavior is a common form of regulation that deals with issues of proper action, speech, or expression. Regulation of costs deals with the acceptable (minimum, maximum) cost of service or product. Cost regulation can come in various forms (e.g. price cap, rate of return). The regulation of content deals with the integrity of a message across various platforms of communication (e.g. books, mass broadcasting, newspapers, internet) and with issues such as the integrity of the message (e.g. advertisement rules, acceptable language, violence, sexuality). The regulation of preferences is manifested most of all via socialization, professionalization, and educational processes. Regulation of technology prescribes the application of a certain technology of production or process (and not others) as a form of control. Finally the regulation of performance is directed towards the achievement of results. Some significant efforts are carried recently in the literature in order to evaluate the costs and benefits of regulating one component of the system instead of others. For example, the literature on performance-based regulation suggests that regulations should be based on achievement of specified results, while leaving it to regulated entities to determine how best to achieve those results (Coglianese and Lazer 2003; May 2007; 2010).

Hybridism abounds and not only in connection to NGOs and third-party regulation. In addition, it is possible to identify four major forms of hybrids that involve both first- and second-, and perhaps also third-party forms of regulation that deal with the issue of *how* to regulate (see Figure 1.3). First is co-regulation, where responsibility for regulatory design or regulatory enforcement is shared by the regulator and the regulatees, often state and civil actors, but also between MaNGOs and CiNGOs and state and MaNGOs. The particular scope of cooperation may vary as long as the regulatory arrangements are grounded in cooperative techniques and the legitimacy of the regime rests at least partly on public–private cooperation. A second form of hybrid regulation is enforced self-regulation, where the regulator compels the regulatee to write a set of rules tailored to the unique set of contingencies facing that firm. The regulator, e.g. a regulatory agency, "would either approve these rules, or send them back for revision if they were insufficiently stringent" (Ayres and Braithwaite 1992: 106). Rather than having the government enforce the rules, most enforcement duties and costs would be internalized by the regulatees, who would be required to establish their own independent compliance administration.

A third form of hybrid regulation is meta-regulation. Unlike enforced self-regulation, it allows the regulatee to determine its own rules. The role of the regulator is confined to the institutionalization and monitoring of the integrity of institutional compliance. In this sense, it is about meta-monitoring (Grabosky 1995). In Christine Parker's formulation, the notion of meta-regulation has been used as a descriptive or explanatory term within the literature on the "new governance" to refer to the way in which the state's role in governance and regulation is changing (Parker 2002). "Meta-regulation" "entails any form of regulation (whether by tools of state law or other mechanisms) that regulates any other form of regulation" (Parker 2007). Thus it might include legal regulation of self-regulation (e.g. putting an oversight board above a self-regulatory professional association), non-legal methods of "regulating" internal corporate self-regulation or management (e.g. voluntary accreditation to codes of good conduct), or the regulation of national law-making by transnational bodies (such as the EU) (Parker 2007). In Bronwen Morgan's formulation, it captures a desire or tendency "to think reflexively about regulation, such that rather than regulating social and individual action directly, the process of regulation itself becomes regulated" (Morgan 2003: 2).

Finally, the fourth form of hybrid regulation is often known as "multi-level regulation." Here regulatory authority is allocated to different levels of territorial tiers – supranational (global and regional), national, regional (domestic), and local (Marks and Hooghe 2001). There are various forms of multi-level regulation depending on the number of tiers that are involved and the particular form of allocation. Regulatory authority can be allocated on a functional basis (whereby regulatory authority is allocated to different tiers according to their capacity to deal with the problem) or on a hierarchical basis (where supreme authority is defined in one of the regulatory tiers), or simply be a product of incremental, path-dependent processes (where the regime is the result of the amalgamation of patches, each designed to solve a particular aspect as it occurred on the regulatory agenda). While much of the discussion on multi-level governance (which is a broader term than multi-level regulation) focuses on the transfer of authority between one tier and another, one should also note that the overall impact of multi-level regulation can be that of accretion (that is, regulatory expansion). Indeed, the possibility that multi-level regulation may involve co-development of regulatory capacities in different tiers is only rarely recognized.

## 1.2   THE REGULATORY AGENCIES

One of the most important indicators of the growth in the scope and depth of regulatory activities in modern society is the proliferation of regulatory agencies as the administrative and intellectual core of national and global systems of regulatory governance. Regulatory agencies are not a new feature of modern systems of governance, but they have become a highly popular form of regulatory governance since the 1990s (see Figure 1.4). A regulatory agency is a non-departmental public organization mainly involved with rule making, which may also be responsible for fact finding, monitoring, adjudication, and enforcement. It is autonomous in the sense that it can shape its own preferences;

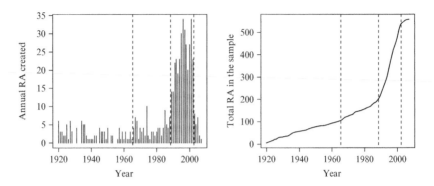

*Note:*    The data cover the creation of agencies in 48 countries and 16 sectors over 88 years (1920–2007).

*Source:*    Jordana et al. (2009).

*Figure 1.4*    *(a) Annual creation of regulatory agencies in the sample. (b) Cumulative annual creation of regulatory agencies, 1920–2007*

of course, the extent of the autonomy varies with its administrative capacities, its ability to shape preferences independently, and its ability to enforce its rules. The autonomy of the agency is also constituted by the act of its establishment as a separate organization and the institutionalization of a policy space where the agency's role becomes "taken for granted." Note that rule making, fact finding, monitoring, adjudication, and enforcement capacities are defining characteristics of regulatory agencies, but also that other organizations, both within and outside the state, can acquire and successfully deploy these characteristics.

As state organizations, regulatory agencies originated in various boards, ad hoc committees, and other pre-modern organizational entities that during the 20th century became the pillars of the modern administrative state. Regulatory agencies became a distinctive feature of the American administrative state in the early 20th century. What other countries often nationalized the US regulated. Indeed, the history of the American administrative state is also the history of the establishment of regulatory agencies. Yet, while the number of regulatory agencies in the US has not grown since the mid-1970s, such agencies have become popular elsewhere in the world. A recent survey of the establishment of regulatory agencies across 16 different sectors in 63 countries from the 1920s through 2007 reveals that it is possible to find an autonomous regulatory agency in about 73 percent of the possible sector–country units that were surveyed (Jordana et al. 2009). The number of regulatory agencies rose sharply in the 1990s. The rate of establishment increased dramatically: from fewer than five new autonomous agencies per year from the 1960s to the 1980s, to more than 20 agencies per year from the 1990s to 2002 (rising to almost 40 agencies per year between 1994 and 1996).

The literature usually distinguishes between two types of regulatory agencies: economic and social. The distinction is not entirely clear cut but it is useful for characterizing the historical context of the establishment of these agencies, their organizational characteristics, and the challenges that they face. In recent years, the regulatory explosion has led to the consolidation of a new type of agency, best called the "integrity agency."

Economic regulatory agencies deal with the functioning of markets and employ a variety of tools to constitute, manage, and supervise them. Issues of competition and costs of service under conditions of concentrated market power on the one hand and restricted options for voice by consumers on the other are major challenges for economic regulatory agencies. Social regulation agencies deal with issues of health, safety, and the environment, and in this sense they are often also called risk-regulation agencies and sometimes protective-regulation agencies. While the stated aim of many economic regulators is to nurture or increase competition, the stated aim of social regulators is to make our lives safer by eliminating or reducing risks or exposure to risks (Breyer 1993: 3). In addition, while economic regulation (with the notable exception of antitrust regulation) is often sector specific, social regulation is usually applied industry-wide, that is, beyond specific sectors. Some countries use social regulation (rather than subsidies) in order to advance goals such as social cohesion and equality. In these cases, the boundaries between the regulatory state and the welfare state are becoming even more blurred (Mabbett, 2011; Haber 2011). Integrity regulatory agencies (or pro-accountability regulation agencies) deal with moral issues in the public sphere and safeguard accountability and other norms of conduct in the public sphere.[7] Examples include autonomous corruption-control bodies, independent electoral institutions, auditing agencies, and human rights ombudsmen.

## 1.3   BEYOND AGENCIES: REGULATORY REGIMES

For certain theoretical, methodological, and empirical purposes, it might be useful to focus on the notion of a regulatory regime rather than solely on regulation as atomistic, stand-alone rule making. The notion of a regulatory regime encompasses the norms, the mechanisms of decision making, and the network of actors that are involved in regulation (Eisner 1993; Drezner 2007). It has many parallels with the notion of "regulatory space" (Hancher and Moran 1989; Scott 2001; Thatcher and Coen 2008). The notion of a regulatory regime is an increasingly popular concept in the study of regulation and regulatory reform, which probably attests to the emergence and consolidation of systemic rule making to govern different issues, arenas, and sectors. The notions of a "regulatory regime" and "international regulatory regime" build on Krasner's definition of a regime as the "principles, norms, rules, and decision-making procedures around which actors' expectations converge in a given issue-area" (Krasner 1982: 185). Steven Vogel applied it to the study of regulation and distinguished between two major components of the regulatory regime. The first component, "regime orientation," indicates "state actors' beliefs about the proper scope, goals, and method of government intervention in the economy and about how this intervention affects economic performance." The second component, "regime organization," captures the particular "organization of those state actors concerned with industry and the relationship of these actors to the private actors" (Vogel 1996: 20–21).

Hood, Rothstein, and Baldwin made the notion of a regulatory regime a central pillar of their risk analysis. Regulatory regime "connotes the overall way risk is regulated in a particular policy domain" (Hood et al. 2001: 8). They identify three major elements of regimes that represent different aspects of the ideal control system. The first is information gathering, to allow monitoring and to produce knowledge about current or changing states of the regime. The second is standard setting, to allow a distinction to be made between more and less preferred states of the regime. The third is behavior modification, to meet the standards, goals, or targets (Hood et al. 2001: 21). The authors make a second important distinction, between the "context" and the "content" of a regime. Regime context means the backdrop or setting in which regulation takes place; it includes the different types and levels of risk being tackled, the nature of public preferences and attitudes to risk, and the way the various actors who produce or are affected by the risk are organized. Regime content refers to three elements of its internal structure: first, the "size" of the policy, which reflects the extent of policy aggregation and the overall regulatory investment; second, the institutional structure of the regulators and especially the distribution of regulatory costs between state and other regulators, and the degree of organizational fragmentation and complexity; and, third, the regulatory style, as expressed by the regulators' attitudes, beliefs, and operating conventions.

## 1.4    THE GOVERNANCE OF REGULATORY REGIMES

Much of the academic and public discussion of regulation nowadays deals with the governance of regulation itself (or regulating regulation) rather than governance via regulation. The growth in the scope and number of regulations raises issues of effectiveness as well as issues of democratic control. This section of the chapter identifies two major challenges of governance: of effectiveness and of democratic legitimacy. The first challenge focuses on the effectiveness of direct regulation, and especially the alleged weakness of systems of command and control with prescriptive rules that tell regulated entities what to do and how to do it. These prescriptive rules tend to be highly particularistic in specifying required actions and the standards to be adhered to, and tend to be backed by state sanctions. At the same time they tend to have clear-cut lines of responsibility and thus accountability (May 2007: 9). Yet clarity, the ability to sanction, and direct accountability all come at a price. Strict authoritarianism, unreasonable rule, and capricious enforcement practices are associated with regulatory formalism, and it is argued that they impose needless costs and generate adversarial relations between regulators and regulatees (Bardach and Kagan 1982). Six shortcomings of regulation are emphasized in this context: (a) expensive and ineffective regulatory strategies; (b) inflexible regulatory strategies that encourage adversarial enforcement; (c) legal constraints on the subjects, procedures, and scope of regulatory discretion; (d) regulatees' resentment, which leads to non-compliance or "creative compliance" (McBarnet and Whelan 1997); (e) strict regulation that often presents an obstacle to innovation; and (f) regulation that often serves to set a lowest common denominator for regulatees to follow rather than supplying incentives for improved standards.

There are five major strategies of response to these weaknesses (Gunningham and Grabosky 1998; Croley 2008). The first, and the most controversial, is the return to "deregulation" and the efforts to ossify rule making. This might result in a race to the bottom or degradation of economic and environmental performances, unmitigated risk, and immoral economies and societies. The second is to turn to "lite" and management-based regulation and to harness economic incentives as much as possible toward politically determined public goods (Coglianese and Lazer 2003; May 2007; Baldwin 2008). The third is to promote responsive regulation (Ayres and Braithwaite 1992; Braithwaite 2005) as well as voluntary, negotiated, and cooperative forms of regulation. The fourth is to improve the regulatory arsenal (for example, employing auctions and using benchmarking) as well as the quality and training of the regulators (Sparrow 2000) and the quality of the regulatory design (Maggetti 2007; Gilardi 2008). The fifth is to institutionalize regulatory impact analysis and cost–benefit techniques (Sunstein 2002; Radaelli and De Francesco 2007). These control measures are becoming increasingly popular, and some countries have even established regulatory agencies to regulate regulation itself (e.g. the Dutch Advisory Board on Administrative Burdens, the British Better Regulation Executive, and the Office of Information and Regulatory Affairs in the United States).

The second challenge stems from the democratic qualities (or more accurately weaknesses) of regulation. Again, more than one democratic challenge is relevant here. First, regulators are not elected and they are accountable to the people only indirectly (Kerwin 1994: 161), leading to arguments about the democratic deficit of regulatory systems (Majone 1999). Regulation, as bureaucratic legislation, impinges on one of the pillars of democratic theory, that is, the doctrine of the separation of powers. The belief that the legislator should legislate, the judiciary should adjudicate, and the executive should govern via the bureaucracy takes regulation to be, at best, a "necessary evil" (Ganz 1997). Yet this "necessary evil" is expanding and diversifying to an extent that raises important challenges for democratic theory and practice. Second, while it is a fundamental idea of law that people should be subject to fixed, known, and certain rules (Raz 1979: 214–15), the sheer numbers of rules and the frequency and the process with which they are changed create a situation where it is beyond the capacity of most if not all individuals to act without legal advice.[8] The large volume of regulations represents a challenge for democratic, judicial, parliamentary, and administrative systems of control (Hewart 1929; Majone 1994, 1997; Dotan 1996; Kerwin 2003; Taggart 2005). Third, the growth of international administrative law – both in the form of regulation by intergovernmental and supranational organization and in the form of both business and international standards – makes supposedly sovereign polities into rule takers rather than rule makers (Braithwaite and Drahos 2000: 3–4). Regionalization, internationalization, and globalization of regulation all raise issues of legitimacy and may lead to new and innovative forms of democratic control over regulatory systems. The fourth democratic challenge is the reinforcement and sometimes the emergence of "private regulatory regimes" and "private governments." These spheres of private control may weaken democratic legitimacy and may change the balance of power between corporations and states (Hall and Biersteker 2002; Haufler 2002).

To deal with these democratic challenges that emerge from the growth in the scope and number of regulations, it is possible to develop and strengthen three systems of control over bureaucratic legislation: parliamentary, judicial, and participatory. The logic of these different systems varies, and so do their aims and degrees of effectiveness. Parliamentary systems of control enforce procedures of *de facto* or *de jure* monitoring and approval mechanisms over bureaucratic legislation. A common procedure of parliamentary control is the obligation to submit bureaucratic legislation to parliamentary approval before its official publication. The scope, mechanisms, and effectiveness of control vary across countries and are very telling as to the political development of the country. Judicial systems of control institutionalize *ex post* judicial review processes over bureaucratic legislation. The review process is triggered by litigation or appeal to either the country's courts or special administrative courts. Empirical studies that cover or sample the volume of judicial review of bureaucratic legislation are rare. Participatory systems of control institutionalize points of access and procedural obligations that require the bureaucratic legislator to publish the intention to legislate, to invite public comments, and to consult affected parties. The rule-making process as set by the American Administrative Procedure Act is one good and pioneering example of a participatory system of control (though not without its limits and flaws).

## 1.5   CONCLUSIONS: UNDERSTANDING REGULATORY GOVERNANCE

This chapter's exploration of the notion of regulation, and indeed the handbook chapters more generally, are based on the observation that we live in the golden age of regulation (Kagan 1995; Braithwaite and Drahos 2000; Ruhl and Salzman 2003; Levi-Faur 2005; Braithwaite 2008). The great financial crisis of 2008 and the sovereign debt crisis that followed it promise that the trend of growth in regulation will be reinforced even more strongly. It is possible to observe more "social" regulations alongside more "economic" regulations; "red tape" alongside "fair tape"; political and civil; national and international. We also observe regulations that hinder competition alongside regulation-*for*-competition, regulations that serve the public interest and regulation that mainly serves private interests. Deregulation, despite its prominence in the scholarly and public discourse, proved to be only a limited element of the reforms in governance. Where it occurred, it was followed either immediately or somewhat later by new regulatory expansion (McGarity 1992; Page 2001; Yackee and Yackee 2010). These observations were made in the so-called "era of deregulation," but they hold even more strongly following the financial crises.

Regulation and governance have become a core concept in the social sciences, and for good reasons. While redistributive, distributive, and developmental policies still abound, the expanding part of governance is regulation, that is, rule making, monitoring, and enforcement. Few projects are more central to the social sciences than the study of regulation and regulatory governance. Regulation, along with the significant issues raised or affected by it, have become central to the work of social scientists from many disciplines, including political science, economics, law, sociology, psychology, anthropology, and history. A strong interest of other professional and scholarly communities, such as physicians, nutritionists, biologists, ecologists, geologists, pharmacists, and chemists, makes regulatory issues even more central to scientists and practitioners (Braithwaite et al. 2007). The financial, ecological, legitimation, and moral crises of our time make regulatory issues even more central then ever before. Thus the demand for better, fairer, more efficient, and more participatory systems of governance promises that regulatory governance will continue to capture the imagination of scholars and dominate the agenda of policy makers. While regulatory governance is hardly a new feature of the social sciences, the issue still attracts less systematic and theoretical attention than it deserves. Attention should focus on the plurality of aspects and forms in which rule making, rule monitoring, and rule enforcement enter into our economic, political, and social life as well as on the creation of regulatory capitalism as a global political-economy order (Levi-Faur, 2011).

## ACKNOWLEDGEMENTS

I would like to acknowledge the useful comments from Avishai Benish, Hanan Haber, Ronit Justo-Hanani, Deborah Mabbett, Christine Parker, and Sharon Yadin. Responsibility for the content is of course mine. Some parts of this research were supported by research grant 2005/7 of the Israel National Institute for Health Policy and Health Services Research.

## NOTES

1. Not that this is only relative. Budgets are transparent to accountants to some degree but not to the public, even the educated public. State budgets omit important elements such as the costs of tax deductions. Transparent and participatory accounting is being called for to narrow the gaps between the rhetoric of democracy and its realities.
2. With the exception of the administrative costs of regulation (costs of fact finding, monitoring, and implementation).
3. "Rule" means the whole or part of an agency statement of general or particular applicability and future effect designed to implement, interpret, or prescribe law or policy (Kerwin 1994: 3).
4. Police patrols represent direct oversight, while "fire alarms" mobilize third parties, including private actors into the regulatory space. See McCubbins and Schwartz (1984).
5. An example of a third-party regulation that is motivated by market considerations is the SGS Corporation. It does inspection, verification, testing, and certification; it has been listed on the Swiss Stock Exchange since 1985 and has more than 46 000 employees, in over 1000 sites around the world. Another is EurepGAP, a private sector body that sets voluntary standards for the certification of agricultural products around the globe. It brings together agricultural producers and retailers that want to establish certification standards and procedures for good agricultural practices (GAP). Certification covers the production process of the certified product from before the seed is planted until it leaves the farm. EurepGAP is a business-to-business label and is therefore not directly visible to consumers. A form of third-party regulation that is socially motivated is the "green" or "social" labels that are offered and promoted by non-governmental, non-profit organizations. A more coercive form of third-party regulation is criminal or civil liabilities of the "third party" in the event that it fails to perform its duties. Indeed, much of the new expansion of regulation in the field of corporate governance is about the expansion of responsibility and demand for accountability from stakeholders who are not necessarily the offending persons but still are in a position to prevent non-compliance.
6. Third-party regulators should not be confused with the notion of "gatekeepers" (Kraakman 1986). These include senior executives, independent directors, large auditing firms, outside lawyers, securities analysts, the financial media, underwriters, and debt-rating agencies (Ribstein 2005: 5–6). Gatekeeping, whether by design or not, is an important element of governance regimes.
7. I owe this point to Avishai Benish.
8. In the US, agency rules have been produced in recent years at a rate of about 4200 a year (Croley et al. forthcoming). According to Coglianese, the volume of regulations issued by specific agencies has experienced a substantial growth. From 1976 to 1996 the overall volume of regulation in the Code of Federal Regulation was almost doubled (Coglianese 2002). In the United Kingdom they are produced at a rate of 3000 or so each year, outnumbering Acts of Parliament by 40 or 50 to one (Page 2001: ix). According to the Australian Parliament the volume of regulations and other statutory instruments is increasing, at the Commonwealth level alone by an annual average of 3000. In Israel they are being produced at a rate of only 800 or so a year, outnumbering Acts of Parliament by a factor of seven to one.

# REFERENCES

Aglietta, M. (1979), *A Theory of Capitalist Regulation: The US Experience*, London and New York: New Left Books (republished by Verso, 1987; originally written in French, 1974).
Ayres, I. and J. Braithwaite (1992), *Responsive Regulation: Transcending the Deregulation Debate*, Oxford: Oxford University Press.
Baldwin, R. (2008), 'Regulation lite: the rise of emissions trading', *Regulation & Governance*, 2 (2), 193–215.
Baldwin, R., C. Scott and C. Hood (1998), *A Reader on Regulation*, Oxford: Oxford University Press.
Bardach, E. and R.A. Kagan (1982), *Going by the Book: The Problem of Regulatory Unreasonableness*, Philadelphia, PA: Temple University Press.
Barkay, T. (2009), 'Regulation and voluntarism: a case study of governance in the making', *Regulation & Governance*, 3 (4), 360–75.
Bernstein, M. (1955), *Regulating Business by Independent Commission*, Princeton, NJ: Princeton University Press.
Biradavolu, Monica Rao, Scott Burris, Annie George, Asima Jena and Kim M. Blankenship (2009), 'Can sex workers regulate police? Learning from an HIV prevention project for sex workers in southern India', *Social Science & Medicine*, 68 (8), 1541–7.
Black, J. (2001), 'Decentring regulation: understanding the role of regulation and self regulation in a "post-regulatory" world', *Current Legal Problems*, 54, 103–47.
Black, J. (2002), 'Critical reflections on regulation', *Australian Journal of Legal Philosophy*, 27, 1–35.
Boyer, R. (1990), *The Regulation School: A Critical Introduction*, New York: Columbia University Press.
Braithwaite, J. (1989), *Crime, Shame and Reintegration*, Cambridge: Cambridge University Press.
Braithwaite, J. (2000), 'The new regulatory state and the transformation of criminology', *British Journal of Criminology*, 40, 222–38.
Braithwaite, J. (2002), *Restorative Justice and Responsive Regulation*, Oxford: Oxford University Press.
Braithwaite, J. (2004), 'Methods of power for development: weapons of the weak, weapons of the strong', *Michigan Journal of International Law*, 26 (Fall), 297–330.
Braithwaite, J. (2005), *Markets in Vice, Markets in Virtue*, Oxford: Oxford University Press.
Braithwaite, J. (2008), *Regulatory Capitalism: How It Works, Ideas for Making It Work Better*, Cheltenham, UK and Northampton, MA, USA: Edward Elgar Publishing.
Braithwaite J. and P. Drahos (2000), *Global Business Regulation*, Cambridge: Cambridge University Press.
Braithwaite, J., C. Coglianese and D. Levi-Faur (2007), 'Can regulation and governance make a difference?', *Regulation & Governance*, 1 (1), 1–7.
Breyer, S. (1993), *Breaking the Vicious Circle: Toward Effective Risk Regulation*, Cambridge, MA: Harvard University Press.
Coen, D. and M. Thatcher (2005), 'The new governance of markets and non-majoritarian regulators', *Governance*, 18, 329–46.
Coglianese, C. (2002), 'Empirical analysis and administrative law', *University of Illinois Law Journal*, 2002, 1111–37.
Coglianese, C. and D. Lazer (2003), 'Management-based regulation: prescribing private management to achieve public goals', *Law and Society Review*, 37, 691–730.
Croley, S. (2008), *Regulation and Public Interests: The Possibility of Good Regulatory Government*, Princeton, NJ: Princeton University Press.
Croley, S., J. Lasken and L. Magill (forthcoming), *What Agencies Do: The Fourth Branch in Operation*, Chicago: American Bar Association Press.
Dejlic, M.-L. and K. Sahlin-Andersson (eds) (2006), *Transnational Governance*, Cambridge: Cambridge University Press.
Dotan, Y. (1996), *Administrative Guidelines*, Jerusalem: Harry Sacher Institute for Legislative Research and Comparative Law, Hebrew University of Jerusalem.
Drezner, D. (2007), *All Politics Is Global: Explaining International Regulatory Regimes*, Princeton, NJ: Princeton University Press.
Eisner, M.A. (1993), *Regulatory Politics in Transition*, Baltimore, MD: Johns Hopkins University Press.
Fischer, E. (2007), *Risk Regulation and Administrative Constitutionalism*, Oxford: Hart Publishing.
Ganz, G. (1997), 'Delegated legislation: a necessary evil or a constitutional outrage?', in P. Leyland and T. Woods (eds), *Administrative Law Facing the Future: Old Constraints and New Horizons*, London: Blackstone Press.
Gilardi, F. (2005), 'The institutional foundations of regulatory capitalism: the diffusion of independent regulatory agencies in Western Europe', *Annals of the American Academy of Social and Political Sciences*, 598, 84–101.
Gilardi, F. (2008), *Delegation in the Regulatory State: Independent Regulatory Agencies in Western Europe*, Cheltenham, UK and Northampton, MA, USA: Edward Elgar Publishing.

Gilardi, Fabrizio, Jacint Jordana and D. Levi-Faur (2007), 'Regulation in the age of governance: the diffusion of regulatory agencies across Europe and Latin America', in A. Graeme Hodge (ed.), *Privatization and Market Development*, Cheltenham, UK and Northampton, MA, USA: Edward Elgar Publishing, pp. 127–47.

Grabosky, P. (1995), 'Using non-governmental resources to foster regulatory compliance', *Governance*, **8**, 527–50.

Gunningham, N. (2009), 'The new collaborative environmental governance: the localization of regulation', *Journal of Law and Society*, **36**, 145–66.

Gunningham, N. and P.N. Grabosky (1998), *Smart Regulation: Designing Environmental Policy*, Oxford: Clarendon.

Haber, H. (2011), 'Regulating-*for*-welfare: a comparative study of "regulatory welfare regimes" in the Israeli, British, and Swedish electricity sectors', *Law & Policy*, **33**, 116–48.

Hall, R.B. and T.J. Biersteker (eds) (2002), *The Emergence of Private Authority in the International System*, Cambridge: Cambridge University Press.

Hancher, Leigh and Michael Moran (eds) (1989), *Capitalism, Culture and Economic Regulation*, Oxford: Clarendon Press.

Haufler, V. (2002), *A Public Role for the Private Sector: Industry Self-Regulation in a Global Economy*, Washington, DC: Carnegie Endowment for International Peace.

Hewart, C.J. (1929), *The New Despotism*, London: Benn.

Hood, C. (2010), *The Blame Game: Spin, Bureaucracy and Self-Preservation in Government*, Princeton, NJ: Princeton University Press.

Hood, C., H. Rothstein and R. Baldwin (2001), *The Government of Risk: Understanding Risk Regulation Regime*, Oxford: Oxford University Press.

Hutter, B. (2001), *Regulation and Risk: Occupational Health and Safety on the Railways*, Oxford: Oxford University Press.

Jacobsson, K. (2004), 'Soft regulation and the subtle transformation of states: the case of EU employment policy', *Journal of European Social Policy*, **14**, 355–70.

Jänicke, M. (2008), 'Ecological modernisation: new perspectives', *Journal of Cleaner Production*, **16**, 557–65.

Jarrell, G.A. (1978), 'The demand for state regulation of the electric utility industry', *Journal of Law and Economics*, **21**, 269–96.

Jordana, J., D. Levi-Faur and X. Fernandez i Marin (2009), 'The global diffusion of regulatory agencies: institutional emulation and the restructuring of modern bureaucracy', Unpublished manuscript.

Kagan R.A. (1995), 'What socio-legal scholars should do when there is too much law to study', *Journal of Law and Society*, **22**, 140–48.

Kerwin, C. (1994; 2003), *Rulemaking: How Government Agencies Write Law and Make Policy*, Washington, DC: Congressional Quarterly Press.

Kraakman, R.H. (1986), 'Gatekeepers: the anatomy of a third party enforcement strategy', *Journal of Law, Economics and Organization*, **2**, 53–104.

Krasner, S.D. (1982), 'Structural causes and regime consequences: regimes as intervening variables', *International Organization*, **36**, 185–205.

Kunreuther, H.C., P.J. McNulty and Y. Kang (2002), 'Third-party inspection as an alternative to command and control regulation', *Risk Analysis*, **22** (2), 309–18.

Laffont, J.-J. (1994), 'The new economics of regulation ten years after', *Econometrica*, **62**, 507–37.

Levi-Faur, D. (1998), 'The competition state as a neomercantilist state: restructuring global telecommunications', *Journal of Socio-Economics*, **27**, 665–85.

Levi-Faur, D. (2005), 'The global diffusion of regulatory capitalism', *Annals of the American Academy of Political and Social Sciences*, **598**, 12–32.

Levi-Faur, D. (2008), 'Regulatory capitalism and the reassertion of the public interests', *Policy and Society*, **27** (3), 181–91.

Levi-Faur, D. (2011), 'Regulatory Capitalism and the Regulatory State', in David Levi-Faur (ed.), *Handbook on the Politics of Regulation*, Cheltenham: Edward Elgar.

Lipietz, A. (1987), *Mirages and Miracles: The Crises of Global Fordism*, trans. D. Macey, London: Verso.

Lobel, O. (2004), 'The renew deal: the fall of regulation and the rise of governance in contemporary legal thought', *Minnesota Law Review*, **89**, 342–70.

Lowi, T.J. (1964), 'American business, public policy, case studies, and political theory', *World Politics*, **16**, 677–715.

Mabbett, D. (2011), 'The Regulatory Rescue of the Welfare State?', in David Levi-Faur (ed.), *Handbook on the Politics of Regulation*, Cheltenham: Edward Elgar.

Maggetti, M. (2007), 'De facto independence after delegation: a fuzzy-set analysis', *Regulation & Governance*, **1**, 271–94.

Majone, G. (1994), 'The rise of the regulatory state in Europe', *West European Politics*, **17**, 77–101.

Majone, G. (1997), 'From the positive to the regulatory state', *Journal of Public Policy*, **17**, 139–67.
Majone, G. (1999), 'The regulatory state and its legitimacy problems', *West European Politics*, **22**, 1–24.
Marks, Gary and Lisbet Hooghe (2001), *Multi-Level Governance and European Integration*, New York: Rowman & Littlefield.
Mattli, W. and T. Büthe (2003), 'Setting international standards: technological rationality or primacy of power?', *World Politics*, **56**, 1–42.
May, J.P. (2007), 'Regulatory regimes and accountability', *Regulation & Governance*, **1**, 8–26.
May, J.P. (2010), 'Performance-Based Regulation', in David Levi-Faur (ed.) *Handbook of the Politics of Regulation*, Cheltenham: Edward Elgar.
McBarnet, D. and C. Whelan (1997), 'Creative compliance and the defeat of legal control: the magic of the orphan subsidiary', in K. Hawkins (ed.), *The Human Face of Law*, Oxford: Oxford University Press, pp. 177–98.
McCubbins, Mathew and Thomas Schwartz (1984), 'Congressional oversight overlooked: police patrols vs. fire alarms', *American Journal of Political Science*, **28**, 165–79.
McGarity, T.O. (1992), 'Some thoughts on "deossifying" the rulemaking process', *Duke Law Journal*, **41**, 1384–1462.
Mitnick, B. (1980), *The Political Economy of Regulation*, New York: Columbia University Press.
Moran, M. (2003), *The British Regulatory State: High Modernism and Hyper-Innovation*, Oxford: Oxford University Press.
Morgan, B. (2003), *Social Citizenship in the Shadow of Competition: The Bureaucratic Politics of Regulatory Justification*, Aldershot: Ashgate.
North, D. (1990), *Institutions, Institutional Change, and Economic Performance*, Cambridge: Cambridge University Press.
Page, E.C. (2001), *Governing by Numbers: Delegated Legislation and Everyday Policy-Making*, Oxford and Portland, OR: Hart Publishing.
Parker, C. (2002), *The Open Corporation: Effective Self-Regulation and Democracy*, New York: Cambridge University Press.
Parker, C. (2007), 'Meta-regulation: legal accountability for corporate social responsibility?', in Doreen McBarnet, Aurora Voiculescu and Tom Campbell (eds), *The New Corporate Accountability: Corporate Social Responsibility and the Law*, Cambridge: Cambridge University Press, 207–37.
Parker, C. and J. Braithwaite (2003), 'Regulation', in P. Cane and M. Tushnet (eds), *The Oxford Handbook of Legal Studies*, Oxford: Oxford University Press, pp. 119–45.
Porter, M. (1991), 'America's green strategy', *Scientific American*, **264** (4), 168.
Power, M. (1997), *The Audit Society: Rituals of Verification*, Oxford: Oxford University Press.
Priest, G. (1993), 'The origins of utility regulation and the "theories of regulation" debate', *Journal of Law and Economics*, **36**, 289–324.
Radaelli, C.M. and F. De Francesco (2007), *Regulatory Quality in Europe: Concepts, Measures, and Policy Processes*, Manchester: Manchester University Press.
Raz, J. (1979), 'The rule of law and its virtue', in *The Authority of Law: Essays on Law and Morality*, Oxford: Clarendon, pp. 210–29.
Ribstein, E.L. (2005), 'Sarbanes–Oxley after three years', *Illinois Law and Economics Working Papers Series*, No. LE05-016.
Ruhl, J.B. and J. Salzman (2003), 'Mozart and the Red Queen: the problem of regulatory accretion in the administrative state', *Georgetown Law Journal*, **91**, 757–850.
Schauer, F. (1992), *Playing by the Rules: A Philosophical Examination of Rule-Based Decision-Making in Law and in Life*, Oxford: Clarendon Press.
Scott, C. (2001), 'Analyzing regulatory space: fragmented resources and institutional design', *Public Law*, Summer, 283–305.
Scott, C. (2004), 'Regulation in the age of governance: the rise of the post-regulatory state', in J. Jordana and D. Levi-Faur (eds), *The Politics of Regulation in the Age of Governance*, Cheltenham, UK and Northampton, MA, USA: Edward Elgar Publishing, pp. 145–74.
Selznick, P. (1985), 'Focusing organizational research on regulation', in R. Noll (ed.), *Regulatory Policy and the Social Sciences*, Berkeley and Los Angeles: University of California Press, pp. 363–7.
Shamir, R. (2005), 'Mind the gap: the commodification of corporate social responsibility', *Symbolic Interaction*, **28** (2), 229–53.
Shamir, Ronen (2008), 'The age of responsibilization: on market-embedded morality', *Economy and Society*, **37** (1), 1–19.
Sharkansky, I. (1982), *The United States Revisited: A Study of a Still Developing Country*, New York: Longman.
Sinden, Amy, Douglas Kysar and David Driesen (2009), 'Cost–benefit analysis: new foundations on shifting sand', *Regulation & Governance*, **3** (2), 48–71.

Sørensen, Eva and Jacob Torfing (2008), *Theories of Democratic Network Governance*, Basingstoke: Palgrave Macmillan.

Sparrow, M.K. (2000), *The Regulatory Craft: Controlling Risks, Solving Problems and Managing Compliance*, Washington, DC: Brookings Institution Press.

Stigler, G.J. (1971), 'The theory of economic regulation', *Bell Journal of Economics and Management Science*, **2**, 3–21.

Sunstein, C.R. (2002), *The Cost–Benefit State: The Future of Regulatory Protection*, Chicago: American Bar Association.

Taggart, M. (2005), 'From "parliamentary powers" to privatization: the chequered history of delegated legislation in the twentieth century', *University of Toronto Law Journal*, **55**, 575–627.

Thatcher, Mark and David Coen (2008), 'Reshaping European regulatory space: an evolutionary analysis', *West European Politics*, **31** (4), 806–36.

Trubek, D. and L.G. Trubek (2005), 'Hard and soft law in the construction of social Europe: the role of the open method of co-ordination', *European Law Journal*, **11**, 343–64.

Vogel, S.K. (1996), *Freer Markets, More Rules: Regulatory Reform in Advanced Industrial Countries*, Ithaca, NY and London: Cornell University Press.

Wilson, J.Q. (1980), *The Politics of Regulation*, New York: Basic Books.

Yackee, J. and S. Yackee (2010), 'Administrative procedures and bureaucratic performance: is federal rule-making "ossified"?', *Journal of Public Administration Research and Theory*, **20** (2), 261–82.

Zedner, L. (2006), 'Liquid security: managing the market for crime control', *Criminology and Criminal Justice*, **6**, 267–88.

# PART II

# THEORIES OF REGULATION FOR THE AGE OF GOVERNANCE

# 2 Bootleggers and Baptists in the theory of regulation

*Bruce Yandle*

The bootlegger and Baptist theory of regulation (B&B) was born in 1983 when I was Executive Director of the U.S. Federal Trade Commission (FTC) (Yandle 1983). Along with other duties, I was responsible for the agency's Consumer Advocacy Program, an activity where the FTC intervened in the regulatory proceedings of other federal agencies in an effort to maintain and enhance the competitiveness of the U.S. economy. The agency's intervention activities revealed a number of instances where seemingly odd interest-group alliances supported the same regulation. This was not the first time I had observed the odd-alliance phenomenon.

The idea that demand for the same regulation could come from two distinctly different interest groups, one that seemed to take moral high ground and another that simply wanted economic rents, had come to me in 1977 when I was a senior economist on the staff of the President's Council on Wage and Price Stability. I was responsible for reviewing and commenting on new regulation proposed by the U.S. Environmental Protection Agency (EPA), the Federal Trade Commission, and the National Highway Traffic Safety Administration. When I reviewed those rules, it became obvious that industry opposition to regulation was far from being monolithic. Almost invariably, there were firms or industry sectors that gained from regulation. For example, in EPA's proposed rules regulating copper smelter emissions, the agency indicated there would never be another U.S. copper smelter once the rules became final. The rules, which set more stringent standards on new smelters than existing ones, were supported by major environmental groups. Later work on the copper smelter episode by Maloney and McCormick (1982) showed that copper producer shareholders earned abnormal positive returns when the smelter rule became final. The major environmental groups celebrated too. The results suggested that both polluters and environmentalists could gain from properly crafted regulation.[1] In my work on the first U.S. auto fuel economy rules, which were supported by environmental groups, I found that General Motors was lobbying for stricter standards while other major auto companies warned of the dire consequences associated with the pending rules. (It turned out that General Motors had led the industry in downsizing its fleet of cars.) I found similar odd alliances in my review of the development of the nation's first water pollution control statutes.

The B&B theory gets its name, of course, from a common phenomenon in the United States in regions that restrict the sale of alcoholic beverages on Sunday. Baptists lobby for the associated regulations; they prefer a world where less alcohol is consumed. Bootleggers, the illegal sellers of alcoholic beverages, support the laws as well. Sunday closing laws shut down legitimate sellers, giving an open field in which bootleggers can sell their wares.

U.S. clean air and clean water statutes had a common characteristic that made them ripe for bootlegger/Baptist cartelization activities. There were stricter standards for new

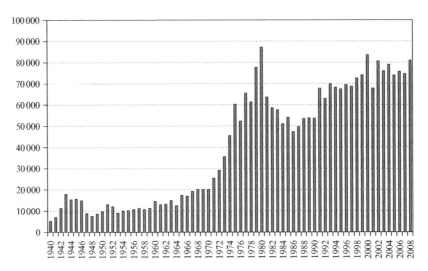

*Figure 2.1*   Federal register *pages, 1940–2008*

sources than for existing sources. Apparently, the existing U.S. copper smelters saw the new rules as a way to cartelize their industry. With rising demand, prices would go up; and, with restricted entry based on meeting stringent standards, profits for industry members would increase. EPA and the environmental groups would happily be the cartel enforcement agents.

My B&B theory was a small part of a growing literature on regulation theory. Efforts by economists and other social scientists to explain the frequency and features of government regulation had moved in lock-step with the rise of regulation in the United States during the 1970s and 1980s. Those two decades saw a dramatic increase in both the number of federal regulatory agencies and the pace at which the new agencies produced regulation. One measure of this activity is seen in Figure 2.1, which reports the annual count of new pages in the *Federal Register*, a daily government publication in which new and revised regulations are published. As shown there, regulation contagion as measured by the *Federal Register* page count emerged around 1970 and peaked in 1981. Of course, one may argue that new and revised regulations are necessary inputs for producing GDP, in which case there would be more pages with more production. Figure 2.2 shows the number of pages per billion dollars of real GDP. Here, we see that a mountain of regulation pages was formed in the 1970s and 1980s.

It was during the 1970s that major new social regulatory agencies were formed. These include the U.S. Environmental Protection Agency, the Consumer Products Safety Commission, the Occupational Safety and Health Administration, and the National Highway Safety Administration. They joined older economic regulatory agencies, such as the Securities and Exchange Commission, the Interstate Commerce Commission (ICC), and the Federal Communications Commission. The new agencies were required by statutes to provide regulatory protection for the environment and for workers in the factories, mines, and other workplaces, to improve conditions that affected occupational health, and to make autos and consumer products safer. As opposed to regulating prices,

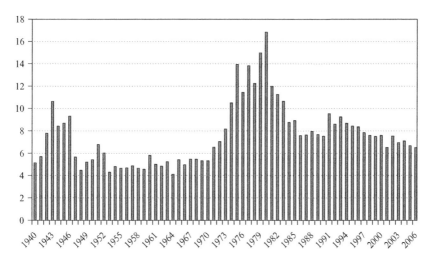

*Figure 2.2* Federal register *pages per billion dollars of real GDP, 1940–2008*

entry, and fitness, the new agencies specified how things would be produced and marketed. The United States, which previously had been primarily regulated by diverse state common law, city ordinances, state statutes, and regional compacts became a code law country for a large category of economic activities.

But, while social regulation was experiencing explosive growth, old-time economic regulation was in a sharp state of decline. Mancur Olson (1984: 249) called attention to this and noted that:

> One striking example has, wondrously, attracted very little journalistic attention. The Carter Administration and its immediate predecessors made great strides in deregulating many industries, such as trucking, airlines, railroads, securities markets, and banking. This deregulation greatly increased the scope of free markets. It would take us far afield to go into the unfolding empirical evidence about the consequences of this deregulation here, but the preliminary indications are that it has greatly increased the efficiency of the American economy. Most strikingly in the area of trucking, the Reagan administration (at least up to the point when this essay is written) has practically stopped this deregulation.

Pages of rules were being printed for the new social regulatory agencies, such as the EPA, but pages of old rules were being removed for the older economic regulators, such as the Interstate Commerce Commission.

My explanation of the timing of the rise of social regulation and decline of economic regulation turns on the emergence of national network TV; this provided for the first time a low-cost way for producers of consumer goods and services to market at low cost to a national market (Yandle 2010a). The rapid rise of national markets for consumer goods at the margin made state and local regulation obsolete. Firms operating in the new national market lobbied for federal laws and regulations. They also lobbied for the elimination of regulations that affected their ability to communicate and ship within the national market. Explaining why there were so many new rules in the decade of the 1970s and 1980s does not explain the lobbying effort for certain common features found in the new regulations that emerged.

Why was command-and-control, technology-based regulation the dominant form of regulation preferred by the new social regulators? Why not economic incentives, taxes, and market processes? Why did most social regulation require less stringent rules of existing firms than for new ones? Why were environmental regulations generally more rigorous for newly developing regions than for older regions? Other theories of regulation cannot answer these questions. But B&B theory helps to answer these questions. So where does B&B fit in the panoply of regulation theories?

## 2.1   THEORIES OF REGULATION

Five theories offer potential explanatory frameworks to use when considering features of regulation: public interest, capture, special interest, money for nothing, and bootleggers and Baptists. The public interest theory is the first and oldest theory of regulation and is not associated with one particular scholar. This theory holds that politicians and their appointees systematically seek to serve a broad public interest, always searching for lower-cost ways to provide public benefits rather than advance the interests of particular groups at the expense of the public generally. If carbon emissions, other pollution, unhealthy working conditions, or teenage smoking is the problem to be addressed, then the legislature seeks to minimize global costs in reducing the cost that pollution, hazardous working conditions, or smoking imposes on the population at large. If the cost of regulating is larger than the cost imposed by harmful activities, no action is taken. Of course, the public interest theory recognizes that politicians are human and, as a result, errors and even deliberate acts of chicanery will occur, but these failings are the exception, not the rule.

Dissatisfaction with the ability of the public interest theory to predict outcomes led to the development of the capture theory, a notion associated with the work of political scientist Marver Bernstein (1955) and economic historian Gabriel Kolko (1963). Capture theory recognizes that politicians and regulators face agency costs and the knowledge problem: There is no clear-cut definition of what might be the public interest for each bill being considered in a legislative session or for each rule a regulator must devise. To help remedy the situation, the dedicated legislator and regulator find an ample supply of advisors who happily recommend how best to vote or act on particular issues. The reason that so much advice is forthcoming rests on a notion that economists call "rent-seeking" behavior (Buchanan et al. 1980). By choosing one regulatory approach versus another, a politician can transfer vast amounts of resources from taxpayers or consumers to the providers of politically favored services.

To illustrate, consider reducing automobile exhaust emissions. How might a regulator make this happen? One approach requires automobile producers to meet a performance standard without specifying how the standard is to be met. Under this approach, which requires monitoring air quality and auto emissions, environmental outcomes matter more than specification of inputs. Placing taxes on emission-generating fuels or on the emissions themselves is another approach. Again, air quality can be monitored and taxes raised or lowered to achieve environmental goals. Finally, the regulator can specify how emissions will be controlled and require all auto producers to follow the same technology-based rules. If one firm is already using the specified technology or has an advantage in building it, then there is no cost imposed on that firm. Instead, the regulation raises rivals' costs (Shalop and Sheffman 1983). Ultimately, the U.S. EPA specified that all automobiles must have catalytic converters to reduce emissions, even if a particular automobile had little emissions. The converters relied on a technology developed by General Motors and brought profits to the patent owner. As air quality improved, GM made more money, and clean air lovers celebrated.

Capture theory may also explain how the railroads won the day when Congress empowered the Interstate Commerce Commission to regulate motor carriers in the Motor Carrier Act of 1935 (49 Stat. 543 (1935)). This occurred after motor carriers began cutting prices for carrying freight and in spite of organized opposition from agricultural and other shipper interests (Felton and Anderson 1989: 10). The rail interests were successful in forcing ICC controls on truckers.

But, while capture theory seems to explain a good bit of regulation, it does not predict which party will capture when more than one is in the struggle, as is generally the case. For that, we must turn to the next theory of regulation. The special interest or economic theory of regulation was developed by the late Nobel laureate George Stigler (1971) and his colleague Sam Peltzman (1976). Stigler suggested that one can make considerable progress in predicting which of several parties will prevail in a political struggle by imagining that the specific content of proposed legislation is simply auctioned off to the highest bidder. By focusing on which parties have the most to lose (or gain) in the struggle, one can begin to understand outcomes. But this is just a first step in the process. In order to be a viable participant in the auction, the agent doing the bidding must know the consensus position of the group it represents. It is costly to organize an interest group, and the larger and more diverse the players the greater the cost. Once organized, a consensus must be found regarding the policy outcome. And that is costly too.

Capture theory can be employed to explain how Eastern high-sulfur coal interests captured key members of Congress when the 1977 Clean Air Amendments were being developed (Ackerman and Hassler 1981). These amendments required the use of scrubbers for removing sulfur oxides from stacks even when cleaner low-sulfur coal from the Western United States might have been used without scrubbers to accomplish the same end. Coal in the Eastern United States was produced by organized labor, represented by the United Mine Workers (UMW) union, while cleaner Western coal was produced by nonunion workers.

Suppose the scrubber case had simply involved pitting Western against Eastern coal producers. The Eastern producers were located in relatively populous states and had been organized and working the halls of Congress for decades. They had more congressmen to confront and more supporting interest groups that wanted to keep local economies humming. The producers were not strictly homogeneous, as some produced metallurgical-grade coal and some were diversified across industries, but the industry was dominated by a small number of large producers. Eastern coal workers had also been organized for decades. When speaking to politicians, the voice of the United Mine Workers came through loud and clear.

Now consider the Western producers. These were comparatively younger firms with unorganized workers located in remote corners of less populous states. They had fewer congressional supporters and less support from local economies that might be disrupted. While the bulk of the market for Western coal was in the East, most consumers and voters were rationally ignorant about where their coal came from. Pushed to pick which region mattered most, concentrated Eastern interests with a lot to lose outweighed scattered Western interests that had yet to enjoy the fruits of an expanded market for their coal. Using this scorecard it is easy to predict Eastern interests would carry the day.

Northwestern Law School professor Fred S. McChesney (1991) developed the fourth theory of regulation to consider. Instead of focusing on political favors that may be provided by politicians, McChesney developed a theory of political wealth extraction; it is damage control with a twist. Consider a group of businesses that have not yet been subject to regulation. The businesses are not organized politically, have no trade association, and provide little in the way of campaign contributions to politicians. In a sense, there is little a politician can do to benefit or harm an unregulated industry. To get the industry's attention, a politician announces that hearings will be held on the possibilities of calling for consumer protection regulation of the industry's main product or services. Several bills are drafted and some have rather draconian proposed rules. Hoping to deflect these pending costs, the industry organizes, hires lobbyists, and makes prudent campaign contributions to strategically important politicians. The politicians relax the threat somewhat, but leave a few clouds in the sky. Regulation has been avoided, but wealth has been extracted.

Finally, as noted earlier, B&B explains how successful lobbying efforts and durable regulation emerge when one interest group, labeled the Baptists, takes the moral high ground while another group, the bootleggers, use the Baptists for cover as they pursue a narrow economic end. For the theory to work, both parties must seek the same end result, and it is clearly not necessary for the two interest groups to communicate or even show up at the same meetings.

The B&B theory combines elements of public interest and special interest theories of regulation and sheds considerable light on a large number of regulatory episodes. Consider for example America's grand experiment with Prohibition, which was finally passed into law in December 1917 after a long struggle by members of temperance leagues nationwide (Boudreaux and Pritchard 1994). Prohibition hindered the production, distribution, sale, and consumption of alcoholic beverages. But two groups had reason to celebrate. Of course, those who favored Prohibition had good reason to cheer. They saw victory, especially when hundreds of breweries and scores of distilleries in cities nationwide were dismantled. What about the bootleggers? They had cause for celebration too. Indeed, according to data on alcohol consumption, average intake actually increased during Prohibition, but not from the same kinds of beverages (Gifford 1977: 66). Beer consumption fell dramatically. The consumption of spirits rose just as dramatically. The cost of monitoring movement of beer barrels was much lower than the cost of tracking equivalent amounts of alcohol in bottles of Scotch and moonshine. And of course, if getting a given volume of alcohol was risky and therefore costly, it made sense to get it in more powerful forms.

There is another bootlegger lurking in the Prohibition story. Until 1916, the federal government received the majority of its revenues from taxes on alcoholic beverages. After entering World War I, the federal government needed more revenue, and an income tax was imposed. The war experience taught the federal government about this reliable revenue source. Prohibition became affordable, and the politicians took the moral high ground. But then something terrible occurred to the reliability of the income tax. The Great Depression arrived and, with it, income tax revenues plummeted. With a government to run and shrinking income tax revenues, the politicians ended the grand experiment with Prohibition in February 1933. Meanwhile, the alcohol industry had been permanently restructured by the good cause, and spirits had become the drink of choice.

## 2.2  WHAT REGULATION DELIVERS

Regulations developed to address a perceived problem always generate benefits for some group and impose costs as well. Sometimes, as in the Prohibition story, the costs and benefits are best seen in relative terms. Generally speaking, regulation is applied uniformly across firms and markets; there is a one-suit-fits-all outcome. But most of the time there are substantial differences in technologies, products, and marketing practices across firms in an industry. Some players in an industry, or some consumers, gain a relative advantage. For example, Prohibition imposed higher costs on the beer industry and beer consumers than on the distilleries and consumers of spirits, and regulation redefined the contours of the industries and markets that were subject to the rules.

Firms are generally quick to recognize the gains that can be secured through regulation. Indeed, success in gaining just the right rules that raise rivals' costs may lead to higher profits than working to increase market share. In 2000, for example, John Deere, with the aid of environmental pressure groups, petitioned the U.S. Environmental Protection Agency to tighten the emission standards on small gasoline engine-driven landscape appliances (Skrzyeki 2000: C1). It so happens that the firm holds patents on a new cleaner engine technology. Deere can easily meet the stricter standards; its competitors cannot. Another interesting coalition emerged when major energy producers joined hands with environmental groups to support the Kyoto Protocol and proposed cap-and-trade legislation for reducing carbon emissions (Yandle, 1999, 2010b; Yandle and Buck 2002).

A somewhat similar situation developed in 2005 when the U.S. Department of Transportation announced new fuel-economy standards for large trucks and SUVs that had been popular with U.S. consumers (Meckler and Lundegaard 2005: B1). (This was prior to the run-up in gasoline prices.) The newly proposed rules allowed vehicle producers to hit an average fuel economy within truck segments, as opposed to achieving an average economy outcome across all vehicles sold. Under the former system, General Motors and Ford, for example, had to sell cheaply some of their less popular, high-fuel-economy vehicles to offset the sales of their more popular, low-fuel-economy SUVs. The differential effects contained in the new rules improved the outlook for General Motors and Ford while taking away an advantage enjoyed by their rival the Toyota Motor Company. (On fuel economy and B&B also see Yandle (2009a).)

Similarly, Senator Charles Schumer (Democrat, New York) assisted one U.S. tobacco company, Phillip Morris, in its drive to have the Food and Drug Administration regulate all tobacco companies (Carney 2006). Phillip Morris, with half of the U.S. market, wanted the FDA to regulate marketing, advertising, and entry of new cigarette companies (Yandle 2009c). In an earlier 2003 effort, Phillip Morris pushed for FDA regulation in an effort to gain federal regulation of health claims for safe cigarettes (Kaufman

2003: A3). Like Deere in its effort to gain a regulatory advantage over its competitors by calling for stricter emission standards, Phillip Morris sought to raise competitors' costs in making health claims. Not surprisingly, it turns out that Schumer was the top recipient of tobacco money of all senators seeking election in 2004.

One should not conclude that B&B theory applies only to the United States or to the modern age (Yandle and Buck 2002; Yandle 2009b, 2010b). Howard Marvel's (1977) analysis of the 18th-century English Factory Acts indicates that the law restricting the use of child labor was supported by the owners of the new water-powered mills. Those same owners were celebrated as enlightened reform social leaders. Even the 1225 Magna Carta contains a specification standard for the width of all woven cloth sold in the realm. The stipulation addressed a consumer protection problem, we are told, as it also happened to fit the looms of the London weavers, who supported the rule, but not those in Norwich (Yandle 1984).

## 2.3  FINAL THOUGHTS

Lessons to be learned from theories of regulation cause us to consider economic logic when seeking to understand regulation and how the rules get formed. The theories say that politicians are like brokers who seek to balance competing demands for valuable political favors. But, for the brokers to survive, the balancing act must generate benefits to interest groups that are appropriately situated. The bootlegger/Baptist theory emphasizes that greater political demand emerges when public interest groups add demand to that of those who seek strictly private interests. The theory helps us to understand the particular features of regulation and how those features may change when "bootleggers" or "Baptists" choose to disappear from the invisible alliance that supported demand for regulation.

## ACKNOWLEDGEMENTS

Sections of this essay are taken from Morriss et al. (2009).

## NOTE

1.  This was the key insight developed by James Buchanan and Gordon Tullock in their seminal piece "Polluters' 'Profit' and Political Response" (1975).

## REFERENCES

Ackerman, Bruce A. and William T. Hassler (1981), *Clean Coal/Dirty Air, or How the Clean Air Act Became a Multibillion-Dollar Bail-Out for High-Sulfur Coal Producers and What Should Be Done about It*, New Haven, CT: Yale University Press.
Bernstein, Marver (1955), *Regulating Business by Independent Commission*, Princeton, NJ: Princeton University Press.

Boudreaux, Donald J. and A.C. Pritchard (1994), 'The price of Prohibition', *Arizona Law Review*, **36**, 1–10.
Buchanan, James M. and Gordon Tullock (1975), 'Polluters' "profit" and political response', *American Economic Review*, **65**, 130–47.
Buchanan, James M., Gordon Tullock and Robert D. Tollison (1980), *Toward a Theory of the Rent-Seeking Society*, Bryan: Texas A&M Press.
Carney, Timothy (2006), 'Schumer's way', *New York Sun*, 19 May.
Felton, John R. and Dale G. Anderson (1989), *Regulation and Deregulation of the Motor Carrier Industry*, Ames: Iowa State University Press.
Gifford, Adams (1997), 'Whiskey, margarine, and newspapers: a tale of three taxes', in William F. Shughart II (ed.), *Taxing Choice*, New Brunswick, NJ: Transaction Press, pp. 55–77.
Kaufman, Marc (2003), 'FDA may receive tobacco authority', *Washington Post*, 3 June, A3.
Kolko, Gabriel (1963), *The Triumph of Conservatism: A Reinterpretation of American History, 1900–1916*, New York: Free Press.
Maloney, M.T. and Robert E. McCormick (1982), 'A positive theory of environmental quality regulation', *Journal of Law & Economics*, **25**, April, 99–124.
Marvel, Howard P. (1977), 'Factory regulation: a new interpretation of early English experiences', *Journal of Law & Economics*, **20**, October, 379–402.
McChesney, Fred S. (1991), 'Rent extraction and interest-group organization in a Coasean model of regulation', *Journal of Legal Studies*, **20**, 73–90.
Meckler, Laura and Karen Lundegaard (2005), 'New fuel-economy rules help the biggest truck makers', *Wall Street Journal*, 24 August, B1.
Morriss, Andrew P., Bruce Yandle and Andrew Dorchak (2009), *Regulation by Litigation*, New Haven, CT: Yale University Press.
Olson, Mancur (1984), 'Ideology and economic growth', in Charles R. Hulten and Isabel V. Sawhill (eds), *The Legacy of Reaganomics*, Washington, DC: Urban Institute Press, pp. 229–51.
Peltzman, Sam (1976), 'Toward a more general theory of regulation', *Journal of Law & Economics*, **19** (2), 211–40.
Shalop, Steven C. and David T. Sheffman (1983), 'Raising rivals' costs', *American Economic Review*, **2** (73), 267–71.
Skrzyeki, Cindy (2000), 'Whose vroom has less fume?', *Washington Post*, 28 January, C1.
Stigler, George J. (1971), 'The economic theory of regulation', *Bell Journal of Economics & Management Science*, **2**, 3–21.
Yandle, Bruce (1983), 'Bootleggers and Baptists: the education of a regulatory economist', *Regulation*, May/June, 12–16.
Yandle, Bruce (1984), 'Intertwined interests, rentseeking, and regulation', *Social Science Quarterly*, **4** (65), 1004–12.
Yandle, Bruce (1999), 'After Kyoto: a global scramble for advantage', *Independent Review*, **1** (6), 19–40.
Yandle, Bruce (2009a), 'America's new fuel economy cartel and freedom to choose', *Regulation*, **3** (32), 6–9.
Yandle, Bruce (2009b), 'Bootleggers, Baptists, and bailed out bankers', *Freeman*, **2** (59), March, available at: http://www/threefreemanonline.org/featured/bootleggers-baptists-and-bailed-out-bankers/ (accessed 5 October 2009).
Yandle, Bruce (2009c), 'The myth of unregulated tobacco', *Freeman*, **3** (59), September, available at: http://www.thefreemanonline.org/featured/the-myth-of-unregulated-tobacco (accessed 16 October 2009).
Yandle, Bruce (2010a), 'National TV broadcasting and the rise and decline of the regulatory state', *Public Choice*, **142** (3–4), 339–53.
Yandle, Bruce (2010b), 'We want to be regulated', *Freeman*, **60** (1), 37–8.
Yandle, Bruce and Stuart Buck (2002), 'Bootleggers, Baptists, and the global warming battle', *Harvard Environmental Law Journal*, **1** (26), 177–229.

# 3 Capturing "capture": definition and mechanisms
*Barry M. Mitnick*

It has been at least since Horace Gray (1940) and Merle Fainsod (1940) that scholars have warned that government regulation tended to serve the interests of regulated parties over more general public interests. Even though modern conceptions of the regulatory state are diverse and evolving (e.g., Jordana and Levi-Faur 2004), the uses of the state by private interests remain prominent features of regulation. A variety of political and bureaucratic processes have been said to be at the root of such outcomes. Huntington (1952) famously characterized the condition of the US Interstate Commerce Commission (ICC) as a "marasmus" in which the railroad industry successfully concentrated and defended regulatory functions within an independent agency strongly supported and influenced by that industry (cf. Kolko 1965 on the early years of the ICC and the critical historiographical literature it generated). Bernstein's (1955) "life cycle" model similarly focused on agency changes that occurred in the evolution of industry support for and defense of its regulation.

The label "capture" has frequently been applied to such situations. A significant problem with the use of the term rests in its casual and sometimes conflicting uses. For example, "capture" has been said to be present, variously, when "regulatory agencies [are] captives of the industries they are supposed to regulate" (Gormley 1982); when regulators identify with the agency or become sympathetic with the agency's problems or become lenient in enforcement (Makkai and Braithwaite 1992); when "regulated groups were able to control or 'capture' the agencies which regulate them" (Berry 1984); when "regulated businesses can take advantage of economic regulation" (Marcus 1984: 73); "when organized interest groups secure regulation that advances their economic interests at the greater expense of citizens generally" (Croley 2011); or when "a single strong firm or industry group gets supportive regulation" (Teske 2004: 37). So does capture involve identification, leniency, sympathy, taking advantage, advancing an economic interest at the expense of the public interest, control, supportive regulation, or whatever "captivity" means? And these are only a few of a host of examples in what has developed as a decades-old literature.

The purpose of this chapter is to analyze the concept of capture and the behavioral and organizational circumstances associated with it. After defining "capture," the chapter sorts the factors discussed by the literature as promoting capture into 12 mechanisms, sorted into six logical groups. Such a categorization potentially permits us to create a normative *theory of fiducial regulation:* If we understand how capture is produced, we may be able to generate a systematic set of design principles that would permit regulatory systems to avoid capture (for one attempt, see Mitnick 2011a, 2011b).

## 3.1   WHAT IS "CAPTURE"?

The largely colloquial term "capture" has served as an imprecise and encompassing label for a wide variety of causal factors, facilitating conditions and contexts, behavior patterns, and outcomes or impacts. The basic defining specification of capture is that it refers to cases in which a regulated industry is able to control *decisions* made about that industry by regulators and/or *performances* by regulators related to the industry. In other words, the industry "captures" regulatory decision making and/or performance so that what regulators decide and/or perform is what industry prefers they decide and/or perform. In short, industry is able to use regulation to steer benefits to itself over other potential targets of those benefits.

Government can provide many such benefits to the private sector, including contracts for services and products, favorable tariffs, forbearance of antitrust prosecutions, tolerance of monopoly or oligopoly, subsidies, favorable tax laws, generous decisions on allocations of public resources, adoption of rules that favor a company or industry over competitors, and so on. These benefits may come as a result of winning a policy battle with competing interests, or may become a permanent benefit locked into place by law and defended aggressively by public agents. Capture, however, reflects a condition that goes beyond incidental influences, victory in particular policy contests, or even substantial and directly profitable public actions.

The concept of "capture" in all its contexts usually requires three defining elements in addition to private control over an area of public decision making and/or performance in order to be recognized as capture: (1) essentiality and/or generality of the benefit, (2) stability or persistence of provision of the benefit, and (3) the public provision of defensive measures or actions that entrench the benefits against actual or potential challenges; such defenses can include the employment of institutional structures or processes that steeply increase the costs of detecting and/or intervening to oppose provision of those sequestered benefits.

In the first condition, capture is not usually appended to situations in which marginal benefits are gained, even if completely dominated by industry. A public utility that pretty much tells the state public utility commission how it will service outages has not captured the commission; the commission may still be negotiating the utility's proposed rate increases. Moreover, the ability to influence public sector decisions and/or performances in one's behalf is not the same as the capture of those decisions and/or performances. Capture presupposes *control* of a wide or general range of valuable, even mission-critical, decision and/or performance contexts; it is a *plenary* condition.

Second, capture is relational and stable. In effect, the benefited party has been absorbed as a participating member of the governance system. The behavior of that system will be seen as predictable, and other parts of the government will want it to be predictable in order to provide predictable interactions on which they can depend in doing their own work. The set of actors that determine how marketing orders for oranges stabilize prices and protect growers and juicers is well known. In addition, the investment necessary to gain capture and maintain capture can be so significant that it will not pay private parties to expend it for time-limited gains.

Finally, it is critical that capture is a term definitionally applied to a relationship with the public sector; except in quasi-public cases, such as private, professional licensing boards established formally as public agents, capture is always of public not private organizations. The key feature, indeed one of its traditional characters, is that the public sector has a monopoly of force. The public sector is so attractive a target not only because it has the deep pockets of revenue and the easy rationales of expenditure of that revenue on what may be claimed are public purposes. But it is also especially attractive because the revenue that is extracted by mandate and the decisions to allocate the revenue or make laws or regulations that apply favorably to actors in the private sector are defended by that monopoly of force. Government is a good partner to capture because it is likely to be able to both fulfill its promises and overwhelm any challenger. Hence capture will always use the powers of the public sector to defend the relationship and/or the continued receipt of the benefit by the favored actor. The defenses can be as simple as constructing what is functionally a levee in the form of the complexity and costs of monitoring for such channeled benefits, and the costs of challenging their provision via the formal administrative process (cf. Mitnick 1981/1993; Levine 1998).

Even if an industry controls regulatory decisions, it may not be able to completely control the behavior of the bureaucratic regulators who implement the decisions and who interface with the industry and to control all contexts of regulatory delivery. This is a common observation in the literature on public policy implementation (e.g., the classic work of Pressman and Wildavsky 1973 [1984]; see also, e.g., Mazmanian and Sabatier 1983). On the other hand, decisions by agency leadership may be little more than symbolic if lower-level regulatory implementation is controlled or systematically influenced by the industry (cf. the situation of state vs. federal strip mining inspectors in some states in the 1980s; Mitnick 1982). Thus control of decisions and control of performances are empirically distinct phenomena, and capture may apply to one or both of them.

Complicating the analysis is the fact that regulatory performances do not always produce the outcomes intended by the regulators or by others who control those performances. It follows that an industry that seems to capture regulatory decisions and/ or regulatory performances may not always achieve the protective benefits that such control should provide. As already noted, implementation issues can intervene and produce effects not intended by any of the participants. Thus one cannot reason backward from impacts to capture, i.e., one cannot confidently infer that "capture" was or was not sought and produced on the sole basis of the impacts of regulation.

Finally, even when industry is able to fully control both regulatory decisions and/or performances and achieve the outcomes intended by such control, there may be no necessary conflict with the public ends espoused by the regulation; public and private interests can conflict, coincide, or overlap (for a discussion, see Ayres and Braithwaite 1992; for a discussion of public interest theory in regulation with comparison to other approaches, see Kalt and Zupan 1984; Levine and Forrence 1990; Christensen 2011). Indeed, the appearances of capture may be unacceptable even when its actual outcomes are not controversial (cf. Mitnick 1975).

## 3.2   CAPTURE MECHANISMS

Capture is not a one-dimensional concept; one cannot simply argue, for example, that the basic mechanism is public corruption. Capture should be understood as a complex set of behavior patterns and relationships that can be produced in many ways, often acting in concert with one another. I have sorted the commonly described contexts of capture – what I will call *capture mechanisms* – into six categories: constitutional, systemic, relational (governance), individual, functional, and chronical. The logic of this sorting is that it goes across levels: from the system level to behavior in the system, to the relationships between actors in the system, to the individuals and roles in those relationships, to the actions conducted in those relationships (e.g., regulation), to factors relating to time and path across all levels. Thus, it covers categories related to the rules of the system (constitutional); behavior in the system of regulation (system); the nature of relationships between regulatory actors, both external and internal to the regulator, especially those that direct or structure behaviors, i.e., relating to governance in the relationship (relational); factors relating to individuals acting in those relationships, i.e., in regulatory roles and bureaucracies (individual); factors relating to the functioning of the regulation itself, such as information flows and regulator competency (functional); and factors related to time and path, such as path dependence (chronical). Twelve mechanisms sort into these categories (on the mechanisms of capture and their discussion, this chapter draws from Mitnick 2011a, 2011b). It is likely that additional mechanisms may be described and later added.

The literature has so far not only lacked a consistent definition of what is and what is not capture, but also generated a confusing mix of mechanisms said to facilitate capture. In order to identify the 12 capture mechanisms, I have sorted a number of the important approaches to treating capture, generalizing their key aspects. If we are to develop a robust descriptive theory of capture (or a normative theory of avoidance of capture, i.e., a theory that relates certain design principles to outcomes that avoid capture), it is essential to not only recognize such alternative paths to capture, but categorize them.

I have deliberately excluded or simplified models that do not provide descriptive theory; positive approaches that incorporate extreme simplification (e.g., assuming that all regulators are elected) can sometimes find interesting empirical support, but are markedly less valuable in trying to design actual policy solutions.

Although it is the interaction of these processes that produces the many manifestations of capture, for the sake of beginning a process of systematic theory-building, we will approach each mechanism as *ceteris paribus*.

### 3.2.1 Constitutional

**Constitutional system biases**
Systematic biases, producing stable protections, i.e., capture, can result when the formal system rules – the constitutional rules, whether established by a formal constitution or via legislative action – have the effect of conferring comparative benefits on some over other actors. In effect, using the common metaphor of a playing field, the rules in place cause the field of competition to be tilted in a way that gives an advantage to one side and/or disadvantages the other. This effect is the counterpart to imbalanced affective access politics (see below), in which one or more groups have enhanced power, yet all groups seek access via the same level constitutional field.

Baron (1997) describes Fujifilm's dominance over Kodak in the Japanese market as resulting from a combination of control over market mechanisms, such as the distribution network for film, and protective treatment of Fujifilm in regulatory contexts – to use the metaphor, the playing field was tilted against Kodak in Japan. When the market is structured by government actions so that some actors retain benefits that exceed the actors' opportunities elsewhere, there exists what Baron (1995) calls a "rent chain."

The stream of research on state capture makes repeated, sometimes explicit references to the capture of the "rules of the game" (see, e.g., Kaufmann 2004: 83). Hellman and Kaufmann (2001, p. 2 of ms.) note that

> state capture refers to corrupt efforts to influence how those laws, rules, and regulations are *formed*. Bribes . . . are the classic examples of grand corruption through which firms can encode advantages for themselves into the basic legal and regulatory structure of the economy.

Thus a characteristic feature of "state capture" is creation of what I have termed constitutional bias.

### 3.2.2   Systemic

#### Imbalanced affective access politics
Classic works by Fainsod (1940), Gray (1940), and McConnell (1966) discussed how biased groups – "parties-in-interest" – gained power, operating as "pressure groups" that sought to control the "access points" to government and shape policy. Questions of who has power and how to limit power often dominated discussions (on power and corporations, see Epstein 1969). Group theorists such as Bentley and Truman understood politics in terms of a process populated by groups rather than in terms of formal institutions.

Later works questioned whether any groups could really sustain such dominance. The pluralist school (e.g., Dahl 1961) argued that groups were functionally small circles of active elites. Because of elections, the elites circulated instead of dominated, so state power would not be systematically biased.

But the issues of concern to some interests never reached the agenda for government action (e.g., Bachrach and Baratz 1970; for a clear exegesis of these arguments, see Cobb and Elder 1972). Democracy in practice was a myth that provided cover for control by a small set of interests so that government programs, including regulatory ones, were, in effect, captured by the benefited parties.

It is difficult to extract a systematic and consistent theory statement from the older literature on pressure groups and power; "pressure" is a vague term; even consideration of the nature and boundary of a group can invite debate. The basic claim is that groups that bias processes and outcomes, acquiring and defending power at the expense of competing groups, are more likely to capture regulation.

I term this general approach *imbalanced affective access politics*. The modifier "affective" is used to reflect bias, i.e., strong preference for or attachment to one position over others in requests for government action. The scale on which groups contend is not balanced – some groups are consistently more powerful than others. I chose to use the modifier "affective" instead of "biased" in order to remove potential confusion with "imbalanced."

One mechanism that attempts to repair such politics uses formal agents to represent interests lacking the capability to compete to bias government action so that it provides private benefit for the group. Such agents can try, in effect, to re-balance competition among groups. They are sometimes termed "proxy advocates" (also "special merit" or public interest counsels, or "consumer advocates"; on these roles, see, e.g., Mitnick and Weiss 1974; Gormley 1982, 1983; Berry 1984; Holburn and Vanden Bergh 2006). Proxy advocates require at least three features in order to be successful: information/expertise in the regulated industry; legal and preferential access; and recognition as substitute players, i.e., as legitimate agents of the interests in question. In particular, proxy advocates solve the agency problems of diffuse groups, and appear to be employed as a way of using their formal role to re-balance advocacy (Holburn and Vanden Bergh 2006).

### Subgovernmental institutionalization

Subgovernments feature a closed system of policy making in which certain actors, for example some interest groups, some institutional actors, and not others, are recognized as legitimate players. Relatively stable expectations develop regarding demands, agenda-building processes, specific role incumbents, negotiating practices, alliances, cultural and normative commonalities, and so on. Although the system may be sustained at least partly by the incentive effects described under incentive-shaped individual decision making, i.e., the effects said to produce iron triangles, subgovernmental networks are virtual institutions that exist across formal governmental agency and process lines.

Subgovernments have been variously described (though not necessarily with the same intended referents) in terms of "issue networks," "policy subgovernments," "advocacy coalitions," and "institutional constellations" (e.g., Heclo 1978; Hamm 1983, 1986; Gormley 1986; Sabatier 1988; Jordana and Sancho 2004; cf. "stakeholder partnerships," Leach et al. 2002; for other systems models of regulation, see, e.g., Krasnow et al. 1982; Meier 1985; Mitnick 1991/1985). Subgovernments can display capture-like stable policy domination by a particular set of actors, critical supportive behaviors by a single major constituency (e.g., Sabatier 1975), or a serial competition in which, as issue and subgovernment membership remains stable, actors compete to dominate policy outcomes. Where contests in the issue area cycle over time, they can reappear with the same set of participants competing to shape the policy outcome. Thus, policy governance is virtual, not bounded by formal institutional lines. *Subgovernmental capture* occurs when the same set of actors dominate decisions and/or performances in the network.

### Regulatory arbitrage

The construction of a system of regulation involves *ex ante commitment*. In addition, acquisition of additional resources and modification of public regulation require coordination and the assent of many actors. Annual budgeting, Civil Service, procurement, and administrative process constraints slow adaptation. Moreover, the government must be transparent, while the regulated actors need only meet reporting requirements. Thus government telegraphs its control strategy, while industry can largely conceal its compliance strategy. As a result, it is unusual for regulation in place to be matched closely with what is needed to assure compliance. The mismatch of regulatory capabilities and resources with regulating needs provides opportunities for the regulated actors to gain advantaged and protected statuses. Furthermore, where the coordinated action of several agencies is required, as may occur in the federal system, such *joint action complexity* multiplies the problems of maladaptation. On the other hand, a firm's strategic response to regulation may require only the firm's own entrepreneurial behavior (sometimes with or through a trade association) (on strategic use of regulation, see, e.g., Mitnick 1981/1993, 1993; Marcus 1984; Wood 1986; Mahon and McGowan 1996; Yandle 2011).

I call the ability of firms to capture benefits within the uncontrolled space created by the agency problems of maladaptive regulation, *regulatory arbitrage*. Although it does not seem to be studied as a systematic problem, it is well understood in particular contexts. For example, the problems of "regulatory lag" (cf. also "regulatory slack") are well understood and widely described in the public utility literature: Public utilities ask for rate increases when their costs increase, but if the regulatory process slows rate adjustments or is insensitive to the true utility cost structure when those costs decrease, utilities will enjoy excessive returns.

### 3.2.3   Relational (Governance)

**External: overhead governance – relational political governance featuring overhead agency controls and channel management**
There is now a very large literature on political control of the bureaucracy (the modern literature on delegation as agency and the modeling of regulatory relationships as agent–principal relationships began with Mitnick 1975, 1980: 326–37 and *infra*). That literature expanded from a focus on how Congress, via tools such as appointments, presumably dominated bureaucratic behavior (Weingast 1981, 1984), to a range of means for shaping a regulatory body's behavior, including budgetary controls, subtle influences identifiable by mapping the policy positions of interested legislators, specification of structural characteristics of administrative instruments, procedural controls, effects on the costs of particular kinds of decision making, Presidential influence, media coverage, signals from wealthy groups rather than overhead ones, effects of multiple principals, actions that affect the reputations of regulators, and other effects (examples of this work, some critical, include McCubbins et al. 1987; Moe 1987; Spiller 1990; Macey 1992; Hammond and Knott 1996; Spence 1997; Waterman and Meier 1998; Waterman et al. 1998; Epstein and O'Halloran 1999; Reenock and Poggione 2004; for discussion of the instruments that manage delegation both in the oversight body and within agencies, see Balla 2011; on relational versus transactional political strategies, see Hillman and Hitt 1999). For some factors, for example budget, this literature does in fact find evidence of political influence, but in some cases the agency can retain discretion (for examples, see Balla 1998; Spence 1999; cf. Carpenter 2001; there are a large number of caveats in the literature about the sources of influences and their effects).

Note that, if it is to be capture, it must go beyond political influence to form a stable relationship with industry that consistently shapes agency decisions and/or performances so as to intendedly benefit that industry. The logic of the iron triangle is based in incentives that guide or distort behaviors. In relational political governance, however, capture is anchored in the basic legitimacy of the overhead controls. Thus, in the Congressional dominance approach, the industry dominates the oversight committee, which then acts with full legitimacy, not just as a sender of incentives.

Carpenter's work on bureaucratic autonomy (2001) provides a nuanced counterpart to the political control stream of work. He demonstrates that some agencies can politically differentiate themselves from political forces that might otherwise control them, can produce entrepreneurial bureaucratic outputs that reflect "unique organizational capacities" (p. 14), and can generate robust "political legitimacy" – taken as equivalent to "reputation." But Carpenter's observations do not challenge the notion that capture or something like it can occur.

**Internal: substitutional governance**
A major theme in explanations of capture relies on replacement of neutral governance by new, stable, and biased role incumbents. The term "revolving door" describes one source for the members of the new regime, the regulated industry itself. Industry members are presumably inclined to serve their industry, and have a sophisticated understanding of the kinds of public actions that would do exactly that. Also, because the regulated industry has an interest in employing able regulators with advanced understanding of the regulations (e.g., Kohlmeier 1969: 73–4; Quirk 1981: 170–72) and of both the formal and the informal contexts in which regulatory decisions are made, they proffer remunerative positions to term-limited and/or ambitious regulators. The assumption is that opportunities for lucrative future employment would promote regulator leniency (see Noll 1971; Mitnick 1980; Quirk 1981; for examples of the revolving door in a variety of regulatory agencies, see Gormley 1979; Krasnow et al. 1982; Skrzycki 2003; but cf. Freitag 1983). Makkai and Braithwaite (1992) identify three capture-related aspects of the revolving door: industry identification; lack of toughness in regulating; and sympathy with the industry's problems. They conclude from their study of Australian nursing home inspectors that the revolving door by itself is too simplistic to offer as a cause of capture; the problem is better understood as situational.

Serious questions have been raised of whether the revolving door really affects policy (e.g., Quirk 1981; Gormley 1983). As noted, it makes sense for firms to hire active, competent regulators; they would be far more useful than those whose ability or commitment to the organization may be questionable. Thus, it is the *regulatory capital* (in analogy to social or human capital) that regulators gain from their time as regulators that has the true value for them, not biased actions on the job or remunerative work after it.

The basic aim of capture in this general case is to replace neutral with biased governance. There are many forms that this can take: biasing existing regulatory managers via incentives; replacing neutral agency managers with biased ones; cutting line regulators so that enforcement becomes delayed and problematic; reducing the level of regulatory expertise in the agency by forcing out experienced regulators, making it less likely that regulatory violations will be recognized and enforcement actions taken; relocating regulators so that they cannot detect violations; delegating regulation to other governments less likely to enforce the regulations because they are more politically sensitive to the regulated industry or less able to enforce them; and so on.

### 3.2.4   Individual

**Incentive-shaped individual decision making**
Literature in this area assumes that regulators are rational in the sense of acting consistently with respect to their goals, and will respond to incentives aimed at those goals. It adopts methodological individualism so that collectives such as organizations are treated as unitary actors; they are what their directing managers are. There are no issues of

implementation, no complexity of joint action. In addition, the usual assumption, often implicit, is that those managers are self-interested.

Most of the institutional/organizational features that structure behaviors are assumed away, with authors relying on the "as if assumption" associated with Milton Friedman's arguments regarding positive economics. For example, Peltzman (1976), building on Stigler (1971), even treats regulators as if they had been merged with legislators and have the same motivations for reelection, an assumption that is in most cases descriptively incorrect. But even simplified models require some institutional framework in order to generate predictions. Thus it is common to assume that legislators are vote-maximizing and seek campaign contributions in order to repeatedly win elections, that regulators receive budgets from the legislatures, and so on.

The self-interest assumption can lead to some shaky logic in setting up the motivations to which incentives are directed. Thus regulators are assumed to want things like an easy managerial life while they are regulators (see Eckert 1973) and lucrative employment when they leave the agency, but those who send them incentives are assumed to have only the firm's or industry's interests as their goals. In other words, the regulators are assumed to be imperfect agents, but their influencers are somehow able to perform as perfect agents.

The individualistic incentives model is said to produce capture via an "iron triangle" that aligns the interests of industry, legislators, and regulators. The logic goes as follows (see Noll 1971; Mitnick 1980, 1991/1985): Legislators arrange to serve on the subcommittees with oversight for the regulated industries in their districts because they seek to be reelected. They need votes and money. The industry can generate both, in part through mobilization of district interests. The legislators are assumed to control the agency's budget, can generate regulatory directives via new legislation (or steer interpretations of existing legislation by threat of new legislation), and can embarrass peak regulators by holding oversight hearings that expose management and regulatory conduct issues. Such hearings threaten *regulatory capital* – regulators won't be able to offer competence and network contacts to future employers. Thus regulators will be especially responsive to legislators and, indeed, will rationally try to anticipate their wishes, rather than suffer the costs of learning those preferences as a result of later legislator interventions.

Regulators require large amounts of idiosyncratic information from the regulated industry in order to regulate. Such knowledge is costly or impossible to obtain from sources other than the industry. The regulators engage in extensive personal interactions with the industry, gain knowledge of industry networks (part of their regulatory capital), and come to see industry managers as decent people trying to be successful. Regulators attend industry association meetings at which they are honored and feted; they receive such positive attention from nowhere else (for examples, see Kohlmeier 1969). Regulators learn of ways in which their regulatory capital can become valuable to them in the future, such as in jobs in the industry or dealing with the industry.

The outcome is capture. Legislators do what industry wants. Regulators do what legislators want. Regulators come to see the world as the industry sees it, develop non-adversarial relationships with industry, recognize personal opportunities in the future, and, eventually, do what industry wants regulation to do.

Later theoretical and empirical research (e.g., Quirk 1981; Berry 1984; Mitnick 1991/1985) challenged the inevitability of this logic. Among factors that can be important are: participation of other actors as regulatory stakeholders, such as citizen groups (e.g., Mitnick 1991/1985; Ayres and Braithwaite 1992); formalized consumer representatives (e.g., Mitnick and Weiss 1974; Berry 1984; Holburn and Vanden Bergh 2006) or "proxy advocates" (Gormley 1982, 1983); maintenance of strongly supportive pro-regulation constituencies (Sabatier 1975); courts willing to go beyond traditional grounds for scope of review; interventions by peak political executives when regulatory crises occur; professionalization in the agencies; and adequate resources, such as overall budget and technical expertise, among others.

**Implementation slippage featuring corruption, expedience, and/or identification processes**
During implementation, capture can occur as regulatory performances become dominated by line regulators who become very responsive to, and/or identify with, the industry with which they work closely.

Capture is facilitated when the same regulators work with only a few firms in one industry, are in direct and repeated contact with the regulated parties (usually the same contact people in the industry), work with the industry at a physical distance from administrative supervision, have come out of or been trained within that industry, lack true professional training and/or professional relationships that can provide prestige or status rewards as well as normative guidance from the profession, lack sources of information on the industry from sources other than the industry itself, see few opportunities for career mobility out of their existing regulatory role relationship (including to higher-paying and/or higher-prestige regulatory positions), and have relatively low compensation (Mitnick 1982; Ayres and Braithwaite 1992; on regulator–industry relationships, cf. Reed 2009).

There are at least three patterns: First, regulators can be directly corrupted or bribed; second, under-resourced regulators faced with complex tasks and deadlines, and constrained to retain good working relationships with personnel in the industry with whom they must interact constantly, economize and simplify regulatory tasks in cooperation with the regulated industry, resulting in reduction in regulatory stringency (see, e.g., Ayres and Braithwaite 1992); third, regulators trained within an industry and lacking competing information sources work in close contact with industry people concerned with the same issues so that, over time, their attitudes and behaviors become indistinguishable from those in the industry. The result in all three cases is capture.

### 3.2.5 Functional

**Information control and impactedness**
In general, the regulated parties control and filter information essential to regulatory decision making; the supply of alternative, potentially competitive information is costly or, in Williamson's term (1975), *impacted*. Hence the capture of information can be equivalent to the capture of the meanings applied in interpretations made as part of regulatory decision making, and, ultimately, to the capture of the process itself.

Technical information can be the source of both quality decision making and defense of decisions that favor some interests over others (e.g., Sabatier 1978; cf. Jenkins-Smith and Weimer 1985 on "analysis as retrograde action"). Gormley (1986) argues that, when technical complexity is high, and accessible largely to the regulated industry, and the salience of the affected issues to the public is relatively low, capture is promoted. If only because of the agency problems involved, government can never be as technically expert as the industry it regulates. The literature also argues that behavior in legislatures that provide critical oversight for regulation may be driven by the sources and availability of reliable information, and affected by the information flows among the participants in policy making, including legislative committees, administrative agencies, interest groups, and other third parties (cf. Hamm 1983; Krehbiel 1991).

In regulation, it has long been argued (e.g., Porter and Sagansky 1976; Mitnick 1980, 1981/1993, 1991/1985; Gormley 1983) that control and strategic manipulation of information can both shape regulatory decisions and outcomes and be used strategically in competition in regulated industries.

**Competency myths**
The classic rationale for delegation to administrative agencies is that they would be populated with a permanent expert staff and would be insulated from corrupting political pressures (see, e.g., Landis 1938). The legislature lacks both the time and the expertise to develop detailed rules to implement regulatory mandates, and so would be obligated to entrust these essential legislative duties to the agency – it was indeed an *agency*. The strictures of judicial review sustain this rationale: The court is loath to substitute its judgment for that of the agency if the agency considers all the issues its regulations and the law say it must consider, and assembles a substantial record reflecting its expert consideration of the case. The ritual of judicial review displays features of what has been labeled "social proof" (e.g., Rao 1994): Credibility that the decision is proper is assigned by the collectivity not on the basis of the actual rationales being compelling, but on social recognition of procedure-following.

The superior expertise of the delegated regulatory agent is one of what I will term *competency myths.* Such myths are necessary to operate coercive systems of regulation that are typically under-resourced; where knowledge linking regulatory controls to impacts is often tenuous; where decisions must sometimes be imposed in fractious environments in ways that suggest that they will be sustained on appeal; where regulation occurs in a distributed, sometimes conflictual environment in which control of the same industry is spread across multiple agencies handling multiple aspects of the industry's behavior; and/or where the agency's competence and effectiveness must be hyped in order to guarantee compliance.

Competency myths are particularly essential when the subject of regulation involves intangibles that cannot be directly validated by consumers (e.g., "credence goods") and in the opposite extreme in which the subject of regulation is so technical and/or abstruse that it requires certification by qualified interpreters of its technical content.

The more technical the nature of the regulated industry, the greater the external need for the agency's regulatory certification, and the more essential it is that the agency either have the actual ability to determine whether the industry's product claims are true and/ or be able to maintain the credible reputation that it has such an ability. Noting that an agency's image or reputation includes performative, moral, and legal-procedural, as well as technical, components, Carpenter (2010) describes the critical role played by the FDA's former reputation for both scientific competence and scientific probity in assuring health product consumers that the scientific status of health-enabling goods claimed to be safe and effective was just that (on competence in regulatory agencies, see Greenwood 1984).

But, at the same time that competency myths support trust in the system, they can also shield agencies from challenges and protect deviant industries from effective regulatory control. Indeed, it is in the interest of capturing industries to construct their regulators in the image of perfect agents (cf. Mitnick 1975).

### "Arational" regulatory process and instrument/tool design

New regulation uses the institutional forms and particular tools or instruments of control that other agencies have used in the past (see institutional theory on mimetic or "isomorphic" behavior; DiMaggio and Powell 1983). After the U.S. Interstate Commerce Commission was made an independent regulatory body in 1889 in response to fears that the incoming President would weaken implementation of the 1887 Act, subsequent regulatory bodies were also created as independent commissions. The rationale for independent design – originally political – was created post hoc. Independence was supposed to foster expert commissioners acting in impartial ways outside immediate political controls. As Huntington (1952) argued, however, the ICC and the transportation industry it regulated developed a mutually supportive relationship protected by the agency's independence.

The use of standardized designs for regulatory instruments, and for the design of the administrative process itself, can benefit industries better able to work with those designs. Regulatory rulemaking can be costly and time-consuming, requiring multiple stages of depositions, briefs, hearings, public notice periods, and so on, creating barriers protecting incumbent firms already enjoying the benefits of regulation ((Mitnick 1981/1993; Levine 1998; on the advantages and limitations of "deep pockets," cf. McCaffrey 1982). The literature on strategic use of regulation (e.g., Mitnick 1981/1993) argues that the ability to participate extensively in rulemaking and other formalized components of the administrative process gives significant advantages to larger firms (but cf. McCaffrey 1982; Carpenter 2004). Such firms can support the necessary response bureaucracy. It follows that larger firms are more likely to be able to dominate and/or capture regulatory decision making and performances than their smaller competitors.

### 3.2.6   Chronical

### Path dependence opportunism

A robust, largely empirical literature in comparative economic systems has developed that investigates the macro conditions, distribution, and societal extensiveness of the systematic steering of the tangible benefits of public action to advantage private parties in certain countries. This literature, often labeled "state capture," has developed largely apart from the much older literature on capture in political science that first observed and theorized about similar phenomena; indeed, there are virtually no citations to the relevant political science literature or even to key works in the strategy literature. State capture has, however, been an important focus of literature that examined the transitioning of communist, centralized economies to more market-driven economies.

Capture was made possible because of opportunistic actions in situations in which both property rights and the nature and source of central controls or regulation were changing. It is at that point that what Kaufmann (2005) defines as "corruption" occurs: "the privatization of public policy." The process of locking in private benefits is facilitated by what is in effect imbalanced affective access politics, as some parties receive differential access and differential benefits – "crony bias" (Hellman and Kaufmann 2002). Unlike imbalanced affective access politics, the privatization of public policy is accompanied by the provision of tangible private, personal benefits to government decision makers, for example bribes; such payments go well beyond reelection assistance such as campaign contributions. Because public policy actions protect private industry, acting at variance to what good governance would require, Kaufmann (2004) labels such behavior "legal corruption."

A significant feature of the state capture approach is its reliance on path dependence – the opportunism occurs, but where or how it is manifested depends on how the system is changing and who controls the supply of private benefits. Thus the mechanism involves the opportunities that path-dependent governmental and societal adjustments allow some actors to capture a benefit flow provided by, or shielded by, government actions.

## 3.3   CONCLUSION

This chapter has provided a general definition of capture and identified 12 mechanisms said to produce capture, sorting them into six logical groups. The ability to understand the mechanisms of capture may provide us with the capability to design regulatory systems that can avoid capture – what I term a normative *theory of fiducial regulation.* I leave presentation of the elements of such a theory to future work (see Mitnick 2011a, 2011b).

## REFERENCES

Ayres, I. and J. Braithwaite (1992), *Responsive Regulation: Transcending the Deregulation Debate*, New York and Oxford: Oxford University Press.

Bachrach, P. and M.S. Baratz (1970), *Power and Poverty: Theory and Practice*, New York: Oxford University Press.

Balla, S.J. (1998), 'Administrative procedures and political control of the bureaucracy', *American Political Science Review*, **92** (3), 663–73.

Balla, S.J. (2011), 'Agency design and oversight: instruments for managing delegation to the bureaucracy', in D. Levi-Faur (ed.), *Handbook on the Politics of Regulation*, Cheltenham, UK and Northampton, MA: Edward Elgar.

Baron, D.P. (1995), 'Integrated strategy: market and nonmarket components', *California Management Review*, **37** (2), 47–65.

Baron, D.P. (1997), 'Integrated strategy, trade policy, and global competition', *California Management Review*, **39** (2), 145–69.

Bernstein, M.H. (1955), *Regulating Business by Independent Commission*, Princeton, NJ: Princeton University Press.

Berry, W.D. (1984), 'An alternative to the capture theory of regulation: the case of state public utility commissions', *American Journal of Political Science*, **28** (3), 524–58.

Carpenter, D.P. (2001), *The Forging of Bureaucratic Autonomy: Reputations, Networks, and Policy Innovation in Executive Agencies, 1862–1928*, Princeton, NJ: Princeton University Press.

Carpenter, D.P. (2004), 'Protection without capture: product approval by a politically responsive, learning regulator', *American Political Science Review*, **98** (4), 613–31.

Carpenter, D.P. (2010), *Reputation and Power: Organizational Image and Pharmaceutical Regulation at the FDA*, Princeton, NJ: Princeton University Press.

Christensen, J.G.C. (2011), 'Public interest regulation reconsidered: from capture to credible commitment', in D. Levi-Faur (ed.), *Handbook on the Politics of Regulation*, Cheltenham, UK and Northampton, MA: Edward Elgar.

Cobb, R.W. and C.D. Elder (1972), *Participation in American Politics: The Dynamics of Agenda-Building*, Boston, MA: Allyn & Bacon.

Croley, S. (2011), 'Beyond capture: Towards a new theory of regulation', in D. Levi-Faur (ed.), *Handbook on the Politics of Regulation*, Cheltenham, UK and Northampton, MA: Edward Elgar.

Dahl, R.A. (1961), *Who Governs? Democracy and Power in an American City*, New Haven, CT: Yale University Press.

DiMaggio, P.J. and W.W. Powell (1983), 'The iron cage revisited: institutional isomorphism and collective rationality in organizational fields', *American Journal of Sociology*, **48**, 147–60.

Eckert, R.D. (1973), 'On the incentives of regulators: the case of taxicabs', *Public Choice*, **14**, Spring, 83–99.

Epstein, D. and S. O'Halloran (1999), *Delegating Powers: A Transaction Cost Politics Approach to Policy Making under Separate Powers*, Cambridge: Cambridge University Press.

Epstein, E.M. (1969), *The Corporation in American Politics*, Englewood Cliffs, NJ: Prentice-Hall.

Fainsod, M. (1940), 'Some reflections on the nature of the regulatory process', in C.J. Friedrich and E.S. Mason (eds), *Public Policy*, vol. 1, Cambridge: Harvard University Press, pp. 297–323.

Freitag, P.J. (1983), 'The myth of corporate capture: regulatory commissions in the United States', *Social Problems*, **30** (4), 480–91.

Gormley, W.T., Jr. (1979), 'A test of the revolving door hypothesis at the FCC', *American Journal of Political Science*, **23**, 665–83.

Gormley, W.T., Jr. (1982), 'Alternative models of the regulatory process: public utility regulation in the states', *Western Political Quarterly*, **35** (3), 297–317.

Gormley, W.T., Jr. (1983), *The Politics of Public Utility Regulation*, Pittsburgh, PA: University of Pittsburgh Press.

Gormley, W.T., Jr. (1986), 'Regulatory issue networks in a federal system', *Polity*, **18** (4), 595–620.

Gray, H.M. (1940), 'The passing of the public utility concept', *Journal of Land and Public Utility Economics*, **16** (1), 8–20. Reprinted in American Economic Association (ed.) (1949), *Readings in the Social Control of Industry*, Philadelphia, PA: Blakiston, pp. 280–303.

Greenwood, T. (1984), *Knowledge and Discretion in Government Regulation*, New York: Praeger.

Hamm, K.E. (1983), 'Patterns of influence among committees, agencies, and interest groups', *Legislative Studies Quarterly*, **8** (3), 379–426.

Hamm, K.E. (1986), 'The role of "subgovernments" in U.S. state policy making: an exploratory analysis', *Legislative Studies Quarterly*, **11** (3), 321–51.

Hammond, T.H. and J. Knott (1996), 'Who controls the bureaucracy? Presidential power, Congressional dominance, legal constraints, and bureaucratic autonomy in a model of multi-institutional policy-making', *Journal of Law, Economics, and Organization*, **12** (1), 121–68.

Heclo, H. (1978), 'Issue networks and the executive establishment', in A. King (ed.), *The New American Political System*, Washington, DC: American Enterprise Institute.

Hellman, J.S. and D. Kaufmann (2001), 'Confronting the challenge of state capture in transition economies', *Finance & Development* (International Monetary Fund), **38** (3).

Hellman, J.S. and D. Kaufmann (2002), 'The inequality of influence', paper presented at the Stanford Corruption Workshop, Stanford University, 2003 January 30–31 (draft dated 2002).

Hillman, A.J. and M.A. Hitt (1999), 'Corporate political strategy formulation: a model of approach, participation, and strategy decisions', *Academy of Management Review*, **24** (4), 825–42.

Holburn, G.L.F. and R.G. Vanden Bergh (2006), 'Consumer capture of regulatory institutions: the creation of public utility consumer advocates in the United States', *Public Choice*, **126** (1/2), 45–73.

Huntington, S.P. (1952), 'The marasmus of the ICC: the Commission, the railroads, and the public interest', *Yale Law Journal*, **61** (4), 467–509.

Jenkins-Smith, H.C. and D.L. Weimer (1985), 'Analysis as retrograde action: the case of strategic petroleum reserves', *Public Administration Review*, **45** (4), 485–94.

Jordana, J. and D. Levi-Faur (eds) (2004), *The Politics of Regulation: Institutions and Regulatory Reforms for the Age of Governance*, Cheltenham, UK and Northampton, MA, USA: Edward Elgar Publishing.

Jordana, J. and D. Sancho (2004), 'Regulatory designs, institutional constellations and the study of the regulatory state', in J. Jordana and D. Levi-Faur (eds), *The Politics of Regulation: Institutions and Regulatory Reforms for the Age of Governance*, Cheltenham, UK and Northampton, MA, USA: Edward Elgar Publishing.

Kalt, J.P. and M.A. Zupan (1984), 'Capture and ideology in the economic theory of politics', *American Economic Review*, **74** (3), 279–300.

Kaufmann, D. (2004), 'Corruption, governance and security: challenges for the rich countries and the world', in *Global Competitiveness Report 2004–05*, Washington, DC: World Bank, Chapter 2.1.

Kaufmann, D. (2005), 'Myths and realities of governance and corruption', in *Global Competitiveness Report, 2005–06*, World Economic Forum (October), 81–98.

Kohlmeier, L., Jr. (1969), *The Regulators: Watchdog Agencies and the Public Interest*, New York: Harper & Row.

Kolko, G. (1965), *Railroads and Regulation, 1877–1916*, Princeton, NJ: Princeton University Press.

Krasnow, E.G., L.D. Longley and H. Terry (1982), *The Politics of Broadcast Regulation*, 3rd edn, New York: St. Martin's Press.

Krehbiel, K. (1991), *Information and Legislative Organization*, Ann Arbor: University of Michigan Press.

Landis, J.M. (1938), *The Administrative Process*, New Haven, CT: Yale University Press.

Leach, W.D., N.W. Pelkey and P.A. Sabatier (2002), 'Stakeholder partnerships as collaborative policymaking: evaluation criteria applied to watershed management in California and Washington', *Journal of Policy Analysis and Management*, 21 (4), 645–70.

Levine, M.E. (1998), 'Regulatory capture', in P. Newman (ed.), *The New Palgrave Dictionary of Economics and the Law*, vol. 3, London and New York: Macmillan Reference and Stockton Press, pp. 267–71.

Levine, M.E. and J.L. Forrence (1990), 'Regulatory capture, public interest, and the public agenda: toward a synthesis', *Journal of Law, Economics, and Organization*, 6, Special issue, 167–98.

Macey, J.R. (1992), 'Organizational design and political control of administrative agencies', *Journal of Law, Economics, and Organization*, 8 (1), 93–110.

Mahon, J.F. and R.A. McGowan (1996), *Industry as a Player in the Political and Social Arena: Defining the Competitive Environment*, Westport, CT: Quorum Books.

Makkai, T. and J. Braithwaite (1992), 'In and out of the revolving door: making sense of regulatory capture', *Journal of Public Policy*, 12 (1), 61–78.

Marcus, A.A. (1984), *The Adversary Economy: Business Responses to Changing Government Requirements*, Westport, CT: Quorum Books.

Mazmanian, D.A. and P.A. Sabatier (1983), *Implementation and Public Policy*, Glenview, IL: Scott, Foresman. Reissued 1989, University Press of America.

McCaffrey, D.P. (1982), 'Corporate resources and regulatory pressures: toward explaining a discrepancy', *Administrative Science Quarterly*, 27 (3), 398–419.

McConnell, G. (1966), *Private Power and American Democracy*, New York: Vintage Books, Alfred A. Knopf.

McCubbins, M.D., R.G. Noll and B.R. Weingast (1987), 'Administrative procedures as instruments of political control', *Journal of Law, Economics, and Organization*, 3, 243–77.

Meier, K.J. (1985), *Regulation: Politics, Bureaucracy, and Economics*, New York: St. Martin's Press.

Mitnick, B.M. (1975), 'The theory of agency: the policing "paradox" and regulatory behavior', *Public Choice*, 24, 27–42.

Mitnick, B.M. (1980), *The Political Economy of Regulation: Creating, Designing, and Removing Regulatory Forms*, New York: Columbia University Press.

Mitnick, B.M. (1981/1993), 'The strategic uses of regulation – and deregulation', *Business Horizons*, 24 (2), 71–83. Revised 1993, in B.M. Mitnick (ed.), *Corporate Political Agency: The Construction of Competition in Public Affairs*, Newbury Park, CA: Sage Publications, pp. 67–89.

Mitnick, B.M. (1982), 'The two-part problem of regulatory compliance: the case of compliance reform and strip mining', in L.E. Preston (ed.), *Research in Corporate Social Performance and Policy: A Research Annual*, vol. IV, Greenwich, CT: JAI Press, pp. 215–42.

Mitnick, B.M. (1991/1985), 'An incentive systems model of the regulatory environment', in M.J. Dubnick and A.R. Gitelson (eds), *Public Policy and Economic Institutions*, vol. 10, Greenwich, CT: JAI Press, pp. 147–204. Originally paper for APSA, 1985.

Mitnick, B.M. (1993), *Corporate Political Agency: The Construction of Competition in Public Affairs*, Newbury Park, CA: Sage Publications.

Mitnick, B.M. (2011a), 'Capturing "capture": developing a normative theory of fiducial regulation', *Jerusalem Papers in Regulation and Governance*, Working Paper No. 32.

Mitnick, B.M. (2011b), 'A normative theory of fiducial regulation', unpublished paper.

Mitnick, B.M. and C. Weiss, Jr. (1974), 'The siting impasse and a rational choice model of regulatory behavior: an agency for power plant siting', *Journal of Environmental Economics and Management*, 1, 150–71.

Moe, T.M. (1987), 'An assessment of the positive theory of "Congressional dominance"', *Legislative Studies Quarterly*, 12 (4), 475–520.

Noll, R.G. (1971), *Reforming Regulation: An Evaluation of the Ash Council Proposals*, Washington, DC: Brookings Institution.

Peltzman, S. (1976), 'Toward a more general theory of regulation', *Journal of Law and Economics*, 19 (2), 211–40.

Porter, M.E. and J. Sagansky (1976), 'Information, politics and economic analysis: the regulatory decision process in the air freight cases', *Public Policy*, **24** (2), 263–307.

Pressman, J.L. and A. Wildavsky (1973) [1984 reissue], *Implementation: How Great Expectations in Washington Are Dashed in Oakland, or, Why It's Amazing that Federal Programs Work at All . . .*, Berkeley: University of California Press.

Quirk, P.J. (1981), *Industry Influence in Federal Regulatory Agencies*, Princeton, NJ: Princeton University Press.

Rao, H. (1994), 'The social construction of reputation: certification contests, legitimation, and the survival of organizations in the American automobile industry: 1895–1912', *Strategic Management Journal*, **15**, Special, 29–44.

Reed, K.K. (2009), 'A look at firm–regulator exchanges: friendly enough or too friendly?', *Business & Society*, **48** (2), 147–78.

Reenock, C. and S. Poggione (2004), 'Agency design as an ongoing tool of bureaucratic influence', *Legislative Studies Quarterly*, **29** (3), 383–406.

Sabatier, P.A. (1975), 'Social movements and regulatory agencies: toward a more adequate and less pessimistic theory of "clientele capture"', *Policy Sciences*, **6** (3), 301–42.

Sabatier, P.A. (1978), 'The acquisition and utilization of technical information by administrative agencies', *Administrative Science Quarterly*, **23** (3), 396–417.

Sabatier, P.A. (1988), 'An advocacy coalition framework of policy change and the role of policy-oriented learning therein', *Policy Sciences*, **21** (2/3), 129–68.

Skrzycki, C. (2003), *The Regulators: Anonymous Power Brokers in American Politics*, Lanham, MD: Rowman & Littlefield.

Spence, D.B. (1997), 'Agency policy making and political control: modeling away the delegation problem', *Journal of Public Administration Research and Theory*, **7** (2), 199–219.

Spence, D.B. (1999), 'Managing delegation ex ante: using law to steer administrative agencies', *Journal of Legal Studies*, **28** (2), 413–59.

Spiller, P.T. (1990), 'Politicians, interest groups, and regulators: a multiple-principals agency theory of regulation, or "let them be bribed"', *Journal of Law and Economics*, **33** (1), 65–101.

Stigler, G.J. (1971), 'The theory of economic regulation', *Bell Journal of Economics and Management Science*, **2** (1), 3–21.

Teske, P. (2004), *Regulation in the States*, Washington, DC: Brookings Institution Press.

Waterman, R.W. and K.J. Meier (1998), 'Principal–agent models: an expansion?', *Journal of Public Administration Research and Theory*, **8** (2), 173–202.

Waterman, R.W., A. Rouse and R. Wright (1998), 'The venues of influence: a new theory of political control of the bureaucracy', *Journal of Public Administration Research and Theory*, **8** (1), 13–38.

Weingast, B.R. (1981), 'Regulation, reregulation, and deregulation: the political foundations of agency clientele relationships', *Law and Contemporary Problems*, **44** (1), 147–77.

Weingast, B.R. (1984), 'The congressional-bureaucratic system: a principal agent perspective (with applications to the SEC)', *Public Choice*, **44**, 147–91.

Williamson, O.E. (1975), *Markets and Hierarchies: Analysis and Antitrust Implications*, New York: Free Press.

Wood, D.J. (1986), *Strategic Uses of Public Policy: Business and Government in the Progressive Era*, New York: Harper Business.

Yandle, B. (2011), 'Bootleggers and Baptists in the theory of regulation', in D. Levi-Faur (ed.), *Handbook on the Politics of Regulation*, Cheltenham, UK and Northampton, MA: Edward Elgar.

# 4 Beyond capture: towards a new theory of regulation
*Steven P. Croley*

The interest group capture theory of regulation has enjoyed unrivaled influence.[1] It occupies, still, a central place in the academic understanding of – given its tenets – the defects of regulatory government. It has, accordingly, provided a foundation for policy arguments to limit the reach of regulatory government. For, on the capture account, sound regulatory government is a naïve aspiration.

Yet the theory has seen criticism as well, broad and deep if unevenly across the social sciences. It rests on a flawed account of interest group formation, and an incomplete account of exactly why interest groups, *qua* groups, participate in regulatory decisionmaking. It also oversimplifies regulatory institutions. Not surprisingly given these defects, its evidentiary base is weak. Its deregulatory policy prescriptions are, therefore, not compelling.

That capture theory has been the focus of critical attention is a testimony to its dominance. It is *the* theory to be evaluated. Thus the challenge for capture theory's critics is: Supply an alternative. Existing critiques have yet to be synthesized; they constitute more or less piecemeal objections, powerful as some may be. Consequently, the lack of a rival theory, not capture theory's irresistibility, explains its resilience. If capture theory is to be replaced rather than displaced, additional conceptual, empirical, and indeed normative theory-building must be undertaken.

The following pages briefly summarize the central claims of the interest group capture theory of regulation, and review illustrative critiques. Having surveyed some of the theory's shortcomings, this chapter then identifies some of the steps to be taken towards constructing an alternative. Centrally, the development of an alternative theory requires increased attention to regulators' decisionmaking processes and methods. Challengers to the interest group theory of regulation must also articulate, convincingly, the marks of desirable regulation, as the endurance of capture theory owes in part to its attractive specificity of what constitutes undesirable regulation.

## 4.1 THE LIMITS OF INTEREST GROUP CAPTURE THEORY

### 4.1.1 Central Themes

A quick review is necessary to lay bare the theory's shortcomings.

The interest group capture theory holds that regulation often/usually/almost always allocates regulatory rents to narrow interest groups.[2] Those groups can extract rents from regulators because they, and mostly/only they, are able to overcome barriers to coordination. They are able to overcome barriers to coordination given the narrowness of their interests and/or given that members of narrow interest groups tend to be few in number, making collective action easier for them relative to those whose interests are diffuse (Olson 1965; Stigler 1971, 1974).[3] The theory is laconic concerning exactly how narrow interest groups secure regulation that benefits them while imposing losses on everyone else. But the general ideas run as follows:

Legislators are motivated to provide regulation favorable to narrow groups to ensure their own electoral survival, legislators' paramount motivation. Because organized groups can supply resources useful to reelection-minded legislators – votes and campaign contributions – legislators support the regulatory policies that narrow interests favor in exchange for groups' political support. As regulatory policymaking frequently takes place at the administrative rather than legislative level, interest groups must secure the support of administrative regulators too. Here capture theory posits that administrators as well will supply regulation favored by narrow interest groups for one or more of three sets of reasons.

First, administrators will provide favorable regulation to avoid sanctions by the leg-islature. Specifically, administrators understand that legislators will punish and reward them – by decreasing/increasing their budgets and the scope of their regulatory authority – depending on whether they deliver favorable regulation to important legislative con-stituencies. Because administrators seek to maximize their own budgets (e.g., Niskanen 1971, 1975), they will comply – thus the iron triangle (e.g., Bernstein 1955; Cater 1964; Freeman 1965), welding agency incentives to provide the regulation interest groups favor to legislators' ability to discipline them. Because legislators have the ability to punish or reward agencies according to their regulatory decisions – "legislative dominance" – agencies follow legislative cues (e.g., McCubbins et al. 1987, 1989).

In addition, or alternatively, administrative regulators are motivated to provide inter-est groups with favorable regulation for their own reasons, not merely to placate their legislative superiors. One strand of capture theory holds that administrators will favor narrow regulatory interests to advance their own professional careers. That is, admin-istrators will supply regulatory favors to improve their prospects of future employment with regulated entities. Because there is a "revolving door" of employment between administrative agencies and the groups they regulate, administrators are solicitous of the interests of their future or hoped-for future employers (e.g., Buchanan and Tullock 1962).

Finally, administrators might favor the regulatory interests of narrow groups because they just cannot help it. This leg of the theory emphasizes that agency regulators often rely on information about regulatory alternatives supplied by regulated parties them-selves. Administrators are thus subject to "informational capture." On one variation of informational capture, agencies have no choice but to rely on information provided by narrow interests, because agencies lack the means to generate information on their own, perhaps especially information concerning regulatory enforcement (e.g., Laffont and Tirole 1993; DeFigueirido 2002; Reenok and Gerber 2007). Administrators are thus biased in favor of regulated parties. On another variation, agency personnel are frequently drawn from the ranks of regulated parties – again the revolving door – such that they are culturally or professionally inclined to view matters from interest groups' vantage points. Here, informational capture becomes in part psychological or epistemic, not solely a product of information asymmetries.

Because the benefits that favored groups receive are more than offset by the losses borne by the unorganized victims of regulation, deregulation is taken to be the central policy implication of the capture account. No regulation would be better than the deadweight losses resulting from the provision of regulatory rents, even given imperfect markets (see generally Huntington 1952; Bernstein 1955; Stigler and Friedland 1962; Kolko 1965; Tullock 1967, 1993; Stigler 1971, 1974, 1975a, 1975b; Krueger 1974; Peltzman 1989; Tollison 1989). The inevitability of socially harmful regulation, given the power of the forces that demand and supply it, argues against regulatory reform.

Suffice it to say that this general account has profoundly shaped contemporary understandings of regulation (see Sabatier 1975 on the rise of capture; Wood and Waterman 1994 on the rise of capture in social sciences; Stewart 1975 and Croley 2010 on the influence on legal discourse; Shleifer 2005 on capture's influence in economics; Hägg 1997 on tracing capture theory's development and influence; and Etzioni 2009 on the consequences of capture generally). Although originally focused on utility and other single-industry regulators, capture theory quickly expanded to extend to all types of regulation (e.g., Abrams and Settle 1978; Bo 2006). As Martimort (1999: 929) observes, "[f]ollowing Stigler (1971), it is now accepted that regulatory capture shapes policy outcomes." Capture theory's development has recently been described as "one of the finest moments of twentieth century economics" (Shleifer 2005: 441).

### 4.1.2   Flaws

Yet the theory's shortcomings are well documented. As capture's critiques often span different disciplines and sub-disciplines (often without reference to one another), however, their power stands to be amplified by compilation. While space and purpose do not allow for exhaustive compilation here (see also Mitnick 2011), select highlights both underscore the need for an alternative theory and foreshadow likely qualities of a successor.

**Conceptual shortcomings**
Interestingly, the theoretical weaknesses of capture theory have been noted almost since its inception (e.g., Posner 1974). And they extend to each of the theory's main premises. To illustrate, while capture theory posits that narrow interests have organizational advantages over broad interests, it provides little account for whether and how organizational advantages translate in the regulatory arena specifically (Croley 2010). For example, if narrow interest organizations participate in regulatory decisionmaking more than broad-based organizations do, it is not clear why policymakers would fail to take that into account (e.g., Denzau and Munger 1986; Arnold 1990). For another example, although members of narrow groups have (by definition) a greater per-capita incentive to contribute to their group activities, it is not clear why members of broad-based groups would not pool their smaller per-capita (though on capture theory's assumption greater overall) resources to form groups to advance their regulatory interests as well. Capture theory also provides an undeveloped account of the political economies of scale or other benefits that lead narrow interests to mobilize for political purposes, and little explanation for why individual firms would bother to form groups at all, rather than pursue their regulatory interests individually. Thus the conceptual gap between an assumed superior ability to mobilize, on the one hand, and the political

fruits of mobilizing, on the other, is never bridged. Capture theory's treatment of interest groups is incomplete.

Capture theory's premises concerning legislative motivation are similarly incomplete. First, the theory contemplates without justification that legislators are so electorally vulnerable that they are always led to trade regulatory benefits for political resources. Some legislative districts are contested; many are not. Further, even election-preoccupied legislators will have some room to pursue other goals. Moreover, the reelection goal is difficult to understand all the way down in non-instrumental terms. That is to say, capture theory does not explain why legislators seek to remain in office at all; presumably they do so to advance some political purpose or agenda. Nor does the theory provide a ready means to distinguish legislators who effectively sell their votes to interest groups from legislators who support interest groups with whom they are, independently, ideologically aligned (e.g., Kollman 1997). The theory's treatment of legislators is thin.

Same but double for capture theory's treatment of administrative regulators. For one thing, the theory's premise that administrators are controlled by legislators is assumed rather than defended. But the opposite assumption – that administrators enjoy substantial autonomy from legislators – is at least as plausible given how outnumbered legislators are, given the more focused expertise many administrators have over legislative generalists, and given that administrators often can create constituencies for their preferred policies (Croley 2008). If principal–agent slack therefore characterizes the relationship between legislators and administrators (e.g., Laffont and Tirole 1991), then that slack would allow administrators to fashion regulatory policies not determined for them by legislators.

That administrators are informationally captured is also suspect. For administrators are sophisticated producers and sophisticated consumers of information. Agency scientists, economists, and other in-house experts develop enormous amounts of information about regulatory alternatives. Agencies also enlist outside experts to provide information about policy alternatives. What is more, information about potential regulatory policy choices is not generated from scratch on the occasion of every new policy initiative. Rather, regulators routinely rely on vast bodies of existing scientific and economic literatures, originally produced by scientists, scholars, and organizations for innumerable purposes unrelated to regulatory policymaking. Administrators seeking information about regulatory alternatives are thus not at the mercy of regulated parties.

Nor is it clear why administrators would be inclined to favor narrow regulatory interests for their own reasons. To begin with, government employment for many line-level regulators is more aptly described as a lobster trap than a revolving door: Most regulators are career government employees, for whom different presidential administrations and legislative majorities come and go. Only a small percentage of regulators have occasion to seek other jobs anywhere, much less from regulated parties. To be sure, political appointees do not regulate indefinitely, but capture theory provides no basis for the assumption that appointees seek post-government employment with regulated parties as opposed to law firms, lobbying firms, consulting firms, and other potential employers with numerous and varied clients. The model of the regulatory commissioner who leaves government to work for the very industry she regulated is highly stylized. Or, put differently, as capture theory expanded to encompass more than utility regulation, its revolving-door premise became increasingly strained, for the behavioral implications of an employment-minded regulator who regulates across many industries are unclear. Moreover, any explicit or implicit promises between employment-minded regulators and regulated firms would plainly violate criminal laws, and thus their enforcement would be problematic anyway. The basis for assuming their enforceability (e.g., Laffont and Tirole 1991) is not apparent.[4]

Furthermore, even assuming regulators who contemplate future employment with regulated parties – in which case "mercenary" rather than "captured" regulators seems apropos – again the behavioral implications are ambiguous. For one thing, as Heyes has shown, if regulators are motivated to maximize their post-government employment prospects, they might do so not by delivering regulatory favors but rather by making regulation complex and opaque, to maximize their future market value (Heyes 2003) (industry might be said to have been captured by regulators, not the other way around). Or administrators contemplating future employment in the private sector might be more strict not less strict on regulated parties, to signal their aggressiveness and/or their intellectual quality (e.g., Che 1995). Note the threat to falsifiability: Depending on the assumed implications of a job-seeking regulator, regulatory leniency or its opposite is predicted.

Capture theory is theoretically indeterminate in other ways as well. For example, while capture theorists often posit that agencies will please interest groups and their legislative patrons in order to maximize their budgets (e.g., Niskanen 1971), administrators might seek to maximize their budgets with the benign aim of performing their regulatory missions well (Levinson 2005). Thus the budget-maximizing administrator is consistent with the capture story, and also consistent with the premise that administrators perform their regulatory missions with zeal. Similarly, some of capture theory's subplots move in opposing directions. For example, the theory often relies on Bernstein's (1955) lifecycle account of regulatory agencies, according to which socially beneficial legislation passed when a given regulatory issue is salient gives way to regulatory decay as legislators turn their attention elsewhere and administrators become captured by the entities they were supposed to regulate. Setting aside that Bernstein's account fails to identify a time span for regulatory decay which impedes its falsification (Sabatier 1975), it runs contrary to the equally frequent suggestion that legislators aim to provide regulatory rents and therefore devise tools to ensure that administrators cooperate to deliver them over the long run (McCubbins et al.1987, 1989). So in one scenario benign legislation yields over time to socially harmful administration, given that legislators cannot control agencies and agencies drift from their desirable missions, while in the other scenario malign legislation is enforced administratively, given that legislators can adopt ex ante controls to ensure administrative favoritism. Thus agency drift, and its absence – and accordingly legislative control, and its absence – may be consistent with capture. The account lacks precision.

### Facts
If capture theory found strong empirical vindication, its conceptual gaps and strained assumptions might be overlooked. Like the theory of gravity, capture theory might be supported by overwhelming evidence even if the links producing its result remain incompletely developed. But it is not. To the contrary, much empirical work calls into question not only capture theory's defining conclusion, but also its behavioral premises.

With respect to the latter, much literature shows, for example, that many broad-based interest groups (whose emergence ironically coincided with the development of capture theory; e.g., Nadel 1971; J. Berry 1977) pursue interests beyond those of their members, advocating for regulatory outcomes that could not plausibly be described as rents (e.g., Walker 1991; J. Berry 1993; Baumgartner and Leech 1998). Thus more than narrow interest groups vie for legislative and administrative benefits. For that matter, more than groups participate in regulatory decisionmaking, subjecting policymakers to the preferences of other entities as well. Moreover, some studies show that greater concentration of economic interests is not correlated with greater political activity (e.g., Lowery and Gray 2004; Hansen et al. 2005).

In addition, legislators have been shown to pursue ideological goals (e.g., Kalt and Zupan 1984, 1990; Poole and Rosenthal 1997; Holburn and Vanden Bergh 2006). Legislative behavior is therefore not reducible to a trade swapping regulatory favors for electoral resources. What is more, no revolving door between regulatory agencies and regulatory industry ensures favorable treatment of narrow interests (e.g., Gormley 1979; Quirk 1981; Freitag 1983; Cohen 1986; Makkai and Braithwaite 1992). Administrators are also demonstrably motivated to advance the mission of their agencies relying on professional norms and the management of information (e.g., W. Berry 1984; Eisner 1993). More than mere budget-maximizers, they can be motivated too by the power of ideas (e.g., Derthick and Quirk 1985).

As for agency information biases, "there is virtually no evidence on how (or whether) asymmetric information fosters regulatory capture" (Bo 2006: 216). Furthermore, administrative regulators prove capable of advancing their visions of sound regulatory policy over their life cycles (e.g., Carpenter 2001) even in the face of contrary pressure from organized interests, in part by enlisting the support of diffuse beneficiaries of regulation (e.g., Sabatier 1975; Croley 2008). All such findings undermine capture theory's premises concerning the mechanisms through which interest groups secure socially harmful regulation.

Finally, many empirical studies show that regulatory outcomes in fact reflect interests beyond those represented by narrow groups. Accordingly, regulatory policy often advances the interests of consumers and other broad-based interests, even where such groups are poorly organized (e.g., Sabatier 1975: regulation of air pollution not consistent with pessimistic capture theory; Weingast 1981: social regulation incongruous with capture's predictions; W. Berry 1984: electricity regulation inconsistent with capture theory; Becker 1986: finding support for Peltzman's (1984) public interest hypothesis of consumer protection over Stigler's (1971) capture theory; Shleifer 2005: regulation of financial markets is beneficial to development of markets and to consumers, and collecting sources; Wallsten 2001: telecommunications regulation can benefit consumers; Holburn and Vanden Bergh 2006: public utility commissions accommodate consumer interests. Nor do narrow interests routinely succeed in their attempts to influence regulatory decisionmakers (e.g., Kaserman et al. 1984: capture theory inconsistent with studied electric utility regulation; Schneiberg and Bartley 2001: rejecting cartel capture theory of state insurance regulation in favor of more powerful explanatory institutionalist factors; Leaver 2009: rejecting version of capture theory according to which regulators are driven by their own pecuniary gain, in favor of assumption that regulators are motivated by reputation). Such findings disconfirm capture theory's policy predictions.

To be sure, one can identify evidence supportive of capture theory (e.g., Yandle 2011). Some empirical studies show that narrow interest groups successfully influence regulatory policymakers (e.g., Grossman and Helpman 1994: finding interest group influence on legislators in context of trade policy; Uphadyaya and Mixon 1995: price of electricity over time confirms regulatory capture; Roberts and Kurtenbach 1998: states with more certified public accountants more likely to see entry regulation; Vukina and Leegomonchai 2006: unregulated contract terms in broiler industry consistent with capture; Drope and Hansen 2008: business associations representing more concentrated industries are more politically active). But, as Bo's recent review of the evidence confirming capture theory aptly concludes (2006: 220) the "empirical evidence on the causes and consequences of regulatory capture is scarce" (Mitchell and Munger 1991; Leight 2010; Christensen 2011).

Furthermore, the policy implications of studies showing narrow group influence are ambiguous in the absence of further evidence that regulation on the whole creates deadweight losses, even if more desirable regulation is imaginable in an ideal world where narrow interests lacked any influence.[5] For regulators might advance narrow group interests in the course of protecting diffuse consumer interests as well, such that regulatory protectionism does not show capture (Carpenter 2004). Moreover, even regulators solicitous of regulated entities may regulate to promote overall welfare and efficiency because under plausible circumstances that is what regulated entities also seek (e.g., Hardy 2006). But, most importantly, deregulation does not follow from imperfect regulation. The policy question is whether regulation is beneficial, all things considered, or whether it is not (and when, and by what metric). The prominence of capture theory is due not to overwhelming supportive evidence, but to the absence of an alternative.

## 4.2   TOWARDS A NEW THEORY OF REGULATION

So the interest group capture theory provides an unsatisfying account of regulation. Not much follows. Showing that the earth is not flat does not make it round. To date, the body of work calling capture theory into question constitutes largely a collection of free-standing critiques, evidence that elements of the interest group capture story are somehow "wrong," to be balanced against contrary evidence that its story is "right." But, while capture theory is routinely set in opposition to the "public interest theory" (e.g., Abrams and Settle 1978; Becker 1986; Laffont and Tirole 1991; Roberts and Kurtenbach 1998; Djankov et al. 2002; Vukina and Leegononschai 2006; Mulherin 2007), there is no alternative, public interest theory of regulation. As Hantke-Domas (2003) has shown, the term "public interest theory" was employed by early advocates of the interest group capture theory as a foil, referencing a competitor theory that did not exist at all (see also Mitnick 1980; Joskow and Noll 1981; Leight 2010). In short, capture theorists made it up. The rubric stuck, but with rare exceptions (Levine and Forrence 1990) "public interest theory" is used to mean simply *not capture*, as opposed to an affirmative account with its own developed premises and causal claims.

Yet the development of an alternative theory of regulation may be possible. In fact, capture theory's shortcomings inform the development of an alternative.

### 4.2.1 Conceptual Considerations

**Purpose and scope**
As capture theory illustrates, a global theory of regulation – one that purports to explain regulation over time, regulatory sub-systems, levels of government, and thus across widely varied regulatory circumstances – may be unlikely to illuminate much (e.g., Sabatier 1975; Ma. Olson 1995; Kosnick 2006). Can one theory of regulation meaningfully illuminate state regulation of fire insurance in the early 20th century (Schneiberg and Bartley 2001), the financing of presidential elections in the 1970s (Abrams and Settle 1978), and contemporary environmental regulation (Zinn 2002), much less business entry regulation across 85 different political systems and cultures (Djankov et al. 2002)?

Maybe. It depends on the purpose of the theory. A universal theory of animal behavior might show, for example, that all animals seek nourishment, adapt to a habitat, and procreate at some critical rate. Such generalizations may be useful for some purposes, yet provide little guidance to those attempting to save the endangered ocelot, or to those seeking more effective fly-fishing techniques. So too the utility of an all-encompassing theory of regulation may be modest for federal policymakers seeking insight about, for example, how to stabilize financial institutions in the wake of the recent financial crisis. If the purpose of a theory of regulation is to identify modest, all-things-equal tendencies of regulatory institutions, then broad-stroke analysis may be sensible. If instead the aim is to provide practical insight for policymakers, generalizations about the consequences of regulation that transcend varying types of regulatory authorities, procedures, and environments find expression at such a high level of generality that they provide little guidance for real-world regulatory policy questions.

A policy-oriented theory of regulation, then, should quickly confront questions of scope, and highlight important distinctions across regulatory environments. An account of federal administrative regulation in the U.S. might distinguish between decisions by administrators within the executive branch of government, on the one hand, and those of independent administrators who have considerable autonomy from the presidential administration, on the other. Likewise, administrative regulators with committed budgets – such as regulators of financial institutions who are funded by fixed and stable assessments upon regulated entities – might behave differently than regulators whose budgets are determined by the budget cycle. In short, regulators operating within different regulatory environments and thus under substantially different constraints should be analyzed at least in part according to those differences. Likewise, proponents of an alternative theory of regulation are well advised to distinguish also among types of regulatory decisions. At least the question is open whether, for example, price regulation and health-and-safety regulation are explicable according to the same fundamental regulatory dynamics.

None of this is to argue against generalization. Of course, the purpose of a theory is to facilitate generalization across cases. All the same, not all generalizations are equally illuminating or plausible, and the boundaries of a useful theory of regulation warrant careful consideration. The most fruitful level of generality is likely to be that (1) which generalizes across comparably situated regulatory decisionmakers, (2) who exercise similar regulatory authority (3) through comparable decisionmaking methods and (4) under similar legal-environmental conditions. As a first cut, proponents of a new theory of regulation might consider whether focusing on particular regulatory phyla provides greater theoretical insight than the more universal strains of interest group capture theory (cf. Bernstein 1961).

**Policy determinants**

To say that capture theory's behavioral premises are implausible begs important questions. For example, if legislators do not in effect simply sell regulatory favors to remain in office, and if some legislators need worry little about reelection in any event, an alternative account must model their (more complex) motivations. Where ideology, beliefs about the proper role of government, and visions of sound regulatory policymaking are taken to motivate legislators, proponents of an alternative theory of regulation must consider *how* these motivations shape regulatory policy.

Whether and how legislators are able to influence administrators in the wake of regulatory delegations also become crucial. Here the methods and limits of legislative control warrant investigative priority. Further, given that administrative decisions seem inexplicable by their desire for future employment, alternative motivations – ideology, a view of what constitutes desirable regulation, a belief in the stated mission of their regulatory agencies, bureaucratic culture, respect of their professional peers, the power of arguments made by those seeking to influence regulatory decisions, or so on – require specification as potential determinants of regulatory outcomes as well (e.g., Leaver 2009).

Whatever administrators' motivations may be, architects of a post-capture theory of regulation must also consider to what extent administrators have the wherewithal to act on them. Just as little follows from the identification of legislative interests wherever legislators lack the means to pursue their interests (because, for example, they cannot control agencies), so too little follows from the specification of administrative motivation unless administrators have methods for advancing those interests. Among students of administrative law, substantial administrative discretion is conventional wisdom (e.g., Magill 2004). But a complete theory of regulation requires some account of the levers through which administrators exercise their regulatory discretion. This issue is addressed further below.

Finally, capture theory's inadequate account of interest group behavior requires more exploration of the role of private parties in regulatory decisionmaking. First, given that the logic of collective action on which the interest group account heavily relies fails to show how narrow interests, and only narrow interests, emerge to participate in regulatory decisionmaking, more conceptual work is necessary to determine whether, why, and how different types of interests mobilize. Furthermore, given that capture theory does not explain why interest groups – as distinct from business firms and other types of organizations – deserve near-exclusive focus as the primary private participants in regulatory politics, proponents of a new theory of regulation should undertake more "census" work to better understand not only which interests participate in regulatory decisionmaking, but also through what organizational form. For example, more research is needed concerning what if anything makes interest groups, as an organizational form, so advantageous for the purpose of affecting regulatory outcomes (Croley 2010). If, for instance, the interest group form proves more advantageous for certain types of interests (e.g., consumers and environmentalists who organize to realize economies of scale across many specific regulatory issues), but not others (e.g., business firms already well positioned to represent their interests independently), more research is necessary concerning the relative importance of interest groups and business firms in the development of regulatory policy.

Here too again, the basic challenge for those who would develop an alternative theory of regulation is to identify not only who participates in regulatory decisionmaking – legislators, administrators, interest groups, business firms, public interest organizations, and others – and what their corresponding regulatory goals are, but also what particular resources each participant uses to advance those aims. With respect to interest groups specifically, if their participation in regulatory decisionmaking does not reduce to providing stick-figure legislators with campaign contributions in exchange for favorable regulatory policy, the alternative channels of their influence must be identified. Likewise, if narrow interest groups do not always (or usually) possess superior information relative to that of other participants in the regulatory process, then what other resources do they enlist to pursue their regulatory goals? To understate, such questions remain unexhausted.

### 4.2.2 Criteria of Desirable Regulation

Whatever its defects, capture theory's message about what makes regulation objectionable is attractively clear: Regulation constitutes the delivery of economic benefits to undeserving interest groups that is not only wasteful but also objectionable from a distributional point of view. Rejecting this conclusion does not establish that regulation is a proper policy response to pressing economic or social problems. Maybe regulation does not usually provide rents to narrow interests, or redistribute wealth from ordinary citizens to powerful interest groups, but wastes lots of resources nonetheless. Thus those who would not only reject capture theory's deregulatory policy orientation but also put something in its place must articulate what is *right* about regulation, where regulation is taken to succeed. What does a regulatory regime not plagued by the defects interest group capture theory envisions look like?

For example, if regulation is taken to be socially desirable because by addressing market failures it creates net social benefits, data about the cost–benefit effects of regulatory decisions allow for the assessment of claims about the beneficial effects of regulation. Or proponents of an alternative picture of regulation may judge regulation according to its distributional effects, and thus the desirability of regulation might be evaluated by whatever criteria are taken to mark a distributional improvement. A new theory of regulation might instead defend regulatory outcomes that reflect the judgment of independent policy experts, or else that enjoy widespread support among citizens. Here again, expert or public support or its absence with respect to a given regulatory initiative is measurable, and thus again the desirability of regulation can be assessed accordingly. The important point is that a new theory of regulation with normative implications must include criteria against which desirable regulatory outcomes can be assessed. Sweeping assertions that regulation inevitably confers illicit rents should not be replaced with broad declarations that regulation advances the public interest. Thus Joskow and Noll (1981: 36) understandably suggest that the so-called public interest theory constitutes "normative analysis as positive theory." They rightly observed that a public interest vision of regulation reincarnates Pigouvian emphasis on regulation (Pigou

1928) to address market failure, although they overstate to say that a public interest view ever postured as positive theory at all.

Meanwhile, the distinction between ideal regulation and successful regulation – that is, between regulatory aspirations and regulatory improvements – must be maintained. Proponents of a new theory of regulation should not commit themselves to regulatory nirvana. From a cost–benefit perspective, for instance, ideal regulation maximizes net social benefits. But ideal is a high standard, and regulation is defensible – because socially useful – where it creates net benefits. Just as markets need not be perfectly competitive to be attractively competitive, so too regulation need not perfectly balance marginal costs and marginal benefits in order to improve social welfare. Similarly, from a point of view that emphasizes public support for regulation, a new regulatory initiative that enjoyed broad though not overwhelming public support may well count as an improvement over the regulatory status quo. And so on.

### 4.2.3 Evidence

Post-capture analyses must also provide reliable expectations about the relationship between the contemplated determinants of regulation, on the one hand, and observed regulatory outcomes, on the other. In short, a new theory of regulation should be subject to confirmation. Happily, considerations of empirical robustness impose welcome discipline on the conceptual development of a new theory, as testability will promote greater specification of what a new theory takes to be the main determinants of regulation.

Yet the post-capture theorist need not start from scratch. If the existing evidence does not vindicate capture theory, what does it suggest? How can that evidence, taken as a whole, best be organized? Is there an alternative account of regulation that better comports with existing evidence? Proponents of a new theory of regulation should reanalyze available data.

Beyond that, proponents of an alternative to the interest group capture story should test falsifiable predictions against newly gathered evidence as well. In the first place, plausible but untested theories will prove unconvincing to those habituated to view regulation as undesirable, and thus will gain few adherents beyond those already dubious of the capture story. Furthermore, precisely because capture theory does not enjoy powerful empirical confirmation, evidence supporting an alternative account will advance the understanding of regulation considerably. Nor is the literature on regulation saturated with empirical studies. It is fair to say that classic pleas for greater empirical research of the regulatory process (e.g., Bernstein 1961) have not been fully answered. Proponents of an alternative theory of regulation would thus make rapid advances with well-designed empirical investigation.

### 4.2.4 Rhetoric

Replacing the interest group capture account of regulatory agencies will also require cogent terminology. For the endurance of capture theory in the face of its weaknesses is due in no small part to the economy of its rhetoric. Its identifying terms not only label an argument, but also succinctly advance one: Regulators are captured. Likewise, capture theory's central if mixed metaphors – a "market" for regulation among participants whose relationship constitutes an "iron triangle" though they move through a "revolving door" – hold compelling grips on scholarly imagination.

But if regulators are not "captured," what are they? And if regulation is not fundamentally the result of an illicit exchange in which regulatory goods are supplied to satisfy interest group demand, proponents of a new theory must communicate the alternative determinants of regulation convincingly. Among other things, a new theory requires succinct expression of the purpose of regulation, as well as a rhetorically compelling account of what motivates regulators. In short, a viable post-capture theory, certainly one ever to have resonance with policymakers, requires evocative articulation.

## 4.3   FROM INTERESTS TO PROCEDURES

More can be said about the building blocks of a new account of regulation. As suggested above, if the shortcomings of the interest group theory of regulation can be reduced to a single failure, that failure would be its conspicuous imprecision about the very production of regulation, that is, about the specific channels through which the preferences of rent-seeking interest groups are converted into concrete regulatory decisions. Although regulatory decisions are commonly the product of complex legal procedures that provide varied opportunities for interested parties to affect regulatory outcomes, those processes are oddly largely elided from the most influential theory of regulation. A new theory should heed calls to put regulatory institutions back in (e.g., Kalt and Zupan 1984; Hägg 1997; Martimort 1999; Russo 2001; Schneiberg and Bartley 2001; Nixon et al. 2002; Helm 2006; Holburn and Vanden Bergh 2006). Unless the procedural rules through which regulations are developed and the environment in which regulation is produced are irrelevant to understanding regulatory outcomes, an assumption capture theory does not vindicate, a new theory of regulation should unpack regulation's machinery.[6]

### 4.3.1   The Regulatory Process

As widely noted if seldom emphasized, regulatory decisionmaking is governed by numerous authorities that constrain the exercise of regulatory authority. A regulatory agency can issue a new rule, for example, only upon following procedures prescribed by the Administrative Procedure Act (APA) and other procedural statutes and executive orders. Among other things, rulemaking procedures require agencies to provide notice of their intent to develop a new rule, and allow opportunities for interested parties to provide argument and information relevant to the proposed rule, and to justify the rule finally developed in light of interested parties' reactions to the agency's proposal.

This notice-and-comment process is open to any interested party. In fact, any party can petition a regulatory agency to initiate a new rule. Rulemaking's openness thus raises central questions about what kinds of interests participate in rulemaking, through what organizational forms, and how such participation affects the development of regulatory rules. Likewise, rulemaking's openness also raises questions about whether and how regulators could deliver regulatory favors only to narrow interest groups, given that rulemaking records can be easily monitored by the public, broad-based interest groups, the press, and the courts.

Participation in rulemaking takes the form of commentary and argumentation by participating parties, whose comments often include data or reference to relevant economic and scientific literature. Comments provided during the development of a rule become part of an agency's rulemaking docket, a public record, and one that can serve as the basis for judicial challenge to a rule later, especially where the agency's final rule failed to consider information or data squarely relevant to its rule. In short, information is the currency of the rulemaking process. As a result, well-informed parties, as opposed to only participants with the most economic resources, may be well positioned to influence the development of a rule. Given the centrality of agency rulemaking to regulatory decisionmaking, proponents of a new theory of regulation should investigate the relationship between the rulemaking process and regulatory outcomes. Any theory of regulation that abstracts away the rulemaking process will be radically incomplete.

Agencies issue regulatory decisions besides rules as well. For example, the agency adjudication process culminates in the issuance of an order. Like rulemaking processes, adjudication procedures too are prescribed by the APA, other procedural statutes, and adjudicating agencies themselves. They too are designed to promote decisionmaking neutrality. In the regulatory arena, administrative law judges typically preside over the adjudication process. The administrative law judge enjoys some degree of independence from the parent agency, and parties may not engage in *ex parte* communications with the presiding judge. Instead, participants submit evidence relevant to the agency's decision into a formal record, which then becomes the basis for the agency's final order. Like rulemaking dockets, the adjudicatory record produced is public, and can form the grounds for judicial challenges to an agency's order.

Agencies also regulate through less formal processes, which result in agency decisions besides notice-and-comment rules and formal orders. Most notably, regulatory agencies often issue "guidances" in the course of implementing regulatory legislation, often to specify enforcement of agency rules. Agencies issue other informal statements, rulings, and opinions too, many of which have regulatory significance. Such informal decisions are perhaps especially worthy of study by developers of a new theory of regulation, given that their issuance is not constrained by strict procedures and thus may reveal much about administrative motivations.

Even where agencies' informal decisions are not governed by the procedural requirements of the APA, other statutes ensure various levels of regulatory transparency. For example, the Sunshine Act requires regulatory commissions to hold meetings in public. The Freedom of Information Act requires agencies to publish or disclose many types of information relevant to regulatory deliberations. The Federal Advisory Committee Act also requires agencies to make public all regulatory policy advice and recommendations they receive, as well as the information on which that advice is based. The National Environmental Protection Act requires agencies contemplating regulatory action that would have a substantial impact on the environment to prepare reports outlining those impacts. Such requirements increase the availability of information about both the impetus for regulatory action and the expected consequences of regulatory policy alternatives.

Nor are regulatory decisions constrained only by legal-procedure requirements narrowly understood. Executive agencies must seek White House approval for many regulatory initiatives. White House review of proposed regulations, according to cost–benefit and other criteria, therefore constitutes another consequential part of the rulemaking process. Because any party that objects to an agency's regulatory decision might bring suit, regulatory agencies must also contemplate courts' likely reactions to their decisions. As the standards of judicial review require courts to consider the evidentiary basis for regulatory decisions as well as whether an agency has acted within the scope of its legal authority, agencies must anticipate judicial reactions to the sufficiency of the information on which their decisions rest. And although agencies do not always know which of their regulatory decisions will be challenged in court – although high-stakes decisions frequently are – the very possibility of judicial review affects agency decisionmaking. Thus, just as a new theory of regulation should incorporate the statutory procedures that condition the exercise of regulatory authority in the first place, such a theory should also accommodate the many procedural feedback effects of executive and judicial review on administrator behavior.

In fact, at bottom all regulatory decisionmaking processes can be well understood, and distinguished, according to how they channel the production and management of information about the consequences of regulatory alternatives. And, just as competition within the marketplace imposes discipline and rewards ingenuity, so too competition among ideas and information constrains but also liberates regulatory decisionmakers, by making certain policy choices less or more defensible. Because regulatory outcomes reflect the regulatory decisionmaking process employed to reach them, a new theory of regulation should incorporate regulatory procedure (and, in turn, legislative[7] and administrative choice of procedure) as one central determinant of regulation.

Here again, developers of a new theory need not start afresh. Much valuable work begins to incorporate administrative procedure as a determinant of regulatory outcomes. For example, W. Berry (1984) has shown that the structure of commissions regulating electricity prices affects the substance of regulatory outcomes, and furthermore that legal intervention in rate-setting procedures by consumers also affects rates. That finding is corroborated by Holburn and Vanden Bergh (2006), who find that ideologically motivated legislatures are more likely to create procedures institutionalizing consumer advocates in utility regulation when legislators' reelection prospects were uncertain. For another example, Nixon et al. (2002) have investigated whether notice-and-comment rulemaking by the Securities and Exchange Commission allows regulated entities to secure regulation favorable to them, concluding it does not. Similarly, Magat, Krupnick, and Harrington (1987), Golden (1998), West (2004), and Kamieniecki (2006) find insubstantial business bias in examined notice-and-comment rulemakings of several agencies. These examples are not exhaustive (e.g., McKay and Yackee 2007), but such studies have not yet been integrated into a fuller account of regulation.

### 4.3.2 Identifying the Benefits of Regulatory Process

Analyses of agency decisionmaking procedures lead quickly to questions about their effects. On many traditional accounts (e.g., Herring 1936; Landis 1938), administrative processes are designed to foster the application of bureaucratic expertise to questions of regulatory implementation and enforcement. Indeed, classically agency authority is taken to be legally legitimate largely on the grounds that administrators are better positioned than legislators to harness expertise relevant to policy implementation (e.g.,

Wilson 1887). Although capture theory holds that matters do not work out so well, if agencies are not inevitably captured, maybe agency decisionmaking methods facilitate the development of desirable regulation after all.

But, again, a theory of regulation that rejects capture theory's distinguishing claim that regulation constitutes the delivery of rents to undeserving interest groups must then specify the benign consequences taken to follow from a robust process. Whatever those consequences are taken to be, proponents of a new theory of regulation should articulate how decisionmaking process rules advance them. Fortunately, the explanatory purchase of administrator motivations, regulatory decisionmaking procedures, and the larger environment in which administrative regulators operate lend themselves to empirical confirmation. Just for example, some regulatory processes – for example, rulemaking – see varying amounts of outside participation. Such variation makes possible investigation of the consequences of participation on the development of agency rules (e.g., Yackee 2006; Yackee and Yackee 2006). Also, whether regulated parties fare better when agencies rely on certain decisionmaking procedures rather than others is susceptible to empirical inquiry. Likewise, agency reactions to executive oversight (e.g., Bressman and Vandenberg 2006) and judicial review can be observed and measured. As existing work shows, the yield from new work examining the relationship between regulatory process and regulatory outcomes would contribute substantially to the understanding of regulation.

Finally, as architects of an alternative theory of regulation devise empirical tests of plausible institutional determinants of regulatory policy, they should develop a vocabulary corresponding to a new framework. For example, accepting the rhetoric of interest group capture commits students of regulation to the question whether administrators are or are not captured. That question should not displace all others, however (cf. Gormley 1986). Rather, architects of a new theory of regulation should investigate the circumstances that lead to greater or lesser agency autonomy or discretion. Similarly, instead of seeking to prove or disprove legislative dominance, proponents of a post-capture theory should instead seek to assess the consequence of legislative feedback, perhaps relative to feedback by the White House, the judiciary, and private participants in regulatory decisionmaking processes. Likewise, proponents of a new theory of regulation should consider how regulators solicit, assess, and manage information, which is not either symmetric or asymmetric, but also contested or uncontested. Thus a new account may see regulation as the coordination of expertise as opposed to the sale of regulatory goods. In short, proponents of a new theory of regulation, most especially one that incorporates the real legal-procedural and other institutional features of regulatory decisionmaking, should not commit themselves to a rhetoric that provides little room for those features.

## 4.4   CONCLUSION

The influence of the interest group capture theory of regulation exceeds its reliability. It does so in part due to the absence of an alternative. While capture theory has seen substantial criticism, its critics have yet to integrate their criticisms, much less to construct a full-fledged alternative account. The development of an alternative requires, among other things, consideration of the purpose and therefore scope of a new theory, a thicker account of administrator motivations, and certainly greater attention to the legal-procedural channels through which regulators exercise regulatory authority. A new theory of regulation also requires a vocabulary capable of challenging capture theory's monopoly on powerful metaphor. Finally, and not least of all, a new theory of regulation according to which regulation may be socially beneficial will require clear articulation of the criteria of beneficial regulation.

## NOTES

1.  This chapter uses "interest group capture" or "capture theory" to refer to a body of literature in political economy according to which organized narrow interest groups secure regulation that advances their economic interests at the greater expense of citizens generally, as explained below. The set of ideas in question is also known as the "economic theory of regulation" and, especially in legal-academic literature, as a facet of "public choice theory." The "special interest theory" is another common rubric. Scholars sometimes distinguish among types of capture – "interest group capture" and "predatory capture," for example (Roberts and Kurtenbach 1998) – but here those distinctions are expressed, following conventional use of the term, as different strands of the same essential picture. While "capture" is sometimes used capaciously to mean any kind of influence by narrow interests on government policy (e.g., Etzioni 2009), here the term labels certain forms of illicit interest group influence on regulatory policy.
2.  It is useful to distinguish between "strong capture," which holds that regulation categorically tends to generate rents, and "weak capture," which holds that powerful interests sometimes exercise socially harmful influence on regulatory policy but does not imply that regulation is on balance socially harmful. See generally Carpenter et al. (forthcoming). This chapter focuses on strong capture.
3.  The premise that narrow interests can overcome obstacles to collective action whereas broad interests cannot is a linchpin of the interest group capture theory. Many have rightly noted the tight connection between Stigler (1971) and Olson (1965). See for example Laffont and Tirole (1991: 1090); Hägg (1997: 343); Bagley and Revesz (2006: 1284); and Bo (2006: 205), among many others. Any weaknesses in the Olsonian account thus plague Stigler's by incorporation.
4.  Moreover, administrators seeking personal economic gain might simply start in the private sector (Meier 1985); public service seems round-about.
5.  See above, note 2.
6.  To give credit where due, much of the positive analysis of regulation moves beyond interests and highlights institutions in the abstract sense. Exploring principal–agent problems, contracting costs, and other transactions costs, positive political theory identifies the implications of strategic interaction among policymakers and interest groups. It does not fully explore actual regulatory decisionmaking processes, however, which it instead abstracts away, and it largely treats governmental institutions – legislatures, agencies, and courts – as monolithic. Positive political theory's important contribution to the study of regulation thus does not typically extend to illuminating the effects of real-world regulatory procedures on regulatory outcomes.
7.  To be sure, regulatory process rules may be partially endogenous to regulatory interests, but it is too much to say they are entirely so. Moreover, the arrow goes both ways; regulatory preferences are endogenous to regulatory structure as well, for different institutional arrangements will reveal the bases and consequences of regulatory alternatives more or less clearly, and in turn create larger or smaller incentives to participate in regulatory decisionmaking.

## REFERENCES

Abrams, Burton A. and R. Settle (1978), 'The economic theory of regulation and the public financing of presidential elections', *Journal of Political Economy*, **86**, 247–52.

Arnold, R.D. (1990), *The Logic of Congressional Action*, New Haven, CJ: Yale University Press.

Bagley, N. and R.L. Revesz (2006), 'Centralized oversight of the regulatory state', *Columbia Law Review*, **106**, 1260–1329.

Baumgartner, F. and B. Leech (1998), *Basic Interests: The Importance of Groups in Politics and in Political Science*, Princeton, NJ: Princeton University Press.

Becker, G. (1986), 'The public interest hypothesis revisited: a new test of Peltzman's theory of regulation', *Public Choice*, **49**, 223–34.

Bernstein, M. (1955), *Regulating Business by Independent Commission*, Princeton, NJ: Princeton University Press.

Bernstein, M. (1961), 'The regulatory process: a framework for analysis', *Law and Contemporary Problems*, **26**, 329.

Berry, J. (1977), *Lobbying for the People: The Political Behavior of Interest Groups*, Princeton, NJ: Princeton University Press.

Berry, J. (1993), 'Citizen groups and the changing nature of interest group politics in America', *Annals of the American Academy of Political and Social Science*, **528**, 30–41.

Berry, W.D. (1984), 'An alternative to the capture theory of regulation: the case of public utility commissions', *American Journal of Political Science*, **28** (3), 524–58.

Bo, E.D. (2006), 'Regulatory capture: a review', *Oxford Review of Economic Policy*, **22** (2), 203–25.

Bressman, Lisa and M. Vandenberg (2006), 'Inside the administrative state: a critical look at the practice of presidential control', *University of Michigan Law Review*, **105**.

Buchanan J. and G. Tullock (1962), *The Calculus of Consent*, Ann Arbor: University of Michigan Press.

Carpenter, D. (2001), *The Forging of Bureaucratic Autonomy: Reputations, Networks and Policy Innovation in Executive Agencies, 1862–1928*, Princeton, NJ: Princeton University Press.

Carpenter, D. (2004), 'Protection without capture: product approval by a politically responsive, learning regulator', *American Political Science Review*, **98** (4), 613–31.

Carpenter, D., S. Croley and D. Moss (forthcoming), *Preventing Capture*.

Cater, D. (1964), *Power in Washington*, New York: Random House.

Che, Y.-K. (1995), 'Revolving doors and the optimal tolerance for agency collusion', *RAND Journal of Economics*, **26** (3), 378–97.

Christensen, Jorgen (2011), 'Competing Theory of Regulatory Governance', in David Levi-Faur (ed.), *Handbook on the Politics of Regulation*, Northampton, NH: Edward Elgar.

Cohen, J. (1986), 'The dynamics of the "revolving door" on the FCC', *American Journal of Political Science*, **30** (4), 689–708.

Croley, S. (2008), *Regulation and Public Interests: The Possibility of Good Regulatory Government*, Princeton, NJ: Princeton University Press.

Croley, S. (2010), 'Interest groups and public choice', in D.A. Forber and A.J. O'Connell (eds), *Reserved Handbook on Public Choice and Public Law*, Cheltenham, UK and Northampton, MA, USA: Edward Elgar Publishing.

DeFigueirido, J. (2002), 'Lobbying and information in politics', *Business and Politics*, **4** (2), 125–8.

Denzau, A. and M. Munger (1986), 'Legislators and interest groups: how unorganized interests get represented', *American Political Science Review*, **80** (1), 89–106.

Derthick, M. and P. Quirk (1985), *The Politics of Deregulation*, Washington, DC: Brookings Institution.

Djankov, S., R. La Porta, F. Lopez-de-Silanes, and A. Shleifer (2002), 'The regulation of entry', *Quarterly Journal of Economics*, **117** (1), 1–35.

Drope, J. and W. Hansen (2008), 'New evidence for the theory of groups: trade association lobbying in Washington DC', *Political Research Quarterly*, **62** (2), 303–16.

Eisner, M. (1993), 'Bureaucratic professionalization and the limits of the political control thesis: the case of the Federal Trade Commission', *Governance*, **6**,127–53.

Etzioni, A. (2009), 'The capture theory of regulation – revisited', *Society*, **46**, 319–23.

Freeman, J. (1965), *The Political Process*, New York: Random House.

Freitag, P. (1983), 'The myth of corporate capture: regulatory commissions in the United States', *Social Problems*, **30** (4), 480–89.

Golden, M. (1998), 'Interest groups in the rule-making process. Who participates? Whose voices get heard?', *Journal of Public Administration Research and Theory*, **8** (2), 245–70.

Gormley, W. (1979), 'A test of the revolving door hypothesis at the FCC', *American Journal of Political Science*, **23** (4), 665–83.

Gormley, W. (1986), 'Regulatory issue networks in a federal system', *Polity*, **18** (4), 595–620.

Grossman, G. and E. Helpman (1994), 'Protection for Sale', *American Economic Review*, **84** (4), 833–50.

Hägg, P. (1997), 'Theories on the economics of regulation: a survey of the literature from a European perspective', *European Journal of Law and Economics*, **4**, 337–70.

Hansen, W., N. Mitchell and J. Drope (2005), 'The logic of private and collective action', *American Journal of Political Science*, **49** (1), 150–67.

Hantke-Domas, M. (2003), 'Public interest theory of regulation: non-existence or misinterpretation', *European Journal of Law and Economics*, **15**, 165–94.

Hardy, D. (2006), 'Regulatory capture in banking', IMF Working Paper WP/06/34.

Helm, D. (2006), 'Regulatory reform, capture, and the regulatory burden', *Oxford Review of Economic Policy*, **22** (2), 169–84.

Herring, P. (1936), *Public Administration and the Public Interest*, New York: McGraw-Hill.
Heyes, A.G. (2003), 'Expert advice and regulatory complexity', *Journal of Regulatory Economics*, **24** (2), 119–33.
Holburn, G. and R. Vanden Bergh (2006), 'Consumer capture of regulatory institutions: the creation of public utility consumer advocates in the United States', *Public Choice*, **126**, 45–73.
Huntington, S. (1952) 'The marasmus of the ICC: the commission, the railroads and the public interest', *Yale Law Journal*, **61** (4), 467.
Joskow, P. and R. Noll (1981), 'Regulation in theory and practice: an overview', in Gary Fromm (ed.), *Studies in Public Regulation*, Cambridge, MA: MIT Press.
Kalt, J. and M. Zupan (1984), 'Capture and ideology in the economic theory of politics', *American Economic Review*, **74** (3), 279–300.
Kalt, J. and M. Zupan (1990), 'The apparent ideological behavior of legislators: testing for principal–agency slack in political institutions', *Journal of Law and Economics*, **33**, 103–31.
Kamieniecki, S. (2006), *Corporate America and Environmental Policy: How Often Does Business Get Its Way?*, Palo Altom, CA: Stanford University Press.
Kaserman, D., R. Kavanaugh and R. Tepel (1984), 'To which fiddle does the regulator dance? Some empirical evidence', *Review of Industrial Organization*, **1** (4), 247.
Kolko, G. (1965), *Railroads and Regulation 1877–1916*, Princeton, NJ: Princeton University Press.
Kollman, K. (1997), 'Inviting friends to lobby: interest groups, ideological bias and congressional committees', *American Political Science Review*, **41** (2), 519–44.
Kosnick, L.-R. (2006), 'Sources of bureaucratic delay: a case study of FERC dam relicensing', *Journal of Law, Economics and Organization*, **22** (1), 258–88.
Krueger, A. (1974), 'The political economy of the rent-seeking society', *American Economic Review*, **64**, 291–303.
Laffont, J.-J. and J. Tirole (1991), 'The politics of government decision-making: a theory of regulatory capture', *Quarterly Journal of Economics*, **106** (4), 1089–1127.
Laffont, J.-J. and J. Tirole (1993), *A Theory of Incentives in Regulation and Procurement*, Cambridge, MA: MIT Press.
Landis, J. (1938), *The Administrative Process*, New Haven, CT: Yale University Press.
Leaver, C. (2009), 'Minimum squawk behavior: theory and evidence from regulatory agencies', *American Economic Review*, **99** (3), 572–617.
Leight, Jessica (2010), 'Public choice: a critical reassessment', in Ed Balleisen and David Moss (eds), *Government and Markets: Toward a New Theory of Regulation*, Cambridge: Cambridge University Press.
Levine, M. and J. Forrence (1990), 'Regulatory capture, public interest and the public agenda: toward a synthesis', *Journal of Law, Economics and Organization*, **6**, 167–203.
Levinson, D. (2005), 'Empire-building in constitutional law', *Harvard Law Review*, **118**, 915.
Lowery, D. and V. Gray (2004), 'A neopluralist perspective on research on organized interests', *Political Research Quarterly*, **57** (1), 164–75.
Magat, W., A. Krupnick and W. Harrington (1987), 'Rules in the making: a statistical analysis of regulatory agency behavior', *Journal of Economics*, **3** (18), 461–4.
Magill, M.E. (2004), 'Agency choice of policymaking form', *University of Chicago Law Review*, **71**, 1383–1447.
Makkai, T. and J. Braithwaite (1992), 'In and out of the revolving door: making sense of regulatory capture', *Journal of Public Policy*, **12** (1), 61–78.
Martimort, D. (1999), 'The life cycle of regulatory agencies: dynamic capture and transaction costs', *Review of Economic Studies*, **66** (4), 929–47.
McCubbins, M., R. Noll and B. Weingast (1987), 'Administrative procedures as instruments of political control', *Journal of Law, Economics and Organization*, **3**, 243–77.
McCubbins, M., R. Noll and B. Weingast (1989), 'Structure and process, politics and policy: administrative arrangements and the political control of agencies', *Virginia Law Review*, **75**, 431–82.
McKay, A. and S. Yackee (2007), 'Interest group comments on federal agency rules', *American Political Research*, **35** (1), 336–56.
Meier, K. (1985), *Regulation: Politics, Bureaucracy, and Economics*, New York: St. Martin's Press.
Mitchell, W. and M. Munger (1991), 'Economic models of interest groups: an introductory survey', *American Journal of Political Science*, **35** (1), 512–46.
Mitnick, Barry (2011), 'Industry capture', in David Levi-Faur (ed.), *Handbook on the Politics of Regulation*, Northampton, NH: Edward Elgar.
Mitnick, B. (1980), *The Political Economy of Regulation*, New York: Columbia University Press.
Mulherin, J. (2007), 'Measuring the costs and benefits of regulation: conceptual issues in securities markets', *Journal of Corporate Finance*, **13**, 421–37.
Nadel, M. (1971), *The Politics of Consumer Protection*, Indianapolis, IN: Bobbs-Merrill.
Niskanen, W. (1971), *Bureaucracy and Representative Government*, Chicago: Aldine Atherton.

Niskanen, W. (1975), 'Bureaucrats and politicians', *Journal of Law and Economics*, **1**, 617–43.

Nixon, D., R. Howard and J. DeWitt (2002), 'With friends like these: rule-making comment submission to the Securities and Exchange Commission', *Journal of Public Administration Research and Theory*, **12** (7), 59–76.

Olson, M. (1965), *The Logic of Collective Action: Public Goods and the Theory of Groups*, Cambridge, MA: Harvard University Press.

Olson, M.K. (1995), 'Regulatory agency discretion among competing industries: inside the FDA', *Journal of Law, Economics, and Organization*, **11** (2), 379–405.

Peltzman, S. (1984), 'Constituent interest and congressional voting', *Journal of Law and Economics*, **27** (10), 181–210.

Peltzman, S. (1989), 'The economic theory of regulation after a decade of deregulation,' *Brookings Papers in Microeconomics*, **1** (41).

Pigou, A. (1928), *A Study in Public Finance*, London: Macmillan.

Poole, K. and H. Rosenthal (1997), *Congress: A Political-Economic History of Roll Call Voting*, Oxford: Oxford University Press.

Posner, R. (1974), 'Theories of economic regulation', *Bell Journal of Economic and Management Science*, **5**, 335–55.

Quirk, P. (1981), *Industry Influence in Federal Regulatory Agencies*, Princeton, NJ: Princeton University Press.

Reenok, C. and B. Gerber (2007), 'Political insulation, information exchange and interest group access to the bureaucracy', *Journal of Public Administration Research and Theory*, **18**, 415–40.

Roberts, R. and J. Kurtenbach (1998), 'State regulation and professional accounting educational reforms: an empirical test of regulatory capture theory', *Journal of Accounting and Public Policy*, **17**, 209–26.

Russo, M. (2001), 'Institutions, exchange relations and the emergence of new fields: regulatory policies and independent power production in America, 1978–1992,' *Administrative Science Quarterly*, **46**, 57–86.

Sabatier, P. (1975), 'Social movements and regulatory agencies: toward a more adequate – and less pessimistic – theory of clientele capture', *Policy Science*, **6** (3), 301–42.

Schneiberg, M. and T. Bartley (2001), 'Regulating American industries: markets, politics, and the institutional determinants of fire insurance regulation,' *American Journal of Sociology*, **107** (1), 101–46.

Shleifer, A. (2005), 'Understanding regulation,' *European Financial Management*, **11** (4), 439–51.

Stewart, R. (1975), 'The reformation of American administrative law,' *Harvard Law Review*, **88**, 1669–1813.

Stigler, G. (1971), 'The theory of economic regulation', *Bell Journal of Economics and Management*, **2**, 3–21.

Stigler, G. (1974), 'Free riders and collective action: an appendix to theories of economic regulation', *Bell Journal of Economics and Management*, **5**, 359–65.

Stigler, G. (1975a), 'Can regulatory agencies protect the consumer?', in *The Citizen and the State: Essays on Regulation*, Chicago: University of Chicago Press.

Stigler, G. (1975b), 'Supplementary note on economic theories of regulation', in *The Citizen and the State: Essays on Regulation*, Chicago: University of Chicago Press.

Stigler, G. and C. Friedland (1962), 'What can regulators regulate? The case of electricity', *Journal of Law and Economics*, **5**, 1–16.

Tollison, R. (1989), 'Chicago political economy', *Public Choice*, **63**, 293–7.

Tullock, G. (1967), 'The welfare costs of tariffs, monopolies and theft', *Western Economics Journal*, **5**, 224–32.

Tullock, G. (1993), *Rent Seeking*, Aldershot, UK and Brookfield, VT, USA: Edward Elgar Publishing.

Uphadyaya, K. and F. Mixon, Jr. (1995), 'Regulatory capture and the price of electricity: evidence from time series estimates', *International Journal of Social Economics*, **22** (1), 16–23.

Vukina, T. and P. Leegomonchai (2006), 'Political economy of regulation of broiler contracts', *Journal of Agricultural Economics*, **5**, 1258–65.

Walker, J. (1991), *Mobilizing Interest Groups in America: Patrons, Professions and Social Movements*, Ann Arbor: University of Michigan Press.

Wallsten, S. (2001), 'An econometric analysis of telecom competition, privatization, and regulation in Africa and Latin America,' *Journal of Industrial Economics*, **41** (9), 1–20.

Weingast, B. (1981), 'Regulation, reregulation, and deregulation: the political foundations of the agency–clientele relationships,' *Law and Contemporary Problems*, **44**, 147–77.

West, W. (2004), 'Formal procedures, informal processes, accountability, and responsiveness in bureaucratic policy making: an institutional policy analysis', *Public Administration Review*, **64** (1), 66–80.

Wilson, W. (1887), 'The study of administration', *Political Science Quarterly*, **2** (2), 197–222.

Wood, B. and R. Waterman (1994), *Bureaucratic Dynamics: The Role of Bureaucracy in a Democracy*, Boulder, CO: Westview Press.

Yackee, J. and S. Yackee (2006), 'A bias toward business? Assessing interest group influence on the US bureaucracy', *Journal of Politics*, **68** (1), 128–39.

Yackee, S. (2006), 'Sweet-talking the fourth branch: the influence of interest group comments on federal agency rule-making', *Journal of Public Administration Research and Theory*, **16** (1), 103–24.

Yandle, Bruce (2011), 'Bootleggers and Baptists in the theory of regulation', in David Levi-Faur (ed.), *Handbook on the Politics of Regulation*, Northampton, NH: Edward Elgar.

Zinn, M. (2002), 'Policing environmental regulatory enforcement: co-operation, capture, and citizen suits', *Stanford Environmental Law Journal*, **21**, 81.

# 5 Institutional design and the management of regulatory governance

*Steven J. Balla*

The delegation of policymaking authority to public bureaucracies is a defining feature of contemporary democratic governance. Such delegation benefits elected officials immensely by, for example, bringing agency expertise to bear on complex economic and social problems (Bawn 1995). Delegation, however, also presents officeholders with the difficult task of influencing the behavior of organizations that possess the ability to act independently of even the most powerful political forces (Carpenter 2001). It is with this task in mind that legislatures and political executives throughout the world have provided themselves with instruments through which to manage delegated authority.

The instruments of managing delegation fundamentally structure the institutional environments within which public bureaucracies craft, implement, and enforce regulatory decisions.[1] Such instruments, for example, establish rules governing the access of citizens, organized interests, and elected officials to regulatory proceedings (Kerwin and Furlong 2011). In allocating access, these instruments have implications for the influence that various types of economic and societal actors exert over regulatory outputs and outcomes (Wood and Waterman 1994). The management of delegated authority is therefore a salient consideration in determining the extent to which regulatory agencies advance the public interest or, alternatively, are captured by specialized industry organizations (Christensen 2011; Croley 2011).[2]

This chapter lays out the behavioral and institutional contours of the management of delegated authority. The focus is mainly on delegation by the United States Congress, although consideration is also given to parliamentary democracies. It is common in research on delegation to distinguish between instruments of agency design and instruments that facilitate oversight of regulatory governance and the bureaucracy in general. In addition, a distinction is made here between instruments that require collective action on the part of elected officials and instruments that are employed by officeholders acting on their own. This latter distinction draws attention to the fact that influencing bureaucratic outputs and outcomes is not the only aim of elected officials who employ instruments of agency design and oversight. Rather, instruments are at times useful to elected officials as means toward other ends, such as bolstering claims for reelection and increasing personal power within political institutions. Given such motivations, the exercise of regulatory governance is inextricably linked to the politics of agency design and oversight.

The presence of disparate instruments and motivations for managing delegation dictates that attention be paid to two questions regarding bureaucratic policymaking. What specifically are the instruments that elected officials have at their disposal for directing administrative agencies? What are the implications of the characteristics and utilization of these instruments for understanding the structure and process of regulatory governance? The first step in addressing these questions is to lay out the range of instruments that elected officials, both in the United States and in parliamentary democracies, use to manage authority delegated to the bureaucracy. Given these options, the second step is to consider the conditions under which particular types of instruments are connected with the advancement of specific economic and societal interests. Through these tasks, the associations between institutional design and bureaucratic decision making can not only be systematically explicated, but also connected back to foundational theoretical perspectives on the participation and influence of various types of stakeholders in regulatory governance.

## 5.1 THEORIES OF REGULATION AND STAKEHOLDER PARTICIPATION AND INFLUENCE

As a means of establishing a broad context for considering and evaluating instruments of managing delegation, it is important at the outset to lay out the principal components of salient theories of regulatory governance. Generally speaking, theories of regulation focus on two main questions. First, what types of actors participate in the making of regulatory decisions? The types of actors with a stake in agency decisions range from business firms targeted by regulations to broad societal constituencies such as consumers, environmentalists, and advocates of the public interest. Second, what is the relative influence that different types of participants exert over regulatory decision making? Theories of regulation offer a variety of perspectives on the extent to which regulatory proceedings are dominated by one type of constituency at the expense of others.

Perhaps the oldest perspective on regulatory governance is the theory of regulation in the public interest. The foundational notion of public interest theory is that regulation generally serves to protect the "public interest against private, especially business, interests" (Christensen 2011: 3). Public interest theory, it is important to recognize, does not assume that action in the public interest occurs in every possible context. Rather, regulatory action is taken specifically in those instances in which the overall costs of regulation are lower than the costs imposed by the targeted activities themselves (Yandle 2011: 6).

Although examples of regulation in the public interest are plentiful, the most dominant paradigm in the study of regulatory governance over the past several decades has been interest group capture theory. Grounded in the public choice tradition (Buchanan and Tullock 1962), capture theory posits that regulation ordinarily operates as a mechanism for transferring resources from broad societal constituencies to narrow economic interests (Yandle 2011). Such rent-seeking behavior is a by-product of the expectation that narrow interests are more likely than broad constituencies to overcome barriers to collective action (Olson 1965; Stigler 1971, 1974).

A classic example of industry capture is nuclear power policymaking in the middle of the twentieth century (Baumgartner and Jones 1993). By the 1950s, scientists and public utilities interested in harnessing nuclear power technology for civilian energy production had found a reliable partner in the United States Atomic Energy Commission (AEC). In a series of decisions that delivered enormous economic rents to industry actors, the AEC, the agency charged with regulating nuclear power production, ordered the construction of more than one hundred nuclear power plants at locations around the country. During this period of rapid expansion, industry mobilization greatly outstripped the activism of the courts, mass media, public utility commissions, and other representatives of broad societal constituencies.

In addition to drawing attention to differential mobilization on the part of industry and society, capture theory posits institutional reasons for the delivery of narrowly constructed regulatory benefits. Agency decision makers typically operate in environments characterized by legislative attention to the design and oversight of regulatory institutions (Croley 2011). The presence of this attention means that agencies have strong incentives to confer benefits upon constituencies aligned with important legislative actors. In the case of nuclear power policy, the Joint Congressional Committee on Atomic Energy served as a powerful institutional advocate for the rapid development of power plants and industry capacity in general (Baumgartner and Jones 1993).

Capture theory has been criticized on a number of grounds that are salient in the context of legislative management of delegated authority (Croley 2011). For example, it is well established that legislators oftentimes do not favor industry interests over broad societal constituencies. In other words, instruments of institutional design and oversight are routinely utilized to steer regulatory benefits to consumers, environmentalists, and advocates of the public interest. By the 1960s, concerns about safety and environmental degradation had compelled legislators to pressure the AEC to bring civilian nuclear operations to a virtual standstill (Baumgartner and Jones 1993). In general, capture theory does not offer an empirically sustainable account of the institutional incentives faced by legislators and regulatory decision makers.

As this discussion indicates, instruments of agency design and oversight carry important implications for advancing theoretical understanding of regulatory governance. Patterns of stakeholder participation and influence are fundamentally connected to such instruments, as well as to the legislative motivations that lead to their deployment. The next task, then, is to classify agency design and oversight, as a means of characterizing the institutional environments within which industry interests and broad societal constituencies compete for regulatory outputs and outcomes.

## 5.2   INSTRUMENTS OF BUREAUCRATIC DESIGN AND OVERSIGHT

Elected officials can influence the exercise of delegated policymaking authority through two basic strategies – the design of bureaucratic structure and process and the oversight of agency decisions. These strategies are distinct, although not perfectly so, in both timing and orientation. Agency design occurs before the bureaucracy acts and shapes the institutional environments within which decision making occurs. An example of this approach is the Administrative Procedure Act of 1946, which requires agencies to provide prior notice of their intention to issue a regulation and to accept public comments on their proposed rules (McCubbins et al. 1987; Kerwin and Furlong 2011). Oversight, in contrast, takes place after the bureaucracy has acted and aims at ensuring that such actions conform to political preferences. Oversight can be carried out by elected officials directly, through mechanisms such as committee hearings and investigations (Aberbach 1990). Alternatively, citizens and organized interests can monitor agency behavior and alert elected officials when bureaucrats make noncompliant or unpopular decisions (McCubbins and Schwartz 1984).

Instruments for managing delegated authority also vary in the extent to which they require collective action on the part of elected officials. On the one extreme, there are instruments that cannot be utilized in the absence of statutory approval. In recent years, about 15 percent of the regulations developed by federal agencies in the United States have been subjected to congressional deadlines (Balla et al. 2007). These deadlines are specified in statutes such as the Energy Independence and Security Act of 2007, which required the National Highway Traffic Safety Administration to provide consumers with information about the fuel efficiency of tires by December 18, 2009.[3] On the other extreme, there are instances in which elected officials take steps on their own to manage the bureaucracy, as in the context of casework conducted on behalf of specific constituents (Johannes 1979). As Representative Michael E. Capuano (Democrat, Massachusetts) states on his website, "My office has helped literally hundreds of persons, citizens and non-citizens, with immigration difficulties."[4] Such assistance has involved intervening with the Departments of State and Homeland Security on behalf of African refugees who find themselves in the midst of bureaucratic proceedings.

The distinction between the archetypes of collective and individual instruments of managing delegated authority exists only as an ideal, in that specific instruments are routinely used in both manners. The Congressional Review Act of 1996 provides Congress with expedited procedures for nullifying agency regulations in the first 60 days after they have been issued. In 2001, the Occupational Safety and Health Administration's ergonomics rule, which had been decades in the making, became the first, and thus far only, regulation to be overturned in this way (Gormley and Balla 2007). Although nullification requires collective action, the Congressional Review Act has also been used by individual legislators as a means of registering dissatisfaction with the direction of agency decision making. In 1997, Representative Joe Scarborough (Republican, Florida) introduced a resolution objecting to the Federal Communications Commission's rules on cable television leased commercial access (Balla 2000).

In the end, the distinction between instruments of collective and individual action is salient not because it offers clear-cut classification, but in that it draws attention to the various goals that elected officials pursue when seeking to manage delegated authority. In addition to pursuing ends directly related to the substance of agency decisions, elected officials also seek to manage the bureaucracy as a means of enhancing their prospects for reelection and gaining power within the political system (Fenno 1978). Given the multifaceted nature of such ends, instruments of agency design and oversight are salient not only in structuring and producing changes in agency behavior, but also in serving the full range of outcomes pursued by elected officials. Table 5.1 lays out the most common and important instruments of managing delegated authority. These instruments are discussed and evaluated in the sections that follow.

### 5.2.1 Agency Design

A common instrument of agency design is assigning a delegated task to a single organization that is favorably disposed toward the underlying goals of elected officials (Moe 1990). This kind of structural arrangement typically reflects an environment where

*Table 5.1   Instruments of managing delegated authority*

| Agency design | Oversight |
| --- | --- |
| ● Assign task to favorably disposed agency | ● Bureaucratic reorganization |
| ● Fragment authority | ● Constituent casework |
| ● Deadlines | ● Resolutions disapproving of agency action |
| ● Hammers | ● Commission studies and reports |
| ● Detailed statutory constraints | ● Hearings and investigations |
| ● Limitation riders | ● Statutory and budgetary changes |
| ● General procedural requirements | |
| ● Specific procedural requirements | |
| ● Comments on proposed rules | |

conflict is muted and a particular organized interest, ordinarily business and industry, is especially influential among elected officials (Macey 1992). Delegation to a single agency therefore is most often associated with the kinds of regulatory proceedings that are the hallmarks of capture theory.

Elected officials employ bureaucratic design not only to facilitate agency action, but also to make it difficult for agencies to follow particular courses. One such instrument is the fragmentation of agenda-setting and policymaking authority across governmental and non-governmental organizations. When Congress established the Consumer Product Safety Commission in 1972, it permitted the agency to issue regulations but limited this authority to standards that had been offered by industry interests, representatives of the general public, and other parties from outside government (Hermanson 1978; McCubbins et al. 1987). In general, when Congress institutes new programs or substantially revises existing ones, it calls for the involvement of more than a single agency in the "overwhelming majority" of the cases (Meier and O'Toole 2006: 56).

Delegation to the bureaucracy can also be managed through the use of statutory deadlines. Although the imposition of deadlines is common throughout the executive branch, certain agencies are especially likely to operate under such constraints. In recent years, three agencies – the Department of Transportation, Department of Homeland Security, and Department of Health and Human Services – have faced deadlines in about one out of every four of their regulatory decisions, a rate that is double the government-wide norm (Balla et al. 2007).

Deadlines are sometimes accompanied by hammers, legislative provisions that automatically take effect if an agency fails to act in a specified period. Hammers are often set so that they are satisfactory to neither elected officials nor the bureaucracy, thereby providing agencies with incentives to finalize decisions in advance of deadlines. The Resource Conservation and Recovery Act, for example, established a total ban on land disposal of wastes in the absence of timely action on the part of the Environmental Protection Agency (Kerwin and Furlong 2011).

A direct instrument for limiting bureaucratic discretion is the enactment of detailed statutory constraints. Elected officials routinely introduce legislation explicitly forbidding agencies from performing particular tasks. In 2007, members of Congress sought to prevent, among many other executive branch actions, the Department of State from making a contribution to the United Nations, the Department of Agriculture from importing certain cattle and beef from Canada, and the Department of the Interior from issuing oil and gas leases on portions of the Outer Continental Shelf.[5]

A related tool for blocking agency action is the limitation rider. Limitation riders are provisions in "general appropriations bills or floor amendments to those measures that prohibit the spending of funds for specific purposes" (Oleszek 2004: 53). On an annual basis, bills proposed by the House Appropriations Committee contain hundreds of such provisions (MacDonald 2007).

Elected officials have placed an array of general procedural hurdles in front of agencies seeking to promulgate regulations. The National Environmental Policy Act (NEPA) of 1969 is a landmark statute in this regard (Kerwin and Furlong 2011). Under NEPA, agencies are required to determine whether prospective rules are likely to have a significant impact on the environment. For regulations judged affirmatively, agencies must then prepare environmental impact assessments, laying out the steps that will be taken to mitigate harmful environmental consequences. Other general procedural mandates include the Paperwork Reduction Act and Regulatory Flexibility Act, both of which were passed in 1980 (Kerwin and Furlong 2011). The Paperwork Reduction Act forces agencies to consider, and if necessary to ameliorate, the paperwork burdens produced by regulations. The key element of the Regulatory Flexibility Act is that agencies are required to analyze the impact of rules on small organizations such as businesses, with an eye toward providing these entities with less burdensome means of complying with executive branch dictates.

In one respect, these procedural requirements have been useful for elected officials seeking to advance the interests of important constituencies by steering the bureaucracy in particular policy directions. NEPA has encouraged agencies from across the government to increase the weight given to environmental considerations in regulatory proceedings. To take one example, after NEPA was passed, the Federal Energy Regulatory Commission became substantially more likely to issue pro-environment hydroelectric licensing decisions (Spence 1999).

From a different vantage point, these procedural requirements have caused rulemaking to become ossified and therefore more difficult for elected officials to meaningfully direct (McGarity 1992). One indicator of ossification is the delays that are frequently associated with the crafting of regulations. Rulemakings at the Environmental Protection Agency average more than 1000 days in length (Kerwin and Furlong 1992). Furthermore, it is not unheard of for rules to take more than ten years to develop (Kerwin and Furlong 2011). These realities imply that procedures are useful both as instruments for facilitating particular types of regulatory decisions and for slowing down or stopping rulemaking altogether.

This same assessment applies to procedural mandates that are more specific in their focus. Elected officials routinely write into statutes detailed instructions for the procedures that particular agencies must follow when crafting regulations. The Federal Railroad Administration, for example, is required to hold public hearings as part of all of its rulemakings. Some statutory instructions apply not just to particular agencies, but to specific regulatory actions. The Price–Anderson Amendments Act of 1988 required the Nuclear Regulatory Commission to conduct a negotiated rulemaking to determine whether radiopharmaceutical licensees should be indemnified (Coglianese 1997).

Elected officials not only enact procedural requirements, but also take advantage of opportunities provided by these mandates and participate directly in agency decision making. For example, it is not uncommon for members of Congress to submit comments on proposed agency regulations, especially when the issues at hand are politically contentious and attract media attention. In 1995, dozens of senators, including majority leader Bob Dole (Republican, Kansas), signed a comment opposing the Food and Drug Administration's proposal to restrict the marketing and sales of cigarettes and smokeless tobacco to individuals under the age of 18 (Kessler 2001).

### 5.2.2   Oversight

One important form of oversight is bureaucratic reorganization. Elected officials can reorganize the executive branch in a number of ways, including the creation of new agencies and elimination of existing ones (McCubbins et al. 1987). Although the Department of Homeland Security stands out as a recent landmark, there has been no shortage of reorganization efforts over time and across policy areas. Between 1946 and 1997, Congress created 182 agencies, including such disparate organizations as Amtrak, the National Military Establishment, and the Federal Mediation and Conciliation Service (Lewis 2003). During this same period, hundreds of bureaucracies were terminated (Lewis 2002). One of these agencies was the Interstate Commerce Commission, which had been regulating the railroad and trucking industries for more than a century when it was dissolved in 1995.

Casework provides elected officials with myriad opportunities to oversee the bureaucracy on a scale that is small and specific, yet salient to electoral calculations. Constituency service fosters oversight in three main ways (Johannes 1979). First, when responding to constituent requests, elected officials are routinely successful in encouraging agencies to take particular courses of action. Second, casework sometimes compels elected officials to engage in other forms of oversight, such as holding hearings, conducting investigations, and introducing legislation. Third, political inquiries can make agency officials aware of problems inside the bureaucracy. As one official put it, "if I see a pattern of abuses, I call one of our field inspectors to check out what's going on" (Johannes 1979: 335).

In contrast to the ubiquity of casework, the prevention of bureaucratic action through the passage of resolutions disapproving of agency rules is extraordinarily unusual. Despite the dim prospects for success, legislators continue to introduce resolutions more than a decade after the Congressional Review Act became law. In 2007, resolutions were introduced disapproving of rules issued by agencies such as the Department of Agriculture and Department of Homeland Security's Citizen and Immigration Services.[6] None of these resolutions were reported out of the committees to which they were assigned, although most of them attracted a number of cosponsors.

When overseeing the bureaucracy, legislators routinely task government organizations with conducting research and producing reports on executive branch policies and programs (McCubbins et al. 1987). The Government Accountability Office supports oversight in a variety of ways, including auditing agency operations and investigating allegations of illegal and improper activities.[7] In 2007, the Government Accountability Office produced over one thousand reports, addressing such disparate topics as the processing of veterans' disability benefits and the management of agricultural quarantine inspection programs. The Congressional Budget Office is charged with tasks that include projecting the budgetary effects of government operations. For example, the agency has estimated that the United States–Peru Trade Promotion Agreement Implementation Act, which President Bush signed into law on December 14, 2007, will have the net effect of reducing deficits by $20 million over the 2008–17 period.[8]

Historically, oversight, as epitomized by hearings, has been considered a "neglected function" (Bibby 1968: 477). In other words, elected officials generally prefer engaging in activities that are salient and visible to their constituents to the mundane work of conducting hearings on executive branch programs. This assessment has come under critical scrutiny in recent years, as there has been a significant increase in the volume of oversight over the past several decades (Aberbach 1990). During the 1960s, congressional committees collectively spent fewer than 200 days per year conducting oversight. By 1983, the level of activity had grown to 587 days. In addition, oversight as a percentage of total committee activity increased from 9.1 percent in 1971 to 25.2 percent in 1983.

One form of oversight that elected officials have never shied away from is high-publicity investigations. At times, investigations are oriented toward spurring the bureaucracy to act. In 1956, the Senate conducted an inquiry into the inadequacies of airpower planning in the Eisenhower administration, highlighting how the United States was falling behind the Soviet Union (Mayhew 1991). In other instances, Congress's focus is on reining in runaway agencies. A classic example occurred in 1987, when Congress conducted a probe into the Iran–Contra Affair, the Reagan administration operation in which weapons were first sold to Iran in exchange for the release of American hostages and then the proceeds of these sales were used to fund Nicaraguan rebels.

When instruments of oversight uncover agencies that are lethargic or overly zealous, one of the remedies that elected officials routinely pursue is statutory and budgetary changes. By shuffling discretionary authority and spending within or across agencies, such changes target specific decisions or entire organizations that are problematic from the perspective of legislators and powerful constituencies. In 1964, the Federal Trade Commission issued a rule requiring cigarette manufacturers to disclose on packages, boxes, cartons, and advertisements that smoking is dangerous to one's health and may cause death from cancer and other diseases (Fritschler and Rudder 2006). A year later, members of Congress held hearings at which tobacco industry representatives testified that there was scientific doubt regarding the adverse effects of smoking and that regulating tobacco would bring great harm to the economy. In the aftermath of these hearings, Congress passed the Cigarette Labeling and Advertising Act, which negated the Federal Trade Commission's rule and prohibited the agency from considering any regulation in this policy area for four years.

### 5.2.3 Neutral Delegation versus Stacking the Deck

An implication of the above considerations is that instruments of managing delegated authority can be divided into those that "increase the transaction costs of agency decision making" and those that increase the "costs of making a *particular* decision" (Spence 1997: 205). For example, comments on proposed regulations are procedurally neutral in that they can be submitted by any party interested in the decisions at hand. Other instruments of agency design, such as mandating the preparation of environmental impact assessments, structure participatory environments to the advantage of specific constituencies. For its part, oversight is naturally oriented toward redirecting regulatory governance in ways consistent with the preferences of particular elected officials and constituencies. In sum, the regulatory regimes envisioned by both public interest theory and capture theory – participation and influence dominated by specific types of stakeholders – are especially likely to be associated with decision-making environments characterized by active oversight and instruments of agency design that stack structures and processes in identifiable substantive directions.

## 5.3    MANAGING DELEGATION BEYOND THE UNITED STATES CONGRESS

In parliamentary systems, the relationship between elected officials and bureaucrats is fundamentally shaped by the absence of a separation between legislative and executive powers. Typically, the locus of policymaking is party leaders who are members of the cabinet (Huber and Shipan 2002), although centralization and ministerial authority vary across parliamentary contexts (Peters 1991). Governments are distinguished, for example, in whether they are headed by a majority party, minority party, or coalition of parties (Peters 1997). Parliamentary systems also diverge in their stability, in terms of both the partisan composition of governments and the distribution of power within governing arrangements (Huber 1998).

Cabinet ministers routinely confront difficulties in managing delegated authority. In the 1980s, officeholders in the government of prime minister Margaret Thatcher were largely stymied in their efforts to rein in the expenditures of the British bureaucracy (Peters 1991). Generally speaking, ministers find it challenging during times of political uncertainty to encourage the bureaucracy to carry out their preferred courses of action (Huber and Lupia 2001). Such difficulties hold even when civil servants view ministerial policies favorably, as bureaucrats face incentives to delay implementation when the prospects for government turnover, and thus political retribution, are particularly pronounced.

Elected officials in parliamentary systems possess many of the same instruments of agency design and oversight as members of Congress. Reorganization has been used in a number of countries as a tool for encouraging bureaucratic action. The "Next Step" reforms in Great Britain sought not only to improve agency innovation, efficiency, and service, but also to transfer policymaking functions to organizations headed by politically appointed chief executives (Huber and Shipan 2002). In addition, statutory constraints are commonly employed as tools for limiting bureaucratic discretion. Ireland's Employment Equality Act of 1998, for example, explicitly defines the words and actions that are construable as sexual harassment (Huber and Shipan 2002).

Some instruments that are often used by members of Congress are not central to agency design and oversight in parliamentary systems. Procedural requirements are not effective long-term strategies for ministers seeking to influence bureaucratic action, as formal structures can be readily revised or eliminated by subsequent governments (Moe and Caldwell 1994). Such changes, although certainly possible in separation of powers systems, are more likely to be implemented in parliamentary democracies, especially in contexts where governing parties are cohesive in their policy preferences.

The reverse also holds, in that elected officials in parliamentary systems possess instruments for managing delegation that are seldom, if ever, utilized by members of Congress. Many of these instruments derive from the exercise of executive power that distinguishes cabinet ministers from legislators in separation of powers systems. For example, ministers have the authority to politicize the bureaucracy through appointments, promotions, and dismissals, although the precise contours of this authority varies across contexts (Mayntz and Derlien 1989; Bernhard 1998; Huber 2000). In Belgium and Great Britain, ministers are relatively circumscribed in their ability to impact the advancement and job security of civil servants (Ridley 1983; Huber and Shipan 2002). In contrast, leaders in Japan's Liberal Democratic Party have historically used personnel decisions to effectively control bureaucratic careers (Ramseyer and Rosenbluth 1993).

In the end, although there is variation across political systems in managing delegated authority, the instruments laid out in Table 5.1 provide a template not just for the United States Congress but for other institutional settings as well. Influencing agency outcomes, securing reelection, and pursuing institutional power are goals that both legislators and cabinet ministers routinely seek to advance through delegation and its management. Agency design and oversight are the main means utilized toward these ends both in parliamentary democracies and in separation of powers systems.

## 5.4 INSTITUTIONAL DESIGN AND THEORIES OF REGULATORY GOVERNANCE

Historically, the management by elected officials of authority delegated to public bureaucracies has been viewed as a kind of all-or-nothing proposition. On the one hand, there are arguments about the information advantages that agencies inherently hold over elected officials and how these advantages readily serve as catalysts for runaway bureaucracies (Niskanen 1971). On the other hand, the case has been made that elected officials possess and do not hesitate to utilize an array of instruments to exercise effective control over agency activities, despite outward appearances to the contrary (Weingast and Moran 1983).

In recent years, research has shifted attention away from blanket claims about political control and agency autonomy toward understanding the conditions under which elected officials delegate policymaking authority to the bureaucracy (Epstein and O'Halloran 1999; Huber and Shipan 2002). This approach emphasizes the importance of cataloging instruments of agency design and oversight, as well as laying out the policy, electoral, and institutional power motivations behind the management of delegated authority. In constructing such a classification, this chapter focuses attention on the characteristics of instruments that are, or are not, associated with the advancement of identifiable economic and societal interests. Specifically, the utilization of both instruments that are procedurally neutral and instruments that are stacked in favor of particular constituencies demonstrates that the preferences and choices of elected officials cannot be meaningfully separated from the structures and processes through which bureaucratic outputs and outcomes are produced.

This connection between institutional design and bureaucratic policymaking is salient in part because of the insight it offers into theories of regulatory governance. Such theories devote substantial attention to developing expectations regarding the participation and influence of different types of stakeholders in regulatory proceedings. In public interest theory, broad constituencies such as consumers and environmentalists are most often the primary beneficiaries of government regulations. Capture theory, in contrast, conceptualizes regulation as a rent-seeking device designed to deliver societal resources to narrow economic interests.

Despite the historical and contemporary importance of these accounts, neither public interest theory nor capture theory has established an empirically sustainable framework for incorporating information about the motivations and institutional environments of legislators and executive decision makers. With these limitations in mind, the distinctions highlighted in this chapter suggest that bringing information about the management of delegation to bear on stakeholder participation and influence can serve as an instrument for moving theories of regulation beyond unconditional statements about industry capture and the public interest. The political management of regulatory governance does not occur solely in institutional settings oriented toward translating the interests of specific economic and societal constituencies into bureaucratic outputs and outcomes. Rather, agency design and oversight vary over time and across political systems in the extent to which they facilitate the pursuit of objectives beyond positions immediately articulated by regulatory stakeholders.

When viewed in this conditional manner, the expectations of public interest theory and capture theory are most likely to be realized in institutional environments characterized by active political oversight and agencies designed to produce decisions and policies stacked in favor of specific constituencies. In contrast, the utilization of instruments that are procedurally neutral, such as public commenting on proposed regulations, is likely, relatively speaking, to be associated with patterns in stakeholder participation and influence that deviate from both industry capture and regulation in the public interest. The identification of such connections between agency design, oversight, and regulatory governance holds the promise of integrating theories of regulation more closely with the study of the management of delegated authority and, more generally, decision making in political institutions.

## ACKNOWLEDGEMENTS

I would like to thank David Levi-Faur and Richard Salt for providing encouragement at various stages in the development of this chapter.

## NOTES

1.  This chapter specifically focuses on political management of policymaking authority delegated to organizations inside government. Regulation consists of one of the central types of public policies that are produced by such bureaucracies. Other research in this volume (Levi-Faur 2011) discusses issues in defining regulation and specifying the organizations that engage in regulatory governance.
2.  The instruments of managing delegation are themselves in part a by-product of the activism and influence

of industry and societal actors. Given this endogeneity, the chapter focuses on identifying patterns of association, rather than making assertions regarding the underlying causal mechanisms at work.
3. Information about this action can be found at http://www.reginfo.gov/public/do/eAgendaViewRule?publ
d=200910&RIN=2127-AK45 (accessed November 23, 2010).
4. This quotation, as well as a number of specific examples of Representative Capuano's casework, can
be viewed at http://www.house.gov/capuano/services/casework_examples.shtml (accessed November 23,
2010).
5. These and other bills can be identified via THOMAS, the Library of Congress's online source for legislative
information (http://thomas.loc.gov/) (accessed November 29, 2010).
6. Information about these resolutions can be found at http://thomas.loc.gov (accessed November 29, 2010).
7. Information about the Government Accountability Office and its activities can be found at http://gao.gov/
(accessed November 29, 2010).
8. This cost estimate is accessible at http://www.cbo.gov/ftpdocs/89xx/doc8910/hr3688.pg.pdf (accessed
November 29, 2010).

# REFERENCES

Aberbach, Joel D. (1990), *Keeping a Watchful Eye: The Politics of Congressional Oversight*, Washington, DC:
Brookings Institution.
Balla, Steven J. (2000), 'Legislative organization and congressional review of agency regulations', *Journal of
Law, Economics, and Organization*, **16**, Fall, 424–48.
Balla, Steven J., Jennifer M. Deets and Forrest Maltzman (2007), 'Outside communications and OMB review
of agency regulations', unpublished manuscript.
Baumgartner, Frank R. and Bryan D. Jones (1993), *Agendas and Instability in American Politics*, Chicago:
University of Chicago Press.
Bawn, Kathleen (1995), 'Political control versus expertise: congressional choices about administrative proce-
dures', *American Political Science Review*, **89**, March, 62–73.
Bernhard, William (1998), 'A political explanation of variations in central bank independence', *American
Political Science Review*, **92**, June, 311–27.
Bibby, John F. (1968), 'Oversight and the need for congressional reform', in Melvin R. Laird (ed.), *Republican
Papers*, Garden City, NY: Anchor Books, pp. 477–88.
Buchanan, James M. and Gordon Tullock (1962), *The Calculus of Consent: Logical Foundations of
Constitutional Democracy*, Ann Arbor: University of Michigan Press.
Carpenter, Daniel P. (2001), *The Forging of Bureaucratic Autonomy: Reputations, Networks, and Policy
Innovation in Executive Agencies, 1962–1928*, Princeton, NJ: Princeton University Press.
Christensen, Jorgen Gronnegaard (2011), 'Public interest regulation reconsidered: from capture to credible
commitment', in David Levi-Faur (ed.), *Handbook on the Politics of Regulation*, Cheltenham, UK and
Northampton, MA: Edward Elgar Publishing.
Coglianese, Cary (1997), 'Assessing consensus: the promise and performance of negotiated rulemaking', *Duke
Law Journal*, **46**, April, 1255–1349.
Croley, Steven (2011), 'Beyond capture: towards a new theory of regulation', in David Levi-Faur (ed.),
*Handbook on the Politics of Regulation*, Cheltenham, UK and Northampton, MA: Edward Elgar Publishing.
Epstein, David and Sharyn O'Halloran (1999), *Delegating Powers: A Transaction Cost Politics Approach to
Policy Making under Separate Powers*, New York: Cambridge University Press.
Fenno, Richard F. (1978), *Home Style: House Members in Their Districts*, Boston, MA: Little, Brown.
Fritschler, A. Lee and Catherine E. Rudder (2006), *Smoking and Politics: Bureaucracy Centered Policymaking*,
6th edn, Upper Saddle River, NJ: Prentice Hall.
Gormley, William T., Jr. and Steven J. Balla (2007), *Bureaucracy and Democracy: Accountability and
Performance*, (2nd edn), Washington, DC: CQ Press.
Hermanson, Judith A. (1978), 'Regulatory reform by statute: the implications of the Consumer Product Safety
Commission's "offeror system"', *Public Administration Review*, **38**, March–April, 151–5.
Huber, John D. (1998), 'How does cabinet instability affect political performance? Portfolio volatility and
health care cost containment in parliamentary democracies', *American Political Science Review*, **92**,
September, 577–91.
Huber, John D. (2000), 'Delegation to civil servants in parliamentary democracies', *European Journal of
Political Research*, **37**, May, 397–413.
Huber, John D. and Arthur Lupia (2001), 'Cabinet instability and delegation in parliamentary democracies',
*American Journal of Political Science*, **45**, January, 18–32.

Huber, John D. and Charles R. Shipan (2002), *Deliberate Discretion? The Institutional Foundations of Bureaucratic Autonomy,* New York: Cambridge University Press.

Johannes, John R. (1979), 'Casework as a technique of U.S. congressional oversight of the executive', *Legislative Studies Quarterly,* **4,** August, 325–51.

Kerwin, Cornelius M. and Scott R. Furlong (1992), 'Time and rulemaking: an empirical test of theory', *Journal of Public Administration Research and Theory,* **2,** April, 113–38.

Kerwin, Cornelius M. and Scott R. Furlong (2011), *Rulemaking: How Government Agencies Write Law and Make Policy,* 4th edn, Washington, DC: CQ Press.

Kessler, David (2001), *A Question of Intent: A Great American Battle with a Deadly Industry,* New York: PublicAffairs.

Levi-Faur, David (2011), 'Regulation and regulatory governance', in David Levi-Faur (ed.), *Handbook on the Politics of Regulation,* Cheltenham, UK and Northampton, MA: Edward Elgar Publishing.

Lewis, David E. (2002), 'The politics of agency termination: confronting the myth of agency mortality', *Journal of Politics,* **64,** February, 89–107.

Lewis, David E. (2003), *Presidents and the Politics of Agency Design: Political Insulation in the United States Government Bureaucracy, 1946–1997,* Stanford, CA: Stanford University Press.

MacDonald, Jason A. (2007), 'Competition, proposal power, and policy-making in the U.S. House of Representatives: limitation riders in House appropriations bills, 1993–2002', unpublished manuscript.

Macey, Jonathan R. (1992), 'Organizational design and political control of administrative agencies', *Journal of Law, Economics, and Organization,* **8,** March, 93–110.

Mayhew, David R. (1991), *Divided We Govern: Party Control, Lawmaking, and Investigations, 1946–1990,* New Haven, CT: Yale University Press.

Mayntz, Renate and Hans-Urlich Derlien (1989), 'Party patronage and politicization of the West German administrative elite, 1970–1987: toward hybridization?', *Governance: An International Journal of Policy and Administration,* **2,** October, 384–404.

McCubbins, Mathew D. and Thomas Schwartz (1984), 'Congressional oversight overlooked: police patrols versus fire alarms', *American Journal of Political Science,* **28,** February, 165–79.

McCubbins, Mathew D., Roger G. Noll and Barry R. Weingast (1987), 'Administrative procedures as instruments of political control', *Journal of Law, Economics, and Organization,* **3,** Autumn, 243–77.

McGarity, Thomas O. (1992), 'Some thoughts on "deossifying" the rulemaking process', *Duke Law Journal,* **41,** June, 1385–1462.

Meier, Kenneth J. and Laurence J. O'Toole, Jr. (2006), *Bureaucracy in a Democratic State: A Governance Perspective,* Baltimore, MD: Johns Hopkins University Press.

Moe, Terry M. (1990), 'The politics of structural choice: toward a theory of public bureaucracy', in Oliver E. Williamson (ed.), *Organization Theory: From Chester Barnard to the Present and Beyond,* New York: Oxford University Press, pp. 116–53.

Moe, Terry M. and Michael Caldwell (1994), 'The institutional foundations of democratic government: a comparison of presidential and parliamentary systems', *Journal of Institutional and Theoretical Economics,* **150,** March, 171–95.

Niskanen, William A., Jr. (1971), *Bureaucracy and Representative Government,* Chicago: Aldine, Atherton.

Oleszek, Walter J. (2004), *Congressional Procedures and the Policy Process,* 4th edn, Washington, DC: CQ Press.

Olson, Mancur (1965), *The Logic of Collective Action: Public Goods and the Theory of Groups,* Cambridge, MA: Harvard University Press.

Peters, B. Guy (1991), 'The European bureaucrat: the applicability of *Bureaucracy and Representative Government* to non-American settings', in Andre Blais and Stephane Dion (eds), *The Budget-Maximizing Bureaucrat: Appraisals and Evidence,* Pittsburgh, PA: University of Pittsburgh Press, pp. 303–53.

Peters, B. Guy (1997), 'Bureaucrats and political appointees in European democracies: who's who and does it make any difference?', in Ali Farazmand (ed.), *Modern Systems of Government: Exploring the Role of Bureaucrats and Politicians,* Thousand Oaks, CA: Sage Publications, pp. 232–54.

Ramseyer, J. Mark and Frances McCall Rosenbluth (1993), *Japan's Political Marketplace,* Cambridge, MA: Harvard University Press.

Ridley, F.F. (1983), 'Career service: a comparative perspective on Civil Service promotion', *Public Administration,* **61,** Summer, 179–96.

Spence, David B. (1997), 'Agency policy making and political control: modeling away the delegation problem', *Journal of Public Administration Research and Theory,* **7,** April, 199–219.

Spence, David B. (1999), 'Managing delegation ex ante: using law to steer administrative agencies', *Journal of Legal Studies,* **28,** June, 413–59.

Stigler, George J. (1971), 'The theory of economic regulation', *Bell Journal of Economics and Management,* **2,** Spring, 3–21.

Stigler, George J. (1974), 'Free riders and collective action: an appendix to theories of economic regulation', *Bell Journal of Economics and Regulation,* **5,** Autumn, 359–65.

Weingast, Barry R. and Mark J. Moran (1983), 'Bureaucratic discretion or congressional control? Regulatory policymaking by the Federal Trade Commission', *Journal of Political Economy*, **91**, October, 765–800.

Wood, B. Dan and Richard W. Waterman (1994), *Bureaucratic Dynamics: The Role of Bureaucracy in a Democracy*, Boulder, CO: Westview Press.

Yandle, Bruce. (2011), 'Bootleggers and Baptists in the theory of regulation', in David Levi-Faur (ed.), *Handbook on the Politics of Regulation*, Cheltenham, UK and Northampton, MA: Edward Elgar Publishing.

# 6 Voluntary programs, compliance and the regulation dilemma
## *Matthew Potoski and Aseem Prakash*

When it comes to enforcing regulations, government regulators and the firms they regulate face a dilemma: while both the government regulators and the firm are jointly better off when they cooperate in regulatory enforcement, each has a short-term incentive or tendency to defect (Scholz 1991; Potoski and Prakash 2004a). Regulated firms can cooperate by making good-faith efforts to comply with regulations and voluntarily disclosing their (accidental) regulatory violations. Firms defect by shirking their obligations to comply with regulations, seeking instead to hide all their regulatory violations. For their part, government regulators can cooperate in regulatory enforcement by forgiving minor regulatory violations and working with firms to solve the root causes of noncompliances. Government regulators can defect by treating all violations as serious and punishing them to the maximum extent allowed by law. The dilemma is that, although cooperation makes both better off, each has powerful incentives to defect, leading to outcomes that make both worse off.

In this chapter we first present the theoretical foundations for this dilemma between firms and government regulators, which we call the regulation dilemma, and show how this dilemma has a structure similar to that of the classic prisoner's dilemma. We then discuss two solutions to the dilemma: harnessing actors' reputations and establishing mechanisms for binding commitments to cooperation. Voluntary programs can help solve this dilemma by signaling attributes about firms' behaviors that regulatory enforcers would not otherwise be able to know. Firms joining a voluntary program pledge to follow the firms' conduct code and, in some cases, to have their compliance with that code audited and verified by external auditors. However, not all voluntary programs are effective at inducing members to follow their codes of conduct, and membership in a voluntary program is not always a more reliable signal about firms' behavior. We conclude the chapter with a brief discussion of what types of voluntary programs can help solve the regulation dilemma.

## 6.1 INFORMATION AND REGULATORY ENFORCEMENT

Spend only a few minutes on any major U.S. highway and it immediately becomes clear that perfect compliance with speed regulations is neither a priority nor a habit for many motorists. Most tend to drive five to ten miles per hour over the speed limit. Arguably, these motorists work under the (usually) safe assumption that the highway police only target the "serious" over-speeders, such as the ones going 15 or 20 miles per hour above the limit. Traffic police or highway patrol officers often enjoy fairly wide discretion in deciding the severity of the infraction and penalties; a driver caught going 20 miles per hour over the limit may be assigned a fine suited for a 10 miles per hour infraction while another 20 miles per hour speeder may be ticketed for the full amount. Police officers enjoy this discretion because Americans generally believe that the severity of the punishment should reflect the reasons for the infraction. A speeding joy rider deserves a bigger fine than someone rushing to work, and someone racing a woman in labor to the maternity ward deserves a free pass.

Across virtually every policy area, inspectors enforcing governmental regulations enjoy some measure of discretion which allows them to calibrate the noncompliance sanctions according to the severity of the transgression and the reasons for noncompliance. Effective calibrations may not be a simple matter: noncompliance stemming from ignorance of what regulations require may be less pernicious in relation to willful ignorance or when the regulation is knowingly disregarded. From the perspective of the government officials enforcing regulations, the challenge is that exercising enforcement discretion calls on them to base judgment on those characteristics of regulatees which are often difficult to observe and verify. The causes of noncompliance would not be a problem if they were fully known to enforcement officials. Benign violations, such as those stemming from genuine accidents or ignorance, justify leniency because more lax punishments are better suited to the crimes. Sinister noncompliance, such as that stemming from willful and recklessly negligent violations, justifies more severe sanctions. A regulation violator may seek leniency claiming benign accident or ignorance, but may in fact have been recklessly careless or willfully ignorant. For deterrence to optimally compel regulatory compliance, the level of punishment must fit not just the infraction, but the reasons why it occurred.

It is fair to say that inspectors enforcing governmental regulations are often not in a position to know the causes of noncompliance, even when it is clear that noncompliance has occurred. These inspectors must still choose some level of sanction knowing well that their mistakes might have perverse consequences on how the regulatees behave in the future. For example, punishing benign (one that is not willful or strategic) noncompliance can undermine incentives for the regulatees to take positive steps to comply with regulations in the future. On the other hand, a lack of adequate sanctioning of willful or sinister noncompliance might create perverse incentives, leading to willful noncompliance in the future.

So far we have been assuming that inspectors themselves detect instances of noncompliance. What about situations where the regulatees self-disclose their noncompliance? How might the inspectors decide on the appropriate level of sanction? Indeed, with governments' enforcement budgets stretched thin, governments may establish policies whereby firms which self-disclose their own violations are sanctioned leniently in relation to those caught through monitoring and inspection processes. But what about a strategic self-disclosure by regulatees? A self-disclosing violator may have done nothing to prevent noncompliance in the first place, and may perhaps have been even more reckless in hopes of future regulatory leniency should a violation occur. Leniency for self-disclosed violations might create a moral hazard problem that encourages reckless behavior leading to sinister violations. Yet punishing self-disclosed violations as severely as those discovered through normal compliance monitoring and inspections reduces incentives for striving for good-faith compliance.

As the above discussion suggests, regulatory compliance presents a dilemma for regulatees (henceforth firms) and government inspectors. For firms, the dilemma is that, while they may make the extra (and good-faith) effort to self-report violations, they may still be sanctioned with full severity because regulators may not deem the firms' self-reporting actions as being genuinely benign. With no way of sorting the sinister violators from the benign, the information-deficient enforcement officials may opt for the safer route: assume all firms have sinister motives, including the ones that self-report violations. Thus, by self-reporting violations, firms acting in good faith might end up creating self-incriminating evidence and still receive the same treatment as those that did not self-report. Consequently, without any credible expectation of regulatory relief, firms can be expected to pause before embarking on the self-reporting path. For government regulatory enforcers, the dilemma is that, while they would like to encourage firms to self-disclose violations, any regulatory relief in lieu of self-disclosure could be exploited by strategic violators. Thus they do not have a credible way to assure good-faith firms that they will be treated differently if they were to self-disclose violations. This creates an adverse selection problem in that good-faith firms select themselves out of the population that self-report violations, leaving the population of self-disclosers to be dominated primarily by strategic firms.

## 6.2   THE REGULATION DILEMMA

The regulation dilemma stems from the style of governments' regulatory enforcement and how firms respond to it. Each can choose a cooperative approach, which would be optimal for both sides, but both have powerful short-run incentives to choose evasive and conflictual approaches. Governments adopting a deterrence enforcement style strive to inspect and audit every firm in order to discover and fully punish every violation, even minor ones.[1] In this approach, the government specifies regulatory standards (such as "best available technology" standards in U.S. air pollution policy) and then inspects and monitors firms, doling out strong sanctions to violators. But deterrence enforcement may not deliver on its objectives. If regulations could be enforced at a low cost, policy objectives would perhaps be met. But governments' enforcement costs are nontrivial, and rigid deterrence enforcement only feeds firms' complaints that high compliance costs hurt productivity and profits (Walley and Whitehead 1994; Jaffe et al. 1995), which in turn raises firms' incentives to evade regulations (Majumdar and Marcus 2001). Further, deterrence enforcement may contribute to the adversarial relationships among regulators, firms, and NGOs (Vogel 1986; Kagan 1991; O'Leary 1993; Reilly 1999; for a critique, see Coglianese 1996).

The cooperative approach to regulatory enforcement seeks to address the drawbacks of deterrence by basing regulatory interactions on a foundation of flexibility and mutual trust between firms and governments. In this approach, regulators do not rigidly interpret the law and penalize firms for every violation. Instead, regulators lower sanctions for self-disclosed violations, particularly minor ones, and provide positive incentives such as technical assistance to help firms achieve compliance.

Just as regulators can choose a regulatory style between deterrence and cooperation, so too can firms choose their compliance style. Firms can choose to respond to government regulations with either sinister evasion or benign self-policing. In the evasion approach,

*Table 6.1   The regulation dilemma*

| | Firm | |
|---|---|---|
| | Evasion | Self-policing |
| Government | | |
| | *Conflictual context* | |
| Deterrence | 2, 2 | 5, 1 |
| | (*a, b*) | (*e, f*) |
| | | *Cooperative context* |
| Flexible enforcement | 1, 5 | 4, 4 |
| | (*c, d*) | (*g, h*) |

firms look for opportunities to skirt regulations to save on compliance costs. In the self-policing approach, firms closely monitor their activities and report and promptly correct regulatory violations. They may hope that only severe violations will be fully sanctioned and that their prompt voluntary disclosures will encourage regulators to take a lenient view of minor ones.

A win–win interaction occurs when government regulators choose cooperative regulatory enforcement and firms choose the self-policing compliance strategy. Regulators win because self-policing lightens their enforcement burden while achieving superior regulatory outcomes. Firms win because the regulatory incentives that governments provide under cooperation (forgiveness for minor violations, technical assistance, flexibility with meeting standards) make compliance easier and improve firms' profits.

The dilemma is that, although cooperation promises superior outcomes, both firms and governments have powerful incentives to behave opportunistically, thus creating lose–lose interactions. Such opportunism generates gains for the performer but still greater losses for the other side. Firms can exploit governments' regulatory relief by sinisterly evading regulations even more effectively, while governments can exploit firms' self-policing by fully punishing regulatory violations that are voluntarily disclosed in good faith. Governments may fear that firms will interpret regulatory relief as permission to circumvent regulations. Moreover, many NGO groups suspect that firms will inevitably abuse such regulatory incentives. Likewise, firms may fear that opportunistic regulators may interpret voluntarily disclosed violations as admissions of guilt that are worthy of substantial punishment, leaving those firms at a competitive disadvantage relative to their more evasive competitors. Consequently, mutual suspicion about the other's opportunism undermines cooperation.

To better illustrate these issues, we recast them into what we call the "regulation dilemma" (Scholz 1991), an extension of the prisoner's dilemma game (Luce and Raiffa 1957; Rapoport and Chammah 1965). Table 6.1 shows the payoff schedule for a hypothetical government and firm in the regulation dilemma. Given interdependence, the outcomes for each player depend on her own and the other's choice (cooperation versus evasion or deterrence). The key point is that, no matter which approach the government chooses, firms are better off evading ($b > f$, $d > h$) and, no matter which approach the firm chooses, the government is better off choosing deterrence ($a > c$, $e > g$). This creates a vicious cycle of opportunism and a series of lose–lose outcomes. Unfortunately, this behavioral equilibrium (Nash equilibrium) is Pareto suboptimal: together they are better off if the government chooses flexible enforcement and the firm chooses to self-police (cooperation: *g*, *h*).

While firms and regulators may prefer cooperation (through self-policing and flexible enforcement, respectively) to conflict (through evasion and deterrence, respectively), each will cooperate only if it is confident the other side will cooperate as well. If each fears the other will exploit cooperation, firms will attempt to evade regulations, and governments will choose deterrence. In fact, both regulators and firms know the other has good reason, at least in the short run, to promise cooperation but deliver deterrence or evasion. Thus, as in the prisoner's dilemma game, both sides end up willingly choosing conflict over cooperation (that is, defection is the dominant strategy), even though both would prefer cooperation to deterrence. In sum, in regulatory enforcement contexts the social benefits reflect the choices of both governments (deterrence versus flexible enforcement) and firms (evasion versus self-policing). For cooperation to succeed, both actors need to credibly assure the other they will not behave opportunistically.

## 6.3 SOLVING THE DILEMMA: BINDING COMMITMENTS AND REPUTATIONS

We can draw on collective action theory to suggest solutions to the collective action problems that arise in complex contracting. Achieving win–win outcomes in a prisoner's dilemma requires the players' incentives be changed so that cooperation becomes both the individually and collectively beneficial outcome for both sides. Here we draw on the collective action literature for guidance in transforming lose–lose conflict into win–win cooperation (Lichbach 1996). One class of solutions is to adjust actors' reputations in response to their cooperative or non-cooperative behavior, burnishing reputations after good behavior and tarnishing them after bad behavior. A second class of solutions is for the actors to adopt binding institutional commitments, such as imposing punishment for non-cooperative behavior (i.e., financial penalties, legal action) or reward for good behavior. These solutions have both internal and external variants. An internal solution uses only the relation between the two parties in the game by looking to restructure the payoffs so that cooperation becomes more likely. An external solution draws on the influence of parties external to the game to achieve cooperation by altering the players' payoffs within the game. Fortunately, these solutions – building a reputation for cooperation and adopting binding institutional commitments – have real-world counterparts that are available to firms and regulators, as we describe below.

### 6.3.1 Reputations

Cooperation in a single-shot prisoner's dilemma is difficult to achieve because, barring external sanctioning, defection always produces higher individual payoffs (though lower collective ones). If a game is played many times, cooperation becomes more likely if the players care about future payoffs and if their strategies in earlier games affect their opponents' strategies in subsequent rounds (Hardin 1982; Axelrod 1984). In such circumstances, the payoffs from strategies in the current round of play reflect not just the payoff from cooperation in the current round, but also the payoffs in later rounds. The tit-for-tat strategy, in which one player reciprocates her partner's move from the previous round in a repeated-play prisoner's dilemma, is a strategy that can be both individually and collectively advantageous. In such cases, defection in the current round may generate a higher payoff in the current round, but may cause greater losses in future rounds if defection induces future-playing partners to be more likely to engage in defection rather than cooperation. When a firm voluntarily behaves cooperatively when defection would have gone undetected, it builds a more credible reputation for the future. Such dynamics work in a manner similar to a "gift exchange," where actors exchange gifts to build the goodwill that facilitates future cooperation (Akerloff 1982).

When the same players interact in repeated instances of a prisoner's dilemma game, cooperative outcomes become possible. In the regulation dilemma, regulators can build a cooperative reputation by forgiving minor offenses. Firms can build a reputation for quickly disclosing and correcting their own violations. Because reputation building takes time and is expensive, the desire to benefit from an existing trustworthy reputation may create incentives to shun opportunism. On the positive side, as trust begets more trust over time and good reputations become solidified, a virtuous circle of cooperation may evolve in place of the vicious circle of opportunism predicted in the simple prisoner's dilemma. A regulator can learn which firms are trustworthy and worthy of regulatory relief and which are more sinister and more deserving of full sanctions.

Reputations can also have an external role in inducing cooperation in single-shot prisoner's dilemma games if players are engaged in subsequent games with other players. Sharing a player's choice of cooperation or defection with the other players in these future prisoner's dilemma games has an effect similar to playing a repeated game against the same player: if players care about future returns it can be rational to cooperate in the first round and then choose the same strategy as the other player in her previous game. If both players choose such a tit-for-tat strategy, where they look to their opponents' actions in previous games to decide on their own strategy in the current game, a virtuous cycle of cooperation becomes possible across multiple, single-shot prisoner's dilemma games.

In the regulation dilemma, reputational effects can shape firm and regulator interaction by providing more information about whether the counterpart will behave cooperatively. Sinister behavior may damage a firm's reputation, making it a less attractive partner for other firms and governments to engage with, while cooperative behavior may signal a more attractive partner. Such external reputational signals are not always clearly communicated. A firm may claim that its regulatory violation was benignly accidental, when in fact it was the result of sinister negligence. The regulator may not have enough information to distinguish between benign and sinister violations. What is required is mechanisms for identifying whether players are cooperative or sinister and for distributing players' choices and reputations across the players in the different games. This could ensure that each player correctly interprets how cooperation and defection are evaluated over future rounds. Cooperation or defection can affect players' payoffs in future rounds where the other party benefits or is sanctioned because of decisions made in previous rounds. Signaling externally what actions have been taken in response to behaviors can lead to more cooperative forms of behavior, especially where parties fear that a long shadow of the future could preclude them from the potential benefits of such exchanges.

### 6.3.2   Voluntary Programs as Binding Commitments

External binding commitments rely on third parties to ensure both sides cooperate (Milgrom et al. 1990; Ostrom 1990). In an externally enforced binding commitment, each side submits its behavior to external monitoring, which verifies whether it is cooperative and sanctions defection. Parties have more incentive to cooperate knowing that they and the other side will be sanctioned for defection. A medieval guild, for example, can be seen as a third party that monitored its members' behavior to ensure they treated customers according to a standard code of conduct. Third parties can be used to monitor each party's behavior to determine whether it is cooperative. However, third parties can raise contracting transaction costs because external enforcement is often costly and requires institutions that are seen by the parties as fair and objective. Voluntary programs have been most prominently studied in environmental areas; consequently, we focus our discussion on voluntary environmental programs, which we elsewhere call "green clubs" (Prakash and Potoski 2006).

Governments can credibly commit to cooperation in advance of regulatory enforcement by establishing regulatory relief programs and compliance audit policies that grant significant immunity to firms whose violations are discovered through self-audits and voluntarily disclosed to regulators. U.S. state environmental protection agencies have created a wide range of environmental leadership programs that offer participating firms regulatory relief benefits for superior environmental performance. Another way that regulators can commit to more cooperation is through policies and laws that offer privilege or immunity protections for firms' compliance self-audits. The Environmental Protection Agency (EPA) (1986, 1995a, 1995b, 1997) and about 25 states provide regulatory relief to firms that promptly disclose and correct violations uncovered through audits. Of course, these policies vary across states (Morandi 1998): some states grant both audit privileges (information gathered in audits is not disclosed to regulatory agencies or to the public) and immunity (from fines and penalties) to self-disclosed information, while others grant only immunity.

For their part, firms can establish credible commitments to cooperation by subscribing to a voluntary program. A voluntary program is a conduct standard that firms pledge to follow. The goal of a voluntary program is to induce participating firms to produce some positive social good beyond what government regulations require. Firms may be willing to do these socially desirable things because they receive pressures from their stakeholders to do so. Membership in a well-regarded voluntary program allows stakeholders to identify firms that are producing social externalities beyond the legal requirements by virtue of their program membership and to differentiate them from non-members that are less likely to produce such social externalities. Firms that join a program enjoy the value of affiliating with the program's brand name. Brand affiliation is an excludable benefit because non-members are unable to receive these benefits. For members, the brand benefits are non-rival because their association with the program does not necessarily diminish the value others receive from the brand. Effective voluntary programs that induce members to produce positive social externalities produce win-all-round outcomes: stakeholders win because firms produce the social externalities they desire, firms win because membership produces goodwill and other rewards from stakeholders, and program sponsors can share some credit for inducing firms to produce positive social externalities.

Even if firms adopt socially desirable policies, they may not have a credible way to signal to stakeholders that they have done so. Stakeholders may not have a low-cost way of differentiating the virtuous firms from others. David Baron (2009) terms unobservable traits of firms as "credence attributes" to emphasize that stakeholders have difficulty verifying firms' behavior. Hence stakeholders may have to spread their goodwill across all firms, an action that would reward the free-riding firms as well as those doing the socially desirable things. Stakeholders may also decide to withhold rewards from all firms, an option that would punish the virtuous firms.

### 6.3.3 Voluntary Programs in Practice

For proponents, voluntary programs are a win–win for firms and governments, especially given the enforcement shortcomings of command-and-control policies. But proponents are right only if the programs identify the cooperating firms. For critics, especially environmental groups, voluntary programs are worse than deterrence-based policies because firms are unlikely to zealously self-police and in fact may use the programs to greenwash their poor environmental performance. Proponents of voluntary programs assume that participating in a program induces firms to self-police their performance, even in the face of short-run incentives to hide regulatory violations. An important question, then, is whether firms that join the voluntary programs actually self-police and disclose pollution violations to regulators. Environmental groups often remain suspicious and, without persuasive evidence confirming that firms become environmentally progressive after joining such programs, they may have good reason.

At first glance, the research on voluntary programs provides fodder for both proponents and critics. Examples of effective and ineffective voluntary environmental programs abound. Ski resorts participating in the Sustainable Slopes Program were not greener than non-participants (Rivera and deLeon 2004; Rivera et al. 2006). Chemical firms participating in the Responsible Care Program did not reduce the emission of toxic chemicals any faster than non-participants (King and Lenox 2000). Participants in the U.S. Department of Energy's Climate Wise Program did not reduce their $CO_2$ emissions any more than non-participants (Welch et al. 2000). On the successful side of the ledger, firms that joined the EPA's 35/50 voluntary program reduced their emissions of toxic pollutants more than the non-participants (Khanna and Damon 1999). Our own work suggests that ISO 14001 improved participating firms' environmental performance (Potoski and Prakash 2005) and compliance with government regulations (Potoski and Prakash 2004b).

Fortunately, the research on voluntary programs has grown to the point that we are now able to draw some preliminary assessments about what separates the successful programs from the failures. A first step is to recognize that voluntary programs, like any social institution, are susceptible to institutional failure. A better understanding of the theoretical basis for such failures can help identify the institutional solutions to mitigate them and thus point to what features voluntary programs need to be successful.

Shirking implies that some participants formally join the program but do not implement and practice the program standards. In doing so, shirkers seek to free-ride on the efforts of other members who build the voluntary program's reputation. While non-members are excluded from enjoying the benefits of program membership, shirkers enjoy the benefits of program participation unless they are discovered and expelled from the program. As word spreads about large-scale shirking, the program's reputation is likely to diminish and its brand reputation to be undermined. Willful shirking is facilitated by information asymmetries between voluntary program participants and program sponsors and/or between participants and program stakeholders. By information asymmetries we mean that voluntary program sponsors and stakeholders cannot observe the levels to which an individual participant is adhering to the program's membership standards because such activities are inherently difficult to observe or are observable only at significant cost. The net effect is that information asymmetries impose costs on program sponsors and stakeholders seeking to differentiate program shirkers from non-shirkers.

For example, suppose a group of firms join a voluntary program that requires them to produce some social externality. Some firms in this group might fail to live up to their obligations, either by intention or by ignorance, yet these firms would continue to receive the benefits of program membership simply because outside stakeholders could not differentiate the shirking firms from the non-shirkers. This problem has serious implications for voluntary programs. Non-shirker members would be less inclined to continue with the program. Eventually, shirking by some program members can threaten the reputation of the program as a whole, making it less attractive for all, and perhaps leading the remaining non-shirkers to select themselves out of the program.

Effective voluntary programs must have monitoring and enforcement mechanisms to curb shirking. Widespread shirking undermines the production of environmental externalities and thereby dilutes the program's credibility. Willful shirking occurs because: (1) the goals of participants and voluntary program sponsors diverge, and (2) participants are able to exploit information asymmetries (regarding their adherence to program standards) between themselves and sponsors and stakeholders. Information asymmetries prevent stakeholders from differentiating program shirkers from non-shirkers. Voluntary programs can mitigate shirking by establishing monitoring and sanctioning mechanisms. A voluntary program with a reputation for effectively policing and sanctioning its participants is likely to have a stronger standing, and therefore a stronger brand reputation, among its firms' stakeholders.

## 6.4   CONCLUSION

Regulatory compliance and sanctioning pose important challenges for firms and regulators. Here we focus on compliance issues rooted in information asymmetries, shirking, moral hazard, and adverse selection, because in our view these are central issues that define regulatory enforcement interactions. For optimal outcomes, both the regulators and the regulatees need to have credible information about their counterparts' incentives, motivations, and constraints. This chapter highlights how voluntary programs can provide one avenue for addressing such governance problems.

On the highways there are no voluntary programs to help police officers determine whether a speeding violation was benign or pernicious. The speeder may certainly plead her case, perhaps by appeal to a clean driving record or exigent circumstances such as medical emergency. The police officer can assess sanction severity, factoring in the plausibility of the speeder's case, but the officer will be relying on his own judgment of the situation, and any misreads will lead to over-punished benign behavior and under-sanctioned transgressions.

Effective voluntary programs provide information about their member firms that regulators would otherwise have difficulty knowing and verifying, such as whether a firm was acting in good faith to avoid regulatory violations. Regulators can leverage this information during enforcement proceedings to better calibrate the level of sanctions to reflect the firms' reasons for noncompliance. Firms participating in well-designed voluntary programs, those with stringent standards and rigorous monitoring and enforcement, are less likely to violate regulations out of sinister neglect. Consequently, regulators have credible reasons to believe that these violations stem from benign causes, such as ignorance or accident, and regulatory relief may not create perverse incentives for the regulatees in the future. This also requires that voluntary programs do not slacken or weaken their institutional requirements in the future, because the benign assessment by the regulators of the participating actors' infractions is predicated on the belief that the firms will continue to participate in the program and that the program will continue to impose stringent obligations on its participants (Potoski and Prakash 2009). If the participants do not follow program obligations in the future, a program seeking to protect its credibility should name the firms that have been expelled or are no longer participating in the program. Thus, to maintain the credibility of the program, sponsors need to be cognizant not only of the program's institutional structure but also of the possibility of internal contamination whereby existing members begin to neglect their obligations to the program.

Our chapter suggests conditions under which voluntary programs can induce compliance. First, in information-scarce environments voluntary programs can provide a low-cost tool for regulatory agencies by signaling which firms are more committed to cooperating with regulatory officials and maintaining their compliance. Information useful to regulators is more scarce, for example, when firms are engaged in technical activities or do much of their work behind closed doors. A voluntary program may provide useful information that is otherwise difficult for government regulators to acquire. The value added of voluntary programs is therefore more limited, at least in a regulatory compliance setting, when the information environment is rich such that firms and government regulators are fully aware of each other's actions and motives. Second, voluntary programs can provide the institutional stability through which firms can build reputations for cooperation. Regulatory enforcement officials can come and go, and their tacit knowledge about which firms have assiduously complied with regulations may not be transferred to the new regulators. An effective voluntary program can codify tacit knowledge, allowing it to be more easily disseminated across enforcement personnel. Of course, many firms and regulatory enforcement officials have successfully built reputations for being cooperative partners. Few doubt, for example, that the ice cream company Ben and Jerry's sterling reputation for corporate good citizenry has not been well earned. Finally, and perhaps most importantly, a voluntary program can be an effective way to boost the credibility of firms' commitments to cooperative behavior. Voluntary programs can sanction firms in ways that governments cannot: a firm that is expelled from a voluntary program for failing to live up to the program's standards may experience a blow to its reputation that more than offsets whatever reputational gains it experienced when it joined the program in the first place. However, voluntary programs are only effective when their members comply with the behavior standards required of membership. In the environmental arena, many voluntary programs have turned out to be "greenwashes," programs that appeared strong on paper, but whose standards were so weakly enforced that participating firms did not improve their performance. Government regulators can look to the voluntary program's institutional design, whether it has effective monitoring and enforcement procedures that ensure participating members are living up to their obligations as program participants.

## NOTE

1.  For discussions of these ideas see Scholz (1991) and Potoski and Prakash (2004a), from which this section draws.

## REFERENCES

Akerloff, G.A. (1982), 'Labor contracts as partial gift exchange', *Quarterly Journal of Economics*, **97** (4), 543–69.
Axelrod, Robert (1984), *The Evolution of Cooperation*, New York: Basic Books.
Baron, D.P. (2001), 'Private politics, corporate social responsibility, and integrated strategy', *Journal of Economics and Management Strategy*, **10** (1), 7–45.
Baron, D.P. (2009), 'Credence standards and social pressure', in Matthew Potoski and Aseem Prakash (eds), *Voluntary Programs: A Club Theory Perspective*, Cambridge, MA: MIT Press.
Coglianese, Cary (1996), 'Litigating within relationships: disputes and disturbances in the regulatory process', *Law and Society Review*, **30**, 735–65.
Environmental Protection Agency (EPA) (1986), 'Environmental auditing policy statement', *Federal Register*, **51**, 25004–06.
Environmental Protection Agency (EPA) (1995a), 'Voluntary environmental self-policing and self disclosure interim policy statement', *Federal Register*, **60**, 16875–8.
Environmental Protection Agency (EPA) (1995b), 'Incentives for self-policing and self disclosure interim policy statement', *Federal Register*, **60**, 66706–09.
Environmental Protection Agency (EPA) (1997), *Audit Policy Interpretive Guidance*, January, available at: http://es.epa.gov/oeca.audpolguid.pdf (accessed 7 January 2000).
Hardin, Russell (1982), *Collective Action*, Baltimore, MD: Johns Hopkins University Press.
Jaffe, Adam, Steven Peterson, Paul Portney and Robert Stavins (1995), 'Environmental regulation and the competitiveness of U.S. manufacturing', *Journal of Economic Literature*, **33** (1), 132–63.
Kagan, Robert K. (1991), 'Adversarial legalism and American government', *Journal of Policy Analysis and Management*, **10** (3), 369–406.
Khanna, M. and L.A. Damon (1999), 'EPA's voluntary 33/50 program: impact on toxic releases and economic performance of firms', *Journal of Environmental Economics and Management*, **37**, 1–25.
King, A. and M. Lenox (2000), 'Industry self-regulation without sanctions: the chemical industry's Responsible Care Program', *Academy of Management Journal*, **43**, August, 698–716.
Lichbach, Mark (1996), *The Cooperator's Dilemma*, Ann Arbor: University of Michigan Press.
Luce, R. Duncan and Howard Raiffa (1957), *Games and Decisions*, New York: Wiley.
Majumdar, Sumit and Alfred Marcus (2001), 'Rules versus discretion: the productivity consequences of flexible regulation', *Academy of Management Journal*, **44** (1), 170–79.
Milgrom, Paul, Douglass North and Barry Weingast (1990), 'The role of institutions in the revival of trade', *Economics and Politics*, **2** (1), 1–23.
Morandi, Larry (1998), *State Environmental Audit Laws and Policies*, Washington, DC: National Conference of State Legislatures.
O'Leary, Rosemary (1993), *Environmental Change: Federal Courts and the EPA*, Philadelphia, PA: Temple University Press.
Ostrom, Elinor (1990), *Governing the Commons*, Cambridge: Cambridge University Press.

Potoski, Matthew and Aseem Prakash (2004a), 'The regulation dilemma and US environmental governance', *Public Administration Review*, **64**, March/April, 137–48.
Potoski, M. and A. Prakash (2004b), 'Green clubs and voluntary governance: ISO 14001 and firms' regulatory compliance', *American Journal of Political Science*, **49** (2), 235–48.
Potoski, M. and A. Prakash (2005), 'Covenants with weak swords: ISO 14001 and firms' environmental performance', *Journal of Policy Analysis and Management*, **24** (4), 745–69.
Potoski, Matthew and Aseem Prakash (eds) (2009), *Voluntary Programs: A Club Theory Approach*, Cambridge, MA: MIT Press.
Prakash, A. and M. Potoski (2006), *The Voluntary Environmentalists*, Cambridge: Cambridge University Press.
Rapoport, Anatol and Albert Chammah (1965), *Prisoner's Dilemma: A Study of Conflict and Cooperation*, Ann Arbor: University of Michigan Press.
Reilly, William K. (1999), 'Foreword', in Ken Sexton, Alfred Marcus, K. William Easter and Timothy D. Burkhardt (eds), *Better Environmental Decisions*, Washington, DC: Island Press, pp. xi–xv.
Rivera, J. and P. deLeon (2004), 'Is greener whiter? The Sustainable Slopes Program and the voluntary environmental performance of western ski areas', *Policy Studies Journal*, **32** (3), 417–37.
Rivera, J., P. deLeon and C. Koerber (2006), 'Is greener whiter yet? The Sustainable Slopes Program after five years', *Policy Studies Journal*, **34** (2), 195–224.
Scholz, John T. (1991), 'Cooperative regulatory enforcement and the politics of administrative effectiveness', *American Political Science Review*, **85** (1), 115–36.
Vogel, David J. (1986), *National Styles of Regulation*, Ithaca, NY: Cornell University Press.
Walley, Noah and Bradley Whitehead (1994), 'It's not easy being green', *Harvard Business Review*, **72** (3), 46–51.
Welch, E.W., A. Mazur and S. Bretschneider (2000), 'Voluntary behavior by electric utilities', *Journal of Policy Analysis and Management*, **19**, Summer, 407–25.

# 7 Competing theories of regulatory governance: reconsidering public interest theory of regulation
*Jørgen Grønnegård Christensen*

Regulation is one of the state's core functions. It is also one of its classical functions. In a historical perspective the state engaged in regulation long before government also took on provision of welfare services to its citizens. Regulation defines the border between state and society, government and market. Therefore regulation represents government's attempt to set limits to the scope of private activities. As broad as this conception is it has one important implication: If the government produces a good or service under its own auspices, for example by a state-owned enterprise or a public hospital, it is not reasonable to speak of regulation. But if a private firm provides the same service, say railroad transportation or hospital treatment within confines defined by legislation, we have to do with regulation. In other words the importance of regulation as an instrument of public policy is highly variable. It is amenable to change when the role of government is reconceived, as has happened with privatizations and pro-market reforms on the one hand and a dedicated effort to protect the environment on the other (Moran 2000).

One of the most fruitful definitions of regulation was phrased by Barry Mitnick: "Regulation is the public administrative policing of a private activity with respect to a rule prescribed in the public interest" (Mitnick 1980: 7). The definition points to three central ideas: Regulation is restrictive and directed towards private activities; it rests on administrative controls undertaken on the basis of general rules; and these rules and their implementation are by implication conducive to the public interest. The definition also raises two questions that have been at the core of political science research in governmental regulation since the early 1980s:

1. What is the role of affected interests in regulatory policy and administration?
2. To what extent does regulatory administration balance the public interest against regulated interests within the private sector?

These questions remain central even if broader conceptions have developed (Chapter 1). The assumption behind governmental regulation is the possibility of protecting the public interest against private, especially business, interests. Yet the risk is that the relationship is turned around as private interests use governmental regulation for rent seeking, typically to protect their business against competition.

Here two possibilities arise. The first is that regulatory administration is captured by regulated interests. As a consequence the administration operates in a way that is systematically biased to the advantage of regulated interests; again the presumption is that they represent private business. The second possibility is that regulatory administration is transformed into the guardian of the public interest. On this presumption law makers have given the administration the mandate to see to it that private interests do not displace the public interest, typically in the form of third-party interests hit by negative externalities.

A considerable research agenda has developed around these themes (Moran 2002). Early research and theory span over both law making and regulatory administration. Contemporary research on regulatory governance places regulatory administration at center stage (Levi-Faur 2011). This chapter sets out the main theoretical models that have been developed in recent decades and then reviews the empirical support for each of them. The review concentrates on the claims of the classical public interest model, the regulatory capture model and the credible commitment model. Their common focus is the role of bureaucracy in regulatory policy and its implementation. What is more, all of them have developed absolutely plausible arguments in support of their positions, "but what is plausible in the abstract may prove false in fact" (Croley 2008: 160).

## 7.1   THE ADMINISTRATIVE PREDICAMENT

In democratic politics law makers interpret the public interest. They are supposed to act on a mandate from the voters. In a representative perspective these decisions are the best approximation to the public interest, as law makers are accountable to the electorate.

Even in this idealized image of representative democracy law makers do not operate in their own capacity. They are dependent on a bureaucracy. The civil service comes into play when new regulatory policy is prepared and again when it is executed. As law makers' informational and organizational capacity is severely constrained it is hardly possible to overestimate the importance of regulatory administration. However, in this conception regulatory administration neither adds to nor subtracts from the policy decided by law makers. The public interest may be served, but it is served exactly as interpreted by law makers.

The perspective appears naïve. Similar naïvety is foreign to the theory of regulatory capture. It echoes neo-classical economics and has found its way into political science analysis of regulation through rational choice theory. Its basic tenets may appear cynical or just realistic, as capture theory rests on the claim that particularistic interests see governmental regulation as a protective shield and that on the whole the state meets their demands. But it does not stop here, as it also questions the neutrality of regulatory administration. For capture theory regulatory administration operates as the willing extension for rent-seeking business. A corollary is the rejection of any idea of regulation in the service of the public interest. Even regulation devised to correct negative externalities in this view is easily thwarted to serve particularistic interests (Stigler 1971; Posner 1974; Peltzman 1976). Thus any idea of "good regulation" is futile or, to quote William Niskanen, "Good regulation is no regulation."[1] So, if politicians are not held up by private interests, self-serving bureaucrats are captured by them.

Credible commitment theory is equally skeptical about classical public interest theory. Still, it moves in another direction than the theory of regulatory capture. The reason is that it differentiates sharply between politicians' behavior when deciding on regulatory policy issues and the behavior of professional regulators within the bureaucracy (Levy and Spiller 1996; Jordana and Levi-Faur 2004). It hypothesizes that politicians will be tempted to give in to short-term concerns if sound regulatory policy runs against their electoral interests. The theory argues that this is particularly relevant when private entrepreneurs invest in long-term projects; if they cannot trust politicians to keep the regulatory regime in force at the time of the investment decision, they run the political risk that the value of their investment is eroded by politicians acting opportunistically. Credible commitment theory sees a solution to such time inconsistency in the proper design of regulatory administration as politicians acknowledge their own frailty and engage in self-binding institutional designs that make it difficult to renege on their initial policy promises. The solution is to delegate decision-making authority to independent regulators or autonomous agencies.

According to credible commitment theory the threat to regulation in the public interest comes from voters rather than from affected interests. It is vote-maximizing politicians' frailty to short-term political loss that induces them to modify regulatory policies that in the long term promote the public interest. Similarly, the relationship to classical public interest theory is subtle. The regulatory bureaucrat of the naïve theory is an ideal-type lawyer dedicated to the subsumption of individual cases under general and precisely phrased individual laws. He does not engage in policy making on his own. Conversely, the regulatory bureaucrat of credible commitment theory is a technocrat, ideally an economist, who applies her analytic insights to the device of solutions furthering the public interest in terms of economic efficiency. The idea is that these analytical skills are applicable both in decisions on individual cases and in the making of general policy. Thus credible commitment theory does not see the motivation of bureaucrats as a potential problem for regulation in the public interest. Here it is in perfect accordance with classical public interest theory.

The three theories cover a long period from the mid-20th to the early 21st century. Common to them is their consistent focus on regulatory administration and governance, that is, the tasks, the organization, and the performance of regulatory authorities. Another commonality is their reliance on the concept of the public interest. Yet for any of the three theories the concept remains elusive, easy to invoke in political discourse but difficult to maintain in operational terms (Mitnick 1980: 242–82; Levine and Forrence 1990; Scharpf 1997: 163–5; Yandle 2011). A solution to this challenge is to distinguish between the interests of regulated business and citizens and those third parties that have a stake in regulatory policy and administration because the regulated activity affects their interests negatively.

## 7.2    COMPETING MODELS

The three theories represent competing models. Their claims differ markedly from each other as set out above. Table 7.1 compares the basic traits of the models.

The difference stems mainly from their often tacit behavioral assumptions. So the theory of public interest regulation shares assumptions with the classical theory of bureaucracy. Here civil servants are office carriers dedicated to carrying out the duties that constitute their particular role or task within a strictly ordered and specialized hierarchy (Weber 1921 [1976]: 124–30, 552–3). Individual decisions are attributed to "either the subsumption under norms or the balancing of means and ends" (Weber 1921 [1976]: 565).

The theory of regulatory capture takes a very different view, be it cynical or just suf-

*Table 7.1    Competing models of regulatory administration*

|  | Public interest regulation | Regulatory capture | Credible commitment |
|---|---|---|---|
| Basic claim | Civil servants act according to general law set out to further the public interest | Civil servants biased in favor of regulated business | Civil servants apply scientific knowledge to further good regulation |
| Behavioral assumption | Civil servants as office carriers | Civil servants self-interest motivated | Civil servants as professional norm abiders |
| Field of relevance | Economic and social regulation | Economic and social regulation | Economic regulation |

ficiently realistic. The main assumption is that public servants, in this case regulatory officials, are self-interest motivated. The negative implication is that they are not bound by norms and official roles. The positive implication is the pursuance of strategies that are beneficial to first of all themselves, but also the agency for which they work. Its behavioral assumption is derived from more general theory as exemplified by William Niskanen's theory of budget-maximizing bureaucracy (Niskanen 1971). When applied to regulatory administration there is an additional assumption, namely that regulated business controls benefits that are so valuable to the bureaucracy and its individual staff that it systematically accommodates business demands. For regulatory bureaucrats the benefits are the prospect of shifts to more lucrative careers outside government or to post-office employment within the regulated industry (Mitnick 1980: 206–14; Levine and Forrence 1990).

Both public interest theory and capture theory derive their underlying assumptions and ensuing empirical predictions from standard political science theory. This is different with the more modern theory of credible commitment. Its behavioral assumptions are rarely explicit and must therefore be construed from the literature. Given the idea of delegating regulatory authority to an agency removed from the executive hierarchy the implicit assumption must be that the agency is led and staffed by experts who abide by professional norms (see e.g. Majone 2001). Compared to the case of public interest theory these expert regulators are equally motivated by other-regarding interests, even though the basis for their decisions is not rule application and rule-abiding behavior. In contrast to capture theory, expert regulators are modeled as benevolent professionals who pursue best-policy solutions even in the absence of clear guidance from the law.

There is some uncertainty as to the empirical scope of any of the three theories. Mostly they direct attention towards economic regulation, for example entry regulation and competition law. But one reason may be purely historical, as both public interest and capture theory developed at a time when social regulation, for example environmental protection, food safety, and consumer protection, figured less prominently on the political agenda. However, there are three important caveats to this.

First, application of rational choice theory led to the prediction that social regulation would be of minor importance as compared to economic regulation because law makers were facing opposition from concentrated business interests. The supporters of regulatory intervention on their side faced severe difficulties in mobilizing support from

*Table 7.2    Validating evidence for the models of regulatory administration*

|  | Public interest regulation | Regulatory capture | Credible commitment |
|---|---|---|---|
| Supporting evidence | Merit bureaucracy | Close cooperation with regulated business | Delegation to independent regulators |
|  | Strict public law regulation of procedures | Exclusion of third-party interests | Staffing with relevant professionals |
|  | Integration into ministerial hierarchy applying strict politics–administration dichotomy | Revolving-doors careers | Exclusion of affected interests |
|  |  |  | Evidence-based decision making |
| Disproving evidence | Interference from political executive | Career transfers rare | Regulatory authorities integrated into executive hierarchy |
|  | Bargaining with external interests | Broad inclusion of affected interests | Institutional integration of affected interests |
|  | Institutional integration of external interests | Strict regulation of decision-making procedures | Political interference in decision making |
|  |  | Decisions against regulated business | De facto bargaining with affected interests |

a public whose members could only expect widely dispersed benefits (Wilson 1980). Second, when capture theorists realized the appearance of a new regulatory trend their impulse was to interpret it as a refined form of creating entry barriers (Peltzman 1998: 334–6). Third, research inspired by credible commitment theory has to a very large extent analyzed the regulation of public service utilities at the stage when market competition was introduced and former state-owned enterprises privatized, and much of the theoretical reasoning behind it focuses on utility regulation (Levi-Faur 2003).

## 7.3    PLAUSIBLE LOGIC, QUESTIONABLE VALIDITY

The basic rationale by each of the competing models rests on venerable political science theory. Each theory identifies plausible political and institutional mechanisms and points at phenomena belonging to real-world politics and administration. This leaves the question to what extent propositions derived from these rival theories find empirical support. Table 7.2 summarizes the evidence.

The theory of public interest regulation presumes the existence of a merit bureaucracy, operating within the strict constraints of public law. Its principles and procedures rest on the non-acceptance of discrimination among regulatees and other affected interests, and it assumes respect for procedures that allow clients first to be heard and second to have their case tried ultimately in the courts. Finally, it assumes the politics–administration dichotomy to describe a behavioral fact.

The theory seems easy to refute. Simple indicators such as interference from the political executive, parliament, or legislative committees raise doubt about its validity and relevance as anything other than an inherently naïve ideal. Equally notable, it is constitutionally acknowledged that much administrative decision making and implementation involve issues to be settled with considerable political discretion exercised by a departmental minister or on his behalf by a civil servant. Similarly, many regulatory issues are technically complex while remaining politically sensitive because law makers neither can nor will specify the rules in the detail needed to reduce them to administrative decisions subsuming individual cases under a legal rule. This opens the way for a combination of political discretion and bargaining or dialogue with regulatees and other stakeholders (Balla 2011).

Hence the theory has for decades been open to an alternative that questions the existence of data supporting its propositions while presenting a logic turning the indicators of disproving evidence into positive propositions. For these reasons capture theory has concentrated on evidence of close, even institutionalized, cooperation between regulatory authorities and regulated business and the simultaneous exclusion of third-party interests from consultation and bargaining. It has also pointed to the possibility of revolving-doors careers where initial employment with a regulatory authority is followed by a lucrative career in the private sector.

Capture theory suggests that the indicators are relatively easily transformed into operational measures, particularly if the focus is on institutional and structural phenomena. However, just as with public interest theory, it is much more difficult to set up behavioral indicators of the prevalence of effective rent seeking by regulated business. Still, in the literature on neo-corporatism, sectorization, quangos and networks in the European context and in the parallel study of iron triangles and pressure group politics in the US, there is evidence to conclude that regulated interests have often had a strong say in their interaction with regulatory administration. Likewise, there is evidence that structural choice often involves institutional provisions embedding regulatory authorities in an environment giving priority to some interests at the expense of others.

This hardly amounts to a confirmation of the capture hypothesis. For one thing, in its most rigorous form it presumes the administration's accommodation of rent-seeking business to be the result of self-seeking bureaucrats' strategy to spur their own careers. Logically, the question has been raised whether this leads to a revolving-doors situation, but appropriate empirical indicators are quite demanding (Mitnick 1980: 8), and the evidence mounted in support of a widespread revolving-doors practice is at best mixed (Mitnick 1980: 214–41). A parallel empirical study came to a similar conclusion for a number of American regulatory agencies (Quirk 1981). Another study displays similar skepticism (Croley 2008: 48–50). If this is the American picture it is even less likely for the European closed career civil service systems as confirmed by studies of for example Danish and French top civil servants (Christensen 2004; Peters 2010: 94–102).

Other indicators undermining the claim of capture theory involve the inclusion of broader and more diverse stakeholders in hearings and bargaining as well as formal procedures regulating administrative decision making in a way to guarantee access to information on both substance and applied procedure. Such procedures are well developed in American federal government owing to the Administrative Procedure Act (Croley 2008; 2011; Balla 2011). Legal provisions guaranteeing open files together with norms ensuring equality before the law that are enforced by the courts are an integral part of European public law.

Research based on credible commitment theory is heavily inspired by the literature on central banks. The indicators it uses to uncover the extent of delegation to independent regulators are parallel to those developed in central bank studies (Cukierman 1992; Gilardi 2008). In the absence of an operational definition, the distinctive mark of an independent regulator becomes the creation of authorities with regulatory tasks that in the American checks-and-balances system are removed from the executive hierarchy with the president as the key office and in the European parliamentary systems agencies that are separate from ministerial departments. Indicators such as appointment procedures, terms of office, and financial status enter into the construction of indices allowing for systematic cross-national and across-time comparisons. Other indicators are staffing with policy experts and exclusion of affected interests from decision-making bodies and from bargaining over rules and individual decisions.

A sizable literature reports support for the theory's claims. It adds that delegation to independent regulators represents a trend that has spread with remarkable speed. It has, the claim is, spearheaded a general movement where law makers delegate administrative implementation to specialized agencies rather than to executive departments (see e.g. Levi-Faur and Jordana 2005). Interestingly, in this line of research, just as in public interest or capture theory, few studies have moved beyond the structural analysis to uncover decision-making behavior by the purported independent regulators.

However, other evidence tends to qualify and even disprove the conclusions reached in the credible commitment, the independent regulator and agency studies. Some involve deeper behavioral analysis, while others include other structural indicators than those relied on in mainstream agency analysis. If we define bureaucratic autonomy as the formal exemption of an agency head from full political supervision by the political executive, i.e. in Europe departmental ministers and in the US the White House, logical next steps are to look for the insertion of an alternative or competing level of political supervision; here it is of particular interest whether affected interests and other stakeholders are integrated into the supervision and control of the agency, maybe even in a way that implies delegation of decision-making authority to them. Another important indicator is whether the agency head in spite of the agency's operation as a non-departmental unit reports to the minister or another political executive or whether regulatory legislation has specified competences for the agency head in his own right, thus carving out a field of authority from which the minister in charge is kept out.

Existing studies are far from clear on these points. Similarly there are several indications of a world of regulatory administration that is much more politically infected than imagined. Politicians in government and parliament have not withdrawn, creating a sphere of non-politics (cf. Lohmann 2006). These are three facts that question the validity of a general trend towards regulatory administration and policy conducted by independent regulators. First, the American use of independent regulatory commissions is often invoked as an example of how American law makers have for a long time acknowledged the credibility-enhancing effect of delegation to independent regulators (Majone 1994). But it is ignored how much independent regulatory commissions and other non-executive agencies are subject to political concern, a fact mirrored in the composition of the commissions and in their political responsiveness (Cushman 1941; Weingast and

Moran 1983; Shapiro 1997; Ingraham 2006). Second, even if Britain is rightly seen as pioneering market-opening reforms since the 1980s, among other things implying the creation of specialized regulatory offices, the precise organization and legal authority of these offices and other agencies have only rarely been subject to close analysis.[2] Third, the delegation of administrative authority to non-departmental agencies is strongly ingrained into the institutional tradition of continental Europe. It has been based on a mixture of credible commitment rationale (the Swedish agency tradition going back to the 17th century) and efficiency-concerned attempts to free ministerial departments from routine matters, for example the Danish (Binderkrantz and Christensen 2009), German (Brecht and Glaser 1940 [1971]: 10; Döhler 2007) and Norwegian (Lægreid et al. 2006) agency traditions.

## 7.4   A FIRST BALANCE

Both regulatory capture and credible commitment theory offer plausible accounts of how regulatory administration is organized and how its political embeddedness may influence its operation. Still, more rigorous studies have hardly produced convincing support. Moreover proponents of the respective theories have widely neglected to subject their propositions to tests using indicators that might challenge their claims. For the classical public interest theory things appear easier, as the theory's claims quite generally are rejected as resting on naïve assumptions. Recent studies take a different perspective (Huber 2007; Croley 2008). Contrary to the original theory they have given up any ambition of defining an abstract public interest, serving as the standard for good regulation. They include in their analysis measures that might question the validity of capture theory and credible commitment theory in their bolder versions. They focus on the inclusion of stakeholders other than affected business in regulatory decision making, for example environmental and consumer groups. Similarly, they look at the application of formal procedures regulating due administrative process in American federal administration; the observance of such procedures might limit the scope for pro-regulatee bias in agency decision making.

Their approach offers a broader basis for a critical evaluation of established theory and the empirical research resting on its claims. This is most directly the case with capture theory. If other interests than those directly affected in private business are heard by regulatory authorities and actually contribute actively to their decisions, the validity of capture theory is brought into doubt. However, such critical evidence also undermines the claims of credible commitment theory. Its principal claim, it should be remembered, is law makers' delegation of regulatory authority to agencies that base their decisions on scientific and professional analysis without inviting any interests, be it regulatees or third parties, to contribute to decision making. The other implication is that contrary to the original, normatively oriented public interest theory the new approach abstains from formulating substantive criteria for the realization of the public interest. Neither economic efficiency nor criteria of environmental sustainability and distributional justice are invoked; rather the criteria advanced focus on political participation and transactions. The ultimate criterion for the realization of the public interest therefore becomes whether regulatory administration makes decisions involving a broad spectrum of insights and stakeholders and adheres to procedures ensuring openness and a second review. These are very political criteria where the concern is to obtain political sustainability and legitimacy in administrative decision making.

These contributions have one serious limitation. It is difficult to generalize their insights, as they are based on a few case studies, all conducted on American data. In Steven Croley's study it is the EPA, FDA and US Forest Service; in Gregory Huber's it is OSHA. There is some basis for expanding the comparative scope of their conclusions, particularly the question of excluding others besides regulatees from participation (capture theory) and the question of an increasing propensity to delegate decision-making authority to independent regulators placed at arm's length from the governmental hierarchy and operating without participation from affected interests (credible commitment theory). In either case, the theories' claim of particular relevance for economic regulation is open to challenge.

## 7.5   THE EUROPEAN EXPERIENCE

In the parliamentary democracies of Western Europe there are three types of central government organizations. Departmental ministries are organized with a department serving the minister. It has a combination of policy- and implementation-related tasks. Depending on the country some tasks are delegated to agencies and collegiate boards. An agency is a sub-departmental unit responsible for policy execution within a part of the department's portfolio; it has its own management, staff, and budget. Such agencies are widespread within regulatory policy areas, but it varies how much countries use them. Up to the British Next Steps reform they were unknown in the UK, while they have been part and parcel of the continental tradition. Collegiate boards are another type of central government unit; a combination of advisory and decision-making responsibilities is delegated to a body consisting of mostly non-ministerial representatives. Again the use of such boards varies from country to country, but they are frequently resorted to in regulatory policy. They are apparently a pan-European phenomenon.

These basic forms shed light on the issues addressed by especially capture and credible commitment theory. First, one question is to what extent regulatory agencies are integrated into the departmental hierarchy. If the agency head reports to the minister through the ministerial department it indicates a strong degree of integration. One implication is that the government appoints and dismisses the agency head, sets its budget, and decides its internal organization; another implication is that the minister can intervene in decision making, be it in questions of general policy or individual cases. In contrast, integration is lower if a board of directors has been inserted so that the agency head reports to it rather than to the minister, with the board of directors assuming the executive tasks of the departmental minister. Table 7.3 shows a diverging practice between four countries. In Denmark and Norway agency integration into the departmental hierarchy is the dominant model. Any difference between agencies responsible for economic as opposed to social regulation has been leveled out. In the Netherlands and Sweden, integration into the hierarchy is much lower. In Sweden it follows from the century-old constitutional order that made agencies independent to protect the interests of the nobility against the king; in the Netherlands it is equally part of a pattern with

*Table 7.3    Basic structure of regulatory administration in four European countries, 1980–2000 (percentages; N in parentheses)*

| | Denmark | | | | The Netherlands | | | | Norway | | | | Sweden | | | |
|---|---|---|---|---|---|---|---|---|---|---|---|---|---|---|---|---|
| | 1980 | | Change[1] 1980–2000 | | 1980 | | Change[1] 1980–2000 | | 1980 | | Change[1] 1980–2000 | | 1980 | | Change[1] 1980–2000 | |
| | Eco reg. | Soc reg. | Eco reg. | Soc reg. | Eco reg. | Soc reg. | Eco reg. | Soc reg. | Eco reg. | Soc reg. | Eco reg. | Soc reg. | Eco reg. | Soc reg. | Eco reg. | Soc reg. |
| Agency head reports to ministerial department | 88 (33) | 94 (17) | +1 (18) | −1 (13) | 19 (72) | 85 (26) | −11 (63) | −57 (39) | 42 (24) | 59 (17) | +26 (24) | +9 (13) | 15[2] (27) | 9[2] (11) | −1 (28) | +18 (22) |
| **Representation on regulatory boards** | | | | | | | | | | | | | | | | |
| Interest organizations | 82 | 85 | −6 | +6 | 56 | 35 | −12 | +25 | 50 | 82 | −12 | +13 | 26 | 58 | +1 | −5 |
| Parliamentary appointees | 9 | 7 | −6 | −2 | 0 | 0 | 0 | 0 | 14 | 6 | −14 | −6 | 19 | 13 | −6 | +20 |
| Judges | 33 | 44 | −6 | +4 | 11 | 6 | 0 | +14 | 25 | 35 | +6 | +5 | 30 | 33 | +50 | 0 |
| N | 55 | 27 | 62 | 44 | 18 | 17 | 9 | 5 | 28 | 17 | 16 | 20 | 27 | 40 | 15 | 15 |

*Notes:*
The data were collected jointly with Kutsal Yesilkagit; see Christensen and Yesilkagit (2006) and Yesilkagit and Christensen (2010).
[1]   Change in percentage points.
[2]   Agency head reports to government, as in Sweden departmental ministers have no direct executive responsibilities.

roots in consociational governance. But the degree of integration has not decreased, and the difference between economic and social regulation had disappeared by 2000.

The second question is how collegiate boards are organized. Delegation of decision-making authority to them is common in both a historical and a contemporary perspective. It allows law makers to limit the authority of departmental ministers and the executive hierarchy in a less ambiguous way than delegation to agencies staffed with policy specialists. Still, it is difficult to say whether such delegation lends support to the capture or the credible commitment theory. Table 7.3 also here gives relevant information. It shows whether among the members there are representatives of interest organizations, representatives appointed by parties in parliament, or members of the judiciary. The diverging patterns are striking. Again Denmark and Norway are similar in their reliance on extensive inclusion of interest organizations and minimal involvement of members appointed by parties. The Netherlands and Norway have decreased interest representation for economic regulation, but increased it for social regulation. In Sweden it remains stable and moderate, but parties to a considerable extent appoint board members. Again, there is no clear difference between boards dealing with economic and social regulation. Finally, boards, in particular in the Scandinavian countries, often have judges as chairmen or members.

This simple analysis of regulatory administration in four European countries with parliamentary democracy shows no signs of a movement from political executive dominance towards its depoliticization. Equally, there is no difference in the administrative set-ups for economic and social regulation where the gradual adaptation of social regulation to the patterns characterizing economic regulation is apparent. Finally, the strong presence of interest organizations questions central elements in credible commitment theory. This is further emphasized by parliament's appointment of board members in Sweden.

Thus there is no unconditional support for the theory of regulatory capture; nor is it possible to reject it. There is clear evidence that organized interests remain involved in regulatory administration, but it is no universal pattern given cross-national variation. Other research indicates that representation has been broadened to include to an increasing extent that organizations working on, for example, environmental and consumers' issues are either in active contact with central government or represented on collegiate boards.[3]

There are limits to any general conclusions drawn from data covering European countries. Nonetheless, if more rigorous definitions of agency independence are applied and if the analysis opens for organizational forms other than the regulatory agency, namely the collegiate board, it is difficult to find support for credit commitment theory. This is even more so as there is no institutional differentiation between economic and social regulation. The implication is not unconditional acceptance of the theory of regulatory capture, although interest group representation is a persistent fact considering the composition of regulatory boards. However, even here caution is appropriate given the remarkable national variation.

The invocation of data from just four, quite similar parliamentary democracies in Northwestern Europe naturally raises the question whether these findings are representative of other European countries. Given the lack of studies using comparable data there is no clear answer to this, but a number of studies on especially British, French, and German practices indicate the existence and persistence of distinct national models. They also indicate the institutionalized involvement of organized interests in even contemporary regulatory policy and administration (see e.g. Black et al. 2005; Coen and Héritier 2006; Thatcher 2007; Busch 2009).

## 7.6 FROM FORMAL STRUCTURE TO ADMINISTRATIVE BEHAVIOR

The competing theories suffer from a common deficiency by relying on structural characteristics, the assumption being that formal structure determines behavior. However, a well-established finding within organizational research is the lacking match between formal prescriptions and behavior. Formally independent authorities may be responsive to political interventions. Similarly authorities formally integrated into the executive hierarchy may display considerable autonomy.

Empirically, either deviation from formal prescriptions occurs. First, it is well established that the Swedish agencies, constitutionally separated from the ministerial departments, are responsive to signals from departmental ministries (Jacobsson 1984). Moreover, through a combination of political appointments and the insertion of boards of directors with party representation, formal agency structure links the agencies to the parliamentary chain of delegation (Christensen and Yesilkagit 2006). Second, formally independent agencies are involved in policy making with ministerial departments and subject to political intervention (Maggetti 2007, 2009; cf. Barth et al. 2003; Busch 2009). Third, Gregory Huber has forcefully shown that American civil servants, be they political appointees or career staff, often work quite independently from their political principals (Huber 2007). Similarly, financial supervisors show considerable de facto autonomy as long as an issue is kept at a low level of political saliency; such autonomy can exist alongside quite closely knit industry networks (Busch 2009: 214–23; see also Quaglia 2008). Finally, a "no-surprises rule" may apply outside Whitehall (Flinders 2008: 54, 147–65).

## 7.7   REHABILITATING PUBLIC INTEREST THEORY?

The argument leads to considerable skepticism towards the validity of credible commitment theory and to reservations as to the full validity of capture theory. Regulatory administration is clearly not delegated to a depoliticized sphere; nor is it tantamount to institutional choices placing implementation under the control of regulated business.

This brings us back to classical public interest theory. It has been dismissed as a manifestation of a sublime normative ideal. The rationale behind credible commitment theory is in clear debt to it. Further, its main problem is the operationalization of the public interest; this turns out to be a problem whether it is conceptualized in economic efficiency, environmental sustainability, or distributional justice terms. Another option is to conceive of it in process terms (Huber 2007; Croley 2008, 2011). Then the focus is not on the results but on the broadness of the interests involved in decision making, the procedures used before conclusions are drawn, and openness as to the decisions made.

The analysis of four European countries together with recent studies of American regulatory administration indicates that the public interest conceived in procedural terms is not treated so badly. One indication is the broad and over time apparently broader inclusion of organized interests; another is the rather frequent use of judges as mediators, umpires, and procedural guardians (see Table 7.3). Other indications of which we lack systematic studies are the presumed strengthening of procedures demanding information of affected groups and access to information, and giving access to formal complaints. These are prescriptions of a general nature, often laid down in administrative procedures and open government acts; they are increasingly and systematically supervised by ombudsmen institutions. This procedural approach is at the core of empirical political science. It is first of all an expansion of the argument advanced by McCubbins et al. (1987) arguing that administrative procedures present an effective strategy for policy makers wanting to install ex ante controls over implementation delegated to the administration. Second, to the extent that long-term changes have taken place opening regulatory administration to the consideration of other than narrow economic interests it demonstrates elected politicians' responsiveness to changes in moods and attitudes both in the business community and among the general electorate (Peltzman 1998). Similarly, the European evidence shows the extent to which policy makers have changed regulatory governance in a way that makes it more inclusive to a broad range of stakeholders. But, in doing so, they have paid their respects to the trajectories of national settings. Finally, it echoes administrative science classics arguing for the relative superiority of procedural rationality as compared to substantive optimality (Weber 1919 [1988]: 549–53; Simon 1955).

In spite of their limits and the limits of the research inspired by them, the theories reviewed in this chapter have together contributed immensely to our understanding of regulatory governance. This research has demonstrated how regulatory governance has adapted to changing economic and societal needs and especially to ever changing political demands. But as the review has laid out it is clear that regulatory governance has a formal as well as an informal side that interact in ways that have yet to be analyzed in depth. It has also made it clear to what extent particular solutions to the challenges of regulatory policy and administration are embedded in traditions and practices that are specific for national political and administrative systems and probably also for particular policy fields.

## ACKNOWLEDGEMENTS

The author wants to thank David Levi-Faur for his comments.

## NOTES

1. Quote by memory from interview on C-SPAN during the 1996 presidential campaign.
2. Compare for example James (2003) with Hogwood et al. (2001), Spiller and Vogelsang (1996) and Flinders (2008).
3. Christiansen and Nørgaard (2003: 88–120) for Denmark; data kindly provided by Gunnar Thesen for Norway; an analysis of Sweden from 1989 shows a similar pattern with marked differentiation between types of interests, but no diachronic data (Petersson 1989).

## REFERENCES

Balla, Steven (2011), 'Agency design and oversight: instruments for managing delegation to the bureaucracy', in David Levi-Faur (ed.), *Handbook on the Politics of Regulation*, Cheltenham, UK and Northampton, MA, US: Edward Elgar.
Barth, James R., D.E. Nolle, T. Phumiwasana and G. Yago (2003), 'A cross-country analysis of the bank supervisory framework and bank performance', *Financial Markets, Institutions, and Instruments*, **12**, 67–120.
Binderkrantz, Anne Skorkjær and Jørgen Grønnegaard Christensen (2009), 'Delegation without agency loss? The use of performance contracts in Danish central government', *Governance*, **22**, 263–93.
Black, Julia, Martin Lodge and Mark Thatcher (eds) (2005), *Regulatory Innovation*, Cheltenham, UK and Northampton, MA, USA: Edward Elgar Publishing.
Brecht, Arnold and Comstock Glaser (1940 [1971]), *The Art and Technique of Administration in German Ministries*, Westport, CT: Greenwood Press.
Busch, Andreas (2009), *Banking Regulation and Globalization*, Oxford: Oxford University Press.
Christensen, Jørgen Grønnegaard (2004), 'Political responsiveness in a merit bureaucracy', in B. Guy Peters and Jon Pierre (eds), *Politicization of the Civil Service in Comparative Perspective*, London: Routledge, pp. 14–40.
Christensen, Jørgen Grønnegaard and Kutsal Yesilkagit (2006), 'Delegation and specialization in regulatory administration: a comparative analysis of Denmark, Sweden and the Netherlands', in Tom Christensen and Per Lægreid (eds), *Autonomy and Regulation*, Cheltenham, UK and Northampton, MA, USA: Edward Elgar Publishing, pp. 203–34.
Christiansen, Peter Munk and Asbjørn Sonne Nørgaard (2003), *Faste forhold – flygtige forbindelser*, Aarhus: Aarhus University Press.

Coen, David and Adrienne Héritier (eds) (2006), *Refining Regulatory Regimes: Utilities in Europe*, Cheltenham, UK and Northampton, MA, USA: Edward Elgar Publishing.
Croley, Steven P. (2008), *Regulation and Public Interests*, Princeton, NJ: Princeton University Press.
Croley, Steven P. (2011), 'Beyond capture: towards a new theory of regulation', in David Levi-Faur (ed.), *Handbook on the Politics of Regulation*, Cheltenham, UK and Northampton, MA, US: Edward Elgar.
Cukierman, Alex (1992), *Central Bank Strategy, Credibility, and Independence*, Cambridge, MA: MIT Press.
Cushman, Robert E. (1941), *The Independent Regulatory Commissions*, New York: Oxford University Press.
Döhler, Marian (2007), *Die politische Steuerung der Verwaltung*, Baden-Baden: Nomos.
Flinders, Matthew (2008), *Delegated Governance and the British State*, Oxford: Oxford University Press.
Gilardi, Fabrizio (2008), *Delegation in the Regulatory State*, Cheltenham, UK and Northampton, MA, USA: Edward Elgar Publishing.
Hogwood, Brian W., David Judge and Murray McVicar (2001), 'Agencies, ministers and civil servants in Britain', in B. Guy Peters and Jon Pierre (eds), *Politicians, Bureaucrats, and Administrative Reform*, London: Routledge, pp. 35–44.
Huber, Gregory A. (2007), *The Craft of Bureaucratic Neutrality*, New York: Cambridge University Press.
Ingraham, Patricia W. (2006), 'Building bridges over troubled waters: merit as a guide', *Public Administration Review*, **66** (4), 486–95.
Jacobsson, Bengt (1984), *Hur styrs förvaltningen?*, Lund: Studentlitteratur.
James, Oliver (2003), *The Executive Agency Revolution in Whitehall*, Houndmills: Palgrave.
Jordana, Jacint and David Levi-Faur (eds) (2004), *The Politics of Regulation*, Cheltenham, UK and Northampton, MA, USA: Edward Elgar Publishing.
Lægreid, Per, Paul G. Roness and Kristin Rubecksen (2006), 'Autonomy and control in the Norwegian civil service: does agency form matter?', in Tom Christensen and Per Lægreid (eds), *Autonomy and Regulation*, Cheltenham, UK and Northampton, MA, USA: Edward Elgar Publishing, pp. 235–67.
Levi-Faur, David (2003), 'The politics of liberalisation: privatisation and regulation- for-competition in Europe's and Latin-America's telecoms and electricity industries', *European Journal of Political Research*, **42**, 705–40.
Levi-Faur, David (2011), 'Regulation and regulatory governance', in David Levi-Faur (ed.), *Handbook on the Politics of Regulation*, Cheltenham, UK and Northampton, MA, US: Edward Elgar.
Levi-Faur, David and Jacint Jordana (2005), 'The rise of regulatory capitalism: the global diffusion of a new order', *Annals of the American Academy of Political and Social Science*, **598**, 12–32.
Levine, Michael E. and Jennifer L. Forrence (1990), 'Regulatory capture, public interest, and the public agenda: toward a synthesis', *Journal of Law, Economics, and Organization*, **6**, 167–98.
Levy, Brian and Pablo T. Spiller (eds) (1996), *Regulations, Institutions, and Commitment*, Cambridge: Cambridge University Press.
Lohmann, Susanne (2006), 'The non-politics of monetary policy', in Barry R. Weingast and Donald A. Wittman (eds), *The Oxford Handbook of Political Economy*, Oxford: Oxford University Press, pp. 523–44.
Maggetti, Martino (2007), 'De facto independence after delegation: a fuzzy-set analysis', *Regulation & Governance*, **1**, 271–94.
Maggetti, Martino (2009), 'The role of independent regulatory agencies in policy-making: a comparative analysis', *Journal of European Public Policy*, **16**, 450–70.
Majone, Giandomenico (1994), 'The rise of the regulatory state in Europe', in W.C. Müller and V. Wright (eds), *The State in Western Europe: Retreat or Redefinition?*, Ilford: Frank Cass, pp. 77–101.
Majone, Giandomenico (2001), 'Two logics of delegation: agency and fiduciary relations in EU governance', *European Union Politics*, **1**, 103–22.
McCubbins, Matthew D., Roger G. Noll and Barry R. Weingast (1987), 'Administrative procedures as instruments of political control', *Journal of Law, Economics, and Organization*, **3**, 243–77.
Mitnick, Barry M. (1980), *The Political Economy of Regulation*, New York: Columbia University Press.
Moran, Michael (2000), 'The Frank Stacey Memorial Lecture: from command state to regulatory state?', *Public Policy and Administration*, **15**, 1–13.
Moran, Michael (2002), 'Understanding the regulatory state', *British Journal of Political Science*, **32**, 391–413.
Niskanen, William A. (1971), *Bureaucracy and Representative Government*, Chicago: Aldine Atherton.
Peltzman, Sam (1976), 'Toward a more general theory of regulation', *Journal of Law and Economics*, **19**, 211–40.
Peltzman, Sam (1998), *Political Participation and Government Regulation*, Chicago: University of Chicago Press.
Peters, B. Guy (2010), *Politics and Bureaucracy*, 6th edn, London: Routledge.
Petersson, Olof (1989), *Maktens nätvärk*, Stockholm: Carlssons.
Posner, Richard A. (1974), 'Theories of economic regulation', *Bell Journal of Economics and Management Science*, **5** (2), 335–58.

Quaglia, Lucia (2008), 'Explaining the reform of banking supervision in Europe: an integrative approach', Governance, **21**, 439–63.

Quirk, Paul J. (1981), *Industry Influence in Federal Regulatory Agencies*, Princeton, NJ: Princeton University Press.

Scharpf, Fritz W. (1997), *Games Real Actors Play*, Boulder, CO: Westview Press.

Shapiro, Martin (1997), 'The problems of independent agencies in the United States and the European Union', *Journal of European Public Policy*, **4**, 276–91.

Simon, Herbert (1955), 'A behavioral model of rational choice', *Quarterly Journal of Economics*, **69**, 99–118.

Spiller, Pablo T. and Ingo Vogelsang (1996), 'The United Kingdom: a pacesetter in regulatory incentives', in Brian Levy and Pablo T. Spiller (eds), *Regulations, Institutions, and Commitment*, Cambridge: Cambridge University Press, pp. 79–120.

Stigler, George T. (1971), 'The theory of economic regulation', *Bell Journal of Economics and Management Science*, **2** (1), 3–21.

Thatcher, Mark (2007), *Internationalization and Economic Institutions*, Oxford: Oxford University Press.

Weber, Max (1919 [1988]), 'Politik als Beruf', in *Gesammelte Politische Schriften*, Tübingen: J.C.B. Mohr.

Weber, Max (1921 [1976]), *Wirtschaft und Gesellschaft*, Tübingen: J.C.B. Mohr.

Weingast, Barry R. and Mark J. Moran (1983), 'Bureacuratic discretion or Congressional control? Regulatory policymaking by the Federal Trade Commission', *Journal of Political Economy*, **91**, 765–800.

Wilson, James Q. (ed.) (1980), *The Politics of Regulation*, New York: Basic Books.

Yandle, Bruce (2011), 'Bootleggers and Baptists in the theory of regulation', in David Levi-Faur (ed.), *Handbook on the Politics of Regulation*, Cheltenham, UK and Northampton, MA, US: Edward Elgar.

Yesilkagit, Kutsal and Jørgen Grønnegaard Christensen (2010), 'Institutional design and formal autonomy: politics versus historical and cultural explanations', *Journal of Public Administration Research and Theory*, **20** (1), 53–74.

# PART III

# HISTORICAL AND COMPARATIVE PERSPECTIVES ON THE REGULATORY STATE

# 8 The rise of the American regulatory state: a view from the Progressive Era

## *Marc T. Law and Sukkoo Kim*

Despite the United States being the world's largest free market economy, government regulation of economic activity is a pervasive feature of the American economy of the early twenty-first century. The foods Americans eat, the cars they drive, the medicines they take, and the financial institutions from which they borrow and to which they lend are all subject to some kind of regulation. While governments from the colonial times played important roles in shaping the allocation of resources, for much of America's history regulation was local and relied on the courts. During the Progressive Era (*circa* 1880–1920), however, the scale and scope of government regulations grew dramatically. State and federal regulatory agencies became the dominant actors in the regulation of economic activities in America.

A key question for social science is why regulation of economic activity exists and why it has grown so dramatically over time. Why and how did the scale and scope of regulation expand? What political and economic forces contributed to the rise to the modern regulatory state, especially during the Progressive Era, the period when centralized state and federal governments became the nexus of regulatory activity?

For economists there are two standard theories of regulation: public interest and capture. The traditional public interest theory argues that government regulation arose to combat market failures, whereas the more recent capture theory claims that producers sought regulation to restrain competition. But what factors account for the major change and growth of regulation during the Progressive Era? Were market failures more prevalent, or were key producers better positioned to "capture" industry rents through regulation? Glaeser and Shleifer (2003) suggest that the emergence of the regulatory state during the Progressive Era was caused by the rise of large, deep-pocket firms that were able to manipulate the courts, the traditional tool of American regulation. In response, governments invented regulatory agencies to complement the court system.

In this chapter we offer a new perspective. Because the use of force by the state is at the heart of all regulation, the scale and scope of regulation in America was intimately tied to the nature and form of the state. Therefore, in order to understand the rise of the modern regulatory state, we must first explore why centralized state and federal governments supplanted the courts and local governments as the loci of regulatory activity. In early America regulation was local and judicial because Americans distrusted centralized powers of government. The common law of nuisance and the *salus populi* (people's welfare) tradition provided the main principles of regulation. Local courts and militia enforced these rules. Novak (1996) argues that local governments effectively used the common law to regulate public safety, trade, space, morality, and public health. While it is beyond the scope of this chapter to explain fully the causes of strong centralized government in America, there are reasons to believe that the causes were multifaceted.

Most importantly, the rise of a more centralized government involved a major Civil War between the states of the North and the South. Accordingly, one theme this chapter explores is how the rise of the modern regulatory state was preceded by a major structural shift in the form of American government during the late nineteenth and early twentieth centuries.

Another theme of this chapter concerns how specialization creates an environment conducive to the rise of regulation. We argue that, once the shift in the balance of power toward centralized state and federal governments set the stage for the rise of the modern regulatory state, regulation became an institutional response to the forces of specialization. In a dynamic market economy, specialization and technological and organizational change tilt the competitive playing field in ways that create new sets of winners and losers among producers and consumers. Regulation emerges in this environment. Sometimes, as the public interest theory suggests, these regulations help markets work better. While specialization increases the gains from trade, it also increases transaction costs, because the more specialized individuals become the less they know about the goods and services produced by others (North and Wallis 1986). Regulation, by creating uniform standards or requiring producers to disclose information about product quality, may reduce informational asymmetries, lower transaction costs, and improve the efficiency of markets. In other instances, however, regulation increases rents of politically organized constituents at the expense of economic welfare. As capture theorists would argue, because regulation can create entry barriers, market participants who are harmed by specialization and technological change have an incentive to seek regulation to thwart new competitors (Stigler 1971; Peltzman 1976). To show how regulation emerges in response to specialization, we will focus on regulations that emerged during the Progressive Era, a period of rapid technological and organizational change, when state and federal regulation of various aspects of the economy began in earnest, and when the foundations of the modern American regulatory state were laid. In particular, we will discuss the adoption and evolution of railroad regulation, meat inspection, antitrust, food and drugs regulation, and occupational licensing regulation.

This chapter will also emphasize the path-dependent nature of regulation in a dynamic market economy. Regulation, once introduced, seldom disappears. While particular statutes may be repealed, or the enforcement of particular regulations may shift from one agency to another, in general regulation tends to "stick." Interests that benefit from regulation become powerful constituencies in favor of its persistence. Additionally, regulation often takes on a life of its own, serving objectives and interests that did not exist when the regulation was initially introduced (see North 1990 for a discussion of path dependence in economic history). We will use the same Progressive Era regulation case studies to show the path-dependent nature of regulatory evolution.

A final theme that we will touch upon in this chapter concerns the federal structure of the American political system and the rise of regulation. A peculiar feature of regulation in contemporary America is that two levels of government (state and federal) sometimes regulate the same activity. Regulation often begins at the state level, diffuses across states, and proceeds upward to the national level. A decentralized process of experimentation across space and over time often accompanies the rise of a particular type of regulation. The emergence of national regulation generally does not preclude state regulation, however. Indeed, in some instances, regulation remains at the state level.

## 8.1 AMERICAN FEDERALISM AND REGULATION

Since the colonies in America evolved independently for over a century and fought for independence from a perceived despotic British government, their first Constitution to form a union, the Articles of Confederation in 1781, provided for an almost non-existent central government: no federal executive, no federal courts, no federal taxes, and no federal coercive authority over states. In six short years, when the Articles proved too weak an instrument to bind the newly formed states, delegates were chosen to amend the Articles. The second Constitution of 1789 established a more powerful central government by instituting the executive branch, federal taxes, federal courts, and federal powers to regulate foreign and interstate commerce. But the fight over the nature and extent of the federal governmental powers implied by the new Constitution continued unabated over the next century.

When Washington became the first president under the new Constitution, the executive branch had little administrative capacity for any kind of regulatory activity: he inherited a foreign office, a treasury board, a secretary of war, and a dozen clerks. When Congress created the Department of Foreign Affairs it even debated whether the president should be given the authority to remove the secretary without the consent of the Senate (White 1948). Washington and Adams, both federalist presidents, with considerable advice from Hamilton, took actions in taxation, banking, finance, public works, and military organization to establish a stronger federal government with centralized powers in the executive branch, but their initiatives were vehemently attacked by antifederalists such as Jefferson and Madison.

Thus, when Jefferson became president in 1801, the federalist movement for a stronger central government came to a halt. Indeed, the hallmark of American government throughout most of the nineteenth century was the devolution and diffusion of powers to states and localities (Skowronek 1982). For example, when bills were proposed to develop the national system of roads funded by the federal government, they were repeatedly vetoed by presidents such as Madison and Jackson, who did so on the ground that federal funding violated the sovereignty of states as guaranteed under the Constitution. The diffusion of political power in America was most profoundly reflected in the locations of its capitals. Unlike their counterparts in Europe and Latin America, national and state capitals in America were primarily located in geographically remote small towns and rural places rather than in major cities (Galiani and Kim forthcoming).

Given the sovereignty of states and localities and the minimal administrative capacities of the federal executive branch during the antebellum period (White 1948, 1951, 1954, 1958), it is not surprising that regulation of the economy was left to the courts. The most important jurisdiction, however, was local and state courts rather than the federal Supreme Court. The original Judiciary Act of 1789 required federal cases to be tried by a district judge and a Supreme Court justice. When they disagreed, the judgment of the district judge prevailed. As a lame-duck president, Adams attempted to strengthen the role of the federal judiciary with the Judiciary Act of 1801, but the Act was promptly repealed and dismantled by Jefferson (Ackerman 2005).

Since the regulation of economic activity was left to state legislatures, local governments, and most importantly their respective courts, regulatory behavior across the states was not uniform. While systematic evidence across the states is still lacking, a historical examination of Massachusetts and Virginia suggests that political and legal institutions in these two states likely diverged from the colonial through the antebellum periods (Kim 2009). In Massachusetts, the state legislatures played a more active role in regulating the economy; additionally, the Massachusetts legal system went from jury-based common law to "instrumental" law. Similar developments did not occur in Virginia. Indeed, with the spread of democracy and the emergence of the Industrial Revolution, state governments throughout the Northeast became more centralized. In these states, legislatures, judges, and justices of state supreme courts played more prominent roles. However, the main tool of regulation remained judicial.

Yet, despite the absence of a federal regulatory state to provide for uniform national regulation, Novak (1996) argues that the US possessed a powerful governmental tradition devoted to the vision of a "well-regulated society" in the nineteenth century. At the heart of this society was "a plethora of bylaws, ordinances, statutes, and common law restrictions regulating nearly every aspect of early American economy and society" (Novak 1996: 1). Moreover, these laws were "the work of mayors, common councils, state legislatures, town and county officers, and powerful state and local judges" (Novak 1996: 1).

In the antebellum era, the demand for regulation was greatest in major urban areas. In 1837, the city of Chicago had no less than 34 regulations, which ranged from the regulation of public highways, gaming, and the selling of spirits, to the burial of the dead. To combat epidemics, cities and states created the medical police and the board of health with broad policing powers. In courts, the common law of public nuisance was used to regulate public safety, noxious trades, adulterated food, obscenity, contagious diseases, theatres, and monopolies. In regulating public safety, especially in the prevention of fire, the common law of public nuisance was used to regulate the manufacture, storage, and sale of gunpowder and the prohibition of wooden buildings in dense urban areas (Novak 1996).

With industrialization and the growth of the modern economy, however, the early American polity, whose powers were situated in localities and the courts, became unsustainable. During the Progressive Era, American political institutions underwent a revolutionary change where political power became centralized in state and federal governments. Yet, owing to the peculiar history of the United States, an important precondition for these developments was the resolution of North–South divisions. With the military victory of the North over the South, Southern insistence on states' rights receded into history and set the stage for the birth of a more centralized federal government (Bensel 1990). Without the military victory by the North, it is very likely that the rise of a strong federal government would have been long delayed. Southern slave owners had strong financial incentives to keep government powers local and state based in order to shield themselves from national anti-slavery influences. Even with the outcome of the Civil War, however, the road to a more centralized federal bureaucracy was difficult, as centralization involved a sharp break from the established political institutions (Nelson 1982; Skowronek 1982). Thus the rise of centralized government also involved the reform of civil administration and the reorganization of the army.

By the late nineteenth century, the Jeffersonian agrarian vision of the primacy of state and local governments had become severely outmoded. The functioning of a modern economy based on manufacturing was much more complicated and beyond the simple understanding of average citizens. While scholars still do not agree on the causes of American political centralization during the Progressive Era, we believe that one of the causes was a response to the greater complexity of the modern economy that required specialized knowledge (Law and Kim 2005). Professionals and specialists were required to understand the causes of diseases and the chemical compositions of food and drugs, as well as pricing practices of chains and large corporations. Not surprisingly, the professionals in the Progressive Era were among the greatest advocates for a more centralized federal government (Skowronek 1982).

Yet, even with the growing powers of the state and federal governments, the early regulatory agencies reflected the historical American distrust of the powers of government. The Massachusetts Board of Railroad Commissioners, an early pioneering regulatory agency entrusted to regulate the state's railroads, possessed limited powers and relied on investigation, appeals to the public, and voluntary cooperation from the regulated (McCraw 1984). While a few Midwestern states created stronger regulatory commissions, many regulatory agencies such as the Securities and Exchange Commission (SEC), as well as the early Food and Drug Administration (FDA), adopted this "sunshine" approach. Finally, perhaps because the weak regulatory system relied on close cooperation from the regulated, regulatory agencies may have been vulnerable to "capture" by the industries that they regulated.

## 8.2   RAILROAD REGULATION

Many scholars trace the beginnings of the modern regulatory state to the emergence of federal regulation of interstate transportation. In 1887 Congress enacted the Interstate Commerce Act (ICA), which gave the federal government sweeping authority to regulate the rates charged by railroads engaged in interstate shipping. The emergence of the ICA followed unsuccessful attempts by several state governments to regulate the railroads. The regulatory agency spawned by the ICA, the Interstate Commerce Commission (ICC), was the first so-called independent regulatory agency. In the twentieth century the ICC eventually obtained authority over interstate trucking. In 1995 the ICA was abolished and its functions were transferred to the Surface Transportation Board.

According to the conventional historiography, the ICA was a political response to agitation by Western farming interests that desired regulation to reduce the monopoly power enjoyed by the railroads. In this pseudo-public interest account of regulatory adoption, the ICA was enacted to solve a market failure arising from the fact that individual railroad companies enjoyed significant market power on particular routes. While there is some truth in this, this account is not completely consistent with the evidence. For one thing, the railroads themselves played an important role in drafting the ICA. Additionally, since Kolko (1965), it has been commonly argued that the ICC's rate-setting power was used to enforce a cartel agreement among competing railroad lines.

In order to understand the forces that led to the adoption of railroad regulation it is important to consider the impact of the expansion of the railroad industry in historical context. During the nineteenth century the US railroad network grew by leaps and bounds. The total miles of railroad track in the US increased from just over 20 miles in 1830 to over 52000 miles in 1870 and in excess of 166000 miles by 1890. While it is important not to overstate the importance of the railroad for overall economic growth of the US economy, it is clear that the development of the railroad industry influenced the geographic distribution of economic activity and the degree of urbanization (Kim 1995; Atack et al. 2010). By connecting far-reaching corners of the country, the railroads facilitated regional specialization and allowed products to be transported more efficiently to urban areas and coastal ports.

Farming interests were most acutely affected by the growth of the US railroad network. This was for several reasons. First, on certain routes, railroad freight charges still consumed a significant portion of the market value of crops. Accordingly, high transportation costs provoked protest on the part of farming interests that were, during this time, becoming increasingly politicized. Second, while competition between railroad lines as well as from canal and river boats kept long-haul prices low, railroads were able to charge near-monopoly prices on short-haul routes. This situation also provoked reaction on the part of farmers and other short-haul shippers who paid more to transport goods for short distances (usually within a state) than long-haul shippers paid to transport goods from the interior to the coast (across several states).

Farmer-based agitation resulted in state-level regulation of railroad rates. Several states enacted laws regulating railroad rates in the 1860s through 1880s, largely in response to the politically influential farm lobby, which desired to use the power of the state to curb the monopoly power enjoyed by railroads over short-haul routes (Kanazawa and Noll 1994). In response to these laws, which appear to have temporarily reduced short-haul freight rates, the railroad industry challenged the constitutionality of state-level railroad rate regulation, claiming that it violated the commerce clause of the Constitution. Two Supreme Court decisions played a key role in shaping the regulation of the railroad industry. In the first case, *Munn v. State of Illinois* (1876), the court ruled that states had the authority to regulate railroad rates and other business activities. This was perceived to be a victory for farming interests. In the second case, *Wabash, St. Louis & Pacific Railroad Company v. Illinois* (1886), the court reversed its earlier position and argued that only the federal government had authority to place "direct" burdens on interstate commerce. The upshot of this decision was that states could regulate rates only on routes within their own state. This implied that interstate railroad rates were not subject to regulation.

The political response to the regulatory vacuum created by the *Wabash* case was the Interstate Commerce Act of 1887. While, as noted earlier, prior scholarship has focused on either the public interest or pure industry capture explanations for the ICA, the most widely accepted view among scholars today is that the ICA was introduced in response to pressure from multiple interest groups. According to Gilligan et al. (1989), the ICA was not purely an attempt to reduce the monopoly power of railroads, nor was it a strict cartel enforcement mechanism. In particular Gilligan et al. argue that the ICA was designed to advance the interests of short-haul shippers and the railroads at the expense of long-haul shippers. In other words, the ICA was designed to placate the two most politically powerful groups at the time: farmers and other short-haul interests (which sought lower short-haul rates) and the railroad companies themselves (which wanted regulation to facilitate collusion over long-haul rates, and to forestall more onerous state-level regulation). These authors demonstrate that the bicameral nature of Congress, in particular the need to obtain majorities in both the House and the Senate, combined with the configuration of interests in the two Congressional chambers, required that any railroad regulation advance the interests of both the railroads themselves (which were influential in the Senate) and the short-haul shippers (who were influential in the House).

Stock market evidence suggests that the passage of the ICA increased the abnormal returns earned by long-haul railroads and reduced the abnormal returns earned by short-haul railroads (Prager 1989; Gilligan et al. 1990). This suggests that both short-haul shipping interests and the long-haul railroads expected to benefit from railroad rate regulation under the ICC. However, in subsequent decades, the ICC was gradually captured, not by the railroads, but by shippers. Indeed, the ICC repeatedly refused to allow the railroads to raise rates in spite of evidence of increasing input costs that significantly reduced railroad profitability (Mullin 2000). Rates were kept low, and eventually the railroads were forced into insolvency (Martin 1971). This does not imply, however, that the influence of the railroads on the ICC was entirely eliminated. Evidence presented by Stigler (1971), for instance, suggests that the railroads were able to use their influence over the ICC to limit the growth of interstate trucking during the early decades of the twentieth century. Regulation, once in place, is often re-adapted to tilt the competitive playing field in response to technological changes. Clearly, however, the role that the ICC played in hindering the growth of interstate trucking was entirely unanticipated by those interests that initially desired railroad regulation.

## 8.3   MEAT INSPECTION AND ANTITRUST

Shortly after the ICA, Congress enacted two additional pieces of legislation that greatly increased the scope of federal regulation of economic activity: the first federal Meat Inspection Act (1891), which gave the US Department of Agriculture broad powers to inspect the safety of meat sold in interstate commerce, and the Sherman Act (1890), the first federal antitrust law.

Far more scholarship has focused on the origins of antitrust regulation than the origins of meat inspection, but the two were products of similar sets of political-economic forces. The late 1880s were a time of significant technological change in the US economy. Falling transportation costs brought about by the emergence of a national rail network, combined with technological changes that created new products and new, large firms, tilted the competitive playing field in ways that disadvantaged smaller producers and traditional products. These forces played a key role in the emergence of both antitrust regulation and meat inspection.

While conventional accounts of the Sherman Act (see Bork 1966, for instance) posit that the law was introduced in order to reduce the market power of trusts and increase economic efficiency, more recent accounts of the Sherman Act and its state-level antecedents argue that antitrust was desired by industry groups representing farmers and small firms that were at a competitive disadvantage relative to the large, multiunit firms (the so-called trusts) that were gaining market share in many industries (DiLorenzo 1985; Stigler 1985; Boudreaux et al. 1995). Evidence provided by these scholars suggests that the trusts did not enjoy significant market power during this time, and that antitrust was generally desired by specific industries and producers that were at a competitive disadvantage relative to the trusts. Among the trusts singled out by advocates of anti-trust regulation were John D. Rockefeller's Standard Oil and the large Chicago meat packing firms (Swift and Armour, for instance).

Let us first consider the role of Standard Oil in creating a demand for antitrust regulation. The nineteenth century witnessed an enormous expansion in the market for oil. On the demand side, the growing consumer demand for oil and oil-related products – most significantly, refined lighting oil – allowed oil refiners to expand output and exploit economies of scale. On the supply side, several technological changes – the replacement of oil barrels with oil tanks, the growth of the railroad network, the invention of tank cars, and the development of oil pipelines – combined with oil discoveries and the expansion of refinery capacity contributed to lower oil prices. Among oil producers at the time, Standard Oil was the industry's leading innovator. It was among the first to replace oil barrels with oil tanks; it aggressively used oil pipelines to link oil-drilling centers to urban markets; additionally, it was able to exploit its significant monopsony power over the railroads to negotiate highly favorable transport rates. As a result of these developments, Standard's share of total oil-refining capacity increased dramatically, from 10 percent in 1870 to more than 90 percent a decade later (Troesken 2002).

In this environment of rapid technological change, smaller refineries were simply unable to compete with Standard Oil and the other industry leaders. Faced with the possibility of extinction, these smaller producers turned to government to tilt the competitive playing field in their favor. Claiming that Standard Oil was using its dominant position to obtain unfair advantages from the railroads, as well as to preclude entry on the part of other oil producers, smaller producers lobbied for state and federal antitrust regulation. At the federal level, small oil producers found a political ally in Senator Sherman. Sherman successfully argued in Congress that, by keeping smaller refiners alive, antitrust regulation would increase competition. The result was the Sherman Act of 1890 (Troesken 2002).

Contemporaneous with the emergence of antitrust laws were meat inspection regulations that mandated inspection of meat products prior to slaughter. Libecap (1992) has noted the connection between these two seemingly disparate regulatory initiatives. Libecap argues that political pressure for meat inspection and antitrust emerged in response to the consolidation of the meat packing industry in large Midwestern centers like Chicago. As a result of the introduction of refrigerated rail cars, it became possible to slaughter meat centrally in Chicago, and transport beef carcasses ("dressed beef") to Eastern markets. This was significantly cheaper than shipping live cattle to Eastern markets (Yeager 1981). According to Libecap, a coalition of interests – specifically, cattle raisers in Western states and local slaughterhouses in Eastern markets – desired meat inspection and antitrust regulation simultaneously. Cattle raisers desired meat inspection and antitrust in order to counter claims that Midwestern cattle was diseased and to reduce the perceived monopsony power enjoyed by the large Chicago packing firms, which were among the largest purchasers of live cattle. Local slaughterhouses desired the two types of regulation in order to substantiate their claims that "dressed beef" was unwholesome, and to reduce the market power enjoyed by the large Chicago packers. The rise of a centralized meat packing industry and the effects of large packinghouses on the competitive playing field therefore also contributed to the emergence of federal meat inspection and federal antitrust regulation.

Early federal antitrust enforcement was haphazard at best. Until the early 1900s, there were relatively few antitrust prosecutions against large corporations. In fact, during the 1890s, labor unions were the most common target of antitrust enforcement under the Sherman Act. Enforcement of the Sherman Act against the "trusts" began under Theodore Roosevelt and continued under William Taft, whose administrations successfully challenged several mergers and forced the break of large companies including Standard Oil and the American Tobacco Company. The scope of antitrust regulation increased with the passage of the Clayton Act and Federal Trade Commission Act, both adopted in 1914. Under the Clayton Act, price discrimination and exclusive dealing were added as potential abuses of a dominant position that may substantially reduce competition. The Federal Trade Commission Act created another antitrust enforcement agency (the Federal Trade Commission or FTC), and gave the commission authority to regulate unfair business practices. While the intent of the FTC Act was to create a strong and independent antitrust enforcement body, in practice the vigilance of antitrust enforcement by the FTC has been dependent on the attitudes of the commissioners, as well as those of the executive office.

## 8.4   FOOD AND DRUGS REGULATION

The last few decades of the nineteenth century also witnessed the emergence of food and drugs regulation. As with antitrust and meat inspection laws, food and drugs regulation began at the state level. State "pure food" laws formed the foundation for subsequent federal regulation of the food and drugs industries. What explains the rise of food and drugs regulation at this time?

Once again, specialization and technological change were important forces driving the adoption of regulation. Specialization and urbanization made households increasingly dependent on impersonal markets for their foods. Technological advances in food processing and manufacturing gave rise to new and unfamiliar food products (e.g. oleomargarine, alum-based baking powders) or food additives (e.g. chemical preservatives) that challenged the dominant position enjoyed by traditional food manufacturers and also made it possible for producers to adulterate (i.e. cheapen through the addition of impurities) food products in ways that consumers could not easily detect. At the same time, these technological changes made it possible for experts to detect food adulteration systematically.

In such an environment, a demand for regulation arose for two reasons. Technological changes that tilt the competitive playing field inevitably generate a desire on the part of incumbent producers for regulation that disadvantages the producers of newer and cheaper substitutes. However, these same technological changes created an asymmetric information problem about the quality of food ingredients. Because food adulteration was not easy for consumers to detect, there was a potentially productive role for regulation of product labels by experts in order to reduce informational asymmetries about food quality (Wood 1986; Young 1989; Goodwin 1999).

The regulations that emerged during this time were a patchwork quilt of state and federal laws that served both objectives. On the one hand, state and federal oleomargarine regulations were clearly producer protection laws that were aimed at protecting dairy interests from the growing popularity of oleomargarine, a cheap and viable substitute for butter in the market for spreadable oils. Laws that taxed oleomargarine sales or oleomargarine producers, or required that oleomargarine be colored pink were introduced at the behest of dairy interests that sought legislative relief from the expanding oleomargarine trade (Dupré 1999). On the other hand, state-level "pure food laws" that required the proper disclosure of product ingredients were introduced to reduce uncertainty about food quality. Evidence presented by Law (2003) suggests that general pure food laws were desired by a coalition of producers of higher-quality products and politically motivated consumers (women's groups and members of the growing home-economics movement) who wanted regulation to solve an asymmetric information problem about product ingredients.

While food regulation began at the state level, it eventually became a federal concern. Several factors contributed to the adoption of federal regulation. First, many food products crossed state borders. Products manufactured in one state are not easily regulated at the state level if sold in another state. Second, within the federal government, bureaucratic entrepreneurs sought to expand the reach of federal authority. In particular, Harvey S. Wiley, the chief of the US Department of Agriculture's Bureau of Chemistry, pushed for an expansion of regulation of food products to the national level (Young 1989; Coppin and High 1999; Carpenter 2001). Finally, certain "crisis" events – specifically the publication of Upton Sinclair's *The Jungle*, with its grisly depictions of the hygienic conditions of slaughterhouses, as well as muckraking journalism about the dangers of patent medicines and proprietary nostrums – played a key role in helping to forge an effective political coalition in favor of federal regulation (Carpenter 2001; Law and Libecap 2006). The culmination of these forces gave rise to the Pure Food and Drugs Act of 1906, which outlawed the adulteration and misbranding of food and drugs products for interstate sale and eventually spawned the creation of the Food and Drugs Administration (FDA), the federal agency that continues to regulate the food and drugs industries.

Early enforcement of the Pure Food and Drugs Act was fraught with difficulties. There is some evidence that enforcement of this law under Wiley may have been used to advantage industries that Wiley himself favored – specifically, straight whiskey manufacturers and food manufacturers that did not use preservatives (Coppin and High 1999). Additionally, because the early FDA was a small agency with relatively weak enforcement powers, its ability to effectively sanction food and drug manufacturers for misbranding and adulteration was limited. Facing such constraints, the FDA gradually changed its enforcement strategy. Instead of inducing compliance with the law by threatening to punish violators, the FDA offered benefits to firms in the way of quality certification and technical assistance in improving food quality. The agency was able to offer these benefits because it had considerable expertise in food science and food manufacturing. Accordingly, the early FDA played an important role in improving food quality and in reducing informational asymmetries notwithstanding the fact that it was a relatively small agency with limited enforcement power (Law 2006).

The impact of the early FDA on the drug industry was far more limited, however. During the late nineteenth and early twentieth centuries, the dominant segment of the drug trade was in so-called patent medicines and proprietary nostrums (Young 1967). The FDA's enforcement work against this industry was devoted to regulating the therapeutic claims printed on the product labels of these products. These efforts were largely unsuccessful because the courts were often inconsistent about whether the FDA had the authority to regulate therapeutic claims, and because the patent medicine industry was large and politically influential. Additionally, because pharmacology was a relatively new science, the FDA did not have much in the way of technical expertise to offer this industry in exchange for regulatory compliance (Law 2006). It was not until the passage of the Food, Drugs, and Cosmetics Act of 1938 that the agency obtained significant regulatory authority over the pharmaceutical industry. The 1938 law required testing of all pharmaceutical products for safety prior to market release. This marked the beginning of modern pharmaceutical regulation.

## 8.5 OCCUPATIONAL LICENSING REGULATION

Contemporaneous with the diffusion of pure food regulation was the adoption of state-level occupational licensing laws. During the late nineteenth and early twentieth centuries, state governments began to adopt laws that regulated occupations ranging from physicians and lawyers to plumbers and beauticians. By the middle of the twentieth century, over 1200 licensing laws were in place, averaging 25 per state, and covering over 75 different occupations. What explains the adoption and diffusion of occupational licensing regulation?

It is commonly argued that occupational licensing represents the canonical case of industry capture of the regulatory apparatus (Friedman and Kuznets 1945; Stigler 1971). Licensing allows incumbent practitioners to establish entry barriers that reduce competition and increase the rents enjoyed by established practitioners, often at the expense of economic efficiency. However, there is an alternative explanation for licensing that yields similar qualitative predictions. Licensing laws often apply to professions – like medicine, for instance – where the quality of professional service is difficult to ascertain *ex ante*. Asymmetric information about professional quality can give rise to a lemons problem, where low-quality practitioners dominate the market (Akerlof 1970). In such an environment, licensing laws that establish minimum standards may indeed reduce entry and raise the income of practitioners, but also improve efficiency by reducing informational asymmetries (Arrow 1963; Leland 1979).

In order to understand the adoption and diffusion of occupational licensing laws in the United States, it is necessary to consider how specialization, technological change, and the growth of knowledge affected the market for professional services. During the nineteenth and twentieth centuries, the scale and scope of scientific knowledge expanded tremendously. Not only did the total stock of knowledge increase, but also scientific knowledge became increasingly specialized. Over time this specialized knowledge found application in occupations like engineering, medicine, dentistry, and architecture.

The implications of this explosion of specialized knowledge were manifold. For one thing, within particular fields, practitioners became more specialized. Second, the benefits of longer, more formal training increased as many occupations became increasingly technical and as universities, colleges, and other institutions emerged to educate individuals who wanted to work in these increasingly technical fields. Finally, occupational specialization and the expansion of scientific knowledge made it harder for consumers to judge the quality of professional services. In fields like medicine, for instance, scientific advances made it more difficult for consumers to know if they were receiving the correct treatment. The heterogeneity of professional quality increased as newly trained technical experts competed with long-standing practitioners. Uncertainty about professional quality therefore increased.

Given this environment, there was a demand for regulation, in part to tilt the competitive playing field, but also to reduce informational asymmetries about professional quality. On the anti-competitive front, there is some evidence that entry into certain occupations was reduced by the licensing regulations. For instance, the adoption and expansion of licensing laws may have reduced entry into medicine, dentistry, architecture, and engineering. However, it is also revealing that the occupations where entry was most restricted were also fields where advances in science and the growth of specialized knowledge were likely to create the most significant informational asymmetries and where the costs of low-quality service were most severe. The evidence also indicates that licensing of these occupations was most likely to be adopted in urban states. During this time, as specialization and the expansion of scientific knowledge were accompanied by urbanization, individuals became less knowledgeable about the goods and services they were purchasing. Additionally, because scientific advances were more likely to occur in cities, informational asymmetries were most likely to be acute in urban areas. Accordingly, it seems plausible that the introduction and diffusion of occupational licensing were also motivated by concerns about asymmetric information (Law and Kim 2005).

While it is difficult to cleanly distinguish these two hypotheses for occupational licensing regulation, three pieces of evidence suggest that the adoption of licensing, at least during the Progressive Era, may have had mostly benign consequences. The first is that, for most occupations, Progressive Era licensing laws did not reduce entry. Accordingly, competition was not significantly hampered by the introduction of occupational licensing. Second, there is evidence that medical licensing may have increased physician quality. In a detailed examination of effects of physician licensing regulation during the early decades of the 1900s, Law and Kim (2005) find that mortality rates for conditions where physician quality may have mattered during this time were lower in places where medical licensing laws were stricter. In particular, they find that maternal and appendicitis mortality rates were lower in places where medical licensing laws were stricter. This suggests that medical licensing may have played a role in improving physician quality. Finally, in an analysis of the effects of the introduction of licensing laws on the representation of minority (female and black) workers in regulated occupations, Law and Marks (2009) find that licensing laws seldom reduced minority representation and sometimes increased it. Specifically, their analysis indicates that the representation of minority workers was enhanced by the introduction of physician, nursing, engineering, and teacher licensing laws. In these increasingly technical fields, licensing may have helped minorities by reducing statistical discrimination against females or blacks. By providing minorities with an observable signal of quality, licensing may have therefore allowed talented women and black workers to enter occupations that would normally have been closed to them. Much of the evidence from the Progressive Era is therefore more consistent with the view that licensing reduced informational asymmetries and helped markets function more efficiently.

Of course, the fact that licensing may have initially improved markets need not suggest that its impact has always been positive. Any regulation that creates entry barriers and yields control over entry to incumbents has the potential to enrich established practitioners at the expense of economic efficiency. Studies of licensing that use more contemporary data suggest that licensing laws generally reduce competition and increase the incomes of incumbent practitioners, often with no offsetting improvement in the quality of professional services (Kleiner 2006). Additionally, the extension of licensing regimes to occupations where there are no obvious informational asymmetries that cannot be addressed adequately through market mechanisms (for instance, funeral directors, manicurists) suggests that the desire to control entry remains an important motivation for licensing.

Nevertheless, the legacy of occupational licensing has been an enduring one. Estimates suggest that over 20 percent of the labor force is currently subject to some kind of state-level licensing regulation (Kleiner 2006). Perhaps the popularity of licensing stems precisely from the fact that it serves twin objectives: on the one hand it reduces informational asymmetries, while on the other it helps incumbent practitioners by reducing competition. By offering potential benefits to both consumers and producers, licensing regimes ensure their own survival.

Finally, it is worth noting that occupational licensing, unlike the other regulatory domains analyzed in this chapter, remains at the state level. Unlike meat inspection, antitrust, railroad regulation, and food and drugs regulation, there are no federal occupational licensing statutes. This is for the reason that concerns about the effects of state-level regulation on interstate commerce are less pertinent for occupational licensing regulation than for the other regulatory areas. When goods produced in one state are purchased and consumed in other states (food and drugs), or when an industry itself literally crosses state boundaries (railroads), it is efficient for regulation to be established and enforced at a federal level. In contrast, when goods and services are produced and consumed within a smaller geographic unit (for instance, the services purchased from professionals like doctors and lawyers tend to be consumed in a given state), and when different jurisdictions have different tastes for regulatory stringency, the state may be the more appropriate regulatory unit. Occupational licensing laws, in fact, are often justified on grounds of setting standards for local safety, and the federal nature of the American political system allows and even encourages different jurisdictions to pursue different policies. While the absence of uniform licensing standards across states may have impeded the geographic mobility of licensed professionals (Pashigian 1979), the federal nature of the American system, combined with the fact that most professional services are produced and consumed locally, has ensured that licensing remains a state-level concern.

## 8.6   CONCLUSIONS

Until the late nineteenth century, regulation in America was largely local and enforced by the courts. Urbanization, industrialization, and most importantly the Civil War provoked a shift in the form of American government that shifted the balance of power towards centralized state and federal governments. In this chapter we argue that an understanding of the rise of the modern American regulatory state first requires an appreciation of how centralized state and federal governments became the nexus of regulatory activity.

Specialization, by creating new and unfamiliar products, gives rise to informational problems. Consumers and producers may desire regulation in order to reduce informational asymmetries and improve efficiency. On the other hand, specialization, by tilting the competitive playing field, creates new sets of winners and losers in the marketplace. The losers in this competitive battle may seek shelter by lobbying for regulation that disadvantages competitors. Our overview of the rise of regulation during the Progressive Era – a period of rapid technological and organizational change in the US economy – illustrates how regulation emerges in response to the forces of specialization. In each of the regulatory domains discussed, specialization and technological advance played a key role in creating a demand for regulation. Accordingly, we believe that specialization and its ripple effects must also play a key role in any account of the emergence and rise of the US regulatory state.

We also argue that regulation, once enacted, tends to stick. Indeed, regulation may ultimately end up serving interests and objectives that played little or no role in its creation. The enduring effects of regulation are often unanticipated by its original sponsors. Our analysis of how specific regulations are shaped over time by competing interests suggests that path dependence is a key aspect of regulatory evolution. Finally, we believe that the federal nature of the American political union has also shaped the rise of regulation in America. In each of the cases analyzed, regulation began at the state level and then diffused across states. While in most instances federal regulation ultimately emerges, in some cases it does not. Whether or not federal regulation arises depends critically on the importance of interstate commerce, as well as the potential for vested interests to use federal regulation to forestall more stringent state laws.

Clearly, our survey of the rise of regulation in America is not exhaustive. Because our focus is the Progressive Era, we have avoided discussing regulatory domains whose genesis lies in other episodes of US economic history (for instance, we do not discuss securities regulation, insurance regulation, banking regulation, or airline regulation). Additionally, there are other hypotheses for the adoption and evolution of regulation (for instance, explanations in which "crises" and other contingent events play a leading role – see Higgs 1987, for example) that we have deliberately sidestepped. Nevertheless, in focusing on how state and federal governments became the loci of regulatory activity in the late nineteenth century, and in examining how a handful of Progressive Era regulations emerged as a response to specialization and technological change and how these regulations evolved through space and time, we believe that we have identified a few key forces behind the rise of the modern American regulatory state.

# REFERENCES

Ackerman, Bruce (2005), *The Failure of the Founding Fathers: Jefferson, Marshall, and the Rise of Presidential Democracy*, Cambridge, MA: Belknap Press of Harvard University Press.
Akerlof, George A. (1970), 'The market for "lemons": quality uncertainty and the market mechanism', *Quarterly Journal of Economics*, **84** (3), 488–500.
Arrow, Kenneth J. (1963), 'Uncertainty and the welfare economics of medical care', *American Economic Review*, **53** (5), 941–73.

Atack, Jeremy, Fred Bateman, Michael Haines and Robert A. Margo (2010), 'Did railroads induce or follow economic growth? Urbanization and population growth in the American Midwest, 1850–1860', *Social Science History*, **34** (2), 171–97.

Bensel, Richard F. (1990), *Yankee Leviathan: The Origins of Central State Authority in America 1857–1877*, Cambridge: Cambridge University Press.

Bork, Robert H. (1966), 'Legislative intent and the policy of the Sherman Act', *Journal of Law and Economics*, **6** (1), 7–14.

Boudreaux, Donald J., Thomas J. DiLorenzo and Steven Parker (1995), 'Antitrust before the Sherman Act', in Fred S. McChesney and William F. Shugart II (eds), *The Causes and Consequences of Antitrust: The Public Choice Perspective*, Chicago: University of Chicago Press, pp. 255–70.

Carpenter, Daniel P. (2001), *The Forging of Bureaucratic Autonomy: Reputations, Networks and Policy Innovation in Executive Agencies, 1862–1928*, Princeton, NJ: Princeton University Press.

Coppin, Clayton A. and Jack C. High (1999), *The Politics of Purity: Harvey Washington Wiley and the Origins of Federal Food Policy*, Ann Arbor: University of Michigan Press.

DiLorenzo, Thomas J. (1985), 'The origins of antitrust: an interest-group perspective', *International Review of Law and Economics*, **5** (2), 73–90.

Dupré, Ruth (1999), 'If it's yellow, it must be butter: margarine regulation in North America since 1886', *Journal of Economic History*, **59** (2), 353–71.

Friedman, Milton and Simon Kuznets (1945), *Income from Independent Professional Practice*, New York: National Bureau of Economic Research.

Galiani, Sebastian and Sukkoo Kim (forthcoming), 'Political centralization and urban primacy: evidence from national and provincial capitals in the Americas'.

Gilligan, Thomas W., William J. Marshall and Barry R. Weingast (1989), 'Regulation and the theory of legislative choice: the Interstate Commerce Act of 1887', *Journal of Law and Economics*, **32** (1), 35–61.

Gilligan, Thomas W., William J. Marshall and Barry R. Weingast (1990), 'The economic incidence of the Interstate Commerce Act of 1887: a theoretical and empirical analysis of the short-haul pricing constraint', *RAND Journal of Economics*, **21** (2), 189–210.

Glaeser, Edward L. and Andrei Shleifer (2003), 'The rise of the regulatory state', *Journal of Economic Literature*, **41** (2), 401–25.

Goodwin, Lorine (1999), *The Pure Food, Drink, and Drug Crusaders: 1879–1914*, Jefferson, NC: McFarland.

Higgs, Robert (1987), *Crisis and Leviathan: Critical Episodes in the Growth of American Government*, New York: Oxford University Press.

Kanazawa, Mark and Roger G. Noll (1994), 'The origins of state railroad regulation: the Illinois state constitution of 1870', in Claudia Goldin and Gary D. Libecap (eds), *The Regulated Economy: An Historical Approach to Political Economy*, Chicago: University of Chicago Press, pp. 13–54.

Kim, Sukkoo (1995), 'The expansion of markets and the geographic distribution of economic activity: trends in US regional manufacturing structure, 1860–1987', *Quarterly Journal of Economics*, **110** (4), 881–908.

Kim, Sukkoo (2009), 'Institutions and US regional development: a study of Massachusetts and Virginia', *Journal of Institutional Economics*, **5** (2), 181–205.

Kleiner, Morris J. (2006), *Licensing Occupations: Ensuring Quality or Restricting Competition?* Kalamazoo, MI: Upjohn Institute.

Kolko, Gabriel (1965), *Railroads and Regulation, 1877–1916*, Westport, CT: Greenwood.

Law, Marc T. (2003), 'The origins of state pure food regulation', *Journal of Economic History*, **63** (4), 1103–30.

Law, Marc T. (2006), 'How do regulators regulate? Enforcement of the Pure Food and Drugs Act, 1907–38', *Journal of Law, Economics, and Organization*, **22** (2), 459–89.

Law, Marc T. and Sukkoo Kim (2005), 'Specialization and regulation: the rise of professionals and the emergence of occupational licensing regulation in America', *Journal of Economic History*, **65** (3), 723–56.

Law, Marc T. and Gary D. Libecap (2006), 'The determinants of Progressive Era reform: the Pure Food and Drugs Act of 1906', in Edward L. Glaeser and Claudia Goldin (eds), *Corruption and Reform: Lessons from America's Economic History*, Chicago: University of Chicago Press, pp. 319–42.

Law, Marc T. and Mindy S. Marks (2009), 'The effects of occupational licensing laws on minorities: evidence from the Progressive Era', *Journal of Law and Economics*, **52** (2), 351–66.

Leland, Hayne (1979), 'Quacks, lemons, and licensing: a theory of minimum quality standards', *Journal of Political Economy*, **87** (6), 1328–46.

Libecap, Gary D. (1992), 'The rise of the Chicago packers and the origins of meat inspection and antitrust', *Economic Inquiry*, **30** (2), 242–62.

Martin, Albro (1971), *Enterprise Denied: The Origins of the Decline of American Railroads*, New York: Columbia University Press.

McCraw, Thomas K. (1984), *Prophets of Regulation*, Cambridge, MA: Belknap Press of Harvard University Press.

Mullin, Wallace P. (2000), 'Railroad revisionists revisited: stock market evidence from the Progressive Era', *Journal of Regulatory Economics*, **17** (1), 25–47.

Nelson, William E. (1982), *The Roots of American Bureaucracy 1830–1900*, Cambridge, MA: Havard University Press.

North, Douglass C. (1990), *Institutions, Institutional Change, and Economic Performance*, New York: Cambridge University Press.

North, Douglass C. and John J. Wallis (1986), 'Measuring the transaction sector of the American economy, 1870–1970', in Stanley Engerman and Robert Gallman (eds), *Long Term Factors in American Economy Growth*, Chicago: University of Chicago Press, pp. 95–148.

Novak, William J. (1996), *The People's Welfare: Law and Regulation in Ninteenth-Century America*, Chapel Hill: University of North Carolina Press.

Pashigian, B. Peter (1979), 'Occupational licensing and the interstate mobility of professionals', *Journal of Law and Economics*, **22** (1), 1–25.

Peltzman, Sam (1976), 'Toward a more general theory of regulation', *Journal of Law and Economics*, **19** (2), 211–40.

Prager, Robin A. (1989), 'Using stock price data to measure the effects of railroad regulation: the Interstate Commerce Act and the railroad industry', *RAND Journal of Economics*, **20** (2), 280–90.

Skowronek, Stephen (1982), *Building a New American State: The Expansion of National Administrative Capacities 1877–1920*, Cambridge: Cambridge University Press.

Stigler, George J. (1971), 'The theory of economic regulation', *Bell Journal of Economics and Management Science*, **2** (1), 3–21.

Stigler, George J. (1985), 'The origins of the Sherman Act', *Journal of Legal Studies*, **14** (1), 1–12.

Troesken, Werner (2002), 'The letters of John Sherman and the origins of antitrust', *Review of Austrian Economics*, **15** (4), 275–96.

White, Leonard D. (1948), *The Federalists: A Study in Administrative History*, New York: Macmillan.

White, Leonard D. (1951), *The Jeffersonians: A Study in Administrative History 1801–1829*, New York: Macmillan.

White, Leonard D. (1954), *The Jacksonians: A Study in Administrative History 1829–1861*, New York: Macmillan.

White, Leonard D. (1958), *The Republican Era, 1869–1901: A Study in Administrative History*, New York: Macmillan.

Wood, Donna J. (1986), *Strategic Uses of Public Policy: Business and Government in the Progressive Era*, Marshfield, MA: Pitman Publishing.

Yeager, Mary (1981), *Competition and Regulation: The Development of Oligopoly in the Meat Packing Industry*, Greenwich, CT: JAI Press.

Young, James H. (1967), *Medical Messiahs: A Social History of Health Quackery in Twentieth Century America*, Princeton, NJ: Princeton University Press.

Young, James H. (1989), *Pure Food: Securing the Federal Food and Drugs Act of 1906*, Princeton, NJ: Princeton University Press.

# 9 Beyond the logic of the market: toward an institutional analysis of regulatory reforms

## Marc Allen Eisner

After nearly a century of regulatory expansion, the United States entered a period of regulatory reform in the mid-1970s. During the previous decade, the case for government regulation came under prolonged scrutiny. Academic analysts and activists from the consumer movement identified serious cases of regulatory failure and compiled case studies that reinforced earlier scholarly works on regulatory capture and life cycles (see Herring 1938; Huntington 1952; Bernstein 1955; Kolko 1963). The critique of regulation was not the sole property of the left. Chicago school economists were developing the economic theory of regulation, modeling regulation as a series of mutually beneficial exchanges between profit-maximizing firms and vote-maximizing legislators (see Stigler 1971). Despite the obvious ideological differences, there was a broad consensus that many regulations protected regulated interests, foisting the costs on to the public. As the arguments against regulation mounted, stagflation created a window of opportunity for policy change (see Derthick and Quirk 1985). Excessive regulation was linked – albeit often only rhetorically – to rising inflation, stagnant growth, and flailing competitiveness. Policymakers concluded that the costs of economic regulations often exceeded whatever benefits might be claimed. Deregulatory initiatives were successfully introduced in commercial banking, communications, and air and surface transportation. In some cases, these initiatives mandated the wholesale elimination of well-established regulatory agencies. When combined with the rejection of Keynesian demand management, the promotion of greater trade liberalization, and welfare reform, deregulation became one of the pillars of neoliberalism. If earlier policy regimes had vested authority in state institutions in the hope of forcing higher levels of corporate accountability and compensating for market failure, these grants had been revoked in the name of efficiency.

Deregulation was only one part of the reform agenda. Beginning in the early 1970s, presidents established ever more demanding systems of regulatory review. Although the Ford and Carter administrations imposed relatively unobtrusive analytical requirements such that agencies could often compose cost–benefit analyses *ex post facto*, the Reagan presidency marked a sea change. In 1981, Reagan's executive order 12291 required agencies to submit regulatory impact analyses grounded in cost–benefit analysis to the Office of Management and Budget's Office of Information and Regulatory Affairs (OMB OIRA). If agencies failed to make the affirmative case that new regulations generated net benefits, OMB OIRA was authorized to prohibit them from publishing notice of rulemaking in the *Federal Register*, thereby stopping the regulatory process (McGarity 1991). Even if the new social regulatory agencies like the Environmental Protection Agency (EPA) and the Occupational Safety and Health Administration (OSHA) survived the deregulatory fervor of the era, they were deeply impacted by the new review requirements. The timing of costs and benefits intrinsic to many social regulatory policies – they imposed large initial compliance costs and generated a flow of benefits that accrued in the distant future – were particularly difficult to justify when discounted to present value. Moreover, the costs of completing the regulatory impact analyses stressed the resources of agencies already working under significant budgetary constraints.

There is much to suggest that the introduction of regulatory review processes reflected both the promotion of market values and presidential efforts to manage inter-branch conflicts (see Percival 1991, 2001). In the 1970s, Congress passed the costliest regulatory statutes in US history. Responding to the above-mentioned critiques of regulatory capture and anxious to assert control over new agencies, legislators wrote exhaustively detailed regulatory statutes that limited the discretionary authority of regulators and, by implication, the capacity of the President to manage the regulatory state. By vesting authority in the OMB within the Executive Office of the President, regulatory review partially redressed the perceived imbalance of power. Although it was convenient in the 1980s to attribute these changes to the Reagan administration's anti-regulatory ethos, these processes were retained, albeit with modifications, by subsequent presidents, regardless of party affiliation and agenda. One can surmise that they were embraced, in part, to mange the balance of power between the President and Congress.

This chapter focuses on deregulation and the role of the market. Advocates of deregulation claimed that the market could produce results superior to the state. And yet, as will be argued below, if we replace the broad and imprecise category of "the market" with a more institutionally rich understanding of economic governance, we discover that deregulation produced results that often bore little resemblance to classical markets. Rather, what emerged was complex governance structures that, in some ways, served coordinative functions comparable to what had existed under regulation. Moreover, these governance decisions were not simply the product of chance or the search for efficiencies. They were shaped by public policy and investment decisions. The following examination proceeds in three stages. First, it explores the limitations of the market–state dichotomy. Second, it turns to consider regulation and deregulation through the lens of governance, with a brief survey of three cases of deregulation in the United States: airlines, surface transportation, and finance. Finally, the discussion concludes with a consideration of the merits of adopting an institutional perspective when considering the dynamics of deregulation.

## 9.1    PUBLIC AUTHORITY AND THE MARKET

Much of our thinking about public policy is shaped by the market–state dichotomy. The market is portrayed as a pre-political world populated by self-interested rational actors engaged in mutually beneficial voluntary transactions. In sharp contrast, the state is a world of coercion. Large bureaucratic organizations impose sanctions to force individuals to do things that they might otherwise choose not to do in hopes of achieving some larger, overarching social goals. The positive theory of market failure offers some technical guidance as to when the state is justified to "intervene" in the market system (see Weimer and Vining 1999: 74–116). That is, interventions are justified if they address various forms of market failure. Of course, even if such justifications exist, critics caution, the costs of government failure may nonetheless surpass the benefits of intervention. As Charles Wolf, Jr. (1990: 6) observed:

> The choice in actuality is among imperfect markets, imperfect governments, and various combinations of the two. The cardinal economic choice concerns the degree to which markets or governments – each with their respective flaws – should determine the allocation, use, and distribution of resources in the economy.

As powerful as the market–state dichotomy has been in structuring our thinking and public discourse about the political economy (Lindblom 1982), the conceptual bifurcation obscures the variety of institutions subsumed by "the market" and the role that the state plays in creating the institutional foundations for the economy. Markets are institutions that facilitate the exchange of property. For property rights to be effective, they must be definable, defensible, and divestible or transferable (Yandle 1999). In each of these dimensions, the state plays a foundational role (e.g., by awarding titles, providing laws that govern transactions, and maintaining institutions for the adjudication of property disputes). Thus, rather than existing as a self-constituting and self-regulating sphere of human action, markets are constituted by public policies and institutions.

We can gain some additional insights into the state–market nexus by exploring the legal foundations of economic activity. The key actors in the economy – corporations, trade associations, labor unions, and banks, for example – are legally constituted entities (see Edelman and Suchman 1997). Consider the corporation. One can model the corporation as a production function, but the corporate charter is a legal document that conveys a particular combination of legal rights and privileges (e.g., limited liability) to organizations that meet particular requirements with respect to organization, governance, and reporting. Banks, as deposit-taking and loan-making institutions, can operate if and only if they are chartered, and this requires meeting legal requirements regarding capitalization, reserves, and governance. Workers may choose to organize, but the process of unionization is heavily regulated in the US by the National Labor Relations Act and the policies of the National Labor Relations Board. In addition to constituting the key organizational actors in the economy, the law delimits the forms of activity and organization that economic actors may employ in their interactions with other actors.

In addition to obfuscating the varied ways in which the state shapes economic behavior, the dichotomous variables of market and state conceal the variety of governance arrangements that are subsumed by "the market." In the past several decades, economic sociologists and political economists have devoted much attention to exploring the different ways in which economic organizations coordinate their behavior and the ways in which law has shaped the evolution of economic governance in different industries and cross-nationally (see Campbell et al. 1991; Hollingsworth and Boyer 1997; Fligstein 2001). Rather than presenting the "market" as a synonym for the economy, it is understood as but one of an array of governance mechanisms that economic actors can use to coordinate their behavior. In its purest form, a market is a decentralized system of exchange linking formally autonomous actors engaged in a self-liquidating transaction. Although it provides an appropriate means of coordinating behavior when transactions involve standardized goods or commodities, a market does not support the long-term coordination of specific parties, nor can it support transactions that involve higher levels of complexity or asset specificity, both of which, under conditions of bounded rationality and informational asymmetry, increase uncertainty and the vulnerability to miscommunication, shirking, and opportunism. Under these conditions, more complex governance mechanisms (e.g., long-term contracting, joint ventures, or, at the extreme, integration) are common. Governance extends to multilateral settings as well. Corporations may seek to coordinate their actions through membership in trade associations or through compliance with the codes issued by standard-setting organizations. They may move toward a weak form of integration through interlocking directorates, research and development alliances, or obligational networks (see Williamson 1985; Alexander 1995).

The evolution of governance regimes – the combination of governance mechanisms in a given industry – cannot be understood without recognizing the role of the state. As noted above, law plays a central role in constituting the economy and facilitating various forms of action. In so doing, it creates an institutional structure within which governance regimes evolve (Campbell and Lindberg 1990). Antitrust laws determine the extent to which firms can coordinate their behavior through associational activities. There is much to suggest that the United States' great merger wave at the turn of the twentieth century was a response to antitrust prohibitions on conspiracies in restraint of trade that effectively foreclosed associational coordination (Bittlingmayer 1996). In contrast, other regulatory policies have explicitly promoted the use of associations to coordinate activities within a given industry (e.g., agricultural marketing associations, labor unions, over-the-counter brokerages). In addition to creating the institutional context within which governance regimes evolve, the state may be an actor, explicitly setting rates, assigning markets, and/or controlling conditions of entry and exit. This brings us necessarily to a discussion of regulation.

## 9.2    REGULATION, DEREGULATION, AND GOVERNANCE

Although much of the work on governance has focused exclusively on the private sector, if we understand governance as the coordination of economic organizations, then we must recognize the important role played historically by regulatory policies. As with private governance mechanisms, regulatory agencies coordinate the behavior of economic organizations, thereby bringing greater stability to the industries in question. This was particularly the case with the economic regulations that were the targets of deregulation in the 1970s and 1980s. The Civil Aeronautics Board determined the terms of competition by controlling entry, assigning route authority, and regulating fares. Carriers did not have to develop their own mechanisms for coordination because regulators executed these functions. A comparable story could be told with respect to the regulation of surface transportation by the Interstate Commerce Commission. In finance, regulations literally created separate sub-industries and through interest rate regulations eliminated price competition (Hammond and Knott 1988).

The examples of regulation as governance can be extended into social regulation. In the 1990s, the Clinton administration's "reinvention of government" initiatives involved the creation of myriad public–private partnerships. For example, Partners for the Environment, a collection of reinvention projects, involved collaboration between the EPA and some 11 000 organizations, including corporations, trade and professional associations, state and local regulators, advocacy groups, and research institutions. Many of these partnerships were designed explicitly to foster coordination among corporate efforts and disseminate best practices. A new regulatory green track, the National Environmental Performance Track (or NEPT), was created in 2000 to give greater compliance flexibility to organizations with a high-quality environmental management system and an exhibited capacity for exceeding regulatory goals. The EPA's Performance Track Participants' Association sponsored annual conferences as vehicles for members to share information and coordinate their practices. While NEPT and the other EPA partnerships did not engage the classical issues addressed by economic regulation, they nonetheless constituted governance mechanisms for firms seeking to coordinate their behavior and manage an uncertain regulatory environment.

Regulations can constitute important governance mechanisms, at the extreme literally dictating the terms of competition and the structure of an industry. Deregulation, in turn, is not fruitfully understood as a return to "the market." Rather, one must explore the way in which changes in policy have stimulated the search for new governance mechanisms and the way this search has been shaped by existing policies and institutions. In some cases, formerly regulated firms may adopt markets as a means of coordinating their behavior. In other cases, they may develop more complex governance structures that may, in important respects, serve functions comparable to those served by previous regulations. The impact of deregulation on the organization of industry is an empirical question that is best understood through the analysis of changes in industry practices and organization. Let us consider, in brief, three cases of deregulation.

### 9.2.1   Deregulation and Commercial Aviation

Beginning in 1940, the Civil Aeronautics Board (CAB) regulated US commercial aviation. It defined industry structure via control over entry into the industry, assignment of route authority, and the regulation of fares. During the 1970s, concerns over CAB performance and the inflationary impacts of economic regulation led to the passage of the Airline Deregulation Act of 1978, which phased out CAB and its regulations (the Federal Aviation Administration retained responsibilities for safety regulation). Advocates of deregulation predicted that deregulation would stimulate new entry, place downward pressure on fares via heightened price competition, and provide an expansion of air travel more generally. These predictions were more than borne out in subsequent decades. Between 1978 and 2005, total passenger miles more than tripled from 188 billion to 584 billion. Deregulation, moreover, had the predicted impact on fares: between 1980 and 2005, inflation-adjusted fares fell by almost 40 percent (US Government Accountability Office 2006: 11).

The governance structures that evolved within a deregulated environment bore little resemblance to what one might characterize as classical markets. Under deregulation, major carriers moved from point-to-point routes to hub-and-spoke systems that offered a number of cost-based benefits. Smaller planes filled to capacity could transport travelers to hubs, reserving larger planes for travel between hubs. Maintenance and services could be consolidated at hubs. Although hub-and-spoke systems allowed for clear efficiencies, there were also strategic concerns at work. Hub airports were usually dominated by one or two airlines that could effectively control travel between locations. The allocation of hubs among legacy carriers was the inheritance of route assignments under regulation. Under the earlier regime, legacy carriers secured exclusive-use gate leases and voice in the approval of subsequent expansions in return for their financing of airport revenue bonds (Morrison and Winston 2000: 4, 22). With deregulation, control over gates became a barrier to entry with significant implications for the survival of new entrants. Although 58 carriers started operation between 1978 and 1990, by 2000 only American West was still in operation, and it merged with US Airways in 2005. Legacy carriers absorbed many of these new carriers, particularly during the 1980s merger wave. As a result of this consolidation and control of hub gates, by the late 1990s a dominant carrier controlled between 70 and 91 percent of the market share at 15 major airports, and between 50 and 70 percent at another six airports (Cooper 2001: 3, appendix 1).

Industry consolidation has been combined with the formation of domestic and international code sharing alliances. Under these alliances, carriers permit each other to market and sell seats on some of their flights by sharing their unique two-letter identification codes. Alliances can provide some clear efficiencies and allow for relatively seamless transportation. But they also support coordination within the industry. When they link commuter airlines to major carriers, they facilitate a loose form of vertical integration without formal consolidation. When they are employed by major airlines (e.g., US Airways and United Airlines), they may allow carriers collectively to capture a larger share of the traffic to a given destination. There are ongoing concerns that commuter lines and some non-legacy entrants may be at a competitive disadvantage if they are not integrated into an alliance (Ito and Lee 2007).

The continued dominance of legacy airlines in a deregulatory environment has been a product of governance decisions. But these decisions have been shaped by public policy in three ways. First, the government is partially responsible for investment in airport expansion and the operation of the air traffic control system. Additional public financing of airport and gate expansion could facilitate entry. However, the inadequacy of funding from the Airport and Airways Trust Fund – diverted to cover regulatory budgets – has rendered airport authorities dependent on major carriers for financing, thereby extending earlier patterns of control. As Elizabeth Bailey (2002: 17) observes, "instead of using regulation to open competition, airport policy has locked in monopoly elements." Second, the consolidation process described above was facilitated by decisions about antitrust enforcement, which lagged in the 1980s (Eisner 1991). Third, the federal government, through the policies of the Pension Benefit Guarantee Corporation (PBGC), has underwritten the profitability of the legacy carriers. As several large carriers used bankruptcy protection to restructure their debt in the wake of the terrorist attacks of September 11, 2001, the PBGC assumed a significant portion of their defined-benefit pension liabilities (some $8.9 billion). These financial rescues carried a significant quid pro quo. As the PBGC provided a subsidy worth billions of dollars, it acquired a major equity stake in the airline industry. As a result of bankruptcy proceedings, the PBGC was awarded a 7 percent stake in US Airways and, more strikingly, a 23.4 percent stake in United Airlines, making it the single largest investor in the airline (US Government Accountability Office 2006: 4). Ironically, under deregulation the state assumed an ownership stake that few would have imagined to be one of the consequences of market-based reforms.

## 9.2.2 Deregulation and the Railroads

The Interstate Commerce Act of 1888 created the Interstate Commerce Commission (ICC) to regulate the railroads. After the passage of the Hepburn Act of 1906, the ICC was granted rate-making powers and assumed the role of a classical economic regulator (i.e., controlling entry, exit, the terms of competition, and pricing). With the passage of the Motor Carriers Act of 1935, the ICC's jurisdiction was extended to interstate trucking, and thus its decisions would have an important impact on shaping the relative fortunes of these two modes of surface transportation. During the post-World War II era, ICC regulation had dire consequences for the performance of the railroads. The ICC set the fares for manufacturing goods high relative to other commodities, thereby allowing trucking to capture a growing share of this lucrative market and leaving the railroads with the low profit margin traffic. The railroads' share of surface rate market (as measured in ton-miles) fell from 65 percent in the immediate postwar period to 35 percent by the 1970s. Rates of return on investments averaged 2 percent during the 1970s, and a wave of bankruptcies (including the Penn Central bankruptcy of 1970 – the largest, thus far, in US history) created great pressure for deregulation (Bailey 1986: 1211–12; Grimm and Winston 2004: 41).

The Railroad Revitalization and Reform Act of 1976 provided some financial assistance for the railroads and, more importantly, made it more difficult to challenge rates set for servicing markets where the railroads did not have market dominance. It also provided the ICC with the discretionary authority to make a finding that regulation was unnecessary for entire categories of traffic, thus creating opportunities for ICC administrators to promote a deregulatory agenda. Four years later, Congress passed the Staggers Rail Act of 1980, permitting railroads to negotiate confidential contract rates with shippers and thus the flexibility to adjust rates to engage in price competition. Maximum rate guidelines were maintained only for shipments that were "captive" to rail (i.e., when there were no other effective means of transporting goods). Ultimately, with the passage of the Interstate Commerce Commission Termination Act of 1995, the ICC was eliminated and its remaining duties were transferred to the newly created Surface Transportation Board.

Advocates of deregulation correctly predicted that market competition would help revitalize the industry while providing reduced rates. Consider the changes during the period 1981 to 2007. Railroads realized productivity gains of 164 percent. In part, this reflected a dramatic reduction in the employed workforce – from 416 251 in 1981 to 186 812 in 2007 – although it was also a product of significant changes in the organization of the industry, a point to be developed below. Inflation-adjusted rail rates fell by 54 percent, and by the end of the period railroads claimed some 41 percent of the surface market, thus reversing a long-term decline. An industry that was mired in bankruptcy in the 1970s realized a 7.4 percent rate of return on investment in the period 2000–06 (Davis and Wilson 2003; Association of American Railroads 2008a). As in the case of airlines, advocates of deregulation would attribute these results to the marvels of the market. Yet, as with the airlines, it is clear that the railroads underwent a transformation in governance that placed minimal reliance on markets qua governance mechanisms.

In a deregulatory environment, the railroad industry experienced three important changes. First, the industry underwent waves of consolidation in the early 1980s and again in the mid-1990s. The 22 class I railroads (a category that includes the largest railroads) were reduced to seven, the largest being the BNSF Railway (formerly the

Burlington Northern and Santa Fe Railway), CSX Transportation (a merger of the Seaboard System Railroad and the Chessie System), and the Union Pacific. The Surface Transportation Board, which has the responsibility of reviewing proposed railroad mergers, rarely raised concerns about consolidation until 2000, when it issued a 15-month moratorium on rail mergers in response to a proposed merger of BNSF and the Canadian National Railway (Madar 2002).

Second, with the elimination of regulatory rate setting, the railroads began to negotiate long-term bilateral contracts with shippers as a means of preventing over-capacity and better aligning physical resources and shipper demands. According to one analysis (Grimm and Winston 2004: 56), 84 percent of the traffic is shipped under contracts with an average duration of 2.4 years, although some contracts are as long as ten years. Within captive markets, 94 percent of shipments occur under long-term contracts. Given the prevalence of long-term contracts, there is little evidence that classical markets are a governance mechanism of choice in the rail industry.

Third, railroads embraced intermodal transportation. That is, containers could be loaded from ships or trucks and transported by flatcar only to be unloaded on to ships or trucks. Railroad participation in intermodal transportation increased dramatically under deregulation, from 3 million trailers and containers in 1980 to in excess of 12 million by 2006 (Association of American Railroads 2008b). Intermodal transportation required heavy railroad investment in "double stack" cars and intermodal terminals, the latter of which was facilitated, albeit only marginally, by the Intermodal Surface Transportation Efficiency Act of 1991, which allowed greater flexibility in the use of federal transportation funds (see US Government Accountability Office 2007b). Additionally, the movement toward intermodal transportation required the development of a network of partnerships with shipping and trucking companies and ports (Stagl 2002), which suggest, that a loose form of integration is evolving across modes of transportation comparable to what has been exhibited in the airlines.

Although these two cases of deregulation involved very different technologies, there are some clear commonalities. As in the case of airline deregulation, the case for deregulating the railroads was premised on a belief in the efficacy of markets relative to state control, and yet the combination of governance mechanisms has little resemblance to classical markets. As in the case of airlines, the industry underwent consolidation that was facilitated by a permissive regulatory environment. Captive shippers raised concerns about the growing consolidation of the rails, and there is clear evidence that they pay a premium relative to shippers that have competitive options. Although captive shippers have the right to appeal rates to the Board, the process is sufficiently costly (some $3 million per litigant) that appeals have been infrequent (US Government Accountability Office 2007a: 41). As in the case of airlines, railroads have adopted non-market governance mechanisms (in this case, long-term bilateral contracting) to stabilize their environments. Through intermodalism, they have increasingly moved toward integrated transportation networks.

### 9.2.3   Deregulation and Finance

The regulatory system for finance that emerged in the early decades of the twentieth century was highly complex, initially consisting of the Treasury Department's

Comptroller of the Currency and, after 1913, the Federal Reserve. The Great Depression marked a watershed in financial regulation. Most importantly, the Glass–Steagall Banking Act (1933) separated commercial and investment banking. It prohibited interest on demand deposits (i.e., checking) and empowered the Fed to regulate interest rates. A newly created Federal Deposit Insurance Corporation insured deposits to prevent bank runs. Parallel institutions were created for credit unions and savings and loans. By the end of the 1930s, regulations had created distinct financial sub-industries, each defined by the products and services it offered, each with its own set of regulators. Interest rate regulations eliminated price competition, and deposit insurance prevented bankruptcies, allowing for remarkable stability in finance (Hammond and Knott 1988). In investment banking, the Securities and Exchange Commission regulated the industry through information disclosure and oversight of exchanges, securities dealers, and self-regulating organizations that functioned as surrogate regulators (see McCraw 1982).

During the 1970s, the financial industry came under increasing stress. Under conditions of high inflation, interest rate regulations made it difficult to attract deposits, and the very regulations that delineated the sub-industries limited the capacity of financial institutions to diversify and pursue new sources of profit. So-called "non-bank banks" (e.g., money market funds) began to offer accounts with higher rates of return. The resulting disintermediation (i.e., the flow of funds outside of regulated financial intermediaries) forced policy changes designed to accommodate market innovations. Although deregulation began incrementally, in the 1980s Congress passed major deregulatory statutes that removed many of the policies and institutions that had promoted financial stability since the New Deal. Although a detailed discussion of these laws is beyond the scope of this chapter (see Worsham 1997), the key statutes deregulated interest rates and provided institutions with far greater latitude in the investments they could make. Ironically, as institutions were assuming greater risks, the laws simultaneously increased the coverage of deposit insurance.

At first glance, one would expect these changes to be particularly beneficial for Savings and Loans (S&Ls), chartered to provide liquidity for housing markets. Inflation had driven the interest rates they had to pay to attract funds well above what could be supported by portfolios of long-term, fixed-rate mortgages. In a deregulated environment, many S&Ls made investments in commercial real estate. But, when the Tax Reform Act of 1986 reduced the tax advantages of these investments, a speculative real estate bubble popped. In the end, some 525 insured S&Ls failed, more than five times the total number since the end of World War II. The Federal Savings and Loan Insurance Corporation (the entity created to insure S&L deposits) fell into bankruptcy, reporting the largest losses ever incurred by a public or private corporation. Ultimately, the costs would exceed $160 billion (see Rom 1996).

Deregulation continued despite the S&L debacle, and the regulatory firewalls established by the New Deal regulations became increasingly porous. Ultimately, Congress passed the Gramm–Leach–Bliley Financial Services Modernization Act of 1999 (GLBA), permitting the consolidation of commercial banks, investment banks, securities firms, and insurance companies in financial holding companies. While GLBA essentially revoked Glass–Steagall, incremental deregulation had already rendered the wall between commercial and investment banking relatively porous. Through mergers and acquisitions, commercial banks had already made forays into investment banking and brokerage activities, creating more diversified financial service companies (see Barth et al. 2000). Formerly separate institutions were now either consolidated or linked through a dense network of commercial relations, many of which fell outside of regulatory oversight.

While the deregulation of air and surface transportation had results that were, on balance, positive, financial deregulation and the changes in the organization of financial markets had tragic consequences. During the 1990s and 2000s, a set of policy decisions created the foundations for a speculative bubble in residential real estate (see Eisner 2011, chapter 10). Changes in the taxation of capital gains, the Federal Reserve's promotion of historically low interest rates, and regulatory pressure for relaxed underwriting standards to expand home ownership created the preconditions for the bubble. Two government-sponsored enterprises (GSEs) – the Federal National Mortgage Association (Fannie Mae) and the Federal Home Loan Mortgage Corporation (Freddie Mac) – securitized mortgages to add liquidity to housing markets. Financial institutions, freed from regulatory constraints, invested heavily in these securities, often hedging the risk with credit-default swaps. Through the process of securitization and the issuance of credit default swaps, a largely unregulated system emerged that was tightly coupled, vulnerable to systemic risk, and, because of its integration into the regulated financial institutions, capable of doing extraordinary damage (see Gelinas 2009).

Real estate markets began weakening in the second quarter of 2006, and as prices declined mortgage defaults increased dramatically. By 2007, the effects spread into a financial system with large investments in mortgage-backed securities, exacerbating what would become the deepest recession since the Great Depression. The collapse forced the failure or near failure of major investment houses and commercial banks, some of which were saved only via large infusions of public funds. The federal government was forced to adopt extraordinary measures to save the GSEs that had securitized mortgages and the American Insurance Group, a major issuer of credit-default swaps. By the end of 2009, the combined costs of the bailout and stimulus package required the largest one-year issuance of debt relative to GDP since World War II (see Congleton 2009). Thus a period that began with an ode to the marvels of the market ended with unprecedented foreclosures and bailouts, somber discussions of bank nationalization, and a search for a new regulatory architecture for finance.

Finance offers a host of lessons, many of which are beyond the scope of this chapter. It clearly illustrates both the way in which public policy and institutions constituted distinct financial industries and the unanticipated effects of deregulation on governance. The shadow banking system that emerged in the gaps created by deregulation was in many ways unanticipated and thus was largely beyond the reach of existing regulatory institutions. More importantly, it shows that economic performance in a deregulated environment is not easily captured by the logic of the market. As the post-2007 crisis reveals, performance and stability are not simply matters of regulation, even if regulation (or the lack of effective regulation) plays a significant role. In this case, changes in the tax treatment of real estate, low interest rates promoted by the Fed, and the social policy goal of expanding home ownership created the preconditions for an asset bubble, whereas the process of deregulation eliminated the regulatory firewalls that might have proven instrumental in limiting the magnitude of the crisis (see Eisner 2011: 180–98).

## 9.3 REGULATORY REFORM FROM AN INSTITUTIONAL PERSPECTIVE

This chapter began with some reflections on the inadequacy of the market–state dichotomy that has been used to frame public discourse about deregulation and regulatory reform more generally. It was argued that law plays a central role in constituting the economy, facilitating the activities of economic actors, and shaping decisions about governance. In this final section, we must turn to a simple question: What is gained by adopting an institutional perspective?

The first response is an empirical one. Classical markets certainly exist and are employed on a regular basis. But, as the above cases suggest, one cannot explain the governance in deregulated industries if one works within the broad terms of "the market" versus the state. The dense organizational networks created in the airlines and the long-term bilateral contracts and intermodal alliances in surface transportation are neither self-liquidating nor anonymous; they cannot be described accurately as markets. Moreover, the control over key assets exerted by legacy airlines and consolidated Class 1 railroads has important implications for the relative power of actors within the respective industries. The category of "the market" is simply too broad and imprecise to capture the wide variety of mechanisms that economic actors use to coordinate their behavior, and this limitation can be addressed by adopting a governance perspective.

The second response involves the implications for public policy. As noted above, policy analysts who work with the broad categories of the market and the state routinely ask when it is justified for the state to "intervene" in the market. The positive theory of market failure has provided the central analytical framework for making these determinations. An institutional perspective takes us beyond such simple questions. The law provides the very foundations for economic activity through its definition of property rights and its role in constituting key economic actors and delimiting the possible relationships among them. To simplify things a bit, there are no markets (in the broadest sense) without the law, and there is no law without the state. Thus, to employ the positive theory of market failure to determine when the government is justified in "intervening" in the economy is, at best, misleading. It would be more accurate to recognize the variety of ways in which public policy shapes the behavior of economic actors, even under conditions of deregulation. As shown above, the financial collapse of 2008 was a product of public policy decisions regarding taxation, interest rates, and access to credit. In sum, law and public policy are as foundational in a deregulated setting as they were under regulation, even if the effects are different.

The third and final response brings us to normative concerns. If we view the market (once again, in its broad sense) as being self-constituting and self-regulating and if we assume that policymakers must have a clear justification (market failure) to intervene, we are simultaneously assuming that market outcomes should be accepted as given. The distributions of wealth, power, and opportunities in society can be cast simply as the emergent properties of voluntary interactions within the market. If one frames deregulation, in turn, as a transfer of control from the state to the market, one may conclude that citizens can no longer harbor expectations of public accountability for the results. Yet, if regulation *and* the collection of governance mechanisms that are employed in a deregulated environment are expressions of public policies and public institutions, it is legitimate to demand that elected officials assume responsibility for ensuring that eco-nomic actors remain accountable to broader social values. These expectations, which were at the core of the regulatory initiatives of the past century, are not vanquished as a result of regulatory reform.

# BIBLIOGRAPHY

Alexander, Ernest R. (1995), *How Organizations Act Together: Interorganizational Coordination in Theory and Practice*, New York: Routledge.
Association of American Railroads (2008a), *The Impact of the Staggers Rail Act of 1980*, Washington, DC: AAR Policy and Economic Department.
Association of American Railroads (2008b), *Rail Intermodal Transportation*, Washington, DC: AAR Policy and Economic Department.
Bailey, Elizabeth E. (1986), 'Deregulation: causes and consequences', *Science*, **234** (4781), 1211–16.
Bailey, Elizabeth E. (2002), 'Aviation policy: past and present', *Southern Economic Journal*, **69** (1), 12–20.
Barth, James R., R. Dan Brumbaugh, Jr. and James A. Wilcox (2000), 'The repeal of Glass–Steagall and the advent of broad banking', *Journal of Economic Perspectives*, **14** (2), 191–204.
Bernstein, Marver H. (1955), *Regulating Business by Independent Commission*, Princeton, NJ: Princeton University Press.
Bittlingmayer, George (1996), 'Antitrust and business activity: the first quarter century', *Business History Review*, **70** (3), 363–401.
Campbell, John L. and Leon N. Lindberg (1990), 'Property rights and the organization of economic activity by the state', *American Sociological Review*, **55** (5), 634–47.
Campbell, John L., J. Rogers Hollingsworth and Leon N. Lindberg (eds) (1991), *Governance of the American Economy*, Cambridge: Cambridge University Press.
Committee for a Study of Competition in the U.S. Airline Industry, Transportation Research Board, National Research Council (1999), *Entry and Competition in the U.S. Airline Industry: Issues and Opportunities*, Washington, DC: National Academy Press.
Congleton, Roger D. (2009), 'On the political economy of the financial crisis and bailout of 2008', *Public Choice*, **140**, 311–12.
Cooper, Mark A. (2001), 'Mergers between major airlines: the anti-competitive and anti-consumer effects of the creation of a private cartel', statement before the Subcommittee on Commerce, Trade and Consumer Protection, Committee on Energy and Commerce, United States House of Representatives, 21 March.
Davis, David E. and Wesley W. Wilson (2003), 'Wages in rail markets: deregulation, mergers, and changing networks characteristics', *Southern Economic Journal*, **69** (4), 865–85.
Derthick, Martha and Paul J. Quirk (1985), *The Politics of Deregulation*, Washington, DC: Brookings Institution.
Edelman, Lauren B. and Mark C. Suchman (1997), 'The legal environments of organizations', *Annual Review of Sociology*, **23**, 479–515.
Eisner, Marc Allen (1991), *Antitrust and the Triumph of Economics: Institutions, Expertise, and Policy Change*, Chapel Hill: University of North Carolina Press.
Eisner, Marc Allen (2011), *The American Political Economy: Institutional Evolution of Market and State*, New York: Routledge.
Fligstein, Neil (2001), *The Architecture of Markets: An Economic Sociology of Twenty-First Century Capitalist Societies*, Princeton, NJ: Princeton University Press.
Gelinas, Nicole (2009), *After the Fall: Saving Capitalism from Wall Street – and Washington*, New York: Encounter Books.
Grimm, Curtis and Clifford Winston (2004), 'Competition in the deregulated railroad industry: sources, effects, and policy issues', in Sam Peltzman and Clifford Winston (eds), *Deregulation of Network Industries: What's Next?*, Washington, DC: AEI–Brookings Joint Center for Regulatory Studies, pp. 41–72.
Hammond, Thomas H. and Jack H. Knott (1988), 'The deregulatory snowball: explaining deregulation in the financial industry', *Journal of Politics*, **50** (1), 3–30.
Herring, E. Pendelton (1938), *Public Administration in the Public Interest*, New York: McGraw-Hill.
Hollingsworth, J. Rogers and Robert Boyer (1997), *Contemporary Capitalism: The Embeddedness of Institutions*, Cambridge: Cambridge University Press.
Huntington, Samuel P. (1952), 'The marasmus of the ICC: the commission, the railroads, and the public interest', *Yale Law Journal*, **61**, April, 467–509.

Ito, Harumito and Darin Lee (2007), 'Domestic code sharing, alliances, and airfares in the U.S. airline industry', *Journal of Law and Economics,* **50** (2), 355–80.

Kolko, Gabriel (1963), *The Triumph of Conservatism: A Reinterpretation of American History, 1900–1916*, New York: Free Press.

Lindblom, Charles E. (1982), 'The market as prison', *Journal of Politics,* **44** (2), 324–36.

Madar, Daniel (2002), 'Rail mergers, trade, and federal regulation in the United States and Canada', *Publius,* **32** (1), 143–59.

McCraw, Thomas K. (1982), 'With the consent of the governed: SEC's formative years', *Journal of Policy Analysis and Management,* **1** (3), 346–70.

McGarity, Thomas O. (1991), *Reinventing Rationality: The Role of Regulatory Analysis in the Federal Bureaucracy*, Cambridge: Cambridge University Press.

Morrison, Steven A. and Clifford Winston (2000), 'The remaining role for government policy in the deregulated airline industry', in Sam Peltzman and Clifford Winston (eds), *Deregulation of Network Industries: What's Next?*, Washington, DC: AEI–Brookings Joint Center for Regulatory Studies, pp. 1–40.

Percival, Robert V. (1991), 'Checks without balance: Executive Office oversight of the Environmental Protection Agency', *Law and Contemporary Problems,* **54** (4), 127–204.

Percival, Robert V. (2001), 'Presidential management of the administrative state: the not-so-unitary executive', *Duke Law Journal,* **51** (3), 963–1013.

Rom, Mark Carl (1996), *Public Spirit in the Thrift Tragedy*, Pittsburgh, PA: University of Pittsburgh Press.

Stagl, Jeff (2002), 'Intermodal alliances: Class 1s have adopted a partnership-promotion philosophy to expand market reach, improve transit times and provide truck-competitive service', *Progressive Railroading,* **45** (4), 27–33.

Stigler, George J. (1971), 'The theory of economic regulation', *Bell Journal of Economics and Management Science,* **2** (1), 3–21.

US Government Accountability Office (2006), *Airline Deregulation: Reregulating the Airline Industry Would Likely Reverse Consumer Benefits and Not Save Airline Pensions*, Washington, DC: Government Accountability Office.

US Government Accountability Office (2007a), *Freight Railroads: Industry Health Has Improved, but Concerns about Competition and Capacity Should Be Addressed*, Washington, DC: Government Accountability Office.

US Government Accountability Office (2007b), *Intermodal Transportation: DOT Could Take Further Actions to Address Intermodal Barriers*, Washington, DC: Government Accountability Office.

Weimer, David L. and Aidan R. Vining (1999), *Policy Analysis: Concepts and Practice*, Upper Saddle River, NJ: Prentice Hall.

Williamson, Oliver E. (1985), *The Economic Institutions of Capitalism*, New York: Free Press.

Wolf, Charles, Jr. (1990), *Markets or Governments: Choosing between Imperfect Alternatives*, Cambridge, MA: MIT Press.

Worsham, Jeffrey (1997), *Other People's Money: Policy Change, Congress, and Bank Regulation*, Boulder, CO: Westview Press.

Yandle, Bruce (1999), 'Grasping for the heavens: 3-D property rights and the global commons', *Duke Environmental Law and Policy Forum,* **10** (1), 13–44.

# 10 The Chinese model of the regulatory state
## *Neil Collins and Jörn-Carsten Gottwald*

'The People's Republic of China puts into practice a Socialist Market Economy' (PRC 1982/2004, Art. 15). The infusion of key elements of markets into a socialist one-party state has created a 'capitalism with Chinese characteristics' (Huang 2008) that defies easy explanation. The 'business of governing business' (Pearson 2005) has followed a distinctive policy process (Heilmann 2008). In the area of financial services, for example, innovations were introduced by Leninist means (Heilmann 2005a, 2005b) in order to preserve the state's interests in key sectors of the economy (Pearson 2007). Clearly, the 'rise of regulatory capitalism' (Levi-Faur and Jordana 2005) has taken a unique turn in the People's Republic of China (PRC). If the primary theoretical challenge is to identify hybrid forms of regulation that cloud the distinctions between the global and the national, it is still important to understand states in which the market and society are themselves subsumed by an all-pervasive political interest. In such cases, ideas of independent agency, due process and market correction act to conceal more than they reveal.

In this chapter we interpret regulation as an outcome of actions within a dynamic and changeable institutional framework (see Vogel 1998; Laurence 2001; Lütz 2002, 2003). Regulation in this sense consists of the formulation, implementation and revision of specific rules for narrowly defined policy fields or aspects of social activity. The rise of the regulatory state in Europe and on a global scale has shown regulation as a process of market creation that has led to divergent outcomes: while generally to be perceived as limiting the scope and depth of government intervention into the economy, it has led to the re-establishment of administrative oversight and control in some cases too (Vogel 1998). In the case of Europe, regulation was hoped to increase the efficiency of decision-making by technocrats within a clearly defined area providing an effectiveness appreci-ated by the people. It was supposed to add legitimacy to the EU in fields beyond the direct reach of the nation-state (Majone 1997). The introduction of regulatory regimes in China shows elements of similarity as well as difference: similarity in the use of regulation to improve efficiency and create new markets; and divergence in allowing for sustaining and improving central authority over particular interests.

China is an inviting candidate for a study of regulation because it has made the setting up of new agencies its default option when faced with pressing policy issues (Yang 2009) and has used the new regulatory structures to signal its commitment to global rules and standards without giving free rein to independent bodies (Peerenboom 2009). According to the World Bank, its regulatory quality has improved to the level of average middle income (Kaufmann et al. 2008: 89) in spite of an incomplete rule of law and deficits in the protection of property rights (Shen and Wang 2009). The equal application of the law to all interests both state and private is far from guaranteed (Landry 2009).

Two areas of regulation, financial services and food safety, are analysed here along two dimensions of regulation: organisation and guiding principles. While food safety is subject to high demands from the domestic population, the reform of financial services has been a corollary of the opening up of the Chinese economy. Closely as banking, securities and insurance are linked with overhauling Chinese state-owned assets, the reform path has been strongly influenced by external demands on the one hand and the strategy to turn state-owned banks and enterprises into global players (Gottwald 2010). In food safety, the state's focus is primarily domestic, the scope of activity is vast and the predominant scale of economic activity is small. Both sectors, however, present potential threats to the 'social harmony' so prized by the Chinese Communist Party (CCP).

## 10.1  THE REGULATION OF FINANCIAL SERVICES

Financial market reform in China has included the establishment of market-oriented regulatory institutions. This process gathered pace under the administration of Zhu Rongji (1998–2003), whose government 'presided over a new, more regulatory approach to economic reform' (Naughton 2008: 102) in general. Regulatory regimes exhibit either a concentration and integration of regulatory powers and competences or a diffusion and segmentation. Unified political finance supervision in the hands of a centralist and unitary government combined with an integrated 'one-shop' financial market supervisor, in charge of both prudential regulation and business conduct, would be the ideal form of a centralised regulatory regime. In contrast, a broad dissemination of regulatory and supervisory functions among various layers of a federalist government structure, plus the existence of a sectoral administrative supervision with a strong role for the central bank in prudential regulation, would define an extreme decentralised regulatory regime. China developed a unique combination of institutional competition under the control of a centralised party-state exerting control over personnel and organisational resources.

### 10.1.1  Organisation

On paper, the PRC has opted for a segmented and sectoral organisation with three formally independent regulatory bodies, the China Securities Regulatory Commission (CSRC), established in 1992, the China Insurance Regulatory Commission (CIRC), established in 1998, and the China Banking Regulatory Commission (CBRC), established in 2003. The central bank, the People's Bank of China (PBOC), which is an organisation directly under the State Council, i.e. the government of the PRC (PRC 2010) and thus not even formally independent, has been providing personnel and functions for these new bodies while preserving the task of implementing monetary policies and supervising financial stability (Schlichting 2008: 35).

The process of reforming the regulatory regime was led by the Communist Party's Central Financial Work Commission, which was dissolved in 2003, when most of its competencies were transferred to the administrative market regulators and the CCP Central Organisation Department.[1] The new regulatory bodies soon engaged in serious turf battles with one another and with other organisations. The institutional fragility of the new structures fostered considerable rivalry. For instance, the relationship between the PBOC and Central Huijin Investment, on the one hand, and the regulatory agencies, on the other, remains strained. While PBOC apparently managed to extend its competencies into the securities area in 2005, the CSRC won the battle on the expansion of the bond market in 2007. New organisations like the National Association of Financial Market Institutional Investors (NAFMII) take on the hybrid function of interest group and regulatory body with the explicit encouragement of the State Council (Anderlini 2010; NAFMII 2010). When the government tightened its control of the economy in 2007/08 and faced the global financial crisis, the role of the regulators seemed to have peaked.

Formally, CSRC, CBRC and CIRC are 'institutions under the State Council' and on the same level as ministries.[2] The CSRC exercises powerful competencies in regulating, supervising, implementing and sanctioning the activities of China's stock exchanges, market participants and intermediaries. Its banking equivalent, the CBRC, separates monetary policies from banking regulation. Reforming the banking sector, especially providing new solutions for the problem of the non-performing loans, is its central task. In addition to the three regulatory agencies, the powerful National Development and Reform Commission (NDRC), the State Asset Supervision and Administration Commission (SASAC), the Ministry of Finance, the People's Bank of China and the Central Huijin Asset Management Corporation are all involved in the policy-making and implementation in the area of financial services. The third regulatory body, the CIRC, is in charge of supervision of the capital-related activities of China's insurance business.

On paper, highest authority for the supervision of financial services, especially the control of the supervisors, rests with the Chinese government, the State Council. The State Council defines the general political aims for the development and regulation of financial services for the administrative market supervisors and self-regulatory bodies. Of course, the State Council has to adhere to the fundamental guidelines of overall economic and social policies – financial market regulation is rather perceived as a means to promote economic growth and social development than as an end in itself. In both areas, the formulation of economic policies as well as the regulatory policies for financial services, supra-ministerial commissions rather than single ministers have played a crucial role.

The National People's Congress (NPC), while the ultimate organ for policy-making according to the constitution of the PRC, is comparatively weak in real terms. In relation to financial services, the legislature is clearly much less central as a forum for policy discussions than the Politburo and its national finance work conference, a high-profile event held every five years to outline central policies for the sector. Main policies are coordinated by the Leading Small Group on Finance and Economics, which brings together the leading cadres from the Central Committee, the State Council, the ministries and other leading organisations (Miller 2008).

### 10.1.2 Guiding Principles

All regulatory regimes enshrine a specific set of ideas and interests, which define a basic understanding about the interactions of state and non-state actors. The elementary distinction is between a primal preponderance of redistribution and market competition, which requires certain governance ideals, and regulatory modes. Financial market regulation is thus embedded in the wider economic structural and process policies. Financial market governance *might* follow the same set of beliefs and policy aims as the overall economic regulation, but it *does not have* to follow the same rules.

## Conflicting imperatives and ongoing internationalisation

In China, the fundamental guiding principles follow a distinct political logic: preserving the dominant position of the CCP by modernising the economy, therefore creating and developing internationally attractive markets for financial services; providing new funds for state-owned banks and enterprises, thereby contributing to the image and the practice of a market economic order; and, finally, turning state-owned enterprises into globally competitive entities. These conflicting imperatives have stymied the first years of regulatory agencies (Heilmann 2001). Even today, they contribute to a strong orientation of regulation in the overall market development, a stronger focus than usually attributed to regulatory agencies. Taking into account the various ministries, commissions and regulatory bodies and a perceived return of ideological divisions in Chinese policy-making, even the most fundamental consensus concerning the introduction of market mechanisms is not beyond doubt. So, while in established market economies the basic distinction can be drawn concerning the objectives of the markets, in China it still is the rather fundamental issue concerning the reach of market mechanisms and the degree of state planning in crucial sectors.

One major principle has been the improvement of corporate governance and the introduction of global best practice. Among others, China's regulators adopted the main principles of the International Organization of Securities Commissions (IOSCO), protection of investors, securing fair, efficient and transparent markets, and the reduction of systemic risks in 2003; the International Financial Reporting Standards in 2007; and the Basel II requirements starting from 2010/11. The World Trade Organization (WTO) commitment to open China's domestic banking market by 11 December 2006 was met, albeit that informal trading barriers seem to have remained. Overall, the guiding principles of the Chinese regulatory framework have moved decisively in the direction of global standards and best practices. It can be reasonably argued, therefore, that, with regard to both regime organisation and orientation, the channels of international influence, such as the exchange of ideas, interaction on a professional level and international role models, have had a significant impact on the new regulations in the Chinese financial markets.

These developments on the level of administrative market supervision have so far had only limited effects on the basic attitudes and ideals concerning the role of the state in China's socialist market economy. According to some observers, the first task of regulation is to ensure that the capital markets develop in accordance with the aims of the government (Zhao 2000). And, even after nearly three decades of structural reforms, 'the fundamental issue is to redefine the role of the state' (OECD 2005). Therefore, the exact role of the Chinese state and the relationship between private, collective and state property is incorporated into the financial service regulation. This continues to raise questions. In addressing the global crisis, the government felt compelled to reject vigorously reports that 'the state advances, private enterprise withdraws'.[3] Conflicting political imperatives still impede clear-cut market-oriented regulation and leave regulatory issues well within the realm of ideological battles concerning the social standing of private entrepreneurs or the legal treatment of private property rights.

Accordingly, regulation of financial services is plagued by the same broad mixture of more or less all governance ideals and regulatory tools imaginable – from anti-corruption movements via court decisions to negotiations and formal self-regulation. According to Western observers at least, there is a clear pattern that indicates the reluctance of the central government to accept a diminished role for the state apparatus in financial services. Be it in the case of China's commercial banks, the qualified domestic institutional investors (QDII) or the floating of non-tradable shares, what might appear to be a clear privatisation turns out to be another twist in preserving the influence of government-controlled organisations on core players in China's financial markets.

**Financial regulation and the party-state**
The party-state control of financial service regulation is based on two main pillars: the *nomenklatura* and cadre system, which provides strong and reliable venues for supervision by managing the individual careers of those active in these fields and centrally allocating the numbers of staff and other resources inside the organisations; and state ownership or at least state control of most financial service enterprises.

Through its *nomenklatura* and *bianzhi* system of staff plans, the Central Organisation Department of the CCP controls human resources management for top positions in regulatory bodies. Besides, the CCP controls the party committees within the enterprises, whose re-establishment seems to have accelerated under the government of Wen Jiabao. The Leninist one-party system thereby easily extends its reach into the arguably most global and most dynamic sector of modern economies, financial services. The close integration of the banking sector into the party-state became obvious during the current financial crisis. First, the Chinese leadership stimulated and then reined in the provision of credit by Chinese banks through informal telephone calls. Second, a conference of the main regulatory bodies led to a new policy linking the financial services industry to the overall strategy of promoting Chinese enterprises abroad, the so-called Go Global Strategy.

When the Chinese leadership designed a 4 trillion RMB yuan (*c.* US$400 billion) macro-economic stimulus package to counter the impact of the financial crisis of 2008, it combined macro-economic measures with party-state intervention. The banks immediately followed the central guidelines and provided roughly 110 per cent more credit in 2009 than the previous year – even against warnings of overheating and a potential rise in non-performing loans. Banks thus added another US$1.4 trillion of stimulus to the government package. In January 2010, when the Chinese leadership had achieved its objectives of keeping GDP growth above 8 per cent, the government simply ordered the banks to change their lending policies. Chinese banks had to oblige no matter how sophisticated was their collaboration with central policy directives. Banks in China ordered branches in various parts of the country to stop lending at all.[4] Only the investment vehicles of local governments proved difficult to rein in. Operating outside the formal regulatory regime, the central leadership acknowledged great difficulties in coming to terms with their extensive investment policies (Shih 2010).

In sum, contrary to the image of 'independent regulatory agencies' in between the state and the market participants, the party's control of the financial industry is pervasive and persistent (Pearson 2005; Anderlini 2009; He 2010). Raising the amount banks have to hold with the central bank and simply ordering bankers to stop lending illustrate perfectly the ambiguous nature of China's socialist market economy (Anderlini et al. 2010).

## 10.2   FOOD SAFETY

Many multinational food companies have responded to China's policy of opening to the world. Among the foreign food companies to take advantage of the continuing economic reforms were the big five chocolate manufacturers – Ferrero, Mars, Cadbury, Hershey and Nestlé. They arrived in the last decade but found themselves managing 'by the seat of their pants when dealing with China's mercurial economic and regulatory environment' (Allen 2010).

The attraction of China for the food sector has been changing, however, even as the regulatory environment has become more comprehensible. The three most significant changes to the food sector since the beginning of the economic opening up are:

- liberalisation of agricultural production based on household units, called the household responsibility system (HRS), which began in 1981;
- elimination of food rationing in urban areas completed in 1993; and
- opening of China's food processing and retailing sector to FDI.

Food availability increased very significantly and consumer buying patterns altered markedly as a result (Dong and Fuller 2010).

Food safety has become a very serious issue after a number of incidents that undermined both Chinese and foreign confidence. In 2008, six children died and nearly 300 000 others were made ill after consuming adulterated milk powder. Similarly, in recent years, noodles containing lead, fake alcohol, soy sauce made from human hair, and eggs with melamine have joined a long list of consumer concerns. Tainted milk powder was at the centre of a previous scandal in 2003 that also prompted regulatory changes though, as will be discussed below, these were thwarted by bureaucratic resistance.

In contrast to financial services, the food producing industry, China's largest sector, is extremely diverse and based on small-scale operations. Similarly, despite the presence of international firms, such as Wal-Mart and Tesco, the retail food sector is highly fragmented. The emphasis on fresh food is high, with some customers shopping for food twice a day. Both the supply and demand sides of food have changed markedly in recent years, adding to the complexity for regulators.

> Next to a proliferation of small private grocery stores, supermarkets, bakeries, poultry stands, and other specialty food outlets, thousands of restaurants and eateries have appeared. [T]he consumption of vegetables has dropped considerably, while . . . meat consumption has doubled– and even tripled in rural areas. . . . The average daily intakes for . . . [dairy and egg products] increased more than threefold between 1982 and 2002. (Zhang et al. 2008: 39–40)

There are nearly half a million food processing factories, of which 80 per cent are food workshops employing fewer than ten people (Engardio et al. 2007: 1). Most processing is completed by hand and produces by-products that are not utilised and constitute an environmental hazard (Luo 2005: 2). For the authorities, these small producers represent a major safety problem (Johnson 2008). For example, given the rise in meat, disproportionately beef, consumption, it is noteworthy that: "the slaughtering, processing and marketing of beef remains . . . extremely primitive. . . . [H]ousehold slaughtering and wet markets still dominate beef processing and distribution in China" (Brown et al. 2002: 269). Chinese regulatory weakness is being presented by some as posing a threat to a globalised food supply chain (Wishnick 2009: 209).

Ominously for the CCP, many of these incidents have triggered domestic public protest and unrest. As Watson points out, authorities are also increasingly faced with a public view fuelled by popular urban legends, such as one about unscrupulous street vendors, that suggest they are more concerned with public order than food safety (Watson 2004). A 2007 survey of Chinese city dwellers for a US food company with manufacturing facilities in the PRC showed that '83% had heard something in the last year about food contamination issues. In addition, 83% responded they are concerned about the safety of food products sold locally'.[5]

Food is also a proxy for discontent for a rural population that resents the growing gap between their lot and that of the ever more prosperous urban dwellers.

> There has been a major shift in farmers' perceptions of the CCP from the time of the Great Leap Forward and Cultural Revolution. . . . [F]armers then viewed the CCP . . . as working in their best interests. . . . [A]s a result of the rural 'reforms', the government could not [now] be seen as being on their side – it could, at best, be regarded as neutral. This change . . . together with a change in leadership styles of Communist officials at various levels of government, have had a huge impact on farmers' perception of and interactions with the state. (Han 2009)

The CCP's representatives, such as local cadres, in the countryside are often officials profiteering from the transfer of agricultural land to industrial use. Regulation can be seen as an additional burden on food producers for the benefit of city consumers. Food safety is, therefore, topical and also provides useful insights into the Chinese approach to regulation.

### 10.2.1   Organisation

China's first comprehensive Food Safety Law (FSL) came into effect in June 2009. The law had been expected for several years, but each of the food scandals caused a delay as the latest lessons were absorbed. Nevertheless, its eventual publication was precipitated by the 2008 milk adulteration scandal. The FSL tries to address the need for specialist agencies in an area of increasing technological sophistication with a level of coordination which critics suggested was lacking previously. Under the new arrangements, the State Council was given the power to establish a national food safety commission. This it did in early 2010, again in the shadow of a renewed scandal centring on milk contamination. The new commission will take an overview of the system, which includes:

- the Ministry of Health (MOH);
- the Ministry of Industry and Information Technology (MIIT);
- the Ministry of Agriculture (MOA);
- the State Administration for Industry and Commerce (SAIC);

- the General Administration of Quality Supervision, Inspection and Quarantine (GAQSIQ); and
- the State Food and Drug Administration (SFDA).

The FSL mandates local government at or above the county level to supervise food safety regulations in the manufacture and trading of food and provides for monitoring of local implementation by the SFDA. Overarching powers in the area of food safety are given to the MOH, which will take control of future food safety incidents. Under Article 8 of the regulations on the implementation of the FSL, medical institutions are also now obliged to notify local authorities of any patient with food-borne diseases, food poisoning or similar conditions in a timely manner. Similarly, food companies must put in place recall procedures, safety training and so on.

The new arrangements are meant to address the uneven enforcement, patchwork of standards and overlapping mandates that typified the former regime. Nevertheless, food safety regulations will be the shared responsibility of a large number of government entities at several levels. The FSL is dealing with a far more diverse and dispersed sector than the regime covering financial services, and the organisational structure reflects this. It still relies on local officials to enforce its national food standards, which include:

- limitations on hazardous ingredients;
- controls on food additives;
- nutritional specifications for foods for vulnerable groups such as infants;
- labelling and instruction requirements; and
- hygiene levels for food production and distribution.

As is common in Chinese legislation, the penalties for breaches are draconian, but the enforcement of previous regulations has been markedly uneven.

### 10.2.2 Guiding Principles

Both President Hu Jintao and Premier Wen Jiabao have signalled unmistakably the central government's concerns with the various food scandals. According to the standard operating procedure following disasters, the leadership 'feels' the people's pain and hounds local officials. In the case of food, however, there was also an important foreign audience in countries that invoked safety concerns to end trade with China. Even Hong Kong, which relies very heavily on mainland sources, has imposed increasingly strict controls on trade. The central aims of the new pan-PRC food safety regime, therefore, are regaining public confidence in China, assuring foreign markets and clarifying lines of responsibility.

The government's analysis appears to be that the food safety problem arises from a combination of insufficient central control and unclear standards and procedures. So the guiding principle, to use May's term, is 'traditional regulation that emphasises enforcement of rules by governmental agencies and penalties for noncompliance with the rules' (May 2007). In contrast to the case of financial services, the PRC largely eschews voluntary approaches, self-auditing, management-based systems or performance-based models, all of which have informed food safety regulation elsewhere. The food safety commission, consisting of three vice-premiers and a dozen minister-level officials, is not a single, powerful body with a large staff akin to the US Food and Drug Administration (FDA), nor is that role assumed by the SFDA. In all, 13 government departments currently have a hand in food safety. In practice, as outlined above, there are six major players. The initial rejection of the American model contrasts with the emulation of the FDA when China upgraded its regulatory framework for the pharmaceutical industry in the late 1990s. In 2003, the SFDA was to receive an American-style comprehensive remit, but this reform was successfully resisted by MOH and other agencies. A potentially significant sign of change in the food safety regime, however, is that Vice-Premier Li Keqiang, whom many observers tip to succeed Wen Jiabao and become China's next premier, heads the new commission on food safety. In the official news report of the commission's first plenary meeting, Li said: 'Food safety is closely related to people's life and health and economic development and social harmony. . . . We should understand the foundation for the country's food safety is still weak and the situation is grave'.[6]

Multinational companies operating in China trumpet the role of supranational institutions, which generate standards about product quality, quality assurance and risk management, and they may exert normative background pressure on the authors of Chinese regulations. For example, some food safety standards attract international accreditation from groups such as the International Federation of Organic Agriculture Movements (IFOAM). In general, officials are also mindful of complying with the new rules and regulations brought about by China's accession to the WTO. The FSL, however, assigns no role to external bodies or to civil society national or international.[7] In general, the involvement of consumer groups, trade unions or producers' associations is weak. The rules, which are still emerging in full detail, are set to be highly prescriptive and top-down. They are also decidedly particularistic, specifying actions, such as product recall, forms of notification and transportation, and standards, in areas such as testing, training and food handling. The assumption is that sticking to the rules will ensure acceptable outcomes.

Unlike its predecessor, the FSL does not exempt 'trusted' companies, which had been left largely unsupervised. For example, many large dairy companies were given inspection-free status by the GAQSIQ, the state body charged with such quality control duties. Nevertheless, the food safety incidents that triggered the new regulations were not the result of a lack of law but a failure of enforcement. As with environmental and other areas based on local implementation:

> local officials are often in cahoots with [errant] factory managers . . . either because the officials have a financial stake in the enterprise or because they are afraid that closing a factory, or making it more expensive to operate, will diminish local employment and lead to social unrest. . . . In other cases, local officials want to do the right thing but are too weak in the face of powerful enterprise managers. (Economy 2007: 29)

Further, the supply chain of law from the NPC to local food producer is very long, and, in practice, locally generated regulations issued by individual departments and local authorities are often poorly formulated and indifferently implemented.

## 10.3   CONCLUSION: THE RISE OF A REGULATORY AUTOCRACY

Observers often question the capacity of the PRC's political system to facilitate reform. Furthermore, the gap between formal provision and actual outcomes in terms of regulation is not confined to food safety or financial services. To take a dramatic example, '[t]he PRC has a comprehensive, sophisticated and complex legal regime dealing with coal mine safety' but a very high level of fatalities even in comparison to other states at similar stages of economic development (Homer 2009: 428). Despite the apparently strong regulatory framework, illegal operations proliferate.

Both the sectors chosen in this study have comparatively recently been the subject of regulatory reform. Obviously, it would be premature to propose a final evaluation of China's regulatory regime for either financial services or food safety so soon after new institutional designs have been put into practice. Nevertheless, some patterns can be discerned and interesting contrasts identified. In financial services, China's choice of the 'three pillars' approach separately regulating banking, securities and insurance reflected the lack of a clear international consensus about which model was 'best'. China's financial system was already well developed albeit very heavily dependent on banks and having a relatively small capital market. The choice of the American model seemed to reassure outsiders in a sector vulnerable to global sentiment. Following the recent economic crisis, which has led to calls for greater regulatory convergence, the choice, on paper at least, seems fortunate. However, China now finds itself under similar pressures as most OECD countries to add a financial stability board to improve macro-regulatory policy.

For food safety, the US example of a single regulator covering most of or the entire sector was contraindicated by the scale, scope and diversity of China's food chain. Food processing, distribution and marketing were underdeveloped, and the practice of regulation seems more important than the design. In both cases, however, the State Council put in place a supervising commission.

The PRC remains a distinctly Leninist state in which one-party rule and significant state control of key sectors of the economy remain even as a market economy is allowed to emerge. The economic reforms have necessitated some accommodations to global governance trends such as substituting regulation for control. Nevertheless, elitism, top-down institutional change and a fear of potential rivals characterise government. New social elites are co-opted, but civil society is tightly controlled. This approach has rendered the CCP both resilient and vulnerable at the same time. Regulatory reform has allowed the adoption of state-of-the-art rules on both food and finance, but these cannot easily be made effective without challenging party control. Party members have their hands on the economic tiller as well as sometimes in the till.

Chinese officials are not accountable to the citizens but to the party-state apparatus at the next higher level. Their performance is assessed for its contribution to the aims of the political elite. Such a line of accountability encourages misreporting and cliques based on patronage rather than the arm's-length relationships that should characterise regulation. While in Western countries the intervention of politics into regulatory affairs has been considered a deviation from the norm (Eisner et al. 2006: 312–14), in the case of China it is part and parcel of everyday regulatory life. This does not, however, imply the day-to-day management to be conducted by the party. But cadre control and lines of communication through party groups allow for the implementation of policies at any time through a trusted channel.

China's opening up towards external global actors has not yet led to a full-fledged capitalist convergence. While significant contributions can be acknowledged, especially in the areas of administrative market supervision and corporate governance, the reliance of the regulatory bodies on CCP political decisions, cadre selection, staffing and departmental planning produces a structural unpredictability. The recurrence of guidance by party commands particularly in the financial sector might prove useful in achieving short-term economic objectives, but it endangers the long-term stability of Chinese regulation. Besides, it throws into question the fundamental achievement of introducing Western-style regulatory bodies: signalling a commitment to incorporating global best practice into China's economic governance. The diffusion of supervisory powers to provincial and local authorities might be a first step towards regulatory federalism and regulatory competition beyond the central party-state. Currently, however, the most obvious danger is local protectionism and reluctance to comply with central directives.

The two sectors examined suggest some differences in approaches to different sectors. In financial services, by introducing regulatory bodies, expert advisory committees and the work of intermediaries, the CCP establishes a venue for limited self-regulation and representation of market participants albeit dominated by state-owned or state-linked corporations. Those venues, though, are limited in scale and scope. They pose little challenge to the overall monopoly of the CCP on policy-making. They definitely have helped to attract foreign capital and expertise to China. There is little reason to believe that, in the short run, these developments might turn into a destabilising force threatening party rule. Food, however, represents far more of a danger, as it is of immediate and daily interest to all citizens, it is crucial to certain localities, and its safety is symbolic of the state's duty of care. It is less easy for the CCP to share responsibility with the industry itself or to encourage the formation of non-governmental partners. As far as regulation has worked, it has added to the legitimacy of the party-state. In food safety as well as in finance, however, failure has led to widespread public discontent which is less directed against the regulatory organisations than against the central authorities in general.

The inadequacy of legislative oversight is a regular criticism of regulatory regimes in the West. The National People's Congress is constitutionally the highest state body in the PRC, but has to follow the guidance of the CCP. It provides a platform for policy pronouncements by the CCP leadership, and in relation to the sectors studied here it played this role. It also dispatched working groups to selected provinces to supervise the detailed formulation of food regulations. Nevertheless, its influence is at best marginal. In this respect the Leninist one-party state, with a clear preference for closed discussion of top policy, shares its approach with more democratic jurisdictions where the regulatory framework is dependent on 'parliamentary acquiescence' to some degree.

A decisive difference between Chinese capitalism and Western examples of regulatory capitalism is that the consumer-electorate in Europe or the US have at least the theoretical possibility of voicing their discontent at regular elections and of relying on courts, the media and political entrepreneurs to ensure they are treated fairly. These levels are completely underdeveloped in China. The failure of regulators in the West to anticipate the problems which led to the current economic crisis has been seen in the PRC as an indication of the greater fitness for purpose of their system. In the short term, there may be merit in their criticism. Ultimately, however, regulation needs public trust, regular feedback and popular legitimacy. The Chinese system is challenged to provide any of these for long.

## NOTES

1. Officially the Organisation Department of the Central Committee of the Communist Party of China, Zhongong Zhongyang Zuzhi Bu. See http://cpc.people.com.cn/GB/64114/75347/75349/index1.html (accessed 20 February 2010).
2. See 'Government of the PRC: institutions directly under the State Council' at http://english.gov.cn/2005-08/07/content_21039.htm (accessed 23 February 2010).
3. See the official explanation regarding the role of the state in the context of the macro-economic stimulus package 'Ruhe kan dai "Guojin Mintui" xianxiang' at http://theory.people.com.cn/GB/10314330.html (accessed 20 February 2010).
4. In a similar case in 2008, banks in Shanghai received phone calls ordering them to stop all lending. Foreign banks asking for a written confirmation were left unanswered. Interviews with Shanghai bank officials, and 'China tightens reins on loans', *Wall Street Journal Asia*, 27 January 2010, available at: http://online.wsj.com/article/SB10001424052748703906204575026350912221106.html?mod=WSJ_hpp_sections_business (accessed 27 January 2010).
5. Reported by Jeffrey Ettinger, president of Hormel Foods Corporation, to the CIES World Food Business Summit, 21 June 2007, Shanghai, China, available at: www.hormelfoods.com/ASSETS/. . ./CIES%20 Speech.pdf.
6. *China National News*, 19 February 2010.
7. The unofficial English translation of the FSL on the US Department of Agriculture web site states: 'Neither the Food Safety Law nor any associated regulations have been notified to the World Trade Organization.' Available at: http://gain.fas.usda.gov/Recent%20GAIN%20Publications/Final%20Food%20Safety%20 Law%20Implementation%20Measures_Beijing_China%20-%20Peoples%20Republic%20of_8-14-2009. pdf.

## BIBLIOGRAPHY

Allen, L.L. (2010), 'Chocolate fortunes: the battle for the hearts, minds, and wallets of China's consumers', *Thunderbird International Business Review*, **52** (1), 13–20.
Anderlini, J. (2009), 'Rule of the iron rooster', *FT Online*, 24 August, available at: http://www.ft.com/cms/s/0/ae083ef2-90de-11de-bc99-00144feabdc0.html?SID=google (accessed 15 February 2010).
Anderlini, J. (2010), 'China ushers in credit default swaps', *FT Online*, 5 November, available at: http://www.ft.com/cms/s/0/23b08c34-e90a-11df-a1b4-00144feab49a.html#ixzz14alK61MN (accessed 8 November 2010).
Anderlini, J., S. Tucker and J. Hughes (2010), *FT.com*, 21 January.
Brown, C.G., J.W. Longworth and S. Waldron (2002), 'Food safety and development of the beef industry in China', *Food Policy*, **27**, 269–84.
Dong Fengxia and F.H. Fuller (2010), 'Dietary structural change in China's cities: empirical fact or urban legend?', *Canadian Journal of Agricultural Economics*, **58** (1), 73–91.
Economy, E.C. (2007), 'China vs. Earth', *Nation*, 7 May, 29.
Eisner, M., J. Worsham and E.J. Ringquist (2006), *Contemporary Regulatory Policy*, London: Lynne Rienner.
Engardio, P., D. Roberts, F. Balfour and B. Einhorn (2007), 'Broken China', *Business Week*, 12 July, 1–2.
Gottwald, J.-C. (2010), 'Cadre-capitalism goes global: financial market reforms and the new role for the People's Republic of China in world markets', in L. Brennan (ed.), *The Emergence of Southern Multinationals*, Basingstoke: Palgrave Macmillan, pp. 285–304.
Han Dongping (2009), 'Farmers, Mao, and discontent in China from the Great Leap Forward to the present', *Monthly Review*, December, available at: http://www.monthlyreview.org/091214dongping.php.
He Nanban (2010), 'Zhongguo Renmin Yinhang, Zhongguo Yinjianhui, Zhongguo Zhengjianhui, Zhongguo Baojianhui chutai jinyibu zuohao jinrong fuwu zhich zhongdian tiaozheng zhenxing he yizhi bufen

xingye channeg guo sheng de zhi', available at: http://www.gzxz.gov.cn/Article/Print.asp?ArticleID=28688 (accessed 20 February 2010).

Heilmann, S. (2001), 'The Chinese stock market: pitfalls of a policy-driven market', *China Analysis*, 15, September.

Heilmann, S. (2005a), 'Regulatory innovation by Leninist means: Communist Party supervision in China's financial industry', *China Quarterly*, **181**, March, 1–21.

Heilmann, S. (2005b), Policy-making and political supervision in Shanghai's financial industry', *Journal of Contemporary China*, **14** (45), 643–68.

Heilmann, S. (2008), 'From local experiments to national policy: the origins of China's distinctive policy process', *China Journal*, **59** (1), 1–30.

Homer, A.W. (2009), 'Coal mine safety regulation in China and the USA', *Journal of Contemporary Asia*, **39** (3), August, 424–37.

Huang Yasheng (2008), *Capitalism with Chinese Characteristics: Entrepreneurship and the State*, London: Cambridge University Press.

Johnson, T. (2008), 'China's troubled food and drug trade', background paper for Council on Foreign Relations, Washington, October, available at: http://www.cfr.org/publication/17545 (accessed 1 February 2010).

Kaufmann, D., A. Kraay and M. Mastruzzi (2008), *Governance Matters VIII: Governance Indicator 1996–2008*, Washington, DC: World Bank.

Landry, P.F. (2009), 'Does the Communist Party help strengthen China's legal reforms?', *China Review*, **9** (1) Spring, 45–71.

Laurence, Henry (2001), *Money Rules: The New Politics of Finance in Britain and Japan*, Ithaca, NY and London: Cornell University Press.

Levi-Faur, D. and J. Jordana (eds) (2005), 'The rise of regulatory capitalism: the diffusion of a new global order', *Annals of the American Academy of Political and Social Science*, **598**, March.

Luo Yunbo (2005), 'Editorial: trends in food R&D in China', *Newsline: International Union of Food Science and Technology Newsletter*, April/May, 2–3.

Lütz, Susanne (2002), *Der Staat und die Globalisierung der Finanzmärkte*, Frankfurt am Main: Campus.

Lütz, Susanne (2003), *Convergence within National Diversity: A Comparative Perspective on the Regulatory State in Finance*, MPIfG Discussion Paper 03/7, Cologne: MPIfG.

Majone, Giandomenico (1997), 'From the positive to the regulatory state: causes and consequences of changes in the mode of governance', *Journal of Public Policy*, **17** (2), 139–67.

May, P.J. (2007), 'Regulatory regimes and accountability', *Regulation & Governance*, **1** (1), March, 8–26.

Miller, A. (2008), 'The Central Committee's leading small groups', *China Leadership Monitor*, **26**, Fall.

NAFMII (National Association of Financial Market Institutional Investors) (2010), 'Responsibilities', available at: http://www.nafmii.org.cn/Channel/350179 (accessed 21 November 2010).

Naughton, B. (2008), *The Chinese Economy: Transition and Growth*, London: MIT Press.

OECD (2005), 'China's Governance in Transition', *Policy Brief*, September, Paris: OECD.

Pearson, M. (2005), 'The business of governing business in China: institutions and norms of the emerging regulatory state in China', *World Politics*, **57** (2), January, 296–325.

Pearson, M. (2007), 'Governing the Chinese economy: regulatory reform in the service of the state', *Public Administration Review*, **67** (4), July/August, 718–30.

Peerenboom, R. (2009), 'Resistance, revision, and retrenchment in the transition to a competitive market economy in China', in J. Gillespie and R. Peerenboom (eds), *Regulation in Asia: Pushing back on Globalization*, Milton Park and New York: Routledge, pp. 114–38.

People's Republic of China (PRC) (1982/2004), *Constitution of the People's Republic of China*.

People's Republic of China (PRC) (2010), *Ministries and commissions directly under the State Council*, available at: http://english.gov.cn/2005-08/05/content_20741.htm (accessed 25 October 2010).

Schlichting, S. (2008), *Internationalising China's Financial Markets*, Basingstoke: Palgrave Macmillan.

Schlichting, S. and J.-C. Gottwald (2008), 'Creating a regulatory regime within Leninist authoritarianism: financial market reforms in the PRC', paper presented to the Association of Asian Studies annual conference, Atlanta, GA, April.

Shen Mingming and Wang Yuhua (2009), 'Litigating economic disputes in rural China', *China Review*, **9** (1), Spring.

Shih, V. (2010), "A reply to my critics on government debt', available at: http://chinesepolitics.blogspot.com/ (accessed 27 October 2010).

Tam Waikeung and Yang Dali (2005), 'Food safety and the development of regulatory institutions in China,' *Asian Perspective*, **29** (4), 5–36.

Vogel, S.K. (1998), *Freer Markets, More Rules: Regulatory Reform in Advanced Industrial Countries*, Ithaca, NY: Cornell University Press.

Watson, J.L. (2004), 'China's Big Mac attack', in James L. Watson and Melissa L. Caldwell (eds), *The Cultural Politics of Food and Eating: A Reader*, Oxford: Wiley-Blackwell, pp. 120–34.

Wishnick, E. (2009), 'Of milk and spacemen: the paradox of Chinese power in an era of risk', *Brown Journal of World Affairs*, Spring, 209–23.

Yang, D. (2009), 'Regulatory learning and its discontents in China: promise and tragedy at the State Food and Drug Administration', in John Gillespie and Randall Peerenboom (eds), *Pushing Back Globalization*, London: Routledge, available at: http://www.daliyang.com/researchpapers.html (accessed 21 January 2010).

Zhang Xiaoyong, H. Dagevos, Yuna He, Ivo van der Lans and Zhai Fengying (2008), 'Consumption and corpulence in China: a consumer segmentation study based on the food perspective', *Food Policy*, **33**, 37–47.

Zhao Yangjun (2000), *Lun zhengquan jianguan*, Beijing: Zhongguo renmin daxue chubanshe.

# 11 The institutional development of the Latin American regulatory state

## Jacint Jordana

In the last three decades Latin American countries have radically transformed their administrative states in the context of a large-scale process of liberalization, privatization and democratization (Bresser Pereira and Spink 1999; Lora 2007; Mainwaring and Scully 2010). Out of this process of transformation a complex structure of regulatory governance emerged that might be best described as the Latin American regulatory state. This radical transformation does not mean that regulatory policies are new to Latin America; nonetheless, the extent of the reforms suggests that something new has emerged in the way new regulatory institutions have been extensively diffused in the region.

In this chapter, we understand regulation to be a public activity aimed at steering the economy and society by constraining, encouraging or designing its functioning. As the development of regulation in most policy domains is extremely interdependent with the capabilities of those administrative units which are responsible for its direct supervision and implementation, we focus basically on the institutional side of regulation. Eventually, the regulatory state might be able to reduce risks, address market failures or expand the public sphere. It is not a neoliberal invention, although it expanded during the neoliberal age (Levi-Faur 2011).

In the following pages we depict the establishment of regulatory institutions in the region after the colonial age, describe a general expansion of regulatory reforms in recent decades, and identify the technocratic and political aspects of the regulatory state. All in all, these elements allow us to distinguish neoliberal imports from historical legacies in the development of Latin American regulatory state. Not focused by the literature, we bring to light that a significant tradition of public regulation already existed in the region, although the impact of neoliberalism allowed strong institutional change in the 1990s. This was in fact a very particular process of institutional amalgamation, strongly related to the political economy of the countries in the region, which also were extremely receptive to the characteristics and singularities of dominant regulatory models in the United States and Europe at that moment.

This chapter, organized in four parts, presents an overview of the regulatory state in Latin America. The details are missing, however, as they are beyond the chapter's scope and extent. We begin by reviewing the origins of the regulatory state in the region and its development up to the 1980s. Second, we focus on the rise of the regulatory state in the region, and examine the mushrooming of autonomous regulatory agencies in many different sectors and countries in recent decades. Third, we discuss the specific political characteristics of the Latin American regulatory state. The chapter concludes by identifying current challenges to the regulatory state in Latin America.

## 11.1   ORIGINS OF THE LATIN AMERICAN REGULATORY STATE

During the colonial age, both economy and society in Latin America were highly regulated, but policies and institutions operated according to the hegemonic logic of the Spanish and Portuguese empires to which they belonged, and were not the creations of embryonic autonomous governments. However, we argue that the emergence of the regulatory state in Latin America dates back at least to the liberal era that followed Latin American countries' achievement of independence, and its development displays a particular path that reflected the region's historical circumstances. In fact, following their independence, already during the nineteenth century we may document relevant cases of public regulation that introduced steering mechanisms in the new Latin American states. By utilizing administrative forms derived from the colonial past, most countries started to produce regulations for the purpose of stimulating certain economic activities or reducing significant social and health risks.

Although many questions remain open and await further research, it is possible to identify a significant influence of Spanish administrative practice during colonial times on Latin American countries (Hanson 1974). In particular, we highlight two special administrative bodies, *superintendencia* and *junta*, which emerged within the Spanish monarchy during the sixteenth century. While the *junta* consisted initially of meetings of experts for the adoption of resolutions on a specific subject, *superintendencia* was a public office exercising special powers to supervise and perform a specific function. In fact, one of the first cases documented by historians refers to the Virrey of Peru as 'Superintendent' – as early as 1575. Over the next two centuries, *superintendencia* was employed for different purposes, and also had a formal meaning as a title within the Spanish public administration. In the eighteenth century, French influence on Spanish administration reshaped the office, making it more precise. Both *superintendencia* and *junta* combined two different functions: to exercise control and supervision over different areas of the public administration, and to undertake highly complex tasks (Pietschmann 1983). In particular during the eighteenth century it was very commonly used by the Spanish colonial administration as a way to modernize public administration and strengthen the managerial and supervisory capabilities of the absolutist state (Céspedes 1953; Pietschmann 1993). Both *superintendencias* and *juntas*, as institutional forms focused on managing specific areas of public concern, were separate from the general structure of public administration. The basic difference between them lay in their composition: while the *supertintendencia* consisted of a single office holder, the *junta* was a collective body composed of several members. Also, the *superintendencia* had a more managerial profile, with its own organizational resources, while the *junta* concentrated more on jurisdictional responsibilities, relying on external managerial resources as and when necessary (Bermejo 1984).

During the nineteenth century state formation in Latin America in most cases involved long periods of political unrest, and almost all Latin American countries retained Spanish colonial laws, delaying the elaboration of new legal codes (Dye 2006). However, state-building in many Latin American states was more effective in the last decades of the nineteenth century. Central governments became stronger and political violence ended, allowing the elimination of traditional forms of public control and the emergence of new regulatory forms (Bethell 1986). In addition, markets became more extended territorially.

Their creation was also stimulated in many countries by political reforms and revisions of legal codes that extended liberal regulatory principles, and by the emergence of new economic elites in the political arena. It was also clear to many contemporary actors in Latin America that states should play 'a crucial role in constituting and safeguarding market relations', to the extent that most emerging domestic markets remained quite weak and underdeveloped (Topik 1999). In this context, the establishment of *juntas* or similar institutions for many different regulatory purposes constituted in many countries a sort of club regulation (Moran 2003) in which economic and social elites, with very limited participation, took part in the process of state construction (Muñoz 1993; Nef 2003). However, supervisory activities remained inexistent or very weak, creating a particular additional obstacle to countries' regulatory development.

As an example of this state of affairs, we can observe the persistence of the *juntas* in the case of food and drug regulation in Peru after the country gained independence in 1821. *Juntas* were usually composed of a mixture of public servants, professionals (doctors and chemists) and some land-owning citizens. They were responsible for setting health standards (which were enforced by public officials), supervising day-to-day activities, and also developing new regulations and policy interventions. These *juntas* had direct sources of funding, as they were allowed to collect special taxes for inspections and fees for licensing medical products, and also to impose fines when regulations were violated. In fact, the *juntas* operated like commissions. The Supreme *Junta* was responsible for public health in the whole country, and also nominated individuals for membership of subordinate *juntas*. The *junta* institutional model survived in Peru throughout the nineteenth century, in spite of renewed food and drug regulations (1839, 1872). In the late nineteenth century, a new ordinance (1884) established a health service within the public administration, although it was subjected to the authority of the *Junta*. Only in the first decades of the twentieth century did the public administration increase its role in these areas, with the establishment of a General Directorate for Health (*Dirección General de Salubridad*) related to the Ministry of Development, which progressively assumed some of the *Junta*'s responsibilities and had some limited supervisory capabilities (Llosa 2006).

A new era in the history of the Latin American regulatory state began after the 1920s, when many countries introduced regulatory innovations strengthening public intervention in many relevant areas (e.g. the elaboration of new banking laws). In the context of the post-First World War era, the export-oriented model of the traditional oligarchies began to break down, and states started to develop more active interventions, relying less on elite 'club' regulation and promoting regulatory institutional innovation among many other administrative reforms (Spink 1999). Such innovation occurred first in the financial area, where recurrent banking crisis and a more sophisticated economic organization played a role, but wider state modernization strategies were also of crucial importance in updating other regulatory frameworks. These innovations combined current foreign models, mainly US-based, with those traditional institutional forms inherited from the colonial age that had remained almost unchanged during the nineteenth century. Not surprisingly, when Latin American governments first created 'modern' regulatory institutions, in many cases they named them *superintendencias*, continuing their local administrative traditions. Thus the link was established and restored, facilitating the blend of historical models with external influences in institutional design.

Here we find also an episode in which the mix of external influence and local origins was made particularly visible. This is the case of the North American consultant missions during the 1920s and early 1930s. In several Andean countries, a Princeton economist, E.W. Kemmerer, helped to reform financial practices in order to ensure that foreign debts were paid on time. The missions advised that regulatory authorities for financial services should be set up, separate from central banks, based on the institutional designs that were dominant at the time in the US. In this sense, Kemmerer's influence was very strong in the adoption of institutional innovations designed according to US standards, although rooted in Latin America's own administrative traditions, which assigned more responsibilities to the agency head, the superintendente, instead of delegating the main responsibilities to commissions. As a consequence, during the 1920s a number of countries, including Mexico, Colombia, Chile, Ecuador, Peru and Bolivia, created banking regulatory agencies in parallel with the establishment of their central banks, also triggered by their neighbours' decisions to reform banking regulation (Seidel 1972; Drake 1989; López and Fernando 2003).

During the import-substitution era in the region, which started in the 1930s, the statist aspect of regulatory activities continued to grow, as government intervention in the market became very intense in many sectors. In addition, initiatives to modernize administration proliferated, seeking greater efficiency and also aiming to separate politics from public management (Spink 1999; Nef 2003). Thus the development of new administrative capacities in Latin America was very significant, expanding the presence of public servants with more technocratic profiles in many different areas of the public sector. In this context, quasi-independent public entities proliferated enormously after the 1940s, giving a strong impetus to the agencification of public administration in many Latin American countries (Thurber 1973). As a consequence, a fragmented and more professional bureaucracy emerged within the developmental state, which in part was devoted to regulating relations between public and private economic activities, protecting domestic markets in order to reduce imports, and favouring export-oriented production. However, the creation of a professional bureaucracy was also associated in several cases with authoritarian regimes. More generally, bureaucrats often tended to protect themselves from political unrest, which also involved an abdication of responsibility for many social and economic problems (for the Brazilian case, see Mattos 2006).

Although the protectionist strategy that dominated economic policy in this period often prevented market competition, it is also worth noting that some pro-market regulations were introduced. Several Latin American states promoted new regulatory tools, mainly under the influence of foreign models. The most important was antitrust regulation, focusing on preventing anti-competitive behaviour. In 1923 Argentina passed the first antitrust legislation in Latin America, and in 1934 Mexico enacted an anti-monopoly law. Years later, Chile (1959), Colombia (1959–64) and Brazil (1962–63) passed legislation to regulate anti-competitive practices (Coate et al. 1992). In addition, the creation of securities commissions in major countries in the region before the 1980s was another indication of the emerging trend towards increasing official supervision of firms and markets. All in all, the regulatory state expanded modestly in the shadow of the developmental state and its distributive policies during this period, becoming more professionalized and abandoning the *junta* model, the Latin American version of the elite regulatory state.

Following the Peruvian case of drug regulation, we can observe clearly the struggle between the two models until the mid-twentieth century. As early as 1922, the public administrative structure became more complex with the creation in Peru of the Pharmaceutical Commission, a more professional entity – also drawn from foreign models – in charge of controlling medicaments and pharmacies and proposing new regulations in the area, which incidentally further marginalized the role of the Supreme *Junta*. Later, the creation of the Public Health Ministry in 1935 involved consolidating food and drugs regulation in a more hierarchic style of public administration, and the closing of the *Junta*. Nevertheless, memories of the *Junta* model persisted , and in 1945 a new National *Junta* of Food and Nutrition was created to make policy proposals in this area, adopting a corporatist rather than an elitist structure and including academics, legislators, technicians, and public servants from diverse ministries. This *Junta* represented an attempt to modernize the original model so that it could operate alongside modern administrative structures, but it was dissolved within a few years (Llosa 2006).

In a context of wider administrative agencification, modern regulatory institutions found a way to expand, principally in the financial and competition areas, where many *superintendencias* continued to be created until the 1980s. However, almost no regulatory agencies existed in the region before the 1980s in the utilities area, as these services in most cases operated as public monopolies. This situation was radically distinct from that in the United States, where the regulatory state had already developed on many fronts before the Second World War, creating a particular mode of governance with a singular character. In this area, until the 1980s Latin America was similar to Europe, where utilities were under public control and social regulation was very weak.

## 11.2    THE RISE OF THE LATIN AMERICAN REGULATORY STATE

It is during the neoliberal decades at the end of the twentieth century that we observe the emergence of a major regulatory impulse for constructing a new regulatory state amid privatizations and deregulatory initiatives. Although not restricted to Latin America, during the early 1990s privatizations swept across the region, propelled by the fiscal crisis and new policy ideas (Levi-Faur 2003). At that time Latin America, like many other regions of the world, experienced radical changes in the way its economies were organized, yet in a more sweeping manner, via the liberalization of different utility sectors and the integration of the region's economy into the world economy (Edwards 1995). Without doubt, privatizations expanded the regulatory state in the region by contributing to opening new markets by creating the need for public intervention to stimulate more competitive environments. However, this causal link did not operate in all cases. Several countries ended up after privatization with private monopolies in under-regulated settings, allowing small social groups to control key economic sectors. In other cases significant regulatory reforms were introduced in many sectors without privatization (Manzetti 2000; Chong and Benavides 2007).

A new regulatory agenda emerged from these transformations: states aimed to open their domestic markets in order to gain access to new ones, fostered internal competition, stimulated private investment, and facilitated technological innovation, expecting to become better regulators. The new regulatory state also expanded to embrace new concerns beyond market efficiency, promoting risk regulation in social and environmental areas, and guaranteeing civic and democratic rights (like the right to information, human rights protection, electoral rights and so forth). The sudden increase in the creation of regulatory institutions in Latin America was impressive. Innovative regulatory designs, often highly sophisticated ones, were also introduced in many different sectors. The creation or reform of autonomous regulatory institutions was seen as the main strategy to develop regulatory reform in the region, as they could help to renovate bureaucracies, to introduce updated regulatory frameworks, to supervise the behaviour of actors in private markets, and also to open regulatory policymaking to more democratic procedures. These changes also had significant effects on policymaking across entire political systems, challenging to some extent the roles of traditional economic and political actors in many regulatory areas.

As indicated, during the 1990s and the early 2000s the number of regulatory agencies in Latin America exploded, making the regulatory state in the region a much more visible and relevant presence. In the financial area regulatory agencies were created or reformed to cover pensions, insurance and stock markets in addition to banks (Demaestri and Guerrero 2006; Brooks 2009). Such growth was also particularly important in the utilities, where market regulation was boosted in different sectors (electricity, water, gas, telecommunications and so on), stimulating an intense diffusion of agency creation (Gutierrez 2003). Also, many agencies were created in the social regulation area, although not so intensively as in the utilities or finance sectors (Gilardi et al. 2006). Agency creation was significant in the environment, but other sectors, such as occupational health, pharmaceutical and food safety, evinced a more modest pattern of diffusion. However, even in these sectors regulation expanded significantly because of the large number of trade agreements that many countries in the region negotiated during this period. Overall, this represented an intense wave of policy and institutional change across the region, in a context of significant economic restructuring and associated public sector reform, which coincided with and contributed to the expansion of regulatory capitalism worldwide (Lora 2007).

A comprehensive cross-regional, cross-national and cross-sectoral study reveals that the growth of specialized regulatory institutions in Latin America since the 1990s has been astounding. The data set for this study includes agencies that meet two criteria: first, they must have an autonomous organizational identity rather than be a unit of a larger ministerial department; and, second, they must focus primarily on regulatory tasks. Also, the unit of analysis is the 'country–sector' case, not actual public organizations, so that what is identified in fact is the number of sectors covered by regulatory agencies – making possible better cross-national and cross-sector comparisons (Jordana and Levi-Faur 2005; Jordana et al. 2011). Figure 11.1 presents the diffusion of regulatory agencies in Latin American countries since 1920, grouping 16 different sectors in four main areas: financial (central banks, banking supervision, pensions, insurance and securities); utilities (telecommunications, electricity, gas, postal and water); social (environment, health, food safety, pharmaceutical, and work safety); and competition. Results show an impressive increase since the late 1980s in all areas, but also significant differences with respect to the financial area. Also it is worth noting that social regulation lags behind all other areas, especially since the 1980s.

This huge diffusion of regulatory agencies in Latin America during the 1990s was

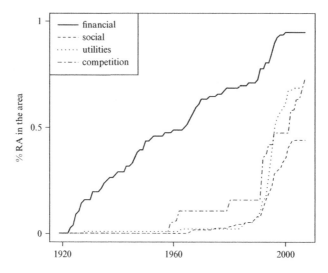

*Source:*   Jordana et al. (2011).

*Figure 11.1*    *Diffusion of regulatory agencies in Latin America (19 countries, 1920–*
*2007) (percentage of sectors covered by a regulatory agency)*

not an isolated phenomenon. At that time, a similar pattern of rapid agency creation
unfolded in Europe and other parts of the world, in both developed and developing
countries, most of them adopting a similar standard design. This wave of institutional
creations with similar designs included the granting of strong organizational autonomy
to regulatory agencies vis-à-vis the traditional state apparatus and political executives, and involved many features of political delegation. Agencies' institutional design
included fixed-term mandates, provisions to prevent the dismissal of staff as a result of
regulatory decisions, successive reappointment of board members, and so forth, in order
to limit political influence on the decisions of the agency.

In Latin America this new institutional design for regulatory agencies was adopted
extensively, although countries varied considerably in the intensity of their impetus to
build new regulatory regimes, and the designs of the regulatory agencies also varied to
a great extent (Jordana and Levi-Faur 2005). Without doubt, the processes of public
sector reform in Latin America that started in the 1980s were behind the regulatory
'explosion' that occurred in the region, but such changes were not homogeneous. In
general, external pressures and foreign models largely facilitated policy diffusion, but
domestic policymakers were often decisive in determining agencies' institutional characteristics in each case (Weyland 2006; Ramió and Salvador 2008).

On the subject of the blend of new and old in the rise of the regulatory state in Latin
America, we might point out that the colonial tradition of *superintendencias* eased the
introduction of new regulatory institutions in many countries. In fact, when Latin
American countries created autonomous organizations for special regulatory purposes
they often named them *superintendencias* rather than 'agencies' or 'commissions', thus
maintaining some resemblance with the administrative forms derived from the colonial

past. This long-standing institutional influence might also have been sustained by the political unrest experienced by most Latin American countries after they gained independence, which impeded administrative and regulatory developments until the late nineteenth century (Przeworski 2009). Thus the colonial institutional heritage was still alive during the twentieth century, and it was combined with institutional models from abroad, particularly North America and to a lesser extent Europe.

In this sense, an institutional characteristic that emerged in many new regulatory agencies in the region was the significant concentration of responsibilities directly in the agency head, which contrasted with the frequent absence – or relatively weak role – of the agency board. This differs clearly from the North American tradition of regulatory commissions, and recalls the organizational character of the historical *superintendencia* model. It is worth noting the residual use of the *junta* model as opposed to the widespread adoption of the *superintendencia* model in many countries in the region during the regulatory revolution of the late twentieth century (however, it is still possible to find in countries such as Ecuador or Guatemala a collective body called *Junta Monetaria*, exercising supreme regulatory authority over finance). In fact, most agencies with regulatory commissions rejected this historical form and adopted foreign models, adjusting them to their particular needs; and their composition in most cases moved beyond the logic of the club regulatory state.

## 11.3   POLITICAL CHARACTERISTICS OF THE LATIN AMERICAN REGULATORY STATE

The Latin American regulatory state is not new but has a long tradition that goes back to the colonial period. Both then and now it is the product of the interaction between foreign and internal influences and their adaptation to the prevailing domestic institutions and constraints. In this sense, regulatory institutions evolved over time in Latin America to fit the particular political characteristics of the region, that is, strong presidential regimes and unstable public administrations. The nature of Latin American political systems, almost all strongly rooted in the conventions of presidential regimes since their independence in the early nineteenth century, and the traditional weakness of hierarchical public bureaucracies (IADB 2006; Longo and Ramió 2008) favoured the salience of administrative units with special purposes, instead of articulating a Weberian model of public administration.

Latin America shares with Western Europe the civil law tradition (Merryman 1985), and its public sector draws on the Napoleonic administrative tradition (Peters 2008). However, Latin American countries never fully realized the European ideal with its well-designed hierarchical structures in the public realm, inspired by the Weberian model. Closer to North American administrative models and practices, the development of the administrative apparatus in Latin American cases did not involve a clear-cut bureaucratic structure but embraced numerous public organizations in addition to the ministries, many of them having direct links to the presidents. Since the 1920s, the administrative state in Latin America has been continuously influenced by North American institutional designs, inducing a significant process of agencification. To some extent the regulatory agencification in the 1990s was a continuation of the fragmented administrative pattern within the state. New regulatory agencies had a different focus and some additional political delegation, but they did not in fact involve a break with the Weberian administrative model to the extent that it had not previously been consolidated in the region. In sum, all these transformations during the past century contributed to the emergence of a distinct version of the regulatory state in Latin America, adapted to its institutional settings while mixing in an intricate way North American institutional models, European common law traditions and Iberian–Napoleonic conceptions of the administrative state.

Unlike in the United States, the embryonic regulatory state in Latin America during the late nineteenth century was not focused on controlling and socializing unfettered markets and robber barons in response to popular pressure, but was mostly used as a market-making and market-enforcing tool to create new opportunities for economic elites in the region, in a way basically influenced by the British club model of the regulatory state but not by the regulatory agencification model that came out of North America. Again, the rise of the Latin American model of the regulatory state at the end of the twentieth century, which included an intense agencification, was not a response to the pressure of popular demands but was a technocratic reform in the context of privatization and liberalization on the one hand and the European and North American influence on the other.

When the developmental state collapsed in most Latin American countries, essentially during the 1980s, macroeconomic stability and democratic transitions were the main priorities of governments. While industry deregulation and trade opening were often the most cited policy objectives, the regulatory state did not emerge in the region as a default option, as Latin America had often previously been considered 'among the world's most regulated market economies, at least on paper' (Manzetti 2000) and the state administrative apparatus lacked political legitimization. Democratization processes, however, stimulated broad and vibrant domestic discussions about policy objectives in those years, and political competition was also an important factor making for policy change (Murillo and Martínez-Gallardo 2007). In fact, many policy changes were triggered more by a major fiscal shortfall resulting from previous ineffective macroeconomic policies than by an ideological shift (Fishlow 1990), which opened a window of opportunity for regulatory technocrats and professionals to foster multiple policy reforms. After some initial deregulation, many elected governments realized that re-regulation was required and new institutions specializing in regulatory governance were needed, but the strong technocratic bias in previous periods of the regulatory state also had an influence on the nature of subsequent developments during the late twentieth century. This was also in line with the need to redefine a solid democratic state able to determine new policy priorities and impose rule compliance. Many governments strongly supported such a move at the time, particularly those of Mexico and Brazil, the two major developmental states in the region with strong bureaucratic backgrounds (Lora 2007; Foxley 2009).

Following the rise of the regulatory state and its expansion to multiple policy areas, regulatory agencies are at the present a tangible reality in all Latin American countries. It is now possible to observe that regulatory institutions often confront significant challenges in coping with the social and political tensions that exist in many different sectors in the region. However, their role as powerful instruments of the state able to govern critical economic sectors has become progressively consolidated. They usually operate in coordination with government units more focused on defining political preferences, such as ministries or parliamentary chambers, but they are also linked internationally to similar institutions in other countries, which is an additional source of legitimacy.

In Latin America most regulatory agencies are autonomous administrative units that sustain their legitimacy by means of their professionalism and the creation of a stable regulatory environment for market operations and long-term investment. Although their recent expansion has included a substantial diffusion of the features of *de jure* political delegation, regulatory agencies often remain under some degree of supervision and guidance by the executive, particularly presidents, so that in many cases they can maintain only a weak *de facto* political delegation (Montoya and Trillas 2009; Jordana and Ramió 2010). The prevalence in most countries in the region of strong presidencies combined with weak legislative chambers usually ensures that the agencies do not have alternative political bases from which to challenge governments, and their only independent support is the professional reputation of their workforces.

Nevertheless, this should not be thought to amount to an institutional failure. To some extent it can be understood as an institutional continuity with the politics of 'remote control' that already existed in the region, corresponding to the characteristics of the traditional *superintendencia* design. Most regulatory agencies in the region actually operate under *de facto* institutional rules that allow delegation to professionals to supervise and control markets without interference, but not to make significant regulatory decisions autonomously. Contributing to defining the Latin American variety of the regulatory state, modern regulatory agencies in the region show some distinctive qualities: strong organizational autonomy, a highly professional identity and technical expertise, pre-eminence of agency heads combined with weak agency boards, and quite limited political delegation (Jordana and Levi-Faur 2006; Jordana and Ramió 2010). In many cases the regulatory agencies also provide considerable stability for civil servants working in them, a characteristic particularly significant in the context of the shortcomings of public administration in Latin America (Echebarría and Cortazar 2007).

## 11.4   CONCLUDING REMARKS

The administrative and regulatory reform of the Latin American states during the 1990s should be understood in the context of the search for a new social and economic equilibrium in the region, wherein regulation has a highly relevant role in making such equilibrium stable and welfare oriented. The liberal regulatory state that was established in the late nineteenth century allowed economic elites to retain effective control and introduce some pro-market regulations. However, this model failed miserably to create more inclusive societies and prosperous economies. By and large, progressive social and political movements during most of the twentieth century could not reverse these circumstances (Draibe and Riesco 2007). Starting in the 1920s, modernization strategies allowed a timid institutionalization of the regulatory state in the shadow of the developmental state, largely propelled by the technocratic side of the state apparatus. However, since the 1980s regulatory reforms have signified an alternative to the liberal state model and an effort to address the weaknesses of Latin American states in controlling, managing and directing markets by means of creating an institutionally robust regulatory state.

This transformation also presents an opportunity to realize the benefits of economic competition and economic freedom. Regulatory agencies have emerged as a distinct institutional alternative, beyond the neoliberal impulse. They are not simply imported designs, but embody a fusion of institutional patterns already existing in the region with a variety of foreign influences. It is important to emphasize that the development of the regulatory state in Latin America is not a consequence of the spread of neoliberalism to the region. It represents a parallel and compensating process, offering the opportunity to balance policies in favour of economic liberalization with policies in favour of citizens, in order to avoid multiple economic, social and political risks (Faundez 2005: 752).

Albeit a technocratic reform in origin, the regulatory state brought some new opportunities to improve the fairness and efficacy of political processes and to limit monopolistic abuses in the region. Most regulatory agencies provided capacities to control market developments, effectively following the activity of major firms operating in their countries, and progressively establishing the 'rules of the game' for them. Obviously, regulatory agencies did not perform successfully in all cases, and many problems of regulatory governance emerged in their interactions. Nevertheless, overall they represented a major improvement of public capabilities, in most cases strengthening state interventions with ever more sophisticated and less distorting policy instruments. The establishment of regulatory agencies also represented an opportunity to improve transparency, the rule of law, participation and accountability in many areas of policymaking. In fact, the amount of information regulatory agencies provided to the public was far greater than that provided under established bureaucratic traditions of Latin American states, which were not very forthcoming in providing public information on their policy deliberations. The introduction of public hearings, the publication of the minutes of their formal meetings, and the procedural consultations all represented administrative innovations introduced by the regulation revolution, which also created new spaces to expand the quality of democratic life. However, without a well-defined schema of anchorage to the wider institutional context in the public realm, regulatory agencies' political base remains weak. In the turbulent political environments of many Latin American countries, this represents a particularly persistent danger to the consolidation of regulatory agencies. It is important that political and legal institutions are capable of monitoring – but also supporting – regulators, reaching the precise equilibrium for each institutional environment. However, many questions about this variety of the regulatory state remain unanswered, in particular regarding its historical dynamic and performance, as well as its adaptations to nations and sectors. Only more focused research could elucidate these issues.

## ACKNOWLEDGEMENTS

I would like to thank Andrea Bianculli, Sergio Costa, David Levi-Faur and Ludolfo Paramio for their useful comments while I was preparing this chapter. I also acknowledge the support provided by the Spanish Ministry of Science and Innovation (Grant CSO2009-11053).

# REFERENCES

Bermejo Cabrero, José Luis (1984), 'Superintendencias en la Hacienda del Antiguo Régimen', *Anuario de Historia del Derecho Español*, **54**, 409–48.

Bethell, Leslie (1986), *The Cambridge History of Latin America, 1870–1930*, vol. 5, Cambridge: Cambridge University Press.

Bresser Pereira, Luiz Carlos and Peter Spink (eds) (1999), *Reforming the State: Managerial Public Administration in Latin America*, Boulder, CO and London: Lynne Rienner.

Brooks, Sarah M. (2009), *Social Protection and the Market in Latin America: The Transformation of Social Security Institutions*, Cambridge: Cambridge University Press.

Céspedes del Castillo, Guillermo (1953), 'Reorganización de la Hacienda virreinal peruana en el siglo XVIII', *Anuario de Historia del Derecho Español*, **23**, 329–70.

Chong, Alberto and Juan Benavides (2007), 'Privatization and regulation in Latin America', in Eduardo Lora (ed.), *The State of State Reform in Latin America*, Palo Alto, CA: Stanford University Press.

Coate, Malcolm B., René Bustamante and A.E. Rodriguez (1992), 'Anti-trust in Latin America: regulating government and business', *University of Miami Inter-American Law Review*, **24**, 37–85.

Demaestri, Edgardo and Federico Guerrero (2006), 'What are the perils of separating banking regulation from the central bank's orbit in Latin America and the Caribbean?', *Journal of Financial Regulation and Compliance*, **14** (1), 70–83.

Draibe, Sonia and Manuel Riesco (2007), 'Latin America: a new developmental welfare state in the making?', in M. Riesco (ed.), *Latin America: A New Developmental Welfare State Model in the Making?*, Houndmills and New York: Palgrave–UNRISD, pp. 21–116.

Drake, Paul W. (1989), *The Money Doctor in the Andes: U.S. Advisors, Investors, and Economic Reform in Latin America from World War I to the Great Depression*, Durham, NC: Duke University Press.

Dye, Alan (2006), 'The institutional framework', in V. Bulmer-Thomas, J. Coatsworth and R. Cortes Conde (eds), *The Cambridge Economic History of Latin America*, vol. II: *The Long Twentieth Century*, Cambridge: Cambridge University Press, pp. 169–207.

Echebarría, Koldo and Juan Carlos Cortazar (2007), 'Public administration and public employment reform in Latin America', in Eduardo Lora (ed.), *The State of State Reform in Latin America*, Washington, DC: The Inter-American Development Bank and Stanford University Press.

Edwards, Sebastian (1995), *Crisis and Reform in Latin America: From Despair to Hope*, Oxford: Oxford University Press.

Faundez, Julio (2005), 'Democratization through law: perspectives from Latin America', *Democratization*, **12** (5), 749–65.

Fishlow, Albert (1990), 'The Latin American state', *Journal of Economic Perspectives*, **4** (3), 61–74.

Foxley, Alejandro (2009), 'More market or more state for Latin America?', in S. Mainwaring and T.R. Scully (eds), *Democratic Governance in Latin America*, Stanford, CA: Stanford University Press.

Gilardi, Fabrizio, Jacint Jordana and David Levi-Faur (2006), 'Regulation in the age of globalization: the diffusion of regulatory agencies across Europe and Latin America', in G. Hodge (ed.), *Privatization and Market Development*, Cheltenham, UK and Northampton, MA, USA: Edward Elgar Publishing.

Gutierrez, Luis (2003), 'Regulatory governance in the Latin American telecommunications sector', *Utilities Policy*, **11**, 225–40.

Hanson, Mark (1974), 'Organizational bureaucracy in Latin America and the legacy of Spanish colonialism', *Journal of Interamerican Studies and World Affairs*, **16** (2), 199–219.

Inter-American Development Bank (IADB) (2006), *The Politics of Policies: Economic and Social Progress in Latin America. 2006 Report*, Washington, DC: IADB and Harvard University Press.

Jordana, Jacint and David Levi-Faur (2005), 'The diffusion of regulatory capitalism in Latin America: sectoral and national channels in the making of a new order', *Annals of the American Academy of Political and Social Science*, **598**, 102–24.

Jordana, Jacint and David Levi-Faur (2006), 'Towards a Latin American regulatory state? The diffusion of autonomous regulatory agencies across countries and sectors', *International Journal of Public Administration*, **29** (4–5), 335–66.

Jordana, Jacint and Carles Ramió (2010), 'Delegation, presidential regimes and Latin American regulatory agencies', *Journal of Latin American Politics*, **2** (1), 3–30.

Jordana, Jacint, David Levi-Faur and Xavier Fernández (2011), 'The global diffusion of regulatory agencies: channels of transfer and stages of diffusion', *Comparative Political Studies*, **44** (10).

Levi-Faur, David (2003), 'The politics of liberalisation: privatization and regulation-for-competition in Europe's and Latin America's telecoms and electricity industries', *European Journal of Political Research*, **42** (5), 705–40.

Levi-Faur, David (2011), 'Regulation and Regulatory Governance', in David Levi-Faur (ed.), *Handbook of the Politics of Regulation*, Cheltenham, Edward Elgar.

Llosa, Alicia C. (2006), '*Boticas y bodegas*: The development of food and drug regulation in Peru', *University of Miami Inter-American Law Review*, **38**, 279–347.

Longo, Francisco and Carles Ramió (eds) (2008), *La profesionalización del empelo público en América Latina*, Barcelona: Fundació CIDOB.

López, Garavito and Luis Fernando (2003), 'Una visión del desarrollo institucional de la Superintendencia Bancaria de Colombia, 1923–2003', in *VV.AA, 80 años de Superintendencia Bancaria en Colombia*, Bogotá: Superintendencia Bancaria.

Lora, Eduardo (ed) (2007), *The State of State Reform in Latin America*, Palo Alto, CA: Stanford University Press.

Mainwaring, Scott and Timothy R. Scully (eds) (2010), *Democratic Governance in Latin America*, Stanford, CA: Stanford University Press.

Manzetti, Luigi (ed.) (2000), *Regulatory Policy in Latin America: Post-Privatization Realities*, Miami: North–South Center Press.

Mattos, Paulo Todescan Lessa (2006), 'A formação do estado regulador', *Novos Estudios*, **76**, 139–56.

Merryman, John Henry (1985), *The Civil Law Tradition: An Introduction to the Legal Systems of Western Europe and Latin America*, Stanford, CA: Stanford University Press.

Montoya, Miguel Á. and Francesc Trillas (2009), 'The measurement of regulator independence in practice: Latin America and the Caribbean', *International Journal of Public Policy*, **4** (1–2), 113–34.

Moran, Michael (2003), *The British Regulatory State: High Modernism and Hyper-Innovation*, Oxford: Oxford University Press.

Muñoz, Oscar G. (ed.) (1993), *Después de las privatizaciones: Hacia el Estado Regulador*, Santiago de Chile: CIEPLAN.

Murillo, Maria V. and Cecilia Martínez-Gallardo (2007), 'Political competition and policy adoption: market reforms in Latin American public utilities', *American Journal of Political Science*, **51** (1), 120–39.

Nef, Jorge (2003), 'Public administration and public sector reform in Latin America', in B. Guy Peters and John Pierre (eds), *Handbook of Public Administration*, London: Sage.

Peters, B. Guy (2008), 'The Napoleonic tradition', *International Journal of Public Sector Management*, **21** (2), 118–32.

Pietschmann, Horst (1983), 'Antecedentes españoles e hispanoamericanos de las intendencias', *Anuario de Estudios Americanos*, **40**, 359–72.

Pietschmann, Horst (1993), 'El desarrollo estatal de Hispanoamérica: enfoques metodológicos', *Chronica Nova*, **21**, 469–92.

Przeworski, Adam (2009), 'The mechanics of regime instability in Latin America', *Journal of Politics in Latin America*, **1** (1), 5–36.

Ramió, Carles and Miquel Salvador (2008), 'Civil service reform in Latin America: external referents versus own capacities', *Bulletin of Latin American Research*, **27** (4), 554–73.

Seidel, Robert N. (1972), 'American reformers abroad: the Kemmerer missions in South America, 1923–1931', *Journal of Economic History*, **32** (2), 520–45.

Spink, Peter (1999), 'Possibilities and political imperatives: seventy years of administrative reform in Latin America', in Bresser Pereira, Luiz Carlos and Peter Spink (eds), *Reforming the State: Managerial Public Administration in Latin America*, Boulder, CO and London: Lynne Rienner, pp. 91–114.

Thurber, Clarence E. (1973), 'Islands of development: a political and social approach to development administration in Latin America', in C.E. Thurber and L.S. Graham (eds), *Development Administration in Latin America*, Durham, NC: Duke University Press.

Topik, Steven (1999), 'The construction of market society in Latin America: natural process or social engineering?', *Latin American Perspectives*, **26** (1), 3–21.

Weyland, Kurt (2006), *Bounded Rationality and Policy Diffusion: Social Sector Reform in Latin America*, Princeton, NJ: Princeton University Press.

# PART IV

# SELECTED ISSUES IN THE STUDY OF REGULATION

# 12 Policymaking accountability: parliamentary versus presidential systems
## Susan Rose-Ackerman

Modern states cannot realistically limit policymaking to the legislature. Pressing contemporary issues are too technically complex, too dynamic, and too numerous for busy, non-expert legislators to resolve in detail. Delegation under broad, framework statutes is essential for effective government, but this does not eliminate the need for democratic responsiveness. Hence committed democrats need to work toward the public accountability of all policymaking – not just in the legislature, but in other institutions as well. Periodic elections are not a sufficient popular check on government. Government accountability is a source of political legitimacy in three distinct senses. Call these performance accountability, rights-based accountability, and policymaking accountability.[1]

The first sense requires the state to carry out public programs competently, using expert professionals as needed and assuring a high level of efficiency and integrity in the public service. Political actors set the goals, and bureaucrats ought to carry them out in a cost-effective way – using their specialized knowledge. The key word is "competence." It implies both the use of experts and the existence of hard-working, well-trained civil servants who do not take bribes, embezzle funds, or create conflicts of interest. Call this *performance accountability*. It requires both transparency and a means of holding officials to account if they perform poorly.

Second, *rights-based accountability* implies legal constraints that protect individuals against the abuses of arbitrary power. It is not conditional on popular sovereignty. These rights may be enforced through a written, constitutional list of rights or by applying judicial concepts of "natural justice" or *principes généraux du droit*. If one accepts the value of a particular set of rights, a government is legitimate only if citizens can monitor the enforcement of such rights and hold government officials to account.

Third, the policymaking process itself should be responsive to democratic values. There are two ways to achieve such accountability. One route is through laws passed by representative assemblies where elections provide the link to public opinion. However, elections are an insufficient check if the legislature delegates policymaking to the government/executive or to independent agencies and private entities. Delegation of policymaking is pervasive in modern democracies, but it needs to be exercised consistent with democratic values. I call this *policymaking accountability*, and my aim is to analyze it and argue for its central importance.

Performance and rights-based accountability are background constraints. Policymaking accountability, however, goes beyond issues of competence, honesty, and the protection of rights. Statutes are frequently vague, unclear, and inconsistent, and they often leave difficult policy issues to the implementation stage. Delegation frequently requires the exercise of substantive policy discretion. Sometimes the executive makes policy on its own without any statutory framework. In all cases, however, officials must use their power consistent with democratic values. Electoral accountability is not sufficient; it is too infrequent and too rough-grained.

Whatever the risks and the countervailing political pressures, legislatures worldwide believe that the benefits of delegation outweigh the costs, and some constitutions require a degree of devolution and delegation through federalism and through constitutionally mandated institutions, such as central banks and broadcasting commissions. Given the ubiquity of delegation, I ask whether administrative law can help assure the democratic character of policymaking.

Administrative law can provide a framework for the achievement of policymaking accountability. Scholars of administrative law need to move away from a primary focus on the formal legality of state actions toward the study of rules and principles that can enhance political accountability and competent policymaking. Protecting the rights of individuals and businesses against an overarching state is not enough. Public law should also help contain excesses of executive power and monitor private or quasi-public entities that carry out public functions.

After a summary of the key aspects of policymaking accountability in section 12.1, section 12.2 outlines four models based on political accountability, expertise, partisan balance, and privatization. With this background, section 12.3 contrasts policymaking accountability and oversight in parliamentary and presidential systems.

## 12.1    KEY ASPECTS OF POLICYMAKING ACCOUNTABILITY

Delegated policymaking is a political act, but public law can help organize and manage the process. In assessing the democratic legitimacy of the policymaking processes, three linked issues frame the reform agenda: the forms of consultation and participation, the role of expertise, and the role of the judiciary and other oversight bodies.

### 12.1.1    Consultation and Participation

Across nation-states, consultation and participation in rulemaking vary in their legal status and in the nature of public input. At one extreme, the law mandates such processes and makes the requirement legally enforceable.[2] At the other, public hearings represent an illegitimate effort to override the political will of the legislature.[3] An intermediate case is one where hearing are permitted but with no legal recourse if they do not occur.[4]

The process of involving the public, business and other private institutions can range from notice and information requirements that cast outsiders in a watchdog role, through acceptance of public comments as part of the rulemaking process, to negotiated consensual rules.[5] The law may require governmental bodies not only to consult but also to explain the reasons for their choices (e.g. 5 USC §553(c)). Consultation may be open-ended or with a closed list of stakeholders. If the law specifies the represented groups, the government may pick the individual participants, or the groups themselves may select them. The state may finance all participation or subsidize only the participation of less wealthy and well-organized groups. Conversely, it can simply make the process available to interested people or groups. The strongest form of public participation is one where a consensus of the stakeholders makes the policy choice, but it raises a host of legitimacy issues (Rose-Ackerman 1994).

### 12.1.2   Expertise

The second dimension concerns the relative status of experts and the analytic techniques they use to assess policy options. If a regulatory policy seeks to correct a market failure, policy analysts often employ cost–benefit analysis or related concepts (Arrow et al. 1996). These are not, however, uncontroversial techniques.[6]

Recently, United States presidents have required cost–benefit analyses of major government regulations under White House oversight.[7] The European Commission is pushing a "Better Regulation" agenda that includes "impact analysis," a general term loosely related to cost–benefit analysis.[8] At one level, advocacy of impact analysis is an unobjectionable call to seek information about costs and benefits before making a policy decision. However, its proponents often presuppose that citizens have accepted particular norms of substantive policy – for example, net benefit maximization – when they, in fact, have not. The project fails to come to grips with the distinction between purely technical issues and those which imply particular normative views of good policy.

### 12.1.3   Judicial Review and Oversight

Government policymaking is subject to oversight in all political systems. The legislature holds hearings on budgets and statutory amendments and can set up special commissions of inquiry. Some systems permit the legislature to veto rules that they find objectionable.[9] Audit, control, and accountability offices are a route for oversight. Supreme audit offices and ombudsmen provide oversight and usually report directly to the legislature. Both are frequently able either to initiate legal challenges directly or to refer cases to the public prosecutor.[10] Beyond specialized oversight bodies, the courts – both special administrative tribunals and ordinary courts – have a central role.

In many systems, however, courts seldom review rulemaking processes. Review involves either challenges to the law as applied in particular cases or constitutional challenges based on failures of performance accountability or rights-based accountability. The judiciary is quite active in reviewing administrative actions but has no authority to review the procedures used to promulgate rules inside the executive or in independent agencies.[11]

The United States is an exception, where federal courts review rulemaking processes under the Administrative Procedures Act and have expanded on the Act's bare-bones procedural requirements.[12] Judicial review checks that the process was sufficient, that the outcome is consistent with the statute, and that the substantive choice is not arbitrary and capricious. The US courts struggle to determine the deference they should give to an agency's interpretation of its underlying statutes.[13] To resolve this difficulty, Justice Breyer proposes a solution that strikes a balance that reflects my own view of the matter. Under his concept of "active liberty," courts should recognize the functional reasons why the legislature delegates policymaking to agencies. The judiciary should then defer to agency interpretations of statutes so long as they seem consistent with what a reasonable member of Congress would want (Breyer 2006).

## 12.2   MODELS OF POLICYMAKING ACCOUNTABILITY

For policymaking outside the legislature, states balance public participation, expertise, politics, private professional norms, and oversight in very different ways. Out of this experience, I distill four stylized models. Call them the political model, the expertise model, the partisan-balance model, and the privatized model. The political model builds in accountability by entrusting the ultimate decision to those with political affiliations. The expertise model delegates authority to neutral or expert decision makers but may require consultation. Under the partisan-balance model, a politically accountable appointment process leads, in the ideal, to neutral, impartial choices. The privatization model delegates policymaking to a quasi-private body that is largely independent of the government.

### 12.2.1   Political Decision Makers

In the political model, the legislature – a political body – delegates policymaking authority to another politically responsible actor, be it the president, the prime minister, or an individual cabinet member. The civil service may help to frame issues, and legislation may require consultation with experts or the public. However, decisions are in the hands of political actors. The route for redress is the ballot box or a lobbying campaign to amend the statute or replace the politically responsible officials. Judicial oversight plays no role so long as constitutional principles are respected.

An extreme form of political delegation is the power of presidents or prime ministers to issue decrees with the force of law in the absence of explicit delegation by statute. The most salient present-day examples are the decree powers of some Latin American presidents and of the Russian president. In most cases, these powers are time limited and must eventually be submitted to the legislature. Even these, more limited, cases, however, give the executive a first-mover advantage (Carey and Shugart 1998; Rose-Ackerman et al. 2011).

### 12.2.2   Expert Decision Makers

Some issues are not politically contentious. The legislature may safely delegate them to experts inside a government department or in an independent body. For example, a statute might appropriate funds for basic scientific research and leave it to an expert agency to apportion the funds. But many policies, although highly dependent on expertise, generate wide-ranging controversy. In these cases, even if experts have the authority to make the final decision, they often engage in formal consultation.

This model, of course, only makes sense when politicians and their constituents believe that experts both have the relevant information and are motivated to act in the public interest as seen by the legislature. To bring expertise in line with political interests, the implementing statute might specify the framework for expert choice. For example, a statute might require the use of both cost–benefit analysis (CBA) and consultation. Experts would promulgate the final rule, but consultation would help them to obtain information on costs and benefits unavailable from published sources. However, the mere use of analytic methods will seldom resolve controversial issues. Analysis, however competent, cannot eliminate deep disagreements over values.[14]

Furthermore, experts may not be immune to improper influence. The pathological version of the expert-led model is regulatory capture where experts tilt their choices in favor of the regulated industry in the hope of subsequent employment or outright bribes (Stigler 1971). More subtle problems arise when the expert's own knowledge is not sufficient to make an informed choice. Then biased consultation, dominated by the regulated industry, could affect the good-faith decisions of experts.

### 12.2.3 Partisan Balance

The partisan-balance model explicitly acknowledges the tension at the heart of modern regulatory policy – the conflict between political accountability and expertise. There are three variants. Call them the *institutional-constraints model,* the *partisan-balancing model,* and the *impartial-generalist model.* The first two are common in the United States; the third is familiar in the UK.

In the first, institutional-constraints, model, political bodies appoint the decision makers. Sometimes, as for US federal judges, the process requires the consent of two or more partisan bodies. In other cases, appointments require a supermajority that incorporates minority party preferences.[15] Although political factors may dominate at the appointment stage, institutional constraints limit the political pressures on sitting officials, once appointed, and prevent narrow self-seeking. These factors may include long or life terms, fixed minimum salaries, earmarked sources of budgetary funds, overlapping terms for multi-member bodies, removal only "for cause," and restrictions on subsequent employment by the regulated industry. In its pure form, the body makes impartial choices even given a purely partisan or self-interested appointment process. Of course, the flip side is the risk that the regulators will have an idiosyncratic, minority view of good policy that they impose on the polity with little hope of correction.

The second, partisan-balancing, model might also include institutional constraints – as in most US independent regulatory agencies. However, it has some distinct characteristics. Its basic form is a multi-member agency which decides policy issues by majority or supermajority vote. To contrast the two models, imagine a multi-member agency whose appointees represent their political supporters, and where political actors can easily remove them. In a two-party state, for example, a five-member commission might be limited to three members from one party. The commission, operating by majority rule, could sideline those affiliated with the minority party, but that could undermine the perceived legitimacy of its rules and policies.

The third, impartial-generalist, model relies on commissions of inquiry composed of people with reputations for probity and no personal stake in the issue. Thus, impartiality results from the appointment of people who claim to be able to consider matters objectively. The danger is that they are also ignorant. Policy recommendations might be neutral but ill informed. To counter this problem, regulated entities and other stakeholders may have a leading role in presenting material to the commission. On the model of a common law judge, experts and groups who have a narrow private interest in the outcome advise the commission but have no decision-making authority.[16]

### 12.2.4   Privatization

Many countries have a long history of using private or quasi-governmental organizations to set standards. Sometimes the nation's courts enforce these standards as law. In Germany, for example, the German Institute for Norms (DIN) operates under a government charter, and it has regulatory powers under a number of statutes (Rose-Ackerman 1995: 63–5). In most countries the professions regulate themselves through associations with exclusive mandates under rules that generally have legal force.[17]

Privatizing policymaking raises delicate questions about the reach of the state. In some cases, a law gives official status to an existing body with a history of self-regulation. In others, a statute creates a new body, sometimes applying the template of an established group to a new regulatory area. A profession may point to a long history of self-regulation and the possession of esoteric knowledge, as with medical doctors or engineers. Even so, the professional association may impose rules that put overly strict limits on entry and overly lax constraints on service quality. Professional norms may conflict with public interest goals.

Under the corporatist or consensual variant, potentially conflicting interests negotiate to make binding regulations, with or without government input. These decisions may have an impact outside of those at the bargaining table. In the labor-management area, the Scandinavian countries provide the archetypal examples where corporatist structures are strong and labor union membership is high. Few workers and businesses lack representation although even there the practice may fall short (Lewin 1994; Gorges 1996). In other countries the national labor union/business bodies have doubtful legitimacy. For example, in Hungary and Poland labor union membership is in decline, and the composition of the national committees is an artifact of the transition process that has not kept pace with evolving economic realities (Rose-Ackerman 2005: 126–62).

## 12.3   POLICYMAKING ACCOUNTABILITY IN PRESIDENTIAL AND PARLIAMENTARY SYSTEMS

Real-world political systems mix and match the above stylized models. Their adoption depends upon politicians' incentives to create accountable institutions. These incentives depend, in part, upon the underlying constitutional structure, for example whether a parliamentary or a presidential system is in place.

### 12.3.1   Parliamentarianism

Consider a simple, archetypal parliamentary system with a one-house legislature that selects the prime minister and the cabinet (the government), perhaps subject to the nominal approval of a non-executive president or monarch. If the parliament loses confidence in the government, it can fall as a result of a vote in the parliament.[18] If parliament delegates policymaking authority to political decision makers, that authority is, in principle, subject to parliamentary oversight.

Because the same coalition controls both the executive and the legislature, the coalition that controls the government has little reason to require direct accountability to the public in ways that would constrain its own discretion (Moe and Caldwell 1994; Rose-Ackerman 1999). The political model dominates; accountability at the ballot box is the main route for public input.

If electoral competition is based on policy promises, not individual favors to constituents, politicians benefit from a professional civil service. Career officials implement the law, but they are under the formal control of the governing coalition and subject to its policy directives. Furthermore, as a practical matter, the government may fall at any time as the result of a no confidence vote. Hence, political change can occur quickly. If political leaders want to ensure that the state functions during transitions, they are likely to support an organizational structure with a thin political layer and a strong professional civil service. Although delegation is by law to politicians, it will often be de facto to professionals in the civil service who focus on performance accountability (B. Ackerman 2000).

The political incentives to avoid direct policymaking accountability to the public must come to terms with the reality of modern welfare states that administer mass benefit systems. Public officials determine the eligibility of thousands of people applying for disability payments, refugee status, permanent residency, or citizenship. This may encourage politicians to seek to control the civil service either through internal controls on recruitment and promotion or through procedures that permit citizens to lodge complaints in court (Mashaw 2006). However, the government would seek to limit the scope of judicial review to individual cases with an emphasis on performance and rights-based accountability.

The politicians who control the government have little incentive to create independent policymaking agencies outside their direct control or to delegate authority to private entities or groups of stakeholders. They will support full delegation to independent bodies only for highly technical issues, in cases where the objects of regulation are politically powerful enough to obtain (or maintain) self-regulatory authority, or when regulation is an unpleasant necessity in a political minefield (Scott 2009). Partisan balance is unlikely to be an attractive option. If the ruling party is divided, however, disgruntled members of parliament who are not in the cabinet may be strong supporters of independent or quasi-independent agencies. The basic policy initiative has strong support from the governing party, but the backbenchers hope to have more influence over an independent agency than a cabinet department (Bertelli 2008). Perhaps for this reason, Britain has about one hundred "independent" agencies although most are nominally under a cabinet department (Ruffert 2007: 29).

Politicians will resist judicial involvement in political issues and, hence, will not want to permit the courts to review policymaking. Neither cabinet officers nor top civil servants favor judicial review of policymaking. The country's administrative procedures act will cover implementation in particular cases, not rulemaking. A ministry may hold hearings and consult broadly if it wishes, but no one has a legal right to demand such processes. Legal consultation requirements are hortatory recommendations to policymakers that are not subject to judicial enforcement. Courts themselves, however, may seek to extend their reach. In fact, several authors point to the active role that courts presently play in reviewing the administration in parliamentary systems with both civil and common law traditions.[19] Nevertheless, review of government policymaking processes remains rare.

However, politicians do not operate in a vacuum. They respond to pressure from powerful interest groups able to affect reelection chances. They may also leave venerable private regulatory bodies in place rather than stir up opposition. As a result, private or quasi-private groups may have the right to issue binding rules governing their profession or industry.

A simple parliamentary system that excludes judicial review of rulemaking has the virtue of simplicity, but it leaves a gaping hole in the legitimacy of public policymaking that is only partially filled by other institutions. It ignores the dangers of delegation, treating them either as problems of secondary importance or as ones best resolved by the legislature.

Perhaps because of the limitation of a pure parliamentary system, most are more complex than the simple form outlined above. Even in the UK other institutions challenge the authority of Parliament, and the European Union has pushed the state toward more oversight by courts and other institutions (Thatcher 2003). Elsewhere, parliamentary systems generally operate under a written constitution with a state structure that Bruce Ackerman (2000) calls "constrained parliamentarianism" that includes oversight requirements that trump the political wishes of sitting politicians. For example, the constitution might mandate an ombudsman, an independent audit office, an independent prosecutor, a constitutional tribunal, or a special administrative court.

### 12.3.2   Presidentialism

Contrast the parliamentary model with a presidential system where the separation of powers is built into the constitutional structure. Different parties may control the legislature and the presidency. This possibility produces political incentives for the legislature to limit and constrain policymaking delegation.[20] The electoral system will help determine party strength, with proportional representation generating stronger parties than first-past-the-post systems of plurality rule (Shugart 1998). However, even with relatively weak parties, the legislature has an interest in controlling executive branch policymaking. Even if the president is from the legislative majority, legislators will seek to constrain the executive and may do this through detailed substantive laws, required procedures, judicial review, and oversight bodies that report to the legislature. It may also create policymaking institutions that are largely outside of presidential control.

In a presidential system with a powerful legislature, one should expect narrower grants of delegated policymaking authority to the executive compared with a parliamentary system. The complex and dynamic nature of most modern statutory initiatives means that the legislature cannot avoid delegation of policymaking, and, once it delegates authority, executive branch policymaking will be more secure than in a parliamentary system because statutes are difficult to change in a system with multiple veto points (Tsebelis 2002). Hence the legislature has an incentive to keep delegation in check. Direct legislative oversight is a partial answer, with the threat of impeachment as the ultimate background constraint, but intrusive, on-going legislative oversight undermines the benefits of delegation. As an alternative, the legislature might create checks that are not under its control but that accomplish much the same purpose. McCubbins and Schwartz (1984) labeled the choice between direct legislative oversight and outside monitoring as a choice between "police patrols" and "fire alarms." They argue that the United States Congress will often select fire alarms. Outsourcing oversight means that Congress has less direct control, but it saves time and money and permits it to react to serious "fires."

The analogy to fire alarms is, however, not completely apt. Congress has an incentive, not just to outsource warnings of emergencies, but also to turn over the day-to-day monitoring of policymaking to those outside government. Those who send fire alarms to the Congress may engage in their own police patrols of agency policymaking. Procedural constraints that ensure broad public input are one way to facilitate oversight of rulemaking. Furthermore, outsiders may bring a court case, not complain to Congress. Hence Congress may incorporate judicial review into statutes so that the courts can monitor compliance with statutory law (Landes and Posner 1975; Mashaw 2006).

Presidents will want to use their policymaking authority to further their own agendas. Given the legislature's efforts to control executive policymaking, the president may fight back by creating oversight bodies and issuing executive orders that do not require legislative approval. Presidents will seek to control and to claim credit for executive branch policymaking (Kagan 2001).

The legislature in a presidential system has an incentive to create bodies that avoid presidential control and are subject to legislative oversight. One example is the US independent regulatory agencies, which are multi-member bodies with partisan balance. They do not report to the president or a member of the cabinet but are accountable to the legislature. Presidents may accept such agencies if they retain some role in appointing members or if they help achieve a substantive policy victory.

One similarity with a parliamentary system exists. The legislature has no incentive to delegate policymaking to private bodies or corporatist institutions except to avoid blame for unpleasant but necessary policy choices. Outside of the blame-shifting cases, delegation of this kind will occur only when the regulated groups are politically powerful as voting blocs or sources of campaign funding.

In a presidential system, the legislature may support aggressive judicial review of the policy choices of executive branch departments and independent agencies to limit the damage caused by policies hostile to legislative interests. The legislature recognizes the value of delegation but seeks to use the courts to constrain its exercise. However, grants of authority to the courts will be ineffective if few plaintiffs are willing to sue. Thus, to facilitate judicial oversight, some statutes require the state to pay the legal fees of successful plaintiffs or otherwise to lower the costs of judicial review (Miller 1987).

Some argue that legislative delegation represents self-serving efforts to shift tough choices out of the hands of lawmakers and onto bureaucrats and the president (Wilson 1980; Fiorina 1982). Others claim that delegation to agencies, especially independent agencies, permits powerful legislators to favor particular narrow interest groups in a less transparent way than by passing an overtly biased statute (Stigler 1971; Posner 1974; Peltzman 1976). These critics claim that single-purpose agencies risk capture by the very industries they are designed to regulate or even that the legislature intended capture when it passed the law.

If judicial review checks these tendencies, why would it be built into the structure of the law? One answer is that legislatures favor judicial review as a way to avoid making the difficult policy choices themselves (Shapiro 2003). Legislators may want to tie their own hands. Because they face pressure from both special interests and ordinary voters, they write statutes that favor interest groups but set standards for judicial review that limit the damage. The legislators can, in David Mayhew's (1974) phrase, "claim credit" for benefiting a powerful constituency while avoiding an overly severe impact on the general public.

Delegating policymaking to politicians in the government is less problematic for legislators in a parliamentary system than it is in a presidential system. Parliaments will have much less interest in controlling the policymaking discretion of the executive than legislatures in presidential systems. In a presidential system, if a statute gives a president or a cabinet member the authority to make policy, this grant is likely to be hedged about with legal specifics and with references to the types of expertise that must be incorporated into policy choices.

## 12.4   CONCLUSIONS

Constitutional structures can influence the political incentives to delegate policymaking to executive departments, independent agencies, and quasi-private bodies. They also provide different motivations for granting oversight responsibilities to courts or other bodies. These contrasting models of democracy do not imply convergence in the institutions and structures of public law. Instead, although all democracies face common problems of legislative drafting, delegation, and oversight, a strong form of convergence seems unlikely.

Policymaking accountability is central to ensuring the democratic legitimacy of modern states, and administrative law is one route to such accountability. To achieve that goal, different models of policymaking accountability mix public accountability and expertise in different ways. All of them are encountered in various forms and combinations in established democracies. Even so, there are important gaps and inconsistencies in existing law and practice.

As an empirical matter, one ought to expect cross-country differences to result from differences in constitutional structures and the incentives they create for politicians. Those interested in strengthening democracy should not be content with the patterns of delegation, consultation, and oversight that arise from the self-interested behavior of politicians in either parliamentary or presidential systems. The executive has wide-ranging policy discretion in all democracies and, in some, private bodies exercise public functions. The modern regulatory, welfare state needs to expand rights to participate beyond a predetermined group of stakeholders and to make these rights legally enforceable in court. These include rights to know about regulatory initiatives, rights to present data and opinions, and rights to public, reasoned decisions both from public agencies and from quasi-private bodies with regulatory functions. These rights will not arise spontaneously, especially in parliamentary systems. They need strong advocates in civil society.

Furthermore, given the complex and wide-ranging nature of many regulations, experts need to review and improve analytic techniques, but they also need to understand their limits. I have argued elsewhere for a strong form of judicial review under statutes that aim to correct market failures. In reviewing rulemaking under these statutes, courts should require CBA unless the substantive statute explicitly outlaws the technique (Rose-Ackerman 1992: 33–42). Judicial review would then evaluate policies in terms of this criterion and remand decisions that appear to be in conflict, recognizing, of course, that all CBAs involve informed judgments about a number of key variables. Agencies could defend themselves by claiming that the statute forbids the use of CBA or that their application of CBA was within the range of acceptable expert policy choice. This proposal is not purely technical. It supports the norm of net benefit maximization but only for statutes aimed at conventional market failures. The proposal is designed to backstop the legislative process by requiring that lawmakers make explicit any efforts to benefit special interests. Without transparent legislative language, the courts would require regulators to balance costs and benefits impartially.

## NOTES

1. For similar taxonomies see Rose-Ackerman (2005: 5–6), Mashaw (2006), and Bovens (2005). See Harlow (2002: 6–24) and Ziller (2008: 84–5) for various definitions of the term "accountability" and the difficulty of finding appropriate parallel terms in different languages.
2. United States Administrative Procedures Act (USAPS), 5 USC §§553, 706.
3. See, for example, the classical German view of the *Rechtsstaat* under which the administration is subordinate to the law and the route for public involvement is through legislative elections based on party competition (Johnson 1983). See Henne (2003) for a review of Rose-Ackerman (1995), which expressed this view.
4. For example, in Argentina (Volosin 2009) and Poland (Dobrowolski et al. 2007).
5. Compare Bignami (2001), who outlines the development of participation rights in the European Union from a focus on enforcement procedures against individuals or firms to the beginnings of participatory processes in the promulgation of general rules.
6. See, for example, Richardson (2000).
7. Exec. Order No. 12866, 3 C.F.R. 638 (1993). The order was "supplemented and reaffirmed" in Exec. Order No. 13563, 14 C.F.R. 3821 (2011). For an overview see Dudley (2009).
8. The initiative was renamed "Smart Regulation" in October 2010. For background see European Commission (2006). The initiative also advocates more participatory processes, less paperwork, simpler rules, and exploration of alternative regulatory models. See also Wiener and Alemanno (2010) and Dorbeck-Jung and Vrielink-van Heffen (2007).
9. The legislative veto was declared unconstitutional by the US Supreme Court, *Immigration and Naturalization Service v. Chadha*, 462 US 919 (1983).
10. For a global overview see J. Ackerman (2010).
11. On the role of the judiciary outside the United States in reviewing administrative decisions see Magill and Ortiz (2010) and Zwart (2010).
12. USAPA §§701–706. Strauss (1996).
13. *Chevron, USA, v. Natural Resources Defense Council*, 467 US 837 (1984); Cohen and Spitzer (1994); Eskridge and Baer (2008).
14. Rose-Ackerman (2011). Adler and Posner (2006) attempt to modify CBA to take account of some of its purported difficulties, but see Sinden et al. (2009) for a critique. See also Nou (2008).
15. For example, in Hungary justices of the Constitutional Court, the ombudsmen, and the president of the Audit Office all must obtain the support of two-thirds of the Parliament (Rose-Ackerman 2005: 57–60).
16. For comparative law discussion of the structure of agencies see Halberstam (2010), Shapiro (2010), and Sossin (2010).
17. For example, in France 11 professions have been granted some degree of public power (OECD 2010: 114). See also Auby (2010) and Barak-Erez (2010).
18. Votes of no confidence can be unconditional or may be valid only if accompanied by an affirmative vote for a new government. The United Kingdom has the former rule; Germany has the latter.
19. Craig (2010); Donnelly (2010); Magill and Ortiz (2010).
20. The literature on this topic is summarized and some of it is reprinted in Rose-Ackerman (2007).

# REFERENCES

Ackerman, Bruce (2000), 'The new separation of powers', *Harvard Law Review*, **113**, 633–729.
Ackerman, John M. (2010), 'Understanding independent accountability agencies', in S. Rose-Ackerman and P. Lindseth (eds), *Comparative Administrative Law*, Cheltenham, UK and Northampton, MA, USA: Edward Elgar Publishing, pp. 265–76.
Adler, Matthew D. and Eric A. Posner (2006), *New Foundations of Cost–Benefit Analysis*, Cambridge, MA: Harvard University Press.
Arrow, Kenneth J., Maureen L. Cropper, George C. Eads, Robert W. Hahn, Lester B. Lave, Roger G. Noll, Paul R. Portney, Milton Russell, Richard Schmalensee, V. Kerry Smith and Robert N. Stavins (1996), 'Is there a role for benefit–cost analysis in environmental health and safety regulation?', *Science*, **272**, 221–2.
Auby, Jean-Bernard (2010), 'Contracting out and "public values": a theoretical and comparative approach', in S. Rose-Ackerman and P. Lindseth (eds), *Comparative Administrative Law*, Cheltenham, UK and Northampton, MA, USA: Edward Elgar Publishing, pp. 511–23.
Barak-Erez, Daphne (2010), 'Three questions of privatization', in S. Rose-Ackerman and P. Lindseth (eds), *Comparative Administrative Law*, Cheltenham, UK and Northampton, MA, USA: Edward Elgar Publishing, pp. 493–510.
Bertelli, Anthony M. (2008), 'Credible governance? Transparency, political control, the personal vote and British quangos', *Political Studies*, **56** (4), 807–29.
Bignami, Francesca (2001), 'Three generations of participation rights before the European Commission', *Law and Contemporary Problems*, **68**, 61–83.
Bovens, Mark (2005), 'Public accountability', in E. Ferlie, Laurence E. Lynn, Jr. and C. Pollitt (eds), *Oxford Handbook of Public Management*, Oxford: Oxford University Press.
Breyer, Stephen (2006), *Active Liberty*, New York: Alfred A. Knopf.
Carey, John M. and Matthew Soberg Shugart (eds) (1998), *Executive Decree Authority*, Cambridge: Cambridge University Press.
Cohen, Linda R. and Matthew L. Spitzer (1994), 'Solving the *Chevron* puzzle', *Law and Contemporary Problems*, **57**, 65–110.
Craig, Paul (2010), 'Judicial review of questions of law: a comparative perspective', in S. Rose-Ackerman and P. Lindseth (eds), *Comparative Administrative Law*, Cheltenham, UK and Northampton, MA, USA: Edward Elgar Publishing, pp. 449–65.
Dobrowolski, Pawel, Lukasz Gorywoda and Agnieszka Janczuk (2007), *Public Hearings in Poland: A Difficult Way to Participatory Democracy in New Member States*, Florence: European University Institute.
Donnelly, Catherine (2010), 'Participation and expertise: judicial attitudes in comparative perspective', in S. Rose-Ackerman and P. Lindseth (eds), *Comparative Administrative Law*, Cheltenham, UK and Northampton, MA, USA: Edward Elgar Publishing, pp. 357–72.
Dorbeck-Jung, B. and M.O. Vrielink-van Heffen (2007), 'EU ways of governing the marketing of pharmaceuticals – a shift towards more integration, better consumer protection and better regulation?', in V. Gessner and D. Nelken (eds), *European Ways of Law: Towards a European Sociology of Law*, Oxford: Hart Publishing.
Dudley, Susan (2009), 'Lessons learned, challenges ahead', *Regulation*, Summer, 6–11.
Eskridge, William N. and Lauren E. Baer (2008), 'The continuum of deference: Supreme Court treatment of agency statutory interpretation from *Chevron* to *Hamdan*', *Georgetown Law Review*, **96**, 1083–1226.
European Commission (2006), *Better Regulation – Simply Explained*, Luxembourg: Office for Official Publications of the European Communities.
European Commission (2010) Communication from the Commission to the European Parliament, the Council et al., *Smart Regulation in the European Union*, COM/2010/0543final. Available at: http://eur-lex.europa.eu/LexUriServ/LexUriServ.do?uri=CELEX:52010DC0543:EN:NOT
Fiorina, Morris (1982), 'Legislative choice of regulatory forms: legal process or administrative process?', *Public Choice*, **39**, 33–66.
Gorges, Michael J. (1996), *Euro-Corporatism? Interest Intermediation in the European Community*, Lanham, MD: University Press of America.
Halberstam, Daniel (2010), 'The promise of comparative administrative law: a constitutional perspective on independent agencies', in S. Rose-Ackerman and P. Lindseth (eds), *Comparative Administrative Law*, Cheltenham, UK and Northampton, MA, USA: Edward Elgar Publishing, pp. 185–204.
Harlow, Carol (2002), 'Accountability in the European Union', in P. Alston and B. de Witte (eds), *Collected Courses of the Academy of European Law*, Oxford: Oxford University Press.
Henne, Thomas (2003), 'Book review: environmental policy in Germany and the United States: *Controlling Environmental Policy* by Susan Rose-Ackerman', *American Journal of Comparative Law*, **51**, 207–28.
Johnson, Nevil (1983), *State and Government in the Federal Republic of Germany*, Oxford: Pergamon.

Kagan, Elena (2001), 'Presidential administration', *Harvard Law Review*, **114**, 2245–319.

Landes, William M. and Richard Posner (1975), 'The independent judiciary in an interest group perspective', *Journal of Law and Economics*, **18**, 875–901.

Lewin, Leif (1994), 'The rise and decline of corporatism: the case of Sweden', *European Journal of Political Research*, **26**, 59–79.

Magill, M. Elizabeth and Daniel R. Ortiz (2010), 'Comparative positive political theory', in S. Rose-Ackerman and P. Lindseth (eds), *Comparative Administrative Law*, Cheltenham, UK and Northampton, MA, USA: Edward Elgar Publishing, pp. 134–47.

Mashaw, Jerry (2006), 'Accountability and institutional design: some thoughts on the grammar of governance', in M.W. Dowdle (ed.), *Public Accountability: Designs, Dilemmas and Experiences*, Cambridge: Cambridge University Press.

Mayhew, David (1974), *Congress: The Electoral Connection*, New Haven, CT: Yale University Press.

McCubbins, Mathew D. and Thomas Schwartz (1984), 'Congressional oversight overlooked: police patrols and fire alarms', *American Journal of Political Science*, **28** (1), 165–79.

Miller, Jeffrey G. (1987), *Citizen Suits: Private Enforcement of Federal Pollution Control Laws*, New York: John Wiley.

Moe, Terry and Michael Caldwell (1994), 'The institutional foundations of democratic government: a comparison of presidential and parliamentary systems', *Journal of Institutional and Theoretical Economics*, **150**, 116–53.

Nou, Jennifer (2008), 'Regulating the rulemakers: a proposal for deliberative cost–benefit analysis', *Yale Law and Policy Review*, **26** (2), 601–44.

OECD (2010), *Better Regulation in Europe: France*, Paris: OECD.

Peltzman, Samuel (1976), 'Toward a more general theory of regulation', *Journal of Law and Economics*, **19**, 211–40.

Posner, Richard (1974), 'Theories of economic regulation', *Bell Journal of Economics and Management Science*, **5**, 335–58.

Richardson, Henry S. (2000), 'The stupidity of cost–benefit analysis', *Journal of Legal Studies*, **29**, 971–1003.

Rose-Ackerman, Susan (1992), *Rethinking the Progressive Agenda: The Reform of the American Regulatory State*, New York: Free Press.

Rose-Ackerman, Susan (1994), 'Consensus versus incentives: a skeptical look at regulatory negotiation', *Duke Law Journal*, **43**, 1206–20.

Rose-Ackerman, Susan (1995), *Controlling Environmental Policy: The Limits of Public Law in Germany and the United States*, New Haven, CT: Yale University Press.

Rose-Ackerman, Susan (1999), *Corruption and Government: Causes, Consequences and Reformi*, Cambridge: Cambridge University Press.

Rose-Ackerman, Susan (2005), *From Elections to Democracy: Building Accountable Government in Hungary and Poland*, Cambridge: Cambridge University Press.

Rose-Ackerman, Susan (ed.) (2007), *Economics of Administrative Law*, Cheltenham, UK and Northampton, MA, USA: Edward Elgar Publishing.

Rose-Ackerman, Susan (2011), 'Putting cost–benefit analysis in its place: rethinking regulatory review', *University of Miami Law Review*, **65** (2), 335–56.

Rose-Ackerman, Susan and Peter Lindseth (eds) (2010), *Comparative Administrative Law*, Cheltenham, UK and Northampton, MA, USA: Edward Elgar Publishing.

Rose-Ackerman, Susan, Diane A. Desierto and Natalia Volosin (2011), 'Hyper-presidentialism: separation of powers without checks and balances in Argentina and the Philippines', *Berkeley Journal of International Law*, **29** (1), 101–88.

Ruffert, Matthias (2007), 'The transformation of administrative law as a transnational methodological project', in M. Ruffert (ed.), *The Transformation of Administrative Law in Europe*, Munich: Sellier, European Law Publishing.

Scott, Colin (2009), 'Agencification, regulation and judicialization: American exceptionalism and other ways of life', in T. Ginsburg and Albert H.Y. Chen (eds), *Administrative Law and Governance in Asia*, London: Routledge.

Shapiro, Martin (2003), 'Judicial delegation doctrines: the US, Britain, and France', in M. Thatcher and A. Stone Sweet (eds), *The Politics of Delegation*, Oxford: Frank Cass.

Shapiro, Martin (2010), 'A comparison of U.S. and European independent agencies', in S. Rose-Ackerman and P. Lindseth (eds), *Comparative Administrative Law*, Cheltenham, UK and Northampton, MA, USA: Edward Elgar Publishing, pp. 293–308.

Shugart, Matthew Soberg (1998), 'The inverse relationship between party strength and executive strength: a theory of politicians' constitutional choices', *British Journal of Political Science*, **28**, 1–29.

Sinden, Amy, Douglas A. Kysar and David M. Driesen (2009), 'Cost–benefit analysis: new foundations on shifting sand', *Regulation & Governance*, **3**, 27–47.

Sossin, Lorne (2010), 'The puzzle of administrative independence and parliamentary democracy in the common law world: a Canadian perspective', in S. Rose-Ackerman and P. Lindseth (eds), *Comparative Administrative Law*, Cheltenham, UK and Northampton, MA, USA: Edward Elgar Publishing, pp. 205–24.

Stigler, George (1971), 'The theory of economic regulation', *Bell Journal of Economics and Management Science*, **2**, 3–21.

Strauss, Peter L. (1996), 'From expertise to politics: the transformation of American rulemaking', *Wake Forest Law Review*, **31**, 745–77.

Thatcher, Mark (2003), 'Delegation to independent regulatory agencies: pressures, functions and contextual mediation', in M. Thatcher and A. Stone Sweet (eds), *The Politics of Delegation*, Oxford: Frank Cass.

Tsebelis, George (2002), *Veto Players: How Political Institutions Work*, Princeton, NJ: Princeton University Press.

Volosin, Natalia (2009), *Administrative Policymaking in Argentina*, working paper, Yale Law School, New Haven, CT.

Wiener, Jonathan B. and Alberto Alemanno (2010), 'Comparing regulatory oversight across the Atlantic: the Office of Information and Regulatory Affairs in the US and the Impact Analysis Board in the EU', in S. Rose-Ackerman and P. Lindseth (eds), *Comparative Administrative Law*, Cheltenham, UK and Northampton, MA, USA: Edward Elgar Publishing, pp. 309–35.

Wilson, James Q. (1980), *The Politics of Regulation*, New York: Basic Books.

Ziller, Jacques (2008), 'Political accountability in France', in H.B. Luc Verhey and Ilse Van den Driessche (eds), *Political Accountability in Europe: Which Way Forward?*, Groningen: Europa Law Publishing.

Zwart, Tom (2010), 'Overseeing the executive: is the legislature reclaiming lost territory from the courts?', in S. Rose-Ackerman and P. Lindseth (eds), *Comparative Administrative Law*, Cheltenham, UK and Northampton, MA, USA: Edward Elgar Publishing, pp. 148–60.

# 13 Law and regulation: the role, form and choice of legal rules
*Margit Cohn*

The centrality of law to the field of regulation has never been challenged, but the debate over its proper role remains open. This debate comprises two types of questions. The first concerns law's content: should law *command* (authorize and enforce), *steer* (subtly direct) or *facilitate* (create mechanisms for the settlement of arrangements through private ordering and other modes of interaction between parties)? The second type of questions is concerned with the role and form of law itself. In which forms do legal rules appear? Does law function as a symbol or threat, while ensuring the legality of regulatory behavior? And how and why do regulators choose one form of law over another?

This chapter is concerned with the latter type of questions. I begin with an overview of the trends in the study of this issue, which is followed by two taxonomies. The first presents the formal variants of law and their binding force; in the second I move beyond the formal concepts of legality and illegality, and consider the role of law-in-action. Moving away from the simplistic distinction between legality and illegality, this taxonomy surveys different ways in which regulators and regulatees may operate within the confines of legality, albeit in the absence of law's central attributes: the provision of clear, detailed frameworks that both empower and limit all participants in the regulatory space. Using the term "fuzzy law," I consider ways in which law may operate as a symbolic threat (as in the developed literature on enforcement), grant extensive freedom to actors in the context of decision-making, or otherwise be only nominally faithful to the legislative mandate model. The chapter ends with a tentative analysis of the strategic elements of the choice between different forms of law. The study of all of these aspects is necessary for a better understanding of the nature and role of law in the field of regulation.

## 13.1 TRENDS IN THE STUDY OF THE ROLE AND FORM OF REGULATION

Although Philip Selznick's classical definition of the term "regulation" does not refer to law as the ordinator of the "activities valued by the community," it does contain a reference to "sustained and focused control," at least a hint of the possible inclusion of law (Selznick 1985: 363). Colin Scott's more recent definition of regulation refers to "norms," yet again rejecting direct reliance on formal law, a strategy explained below and credited to the growing diffusion of forms and frameworks of action (Scott 2001: 331). Indeed, social, cultural or other norms that have no legal content may be highly instrumental in directing regulatory behavior, but neither Selznick nor Scott would deny the role of law in its various forms in the design and application of regulatory schemes. The creation and application of legal rules is one of the essences of regulation: so much so that several books are dedicated to this aspect or grant it special attention within a general analysis of the discipline (e.g. Ogus 1994; Baldwin 1995; Black 1997; Kerwin 1999; Morgan and Yeung 2007).

Classical studies of regulation have assumed that regulation was initially formed by law, or translated into legalese once designed, and that regulators are required to follow the law to the letter: they are both required to implement its empowering provisions and limited by it. Yet, despite the reliance on the legislative mandate model, not all regulatory arrangements must rely on statute for their existence. When the regulator is a government ministry or located in a government department, its existence precedes statute law and can be derived from the constitution or constitutional arrangements; it need not rely on statute for its existence. Its powers may also derive from general sources, at best traced back to the constitution. For example, the design and implementation of policy regarding the allocation of funds within a regulator's budget and the treatment of applicants wishing to receive a license can both be applied in the absence of a detailed direction in statute.

Discussions of the transformation of the role of law in the context of regulation have been part of the study of the evolution of economic and social governance from state-centered to fragmented, hybrid forms of decision-making, now central to the study of regulation and well analyzed in this handbook (and elsewhere, e.g. Lobel 2004; Scott 2004; Levi-Faur 2005; Parker 2008). The rise of attention to this fragmentation process is paralleled by research on the form and role of law in regulation. State-centrist modes of governance needed less statute law than agency-based regulation, although statute was required in certain areas discussed below. Independent agencies, on the other hand, were created by statute, which also delineated their powers and retained the status of over-arching ordinator. Therefore the regulatory state generated "more rules" not only owing to the requirement to oversee previously state-granted services (Vogel 1996); statute law became essential to the project itself.

The survey begins with Richard Stewart's seminal 1975 article, which analyzed different underlying models, or theories, of administrative action at large (since American administrative law is mainly concerned with government agencies, this influential study is highly relevant to the field of regulation). Under the first, traditional "transmission belt" model, agencies operate under the aegis of statutory direction and cannot interfere with private rights and interest in the absence of statute; delegation is considered anathema to the separation of powers ideal; and courts retain a central role in ensuring agency fidelity to statute. The rise of the alternative, "interest representation" model, no doubt influenced by the social sciences, came to answer some of the inadequacies of the traditional model, mainly its weakness in practice. This alternative model stresses the role of ensuring participation, buttressed by procedural mechanisms inserted in legal frameworks, but carries its own difficulties (Stewart 1975).

This seminal study and the rich study of decision-making in the social sciences draw on pluralist accounts of societies, under which simple "top-down" models could not be sustained. Nonet and Selznick's "responsive law" was offered as an evolutionary improvement over two other forms of law, repressive (power-centered, order-oriented, subordinate to politics, with emphasis on coercion, exception of rulers from law's application, and participation only by submission) and autonomous (procedure-centered, legitimacy-oriented, with emphasis on rules, many of procedural nature, with law being ostensively separate from politics, and participation via institutional frameworks). "Responsive" law is, alternatively, centered on substantive justice, and is competence-oriented, aimed at achieving defined purposes by integrating legal and political aspirations. Responsive law is also designed and implemented through enlarged participation and by positive search for alternatives to replace coercion (Nonet and Selznick 1978).

Ayres and Braithwaite's *Responsive Regulation* (1992) similarly explores alternatives to law-as-coercion in the field of regulation. This highly influential book, aimed at transcending "the intellectual stalemate between those who favor strong regulation of business and those who advocate deregulation" (p. 3), expands the horizons of policy design, recognizing, through the "pyramid" image, that reality challenges assumptions about the actual dominance of law-as-coercion (see further below).

Teubner's parallel, but quite distinct, call for "reflexive" law is based on systems theory, which emphasizes the autonomy and "closed" nature of social subsystems, the legal subsystem included. Subsystems evolve in self-referential ways rather than by interconnection; at best, isolated "couplings" or connective events may occur. Since law is an isolated, self-reflecting system, calls for law to direct the regulatory sphere are doomed to fail. At best, law, owing to its inherently coordinative nature, may provide methods of "democratic self-regulatory mechanisms" (Teubner 1983: 275; see also Teubner 1986, 1993). Essentially, this call for "discursive structures" replaces excessive reliance on a single version of substantive legal rationality with a vision of participatory governance.

Despite their differences (Parker 2008), both "responsive" and "reflexive" theories emphasize the function of law as setting the procedural rules of the regulatory game. This emphasis is echoed in the literature conceptually connected with network theory. Emphasis here is set on the communicative nature of regulation as enabling "conversations" between participants and on the "facilitative" role of law as promoter of such conversations, operating indirectly in a "decentred" sphere, in which fragmentation and interdependency are dominant (Black 1998, 2002a, 2002b). Under the more recent "new governance" model, which encapsulates and solidifies much of the former analysis, the diffusion of power centers is identified, if not celebrated, and law is regarded as the facilitator of participant interaction (e.g. Lobel 2004; Schmidt 2004; Morgan and Yeung 2007; Parker 2008).

Some of this rich body of literature does not deny the nature of law as "hard," a set of rules that should be followed; it calls for a renewed content of this law. Law that sets facilitating processes, or offers model codes of behavior that may be transformed by party consent, still sets ground rules that are to be followed and enforced. Regulation may coerce or facilitate, impose obligations and duties or enable conversations; law may express any of these regulatory strategies, but it should still be obeyed.

Others view the departure from law as more radical. The term "soft law" is often used in studies of governance, including Oren Perez's (Chapter 25) (see also Lobel 2004: 388–95; Mörth 2004; Trubek 2006). The term has received much attention also in the context of transnational and international law (recently, Shaffer and Pollack 2010), and connotes the existence of different levels of flexibility, openness, non-coerciveness, informality and a-legality. The term itself, however, is just as "soft" as its subject; as Lobel notes, "soft law" carries different meanings, embracing modes of private voluntary ordering, consensual regulator–regulated action or weak forms of coercion and enforcement. These are sometimes only tenuously linked to law, sometimes independent of law, assuming law facilitates or tolerates these arrangements, and sometime fully backed by law that prescribes "soft" processes.

Discussion of all of these transformations and permutations would benefit from some ordering. Some analyses of the different dimensions of rules exist: they recognize and classify rules according to legal form or status (statute, secondary legislation, and further down the formal hierarchy), substance (the content of the rules), character (permissive or mandatory), sanction attached and specificity or precision (Baldwin 1995: 8; Black 1995: 96–7). The rest of the chapter builds on this limited existing literature.

## 13.2   LEGAL RULES: A FORMALISTIC TAXONOMY

In this section I classify the different types of rules according to the identity of their authors and their binding force. This part is not concerned with the analysis of law-in-action, which rightfully supplements formalistic analysis in the field of regulation, and is discussed in section 13.3 and elsewhere in this handbook.

The overview is based on two distinctions. The first is formalistic – the classical distinction between domestic law and transnational law. The second concerns the binding force of a legal measure. Here, I distinguish between "direct binding force," occurring when the rule must be obeyed by the persons and entities to which it is directed, its breach resulting in direct penal or civil liability towards state organs, and "indirect binding force," a collection of situations in which the legal rule has strong persuasive force that may, and often does, shape the behavior of participants in the regulation game (for the different types of rules discussed below see Table 13.1).

### 13.2.1   Domestic Rules

Legal rules made within national systems carry different normative status. The highest in status are constitutions and, when recognized by the system, their surrounding penumbrae or interpretations which build on the spirit of the text or of the nation. A constitution may directly grant regulatory powers, clearly so when it defines the powers of the executive. For example, Article II of the US Constitution entrusts the President of the United States, inter alia, with the office of Commander in Chief of the Army and Navy of the United States, thus granting the holder of the office direct regulatory powers in this field of governance. Much can also be drawn from the interpretation of open-ended clauses in the constitution. In the US Constitution, the "take-care" clause has been relied upon in a variety of cases to justify action that extends beyond the mere execution of statutes, and the debate over the nature of the "vesting clause," which can be interpreted prescribing all the specific granted powers in the Article as mere examples of a broader remit of power (e.g. Calabresi and Prakash 1994; Froomkin 1994; Calabresi and Yoo 2008).

Executive powers can also be gleaned from nebulous constitutional-type sources, as "inherent" powers, the spirit of the constitution or its penumbra. In the US, these have tended to be supported in emergency contexts, rather than in more mundane regulatory contexts, and, earlier in the 20th century, as the basis for the seizure of oil-rich lands (for recent examples in the national security context see Yoo 2006, 2010). However, the idea of inherent powers that do not derive from statute is part of many Western countries'

*Table 13.1   Regulation, legal measures: a formalistic taxonomy*

| Source and force | | Details |
|---|---|---|
| *Domestic* | | |
| Directly binding | Constitution | Direct empowerment. |
| | | Open-ended interpretable provisions. |
| | | Provisions or concepts recognizing extra-statutory powers of the central executive. |
| | | Constitution "emanations" and inherent powers. |
| | Statute law | Legislative mandate. |
| | Incorporated Transnational arrangements in dualistic systems | Ratified conventions and agreements, incorporated by statute into domestic law. |
| | Secondary legislation | Regulations, orders and decrees, promulgated under statute by central government, agencies and other public bodies. |
| | Individual measures | Permits, franchises and licenses granted under statute. |
| | Judicial decisions | Binding on parties. |
| Indirectly binding under contract law | Tertiary rules | Internal codes of conduct, circulars and policy statements. |
| | Regulator–regulated arrangements | Contracts and other consensual arrangements. |
| | Private ordering, backed by contract law | Voluntary codes of conduct. |
| Indirectly binding, precedent/persuasive force | Judicial decisions | Indirect effect on future arrangements and third parties. |
| *Transnational* | | |
| Directly binding | Treaties and conventions, when ratified (in monist systems) or ratified and incorporated in domestic law (in dualist systems) | Multilateral/bilateral treaties and conventions. |
| | International customary law | Principles recognized universally applicable (marginal). |
| | Judicial decisions of transnational courts, when national law incorporates binding force | Binding on parties. |
| Indirectly binding, persuasive force | Transnational arrangements in dualistic systems, when unincorporated | |
| | Judicial decisions | Indirect effect on future arrangements and third parties. |

constitutional frameworks and, in Israel, is explicitly recognized in Section 32 of the Basic Law: The Government (Cohn 2002).

Second in status, statutes are usually postulated in the literature as detailed legislative mandates set at the apex of a regulatory regime, which provide complete regulatory frameworks. According to such accounts, the typical legislative mandate: establishes the regulatory body; often defines the regulatory purpose; subjects regulatees to a set of duties and obligations; grants regulatory powers to the regulator, thus enabling it to monitor, supervise, license and perform defined functions regarded as necessary to ensure proper activity in the regulated sector; and authorizes the regulator and law-enforcing bodies to enforce activity, inter alia by applying criminal and sometimes also civil penalties, as defined in the statute.

Statute law is essential to the imposition of some regulatory elements. When the regulator is an independent agency – a legal entity which is separate from central government – its existence must derive from the statute that created it. Independent regulators organized as private corporations have almost disappeared, remaining only in some pockets of self-regulatory agencies, such as bar and law societies. The attention to the legislative mandate, especially evident in the American context, may be explained by the prevalence of independent regulatory agencies in the regulatory sphere of the United States and the rise of this institutional form elsewhere, replacing Weberian bureaucracy (e.g. Gilardi 2005; Jordana and Levi-Faur 2005; Levi-Faur 2005; Black 2007: 60–61). The privatization of sectors and services previously provided by government is a second cause for the centrality of the legislative mandate. The privatization process, from the sale of shares to post-privatization sector activity, is often effected by statute. Under the British model, each sector was privatized by a specific statute, and the privatization statute usually remained the source of legal authority to regulate the sector (e.g. Veljanowski 1991: 11). This form may be common in other systems that entered "the regulation game" via the privatization portal (but see below: privatization may be also effected using private law measures).

Further, under common law, statute law is necessary for the imposition of duties, penalties, and essential parts of any regulatory scheme which has at least some command and control features. Such measures directly affect individual rights and other protected values; legal systems that adhere to liberal and constitutional ideologies require that intervention in individual liberty and property be sanctioned by the people, represented by the legislature. Such a requirement of legality can derive from the constitution or from general principles of legality developed in public law.

Statute law can be an advantageous option to both regulators and regulatees even when not essential. Indeed, the existence of an overarching legislative mandate is considered as the first condition for "good" and legitimate regulation (Baldwin and McCrudden 1987: 33–35; Baldwin 1995: 41–43). Statute law potentially promotes several basic values. First is the democratic principle, which operates throughout the system to require that all rules burdening the citizens should be issued by their representatives. Statute further offers visibility and easy access, which enable regulatees to plan their action. The democratic principle can be restated with a focus on participation, emphasizing the value of market and consumer participation in the making of the rules. Further, accountability and review mechanisms benefit from statute law, as it provides reviewers with yardsticks against which regulatory behavior can be checked.

Secondary legislation, promulgated under empowering provisions set in a statute, is third in status and carries several titles: regulation, order, decree and bylaw are the most common (not all of these measures contain regulatory provisions, although many do). The legal status of such secondary legislation stems from the empowering statute; they cannot extend beyond the grant of power in the legislative mandate, but are just as legally binding as their parent statute. Promulgators of secondary legislation may be agency heads, but just as common are rules enacted by government ministers, even when an agency operates alongside the ministry. In certain cases, even self-regulated sectors may be granted power to promulgate such binding rules.

Tertiary rules, such as guidelines, circulars and codes of conduct, are directed internally and do not derive from explicit authorization in statute (Baldwin and Houghton 1986; Baldwin 1995). They cannot contradict statute, and have no binding legal effect beyond the organization, although they do reflect patterns of behavior that can affect third parties on a regular basis and can be relied upon in court as proof of such patterns.

Further, private law arrangements between regulators and regulatees, mainly contracts and other consensual arrangements, may supplement and even create regulatory arrangements (Daintith 1979; Harden 1992; Collins 1999; Davies 1999). Voluntary codes of conduct and other forms of private ordering may be made in the absence of government or agency direction and are presented as the epitome of "soft law" (as in Wellens and Borchardt's definition of the term; 1989: 274). Their binding force may derive from contract law, which protects properly made consensual arrangements, but, when they are not linked with a statute, their force has little to do with the public element of regulation.

The judiciary can operate as an alternative rulemaking forum in common-law systems (e.g. Rose-Ackerman 2011). By settling disputes between individual parties, domestic courts not only directly impact on the dispute itself, but form standards and rules in piecemeal fashion, fleshing out and interpreting primary and secondary legislation and gradually creating rules of administrative law that set limits to the exercise of discretion (Baldwin and McCrudden 1987, Chapter 4). Judiciaries may also be the authors of detailed regulatory frameworks, extending their function beyond their primary role as settlers of particular disputes. "Micromanaging" regulatory action, courts can make policy by issuing rules of conduct, inter alia in the guise of rules designed to ensure regulators' immunity from future review (e.g. Feeley and Rubin 1998). In systems which accord decisions delivered by high courts the force of judicial precedent, such decisions can shape future arrangements; this type of indirect binding, when highly detailed, has a significant effect on the design and implementation of regulation.

### 13.2.2   Transnational Rules

The term "transnational" is consciously used here to connote all types of legal arrangements made beyond the confines of a single state. The well-established discipline of international law distinguishes between customary international law, the collection of universal rules that are deemed binding on all states without the requirement of any formal incorporation, and treaty law, written agreements that apply to a number of states, ranging from multi-state, via regional, to bilateral (Brownlie 2008: 6–14). The term "transnational" covers all of these measures, as well as different types of private ordering and arrangements which originate neither from the collaboration of states nor from bodies whose members are state-based.

Sorted according to their binding force in the domestic arena, I begin with treaties and conventions, measures that are now central to many areas previously regulated only domestically, such as the protection of the environment, health, labor, international trade, communications and aviation. The binding force of such treaties, when formally ratified by the state (a stage that supplements mere signature), will be self-executing, or directly binding in domestic law, only in states that practice monism, as in the United States and France. Under this constitutional rule, treaties ratified according to the constitution are integrated into domestic law by the mere act of ratification. In dualist states, such as the United Kingdom and Israel, a convention will be binding only when incorporated by statute or by regulations under statute (Brownlie 2008: 31–3). When unincorporated, direct responsibility for its breach lies in the international sphere only, but it still retains a strong persuasive power which shapes internal decisions and thus has a strong indirect binding effect.

Customary international law, deemed to bind all states without any formal requirement, is mainly concerned with political fields such as the creation of states, the immunity of heads of state, and the law of war, and has a marginal role in regulation (but see a recent decision of the International Court of Justice, ruling that the preparation of an environmental impact assessment when a significant risk resulting from a proposed industrial activity is possible is "a requirement under general international law" (*Argentina v. Uruguay* 2010, para. 204).

Regional arrangements provide an additional important layer of transnational rules. The European Union, the most far-reaching and stable of such frameworks, binds its members to regulations (detailed arrangements) and directives (measures setting principles that allow discretion in application). Recommendations and opinions issued by EU institutions have no binding force, but may shape particular decisions of the European Court of Justice and of other EU institutions (Article 288, Treaty on the Functioning of the European Union (EU Treaty) (2008); Craig and de Búrca 2008: 83–6). The EU treaties contain several binding principles, including the requirement to secure free movement of goods, persons, services and capital (Article 26 and throughout, EU Treaty), which have implications for all regulatory arrangements of the member states, and broad principles for the application of policy in a variety of sectors, which carry a declaratory force but direct decision-making, as in the case of energy policy (Article 194, EU Treaty).

Judicial decisions rendered by courts created under transnational arrangements may have implications for regulation, but this role may be of a different nature in comparison to decisions delivered by domestic courts. The binding force of such courts depends on the terms of the arrangement and the extent of incorporation in domestic law. For example, members of the EU and signatories of the European Convention on Human Rights are bound in the domestic sphere by decisions of the respective courts, so far as this body of transnational law is incorporated into domestic law. Even when unincorporated, decisions carry a strong persuasive effect, which is also evident with regard to the effect of a decision on future regulatory behavior.

## 13.3 LEGALITY, ILLEGALITY AND THE ROLE OF LAW

The formalistic taxonomy above assumes a dichotomy between legality and illegality, and draws its legitimacy from the simplistic idea that statute law should and can provide detailed direction to actors. Of course, this distinction has never been clear-cut for a number of inherent reasons: the indeterminacy of the text, different modes of its application, and possible attitudinal changes in time and place, essentially render the search for pure legality an impossible one. Further, realities justify the rejection of a form of absolute legality, to be expressed by a fully detailed statute, implemented and enforced to a tee. In this section I offer an overview of the different roles of law, in which its "fuzziness" enables actors to act within the confines of legality, but without the strict constraints dictated by the edicts of absolute legality (Table 13.2). I do not discuss "pure illegality," or breach of law, since in such cases the question of the legitimacy of the action is settled. The open-ended cases, to be now discussed, offer better prospects for actors who wish to advance their interests without risking their legal integrity.

First is the absence of legislative mandate. As discussed above, regulation administered by central government need not rely on statute, as long as it does not impose criminal or civil liability or is not otherwise strongly restrictive of human behavior. In such cases, regulation may rely on constitutional sources, such as Article II of the US

*Table 13.2   The role of law in regulation: fuzzy practices*

| Type | Nature | Details/examples |
| --- | --- | --- |
| "Absence" of law | No legislative mandate, but various legal power sources | Constitutional sources (constitutional provisions, prerogative, inherent executive powers). Budget/appropriation laws. Private law powers (contract, consensual arrangements), unilateral state action (subsidies), market and finance transactions, private ordering and self-regulation. |
| Sweeping delegation/ discretion | Broad empowering statutes | Absence of direction in delegation/ discretion. |
| Lopsided mandate | Statute chosen only if necessary by law, or in order to empower and not limit | Frameworks intentionally impartial re state power. |
| Selective enforcement/ creative compliance | Extensive informal enforcement; law as "last resort"/"benign big gun" | Negotiated, consensual arrangements in lieu of prosecution. |
| Extra-statutory parallel arrangements | Introduction of parallel schemes outside of law | Incentive programs complementary to statutes. |
| Pastiche law | "Dead letter" law, unimplemented statute | Laws enacted under pro-legislation pressure with insufficient further support. |

Constitution, discussed above. Much of constitution-derived action pertains to high policy such as external relations and national security, but other areas, such as the taking of oil-rich lands and the creation of native American reservations, have been recognized as drawing on a vague constitutional basis (*United States v. Midwest Oil* 1915). Importantly, presidential executive orders, the legal/constitutional source of which is still debated (e.g. Mayer 2002; Howell 2003; Rose-Ackerman 2011), set the contours of the Office of Management and Budget in the White House and famously set requirements for cost–benefit analysis by major agencies (for the first executive orders on both issues see E.O. 11541 (1970) and E.O. 12291 (1981), both replaced since). In the UK, the royal prerogative remains the basis for the regulation of the civil service and the passport regime, and, in Israel, Section 32 of the Basic Law: The Government authorizes the government to act in the absence of statute, as long as no individual right is implicated; this provision has been relied upon, inter alia, as a basis for the operation of subsidy regimes (*Gross v. Ministry of Education* 1991).

Private law powers offer an additional basis for regulatory action in the absence of statutes. For example, when regulation is introduced after privatization, much of the regulatory regime may be found in the contract of sale of shares; agreements between regulators and regulatees are common features in regulatory frameworks, often fleshing out a rather thin statute or operating in the absence of explicit empowerment; and private ordering may rely on no legislative mandate.

Second are sweeping, open-ended grants of delegation and discretion. Such grants are common features of the legislative mandate. Statutes often grant discretion, delegate rulemaking powers, and empower regulators to delegate defined powers to agency employees or others (e.g. delegation of search and inspection powers). Public lawyers and political scientists have explored the extent of delegation and discretion, argued for their necessity in today's complex fast-changing world and, in certain cases, for their political necessity in unresolved issues (Davis 1969; Fiorina 1981; Aranson et al. 1982; Galligan 1986; Huber and Shipan 2002; Rose-Ackerman 2011). The enaction of an umbrella law that lacks direction and offers regulators a de facto free hand is not dictated by the above needs and does not impose a strict legality rule; in such cases law operates merely as a mechanism for the grant of legitimacy, since most modes of behavior will be found within its confines.

Further, certain legislative mandates may provide only parts of a regulatory regime. Such is the case when legislation is passed to answer pressing needs, rather than to provide a full framework of action, or when the statute is limited to fields of action that necessitate legislation. For example, a privatization statute may authorize privatization or sale of shares, but refrain from setting limits on post-privatization supervision of the privatized concern, despite its subjection to some form of regulation; a statute may grant supervision/command and control powers, since they cannot be invoked in its absence, but neglect to introduce other provisions – the outcome usually being that such powers can be invoked without statute-based restrictions. Such "lopsided statutes" are then supplemented by a variety of non-statutory practices.

Fuzziness is central to the literature on enforcement, which is by far the most developed in the context of analysis of law-in-action. Informal modes of enforcement include bargaining, negotiation and persuasion (Bardach and Kagan 1982; Hawkins 1984, 1986: 1168–71; Hawkins and Thomas 1984). Ayres and Braithwaite's "enforcement pyramid" likewise presents a scale ranging from persuasion (the most common strategy), through the issuing of warning letters, and the imposition of civil penalties, criminal penalties and license suspension, and ending with license revocation (Ayres and Braithwaite 1992: 35).[1] Much of this literature views these latter practices as skirting the limits of legality or as quasi-legal practices (e.g. action "in the shadow of the law," Veljanowski 1991: 22; Teubner 1987: 34). Similar scales or pyramids can be drawn also in the context of rule-making. A statute may be found at the apex of this pyramid, below it secondary legislation, then tertiary rules and, finally, types of non-statutory powers, to be now discussed. Note, however, that this structure need not necessarily be in pyramid form; the two lowest strata may not be the most common.

In the context of compliance, still part of the enforcement study, market behavior which is contrary to the spirit of the law but still "perfectly legal" by conforming with the letter of the law has been coined "creative compliance" and discussed in the context of tax evasion (McBarnet 1988; McBarnet and Whelan 1991, 1999). Agency non-compliance with statute need not be downright illegal; agencies may be "shirking by undersupplying policy outcomes; pursuing policy objectives that are inconsistent with the preference of elected political officials; or creating new, organized political interests" (McCubbins et al. 1987: 23), all of which can be achieved without stepping out of the zone of legality.

Moving to other forms of fuzziness, some allocative powers may be employed even when statute provides a seemingly overarching framework. For example, ex gratia payments and various types of support may be granted in addition to statutory arrangements. Legal limits to such activity may be set when a strict residuality doctrine, under which no supplementary powers may be invoked once a statute governs the area, rules out parallel arrangements, but such a rule is often weak and applied sparingly (Cohn 2005).

Finally, despite the existence of statute, regulation de facto may have little to do with the statute. This may happen when pro-legislation forces render legislation necessary or advantageous. Legislation may be a political show of power in response to crises or issues that attract strong pro-legislation forces. States may, for example, legislate a detailed law to "fight" road accidents, or an anti-pollution law in response to their duties under transnational law, without intending to follow its edicts; alternatively, the transformation of law to "dead letter law" may be gradual, for example when "benign big guns" lose their force owing to disuse. Under these conditions, legislation is no more than "pastiche," and the rules are to be found elsewhere.

In all such cases in which statute law cannot be viewed as the single and all-encompassing source of power, regulators may rely on non-statutory powers that enable such practices, as exemplified in the literature on regulatory enforcement mentioned above. Importantly, the role of formal law is redefined in such cases: from central ordinator to provider of a fuzzy source of legitimacy, which allows the development of alternative, but not illegal, modes of behavior.

## 13.4 CONCLUDING REMARKS: ON THE CHOICE OF LEGAL FORM

The choice of legal form of a regulatory regime is a strategic decision that impacts on the extent and type of available powers and on further developments of these regimes, as well as on, as some assume, the success and efficiency of a policy package. This section is concerned with the *choice* of the legal status of the rule, setting aside questions of rule content and, indeed, its implementation and enforcement.

Designers of regulatory frameworks may be able to choose between a detailed statutory arrangement, the grant of discretion/delegation of rulemaking powers, and non-statutory mechanisms. Legal systems may set constraints on this choice. As discussed above, certain rules – those setting criminal and other sanctions, or creating new independent agencies – require a statutory basis. In certain systems these provisions must be specifically embedded in statute; in others, secondary legislation may suffice.

When a full choice exists, its analysis can follow several paths. The first is normative in nature. Statute law is considered the highest form of legal regulatory organization, as it has the best potential to achieve several important values. As above, the legislative process injects democratic legitimacy and enables participation; once legislated, statute is readily accessible and, being written, offers clarity, promoting the ability both of regulatees and of the public at large to plan ahead; further, statute law both legitimizes and assists the application of accountability and review mechanisms, again owing to the existence of an accessible, relatively clear set of rules (Baldwin and McCrudden 1987; Cohn 2001). Further normative studies explain the benefits of delegation of rulemaking power, thereby forwarding "managerial" justifications for the growth of secondary legislation. The classic literature points at agency/executive expertise, efficiency, inability of legislatures to address all issues owing to "the explosion" of areas to be regulated, the need for speedy adaption of existing rules, and the like (Davis 1969; Aranson et al. 1982; Baldwin 1995). Black (1995) offers several considerations to be taken into account by regulators, including certainty and flexibility, inducing compliance, and exercising control. This public interest-focused model also strongly implies that the rule type should be tailored according to the sector's specificities.

Under a second, much travelled path, the choice of rule type is assessed as a strategic decision. The vast literature on the politics of delegation/discretion is joined by interconnecting analyses that focus on the choice of detail or the clarity of rules. Models may be legislative-centered, when they consider the benefits accrued by legislators, weighing, for example, benefits for the legislator, decision-making costs, responsibility shifting, ideology and uncertainty (e.g. Fiorina 1981); others approach the issue under the assumption of agency and executive dominance, and offer more complex accounts of inter-branch dynamics, from analyses that map the interests of a variety of actors (e.g. Aranson et al. 1982) to models that identify various factors that operate as determinants of the degree of discretion granted to agencies (such as the degree of inter-branch conflict, the ability to rely on ex-statutory checking mechanisms over the executive, and the capacity of the legislature to enact its policy preferences; e.g. Epstein and O'Halloran 1994, 1999; Huber and Shipan 2002). These studies are concerned with the degree of detail, delegation and discretion granted in statute, and at least indirectly address the question of choice between primary and secondary legislation. The literature on the choice of non-statutory arrangements is more limited, but applies similar interest-oriented models (e.g. Cohn 2002).

A third direction of study provides tools for analysis of the choice of rule type, mapping the different considerations to be taken into account. Here one can draw on Kagan's (1994) taxonomy of factors, originally created in the context of the study of regulatory enforcement, which are divided into four groups (legal design, task environment, political environment, and leadership factors). Harmathy's list contains everything from global politics to methods of micro-economic planning, spanning political ideology, specific characteristics of the policy field, institutional structure, systemic influence and constitutional provisions (Harmathy 1988). Cohn (2002) offers a three-dimensional grid of factors influencing fuzziness, under which different combinations of organizational-level factors (global, national, sectoral), market-level factors (structure, culture) and legal factors (structure, culture) can be considered to assess the social forces affecting the choice of form of law.

Sector-specific analyses may identify trends in choice of rule type. For example, Daintith's edited volume (1988), which offered a comparative analysis of regulatory frameworks in two sectors, the energy sector and the manpower sector in five European states between 1973 and 1982, found, inter alia, that regulation of the energy sector tends to be less formal than regulation of the workplace. Barely one-quarter of the measures applicable in the energy sector originated from parliament, while the ratio in the manpower sector was over 50 percent (Jarass 1988: 92).

To conclude: while law is an essential part of any regulatory regime, its functions and forms are many and malleable. This chapter surveys this complex terrain by mapping the formal variants of law, the roads which can be taken by participants in the regulatory sphere who wish to maintain legality but limit the role of law as sole ordinator, and the paths available to designers of regulatory frameworks and regulators with regard to the form of law. The central role of law as a legitimating and empowering agent justifies a continued attention to this aspect.

## ACKNOWLEDGEMENTS

I thank Moshe Hirsch and David Levi-Faur for invaluable comments and suggestions. The usual caveat applies.

## NOTE

1.  This, of course, applies to licensing regimes. In others, criminal sanctions can be found at the top of the pyramid. Ayres and Braithwaite's "enforcement strategies" pyramid (1992: 39) considers the content, not the type of legal rule applied. The distinction between content and form is central to this chapter.

## REFERENCES

Aranson, P.H., E. Gellhorn and G.O. Robinson (1982), 'A theory of legislative delegation', *Cornell Law Review*, 68, 1–67.
Ayres, I. and J. Braithwaite (1992), *Responsive Regulation: Transcending the Deregulation Debate*, New York: Oxford University Press.
Baldwin, R. (1995), *Rules and Government*, Oxford: Clarendon.
Baldwin, R. and J. Houghton (1986), 'Circular arguments: the status and legitimacy of administrative rules', *Public Law*, **1986**, 239–84.
Baldwin, R. and Christopher McCrudden (1987), *Regulation and Public Law*, London: Weidenfeld & Nicolson.

Bardach, E. and R.A. Kagan (1982), *Going by the Book*, Philadelphia: Temple University Press.
Black, J.M. (1995), '"Which arrow?" Rule type and regulatory policy', *Public Law*, **1995**, 94–117.
Black, J.M. (1997), *Rules and Regulators*, Oxford: Clarendon Press.
Black, J.M. (1998), 'Regulation as facilitation: negotiating the genetic revolution', *Modern Law Review*, **61**, 621–59.
Black, J.M. (2002a), 'Regulatory conversations', *Journal of Law and Society*, **29**, 163–96.
Black, J.M. (2002b), 'Decentring regulation: understanding the role of regulation and self-regulation in a post-regulatory world', *Current Legal Problems*, **2002**, 103–46.
Black, J.M. (2007), 'Tensions in the regulatory state', *Public Law*, **2007**, 58–73.
Brownlie, I. (2008), *Principles of Public International Law*, 7th edn, Oxford: Oxford University Press.
Calabresi, S.G. and S. Prakash (1994), 'The president's power to execute the laws', *Yale Law Journal*, **104**, 541.
Calabresi, S.G. and C.S. Yoo (2008), *The Unitary Executive: Presidential Power from Reagan to Bush*, New Haven, CT: Yale University Press.
Cohn, M. (2001), 'Fuzzy legality in regulation: the legislative mandate revisited', *Law and Policy*, **23**, 469–97.
Cohn, M. (2002), *General Powers of the Executive Branch*, Jerusalem: Harry Sacher Institute.
Cohn, M. (2005), 'Medieval chains, invisible inks: on non-statutory powers of the executive', *Oxford Journal of Legal Studies*, **25**, 97–122.
Collins, H. (1999), *Regulating Contracts*, Oxford: Oxford University Press.
Craig, P. and G. de Búrca (2008), *EU Law*, 4th edn, Oxford: Oxford University Press.
Daintith, T. (1979), 'Regulation by contract: the new prerogative', *Current Legal Problems*, **32**, 41.
Daintith, T. (ed.) (1988), *Law as an Instrument of Economic Policy: Comparative and Critical Approaches*, Berlin: de Gruyter.
Davies, A.C.L. (1999), 'Using contracts to enforce standards: the case of waiting times in the National Health Service', in C. McCrudden (ed.), *Regulation and Deregulation*, Oxford: Clarendon Press.
Davis, K.C. (1969), *Discretionary Justice: A Preliminary Inquiry*, Westport, CT: Greenwood Press.
Epstein, D. and S. O'Halloran (1994), 'Administrative procedures, information, and agency discretion', *American Journal of Political Science*, **38**, 697–722.
Epstein, D. and S. O'Halloran (1999), *Delegating Powers: A Transaction Cost Politics Approach to Policymaking under Separate Powers*, Cambridge: Cambridge University Press.
Feeley, M.M. and E.L. Rubin (1998), *Judicial Policy Making and the Modern State: How the Courts Reformed America's Prisons*, Cambridge: Cambridge University Press.
Fiorina, M.P. (1981), 'Legislative choice of regulatory forms', *Public Choice*, **39**, 33–66.
Froomkin, A.M. (1994), '*The imperial presidency's new vestments*', *Northwestern University Law Review*, **88**, 1346–76.
Galligan, D.J. (1986), *Discretionary Powers: A Legal Study of Official Discretion*, Oxford: Clarendon Press.
Gilardi, F. (2005), 'The institutional foundations of regulatory capitalism: the diffusion of independent regulatory agencies in Western Europe', *Annals of the American Academy of Political and Social Sciences*, **598**, 84–101.
Harden, I. (1992), *The Contracting State*, Buckingham: Open University Press.
Harmathy, A. (1988), 'The influence of legal systems on modes of implementation of economic policy', in Daintith (ed.), *Law as an Instrument of Economic Policy: Comparative and Critical Approaches*, Berlin: de Gruyter, pp. 245–66.
Hawkins, K. (1984), *Environment and Enforcement: Regulation and the Social Definition of Pollution*, Oxford: Clarendon Press.
Hawkins, K. (1986), 'On legal decision-making', *Washington and Lee Law Review*, **42**, 1161–1242.
Hawkins, K. and John M. Thomas (eds) (1984), *Enforcing Regulation*, Boston: Kluwer-Nijhoff.
Howell, W.G. (2003), *Power without Persuasion: The Politics of Direct Presidential Action*, Princeton, NJ: Princeton University Press.
Huber, J.D. and C.R. Shipan (2002), *Deliberate Discretion? The Institutional Foundations of Bureaucratic Autonomy*, Cambridge: Cambridge University Press.
Jarass, H.D. (1988), 'Regulation as an instrument of economic policy', in T. Daintith (ed.), *Law as an Instrument of Economic Policy: Comparative and Critical Approaches*, Berlin: de Gruyter, pp. 75–96.
Jordana, J. and D. Levi-Faur (2005), 'The diffusion of regulatory capitalism in Latin America: sectoral and national channels in the making of a new order', *Annals of the American Academy of Political and Social Sciences*, **598**, 102–24.
Kagan, R.A. (1994), 'Regulatory enforcement', in D.H. Rosenbloom and R.D. Schwartz (eds), *Handbook of Regulation and Administrative Law*, New York: Marcel Dekker.
Kerwin, C.M. (1999), *Rulemaking: How Government Agencies Write Law and Make Policy*, 2nd edn, Washington, DC: CQ Press.
Levi-Faur, D. (2005), 'The global diffusion of regulatory capitalism', *Annals of the American Academy of Political and Social Sciences*, **598**, 12–32.

Lobel, O. (2004), 'The renew deal: the fall of regulation and the rise of governance in contemporary legal thought', *Minnesota Law Review*, **89**, 342–470.

Mayer, K. (2002), *With the Stroke of a Pen*, Princeton, NJ: Princeton University Press.

McBarnet, D. (1988), 'Law, policy, and legal avoidance: can law effectively implement egalitarian policies?', *Journal of Law and Society*, **15**, 113–21.

McBarnet, D. and C. Whelan (1991), 'The elusive spirit of the law: formalism and the struggle for legal control', *Modern Law Review*, **54**, 848–71.

McBarnet, D. and C. Whelan (1999), 'Challenging the regulators: strategies for resisting control', in C. McCrudden (ed.), *Regulation and Deregulation*, Oxford: Clarendon Press.

McCubbins, M.D., R.G. Noll and B. Weingast (1987), 'Administrative procedures as instruments of political control', *Journal of Law, Economy and Organization*, **3**, 243–77.

Morgan, B. and K. Yeung (2007), *An Introduction to Law and Regulation*, Cambridge: Cambridge University Press.

Mörth, U. (ed.) (2004), *Soft Law in Governance and Regulation: An Interdisciplinary Analysis*, Cheltenham, UK and Northampton, MA, USA: Edward Elgar Publishing.

Nonet, P. and P. Selznick (1978), *Law and Society in Transition: Towards Responsive Law*, New York: Harper.

Ogus, A. (1994), *Regulation: Legal Form and Economic Theory*, Oxford: Clarendon Press.

Parker, C. (2008), 'The pluralization of regulation', *Theoretical Inquiries in Law*, **9**, 349–69.

Rose-Ackerman, S. (2011), 'Accountable Regulation: Parliamentary versus Presidential Systems', in D. Levi-Faur (ed.), *Handbook on the Politics of Regulation*, Cheltenham: Edward Elgar.

Schmidt, P. (2004), 'Law in the age of governance', in J. Jordana and D. Levi-Faur (eds), *The Politics of Regulation: Institutions and Regulatory Reforms for the Age of Governance*, Cheltenham, UK and Northampton, MA, USA: Edward Elgar Publishing.

Scott, C. (2001), 'Analysing regulatory space: fragmented resources and institutional design', *Public Law*, **2001**, 283–305.

Scott, C. (2004), 'Regulation in the age of governance: the rise of the post-regulatory state', in J. Jordana and D. Levi-Faur (eds), *The Politics of Regulation: Institutions and Regulatory Reforms for the Age of Governance*, Cheltenham, UK and Northampton, MA, USA: Edward Elgar Publishing.

Selznick, P. (1985), 'Focusing organizational research on regulation', in R.Q. Noll (ed.), *Regulatory Policy and the Social Sciences*, Berkeley: University of California Press.

Shaffer, G.C. and M.A. Pollack (2010), 'Hard vs. soft law: alternatives, complements, and antagonists in international governance', *Minnesota Law Review*, **94**, 706–99.

Stewart, R.B. (1975), 'The reformation of American administrative law', *Harvard Law Review*, **88**, 1667–1813.

Teubner, G. (1983), 'Substantive and reflexive elements in modern law', *Law and Society Review*, **17**, 239–85.

Teubner, G. (1986), 'After legal instrumentalism? Strategic models of post-regulatory law', in G. Teubner (ed.), *Dilemmas of Law in the Welfare State*, Berlin: de Gruyter, pp. 299–325.

Teubner, G. (1987), 'Juridification: concepts, aspects, limits, solutions', in G. Teubner (ed.), *Juridification of Social Spheres*, Berlin: de Gruyter, pp. 3–48.

Teubner, G. (1993), *Law as an Autopoietic System*, trans. A. Bankowska and R. Adler, ed. Zenon Bankowski, Oxford: Blackwell.

Trubek, L.G. (2006), 'New governance and soft law in health care reform', *Indiana Health Care Law Review*, **3**, 139–70.

Veljanowski, C. (1991), 'The Regulation Game', in C. Veljanowski (ed.), *Regulators and the Market*, London: IEA, pp. 3–22.

Vogel, S.K. (1996), *Freer Markets, More Rules: Regulatory Reform in Advanced Industrial Countries*, Ithaca, NY: Cornell University Press.

Yoo, J. (2006), *The Powers of War and Peace: The Constitution and Foreign Affairs*, Chicago: University of Chicago Press.

Yoo, J. (2010), *Crisis and Command: A History of Executive Power from George Washington to George W. Bush*, New York: Kaplan.

Wellens, K.C. and G.M. Borchardt (1989), 'Soft law in European community law', *European Law Review*, **14**, 267–321.

## Executive Orders

Exec. Order 11541, 35 FR, 3 CFR, 1966-1970 Comp., p. 939 (1970).

Exec. Order 12291, 46 FR 13193, 3 CFR, 1981 Comp., p. 127.

## Judicial Decisions

Case Concerning Pulp Mills on the River Uruguay (*Argentina v. Uruguay*), 20 April 2010, at http://www.hague-
    justiceportal.net/Docs/Court%20Documents/ICJ/Argentine_Vs_Uruguay_judjment.pdf.
HCJ 381/91 *Gross v. Ministry of Education*, 46(1) P.D. 53.
*United States v. Midwest Oil*, 236 US 459 (1915).

# 14 The independence of regulatory authorities
*Fabrizio Gilardi and Martino Maggetti*

## 14.1 INTRODUCTION

The thesis of the "rise of the regulatory state," put forward most forcefully by Majone (1994, 1997) well over a decade ago, has proved to be more accurate than many skeptics thought. Regulation has indeed become one of the main governance forms, and the breadth of its spread, across both policy areas and countries, has led some authors to conclude that we are witnessing the rise of a new type of political economy, namely "regulatory capitalism" (Levi-Faur 2005, 2006a).

This powerful trend is epitomized by the worldwide establishment and strengthening of independent regulatory agencies, that is, regulators that are not under the direct control of elected politicians. More precisely, they are highly specialized bodies that hold considerable public authority while enjoying the highest discretionality in the public sector (Majone 1996), because they are institutionally and organizationally disaggregated from the ordinary bureaucracy (Verschuere et al. 2006) and constitutionally separated from elected politicians (Thatcher 2002). This type of regulatory authority was once confined to specific sectors (such as financial markets) or countries (the United States), but it has now become common in many policy areas and all countries (Jordana et al. forthcoming). Prominent examples include the Financial Services Authority in Britain, the Food and Drug Administration in the United States, and the Bundeskartellamt in Germany. This phenomenon is not an academic curiosity; its consequences are concrete and wide-ranging. The spread of independent regulators means that more and more aspects of our lives are shaped by decisions made by institutions that are not elected and that are not under the direct control of elected officials, which has important implications for the democratic accountability of policy-making.

This chapter offers a theoretical and empirical assessment of the main feature of this type of regulatory institutions, namely their independence. We first discuss the distinction between formal and informal (or de facto) independence, and we show how they can be conceptualized and measured. We argue that both dimensions are important and capture different facets of the independence of regulators. We then present data on these two dimensions, and we discuss the main arguments that have been developed to account for cross-national and cross-sectional variations in European countries. In particular, we show that formal independence is not always associated with de facto independence and that, on the other hand, some regulators can be independent in practice without being independent on paper. The conclusion underlines the relevance of regulatory independence, and of its study, for enhancing our understanding of the ongoing processes of re-regulation and agencification in contemporary political economies.

## 14.2   CONCEPTUALIZATION AND OPERATIONALIZATION

There is no consensus on how independence should be conceptualized and operationalized, and studies use various strategies to capture the idea that some regulators are more strongly insulated from external influence (Verhoest et al. 2004). We consider that independence requires the presence of two components (Maggetti 2007). First, independence means self-determination, namely the faculty of actors to judge their own interests and values (Dahl 1989). When applied to political institutions, this dimension can be measured by the extent to which their interests and values are distinguishable from those of other social forces (Huntington 1968). At the same time, the deployment of autonomy also requires the ownership of one's actions (Walzer 1983), so that political institutions can be considered autonomous only when they can translate their own interests and values (e.g., preferences) into (authoritative) actions, without external constraints (Nordlinger 1981). The concept of organizational autonomy should not be understood in an absolute but in a relative sense (Sartori 1973). Organizations are not self-referential autopoietic systems (Teubner 1988), but need to be considered open systems (Kickert 1993). Thus public sector agencies are neither fully autonomous from nor fully dependent upon their environment, and their preferences and behavior are always shaped by their social interactions with other actors. Our conceptualization of autonomy points out the extent to which preferences and consequent organizational activity are mostly endogenously formed or, conversely, externally affected. The underlying assumption is that these (relative) levels, situated on a continuum between the two extremes, may vary significantly among agencies. They are shaped by statutory provisions but are not fully determined by them. Accordingly, we distinguish between the formal and the de facto independence of regulators.

The concept of formal independence was originally developed in the literature on central banks (Rogoff 1985). In its most encompassing version, central bank independence comprises two elements (Alesina and Summers 1993): political independence, defined as the ability to select policy objectives without influence from the government, and economic independence, that is, the ability to use instruments of monetary policy without restrictions. The various existing indices of central bank independence are usually based on statutory prescriptions, such as the procedure for appointing the members of the board, the approval requirements for monetary policy decisions, the prior definition of monetary objectives in the central bank statute, and the budgetary arrangements (Cukierman 1992; Cukierman et al. 1992; Alesina and Summers 1993).

Gilardi (2002, 2005a, 2008) drew inspiration from this approach to assess the formal independence of other regulatory agencies. To do so, he considered a series of prescriptions, enshrined in the constitutions of agencies, that should guarantee their independence from elected politicians. The operationalization of formal independence put forward by Gilardi is summarized in the first half of Table 14.1. The first dimension refers to the status of the agency head and/or management board. Crucial information here is the length of the term of office (longer terms increase independence), whether agency officials are appointed by a single actor such as a minister or by a more encompassing procedure, whether they can be dismissed, whether the appointment is renewable, whether it is compatible with other public offices, and finally whether the independence of officials is an explicit requirement. The second dimension is the relationship between the agency

*Table 14.1   Operationalizing the independence of regulatory authorities*

| Formal | Chairperson and management board | Term of office. |
|---|---|---|
| | | Appointment procedure. |
| | | Dismissal procedure. |
| | | Renewability of appointment. |
| | | Compatibility with other offices. |
| | | Formal requirements of independence. |
| | Relationship with elected politicians | Independence formally stated. |
| | | Formal obligations. |
| | | Overturning of decisions. |
| | Finances and organization | Source of the budget. |
| | | Agency's internal organization. |
| | | Control of human resources. |
| | Regulatory competencies | Rule-making. |
| | | Monitoring. |
| | | Sanctioning. |
| De facto | From politicians | Frequency of revolving door. |
| | | Frequency of contacts. |
| | | Influence on budget. |
| | | Influence on internal organization. |
| | | Partisanship of nominations. |
| | | Political vulnerability. |
| | | External influence on regulation. |
| | From regulatees | Frequency of revolving door. |
| | | Frequency of contacts. |
| | | Adequacy of budget. |
| | | Adequacy of internal organization. |
| | | Professional activity of chairperson/board members. |
| | | External influence on regulation. |

*Source:*   Gilardi (2008); Maggetti (2007, 2009).

and elected politicians, namely whether the independence of the authority is formally stated, what its formal obligations are, and under which conditions its decisions can be overturned. The third dimension considers the financial and organizational independence of the agency, which depends on whether the budget comes from the government or from other sources (such as fees levied on the regulated firms) and on whether the agency is free to organize its internal structures and to determine its staff policy (for instance, salary structures). The final dimension captures the competencies that are delegated to the authority. The coding scheme put forward by Gilardi is to some extent arbitrary, and recent work has tried to improve upon it. Hanretty and Koop (2009), for instance, have used item-response methods to derive data-driven measures of independence. The resulting index is quite strongly correlated with Gilardi's, but such efforts to develop a more systematic way to measure independence are certainly welcome.

The formal aspects of independence are without any doubt important. In particular, they are the primary dimension that political principals can control when delegating powers to regulatory authorities. However, they are obviously not everything, and there is little reason to believe that formal independence automatically translates into independence in practice. Thus it is important that the de facto independence of regulators is also taken into account. We use the term "de facto independence" to connote the extent of regulators' effective autonomy as they manage their day-to-day regulatory actions. The term "independence" is thus intended to stress both the extent and the degree of the institutionalization of the discretion conveyed to these agencies. It is important to add that the level of agencies' de facto independence should be conceived not only with reference to elected politicians, but also with respect to representatives of the sectors targeted by regulation, which constitute the "second force" in regulation (Thatcher 2005), and which also have both incentives and resources to mold the regulatory action of agencies, as argued most forcefully by the "capture theory" of regulation (Stigler 1971). Independent regulators can thus be considered "intermediary organizations" that act as mediators between the heterogeneous and conflicting interests of the politicians and the regulatees (Braun 1993). Therefore we suggest that the de facto independence of formally independent regulatory agencies can be seen as the combination of two necessary components, namely the (relative) self-determination of agencies' preferences and the (relative) lack of restrictions when enacting their regulatory activity, with respect to both elected politicians and regulatees. The operationalization of this concept, which cannot be reported in detail here owing to space constraints, requires assigning indicators to assess the position of each component on an ordinal scale of de facto independence, for each one of the two dimensions, to obtain one aggregate measure that accounts for each double relationship (Maggetti 2007). The main information is summarized in the second half of Table 14.1.

## 14.3   EMPIRICAL RESEARCH

Empirical research on the formal independence of regulators has examined the sources of cross-national and cross-sectoral variations on this dimension (Gilardi 2002, 2005a, 2008). The top panel of Figure 14.1 shows that there are indeed considerable differences between countries, both for the average independence of regulators within the country and for their heterogeneity. While the median independence score of regulators is less than 0.3 in Germany and Austria, it is over 0.6 in Ireland and Italy, with the other countries in between. On the other hand, the formal independence of regulatory authorities tends to be much more similar in Norway, France, and the UK than in Austria, Italy, and Portugal, which points to a greater coherence of the institutional structures of regulators in the former than in the latter group of countries. The bottom panel of Figure 14.1 shows that significant variations also exist across sectors. Regulatory authorities in the energy, telecoms, and financial sectors are quite uniformly more independent than their counterparts in food safety and environmental protection. Interestingly, some pharmaceuticals regulators are quite independent while others are not, and competition authorities tend to have an average degree of independence, with a few exceptions.

Why does the formal independence of regulators differ so much, both across and within countries? While national specificities and historical legacies are certainly important (see, e.g., Thatcher 2002), it has also been argued that three more general explanations may

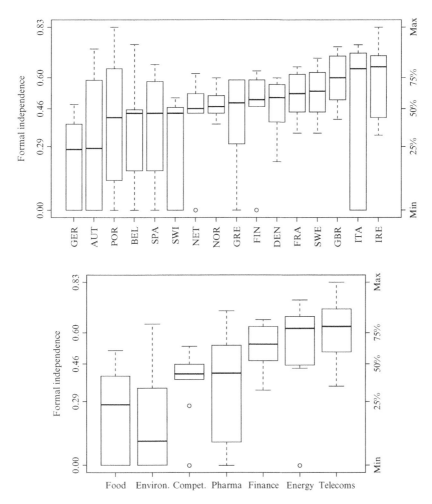

*Note:* The solid line indicates the median value; boxes and whiskers extend, respectively, from the 25th to the 75th percentile and from the minimum to the maximum. The y-axis labels correspond to the minimum, maximum, and 25th, 50th, and 75th percentiles in the whole sample.

*Source:* Gilardi (2008).

*Figure 14.1 The formal independence of regulators in 16 countries and seven sectors*

be relevant, namely the (perceived) need for policy-makers to improve the credibility of their regulatory commitments, their desire to cope with political uncertainty, and the constraints set by the institutional framework (Gilardi 2008). The credibility argument considers that policy-makers may be unable to achieve their goals unless their regulatory promises are credible. This applies especially in the case of utilities reforms, the goal of which was to create a market in sectors previously characterized by the presence of a state-owned monopolist. The achievement of this goal presupposes that private investors can be persuaded to enter the newly opened market, which requires certain assurances that the regulatory set-up will be unbiased and protected from political manipulation. Delegation of regulatory competencies to independent regulatory agencies can be a means to achieve this goal. Relatedly, policy-makers may be interested in preventing political alternation in government from affecting regulatory policies. Again, granting independence to regulators can be a means to this end. Finally, the institutional context may affect these two dynamics. Because veto players make policy change more difficult (Tsebelis 2002), they could be a functional equivalent of regulatory independence with respect to both credibility and political uncertainty pressures.

Using the data shown in Figure 14.1 as the dependent variable, Gilardi (2002, 2005a, 2008) found empirical support for these arguments. The strongest finding is that utilities regulators, and to a lesser extent other economic regulators, are on average significantly more independent than authorities in so-called social regulation (food safety, pharmaceuticals, environment). Furthermore, regulators tend to be more independent in countries with fewer veto players and where political uncertainty is high. These findings support the argument that credibility, political uncertainty, and veto players are important factors for the formal independence of regulators. However, an important problem is that the data capture only a snapshot of the formal independence of regulatory agencies. While it does not vary dramatically from year to year, formal independence can nevertheless change, and longitudinal data on this dimension would be extremely useful. The new survey by Hanretty and Koop (2009) covering 175 regulators worldwide is thus welcome.

A second question is why formally independent regulators have spread so widely, especially since the 1990s. While many countries have experienced similar pressures, such as technological changes and wide-ranging market reforms (Levi-Faur 2003), that may have led them to adopt similar solutions, recent studies have stressed that the adoption of regulatory independence has been strongly influenced by a horizontal process of interdependent diffusion, in which the introduction of an independent regulator in one country and sector has been shaped by prior decisions in other countries and/or sectors, leading to the identification of both national and sectoral patterns of diffusion (Levi-Faur 2006b). In this perspective, Gilardi (2005b, 2008) emphasized that, despite the rationalistic considerations outlined above, the idea of regulatory independence has progressively acquired considerable legitimacy as a socially approved means to organize regulatory policies. This argument essentially means that the burden of proof has shifted. While at the beginning of the process it was the introduction of an independent regulator that needed to be more strongly justified, later on this became the default solution, at least in some sectors such as utilities, and a stronger argument was needed to prevent the setting up of independent regulators than for their introduction.

Gilardi (2008) based his analysis on a rather crude operationalization (though quite standard in the earlier diffusion literature) of these normative dynamics, namely the number of prior adoptions. Controlling for many factors, the probability that an independent regulatory authority is introduced increases with the number of existing independent regulators in other countries and sectors. Recently, these arguments have been expanded by Jordana et al. (forthcoming), who distinguished explicitly between diffusion patterns within and across both countries and sectors, as well as between different stages in the process (i.e., incubation, take-off, and saturation). Their analysis relies on the most comprehensive dataset to date (48 countries and 16 sectors since the 1920s) and shows that, while some channels of diffusion, such as national transfer (within countries, across sectors), matter at all stages, others play a role only in some. In particular, sectoral (within sectors, across countries) and supranational (across sectors, across countries) channels matter more in the incubation and take-off stages, some inter-governmental channels (all sectors in other OECD countries) in only the take-off stage, and others (all sectors in European Union member states) in the take-off and saturation stages. Although the interpretation of these findings is not entirely straightforward, it is a definite step forward for our understanding of how regulatory independence has diffused worldwide. Specifically, the findings permit us to delimit more precisely the scope of credible commitment theory, which Christensen discusses critically in Chapter 7. Credibility arguments seem to be relevant not so much for the creation of independent regulators, which takes place in an international diffusion process, but rather for the variation in the level of formal independence granted to regulatory agencies. This distinction can address some of the concerns raised by Christensen (2011), for instance the fact that the independent regulator model, contrary to credibility arguments, has also spread within social regulation.

These findings pertain only to the formal aspects of independence, but, as we argued earlier, the informal dimensions of independence should also be taken into account. Because any organizational framework allows a certain amount of discretion (Friedberg 1997; March and Sutton 1997), there exists a potential gap between formal and informal structures, and the latter may be more important than the former for organizational outcomes (Downs 1967). Bureaucratic delegation of regulatory competencies from political decision-makers (the "principal" or the "trustor") to agencies (the "agent" or the "trustee"), though backed by law and highly formalized, invariably relies upon an incomplete contract, since it is impossible to spell out in explicit detail all the precise obligations of the agent throughout the life of the contract, and the cost of monitoring the whole process would be prohibitive (Williamson 1985; Balla 2011). In fact, a number of studies suggested that statutory prescriptions correspond only partially to regulators' actual practices (Stern 1997; Stern and Holder 1999; Thatcher 2002; Wilks and Bartle 2002; Yesilkagit and van Thiel 2008).

In particular, Maggetti (2007) demonstrated that formal independence is neither a necessary nor a sufficient condition for explaining variations in regulators' de facto independence from political decision-makers and from the regulated industries. The disjuncture between formal and de facto independence is evident in Figure 14.2, which shows the relationship between these two dimensions for 16 regulators. There is a weakly positive but statistically non-significant relationship between the two dimensions,[1] and, with a couple of exceptions, regulators tend to be either formally more than de facto independent or, interestingly, the other way around. Thus the German finance regulator (BAFIN) and the Swedish competition authority (KKV) seem to be more independent in reality than they are on paper, while the Swedish finance regulator (FI) and the Dutch telecom agency (OPTA) enjoy high formal independence, which however does not seem to translate into real independence in practice.

Our knowledge of the determinants of de facto independence is still in its infancy. However, there are indications of a systematic association between agencies' high de facto independence from politicians and their institutional age or the presence of several

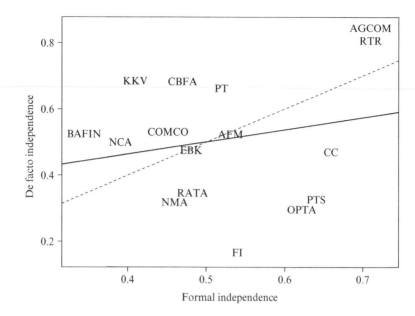

*Note:* The solid line is the regression line; the dashed line is the y = x line. AFM: finance (Netherlands); AGCOM: telecom (Italy); BAFIN: finance (Germany); CBFA: finance (Belgium); CC: competition (UK); COMCO: telecom (Switzerland); EBK: finance (Switzerland); FI: finance (Sweden); KKV: competition (Sweden); NCA: competition (Norway); NMA: competition (Netherlands); OPTA: telecom (Netherlands); PT: telecom (Norway); PTS: telecom (Sweden); RATA: finance (Finland); RTR: telecom (Austria).

*Source:*   Maggetti (2009).

*Figure 14.2*   *Formal and informal independence from elected politicians for 16 regulatory authorities*

veto players in the political system, the latter element in combination with high formal independence. This means that the presence of multiple veto players fosters the formal independence of agencies, as it becomes more difficult for divided principals to sway their regulatory action, which is what veto players theory expects (Tsebelis 2002). Moreover, independent regulators may follow a process of autonomization as they age, in line with the literature about the life cycle of agencies (Martimort 1999). Concerning the relationship with regulatees, it appears that the most de facto independent regulators are those that participate intensely in networks of regulators. These agencies are reinforced by the diffusion of expertise and information coming from other regulators, while gaining potential allies when dealing with third parties. Finally, the relationship between agencies and politicians and, respectively, the relationship between agencies and those being regulated are mutually related. An agency cannot be a servant of two masters: if it is scarcely independent from the politicians, it should be highly independent from those being regulated.

To sum up, the analysis shows that regulators are neither systematically under direct political control nor systematically captured by the regulated industries. These findings challenge a crucial argument of the economic theory of regulation (Stigler 1971) and corroborate the critical assessment of this theory by both Croley (2011) and Christensen

(2011). Furthermore, they lend support to the view that independent regulators are key actors in the context of regulatory capitalism (Levi-Faur 2005).

The development of the regulatory state, and especially the process of agencification, is also expected to have an impact on the transformation of policy-making styles in Europe (Majone 1997; Moran 2002). A common finding is that the expansion of regulatory governance leads to unintended consequences and to the alteration of the modes of political interaction (McGowan and Wallace 1996; Pollitt and Bouckaert 2004). For instance, Wilks and Bartle (2002) show that the design of competition agencies had a symbolic component. They were not expected to be factually dynamic in rule-making or implementation, yet they gradually redefined their roles so as to exert a material impact on market economies. There is also evidence that contextual factors shape the functioning of agencies and the effectiveness of regulatory reforms, implying potential implementation problems (Hood et al. 2001; Pollitt et al. 2001; Christensen and Laegreid 2006). Finally, some studies emphasized the changes introduced by independent regulators in national decision-making processes, which have dramatically opened up, in contrast to closed processes before delegation (Coen and Thatcher 2005; Thatcher 2005).

Evidence from our previous research, based on a comparison of financial and competition regulators in the Netherlands, Sweden, and Switzerland (Maggetti 2009), reveals that independent regulators play a central role in law-making related to their area of competence (more than expert commissions, organized interest representatives, and ordinary agencies subordinated to the ministerial level). Not only are agencies in charge of implementing the new rules, but they also affect the entire policy-making process, especially agenda-setting and pre-parliamentary negotiations. This point corroborates the arguments about the rise of an age of "regulocracy" (Levi-Faur 2005) and "agencification" (Christensen and Laegreid 2006). At the same time, it suggests that the activity of independent regulators is not limited to market supervision and technical regulatory functions, but that regulators also are developing a key political role. Moreover, it appears that the level of de facto independence from politicians may positively affect their influence in policy-making, in combination with other variables, namely the non-professionalization of the legislature. This was the case for the Swiss Federal Banking Commission during the revision of the Stock Exchange Act of 2006 and the Swiss Competition Commission during the revision of the Act on Cartels of 2003. When non-professional legislators, who suffer from a lack of material and symbolic resources, have to cope with an independent regulator that might challenge the later stages of the policy-making process, they will have strong incentives to include *ex ante* this agency in policy-making for obtaining relevant information and to overcome any possible conflict or resistance during the implementation process.

Having said that, it is necessary to ask whether and to what extent independent regulators can still deliver what they promise. In this context, we should adopt the presumed benefits of delegation as an analytical benchmark, namely the increase of policy credibility (through independence) and the enhancement of decision-making efficiency (through expertise) (Majone 2001). The problem is that the study of agencies' performances has proved to be inconclusive (Verhoest 2005). First, it is difficult to assess the impact of independent regulators because their constitutional goals are varied, mixed, broad, unclear, or at least blurred, in short less intelligible than those of central banks;

they indeed constitute the type of public sector organizations that display the highest level of goal ambiguity (Chun and Rainey 2005). Second, the concepts of "regulatory quality" and "public interest" have to be considered empirically sensitive to the subjective understandings of the different actors involved, such as political decision-makers, civil servants, experts, producers, consumers, and citizens (Radaelli and De Francesco 2007). Third, the study of agencies' outcomes suffers from crucial identification problems, mainly owing to the disregard of the complex causal structure behind correlational findings and to the limits of existing and available data, which is largely based on retrospective and subjective recalls of informants (March and Sutton 1997).

To contribute to this debate, and given the difficulty of directly measuring regulatory performances, another, indirect type of regulatory outcome can be examined: the evaluation of agencies in the media (Maggetti 2010). Media coverage cannot be equated to regulatory performance, but it is a condition for accountability and, eventually, legitimacy. The media provide information to citizens, enhance transparency, and perform a fire-alarm function for policy-makers by constituting a linkage mechanism between the bureaucracy and its principal (Hopenhayn and Lohmann 1996; Waterman et al. 1998). A most likely case, the British Competition Commission, and a least likely one, the Swiss Competition Commission, were examined in terms of the media evaluation of their credibility and efficiency, with a content analysis of the major national newspapers during the period 2006–07 (Maggetti 2010). Results show that, against some pessimistic expectations, factually independent regulators can benefit from a positive media evaluation of credibility, as was the case of the British Competition Commission. However, even de facto independence from elected politicians – entailing a broad delegation of regulatory competencies, extensive regulatory discretion vis-à-vis the elected politicians, and relative freedom from *ex post* controls – seems insufficient to secure credible commitments towards the media: the case of the Swiss Competition Commission suggests that perceived autonomy from the regulated industries is another plausibly necessary condition. In addition, even in the very favorable case of the British Competition Commission, the media evaluation of efficiency is negative, casting doubts on the new public management's ambition of reconciling bureaucratic autonomy with decision-making efficiency gains.

## 14.4   CONCLUSIONS

In this chapter, we discussed the conceptualization, operationalization, and measurement of the formal and de facto independence of regulatory agencies. We also provided theory and empirical evidence for several arguments about the determinants of independence and the relationship between its two dimensions. Formal independence represents the key variable for explaining the process of delegation of regulatory authority from governments to independent regulators and for examining the shapes and colors of the worldwide diffusion of this particular type of public sector organization. On the other hand, de facto independence is a decisive factor – complementary to the former – for investigating the consequences of establishing independent regulators on the effectiveness of regulatory governance and the transformation of policy-making.

In particular, the main insights are as follows. On the one hand, the formal independence of regulators tends to be greater in economic regulation than in social regulation, in countries where there is higher political uncertainty owing to frequent alternation between governments with different preferences, and few veto players, suggesting that an institutional context protecting the status quo is a functional equivalent of delegation (Gilardi 2002, 2005a, 2008). Beyond these common pressures, it is worth noting that independent regulators have diffused across countries and sectors following a mechanism of emulation, as they have become a socially valued organization for implementing regulatory governance (Gilardi 2005b, 2008). On the other hand, de facto independence from politicians and from those being regulated appears to be positively affected by the age of agencies and the presence of several veto players, as well as by the participation in networks of regulators (Maggetti 2007). De facto independence from politicians, in turn, positively affects the influence of independent regulators in domestic law-making (Maggetti 2009) and possibly represents a necessary but insufficient condition for a positive media evaluation of credibility (Maggetti 2010).

These insights shed considerable light on the unfolding of regulatory governance by independent regulators. Nonetheless, further research is needed, especially to refine and adapt our measures of independence and to better understand the effects of formal and de facto independence on regulatory outcomes. In particular, to what extent formal and de facto independence influence the performance of regulators remains a largely unanswered question. Even the conceptualization and operationalization of agencies' performance is problematical, given the high level of goal ambiguity characterizing regulatory mandates (Chun and Rainey 2005). Furthermore, the concepts of "regulatory quality" and "public interest" are sensitive to the subjective understandings of the different actors involved, such as political decision-makers, civil servants, experts, producers, consumers, and citizens (Radaelli and De Francesco 2007; Christensen 2011). In that regard, if we take the "crucial case" of the British Financial Services Authority (FSA), it seems that independence is insufficient to prevent regulatory failure. The FSA is a formally and factually independent regulatory agency that employs more than 2500 people and possesses important regulatory powers. It regulates a crucial sector of a leading country that is widely recognized as a trend-setter in regulatory governance, at least in Europe. Yet not only was it publicly blamed for its allegedly "light-touch" regulatory approach and failure to prevent the 2008–10 financial crisis, but, according to the envisaged reform of financial supervision, it will be dismembered and its competencies will be divided between a number of new and old agencies. In fact, the performance of integrated supervisors with broad and consolidated competencies – fiercely independent from the ministry – proved to be not up to expectations. Structural weaknesses stemming from unclear objectives and extended moral hazard seem to surpass efficiency gains (Abrams and Taylor 2000). However, a number of elements suggest that policy-makers will rather reinforce regulatory governance by independent regulators, by improving their design and coordination. On the one hand, new and more appropriate sector-specific agencies are being created. On the other, the trend of agencification continues with the recent institutionalization of European networks of independent regulators, and with the establishment of numerous independent agencies at the European level (Wonka and Rittberger 2010).

## ACKNOWLEDGEMENTS

We are grateful to David Levi-Faur for helpful comments.

## NOTE

1. De facto independence = 0.32(0.23) + 0.37(0.43) × formal independence (OLS estimates, standard errors in parentheses, $R^2 = 0.05$).

## REFERENCES

Abrams, Richard K. and Michael W. Taylor (2000), *Issues in the Unification of Financial Sector Supervision*, Washington, DC: International Monetary Fund.
Alesina, Alberto and Lawrence H. Summers (1993), 'Central bank independence and macroeconomic perform- ance: some comparative evidence', *Journal of Money, Credit, and Banking*, **25** (2), 151–62.
Balla, Steven J. (2011), 'Agency Discretion and Oversight: Instruments for Managing Delegation to the Bureaucracy', in David Levi-Faur (ed.), *Handbook on the Politics of Regulation*, Cheltenham: Edward Elgar.
Braun, Dietmar (1993), 'Who governs intermediary agencies? Principal–agent relations in research policy- making', *Journal of Public Policy*, **13** (2), 135–62.
Christensen, Jørgen Grønnegaard (2011), 'Public Interest Regulation Reconsidered: From Capture to Credible Commitment', in David Levi-Faur (ed.), *Handbook on the Politics of Regulation*, Cheltenham: Edward Elgar.
Christensen, Tom and Per Laegreid (eds) (2006), *Autonomy and Regulation: Coping with Agencies in the Modern State*, Cheltenham, UK and Northampton, MA, USA: Edward Elgar Publishing.
Chun, Young Han and Hal G. Rainey (2005), 'Goal ambiguity and organizational performance in U.S. federal agencies', *Journal of Public Administration Research and Theory*, **15** (4), 529–57.
Coen, David and Mark Thatcher (2005), 'The new governance of markets and non-majoritarian regulators', *Governance*, **18** (3), 329–46.
Croley, Steven (2011), 'Beyond Capture: Towards a New Theory of Regulation', in David Levi-Faur (ed.), *Handbook on the Politics of Regulation*, Cheltenham: Edward Elgar.
Cukierman, Alex (1992), *Central Bank Strategy, Credibility, and Independence: Theory and Evidence*, Cambridge, MA: MIT Press.
Cukierman, Alex, Steven B. Webb and Bilin Neyapti (1992), 'Measuring the independence of central banks and its effect on policy outcomes', *World Bank Economic Review*, **6** (3), 353–98.
Dahl, Robert A. (1989), *Democracy and Its Critics*, New Haven, CT: Yale University Press.
Downs, Anthony (1967), *Inside Bureaucracy*, Boston, MA: Little, Brown.
Friedberg, Erhard (1997), *Le pouvoir et la règle: dynamiques de l'action organisée*, Paris: Seuil.
Gilardi, Fabrizio (2002), 'Policy credibility and delegation to independent regulatory agencies: a comparative empirical analysis', *Journal of European Public Policy*, **9** (6), 873–93.
Gilardi, Fabrizio (2005a), 'The formal independence of regulators: a comparison of 17 countries and 7 sectors', *Swiss Political Science Review*, **11** (4), 139–67.
Gilardi, Fabrizio (2005b), 'The institutional foundations of regulatory capitalism: the diffusion of independent regulatory agencies in Western Europe', *Annals of the American Academy of Political and Social Sciences*, **598**, 84–101.
Gilardi, Fabrizio (2008), *Delegation in the Regulatory State: Independent Regulatory Agencies in Western Europe*, Cheltenham, UK and Northampton, MA, USA: Edward Elgar Publishing.
Hanretty, Chris and Christel Koop (2009), 'Statutory interpretation, appointment method, and agency inde- pendence', European University Institute.
Hood, Christopher, Henry Rothstein and Robert Baldwin (2001), *The Government of Risk: Understanding Risk Regulation Regimes*, Oxford: Oxford University Press.
Hopenhayn, Hugo and Susanne Lohmann (1996), 'Fire-alarm signals and the political oversight of regulatory agencies', *Journal of Law, Economics, and Organization*, **12** (1), 196–213.
Huntington, Samuel P. (1968), *Political Order in Changing Societies*, New Haven, CT: Yale University Press.
Jordana, Jacint, David Levi-Faur and Xavier Fernandez i Marin forthcoming. 'The global diffusion of regulatory agencies: channels of transfer and stages of diffusion'.

Kickert, Walter J.M. (1993), 'Autopoiesis and the science of (public) administration: essence, sense, and nonsense', *Organization Studies*, **14** (2), 261–78.

Levi-Faur, David (2003), 'The politics of liberalisation: privatisation and regulation-for-competition in Europe's and Latin America's telecoms and electricity industries', *European Journal of Political Research*, **42**, 705–40.

Levi-Faur, David (2005), 'The global diffusion of regulatory capitalism', *Annals of the American Academy of Political and Social Sciences*, **598**, 12–33.

Levi-Faur, David (2006a), 'Regulatory capitalism: the dynamics of change beyond telecoms and electricity', *Governance*, **19** (3), 497–525.

Levi-Faur, David (2006b), 'Varieties of regulatory capitalism: getting the most out of the comparative method', *Governance*, **19** (3), 367–82.

Maggetti, Martino (2007), 'De facto independence after delegation: a fuzzy-set analysis', *Regulation & Governance*, **1** (4), 271–94.

Maggetti, Martino (2009), 'The role of independent regulatory agencies in policy-making: a comparative analysis', *Journal of European Public Policy*, **16**, 445–65.

Maggetti, Martino (2010), 'Are regulatory agencies delivering what they promise?', in Per Laegreid and Koen Verhoest (eds), *Governance of Public Sector Organizations: Autonomy, Control and Performance*, Houndmills: Palgrave Macmillan.

Majone, Giandomenico (1994), 'The rise of the regulatory state in Europe', *West European Politics*, **17** (3), 77–101.

Majone, Giandomenico (1996), 'Temporal consistency and policy credibility: why democracies need non-majoritarian institutions', European University Institute.

Majone, Giandomenico (1997), 'From the positive to the regulatory state: causes and consequences of changes in the mode of governance', *Journal of Public Policy*, **17** (2), 139–67.

Majone, Giandomenico (2001), 'Two logics of delegation: agency and fiduciary relations in EU governance', *European Union Politics*, **2** (1), 103–21.

March, James G. and Robert I. Sutton (1997), 'Organizational performance as a dependent variable', *Organization Science*, **8** (6), 697–706.

Martimort, David (1999), 'The life cycle of regulatory agencies: dynamic capture and transaction costs', *Review of Economic Studies*, **66**, 920–47.

McGowan, Francis and Helen Wallace (1996), 'Towards a European regulatory state', *Journal of European Public Policy*, **3** (4), 560–76.

Moran, Michael (2002), 'Review article: understanding the regulatory state', *British Journal of Political Science*, **32**, 391–413.

Nordlinger, Eric A. (1981), *On the Autonomy of the Democratic State*, Cambridge, MA: Harvard University Press.

Pollitt, Christopher and Geert Bouckaert (2004), *Public Management Reform: A Comparative Analysis*, Oxford: Oxford University Press.

Pollitt, Christopher, Karen Bathgate, Janice Caulfield, Amanda Smullen and C. Talbot (2001), 'Agency fever? Analysis of an international policy fashion', *Journal of Comparative Policy Analysis*, **3** (3), 271–90.

Radaelli, Claudio M. and Fabrizio De Francesco (2007), *Regulatory Quality in Europe: Concepts, Measures, and Policy Process*, Manchester: Manchester University Press.

Rogoff, Kenneth (1985), 'The optimal degree of commitment to an intermediate monetary target', *Quarterly Journal of Economics*, **100**, 1169–89.

Sartori, Giovanni (1973), 'What is "politics"', *Political Theory*, **1** (1), 5–26.

Stern, Jon (1997), 'What Makes an Independent Regulator Independent?', *Business Strategy Review*, **8** (2), 67–74.

Stern, Jon and Stuart Holder (1999), 'Regulatory governance: criteria for assessing the performance of regulatory systems', *Utilities Policy*, **8** (1), 33–50.

Stigler, George J. (1971), 'The theory of economic regulation', *Bell Journal of Economics and Management Science*, **2** (1), 1–21.

Teubner, Gunther (1988), *Autopoietic Law: A New Approach to Law and Society*, New York: W. de Gruyter.

Thatcher, Mark (2002), 'Delegation to independent regulatory agencies: pressures, functions and contextual mediation', *West European Politics*, **25** (1), 125–47.

Thatcher, Mark (2005), 'The third force? Independent regulatory agencies and elected politicians in Europe', *Governance*, **18** (3), 347–73.

Tsebelis, George (2002), *Veto Players: How Political Institutions Work*, Princeton, NJ: Princeton University Press.

Verhoest, Koen (2005), 'Effects of autonomy, performance contracting, and competition on the performance of a public agency: a case study', *Policy Studies Journal*, **33** (2), 235–58.

Verhoest, Koen, B. Guy Peters, Geert Bouckaert and Bram Verschuere (2004), 'The study of organizational autonomy: a conceptual review', *Public Administration and Development*, **24**, 101–18.

Verschuere, Bram, Koen Verhoest, Falke Meyers and B. Guy Peters (2006), 'Accountability and accountability arrangements in public agencies', in Tom Christensen and Per Laegreid (eds), *Autonomy and Regulation: Coping with Agencies in the Modern State*, Cheltenham, UK and Northampton, MA, USA: Edward Elgar Publishing.

Walzer, Michael (1983), *Spheres of Justice: A Defense of Pluralism and Equality*, New York: Basic Books.

Waterman, Richard W., Amelia Rouse and Robert Wright (1998), 'The venues of influence: a new theory of political control of the bureaucracy', *Journal of Public Administration Research and Theory*, **8** (1), 13–38.

Wilks, Stephen and Ian Bartle (2002), 'The unanticipated consequences of creating independent competition agencies', *West European Politics*, **25** (1), 148–72.

Williamson, Oliver E. (1985), *The Economic Institutions of Capitalism*, New York: Free Press.

Wonka, Arndt and Berthold Rittberger (2010), 'Credibility, complexity and uncertainty: explaining the institutional independence of 29 EU agencies', *West European Politics*, **33** (4), 730–52.

Yesilkagit, Kutsal and Sandra van Thiel (2008), 'Political influence and bureaucratic autonomy', *Public Organization Review*, **8** (2), 137–53.

# 15 The regulatory rescue of the welfare state
## *Deborah Mabbett*

For many researchers immersed in the world of regulatory governance, the very title of this chapter poses a challenge. Surely the regulatory state is concerned with the operation of markets, whereas the welfare state is concerned with the redistribution of market output through taxing and spending? The former adopts economic efficiency and procedural fairness as its central norms; the latter promotes various forms of social equality. For the regulatory state, rules are the central instruments of policy; for the welfare state, the government budget serves as the focus of policy-making and the measure of activity.

This perspective on the regulatory state, defined almost in opposition to the welfare state, has been developed most strongly by Majone (1993) in the context of the development of social regulation in the EU. But it can be found in other accounts of the role of the regulatory state in 'building' markets, a role which is contrasted with the welfare state roles of redistribution through transfer payments and service provision by public bureaucracies (Sbragia 2000). Characteristic of the regulatory state are non-majoritarian institutions in which technical experts search for socially optimal solutions; the redistributive welfare state, by contrast, is seen as the central policy domain of majoritarian political contestation, in which conflicting interests are represented and policy outcomes depend on negotiation and coalition formation.

The difference between the regulatory state and the welfare state can therefore be framed in terms of two contrasting pairs of policy area and policy process, or 'types of policy' and 'types of politics' (Lowi 1972: 300). The paradigmatic regulatory type of policy is market coordination (setting standards, combating information asymmetries, ensuring access), and its type of politics is non-majoritarian, technical and supranational. The welfare state pairing has tax-benefit redistribution as its paradigmatic type of policy, and the dominant type of politics is majoritarian, party-political and national.

The first two sections of this chapter challenge both parts of this characterisation of the welfare state. Section 15.1 shows that the welfare state encompasses many more types of policy than redistribution. In particular, welfare states are constituted as much by their structures of labour market regulation as by their patterns of government expenditure and taxation (Esping-Andersen 1990, Part 2). Of course, labour market regulation is different to utilities or competition regulation, because it is explicitly organised around conflicting interests, indeed around the most politically salient class conflict: that between capital and labour. It is often governed by a corporatist structure of interest representation which stands in stark contrast to the dominance of impartial experts in other market-regulatory bodies. But the difference should not be overstated. In the late-nineteenth-century heyday of innovation in employment regulation, the 'labour question' engaged experts and brought forth proposals for achieving socially optimal arrangements. These ideas find counterparts in current regulations to enhance efficiency in employment relationships.

Section 15.2 demonstrates that characteristic features of policy-making in the regulatory state may also be found in the welfare state. The type of politics found in welfare policy-making is often technical and consensual. Once we go looking for regulatory policy-making, we can find numerous applications to welfare sectors. This is not just a matter of having a hammer and seeing nails everywhere. Regulatory techniques shape the way in which social policy problems are defined, in particular by highlighting efficiency goals but also through the international dissemination of norms, including rights. The use of regulatory venues also means that social policies are not necessarily shaped around majoritarian political support, which may restrain their redistributive impact but may also mean that disadvantaged minorities are provided for.

Section 15.3 turns to the supranational dimension of welfare state policy-making. In the era of 'embedded liberalism' (Ruggie 1982), organisations such as the International Labour Organization (ILO) promoted a standard set of social policy institutions as part of a vision of how a modern nation state should be constituted (Meyer et al. 1997). In the era of neoliberalism, we might expect to see the transnational dissemination of social policy in decline, but this is not the case. Instead, social policy is reconstituted and reappears in supranational domains via regulatory regimes. We find familiar social policies reframed as correctives to market failures in the work of organisations like the European Commission, the OECD and the World Bank. Also evident is an expansion in the international dissemination of expressions of social rights, solidifying expectations that social provisions will be maintained and providing the focus for monitoring and analysis by 'integrity agencies' (Levi-Faur 2011).

When the regulatory state and the welfare state are characterised as opposing pairs of policy and politics, the inference is readily drawn that the international integration of markets in goods and services, and the accompanying development of supranational regulatory institutions, is a threat to welfare states. By tracing the efficiency-promoting content of welfare policies and the role of regulatory techniques in their dissemination, we gain a different understanding of the impact of supranational integration and can better appreciate the resilience of welfare states in the face of economic pressures.

## 15.1    THE REGULATORY STATE INSIDE THE WELFARE STATE

In understanding the evolution of the regulatory state, the central process has been the wave of privatisation of state-owned enterprises that started in the 1980s and was rapidly diffused around the world (Levi-Faur 2005). Privatisation was accompanied by the establishment of a new type of regulatory body: an independent agency, staffed by experts and charged with creating conditions that would emulate the efficient outcomes of a competitive market. State-owned trading enterprises (public utilities, airlines, etc.) were not part of the welfare state as it is conventionally understood (measured as government spending on welfare services and social transfer payments), although they pursued social mandates, particularly to do with maintaining employment. Their privatisation had little direct effect on the welfare state, although it helped to weaken the corporatist regulation of the labour market.

Privatisation came to have a direct impact on the welfare state when governments moved to reform the provision of public services by involving private providers through 'contracting-out' and 'quasi-market' arrangements. This mode of privatisation differed from the privatisation of trading enterprises in that governments remained the major purchasers of services. Thus the size of government measured in financial terms (the size of the government budget) was not reduced by this type of reform, although the role of government as a provider *was* reduced, as is reflected in data on public sector employment (Grout and Stevens 2003, Table 1).

The splitting of purchasers from providers has contributed to the entry of the regulatory state into the welfare state, as reflected in the proliferation of regulatory bodies within government (Hood et al. 1999). Regulatory techniques include contracts that specify performance requirements and link payments to outputs, in contrast to previous 'demand-driven' financial arrangements. Competition among providers is promoted, and even required as a consequence of commitments to market integration within the EU and more widely under the GATS. New regulatory approaches have brought more formal systems of monitoring, benchmarking and auditing in place of previous reliance on professional self-government in welfare services.

These developments have affected the 'budgetary' welfare state, where governments make transfer payments and purchase services. Welfare states are also constituted by characteristic patterns of labour market regulation. Esping-Andersen (1990) distinguished the minimal regulation (low minimum wage, limited employment protection) found in liberal market economies from the status-protecting regulations governing employment relationships in much of continental Europe and from the Scandinavian model of promoting equality by achieving high employment rates and a relatively compressed wage structure. Others have identified other regulatory strategies. For example, Castles (1985) showed how immigration control and trade protection could provide the foundations of a 'wage-earners welfare state'.

Labour market regulation has visible and salient distributional effects, and engages parties (employers and unions) with clearly conflicting interests. Labour market regulatory bodies have generally been constituted with corporate representation of those interests, through the participation of organised labour and employer groups. Furthermore, while governments have often tried to engineer regulatory arrangements to secure industrial peace and to counter inflation, they have rarely been able to enter the fray without a high degree of politicisation attaching to their interventions. This is because the central cleavage in the labour market has also been the central political cleavage for most developed countries. Trade unions have been affiliated to the political left and often have close ties to left-wing governments, while employers' organisations have supported right-wing governments.

However, there has also been a persistent efficiency-promoting dimension to labour market regulation. For the fledgling field of social research in the nineteenth century, the 'labour question' was the central issue. Social scientists looked for ways to organise and regulate the labour market, not only to restrain the growth of class consciousness and the rise of socialism, but also to remedy consequences of industrialisation that were seen as perverse and counterproductive. They did not use the language of 'market failure', but some of the phenomena that concerned them can be framed as such. For example, 'sweating' (the employment of workers for long hours at very low rates of pay) was driven by a disequilibriating market dynamic, whereby, as wages fell, desperate families supplied more and more labour (specifically, women and children) in order to meet their income needs. The implication drawn by contemporary commentators was that regulating for a 'family wage' would stabilise and equilibrate the market.

Another recognised 'market failure' was that employers of wage labour had little incentive to ensure the long-term reproduction and maintenance of the labour force, once workers became mobile and were not bound to one master. Regulations prohibiting child labour and limiting factory work by women drew on this type of argument. Modern successors to this thinking are reflected in regulations to promote 'family-friendly' employment. While much of the policy discourse of the time seems highly moralising to modern eyes, it was recognisably based on a search for policies that would produce 'positive-sum' outcomes, maximising the size of national income.

The erosion of corporatist approaches to labour market regulation – in particular, the decline of trade union membership and national collective bargaining – has been well documented (Iversen 1999). However, there remains an abundance of non-partisan regulation in employment, for instance through provisions on health and safety and gender equality (Majone 1993). A striking example arose when the 1997 Labour government in the UK ventured to introduce a national minimum wage. It adopted a technical, depoliticised solution to the question of how to set and uprate the wage, establishing a Low Pay Commission to make recommendations which the government has, since its inception in 1999, always accepted. The Commission has employer and union representatives but also academic members. It has actively promoted analyses of the effects of the minimum wage which argue that its distributional impact on household income and poverty is limited, but that there are good market-regulatory reasons for having a minimum wage: to prevent abusive employment and to promote more stable and productive employment relationships (Metcalf 2008).

These examples serve to illustrate that regulation in the labour market, while differently constituted in different welfare regimes, is not necessarily structured around politically salient, class-conscious divides. More generally, there is no clear distinction between the policy areas to which regulation is applied and the policy areas that are salient for the classification and operation of welfare states.

## 15.2    THE REGULATORY LENS ON WELFARE STATE POLICY-MAKING

The previous section has shown that 'regulation' as a description of a type of policy, in which rule-making for market transactions occurs, does not delineate a policy sphere which is separate from the welfare state. On the contrary, welfare states are partly constituted by market-regulatory arrangements, and welfare state reform processes are closely linked to the rise of the regulatory state. This section discusses the regulatory techniques used in welfare policy-making. The basic point is that welfare state policy-making is not always (or even mostly) a domain of politicised debate with high levels of public engagement. On the contrary, many areas are as esoteric as the finer points of the regulation of privatised utilities. Furthermore, it is not even obvious that redistribution is correlated with high politicisation. Groups with strong interests in maintaining the welfare state sometimes advocate depoliticising strategies, for example by pressing for automatic indexation of benefits or seeking the creation of an independent agency to administer provisions.

As noted above, central to the evolution of the regulatory state has been the creation of independent agencies in which specialised knowledge and competence are brought to bear on the task of combating market failure and promoting allocative efficiency. Thus there are three characteristic aspects to regulatory policy-making: an institutional aspect (delegation out of the political arena), the use of technical expertise, and the formulation of the policy problem (promoting efficiency) (Mabbett and Schelkle 2009). This section examines the extent to which these features are found in welfare state policy-making.

The development of the social sciences saw the introduction of the analytical techniques that we now regard as characteristic of regulatory policy-making, notably the use of social statistics. Systematic counting of the population and measurement of its living conditions structured the analysis of social conditions and shaped the proposed solutions. Sociologists such as Nikolas Rose (1991) have examined how quantification shaped social understandings and political discourses. Rose notes the paradox that, while social researchers drew political attention to poverty and contributed to the mobilisation of public opinion, their use of statistical methods also 'promise[d] a "de-politicization" of politics, redrawing the boundaries between politics and objectivity by purporting to act as automatic technical mechanisms for making judgements, prioritizing problems and allocating scarce resources' (Rose 1991: 674).

Statistical analysis yielded, inter alia, the idea of social insurance, a mechanism whereby a class of people could raise its own security and well-being by contributing to a common pool, from which those affected by misfortune could draw. *Ex post*, social insurance was redistributive, but, *ex ante*, statistical analysis demonstrated how such schemes could be actuarially fair. Through such processes, the political could be made technical. 'Arguments about numerical quotas, availability pools and demographic imbalance become a substitute for democratic discussion of the principles of equity and justice' (Prewitt, quoted in Rose 1991: 680).

Whereas theories of working-class mobilisation emphasise the electoral success of social democratic parties in explaining the origins of the welfare state (Korpi 2006), accounts which pay more attention to the production of social knowledge remark on the absence of a party-political aspect to many early welfare state-building initiatives. For example, Kuhnle's (1996: 244) account of early Norwegian social policy highlights that

> a common view [among participants at the time] was that social policymaking was or ought to be lifted above the party political struggle in Norway. . . . Irrespective of party adherence, politicians met to work jointly for the implementation of social legislation, according to a contemporary analysis.

One implication is that social programmes, far from being populist in appealing to the majority of the population, are often depoliticised, in the sense of being removed from salient class conflicts. The creation of autonomous bodies, both for policy formulation and for administration, can also play a part in this. Expert commissions have played a large role in the formulation of social policy in Scandinavia throughout recent history (Kuhnle 1996: 241–4). Working groups have been established to achieve cross-party consensus: a notable example is the Swedish pension reform of 1994 (Brooks and Weaver 2005). Other instances where independent bodies have been created to bring expertise to policy-making and increase the perceived security and reliability of social commitments include the US Social Security Administration, which manages earmarked social security contributions, taking it out of the domain of budgetary contestation (Patashnik 1997). With the spread of quasi-markets and privatisation in health care, the last two decades have seen the establishment of numerous regulatory authorities. For example, the UK's National Institute for Health and Clinical Excellence (NICE, established in 1999) describes itself on its website as 'an independent organisation responsible for providing national guidance on promoting good health and preventing and treating ill health'. It develops clinical guidelines on the most cost-effective treatments for conditions, and assesses the cost-effectiveness of new drugs and other health technology innovations. Its German counterpart, AQUMED, hosts an international regulatory network called Guidelines International Network (GIN), established in 2002, which brings together similar agencies from other countries. Another network, Health Technology Assessment (HTA) International, includes the major pharmaceutical companies among its members as well as HTA regulatory bodies from 16 countries.

It is arguable that the whole structure of social provision in the welfare states of advanced countries rests on processes of rule-based delegation. Parliaments do not review the entitlements of individuals: they set rules instead. Direct intervention by politicians in determining individual benefits is generally impugned as 'clientelism'; in other words, as an inappropriately high level of political engagement in the redistribution of resources. Delegation through rules is taken a step further in instances of 'automatic government' (Weaver 1988), for example where the legislature agrees on a technical scheme for uprating benefits in line with inflation. The use of these devices suggests that, while the welfare state can be seen as a political resource for assembling constituencies and 'buying votes', politicians see limits to the potential for gaining credit by distributing benefits.

In the best regulatory tradition, social policy agencies promulgate technical analyses and attempt to eliminate distributional contestation from their domain of decision-making. One technique for the agency is to narrow and 'partition' the policy area, so that the participants in the regulatory part of the process see their task as one of finding efficient solutions, while the resolution of distributional issues is assigned to another policy process with different participants (Mabbett 2009). The idea that pension provision should be understood as consisting of distinct 'pillars' provides a good example of partitioning. In an influential report, the World Bank (1994: 234) argued that 'a different government role is appropriate for each [pillar]'. The Bank advocated that the first, budgetary, pillar should be focused on redistribution, instead of also addressing the savings function. This meant that the functional logic of the budgetary pillar would conform to the institutional setting of parliamentary politics, which is able to make majoritarian decisions over redistribution. In the second and third pillars, provision would be 'actuarially fair' rather than redistributive, so governments would have a regulatory role which could be delegated to an independent agency.

## 15.3    THE INTERNATIONAL DIMENSION

One noticeable feature of looking at welfare state policy-making through a regulatory lens is that cross-national and supranational aspects are highlighted. It is characteristic of regulatory policy domains both that supranational networks are created and that policies are transferred from country to country. Privatisation and the creation of independent regulatory agencies exhibit striking patterns of diffusion across countries (Levi-Faur 2005). Welfare states also exhibit diffusion patterns in measures ranging from the introduction of social insurance to the adoption of welfare-to-work programmes. Freeman and Moran (2000) remark on the internationalisation of policy-making in health care, for example through the international networks developed by pharmaceutical regulators. In pensions, the construction of a regulatory domain, particularly around the third pension pillar, has been accompanied by the worldwide promulgation of a pension reform programme based on the World Bank's 1994 report (Orenstein 2005).

Yet it seems almost paradoxical to emphasise the cross-national and supranational aspect to welfare state policy-making when there is abundant evidence of the idiosyncrasy of national welfare states. Furthermore, by contrast with market-regulatory policy domains, where strong interests in market integration drive supranationalism forward, there is no obvious interest-based driver for international networking in social policy. Supranational communication does not come easily: among welfare administrators, one often finds blank-faced incomprehension of other countries' procedures and a general conviction that one's own national system is 'better'. This reflects the primacy of communication with clients in social policy: everyday 'street-level' practice is highly localised.

Nonetheless, there are persistent and pronounced elements of supranationalism in welfare state policy-making. Meyer et al. (1997) give a compelling account of the incorporation of the welfare state into prevailing norms of what constitutes a nation state. Their argument is that the policies and structures that are seen as the normal apparatus of the nation state are constructed and propagated through global processes. Instead of seeing the welfare state as the organic expression of the solidarity of a community, they show how its characteristic features are introduced into unlikely social settings through the creation of distinctive state institutions, starting with the construction of members of the polity as 'citizens' with 'rights' and going on to the identification of certain categories of citizen as needy, vulnerable or deserving (Meyer et al. 1997: 145–6). Actors engaged in building nations and achieving their recognition in the international system are receptive to internationally transmitted norms about how a state is constituted, resulting in copying or 'isomorphism' of institutions across polities.

International organisations play a role in this transmission mechanism, presenting models of government structures and policies and collecting data, which both has an organisational effect itself and facilitates comparison across countries. For example, the ILO has many of the characteristics of a supranational regulatory body. It formulates standards in the form of conventions, collects cross-national statistics and provides technical assistance. Strang and Chang (1993: 242) argue that ILO conventions 'offer a script or model that actors can draw upon to design policy'. Evidence for this comes from direct references to conventions in national legislation, along with case studies of reform processes where ILO conventions have been invoked. Conventions may also provide a ready-made policy rationale, to the extent that conformity with international standards is a reason for policy in itself.

However, unlike the regulatory networks that have developed out of market-oriented reforms in recent years, the ILO has a corporatist structure, with each state sending trade union and employer representatives along with government officials, and it has, for much of its history, been affected by dissension over convention standards. Seekings (2008) documents how the ILO promoted the German model of social insurance despite Danish and British attempts to make the case for tax-financed systems. He also finds the ILO to have been resolutely 'workerist', limiting the relevance of its prescriptions in countries where formal employment is low. From a regulatory perspective it is easy to understand why the ILO was both workerist and social insurance-oriented. It sought to formulate prescriptions which could attract the support of employers as well as unions (and governments). Employers have often supported social insurance when benefits are confined to the contributing workforce and can be negotiated over as part of the remuneration package (Swenson 1991). As the ILO has moved away from workerism and insurance, to address problems of poverty more directly, it has been less and less able to achieve unanimous support for conventions, and its influence has waned.

Consensual supranational policy exchanges on social policy rely on the adoption of a highly functionalist language, portraying the favoured policies of the day as promoting economic growth and development. Intergovernmental venues provide occasions on which states present themselves as unitary, rational and responsible. In these venues, states declare 'standardized purposes like collective development, social justice and individual rights', and they present themselves as having 'policy technologies for the rational means–ends accomplishment of goals' (Meyer et al. 1997: 153). Activities in these venues often appear decoupled from the political realities of national policy-making, raising a basic question about how important supranational policy-making is. Guiraudon (1998) has addressed this question in a study of the influence of supranationalism on the granting of social rights to migrants. The puzzle is that migrants generally do have social rights, yet political pressures in national venues would often point to the denial of access to welfare for migrants. One explanation for this is that governments comply with supranational agreements, suggesting that participation in supranational venues shapes the way that rights are structured in the welfare state.

It is well known that the EU requires its members not to discriminate against other countries' nationals in their social provisions, but this is often seen as an alien imposition of the EU regulatory state that undermines national welfare states (Ferrera 2005; Leibfried 2005). Guiraudon suggests that EU regulation is part of a wider process whereby 'international institutions and transnational actors were able to diffuse shared understandings about the treatment of foreigners so as to change and shape the views of domestic state and societal actors' (1998: 280). Forensically tracing through how these norms are transmitted, Guiraudon draws a distinction between open and closed policy domains. 'The impact of international-level variables should be strongest when domestic pressure is low and debate is contained within the gilded doors of official buildings' (1998: 286). Foreigners' rights have been protected when the policy debate has been kept closed; opening the debate and widening publicity on the issue tends to be detrimental to the status of foreigners (1998: 290). Guiraudon argues that immigrants' rights are subject to a political cycle, threatened near to elections as politicians make populist appeals, but secured after elections when political time horizons are longer. Just as regulatory institutions for monetary policy can be seen as dampening the political business cycle in the interests of economic stability and growth, so one can see the embedding of rights as a counterweight to political opportunism that will tend to produce more social stability and cohesion in the long term.

It is striking that Guiraudon's account portrays 'rights language' as a depoliticising strategy, given that rights claims are also used to mobilise identity groups, as reflected in women's rights and disability rights campaigns. The relationship between rights and the characteristic patterns of regulatory policy-making remains an open question. There are obvious differences between rights claims and regulatory proposals: for example, the former tend to be made and mediated by lawyers, whereas the latter are dominated by economists. However, rights claims, particularly when promulgated at the international level, have a striking capacity to reframe policy issues in a way that shifts them away from domestic political contestation. While social rights are claims on resources which will be exercised in competition with other claims, their formulation avoids the frame of redistribution. For example, Strang and Chang suggest that ILO conventions on workers' rights shift policies symbolically 'out of the realm of zero-sum, partisan politics and into the realm of fundamental, universally-recognised rights' (1993: 242–3). This suggests that supranational communication has a depoliticising function: if a claim can be formulated in a way that can be understood in international fora, it is by that very process transformed from being a redistributive claim into a proposition about the legitimacy of the state itself.

The wider implication is that the 'redistributiveness' of a policy is not an inherent structural feature, as it might be understood by an economist calculating winners and losers, but a construction which depends on the policy domain in which resources are being claimed. A claim exercised in the tax or benefit system is therefore instantly classifiable as redistributive, even if it might have positive-sum aspects (such as facilitating a person's return to work, or maintaining macroeconomic stability by preventing home owners defaulting on their mortgages). Conversely, a claim made in the international arena is not made in the realm of partisan politics, and thereby escapes partisan political scrutiny.

## 15.4   CONCLUSION

One conclusion from this discussion is, by now, a familiar one. Market-regulatory policies reach deep into the heart of the welfare state, and the supranational regulation of market integration has pronounced implications for social policy, even while its proponents seek to preserve national welfare state competences. Majone's account of regulatory legitimacy as derived from solving 'positive-sum' problems and staying away from redistributive issues does not describe the current state of affairs in the EU (as Majone 2005 indeed acknowledges). The supranational regulatory state is directly implicated in policy-making in the welfare state, exerting a strong impact on welfare state ideas and institutions. For many commentators, this development is (a) undemocratic and (b) likely to have a detrimental effect on levels of redistribution, since these depend on national processes which produce solidarity. This conclusion considers these two concerns in turn.

One response to the first concern is to question the value attached to majoritarian democracy. This is the position taken by many advocates of social rights, who see them as countering the flaws of national political systems and providing the basis for a more robust deliberative democracy (Fredman 2008). It is argued that non-majoritarian strategies such as the promulgation of rights are not necessarily undemocratic, if one has a more ambitious definition of democracy than the current mode of government in developed Western states. Rose, having documented the role of statistical measurement and technique in the foundation of the welfare state, also implicitly criticises the reification of existing democracies, arguing that they are already too reliant on regulatory techniques for the exercise and justification of power, specifically on technologies for measuring, monitoring and controlling social entities (1991: 691). Students of social policy might draw a different implication: that the development of the welfare state does not have to be reliant on majoritarian rule and that socially excluded minorities who lack political as well as economic power might nonetheless receive fair(ish) allocations of public goods and social services in existing democracies because of the responsiveness of public policy to social research. This would help to explain the ongoing engagement of researchers and policy activists with surveying, measuring and publicising poverty and exclusion.

A different defence of the regulatory state against the claim that it is undemocratic can be formulated as follows. Presently existing democracies are organised around states, but choices made by citizens in these states are constrained by the policies of other states. Thus many of the policies that citizens might support cannot be adopted without resolving collective action problems between states. If supranational regulation can overcome these problems and organise international collective action, the result is more empowering of national democracy, not less. This type of argument would be most convincing if supranational regulation could be shown to prevent 'race to the bottom' dynamics in welfare provision. Critics argue that it does not do so because it has a market-integrative bias (Scharpf 1999). The era of embedded liberalism is over: market integration is no longer constrained by the quest to safeguard domestic stability (cf. Ruggie 1982: 393). In the era of neoliberalism, the welfare state is trampled under the forward march of global capitalism.

The analysis of regulatory capitalism challenges the claim that we have entered a neoliberal era marked by the decline of public authority, replaced by the rule (or misrule) of anonymous markets. Instead, it is argued that states and other collective actors reconstitute market relationships in the course of formulating regulations to promote efficiency and manage risk. One implication is that the loss of redistributive capacity that comes with market integration can be at least partially countered by the reconstitution of social policy as efficiency-enhancing policy, through the use of regulatory techniques. Efficiency explanations can be 'discovered' for large parts of the welfare state: for example, companies incur lower health care costs in the social insurance systems of Europe than in the private insurance system of the US, and thus reconcile competitiveness and distributional fairness. Welfare-to-work programmes aim to reform social assistance provision into 'productive' policies, and so on.

Jonah Levy (1999) has pointed out that West European welfare states, in particular, seem to have a large potential for 'vice-into-virtue' reforms, whereby efficiency and distributional fairness can both be enhanced by suitably designed measures. However, he also notes that these reforms are accompanied by an erosion of the political salience of the welfare state. 'With welfare expansion giving way to restructuring and retrenchment, leftist governments have lost their most prized policy instrument' (1999: 239–40). Rather than wishing to retain control of instruments of social policy, seeing them as valuable political resources for satisfying domestic constituencies, the politics of vice-into-virtue may call for downplaying distributional conflicts, for consensus formation and blame avoidance.

The argument is a familiar one from the literature on the politics of retrenchment, which postulates that the welfare state has gone from being a resource for national politics, allowing parties to mobilise their supporters behind proposals and to 'buy in' key groups, to a burden on governments which they manage at least in part through delegation strategies (Pierson 1996). One implication is that governments have little reason to resist the regulatory takeover of the welfare state, and may even facilitate it as a mechanism for reforming and reducing fiscal burdens and allowing them to shift political contestation to more tractable domains. Furthermore, the domestic popularity of market-oriented social policy reforms suggests that welfare states are not simply victims of wider processes; on the contrary, domestic sources of pressure for welfare state reform contribute to the active engagement of governments in regulatory state-building and its extension into welfare policy areas (Iversen and Wren 1998).

This chapter has argued that social policy is reconstituted in the regulatory state as a technical domain of efficiency-enhancing policy. This reconstituted policy domain is certainly less open to political contestation and less inviting as a flagship of left-wing politics than its predecessor. Some readers may feel that the processes described here are not so much rescue as capture, imprisoning the welfare state in a narrow normative frame that consolidates its role as handmaiden of capital and undermines other value bases. It remains that social programmes and expenditures have largely survived the intensified processes of market integration that have occurred in the last few decades, and identifying the affinities between the regulatory state and the welfare state helps to explain how.

## ACKNOWLEDGEMENTS

Many thanks to David Levi-Faur, Hanan Haber and Waltraud Schelkle for detailed comments on earlier drafts of this chapter. This chapter was largely prepared while I was on research leave at the Hanse-Wissenschaftskolleg, and I am very grateful for the facilities and resources provided there.

## REFERENCES

Brooks, S.M. and R.K. Weaver (2005), 'Lashed to the mast? The politics of notional defined contribution pension reforms', Center for Retirement Research Working Paper 2005–04, Boston College.
Castles, F. (1985), *The Working Class and Welfare*, Sydney: Allen & Unwin.
Esping-Andersen, G. (1990), *The Three Worlds of Welfare Capitalism*, Cambridge: Polity.
Ferrera, M. (2005), *The Boundaries of Welfare: European Integration and the New Spatial Politics of Social Protection*, Oxford: Oxford University Press.
Fredman, S. (2008), *Human Rights Transformed: Positive Rights and Positive Duties*, Oxford: Oxford University Press.
Freeman, R. and M. Moran (2000), 'Reforming health care in Europe', *West European Politics*, **23** (2), 35–58.
Grout, P. and M. Stevens (2003), 'The assessment: financing and managing public services', *Oxford Review of Economic Policy*, **19** (2), 215–34.
Guiraudon, V. (1998), 'Citizenship rights for non-citizens: France, Germany, and The Netherlands', in C. Joppke (ed.), *Challenge to the Nation-State*, Oxford: Oxford University Press.

Hood, C., C. Scott, O. James, G. Jones and T. Travers (1999), *Regulation inside Government: Waste-Watchers, Quality Police, and Sleaze-Busters*, Oxford: Oxford University Press.

Iversen, T. (1999), *Contested Economic Institutions*, New York: Cambridge University Press.

Iversen, T. and A. Wren (1998), 'Equality, employment and budgetary restraint: the trilemma of the service economy', *World Politics*, **50**, 507–46.

Korpi, W. (2006), 'Power resources and employer-centred approaches in explanations of welfare states and varieties of welfare capitalism', *World Politics*, **58**, 167–206.

Kuhnle, S. (1996), 'International modelling, states and statistics: Scandinavian social security solutions in the 1890s', in D. Rueschemeyer and T. Skocpol (eds), *States, Social Knowledge and the Origins of Modern Social Policies*, Princeton, NJ: Princeton University Press.

Leibfried, S. (2005) 'Social policy: left to the judges and the markets?', in H. Wallace, W. Wallace and M. Pollack (eds), *Policymaking in the European Union*, Oxford: Oxford University Press.

Levi-Faur, D. (2005), 'The global diffusion of regulatory capitalism', *Annals of the American Academy of Political and Social Science*, **598**, March.

Levi-Faur, D. (2011), 'Regulation and regulatory governance', in D. Levi-Faur (ed.), *Handbook on the Politics of Regulation*, Cheltenham: Edward Elgar.

Levy, J. (1999), 'Vice into virtue? Progressive politics and welfare reform in continental Europe', *Politics and Society*, **27** (2), 239–73.

Lowi, T.J. (1972), 'Four systems of policy, politics, and choice', *Public Administration Review*, **32** (4), 298–310.

Mabbett, D. (2009), 'Supplementary pensions between social policy and social regulation', *West European Politics*, **32** (4), 774–91.

Mabbett, D. and W. Schelkle (2009), 'The politics of conflict management in EU regulation', *West European Politics*, **32** (4), 699–718.

Majone, G. (1993), 'The European Community between social policy and social regulation', *Journal of Common Market Studies*, **31** (2), 153–70.

Majone, G. (2005), *Dilemmas of European Integration*, Oxford: Oxford University Press.

Metcalf, D. (2008), 'Why has the British national minimum wage had little or no impact on employment?', *Journal of Industrial Relations*, **50** (3), 489–512.

Meyer, J.M., J. Boli, G.M. Thomas and F.O. Ramirez (1997), 'World society and the nation-state', *American Journal of Sociology*, **103** (1), 144–81.

Orenstein, M.A. (2005), 'The new pension reform as global policy', *Global Social Policy*, **5** (2), 175–202.

Patashnik, E. (1997), 'Unfolding promises: trust funds and the politics of precommitment', *Political Science Quarterly*, **112** (3), 431–52.

Pierson, P. (1996), 'The new politics of the welfare state', *World Politics*, **48**, 143–79.

Rose, N. (1991), 'Governing by numbers: figuring out democracy', *Accounting, Organizations and Society*, **16** (7), 673–92.

Ruggie, J.G. (1982), 'International regimes, transactions, and change: embedded liberalism in the postwar economic order', *International Organization*, **36** (2), 379–415.

Sbragia, A. (2000), 'Governance, the state, and the market: what is going on?', *Governance*, **13** (2), 243–50.

Scharpf, F. (1999), *Governing in Europe: Effective and Democratic?*, Oxford: Oxford University Press.

Seekings, J. (2008), 'The ILO and social protection in the global South, 1919–2005', ILO Century Project (website).

Strang, D. and P.M.Y. Chang (1993), 'The International Labor Organization and the welfare state: institutional effects on national welfare spending, 1960–80', *International Organization*, **47** (2), 235–62.

Swenson, P. (1991), 'Bringing capital back in, or social democracy reconsidered: employer power, cross-class alliances, and centralization of industrial relations in Denmark and Sweden', *World Politics*, **43**, 513–44.

Weaver, K. (1988), *Automatic Government: The Politics of Indexation*, Washington, DC: Brookings Institution Press.

World Bank (1994), *Averting the Old Age Crisis*, Washington, DC: World Bank.

# 16 The regulation of privacy
## Andreas Busch

The debate about the regulation of privacy has in recent years above all been linked to technological developments and their uses. From the 1960s onwards, the emergence and spread of computers, data banks, telecommunication, and eventually the internet have led to several waves of concerned public debate about the impact they have on privacy, society, and the state (see as representative publications Packard 1964; Miller 1971; Burnham 1983; Sykes 1999; O'Harrow 2006). In this perspective, individual privacy is threatened by person-related information which can be stored electronically and easily transmitted. Such information has increased massively in recent years; the capacity for cheap storage has grown even more quickly, and, since such information can be digitally processed and cross-linked, new data can be generated from very diverse sources of information, giving them a new quality and allowing very detailed portraits of individual people, their preferences and their characteristics to be created. Regulatory challenges in this field thus include the questions of who is allowed to collect and store such data, by whom and for what purposes they can be retrieved, and what legitimate uses they can be put to. In several countries, disputes about the power of internet search giant Google (whose corporate aim it is 'to organize the world's information and make it universally accessible and useful' and whose activities range from scanning books to filming streets) have recently indicated the growing fears of citizens and their representatives about losing control over valued person-related information, moving the issue of regulation in this field up on the political agenda.

Looking at privacy from that angle one could be led to believe that it is a new and modern concept. Indeed it was long assumed that primitive societies neither knew nor demanded privacy. In the late 1940s, anthropologist Margaret Mead, in her famous study on *Coming of Age in Samoa*, argued that, in a society which lived in houses without walls, where there were no separate sleeping quarters, and little clothing was worn, 'there is no privacy and no sense of shame.'[1] But further research has shown this view to be factually not correct. Even primitive societies had 'distance' and 'avoidance' rules to provide for some degree of individual privacy. Privacy norms were thus not absent; they were just harder to realise under the living, working and economic conditions of primitive societies (cf. the summary of research in Westin 1967: 13–18). While privacy is a basic human need and constitutive for the individual, without a society there would be no intrusion and hence no need for privacy as protection against intrusion. Since societies differ, however, the desire or need for privacy varies historically (Moore 1984, chap. 1), and demand for privacy has grown substantially in the process of modernisation. Nuclear families living in individual households, urbanisation and the anonymity of city life, mobility in work and residence, and the weakening of religious authority – all these factors contributed to this development since they increased chances for privacy. At the same time, however, countervailing forces developed as well: greater population density and new technical instruments made possible new ways to encroach upon privacy or engage in surveillance.

Despite the intense debates about privacy in recent decades, a generally accepted definition has so far failed to emerge. 'Few values so fundamental to society as privacy have been left so undefined in social theory or have been the subject of such vague and confused writing by social scientists,' Westin (1967: 7) remarked in his seminal study on the subject many years ago. And, more than four decades later, a major study still starts by admitting that privacy 'is a concept in disarray. Nobody can articulate what it means' (Solove 2008: 1). The main reason for this situation is that privacy is negatively defined as an absence of intrusion and that such intrusion can both come from many directions and vary in its subjectively perceived intensity. Characterisations of privacy are manifold (cf. the discussions in Allen 2005; Waldo et al. 2007; Solove 2008) and range from an encompassing 'right to be let alone' (on which see originally Warren and Brandeis 1890) to control over one's own body, including the intimate and personal aspects of conducting one's life and sexuality, and from control over personal information and protection of one's reputation to protection from interrogation and searches by public authorities. This non-exhaustive list combines personal, social, and political aspects, indicating the breadth of the debate.

Almost as varied have been the academic disciplines that have debated privacy over the last decades. Legal scholars have discussed the extent to which the protection of privacy is granted by constitutional protection, how it relates to the right to free speech, or how the law of torts relates to the issue (Prosser 1960). Feminist scholars have argued that existing legal provisions protecting family matters from state interference in the name of privacy can seriously disadvantage women seeking protection from abuse (Schneider 1991; see also Gavison 1992). In political philosophy, liberal thinking has been predominant, regarding privacy as a property of the individual, important for his or her self-interest mainly for self-development and/or the establishment of intimate or human relationships (Rössler 2005). But this has been criticised by authors from a communitarian perspective who argue that privacy should not be an 'unbounded or privileged good' (Etzioni 1999: 195) because an exclusive focus on individual rights can harm the needs and values of society.

This chapter looks at the regulation of privacy through a perspective of 'data protection' (Bennett 1992), because use of modern technology is the main threat to privacy understood as 'the claim of individuals, groups, or institutions to determine for themselves when, how, and to what extent information about them is communicated to others' (Westin 1967: 7). The chapter surveys attempts to protect privacy through regulation both on the international and on the national level, and analyses actors and the tools they use. In recent years, conflicts about the regulation of privacy have emerged also on the international level because of different approaches, priorities and values, and a number of them are described and analysed in section 16.3. Section 16.4 looks at the challenges for the regulation of privacy in the 21st century.

## 16.1 INTERNATIONAL SOURCES OF REGULATING PRIVACY

Since digital data move with ease across national borders and around the globe, the international level would seem to be the right place for the regulation of privacy. Indeed several international bodies have made attempts at drawing up guidelines and agreeing on common frameworks in recent decades.[2] Political agency has varied in this field over time, but generally one can say that the proliferation of rules protecting privacy owes a lot to the initiatives of the network of national data protection commissioners from the 1970s onwards who overcame initial resistance from national governments and industry interests (Newman 2008). Economic interests in lowering transaction costs of trade through harmonisation of national rules then supported the creation of international level rules, while civil rights action groups supported the defence of privacy protection standards against law enforcement interests in weakening them, especially in anti-terrorism after 9/11.

The Council of Europe (CoE) was the first international organisation to guarantee 'the right to respect for his private and family life, his home and his correspondence' to everyone in Article 8 of its 1950 European Convention on Human Rights (ECHR). Out of this right to privacy and discussions in the CoE's Parliamentary Assembly in 1968 about how it was to be protected in the face of emerging modern technology grew two resolutions of the CoE's Committee of Ministers in 1973 and 1974 establishing principles of data protection for computerised 'data banks' in the public and private sectors. While these resolutions were not legally binding for the member states, many of them started to enact national data protection laws and/or incorporated data protection as a fundamental right into their constitutions.[3] The international Convention for the Protection of Individuals with Regard to Automatic Processing of Personal Data was adopted by the CoE in 1980 and opened for signature on 28 January 1981 (Council of Europe 1981). It entered into force on 1 October 1985.[4]

The Convention contains basic principles for data protection which every participating country should consider in its domestic legislation. This common core contains basic information privacy principles, namely that personal data should be obtained and processed fairly and lawfully, be stored only for specified and legitimate purposes, not be excessive in relation to those purposes, be accurate and kept up to date, and permit identification of the data subjects for no longer than is required (Article 5). In addition, data security and protection against unauthorised access is called for, and individuals are vested with rights regarding data files which contain their data. Furthermore, the Convention contains regulations regarding transborder data flows (establishing the principle of free flow of data between contracting parties) and rules for mutual assistance between the contracting parties.

As the CoE has no supranational legal structure, it has no mechanism for enforcing compliance with the rules set out in the Convention; other weaknesses of the 1981 Convention include that many of the terms used are left undefined (which has not helped in the harmonisation of national data protection legislation) and that it does not include provisions for the transfer of data to non-contracting parties.[5] Nevertheless the 1981 Convention is 'a key reference point' (Bygrave 2008: 26) on the international level, influential in shaping the debate about data protection in Europe and beyond – and not least in the newly democratising countries of Central and East Europe after 1990, almost all of which signed and ratified the Convention.

The Organisation for Economic Co-operation and Development (OECD) had been invited to cooperate in the drafting of the CoE convention, and representatives of the organisation and its four non-European member countries (Australia, Canada, Japan and the United States) participated in the work of the CoE's drafting committee. The

OECD, as an organisation of economically advanced liberal democracies which included important data-processing countries among its members, had already taken an early interest in the issue (cf. Niblett 1971). In 1978, it set up its own group of experts to draw up guidelines which would help to harmonise the different national data protection legislations. Since this forum included the United States as the country with the dominant data-processing industry, negotiations were difficult (Bennett 1992: 136f.). But it was possible for the group to agree on certain principles, finishing a draft in 1979 that was adopted in September 1980. The Guidelines on the Protection of Privacy and Transborder Flows of Personal Data (Organisation for Economic Co-operation and Development 1981) contain eight specific 'basic principles', namely collection limitation, data quality, purpose specification, use limitation, security safeguards, openness, individual rights, and accountability (OECD, 1981, Part Two). There are evident parallels to the CoE Convention, and similarly the wording is somewhat vague, leaving room for interpretation (which was probably necessary to reach agreement). As the guidelines are explicitly labelled as 'minimum standards' and since they are voluntary and not legally binding, their enforceability is even weaker than that of the CoE Convention. Not all member states even adopted legislation or created data protection authorities, opting instead for the expressed preference for self-regulation (Article 19b). But, despite these shortcomings, the OECD guidelines have been influential, especially for the data protection legislation outside Europe, in countries like Japan, Australia, New Zealand, Canada and Hong Kong (Bygrave 2008: 28).

As the issue of transborder data flows became more important, the OECD in 1985 adopted a Declaration on Transborder Data Flows which pledged support for international exchange of data and information and opposed 'unjustified barriers' to it; and in 1998 a Declaration on the Protection of Privacy on Global Networks followed, acknowledging the different approaches taken by member countries in their data protection policies while confirming the importance of effective privacy protection for the future development of e-commerce. The OECD even set up an online Privacy Statement Generator which allowed easy compilation of a specific privacy statement for websites.[6]

While the focus of the OECD was clearly on privacy with a view to commercial and economic issues, the United Nations' Guidelines Concerning Computerized Personal Data Files were primarily motivated by human rights considerations. Following from the Universal Declaration of Human Rights (1948), which contained privacy protection provisions in its Article 12, the guidelines adopted by the General Assembly on 14 December 1990 contained principles that formulated 'minimum guarantees that should be adopted in national legislations'. Again similarities exist with the CoE Convention and the OECD Guidelines, but two innovations are the 'principle of accuracy', which calls for data holders 'to conduct regular checks on the accuracy and relevance of the data recorded', and the application of the guidelines to personal data files kept by governmental international institutions. The most important fact, however, is that with the UN taking up a stance on privacy the topic had clearly started to move beyond the developed Western world.

During the 1990s, the increasing use of the internet brought the issues of electronic commerce and the privacy implications of transborder data flows on the agenda. In 1995, the European Union passed its Directive on the Protection of Personal Data with Regard to the Processing of Personal Data and on the Free Movement of Such Data

(95/46/EC) which harmonised data protection regulations across the then 15 member states (European Union 1995).[7] This directive had been discussed over a couple of years and was a consequence of the completion of the Union's single internal market in goods and services in 1992. Since the European Union is a supranational body, its directive was legally binding and enforceable, which set it apart from the international rules discussed so far. It also had substantial reverberations beyond Europe. Since Article 25 of the directive included restrictions on the transfer of personal data to third countries which did not have an 'adequate level of protection', areas outside Europe with significant data processing industries feared that they might be cut off from European business. Most prominently the Asia-Pacific Economic Cooperation (APEC), an intergovernmental organisation of 21 Pacific Rim countries including Australia, Canada, Japan, South Korea, Taiwan and the United States, started to work on a Privacy Framework in 1998 which was adopted in late 2004 (Asia-Pacific Economic Cooperation 2004). The APEC Framework, too, builds on privacy principles; however, compared to the CoE and EU approaches, several elements are missing (such as the purpose specification and the openness principle), and no rules about data exports to countries with lower data protection standards are set. The APEC Framework thus seems less motivated by human rights protection than by economic interests and sets a comparatively 'low standard' of data protection (Greenleaf 2005). In Africa, legal regimes for data privacy are least developed: the African Charter on Human and People's Rights (1981) omits mentioning a right to privacy in its catalogue of basic human rights, and none of the African countries has enacted comprehensive data privacy laws, although South Africa has started to make steps towards one (Waldo et al. 2007: 394).

## 16.2   NATIONAL TOOLS OF REGULATING PRIVACY

Despite the efforts at harmonisation on the international level, different national approaches to the regulation of privacy still dominate in the early 21st century. Moreover, these national regimes do not necessarily follow a rational blueprint – indeed, they sometimes rather resemble a patchwork quilt, having evolved over the decades and adapted step by step to technological progress rather than making a clean regulatory break by imposing a new and consistent approach. This section gives an overview of the principal tools available for the regulation of data privacy on the national level, and characterises the basic approaches that can be distinguished.

Regulation theory distinguishes between performance- or principles-based and rules-based regulation (see Chapter 27; also Australian Law Reform Commission 2008, vol 1: 234ff.). Both approaches have advantages and disadvantages. Performance-based regulation sets an overall objective rather than detailing steps that must be complied with. It can thus be described as focused on outcomes, with the advantages of flexibility but at the cost of potential ambiguity and imprecision.[8] Rules-based regulation, in contrast, provides for clarity about the actions regulatees have to perform, creating certainty of expectations for all sides concerned. On the other hand, such an approach may invite 'box ticking', and may appear rigid in the face of shifting circumstances, thus disconnecting the situation from the desired outcomes.

In privacy regulation, both performance-based and rules-based regulation can be found. Bennett and Raab (2006) find the three main classes of policy tools in this area to be legal instruments and regulatory agencies, self-regulatory instruments, and technological instruments. Relating them to the theoretical distinction introduced above, we find that both the first and the second bridge rules- and performance-based regulation (since legislation as well as self-regulation can follow either strategy), and the third is highly privacy-specific and cannot be mapped on to the distinction.

Legal instruments regulating privacy vary in two dimensions, namely their focus on either performance or rules, and the degree to which they are comprehensive or issue-specific. In the form of 'fair information practices' (FIP), performance-based regulation emerged first in the United States in the early 1970s. The Advisory Committee on Automated Personal Data Systems established by the US Department of Health, Education and Welfare (HEW) contained the first such code, and defined the core of a policy solution to personal data protection in terms of fairness and hence justice (Regan 2008: 55f.). This approach has proven influential in subsequent years in shaping the information practices of numerous private and governmental institutions, and it became the dominant US approach to information-privacy protection for the next decades (Westin 2003: 436). Privacy principles can be defined as an attempt to balance competing business and consumer interests in the private sector (and bureaucracy and citizen interests in the public sector) based on general considerations of justice. To implement such principles and put them into practice, however, requires further steps, namely either legislation or agency regulation, or self-regulation. While some legislation in this field exists in all countries, it varies considerably in character: there are privacy laws that cover both private and public sectors (dominant for example in European countries); and there are cases where a multitude of privacy laws exists that regulates only very specific areas (for example the United States Video Privacy Protection Act of 1988 which provides rules only for the use of video rental information). For the implementation of such legislation, governments normally set up or designate an agency responsible for its implementation – usually called the 'Privacy Commissioner', 'Data Commissioner' or 'Data Protection Commissioner'.[9] The degree of resources devoted to such an agency, its independence from the national executive, and the degree to which they are active participants in the national regulatory debates, however, vary considerably between countries (Bennett 1992; Bennett and Raab 2006; Newman 2008).

Self-regulation is a mode of regulation that works without direct government involvement, but may exist 'in the shadow of public power' (Newman and Bach 2004). Industry is usually the initiator of self-regulation, and the likelihood of using this instrument is linked to the structure of sectoral interest representation. If strong associations exist that have the dominant firms on board, the adoption, implementation and enforcement of rules will be easier than if several associations compete for industry representation and/ or dominant firms remain absent. Authored by industry, self-regulation will normally consist of codes of practice of different varieties, but, in contrast to the privacy principles discussed above, they will be much more specific in the level of detail they employ (Bennett and Raab 2006, chap. 6). Doubts exist, however, about the effectiveness of self-regulation in the field of privacy protection, with respect to both the underlying theory and the practical experience (Papakonstantinou 2002: 143).

Regulation through technology is a third principal regulatory instrument that is highly specific as it builds privacy rules into the machinery and protocols of the communication flows dealing with personal data. Such 'privacy-enhancing technologies' (PETs)[10] include public key encryption, anonymisation servers, software that blocks cookies for browsers, or the use of privacy preferences such as P3P to ensure users' informed consent to a website's privacy policy. In spite of the obvious benefits, PETs have not (yet?) been widely implemented, and further research into them has been called for (Royal Academy of Engineering 2007: 40–43).

The instruments described in this section constitute a toolbox from which governments can choose in their attempt to regulate the field of person-related data privacy. In spite of the commonality of the challenge, however, countries' regulatory approaches continue to differ. No best practice has emerged so far, and, while the piece-by-piece emergence of regulation over time may have contributed to this situation, it also points to differences in the fundamental approaches to the regulation of person-related privacy. In Europe, differences have narrowed substantially through the adoption of the EU Data Protection Directive in 1995; but a substantial divergence exists with the United States which can perhaps most succinctly be summarised as a human rights approach versus a property rights approach (cf. Zwick and Dholakia 2001; Kobrin 2004). The European approach sees privacy as a fundamental human right, which is a precondition for the individual's autonomy and thus cannot be traded away. The burden of protection rests not with the individual, but with society. Explicit statutes and regulatory agencies to oversee enforcement are the chosen mechanisms for this, and protection can be seen as being proactive, not reactive. Historical experiences with dictatorships such as that of the Nazis (who used census data for the Holocaust) and repressive regimes in East Europe have sensitised Europeans to the importance of data protection. In contrast, the absence of such experiences, combined with a tradition of distrust against government, led to a preference for markets and self-regulation in privacy in the United States. Privacy is seen as a property right rather than a human right, a commodity that is tradeable, and the legal system treats it like private property. Therefore the private sector and free market are seen as the most effective mechanisms for protecting privacy, with the focus being more on the consumer than the citizen. Consequently protection is often more reactive than proactive.

## 16.3 INTERNATIONAL DISPUTES ABOUT REGULATING PRIVACY

The different approaches taken to the protection of person-related data on both sides of the Atlantic have contributed to disputes in this area since the 1990s. Their root cause, however, lies primarily in competing economic interests and different security strategies that became evident because of the massive growth of electronic commerce and the fight against international terrorism after 9/11. But already long before that, differences had emerged. Given their early advantage in the IT industry in the 1960s and 1970s, United States' representatives had been sceptical about European moves towards data protection in the 1970s, at least as far as transborder data flows were concerned. Already on the occasion of an OECD workshop in 1977, sharp contrasts had emerged between the US and European approaches to international data protection. Europeans saw the American championing of freedom of information and free flows of data across national borders primarily as designed to protect the advantage of the US data processing industry, while Americans suspected Europeans of erecting protectionist barriers to trade in the name of protecting privacy (Bennett 1992: 137; see also Bygrave 2008: 21).

Since the mid-1990s, past suspicions have turned into concrete conflicts across the Atlantic. Starting in the area of economic interests, their focus has shifted to issues of security policy over the last decade, thus demonstrating that the regulation of privacy is an issue which has been broadening in scope and importance. The expansion of electronic commerce, with double-digit growth rates continuously surpassing those of overall economic activity, put the issue of access to electronic markets high on the agenda of policy makers: in 2001, total e-commerce (including business-to-business transactions) amounted to $1080 billion in the United States, and $430 billion in Europe,[11] making access to overseas markets a matter of supreme economic importance. But access to the promising European market was threatened for the United States by adoption of the 1995 EU Data Protection Directive,[12] which limited transfer of personal data to countries with an 'adequate level of protection'. Despite the warnings in a legal study on privacy protection in the United States commissioned by the European Commission (Schwartz and Reidenberg 1996), the US government initially did not take the threat of trade disruption in e-commerce seriously; thus negotiations between the two sides only began shortly before the directive was about to enter into effect in October 1998. For a year, they were stuck as each side demanded the other adapt to its own modus operandi: EU officials wanted the United States to introduce appropriate formal legislation and authorities to protect privacy; US representatives insisted that their strategy to rely on independent privacy auditing agencies awarding seals for websites was the only possible solution to the conflict.[13] The logjam in the negotiations was only overcome when American lead negotiator David Aaron suggested the concept of a 'Safe Harbor' – a set of principles to which companies would be able to subscribe and which would be considered 'adequate' under the EU directive. On this basis – and the assurances of the Federal Trade Commission to initiate legal action if companies failed to comply with their obligations – a compromise was struck which became known as the Safe Harbor agreement.[14] In July 2000, the EU Commission issued a decision certifying the adequacy of the agreement with respect to the Data Protection Directive.

Only a year later, after the terrorist attacks of 11 September 2001, the focus of transatlantic disputes about person-related data regulation shifted from the economic to the security sphere. Negotiated compromise gave way to unilateral imposition of preferences, and the hopes expressed in academic literature that Safe Harbor had set an example for solving the problem of regulatory spill-over across jurisdictions and would become a model of future solutions for problems of this kind (Farrell 2003: 297) became dubious as two more conflicts emerged. The first was a dispute about airline passenger name records (PNRs), which included confidential information such as home addresses, credit card details, religious meal preferences and physical or medical conditions (Lyon 2003: 126ff.). After the US Congress passed the Aviation and Security Act in November 2001, airlines flying from, to or through the United States were required to give the US Bureau of Customs and Border Protection electronic access to PNR data contained in their reservation and departure control systems. Since these were personal data protected under the EU directive, airlines had the choice to either breach US law or European law and face the respective consequences, ranging from penalties to landing rights withdrawal.

Negotiations between the EU and the US took place, but analysis makes clear that the two sides did not reach a compromise but the US side largely prevailed with its demands (Busch 2006: 312–14). When the EU Commission issued an adequacy ruling for the PNR agreement in May 2004, the European Parliament decided to take the Commission to the European Court of Justice to demand an annulment of both the agreement and the ruling, thus adding an intra-European dimension to the conflict.

In 2006, another transatlantic dispute arose over person-related data and privacy. Through investigative reporting by the *New York Times* (Lichtblau and Risen 2006), it emerged that since late 2001 the US administration had gained access to the data of worldwide financial transactions held by the Society for Worldwide Interbank Financial Telecommunication (SWIFT) for the purposes of the Terrorist Finance Tracking Program. SWIFT is an industry-owned cooperative incorporated under Belgian law that has been providing services to the international financial industry through a transfer message service since its foundation in 1973. With over 8000 customers in more than 200 countries, it routes up to 12 million transactions per day, with a volume of up to 6 trillion US dollars. The data had been subpoenaed in the United States, where one of the two data centres of SWIFT happened to be located. As the huge data transfer had been kept secret, the reaction across Europe was one of indignation from governments and privacy supporters, but also from business associations that feared the data might be used for the purposes of industrial espionage. Reactions included the decision by SWIFT to subscribe to the Safe Harbor agreement and to move its data centre out of the US, while negotiations between the EU and the United States resulted in the Europeans agreeing in principle to the use of financial data for anti-terrorism purposes if a degree of data protection was ensured. However, both the PNR case and the SWIFT case became politicised because of growing worries in Europe about the increasingly restrictive stance of anti-terrorism policy and the extension of police and secret service powers. The European Parliament took up these complaints, and through its increased powers under the Lisbon Treaty was able to vote down existing agreements with the United States in early 2010, thus forcing a renegotiation.

## 16.4   CHALLENGES FOR REGULATING PRIVACY IN THE 21ST CENTURY

As a political issue, the regulation of privacy is more likely to gain in salience than to lose in the years to come. This is due to the increased importance of the issue on the international level, as described in the previous section, but also to growing demand from the population to protect privacy better, as demonstrated by opinion polls. Irrespective of the different regulatory approaches across the Atlantic, citizens both in Europe and in the United States feel that their privacy is increasingly under threat. In the United States in the 1990s, the share of respondents who were 'very' or 'somewhat' concerned about their personal privacy rose from 80 per cent in 1990 to 94 per cent in 1999; in 2002, 34 per cent of respondents felt 'basically safe' about their right to privacy, and 65 per cent thought it was either 'under serious threat' or had 'already been lost'; by 2005, the respective numbers had dropped to 16 per cent and risen to 82 per cent (National Research Council 2008: 288, 290). In the European Union, concern about data privacy varies considerably between countries, with a mean of 64 per cent being 'very' or 'fairly' concerned about data privacy (with variations ranging from 32 per cent in the Netherlands to 86 per cent in Germany and Austria); over the past decade, concern has clearly been on the increase, with particularly strong increases in countries where citizens had previously been highly concerned about the issue (Gallup Europe and European Commission 2008: 7–9). In Europe, recent worries about privacy protection have helped spawn a new political movement in the shape of the Pirate Party, which has an international umbrella organisation that helps coordinate the national parties.[15] Starting in Sweden in 2006, Pirate Parties have started to contest elections, and in 2009 won two seats in the European Parliament election (from 7.13 per cent of the vote in Sweden) as well as polling 2 per cent in the German general election (making it the strongest party not to enter parliament).

In the decades since the 1970s, data protection legislation has spread across the globe from its origins in West Europe to North and South America, East and Central Europe, Australasia, the Middle East and Asia (see the helpful overview in Bennett and Raab 2006: 127). Much of that legislation has been influenced by diffusion, policy learning, and a network of policy experts largely consisting of data protection commissioners, and this at an early point led scholars to diagnose policy convergence, which was expected to continue as privacy legislation spread to more countries (Bennett 1992, chaps 3, 4). The United States' privacy standards especially were expected to see some ratcheting up through a variety of mechanisms such as EU collective action and market clout, firms' desire to expand their markets and the constraints of supranational trade rules (Regan 1993; Shaffer 2000). Some projected that the EU Data Protection Directive would establish itself as a global standard (Heisenberg and Fandel 2004).

In reality, things have moved far more slowly than had been expected. This may have been influenced by the international fight against terrorism since 2001, which saw a strengthening of state law enforcement and secret service powers – not least in information technology and surveillance capabilities – around the world, accompanied by (as critics state) a weakening of privacy and data protection (Klosek 2007; National Research Council 2008). But besides that, divergent economic interests as well as the slow march of international negotiations have also hampered convergence developments more than had been expected. European standards of data protection as embodied in the 1995 EU directive have for example influenced Australian privacy legislation (Westin 2003). However, as information becomes a key asset in the twenty-first century world economy, OECD countries' role in the global IT industry is changing, and with it the regulatory landscape. As countries such as the BRIC economies develop their IT industry capabilities and compete in the worldwide market for data processing, the question of privacy standards gains new importance. The race for the setting of a global standard in this field is dominated by two competing approaches, namely the European and the United States' ones outlined above. Both sides are positioning themselves, and the United States has been using its membership of APEC to influence that organisation's Privacy Framework to advocate its own (and, compared to the European level, lower) standards of privacy protection (Greenleaf 2003, 2005) and help create a competitor for the EU directive.

Regulatory competition can lead to different dynamics which can either lead to tighter regulation (a 'race to the top') or lighter regulation (a 'race to the bottom') (Vogel 1986).

But which of the two dynamics is likely to prevail in the competition for an international standard in privacy regulation? While a lower standard, in so far as it carries lower compliance costs, may bring a cost advantage to national industry and thus help compete in the marketplace, this need not be an advantage in the competition for setting an international standard. For regulatory standards are a public good which creates a common point of reference and can contribute to overall market growth. In banking regulation, for example, agreements about minimum capital adequacy standards and their quick international dissemination have shown that tighter regulation may actually become a market advantage (Genschel and Plümper 1997). As a consequence, a rationale exists for non-OECD economies such as India which compete for outsourcing of North American and European data processing to adopt the tighter European standards of privacy protection, which would help them gain access to that particular market. However, whether the market logic that underlies the process outlined here will prevail remains to be seen. Others have pointed to factors impeding convergence on an international standard, including the lack of an international organisation sufficiently strong to bridge the differences in national approaches (Bygrave 2004: 347–8) and the importance of legal transplantation between national legal systems (Reidenberg 2000: 1370f.). In addition, the possible influence on such a process through political pressure is an aspect that should not be discounted when trying to make probability assessments about future developments, especially in an area that is of such strategic and economic importance as regulation affecting the international exchange of data and information.

## ACKNOWLEDGEMENTS

Research for this chapter was supported by ESRC grant RES-062-23-0536 and by a fellowship at the Hanse Institute for Advanced Study in 2009. Both are gratefully acknowledged.

## NOTES

1. Quoted after Westin (1967: 12).
2. A recent summary of international agreements to protect personal data can be found in Bygrave (2008). A comprehensive review of transnational policy instruments in this area is chapter 4 of Bennett and Raab (2006). Excellent sources for information about international privacy law are Solove et al. (2006) and Electronic Privacy Information Center (2007).
3. See the Explanatory Report about Convention 108 at http//conventions.coe.int/Treaty/EN/Reports/HTML/108.htm (accessed 19 February 2010).
4. As of February 2010, 41 of the 47 member states had signed and ratified the convention. Russia, Turkey and Ukraine had signed but not ratified it, and Armenia, Azerbaijan and San Marino had done neither.
5. This latter deficiency has been corrected by explicitly adding a protocol addressing the subject of transborder data flows in 2001 (Council of Europe 2001) which makes these subject to the non-contracting countries possessing an 'adequate level of protection' (Article 2, Para. 1).
6. The generator is available at http://www2.oecd.org/pwv3/ (accessed 20 February 2010). The other documents cited are printed or reprinted in Organisation for Economic Co-operation and Development (2002, 2003).
7. For an analysis, see for example Klosek (2000, chap. 3).
8. See Black (2008) on the dependence of such an approach on pre-existing trust between the parties involved.

9.  The United States is the only OECD country without such an agency; in Japan, 'competent ministers' for the implementation of the data protection act are designated by the prime minister.
10. For an inventory of PETs see Organisation for Economic Co-operation and Development (2003, chap. 12); for a discussion of them see Bennett and Raab (2006, chap. 7). See Brands (2000) for a concrete example.
11. Data after UNCTAD (2004) and *The Economist*, 15 May 2004, p. 9.
12. A succinct summary of the directive can be found in Heisenberg (2005: 27–32).
13. For a detailed analysis of the case, see Regan (2003) and Heisenberg (2005).
14. Details can be found at http://www.export.gov/safeharbor/ (accessed 3 March 2010).
15. See http://en.wikipedia.org/wiki/Pirate_Parties_International for an introductory overview (accessed 2 March 2010).

# REFERENCES

Allen, Anita L. (2005), 'Privacy', in Hugh LaFollette (ed.), *The Oxford Handbook of Practical Ethics*, Oxford: Oxford University Press, pp. 485–513.
Asia-Pacific Economic Cooperation (2004), *APEC Privacy Framework: 16th APEC Ministerial Meeting*, Santiago, Chile, 17–18 November, available at: www.apec.org/.
Australian Law Reform Commission (2008), *For Your Information: Australian Privacy Law and Practice*, report, Canberra: Law Reform Commission.
Bennett, Colin J. (1992), *Regulating Privacy: Data Protection and Public Policy in Europe and the United States*, Ithaca, NY: Cornell University Press.
Bennett, Colin J. and Charles D. Raab (2006), *The Governance of Privacy: Policy Instruments in Global Perspective*, 2nd edn, Cambridge, MA and London: MIT Press.
Black, Julia (2008), *Forms and Paradoxes of Principles-Based Regulation*, LSE Law, Society and Economics Working Papers, 13-2008, London: London School of Economics and Political Science.
Brands, Stefan A. (2000), *Rethinking Public Key Infrastructures and Digital Certificates: Building in Privacy*, Cambridge, MA and London: MIT Press.
Burnham, David (1983), *The Rise of the Computer State*, London: Weidenfeld & Nicolson.
Busch, Andreas (2006), 'From safe harbour to the rough sea? Privacy disputes across the Atlantic', SCRIPTed: *A Journal of Law and Technology*, 3 (4), 304–21, available at: www.law.ed.ac.uk/ahrc/script%2Ded/vol3-4/busch.asp.
Bygrave, Lee A. (2004), 'Privacy protection in a global context – a comparative overview', *Scandinavian Studies in Law*, 47, 319–48.
Bygrave, Lee A. (2008), 'International agreements to protect personal data', in James B. Rule and Graham Greenleaf (eds), *Global Privacy Protection*, Cheltenham, UK and Northampton, MA, USA: Edward Elgar Publishing, pp. 15–49.
Council of Europe (1981), *Convention for the Protection of Individuals with Regard to Automatic Processing of Personal Data*, Convention 108, Strasbourg: Council of Europe.
Council of Europe (2001), *Additional Protocol to the Convention for the Protection of Individuals with Regard to Automatic Processing of Personal Data Regarding Supervisory Authorities and Transborder Data Flows*, Convention 181, Strasbourg: Council of Europe.
Electronic Privacy Information Center (2007), *Privacy and Human Rights 2006: An International Survey of Privacy Laws and Developments*, Washington, DC: Electronic Privacy Information Center and Privacy International.
Etzioni, Amitai (1999), *The Limits of Privacy*, New York: Basic Books.
European Union (1995), 'Directive 95/46/EC of the European Parliament and of the Council on the protection of personal data with regard to the processing of personal data and on the free movement of such data', *Official Journal of the European Communities*, L 281/31.
Farrell, Henry (2003), 'Constructing the international foundations of e-commerce – the EU–US Safe Harbor arrangement', *International Organization*, 57 (2), 277–306.
Gallup Europe and European Commission (2008), *Data Protection in the European Union: Citizens' Perceptions: Analytical Report*, Brussels: Gallup Europe and European Commission.
Gavison, Ruth (1992), 'Feminism and the public/private distinction', *Stanford Law Review*, 45, 1–45.
Genschel, Philipp and Thomas Plümper (1997), 'Regulatory competition and international co-operation', *Journal of European Public Policy*, 4 (4), 626–42.
Greenleaf, Graham (2003), 'APEC privacy principles: more lite with every version', *Privacy Law and Policy Reporter*, 10 (6), available at: www.austlii.edu.au/au/journals/PLPR/2003/50.html.

Greenleaf, Graham (2005), 'APEC's privacy framework: a new low standard', *Privacy Law and Policy Reporter*, **11** (5), available at: www.austlii.edu.au/au/journals/PLPR/2005/1.html.

Heisenberg, Dorothee (2005), *Negotiating Privacy: The European Union, the United States, and Personal Data Protection*, Boulder, CO: Lynne Rienner Publishers.

Heisenberg, Dorothee and Marie-Hélène Fandel (2004), 'Projecting EU regimes abroad: the EU Data Protection Directive as global standard', in Sandra Braman (ed.), *The Emergent Global Information Policy Regime*, International Political Economy Series, Basingstoke: Palgrave Macmillan, pp. 109–29.

Klosek, Jacqueline (2000), *Data Privacy in the Information Age*, Westport, CT: Quorum Books.

Klosek, Jacqueline (2007), *The War on Privacy*, Westport, CT: Praeger Publishers.

Kobrin, Stephen J. (2004), 'Safe harbours are hard to find: the trans-Atlantic data privacy dispute, territorial jurisdiction and global governance', *Review of International Studies*, **30** (1), 111–31.

Lichtblau, Eric and James Risen (2006), 'Bank data sifted in secret by US to block terror', *New York Times*, 23 June, p. 1.

Lyon, David (2003), *Surveillance after September 11: Themes for the 21st Century*, Cambridge: Polity Press.

Miller, Arthur Raphael (1971), *The Assault on Privacy: Computers, Data Banks, and Dossiers*, Ann Arbor: University of Michigan Press.

Moore, Barrington, Jr. (1984), *Privacy: Studies in Social and Cultural History*, Armonk, NY and London: M.E. Sharpe.

National Research Council (ed.) (2008), *Protecting Individual Privacy in the Struggle against Terrorists: A Framework for Program Assessment*, Washington DC: National Academies Press.

Newman, Abraham L. (2008), *Protectors of Privacy: Regulating Personal Data in the Global Economy*, Ithaca, NY: Cornell University Press.

Newman, Abraham L. and David Bach (2004), 'Self-regulatory trajectories in the shadow of public power: resolving digital dilemmas in Europe and the United States', *Governance*, **17** (3), 387–413.

Niblett, G.B.F. (1971), *Digital Information and the Privacy Problem*, OECD Informatics Studies, vol. 2, Paris: Organisation for Economic Co-operation and Development.

O'Harrow, Robert (2006), *No Place to Hide: Behind the Scenes of Our Emerging Surveillance Society*, New York: Free Press.

Organisation for Economic Co-operation and Development (1981), *Guidelines on the Protection of Privacy and Transborder Flows of Personal Data*, Paris and Washington, DC: Organisation for Economic Co-operation and Development.

Organisation for Economic Co-operation and Development (2002), *OECD Guidelines on the Protection of Privacy and Transborder Flows of Personal Data*, Paris: Organisation for Economic Co-operation and Development.

Organisation for Economic Co-operation and Development (2003), *Privacy Online: OECD Guidance on Policy and Practice*, Paris: OECD.

Packard, Vance Oakley (1964), *The Naked Society*, London: Longman.

Papakonstantinou, Vagelis (2002), 'Self-regulation and the protection of privacy', *Frankfurter Studien zum Datenschutz*, vol. 22, Baden-Baden: Nomos.

Prosser, William (1960), 'Privacy', *California Law Review*, **48** (3), 383–423.

Regan, Priscilla M. (1993), 'The globalization of privacy: implications of recent changes in Europe', *American Journal of Economics and Sociology*, **52**, 257–74.

Regan, Priscilla M. (2003), 'Safe harbors or free frontiers? Privacy and transborder data flows', *Journal of Social Issues*, **59** (2), 263–82.

Regan, Priscilla M. (2008), 'The United States', in James B. Rule and Graham Greenleaf (eds), *Global Privacy Protection*, Cheltenham, UK and Northampton, MA, USA: Edward Elgar Publishing, pp. 50–79.

Reidenberg, Joel R. (2000), 'Resolving conflicting international data privacy rules in cyberspace', *Stanford Law Review*, **52**, 1315–71.

Rössler, Beate (2005), *The Value of Privacy*, Cambridge and Malden, MA: Polity.

Royal Academy of Engineering (2007), *Dilemmas of Privacy and Surveillance: Challenges of Technological Change*, London: Royal Academy of Engineering.

Schneider, Elisabeth M. (1991), 'The violence of privacy', *Connecticut Law Review*, **23**, 973–99.

Schwartz, Paul M. and Joel R. Reidenberg (1996), *Data Privacy Law: A Study of United States Data Protection*, Charlottesville, VA: Michie.

Shaffer, Gregory (2000), 'Globalization and social protection: the impact of EU and international rules in the ratcheting up of US privacy standards', *Yale Journal of International Law*, **25** (1), 1–88.

Solove, Daniel J. (2008), *Understanding Privacy*, Cambridge, MA: Harvard University Press.

Solove, Daniel J., Marc Rotenberg and Paul M. Schwartz (2006), *Information Privacy Law*, 2nd edn, New York: Aspen Publishers.

Sykes, Charles J. (1999), *The End of Privacy*, New York: St. Martin's Press.

UNCTAD (2004), *E-Commerce and Development Report 2004*, New York and Geneva: United Nations.

Vogel, David (1986), *National Styles of Regulation: Environmental Policy in Great Britain and the United States*, Cornell Studies in Political Economy, Ithaca, NY: Cornell University Press.

Waldo, James, H.S. in and L.I. Millett (eds) (2007), *Engaging Privacy and Information Technology in a Digital Age,* Washington, DC: National Academies Press.

Warren, Samuel D. and L.D. Brandeis (1890), 'The right to privacy', *Harvard Law Review*, **IV** (5), 193–220.

Westin, Alan F. (1967), *Privacy and Freedom*, New York: Atheneum.

Westin, Alan F. (2003), 'Social and political dimensions of privacy', *Journal of Social Issues*, **59** (2), 431–53.

Zwick, D. and N. Dholakia (2001), 'Contrasting European and American approaches to privacy in electronic markets: property right versus civil right', *Electronic Markets*, **11** (2), 116–20.

# PART V

# REGULATING OLD AND NEW MEDIA

# 17 Regulating the media: four perspectives
## *Amit M. Schejter and Sangyong Han*

The media of mass communications are social institutions with the technological capacity to disseminate mass-produced messages (Turow 1992). In contemporary society they have become the chief distributors of symbolic content. Media regulation is the authoritative establishment of the quantity, quality and type of messages that they can or are required to distribute in a given social order. As a result, and within the context of defining the term "regulation" as set in Chapter 1 of this volume (Levi-Faur 2011) it is unworkable to discuss media regulation within a narrow definition of "regulation" that is limited to secondary legislation, as media regulation is a central and all-encompassing activity determining the extent of free expression in a given society, and all legal, economic and social means of governance can be employed in order to reach the same ends.[1] The means for media regulation differ among political systems as contemporary media regulation emerges from patterns embedded in deep-seated ideological traditions.

In order to analyze the different models of media regulation, both historically and contemporarily, this chapter identifies four perspectives employed to justify it: economic, technological, cultural and democratic. These four perspectives correspond to some extent to the chronological development of media regulation, as media regulation is as old as the media themselves. The chapter analyzes each of these perspectives, sets them within their historical context and ideological underpinnings, and provides examples for the development and changes in media regulation as they pertain to each of them.

## 17.1 THE ROOTS OF MEDIA REGULATION

Despite its early Asian beginnings, printing technology in its modern form was introduced in Europe (Green 2003a), where it was met by strictly governed authoritarian hierarchical societies controlled by the monarchy and the church (Siebert et al. 1956). The founding of the United States and the eventual ratification of the Bill of Rights (and within it the First Amendment to the Constitution, which promised unlimited press freedom) set press regulation on a different and free-of-government-intervention course in the Americas, inspired by the French Revolution. In Europe, however, including in post-revolutionary France itself, the adoption of a free press paradigm had a rocky beginning and suffered almost immediate setbacks (Walton 2009). The same can be said of the United Kingdom, in which the liberal ideas of the 17th and 18th centuries, advocating freedom of expression as an individual natural right and as an exercise without which the truth cannot be tested, contributed to the erosion of press controls; however, in lack of constitutional safeguards the actual defense of free speech amounted for decades to little more than "the right to write or say anything which a jury, consisting of twelve shopkeepers, think it expedient should be said or written" (Dicey 1959 as cited in Barendt 2005: 40). Unlike the Western individualistic and emancipatory ideals,

Asian conceptions of free speech emanated from consensual and group-oriented roots (Hsiung 1985). As a result, "the 'Asian-values' school has used this line of reasoning to equate press freedom with press-government harmony" (Gunaratne 1999: 206). Critical observers of the endorsement of "Asian values" find them inherently rooted in the pre-modern social-political system of the oriental monarchy, thus not only obsolete, but also susceptible to be employed by authoritarian elites in the same confounding manner as "Western values" had been used in the West (Sen 1997; Li 1999).

### 17.1.1   Media Regulation as Economic Regulation

Information products embody unique characteristics, which differentiate them from an economic perspective from tangible products. Information is a public good; thus its sharing does not eradicate its value (Owen 2002). Still, an economy to which information goods are central, what is commonly referred to as an "information society," is based on the understanding that information is a commodity (Schement and Liverouw 1988). The distinction between "information products" and "information economics" and the economics of tangible goods, however, was not recognized initially when an economic perspective was employed to regulate newspaper markets in the US.

Newspapers, the first "mass" medium, emerged initially as political pamphlets. The industrialization of the newspaper with the invention of the "penny press" led to its transition into a commercial medium[2] that enjoyed extensive freedoms, and news became a mass commodity (Hamilton 2004). In 1934 the United States Supreme Court agreed to review antitrust complaints against the press and determined that the business of news-papers was not exempt from such scrutiny. Thus an economic rationale and procedure opened the door to government oversight of an industry perceived until then best exempt from government regulation.

Unlike the printed press in the US, which emerged through unregulated private enterprise that limited government intervention to the "economic" frame, broadcasting was launched as a private enterprise and has been subject to licensing since 1912 and subjected to regulations aimed at ensuring that it serves the "public interest" since 1927. This determination allowed the Federal Communications Commission (FCC), an economic regulator (Yandle 2011) created by the Communications Act in 1934,[3] to manage electronic media regulation, in addition to other considerations, as an "economic" issue and use the "economic rationale" to regulate speech. Broadcasting licenses were at first granted on a local basis, creating "broadcasting markets," and early policy determined by the FCC that it would not be in the public's interest for a private organization to be granted more than one broadcast license for each such market. The FCC rationalized the rule at first as necessary in order to protect the public from the dangers emanating from the concentration of economic power.

From a narrow focus on concentration, economic media regulation expanded to include enhancement of competition. The 1934 Communications Act "expressly forbids ownership or control of stations where the purpose or the effect thereof might be to sub-stantially lessen competition or to restrain commerce" (*Superior Oil Company v. Federal Power Commission*), and the context of the Communications Act and its language focus on the economic rationale for ownership regulation, as was constantly repeated in its interpretation by the courts during the Act's early years. The economic perspective with regard to the electronic media, however, was mostly an American paradigm for most of the 20th century, as the electronic media in the rest of the world were in the hands of governments. The late-20th-century emergence of private media across the globe introduced regulations embedded in the economic perspective in other countries as well. Those were mostly focused on the governance of the different markets commercial media created – the market for content, the market for distribution and the market for advertising. The former two led to regulatory control of horizontal and vertical mergers, while the latter, though an economic activity, led to the development of a distinct arena of regulation, which is invoked by cultural concerns as well (Ginosar 2011).

### 17.1.2  Media Regulation as a Technological Challenge

One perspective that has historically been shared by governments and lawmakers in the US with those in other countries is the technological, an angle that developed into a justification for content control both directly and indirectly. Content can be affected both directly and indirectly, as intended and as unintended, as a result of technological and technical determinations (Turow 1992: 28). The technological perspective was first rooted in the unique physical attributes of the broadcasting medium. The reliance on a new technology, the radio, and on a new distribution medium, the electromagnetic spectrum, challenged governing bodies worldwide. The appearance of subsequent technological developments such as cable distribution of video, satellite distribution, and content service over mobile telephone devices and ultimately the emergence of digital distribution and the Internet, each in its time, served as the justification for the creation of new rules, which were aimed at and eventually had an immediate effect on the distribution of information and ideas.

The first technologically induced radio law in the United States was enacted in 1910. However, it did not target content, as it pertained to the need of ocean vessels to carry emergency communications (Douglas 1987: 220). Its immediate successor, the Radio Act of 1912, while again targeting emergency communications, empowered the Secretary of Commerce with the authority to license the airwaves (Douglas 1987: 234). The road to introducing content-related considerations to the licensing process was not long. In 1927 the US Congress passed a new Radio Act, which was described by its initiator, Secretary of Commerce Herbert Hoover, as making it possible to "clear up the chaos of interference" (as cited by McChesney 1993: 18) but addressed radio as a medium carrying content that needed to serve the "public interest, convenience and necessity." Similarly, the first British media law driven by technological considerations, the Cinematograph Act of 1909, was also not content directed, as it aimed at protecting the well-being of movie theater audiences, by addressing safety concerns arising from the flammable nature of early film (Goldberg et al. 2009: 9). By 1912, however, concerns for public morality became the impetus for the establishment of the British Board of Film Classification, whose regulatory powers were content directed (Goldberg et al. 2009: 342).

One effect of the technological perspective was the evolution of policies aimed at diversifying content over the airwaves. In the US, the FCC adopted the "fairness doctrine" that required licensees to broadcast programming of a political-controversial nature and to do so while allowing opposing viewpoints the opportunity to be heard. The Supreme Court's decision in 1969 in which the (now defunct) doctrine was upheld as constitutional cited scarcity of broadcast frequencies as the reason for the ruling. Since broadcasters utilized a resource which was scarce to others, it was deemed pertinent that the government could proactively deny them the right to censor. Scarcity was also the reasoning behind the introduction of the broadcasting regime in the UK (Goldberg et al. 2009: 304), although the eventual regulatory system that emerged as a result was very different than that in the US. Another technology-related phenomenon was recognized and cited by UK regulators in the 1920s: the perceived power of the media over a mass audience (Goldberg et al. 2009: 304). Concerns regarding the impact of media appeared in the US as well. However, they were first expressed only in 1978 when the Supreme Court justified the need for regulation of indecent content in broadcast media, citing the intrusive nature of radio and the presence of children, to whom broadcasting is uniquely accessible even when they are too young to read. The identical assumption that the media are powerful and the spectrum is scarce had also been the driving force behind media regulation in other countries, such as New Zealand (Brown and Price 2006).

Technologically driven regulation has often led to the creation of multiple regulatory regimes (and even regulatory agencies) within legal systems. In the 1980s and 1990s, countries such as South Korea and Israel established separate regulators for cable and broadcast television (Kwak 1999; Schejter 2009). In the United Kingdom, on the other hand, all commercial television services were regulated in the 1990s under the same regulatory authority, regardless of their form of distribution. Commercial radio in the UK was regulated under a separate umbrella, while in Israel it was regulated within the same framework as commercial television. In the US, there has always been only one regulatory agency overseeing both media and telecommunications, but the technological distinctions between the printed press, the broadcasting industry and the cable industry led to three distinct regulatory philosophies, each enjoying different degrees of freedom (Pool 1983). As a result, US courts have determined that rules pertaining to political fairness, for example, can be imposed only on broadcasters but not on newspapers, and their application to cable was limited to local cable channels. Technological differences, however, did not have such an effect universally, which demonstrates how technology is but a perspective, not a determinant of a single regulatory response. Article 5(1) of the German Basic Law, for example, guarantees "freedom of the press and freedom of reporting by means of broadcast and films."[4] One reason for these differences in structural regulatory determinations may be that US law had made the technological differences between the media a cornerstone of media regulation, as all media were inherently market based and privately owned, while European governments asserted early on that broadcasting was too important to be left in the hands of the market (Levy 1999) and managed the broadcasters by themselves. Consequently, since the introduction of new media technologies such as cable and eventually the Internet was virtually simultaneous with the transition to a regulated media market in Europe, it allowed for the emergence of technologically neutral regulatory regimes, even though at first the transnational nature of the latter suggested it might be ungovernable (Murray 2011).

Technology has also been the driving force behind the establishment of transnational regulatory regimes such as the European Union's (EU) Directive on Television without Frontiers (TWF), which was a response to the transnational nature of satellite broadcasting (Harrison and Woods 2007: 52). However, the adoption of a technologically neutral framework by the EU led to the rewriting of the directive in an attempt to overcome traditional distinctions between broadcasting technologies. The new Audiovisual without Frontiers (AWF) Directive[5] distinguishes "linear audiovisual media services" (analog and digital television, live streaming, webcasting, and near video-on-demand) from "nonlinear audiovisual media services" (on-demand services). Because "nonlinear services" are distinct from "linear services" in the user's choice and control and in their impact on society, the directive imposes lighter restrictions on them. Yet newspapers and magazines do not fall into the jurisdiction of the directive (Schejter 2008).

### 17.1.3   Media Regulation as Cultural Paternalism

The paternalistic perspective of media regulation is most commonly associated with the emergence of the media in the UK. It is a perspective deemed to "guide and protect" the majority to adopt the ways of the minority by emphasizing what "ought" to be communicated (Williams 1976). Raymond Williams, who first identified this perspective, rejected technology as the shaping force behind media regulatory structures and claimed they are subordinated to the social and economic structure, which is primarily capitalist, but in the UK is modified by the "paternalistic" view of the public interest (St. Leger 1980). Similar conceptions of the role of the media were eventually adopted in former British colonies such as Australia where the right to broadcast was assigned to national organizations operating in the "public interest" or to private individuals who were licensed to operate their stations as "public trustees." Since those private enterprises were suspect as for their capability to provide what the public "needs" over what the public "wants", extensive control and scrutiny by a public body were deemed to be necessary to ensure that private broadcasters lived up to their public trustee status (Albion and Papandrea 1998: 3). Similarly, the British public broadcasting ethos has made its way into the former colonies of Hong Kong, Singapore, Malaysia and India (Green 2003b).

The notion that broadcasters need to adhere to close state supervision and to assume "public service" responsibilities that are cultural was widespread all across Western Europe from the inception of broadcasting and well into the 1990s and beyond. The "public service" role may have changed over the years and may have been tweaked to meet changing social, political and economic conditions, but by the 1990s it had embodied a number of accepted principles: public accountability; public finance; regulated content; universal service; regulated entrance (Siune and Hulten 1998); a comprehensive coverage remit; a generalized "broadly worded" mandate; pluralism; a cultural mission; a central place in politics both as highly politicized organizations and as reporters of the political process; and non-commercialism (Blumler 1992). Within this "interventionist" culture and clear sense of social purpose, Blumler assembled a list of "vulnerable values" protected by media policies across Europe, which were created as a reaction to the loss of the monopoly status of public service broadcasting. Generally, those "values" were identified as: program quality; maintenance of cultural diversity; cultural identity; independence from commercial influence; safeguarding the integrity of the civic community; protecting the young; and maintaining standards. Ang (1991) perceives broadcasting in Europe as a "servant of culture" (p. 101) and argues that these high-minded national cultural ideals may have been the destructive force behind its decline. Ang's predicament notwithstanding, European public broadcasters have long struggled to maintain their unique position and were successful in pushing through the institutions of the European

Union a protocol appended to the 1999 Amsterdam treaty, which defined the mission of public broadcasting as "directly related to the democratic, social, and cultural needs of each society and to the need to preserve media pluralism" (Schejter 2008). Still, some observers note that the transition to a single European market has in fact "gone hand in hand with an erosion of the cultural dimension upon which the European public service tradition has been based" (Burgelman and Pauwels 1992), and the adoption of the new AWF Directive has led to further devaluation of cultural objectives (Burri-Nenova 2007). At the same time the public service model was the dominant broadcasting model adopted by post-communist European countries (Harcourt 2003).

The cultural paradigm, although traditionally associated with Europe, has both been exported to and independently emerged elsewhere. Reviewing African media policies, Eko (2003) notes that the colonial heritage of African nations has also led to the adoption of the colonialists' view of the media, in particular the establishment of broadcasters in the "public service" mode. Interestingly, Eko refers to these entities as "governmental public broadcasters," a characterization that distances them from the "cultural paternalism" paradigm to one more associated with state control or "authoritarianism." In the meantime, a similar regulatory philosophy on the border between cultural paternalism and authoritarian state control developed in the early days of Japanese radio. Advertising was banned to ensure the burgeoning medium's reliance on the government, and the government maintained strict controls on all aspects of broadcasting. However, the justification for this control was cited as defense of the "Japanese character" of a working people who are "unlike Westerners" (Green 2003a). Kwak (1997) claims that at the end of the day the dominant common Confucian cultural values have been reflected in the practice of broadcast regulation in Japan, as well as in Korea and Hong Kong.

### 17.1.4   Media Regulation as Promoter of Democracy

Freedom of expression, as noted, is at the root of media regulation. While economic and technological justifications have traditionally played a role in regulatory design, more often than not the regulatory effort focused on the control of content as governments assumed the role of determining if and which type of content would be allowed. Napoli (1999) identifies three fundamental differences between communications regulation and the regulation of other industries: the unique potential for social and political impact; the ambiguity of classification of decisions along economic or social regulatory lines; and the potential overlap and interaction between economic and social concerns within individual decisions. All three point to the inherent tension between applying regulatory constraints on the media for whatever reason and the consequences such action has on the social role the media play in society and, as a result, on the health of democracy.

Thus, as Curran and Seaton (2003) note, the prevailing myth regarding freedom of expression in the United Kingdom, for example, is that the British press gained its "freedom" from government sometime in the mid-19th century. However, while the printed press enjoyed growing freedoms from government starting in the mid-19th century, it transited into a new market-controlled system, which established limitations of its own on press freedoms that have even been considered as "more effective than anything that had gone before" (Curran and Seaton 2003: 5). A similar fallacy equating the mere relaxation of government controls on the media and their subjugation to market rules as setting them free was also at the basis of the classic analysis of press systems offered in the mid-20th century by Siebert et al. (1956) in *Four Theories of the Press*, regarded as the single most influential volume in contemporary media studies (Nordenstreng 1998). In addition to failing to see the role of the market in regulating media (rather than "freeing" it), analyses based on *Four Theories* fail to identify regulatory mechanisms that are designed to enhance democracy, not only to leave it be.

An example of such an effort is the development of "diversity" as a component of the "public interest" standard in US media governance. First appearing in the Radio Act of 1927, the "public interest" was merely a term plugged into the legislation for lack of a more coherent and finely defined standard over which members of Congress could agree (Krasnow and Goodman 1998). But, over the years, it was explicated by the FCC, which determined that it meant maintaining and fostering "competition," "diversity" and "localism" – three concepts it believed to extend directly from the public interest (Napoli 2001). Diversity, as a policy goal, is often described as "competition in the marketplace of ideas" (Kwerel et al. 2002: 350) and is operationalized by policies aimed at ensuring public access to a wide range of viewpoints and opinions as well as to a large number of sources for information. The diversity principle in the US is associated with the Supreme Court's position that the First Amendment is based on an assumption that diverse and antagonistic sources of information are essential to the public welfare.

A combination of the conventional notion that electronic media have a powerful effect, of the fact that they play a role in the sustenance of a democratic public sphere and of the idea that "elections are won by the press" (Barendt 1998) has led to the development of rules regarding media usage during elections. In the US, these rules are mostly limited to post factum rectifications of perceived advantages given to one candidate for office over another.[6] In the United Kingdom each of the commercial and public broadcasting regulators is required to adopt a code of practice with respect to the participation of candidates in programming during the election period. Paid advertising, however, is prohibited, and, while in the US candidates can virtually purchase as much airtime as they wish, in the UK they are limited to a very limited number of "party election broadcasts." In Australia political advertisements need to be truthful (Orr et al. 2003), and the role of banning the untruthful is in the hands of the self-regulatory body of commercial broadcasters, the Federation of Australian Commercial Television Stations (Bamford 2002). In Canada, fairness during election times is governed through a mandate on all broadcasters to make a minimum of paid prime time broadcasting available to the eligible political parties.

Governing media in a democracy supporting perspective is not limited to the political sphere. In addition to diversity of opinion, other forms of diversity can be supported by concerned regulatory regimes. One area, which is addressed in many systems, is the provision of minority voice and representation, which at times conflicts directly with the acculturating role assigned to the media in the name of national unity. The need to provide for minority voices has been recognized internationally. The normative aim of minority media rights is for "autonomous ethnic minority media which can speak for, and to, their own community; . . . minority media which can generate a dialogue between . . . minority communities; and between these and dominant . . . communities" (Husband 1994: 11). Still, minorities' "self-presentations remain minuscule in comparison with the electronic media output of majority culture" (Browne 2005: 3). The US legal system never created a mechanism of positive content regulation to ensure diversity in programming (Freedman 2005), and minority representation was supposed to be achieved through diversity in ownership (Mason et al. 2001), applying an "economic" rather than a "democratic" perspective. In 1990, the Supreme Court found that the government had a "compelling interest" in promoting diversity of viewpoints through broadcasting, and that this objective could be achieved by encouraging minority ownership of media outlets. This determination was later somewhat mitigated and never fully prompted action by the FCC. In Australia, the Special Broadcasting Service (SBS), incorporated in 1991, is to provide "multilingual and multicultural radio services that inform, educate, and entertain all Australians and in doing so, reflect Australia's multicultural society" (SBS 2005). The Australian Broadcasting Corporation (ABC), the public service broadcaster, is required to "reflect the cultural diversity of the Australian community." However, this requirement was not geared toward Aborigines or their culture, but rather to immigrant groups (Jupp 2001). In more uniformly cultural settings, such as in the post-Soviet European republics, minority programming is little promoted in mainstream media (OSI 2005), while in long-established systems such as those in the UK and France the reference to minority broadcasting is all but marginal and on a regional basis (Schejter et al. 2007).

## 17.2   CURRENT TRENDS AND FUTURE CHALLENGES

The media landscape is undergoing changes challenging all of the four historical perspectives. The changes affecting this process include:

- democratization in previously totalitarian regimes;
- the rise of neo-liberalism and its global diffusion; and
- the emergence of global markets for media fare.

The control mechanisms set on media are challenged, as are the economic justifications for media regulation, and the ability to enforce cultural goals and regulatory structures on content that negates national boundaries.

These have taken place parallel to technological changes:

- an abundance of media content that audiences can access;
- a diminishing need to rely on content delivery over the airwaves for stationary devices;
- the transition to digital and Internet protocol-based delivery systems;
- a growing mobile entertainment industry; and
- a blurring of the traditional boundaries between information services and entertainment.

The new technological reality raises challenges from all perspectives. *Economically* there are calls to leave the future of the media sphere in the hands of the market (Blackman 1998), even suggesting that no government regulation will be further needed in light of the decentralized nature of new media (Negroponte 1995). Others assert that the economic framework is not sufficient to encounter the needs of a functioning market

(Shelanski 2006) and that government still has a role in regulating the media (Abramson 2001). New *technologies* have allowed countries to adopt rules that significantly reduce freedom of expression, most notably in Asia (Gomez 2004), although not uniformly (Skoric 2007). *Cultural* effects of the new media environment call for prescriptions to enhance the role of non-commercial media within this new environment (Goodman 2009) and to further protect children from the new dangers it imposes (Montgomery 2009). Late-20th-century deregulation has led to warnings that this regulatory oversight could lead to unhealthy consequences for *democracy* in the long run and that communication theory can contribute to bridge normative gaps that economic analysis alone cannot offer (Brennan 1992).

At this developed stage in the history of media regulation, it is clear that normative choices truly determine which perspective is adopted in each locale. An informed and educated citizenry should be able to seize this opportunity and ensure that the change works to favor civil empowerment over economic and technological determinism and open and egalitarian cultural exchange over top-down paternalistic imposition.

## NOTES

1. There are other methods to control free expression or to enhance it, ranging from the incarceration of anti-government political activists to the teaching of the importance of free speech within the educational system; however, the media are the central arena to which all actions eventually merge.
2. Although, as Altschull (1984) notes, no causal connection between the expansion of the advertising industry and the penny press has been proven (p. 27), and, as Nerone (1987) contends, the emergence of the penny press was influenced by the political and economic environment and was not a result of a determined decision on the part of the newspapers to become more commercial.
3. As an heir to the Federal Radio Commission formed under the previous Radio Act in 1927.
4. https://www.btg-bestellservice.de/pdf/80201000.pdf.
5. http://eur-lex.europa.eu/LexUriServ/LexUriServ.do?uri=CONSLEG:1989L0552:20071219:EN:PDF.
6. With the exception of the right to purchase airtime on radio or television that is secured for candidates to federal positions.

## REFERENCES

Abramson, B.D. (2001), 'Media policy after regulation?', *International Journal of Cultural Studies*, 4 (3), 301–26.
Albion, R. and F. Papandrea (1998), *Media Regulation in Australia and the Public Interest*, Melbourne, Victoria: Institute of Public Affairs.
Altschull, J.H. (1984), *Agents of Power: The Media and Public Policy*, White Plains, NY: Longman.
Ang, I. (1991), *Desperately Seeking the Audience*, London: Routledge.
Bamford, D. (2002), 'Current issues in Australian electoral law', *Election Law Journal*, 1, 253–8.
Barendt, E. (1998), 'Judging the media: impartiality and broadcasting', *Political Quarterly*, 69 (B), 108–16.
Barendt, E. (2005), *Freedom of Speech*, 2nd edn, New York: Oxford University Press.
Blackman, C.R. (1998), 'Convergence between telecommunications and other media – how should regulation adapt?', *Telecommunications Policy*, 22, 163–70.
Blumler, J. (ed.) (1992), *Television and the Public Interest: Vulnerable Values in West European Broadcasting*, London: Sage Publications.
Brennan, T.J. (1992), 'Integrating communication theory into media policy: an economic perspective', *Telecommunications Policy*, 16 (6), 460–74.
Brown, R. and S. Price (2006), *The Future of Media Regulation in New Zealand: Is There One?*, Wellington: Broadcasting Standards Authority.
Browne, D. (2005), *Ethnic Minorities, Electronic Media and the Public Sphere: A Comparative Study*, Cresskill, NJ: Hampton Press.

Burgelman, J.C. and C. Pauwels (1992), 'Audiovisual policy and cultural identity in small European states: the challenge of a unified market', *Media Culture Society*, **14**, 169–83.

Burri-Nenova, M. (2007), 'The new audiovisual media services directive: television without frontiers, television without cultural diversity', *Common Market Law Review*, **44**, 1689–725.

Curran, J. and J. Seaton (2003), *Power without Responsibility: The Press, Broadcasting and New Media in Britain*, 6th edn, London: Routledge.

Douglas, S.J. (1987), *Inventing American Broadcasting, 1899–1922*, Baltimore, MD: Johns Hopkins University Press.

Eko, L. (2003), 'Between globalization and democratization: governmental public broadcasting in Africa', in M. McCauley, E. Peterson, L. Artz and D. Halleck (eds), *Public Broadcasting and the Public Interest*, Armonk, NY: M.E. Sharpe, pp. 175–91.

Freedman, D. (2005), 'Promoting diversity and pluralism in contemporary communications policies in the US and UK', *International Journal on Media Management*, **7** (1&2), 16–23.

Ginosar, A. (2011), 'The Regulation of Advertising', in D. Levi-Faur (ed.), *Handbook on the Politics of Regulation*, Cheltenham, UK: Edward Elgar.

Goldberg, D., G. Sutton and I. Walden (2009), *Media Law and Practice*, New York: Oxford University Press.

Gomez, J. (2004), 'Dumbing down democracy: trends in Internet regulation, surveillance and control in Asia', *Pacific Journalism Review*, **10** (2), 130–50.

Goodman, E. (2009), 'Public service media 2.0', in A. Schejter (ed.), *. . . And Communications for All: A Policy Agenda for a New Administration*, Lanham, MD: Lexington Books, pp. 263–80.

Green, A. (2003a), 'The development of mass media in Asia-Pacific', *International Journal of Advertising*, **22** (2), 273–301.

Green, A. (2003b), 'The development of mass media in Asia-Pacific', *International Journal of Advertising*, **22** (2), 413–30.

Gunaratne, S.A. (1999), 'The media in Asia: an overview', *International Communication Gazette*, **61** (3–4), 197–223.

Hamilton, J. (2004), *All the News that's Fit to Sell*, Princeton, NJ: Princeton University Press.

Harcourt, A. (2003), 'The regulation of media markets in selected EU accession states in Central and Eastern Europe', *European Law Journal*, **9** (3), 316–40.

Harrison, J. and L. Woods (2007), *European Broadcasting Law and Policy*, Cambridge: Cambridge University Press.

Hsiung, J. (1985), *Human Rights in East Asia: A Cultural Perspective*, New York: Paragon House Publishers.

Husband, C. (1994), 'General introduction: ethnicity and media democratization within the nation state', in C. Husband (ed.), *A Richer Vision: The Development of Ethnic Minority Media in Western Democracies*, London: John Libbey.

Jupp, J. (2001), 'The institution of culture: multiculturalism', in T. Bennet and D. Carter (eds), *Culture in Australia: Public, Policies, Programs*, Cambridge: Cambridge University Press, pp. 259–77.

Krasnow, E.G. and J.N. Goodman (1998), 'The "public interest" standard: the search for the Holy Grail', *Federal Communications Law Journal*, **50** (3), 605–35.

Kwak, K.-S. (1997), 'Structural and cultural aspects of the regulation of television broadcasting in East Asia: a comparative study', *International Communication Gazette*, **59** (6), 429–43.

Kwak, K.-S. (1999), 'The role of the state in the regulation of television broadcasting in South Korea', *Media International Australia Incorporating Culture & Policy*, **92**, 65–79.

Kwerel, E., J. Levy, R. Pepper, D. Sappington, D. Stockdale and J. Williams (2002), 'Economic issues at the Federal Communications Commission', *Review of Industrial Organization*, **21** (4), 337–56.

Levi-Faur, D. (2011), 'Regulation and Regulatory Governance', in D. Levi-Faur (ed.), *Handbook on the Politics of Regulation*, Cheltenham, UK: Edward Elgar.

Levy, David (1999), *Europe's Digital Revolution: Broadcasting Regulation, the EU and the Nation State*, London: Routledge.

Li, X. (1999), '"Asian values" and the universality of human rights', *Business and Society Review*, **102** (1), 81–7.

Mason, L., C. Bachen and S. Craft (2001), 'Support for F.C.C. minority ownership policy: how broadcast station owner race or ethnicity affects news and public affairs programming diversity', *Communication Law & Policy*, **6** (1), 37–73.

McChesney, R. (1993), *Telecommunications, Mass Media, and Democracy: The Battle for the Control of U.S. Broadcasting, 1928–1935*, New York: Oxford University Press.

Montgomery, K. (2009), 'Creating a media policy agenda for the digital generation', in A. Schejter (ed.), *. . . And Communications for All: A Policy Agenda for a New Administration*, Lanham, MD: Lexington Books, pp. 281–300.

Murray, A.D. (2011), 'Internet regulation', in D. Levi-Faur (ed.), *Handbook on the Politics of Regulation*, Cheltenham, UK: Edward Elgar.

Napoli, P.M. (1999), 'The unique nature of communications regulation: evidence and implications for communications policy analysis', *Journal of Broadcasting & Electronic Media*, **43** (4), 565–81.

Napoli, P. (2001), *Foundations of Communication Policy*, Cresskill, NJ: Hampton Press.

Negroponte, N. (1995), *Being Digital*, New York: Alfred A. Knopf.

Nerone, J. (1987), 'The mythology of the penny press', *Critical Studies in Mass Communication*, **4**, 376–404.

Nordenstreng, K. (1998), 'Beyond the four theories of the press', in J. Servaes and R. Lie (eds), *Media and Politics in Transition*, Leuven, Belgium: Acco, pp. 97–109.

Orr, G., B. Mercurio and G. Williams (2003), 'Australian electoral law: a stocktake', *Election Law Journal*, **2**, 383–402.

OSI (2005), *Television across Europe: Regulation, Policy, and Independence*, report, Budapest and New York: Open Society Institute.

Owen, B. (2002), 'Media as industry: economic foundations of mass communications', in *The Right to Tell: The Role of Mass Media in Economic Development*, Washington, DC: World Bank, pp. 167–86.

Pool, I. (1983), *Technologies of Freedom*, Boston, MA: Belknap Press.

SBS (2005), *Special Broadcasting Service: Annual Report*, available at: www20.sbs.com.au/sbscorporate/media/documents/777101_front_section.pdf (accessed 27 March 2010).

Schejter, A. (2008), 'European Union: communication law', in W. Donsbach (ed.), *The International Encyclopedia of Communication*, Oxford: Blackwell Publishing, pp. 1609–15.

Schejter, A. (2009), *Muting Israeli Democracy: How Media and Cultural Policy Undermine Free Expression*, Urbana: University of Illinois Press.

Schejter, A., J. Kittler, M. Lim, M. Balaji and A. Douai (2007), '"Let's go down, and there confuse their language, that they may not understand one another's speech": developing a model for comparative analysis and normative assessment of minority media rights', *Global Media Journal*, **5** (10).

Schement, J.R. and L. Liverouw (eds) (1988), *Competing Visions, Complex Realities: Social Aspects of the Information Society*, Norwood, NJ: Ablex.

Sen, Amartya (1997), 'Human rights and Asian values', *New Republic*, **217** (2–3), 33–40.

Shelanski, H.A. (2006), 'Antitrust law as mass media regulation: can merger standards protect the public interest?', *California Law Review*, **92**, 371–421.

Siebert, F., T. Peterson and W. Schramm (1956), *Four Theories of the Press: The Authoritarian, Libertarian, Social Responsibility, and Soviet Communist Concepts of What the Press Should Be and Do*, Urbana: University of Illinois Press.

Siune, K. and O. Hulten (1998), 'Does public broadcasting have a future?', in D. McQuail and K. Siune (eds), *Media Policy: Convergence, Concentration and Commerce*, London: Sage, pp. 23–37.

Skoric, M.M. (2007), 'Is culture destiny in Asia? A story of a tiger and a lion', *Asian Journal of Communication*, **17** (4), 396–415.

St. Leger, F.Y. (1980), Book review, *Community Development Journal*, **15** (3), 229–30.

*Superior Oil Company v. Federal Power Commission*, 425 U.S. 971 (1976).

Turow (1992), *Media Systems in Society: Understanding Industries, Strategies and Power*, White Plains, NY: Longman.

Walton, C. (2009), *Policing Public Opinion in the French Revolution: The Culture of Calumny and the Problem of Free Speech*, New York: Oxford University Press.

Williams, R. (1976), *Communications*, 3rd edn, London: Penguin.

Yandle, B. (2011), 'Bootleggers and Baptists in the theory of regulation', in D. Levi-Faur (ed.), *Handbook on the Politics of Regulation*, Cheltenham, UK: Edward Elgar.

# 18 The regulation of advertising
## *Avshalom Ginosar*

Academic discussion on advertising regulation is characterized by its multi-disciplinary nature. It engages scholars from disciplines such as economics, law, communications, public policy, decision making and marketing. Consequently there is no unified body of literature on the subject and there is no single framework for studying and analyzing it or for comparing different regulatory regimes across different countries, media, technologies and/or eras. Creating such an integrative model, based on studies from various academic disciplines, was first suggested by Rotfeld and Stafford (2007), who recommended developing an interdisciplinary course of research based on the interface between advertising and public policy. In accordance with this idea, this chapter suggests an analytical framework that aims to cover various aspects of advertising regulation (see Figure 18.1). The framework is based on four main distinctions: (1) the *content* of regulation, which deals with the variety of advertising topics that might be subject to regulation (such as the obligation to identify commercial messages and separate them from editorial content, the maximum amount of advertising, the prohibition of offensive advertising content, etc.); (2) the *level* of regulation, which addresses the distinction between national and supranational regulation; (3) the *mode* of regulation, which reflects the differences between statutory-compulsory regulation and voluntary or self-regulation; (4) the *technological* distinction, which refers to differences in advertising regulation between traditional media (such as print, radio and television) and new media (the Internet and mobile phones) and

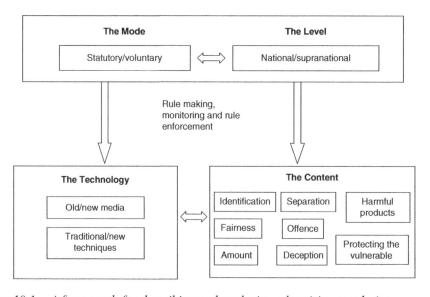

*Figure 18.1   A framework for describing and analyzing advertising regulation*

to the difference in regulation between traditional advertising practices (such as spot-advertising in television) and new techniques (such as "pop-ups" in digital advertising).

Advertising regulation can be traced back to the very beginning of the twentieth century (Hansen and Law 2008), and yet the problematic effects of advertising have been identified since the very beginning of the industry (Pollay 1986) and have varied across states, regimes and eras. Therefore this framework suggests that an analysis of a certain regime and/or the comparison between such regimes should take into consideration all of the above factors. This chapter consists of five sections. The first presents three perspectives on advertising: economic, societal and cultural. Each offers different justifications for regulation and introduces different issues to be regulated. The second section deals with the mode of regulation, the third with the level of regulation, the fourth with the technological aspect, and the fifth section concludes.

## 18.1   THREE PERSPECTIVES ON ADVERTISING REGULATION

The content of advertising regulation is affected by different types of criteria. There are three main ones: economic, societal and cultural (Kirkpatrick 2007). Accordingly, this section presents three perspectives of advertising regulation based on these three.

### 18.1.1   The Economic Perspective

Economists point at two main issues regarding the effect of advertising on the economy: (a) the link between the amount of advertising in a certain market/industry and the extent to which competition exists in that market; (b) the link between the informative function of advertising and product prices. Both are related to the concerns regarding the truthfulness of commercial messages.

Brown (1948 in Litman 1999) asserts that the public's chief interest lies in the promotion of competition through advertising. Yet there are two competing theoretical views regarding the relation between advertising and competition. The first holds that advertising encourages brand loyalty by differentiating products, and thus reduces competition by creating entry barriers and de facto monopolistic behavior. The other view stresses that advertising increases competition by providing consumers with various types of information, increases rivalry among firms and encourages the entry of new firms (Eckard 1987). However, Comanor and Wilson (1979) demonstrate that advertising's effects on competition differ across sectors. In their opinion, restrictive policy towards advertising might improve social welfare when addressing industries in which advertising negatively affects competition. However, at the same time, this may sabotage the availability of product information, which is considered the most harmful regulatory policy towards advertising (Rubin 2004). Thus fruitful regulation is regulation that succeeds in decreasing the volume of advertising, when it negatively affects competition, without limiting the availability of product information.

Advertising affects not only competition but also the prices of products. The lack of information about possible products or of different sellers might add costs to the consumer, such as in the extra time dedicated to searching for that information. Good advertising reduces costs (Nelson 1974; Erlich and Fisher 1982; Ekelund et al. 1995). This premise implies that restrictive regulation on advertising might raise the price of goods. However, the effects of regulation on prices are controversial. Applegate (2009) argues that advertising, while encouraging the creation of monopolies, enables manufacturers to increase prices and to pass on their advertising expenditures to consumers. In contrast, Hollifield (2009) indicates that in some sectors or product categories, if advertising causes an increase in sales, manufacturers and retailers cut prices. Either way, true and accurate information about price is useful for consumers, and so regulatory authorities should encourage the dissemination of it (Rubin 2004). Proper information includes not only the product's price but the full information about payment options, discounts and so on.

Insufficient or incorrect information about products affects consumers' trust, impedes advertising credibility and reduces marketplace efficiencies (Resnik and Stern 1977; Pollay and Mittal 1993). The direct goal of regulation should be to secure the provision of reliable and necessary data in order to serve consumers and enhance competition in the market as well (Pitofsky 1977). Therefore it is not surprising that historically both industrial and consumer groups initiated regulation on the integrity of commercial messages. These different groups in the United States have struggled for decades in order to gain an influence on legislators and regulators who then shaped the "truth in advertising" regulation (Tedlow 1981; Stole 2000; Hansen and Law 2008).

In sum, the economic perspective addresses advertising's effects on markets. It approves of regulation regarding the truthfulness of the commercial messages, while it reflects different views regarding regulation on the amount of advertising.

### 18.1.2   The Societal Perspective

There are two main types of societal criticisms of advertising: the first addresses the coercive and manipulative nature of advertising and its power to force consumers to buy products they do not need or want; the second addresses the offensive nature of advertising which leads to consumption of harmful products or services. These criticisms are based on the view that advertising gives priority to private (commercial/industrial) at the expense of public (consumer/social) interests. Therefore regulation is supposed to promote public interests and improve social welfare.

One of the most influential publications about the manipulative nature of advertising is Vance Packard's *The Hidden Persuaders* (1981), first published in 1957. This book was considered the first exposure of advertising's subliminal techniques of persuasion. In fact, Packard highlighted different advertising techniques which are based on the fact that "individuals do not always have access to their *conscious* thoughts and can be persuaded by *supraliminal* messages without their knowledge" (Nelson 2008: 113). Packard (1981) approved of prohibitive regulation of such practices. Fifty years later, Nelson (2008) indicates that nowadays the advertising industry uses the same strategies Packard emphasized, but adds new methods in which "consumers are exposed to masked commercial messages that are not legally defined as commercial messages" (p. 113). Scholars like Rotfeld and Taylor (2009) argue that, even if advertising techniques are not as deceitful as described by Packard, the public might demand regulation which treats them as if they were.

The promotion of harmful and immoral products is a common justification for advertising regulation. Boddewyn (1991) named these the "soft issues" of advertising. They are more difficult to define and control and they change over time or across nations and cultures. For example, Shao and Hill (1994) found a difference between developed countries, in which constraints on advertising "sensitive products" are within legal frameworks, and developing nations, where these constraints are rooted in social codes.

Cigarettes and alcohol are good examples of "sensitive products" which remain at the center of public and political debate. This debate reflects much wider and deeper disputes about regulation and morals, religion, science, public health, decency and so on. This is a conflict between value systems: while the tobacco and alcohol industries use the constitutional right to free speech (in the US) as one of their main arguments against regulation, their opponents (from public interest groups) emphasize religious, social and/or health arguments to justify regulation (Schuster and Powell 1987; Saffer and Chaloupka 2000; Pennock 2007). Pennock (2007) demonstrates how, in the first half of the twentieth century, religious-moral arguments dominated the struggle for regulation, while in the second half of the century arguments based on science and public health were more common. The scientific evidence regarding the effects of tobacco on adolescents' health, and the findings about the effects of advertising on children and adolescents' consumption of cigarettes and alcohol (Nelson 2010) made it easier for the FDA to issue in 1996 regulation restricting the sale and distribution of tobacco products to children and adolescents (Kessler et al. 1996).

Another example of a "sensitive product" is food. The main concern is misleading information about ingredients and the nutritional values of food (Andrews et al. 1998). However, a much more significant concern is about the advertising of fast/fatty food aimed at children and adolescents, which is associated with the worldwide epidemic of child obesity (Kunkel and Gantz 1992; Story and French 2004; Kelly et al. 2007). Several studies revealed a link between the extent to which children are exposed to fat-food advertisements and the extent to which they consume such food. Consequently, many researchers see regulatory restrictions on fat-food advertising aimed at children as necessary in the public interest (Robinson 1999; Coon et al. 2001; Lobstein and Dibb 2005; Kelly et al. 2007).

Some scholars emphasize the cultural aspect of advertising aimed at children and frame it as the "commercialization of childhood" (Gray 2005), while others stress the psychological aspect: citing the fact that children under the age of eight are unable to understand the intent of advertisements. Therefore advertising aimed at children can be viewed as exploitation (Story and French 2004). These issues have stood at the core of a long regulatory struggle in the US, which began in the early 1970s, when groups advocating children's rights called for federal agencies to prohibit or limit television advertising directed at children. In 1974, the first federal restrictions were issued by the Federal Communications Commission (FCC), imposing both a limitation on the amount of advertising aimed at children and a clear separation between program content and commercial messages. In response, the American advertising industry launched self-regulatory policies. Four years later, the Federal Trade Commission (FTC) proposed banning, or severely restricting, all television advertising for children. The proposal was followed by a negative and aggressive campaign by the broadcasting and advertising industries based on First Amendment protection and made the Congress disapprove of the FTC's proposal. During the 1980s, with the deregulation wave of the Reagan administration, the FCC lifted all the restrictions on advertising directed at children that were established a decade earlier, and only in 1990, following pressure by children's rights advocacy and consumer groups, were they restored (Story and French 2004).

Similar regulatory struggles occurred in other countries as well. In Europe, Sweden and Norway enforced the most stringent rules against advertising for children younger than 12. Other countries, such as Belgium and Greece, also had restrictions (Bandyopadhay et al. 2001). It is worth noting that regulating advertising to children is only one example of the aim to protect vulnerable groups, such as the elderly, the sick and the recently bereaved (Boddewyn 1982).

In short, the societal perspective employs public interest justifications for advertising regulation while addressing either sensitive products or specifically vulnerable groups.

### 18.1.3   The Cultural Perspective

The cultural perspective considers values rather than interests to be the major justification for regulating advertising. The assumption is that advertising does not merely reflect a culture and/or a certain society's values but affects culture and values as well (Pollay and Gallagher 1990). The American historian David Potter, in his book *People of Plenty*, states: "the most important effects of this powerful institution [advertising] are not upon the economics of our distributive system; they are upon the values of our system" (Potter 1954 in Berger 2004: 27). As many sociologists and communication scholars argue, the values that the advertising industry promotes are of "the consumer culture." Michael Schudson (1984) argues that

> a consumer culture is taken to be a society in which human values have been grotesquely distorted so that commodities become more important than people or, in alternative formulation, commodities become not ends in themselves but overvalued means for acquiring acceptable ends like love and friendship. (p. 7)

Similarly, Pollay (1986) claims that advertising's fundamental impact is that "people keep productive in order to keep consuming, to work in order to buy" (p. 25). In other words, consumer culture is based on the ideas that: (a) consuming and purchasing goods have become values in themselves; (b) products are seen as means to happiness in life; (c) advertising influences people to find life's meaning in the products they purchase; and (d) a link can be found between advertising and materialistic values (Belk and Pollay 1985; Richins 1987).

An empirical study that investigated two television advertising campaigns in Hong Kong from the 1970s and early 1980s for banking services demonstrated how advertising changes social and cultural values from traditional Chinese values, such as saving and hard work, to more Western consumer values of spending and attaining material possessions (Wong 2000). Nevertheless, cultural differences between societies affect advertising as well. Han and Shavitt (1994), for example, demonstrate how cultural differences in an individualism–collectivism dichotomy between two societies, the US and Korea, play an important role in the persuasion processes, influencing the prevalence and effectiveness of different types of advertisements.

One of the most controversial examples which reflects the link between advertising and values is sex in advertising. Traditional criticism of the use of sex in advertising concerns the religious-puritan moral perspective. Liberals and feminists share this objection, although for different reasons. One side claims that advertising creates an ideal image of a woman's body (tall, thin, blond, etc.) which is quite different from the average woman's body. It is argued that women are presented only as sexual objects, which distorts not only sexual relationships but family and other social values as well (Kilbourne 2005). On the other side, Reichert (2009) argues that sex in advertising can be a "very effective strategy if it is relevant to the product it is promoting, if it is not sexist, and if it does not target susceptible populations" (p. 117).

It might be argued that, from the cultural perspective, advertising regulation is a product of a struggle over contradicting values within each culture. In a globalized world it reflects a struggle over values between different cultures as well.

## 18.2   THE MODE OF REGULATION

As early as the late 1880s, local coalitions of manufacturers, advertisers and publishers in the United States began fighting against false and misleading advertising. These groups – such as the Association of Advertising Clubs – monitored advertising claims and tried to educate firms about the benefits of truthful advertising (Hansen and Law 2008). This first attempt at self-regulating advertising was initiated for two interrelated reasons: (a) the huge growth in the volume of advertising and in the numbers of advertising agencies in the late nineteenth century (Pope 1974); (b) the industry's acknowledgement of its own interest in increasing the credibility of advertisements, in order to enhance advertising's effects on consumers (Miracle and Nevett 1988). It should be noted that it was not until 1910 that these groups begin to press for state regulation. As with self-regulation, state regulation in the United States was shaped in response to deceptive advertisements. The calls for state regulation were initiated by the industry and by consumer groups, which both struggled to influence the legislators (Tedlow 1981).

Ever since that early period, the co-existence of the two modes of regulation in the advertising industry – self-regulation and state regulation – has been common worldwide. The main reason industry tried to self-regulate was the desire to minimize state regulation, because it was felt that state regulation served only the public interest at the expense of the industry (Labarbera 1980). However, self-regulation has several other advantages over state regulation: it is faster, cheaper, more efficient and more effective, and at the same time strengthens the credibility of advertising (Labarbera, 1980, 1983; Boddewyn, 1985).

It is reasonable to assume that, in order to strengthen the mechanisms of self-regulation and to get political and public support for them, the industry will attempt to preserve ethical principles dealing with "questions of what ought to be done, not just with what legally must be done" (Cunningham 1999: 500). Nevertheless, empirical research conducted by Davis (1994) reveals that most advertising professionals are primarily influenced by legal considerations, and not by ethics, which are the basis of self-regulatory codes. Therefore, self-regulation is often treated by the public, politicians and regulators in a skeptical manner. While some, like Boddewyn (1989), see it as a useful, if imperfect, form of control, others, like Hill and Beaver (1991), argue that it fails to develop consistent and enforceable standards which are fair to all. However, there are several ways to overcome these problems: the participation of consumers and other public representatives as members of the industry's self-regulation organizations (Boddewyn 1985); close cooperation between advertisers, advertising agencies and media within these organizations (Harker 1998); and the existence of an efficient funding system and written ethics codes (Harker 2003).

Despite these proposed remedies, some critical scholars (like Rotfeld 1992) suggest that considering self-regulation's weaknesses, strong and efficient government regulation is imperative. Accordingly, advertising regulation worldwide is complex. It includes legal considerations (state-compulsory mode), ethical codes (self-regulatory mode) and co-regulation (various types of hybrid modes) (Boddewyn 1985; Petty and Kopp 1995; Harker 2003). While in some cases state regulation and self-regulation act separately yet side by side, there is a growing trend for co-regulatory systems. The most distinctive example is in the United Kingdom, where the state regulator (Ofcom) supports and legitimizes self-regulatory organizations (Dacko and Hart 2005). The role of self-regulation within these mixed systems is to internalize the standards that state laws express (Boddewyn 1989). In this way, the gaps left by weak or unenforced laws are filled (Burleton 1982), or there is a reaction "to the level and types of government regulation, as they vary over periods and time" (Miracle and Nevett 1988: 116). When the synchronization between state and self-regulation is at its optimum level, in such a way that each system compensates for the weaknesses of the other, the regulatory system is more acceptable (Harker 1998).

This complexity of regulatory systems increased with the spread of the Internet and online advertising. Traditionally, these were self-regulated, but the growing concerns about the effects of them have led to worldwide thought being given to establishing new types of mixed-system regulation. This topic is discussed in section 18.4.

## 18.3    THE REGULATION OF ADVERTISING IN A GLOBAL WORLD

Traditionally, advertising regulation in its two modes, state regulation and self-regulation, has acted at the national level. However, since the early 1900s, several efforts have been made to set or coordinate international standards. It should be noted that the first attempts at the supranational level – just as at the American national level – were made by the industry itself, meaning the establishment of international self-regulation advertising codes. The earliest of these, in 1911, was made by the Associated Advertising Clubs of the World, which accepted the Truth in Advertising Resolution. The International Chamber of Commerce (ICC) issued the first Code of Advertising Practices in 1937. Similarly, the International Advertising Association (IAA) has tried for several decades to promote the internationalization of advertising regulation (Cunningham 2000). Many years prior to the intensive globalization period, these early attempts were explained as efforts "to provide a globally accepted framework for responsible creativity and communication" (ICC 2006: 8). The ICC Code focuses on the industry's responsibility towards consumers worldwide and aims at minimizing the need for "detailed governmental and/ or intergovernmental legislation or regulation" (p. 9).

Since the 1980s, developments in the international political and economic environments have intensified these efforts, that is, the process of globalization, the spread of democracy, significant economic growth in many countries, new technologies and media, and the breaking of cultural barriers (Boddewyn 1982, 1989; Gao 2005). One effect of these developments is that local advertising agencies have started acting internationally and have been forced to adjust their modes of activity to various national regulatory systems and to different codes of standards (Boddewyn 1988; Papavassiliou and Stathakopoulos 1997). A significant example is the European Union (EU), in which standardization and harmonization of advertising rules and regulation have been emerging since the late 1970s, when the European Commission prepared its proposal for the Directive on Misleading and Unfair Advertising (Greer and Thompson 1985; Miracle, et al. 1988), and in a more intensified manner since the 1980s (Cunningham 2000). Other regions in the world might take the same path. Gao (2005), for example, suggests harmonizing advertising regulation in "Greater China" (China, Hong Kong and Taiwan) and suggests similar processes in two other geographical areas: the Middle East and Latin America.

Both the EU example and the ICC's advertising code reflect the course of internationalization. However, there are institutional and substantial differences between these two examples. In the EU, national statutory regimes should be adapted to a statutory supranational regime. In addition and independently, self-regulation exists at both national and European supranational levels. As to the other example, the ICC Code's main target is for international self-regulation to replace or at least minimize the statutory regimes at both levels. That is, the first establishes a mix of regulatory systems, while the latter pushes towards a more unified international regulatory system, based on voluntary self-regulation.

The globalization and regionalization of advertising standards might move in opposite directions as "a race to the bottom," which is the lowering of standards in order to compete (Spar and Yoffie 2000), or "a race to the top," in which states and international organizations raise or adapt their regulatory standards to match those of the dominant regional economy (Vogel 1995). Vogel and Kagan (2004) argue that the EU has been a major force in driving all member states towards higher regulatory standards. Yet the direction of these processes – to the top or to the bottom – is not conclusive and should be subject to an empirical investigation in each case.

## 18.4   NEW MEDIA, NEW TECHNIQUES, NEW REGULATION

The link between technological developments and regulatory reform in the communication sector is not a new phenomenon. The allocation of frequencies for radio and television has been for many years the main justification for limiting the number of firms in the industry and for public ownership or public conducting of the communication market. Since the 1980s, the new cable, satellite and digital technologies have weakened this justification and have led to a more tolerant public attitude towards private operators, particularly in Europe (Motta and Polo 1997). Harcourt (2005) indicated that the digital revolution of the 1990s was an important catalyst in changing media regulation. Van Cuilenburg and McQuail (2003) point at the technological convergence of media platforms as the motivation for reforming media regulation. The emergence of the Internet as a major medium is currently an example of this link between technological development and public policy reform (Farrall 2007). As a new medium it challenges advertising in two main ways: first, the mode of regulation (who regulates?) and, second, the content of regulation (what should be regulated?).

The Internet innovators and their companies, supported by market-led governments, have created co- or self-regulatory institutions for all areas of activity on the Internet, including marketing and advertising. Several studies demonstrate that marketers and the Internet users alike prefer less governmental regulation of online advertising and support self-regulation (Schlosser et al. 1999; Bush et al. 2000). However, it is commonly held in the literature that the nature of the Internet dictates a new regulatory approach in which consumers are important and equal members in a new "regulatory partnership" with the private and public sectors and civil society. Marsden (2008) calls this new type of system "multi-stakeholder governance," and Murray (2011) refers to a "community-based regulation" in which the power to shape the regulatory environment does not rest with the regulator alone. Accordingly, various countries have shaped different models. For example, the Dot Com Disclosures Guidelines published in May 2000 by the American Federal Trade Commission (FTC) are similar to the policy for the traditional media (Keaty et al. 2002). The main goal of the European Audio-Visual Media Service Directive (AVMSD) of 2007 was the creation of unified regulatory standards to all "audiovisual media services, both television broadcasting and on-demand audiovisual media services" (AVMSD, provision 7). Advertising standards are part of the EU's unified regulatory system (Ginosar and Levi-Faur 2010). In the US and in Australia, online advertising regulation is based on state intervention, but in other countries, such as the United Kingdom and New Zealand, self-regulatory organizations work alongside the state (Loosley et al. 2004). The above examples indicate that, although in the first stage of the Internet online advertising (like other issues on the Internet) was not regulated, there is a tendency to move into a new phase in which advertising on the Internet is regulated but by different modes across countries.

As to the content of regulation, while all the traditional regulatory issues are relevant to Internet advertisement, the technological opportunities of the new media give these issues broader meanings (McAllister and Turow 2002). Three distinctive examples are: (a) the blurring between editorial and commercial contents (embedded advertising); (b) "purchased search engine results" (a payment by an advertiser to the search engine operator in order to advance the advertiser's site) (Keaty et al. 2002); and (c) targeting advertising (the matching between consumers and products) (Davis 2009). These examples represent the more intrusive nature of Internet advertising, which creates more concerns for consumers. Goldfarb and Tucker (2011), for example, found that consumers dislike having data collected about their browsing behavior for the purpose of targeted advertising, and express dislike of highly visible ads, which they find intrusive. Therefore they recommend that regulators should consider these two potential sources of consumer resistance when shaping new restrictions.

Since regulating Internet advertising is relatively new, there is no one accepted approach nor accepted worldwide guidelines yet, and consequently there is much variety. Harker (2008) indicates that there is a continuum, ranging from regimes of no control at all to those characterized by very heavy regulation. Ang (1997) found that the dominant factor which affects online advertising regulation and might explain this variety of regimes is the culture of each society rather than technology or law.

## 18.5 CONCLUSIONS

This chapter brings together four main dimensions of advertising regulation: content, mode, level and technology. Each represents a different public concern. These concerns have changed only marginally over more than a century, since the birth of modern advertising. Therefore the content dimension reflects the more stable issues of advertising regulation, such as the integrity of the commercial messages and the effects of advertising on the economy, on social and cultural values, on the individual consumer's welfare and on certain vulnerable groups. In contrast, the other three dimensions demonstrate the dynamic nature of advertising regulation. They reflect how it has faced various challenges: the shift from separate modes of state and self-regulation towards co-regulation and various types of hybrid modes; the growing part of various types of supranational regulatory systems that co-exist with the traditional national-level regulation; and the adaptation of advertising regulation to new media, particularly the Internet.

The fact that the basic justifications for advertising regulation have not been changed during the last century in spite of the technological and economic changes during that period means it is reasonable to assume that these justifications will not be dramatically changed during the twenty-first century either. Yet technological developments of the Internet and cellular telephony, the empowerment of consumers, the growing awareness regarding privacy on the Internet, and the continuing process of globalization might change the architecture of advertising regulation. It might be a multi-faced architecture, consisting of: (a) different modes (probably various new types of hybrid regulatory systems); (b) a multi-level nature (local, regional, national and international); (c) multi-media regulation (traditional media as well as the Internet and mobile phones); and (d) multi-stakeholder partnerships (industrial, public, statist and consumers). This new structure might call for a more universal definition of which commercial messages fall under regulation. Yet it ought to be less dependent on technology, geography and institutional settings.

## REFERENCES

Andrews, J.C., R.G. Netemeyer and S. Burton (1998), 'Consumer generalization of nutrient content claims in advertising', *Journal of Marketing*, **62**, 62–75.

Ang, P.H. (1997), 'How countries are regulating Internet content', paper presented at the Internet Society Annual Conference, Kuala Lumpur, Malaysia.

Applegate, E. (2009), 'Advertising makes products more expensive', in C.J. Pardun (ed.), *Advertising and Society*, Oxford: Blackwell.

Bandyopadhay, S., G. Kindra and L. Sharp (2001), 'Is Television Advertising Good for Children? Areas of Concern and Policy Implications', *International Journal of Advertising*, **20** (1), 1–20.

Belk, R.W. and R.W. Pollay (1985), 'Materialism and magazine advertising during the twentieth century', *Advance in Consumer Research*, **12**, 394–8.

Berger, A.A. (2004), *Ads, Fads, and Consumer Culture*, Lanham, MD: Rowman & Littlefield.

Boddewyn, J.J. (1982), 'Advertising regulation in the 1980s: the underlying global forces', *Journal of Marketing*, **46**, 27–36.

Boddewyn, J.J. (1985), 'Advertising self-regulation: private government and agent of public policy', *Journal of Public Policy & Marketing*, **4**, 129–41.

Boddewyn, J.J. (1988), *Advertising Self-Regulation and Outside Participation: A Multinational Comparison*, Westport, CT: Quorum Books.

Boddewyn, J.J. (1989), 'Advertising self-regulation: true purpose and limits', *Journal of Advertising*, **18** (2), 19–28.

Boddewyn, J.J. (1991), 'Controlling Sex and Decency in Advertising around the World', *Journal of Advertising*, 20, 4, 25–35

Burleton, E. (1982), 'The self-regulation of advertising in Europe', *Journal of Advertising*, **1**, 333–44.

Bush, V.D., B.T. Venable and A.J. Bush (2000), 'Ethics and marketing on the Internet: practioners' perceptions of societal, industry and company concerns', *Journal of Business Ethics*, **23**, 237–48.

Comanor, W.S. and T.A. Wilson (1979), 'The effects of advertising on competition: a survey', *Journal of Economic Literature*, **17** (2), 453–76.

Coon, K.A., J. Goldberg, B.L. Rogers and K.L. Tucker (2001), 'Relationship between use of television during meals and children's food consumption patterns', *Pediatrics*, **107** (1) 1–9.

Cunningham, A. (2000), 'Advertising self-regulation in broader context: an examination of the European Union's regulatory environment', *Journal of Promotion Management*, **5** (2), 61–83.

Cunningham, P.H. (1999), 'Ethics of advertising', in J.P. Jones (ed.), *The Advertising Business*, London: Sage, pp. 499–513.

Dacko, S.G. and M. Hart (2005), 'Critically examining theory and practice: implications for co-regulation and co-regulating broadcast advertising in the United Kingdom', *International Journal on Media Management*, **7** (1&2), 2–15.

Davis, E.S. (2009), 'The online advertising industry: economics, evolution, and privacy', *Journal of Economic Perspectives*, **23**, 37–60.

Davis, J.J. (1994), 'Ethics in advertising decision making: implications for reducing the incidence of deceptive advertising', *Journal of Consumer Affairs*, **28** (2), 380–402.

Eckard, E.W. (1987), 'Advertising, competition, and market share instability', *Journal of Business*, **60** (4), 539–52.

Ekelund, R.B., Jr., F.G. Nixon, Jr. and R.W. Ressler (1995), ' Advertising and information: an empirical study of search, experience and credence goods', *Journal of Economic Studies*, **22** (2), 33–43.

Erlich, I. and L. Fisher (1982), 'The derived demand for advertising', *American Economic Review*, **72**, 366–88.

Farrall, K. (2007), 'Cascading network: electronic communication and the diffusion of social instability', paper presented at the annual meeting of the International Communication Association, San Francisco, CA.

Gao, Z. (2005), 'Harmonious regional advertising regulation? A comparative examination of government advertising regulation in China, Hong Kong, and Taiwan', *Journal of Advertising*, **34** (3), 75–87.

Ginosar, A. and D. Levi-Faur (2010), 'Regulating product placement in the EU and Canada: explaining regime change and diversity', *Journal of Comparative Policy Analysis*, **12** (5), 467–90.

Goldfarb, A. and Tucker, C. (2011), 'Online display advertising: targeting and obtrusiveness', available at: http://www.rotman.utoronto.ca/~agoldfarb/GoldfarbTucker-intrusiveness.pdf.

Gray, O. (2005), 'Responsible advertising in Europe', *Young Consumers: Insight and Ideas for Responsible Marketers*, **6** (4), 19–23.

Greer, T.V. and P.R. Thompson (1985), 'Development of standardized and harmonized advertising regulation in the European Economic Community', *Journal of Advertising*, **14** (2), 23–32.

Han, S. and S. Shavitt (1994), 'Persuasion and culture: advertising appeal in individualistic and collectivistic societies', *Journal of Experimental Social Psychology*, **30**, 326–50.

Hansen, Z.K. and M.T. Law (2008), 'The political economy of truth-in-advertising regulation during the Progressive Era', *Journal of Law and Economics*, **51**, 251–69.

Harcourt, A. (2005), *The European Union and the Regulation of Media Markets*, Manchester and New York: Manchester University Press.

Harker, D. (1998), 'Achieving acceptable advertising: an analysis of advertising regulation in five countries', *International Marketing Review*, **15** (2), 101–18.

Harker, D. (2003), 'Towards effecting advertising self-regulation in Australia: the seven components', *Journal of Marketing Communications*, **9**, 93–111.

Harker, D. (2008), 'Regulating online advertising: the benefit of qualitative insights', *Qualitative Market Research: An International Journal*, **11** (3), 295–315.

Hill, R.P. and A.L. Beaver (1991), 'Advocacy groups and television advertisers', *Journal of Advertising*, **20** (1), 18–27.

Hollifield, C.A. (2009), 'Advertising lowers prices for consumers', in C.J. Pardun (ed.), *Advertising and Society*, Oxford: Blackwell.

International Chamber of Commerce (ICC) (2006), *Advertising and Marketing Communication Practice: Consolidated ICC Code*, Document No. 240-46/330, Paris: ICC.

Keaty, A., R.J. Johns and L.L. Henke (2002), 'Can Internet service providers and other secondary parties be held liable for deceptive online advertising?', *Business Lawyer*, **58** (1).

Kelly, B., B. Smith, L. King, V. Flood and A. Bauman (2007), 'Television food advertising to children: the extent and nature of exposure', *Public Health Nutrition*, **10** (11), 1234–40.

Kessler, D.A., A.M. Witt, P.S. Barnett, M.R. Zeller, S.L. Natanblut, J.P. Wilkenfeld, C.C. Lorraine, L.G. Thompson and W.B. Schultz (1996), 'The Food and Drug Administration's regulation of tobacco products', *New England Journal of Medicine*, **335**, 988–94.

Kilbourne, J. (2005), 'What else does sex sell?', *International Journal of Advertising*, **24** (1), 119–22.

Kirkpatrick, J. (2007), *In Defense of Advertising*, Claremont, CA: TLJ Books.

Kunkel, D. and W. Gantz (1992), 'Children's television advertising in the multichannel environment', *Journal of Communication*, **42** (3), 134–52.

Labarbera, P.A. (1980), 'Analyzing and advancing the state of the art of advertising self-regulation', *Journal of Advertising*, **9** (4), 27–38.

Labarbera, P.A. (1983), 'The diffusion of trade association advertising self-regulation', *Journal of Marketing*, Winter.

Litman, J. (1999), 'Breakfast with Batman: the public interest in the advertising age', *Yale Law Journal*, **108**, 1717–31.

Lobstein, T. and S. Dibb (2005), 'Evidence of a possible link between obesogenic food advertising and child overweight', *Obesity Review*, **6**, 203–08.

Loosley, R., S. Richards and J. Gregory (2004), 'The effect on brand management when a business migrates onto the Internet: a legal perspective', *Journal of Brand Management*, **11** (3), 183–96.

Marsden, C.T. (2008), 'Beyond Europe: the Internet, regulation, and multistakeholder governance – representing the consumer interest?', *Journal of Consumer Policy*, **31**, 115–32.

McAllister, M.P. and J. Turow (2002), 'New media and the commercial sphere: two intersecting trends, five categories of concern', *Journal of Broadcasting & Electronic Media*, **46** (4), 505–14.

Miracle, G.E. and T.R. Nevett (1988), 'Improving NAD/NARB self-regulation of advertising', *Journal of Public Policy & Marketing*, **7**, 114–26.

Miracle, G.E., R. Rijkens and A. Tempset (1988), 'The saga of the Directive on Misleading Advertising', *International Journal of Advertising*, **7**, 118–29.

Motta, M. and M. Polo (1997), 'Concentration and public policies in the broadcasting industry: the future of television', *Economic Policy*, **25**, 295–334.

Murray, A.D. (2011), 'Internet Regulation', in D. Levi-Faur (ed.), *Handbook on the Politics of Regulation*, Cheltenham, UK: Edward Elgar.

Nelson, J.P. (2010), 'What is learned from longitudinal studies of advertising and youth drinking and smoking? A critical assessment', *International Journal of Environmental Research and Public Health*, **7**, 870–926.

Nelson, M.R. (2008), 'The hidden persuaders: then and now', *Journal of Advertising*, **37** (1), 113–26.

Nelson, P. (1974), 'Advertising as information', *Journal of Political Economy*, **81**, 729–54.

Packard, V. (1981), *The Hidden Persuaders*, Harmondsworth: Penguin Books.

Papavassiliou, N. and V. Stathakopoulos (1997), 'Standardization versus adaptation of international advertising strategies: towards a framework', *European Journal of Marketing*, **31** (7), 504–27.

Pennock, P.E. (2007), *Advertising Sin and Sickness: The Politics of Alcohol and Tobacco Marketing 1950–1990*, Dekalb: Northern Illinois University Press.

Petty, R.D. and R.J. Kopp (1995), 'Advertising challenges: a strategic framework and current review', *Journal of Advertising Research*, April, 41–54.

Pitofsky, R. (1977), 'Beyond Nader: consumer protection and the regulation of advertising', *Harvard Law Review*, **90** (4), 661–701.

Pollay, R.W. (1986), 'The distorted mirror: reflections on the unintended consequences of advertising', *Journal of Marketing*, **50**, 18–36.

Pollay, R.W. and K. Gallagher (1990), 'Advertising and cultural values: reflections in the distorted mirror', *International Journal of Advertising*, **9**, 359–72.

Pollay, R.W. and B. Mittal (1993), 'Here's the beef: factors, determinants, and segments in consumer criticism of advertising', *Journal of Marketing*, **57** (3), 99–114.

Pope, D. (1974), 'The development of national advertising, 1865–1920', *Journal of Economic History*, **34** (1), 295–6.

Reichert, T. (2009), 'Sex in advertising: no crime here!', in C.J. Pardun (ed.), *Advertising and Society*, Oxford: Blackwell.

Resnik, A. and B.L. Stern (1977), 'An analysis of information content in television advertising', *Journal of Marketing*, January.

Richins, M. (1987), 'Media, materialism, and human happiness', *Advance in Consumer Research*, **14**, 352–6.

Robinson, T.N. (1999), 'Reducing children's television viewing to prevent obesity', *Journal of American Medical Association*, **282**, 1561–7.

Rotfeld, H.J. (1992), 'Power and limitations of media clearance practices and advertising self-regulation', *Journal of Public Policy & Marketing*, **11** (1), 87–95.

Rotfeld, H.J. and M.R. Stafford (2007), 'Toward a pragmatic understanding of the advertising and public policy literature', *Journal of Current Issues and Research in Advertising*, **29** (1), 67–80.

Rotfeld, H.J. and C.R. Taylor (2009), 'The advertising regulation and self-regulation issues ripped from the headlines with (sometimes missed) opportunities for disciplined multidisciplinary research', *Journal of Advertising*, **38** (4), 5–14.

Rubin, P.H. (2004), 'Regulation of information and advertising', Working Paper No. 04-05, available at: http://ssrn.com/abstract=498683.

Saffer, H. and F. Chaloupka (2000), 'The effect of tobacco advertising bans on tobacco consumption', *Journal of Health Economy*, **19** (6), 1117–37.

Schlosser, A.E., S. Shavitt and A. Kanfer (1999), 'Survey of Internet users' attitude towards Internet advertising', *Journal of Interactive Marketing*, **13** (3), 34–54.

Schudson, M. (1984), *Advertising, the Uneasy Persuasion: Its Dubious Impact on American Society*, New York: Basic Books.

Schuster, C.P. and C.P. Powel (1987), 'Comparison of cigarette and alcohol advertising controversies', *Journal of Advertising*, **16** (2), 26–33.

Shao, A.T. and J.S. Hill (1994), 'Global television advertising restrictions: the case of socially sensitive products', *International Journal of Advertising*, **13**, 347–66.

Spar, D.L. and D.B. Yoffie (2000), 'A race to the bottom or governance from the top?', in A. Prakash and J.A. Hart (eds), *Coping with Globalization*, London: Routledge, pp. 31–5.

Stole, I.L. (2000), 'Consumer protection in historical perspective: the five year battle over federal regulation of advertising, 1933 to 1938', *Mass Communication & Society*, **3** (4), 351–72.

Story, M. and S. French (2004), 'Food advertising and marketing directed at children and adolescents in the US', *International Journal of Behavioral Nutrition and Physical Activity*, **1** (3).

Tedlow, R.S. (1981), 'From competitor to consumer: the changing focus of federal regulation of advertising, 1914–1938', *Business History Review*, **55** (1), 35–58.

Van Cuilenburg, J. and D. McQuail (2003), 'Media policy paradigm shifts: towards a new communication policy paradigm', *European Journal of Communication*, **18** (2), 181–207.

Vogel, D. (1995), *Trading up: Consumer and Environmental Regulation in a Global Economy*, Cambridge, MA: Harvard University Press.

Vogel, D. and R.A. Kagan (2004), 'Introduction', in D. Vogel and R.A. Kagan (eds), *Dynamics of Regulatory Change: How Globalization Affects National Regulatory Policies*, Berkeley, Los Angeles and London: University of California Press, pp. 1–41.

Wong, W.S. (2000), 'The rise of consumer culture in a Chinese society: a reading of banking television commercials in Hong Kong during the 1970s', *Mass Communication & Society*, **3** (4), 393–413.

# 19 Internet regulation
## Andrew D. Murray

Cyberspace is both familiar and foreign. It is a place we are all extremely familiar with, a place we visit often on a daily basis, yet it is a place with social conventions very unlike our Realspace world. While we are able to socialise in both environments, often adopting different personas for different online and offline roles or activities, it is more difficult for regulators to design the correct regulatory response to online regulatory challenges or failures. This is because regulation in Realspace reflects the socio-political ordering of the regulatory environment it seeks to exert control over: in Realspace we discuss regulation in terms of the regulatory state or even the post-regulatory state (Levi-Faur, 2011). In Cyberspace there is no state, only nodes (Shearing and Wood 2003): this lack of social cohesion disrupts political organisation and ultimately attempts at external regulation.

If we think of primary Realspace regulation in the form of law we find in the modern environment a multi-layered legal system, but one in which primary legislative responsibility rests with the sovereign government of any territory. This creates a commonality between the regulator and the regulatee based on their shared dependency upon and responsibility for a geographically defined community (Galligan 2007, chap. 5). Thus members of the macro-community of UK citizens share responsibility for social and economic ordering within the UK and, more importantly, share the consequences of regulatory failure. For example, a real-world macro-community collectively shares the consequences of anti-social behaviour such as theft or violence against the person. It is therefore in the interest of community members to assist lawmakers in supporting initiatives designed to reduce anti-social behaviour, such as the Anti-Social Behaviour Act 2003, and to assist law enforcement authorities in detecting and prosecuting anti-social behaviour. The same is true with market regulation in real-world macro-communities. It is in the interests of most market participants to allow for market transparency. This permits fair transactions in which neither party unduly takes advantage of market conditions to defraud or even simply mislead the other party. A lack of market transparency leads to a lack of confidence in market participants and risks market failure. When one ventures online, though, the cohesive elements of real-world macro-communities are lost. The act of entering Cyberspace seems to drive us to shed our social responsibilities and duties. There is extensive anecdotal evidence to support this proposition, including the very high levels of anti-social and illegal activities seen online such as file sharing in breach of copyright, the consumption of indecent and obscene content and high levels of insensitive or harmful speech. Similarly the extensive nature of the available market and spooky economics such as Chris Anderson's *The Long Tail* (2007) cause a breakdown in traditional market controls. With digital goods being in limitless supply and with the distribution cost of physical goods being dramatically reduced through centralised storage and distribution warehouses, online retailers can offer a wider variety of goods and services than their offline counterparts at lower cost. In particular, Anderson points out that the zero sum cost of production and distribution of marginal digital goods leads to an inevitable movement towards content being made available free of charge (Anderson 2009).

These movements lead to a disintegration of the connective threads which bind individuals together as a socio-political body in Realspace. This disintegration of social connectivity has been catalogued by a number of leading sociologists. In his 2001 book *The Internet Galaxy*, Manuel Castells describes the move from the cohesive communities and diasporas of Realspace to the fractured, new communities found in Cyberspace as 'the culmination of an historical process between locality and sociability in the formation of community' (Castells 2001: 116), while Frank Webster harnesses the concept of 'entering the world of strangers' to describe the move from a Realspace community of neighbours to a Cyberspace community of strangers (Webster 2002: 208). For lawyers and regulators, though, the most interesting formulation of this common theme is probably Cass Sunstein's. In his 2001 book *Republic.com*, Sunstein posited that the 'communities of strangers' identified by Webster and Castells would lead to the formation of self-reinforcing micro-communities surrounding single issues. He began his argument by identifying a particular threat of Nicholas Negroponte's *Daily Me* analysis, which argues that the nature of digital content allows for the creation of personalised unique content (Negroponte 1995: 152–4). Sunstein says the *Daily Me* will allow citizens to 'filter what they see', which Sunstein warns undermines democratic discourse, as

> people must be exposed to material they would not have chosen in advance. Unplanned, unanticipated encounters are central to democracy itself. Such encounters often involve topics and points of view that people have not sought out and perhaps find quite irritating. They are important partly to ensure against fragmentation and extremism, which are predictable outcomes of any situation in which like-minded people speak only to themselves. (Sunstein 2001: 8–9)[1]

Sunstein develops this theory of fragmentation in chapter 3. Here he notes that the self-reinforcing nature of the *Daily Me* risks breakdown of social cohesion:

> [P]eople of certain interests and political convictions tend to choose sites and discussion groups which support their convictions. . . . Many of those with committed views on one or another topic – gun control, abortion, affirmative action – speak mostly to each other. (Sunstein 2001: 58–9)

In Sunstein's terms this leads to a Balkanisation of the internet: a network where 'diverse groups are seeing and hearing quite different points of view, or focussing on quite different topics', meaning that 'mutual understanding might be difficult and it might be increasingly hard for people to solve problems that society faces together' (Sunstein 2001: 61).

Although Sunstein may have slightly overplayed the threat the internet poses to democracy and democratic discourse,[2] there is no doubt that he captured the process of online individualisation. This reflects the move from Realspace macro-communities to online micro-communities. When one 'visits' Cyberspace one feels no connection to the macro-community of internet users; rather one feels community affiliation, if at all, to the space one inhabits – the community of online file sharers, the community of right-wing political bloggers, the community of sexual fetishists or the community of commercial traders. Individuals seek to obtain the best regulatory settlement *for their community* rather than for the macro-community at large. In short, there are no common values which are shared by all internet users and which may be used to encourage control of anti-social or harmful behaviour. File sharers, although aware of the anti-social aspects of their behaviour, feel no responsibility to the wider macro-community to mitigate their behaviour. Likewise, sexual fetishists who may wish to access and trade obscene content do not feel their behaviour is harmful to others, as it is contained 'within the community', where self-reinforcing communications encourage them to continue to act. There is a complete breakdown between the traditional relationship between the community as a political actor and the individual as part of the community and the role and force of regulation or governance. The concept of the state as regulator (either the regulatory state or the post-regulatory state) is rendered nugatory as the node (or rather the community of nodes) replaces the state as the socio-political entity to which the individual pledges allegiance. No longer do individuals share concerns with their neighbours. Now they merely collect as strangers with common interests. This is the challenge faced when one comes to regulate online activity: how does the wider community enforce its social values on an errant micro-community when the members of that community feel they are a community of themselves and not part of the wider macro-community?

## 19.1  THEORY ONE: SELF-REGULATION

This led to the initial suggestion that the internet as a non-geographical space with no regard for traditional borders or boundaries and with its unique micro-community structure was a place unsuitable for traditional forms of regulation. In his now infamous 1996 *Declaration of Independence for Cyberspace*, internet activist and EFF founder John Perry Barlow encapsulated this movement by imitating the US Declaration of Independence:

> Governments of the Industrial World, you weary giants of flesh and steel, I come from Cyberspace, the new home of Mind. On behalf of the future, I ask you of the past to leave us alone. You are not welcome among us. You have no sovereignty where we gather.
>
> We have no elected government, nor are we likely to have one, so I address you with no greater authority than that with which liberty itself always speaks. I declare the global social space we are building to be naturally independent of the tyrannies you seek to impose on us. You have no moral right to rule us nor do you possess any methods of enforcement we have true reason to fear.
>
> Governments derive their just powers from the consent of the governed. You have neither solicited nor received ours. We did not invite you. You do not know us, nor do you know our world. Cyberspace does not lie within your borders. Do not think that you can build it, as though it were a public construction project. You cannot. It is an act of nature and it grows itself through our collective actions. (Barlow 1996)

This statement encapsulates several foundational theories which would form the Cyberlibertarian School. The first is that traditional Realspace governments lack legitimacy in Cyberspace. This is based upon the assumption that Realspace governments draw legitimacy from a social contract with those who are governed. Although an extremely narrow view of legitimacy, which reflects only one view of the relationship between governments and those they govern, the Cyberlibertarian School focused on this relationship, as they wished to explore how the disassociation of community from geography affected the legitimacy of external lawmaking. They believed that, with no one Realspace government in a position to legitimately exert control over all the citizens of Cyberspace, and with no possibility of Realspace governments targeting only their citizens in Cyberspace owing to the nature of the place as one which 'does not lie within borders', any form of external intervention by Realspace governments would be illegitimate. The second is that Realspace governments have no ability to control the actions of individuals within Cyberspace owing to the borderless nature of the environment. This assumption was at the heart of the Cyberlibertarian School. It was premised upon the thesis that territorial borders delineate the effective boundaries of legal enforcement procedures. Thus if a citizen of the United Kingdom carries out an illegal act, such as the offering for sale of obscene material within the UK, he may expect enforcement through the UK criminal justice system: to be investigated by UK police officers and prosecuted before the UK courts before being fined or imprisoned in a UK prison. If that same citizen was to carry on his activity in France the UK criminal justice system would have no say over investigation and prosecution of his actions: it would be within the purview of the French criminal justice system. The Cyberlibertarian School believed that, as Cyberspace 'floated above Realspace' and did not respect Realspace borders, laws passed by states' regulators, sovereign only within their own borders, were doomed to fail. This is most clearly encapsulated in the classic Cyberlibertarian text 'Law and borders: the rise of law in Cyberspace' (Johnson and Post 1996).

Here Johnson and Post set out the legal argument for Cyberlibertarianism:

> Cyberspace radically undermines the relationship between legally significant (online) phenomena and physical location . . . efforts to control the flow of electronic information across physical borders – to map local regulation and physical boundaries onto Cyberspace – are likely to prove futile, at least in countries that hope to participate in global commerce. Individual electrons can easily, and without any realistic prospect of detection, 'enter' any sovereign's territory. The volume of electronic communications crossing territorial boundaries is just too great in relation to the resources available to government authorities to permit meaningful control. (Johnson and Post 1996: 1370, 1372)

This lack of ability to police borders divests efforts to control the activities of citizens online of any relationship with a physical territory or, more pertinently, with the residents or citizens of that territory. This means that

> the global computer network is destroying the link between geographical location and: (1) the *power* of local governments to assert control over online behavior; (2) the *effects* of online behavior on individuals or things; (3) the *legitimacy* of the efforts of a local sovereign to enforce rules applicable to global phenomena; and (4) the ability of physical location to give *notice* of which sets of rules apply. (Johnson and Post 1996: 1370)

This concept was attacked by a number of commentators, who suggested that Johnson and Post had failed to take account of the international nature of law in the late 20th century. Drawing upon the international nature of legal settlements such as the law of sea, aviation law, the laws and principles of human rights and environmental law, they pointed out that it was the nature of law in the modern global environment to display pluralistic characteristics; therefore to say Cyberspace was effectively ungovernable owing to its nature as a global communications media was naïve. This counter-argument was best encapsulated in Jack Goldsmith's paper 'Against cyberanarchy' (Goldsmith 1998), where he argued that the Cyberlibertarian argument is 'in the grip of a nineteenth century territorialist conception of how "real space" is regulated and how "real-space" conflicts of law are resolved'. This conception, he notes, 'was repudiated in the middle of this century' (Goldsmith 1998: 1205). Goldsmith argues that the concept of law tied to a bordered territory is no longer applicable, and further that Cyberspace transactions are no different to other forms of transnational transactions, as both involve 'people in real space in one territorial jurisdiction transacting with people in real space in another territorial jurisdiction in a way that sometimes causes real-world harms' and 'in both contexts, the state in which the harms are suffered has a legitimate interest in regulating the activity that produces the harms' (Goldsmith 1998: 1200).

Goldsmith therefore convincingly disassembled the Cyberlibertarian argument and soon thereafter it became eclipsed by the Cyberpaternalist argument, but before leaving Cyberlibertarianism behind one should ask 'How did the Cyberlibertarians envisage a legitimate functioning system of governance for Cyberspace would emerge?' This is clear in both the work of Barlow and of Johnson and Post. Barlow alludes to it in his *Declaration of Independence*: 'We are forming our own Social Contract. This governance will arise according to the conditions of our world, not yours.' This concept is made flesh by Johnson and Post, who see the only legitimate form of Cyberspace governance as responsible self-regulation. In this Johnson and Post see a parallel with the development of *Lex Mercatoria* in medieval Europe. There too a body of individuals were engaged in transactions outwith the traditional boundaries of states, and in that case self-regulation flourished supported by a strong enforcement procedure developed from within the community. Unfortunately Johnson and Post were drawing upon a false analogy. The community of traders who formed the *Lex Mercatoria* were a homogeneous community who shared a common set of goals and experiences, whereas the macro-community of internet users is heterogeneous. There was no commonality of goals or experiences which would allow an internet form of *Lex Mercatoria* to emerge.

## 19.2   THEORY TWO: DESIGN-BASED REGULATION

The concept of governance achieved through changes at the technical protocol level of the internet formed the foundation of the Cyberpaternalist School. This school emerged in a number of papers published in 1998 and 1999, including Jack Goldsmith's 'Against cyberanarchy' (1998), Joel Reidenberg's '*Lex Informatica*' (1998) and famously Lawrence Lessig's 'The law of the horse: what cyberlaw might teach' (Lessig 1999a). The Cyberpaternalist approach married Goldsmith's argument that effective and legitimate law may be affected without a jurisdictional foundation to Johnson and Post's argument that standards may be applied though technical protocols. The Cyberpaternalist School found its voice in Reidenberg's classic 1998 paper '*Lex Informatica*'. Here Reidenberg built upon Johnson and Post's argument that self-regulation may form in Cyberspace in a manner similar to the development of *Lex Mercatoria*. Reidenberg though was not arguing for the organic development of self-regulatory constructs within Cyberspace;

rather he used the example of *Lex Mercatoria* to illustrate how effective external regulation could be imposed on 'sovereign Cyberspace'.

Reidenberg argues that the design of network protocols may regulate as effectively as, or even more effectively than, traditional state-based laws. Reidenberg points out that changes may be implemented directly by network designers, or may be mandated by traditional Realspace lawmakers who may direct changes in the network protocols: thus 'policy choices are available either through technology itself, through laws that cause technology to exclude possible options, or through laws that cause users to restrict certain actions' (Reidenberg 1998: 565). Reidenberg identifies six ways in which traditional policymakers and lawmakers may influence or mandate the development of *Lex Informatica*: (1) the bully pulpit, (2) participation, (3) funding, (4) procurement, (5) regulated behaviour and (6) regulated standards (Reidenberg 1998: 581). Each is more directive than the previous, with the bully pulpit representing the influence lawmakers and policymakers exert on civil society, and regulated standards ultimately reflecting the ability of lawmakers to control software and hardware developers through law mandating such approaches as disconnection strategies against file sharers or filtering technologies to prevent the distribution of child abuse images such as the BT Cleanfeed system used in the UK.

Reidenberg's concept of governance through directed or mandated changes to network infrastructure was most famously adopted by Lawrence Lessig in his paper 'The law of the horse: what cyberlaw might teach' (1999a) and his subsequent book *Code and Other Laws of Cyberspace* (1999b). *Code* became the central rallying point for the Cyberpaternalist School. A bestseller, *Code* is among the few academic law books which found a market beyond legal practice and legal scholarship. The simple, effective message of *Code* reached out to technologists, software designers, activists and even the average internet user. The heart of *Code* is found in its title. Lessig very deliberately entitled his book *Code and Other Laws of Cyberspace*, for in this title he captures the pre-eminence of code-based or *Lex Informatica* systems of control and governance in the online environment.

Lessig gives pre-eminence to his new theory, which he entitles the New Chicago School to differentiate it from the 'Old' Chicago School which places pre-emphasis on law and economic theory (Lessig 1998). He identified four modalities of regulation which collectively act as a constraint on action: laws, norms, markets and architecture. Each has a distinct but equally effective ability to control an outcome or action. Law (in its traditional, or Austinian, sense) directs behaviour by threatening sanctions *ex post* if those orders are not obeyed. Norms constrain an individual's behaviour, but not through the centralised enforcement of a state. They constrain because of the enforcement of a community: examples would include an audience reaction to a comedian's racist jokes or the intervention of the community to tell an anti-social fellow train traveller to turn down his or her loud music. Markets regulate through the device of price. For example, the market constrains my ability to trade hours of teaching for a new car. Clearly this is a different form of regulation from the first two. Whereas both laws and norms see normative standards enforced by an *ex post* sanction, markets constrain *ex ante*. I cannot choose to break the normative rule and take the risk of being caught and sanctioned; instead the market indicator (price) is set *ex ante*. This does not mean that markets are not subject to manipulation, just that the normative standard and

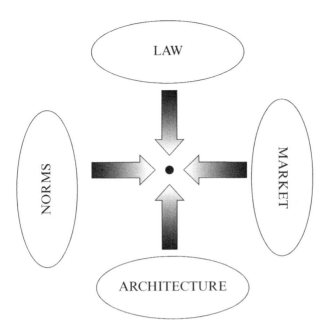

*Figure 19.1    The New Chicago School: Lessig's modalities in action*

the application of the control mechanism are both set *ex ante*. Finally Lessig identifies architecture as the final regulator. This is 'the world as I find it, understanding that as I find it, much of this world has been made' (Lessig 1998: 663). Lessig gives examples such as:

> That I cannot see through walls is a constraint on my ability to snoop. That I cannot read your mind is a constraint on my ability to know whether you are telling me the truth. That I cannot lift large objects is a constraint on my ability to steal. That it takes 24 hours to drive to the closest abortion clinic is a constraint on a woman's ability to have an abortion. That there is a highway or train tracks separating this neighborhood from that is a constraint on citizens to integrate. These features of the world – whether made, or found – restrict and enable in a way that directs or affects behavior. They are features of this world's architecture, and they, in this sense, regulate. (Lessig 1998: 663)

Collectively, Lessig argues, these four modalities function together, controlling the individual, or 'pathetic dot' (as seen in Figure 19.1): they 'constitute a sum of forces that guide an individual to behave, or act, in a given way – the net, as Robert Ellickson might describe it, of the regulatory effect to some behavioural end' (Lessig 1998: 663).

The key to the New Chicago School is Lessig's argument that all regulation is a mix of the direct and the indirect:

> In its direct aspect, the law uses its traditional means to direct an object of regulation (whether the individual regulated, norms, the market, or architecture); in its indirect aspect, it regulates these other regulators so that they regulate the individual differently. In this, the law uses or co-opts their regulatory power to law's own ends: modern regulation is a mix of the two aspects. (Lessig 1998: 666–7)

Thus Lessig argues that the modern regulatory state is not an Austinian state but is a post-regulatory state using indirect controls as much as, if not more than, direct legal control. Lessig has many examples to support this thesis, including rules on smoking, the use of seat belts and fitting of airbags, drugs policy and disability access. The New Chicago School is not, though, a theory or school of internet regulation; rather it may be seen as a general theory of regulation, a development of the work of Robert Ellickson in *Order without Law* (1991).

The link between the New Chicago School and internet regulation is made clear in *Code and Other Laws of Cyberspace*. Applying Reidenberg's *Lex Informatica* theory, Lessig suggests that Cyberspace is different from Realspace in a regulatory sense. In Realspace, architectural controls are constrained by basic physical laws. We can either regulate, by designing a change in the environment, or we can leave the universal laws in place. To make a change in the design or architecture of Realspace involves considerable investment, as one must overcome the settled position; thus to use architecture to constrain speeding motorists involves a considerable investment (in both time and money) to build traffic calming measures. In Cyberspace when one escapes the basic carrier level of cables, servers and routers, there is no predesigned environment. We design that environment to achieve whichever ends we want, and we do so by designing the software which manages the environment. We can design software that allows for privacy or which removes it; we can design software which will filter content or which will not; we can design software which allows files to be shared across peers or which does not. In Lessig's words:

> We can build, or architect, or code Cyberspace to protect values that we believe are fundamental, or we can build, or architect, or code Cyberspace to allow these values to disappear. There is no middle ground. There is no choice that does not include some kind of *building*. Code is never found; it is only ever made, and only ever made by us. (Lessig 1999b: 6)

The Cyberpaternalist School sees code as a potentially perfect, covert regulator. It is potentially perfect, as it regulates *ex ante* and there is little the user can do but comply with the environment as he finds it (unless he has programming skill to change it). It is covert, as the code remains hidden from view; thus regulatees are unaware of the effect the code is having on controlling their actions or decisions, or potentially even that they are being controlled at all. This is extremely threatening to autonomy and personalised decision making (Lessig 1996: 1408). For Cyberpaternalists such as Lessig the solution is to make lawmaking, both online and offline, open to greater scrutiny. As with open-source software, open-source regulation, or to be more precise regulation subject to public scrutiny, is the best system. For Lessig doing nothing is not an option or the invisible hand of commerce will regulate in a manner which best suits its aims and objectives. As a result Lessig both calls his reader to action and places confidence in political lawmaking processes, what he calls East Coast Code – code made in Washington, DC rather than in Silicon Valley (Lessig 1999b: 222–31). For the remains of the Cyberlibertarian School, this is a dangerous argument. In his book review of *Code and Other Laws of Cyberspace*, David Post argues that this is a false narrowing of choice. He cites the success of the English language in developing complex regulatory rules for grammar and syntax and that those developed without political involvement and free from the hand of commerce. As he notes:

We do not have, and we do not want, the Ministry of Semantic Propriety, or our elected representatives, or specially-constituted board of experts, or even the law professors, to make a 'plan' about the proper direction(s) that English may take and to make decisions for us in accordance with that plan. We do not, in fact, have, or need, a 'plan' at all. We are, and should be, deeply suspicious of those who claim to have such a plan, and positively terrified of those who assert that they need to enlist the coercive powers of the State to implement that plan. (Post 2000: 1457)

Post therefore argues that internet regulation need not be directed paternalistically. He disagrees with Lessig that left 'unregulated' the invisible hand of commerce will direct the future direction of internet regulation. Remaining true to his Cyberlibertarian ethos he argues that we should keep the state, in the form of East Coast Code, out of Cyberspace. Regulation, in his view, is best nurtured from the seeds of self-regulation and self-ordering rather than as an imposed settlement, whether this is in the form of East Coast or West Coast intervention. His views lead to the final approach: network communitarianism.

## 19.3   THEORY THREE: COMMUNITY-BASED REGULATION

There is a subtle but important difference between the self-regulation argument of the Cyberlibertarian School and the community-based regulation of the Network Communitarian School. The Network Communitarian School has evolved as a counterpoint to the Cyberpaternalist School. It, like Cyberlibertarianism, focuses on the communicative power of the network, but unlike Cyberlibertarianism does not believe that only internal self-regulatory constructs may be effective in the online environment.

Network communitarianism believes that the Cyberpaternalist model fails to account for the complexities of information flows found in a modern telecommunications/media system such as the internet. The main influences on network communitarianism are actor network theory (ANT) and social systems theory (SST). A key concept of ANT is that social communications are made up of parallel transactions between the material (things) and semiotic (concepts), which together form a single network. This has the potential to be particularly powerful when applied to the internet. The internet is the largest person–to-person communication network yet designed. It allows individuals to move social transactions in space and time, and it allows transactions between people with shared experiences who are geographically remote and between people with no common history who are geographically close. The potential for new networks to form, dissolve and reform on the internet is massive, leading one to reconceptualise the internet not merely as a communications/media tool but as a cultural/social tool (Mansell 2002). SST shares some roots with ANT but is quite distinct. SST attempts to explain and study the flow of information within increasingly complex systems of social communication. Niklaus Luhmann attempts to explain how communications affect social transactions by defining social systems as systems of communication, and society as the most encompassing social system. A system is defined by a boundary between itself and its surrounding environment, dividing it from the infinitely complex, or chaotic, exterior. The interior of the system is thus a zone of reduced complexity. Communication within a system operates by selecting only a limited amount of all information available outside.

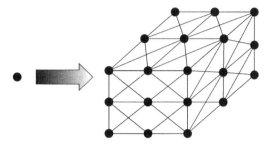

*Figure 19.2    From the pathetic dot to the active dot matrix*

This process is also called reduction of complexity. The criterion according to which information is selected and processed is meaning (Luhmann 2004). Like ANT, SST is an attempt to map and study the complex process of social interactions in the increasingly complex and connected environment of modern society. Whereas ANT is about the evolution and formation of networks, SST is about the filtering of information flows in the decision-making process and the communication of ideas and concepts between systems.

Although these theories are quite distinct, network communitarianism argues that taken together they can illuminate much of our understanding of communications and social interaction in a networked environment such as the internet with a variety of actors, both human and non-human (Teubner 2006). This is what the current author attempts in *The Regulation of Cyberspace* (Murray 2007: 22–54, 233–51). There I re-examine the New Chicago model, in which a pathetic dot is found to reside among four regulatory modalities which act as a constraint on the choice of actions of that dot, and find that in applying the principles of ANT and SST we can consider the dot rather differently. The dot is in ANT terms a material node in the network, while in SST terms it is part of a system. In either term the dot is not isolated. It forms part of a matrix of dots, or to put it another way the dot, which is designed to represent the individual, must always be considered to be part of the wider community. It is here that traditional Cyberpaternalism runs into difficulty, for when one examines the modalities of regulation proposed by Lessig we find that, of the four, three of them, laws, norms and markets, are in fact a proxy for community-based control. Laws are passed by lawmakers elected by the community, markets are merely a reflection of value, demand, supply and scarcity as reflected by the community in monetary terms, and norms are merely the codification of community values. I therefore term these 'socially mediated modalities', reflecting an active role for the dot in the regulatory process: far from being a 'pathetic dot' which was the subject of external regulatory forces, the dot was in fact an 'active dot' taking part in the regulatory process (Murray 2007: 233–51).

There are two key distinctions between the classic Cyberpaternalist model and the new network communitarian model. The first is to replace the isolated pathetic dot with a networked community (or matrix) of dots which share ideas, beliefs, ideals and opinions (Figure 19.2). The second is to recognise that the socially mediated modalities of law, norms and markets draw their legitimacy from the community (or matrix of dots), meaning the regulatory process is in nature a dialogue not an eternally imposed set of constraints (Figure 19.3).

How does this affect our understanding of internet regulation? Firstly it suggests that

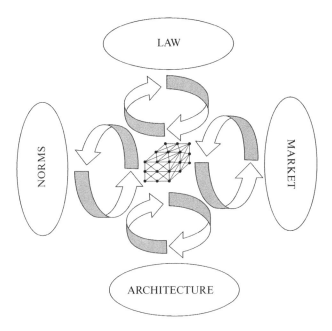

*Figure 19.3    Network communitarian regulatory discourse*

regulation in the online environment is little different to regulation in the real world. Regulation is a process of discourse and dialogue between the individual and society. Sometimes society, either directly through the application of norms or indirectly by distilling its opinions, norms or standards down to laws, wishes to force a change in the behaviour of the individual. But sometimes it is the regulatory settlement itself which is challenged by society when there is no longer any support for it. This is most clearly illustrated by the fact that the UK enforcement authorities have declined to prosecute individuals under either the Customs Consolidation Act or the Obscene Publications Act 1959 for privately viewing obscene material using an internet connection. We, the community of dots, have collectively decided that the viewing of pornography by internet connection is no longer to be viewed as morally objectionable and have communicated this decision both by driving the market for material of this type and by communicating to our lawmakers where a line is to be drawn. We wish to sanction and criminalise those who possess or trade in images of child pornography (including pseudo-images) and those who possess or trade in images of sexual violence, harm, bestiality and necrophilia (Murray 2009). Thus the regulatory settlement is not imposed upon us; if it were we would all avoid the viewing of obscene material for fear of prosecution under the Obscene Publications Acts. Rather there is part of a dialogue in which the regulatory settlement evolves to reflect changes in society.

This may also explain why digital rights management systems (DRMs) failed to have the desired effect. DRMs were viewed by the majority of music consumers to be an unreasonable, and sometimes damaging, restriction on their freedom to enjoy something they viewed, having paid to purchase it, as their property. When Cactus Data Shield prevented them from playing their new CD on their old CD player, when Apple FairPlay restricted them to having five authorised computers (a problem in an extended family) or worst of all when Sony Extended Copy Protection was shown to leave their PCs vulnerable to attack, consumers reacted in the way one would expect: they collectively used their market power to respond. The industry could not force its DRM technology on us because we can withhold our market support for them. In network communitarian theory the power to determine the regulatory environment does not rest with the regulator alone.

## 19.4   CONCLUSION

It is difficult to draw conclusions on the nature and politics of internet regulation or regulation in the wider communications sphere based on the current models, which remain in opposition to one another. If Cyberpaternalism is right we should expect to see greater controls emanating from both East Coast codemakers and West Coast codemakers. Anecdotally there is evidence in support of this, as we rely to a greater extent on tied devices such as Apple's iPhone and other smartphones and closed devices such as netbooks, tablets and games systems. This has led Jonathan Zittrain to suggest a future where without intervention the invisible hand will partition off much of the internet into walled gardens or closed systems, reducing consumer choice and control (Zittrain 2008). However, tied devices do not lead to closed political systems. We remain able to communicate via open devices: PCs, email, social networking tools and messaging systems. The power of the human network has proven decisive again and again in bringing about change and, given the connective nature of modern Realspace, network communitarianism may be about to move into the mainstream (Lehmkuhl (2008); Schulte (2009); Stevens and Neumann (2009)).

## NOTES

1. A second edition, *Republic.com 2.0*, was published in 2007. References here are to the first edition as the source of the discussion.
2. See critiques in Nadel (2002) and Chander (2002).

## BIBLIOGRAPHY

Anderson, Chris (2007), *The Long Tail: How Endless Choice Is Creating Unlimited Demand*, New York and London: Random House.
Anderson, Chris (2009), *Free: The Future of a Radical Price: The Economics of Abundance and Why Zero Pricing Is Changing the Face of Business*, New York and London: Random House.
Barlow, John Perry (1996), *A Declaration of Independence for Cyberspace*, available at: http://homes.eff.org/~barlow/Declaration-Final.html (accessed 17 November 2009).
Castells, Manuel (2001), *The Internet Galaxy: Reflections on the Internet, Business, and Society*, Oxford and New York: Oxford University Press.
Chander, Anupam (2002), 'Whose Republic?', *University of Chicago Law Review*, **69**, 1479–1500.
Ellickson, Robert (1991), *Order without Law: How Neighbors Settle Disputes*, Cambridge, MA: Harvard University Press.
Galligan, Dennis (2007), *Law in Modern Society*, Oxford and New York: Oxford University Press.

Goldsmith, Jack (1998), 'Against cyberanarchy', *Chicago Law Review*, **65**, 1199–1250.
Johnson, David R. and David G. Post (1996), 'Law and borders: the rise of law in Cyberspace', *Stanford Law Review*, **48**, 1367–1401.
Lehmkuhl, Dirk (2008), 'Control modes in the age of transnational governance', *Law & Policy*, **30**, 336–63.
Lessig, Lawrence (1996), 'The zones of Cyberspace', *Stanford Law Review*, **48**, 1403–11.
Lessig, Lawrence (1998), 'The New Chicago School', *Journal of Legal Studies*, **27**, 661–91.
Lessig, Lawrence (1999a), 'The law of the horse: what cyberlaw might teach', *Harvard Law Review*, **113**, 501–49.
Lessig, Lawrence (1999b), *Code and Other Laws of Cyberspace*, New York: Basic Books.
Levi-Faur, David (2011), 'Regulation and Regulatory Governance', in David Levi-Faur (ed.), *Handbook on the Politics of Regulation*, Cheltenham, UK and Northampton, Mass., US: Edward Elgar.
Luhmann, Niklaus (2004), *Law as a Social System*, trans. Klaus Ziegert, Oxford and New York: Oxford University Press.
Mansell, Robin (ed.) (2002), *Inside the Communication Revolution: Evolving Patterns of Social and Technical Interaction*, Oxford and New York: Oxford University Press.
Murray, Andrew D. (2007), *The Regulation of Cyberspace: Control in the Online Environment*, Abingdon and New York: Routledge.
Murray, Andrew D. (2009), 'The reclassification of extreme pornographic images', *Modern Law Review*, **72**, 73–90.
Nadel, Mark (2002), 'Customized filtering and extremist enclaves in Republic.com', *Stanford Law Review*, **54**, 831–86.
Negroponte, Nicholas (1995), *Being Digital*, New York and London: Vintage.
Post, David G. (2000), 'What Larry doesn't get: code, law, and liberty in Cyberspace', *Stanford Law Review*, **52**, 1439–59.
Reidenberg, Joel (1998), '*Lex Informatica*: the formulation of information policy rules through technology', *Texas Law Review*, **76**, 553–93.
Schulte, Stephanie (2009), 'Self-colonizing eEurope: the information society merges onto the information superhighway', *Journal of Transnational American Studies*, **1** (1).
Shearing, Clifford and Jennifer, Wood (2003), 'Nodal governance, democracy, and the new "Denizens"', *Journal of Law and Society*, **30**, 400–419.
Stevens, Tim and Peter R. Neumann (2009), *Countering Online Radicalisation: A Strategy for Action*, London: International Centre for the Study of Radicalisation and Political Violence.
Sunstein, Cass (2001), *Republic.com*, Princeton, NJ: Princeton University Press.
Teubner, Gunther (2006), 'Rights of non-humans? Electronic agents and animals as new actors in politics and law', *Journal of Law and Society*, **33**, 497–521.
Webster, Frank (2002), *Theories of the Information Society*, 2nd edn, New York and London: Routledge.
Zittrain, Jonathan (2008), *The Future of the Internet and How to Stop It*, London and New Haven, CT: Yale University Press.

# PART VI

# RISK REGULATION

# 20 Risk regulation and precaution
*Dieter Pesendorfer*

Controlling risks is a concern central to any regulation. Specific levels of risk taking and uncertainties are inherent to all social situations and decision-making, including non-decisions. Yet individuals and collective actors react in different, culturally framed and inconsistent ways to whatever they identify as safe enough or too dangerous. Reactions to harm, threats and dangers can be perceived, for example, as rational, irrational, appropriate, insufficient or ignorant depending on individual assumptions and abstract commitments to fundamental values which are by definition open for interpretation. It is common sense that risks and corresponding alternative decisions are related to possible gains and losses. Risk regulation should try to avoid, to minimize or to reduce the most severe harm in a rational, efficient and effective manner. As risk taking is a precondition for and inherent to development and progress and always includes the possibility of failure, the right level of regulation is crucial, and the overall design in risk regulation establishes path dependencies of economic development and innovation and therefore contributes to the overall level of risk in a society.

With nascent capitalism a new climate of risk taking has emerged since the Renaissance. Insurance business and risk management based on a rational-mathematical analysis of the probability of certain kinds of harm from alternative decisions were established (Bernstein 1996; Jaeger et al. 2001). Driven by rapid societal and economic transformations the decades since the 1960s then brought about strong concerns, particularly in rich Western societies, with insufficient regulation of all kinds of risks, accompanied by a growing distrust of specific industry sectors, science, experts and regulators that could not be overcome by new tools such as risk assessment and cost–benefit analysis (recently relabelled as benefit–cost analysis). Faced with numerous transnational and global risks with catastrophic potential and several major accidents, modern societies have been described as 'risk societies' in a 'world risk society' (Beck 1986, 1999) and, with regard to risk management, as 'post-trust societies' (Löfstedt 2009), in which decision-makers as well as the public got preoccupied with risk, yet with fundamental differences between the poorest and richest countries. In the wealthy countries the rapidly increasing number of risk regulations with all kind of shortcomings and inconsistencies as well as new and persistent problems led to demands for more effective risk regulation, a better use of science in risk assessment and a more systematic evaluation of benefits and costs of measures to maximize what risk regulation can achieve (Breyer 1993).

For some of the most serious, but uncertain, threats to humans and the environment the precautionary principle emerged in the 1980s as a new idea in international environmental law. Compared to traditional risk regulation, mostly dependent on 'hard scientific facts' for legitimating action and focusing on the idea of prevention of well-known possible effects and related probabilities, precautionary public policy empowers regulators explicitly to take early action in situations of severe harm. Successfully incorporated into a large number of international treaties, agreements, policy declarations and recommendations as well as in numerous national legal systems this principle won many supporters, who have interpreted it as a cornerstone of sustainable development strategies with general importance and relevance in all areas of risk regulation. Precautionary public policy became part of discussions about overcoming the traditional technocratic model of risk governance and establishing a more transparent and adequate model that reflects the normative ideas underlying 'good governance' and 'better regulation' and takes the interests of future generations into account. In the light of past regulatory failures great expectations were held out for the principle's implementation, as a radical shift or at least the 'best practice' in risk regulation. Its new legal status promised the enacting of 'the most radical idea for rethinking humanity's relationship to the natural world since the 18th-century European Enlightenment', resulting in a 'great shift from a risk-taking age to a risk-prevention era' (Rifkin 2004).

However, the precautionary principle has frequently been the subject of major critique and vigorous opposition. For moderate critics it adds nothing new to sound risk regulation or should play only a very limited role; for most radical opponents it poses a serious and unacceptable threat to democracy, development, innovation and wealth. 'All the fears of our age seem to have found shelter in the word "precaution"', proclaimed Dupuy and Grinbaum (2004: 9). Others warned that the principle would only lead to unjustifiable 'aggressive regulation' and 'laws of fear' (Sunstein 2005). Because of its potential abuse through irrational, populist and protectionist measures the precautionary principle turned into the most controversial principle in risk regulation. As a result numerous academic and political discussions about its meanings, scope and application as well as legal disputes and court cases led to ongoing debates and a vast body of literature on consequences of its achieved status and reformulations and refinements which have affected and will continue to affect risk regulatory practices.

This chapter provides a broad overview and a critical discussion of the principle and general patterns of its implementation and application to identify underlying changes in risk regulatory practices. After a short section on the need for precaution and a discussion of the role of principles in risk regulation it proceeds with the history of the principle and its successful global diffusion, before discussing the controversies about meanings and definitions. It will be argued that the moderate versions adopted in international environmental law and at the EU level and political and legal clarifications have especially led to an increased similarity in risk regulatory practices between countries which adopted the precautionary principle and those opposing that idea. With regard to (serious) risks most countries in the world have been moving towards a strict separation of risk assessment and risk management and a systematic use of benefit–cost analysis which makes a real change. It is expected that risk regulation will remain politically and controversial despite the various attempts to depoliticize risk governance.

## 20.1    WHY PRECAUTION?

Today's most significant problems in risk regulation have highly complex problem structures and a transnational or global dimension. More than ever and even with all scientific progress there is great uncertainty about responses of complex biological, ecological, economic, social and political systems. In many cases the consequences of human action occur with a delay in time. When 'full' scientific evidence becomes available it might well be too late for action, or costs of adoption measures might have become significantly higher. Popular examples are the extinction of species and biodiversity, climate change, bioaccumulation of certain hazardous chemical substances, genetically modified organisms (GMOs), nuclear power or nanotechnology. As these examples indicate, action is limited not only by a lack of knowledge caused by complex natural and societal systems but also by powerful economic and political interests. Many cases moreover demonstrate that uncertainty can even increase with further research if new information reveals the presence of previously unknown or understated uncertainties. For advocates the precautionary principle's application is one crucial possibility to deal with complex problems of risk which can help to overcome the weaknesses of traditional approaches (Tickner 2003). Principles might be seen as rather weak and unimportant compared to other factors affecting risk regulation, so why did precaution become so important and how do principles in general affect action?

Controversies about the role of precaution in risk regulation are a logical consequence of serious interest conflicts related to expectations about significant gains and losses of risk taking in the contested areas in which this principle has become most relevant. They also result from the increased role of the global context in risk regulation. However, a part of the discussion is related to legal interpretations about the role of principles in general and consequences of their application in different jurisdictions. All policies are based on general goals, principles, approaches and rules which structure political action and contribute to specific policy styles. Democracies are based on principles such as freedom, justice, security and solidarity. Modern liberal economies have principles such as economic growth, welfare, trade openness and even full employment. In risk regulation several additional principles have been established such as the cooperation, the polluter-pays, the common burden, the proportionality in cost and gain and the sustainability principles. All principles have in common that they do not necessitate a particular direction, which is different to rules which simply fix the direction of action whenever they apply. While rules, structured hierarchically, must not contradict each other, principles not only can but frequently do contradict each other. In such cases the right balance between competing objectives must be chosen and consistency in application assured (Sands 1995).

Principles are based on common sense and political, moral and ethical assumptions (the latter three especially have become highly relevant in areas of risk regulation, which led, for example, to debates about how to incorporate moral and ethical concerns into risk governance). The interpretation of principles varies between different cultures as well as among individuals in a given society. Theoretically they have practical consequences. Incorporated into legal obligations they have to be taken into consideration by decision-makers, and they become relevant for courts.

## 20.2 HISTORY AND DEVELOPMENT OF THE PRECAUTIONARY PRINCIPLE

Giving priority to human health and the environment and therefore weakening business interests as demanded in strong interpretations of precaution (see below) would indeed be a radical change from traditional risk regulation. However, the history of precautionary risk governance is much less radical. Emerging from clean air legislation debates in West Germany the precautionary principle (*Vorsorgeprinzip*) was incorporated into the federal government's first environmental programme (1971). The Air Pollution Control Act 1974 was the first law referring to the principle, followed by further laws in the following decades. Originally understood similarly to prevention, the principle's meaning extended quickly to 'acting when conclusively ascertained understanding by science is not yet available'. However, risk regulatory practice was not radically different to that of other countries, as decision-makers and courts took the technological development, scientific knowledge, proportionality and technical and administrative feasibility of measures into account (Boehmer-Christiansen 1994; Jordan and O'Riordan 2004).

From the late 1970s the term 'precautionary principle' spread to neighbouring countries and became part of discussions on several regional environmental agreements. Poland (1980) and Switzerland (1985) were early adopters. During the 1990s, a large number of EC/EU member states too incorporated the principle into national legislation. Among those countries were Austria (1990), Belgium (1999), Denmark (1993), France (1995), Greece (1994), Italy (1997), Portugal (1995), Sweden (1998) and the United Kingdom (1990). A number of applicant countries, including Hungary (1995) and Rumania (1995), also adopted laws referring to the principle, while in other European countries, including the Netherlands, Ireland and Spain, opposition from key actors stopped initiatives. Outside Europe several countries, including Australia (1991), Canada (1999), India (Marchant and Mossman 2004: 6), Japan (1994), Mexico (1996) (Pesendorfer 2009) and New Zealand incorporated the principle into domestic laws. France was then the first and so far the only country to incorporate a reference to precaution into the constitution, namely in 2005 in the annexed environmental charter (Godard 2006).

The increasing notion of the term 'precautionary principle' and the underlying policy learning were supported by 'precautionary-type' policies in many countries – the Swedish chemicals policy is a frequently mentioned early case, with Sweden sometimes even held as the real inventor or at least as important as Germany in developing the principle's core elements and features in the late 1960s. For other countries, roots of precaution have been tracked too (e.g. Löfstedt 2004; de Sadeleer 2007). In short, especially throughout the 1990s a fast-increasing number of countries around the world adopted the precautionary principle. However, the probably incomplete overview of countries with a reference to a precautionary principle is just an indicator for an assumed policy change in risk regulation, but this information as such does not allow conclusions about the scope of changes with regard to similarity in risk regulatory practices (Wiener 2004: 76). The Netherlands, for example, as a country without a direct reference to precaution in domestic laws, has not only been a strong supporter of the idea and incorporated the principle into many policy declarations and plans, but established a precautionary practice in various areas of risk regulation, supported by several court decisions (Pesendorfer 2009). Moreover for countries without a reference to the principle in domestic laws precaution became relevant via international environmental law, as most countries ratified treaties or conventions calling for precautionary action.

As an international environmental principle the precautionary principle emerged in the context of the UN World Charter for Nature (1982), the Vienna Convention for Protection of the Ozone Layer (1985) and the soft law adopted by the North Sea

Conferences (1984 Bremen, 1987 London, 1990 The Hague, 1995 Esbjerg, 2002 Bergen Declarations). The principle was listed in the Brundtland Report (Annexe 1) by the World Commission on Environment and Development (1987), and the 1992 United Nations Rio Declaration on Environment and Development recommended that the 'precautionary approach shall be widely applied by states according to their capabilities' (Principle 15). In February of the same year, the Treaty on European Union signed at Maastricht formulated the goal that the Community's environmental policy 'shall be based on the precautionary principle' (Article 130r(2); ex-Article 174(2) Amsterdam, now Article 191(2) of the Lisbon Treaty). Precaution was additionally incorporated into EU secondary law (in the areas of animal health, antibiotics, biocides, biotechnology, chemical substances, fishery products, general food law, habitats, integrated pollution control, water protection and waste management). The Agreement on the European Economic Area referred to the principle in Article 44. At the international level it became part of a number of conventions in the areas of biodiversity and GMOs, chemicals policy, clean air policy, climate change, marine pollution and waste management. Additionally the principle found support in policy recommendations by UN organizations (e.g. UNEP Governing Council Decision 15/27 1989, 1990 UNECE Bergen Ministerial Declaration on Sustainable Development in the ECE Region, 1993 UNEP Caribbean Environment Programme), the OECD (1990 Recommendation on Integrated Pollution Prevention and Control, 1991 declaration by environment ministers, 2001 Environmental Strategy for the 1st Decade of the 21st Century), the WHO (numerous recommendations since 1990, especially from WHO Europe), the FAO (1996 FAO Technical Guidelines for Responsible Fisheries) and the European Environment Agency (Pesendorfer 2009).

Given this 'success' story, the precautionary principle's legitimacy quickly increased. In many cases it was seen as a way to overcome inaction by states based on the excuse of incomplete scientific knowledge. For transition or developing countries the precautionary principle became also an attractive idea to legitimate action in a general situation of limited resources for research.

## 20.3 CONTROVERSIES ABOUT TERMS, MEANINGS, AND WEAK AND STRONG PRECAUTION

The debate on the core question of how precaution might be or should be applied in law- and policy-making has remained controversial. In evaluating the overall effects of precaution, opinions range from unjustified protectionist measures to purely rhetorical or symbolic to practical success. Some argue that the legal status of the principle and experiences with its implementation have proven that it is sound, workable, legitimate and meaningful (Fisher et al. 2006), while others conclude 'that it provides an open invitation for arbitrary and unreasonable decisions by both regulators and judges' (Marchant and Mossman 2004: 65).

Controversies start with the principle's definition. The differences in understandings of the precautionary principle(s) have been summarized in three categories: those saying that 'uncertainty does not justify inaction', those saying that 'uncertainty justifies action' and those calling for 'shifting the burden of proof' (Wiener 2007). For many critics the differences in the various definitions are too great and make the principle arbitrary and capricious. Proponents argue that the principle is not only simple and clear enough, but already established as customary law (McIntyre and Mosedale 1997; Dupuy 2007).

As with the principle of sustainability, various – although not that many – definitions of the precautionary principle have emerged. International declarations and conventions led to some refinements but also to different understandings. The most important differences are between weak and strong definitions. The latter demand precautionary action when there is a serious threat. The weak versions often use the terms 'precautionary measures' or 'precautionary approach' as substitutes for 'precautionary principle', signalling that these measures are preliminary (see below). Strong versions, included in early versions such as the soft law adopted by the North Sea Conferences, have mainly been advocated by NGOs and some academics.

The Rio Declaration (1992) included the 'precautionary approach' as Principle 15 in a weak form by linking its 'wide application' to action capabilities of states and cost-effective measures. Similarly the Framework Convention on Climate Change (1992) called for precautionary measures which 'should be cost-effective so as to ensure global benefits at the lowest possible cost'. The Kyoto Protocol (adopted in 1997, in force since 2005) calls in Article 3.3 for precautionary measures and adds to the Framework Convention that 'different socio-economic contexts' should be taken into account. The Cartagena Protocol on Biosafety (adopted in 2000, in force since 2003) and the Stockholm Convention on Persistent Organic Pollutants (2001) both refer to Article 15 of the Rio Declaration within their Article 1 'Objective'.

Another famous definition comes from the so-called Wingspread Statement on the Precautionary Principle drafted and finalized by 32 authors (mostly academics) in 1998:

> When an activity raises threats of harm to human health or the environment, precautionary measures should be taken even if some cause and effect relationships are not fully established scientifically. In this context the proponent of an activity, rather than the public, should bear the burden of proof.[1]

Additionally the Statement demanded 'open, informed and democratic' risk governance and 'an examination of the full range of alternatives, including no action'. This definition was subject to much criticism, as it missed the word 'serious' before 'threats of harm' and because it called for democratic participation and a shift of the 'burden of proof', which is often interpreted as 'invitation for overregulation' (Wiener 2007: 606). The latter demand has its origin in the Swedish chemicals policy adopted in the early 1970s and has quite a tradition for products such as drugs, pesticides or food additives with specific hazardous properties. It especially found support among a larger number of academics and many consumer and environmental protection NGOs. But it also became a core element in the EU's biotechnology, chemicals and food policies.

The EU provided no definition of the precautionary principle within the Maastricht Treaty or in subsequent treaty reforms. As the principle was listed in the title on the environment, it was partly interpreted as applying only to that area. However, as since 1997 it has been a Treaty requirement that 'environmental protection requirements must be integrated into the definition and implementation of the Community policies' (ex-Article 6 TEU, Article 11 Lisbon Treaty) it became relevant and a key tenet for all areas of risk regulation. The EU Commission reacted to criticism against the 'too ambitious' and vague concept, its potential conflict with WTO rules and the ongoing debates about the scope of the principle with a communication. According to this document the precautionary principle applies 'where preliminary objective scientific evaluation indicates that there are reasonable grounds for concern' (European Commission 2000).

Although the principle's definitions in international law and within the EU are moderate, they attracted serious concerns. Majone (2002: 90f.) and many others argued that the EU Commission's position would not be accepted by other WTO member states and that the EU would 'risk international isolation'.

## 20.4 'UTOPIA AND JUNK SCIENCE' VERSUS 'BETTER SAFE THAN SORRY': PRECAUTION IN PRACTICE

Majone (2002) listed five major shortcomings of the precautionary principle as formulated by the European Union. Besides lacking a sound legal foundation, it has potential to 'distort regulatory priorities' and 'to justify protectionist measures'. It would endanger international regulatory cooperation 'and it may have undesirable distributive consequences'. Altogether, he concluded, 'the precautionary approach is deeply ambiguous, and . . . this ambiguity is abetted by a lack of clear definitions and sound logical foundations' (Majone 2002: 90; see also Majone, Chapter 21). The most common critique is that the principle is anti-scientific and adds little or nothing to standard risk assessment and management. It would be about values and emotions but not science. The 'most reliable science' would be replaced by 'the most radical science' (Morris 2000: 19). Claims made under the precautionary principle would be unfalsifiable and open the way for speculation and 'junk science'. If implemented, it would strangle technological and economic progress and only create a litigious society. In the worst case it would direct to overregulation of insignificant or even non-existent risks. The principle would neglect risk–risk trade-offs, and its application would stop progress and innovation. In its strong version it would not lead 'in bad directions' but 'in no direction at all' (Sunstein 2003). Slogans such as 'better safe than sorry', used by NGOs, have been criticized for ignorance and as unacceptable demands to stop everything that could cause harm. A paranoid 'no risk principle', critics continue, such as the NGOs' demand for 'a toxic-free environment', is impossible because a world without risks is impossible (and in case of the example an environment without toxics never existed). Similar allegations have been inherent in risk regulation conflicts for a long time, but they became stronger related to debates about sound, biased, junk, corrupt, business-dependent and critical science.

Advocates of precaution argue that the principle's application is feasible and necessary in science-based decisions about risk because humans' ability to predict, calculate and control the impacts of certain activities is limited. Nobody actually believes in a society without any risk. The NGO slogan directly addressed the traditional 'rational' assumptions of 'What you do not know is safe' resulting in ignorance or denial of many risks and 'late lessons from early warnings'. Advocates stress the fact that in cases of uncertainty 'a number of perspectives may constitute equally valid interpretations of the available evidence' and this creates a situation of 'pluralistic realism' (Stirling 2003: 41). Reversing the anti-science argument to the critics is also part of the confrontation. On the basis of experiences in chemicals regulation Quijano (2003: 22), for example, demands 'true science', which he opposes to the 'pseudo-science of economic interests'. Unsurprisingly a closer look at risk regulatory issues reveals that advocates of a (strong) precautionary principle do not just call for a stop to an activity, but are pushers for alternative activities and underlying innovations (e.g. green chemicals versus many current chemical products; organic farming versus agricultural biotech products; renewable energy sources versus nuclear power). In short, the real conflicts about precautionary public policy are about antagonistic goals.

Several precautionary measures have been criticized as protectionist, establishing unjustifiable barriers to trade (e.g. GMO regulations, including the EU's de facto moratorium on approving new GM products between 1998 and 2004 and the creation of GM-free zones, Mexico's moratorium on GM products 1998–2004, food safety regulations, chemical regulations). After the EU introduced its moratorium the US claimed that this also had negative effects on African countries. There was a general accusation that precautionary regulation would disadvantage developing countries (one example was DDT use in controlling malaria in Africa, which was affected by EU food safety standards). However, the main conflicts arose between the US and the EU, since the Europeans emerged as the main advocate of the contested precautionary principle. Between the 1960s and 1980s the US had the leadership and influenced many early precautionary measures in the European Community. But since the 1990s the US approach has shifted, including the decisions by the Bush administration not to ratify the Cartagena and Kyoto protocols and its generally strong opposition to the principle. More and more a 'transatlantic divide' was observed. Especially with regard to climate change, biodiversity, green biotechnology and chemicals, it has been broadly debated whether there has been a completely different understanding of regulating risks in the EU as compared to the rest of the world in recent years (Jasanoff 2003; Jordan and O'Riordan 2004; Vig and Faure 2004; Ashford 2007). In opposition to the EU the US government argues 'that precaution is a sensible idea, but there are multiple approaches to implementing precaution in risk management. There is no such thing as a universal "precautionary principle" in regulatory policy' (Graham 2004: 1). However, the differences are not that great overall. Harremoës et al. (2002) point at the US's promotion of similar ideas under the label 'precautionary prevention'. As Wiener (2004, 2007) shows, the level of precaution varies across different areas, with sometimes the US (not only in security policy or with regard to pre-emptive war) and sometimes the EU being more precautionary.

Within the WTO framework, Article XX of the General Agreement on Tariffs and Trade (GATT) allows governments to act on trade in order to protect human, animal or plant life or health, provided they do not discriminate or use this as disguised protectionism. In addition there are two specific WTO agreements dealing with food safety and animal and plant health and safety and with product standards. The WTO Sanitary and Phytosanitary (SPS) Agreement (Article 3.3) allows member states to introduce stricter standards to those in international standards, guidelines or recommendations 'if there is a scientific justification' and if there is no inconsistency with any other provision of the Agreement. Article 5.7 specifies:

> In cases where relevant scientific evidence is insufficient, a Member may provisionally adopt sanitary or phytosanitary measures on the basis of available pertinent information, including that from the relevant international organizations as well as from sanitary or phytosanitary measures applied by other Members. In such circumstances, Members shall seek to obtain

the additional information necessary for a more objective assessment of risk and review the sanitary or phytosanitary measure accordingly within a reasonable period of time.

Additionally the WTO Technical Barriers to Trade (TBT) Agreement tries to ensure that regulations, standards, testing and certification procedures do not create 'unnecessary obstacles'.

In the rulings of the WTO Panel and Appellate Body it was confirmed that member states can adopt precautionary measures if they are justified by a prior risk assessment and sufficient scientific evidence. Measures must be provisional in nature and there must be evidence that further research is deployed with the goal of reducing uncertainty to an acceptable level 'within a reasonable period of time'. WTO disputes made clear that decisions about justifiable, reasonable precautionary measures can only be taken on a case-by-case judgement. Now after several trade conflicts at the WTO level and controversies between WTO member states[2] and based on decisions by WTO dispute settlement bodies and EU court rulings it also became clear that the moderate version of the precautionary principle is possible and sound precautionary measures on case-specific factors can be taken if a scientific risk assessment has been carried out before and clear evidence of harm is given (Stokes 2008).

## 20.5 THE OVERALL ROLE AND FUTURE OF PRECAUTION IN RISK REGULATION

The international debate led to an ongoing transatlantic dialogue on risk regulation practices, which resulted in the conclusion that most countries in the world, including the EU, are moving towards benefit–cost approaches in risk regulation which reduce the differences between countries using standard practices and countries calling for a precautionary approach/principle. More recent developments such as the international and European debates about the EU's chemicals policy change or the establishment of a Chemicals Agency and food safety agencies were less concerned about the principle than about real consequences on industry's competitiveness and regulatory competition (Pesendorfer 2006, 2007). Concerning biotechnology, precautionary measures (in line with the Cartagena Protocol) are now broadly accepted, as their preliminary application includes continued further research (e.g. field trials), which is also supportive and welcome for market creation. Many proponents of nanotechnology already drew a lesson from biotechnology and adopted a more proactive approach towards challenges deriving from precaution to avoid any delays in technology development. In short, precaution in its moderate version became one of the core principles in today's risk regulation. A strict and rigid implementation of the precautionary principle remains a concern for many critics and highly problematic for political, legal, economic, scientific and technical reasons. Science, uncertainty, 'true' facts and bias are crucial factors in every debate about risk in complex social formations based on antagonistic goals. Yet some still hope that initiatives to eliminate the use of the term 'precautionary principle' will succeed. The OECD (2002) started advocating a 'precautionary approach' or just 'precaution' without any additional terms as a part of standard risk analysis and risk assessment and explicitly limited to 'preliminary measures'. The UK House of Commons

Science and Technology Committee (2006) recommended that 'the use of the term "precautionary principle" should cease in view of the lack of clarity surrounding its meaning'. The Codex Alimentarius Commission discussed the incorporation of the principle into its guidelines for several years, but in 2007 the Codex Commission decided against such a change 'when the "Working Principles for Risk Analysis for Food Safety for Application by Governments" was finally adopted'.[3] On the other side, critics such as Sunstein (2007) concluded that there remain significant areas where governments need to take radical measures for which a 'catastrophic harm precautionary principle' might be useful.

However, with regard to risks, most countries in the world have been moving towards a strict separation of risk assessment and risk management and a systematic use of benefit–cost analysis, which makes the real change. In some areas such as food safety or chemicals policy new independent agencies have been founded to depoliticize risk assessment. In some cases the new governance paradigm led to more transparent risk governance processes, but in many other cases governments used participation just for educating 'the public in scientific rationalities' or 'as a simple exercise in democratic legitimation and trust enhancement' (Everson and Vos 2009: 15) or to avoid implementation deficits and to increase competitiveness by creating a business-friendly framework of 'better regulation' (Pesendorfer, 2006). In short, risk regulation will remain political and controversial despite the depoliticization intended by the changes in risk governance.

## NOTES

1. http://www.sehn.org/wing.html (accessed May 2010).
2. http://www.wto.org/english/news_e/news00_e/sps_e.htm (accessed May 2010).
3. http://www.nutraingredients.com/Regulation/Precautionary-principle-left-out-by-Codex (accessed May 2010).

## REFERENCES

Ashford, Nicholas A. (2007), 'The legacy of the precautionary principle in US law: the rise of cost–benefit analysis and risk assessment as undermining factors in health, safety and environmental protection', in Nicolas de Sadeleer (ed.), *Implementing the Precautionary Principle: Approaches from the Nordic countries, EU and USA*, London: Earthscan, pp. 352–78.
Beck, Ulrich (1986), *Risikogesellschaft auf dem Weg in eine andere Moderne,* Frankfurt am Main: Suhrkamp.
Beck, Ulrich (1999), *World Risk Society,* Cambridge: Polity Press.
Bernstein, Peter L. (1996), *Against the Gods: The Remarkable Story of Risk,* New York: Wiley.
Boehmer-Christiansen, Sonja (1994), 'The precautionary principle in Germany – enabling government', in Timothy O'Riordan and James Cameron (eds), *Interpreting the Precautionary Principle*, London: Earthscan, pp. 31–60.
Breyer, Stephen (1993), *Breaking the Vicious Circle: Toward Effective Risk Regulation,* Cambridge, MA: Harvard University Press.
de Sadeleer, Nicolas (ed.) (2007), *Implementing the Precautionary Principle: Approaches from the Nordic Region and the EU*, London: Earthscan.
Dupuy, J. and A. Grinbaum (2004), 'Living with uncertainty: toward the ongoing normative assessment of nanotechnology', *Techné,* **8** (2), 4–25.
Dupuy, Pierre-Marie (2007), 'Formation of customary international law and general principles', in Daniel Bodansky, Jutta Brunnée and Ellen Hey (eds), *The Oxford Handbook of International Environmental Law,* Oxford: Oxford University Press, pp. 449–66.

European Commission (2000), *Communication on the Precautionary Principle*, 02.02.2000, COM(2000) 1, Brussels: Commission of the European Communities.

Everson, Michelle and Ellen Vos (2009), 'The scientification of politics and the politicisation of science', in Michelle Everson and Ellen Vos (eds), *Uncertain Risks Regulated*, Abingdon: Routledge-Cavendish, pp. 1–17.

Fisher, Elizabeth, Judith S. Jones and René von Schomberg (eds) (2006), *Implementing the Precautionary Principle: Perspectives and Prospects*, Cheltenham, UK and Northampton, MA, USA: Edward Elgar Publishing.

Godard, Olivier (2006), 'The precautionary principle and catastrophism on tenterhooks: lessons from a constitutional reform in France', in Elizabeth Fisher, Judith S. Jones and René von Schomberg (eds), *Implementing the Precautionary Principle: Perspectives and Prospects*, Cheltenham, UK and Northampton, MA, USA: Edward Elgar Publishing, pp. 63–87.

Graham, John D. (2004), 'The perils of the precautionary principle: lessons from the American and European experience', Heritage Lectures No. 818, Heritage Foundation.

Harremoës, Poul, David Gee, Malcolm MacGarvin, Andy Stirling, Jane Keys, Brian Wynne and Sofia Guedes Vaz (eds) (2002), *The Precautionary Principle in the Twentieth Century: Late Lessons from Early Warnings*, London: Earthscan.

House of Commons Science and Technology Committee (2006), *Scientific Advice, Risk and Evidence Based Policy Making: Seventh Report of Session 2005–06*, London: Stationery Office.

Jaeger, Carlo C., Ortwin Renn, Eugene A. Rosa and Thomas Webler (eds) (2001), *Risk, Uncertainty, and Rational Action*, London: Earthscan.

Jasanoff, Sheila (2003), 'A living legacy: the precautionary ideal in American law', in Joel A. Tickner (ed.), *Precaution, Environmental Science and Preventive Public Policy*, Washington, DC: Island Press, pp. 227–40.

Jordan, Andrew and Timothy O'Riordan (2004), 'The precautionary principle: a legal and policy history', in Marco Martuzzi and Joel A. Tickner (eds), *The Precautionary Principle: Protecting Public Health, the Environment and the Future of Our Children*, Copenhagen: World Health Organization Europe, pp. 31–48.

Löfstedt, R.E. (2004), 'The swing of the regulatory pendulum in Europe: from precautionary principle to (regulatory) impact analysis', *Journal of Risk and Uncertainty*, **28** (3), 237–60.

Löfstedt, Ragnar E. (2009), *Risk Management in Post-Trust Societies*, London: Earthscan.

Majone, Giandomenico (2002), 'What price safety? The precautionary principle and its policy implications', *Journal of Common Market Studies*, **40** (1), 89–109.

Marchant, Gary and Kenneth Mossman (2004), *Arbitrary and Capricious: The Precautionary Principle in the European Union Courts*, Washington, DC: AEI Press.

McIntyre, Owen and Thomas Mosedale (1997), 'The precautionary principle as a norm of customary international law', *Journal of Environmental Law*, **9** (2), 221–41.

Morris, Julian (2000), 'Defining the precautionary principle', in Julian Morris (ed.), *Rethinking Risk and the Precautionary Principle*, Oxford: Butterworth-Heinemann, pp. 1–21.

OECD (2002), *Uncertainty and Precaution: Implications for Trade and Environment*, Paris: OECD.

Pesendorfer, Dieter (2006), 'EU environmental policy under pressure: chemicals policy change between antagonistic goals?', *Environmental Politics*, **15** (1), 95–114.

Pesendorfer, Dieter (2007), 'Regulatory competition and toxic substances: is EU risk regulation diverging from the rest of the world?', in Larisa Deriglazova and Anselm Skuhra (eds), *EU and Russia: Face to Face*, Tomsk: Tomsk State University Publishing House, pp. 288–301.

Pesendorfer, Dieter (2009), 'Converging ideas about risk regulation? The precautionary principle in national legal systems', in 'Environmental policy convergence in Europe: the impact of international institutions and trade on policy convergence', ENVIPOLCON Qualitative Study Report, Konstanz.

Quijano, Romeo (2003), 'Elements of the precautionary principle', in Joel A. Tickner (ed.), *Precaution, Environmental Science and Preventive Public Policy*, Washington, DC: Island Press, pp. 21–7.

Rifkin, Jeremy (2004), 'A precautionary tale', *Guardian*, 12 May.

Sands, Philippe (1995), *Principles of International Environmental Law*, Manchester: Manchester University Press.

Stirling, Andy (2003), 'Risk, uncertainty and precaution', in Frans Berkhout, Melissa Leach and Ian Scoones (eds), *Negotiating Environmental Change: New Perspectives from Social Science*, Cheltenham, UK and Northampton, MA, USA: Edward Elgar Publishing, pp. 33–76.

Stokes, E. (2008), 'The EC courts' contribution to refining the parameters of precaution', *Journal of Risk Research*, **11** (4), 491–507.

Sunstein, Cass R. (2003), 'Beyond the precautionary principle', *University of Pennsylvania Law Review*, **151** (3), 1003–58.

Sunstein, Cass R. (2005), *Laws of Fear: Beyond the Precautionary Principle*, Cambridge: Cambridge University Press.

Sunstein, Cass R. (2007), *Worst-Case Scenarios*, Cambridge, MA and London: Harvard University Press.

Tickner, Joel A. (ed.) (2003), *Precaution, Environmental Science, and Preventive Public Policy*, Washington, DC and London: Island Press.

Vig, Norman J. and Michael G. Faure (eds) (2004), *Green Giants? Environmental Policies of the United States and the European Union*, Cambridge, MA: MIT Press.

Wiener, Jonathan B. (2004), 'Convergence, divergence, and complexity in US and European risk regulation', in Norman J. Vig and Michael G. Faure (eds), *Green Giants? Environmental Policies of the United States and the European Union*, Cambridge, MA: MIT Press, pp. 73–109.

Wiener, Jonathan B. (2007), 'Precaution', in Daniel Bodansky, Jutta Brunnée and Ellen Hey (eds), *The Oxford Handbook of International Environmental Law*, Oxford: Oxford University Press, pp. 597–612.

# 21 Strategic issues in risk regulation
## Giandomenico Majone

## 21.1 INTRODUCTION: THE INFEASIBILITY OF A NO-RISK APPROACH

The issue of risk looms so large in contemporary public discourse and in popular perception that some authors speak of a "risk society," where problems of risk distribution replace the problems of wealth distribution that characterized industrial society. It is any rate certain that the political significance of risk regulation will keep growing, in parallel with advances in technology, and with the expansion of international trade – as shown in the following pages. It is often alleged that irrationality and bias in risk perception prevent a rational approach to the setting of regulatory priorities. In particular, the tendency to overestimate low-probability events can have substantial impact on government policy. Hence how the government should respond to public (mis)perceptions is a central question for the politics of risk regulation. Some democratic theorists would go as far as suggesting that public policy should always reflect the preferences of the voters. In the case of risk regulation, however, such a position is difficult to defend: if the general public *underestimates* a certain risk, one presumably would not expect the government to remain idle and let citizens incur risk unknowingly (Viscusi et al. 1996: 656–60).

A more reasonable approach to the question of regulatory priorities recognizes that legislators, judges, regulators, and public opinion all have important, but distinct, roles in the process of risk regulation. The early history of risk regulation provides an instructive example of how public opinion can actually be ahead of regulators and legislators in recognizing the inevitability of a tradeoff between risk reduction and the cost of control. In 1977 the U.S. Food and Drug Administration (FDA) banned the use of saccharin after a Canadian study showed a significant increase in bladder tumors among male rats exposed to high levels of saccharin consumption. According to the FDA, the ban was made necessary by the wording of the Delaney anti-cancer clause of the 1958 Food Additives Amendment (see section 21.2). However, the proposed ban was very controversial because no acceptable saccharin substitute existed at that time. The weight of medical testimony before congressional subcommittees was that saccharin was probably a weak carcinogen, but that a ban on saccharin could also pose risks, especially if saccharin users responded by substantially increasing their consumption of sugar. Despite congressional awareness of these facts, congressional hearings failed to produce any definite conclusion. The only outcome was continuing postponement of the ban, coupled with labeling requirements. The FDA did try, however, to modify in practice a conceptually flawed, but legally binding, no-risk decision rule.

Three important lessons can be drawn from this episode. First, it is clear that risk regulators operate on the basis of great, and in many cases irreducible, uncertainty. Such uncertainty is too important to be treated in a purely intuitive and qualitative way;

rather, it should be expressed in terms of numerical probabilities. These probability estimates are necessarily subjective but they are explicit, hence open to scrutiny by third parties, and can be revised in a logically consistent way when new information becomes available (Majone 2005: 138–42). A second lesson is that a zero-risk approach, such as is implied by the Delaney clause, is practically and conceptually untenable. Since the FDA's saccharin ban, the capacity to detect chemicals in foods in quantities as small as parts per trillion has been perfected. This means that

> the FDA was hostage to progress in analytical chemistry: As scientists improved their ability to detect cancer-causing chemicals, the FDA would be obliged to ban those chemicals (and the foods that contained them). . . . Cancer was a risk, the FDA was told, that it was impermissible to run, whatever the costs. (Wilson 1989: 340)

Finally, what is particularly remarkable in the saccharin ban case is the widespread opposition to a regulatory decision which took into account the remote risk posed by a product, but not its actual benefits. As mentioned earlier, people often overestimate events associated with lower-probability events, while ignoring potential benefits. But in this case we have the reverse situation: a public acceptance of some risk for the sake of well-understood benefits. Moreover, the demonstration that people are prepared to trade off risks and health benefits, as long as both sides of the equation are well understood, triggered an institutional learning process that has significantly improved the foundations of risk regulation.

## 21.2   THE CONCEPTUAL DEVELOPMENT OF RISK REGULATION

It is convenient to trace this learning process of American courts, legislators, and policy-makers through a sequence of four regulatory principles: prohibitions; lowest feasible risk; elimination of significant risk; balancing costs and benefits of risk reduction. This survey reveals a clear trend in the direction of broader inclusion of relevant factors, and of greater consistency in putting together the various elements of the regulatory problem.

### 21.2.1   Prohibitions

Prohibitions represent one of the earliest and least sophisticated approaches to risk regulation. In some cases an outright ban may be the most appropriate regulatory response, but the appropriateness of such a radical measure has to be proved rather than assumed. The best illustration of the limits of this approach is provided by the already mentioned Delaney clause, which appears in the Food Additives Amendment added to the Federal Food, Drug, and Cosmetic Act in 1958. The Amendment directs the FDA to refuse approval of any food additive not shown to be safe. To this general instruction the Delaney clause adds the proviso:

> No additive shall be deemed to be safe if it is found to induce cancer when ingested by man or animal, or if it is found, after tests which are appropriate for the evaluation of the safety of food additives, to induce cancer in man or animals. (cited in Mashaw et al. 1998: 128)

According to FDA officials, this proviso authorizes the agency to exercise scientific judgment in determining whether a test is an appropriate one, and whether the results demonstrate induction of cancer. Once the agency has made its determinations concerning these two matters, however, no further inquiry is allowed. For example, the agency may not establish a maximum level of safe use, or authorize further use of an additive based on a judgment that the benefits of continued use outweigh the risks involved. At the time of the announcement (March 9, 1977) no other non-nutritive sweetener was approved for use in the United States. Hence there was a widespread criticism of the ban: congressmen reportedly received more mail on saccharin than on any other issue since the Vietnam war. Representatives of health organizations testified at congressional hearings that saccharin provided enormous health benefits to persons, such as diabetics, who must restrict the intake of sugar. Responding to these concerns, Congress commissioned two studies by the National Academy of Sciences, to assess the scientific evidence concerning saccharin's safety, and to evaluate the law's current food safety standards and suggest alternative approaches. The Academy's studies did not lead to any radical amendment of the legislation, but the FDA found other means of avoiding a ban if a food additive presented only slight risks or offered substantial benefits. Thus the agency has sometimes concluded that a substance is not a "food additive," and hence subject to the Delaney clause, even though it occurs in food, arguably through human agency (Mashaw et al., 1998: 129–34). Proceeding in this fashion, by the mid-1980s the agency had effectively narrowed the application of the clause to direct food additives.

In retrospect, we can see that the drafters of the clause assumed that only a few additives caused cancer, but that they were extremely dangerous. By the 1980s it was clear that many substances are carcinogenic, but many of them create exceptionally minor risks. The new information severely undermined the original assumption, suggesting that a prohibition may well cause more deaths than it prevents. This is because vastly improved detection techniques prevent basically safe, but weakly carcinogenic, substances from coming on the market, whereas cruder and older technology used to test previously authorized substances allowed them to be approved. The result is less rather than more safety.

### 21.2.2 Least Feasible Risk

According to this principle, human exposure to health risks should be reduced to the lowest possible level. This is a sort of second-best rule. The best regulatory policy would be one that ensures a risk-free working and living environment, but because of technical and economic constraints a risk-free environment is unattainable: hence the need of a second-best rule. Thus, section 6(b)(5) of the 1970 Occupational Safety and Health Act directs the U.S. Occupational Safety and Health Administration (OSHA), in regulating worker exposure to toxic substances, to set standards that "most adequately assure, *to the extent feasible* . . . that no employee will suffer material impairment of health or functional capacity even if such employee has regular exposure to the hazard . . . for the period of his working life" (cited in Mendeloff 1988: 83–4, emphasis added).

Trade union representatives claimed that this instruction obliged OSHA to mandate the use of whatever available technology an industry could afford without bankrupting itself. A body of analysis and case law has emerged to clarify the meaning of "feasibility" in this context. According to some court decisions, a standard may be considered technologically feasible even if no existing devices would allow industry to comply with the standard, as long as there is evidence that companies "acting vigorously and in good faith" can develop the technology. This "technology forcing" approach implies that regulatory agencies are not limited to setting standards based on existing devices, but may require improvements in existing technology, or even the development of new technology. This may be quite expensive, so the issue of technical feasibility is inseparable from the issue of economic feasibility, and economic feasibility has been interpreted quite broadly: a standard is to be considered infeasible only if it would cripple or bankrupt an entire industry, rather than some technologically backward firms.

The least-feasible-risk approach is far from any sort of balancing of marginal costs and benefits. In fact, marginal considerations are rejected on the ground that the two sides of the equation are incommensurable. But, even if one assumes that health benefits ought to be considered above all other considerations, serious conceptual problems remain. The approach fails to consider possible alternatives to standards, such as information disclosure or greater reliance on liability rules. It also omits any consideration of probabilities of possible events, so that standards are set without any knowledge of the expected number of deaths or accidents prevented. On the other hand, the reference to industry viability means that very dangerous occupations in marginally profitable industries may be unregulated, while other jobs may be made so safe at such high cost that employment levels and wages shrink – an instance of over-regulation leading to under-regulation (Mendeloff 1988).

### 21.2.3    The Significant-Risk Doctrine

Federal courts have generally upheld OSHA's standards. The striking exception was the benzene standard, which reduced the occupational exposure to this carcinogen from 10 parts per million (ppm) to 1 ppm. In *American Petroleum Institute v. OSHA* (1978), the Fifth Circuit Court of Appeals held the regulation invalid on the ground that the agency had not shown that the new exposure limit was reasonably necessary and appropriate to provide safe or healthful employment, as required by the statute. Specifically, the court argued that OSHA had failed to provide substantial evidence that the benefits to be achieved by the stricter standard bore a reasonable relationship to the costs it imposed. The court added:

> This does not mean that OSHA must wait until deaths occur as a result of exposure levels below 10 ppm before it may validly promulgate a standard reducing the permissible exposure limit. Nevertheless, OSHA must have some factual basis for an estimate of expected benefits before it can determine that a one-half billion dollar standard is reasonably necessary. (cited in Mendeloff 1988: 116–17)

What the court required was some sort of quantification of risk as a necessary step to calculate the expected number of lives saved by the regulation and to carry out a benefit–cost test of the new standard. Unlike other agencies such as the Environmental Protection Agency (EPA) and the Food and Drug Administration (FDA), OSHA had always maintained that quantitative risk analysis is meaningless. As Mendeloff notes, OSHA's reluctance to follow the example of the EPA and the FDA reflected trade union pressures, combined with staff preferences for protection, to override any interest in the use of more analytic approaches. It was feared that, if the agency performed quantitative risk assessments, these might be used as a weapon by those who opposed strict standards. On the other hand, an agency like the EPA, with a much broader mandate, is aware that not every risk can be reduced to the lowest feasible level.

The court's decision stunned OSHA's leaders, who viewed it as a challenge to their regulatory philosophy and to their idea of the agency's mission. They decided to appeal the decision. In *Industrial Union Department (AFL-CIO) v. American Petroleum Institute* (1980), a badly split Supreme Court upheld the Fifth Circuit's decision, but expressed no opinion about the requirement of a cost–benefit assessment. Justice Powell did however note that

> a standard-setting process that ignored economic considerations would result in a serious misallocation of resources and a lower effective level of safety than could be achieved under standards set with reference to the comparative benefits available at a lower cost. (cited in Mashaw et al. 1998: 815)

Expressing the view of a four-judge plurality, Justice Stevens explicitly rejected the lowest-feasible-risk approach:

> We think it is clear that the statute was not designed to require employers to provide absolute risk-free workplaces whenever it is technologically feasible to do so, so long as the cost is not great enough to destroy an entire industry. Rather, both the language and structure of the Act, as well as its legislative history, indicate that it was intended to require the elimination, as far as feasible, of *significant* risks of harm. (cited in Graham et al. 1988: 100, emphasis added)

Justice Stevens insisted that "safe" is not the same as risk-free, pointing to a variety of risks in daily life that people find acceptable. Hence, before any decision is taken, the risk from a toxic substance must be quantified sufficiently to enable the agency to characterize it as significant "in an understandable way." OSHA was not required to support its finding that a significant risk existed with anything approaching scientific certainty. So long as the determination is supported by a body of reputable scientific thought, the agency was free to use conservative assumptions in interpreting the data. The question was not whether the standard of 1 ppm was "correct," but whether sufficient justification for this determination had been provided. OSHA's standard-setting process was flawed because from the government's generic carcinogen policy the agency had simply concluded that, in the absence of definitive proof of a safe level, it must be assumed that *any* level above zero presented *some* increased risk of cancer. But, as the justices pointed out:

> In view of the fact that there are literally thousands of substances used in the workplace that have been identified as carcinogens or suspect carcinogens, the Government's theory would give OSHA power to impose enormous costs that might produce little, if any, discernible benefit. (cited in Mashaw et al. 1998: 813)

Thus the significant-risk doctrine raised the crucial issue of regulatory priorities. Most risks are regulated in response to petitions or pressures from unions, public-health groups, environmentalists, and other political activists, with little analysis by the agency of other possible regulatory targets. Given that resources are always limited, the opportunity cost of a regulation is the number of lives that could be saved by using the same resources to control other, perhaps more significant, risks. By requiring OSHA to show significant risk as a prelude to standard setting, the justices were insisting on some analysis in priority setting: regulatory priorities should be directed toward the most important risks – which are not necessarily those that are politically most salient. *Industrial Union Department (AFL-CIO) v. American Petroleum Institute* is a landmark case also from the point of view of the methodology of risk analysis. The Supreme Court not only confirmed the legitimacy of quantitative risk assessment; it effectively made reliance on the methodology obligatory for all American agencies engaged in risk regulation. In most subsequent disputes over regulatory decisions to protect human health, the question has not been whether a risk assessment was required but whether the assessment offered by the agency was plausible. This historical background may explain American advocacy of science-based risk assessment at the international level (Majone 2006), as well as that country's opposition to the precautionary principle as interpreted by the European Commission (see section 21.3).

### 21.2.4   Balancing Costs and Benefits

Until the 1970s judicial review was the only effective control on the quality of the decision-making process of American regulatory agencies. Congress can pass legislation requiring that an agency take a particular type of action, but congressional oversight is output- rather than process-oriented, and there is no need for congressional approval for a regulatory agency to take action, provided that it can survive judicial review. But judicial oversight, too, suffers from serious shortcomings. First, it is only exercised *ex post*–though it is true that a judicial doctrine like the significant-risk doctrine will influence a stream of future agency decisions. Also, the principle of separation of powers prevents any sustained interaction between courts and agencies before proceedings are formally initiated. Again, there is a serious mismatch between the leisurely time of judicial decision-making and the hectic pace of agency rule-making, while heavy reliance on judicial review may create an adversarial atmosphere which does not always facilitate the achievement of regulatory objectives.

From the point of view of policy learning, the most serious limitation of judicial review, however, is the unpredictability of court decisions. In the benzene case, for example, the Supreme Court criticized the logic of the least-feasible-risk decision rule, and effectively mandated the use of quantitative risk assessment, while taking no position on the issue of whether an agency should undertake a formal cost–benefit analysis to justify its decisions. But only a year later the court, in the cotton-dust case (*American Textile Mfrs. v. Donovan,* 1981), held explicitly that OSHA standards need not show a positive cost–benefit ratio; they must only be shown to be technologically achievable and "affordable." The decision on the cotton-dust standard seemed to interrupt an ongoing learning process, and for this reason it has been severely criticized by students of the regulatory process. With the great expansion of environmental, health, and risk regulation in the 1970s the need to calculate more precisely the costs of the proliferating regulations, and the corresponding benefits, became increasingly evident. According to many advocates of regulatory reform, only the executive could provide a continuous and systematic oversight of the regulatory process. Important steps to improve the quality of federal regulation were taken under President Carter, when the notion of a "regulatory budget" was first introduced. The oversight mechanism was perfected in the late 1980s, during the second term of the Reagan administration. The Office of Management and Budget (OMB), in the president's Executive Office, was given responsibility for setting the budgets of all regulatory agencies, and for monitoring the rule-making process. Instead of simply imposing a cost-effectiveness requirement, Reagan moved to a fully fledged cost–benefit test with his Executive Order No. 12291 of 1981: regulatory action was not to be undertaken unless the potential benefits to society outweighed the potential costs; and, among alternative approaches to any given regulatory objective, the alternative involving the least net cost to society had to be chosen.

Executive Order No. 12498 of 1985 added to the oversight process – the review by OMB of the regulation proposed by an agency, and of the analysis supporting it – the development of a formal planning process whereby the agencies would have to clear a regulatory agenda (a "regulatory calendar") with OMB. Although the Budget Office has frequently been unable to enforce completely the cost–benefit test because of conflicts with the agency's legislative mandate, the quality of rule-making has improved significantly over the last two decades. The usefulness of the regulatory oversight process designed by the Reagan administration explains why subsequent administrations, Democrat as well as Republican, have continued to use it in a form that has not substantially changed from the original model. In the meantime, Congress was also undergoing a learning process, resulting in a more balanced appreciation of the many dimensions of risk regulation. The legislators came to accept the view that regulations should be based on an accurate assessment of the risks involved, rather than on worst-case scenarios, and that regulatory agencies should proceed with regulations only if the benefits exceeded the costs.

This survey of conceptual and institutional developments in the United States reveals a steady improvement in the understanding of the various dimensions of risk regulation. The progress from the early reliance on outright bans or simple "feasibility" tests to the application of key principles of risk and cost–benefit analysis, not only to agency rule-making but also to the enabling legislation, is an outstanding, and in many respects unique, example of policy learning. This learning process has been made possible by the interaction among different, partly cooperating, partly competing institutions. A more detailed study would also reveal the importance of a style of policy discourse that puts a high premium on reliable quantitative information and on analytic sophistication. Invaluable as the American experience has been for policymakers elsewhere, a discussion of the foundations of risk regulation would be incomplete without mentioning a quite different approach: the precautionary approach, which despite its conceptual flaws has many advocates, particularly in Europe.

## 21.3 THE PRECAUTIONARY PRINCIPLE: AN IDEA IN SEARCH OF A DEFINITION

In striking contrast to the learning process discussed above, the advocates of the precautionary principle (PP) still subscribe, more or less explicitly, to the old least-feasible-risk (or even no-risk) approach. It has been maintained that the PP should become a "full-fledged and general principle of international law" (Commission of the European Communities 2000: 13). In fact, the precautionary principle is an idea (perhaps a state of mind) rather than a clearly defined concept, or a guide to consistent policymaking; an authoritative and generally accepted definition is nowhere to be found. The principle is of German origin (*Vorsorgeprinzip*) and has been used in that country since the 1980s in order to justify a number of developments in environmental law. An eminent legal scholar has distinguished no fewer than 11 different meanings assigned to the PP within German policy discourse (Rehbinder 1991). In the 1997 treaty establishing the European Community (in place of the old European Economic Community), the principle is mentioned only in Article 174(2), which provides that Community environmental policy "shall be based on the precautionary principle and on the principles that preventive action should be taken, that environmental damage should as a priority be rectified at the source and that the polluter should pay." No definition of the precautionary principle is offered in this article or anywhere else in the treaty.

Unsurprisingly, interpretations of the meaning of the principle vary considerably. The consequences of this ambiguity are particularly serious when the precautionary approach is considered not as an exceptional measure but as a guide in preparing proposals for legislation, or even as a general principle of international law. The attempt to control poorly understood, low-level risks necessarily uses up resources that in many cases could be directed more effectively towards the reduction of well-known, large-scale risks. Even if a society is willing to pay a higher cost to protect an interest to which it attaches a priority, such as the environment or health, it is still the case that some environmental or risk regulations might be too expensive. Precautionary measures – taken on an ad hoc basis, often in response to political pressures – tend to distort regulatory priorities and thus to compromise the consistency of regulatory policies. Like the minimax rule in decision theory, the PP tends to focus the attention of regulators on some particular events and corresponding losses, rather than on the entire range of possibilities (Majone 2005: 138–42). As a consequence, regulators will base their determinations on worst cases, rather than on the weighted average of all potential losses and benefits. Another serious conceptual flaw is the artificial distinction between situations where the level of scientific information is sufficient to permit a formal risk assessment, and situations where scientific information is said to be insufficient, inconclusive, or uncertain. In reality, these are two points on a knowledge–ignorance continuum rather than two sharply distinct situations. The normal state of affairs is neither scientific certainty nor complete ignorance, and for this reason a sensible decision rule is one that uses all the available information, weighted by its reliability (coded in terms of subjective probabilities), instead of privileging some particular risk.

Some interpretations of the precautionary approach are unobjectionable, but also unhelpful. It is certainly correct to say that lack of full scientific certainty should not be used as an excuse for regulatory inertia (Principle 15 of the Declaration of the 1992 UN Conference on Environment and Development), but, since risk regulators can never rely on scientific certainty, the statement does not provide any useful guidance. Much more worrisome is the claim that the PP entails the principle of reversal of the burden of proof, according to which it is up to the developer of a new product or process to prove that the product or process poses no health or environmental risk. Thus, according to the European Commission's Communication on the PP:

Community rules . . . enshrine the principle of prior approval (positive list) before the placing on the market of certain products, such as drugs, pesticides or food additives. This is one way of applying the precautionary principle. . . . In this case the legislator, by way of precaution, has clearly reversed the burden of proof by requiring that the substances be deemed hazardous until proven otherwise. (Commission of the European Communities 2000: 21)

Since no absolute proof of safety is possible, acceptance of this interpretation of the PP is equivalent to advocating a zero-risk approach and effectively stopping technical innovation.

The consequences of relying on the PP in international economic relations can also be quite serious. A clear example is the controversy over the use of growth hormones in cattle raising, which for years has opposed the European Community (EC) to some of its major trading partners. In 1998 the Appellate Body of the World Trade Organization (WTO) concluded that, in prohibiting the importation of U.S. and Canadian beef, the EC had failed to base its measure on a risk assessment and decided against the EC. A key finding that persuaded the Appellate Body was that the carcinogenic risk from banned hormone-treated beef was no greater than the carcinogenic risk from antibiotic-treated pork, grown in Europe, which was not banned. This finding seemed to support the contention of the United States and Canada that the EC ban was in fact a disguised restriction on trade aimed at reducing beef surpluses in the EC member states. In sum, while the PP is too ill defined to serve as a general principle of international economic law, this ambiguity may be used for protectionist purposes.

## 21.4   THE INTERNATIONAL REGULATION OF RISK

Regulatory science and risk assessment are playing an increasingly significant role in the regulation of risks connected with international trade. Thus, the WTO Agreement on the Application of Sanitary and Phytosanitary Measures introduced a new science-based regime for disciplining health regulations which may affect international trade in agricultural products and foodstuffs. Annex A to the agreement defines a sanitary or phytosanitary (SPS) measure as any measure applied to protect animal or plant life or health from a variety of risks, including risks arising from additives, contaminants, toxins or disease-causing organisms in foods, beverages or feedstuffs. Article 2(2) of the agreement states, *inter alia*, that members of WTO shall ensure that any SPS measure "is based on scientific principles and is not maintained without sufficient scientific evidence, except as provided for in paragraph 7 of Article 5." Article 5 deals with risk assessment as a method for determining the appropriate level of health protection. Risk assessment – conducted according to the criteria and taking into account the factors mentioned in the same article – is the standard by which SPS measures are to be judged as necessary and justified. As interpreted by the WTO Appellate Body, Article 5 says that there must be a rational relationship between the SPS measure and the risk assessment. Where relevant scientific evidence is insufficient, a member state may provisionally adopt a measure "on the basis of available pertinent information. . . . Members shall seek to obtain the additional information necessary for a more objective assessment of risk and review the sanitary or phytosanitary measure accordingly within a reasonable period of time." Moreover, if a country wishes to adopt a higher level of protection than what is provided by international standards it must provide scientific justification.

The SPS Agreement is a good illustration of the importance of *procedural* harmonization in the international regulation of risk. The purpose of harmonization is to make the regulatory requirements of different jurisdictions more similar, if not identical, in some relevant aspects. Procedural harmonization refers to the harmonization of institutional structures, decision-making procedures, or methodologies. In addition to the WTO SPS Agreement, other examples of this type of harmonization are provided by some provisions of the North American Free Trade Agreement (NAFTA) requiring that certain procedures for enforcement of domestic laws, including appellate review, be harmonized. In case of the NAFTA environmental side agreement, for instance, it would have been inappropriate to impose on Mexico the same environmental standards used in Canada or in the United States, i.e., "output harmonization" (Leebron 1996). Instead, Article 3 of the agreement recognizes "the right of each Party to establish its own levels of domestic environmental protection," while Article 5 requires that "each Party shall effectively enforce its environmental laws and regulations through appropriate government action," and Article 6 requires that "interested persons" be able to request a party's regulatory authorities to investigate possible violations of *domestic* environmental laws and regulations.

## 21.5   THE POLITICS OF RISK REGULATION

As mentioned in section 21.1, people tend to overestimate risks associated with low-probability events, such as botulism and floods, and to underestimate the risks associated with higher-probability events, such as the risk of being killed in a car accident, or risks of cancer, heart disease, and stroke. Moreover, risk perceptions can vary greatly even among neighbouring countries: in the past, cyclamates were permitted and saccharin was banned in Canada, while cyclamates were banned and saccharin was effectively permitted in the U.S.A. – until acceptable substitutes became available. During the BSE ("mad cow" disease) crisis the European Union imposed a ban on exports of beef from the United Kingdom, while the product was permitted for sale within the U.K. (Hood et al. 2001: 3–5). Other examples are the EU's precautionary ban on imports of milk and beef containing growth hormones, products that are consumed daily by millions of Americans and Canadians, and the ban by France and other EU countries on the importation of chrysotile asbestos from Canada, which most experts believe to be virtually harmless if left in place. In cases directly affecting international trade, such differences are openly debated in the WTO and other international forums; and it often happens that within particular risk domains, such as chemicals or air and sea transport, there is a strong international exchange of knowledge and views. Paradoxically, there seems to be little cross-domain exchange within countries. The result

> is a policy and intellectual "archipelago" of risk domains isolated from one another, with very different policy stances across the various domains. For some hazards, governments adopt heavy-duty, anticipative, and intrusive regulatory arrangements. . . . For other hazards, such as smoking, much lighter and more reactive approaches are adopted. (Hood et al. 2001: 7)

The segmentation of risk domains observed by Christopher Hood and co-authors is explained, in part, by the fact that scientific uncertainties and worst-case scenarios produce public pressure, which in turn may focus the attention of both legislators and regulators on those substances or activities that catch the public eye. The question raised in section 21.1, therefore, is crucially important: How should policymakers respond to public (mis)perceptions of risk, and what weight, if any, should be attached to such social and political data relative to scientific, technical, and economic data? Justice Stephen Breyer of the U.S. Supreme Court has argued that not every risk-related matter "need become a public issue. A depoliticized regulatory process might produce better results, hence increased confidence, leading to more favorable public and Congressional reactions" (Breyer 1993: 55–6). Biased public perceptions create what Breyer calls a "vicious circle" – public perceptions influence legislators, legislators help to shape public perceptions, and both influence the response of regulatory agencies. He suggests breaking this vicious circle by institutional changes, such as creating a mission-oriented, independent agency commanding significant prestige and authority. This super-agency would have

> the mission of building an improved, coherent risk-regulating system adaptable for use in several different risk-related programs; the mission of helping to create priorities within as well as among programs; and the mission of comparing programs to determine how better to allocate resources to reduce risks. (Breyer 1993: 60)

The author envisages a centralized administrative group that "could usefully try to make explicit, and more uniform, controversial assumptions that agencies now, implicitly and often inconsistently, use in reaching their decisions." This elite group could also help develop models that aim to achieve higher-quality analysis and better results, and "might create a 'risk agenda' that helps to prioritize different programs, and different activities within programs, and that looks for tradeoffs among programs that will lead overall to improved health or safety" (Breyer 1993: 65–7). This group of experts would not directly regulate, but accomplish its ambitious tasks primarily by argument and persuasion. It is hard, however, to see how such a group, with no rule-making power and thus taking no responsibility for the final regulatory outcomes, could acquire sufficient legitimacy to change public perceptions and reform the decision-making processes of existing agencies.

In a democracy depoliticization can only be carried so far, especially in sensitive areas like health and environmental risk. We are faced with a real dilemma: on the one hand, risk regulation should be responsive to the preferences of the citizens, like any other public policy; on the other hand, the regulator's task is to issue regulations that are needed to control the "real" risk levels, as indicated by the best available scientific evidence, not to respond to biased perceptions. Even less is it the regulator's responsibility to balance conflicting societal values, such as safety and economic efficiency. Such balancing is the exclusive responsibility of democratically accountable policymakers. Hence, the dilemma can be resolved only by acknowledging that regulators, politicians, and public opinion have important, but distinct, roles to play in risk regulation. In particular, an elected policymaker should have the right to override an agency's decision if he or she is convinced that societal welfare is thereby promoted. But such interventions into the regulatory process ought to be completely transparent, and follow well-defined and publicly known procedures. Overriding agency decisions should be neither too easy (for in this case agency independence would be an empty concept) nor too difficult – so that basic principles of democratic accountability may not be sacrificed in favour of narrow regulatory principles.

A good example is provided by the procedures which the German government must follow when it wishes to overrule a decision of the antitrust regulator, the Federal Cartel Office. The procedures are such that they entail high political costs and make the interference plain for all to see. If the Cartel Office refuses to authorize a merger on the grounds that the merger is likely to lead to the creation or strengthening of a dominant position, the economics minister can evaluate advantages and disadvantages of the merger from the perspective of the entire economy. In addition, the minister must obtain the opinion of another independent body, the Monopoly Commission. Because of these strict requirements, few decisions of the Cartel Office have ever been overruled by the political authority. It is submitted that this example could provide a relevant model also for risk regulation. The procedural approach exemplified by the German case seems to be more realistic than the depoliticization proposed by Justice Breyer as a way of breaking the vicious circle created by biased perceptions of risk. In fact, the evidence presented in section 21.2 strongly suggests that, in situations characterized by a high level of uncertainty, procedural rationality (how decisions are made) is at least as important as substantive rationality (what decisions are made).

The great scientific uncertainty under which risk regulators must decide has been a recurring theme in this chapter. Since technological progress is one of the most important causes of scientific uncertainty, we cannot expect to ever reach a sufficient level of information. It is rather the style and methods of regulation that will have to change. Take the case of nanotechnology. There is a growing consensus that regulatory action is needed, not only to ensure that any potential hazards posed by this new technology are adequately controlled, but also as an important prerequisite for the social acceptance of the technology. At the same time, the high level of uncertainty about such basic factors as the definition of what constitutes a new nanomaterial, and about the reliability of methods of testing either the materials or their effects in terms of exposure and toxicity, seems to preclude recourse to command-and-control methods of regulation (Bowman and Hodge 2009). Even if government involvement in the regulation of nanotechnology is eventually inevitable, the most promising path is through a co-regulatory approach, in which each party – government, industry, and consumers – has a hand in defining not only the means and procedures by which the goal is to be achieved but the details of the goal itself.

## REFERENCES

Bowman, D.M. and G.A. Hodge (2009), 'Counting on codes: an examination of transnational codes as a regulatory governance mechanism for nanotechnologies', *Regulation & Governance*, **3**, 145–64.
Breyer, S.W. (1993), *Breaking the Vicious Circle*, Cambridge, MA: Harvard University Press.
Commission of the European Communities (2000), *Communication on the Precautionary Principle*, COM (2000) 1, Brussels: Commission of the European Communities.
Graham, J.D., L.C. Green and M.J. Roberts (1988), *In Search of Safety*, Cambridge, MA: Harvard University Press.
Hood, C., H. Rothstein and R. Baldwin (2001), *The Government of Risk*, Oxford: Oxford University Press.
Leebron, D.W. (1996), 'Lying down with Procrustes: an analysis of harmonization claims', in J.N. Bhagwati and R.E. Hudec (eds), *Fair Trade and Harmonization*, vol. 1, Cambridge, MA: MIT Press, pp. 41–118.

Majone, G. (2005), *Dilemmas of European Integration: The Ambiguities and Dilemmas of Integration by Stealth*, Oxford: Oxford University Press.

Majone, G. (2006), 'The internationalization of regulation: implications for developing countries', in M. Minogue and L. Carino (eds), *Regulatory Governance in Developing Countries*, Cheltenham, UK and Northampton, MA, USA: Edward Elgar Publishing, pp. 39–60.

Mashaw, J.L., R.A. Merrill and P.M. Shane (1998), *Administrative Law*, 4th edn, St. Paul, MN: West Group.

Mendeloff, J.M. (1988), *The Dilemma of Toxic Substance Regulation*, Cambridge, MA: MIT Press.

Rehbinder, E. (1991), *Das Vorsorgeprinzip im internationalen Vergleich*, Baden-Baden: Nomos.

Viscusi, W.K., J.M. Vernon and J.E. Harrington, Jr. (1996), *Economics of Regulation and Antitrust*, Cambridge, MA: MIT Press.

Wilson, J.Q. (1989), *Bureaucracy*, New York: Basic Books.

# PART VII

# POLITICS OF REGULATORY ENFORCEMENT AND COMPLIANCE

# 22 The politics of civil and criminal enforcement regimes
## *Michelle Welsh*

Often the response to a financial crisis, large corporate collapse or perceived failure in corporate regulation is a call to provide regulators with greater enforcement powers. Increasingly legislatures consider the provision of civil penalty regimes either as an alternative to or in addition to criminal sanctions for corporate misconduct.

Frequently the introduction of a civil penalty regime is justified because the regulator has experienced difficulty in obtaining criminal convictions. Theoretically civil penalty orders are easier to obtain than criminal sanctions. The introduction of civil penalties is desirable from the regulators' perspective because it can increase the range of available enforcement mechanisms in a manner envisaged by responsive regulation theory (Ayres and Braithwaite 1992).

The opposing argument is that civil penalties are not desirable because they allow the state to bypass the limits imposed by criminal procedure in order to achieve a regulatory result. No penalty of any kind should be imposed without the protection of the rules of the criminal law. If regulators are provided with civil penalty regimes the risk is that they will use them at the expense of criminal prosecutions.

This chapter examines the policy and political tradeoffs faced by legislatures when they consider whether or not to introduce a criminal enforcement regime, a civil penalty regime or both. In addition this chapter examines the dilemma faced by regulators who have been provided with overlapping criminal sanctions and civil penalties. When faced with an alleged contravention of the law these regulators are required to determine which of these two regimes will provide the appropriate regulatory response. This determination will have implications for regulatees, as well as the broader community.

## 22.1   CIVIL PENALTIES AND CRIMINAL SANCTIONS

Civil penalty regimes are similar to criminal enforcement regimes in that they allow regulators to apply for court-ordered punitive penalties. However, the rules of evidence and procedure are the civil rules, and the civil standard of proof applies. The penalties that can be imposed under a civil penalty regime are not as severe as those that can be imposed under a criminal regime. The types of sanctions available under a civil penalty regime include pecuniary penalties, disqualification orders and compensation orders. Some civil penalty regimes determine the maximum pecuniary penalty that may be imposed. Other regimes provide for pecuniary penalties to be assessed as a multiple of the benefit gained from the contravening conduct. Incarceration, which is available under a criminal regime, is never available under a civil penalty regime.

Regulators are charged with the responsibility of investigating suspected contraventions of the laws they administer. Usually civil penalty applications are initiated by the regulator who investigated the suspected contravention. By contrast, in many jurisdictions, a criminal prosecution will be launched by an independent public prosecutor, following a referral from the regulator.

## 22.2    THE INTRODUCTION OF CIVIL PENALTY REGIMES: THE LEGISLATURE'S DILEMMA

Legislatures introduce civil penalty regimes for a variety of reasons, one of which is that the criminal law is often perceived to be an inadequate enforcement mechanism, especially for contraventions of corporations and securities laws. Another reason cited for the introduction of civil penalty regimes is the belief by some that criminal sanctions are not appropriate for these types of contraventions. Many legislatures favor the use of overlapping civil penalty and criminal regimes so that regulators are provided with an increased range of enforcement options, allowing them to adopt a strategic approach to regulation.

The criminal law is seen to be an inadequate control mechanism for contraventions of corporations and securities laws by those who believe that the detection and conviction rates for these types of contraventions are not high enough (Mann 1992: 1798). Detection of corporate crime can be difficult in situations where the only evidence of a contravention is in the hands of the contravening corporation or its officers. This evidence may be destroyed easily if an investigation is threatened. In many cases corporate criminals are powerful and well resourced and are therefore able to take advantage of the vagaries of the law (Tomasic 1994: 263).

The need to prove the breach beyond reasonable doubt adds to the difficulty of obtaining criminal convictions. If an offender is prosecuted and convicted, the sanction imposed sometimes bears little relation to the harm inflicted or the profits made from the contravening conduct. After a cost–benefit analysis some firms may decide that it is better to violate the law in situations where the risk of discovery is low and, even if discovered, the benefits of the crime outweigh the fine that may be imposed (Simpson 2005: 48–9).

The low detection rates, the evidentiary requirements of the criminal law, and the low sanctions that have been imposed in some cases have greatly reduced the effectiveness of regulation in the companies and securities area. The perceived inadequacies of the criminal justice system in relation to contraventions of corporate and securities laws can undermine the criminal law as an effective mechanism for the control of corporate misconduct and can erode the public's confidence in the legal system (Bosch 1992: 1; Miller 1995: 162).

Civil penalty regimes can overcome the difficulties associated with criminal sanctions and can increase the deterrent effect of the law. This is because civil penalties are perceived to be easier to obtain, and are therefore cheaper and more efficient, than traditional criminal penalties (Mann 1992: 1798; Gillooly and Wallace-Bruce 1994: 270). The certainty of a sanction being imposed is potentially greater under a civil penalty regime than under the criminal regime (Simpson 2005: 78). This increased certainty arises because of the difference between the civil and criminal rules of evidence and procedure.

However, there is a debate in the literature concerning the acceptability of using the civil rules of evidence and procedure to determine liability to what are in effect penal sanctions. The object of many civil penalty regimes "seems to be to achieve the state's regulatory purpose unimpeded by the 'technical' limits imposed by criminal law or criminal procedure" (Goldstein 1992: 1895). Whilst it is true that incarceration is not an option under a civil penalty regime, defendants can suffer severe hardship from the imposition of large pecuniary penalties or disqualification orders. In reality, there is little difference between a criminal fine and a pecuniary penalty imposed under a civil penalty regime.

A person subject to a civil penalty order may suffer as much stigma as, or even greater stigma than, a convicted criminal. The stigma attached to a criminal conviction is not dependent upon it being labeled as criminal. It depends upon the nature and seriousness of the contravening conduct and the degree of publicity the matter attracts, rather than the classification of the offending behaviour as civil or criminal (Gillooly and Wallace-Bruce 1994: 270–71). For these reasons it has been argued that civil penalties should not be imposed without the protection normally afforded a person subject to a criminal prosecution. Regardless of the modifications that are made to the civil rules in order to take account of the severity of the penalties imposed, these modified rules will offer less protection than traditional criminal rules. Therefore there is a risk that penalties may be wrongly imposed. "Deterrence is not enhanced by punishing the innocent, and even if it were, deterrence would then be bought at too high a price" (Gillooly and Wallace-Bruce 1994: 271).

Legislatures considering the introduction of civil penalties must balance the need to provide effective alternatives to criminal sanctions with the need to provide defendants with adequate protection. As stated previously, owing to the fact that civil penalties are perceived to be easier to obtain than criminal sanctions, the risk is that regulators who are provided with overlapping criminal sanctions and civil penalties may stop utilizing criminal sanctions and may instead utilize civil penalties as a means of bypassing the protections offered to defendants by the criminal law. The counter-argument is that diminishing the role of the criminal law is desirable and appropriate. The criminal law is the strongest punishment that society can inflict on its citizens and it should be reserved for the most serious contraventions of the law. Labeling too many contraventions "criminal" means that the special nature of the criminal law is lost (Australian Law Reform Commission 2003, para. 3.37). "The criminal law should be reserved to prohibiting conduct that society believes lacks any social utility" (Coffee 1992: 1876). The introduction of civil penalties for less serious offences widens the range of the enforcement regimes available to the regulator and allows criminal sanctions to be retained for the most egregious conduct (Zimring 1992: 1905; Gething 1996: 376; Goldwasser 1999: 212; Australian Law Reform Commission 2003, para. 3.103).

The need for regulators to be armed with a range of enforcement mechanisms is supported by responsive regulation theory. Responsive regulation theory underpins civil penalty regimes. This theory recognizes that it is not possible for any regulatory agency to detect and enforce every contravention of the law that it administers. The goal of responsive regulation theory is to "stimulate maximum levels of regulatory compliance" (Gilligan 1999: 426) by encouraging actors to comply with the law voluntarily.

Responsive regulation theory is represented graphically by the pyramid model that was developed and expanded by John Braithwaite and Ian Ayres. Responsive regulation theory relies on the premise that the actions of individuals will be motivated by different factors and that a successful regulatory agency will need to have a range of enforcement options available to it to enable it to deal with actors who are subject to those different motivational factors. Some business actors will be motivated purely by economic factors, while others' actions will be determined by a sense of social responsibility. Some will be induced to act by a combination of these and other factors. Moreover the motivational factors influencing the behaviour of individual actors will change over time. Responsive regulation theory requires regulators to be armed with a wide range of sanctions to deal with these differing motivational factors (Braithwaite 1985; Ayres and Braithwaite 1992).

Apart from the requirement to deal with actors motivated by different factors there are other reasons regulators need to be armed with a range of sanctions. Difficulties can arise if a regulator has a single enforcement option, especially when it is severe. Regulators with one severe enforcement option can use it in relation to the most serious offences only. Such regulators have no appropriate enforcement mechanism at their disposal when less serious offences occur. When only one drastic enforcement mechanism is available a regulator may find that it lacks credibility because the regulated community will ignore its demands to comply with the law, knowing that the regulator is unlikely to take action, except in the most blatant of cases (Ayres and Braithwaite 1992: 36).

If a regulator has at its disposal a variety of enforcement mechanisms its choice is not limited to "low-cost, low-impact remediation and high-cost, high-impact criminal sanctions" (Lochner and Cain 1999: 1901–02). The provision of a range of enforcement options that include civil penalties can protect society from both under-enforcement and over-enforcement (Mann 1992: 1865; Simpson 2005: 74). Civil penalties protect against under-enforcement because they allow the regulator to take enforcement action in situations where the conduct is not severe enough to justify the commencement of a criminal prosecution. If civil penalties did not exist these contraventions could be subjected only to a civil action for damages (Mann 1992: 1865). In addition civil penalties protect against over-enforcement by providing a non-criminal sanction for those contraventions that involve conduct that is not genuinely criminal. Without civil penalties these contraventions would be treated as criminal or not punished at all (Mann 1992: 1865).

Providing regulators with overlapping criminal sanctions and civil penalties raises the possibility of regulatory capture. Regulatory capture can occur if the regulator becomes subject to the influences of powerful regulated parties to such an extent that the regulator exercises its discretion in favor of those regulated parties, rather than in the public interest (Baldwin and Cave 1999: 20). If a regulator that has at its disposal overlapping criminal sanctions and civil penalties is captured, it will exercise its discretion in accordance with the preference that has previously been expressed by the regulated community (Simpson 2005: 87).

Members of the regulated community facing possible enforcement action by a regulator clearly have an interest in the exercise of the regulator's discretion to pursue either criminal sanctions or civil penalties. In most cases it would be expected that members of the regulated community would prefer to be subjected to a civil penalty application rather than a criminal prosecution. However, this is not always the case. In some circumstances a criminal prosecution may be preferred. This could occur, for example, if the regulatee were a corporation and the most severe penalty available was either a criminal fine or a pecuniary penalty under a civil penalty regime. In that case the corporation would have a greater chance of defending the criminal prosecution than the civil penalty application because of the protections afforded by the criminal rules of evidence and procedure.

There are many policy and political factors that legislatures must consider when they are determining whether or not to introduce civil penalty regimes. Despite policy disincentives for the introduction of civil penalties, increasingly legislatures are choosing to introduce them in an effort to address public concern regarding the perceived inadequacy of the criminal law. In the United States, civil penalties have replaced criminal sanctions in some critical, volatile and controversial areas of law enforcement (Clements 1988: 361; Mann 1992: 1798). For example, civil penalties are utilized as enforcement mechanisms in the United States in workplace safety, health care, environmental, and corporations and securities laws (Brown 2001: 1327–8).

Civil penalties are available under a variety of legislative instruments in the United Kingdom, including taxation (Davison 2009), environmental protection (Parpworth and Thompson 2009) and corporations and securities laws. Many regulators in the United States and the United Kingdom are provided with overlapping criminal sanctions and civil penalties.

The use of civil penalties in the United States and the United Kingdom is mirrored in Australia. Civil penalties as regulatory instruments have been available in Australian legislation for more than 100 years, and their use is increasing. Civil penalty provisions can be found in many areas of regulation as diverse as taxation, social security, the provision of financial services, the regulation of food technology, insurance, broadcasting, immigration, and the licensing of nursing homes, airlines, navigation and fishing (Australian Law Reform Commission 2003, para. 5.1). Recently civil penalty provisions have been introduced to regulate promoters of tax exploitation schemes and to ensure compliance with the Occupational Health and Safety (Commonwealth Employment) Act 1991 (Cth) and the Therapeutic Goods Amendment Act 2006 (Cth). In many of these cases civil penalty provisions were introduced because the relevant regulatory agency had experienced difficulty in obtaining criminal convictions.[1]

The Australian Securities and Investments Commission (ASIC) is the regulator of corporate law in Australia. It has at its disposal a variety of enforcement mechanisms, including criminal sanctions and civil penalties. Civil penalties were introduced into the predecessor to the Australian Corporations Act 2001 (Cth) in 1993. Initially civil penalties applied to the statutory directors' duties and a limited number of other provisions of the Corporations Act 2001 (Cth). Since their introduction the reach of civil penalties has expanded, and they now cover a diverse range of provisions. Some of the provisions that are subject to the civil penalties are also subject to criminal sanctions.

The Australian civil penalty regime was introduced for the purpose of overcoming apparent deficiencies in the law relating to the enforcement of the statutory directors' duties (Australian Law Reform Commission 2003, para. 2.62).[2] Prior to the introduction of the civil penalty provisions, directors who contravened the directors' duty provisions were subject to a range of criminal sanctions. These criminal sanctions were seen to be deficient for a variety of reasons, including an apparent reluctance on the part of the courts to impose custodial sentences, even though the regime allowed for the imposition of them. In some cases where a custodial sentence may have been appropriate the courts had been inclined to impose modest fines. This led to community discontent and to a belief by some that the law had fallen into disrepute (Australian Law Reform Commission, para. 13.6).

When the civil penalty provisions were introduced it was anticipated that the regulator would make great use of them. However, in the early years it was noted that there was a marked disparity between the intrinsic enforcement capabilities of the civil penalty provisions and the enthusiasm of regulators to use them (Moodie and Ramsay 2002: 62). A study examining the reasons ASIC had made little use of these provisions between 1993 and 1999 found that the lack of use by ASIC of the civil penalty regime could be explained by a variety of factors. These factors included the financial constraints placed on ASIC, ASIC's enforcement culture, and the variation in skill and experience of ASIC's enforcement personnel. Many of the enforcement officers at ASIC came from a criminal law background and had a tendency to prefer criminal actions rather than civil penalties (Gilligan et al. 1999: 31–6). Changes were made to the civil penalty regime in 2000, and the use of these provisions has increased (Welsh 2009a).

## 22.3   THE USE OF CIVIL PENALTY REGIMES – THE REGULATOR'S DILEMMA

Many regulators are provided with overlapping criminal and civil penalty sanctions. When faced with an alleged contravention of the law these regulators must determine which of these enforcement regimes will provide the appropriate regulatory response. There are opposing views in the literature as to the strategies that are likely to be adopted by regulators who have overlapping criminal and civil penalty regimes at their disposal. One view is that, owing to the fact that civil penalties are perceived to be easier to obtain than criminal sanctions, regulators who have at their disposal overlapping criminal sanctions and civil penalties are likely to utilize civil penalties in preference to criminal sanctions (Mann 1992: 1863). The view that an expanded use of civil penalties will result in a decreased use of criminal sanctions is supported by responsive regulation theory.

If a regulator were to utilize the enforcement mechanisms at its disposal in a manner envisaged by responsive regulation, two consequences would follow. First, in the majority of cases the regulator would commence with the least severe enforcement mechanism available and consider whether it provided an appropriate regulatory response, prior to considering more severe enforcement mechanisms. Second, most enforcement activity would involve the use of less severe enforcement mechanisms, with the use of enforcement mechanisms decreasing as the severity of the enforcement mechanism increased. In the context of overlapping criminal sanctions and civil penalties this means that regulators would issue more civil penalty applications than criminal prosecutions. Criminal prosecutions would be reserved for the worst cases.

The opposing view is that, owing to bureaucratic incentives, regulators who have at their disposal overlapping criminal sanctions and civil penalties are likely to display a preference for criminal prosecutions (Coffee 1992: 1889). Bureaucratic incentives to utilize criminal sanctions arise as a result of the publicity and public drama that surround a criminal prosecution. Regulators who obtain criminal convictions are more likely to be regarded as tough enforcers than those who obtain civil penalty orders. A perception as a tough enforcer is desirable because it can lead to the obtaining of greater levels of funding and the maintenance of staff morale and can assist in the recruitment of new staff. Enforcement officers employed by regulatory agencies are likely to prefer criminal prosecutions because they are likely to believe that the laws they enforce are important and contraventions of them should be regarded as crimes (Coffee 1992: 1888–90).

Regulators who adopt a deterrence-based strategy are likely to utilize criminal sanctions in preference to civil penalties. Deterrence theorists assume that regulated persons are self-interested rational actors who take advantage of opportunities to maximize their own outcomes. Corporate decision-makers weigh the benefits of non-compliance against the probability and costs of punishment (Simpson 2005: 94). Deterrence theory assumes that these persons will comply with the law when the cost of non-compliance outweighs the benefits to be gained (Scholz 1984: 179).

A deterrence strategy requires that offenders be watched closely, all suspicious signs be investigated and the letter of the law be enforced meticulously (Scholz 1984: 182). It calls for command-and-control regulation where penalties are threatened for non-compliance and violators of the law are punished (Job et al. 2007: 87). The use of harsh sanctions and strict penalties is often justified by deterrence theory. Harsher penalties provide the most powerful deterrents (Szott Moohr 2003: 35; Simpson 2005: 17). A deterrence approach supports the commencement of a criminal prosecution in all situations where the available evidence will support one.

Research has been conducted by the author into ASIC's use of overlapping criminal and civil penalty regimes (Welsh 2009a). The research examined ASIC's use of these enforcement regimes in relation to contraventions of certain directors' duty provisions between 2000 and June 2009. The provisions examined were the directors' duty provisions that are capable of being enforced by both the civil penalties and criminal sanctions.

The data collected reveal that ASIC commenced court-based enforcement actions alleging a contravention of these directors' duty provisions on 97 occasions between 2001 and June 30, 2009. ASIC had the choice of a criminal prosecution or a civil penalty application in all of those cases. Ninety-five criminal prosecutions and two civil penalty applications were commenced. This result is surprising given that one of the reasons for the introduction of the civil penalty regime was to overcome difficulties with the criminal enforcement regime.

During this same period ASIC commenced 16 civil penalty applications alleging that a contravention of the directors' statutory duty of care and diligence had occurred. ASIC did not have the choice of a criminal prosecution in all of these cases because this duty is not subject to the criminal enforcement regime. The most severe sanctions available for contraventions of this duty are those that are available under the civil penalty regime.

ASIC is an example of a regulator that has at its disposal overlapping criminal sanctions and civil penalties. This regulator has displayed a clear preference for criminal sanctions in situations where it has the choice between those sanctions and civil penalties. It had that choice on 97 occasions and it issued only two civil penalty applications. The other 16 civil penalty applications issued by ASIC during the relevant period were issued in situations where ASIC could not have commenced a criminal prosecution.

The decision to instigate a criminal prosecution or a civil penalty application is made by ASIC in consultation with the Commonwealth Director of Public Prosecutions (CDPP). Potential contraventions of the directors' duty provisions are investigated by

ASIC. Once the investigation stage is complete, ASIC is required to consult with the CDPP. ASIC must not issue a civil penalty application until the CDPP has ruled out the possibility of obtaining a criminal conviction (ASIC and CDPP 2006, para. 4.1). Both ASIC and the CDPP have stated publicly that whenever sufficient evidence is available to support a criminal prosecution then one will be commenced in preference to a civil penalty application (Welsh 2009a).

There are several reasons ASIC and the CDPP have adopted a preference for criminal prosecutions in situations where there is a choice between civil penalties and criminal sanctions. The regulators appear to have adopted a deterrence-based approach. Such an approach supports the use of criminal sanctions instead of civil penalties, whenever they are available.

Another reason why ASIC and the CDPP have adopted a preference for criminal prosecutions is because this attitude reflects the desire of the public that corporate officers who contravene corporations and securities laws should be subjected to criminal prosecutions. The public desire for criminal prosecutions is evident from the criticism that has been directed at ASIC following some civil penalty applications. For example, in one of the two cases where ASIC issued a civil penalty application in a situation where a criminal prosecution may have been available, it was subject to much criticism in the media[3] and in academic writings (Comino 2006, 2007; Overland 2006). In addition to facing criticism from the media and the academy, ASIC has been required to justify to the Australian Parliament some of its enforcement decisions to institute civil penalty proceedings instead of criminal prosecutions (Welsh 2009b: 386–7).

The criticism directed towards ASIC following some decisions to institute civil penalty proceedings rather than criminal prosecutions results from public discontent over the perceived lenient treatment of corporations and corporate officers who are subjected to civil penalty applications instead of criminal prosecutions. ASIC is not alone in facing this criticism. Another recent example of public discontent with civil penalties in the Australian context is the public debate surrounding the enforcement of cartel misconduct under the Australian Competition and Consumer Act 2010 (C'th) (formerly the Trade Practices Act). The Australian cartel misconduct provisions are similar to the antitrust provisions in the United States. These provisions are enforced by the Australian Competition and Consumer Commission (ACCC).

Prior to July 2009, contraventions of the cartel misconduct provisions were enforced by a civil penalty regime. Criminal penalties were not available. For some time it had been argued that these penalties were not capable of providing an effective deterrent against cartel conduct (Clarke 2005). The debate in Australia was heightened in 2007 by the media outcry that followed a particularly high-profile civil penalty application. This case resulted in renewed calls in certain sectors for the introduction of criminal penalties (Beaton-Wells and Brydges 2008: 6). Criminal penalties for cartel misconduct were introduced in July 2009 as a supplement to the existing civil penalties. It was argued that criminal penalties, and in particular the threat of incarceration, would provide an effective deterrent to cartel behavior for hard-core breaches (Australian Trade Practices Review Committee 2003: 153, 163).

A public desire for criminal prosecutions is not unique to Australia. In 2003 Szott Moohr wrote about a similar desire that was evident in the United States following some high-profile corporate collapses. Szott Moohr stated that:

[a]s the Enron scandal unfolded, government and industry officials, editorial writers, Enron employees and retirees, and the general public spoke with one voice: those responsible should be punished. In the months that followed Enron's disclosures, a flood of reports about executive malfeasance at other corporations – WorldCom, Adelphia, Tyco, and others – increased the demand for criminal sanctions. (Szott Moohr 2003: 938)

Public desire for criminal prosecutions following corporations and securities violations was evident again in many jurisdictions, including the United States, following the corporate collapses associated with the recent global financial crises.

Many of the bureaucratic incentives identified by Coffee that lead to the utilization of criminal sanctions in preference to civil penalties apply to ASIC. Like many regulators, ASIC operates in an environment where vigorous public and political debate about its actions needs to be taken into consideration. The environment in which ASIC works requires it to provide strong justification for any decision not to prosecute criminally.

## 22.4   CONCLUSION

Before legislatures introduce civil penalty regimes they are required to balance competing considerations. Often civil penalties are called for following financial crises, corporate collapses or other perceived failures in corporate regulation. Usually the call for the introduction of these penalties is accompanied by a claim that existing criminal regimes have failed to protect financial markets and members of the public from corporate misconduct.

Opponents of civil penalties argue that these penalties are dangerous because they expose corporate entities and officers to the risk of the imposition of severe penalties, without the protection of rules that are normally associated with criminal enforcement regimes. Civil penalties should not be introduced because the civil rules of evidence and standard of proof may lead to penalties being imposed wrongly. Despite these risks the use of civil penalty provisions is increasing in the United States, the United Kingdom and Australia.

In many cases legislatures are introducing overlapping criminal sanctions and civil penalties. Regulators who have at their disposal overlapping sanctions and penalties are required to determine which of these enforcement regimes is appropriate, when they are faced with an alleged contravention of the law that they administer. This increases the possibility of regulatory capture, and these regulators may reduce the number of criminal prosecutions in favour of civil penalty applications. The counter-argument is that bureaucratic incentives will mean that these regulators will issue more criminal prosecutions than civil penalty applications.

ASIC is an example of such a regulator. It has been provided with overlapping criminal sanctions and civil penalties for contraventions of some of the statutory directors' duties. Despite the fact that these civil penalty provisions were introduced because of perceived inadequacies with the criminal enforcement regime, ASIC issues many more criminal prosecutions than civil penalty applications in situations where both of these enforcement regimes are available. ASIC has made use of the civil penalty regime, but that use has been limited largely to situations where criminal sanctions are not available.

There are various reasons why ASIC favors criminal sanctions over civil penalty applications. One of those reasons is that ASIC operates in an environment which requires it to take into consideration vigorous public and political debate about its actions. When choosing between the available enforcement options, ASIC would be aware that it may be required to provide strong justification for any decision not to prosecute criminally. The public desire for persons who commit corporate malfeasance to be subject to criminal prosecutions is not limited to Australia.

The study of ASIC's use of overlapping criminal sanctions and civil penalties provides an interesting illustration of one regulator's enforcement strategies. However, the data examined does not allow for predictions to be made as to the approach that may be adopted by other regulators in similar circumstances. Further studies of a number of regulators would need to be undertaken before such predictions could be made.

## NOTES

1. See Helen Coonan, Minister for Revenue and Assistant Treasurer, 'Crackdown on promoters of tax avoidance and tax evasion schemes' (press release, 5 December 2003), Department of Treasury, http://parlsec.treasurer.gov.au/DisplayDocs.aspx?doc=pressreleases/2003/117.htm&pageID=003&min=hlc&Year=2003&DocType=0 C117/03 (accessed 17 December 2007); Explanatory Memorandum, Tax Laws Amendment (2006 Measures No. 1) Bill 2006 (Cth) [3.147]; Tooma (2006: 59); Explanatory Memorandum to the Occupational Health and Safety (Commonwealth Employment) Amendment (Employee Involvement and Compliance) Bill 2004 (Cth), vi; Explanatory Memorandum to the Therapeutic Goods Amendment Bill 2005 (Cth), 4.
2. See Commonwealth of Australia, *Parliamentary Debates*, Senate, 28 November 1991, 3611 [55] (Senator Richardson). See also Tomasic (1994: 267–8).
3. See *ASIC v Vizard* (2005) 54 ACSR 394 and ASIC Media Releases 05/190, 05/215. Examples of the comments in the press include "Inside business," ABC TV, 24 July 2005, transcript available at: http://www.abc.net.au/insidebusiness/content/2005/s1421030.htm (accessed 18 December 2007); J. Sexton, 'Vizard was too well connected for jail', *Australian* (Sydney), 6 July 2001, 1; B. Frith, 'The unbearable lightness of sentencing', *Australian* (Sydney), 22 July 2005, 22; T. McCrann, 'Why it's a mistake to civilise the criminal', *Weekend Australian* (Sydney), 23 July 2005, 34; Richard Gluyas, 'Hanging judge did our crime-deaf watchdog's job', *Australian* (Sydney), 29 July 2005, 4; J. McCullough, 'One law for rich, another for richer', *Courier Mail* (Brisbane), 30 July 2005, 27; and R. Gluyas and B. Speedy, 'ASIC should have tried to jail Vizard', *Australian* (Sydney), 30 July 2005, 8.

## REFERENCES

ASIC and CDPP (2006), *Memorandum of Understanding*, 1 March.
Australian Law Reform Commission (2003), *Principled Regulation: Federal Civil and Administrative Penalties in Australia*, Report No. 95, Sydney: Australian Law Reform Commission.
Australian Trade Practices Review Committee (2003), *Review of the Competition Provisions of the Trade Practices Act*.
Ayres, I. and J. Braithwaite (1992), *Responsive Regulation: Transcending the Deregulation Debate*, New York: Oxford University Press.
Baldwin, R. and M. Cave (1999), *Understanding Regulation: Theory, Strategy and Practice*, New York: Oxford University Press.
Beaton-Wells, C. and N. Brydges (2008), 'The cardboard box cartel case: was all the fuss warranted?', *Australian Business Law Review*, **36**, 6–28.
Bosch, H. (1992), 'Bosch on business', *Information Australia*, **1**.
Braithwaite, J. (1985), *To Punish or Persuade: Enforcement of Coal Mine Safety*, Albany: State University of New York Press.
Brown, D. (2001), 'Street crime, corporate crime and the contingency of criminal liability', *University of Pennsylvania Law Review*, **149**, 1295–1360.

Clarke, J. (2005), 'Criminal penalties for contraventions of Part IV of the Trade Practices Act', *Deakin Law Review*, **10** (1), 141–76.

Clements, E. (1988), 'The seventh amendment right to jury trial in civil penalties actions: a post-*Tull* examination of the Insider Trading Sanctions Act of 1984', *University of Miami Law Review*, **43**, 361–418.

Coffee, J. (1992), 'Paradigms lost: the blurring of the criminal and civil law models – and what can be done about it', *Yale Law Journal*, **101**, 1875–94.

Comino, V. (2006), 'Civil or criminal penalties for corporate misconduct: which way ahead?', *Australian Business Law Review*, **34**, 428–46.

Comino, V. (2007), 'The enforcement record of ASIC since the introduction of the civil penalty regime', *Australian Journal of Corporate Law*, **20** (2), 183–213.

Davison, J. (2009), 'The new VAT penalty regime', *VAT Digest*, **72**, 2–15.

Gething, M. (1996), 'Do we really need criminal and civil penalties for contraventions of directors' duties?', *Australian Business Law Review*, **24**, 375–90.

Gilligan, G., H. Bird and I. Ramsay (1999), 'Civil penalties and the enforcement of directors' duties', *University of New South Wales Law Journal*, **22** (2), 417–61.

Gillooly, M. and N.L. Wallace-Bruce (1994), 'Civil penalties in Australian legislation', *University of Tasmania Law Review*, **13** (2), 269–93.

Goldstein, A.S. (1992), 'White-collar crime and civil sanctions', *Yale Law Journal*, **101**, 1895–1900.

Goldwasser, V. (1999), 'CLERP 6 – implications and ramifications for the regulation of Australian financial markets', *Companies and Securities Law Journal*, **17**, 206–19.

Job, J., A. Stout and R. Smith (2007), 'Culture change in three taxation administrations: from command-and-control to responsive regulation', *Law and Policy*, **29** (1), 84–101.

Lochner, T. and B.E. Cain (1999), 'Equity and efficacy in the enforcement of campaign finance laws', *Texas Law Review*, **77**, 1891–1942.

Mann, K. (1992), 'Punitive civil sanctions: the middleground between criminal and civil law', *Yale Law Journal*, **101**, 1795–1874.

Miller, S. (1995), 'Corporate crime, the excesses of the 80's and collective responsibility: an ethical perspective', *Australian Journal of Corporate Law*, **5**, 139–53.

Moodie, G. and I. Ramsay (2002), 'The expansion of civil penalties under the Corporations Act', *Australian Business Law Review*, **30** (1), 61–7.

Overland, J. (2006), 'Two steps forward, one step back: assessing recent developments in the fight against insider trading', *Company and Securities Law Journal*, **24**, 207–22.

Parpworth, N. and K. Thompson (2009), 'Fly-tipping: a real environmental crime', *Journal of Planning and Environmental Law*, **9**, 1133.

Scholz, J. (1984), 'Cooperation, deterrence, and the ecology of regulatory enforcement', *Law and Society Review*, **18**, 179–224.

Simpson, S. (2005), *Corporate Crime, Law and Social Control*, New York and Cambridge: Cambridge University Press.

Szott Moohr, G. (2003), 'An Enron lesson: the modest role of criminal law in preventing corporate crime', *Florida Law Review*, **55**, 937–76.

Tomasic, R. (1994), 'Corporate crime', in Duncan Chappell and Paul Wilson (eds), *The Australian Criminal Justice System: The Mid 1990s*, Sydney and Austin, TX: Butterworths, p. 253.

Tooma, R. (2006), 'Deterring promoters of tax exploitation schemes: lessons from continuous disclosure', *Australian Business Law Review*, **34**, 58–74.

Welsh, M. (2009a), 'Civil penalties and responsive regulation: the gap between theory and practice', *Melbourne University Law Review*, **33** (3), 908–33.

Welsh, M. (2009b), 'The regulatory dilemma: the choice between overlapping criminal sanctions and civil penalties for contraventions of the directors' duty provisions', *Company and Securities Law Journal*, **27**, 370–88.

Zimring, F. (1992), 'The multiple middlegrounds between civil and criminal law', *Yale Law Journal*, **101**, 1901–08.

# 23 The pragmatic politics of regulatory enforcement
## *Salo Coslovsky, Roberto Pires, and Susan S. Silbey*

This chapter describes regulatory enforcement as an intrinsically political endeavor. We argue that regulatory enforcement, as enacted daily by front-line enforcers around the world, consists of the production of local agreements and arrangements that realign interests, reshape conflicts, and redistribute the risks, costs, and benefits of doing business and complying with the law. We argue that, through their transactions, both the regulators and the regulated reshape both their interests and the environment in which they operate, reconstructing their perceptions of and preferences for compliance. We call this phenomenon the "sub-politics of regulatory enforcement," and claim that it provides a springboard for a pragmatic approach to better regulation.

We begin by tracing the trajectory of the field of regulatory enforcement to identify some of its current boundaries. Next, we explore recent research on inspectors and street-level regulatory agents, introducing the notion of "sub-politics of regulatory compliance." This construct evokes a conception of politics that differs from the idea that predominates in the regulatory enforcement literature. Contrary to those who see enforcement styles and strategies as independent variables determining compliance, we posit that enforcement agencies and regulated entities engage in an indeterminate exploration of their institutional surroundings to create legal, technological, and managerial artifacts and agreements to address practical problems of doing business and complying with law. These agents move beyond imposing fines, issuing warnings, or educating their subjects. Rather, they engage in what we describe as a terrain of sub-politics by building agreements that reshape conflicts and reapportion risks, costs, and benefits among various agents so as to make compliance tolerable, sometimes even advantageous, to all involved. We conclude with a discussion of theoretical implications and suggestions of potentially new directions for research on the politics of regulatory enforcement and compliance.

## 23.1 RULEMAKING VERSUS RULE ENFORCEMENT

Much of the literature on regulation treats rulemaking as inherently separate from rule enforcing. Indeed, there are several reasons for such a distinction. Ideally, rules are abstract and universalistic and assign general, publicly available rights and responsibilities. In states claiming to operate under the rule of law, regulations are produced through visible and participatory processes based on public consultation and open debate. Conversely, enforcement acts are concrete and particularistic; they take place in private settings far from public scrutiny, and result from an exercise in interpretation in which enforcers assign legal labels to facts on the ground.

Still, this distinction is not absolute. Crucially, it is inaccurate to claim that rulemaking is political while rule enforcing is the mechanical application of predetermined and unambiguous rules. Enacted policies are the consequence of competing interests, often embedding oppositions within the law (Kolko 1965; Silbey 1984). Even where the authorizing mandate is uncontroversial, ambiguity is likely to prevail in prescriptive rules, and thus enforcers will always find interstitial room for maneuver, moving beyond interpretation to engage either overtly or covertly in the prioritization and redistribution of power and resources (Davis 1972).

The political nature of enforcement is well known to those being regulated. As stated by Scott (1969: 1142, emphasis in the original):

> A large portion of individual demands, and even group demands . . . reach the political system, not before laws are passed, but rather at the enforcement stage . . . [and while] . . . influence before the legislation is passed often takes the form of "pressure-group politics"; *influence at the enforcement stage . . . has seldom been treated as the alternative means of interest articulation which in fact it is.*

Interestingly, the elision of politics from enforcement tracks the evolution of studies of implementation, an activity that was once seen as "technical" while the policy deliberations that preceded it were considered "political." Pressman and Wildavsky, in their classic study *Implementation* (1973), lamented that faulty technical implementation subverted legitimate political goals, or, as they put it, "how great expectations in Washington are dashed in Oakland." Ultimately, Pressman and Wildavsky identified such a large number of occasions on which public policies could be derailed during implementation that they expressed surprise that government programs worked at all. Lack of adequate funding is a common concern, but, as suggested by Freundenburg and Gramlin (1994), bureaucratic slippage, which they define as "the tendency for broad policies to be altered through successive reinterpretation" (p. 214), is an even more insidious source of variation between plan and reality. For this reason, scholars ought to "devote far greater attention to the 'details' of implementation," since these details "have the distinct potential to be not just administrative, but effectively political" (1994: 214).

Nowhere is the view that rule enforcement is inherently political clearer than in studies of front-line organizations where street-level bureaucrats go beyond implementing to actually making policy. "The decisions of street-level bureaucrats, the routines they establish, and the devices they invent to cope with uncertainties and work pressures, effectively *become* the public policies they carry out" (Lipksy 1980: xii, emphasis in original).[1] Enforcement agents, just like policy- and rulemaking agents, engage in the allocation and redistribution of resources, inevitably benefiting some groups or interests over others. "Choosing among courses of action and inaction, individual law enforcement officers become the agents of clarification and elaboration of their own authorizing mandates. Bureaucrats become lawmakers, freely creating . . . law beyond written rules or courtroom practices" (Silbey 1980–81: 850).

Despite these long-standing observations, the politics of regulatory enforcement remains understudied. In a review, Schneiberg and Bartley (2008) suggest that future work on regulatory dynamics in the contemporary world should "address how rules, models, and conceptions of compliance get reshaped in the process of implementation" because "legal and organizational blueprints rarely emerge unscathed from a trip from one setting to another" (p. 49).

## 23.2   UNPACKING ENFORCEMENT

The bulk of the literature that addresses regulatory enforcement focuses primarily on a deceptively straightforward question, namely "When enforcing the law, what is it that regulators actually do?" To answer this question, researchers have strived to establish a consensually agreed taxonomy of regulatory practices and consequences, with the main challenge concerning the mode of aggregation. Empirically, the only observable manifestation of regulatory enforcement is the "enforcement act," i.e. the discrete signal conveyed by a law enforcement official when interacting with the regulated enterprise. Examples include verbal admonishments, written warnings, and the imposition of a fine, and the universe of these acts is immense. Hunter and Waterman (1992) studied how the US Environmental Protection Agency (EPA) enforces water regulations and discovered that EPA agents deploy at least 60 different techniques.

Clearly, none of these enforcement acts means much by itself, when considered in isolation from other acts and from the context in which it is deployed. Ultimately, the challenge is to make a forest out of these trees. To accomplish this goal, scholars of regulatory enforcement aggregate the enforcement acts performed by a given unit of analysis – ranging across individual inspectors (May and Burby 1998; May and Winter 2000; Locke et al. 2009), enforcement agencies (Silbey 1980–81; Hawkins 1984; Braithwaite 1985), countries (Kelman 1981; Badaracco 1985; Brickman et al. 1986; Vogel 1986), and major political and legal traditions (Piore and Schrank 2006) – into either static, hard-wired "styles" and/or dynamic, interactional "strategies."

To this end, and historically, scholars of regulatory enforcement started out by assuming a uni-dimensional space that led to early distinctions between means-oriented and result-oriented approaches (Bardach and Kagan 1982). Subsequently, others separated the arm's length detection and punishment of violations (the so-called "deterrence," "sanctioning," "adversarial," or "policing" model of enforcement) from the transactional processes of cooperation and negotiation (the "compliance," "cooperation," "pedagogic," "bargaining," or "persuasive" model) (Hawkins 1984; Braithwaite 1985; Day and Klein 1987; Hutter 1989; Hunter and Waterman 1992; Zinn 2002; Piore and Schrank 2006; Locke et al. 2009). Eventually, researchers started plotting phenomena on a multi-dimensional space that took into account how enforcers interpret the legal code (ranging from a narrow-legalistic code to a broad, general mandate) and how facilitative (or "friendly") the enforcers are, i.e. whether they emphasize correction or punishment (Braithwaite et al. 1987; May and Burby 1998; May and Winter 2000).

As part of this same program, some researchers incorporated contextual variables into their models and thus, instead of attempting a taxonomy of static styles, have described, and prescribed, dynamic strategies in which regulatory agents act in a way that counterbalances the enterprises' intrinsic inclinations and prior responses (Sparrow 2000; Baldwin and Black 2008). While identifying and then assessing these strategies, some suggest that enforcers temper their cooperation with the credible threat of punishment (Zinn 2002), follow a tit-for-tat approach (Scholz 1984), or adopt an escalating strategy, in which the remedy is tailored to offset the nature of the violations and the prior responses from the regulated enterprise (Ayres and Braithwaite 1992). Ultimately, this debate created a conceptual vocabulary lacking mutually exclusive categories to characterize a range of enforcement practices, from accommodative, flexible, persuasive, and creative to insistent, strict, legalistic, retreatist, and more.

Despite important advances, the effort to identify enforcement strategies correlated with degrees of regulatory conformity is undermined at its origin. First, there is a significant amount of measurement error and limited generalizability. As mentioned earlier, this literature pivots on the challenge of aggregation, i.e. collating discrete enforcement acts so they can be catalogued as styles or strategies. However, some enforcement acts may be misleading and difficult to code. An instance of "strict enforcement" – such as referral to criminal prosecution – may not be strict if everyone involved knows that the prosecutor is unlikely to indict. Likewise, criminal prosecution could mean interminable delay and thus, instead of being a sign of severity, such a referral would be a boon to the defendant, creating opportunity to gather profit that exceeds the ultimate losses (cf. Ewick 1985). And then, even if any given enforcement act can be usefully coded, other aggregation problems arise. The same inspector can be strict today and lenient tomorrow, focused on deterrence when dealing with a large corporation and focused on compliance when dealing with a mom-and-pop shop, or vice versa. Analogously, the same bureaucracy can harbor people with different orientations. This means that aggregation forcibly eliminates certain details, inadvertently obscuring the existence of internal variation, pockets of deviance, and the interaction among different styles or strategies.

Second, the existing literature assumes that enforcement relationships are dyadic and mutually exclusive, i.e. each enforcement agent is supposed to engage with one regulated enterprise at a time and in the absence of any other intervening institution. This view describes two parties to each transaction communicating exclusively through discrete enforcement acts. This assumption makes some amount of aggregation possible, but it obscures the possibility of agency that is intrinsic to front-line work, as will be described below.

Finally, the existing approach does not take sufficient account of the conflicting interests, ambiguities, and indeterminacies embedded in regulatory law itself. At a broader level, the literature on regulation rarely provides general or contextualized accounts of how interests are formed, channeled, and reshaped through regulatory enforcement, and how the desirability of compliance can be constructed as a result of ongoing and evolving transactions between regulators and those being regulated. In other words, existing attempts at understanding regulatory enforcement too often overlook the politics of regulatory enforcement.

## 23.3   THE (SUB)POLITICS OF REGULATORY ENFORCEMENT

Surely, existing analyses have paid some attention to a certain "politics of regulatory enforcement." However, where there has been notice, the "politics of regulatory enforcement" has been defined narrowly as the enabling or constraining environment in which inspectors and their counterparts work. As part of this effort, researchers have compiled a long list of variables that determine the styles and strategies that regulators will adopt and the likelihood that they will be effective in fostering compliance. This list includes: the characteristics of the legal regimes in which relevant actors operate, for example civil law versus customary law (Hawkins 1992, 2002; Braithwaite 2006); the prevailing political-cultural traditions and conceptions of state–society relationships, for example liberal versus corporatist (Kelman 1984; Piore 2004); the local political environment, for example conflictive or insulated, and the degrees to which regulators may be explicitly or tacitly captured by the regulated (Marvel 1977; Hawkins and Thomas 1984; Silbey 1984); characteristics of the regulated industries and their production processes, for example firm size and number of firms (Shover et al. 1984; Lee 2005; Weil 2005); firms' internal management systems (Gunningham et al. 2003); and types of relationships and networks linking the various actors involved, including business associations, NGOs, trade unions, and others (Ayres and Braithwaite 1992).

The attention paid to these contextual variables notwithstanding, the existing literature has often overlooked the processes through which the different actors construct and reformulate their alliances, preferences, and willingness to comply. In other words, it has overlooked what, following Vries (2007), we call "the sub-politics of regulatory enforcement." The labor inspectors we study are involved in politics "because they . . . translate[d] a wide range of conflicting views and interests into a common good." But, "for the simple reason that their political work took place outside the official institutions and arenas of state politics, we may qualify their role as a 'sub-political' one" (Vries 2007: 798).

The next section moves into this neglected space with two cases illustrative of what has been repeatedly found in the enforcement of labor, as well as environmental regulations, in countries such as Brazil (Coslovsky 2009; Pires 2009). These cases show how regulators, regulated enterprises, and other parties and institutions co-produce local agreements and arrangements that can facilitate or hinder compliance (cf. Jasanoff 1996). In other words, we describe how these labor inspectors engage in the sub-politics of regulatory enforcement.

## 23.4   THE ENFORCEMENT OF LABOR REGULATIONS IN BRAZIL

This section reports on two cases involving respectively the enforcement of wages and hours, and occupational health and safety regulations in Brazil. The first case concerns the temporary employment of low-skilled workers during carnival in Salvador, Bahia. For six consecutive days in February or March every year, an estimated 1.2 million people occupy 26 kilometers of streets in Salvador to celebrate carnival. This activity generates upwards of US$250 million in revenue and creates 130 000 to 185 000 additional jobs in the city (Secult/Seplan-BA 2007). Approximately 70 000 of these people are recruited among the low-skilled to act as *cordeiros* (rope-holders) for one of the many *trios elétricos* (roving carnival bands). Their job is to lock arms with each other around a thick rope and form a compact human shield that encircles paying customers, separating them from the non-paying audience. Not surprisingly, most of these workers are hired informally and granted none of the guarantees prescribed by Brazilian labor laws.

Employers in the sector operate in highly competitive markets and are chronically pressed to reduce costs. They perceive existing wage and hour regulations as burdensome, claiming that formalization of contracts and compliance with wage and hour regulations are likely to drive them out of business. To preserve profits, many of them recruit their workers through labor contractors who ignore practically all Brazilian labor laws.

As a result, actual work conditions tend to be precarious, the non-payment or underpayment of wages is widespread, and workers are not afforded safe working conditions or access to grievance mechanisms through which to seek redress.

In response to this situation, in 2003, labor inspectors moved in to impose fines on individual violators. Inspected firms pushed back and pointed out that compliance posed economic risks when competitors did not also comply. Thanks to this initial exchange, inspectors learned that regulatory infringements were so widespread that they could not be fixed one firm at a time. To move forward, inspectors decided to check on carnival promoters during the festivities to fine large numbers of violators simultaneously. Thanks to this aggressive and coordinated move, firms that had previously ignored warnings or refused to talk agreed as a group to start meeting with the labor inspectors.

These meetings, held in 2004, were heated, often hostile. Firms raised multiple justifications for existing practices, and inspectors responded with an equally diverse set of arguments for improving labor conditions. Thanks to this collective engagement in a process of justification and reason-giving, the firms, regulators, representatives from local business, and workers' associations exchanged what turned out to be pertinent technical, legal, and commercial information, developing through the discussions a shared account of local market conditions. For instance, inspectors found out that carnival promoters often had problems with *cordeiros* who abandoned their post for better jobs during the festivities, got drunk or otherwise intoxicated during their shifts, or even mugged or intimidated paying customers.

Eventually, participants started to inch towards a mutually acceptable solution. Inspectors recognized that it was unreasonable to require carnival promoters to process all the paperwork to formally hire and then fire tens of thousands of workers within a single week. Likewise, employers accepted that they could not continue to avoid all provisions of the labor laws and that workers merited some protections. Together, inspectors and carnival promoters developed a standardized contract that reproduced many of the mandatory provisions already included in Brazilian labor laws but with modifications appropriate to the brief employment relationship typical of this industry. These service provision contracts (SPCs) stipulated minimum daily wages, a minimum number of breaks during the shift, the provision of food, gloves, and other protective equipment to *cordeiros*, and insurance against accidents. These contracts also automatically lapsed at the end of carnival. Early adopters soon realized that their workers provided better services, and some of these enterprises started advertising services of higher quality to their prospective customers. Since 2005, more than 25000 SPCs have been signed each year, and just about all contracting parties have found themselves to be better off.

The second case examines the enforcement of health and safety regulations in the auto-parts industry, in Minas Gerais. The wave of trade liberalization that swept the world during the 1990s increased pressure on manufacturers in all sectors to reduce costs and increase productivity. This trend was particularly acute in the auto-parts industry, which had undergone significant restructuring worldwide in previous decades, including the widespread adoption of just-in-time production strategies (Tewari 2006).

In Brazil, auto-parts manufacturers, an industry that employs an estimated 310000 people, responded to these pressures by increasing production targets and "sweating" their labor. A large proportion of these firms use punch-presses, the equipment that stamps auto-parts out of sheet metal. These machines are intrinsically dangerous, and occupational accidents in this industry, including the laceration and amputation of fingers, hands, and arms, soared to the point where they represented 48 per cent of all industrial machine accidents in the country (Piancastelli 2004). To a large extent, the problem rested on the absence or obsolescence of safety devices. A contemporary study found that none of the punch-presses traded in Sao Paulo state had adequate protection to minimize workplace accidents (Mendes 2001). And yet manufacturers resisted upgrading their machines as mandated by labor regulations not only because of the large capital investment required, but also because they feared that safety devices would reduce overall productivity.

For some time, labor inspectors tried to crack down on these violations and to entice firms to replace obsolete punch-presses with new ones. This effort mostly foundered, so a team of labor inspectors reached out to labor prosecutors and researchers from FUNDACENTRO, a health and safety institute associated with the Ministry of Labor, to explore alternative approaches to improving safety conditions. These officials soon realized that they did not know much about the design and functioning of punch-presses, which safety devices actually existed, and whether worker safety could be improved without compromising productivity. According to a labor inspector, "we studied the functioning of these machines, the catalogues of protective equipment producers, all in order to know the best alternatives to manage productivity loss."

Instead of pursuing what seemed like the utopian goal of replacing all existing machines with newer and safer models, the regulators searched for more efficient protective devices, conducted ergonometric studies, and tried to convince public banks and financial authorities to provide subsidized credit for retrofitting existing machines. Eventually, they developed a set of comprehensive protection kits that effectively improved worker safety without compromising overall productivity. In 2003, the number of accidents recorded in the auto-parts industry fell by 66 percent when compared to 2001 figures. By 2005, 70 percent of the 350 firms inspected in the Belo Horizonte metropolitan area had adopted adequate protection for their punch-presses.

Together, these two cases illustrate how far regulatory enforcement agents can move from conventional practices of visiting firms, detecting violations, and issuing citations. As these cases show, the agents also explore options, convene allies, enable collective action, and create room for maneuver within prevailing statutes to propose innovative routes to compliance. In one instance they developed novel legal contractual forms, namely the service provision contract for *cordeiros* in Bahia. In another instance, they helped fairly sophisticated auto-parts firms develop safety devices that protected workers while preserving productivity. Importantly, these arrangements also required the inspectors to recruit additional institutional allies such as FUNDACENTRO (punch-presses), labor prosecutors (service provision contracts), and others. Clearly, this kind of intervention is not captured by existing portrayals of regulatory enforcement agents either enacting particular styles or pursuing a recognized strategy – whether of deterrence or education. They certainly use the "standard" tools of the trade, but they also go beyond the conceptions of politics as a competitive game and enforcement as conformity with legal instruction that underlie the existing literature. Rather, they engage in a type of sub-politics of regulatory enforcement that stimulates participation in local agreements, in the process constructing novel legal, technological, and managerial objects and arrangements that can travel beyond the local origin. More pointedly, these agents go beyond existing conceptions of regulatory enforcement as a zero sum outcome and transform compliance with the law into a positive sum.

## 23.5   PRAGMATISM AND THE SUB-POLITICS OF REGULATION: CONCLUDING REMARKS ON THE RELEVANCE OF POLITICAL AND LEGAL THEORY

Although the existing literature on regulatory enforcement certainly recognizes that enforcement agents have at their disposal a multitude of tools, tactics, and strategies, it too often embeds the conception of the multi-dexterous agent within a narrowly instrumental conception of law and of actors as proto-rational calculators. These enlightenment conceptions depict laws as expressions and uses of state power for purposively organizing social relations to produce specific conditions. In constitutional polities, laws – whether expressions of popular or merely elite will – are created through predictable and visible processes of legislature, court, or regulatory agency. The resulting decisions are purported to be binding for all members because that is what constitutionally established democratic institutions and procedures are for: the people rule themselves, take responsibility for their own laws, and – as rational beings – conform to the law or are held responsible when they fail to do so.

Eschewing equally valid conceptions of law as symbolic articulations of general or group norms (Gusfield 1963, 1981; Edelman 1964), or as available devices for diverse and unpredictable uses (Silbey and Bittner 1982), the regulation literature has cornered itself into narrow models of competitive politics, albeit with a long and prestigious lineage from Hobbes to Weber and Schumpeter, the founders of what turn out to be forms of naïve rationalism and democratic elitism. This historical understanding of politics is modeled on a conception of human agency that identifies action with the execution of an individual's (or a collectivity's aggregated) will: preferences, interests, aims, and plans (Unger 1975 [1981]). This pervasive, if often subtly, instrumental conception of law limits our understandings of regulation, by making it coincident with conceptions of politics as the activities of "only the leadership, or the influencing of the leadership, of a political association, hence today, of a state" (Weber 1946 [1917]: 506).

For analyses of regulatory enforcement, however, this political theory seems to make a crucial but unsubstantiated assumption that will formation and the execution of decisions are clearly separated, conceptually as well as temporally, with processes of will formation preceding execution (Vries 2007). Drawing from this prevalent conception of politics, discussions of regulatory efficacy – as we discussed at the outset – focus on practices, styles, and strategies as the means through which regulatory and policy goals, functioning as predetermined conceptions of compliance, are achieved. With such an instrumental conception of policy and action, it is not surprising that researchers looking for consistency between law and action declared through the 1980s and beyond that the regulatory state was a failure (Sunstein 1990). A consensus developed among mainstream scholars that things never quite work out as they ought when legislation is translated into administration. Rather than focus on what kind of practices were nonetheless achieved, the research depicting regulatory inadequacies became fodder for normative projects decrying public regulation alongside policy to deregulate (Besley and Burgess

2004; Botero et al. 2004; Alesina et al. 2005). While scholars may have sought regulatory reform, their work was appropriated to fuel regulatory retreat.

In contrast to the efforts to document the ways in which law enforcement meets or escapes authorizing regulations, the empirical material we presented above and elsewhere (Pires 2008; Coslovsky 2009) takes up the focus abandoned by earlier research to observe what is actually accomplished through regulatory enforcement and how what is done is actually performed. Specifically, we described a process of regulatory enforcement that is more dispersed and not necessarily limited within the confines of the state or predetermined procedures. The examples suggest the co-production of compliance at the local level and not the execution of predetermined mandates. The solutions devised in each case did not result from the mere accumulation of preferences and interests of the different actors involved, or from a simple compromise among the parties. Of course, these were present, but the actual solutions for each case involved exploration, discovery, invention, and agreement around the creation of new technological, managerial, and legal solutions, some institutionalized in contracts and organizations, and others incorporated almost seamlessly into the production process.

This type of regulatory enforcement evokes a different conception of politics, one that has equally deep and generative roots in Aristotle and more contemporarily in Arendt, Habermas, and most importantly Dewey. Without insisting that these theorists can be made mutually consistent, their work, individually and collectively, offers an alternative to the model of law as prescription and governing agents as means–end calculators. According to Aristotle, politics refers to any form of governance that explicitly takes into account the plurality of interests and opinions among participants. Politics, in this pragmatic sense, involves the search for actions that can reconcile conflicting experiences. Dewey (1927) analogized this conception of politics to scientific experimentalism, where policies, decisions, and actions are revisable in light of experience and new evidence. Dewey believed that democracy was a form of politics uniquely suited to the 20th century precisely because "the democratic community replicates the community of broadly conceived scientific inquiry that serves as the prototype of instrumental reasoning" (quoted in Westbrook 1998: 130). Importantly, for Dewey, instrumental reasoning means something quite different than the standard rational calculation model. He is invoking not only a more capacious notion of politics but also a conception of empirical and collaborative reasoning far from the legalistic model of command and control characteristic of more traditional conceptions of politics, law, and regulation. For Dewey, instrumental reasoning refers to processes in which "free and creative individuals, in democratic as in scientific communities, collectively test hypotheses to find out what works best. These communities set their own goals, determine their own tests, and evaluate their results in a spirit of constructive cooperation" (Kloppenberg cited in Westbrook 1998: 130). This conception of politics, and by implication regulatory enforcement, includes and goes beyond the give-and-take of "normal" politics, or the command and control of legal prescription and agent implementation; it requires creativity, flexibility, and joint problem-solving in the construction and articulation of new solutions and policies for emergent collective problems.

Although one can understand law as a tool, an instrument for both enabling and confining action, it is also a system of meanings (Ewick and Silbey 1998). Rather than beginning with the notion that law exists independently and outside of the subjects it purportedly regulates (e.g. persons, workplaces, firms, and business associations), the examples we presented above of the sub-politics of regulation illustrate the practices through which agents and firms collaboratively crafted distinctive institutions (new forms of contract, new packages of safety equipment, new labor and management collaborations) and new forms of subjectivity. Moreover, the negotiations that developed between agents and firms did not merely re-inscribe moral values or economic interests that existed independently or prior to the enforcement collaboration. Neither the law nor the regulations guided agents that ran like trains on their tracks. Rather, as noted in the classic studies of routine regulatory enforcement, the agents' decisions "effectively [became] the public policies they [are empowered] to carry out" (Lipsky 1980: xii), and "the individual law enforcement officers [became] the agents of clarification and elaboration of their own authorizing mandates" (Silbey 1980–81: 850).

As an important corollary, the interests and aspirations exchanged and negotiated among agents and the firms did not exist in pristine independence of the aspirations and purposes encoded in law. The goals of any law (e.g. labor regulations and standards) are a significant part of the commonly circulating understandings of what constitutes labor or workplace safety (Gray 2002, 2009). What we expect of each other, of the state, and of business is in part shaped by law, even if those goals are not fully achieved in practice. In both its ideals and its practices (Silbey 1985), law is part of everyday social transactions without which those relations would not be decipherable or interpretable.

This pragmatic, cultural perspective on the sub-politics of regulation challenges the conception of policy as a linear aggregation of individual actions. As Dewey and Habermas suggest, the law is not the outcome of independently self-determining individuals collecting their wills for mutually self-interested ends. This pragmatic framing argues that the interests, desires, and compliant or resistant actions are mediated (produced and articulated) through legal (and non-legal) symbols, institutions, and organizations without which they are indecipherable and meaningless. This is a reciprocal and recursive process of mutual construction; neither legal regulations nor their implementation exists independently of the social relations (transactions and subjectivities) which they help to compose and in which they are embedded.

Of course, there are dangers in the kind of emergent, pragmatic, and collaborative problem-solving we have described as the pattern of Brazilian labor regulation. At its extreme, it hints at ungoverned power, lawlessness, and unlimited discretion. Recall, however, that these regulatory successes were achieved through painstaking, sometimes hostile negotiations and sometimes participatory deliberations. No one agent or group acted independently or autonomously, although the labor inspectors certainly had some authority to do so. These observations demand further inquiry, in which we and others are actively engaged.[2] For example, Pires (2009) investigated the conditions under which the same Brazilian labor inspectors use their discretion to serve, rather than to thwart, the public interest, calling attention to the possibility of "flexible bureaucracies" as organizations that reconcile accountability of bureaucratic behavior with creativity and innovation. Likewise, Coslovsky (2009) examined how Brazilian prosecutors use their discretion to enforce labor and environmental laws in a way that preserves, and in some cases even enhances, the competitiveness of offending firms. He identifies an internal ideological dispute between conservative and reformist prosecutors within the procuracy, as well as the reformists' reliance on NGOs and community groups for political backing, technical data, and logistical support, as overlooked sources of accountability that ensure that discretion will be used to advance the public good. Rodrigo Canales (2011) has followed the work of micro-credit loan officers in Mexico, documenting the ways in which greater financial stability and economic productivity are achieved when loan offices include agents who vary in their strategies, some legalistic and following the letter of the law, and others using discretion to respond to individual needs and situations. Finally, Huising and Silbey (2011) and Haines (2011) examine front-line officials operating in a variety of settings, identifying an emerging "sociological citizenship" among those who apprehend "the relational interdependence that constitutes [their] life-world" and use "this systemic perspective to meet occupational and professional obligations" (Silbey et al. 2009: 223).

In conclusion, we reiterate that this cultural, essentially pragmatic conception of the sub-politics of regulation has a rich and diverse genealogy. Studies of regulatory enforcement would clearly benefit by careful excavation and recuperation. Hirschman (1995) offered just such a pragmatic account. In contrast to conventional views of politics that assumed a shared idea of the common good as a prerequisite for policy, Hirschman argued that the common good is itself the result of a process of reconciliation among the various groups or actors touched by local problems. "Diverse groups hold together because they practice politics, not because they agree about 'fundamentals,'" (Dubiel quoted in Hirschman 1995: 238-9). According to this proposition, the meanings and practices required for compliance with the law by firms and economic actors are not some mysterious quality that precedes or soars above politics: it is the activity of politics, sub-politics, itself.

## NOTES

1. However, Lipsky (1980) also claims that front-line officials are so overwhelmed with the demands of the job that they are forced to renounce their discretion (and public spirit) and adopt coping routines. In the end, they affect policy, but not in a conscious and proactive manner – indeed, this is the "dilemma of the individual in public service."
2. See Noonan et al. (2009) for a discussion of how welfare programs can be adaptive and responsive and yet meet rule-of-law criteria.

## BIBLIOGRAPHY

Alesina, A., S. Ardagna, G. Nicoletti and F. Schiantarelli (2005), 'Regulation and investment', *Journal of the European Economic Association*, **3** (4), 791-825.
Ayres, I. and J. Braithwaite (1992), *Responsive Regulation: Transcending the Deregulation Debate*, Oxford: Oxford University Press.
Badaracco, J. (1985), *Loading the Dice: A Five-Country Study of Vinyl Chloride Regulation*, Boston, MA: Harvard Business School Press.
Baldwin, R. and J. Black (2008), 'Really responsive regulation', *Modern Law Review*, **71** (1), 59-94.
Bardach, E. and R. Kagan (1982), *Going by the Book: The Problem of Regulatory Unreasonableness*, Philadelphia, PA: Temple University Press.
Besley, T. and R. Burgess (2004), 'Can labor regulation hinder economic performance? Evidence from India', *Quarterly Journal of Economics*, **119** (1), 91-134.
Botero, J.C., S. Djankov, R. La Porta, F. Lopez-de-Silanes and A. Shleifer (2004), 'The regulation of labor', *Quarterly Journal of Economics*, **119** (4), 1339-82.
Braithwaite, J. (1985), *To Punish or Persuade: Enforcement of Coal Mine Safety*, Albany: State University of New York Press.
Braithwaite, J. (2006), 'Responsive regulation and developing economies', *World Development*, **34** (5), 884-98.

Braithwaite, J., J. Walker and P. Grabosky (1987), 'An enforcement taxonomy of regulatory agencies', *Law and Policy*, **9** (3), 323–51.

Brickman, R., S. Jasanoff and T. Ilgen (1986), *Controlling Chemicals: The Politics of Regulation in Europe and the United States*, Ithaca, NY: Cornell University Press.

Canales, R. (2011), 'Rule bending, sociological citizenship, and organizational contestation in microfinance', *Regulation & Governance*, **5** (1), 90–117.

Coslovsky, S. (2009), 'Compliance and competitiveness: how prosecutors enforce environmental and labor standards and encourage economic development in Brazil', Ph.D. dissertation, Department of Urban Studies and Planning, Massachusetts Institute of Technology, Cambridge, MA.

Davis, K.C. (1972), *Discretionary Justice*, Baton Rouge: Louisiana State University Press.

Day, P. and R. Klein (1987), 'The regulation of nursing homes: a comparative perspective', *Milbank Quarterly*, **65** (3), 303–47.

Dewey, J. (1927), *The Public and Its Problems*, New York: H. Holt.

Edelman, M. (1964), *The Symbolic Uses of Politics*, Urbana: University of Illinois Press.

Ewick, P. (1985), 'Redundant regulation: sanctioning broker-dealers', *Law and Policy*, **7** (4), 421–45.

Ewick P. and S. Silbey (1998), *The Common Place of Law: Stories From Everyday Life*, Chicago: University of Chicago Press.

Freundenburg, W.R. and R. Gramlin (1994), 'Bureaucratic slippage and failures of agency vigilance: the case of the environmental studies program', *Social Problems*, **41** (2), 214–31.

Gray, G.C. (2002), 'A socio-legal ethnography of the right to refuse dangerous work', in A. Sarat and P. Ewick (eds), *Studies in Law, Politics and Society*, **24**, 133–69.

Gray, G.C. (2009), 'The responsibilization strategy of health and safety: neo-liberalism and the reconfiguration of individual responsibility for risk', *British Journal of Criminology*, **49** (3), 326–34.

Gunningham, N., R. Kagan and J. Thornton (2003), *Shades of Green: Business, Regulation, and Environment*, Stanford, CA: Stanford University Press.

Gusfield, J. (1963), *Symbolic Crusade: Status Politics and the American Temperance Movement*, Urbana: University of Illinois Press.

Gusfield, J. (1981), *The Culture of Public Problems*, Chicago: University of Chicago Press.

Haines, F. (2011), 'Addressing the risk, reading the landscape: the role of agency in regulation', *Regulation & Governance*, **5** (1), 118–44.

Hawkins, K. (1984), *Environment and Enforcement: Regulation and the Social Definition of Enforcement*, Oxford: Clarendon Press.

Hawkins, K. (ed.) (1992), *The Uses of Discretion*, Oxford: Clarendon Press.

Hawkins, K. (2002), *Law as Last Resort: Prosecution Decision-Making in a Regulatory Agency*, Oxford: Oxford University Press.

Hawkins, K. and J. Thomas (1984), *Enforcing Regulation*, Boston, MA: Kluwer-Nijhoff Publishing.

Hirschman, A.O. (1995), *A Propensity to Self-Subversion*, Cambridge, MA: Harvard University Press.

Huising, R. and S.S. Silbey (2011), 'Governing the gap: forging safe science through relational regulation', *Regulation & Governance*, **5** (1), 14–42.

Hunter, S. and R.W. Waterman (1992), 'Determining an agency's regulatory style: how does the EPA Water Office enforce the law?', *Western Political Quarterly*, **45** (2), 401–17.

Hutter, B.M. (1989), 'Variations in regulatory enforcement styles', *Law and Policy*, **11** (2), 153–74.

Jasanoff, L. (1996), 'Beyond epistemology: relativism and engagement in the politics of science', *Social Studies of Science*, **26**, 393–418.

Kelman, S. (1981), *Regulating America, Regulating Sweden: A Comparative Study of Occupational Safety and Health Policy*, Cambridge, MA: MIT Press.

Kelman, S. (1984), 'Enforcement of occupational safety and health regulations: a comparison of Swedish and American practices', in K. Hawkins and J.M. Thomas (eds), *Enforcing Regulation*, Boston, MA: Kluwer-Nijhoff Publishing, pp. 97–120.

Kolko, G. (1965), *Railroads and Regulation, 1877–1916*, Princeton, NJ: Princeton University Press.

Lee, E. (2005), 'Why did they comply while others did not? Environmental compliance of small firms and implications for regulation', Ph.D. dissertation, Department of Urban Studies and Planning, Massachusetts Institute of Technology, Cambridge, MA.

Lipsky, M. (1980), *Street-Level Bureaucracy: Dilemmas of the Individual in Public Services*, New York: Russell Sage Foundation.

Locke, R., M. Amengual and A. Mangla (2009), 'Virtue out of necessity? Compliance, commitment and the improvement of labor conditions in global supply chains', *Politics and Society*, **37** (3), 319–51.

Marvel, H. (1977), 'Factory regulation: a reinterpretation of early English experience', *Journal of Law and Economics*, **20** (2), 379–402.

May, P.J. and R.J. Burby (1998), 'Making sense of regulatory enforcement', *Law and Policy*, **20** (2), 157–82.

May, P.J. and S. Winter (2000), 'Reconsidering styles of regulatory enforcement: patterns in Danish agro-environmental inspection', *Law and Policy*, **22** (2), 143–73.

Mendes, R. (2001), *Máquinas e acidentes de trabalho*, Brasilia: MTE/SIT, MPAS, available at: http://www.segurancaetrabalho.com.br/download/maquinas-rene_mendes.pdf (accessed 6 June 2008).

Noonan, K.G., C. Sabel and W. Simon (2009), 'Legal accountability in the service-based welfare state: lessons from child welfare reform', *Law and Social Inquiry*, **34** (3), 523–68.

Piancastelli, C. (2004), 'Projeto Prensas', paper presented at XXII ENAFIT (Encontro Nacional dos Auditores Fiscais do Trabalho).

Piore, M. (2004), 'Rethinking international labor standards', in W. Milberg (ed.), *Labor and the Globalization of Production: Causes and Consequences of Industrial Upgrading*, Houndmills: Palgrave Macmillan, pp. 249–65.

Piore, M. and A. Schrank (2006), 'Trading up: an embryonic model for easing the human costs of free markets', *Boston Review*, **31** (5), 11–14.

Pires, R. (2008), 'Promoting sustainable compliance: styles of labour inspection and compliance outcomes in Brazil', *International Labor Review*, **147** (2–3), 199–229.

Pires, R. (2009), 'Flexible bureaucracies: discretion, creativity, and accountability in labor market regulation and public sector management', Ph.D. dissertation, Department of Urban Studies and Planning, Massachusetts Institute of Technology, Cambridge, MA.

Pressman, J.L. and A.B. Wildavsky (1973), *Implementation: How Great Expectations in Washington Are Dashed in Oakland*, Berkeley: University of California Press.

Schneiberg, M. and T. Bartley (2008), 'Organizations, regulation, and economic behavior: regulatory dynamics and forms from the 19th to 21st century', *Annual Review of Law and Social Science*, **4**, 31–61.

Scholz, J. (1984), 'Cooperation, deterrence, and the ecology of regulatory enforcement', *Law and Society Review*, **18** (2), 179–94.

Scott, J.C. (1969), 'Corruption, machine politics, and political change', *American Political Science Review*, **63** (4), 1142–58.

Secult/Seplan-BA (2007), 'Relatório Impacto do Carnaval de 2007 em Salvador', Secretaria de Estado de Cultura da Bahia and Secretaria de Estado de Planejamento da Bahia.

Shover, N., J. Lynxwiler, S. Groce and D. Clelland (1984), 'Regional variation in regulatory law enforcement: the Surface Mining Control and Reclamation Act of 1977', in K. Hawkins and J.M. Thomas (eds), *Enforcing Regulation*, Boston, MA: Kluwer-Nijhoff Publishing, pp. 121–44.

Silbey, S.S. (1980–81), 'Case processing: consumer protection in an attorney general's office', *Law and Society Review*, **15** (3–4), 849–81.

Silbey, S.S. (1984), 'The consequences of responsive regulation', in K. Hawkins and J.M. Thomas (eds), *Enforcing Regulation*, Boston, MA: Kluwer-Nijhoff Publishing, pp. 147–70.

Silbey, S.S. (1985), 'Ideals and practices in the study of law', *Legal Studies Forum*, **IX** (1), 7–22.

Silbey, S.S. and E. Bittner (1982), 'The availability of law', *Law and Policy*, **4** (4), 399–434.

Silbey, S.S., R. Huising and S. Coslovsky (2009), 'The sociological citizen: recognizing relational interdependence in law and organizations', *Année Sociologique*, **52** (1), 201–29.

Sparrow, M. (2000), *The Regulatory Craft: Controlling Risks, Solving Problems, and Managing Compliance*, Washington, DC: Brookings Institution Press.

Sunstein, C.R. (1990), *After the Rights Revolution: Reconceiving the Regulatory State*, Cambridge, MA: Harvard University Press.

Tewari, M. (2006), 'Industrial upgrading and the "double-binds" of FDI policies: illustrations from India's automobile industry', draft paper.

Unger, R.M. (1975) [1981], *Knowledge and Politics*, New York: Free Press.

Vogel, D. (1986), *National Styles of Regulation: Environmental Policy in Great Britain and the United States*, Cornell Studies in Political Economy, Ithaca, NY: Cornell University Press.

Vries, G. (2007), 'What is political in sub-politics? How Aristotle might help STS', *Social Studies of Science*, **37** (5), 781–809.

Weber, M. (1946) [1917], 'Politics as a vocation', in H.H. Gerth and C. Wright Mills (eds), *From Max Weber: Essays in Sociology*, New York: Oxford University Press.

Weil, D. (2005), 'Public enforcement/private monitoring: evaluating a new approach to regulating the minimum wage', *Industrial and Labor Relations Review*, **58** (2), 238–57.

Westbrook, R. (1998), 'Pragmatism and democracy: reconstructing the logic of John Dewey's Faith', in M. Dickstein (ed.), *The Revival of Pragmatism: New Essays on Social Thought, Law and Culture*, Durham, NC: Duke University Press, pp. 128–40.

Zinn, M.D. (2002), 'Policing environmental regulatory enforcement: cooperation, capture, and citizen suits', *Stanford Environmental Law Journal*, **21** (1), 81–174.

# 24 Five models of regulatory compliance motivation: empirical findings and normative implications
## *Yuval Feldman*

In recent years, the influence of psychology on legal policy making has been on the rise (for a review see Korobkin and Ulen 2000; Bilz and Nadler 2009). Among the various aspects of psychology discussed in the interaction between psychology and the law, motivation seems to be among the most important ones, albeit not among the ones most discussed. The focus of this chapter will be on the contribution of behavioral studies to the understanding of compliance motivation (e.g. MacCoun 1993). This chapter will suggest that five distinctive assumptions of human motivation can be identified among the existing regulatory models.

After laying the ground for the differences between the models, the chapter will go on to discuss a few drawbacks to the suggested taxonomy. First, the mutual exclusivity of these models will be challenged, suggesting the complexity that the behaviorally informed legal policy maker might face. Second, as people may be motivated to comply with more than one motivation, targeting one motivation may cause an adverse effect on the other motivations. Third, by taking motivation into account when shaping regulation, the legal policy maker may be forced to speak with many voices as not everyone is motivated by the same motivation in every situation. With the limited ability to predict *ex ante* to which type of person a given regulation is targeted, the challenge of responsive regulation might prove to be especially difficult. The chapter will conclude with some preliminary suggestions for a responsive regulatory design, which would account for the different motivations, as well as for the complexities that might arise when one takes motivation into account.

## 24.1 FIVE MOTIVATION-RESPONSIVE REGULATORY APPROACHES

As stated in the introduction, the major theme of this chapter is to attempt to distinguish between the competing models of human compliance motivation and the ability to frame legislation which will be responsive to these distinctive motivations. Such a taxonomy is not new to the psycho-legal literature and is partly based on existing social influence models as well as moral reasoning models that are well recognized within social psychology (e.g. Tapp and Kohlberg 1971). The general idea of this type of scholarship is related to the perspective that, in different contexts, people process information and choose a course of action using alternative modes of conduct. An alternative perspective is that people differ in the dominant motivation that guides them, a view which gives the suggested taxonomy an obvious shift (Feldman and MacCoun 2005).

### 24.1.1   The Incentive-Driven Individual

The first regulatory approach targets the calculative or the incentive-driven individual. According to this model, the dominant motivation of the individual is based on a cost–benefit calculation; hence the approach of the regulator should focus on deterring the bad apples and providing incentives to the good apples. On many accounts, the literature that discusses this approach is the richest one, given the centrality of both deterrence and incentives within legal scholarship (see generally Zimring and Hawkings 1973; Tittle 1980).

Within the deterrence literature, much attention has been given to the question of whether deterrence really works. Many scholars have argued that perceptions of the severity and certainty of punishment have no effect on delinquent behavior (Paternoster and Iovanni 1986: 768). Many others have demonstrated empirically the limits of deterrence in explaining both self-reported and actual compliance (e.g. Braithwaite and Makkai 1991). Other scholars have suggested that deterrence does not really work, simply owing to the fact that people have little awareness of the law in the books (Robinson and Darley 2004). Therefore, according to this approach, the ineffectiveness of deterrence could be explained on the grounds of cognition rather than on the grounds of motivation.

A different methodological approach was taken by MacCoun and Reuter (2001), who used a cross-national study to demonstrate that increases or decreases in a punishment make no difference to the rate of marijuana use. In contrast, other scholars have suggested that the insensitivity to punishment is limited only to some aspects of deterrence. A common argument within this body of literature is that people are not very sensitive to the severity of a punishment, but rather to its probability of detection (Doob and Webster 2003). Other analyses which reviewed much of the literature for and against deterrence concluded that, using the right measurements, deterrence is an important policy tool (Nagin 1998).

### 24.1.2   The Reason-Driven Individual

The second regulatory approach assumes a reason-driven individual. According to this approach, the main assumption about human motivation is of an individual who looks to regulators to be convinced of the wisdom of engaging in constructive and efficient behavior while abstaining from destructive behavior. According to this informational account of the law, the legislative process aggregates information to produce a decision that is superior to the opinion of any individual legislator. As a result, if a legislative body prohibits public smoking, people might be less likely to smoke publicly because the process of enacting the legislation leads people to update their beliefs (Dharmapala and McAdams 2003).[1] Kagan et al. (2003) have taken a somewhat different view of informative functioning in an environmental context. They show how the law clarifies the boundary between activity which is harmful to the environment and activity which should be tolerated. An additional context, where the substantive focus of the policy maker was aimed toward information processing by the individual, is in the legislation of traffic laws. In this area, it is common to view informative campaigns that attempt to use scientific knowledge to increase people's response to these laws (LaTour and Zahra

1988; Tay 2005). This model also resembles Gray and Silbey's (2010) taxonomy of how regulators are being perceived in various organizations. One of the models, the regulator as an ally, primes on the perceived expertise and knowledge of regulators by the people they regulate.

### 24.1.3   The Socially-Oriented Individual

The third regulatory approach assumes that the dominant compliance motivation is related to the social identity of the individual. In that approach, most of the attention is focused on communicating to the individual the prevailing norm. Thus the effort of the policy maker would shift from communicating the wisdom of the law itself to the identity or quantity of others who engage in the law-abiding behavior.

The importance of group identity and the individual's need to belong is beyond debate in psychology (Baumeister and Leary 1995). Group identity motivation is widely recognized in the social dilemma context as a way to countervail the self-interest of the individual (Brewer and Kramer 1986; Jackson 2002). In the context of public goods, Tyran and Feld have demonstrated through experiments that people are conditional cooperators and want to engage in legal compliance when they have a reason to believe that others would do the same (Tyran and Feld 2002). Similarly, Kahan has suggested a somewhat different non-identity view as to why people would care about what others are doing. According to his approach, the individual needs to believe that other members of society share his or her commitment to the law in order to maintain his or her own commitment to society and its rules (Kahan 2001). According to this approach, the focus is neither on reputation nor on identity but rather on the fear of being the only "sucker" who obeys the law (Scholz and Lubell 1998; Biel et al. 1999).

Within this regulatory approach, a fast-growing body of literature focuses on the expressive function of the law and emphasizes the social-norms-mediated approach to legality (Sunstein 1996; Cooter 2000). McAdams's attitudinal theory of expressive law suggests that enacting law solves a pluralistic ignorance problem by signaling the underlying attitudes of a community or society. Under this approach, the main legal motivation of people is to seek the approval of others, so that the information signaled by legislation provides a guide for engaging in socially approved behavior (McAdams 2000).

It should be admitted that, while many legal economists have shared the view that the content of the prevalent social norm is crucial for the motivation to engage in legal compliance, their view of why it is important to the individual is obviously different from that of psychologists. For example, Posner (1997), returning to his famous model of signaling, discusses how such a high percentage of taxes is collected while the probability and size of sanctions are low. By paying taxes, individuals signal to their surroundings that they belong to a good type of people or the various models of using shame to increase compliance (see also Kahan and Posner 1999). Thus, while such economic approaches focus on the approval of others, many of them treat this approval in using models of reputation (hence resembling the calculative model as discussed above) rather than as an endogenous desire to belong.

### 24.1.4   The Moral-Oriented Individual

The fourth regulatory approach assumes that an individual is mainly motivated by morality and fairness. Given the assumed care for morality by the individual, the legal policy maker should design the law in a way that would emphasize its moral virtue, (i.e. potential harm to others that would be prevented by compliance) (Tapp and Levine 1970; Robinson and Darley 1997).

A concept highly related to morality is fairness, which was widely recognized as an important antecedent of human behavior that could sometimes overcome self-interest (Kahneman et al. 1986; Fehr and Schmidt 1999). Within the concept of fairness, there are a number of sub-concepts which received much attention in the literature. One of the well-known distinctions in this context is between procedural and distributive justice. Distributive justice focuses on the substance of the law – that people will comply more when they think the individual gets from the law what he or she is entitled to or that an individual gets the punishment that he or she deserves (Carlsmith et al. 2001). In this way, there is a marked similarity between the effect of morality and the effect of distributive justice on one's motivation to comply. In contrast, procedural justice focuses on how decisions are being made in terms of neutrality and voice, regardless of the content of the decision or the law. Procedural justice is one of the most studied concepts within the psycho-legal scholarship. Starting from the work of scholars such as Thibaut and Walker (1975), Lind and Tyler (1988), and Leventhal et al. (1980), a list of requirements has been suggested that needs to be satisfied for people to experience procedural justice, among them consistency, accuracy, and representativeness. Even without reference to its effect on legitimacy, the concept of procedural justice has both instrumental views and intrinsic ones. One of the leading scholars who explored the contribution of procedural justice legal compliance is Tom Tyler (1990, 1992). In his widely cited book *Why People Obey the Law*, Tyler suggests that procedural fairness, the way people are treated by authorities, is the main motivation for legal compliance (see also Tyler and Darley 2000; Sunshine and Tyler 2003). The unique contribution of morality to legal compliance was demonstrated in various legal contexts, even in areas which are usually viewed as economic ones, such as taxation (see Wenzel 2005).

### 24.1.5   Citizenship-Oriented Individual

According to the last model, the citizenship-oriented individual obeys the law simply because he or she believes that the sovereign authority is entitled to create rules and that rules need to be obeyed because this is what good citizens do regardless of the law's content (Scholz and Pinney 1995).

The main feature of legislation that needs to be responsive to this assumption of human motivation is its legitimacy. According to many accounts of legitimacy, the content of the law seems to be secondary to the perception that the law was formulated and executed with full authority. Here too, the distinction from the moral individual model might be problematic, as presumably immoral rules are unlikely to be seen as legitimate. Nonetheless, it seems that there is a genuine gap between obeying the law because it gives individuals moral commands or restraints and obeying the law because the authority is entitled to compel its citizens to do so. Indeed, within the concept of legitimacy, there are scholars who focus more on the legalistic and institutional perspectives, while others give more weight to the content of the law (Strauss 2005). Fagan and Tyler (2008) discuss the gap between the various perspectives of legitimacy, demonstrating the differences between its sociological, legal, and moral aspects.

Indeed, the ability to speak about legitimacy as a distinctive concept to the moral nature of the law's content seems to lie at the heart of the discussion of citizenship as a mutually exclusive model. Some researchers make a stronger claim for the relationship between legitimacy and values, noting that the differences between the morals and citizenship are less likely to be separated (see Tyler and Darley 2000). Given that procedural justice is seen by many as the main indicator of legitimacy, however, there is room to make the separation between the content of the law and the procedure through which it is enacted and enforced. On many accounts, when an individual is obeying the law owing to an obligation, rather than under a belief in the morality of the law, there is a greater chance that that the individual will obey the law, even when he or she does not fully agree with its content (Kelman 2001).

### 24.1.6 Mutual Dependency of the Models

The five models discussed thus far are different from each other on many counts. Some of the models focus mainly on the framing of the law, where the legal policy maker only needs to prime certain aspects that would trigger compliance but no real change in the legal policy is required (i.e. deterrence models' emphasis on enforcement and sanctioning). Nonetheless, some of the other models, for example the citizenship and to some extent the moral-related models, require that the policy maker will be perceived by the public as legitimate and hence a broader institutional change is required. Finally, some models such as the informative and the social model tend to be context specific, and the required behavior by the regulator will be more likely to focus on a specific law or a group of laws. Thus a legal policy maker who is interested in being responsive to the different compliance motivations needs to account not only for the different aspects of the law that need to be emphasized and communicated but also for a broader institutional adjustment which some of those models require. This task becomes even more complex given the wealth of empirical research that suggests cross-over between the models. Hence the question is whether the law could really react to each of these motivations without altering the efficacy of its other motivations.

One of the most intuitive demonstrations for mutual influence among the models could be seen from the inter-relationship between the informative model and the other models. For example, information expressed in the substance of the law (e.g. smoking is unhealthy) is likely to be relevant to the social model (because most people want to be healthy), as well as to the morally driven individual (secondary smoking) and the citizenship-oriented individual (the government has legitimacy to protect the health of its citizens). Furthermore, this last concept of legitimacy is in itself a concept which could be theoretically tied not only to the citizenship model but to the other models as well. According to many accounts, legitimacy is related to justice principles (Hegtvedt and Johnson 2000; Mueller and Landman 2004). On other accounts, however, legitimacy is also part of the reason-driven individual who recognizes the importance of compliance to the social order of society, regardless of the content of the law (Suchman 1995). Kelman and Hamilton (1989) have suggested a typology of compliance motivation, which relates legitimacy to different accounts depending on the situation and the individual. The first type, according to their taxonomy, is rule orientation, where fear of punishment is the main legitimizing power of the sovereignty (in our terminology, calculative). According to their second model, the rule-oriented legitimacy is related to identification with the authority (in our terminology, both social and citizenship). Lastly, the value-oriented legitimacy is related to shared morality and therefore requires examination of the moral content of the law. Similar confusion could be shown with regard to procedural justice, which is also associated with many of the models besides its obvious association with legitimacy and the moral individual, as suggested above. Furthermore, according to van den Bos et al. (2001), procedural justice is a proxy people use to evaluate the likelihood of getting positive results, thus suggesting a relevancy for the calculative individual. Other accounts suggest that procedural justice is used by people to evaluate their social role in the group, hinting toward the socially sensitive individual (Tyler and Lind 1992).

Even deterrence, which seems to be a clear regulatory tool which is supposed to interact solely with the calculative individual, was shown to interact with other models as well. Paternoster et al. (1983) showed that perceived punishment is a significant predictor of an act's perceived morality. This suggests that formal deterrence is needed to maintain the credibility of informal sanctions. Similarly, in an experimental setting, Schwartz and Orleans (1967) demonstrated in the context of tax compliance that people in the "fear-of-punishment" group were more likely to feel a moral duty to pay taxes than those in the control group.

In sum, while we demonstrated that these five motivations are separated conceptually, restricting legal intervention to one model is close to impossible. The dependency between the models and their mutual influence makes the regulatory challenges that will be discussed in section 24.2 even more intriguing.

## 24.2   IS BEHAVIORALLY-INFORMED REGULATION FEASIBLE?

The classical argument for the importance of understanding motivation in legal compliance is related to the advantage of intrinsic over extrinsic motivation. This argument suggests that, when people are motivated by intrinsic motivation, the enforcement not only is cheaper but also might lead people to behave in ways which could not be achieved by mere deterrence. In many areas where behavior beyond compliance is desirable, there is a clear advantage for the non-instrumental motivation to human behavior, especially according to the third, fourth, and fifth models (Tyler et al. 2008). This advantage seems to be the main justification for attempting to adapt to the motivation which is most likely to be dominant in any given situation. Designing a law which will be viewed as just, reasonable, or legitimate is likely to cause people to rely on their intrinsic motivation when complying with the law.[2] This classical view suffers, however, from a few problems that will be briefly addressed in this section.

First, individual differences as well as situational differences exist in the context of compliance motivation, as suggested. While it might be possible to adapt the regulation to the likely dominant motivation in any given situation, it is much harder to adapt the regulation *ex ante* to the motivations of different individuals. As long as some of the people are expected to be calculative, one could not really avoid the use of instrumental sanctions, even if its usage is more costly.

Second, there is a gap between one's own motivation and that of one's perception of the compliance of others. For example, Sanderson and Darley (2002) have shown that there is a stable gap between what people say motivates them (mostly internal factors) and what they think motivates others (the fear of punishment) (Feldman and Lobel 2010). According to our third model, that people are willing to comply if they think that others will similarly comply, the policy maker has to take into account not only what motivates the individual, but also what he or she *thinks* motivates others. In that regard, this gap creates a paradoxical situation where deterrence may need to be used not to motivate people, but rather to make them believe that others will obey, even when they themselves could have been motivated by internal factors.

These challenges might suggest that the safest regulatory approach is to focus on the common denominator that a fear of punishment is the way to avoid the need to take a specific motivation into account. The use of incentives as either the main or the sole approach might be seen as the lesser evil in comparison to the complexity and uncertainty associated with targeting the presumed motivation of the individuals we wish to regulate. While this approach is not without value and is in fact well established within the legal scholarship (the bad man of Holmes) (Holmes 1897), its costs were demonstrated in a rich and diverse theoretical and empirical literature, which will be explored in section 24.2.1.

### 24.2.1 Why Playing it Safe Might Not Work

Aside from the quality of performance, which is expected to be better according to the four non-calculative models, as discussed above, a wealth of research attacks the negative impact of punishment (Allen et al. 1981) as well as the incentives. According to the "crowding out" theory, exposing people to external motivation (either positive or negative) undermines their internal motivation (Deci 1971; Frey and Jegen 2001). Frey is one of the leading economists to explore possible psychological mechanisms underlying the destructive potential of the law on norms, marked by the crowding out of internal and non-calculative motivations that can occur when external motivation is introduced. Frey found that residents were more likely to oppose a nuclear plant in their neighborhood if they were offered compensation (Frey 1998). Fehr and Falk (2002) show that using incentives could reduce the performance of agents as well as their compliance with various rules.

The related "fine is a price" mechanism describes a phenomenon that Gneezy and Rustichini (2000) documented in the context of daycare centers that assessed fines upon parents who were late in picking up their children at the end of the day. Imposing a fine on late parents was found to be counterproductive, resulting in an increased number of late pickups. Apparently, the fine led parents to feel licensed to arrive late. In another study on the potentially disruptive effect of laws, a related theory in the context of prosocial behaviors suggests that both rewards and punishments were shown to trigger an over-justification effect, where the fact that external rewards were present was likely to cause people to question whether "true motivation" was present (Bénabou and Tirole

2006). This effect is more likely to occur when done in public rather than in private (Ariely et al. 2007[3]).

A related fear comes from the documented negative effect of regulation on trust. Falk and Kosfeld (2004) have demonstrated experimentally that, when a principal signals distrust to an agent, the agent's performance is reduced. Along those lines, Blair and Stout (2001) have demonstrated the inadvertent effect of regulation and monitoring on the behavior of the executive, which exists in current corporate law. They suggest that the mistrust signaled through harsh regulation serves as a self-fulfilling prophecy. A policy that threatens people overlooks the possibility that threatened punishment is perceived as a signal that noncompliance is widespread (DePoorter and Vanneste 2005). In this way, incentives can crowd out altruism because they eliminate the opportunity to demonstrate altruism and good will by signaling to others that few people are similarly contributing.

In sum, this short review suggests that playing it safe and focusing only on the calculative model is likely to harm, at least theoretically, the functioning of most other models reviewed thus far.

## 24.3    CONCLUSION

To address some of the concerns raised in section 24.2, this section of the chapter will propose some preliminary suggestions for a regulatory design that would be responsive to the different models of human motivation and at the same time sensitive to the specific context and the likely audience of the regulation in question. For example, when the regulated activity carries great potential for immediate harm to others, it might be the case that taking the safest approach and focusing on deterrence might be more justifiable. On the other hand, if the regulated behavior is such that the goodwill of the people is required and that their behavior beyond compliance is necessary, then the reliance on deterrence is not desirable, and greater focus should be placed on attempting to target people with the regulatory measure that supports their dominant motivation. Additional considerations that could be taken into account are enforceability of the targeted behavior. When enforcement is less costly, then the need for focusing on the other models is reduced. Furthermore, when the quality of regulated behavior is more important than ensuring that it occurs, then the harm which might arise from ignorance of the other models or even harming them, through various crowding-out mechanisms, is even more important. Finally, given the differences between individuals suggested above, preliminary analysis of attitudes of the target population could shed light on the likely effect of each of the models on the aggregated compliance behavior (Feldman 2011).

Another possible solution is the preventative approach, which shares the instrumental view of compliance motivation but is less likely to distract from other compliance motivations (Katyal 2002). Such an approach is represented by Cheng (2006), who focuses on a structural law approach whereby the policy maker makes the socially undesirable behavior more costly by design rather than by enforcement. Thus, according to such an approach, the solution to mail theft would not be to impose fines, but rather to make the boxes less accessible to unauthorized individuals. Similar tactics can be seen in the method of tax withholding rather than by deterring tax evaders, or by using technological design to prevent file sharing rather than by penalizing individuals. Thus, while this approach does not focus on enforcement, it does share in many senses the behavioral perspective that the individual is instrumental and would have violated the law if not for the costs of the violation. Furthermore, this instrumental approach might be less likely to crowd out motivations than other models.

Nevertheless, while many have argued against the effectiveness of deterrence, abandoning it as a sole regulatory tool does not imply that the assumption of the calculative individual has been abandoned. For example, under the same assumption on human motivation, various modern methods of governance have been created, such as environmental taxation (Revesz and Stavins 2004), as well as various forms of self-governance programs which do not always carry direct sanctions (King and Lenox 2000). Taxation and to a lesser extent self-regulation, while deviating from the traditional command-and-control method, still share, for the most part, the same calculative view of human motivation. Other scholars have suggested that the concept of deterrence should not be abandoned but rather revisited, taking a broader perspective accounting for various social factors and sanctions that might make deterrence more effective (Kahan 1997; McAdams 2000). In that regard, the environmental field has been an especially interesting context, where deterrence has been used in a more sophisticated way, through various regulations that force the organization to publicize its emission levels and face sanctions from the public (Pedersen 2001; Feldman and Perez 2009).

Finally, focus should be given to some of the models reviewed in this chapter which are less likely to interfere with other models and are less likely to carry with them inadvertent effects, as was demonstrated with regard to sanctions or incentives. For example, the concept of procedural justice, widely studied by scholars such as Tyler and others, is likely to increase legitimacy and compliance with less likelihood of interfering with effective functioning of deterrence. Similarly, the concept of informing people of the harm associated with their behavior might be relevant for some people without causing others to resent the law more. Nevertheless, even with those approaches, some scholars have suggested the possibility that focusing on aspects such as morality might give people the impression that the state is unable to enforce the law and therefore might have a backfire effect (Bardach 1989). Thus the legal policy maker should at best aim to find the policy which will target as many motivations as possible, while at the same time recognizing the improbability of complete success in this mission.

## ACKNOWLEDGEMENTS

Thanks to Assaf Unger, Arik Ben Simchon, Naama Holzman, Ido Novogrozki for their research assistance.

## NOTES

1. This model also targets the socially oriented individual discussed in section 24.1.3.
2. Admittedly, there is a reason to suspect that being motivated by morality is not the same intrinsic motivation as being motivated by citizenship or reason. On many accounts, such as willingness to pay, endurance,

and consistency, these models are not expected to trigger similar levels of motivation in accounting for legal motivation on most aspects.
3. Discussing the notion of image motivation, where crowding out occurs mainly in the presence of others.

# REFERENCES

Allen, H.E., P.C. Friday, J.B. Roebuck and E. Sagarin (1981), *Crime and Punishment: An Introduction to Criminology*, New York: Free Press.
Ariely, Dan, Anat Bracha and Stephan Meier (2007), 'Doing good or doing well? Image motivation and monetary incentives in behaving prosocially', *American Economic Review*, **99** (1), 544–55.
Bardach, Eugene (1989), 'Moral suasion and taxpayer compliance', *Law and Policy*, **11** (1), 49–69.
Baumeister, R.F. and M. Leary (1995), 'The need to belong: desire for interpersonal attachments as a fundamental human motivation', *Psychological Bulletin*, **117** (3), 497–529.
Bénabou, R. and J. Tirole (2006), 'Belief in a just world and redistributive politics', *Quarterly Journal of Economics*, **121** (2), 699–746.
Biel, Andres, Chris von Borgstede and Ulf Dahistrand (1999), 'Norm perception and cooperation in large scale social dilemmas', in Margaret Foddy, Michael Smitson, Sherry Schnider and Michael Hogg (eds), *Resolving Social Dilemmas*, Hove: Psychology Press, p. 245.
Bilz, Kenworthey and Janice Nadler (2009), 'Law, psychology and morality', in D. Medin, L. Skitka, C.W. Bauman and D. Bartels (eds), *Moral Cognition and Decision Making: The Psychology of Learning and Motivation*, vol. 50, San Diego, CA: Academic Press.
Blair, M.M. and L.A. Stout (2001), 'Trust, trustworthiness, and the behavioral foundations of corporate law', *University of Pennsylvania Law Review*, **149**, 1735.
Braithwaite, J. and T. Makkai (1991), 'Testing an expected utility model of corporate deterrence', *Law and Society Review*, **25**, 7–40.
Brewer, M.B. and R.M. Kramer (1986), 'Choice behavior in social dilemmas: effects of social identity, group size and decision framing', *Journal of Personality and Social Psychology*, **50**, 543–9.
Carlsmith, Kevin M., John M. Darley and Paul H. Robinson (2002), 'Why do we punish? Deterrence and just deserts as motives for punishment', *Journal of Personality and Social Psychology*, **83** (2), 284–99.
Cheng, E. (2006), 'Structural laws and the puzzle of regulating behavior', *Northwestern University Law Review*, **100** (2), 655.
Cooter, R.D. (2000), 'Three effects of social norms on law: expression, deterrence, and internalization', *Oregon Law Review*, **79** (1).
Deci, E.L. (1971), 'Effects of externally mediated rewards on intrinsic motivation', *Journal of Personality and Social Psychology*, **18**, 105.
DePoorter, Ben and Sven Vanneste (2005), 'Norms and enforcement: the case against copyright litigation', *Oregon Law Review*, **84**, 1127–57.
Dharmapala, D. and R.H. McAdams (2003), 'The Condorcet jury theorem and the expressive function of law: a theory of informative law', *American Law and Economics Review*, **5** (1), 1–31.
Doob, Anthony N. and Cheril Marie Webster (2003), 'Sentence severity and crime: accepting the null hypothesis', *Crime and Justice*, **30**, 143.
Fagan, Jeffrey and Tom R. Tyler (2008), 'Legitimacy and cooperation: why do people help the police fight crime in their communities', *Ohio State Journal of Criminal Law*, **6**, 231.
Falk, Armin and Michael Kosfeld (2004), 'Distrust – the hidden cost of control', IZA Discussion Paper No. 1203.
Fehr, Ernst and Klaus M. Schmidt (1999), 'A theory of fairness, competition, and cooperation', *Quarterly Journal of Economics*, **114** (3), 817–68.
Fehr, Ernst and Armin Falk (2002), 'Psychological foundations of incentive', IZA Discussion Paper No. 507, CESifo Working Paper Series No. 714, and Zurich IEER Working Paper No. 95.
Feldman, Yuval (2011), 'The complexity of disentangling intrinsic and extrinsic compliance motivations: theoretical and empirical insights from the behavioral analysis of law', *Washington University Journal of Law and Policy*, 9 March, symposium on 'For Love or Money'.
Feldman, Yuval and Robert J. MacCoun (2005), 'Some well-aged wines for the "new norm" bottles: implications of social psychology to law and economics', in Francesco Parisi and Vernon Smith (eds), *The Law and Economics of Irrational Behavior*, Stanford, CA: Stanford University Press.
Feldman, Yuval and Perez, Oren (2009), 'How law changes the environmental mind: an experimental study of the effect of legal norms on moral perceptions and civic enforcement', *Journal of Law and Society*, **36**, 501–35.

Feldman, Yuval and Orly Lobel (2010), 'The incentives matrix: the comparative effectiveness of rewards, liabilities, duties and protections for reporting illegality', *Texas Law Review*, **87**, 1151–1211.

Frey, Bruno S. (1998), 'Institutions and morale: the crowding-out effect', in Avner Ben-Ner and Louis Putterman (eds), *Economics, Values, and Organization*, Cambridge: Cambridge University Press.

Frey, B.S. and R. Jegen (2001), 'Motivation crowding theory: a survey of empirical evidence', *Journal of Economic Surveys*, **15** (5), 589–611.

Gneezy, Uri and Aldo Rustichini (2000), 'A fine is a price', *Journal of Legal Studies*, **29** (1).

Gray, G. and S. Silbey (2010), 'Inside the organization: the social construction of compliance', paper presented at the annual meeting of the Law and Society Association, Chicago, 27 May.

Hegtvedt, Karen A. and Cathryn Johnson (2000), 'Justice beyond the individual: a future with legitimation', *Social Psychology Quarterly*, **63**, 298–311.

Holmes, Oliver Wendell (1897), 'The path of the law', *Harvard Law Review*, **10**, 457.

Jackson, J.W. (2002), 'Reactions to social dilemmas are influenced by group identification motives', in Serge P. Shohov (ed.), *Advances in Psychology Research*, vol. 16, Hauppauge, NY: Nova Science, pp. 167–83.

Kagan, Robert A., Neil Gunningham and Dorothy Thoronton (2003), 'Explaining corporate environmental performance: how does regulation matter?', *Law and Society Review*, **37** (1), 51–90.

Kahan, Dan M. (1997), 'Response: between economics and sociology: the new path of deterrence', *Michigan Law Review*, **95**, 2477.

Kahan, Dan M. (2001), 'Trust, collective action, and law', *Boston University Law Review*, **81**, 333.

Kahan, D.M. and E.A. Posner (1999), 'Shaming white-collar criminals: a proposal for reform of the federal sentencing guidelines', *Journal of Law and Economics*, **42**, 365.

Kahneman, D., Jack L. Knetsch and Richard Thaler (1986), 'Fairness as a constraint on profit seeking: entitlements in the market', *American Economic Review*, **76** (4), 728–41.

Katyal, N.K. (2002), 'Architecture as crime control', *Yale Law Journal*, **111**, 1039.

Kelman, Herbert C. (2001), 'Reflections on social and psychological processes of legitimization and delegitimization', in J.T. Jost and B. Major (eds), *The Psychology of Legitimacy: Emerging Perspectives on Ideology, Justice, and Intergroup Relations*, New York: Cambridge University Press, pp. 54–73.

Kelman, H.C. and V.L. Hamilton (1989), *Crimes of Obedience*, New Haven, CT: Yale University Press.

King, Andrew A. and Michael J. Lenox (2000), 'Industry self-regulation without sanctions: the chemical industry's responsible care program', *Academy of Management Journal*, **43** (4), 698–716.

Korobkin, R.B. and T.S. Ulen (2000), 'Law and behavioral science: removing the rationality assumption from law and economics', *California Law Review*, **88** (4), 1051.

LaTour M. and S. Zahra (1988), 'Fear appeals as advertising strategy: should they be used', *Journal of Services Marketing*, **2**.

Leventhal, G.S., W.R. Fry and J. Karuza (1980), 'Beyond fairness: a theory of allocation preferences', in G. Mikula (ed.), *Justice and Social Interaction*, New York: Springer, pp. 176–218.

Lind, E.A. and T.R. Tyler (1988), *Social Psychology of Procedural Justice*, New York: Plenum Press.

MacCoun, R.J. (1993), 'Drugs and the law: a psychological analysis of drug prohibition', *Psychological Bulletin*, **113**, 497–512.

MacCoun, R. and P. Reuter (2001), 'Evaluating alternative cannabis regimes', *British Journal of Psychiatry*, **178**, 123–8.

McAdams, R.H. (2000), 'An attitudinal theory of expressive law', *Oregon Law Review*, **79**, 339–90.

Mueller, C.W. and M.J. Landman (2004), 'Legitimacy and justice perceptions', *Social Psychology Quarterly*, **67**, 189–202.

Nagin, Daniel S. (1998), 'Criminal deterrence research at the outset of the twenty-first century', *Crime and Justice*, **23**.

Paternoster, R. (1983), 'Perceived risk and social control: do sanctions really deter?', *Law and Society Review*, **17**, 457.

Paternoster, R. and L. Iovanni (1986), 'The deterrent effect of perceived severity: a reexamination', *Social Forces*, **64** (3), 751–77.

Paternoster, R., L. Saltzman, G. Waldo and T. Chiricos (1983), 'Perceived risk and social control: do sanctions really deter?', *Law and Society Review*, **17**, 457–80.

Pedersen, William F. (2001), 'Regulation and information disclosure: parallel universes and beyond', *Harvard Environmental Law Review*, **25**, 151–211.

Posner, E.A. (1997), 'The legal construction of norms: law and social norms: the case of tax compliance', *Virginia Law Review*, **86**, 1781–83.

Revesz, Richard L. and Robert N. Stavins (2004), 'Environmental Law and Policy', 13 September, NYU Public Law Research Paper 82, NYU Law and Economic Research Paper 04-015, Harvard Public Law Working Paper No. 102, and KSG Working Paper No. RWP04-023.

Robinson, P.H. and J.M. Darley (1997), *Justice, Liability, and Blame: Community Views and the Criminal Law*, Boulder, CO: Westview Press.

Robinson, P.H. and J.M. Darley (2004), 'Does criminal law deter? A behavioral science investigation', *Oxford Journal of Legal Studies*, **24**, 173–205.

Sanderson, C.A. and J.M. Darley (2002), 'I am moral, but you are deterred: differential attribution about why people obey the law', *Journal of Applied Social Psychology*, **32**, 375–88.

Scholz, John and Neil Pinney (1995), 'Duty, fear and tax compliance: the heuristic basis of citizenship behavior', *American Journal of Political Science*, **39**, 490.

Scholz, John and Mark Lubell (1998), 'Trust and taxpaying: testing the heuristic approach', *American Journal of Political Science*, **42**, 398.

Schwartz, R.D. and S. Orleans (1967), 'On legal sanctions', *University of Chicago Law Review*, **34**, 274.

Strauss, David A. (2005), 'Reply: legitimacy and obedience', *Harvard Law Review*, **118**, 1854.

Suchman, M.C. (1995), 'Managing legitimacy: strategic and institutional approaches', *Academy of Management Review*, **20**, 571–610.

Sunshine, Jason and Tom R. Tyler (2003), 'The role of procedural justice and legitimacy in shaping public support for policing', *Law and Society Review*, **37** (3), 513–48.

Sunstein, C. (1996), 'Law, economics and norms: on the expressive function of the law', *University of Pennsylvania Law Review*, **144**, 2021–53.

Tapp, June L. and Felice J. Levine (1970), 'Persuasion to virtue – a preliminary statement', *Law and Society Review*, **4**, 565.

Tapp, J.L. and L. Kohlberg (1971), 'Developing senses of law and legal justice', *Journal of Social Issues*, **27** (2), 65–91.

Tay, Richard (2005), 'The effectiveness of enforcement and publicity campaigns on serious crashes involving young male drivers: are drink driving and speeding similar?', *Accident Analysis and Prevention*, **37** (5), 922–9.

Thibaut, G. and L. Walker (1975), *Procedural Justice: A Psychological Analysis*, Hillsdale, NJ: Erlbaum.

Tittle, C.R. (1980), *Sanctions and Social Deviance: The Question of Deterrence*, New York: Praeger.

Tyler, T.R. (1990), *Why People Obey the Law*, New Haven, CT: Yale University Press.

Tyler, T.R. (1992), 'The psychological consequences of judicial procedures: implications for civil commitment hearings', *Southern Methodist University Law Review*, **46**, 401–13.

Tyler, T.R. and E.A. Lind (1992), 'A relational model of authority in groups', in M. Zanna (ed.), *Advances in Experimental Social Psychology*, **25** (1), 115–92.

Tyler, T.R. and J.M. Darley (2000), 'Building a law-abiding society: taking public views about morality and the legitimacy of legal authorities into account when formulating substantive law', *Hofstra Law Review*, **28**, 707.

Tyler, Tom R., John Dienhart and Terry Thomas (2008), 'The ethical commitment to compliance: building value-based culture', *California Management Review*, **50** (2), 31–51.

Tyran, J.-R. and Lars Feld (2002), 'Why people obey the law: experimental evidence from the provision of public goods', CESifo Working Paper No. 651(2), January, Centre for Economic Studies and Institute for Economic Research, Munich, pp. 1–33.

van den Bos, K., E.A. Lind and H.A.M. Wilke (2001), 'The psychology of procedural and distributive justice viewed from the perspective of fairness heuristic theory', in R. Cropanzano (ed.), *Justice in the Workplace*, vol. 2: *From Theory to Practice*, Hove: Psychology Press, pp. 49–66.

Wenzel, Michael (2005), 'Motivation or rationalisation? Causal relations between ethics, norms and tax compliance', *Journal of Economic Psychology*, **26** (4), 491–508.

Zimring, F. and G. Hawkings (1973), 'Deterrence: the legal threat in crime control', *Chicago Journal of Social Issues*, **27**, 66–91.

# 25 Between soft law and greenwash: the compliance dynamic of civil forms of environmental regulation
*Oren Perez*

Over the last few years, the environmental regulation system has undergone radical changes. Various private normative schemes, including voluntary corporate codes,[1] environmental management systems,[2] "green label" schemes,[3] environmental reporting standards,[4] green financial schemes and green indexes,[5] have taken an increasingly important role in the environmental regulatory field.[6]

One of the key questions raised by this phenomenon is the issue of efficacy. To what extent do these multiple instruments of private ordering have a meaningful social effect? This question has to be considered in the context of the recurring accusation that these "soft" instruments are nothing but a "greenwash" ploy: a façade of environmental regulation, whose only objective is to enable corporations to continue without disruption with their ecologically destructive practices (Waddock 2008: 105; Schwartz and Tilling 2009: 296).[7] The "greenwash"/private regulation conundrum reflects a broader dilemma concerning the circumstances under which firms will take environmental actions that go beyond what is prescribed by law.

The chapter begins by outlining the evolving terrain of private environmental ordering. It argues that these new forms of private governance have taken on a globalized "face" – a process that began in the mid-1990s. The chapter first discusses the unique features of this emerging field of transnational private governance, highlighting, in particular, the multiple links and cross-sensitivities between the distinct schemes, which create a novel ensemble regulatory structure. The chapter then discusses the efficacy puzzle, contrasting between different theoretical accounts of compliance. It argues that the commonly used concepts of "soft law" and "greenwash" do not capture the complex social dynamic underlying these new forms of governance and that it is wrong to dismiss these instruments as "cheap talk." The chapter concludes with a brief exploration of the future of private regulation in the global sphere.

## 25.1 ENVIRONMENTAL "PRIVATE ORDERING" AS A GLOBALIZED, INTERTWINED PROCESS

The emergence of private environmental schemes with global reach is a relatively new phenomenon. From the beginning of the 1980s to the mid-1990s the field of private governance was highly fragmented, consisting of segregated contractual arrangements and uncoordinated organizational routines. However, since the mid-1990s the nature of the field has changed: new centers of global governance have emerged, transforming the field into a much more ordered domain. This change influenced all the facets of the governance game – from the norm-production process to implementation and enforcement. As

I will demonstrate below, a unique feature of this emerging field of private governance is the multiple links and cross-sensitivities between the distinct regimes, forming what I call an ensemble regulatory structure. By ensemble regulation I refer to a collection of autonomous regulatory schemes that form a regulatory network, clustering around a common core of basic principles, and exhibiting positive enforcement and normative externalities. There are, in other words, positive complementarities among the ensemble's sub-systems with respect both to their impact on firms' behavior and their underlying normative commitments.

It is beyond the scope of this chapter to give a detailed historical account of this transformative process. The following three examples are therefore illustrative and non-exhaustive. Consider first the global market for environmental management systems (EMS), which is dominated today by the ISO 14001 environmental management system.[8] ISO 14001 is a set of procedures and organizational practices which are used to assist an organization in achieving its environmental goals through a process of continual improvement. The standard gives the organization the freedom to choose between self-certification and third-party certification and evaluation. Nonetheless, one of the unique features of the ISO 14000 series is the comprehensive system of third-party certification and auditing that evolved around it. This private enforcement system draws on the institutional support of the International Organization for Standardization, and the national standards institutions affiliated with it, and is perceived – despite various limitations – as relatively trustworthy and efficient (Potoski and Prakash 2005).

Before the publication of ISO 14001, countries employed numerous and often conflicting sets of environmental management programs (Melnyk et al. 2003: 330). ISO 14001 has however quickly positioned itself as the most prominent global EMS standard (Albuquerque et al. 2007). The standard has received strong support from large multinational enterprises (MNEs), especially in environmentally conscious countries (Nishitani 2010). Up to the end of December 2008, 188815 certificates had been issued in 155 countries, reflecting a steady year-to-year increase (ISO 2009: 12; Perkins and Neumayer 2010). The adoption of ISO 14001 as the EMS of the EU EMAS scheme is another reflection of its global success.[9]

Another example of the globalization of private environmental standards is the field of sustainability reporting, which has undergone a similar transformation from fragmented self-regulation to centralized global governance. Firms, especially MNEs, have been publishing non-financial information since the 1980s. However, these social–environmental reports varied greatly in their style and form (Maltby 1997; UNCTAD 2003, paras 34, 38; Waddock 2008: 93). While there was a process of convergence and reciprocal learning between firms (Tile 2001), there was no central coordination.

The disordered landscape of the 1990s was transformed over the last ten years into a much more ordered domain, with the emergence of global private codes that set out clear rules for sustainability reporting and external assurance. The most important code is the set of reporting standards produced by the Global Reporting Initiative (GRI). The GRI published its first set of guidelines for sustainability reporting in 2002; the last version was published in 2006.[10] The objective of the GRI Guidelines is to provide a "trusted and credible framework for sustainability reporting that can be used by organizations of any size, sector, or location" and could facilitate open dialogue about sustainability using a "globally shared framework of concepts, consistent language, and metrics."[11] The 2006

Guidelines require organizations to provide information on the economic, environmental and social aspects of their activities.[12] This choice is supported by the idea that "*achieving sustainability* requires balancing the complex relationships between current economic, environmental, and social needs in a manner that does not compromise future needs" (emphasis added).[13] The GRI Guidelines dominate the global market of sustainability reporting, having a particularly strong influence over the disclosure practices of MNEs (KPMG 2008).[14]

This process of global convergence was supported by two intertwined processes. First, there was the incorporation of disclosure requirements in other private corporate social responsibility (CSR) instruments. Thus, for example, ISO 14001, the EU EMAS scheme and Responsible Care include extensive disclosure requirements. Disclosure requirements also form part of the ranking criteria used by FTSE4Good and the Dow Jones Sustainability Index (DJSI).[15] The 2006 Equator Principles require each subscribing institution to publish an annual report elaborating on the way it has implemented the principles (principle 10).

Governmental intervention has provided a second line of support. National securities regulators have recognized that the disclosure requirements of securities laws require more extensive disclosure of environmental data, owing to the recognition that environmental data is necessary to a proper assessment of firms' economic situation.[16] Mandatory environmental disclosure programs, such as the US Toxics Release Inventory (TRI) program, the European Pollution Emissions Register (EPER) and the Canadian National Pollutant Release Inventory (NPRI) provided another source of support, by further extending firms' disclosure obligations.[17] The GRI scheme goes, however, beyond the requirements of these two types of state-sponsored disclosure programs, by extending the disclosure requirements to ethical and labor issues, by expanding the scope and scale of the ecological data that must be disclosed and by not basing the disclosure requirement on an economically defined notion of materiality.

The GRI Guidelines offer two complementary compliance mechanisms (GRI 2006: 1–4). First, the GRI secretariat offers to check the reporter self-declaration of its reporting. A second alternative is to have the report reviewed by a third party. The growth of the market of sustainability reporting has also generated demand for independent external assurance (Simnett et al. 2009). Two prominent global codes that seek to regulate the emerging field of external assurance are the International Standard on Assurance Engagements (ISAE 3000) promulgated by the International Auditing and Assurance Standards Board[18] and AccountAbility AA1000 Assurance Standard.[19] The GRI Guidelines also include various references to other external standards.[20]

A third example of private ordering "going global" is the field of sustainability indexes. These indexes should be considered in the broader context of the new ethical investment movement. Ethical investment is the "process of identifying and investing in companies that meet certain baseline standards or criteria of Corporate Social Responsibility" (Social Investment Forum 2006: 2). From a legal perspective, ethical investment represents a form of private rule-making, in which private investors contract with financial institutions to invest on their behalf, subject to certain investment rules that are designed by the financial institution. It is thus a process of both *self-regulation* and *standard contracting*. This process has evolved in a highly fragmented environment (EU Commission 2001: 22), with each financial institution devising its own set of investment criteria, sometimes relying on external consultancies. This disordered picture has changed with the evolution of new centers of governance. I will focus here on the role of sustainability indexes in this new emerging field of governance.[21]

The primary providers of sustainability indexes are the Dow Jones indexes and the FTSE Group, the world leaders in the stock index market.[22] The Dow Jones Sustainability Indexes track the financial performance of the leading sustainability-driven companies worldwide. The first index in this "family" – the Dow Jones Sustainability World Index (DJSI World) – covers the top 10 percent of the leading sustainability companies out of the biggest 2500 companies in the Dow Jones Global Total Stock Market Index. Since the launch of the DJSI World in 1999, other indexes have been added to the series.[23] The FTSE4Good Index Series was launched in July 2001. It was designed to "measure the performance of companies that meet globally recognised corporate responsibility standards, and to facilitate investment in those companies."[24] The Dow Jones and FTSE indexes focus on positive criteria to select companies, although both also employ certain negative criteria (excluding certain industries, such as tobacco producers and companies manufacturing whole weapons systems).[25]

The Dow Jones Sustainability Indexes and the FTSE4Good Indexes influence the corporate world in several different ways.[26] First, the methodologies used by the two index families to select and rank companies and their ultimate selections constitute a normative benchmark for the whole ethical investment market. Second, the ranking and the continuous engagement of the index teams with participant firms influence firms' behavior. Finally, the normative benchmark developed by the indexes influences the thematic horizon of CSR discourse as a whole.[27]

The ranking criteria used by both indexes include various references to other global codes. Thus, for example, both indexes refer to EMS and environmental disclosure in their ranking criteria. The FTSE4Good Inclusion Criteria state, for example, that high-impact companies with ISO certification and EMAS registrations are considered to meet several core indicators, which are required from such companies (FTSE 2006: 3). High-impact companies are also required to publish an environmental report, which needs to be sufficiently detailed (FTSE 2006: 3). The Dow Jones ranking process, as reflected in the corporate sustainability assessment questionnaire which is sent to firms as part of the ranking process, similarly emphasizes the existence of a certified EMS requirement and the firm's commitment to environmental (and social) reporting.[28]

Table 25.1 captures the global convergence process depicted above.

## 25.2 PRIVATE ENVIRONMENTAL GOVERNANCE: GREENWASH OR ALTERNATIVE REGULATION

I argued above that the over-used notions of "soft law" and "greenwash" do not capture the complex social dynamic generated by the new universe of private environmental governance. The debate about the effectiveness of these private schemes is informed by two key conceptual contrasts: the distinction between the logics of "consequences" and "appropriateness" (March and Olsen 1998, 2004) and the contrast between individualism and institutionalism (Ghoshal 2005: 85; Rocha and Ghoshal 2006).

The foregoing distinct theoretical positions lead to different hypotheses regarding

*Table 25.1    The universe of global private environmental ordering (partial picture)*

| Field | Past governance structure | Current governance structure: global code | Level of specificity | Responsible organization | Compliance mechanisms |
|---|---|---|---|---|---|
| Environmental management | Uncoordinated, organizational management schemes | ISO 14001, Responsible Care | High | International Organization for Standardization, International Council of Chemical Associations (ICCA), | Private external verification (relatively robust in the case of ISO 14001) |
| Environmental impact assessment in the private financial sector | Uncoordinated, organizational risk-assessment schemes | Equator Principles[1] | High | Joint governance by participating banks | Voluntary reporting mechanism (http://www.equator-principles.com/reporting.shtml) |
| Sustainability reporting | Uncoordinated, organizational disclosure formats | GRI Guidelines | High | Global reporting initiative | GRI (documents check), private external assurance (drawing on global codes) |
| Assurance practices | None | ISAE 3000, AA1000 Assurance Standard | High | the International Auditing and Assurance Standards Board; AccountAbility | None |
| Sustainability indexes | None | FTSE4-Good, DJSI | High | FTSE, Dow Jones | Private compliance governed by FTSE and Dow Jones and drawing on external consultants (Eiris and SAM) |
| Green labels: sustainable forests | None | Forest Stewardship Council global label[2] | High | Forest Stewardship Council | Independent certification bodies accredited by the Forest Stewardship Council |

*Notes:*
1. There are close links between the Equator Principles and the GRI Financial Services Sector Supplement (see, e.g., FS2, Procedures for assessing and screening environmental and social risks in business lines).
2. There is some competition between ISO 14001 and the FSC rules; see Stringer (2006).

the potential impact of soft regulation. Weaving together the individualist perspective and the assumption that the logic of "consequences" dominates the corporate order (the "economic optimizer" model) leads to a highly skeptical view of the capacity of soft law instruments to trigger substantial behavioral impacts.[29] First, it is assumed that firms will not be willing to bear the costs of joining some voluntary scheme unless these initial costs can be economically justified (e.g., by prospective efficiency or reputational gains). Second, joining a voluntary program does not in itself guarantee that the firm will comply with its provisions. If a firm can benefit, for example, from the reputation associated with ISO 14001 certification or inclusion in FTSE4Good or DJSI without making any real changes to its behavior it will (presumably) take this option. The question whether firms will follow this path depends solely on the strength of the enforcement framework associated with these private regimes, i.e., it can be answered solely through a calculus of (economic) "incentives." Economists thus distinguish between economically justified CSR – strategic CSR – and altruistic CSR, which requires firms to forgo profits (Lyon and Maxwell 2008: 241; Reinhardt et al. 2008: 219). From the perspective of agency cost theory, altruistic CSR is viewed as a case of corporate governance failure, generated by the ability of under-monitored managers to use corporate resources to advance their ideological agenda.[30]

The economic optimizer model does not deny, though, the possibility that some voluntary codes will yield beyond-compliance actions. However, such result must be grounded in economic calculation. Thus, for example, Potoski and Prakash's "green club" model suggests that firms may certify to ISO 14001 because of the standard's contribution to firms' reputations. Because the ISO 14001 scheme is associated with a relatively effective system of external verification, firms cannot capture the standard's reputational benefits without making real effort to implement the standard (Prakash and Potoski 2006).

Stakeholder theory offers another explanation for the possible efficacy of soft law instruments, by highlighting the way in which external stakeholders may influence the firm's internal dynamic. Gunningham et al. argue in this context that firms operate under "multifaceted 'license to operate,'" reflecting the multiple claims (economic, social and legal) they have to deal with (Gunningham et al. 2004: 329). The adoption and implementation of soft law obligations constitute a rational response (economic-wise) to these pressures (Donaldson and Preston 1995: 75; Gunningham et al. 2004: 326–8).[31]

In contrast to the foregoing models the institutionalist and pluralistic-self schools take a more nuanced approach to the question of the potential effect of soft law instruments, postulating further paths through which they can influence the corporate dynamic. I want to highlight in this context two ideas: first, an alternative model of the firm – the *polyphonic model* – and second the unique *ensemble structure* of the global private regulatory order.

The polyphonic model conceptualizes the firm as a dynamic, self-organized decisions-processing system, which can accommodate multiple logics.[32] The calculative logic of profit maximization, while important, constitutes only one of these co-occurring logics. One of the key issues highlighted by the polyphonic model is the reciprocal interaction between the firm's structure and culture and the attitudes and beliefs of the employees. The firm is depicted as an autonomous social system that interacts with the workers in a reciprocal process of structural coupling. In this context the polyphonic model draws on a pluralistic concept of the self which takes into account the possibility that managers, employees and shareholders may be driven by a complex set of motives (Ghoshal 2005; Perez 2008: 157–62; Richardson 2008: 180–85).

The polyphonic model provides a more open-ended framework for thinking about the reasons causing firms to adopt voluntary schemes and the impact of such schemes on firms' behavior and internal structure. In particular, the model seeks to unfold the institutional dynamic generated by the adoption of voluntary schemes. By introducing new routines into the organization, standards such as ISO 14001, the Equator Principles or the GRI Sustainability Reporting Guidelines can change the firm's internal dynamic, moving it into a new equilibrium trajectory, which enmeshes together environmental and economic goals and reflects greater organizational sensitivity to ecological concerns. The various routines underlying the ISO 14001 EMS, for example, ensure that environmental concerns will receive a stronger presence in the firm's decision-making process, allowing for the discursive expression of motivations and ideas that may have been suppressed under the previous regime (Perez et al. 2009). New routines for selecting, ordering and processing information change the organization's cognitive horizon, enabling the generation of environmentally related data which would not have been available to the organization beforehand.

Another important process highlighted by the polyphonic model is the potential virtuous cycle that the adoption of voluntary schemes such as ISO 14001 can generate between the new organizational reality and the motivations and beliefs of the employees.[33] There is in this context a potential amplifying feedback between the organizational and individual levels, in which the transformation of the institutional culture facilitates changes at the psychic level (e.g., in terms of environmental commitment and loyalty to the organization), which in turn supports the institutional changes instigated by the voluntary standard (e.g., by increasing the employees' willingness to invoke the new conceptual apparatus introduced by the standard and to implement its routines).

This virtuous cycle between the organizational and individual levels can unleash economic resources which were not available in the previous organizational setting, both by affecting the employees' internally driven willingness to engage in pro-environmental behaviors and by increasing employees' commitment to the organization.[34] These two processes explain the capacity of voluntary green standards to effectuate enduring changes within firms and also provide additional explanation for the ability of firms to bear the costs of certification (e.g., ISO 14001) without sacrificing profits. The endorsement of private green schemes can thus form an important part in the creation of a corporate culture that draws on social norms, rather than relying exclusively on economic incentives (Ariely 2008: 80–83; Perez et al. 2009: 597–601).

Adopting an institutionally sensitive frame of observation also highlights the importance of the broader institutional setting in which distinct CSR instruments operate. In particular it calls our attention to the way in which the ensemble structure of the new global private order intervenes in the processes that take place within "CSR" firms. First, the cross-linkages between the different standards create a system of positive enforcement externalities, in which the compliance mechanisms of each regime also serve as an enforcement agent of the other regimes in the network, generating an amplified compliance effect. The consequence of this effect is that firms entering into the world of CSR will find it increasingly difficult to reap the reputational gains associated with voluntary CSR codes without undertaking real organizational efforts.[35] Once a firm starts publishing environmental reports drawing on the GRI Guidelines, adopts a certified EMS (ISO 14001 or Responsible Care) and enters the reputable list of either FTSE4Good or DJSI, it becomes increasingly difficult for it to renege on its multi-dimensional promises.

But the ensemble structure of this new private order has another more subtle effect. There is a positive feedback between the multi-focal invocation of the idea of sustainability across the ensemble, the normative standing of the idea as a moral-political principle and the moral legitimacy of the ensemble and each of its constituent regimes. The mutual engagement with the concept of sustainability through the distinct regime-spaces and the normative cross-reference it facilitates are thus a source of positive normative externality.

Which of these alternative accounts of the social dynamic underlying the world of private environmental governance is more accurate? Unfortunately the current empirical literature does not provide a conclusive answer to this question. There are good indications within the literature that some of these soft legal instruments succeed in effectuating social change. Thus, for example, various studies have documented the positive effect of ISO 14001 on firms' environmental commitment and ecological footprint (Prakash and Potoski 2006; Perez et al. 2009; Chatterji and Toffel 2010). Other studies have pointed, although more tentatively, to the positive influence of sustainability indexes on firms' CSR profile (Slager 2009; Chatterji and Toffel 2010). However, the exact causal dynamic underlying these success stories remains unclear; unfolding it faces difficult methodological challenges (Borck et al. 2008). There are relatively few studies that attempt to unfold the internal institutional dynamic of firms that adopt voluntary codes (Perez et al. 2009; Slager 2009). It is also clear that the social impact of different programs may be dissimilar, thus calling for contextual research and differentiated policy reactions (Borck and Coglianese 2009). One of the key challenges for future research lies in the development of better understanding of the internal dynamic of organizations, as they react to private environmental programs, drawing on multi-dimensional research techniques (Fine and Elsbach 2000; Hancke 2009).

## 25.3   CONCLUSIONS

The new universe of private environmental governance has created an intricate network of governance, which not only is intensely inter-connected but also interacts with the public regulatory system in various ways. Public regulators are drawing on private standards not only as sources of inspiration but also as alternative forms of governance. It is tempting, in the aftermath of the 2009 financial crisis, to dismiss this universe of private governance as irrelevant and non-credible. This would be a mistake, I believe, first, because it disregards the positive enforcement and normative externalities generated by the ensemble structure of this field of governance and, second, because it underestimates the virtuous, reciprocal dynamic that the adoption of voluntary codes may instill in the firms adopting them.

The expansion of private regulation over the last decade represents a robust social process, which is likely to further expand in the next decade. The ISO CSR standard (ISO 26000)[36] and the DuPont and Environmental Defense framework for the responsible development, production, use and disposal of nano-scale materials[37] are just two examples of new possible entrants into this network. In parallel, existing schemes, such as ISO 14001 and GRI, are constantly expanding. While this chapter has argued that it is a mistake to dismiss these soft legal instruments as cheap talk, highlighting their steering capacity, it should also be noted that these instruments remain constrained by the current capitalist order. These intertwined schemes can deliver incremental changes, supplementing governmental intervention. Any radical changes to the way in which corporations manage the environmental aspects of their behavior will require global, coordinated political action that will challenge the current political-economic order – rethinking the place of nature within the global social order.

## NOTES

1. E.g., OECD Guidelines of Multinational Enterprises, the International Chamber of Commerce Business Charter for Sustainable Development.
2. E.g., ISO 14001, the EU EMAS scheme and the Responsible Care program.
3. E.g., the Forest Stewardship Council certification scheme, the US Energy Star program.
4. E.g., the Global Reporting Initiative Sustainability Reporting Guidelines (GRI), the AA1000 Assurance Standard.
5. Green financial schemes include codes regulating lending practices and "ethical" investment standards. Green indexes include, e.g., the Dow Jones Sustainability Indexes and FTSE4Good series.
6. Some of the foregoing instruments, such as the GRI, also cover non-environmental issues. There are similar instruments covering other aspects of the corporate responsibility issue, such as the SA8000 standard, dealing with human rights of workers (http://www.sa-intl.org/).
7. For a definition of greenwash see CorpWatch, 'Greenwash Fact Sheet', 22 March 2001, available at: http://www.corpwatch.org/article.php?id=242, and Lyon and Maxwell (2007).
8. ISO 14001 was released in 1996 (and revised in 2004); ISO 14001 (2004): Environmental management systems – requirements with guidance for use. Further guidelines regarding the implementation of the ISO 14001 EMS are included in ISO 14004 (2004): Environmental management systems – general guidelines on principles, systems and support techniques.
9. See http://ec.europa.eu/environment/emas/index_en.htm.
10. GRI, *Sustainability Reporting Guidelines* (Amsterdam: Global Reporting Initiative, 2002); GRI, *RG – Sustainability Reporting Guidelines* (Amsterdam: Global Reporting Initiative, 2006). In the following discussion I will refer to the 2006 text.
11. Ibid.
12. 2006 Guidelines, at 8, 25–34; 2002 Guidelines, at 9, 34.
13. 2002 Guidelines, at 9; see also 2006 Guidelines, at 8.
14. For a comprehensive list of firms using the GRI Guidelines see http://www.globalreporting.org/GRIReports/GRIReportsList/.
15. The FTSE4Good Inclusion Criteria require high-impact companies to publish an environmental report (FTSE 2006: 3). The DJSI Corporate Sustainability Assessment Criteria also include a requirement of environmental (and social) reporting (see http://www.sustainability-index.com/07_htmle/assessment/criteria.html).
16. See, e.g., *EPA Enforcement Alert*, **4** (3) October 2001, available at: www.epa.gov/compliance/resources/newsletters/civil/enfalert; and Perez (2006).
17. See respectively http://www.epa.gov/tri/, http://eper.eea.eu.int/eper/ and www.ec.gc.ca/pdb/npri; UNEP et al. (2003: 110–12); and Brehm and Hamilton (1996: 445). Several European countries have taken a more radical step, adopting regulations requiring large or state-owned companies to publish sustainability reports; see, e.g., the Danish initiative, available at: http://www.eogs.dk/graphics/Samfundsansvar.dk/Dokumenter/Proposal_Report_On_Social_Resp.pdf, and the Swedish initiative, available at: http://www.sweden.gov.se/content/1/c6/09/41/25/56b7ebd4.pdf.
18. See http: http://www.accountability21.net/uploadedFiles/Issues/ISAE_3000.pdf and http://www.ifac.org/IAASB/.
19. See www.accountability.org.uk.
20. Thus, for example, the guidelines require organizations to list all the external economic, environmental

and social codes to which the organization subscribes or that it endorses, including any environment-related performance or certification system (GRI 2006: 23, 27).

21. Other sources of governance are transnational networks involving different stakeholders, UNEP new Principles for Responsible Investment, and public regulation. See further Perez (2008).

22. Some other noteworthy social–environmental indexes are the FTSE KLD 400 Social Index (formerly known as the Domini Index), the Vigeo Index series, the Australian SAM Sustainability Index (AuSSI), the Canadian the Jantzi Social Index, and the Calvert Social Index; see http://www.kld.com/indexes/ds400index/index.html, http://www.vigeo.com/csr-rating-agency/index.php?lang=en, http://www.aussi.net.au/, http://www.jantzisocialindex.com, http://www.calvertgroup.com/sri-index.html. Other related players are ranking initiatives, such as CRO's 100 Best Corporate Citizens (http://www.thecro.com), Global 100: The Definitive Corporate Sustainability Benchmark (http://www.global100.org/) and Business in the Community Corporate Responsibility Index (http://www.bitc.org.uk/). I think that the fact that the FTSE4Good and DJSI are not just ranking exercises, but actually act as a focal source for financial decisions, makes them more influential. Also, the institutional structure in which they are embedded is much more developed.

23. For the full list see http://www.sustainability-index.com/07_htmle/indexes/overview.html.

24. See http://www.ftse.com/Indices/FTSE4Good_Index_Series/index.jsp. The FTSE4Good Index Series encompasses four tradable and five benchmark indices, representing Global, European, US, Japan (benchmark only) and UK markets. The FTSE group launched two additional indexes: FTSE4Good Environmental Leaders Europe 40 Index and FTSE4Good IBEX Index.

25. For a detailed description of the selection methodologies of both index families see FTSE (2006); Dow Jones (2010).

26. The social impact of sustainability indexes has not been studied extensively so far, so the following claims should be seen as plausible hypotheses, calling for further empirical research.

27. A good example of this phenomenon is inclusion of new climate change criteria in the FTSE4Good criteria in 2007.

28. See SAM Research Corporate Sustainability Assessment Questionnaire (2009), paras 38–41.

29. For studies using the economic viewpoint see Kollman and Prakash (2002: 48), Coglianese and Lazer (2003: 707) and Prakash and Potoski (2006: 41, 79).

30. From this perspective, altruistic CSR is no different from the "greed capitalism" which characterized the 2009 financial crisis; the solutions are also similar: the adoption of organizational or incentive-based mechanisms, ensuring that the incentives of the firm's managers and shareholders are aligned (Bebchuk and Spamann 2009; Stiglitz 2009).

31. Stakeholder theory has also a normative facet, which argues – contra to the agency cost model – that managers ought to pursue the interests of multiple stakeholders, not just those of the shareholders (Donaldson 1999: 238).

32. The model draws on Niklas Luhmann's communication-based theory of social systems (Luhmann 1995) and on Richard Nelson's concept of "social technologies" (Nelson 1991; Nelson and Sampat 2001). For further elaboration of this model, and application in the context of ISO 14001, see Perez et al. (2009).

33. This idea is mentioned by other CSR scholars (Portney 2008: 264, 266; Reinhardt et al. 2008: 226). However, these authors do not offer a detailed socio-psychological model that can explain the mechanics of this virtuous cycle.

34. For empirical analysis supporting this claim see Perez et al. (2009).

35. This cross-regime effect is neglected by some authors; see, e.g., Schwartz and Tilling (2009: 296).

36. See http://www.iisd.org/standards/csr.asp.

37. See http://www.edf.org/article.cfm?contentID=4821.

# REFERENCES

Albuquerque, Paulo, Bart J. Bronnenberg and Charles J. Corbett (2007), 'A spatiotemporal analysis of the global diffusion of ISO 9000 and ISO 14000 certification', *Management Science*, **53** (3), 451–68.

Ariely, Dan (2008), *Predictably Irrational: The Hidden Forces That Shape Our Decisions*, London: HarperCollins.

Bebchuk, Lucian A. and Holger Spamann (2009), 'Regulating bankers' pay', *Georgetown Law Journal*, **98** (2), 247–87.

Borck, Jonathan C. and Cary Coglianese (2009), 'Voluntary environmental programs: assessing their effectiveness', *Annual Review of Environment and Resources*, **34**, 305–24.

Borck, Jonathan C., Cary Coglianese and Jennifer Nash (2008), 'Evaluating the social effects of environmental leadership programs', *Environmental Law Reporter*, **38**, 10697.

Brehm, J. and J.T. Hamilton (1996), 'Noncompliance in environmental reporting: are violators ignorant, or evasive, of the law?', *American Journal of Political Science*, **40** (2), 444–77.

Chatterji, Aaron K. and Michael W. Toffel (2010), 'How firms respond to being rated', *Strategic Management Journal*, **31** (9), 917–45.

Coglianese, Cary and David Lazer (2003), 'Management-based regulation: prescribing private management to achieve public goals', *Law and Society Review*, **37**, 691–730.

Donaldson, Thomas (1999), 'Making stakeholder theory whole', *Academy of Management Review*, **24** (2), 237.

Donaldson, Thomas and Lee E. Preston (1995), 'The stakeholder theory of the corporation: concepts, evidence', *Academy of Management Review*, **20** (1), 65.

Dow Jones (2010), *Dow Jones Sustainability World Index Guide Book: Version 11.4*, November, New York: Dow Jones Sustainability Indexes.

EU-Commission (2001), Green paper on promoting a European framework for corporate social responsibility.

Fine, Gary Alan and Kimberly D. Elsbach (2000), 'Ethnography and experiment in social psychological theory building: tactics for integrating qualitative field data with quantitative lab data', *Journal of Experimental Social Psychology*, **36** (1), 51–76.

FTSE (2006), *FTSE4Good Index Series Inclusion Criteria*, London: FTSE the Index Company.

Ghoshal, Sumantra (2005), 'Bad management theories are destroying good management practices', *Academy of Management Learning and Education*, **4** (1), 75–91.

GRI (2006), *Sustainability Reporting Guidelines – G3*, Amsterdam: Global Reporting Initiative.

Gunningham, Neil, Robert A. Kagan and Dorothy Thornton (2004), 'Social license and environmental protection: why businesses go beyond compliance', *Law and Social Inquiry*, **29** (2), 307.

Hancke, Bob (2009), *Intelligent Research Design: A Guide for Beginning Researchers in the Social Sciences*, Oxford: Oxford University Press.

ISO (2009), The ISO Survey – 2008.

Kollman, Kelly and Aseem Prakash (2002), 'EMS-based environmental regimes as club goods: examining variations in firm-level adoption of ISO 14001 and EMAS in U.K., U.S. and Germany', *Policy Sciences*, **35**, 43–67.

KPMG (2008), *KPMG International Survey of Corporate Responsibility Reporting 2008*, Amsterdam: KPMG International.

Luhmann, Niklas (1995), *Social Systems*, Stanford, CA: Stanford University Press.

Lyon, Thomas P. and John W. Maxwell (2007), 'Greenwash: corporate environmental disclosure under threat of audit', Indiana University, Kelley School of Business Working Paper, 23 May.

Lyon, Thomas P. and John W. Maxwell (2008), 'Corporate social responsibility and the environment: a theoretical perspective', *Review of Environmental Economics and Policy*, **2** (2), 240–60.

Maltby, Josephine (1997), 'Setting its own standards and meeting those standards: voluntarism versus regulation in environmental reporting', *Business Strategy and the Environment*, **6**, 83–92.

March, James G. and Johan P. Olsen (1998), 'The institutional dynamics of international political orders', *International Organization*, **52**, 943–69.

March, James G. and Johan P. Olsen (2004), 'The logic of appropriateness', ARENA Working Papers WP 04/09.

Melnyk, S.A., R.P. Sroufe and R. Calantone (2003), 'Assessing the impact of environmental management systems on corporate and environmental performance', *Journal of Operations Management*, **21**, 329–51.

Nelson, Richard R. (1991), 'Why do firms differ, and how does it matter?', *Strategic Management Journal*, **12**, 61.

Nelson, Richard R. and Bhaven N. Sampat (2001), 'Making sense of institutions as a factor shaping economic performance', *Journal of Economic Behavior and Organization*, **44**, 31–54.

Nishitani, Kimitaka (2010), 'Demand for ISO 14001 adoption in the global supply chain: an empirical analysis focusing on environmentally conscious markets', *Resource and Energy Economics*, **32** (3), 395–407.

Perez, Oren (2006), 'Facing the global hydra: ecological transformation at the global financial frontier: the ambitious case of the Global Reporting Initiative', in C. Joerges and E.-U. Petersmann (eds), *Constitutionalism, Multilevel Trade Governance and Social Regulation*, Oxford: Hart.

Perez, Oren (2008), 'The new universe of green finance: from self-governance to multi-polar governance', in O. Dilling, M. Herberg and G. Winter (eds), *Responsible Business: Self-Governance in Transnational Economic Transactions*, Oxford: Hart.

Perez, Oren, Yair Amichai-Hamburger and Tammy Shterental (2009), 'The dynamic of corporate self-regulation: ISO 14001, environmental commitment, and organizational citizenship behavior', *Law and Society Review*, **43** (3), 593–630.

Perkins, Richard and Eric Neumayer (2010), 'Geographic variations in the early diffusion of corporate voluntary standards: comparing ISO 14001 and the global compact', *Environment and Planning A*, **42** (2), 347–65.

Portney, Paul R. (2008), 'The (not so) new corporate social responsibility: an empirical perspective', *Review of Environmental Economics and Policy*, **2** (2), 261–75.

Potoski, Matthew and Aseem Prakash (2005), 'Covenants with weak swords: ISO 14001 and facilities' environmental performance', *Journal of Policy Analysis and Management*, **24** (4), 745–69.

Prakash, Aseem and Matthew Potoski (2006), *The Voluntary Environmentalists: Green Clubs, ISO 14001, and Voluntary Environmental Regulations*, Cambridge: Cambridge University Press.

Reinhardt, Forest L., Robert N. Stavins and Richard H.K. Vietor (2008), 'Corporate social responsibility through an economic lens', *Review of Environmental Economics and Policy*, **2** (2), 219–39.

Richardson, Benjamin J. (2008), *Socially Responsible Investment Law: Regulating the Unseen Polluters*, Oxford: Oxford University Press.

Rocha, Hector O. and Sumantra Ghoshal (2006), 'Beyond self-interest revisited', *Journal of Management Studies*, **43** (3), 585.

Schwartz, Birgitta and Karina Tilling (2009), '"ISO-lating" corporate social responsibility in the organizational context: a dissenting interpretation of ISO 26000', *Corporate Social Responsibility and Environmental Management*, **16** (5), 289–99.

Simnett, Roger, Ann Vanstraelen and Wai Fong Chua (2009), 'Assurance on sustainability reports: an international comparison', *Accounting Review*, **84** (3), 937–67.

Slager, Rieneke (2009), 'What gets measured gets managed – exploring the link between sustainability indices and responsible corporate behaviour', Oikos PRI Young Scholars Academy 2009: Responsible Investment: Integration, Engagement, Transparency.

Social Investment Forum (2006), *2005 Report on Socially Responsible Investing Trends in the United States: 10-Year Review*, Washington, DC: Social Investment Forum.

Stiglitz, Joseph (2009), 'Regulation and failure', in D. Moss and J. Cisternino (eds), *New Perspectives on Regulation*, Cambridge, MA: Tobin Project.

Stringer, C. (2006), 'Forest certification and changing global commodity chains', *Journal of Economic Geography*, **6** (5), 701.

Tile, Carol Ann (2001), 'The content and disclosure of Australian corporate environmental policies', *Accounting, Auditing and Accountability Journal*, **14** (2), 190–212.

UNCTAD (2003), *Disclosure of the Impact of Corporations on Society: Current Trends and Issues*, Geneva: UNCTAD Secretariat.

UNEP, World Bank and World Resources Institute (2003), *World Resources 2002–2004: Decisions for the Earth: Balance, Voice, and Power*, Washington, DC: World Resources Institute.

Waddock, Sandra (2008), 'Building a new institutional infrastructure for corporate responsibility', *Academy of Management Perspectives*, **22**, 87–108.

# PART VIII

# TOWARD BETTER
# REGULATION?

# 26 The new regulatory orthodoxy: a critical assessment
*Tom Christensen and Per Lægreid*

Over the last 25 years the traditional model of hierarchical and integrated government has been challenged by structural fragmentation inspired by the New Public Management (NPM) reforms (Christensen and Lægreid 2001; Pollitt et al. 2001; Pollitt and Bouckaert 2004). A central aspect of this development in many countries has been a change in how regulatory activities are organized. Regulation based on central command and control from the top has been weakened in favour of more regulation by autonomous regulatory agencies (Levi-Faur 2005). The new international regulatory orthodoxy, enhanced by the emergence of a universal reform model, holds that the creation of autonomous agencies will improve regulatory performance and efficiency without having negative side-effects on accountability, transparency and democratic legitimacy (Majone 1994, 1997; Self 2000; Pollitt et al. 2004). This chapter asserts that these expectations are not established as evidence-based facts but need to be examined through empirical studies. The causes and effects of this development in regulatory policy are still unclear.

We will focus on the dynamic interplay between the increase in the autonomy of regulatory agencies and political control of those agencies. The general research issues are the weak empirical foundations of regulatory reforms, the complex trade-off between political control and agency autonomy, the dual process of deregulation and reregulation, the problems of role-specialization and coordination, and the question of 'smart practice' in regulatory policy and practice.

Our argument is that agencification and regulation operate in tandem. Autonomous organizations need regulation, and regulation flourishes with the establishment of autonomous organizations. Likewise, vertical structural specialization is coupled to reregulation, i.e. political executives and ministries both let go and tighten the reins at the same time, both towards autonomous bodies and towards regulatory agencies with increased autonomy. So deregulation and reregulation deal with two relationships: ministry–agency and agency–regulatee.

The NPM-inspired regulatory model, with its autonomous agencies, has been a main tool of governance in the USA for a long time (Eisner 1994). It was once seen as an expression of 'American exceptionalism', but this is no longer the case. The Regulatory State has spread to Europe and elsewhere and tends to favour regulation over other means of policy-making. It is more a rule-making and rule-following state than a taxing and spending state. It involves a shift from direct to indirect government, and important policy-making powers are delegated to independent technocratic bodies with considerable political leeway. The government is kept at arm's length from direct intervention in the economy but has a well-developed new regulatory role (McGowan and Wallace 1996). The agency model is different from the traditional integrated bureaucratic model in that it combines expertise, autonomy and specialization of tasks in a narrow range of policy issues (Majone 1997), but because it is based on the assumption of a special need for professional autonomy it also entails more autonomy from ministries. There is separation both on a vertical dimension between agencies and ministries and on a horizontal dimension between different agencies responsible for different tasks, making both ministries and agencies more specialized. This creates a lot of organizational complexity, potentially requiring more coordination (Gregory 2003).

Agency autonomy is an ambiguous and multidimensional concept that is not linked to agencies' formal legal status in a straightforward way. There are differences between formal autonomy, legal autonomy and de facto autonomy. De facto autonomy, which we focus on in this chapter, is about absence of external interference as well as actual capability to exploit available discretion or leeway (Olsen 2009b). Formal independence is neither a necessary nor a sufficient condition for explaining variation in the de facto autonomy of agencies (Maggetti 2007). Carpenter (2001) argues that agency autonomy lies less in fiat than in leverage and asserts that there are generally three conditions for agency autonomy: political differentiation from the political executive; independent organizational capacity; and political legitimacy generated by a strong organizational reputation embedded in an independent power base.

Regulatory agencies are a sub-group of central agencies, and one of their main tasks is to control the power of the market, ensure fair competition, and protect consumers and citizens by guiding and implementing policy regulation, but also to regulate the activities of other public bodies. One of their features is that they often seem to be constitutional hybrids having both statutory power and incorporated status. These bodies carry out regulation using their own delegated regulatory power, resources and responsibilities. They are neither directly elected by the people, nor directly managed by elected officials (Thatcher and Stone Sweet 2002; Gilardi 2004), but derive some of their authority and legitimacy from such sources. Generally, regulatory agencies are seen as having more formal autonomy than agencies with managerial tasks.

We will first give a brief introduction to the new regulatory reform advocated by the OECD and other international organizations and then examine how it works in practice. We will examine the problem of balancing autonomy and control in NPM-based regulatory reform by going beyond the question of formal legal autonomy and address the de facto autonomy and control of the regulatory agencies. This will be done by discussing whether civil servants in central agencies in practice meet the requirements of the new regulatory model with regard to their contact patterns, decision-making behaviour and influence. We cover both the process of regulatory reorganization and decision-making within established regulatory structures. The main picture is that there is a loose coupling between the new regulatory policy ideal and a) specific regulatory policy in different countries and policy areas and b) the regulatory practice in individual cases. We will argue that regulatory practice is much more complex than the new regulatory model suggests and that the degree of political salience is an important explanatory factor.

Second, we will discuss how the new NPM-inspired regulatory model embracing agency autonomy corresponds with regulatory challenges in the post-NPM era where there has been an enhanced focus on political control. A main question is how the role of the regulatory agencies changes under post-NPM reforms. We will address how 'whole-of-government'-inspired post-NPM reform initiatives might change the regulatory model through processes of reregulation, either at a distance or as centralization.

A central argument will be that there is a sedimentation or layering process going on in which new reform initiatives are added to old ones rather than replacing them (Christensen and Lægreid 2008c; Olsen 2009a).

## 26.1 THE NEW REGULATORY ORTHODOXY

A broad and comprehensive programme of regulatory reform launched internationally in recent years (OECD 1997, 2002) has affected many countries. This reform programme, which intends as one of its main goals to foster competition by use of central oversight units independent from political executives, has entailed a fundamental review of supervisory agencies. Governments around the world have been formulating a new regulatory policy aimed at making supervisory bodies stronger and more autonomous. One of the chief features of this new policy is the regulation of market actors, but it also has implications for a broad range of regulatory agencies and activities.

The new regulatory model took it more or less for granted that the traditional integrated, reactive, ad hoc and piecemeal approach, which balances different values and goals, should be replaced by comprehensive, proactive and systematic regulatory reforms. The new recipe, labelled by Pollitt (2003b) as the 'practitioners' model', is to separate the regulatory role of the state from its roles as owner, policy-maker and commercial actor, to upgrade competition policy to make it the main goal, to deregulate and liberalize state monopolies, to reduce state ownership, to commercialize public services, and to improve the performance, efficiency and effectiveness of public spending. It holds that competitive neutrality, autonomy and clear division of labour are essential for increasing legitimacy, and the government should retain less public control in the liberalization process.

The recommendation was to separate the regulatory function from the commercial one, to enhance a business perspective and to reduce the potential for ministerial intervention by making agencies more autonomous and professional (Pollitt and Talbot 2004). Consensus-based decision-making should be replaced by evidence-based decision-making. Political intervention in particular decisions should also be replaced by the establishment of separate expert-based appeal bodies outside the ministries.

Previous regulatory reforms were criticized for being partial and piecemeal, and the policy recommendation was to strengthen the independence and authority of the regulatory agencies by reducing the opportunities for appealing decisions to the minister and reducing the ministry's scope for instructing the agencies. The official *raison d'être* for autonomous agencies is that structural separation, more managerial autonomy and managerial accountability for results will improve performance (OECD 2002; James 2003; Pollitt et al. 2004). The new regulatory orthodoxy is that formally autonomous regulatory agencies should be designed to improve the credibility and efficiency of regulatory activity by insulating them from short-term politics and by providing technical expertise (Maggetti 2007).

One main question related to this regulatory reform concerns the complex trade-off between political control and agency autonomy. How far can one go under the new regulatory regime in increasing an agency's independence without losing political control? Through the process of modernization attempts have been made to satisfy both demands simultaneously by finding an optimal blend of autonomy and control. The question is how a balance can be achieved in practice and how stable such a balance will be. The political executive would like to decentralize decisions in individual cases, while at the same time striving for stronger central coordination of regulatory policy and stronger strategic management (OECD 2003a). We challenge the assumption that such rational-choice-inspired reforms will enhance political control. It is argued that it is difficult to accommodate political accountability and control at the same time as professionalization, autonomization, deregulation and market orientation gain momentum (Christensen and Lægreid 2003).

An important question is what the preconditions are for smart practice and how such a policy might result in better regulatory practice. The official practitioners' regulatory model seems to indicate that increased vertical differentiation or structural devolution, implying a hands-off attitude from the political executives, will potentially enhance the efficiency and credibility of regulation. The same argument is applied to increased horizontal differentiation, through non-overlapping roles and functions. Another question is why regulatory agencies need special professional autonomy, and more than other agencies. Is this showing an anti-democratic or anti-political trend typical for NPM (Christensen and Lægreid 2001)? As will be illustrated, the new regulatory practice actually combines old and new regulatory policy, and we will analyse whether this hybrid in fact produces better regulatory practice than sticking to a more pure form.

## 26.2   THE NEW REGULATORY ORTHODOXY IN PRACTICE

This change from a unified central administration with mixed roles under ministerial rule to a separation of the different functions and tasks and their allocation to more autonomous bodies has rather weak empirical foundations, and there is generally little systematic documentation of the effects of such reforms. Some more general studies seem to indicate that public choice-related arguments for increasing political control through vertical structural specialization and single-purpose organizations are difficult to fulfil in practice (Boston et al. 1996; Pollitt and Bouckaert 2004). Creating separate, specialized agencies can contribute to a clearer demarcation of responsibilities and roles and greater credibility, efficiency and predictability, but it may also result in increased complexity, problems of coordination, higher transaction costs and reduced potential for effective political control and accountability (Christensen and Lægreid 2001, 2007a). We will illustrate some general points by discussing examples mainly from the Norwegian experience.

First, something happens to the new regulatory orthodoxy when it moves into domestic political administrative systems. One example of this is what happened when the Norwegian Conservative-Centre government in 2003 proposed a regulatory agency reform inspired by the OECD model (OECD 2003b; Christensen and Lægreid 2007b). The minority government proposal was to make the regulatory agencies more independent and the role of a regulatory agency more specialized and unambiguous (St.meld. no. 17 2002–03). It was proposed that there should be a general principle of non-interference from political executives in single cases in the regulatory agency and that the appeal cases should be moved out of the ministries. Another main element was to move a number of regulatory agencies out of the capital. After a tug-of-war between the minority government and the opposition in Parliament, a compromise was reached. The relocation part was agreed on, but it was decided that the main overall devolution principle should not be applied to all regulatory agencies and there should be no change for the appeal cases. Thus the regulatory agency reform also implied increased complexity, since the aim of an unambiguous principle of structural devolution is obscured by the compromise reached, thereby also combining a traditional culture of control with a new culture of autonomy. The policy adopted is more of a hybrid where the new regulatory features are important, but not dominant, so the new model may be changed and transformed in political processes. The new regulatory orthodoxy model is modified with the national adaptation process.

Second, there might be a loose connection between the general regulatory reforms and what happens in specific policy areas. It is important to distinguish between the overall regulatory policy on the one hand and sector-specific reform processes on the other hand. The new regulatory policy is not a template that is applied in a standardized way across different policy areas. In fact there are great variations – from the 'hard' and competitive areas of business, utilities and transportation in which the practitioners' model to a great extent is applied, to the softer areas of the welfare state such as health care and education (Jordana and Levi-Faur 2004). But even in harder policy areas one can experience gaps between ideal and practice. One illustration of this is the area of internal security (Lægreid and Serigstad 2006). In this case in Norway there was a tug-of-war between the Ministry of Defence and the Ministry of Justice over how to organize for internal security, and the result was an ambiguous compromise. In the US, too, there is tension between the Department of Homeland Security and the military part of the anti-terrorist organization (Kettl 2004; Hammond 2007). The same type of processes happened in the area of food safety regulation, where there were attempts to balance the values and interests of public health and the business interests of the agricultural sector (Elvbakken et al. 2008). Tasks matter when applying the regulatory model (Pollitt et al. 2004), but so does underlying cultural path-dependency.

Third, there might be a loose connection between the new regulatory policy and the actual practice and daily work of handling specific cases in regulatory agencies. Two different cases from the Norwegian context illustrate this ambiguity. One example is the system of regulation in the post and telecommunications sector in Norway, which is now set up very much in accordance with the official and ideal model of the OECD. The different actors further their roles and interests according to this model, but this is not a model that always results in an objective and purely professionally based practice. When the different actors disagree, because they play different roles, and conceptually driven cooperation is difficult to obtain, the ministry has to balance the different definitions and interpretations. It does that in a political-administrative context that results in a compromise that is politically possible under the circumstances, as illustrated by the Teletopia case in which a small new telephone operator tried to get access to the network of the former big monopoly Telenor. The former monopolist appealed to the ministry to overturn the decision of the regulatory agency, and the ministry ruled in favour of Telenor (Christensen and Lægreid 2007b).

Another example is related to the Norwegian Competition Authority (NCA) (Christensen and Lægreid 2008a). This case demonstrates how difficult it is for the NCA to fulfil its role objectively and independently as a competition authority, since its work and practice are complicated by the need to respond to external pressure, as illustrated in the merger of the airlines SAS and Braathen. Clearly the process was characterized by environmental pressure, anticipated reactions, and negotiations, while the NCA's initial attempt to proceed according to the rules received little support from the political executive. Another example is the merger of the two largest financial institutions in Norway in 2003. As in the first case, the NCA again experienced a lot of pressure, revealing that many political actors were less concerned about competition policy than about creating a major Norwegian financial company. This time, however, the NCA had more control over the negotiation process. Anticipating that the Ministry of Finance would agree to the deal anyhow, the NCA obviously thought it would be wiser to give its conditional approval than to adhere rigidly to the provisions of the law on competition. By imposing certain conditions, it would appear to be upholding some of the principles of competition to a greater extent that in the first case.

A main observation from these cases is that one cannot easily infer from the new regulatory models and formal structure to practice. There is a rather loose coupling between comprehensive policy programmes and specific reorganizations in certain policy areas, and agency status in itself is a highly uncertain predictor of steering relationships (Pollitt et al. 2004). The legal status and formal powers of the regulatory agencies represent broad categories that allow for huge variations in practice. Contrary to the OECD's assumption, actual regulatory practice does not always concur with regulatory orthodoxy.

At the macro level, the new international regulatory doctrines are modified, translated and transferred into hybrids when they encounter domestic political administrative cultures and structures. The result is a less radical compromise between this new approach to regulation and the traditional domestic way of regulating.

On the meso level it is difficult to implement the new regulatory policy through interagency cooperation and mergers. The overall reform has to pass a compatibility test when it faces the different policy areas, and sector-specific path-dependencies constrain adaptation in different policy areas. There is an unstable balance between political control and agency autonomy, and it is difficult to find a sustainable organizational form. In practice it is not easy to live up to the organizational model espoused by the new regulatory policy.

On the micro level, which concerns the handling of individual cases in practice, there are further problems of matching administrative practice with the new regulatory orthodoxy. Even in the core of the new regulatory policy, represented by regulatory agencies in the economic field, it is hard to live up to the new doctrines in practice. The cases dealt with by the competition authority illustrate the complicated interaction between political signals and professional decision-making. In some cases political and managerial executives can form a powerful alliance; in other cases there might be a complex interplay between environmental pressure, professional attitudes and political considerations. The case of regulation in the post and telecommunications sector shows both how there are internal professional disagreements in the regulatory agency and how the different actors have furthered their own roles and interests according to the new regulatory model. When different actors disagree because they play different roles, conceptually driven cooperation is difficult to achieve, and the ministry has the task of balancing the different definitions and interpretations. New institutional autonomy reverts to traditional hierarchical decisions, based on balancing different decision-making premises.

These case-based illustrations can be supplemented by survey data. A survey of civil servants in Norwegian central agencies conducted in 2006 examines whether the new regulatory model corresponds with regulatory practice. A general finding is that there is a relatively close relationship between agencies in general and their parent ministry and political executives (Christensen and Lægreid 2008b). In contrast to the new regulatory orthodoxy, the central agencies in general are not isolated from their administrative and political superiors. This is the case for civil servants working with both regulatory tasks and other tasks. They pay a particularly large amount of attention to signals from the administrative leadership in their parent ministry, have well-developed contact patterns upwards and generally assess their superior as having an important role to play when central decisions are made within their own field of work. One main finding is, therefore, that regulatory practice is much more complex than the practitioners' model suggests. One of the most important factors for explaining the relationship between agencies and political and administrative superiors is the degree of political salience of the issues concerned (Pollitt 2003b; Christensen and Lægreid 2009).

Another broad survey of Norwegian state agencies carried out in 2004 reveals that regulatory tasks represent a major activity for state agencies in Norway, but also that the majority of the agencies have not become 'single-purpose organizations' but combine regulatory tasks with other tasks in more traditional integrated organizational forms. The external control by both the executive and the legislative bodies over the agencies is rather significant (Lægreid et al. 2008). Moreover, contrary to what we would expect, given current regulatory orthodoxy, regulatory agencies are controlled to a larger extent than other agencies. Over the last two decades of NPM it has become increasingly clear that vertical structural specialization and deregulation have come to be coupled with reregulation and more scrutiny and control (Christensen and Lægreid 2006). Generally agency autonomy is greater in operational matters and in personnel and financial issues than in strategic and policy matters, reflecting a long administrative tradition in Norway (Lægreid et al. 2006).

The selected illustrations show that the regulatory policy field is politically controversial and complex and that there are a lot of cultural constraints governing how civil servants in regulatory agencies work in practice. Individual cases of reorganization or regulation cannot be viewed in isolation simply as examples of the technicalities of implementation but need to be treated as political cases, involving political steering and negotiations, external pressure and historical-institutional constraints. In practice the new regulatory orthodoxy may be more a question of arena-shifting than depoliticization (Flinders and Buller 2006). The cases reveal that in practice it is hard to implement the new regulatory policy programme and simultaneously live up to the official formal governance model of frame-steering and performance management (Pollitt et al. 2004). Neither does the OECD model fit in very well with how the government's comprehensive regulatory reform programme is being implemented in specific policy areas. Political executives cannot freely select desirable reform measures, and the objectivity of professional-judicial processes and considerations is often disputed and negotiable. Regulatory practice is more diverse and context-dependent than the official model implies.

An examination of the formulation of regulatory policy, the implementation of the policy programme in specific policy areas and how relations between ministries and agencies work in practice reveals a complex interaction between external pressure from the doctrines of dominant international agencies, the domestic administrative and institutional context, and political choices made by government executives and political leaders (Christensen and Lægreid 2001).

In practice, it would be fair to say that the official model is more a special case that seems to work pretty well under specific conditions, such as in situations with low political salience. When these preconditions are not fulfilled, however, it tends to run into trouble (Pollitt 2003b). The lesson is that context matters and that there is no best way of governing agencies. In this perspective regulatory practice will be context-dependent. The overall outcome of the regulatory policy is some convergence in formal regulatory institutions, but with significant differences in the mechanisms of reform, national strategies and informal institutions (Thatcher 2007). The organizational structure, the daily practical work and the steering of agencies are not standardized.

## 26.3 REGULATORY CHALLENGES UNDER POST-NPM REFORMS

The NPM regulatory reform wave advanced the autonomy argument, stressing vertical structural specialization and increased distance to executive politicians, while post-NPM reforms, which started in the late 1990s in some countries that had been NPM trailblazers, have revived the control and coordination aspects (Christensen et al. 2007). The NPM reforms combined vertical specialization with extensive use of the principle of 'single-purpose organizations' or horizontal specialization, creating a fragmented system which, it was argued, catered to 'role purity' (Gregory 2001). Post-NPM reforms introduced a combination of a) vertical integration via stronger central control measures and making more capacity available to the political executive and b) more horizontal collaboration and coordination in the form of networks, teams, projects and eventual mergers (Gregory 2003; Halligan 2006; Christensen and Lægreid 2007c). This generation of reforms, which followed in the aftermath of NPM, has been labelled 'whole-of-government' or 'joined-up-government' reform programmes (Pollitt 2003a).

When the first post-NPM measures emerged in the UK, Australia and New Zealand, they could primarily be seen as a reaction to the effects and implications of NPM-related reforms (Gregory 2003; Christensen and Lægreid 2007b; Halligan 2007). Two types of challenges seemed to be important. One was the undermining of control and central capacity that NPM brought. Now it was time for the executive politicians to take back some of that control and increase their own capacity to solve cross-sectoral societal problems. The measures used were to vertically reintegrate some of the agencies and enterprises, either by dissolving some agencies and integrating their activities in the ministries or by establishing more control measures and constraints. Another measure was to strengthen overall administrative or political capacity close to the political executive (Halligan 2006).

When the post-NPM reforms were introduced, the balance tipped back somewhat towards more control, but it did not restore the situation that had existed under the 'old public administration' (Christensen and Lægreid 2007b). This was partly due to the fact that changing some of the vertical structural specialization was both politically and administratively difficult. Post-NPM plays out more along the horizontal dimension, with more structural and cultural integration, and has added to and modified the NPM reforms, making the system even more structurally and culturally complex. The development has been from simple integration (old public administration) through complex, fragmented and unbalanced complexity (NPM) to integrated and more balanced complexity concerning political control and autonomy (post-NPM).

A study of post-NPM administrative reforms in Norway in the fields of immigration, hospitals and welfare administration reveals that the reforms are designed by combining NPM and post-NPM reform elements in a complex mix (Christensen and Lægreid 2008c). The different reform initiatives do not replace one another but rather supplement one another in a sedimentation process. What we see is a layering in which the new NPM-inspired regulatory orthodoxy is added to the old regulatory administrative model, and when the post-NPM movement comes along this is superimposed on an already rather complex system, resulting in increased complexity and hybridization of the regulatory system. The NPM-inspired regulatory model is by no means dead, but it has been modified and complemented by post-NPM features.

The need for 'whole-of-government' regulatory approaches has been illustrated by the international financial crisis that started in 2008. One of the arguments behind the practitioners' model was that the deregulation of former public monopolies, privatization and marketization created a demand for regulation and control of markets. One important tool was to establish autonomous regulatory agencies. Deregulation and privatization went in tandem with reregulation and agencification (Christensen and Lægreid 2006). The slogan was more markets and more rules (Vogel 1996). The financial crisis has, however, revealed that the practitioners' model was not able to handle the 'wicked issues' that did not follow sector-specific policy areas within and across countries. Such cross-sectoral regulatory failures are also obvious regarding the challenge of climate change (Lodge and Wegrich 2010). When the problems blur the boundaries between countries, administrative levels and policy areas there is a need for regulatory approaches that are able to handle the different horizontal coordination challenges and reinvolve the central political leadership.

One of the main challenges in this complex regulatory landscape is the issue of accountability, which tends to become increasingly ambiguous. Thus one challenge facing civil service systems in the post-NPM generation of reform is balancing the need for both flexibility and accountability. One perspective is that this new set of reforms is partly a reaction to problems of control and accountability generated by the first generation of NPM reforms, and that the new balance of control and autonomy opens up new accountability issues (Christensen and Lægreid 2001). Another perspective is that accountability was actually already a problem in the old, more trust-based public management systems and that NPM brought more unambiguous and transparent accountability instruments. According to this perspective, post-NPM reforms are simply fine-tuning or rebalancing this system.

The question of accountability is also closely related to power relations. Increased agencification often means transferring power from political executives to managers, and 'regulocrats' are emerging as a new group of highly influential bureaucrats in regulatory agencies that enjoy broad institutional autonomy (Levi-Faur et al. 2005). The 'logic of discipline' that strengthens the power of technocrats who were shielded from political influence tended to undermine democratic accountability and often did not work in practice (Roberts 2010). One observation is that power relations seem to be changing faster than accountability relations (Christensen and Lægreid 2003). The political leadership often finds itself in situations where it has responsibility without the corresponding power and control. Conversely, many autonomous agencies may gain more power without necessarily becoming more accountable. The trend in the post-NPM reforms to strengthen the centre can be seen as an effort to redress the balance.

## 26.4   CONCLUSION

We have revealed that, owing to new regulatory reforms and the spread of the agency form as a best practice, regulatory models are in a state of transition. But there is weak comprehensive evaluation of such regulatory reforms across different countries, and systematic evidence for some of the promised benefits of the reforms is very patchy. It is not an evidence-based fact that non-majoritarian regulatory agencies have achieved more de facto autonomy. In practice it is difficult to find a stable balance between political control and agency autonomy. One reason for this is probably that the reformers often do not understand well the complex dynamics of regulatory reforms as a mixture of society-driven, government-driven and institution-driven processes. Formal agency status is a highly uncertain predictor for steering relationships, and it is necessary to go behind the regulatory rhetoric and the legal status of regulatory agencies to understand how they work in practice (Pollitt 2003b; Christensen and Lægreid 2007a; Olsen 2009b). Certain reform effects are often promised and anticipated, but, although their appearance is seldom reliably documented and evidence of success is lacking, the reform dynamic enables them to continue to spread (Pollitt and Bouckaert 2004: 140). However, there is also a learning process going on in some countries that is prompting them to adjust their reform paths and practices.

The extent to which regulatory reforms and agencification will corrode traditional values of fairness and impartiality or else enhance credibility and reduce political opportunism remains to be seen. One hypothesis is that norms of fairness, equity, predictability and impartiality will remain in tension with demands for greater flexibility and managerial discretion (Pollitt 2003b). The challenge of finding a sustainable balance between centralization and decentralization, between political control and agency autonomy, and between coordination and specialization is a never-ending story, for we are dealing with multi-functional systems which have to balance partly conflicting norms and values that vary across political-institutional contexts and over time.

A lesson from this analysis is that there is no easy solution or one ideal type of regulatory system. Regulatory autonomy is in practice changing the trade-offs between different external dependencies rather than being a development from all external influence, as suggested by the new regulatory orthodoxy (Olsen 2009b). The ideals of efficiency, adaptability and flexibility of the civil service on the one hand and a sense of collectivity, shared values and mutual trust relations between civil servants and political and managerial executives on the other hand mean that there is a difficult trade-off between managerial delegation and agencification on the one hand and political control and accountability on the other hand. How to balance fragmentation and integration, autonomy and control, individualization and common identities, and market pressure and cultural cohesion remains a major challenge for regulatory reformers.

# REFERENCES

Boston, J., J. Martin, J. Pallot and P. Walsh (1996), *Public Management: The New Zealand Model*, Auckland: Oxford University Press.
Carpenter, D.P. (2001), *The Forging of Bureaucratic Autonomy*, Princeton, NJ: Princeton University Press.
Christensen, T. and P. Lægreid (eds) (2001), *New Public Management: The Transformation of Ideas and Practice*, Aldershot: Ashgate.
Christensen, T. and P. Lægreid (2003), 'Coping with complex leadership roles: the problematic redefinition of government-owned enterprises', *Public Administration*, 81 (4), 803–31.
Christensen, T. and P. Lægreid (2006), 'Agencification and regulatory reform', in T.Christensen and P. Lægreid (eds), *Autonomy and Regulation: Coping with Agencies in the Modern State*, Cheltenham, UK and Northampton, MA, USA: Edward Elgar Publishing.
Christensen, T. and P. Lægreid (2007a), *Transcending New Public Management: The Transformation of Public Sector Reforms*, Aldershot: Ashgate.
Christensen, T. and P. Lægreid (2007b), 'Regulatory agencies – the challenge of balancing agency autonomy and political control', *Governance*, 20 (3), 497–519.
Christensen, T. and P. Lægreid (2007c), 'The whole-of-government approach to public sector reform', *Public Administration Review*, 67 (6), 1057–64.
Christensen, T. and P. Lægreid (2008a), 'Modern regulatory policy – ideas and practice', *Policy and Society*, 6 (4), 19–39.
Christensen, T. and P. Lægreid (2008b), 'The regulatory orthodoxy in practice', in U. Sverdrup and J. Trondal (eds), *The Organizational Dimension of Politics*, Oslo: Fagbokforlaget.
Christensen, T. and P. Lægreid (2008c), 'Transcending New Public Management – a transformative approach to increased complexity and the challenge of balancing autonomy and control', paper presented at the Scancor 20th anniversary conference, Stanford, 20–22 November.
Christensen, T. and P. Lægreid (2009), 'Organizing immigration policy – the unstable balance between political control and agency autonomy', *Policy and Politics*, 37 (2), 161–77.
Christensen, T., A. Lie and P.Lægreid (2007), 'Still fragmented government or reassertion of the centre?', in T. Christensen and P. Lægreid (eds), *Transcending New Public Management: The Transformation of Public Sector Reform*, Aldershot: Ashgate.
Eisner, M.A. (1994), 'Discovering patterns in regulatory history: continuity, change and regulatory regimes', *Journal of Policy History*, 6 (2), 157–87.
Elvbakken, K.T., P. Lægreid and L. Rykkja (2008), 'Regulation for safe food: a comparison of five European countries', *Scandinavian Political Studies*, 31 (2), 109–32.
Flinders, M. and J. Buller (2006), 'Depolitization, democracy and arena shifting', in T. Christensen and P. Lægreid (eds), *Autonomy and Regulation: Coping with Agencies in the Modern State*, Cheltenham, UK and Northampton, MA, USA: Edward Elgar Publishing.
Gilardi, F. (2004), 'Institutional change in regulatory policies: regulation through independent agencies and the three new institutionalisms', in J. Jordana and D. Levi-Faur (eds), *The Politics of Regulation*, Cheltenham, UK and Northampton, MA, USA: Edward Elgar Publishing.
Gregory, R. (2001), 'Transforming government culture: a skeptical view of New Public Management', in T. Christensen and P. Lægreid (eds), *Autonomy and Regulation: Coping with Agencies in the Modern State*, Cheltenham, UK and Northampton, MA, USA: Edward Elgar Publishing.
Gregory, R. (2003), 'All the king's horses and all the king's men: putting New Zealand's public sector back together again', *International Public Management Review*, 4 (2), 41–58.
Halligan, J. (2006), 'Theoretical faith and practical works: de-autonomization and joining-up in the New Zealand state sector', in T. Christensen and P. Lægreid (eds), *Autonomy and Regulation: Coping with Agencies in the Modern State*, Cheltenham, UK and Northampton, MA, USA: Edward Elgar Publishing.
Halligan, J. (2007), 'Reform design and performance in Australia and New Zealand', in T. Christensen and P. Lægreid (eds), *Transcending New Public Management: The Transformation of Public Sector Reform*, Aldershot: Ashgate.
Hammond, T.H. (2007), 'Why is the intelligence community so difficult to redesign? Smart practices, conflicting goals, and the creation of purpose-based organizations', *Governance*, 20 (3), 401–22.

James, O. (2003), *The Executive Agency Revolution in Whitehall*, London: Palgrave.

Jordana, J. and D. Levi-Faur (2004), 'The politics of regulation in the age of governance', in J. Jordana and D. Levi-Faur (eds), *The Politics of Regulation: Institutions and Regulatory Refoms in the Age of Governance*, Cheltenham, UK and Northampton, MA, USA: Edward Elgar Publishing.

Kettl, D. (2004), *System under Stress: Homeland Security and American Politics*, Washington, DC: CQ Press.

Lægreid, P. and S. Serigstad (2006), 'Framing the field of homeland security', *Journal of Management Studies*, **43** (6), 1395–1413.

Lægreid, P., P.G. Roness and K. Rubecksen (2006), 'Autonomy and control in the Norwegian civil service: does agency form matter?', in T. Christensen and P. Lægreid (eds), *Autonomy and Regulation: Coping with Agencies in the Modern State*, Cheltenham, UK and Northampton, MA, USA: Edward Elgar Publishing.

Lægreid, P., P.G. Roness and K. Rubecksen (2008), 'Controlling regulatory agencies', *Scandinavian Political Studies*, **31** (1), 1–26.

Levi-Faur, D. (2005), 'The global diffusion of regulatory capitalism', *Annals of the American Academy of Political and Social Sciences*, **598**, 1–21.

Levi-Faur, D., J. Jordana and F. Gilardi (2005), 'Regulatory revolution by surprise: on the citadels of regulatory capitalism and the rise of regulocracy', paper presented at the 3rd ECPR Conference, Budapest, 8–10 September, Section 3: "Regulation in the age of governance."

Lodge, M. and K. Wegrich (2010), 'Letter to the editor of *Public Administration Review* in response to a recent symposium of financial regulatory reform', *Public Administration Review*, **70** (2), 336–41.

MacGowan, F. and H. Wallace (1996), 'Towards a European Regulatory State', *Journal of European Public Policy*, **3** (4), 560–76.

Maggetti, M. (2007), 'De facto independence after delegation: a fuzzy-set analysis', *Regulation & Governance*, **1** (4), 271–94.

Majone, G. (1994), 'The rise of the Regulatory State in Europe', *West European Politics*, **17** (3), 77–101.

Majone, G. (1997), 'From the positive to the Regulatory State – causes and consequences from changes in the modes of governance', *Journal of Public Policy*, **17** (2), 139–67.

OECD (1997), *Report on Regulatory Reform*, Paris: OECD.

OECD (2002), *Distributed Public Governance: Agencies, Authorities and other Autonomous Bodies*, Paris: OECD.

OECD (2003a), *Public Sector Modernization: Changing Organizations*, Paris: OECD/PUMA.

OECD (2003b), *Norway: Preparing for the Future Now*, Paris: OECD.

Olsen, J.P. (2009a), 'Change and continuity: an institutional approach to institutions and democratic government', *European Political Science Review*, **1** (1), 3–32.

Olsen, J.P. (2009b), 'Institutional autonomy', in P.G. Roness and H. Sætren (eds), *Change and Continuity in Public Sector Organizations: Essays in Honour of Per Lægreid*, Bergen: Fagbokforlaget.

Pollitt, C. (2003a), 'Joined-up government', *Political Studies Review*, **1** (1), 34–49.

Pollitt, C. (2003b), *The Essential Public Manager*, Maidenhead: Open University Press.

Pollitt, C. and G. Bouckaert (2004), *Public Management Reform*, Oxford: Oxford University Press.

Pollitt, C. and C. Talbot (eds) (2004), *Unbundled Government*, London: Routledge.

Pollitt, C., K. Bathgate, J. Caulfield, A. Smullen and C. Talbot (2001), 'Agency fever? Analysis of an institutional policy fashion', *Journal of Comparative Policy Analysis*, **3** (3), 271–90.

Pollitt, C., C. Talbot, J. Caulfield and A. Smullen (2004), *Agencies: How Governments Do Things through Semi-Autonomous Organizations*, London: Palgrave.

Roberts, A. (2010), *The Logic of Discipline. Global Capitalism and the Architecture of Government*. Oxford: Oxford University Press.

Self, P. (2000), *Rolling back the State: Economic Dogma and Political Choice*, New York: St. Martin's Press.

St.meld. no. 17 (2002–03), *Om statlige tilsyn* [On regulatory agencies], White Paper, Norwegian Government.

Thatcher, M. (2007), 'Reforming national regulatory institutions: the EU and cross-national variety in European network industries', in R. Hanche, M. Rhodes and M. Thatcher (eds), *Beyond Varieties of Capitalism*, Oxford: Oxford University Press.

Thatcher, M. and A. Stone Sweet (2002), 'Theory and practice of delegation to non-majoritarian institutions', *West European Politics*, **25** (1), 1–22.

Vogel, D. (1996), *Freer Markets, More Rules: Regulatory Reform in Advanced Industrial Countries*, Ithaca, NY: Cornell University Press.

# 27 Performance-based regulation

## Peter J. May

Performance-based regulation is predicated on the notions that regulation should focus on achievement of regulatory objectives and leave it to regulated entities to determine how best to achieve them. In emphasizing objectives, the performance-based approach differs from other regulatory approaches that are based on specification of technologies (technology-based regulation), processes (systems-based regulation), or prescribed means (prescriptive regulation). The performance-based approach has been widely adopted throughout the world to regulate air and water quality, building and fire safety, consumer product safety, food safety, forest practices, nuclear power plant safety, pipeline safety, public health, transportation safety, energy utilization, and worker safety (see Organisation for Economic Co-operation and Development 2002; Deighton-Smith 2008).

Any depiction of performance-based regulation is complicated by the fact that the concept can be and has been applied in a variety of ways and with different degrees of regulatory comprehensiveness. As discussed by Coglianese et al. (2003), performance-based regulations differ with respect to the generality of the performance objective, the extent to which performance is quantified, and the mechanisms for monitoring or predicting performance. Regardless of the form it takes, performance-based regulation cannot be considered as separate from the broader regulatory system. Like other forms of regulation, performance-based regulation requires the setting of standards for compliance, establishing a monitoring and enforcement system, and applying sanctions when violations are detected. Given the variation in regulatory comprehensiveness and different methods for carrying out the implementation tasks, there is a large array of potential performance-based regulatory regimes.

A variety of claims have been made about the benefits of the performance-based approach, though few of these have been substantiated (see Office of Technology Assessment 1995; Coglianese et al. 2003). The performance-based approach is appealing because it holds the prospects for increased flexibility in how regulated entities meet regulatory objectives. This, in turn, may promote more cost-effective and innovative solutions. Because particular methods or technologies are not prescribed, performance-based approaches provide a more level playing field in the choice of products or technologies. This means particular suppliers or producers are not favored over others.

Performance-based regulatory regimes alter key regulatory responsibilities. Regulated entities take the lead in determining compliance, whereas traditionally regulatory enforcement personnel perform this function. This reversal of regulatory roles changes the required skills of regulatory enforcers from those of inspecting specific items to those of certifying performance. This also raises fundamental issues concerning regulatory accountability. Holding officials accountable for their actions is a key tenet of democratic governance (more generally see Behn 2001; Gormley and Balla 2004). At issue is how that accountability in performance-based regulatory regimes is achieved when non-governmental actors assume important roles that are normally undertaken by public officials.

This chapter discusses various aspects of performance-based regulation. The variety of different forms of the approach is first discussed. This draws attention to variation in the degree of specificity of performance goals and the creation of hybrid regulatory regimes that blend performance-based and other forms of regulation. The subsequent review of experience with various forms of performance-based regulatory regimes suggests some of the potential pitfalls and issues involved in implementing this form of regulation. The conclusions consider the future prospects for performance-based regulation.

## 27.1 VARIETIES OF PERFORMANCE-BASED REGULATION

The variety of forms of performance-based regulation is a function of two sets of considerations. One is the different degrees of regulatory comprehensiveness and associated variation in specificity of regulatory performance. The second is brought about by the blending of performance-based approaches with combinations of traditional prescriptive regulation, systems-based approaches, and risk-based approaches. These are considered here with respect to variation in performance provisions and in regulatory mixes.

### 27.1.1 Variation in Performance Provisions

Expectations regarding performance enter at multiple stages in performance-based regulatory regimes. The broadest level consists of statements about desired outcomes that constitute the goals to be achieved. Next is the characterization of desired levels of achievement of those goals that constitute acceptable performance – performance standards. Finally, there is the assessment of actual or expected performance – performance assessment. Each of these can differ in level of specificity and quantification.

Statements of outcomes provide the goals or intent of a regulation as would normally be specified in legislation or the regulation itself. These can be stated with varying degrees of comprehensiveness in referring to either a broad or narrow spatial distribution (e.g., the scale of a given air quality attainment area), a system as a whole or parts of it (e.g., a building or building component), or a broad or narrower target group (e.g., all workers or particular classes of workers). There can be a single goal, such as avoiding adverse health impacts, or there can be multiple goals of protecting life and property from harm. Each of the performance goals can be stated with differing levels of specificity.

The characterization of desired level of achievement is the standard against which compliance is gauged. Identifying relevant measures of performance and standards for desired levels of performance are much more difficult than stating performance objectives (see Gormley 2000). Numerous examples exist of the difficulties of translating vague performance objectives for regulations into meaningful standards. One example, which perhaps is the first quantitative performance standard in the United States, is the creation in 1914 of a voluntary federal drinking water quality standard that specified maximum coliform bacteria levels for municipal water supplies (see Gurian and Tarr 2001). As was the case for the original drinking water quality standard, the establishment of desired performance standards has engendered controversy within a variety of regulatory arenas in the United States. Marc Landy and his colleagues (1994: 49–88; also see Powell 1999: 267–84) discuss the difficulties in 1979 of revising the ozone standard to meet the legislative requirement under the Clean Air Act of protecting the public health with an adequate margin of safety. At issue were what constituted public health and relevant "sensitive populations," what constituted an adequate margin of safety, and how any particular standard could be defended against likely legal challenges.

Standards can be expressed in quantitative or qualitative terms. The ozone standard illustrates use of a quantitative measure in that it specifies exposure levels for a particular duration of time at particular measurement sites. The establishment of the standard engendered debate over the relevant metric for measuring exposure, the level at which exposure is harmful to health, and the duration of that exposure that would be harmful, allowing for the legislatively mandated margin of safety. An example of a qualitative expression of a standard is the International Code Council's performance-based fire safety objective. The objective of preventing unwanted ignition by building equipment and systems is one of several performance requirements for which relevant equipment "shall be installed so that they will not become a source of ignition" (International Code Council 2001, provision 601.3.2, p. 21). This can be contrasted with prescriptive-code fire safety provisions that specify particular shielding requirements, distances from walls, and so on.

Another set of considerations for performance-based regulations is the way that performance is assessed. The basic distinction is whether performance can be directly observed and measured, or whether it requires other forms of assessment. Direct observation requires actual measurement of performance to gauge adherence to a given performance standard. This is common practice for assessing potential contamination of drinking water, air quality emissions, and water quality effluents. For many instances it is not possible to undertake direct assessment of outcomes since they are unobservable harms to be prevented. For example, the safety of a nuclear power plant cannot be directly observed, nor can the safety of a building with respect to earthquakes, fire, or other potential harms.

When performance cannot be observed, it must be predicted. One approach involves probabilistic risk assessment analysis, as has been applied in the nuclear power industry. This entails tests or assessments of elements of the facility with particular attention to those elements that are most critical. Another approach is the use of computer models to simulate the performance of the system for varied situations. This requires an understanding of the performance characteristics of the system in question. The obvious issues for any prediction are the uncertainty associated with the prediction and the validity of the prediction method.

The fire-related life losses for the World Trade Center after the terrorist attacks on September 11, 2001 underscore the lack of reliable methods for predicting the performance of fire protective systems as part of performance-based fire safety regulations. Although there are a number of computer programs for modeling the ignition and spread of fire and guidelines have been produced by the American Society of Fire Protection Engineers for carrying out such evaluations, much of the commentary in technical forums about predictive modeling underscores the difficulties and inherent limits. The prediction difficulties in part stem from the complexity of potential ignition sources, spread, and other physical and engineering factors. One complicating factor, particularly evident in the World Trade Center 9/11 experience, is the unpredictability of human behavior in responding to fires.

### An example: building safety regulation

One of the widest applications of the use of the performance-based approach across the world is the regulation of the safety of buildings. The primary emphasis of building regulation is protecting the health and safety of building occupants. This is typically accomplished through regulatory controls concerning the design and construction of buildings with respect to fire safety, structural integrity, energy use, heating and ventilation, and so on (see Meacham et al. 2005). Until the past decade, the regulation of building safety has developed throughout the world as one of the more rule-bound and prescriptive aspects of protective regulation.

Under the prescriptive approach, the typical prescriptive building code provision addresses requirements for a component (i.e., a wall, partition, or floor) in specifying required practice (i.e., nailing pattern, bolting or bracing), materials, or both. The complexity of prescriptive building codes has exacerbated code enforcement in that building inspectors cannot possibly enforce all provisions. As a consequence, inspectors must choose the provisions that they deem it most important to enforce. Inevitably this has led to inconsistencies in enforcement practices among jurisdictions and among inspectors that frustrate contractors (see May and Wood 2003). The cumbersome nature of the code provisions and their enforcement has been widely criticized within the building industry. Critics argue that the overly prescriptive and redundant code provisions add to the costs of construction and limit innovation in development of new building practices.

The use of performance-based codes is appealing because it provides greater flexibility in regulating the safety of non-traditional and older structures. Prescriptive fire and building codes are difficult to apply in these circumstances. Prescriptive-code provisions are poorly suited for construction involving the use of exotic materials or for buildings that have odd configurations. Consider, for example, the pyramid-shaped Luxor Hotel in Las Vegas, which employed a non-traditional configuration and was built with non-standard building materials. Prescriptive seismic provisions of building codes are difficult to apply to the rehabilitation of buildings that were constructed prior to the advent of modern seismic codes. Performance-based codes are appealing for these circumstances because they provide an alternative framework for determining compliance with fire and building safety provisions.

Recognizing the deficiencies of the prescriptive approach and the increasing complexities of code provisions, a trickle of efforts that began in the 1970s and gathered momentum in a variety of forums since then has led to a rethinking of the philosophy of building and fire codes in the United States and a number of other countries. As discussed by Brian Meacham and his colleagues (2005), the basic framework in most countries employing this approach consists of a set of statements about goals, delineation of what this means in terms of "functional performance" for different types of structures, delineation of criteria for assessing performance (performance standards), and methods for verifying compliance with those standards. Compliance is gauged in terms of the degree to which a given structure adheres to the overall performance objectives as determined by compliance with the relevant performance standards. This is far different than the

*Table 27.1   Variation in performance-based regulatory regimes*

| | Regulatory regimes | | |
| --- | --- | --- | --- |
| | Prescriptive regulation | Performance-based regulation | Hybrid regulatory provisions |
| Regulatory foci | Prescribed actions. | Objectives or outcomes. | Mixed foci – aspects of actions, processes, and outcomes. |
| Compliance determination | Adherence to prescribed actions. | Achievement of desired results. | "Deemed to comply" alternative provisions. Performance of production systems. Performance in reducing risks. |
| Nature of rules and standards | Particularistic and detailed specifications. | Goal-oriented outcome specifications. | Delineation of "acceptable alternatives" or "codes of practice". Performance standards for production systems. Risk-based priorities for standard setting and enforcement. |

traditional, prescriptive approach that gauges compliance in terms of use of prescribed materials and construction methods.

### 27.1.2   Variation in Regulatory Mixes

Aspects of prescriptive, process-based, and risk-based approaches have been incorporated as part of performance-based approaches to create hybrid performance-based regulatory regimes. The process-based overlay focuses attention on aspects of production or management systems (see Coglianese and Lazer 2003). The risk-based overlay draws attention to those aspects of performance that relate to the greatest risks (see Black and Baldwin 2010). As with any performance-based approach, the main emphasis of the hybrid approaches is regulating for results. But the compliance determinations and nature of the rules and standards differ in allowing or mandating alternative mechanisms. Table 27.1 summarizes the key elements of prescriptive-based regulatory regimes, performance-based regulatory regimes, and hybrid provisions that have been applied to performance-based regulatory regimes. The latter are discussed in what follows.

Prescriptive provisions often serve as a backstop to the performance-related provisions. These help address situations that are relatively simple to assess and for which the conduct of a performance assessment would be inappropriate or overly expensive. Thus, for example, most performance-based building codes contain "deemed to comply" provisions that specify that use of a given material or following a particular approach meets the performance standard (see Meacham et al. 2005; Deighton-Smith 2008). Codes of practice, which have been employed in a number of countries, provide a similar "acceptable alternative" approach to performance-based approaches for such tasks as the regulation of worker health and safety (see Gunningham and Johnstone 1999: 27–8).

Performance-based regulation has also been used in conjunction with process-based regulation, which is also known as system-based regulation and management-based regulation. Adherents of the system-based approach argue that regulatory goals can be achieved by instituting the appropriate systems for monitoring production processes by firms rather than attempting to evaluate the outputs or outcomes of those processes (see Coglianese and Lazer 2003). The overall logic of this approach is that prescriptive regulation falls short because the production systems of firms are too complicated to be able to effectively prescribe regulatory fixes. Combining performance-based and process-based regulatory provisions leads to a hybrid regulatory regime that entails monitoring both the adequacy of production processes and the outputs of those processes.

An example of this is the hazard analysis and critical control point (HACCP) approach to regulating meat and poultry safety in the United States, as has been adopted in a number of other countries. Meat and poultry processors are required to identify potential sources of contamination within processing plants, to monitor those critical control points, to institute additional controls that are aimed at preventing contamination, and to test for the presence of *E. coli* and of *Salmonella* (see Coglianese and Lazer 2003). The process-based regulatory philosophy is evident in requiring firms to identify potential food-safety hazards and critical control points in meat and poultry production and processing. The performance-based approach is evident with the establishment by the firm of critical limits of a hazard for each critical control point and the requirements for testing for the presence of specified bacteria.

A different combination of regulatory approaches is the matching of performance-based and risk-based regulation as has been undertaken by the U.S. Nuclear Regulatory Commission in regulating the safety of nuclear power plants. The risk-informed approach is in essence a systems-based regulatory approach that also includes performance outcomes. It evolved from the efforts to develop and employ probability-based risk analyses in setting standards and evaluating nuclear power plant performance (see Golay 2000). The risk-informed approach shifts the emphasis from detailed inspections of nuclear power plants to greater emphasis on establishing adequate safety systems by nuclear power plant operators as overseen by Nuclear Regulatory Commission inspectors. A similar approach has been used in the United States for the regulation of aspects of chemical plant safety (see Chinander et al. 1998). More generally, Black and Baldwin (2010) discuss how "really responsive risk-based regulation" can be employed in selecting performance objectives, in specifying performance standards, and in choosing enforcement targets.

Each of the hybrid performance-based regulatory regimes highlights different aspects of risk, processes, and outcomes. Regardless of the specific form that a hybrid regime takes, the issues surrounding specification of desired performance and assessment of it loom greatly.

## 27.2    EXPERIENCES WITH PERFORMANCE-BASED REGULATION

Despite the variety of ways that performance-based approaches have been incorporated into different regulatory provisions around the world, there have been limited systematic efforts to assess the approach. In summarizing the results of a workshop convened in 2002 of regulators from various federal agencies in the United States, Coglianese et al. observe: "Participants noted a general absence of empirical studies evaluating the effectiveness of performance-based standards, let alone systematic work showing when, where, and how well performance-based standards work in various regulatory settings" (2003: 714). In reviewing a range of performance- and process-based regulatory regimes, Deighton-Smith (2008) suggests that the lack of critical assessment has led to indiscriminate adoption of these regulatory approaches.

### 27.2.1 Leaky Buildings and Performance-Based Regulation

New Zealand's performance-based regulation of building safety that was introduced in 1992 is instructive since it is one of the more extensive efforts to apply the performance-based approach. The experience with the New Zealand regime was not positive. A major crisis in building quality that became known as "the leaky building" crisis was exacerbated by the change from a prescriptive to a performance-based regime. As documented by May (2003), the lack of accountability of key players was a key factor in undermining the effectiveness of the performance-based regulatory regime.

New Zealand's Building Act of 1991 provided broad objectives of protecting people, their health and safety, and the environment, with more detailed sub-objectives that identified desirable building performance. These and other provisions embraced the New Right's faith in the market and limited governmental intervention that were themes of a variety of reforms in New Zealand at the time. Consistent with the philosophy of reducing the dependency of citizens on the state, the Act introduced a strong dose of "buyer beware" provisions in requiring owners to acknowledge the presence of buildings in sites that may be vulnerable to natural hazards, in putting the responsibility of choosing those who certify compliance onto owners, and in not providing owners specific legal protections for building deficiencies. Market-like mechanisms were introduced by encouraging innovation in development of building materials and by allowing certification of compliance with desired building performance characteristics to be undertaken either by private inspectors or by local authorities.

As the *New Zealand Herald* labeled the problem in a series of two dozen articles appearing in 2002 and 2003, the "leaky building crisis" was not the typical story of shoddy construction or localized failures in building inspection that move the mundane aspects of building regulation into the public consciousness. The problems were pervasive and eventually fostered a crisis for many homebuyers, the central government, and the building industry. Beginning in the mid-1990s, condominiums and homes built with a particular type of exterior cladding revealed evidence of moisture entering into the membrane of a structure that led to cracking and, in some cases, eventual partial or total collapse of a building. Various investigations and media coverage suggest up to 20 000 homes and hundreds of multi-unit buildings were affected, many of which had to be abandoned as uninhabitable. A number of major construction firms were forced into receivership because of the anticipated costs of repairing damage to structures they had built. The insurance market for professionals who certify building compliance dried up, leading to an implosion of private firms who performed this function, including the second largest firm in Auckland. Numerous lawsuits were brought against builders and local councils by owners of damaged buildings, many of which still have not been resolved.

Shortfalls at each of three levels of accountability entered into the New Zealand "leaky building" case. One is a shortfall in legal accountability resulting from the specification of goals for which the goal of "durability of structures" was insufficiently precise (New Zealand Building Industry Authority 2002). This led to inconsistencies in interpretation of the provisions by local building authorities especially as they applied to new building materials that were the source of many of the leaks when improperly applied.

A second shortfall was a lapse in bureaucratic accountability that resulted from lessening reliance on the bureaucratic controls as a means for ensuring adequate construction of buildings. Indeed, the 1991 Act did not require inspections of building during construction, although local governments could require them. Among other considerations, one of the major reviews highlighted how the new regime resulted in changes in responsibilities, "with clarity of lines of responsibility now blurred" with respect to who was providing assurance to the public (New Zealand Building Industry Authority 2002: 38). The report specifically draws a contrast with clearer lines of responsibility and accountability under the previous regime. Not surprisingly, the 2004 Building Act revisions tightened bureaucratic accountability, with emphasis on greater specification of performance standards, stronger monitoring of building inspection practices, and tighter licensing provisions for professionals who certify building compliance.

The shortfall in bureaucratic oversight would not have been as problematic if builders and those who certify compliance with codes were fulfilling their professional obligations. Lapses in professional accountability – as fostered by professional associations, licensing boards, or peer reputations – provided a third source of accountability shortfalls. Reviews of the crisis highlighted the lack of licensing requirements for builders that exacerbated the weaknesses in regulatory oversight. The use of third-party inspectors for compliance with building provisions was particularly problematic, as subsequent findings suggested they were not well trained or adequately certified by the Building Industry Authority.

### 27.2.2   Performance-Based Regulation and Accountability

Ensuring accountability is a fundamental issue for any form of regulation. The relevant foci are the mechanisms for guaranteeing that the responsibilities of various players, including regulated entities, are adequately carried out (see Scott 2000; Behn 2001). The accountability bases, limits, and biases differ among regulatory approaches. These are summarized in Table 27.2 for prescriptive and performance-based regulation. The latter accountability considerations are of particular concern since, as illustrated by New Zealand's "leaky building" crisis, accountability can be the Achilles' heel of performance-based regulation.

Prescriptive-based regulatory regimes attempt to achieve accountability by mandating adherence to prescribed rules. The sheer number of rules that often exist serves as a limiting factor given that no inspector can ensure adherence with all of the rules. Instead, inspectors are typically biased towards monitoring adherence to rules for which compliance is easy to observe. As a consequence, accountability under such systems can be

*Table 27.2    Accountability considerations*

| Considerations | Form of regulation | |
|---|---|---|
| | Prescriptive regulation | Performance-based regulation |
| Primary basis for accountability | Monitoring for adherence to prescribed rules. | Monitoring for adherence to performance goals. |
| Limits | Numerous rules that cannot all be enforced. | Inability to observe or predict results. |
| Biases | Adherence to easily observable items. | Reliance on experts and professional judgment. |
| Potential negative consequences | Haphazard and misplaced enforcement. | Misjudged quality of regulatory performance. |

haphazard and misplaced, with little attention to the end result (see Bardach and Kagan 1982; Sparrow 2000).

Performance-based approaches seek accountability for results. As discussed in this chapter, determining compliance is difficult when regulatory outcomes cannot easily be observed or predicted. In such circumstances, much of the compliance determination rests on professional judgment (e.g., in modeling results or interpreting performance predictions) and the skills of experts who are knowledgeable about the subject. But herein lies the rub. There is typically little basis for gauging the professional judgments or assessing the conclusions of experts. When such expertise is inadequate, as was the case in New Zealand's performance-based building safety regime, shortfalls in regulatory performance arise. As observed by May (2003), the case of performance-based regulation of buildings in New Zealand illustrates a leaky regulatory regime. The regime allowed for flexibility without adequate accountability. The problems were systemic, caused by a regulatory regime that placed too much faith on self-correction of the marketplace as a means of control and too little emphasis on accountability for results.

## 27.3   CONCLUSIONS

Performance-based regulation has the prospects for overcoming the restrictions of prescriptive regulation. The attention to results, rather than prescribed actions, emphasizes achievement of regulatory objectives. The ability of regulated entities to choose how to achieve those results provides greater flexibility and opens up possibilities for more cost-effective compliance solutions. These prospects have led regulators across the globe to experiment with performance-based regulatory approaches, leading to wide adoption of the approach for many regulatory sectors.

Increasingly, public administration and regulatory scholars have suggested adoption of performance-based approaches for dealing with thorny problems. Karkkainen et al. suggest "a model of environmental regulation that promises to be at once more flexible, democratic, and effective than the familiar methods of central command or market-based control" that is based on locally determined environmental performance standards (2000: 692). Pomeranz et al. (2009) suggest the use of performance targets regarding childhood obesity against which junk food manufacturers could be evaluated as contributing to the obesity epidemic. Similarly, Sugarman (2009) discusses how performance-based standards could be applied to food makers, retailers, or both in dealing with high levels of salt in humans and its contribution to high blood pressure.

Many of the efforts to employ performance-based regulatory approaches are still in their infancy. Few constitute standalone regulatory regimes. Most of the criticisms that have been raised about the performance-based approach revolve around the uncertainties that are fostered by vague performance goals or standards, and the inability to adequately quantify or otherwise measure performance (see Coglianese et al. 2003; Deighton-Smith 2008). These criticisms mirror the challenges of moving from the concepts of performance-based regulation to workable performance-based regulatory regimes. Meacham et al. depict these challenges for performance-based approaches to building regulation as follows: "There remain significant gaps in the knowledge, understanding and application of performance building regulatory and design concepts, and research and development is needed in several areas to increase their effectiveness, from the overall regulatory framework to addressing specific emerging issues" (2005: 103).

Implementation of performance-based regulation requires meaningful performance standards, an ability to gauge adherence to them, and new skill sets for regulatory enforcement agencies. As illustrated by the saga of leaky buildings in New Zealand, substantial gaps in regulatory compliance can result from weak performance-based regulatory regimes. Professional judgment and the exercise of professional responsibility are important accountability mechanisms for performance-based regimes. When such expertise is lacking, as was the case in New Zealand's performance-based building safety regime, there is a clear mismatch in regulatory design. One challenge for regulatory designers is figuring out how to compensate for the lack of the requisite professional expertise. New Zealand officials added prescriptive requirements as part of their reform of the performance-based approach to building regulation without giving up on the basic performance notions. It may be possible to strengthen a sense of professional accountability through education programs or through increased legal liability for failure to meet codes of conduct.

These concerns about accountability underscore the importance of finding the right fit between the regulatory circumstances and the design of performance-based regulatory regimes. Coglianese and Lazer (2003) suggest performance-based approaches are more appropriate when it is possible to gauge regulatory outcomes and when there is a diversity of regulated entities. The former is a necessary condition for application of the approach. The latter reflects the comparative advantage of the approach in allowing diverse regulated entities to determine the best approach to regulatory compliance. When the requisite professional expertise is lacking, there may be little choice but to revert to a largely prescriptive regime.

Despite their appeal, it is doubtful that performance-based regulatory approaches will wholly supplant traditional regulation that is based on prescriptive requirements. Prescriptive provisions help address situations that are relatively simple to assess and for which the conduct of a performance assessment would be inappropriate or overly expensive. They are also a necessary backstop for situations for which the potential harm from failure to comply would be catastrophic, as in the case of nuclear power plant safety. Nonetheless, performance-based approaches should be embraced as one of the key elements of the regulatory toolkit. They hold much promise and provide a wide array of possibilities for innovative regulatory regimes when paired with the appropriate combination of prescriptive, systems-based, and risk-based provisions.

## ACKNOWLEDGEMENTS

The author thanks David Levi-Faur for encouraging this contribution and Ashley Jochim and Barry Pump for research assistance. The contribution is part of research undertaken under the auspices of the Donald R. Matthews Endowment.

## REFERENCES

Bardach, Eugene and Robert A. Kagan (1982), *Going by the Book: The Problem of Regulatory Unreasonableness*, Philadelphia, PA: Temple University Press.
Behn, Robert D. (2001), *Rethinking Democratic Accountability*, Washington, DC: Brookings Institution Press.
Black, Julia and Robert Baldwin (2010), 'Really responsive risk-based regulation', *Law and Policy*, **32** (3), 183–213.
Chinander, Paul R., Paul R. Kleindorfer and Howard C. Kunreuther (1998), 'Compliance strategies and regulatory effectiveness of performance-based regulation of chemical accident risks', *Risk Analysis*, **18** (2), 135–43.
Coglianese, Cary and David Lazer (2003), 'Management-based regulation: prescribing private management to achieve public goals', *Law and Society Review*, **37** (4), 691–730.
Coglianese, Cary, Jennifer Nash and Todd Olmstead (2003), 'Performance-based regulation: prospects and limitations in health, safety, and environmental protection', *Administrative Law Review*, **55** (4), 705–28.
Deighton-Smith, Rex (2008), 'Process and performance-based regulation: challenges for regulatory govern-ance and regulatory reform', in Peter Carroll, Rex Deighton-Smith, Helen Silver and Chris Walker (eds), *Minding the Gap: Re-visiting the Promise and Performance of Regulatory Reform in Australia*, Canberra: ANU E Press, chap. 7, available at: http://hdl.handle.net/1885/47098 (accessed 3 August 2009).
Golay, M.W. (2000) 'Improved nuclear power plant operations and safety through performance-based safety regulation', *Journal of Hazardous Materials*, **71** (1–3), 219–37.
Gormley, William T., Jr. (2000), *Environmental Performance Measures in a Federal System*, Research Paper No. 13, Washington, DC: National Academy of Public Administration, available at: www.napawash.org.
Gormely, William T., Jr. and Steven J. Balla (2004), *Bureaucracy and Democracy: Accountability and Performance*, Washington, DC: CQ Press.
Gunningham, Neil and Richard Johnstone (1999), *Regulating Workplace Safety, Systems and Sanctions*, Oxford: Oxford University Press.
Gurian, Patrick and Joel A. Tarr (2001), 'The first federal drinking water quality standards and their evolution: a history from 1914 to 1974', in Paul S. Fischbeck and R. Scott Farrow (eds), *Improving Regulation: Cases in Environment, Health, and Safety*, Washington, DC: Resources for the Future, pp. 43–69.
International Code Council (2001), *ICC Performance Code for Buildings and Facilities*, Whittier, CA: International Conference of Building Officials.
Karkkainen, Bradley C., Archon Fung and Charles F. Sabel (2000), 'After backyard environmentalism: toward a performance-based regime of environmental regulation', *American Behavioral Scientist*, **44** (4), 692–711.
Landy, Marc K., Marc J. Roberts, Stephen R. Thomas with Valle Nazar (1994), 'Revising the ozone standard', in M. Landy, M. Roberts and S.R. Thomas (eds), *The Environmental Protection Agency: Asking the Wrong Questions from Nixon to Clinton, expanded edn*, New York: Oxford University Press, pp. 49–88.
May, Peter J. (2003), 'Performance-based regulation and regulatory regimes: the saga of leaky buildings', *Law and Policy*, **25** (4), 381–401.
May, Peter J. and Robert C. Wood (2003), 'At the regulatory frontlines: inspectors' enforcement styles and regulatory compliance', *Journal of Public Administration Research and Theory*, **13** (2), 117–39.
Meacham, Brian, Robert Bowen, Jon Traw and Amanda Moore (2005), 'Performance-based building regula-tion: current situation and future needs', *Building Research and Information*, **33** (2), 91–106.
New Zealand Building Industry Authority (2002), *Report of the Overview Group on the Weathertightness of Buildings to the Building Industry Authority*, Hunn Report, submission of 31 August, Wellington: Building

Industry Authority, available at: http://www.bia.govt.nz/publicat/pdf/bia-report-17-9-02.pdf (accessed 2 April 2003).

Office of Technology Assessment, U.S. Congress (1995), *Environmental Policy Tools: A User's Guide*, OTA-EVN-634, Washington, DC: U.S. Government Printing Office.

Organisation for Economic Co-operation and Development (2002), *Regulatory Policies in OECD Countries: From Interventionism to Regulatory Governance*, Paris: OECD.

Pomeranz, Jennifer L., Stephen P. Teret, Stephen D. Sugarman, Lanie Rutkow and Kelly D. Brownell (2009), 'Innovative legal approaches to address obesity', *Milbank Quarterly*, **87** (1), 185–213.

Powell, Mark R. (1999), *Science at the EPA: Information in the Regulatory Process*, Washington, DC: Resources for the Future.

Scott, Colin (2000), 'Accountability in the regulatory state', *Journal of Law and Society*, **27** (1), 38–60.

Sparrow, Malcolm K. (2000), *The Regulatory Craft: Controlling Risks, Solving Problems, and Managing Compliance*, Washington, DC: Brookings Institution.

Sugarman, Stephen D. (2009), 'Salt, high blood pressure, and performance-based regulation', *Regulation and Governance*, **3** (1), 84–102.

# 28 The evolution of cost–benefit analysis in US regulatory decisionmaking
## Stuart Shapiro

The possibility of bias in regulatory analysis threatens its viability as a decision making tool. (McGarity 1987)

It is time for progressive groups as well as ordinary citizens to retake the high ground by embracing and reforming cost–benefit analysis. (Revesz and Livermore 2008)

## 28.1 INTRODUCTION

The use of cost–benefit analysis (CBA) in United States regulatory policy is approaching its fourth decade. Over the past 30 years, CBA has been at the center of intense controversy. Supporters of regulation have blamed CBA for deregulation and for playing an important role in reducing environmental protections and American health and safety. Opponents of regulation have regularly called for greater use of CBA, citing the immense cost that regulation imposes upon American business.

Through all of this fiery rhetoric, however, something remarkable is emerging. Cost–benefit analysis is now firmly entrenched in the regulatory process, and few predict that this will change in the decades ahead. Agencies that once fought having to conduct analyses now do so regularly. And the academic community, particularly legal scholars, has begun to focus on improving cost–benefit analysis rather than removing it from the regulatory process.

While CBA still has its strident opponents, they are becoming increasingly marginalized in the debate over its use. Now the focus on CBA primarily concerns how to incorporate distributional concerns and insights from behavioral economics into its use. Supporters of regulation are now weighing in on these debates rather than merely arguing that CBA is inherently biased against regulation.

How did we get here and what does this evolution mean for the future of cost–benefit analysis? This chapter traces the evolution of cost–benefit analysis in the United States regulatory process from controversy to something closer to consensus. Particular attention is given to the important role of the new administrator of the Office of Information and Regulatory Affairs (OIRA), Cass Sunstein, because his appointment signals an important new stage in the debate over analysis.

The chapter proceeds as follows. Section 28.2 covers the rancorous debate over cost–benefit analysis after it was adopted by Ronald Reagan in 1981. It also chronicles the Clinton administration's acceptance of CBA and pro-regulation advocates' reaction – an increased stridency in the calls for CBA's elimination. Section 28.3 covers the evolution of a pro-regulation, pro-cost–benefit-analysis argument and its eventual ascendance. Finally, Section 28.4 takes stock of where cost–benefit analysis stands in the Obama administration and how it is likely to evolve as its role in the regulatory process approaches middle age.

## 28.2   THE EARLY HISTORY OF COST–BENEFIT ANALYSIS

While the implementation of CBA is generally associated with the Reagan administration and Executive Order (E.O.) 12291, it has its genesis in the three presidencies of the 1970s. President Nixon implemented "quality of life reviews," requiring that, before agencies adopt regulations, they consider alternatives. President Ford required agencies to produce "inflation impact statements" in limited circumstances. Finally, requirements most closely resembling CBA were instituted under President Carter (Weidenbaum 1997).

Carter created the Regulatory Analysis Review Group (RARG) and for the first time, in Executive Order 12044,[1] required an economic analysis for any regulation with a likely impact of more than $100 million. Agencies were required to choose "the least burdensome of acceptable alternatives." There were no requirements that agencies balance costs and benefits, however; and there was no authority within the RARG or within the Office of Management and Budget (OMB) to reject rules that failed cost–benefit criteria (Weidenbaum 1997).

All of this changed when President Reagan took office. Reagan had campaigned on a deregulatory platform (Revesz and Livermore 2008) and wasted little time issuing Executive Order 12291 and repealing the Carter Order (E.O. 12044).[2] The new E.O. vested OIRA with the authority to review agency regulations and required agencies to produce regulatory impact analyses on regulations with a likely annual impact of $100 million or more.[3] Agencies were also required to show that the benefits of their regulations exceeded the costs and to provide detailed justifications for the regulations if they did not. If regulations failed to meet the criteria set out in the E.O., OIRA had the authority to return the regulations to the agencies.

Initial debates on OIRA focused on the right of the President to oversee agency decisionmaking. Debates over CBA soon followed. Academic supporters of CBA were largely those who had served in the Reagan or Bush administrations. Demuth and Ginsburg (1986) argued that analysis and executive regulatory review were complementary because they both encouraged accountability and a broad, balanced view of regulatory decisions. The academic defenses of CBA were not nearly as numerous as the critiques, which began to emerge in the 1980s and fully flowered in the 1990s. Many of the critiques were institutional in nature, criticizing OIRA for a lack of transparency and for killing regulations by taking years to review them (Friedman 1995). However, there were many criticisms that focused on the nature of CBA itself. These included three types of arguments.

The first asserted that CBA was merely a cover for political goals. Olson (1984) wrote:

> As one key OMB official notes, "debate on the merits of economic analysis doesn't help resolve the real issues where OMB has budgetary, philosophical, or political problems with a rule; the regulatory analysis is used as a key in holding up or changing EPA [Environmental Protection Agency] action."

McGarity (1987) and Friedman (1995) later provided some evidence for Olson's claim. Friedman wrote: "[t]he analytical legitimacy of cost–benefit analysis appears to have been a charade. [OIRA official Jim] Tozzi[4] acknowledged [in an interview with the author] that costs and benefits were not actually compared."

Second, some argued that CBA was inherently anti-regulatory and ethically wrong. Kelman (1981) wrote a widely cited ethical critique of CBA, specifically challenging CBA's monetization of environmental goods and public health. Kelman argued that CBA inevitably supported some policy choices that were not moral, including persecuting the innocent and stifling dissent. He also argued that monetization of policy impacts was often impossible and devalued the things being monetized. McGarity (1987) echoed some of Kelman's arguments in an attempt to put together the first comprehensive list of criticisms (and strengths) of CBA. The criticisms included valuing mortality risks, discounting future effects, and ignoring distributional impacts. It is this ethical argument that would become most prominent among CBA opponents in the 1990s and 2000s.

Finally, there were arguments made that CBA delayed the regulatory process. In a 1992 article, McGarity coined the term "ossification of the rule-making process." Referring to stringent judicial review of agency regulations and the preponderance of analytical requirements imposed upon agencies that engage in rulemaking, McGarity contended that the rulemaking process had become so protracted and burdensome that agencies were avoiding rulemaking altogether. Mashaw and Harfst (1990) had made a similar point in examining the movement of the National Highway Traffic and Safety Administration (NHTSA) away from rulemaking and toward recalls of automobiles.

The institutional criticisms of OIRA had the largest and most immediate practical impact. In a letter to Congress, OIRA Administrator Wendy Gramm (1986) pledged to increase the transparency at OIRA and to ensure timely reviews of regulations. These changes were cemented in executive order under President Clinton in 1993. While the institutional critique would continue to surface occasionally (Bressman and Vandenbergh 2006) over the ensuing two decades, much of the legal and academic literature on OIRA review focused on cost–benefit analysis and the specific criticisms listed above.

The criticisms of CBA intensified after Bill Clinton became President. Clinton, contrary to the expectation of supporters of regulation, retained cost–benefit analysis in the regulatory process (Revesz and Livermore 2008). Clinton issued Executive Order 12866[5] to govern regulatory review. The new E.O. changed some of the language from the Reagan executive order (requiring that benefits of a regulation justify the regulation's cost rather than the formulation in the Reagan E.O., which required that benefits exceed the costs) and added "reduction of discrimination or bias" as one of the benefits to be considered as part of a regulatory analysis.

As Friedman (1995) writing early in the Clinton era noted, "Clinton, a moderate Democrat, may institutionalize regulatory reform far more effectively than the antiregulation Reagan, a conservative Republican." This institutionalization occurred without the support of the pro-regulation community (Revesz and Livermore 2008). However, with the institutional arguments against OIRA weakening because of efforts to make it more transparent and its reviews more timely, and presidential oversight of agency rulemaking becoming generally accepted,[6] supporters of regulation trained their fire on the probity of cost–benefit analysis.

The anti-CBA literature that developed during this period focused on the analytical legitimacy of cost–benefit analysis. Criticisms of particular aspects of CBA – such as the discounting of future values, the treatment of uncertainty, and the techniques for calculating the values of risk reduction (commonly expressed as the "value of a statistical life

(VSL)")[7] – were merged together to argue that CBA should play no role in the regulatory process (see e.g. Heinzerling 1997, 1999, 2000). Dreisen (2006) argued that these aspects inevitably biased CBA against regulation.

While supporters of regulation focused on arguing for the elimination of cost–benefit analysis, supporters of CBA worked on suggesting improvements. Elliott (1994) argued that analysis did improve rules and noted that 80 percent of issues raised by OMB had not been considered by EPA.[8] This showed, according to Elliott, that OMB (and by extension cost–benefit analysis) could add value, but that the issues were often raised too late in the regulatory process to make a difference. Hahn and Litan (2005) argued that CBA was imperfectly applied by federal agencies and OIRA and produced numerous suggestions for strengthening its role in the regulatory process.

One academic[9] exception to the dichotomy between pro-regulation and anti-regulation voices on cost–benefit analysis was Cass Sunstein. Sunstein, a law professor at the University of Chicago, is a well-known supporter of the idea that government should play a significant role in the regulation of the economy (Sunstein 2004). At the same time, Sunstein is a fervent advocate of cost–benefit analysis. This pro-regulatory argument in favor of cost–benefit analysis subjected Sunstein to criticism from other supporters of regulation (Sinden 2004). However, over the course of the George W. Bush administration, Sunstein would gain adherents and then would be appointed by President Obama as the Administrator of OIRA. This appointment marked the ascendance of a pro-regulatory CBA argument.

## 28.3   THE DEVELOPMENT OF THE PRO-CBA, PRO-REGULATION ARGUMENT

Sunstein emphasized several aspects of the debate on cost–benefit analysis that had not been discussed by either side. First and most prominently, Sunstein drew on the relatively new field of behavioral economics to justify cost–benefit analysis. Behavioral economics is concerned with the effects of bounded rationality on the decisions made by economic actors. The pioneering work in the field was done by Amos Tversky and Daniel Kahneman.[10] Behavioral economists have shown that individuals often rely on biases and heuristics to assist in decisionmaking. These biases and heuristics often lead individuals to make decisions that are not in their own interest. More importantly, from Sunstein's perspective, these heuristics and biases lead individuals to advocate for policies that are not necessarily in their interests.

Sunstein views CBA as a corrective for this. "Cost-benefit analysis . . . is most plausibly justified on cognitive grounds – as a way of counteracting predictable problems in individual and social cognition." Sunstein outlines six problems "in the public demand for regulation." These include what Sunstein terms the "availability heuristic," "informational and reputational cascades," the phenomenon of "dangers on-screen and benefits off-screen," "health–health tradeoffs," emotions and alarmist bias, and "separate evaluation and incoherence." He shows how these biases lead to consumer demand for regulations that at best will not improve their welfare and at worst may actually harm it. "Cost-benefit analysis is best taken as a pragmatic instrument, agnostic on the deep issues and designed to assist people in making complex judgments where multiple goods are involved." (Sunstein 2001a). This argument was echoed by Adler and Posner (2001) in an essay arguing that cost–benefit analysis corrects for "distorted preferences" or preferences that do not enhance the individual's welfare. Adler and Posner specifically call for agencies to ignore or discount such distorted preferences.

In another article, Sunstein (2001b) argues:

> The best defense of CBA relies not on controversial claims from neo-classical economics but on a simple appreciation of how we all make mistakes in thinking about risks. . . . Properly understood CBA should help us save lives, not only money. . . . What is most important here is to see that the case for cost–benefit analysis does not rest only or even mostly on economic grounds and that people of widely divergent views can support a suitably specified form of CBA. The emerging questions involve not whether to do CBA, but how; it is to those questions that we should now be turning.

Sunstein (2002b) also argued for CBA as a pro-democratic reform that enhanced the transparency of agency decisionmaking:

> There are democratic advantages as well . . . interest groups often manipulate policy in their preferred directions, sometimes by exaggerating risks, sometimes by minimizing them, sometimes by utilizing heuristics and biases strategically so as to mobilize public sentiment in their preferred directions. An effort to produce a fair accounting of actual dangers should help to diminish the danger of interest group manipulation.

This transparency argument had been made occasionally in the past by advocates of cost–benefit analysis (Arrow et al. 1996), but it had never been made by a supporter of government regulation, nor had the argument been explicitly based on the findings of behavioral economics.

Finally, Sunstein (2002b) synthesized the growing acceptance of cost–benefit analysis by Congress and by the courts. Employing what Sunstein called "cost–benefit default principles," courts had evinced some growing acceptance of cost–benefit analysis as a technique for agency decisionmaking. These principles can certainly be interpreted as allowing agencies to ignore de minimis risks, consider costs of their actions, decline to over-regulate, and balance benefits and costs. Indeed, Sunstein postulates that the principles may even require agencies to conduct CBA.

While Sunstein was developing a pro-regulation argument for cost–benefit analysis,[11] the George W. Bush administration was provoking a strong reaction from many of the same advocates who had fought CBA during the previous several administrations. Heinzerling along with Frank Ackerman produced a frequently cited book (Ackerman and Heinzerling 2004) decrying CBA in its entirety, and pro-regulatory organizations like OMB Watch and the Center for Progressive Reform echoed many of the arguments made by Heinzerling and Ackerman. Sinden et al. (2009), responding to Adler and Posner's call for "New Foundations of Cost–Benefit Analysis," argue that the theoretical and practical weaknesses of CBA are too great to be mended and that CBA should be replaced by feasibility analysis.

Bush's first OIRA Administrator was the controversial John Graham, who was often the subject of considerable vitriol from OMB Watch and the Center for Progressive Reform. Graham, however, echoed some of Sunstein's arguments about the potential for cost–benefit analysis to serve a pro-regulatory aim. He pioneered the "prompt letter" from OIRA, which used analysis to push agencies to pursue regulatory initiatives. After leaving OIRA, he cited several instances during his tenure when OIRA argued in favor of regulation because of the results of cost–benefit analysis. Graham also argued that there was a need for cost–benefit analysis to take greater account of distributional concerns, particularly the impact of regulations on the poorest members of society (Graham 2008).

In this last point, Graham found support from other academic voices that could not be easily characterized as anti-regulation. Adler (2006) argued that equity is a distinct consideration that should be added to considerations of efficiency and that the currency for equity should be well-being. Equity analysis should inform all natural hazards policy and choices about how to structure preparedness, response, and recovery. He believes that equity analysis should be focused on avoiding poverty (reducing death, physical injury, etc.).

Farrow (2009) put forward another way to incorporate equity into CBA. He argues that, since redistribution is often seen as the central issue in government policy, analysis of regulatory impact must include it. He calls on OIRA to improve its guidance on distributional analysis and provides several suggestions, including analysis of impact on particularly disadvantaged groups and that OIRA conduct sensitivity analysis on the current assumption that the marginal utility of income is constant across income levels.[12] Any such analysis would add support for regulations that distribute income from wealthier individuals to poorer ones.

Sunstein echoed these calls, saying that, "[i]n addition to knowing the benefits and costs of regulation, it is necessary to know who bears those costs and enjoys those benefits" (2002b). Sunstein recommended that "[e]xisting executive orders calling for CBA . . . be amended to require a distributional analysis as well" (2002a). Since one of the chief criticisms of the nature of CBA had been its reliance on willingness-to-pay measures of welfare and the bias that these measures had against those with lower incomes, a change in CBA to incorporate distributional equity would go a long way to answering these critics.

While the academic debate was slowly evolving, the "facts on the ground" were changing more rapidly. Agencies throughout the federal government were conducting cost–benefit analyses of their regulations, and the techniques they were using were rapidly becoming more sophisticated. EPA alone spent millions of dollars on CBAs (Adler and Posner 1999) and created its own guidelines for analysis (Revesz and Livermore 2008).

Outside of the United States, cost–benefit analysis has had a growing role in the regulatory process emerging in the European Union. Wiener (2006) writes:

> Europe and America now appear to be converging on the analytic basis for regulation. In a process of hybridization, European institutions are borrowing "Better Regulation" reforms from both the US approach to regulatory review using benefit–cost analysis and from European member states' initiatives on administrative costs and simplification; in turn the European Commission is helping to spread these reforms among the member states.

This movement of CBA to Europe is a further indication of the growing breadth of support for it and its likely permanence in the United States.

The European Union formally began impact assessments in 2002. European Commission directorates conduct impact assessments. Starting in 2006, these assessments were reviewed by an Impact Assessment Board in the Office of the Secretary-General. This system means that legislation (in addition to administrative action) in the EU is subject to impact assessment (Wiener and Alemanno 2010).[13]

Two important works were published that signaled an important landmark in the debate over cost–benefit analysis. In *Retaking Rationality,* Revesz and Livermore (2008) issued a rebuke to pro-regulation forces who had argued against cost–benefit analysis. They said, "Now is a good time for liberals to enter the conversation. . . . [I]t was more politically expedient for progressives to issue blanket criticisms than develop more nuanced positions. But entrenchment in that position cost proregulatory groups."

Revesz and Livermore argued that, by adopting a strict anti-CBA position, pro-regulation forces had allowed opponents of regulation to paint them as anti-rational. They went on to explain:

> Yet cost–benefit analysis is only inherently antiregulatory if proregulatory groups are gulled into passivity by that belief. Proregulatory groups must shake off their torpor. Their opposition to cost–benefit analysis, even if it was understandable at the outset[,] has become very counterproductive.

Revesz and Livermore argued that there are many ways to reform cost–benefit analysis to ensure that it leads to fairer (pro-regulation) outcomes and urged liberals to make these arguments.

The second work was in many ways even more groundbreaking. Lisa Heinzerling, who had been a leader of the critics of cost–benefit analysis, cooperated with two economists and supporters of cost–benefit analysis, Winston Harrington and Richard Morgenstern, to edit the volume *Reforming Regulatory Impact Analysis* (2009). The introductory chapter acknowledges the seeming permanence of cost–benefit analysis on the regulatory landscape. After a series of case studies, Heinzerling and her two co-authors offer a number of recommendations. These recommendations overlap considerably with the recommendations of Revesz and Livermore and, more importantly (since he is the new Administrator of OIRA), with those that Sunstein had made in various works.

Then, in February 2009, President Obama appointed Cass Sunstein as OIRA Administrator. After a contentious confirmation process, Sunstein was confirmed by the Senate in September 2009.[14] The appointment of Sunstein signals a commitment by President Obama to cost–benefit analysis. While a new executive order governing regulatory review is still pending as of this writing, Sunstein's appointment ensures that any such order will preserve a prominent role for cost–benefit analysis in the Obama administration.[15]

Much of this direction is evident in the 2009 report to Congress from OMB on the costs and benefits of federal regulations. This report is the first of the annual reports to Congress issued since Sunstein was confirmed as Administrator of OIRA. The report carefully catalogs the ways in which behavior systematically deviates from rationality and calls for reforms in regulation to account for these deviations. Such reforms include an emphasis on disclosure as a regulatory tool, the use of default rules and simplification, making costs of social harms more salient, and influencing social norms.

*Table 28.1    Historical developments in the use of CBA in the United States regulatory process*

| Date | Development |
|------|-------------|
| 1970s | Presidents Nixon, Ford, and Carter begin use of CBA. |
| 1981 | President Reagan issues Executive Order 12291 and requires CBA for certain rules. |
| 1993 | President Clinton rescinds E.O. 12291 and replaces it with E.O. 12866, reaffirming the use of CBA but modifying the requirement. |
| 2001 | President Bush appoints John Graham as OIRA Administrator. |
| 2006 | President Bush issues E.O. 13422 modifying E.O. 12866. |
| 2009 | President Obama repeals E.O. 13422, and appoints Cass Sunstein as OIRA Administrator. |

## 28.4    THE FUTURE OF CBA IN THE REGULATORY PROCESS

It has been said that President's Clinton's issuance of Executive Order 12866 cemented the role of presidential review in the regulatory process (Blumstein 2001). Throughout Clinton's presidency and the presidency of George W. Bush, however, the debate on the other crucial piece of E.O. 12866, cost–benefit analysis, grew in its intensity. President Obama's appointment of Sunstein and probable issuance of a new executive order with cost–benefit analysis contained in it[16] will in all likelihood do for cost–benefit analysis what President Clinton did for executive review: render it a part of the regulatory process that is taken for granted.

What does this mean for the future of cost–benefit analysis and for the future of the regulatory process? For the early proponents of CBA who had hoped that CBA would lead to deregulatory outcomes, the permanent ascendance of CBA is hardly an unmitigated victory. In order to ensure that CBA stayed in the regulatory process, both the technique and its application required and will continue to require modification. Part of this modification occurred when President Clinton changed the requirement that regulations have benefits that "exceed" their costs to a requirement that benefits "justify" their costs.

The recent work by Revesz and Livermore (2008) and by Harrington et al. (2009) signals the other adaptations that we are likely to see in the application of CBA. Among these suggestions are the listing of benefits and costs in a non-monetized manner, greater and more transparent consideration of alternative policy options (Harrington et al. 2009), greater accounting of ancillary benefits, decreased use of intergenerational discounting (Revesz and Livermore 2008), and analyses of deregulatory options with the same rigor as regulatory ones (Revesz and Livermore 2008; Harrington et al. 2009). All of these changes will lead to analyses that are at least as likely to favor regulation as deregulation, and few of them (if any) would be opposed by economists.

The result predicted by Revesz and Livermore, which I find entirely reasonable, will be a CBA that is used to argue for regulation as often as it is used to argue against it. An interesting question is whether CBA will lose some of its original supporters once it is seen as a tool that can be used to defend regulation as easily as attack it. In any case, the policy battles over cost–benefit analysis in the next decade are likely to be fights over techniques and specifics rather than over the merit of CBA itself. Indeed, one might see CBA used by agencies not previously required by law to use it if a consensus emerges that CBA is a valuable tool.[17]

However, there are still two criticisms of CBA and its use that have not been effectively answered by those who support it (either those pro-regulation supporters of CBA or those anti-regulation supporters of CBA). The first of these, mentioned above, is that CBA, as currently utilized, is merely a cover for political goals. Olson (1984) first made this point, but several other scholars have recently emphasized it.

Shapiro (2005) argued that the coupling of the enforcement of CBA with executive review inevitably forced CBA to take a backseat when the results of analysis conflicted with political priorities. Wagner (2009) writes: "RIAs may serve primarily as a mechanism for promoting agency decisions rather than scrutinizing them." She contends: "[t]hat the RIA offers nothing to policy analysis is, in fact, precisely the point; in other words, the point is to protect the rulemaking, not to open it up to attack." These recent arguments echo the concerns that Olson (1984) raised a generation earlier that CBA was used primarily to provide cover for political goals.

If there is general agreement regarding the worthiness of CBA, focus may turn to this issue of whether CBA can achieve its potential in its current institutional structure or whether it is inevitable that CBA, as constructed, will be intertwined with and subverted by politics. Some have argued that only if responsibility for conducting and/or overseeing regulatory analysis is removed from the executive branch, which also has responsibility for issuing regulations, will analysis play a role in guiding regulatory decisions. This argument leads naturally to calls for a Congressional office akin to the Government Accountability Office (GAO) to play a role in supervising the conduct of CBA (Niskanen 2003). I expect the institutional location and setting of cost–benefit analysis to be a primary debate in U.S. regulatory politics in the decade to come.

This debate will also surround the growth of CBA in Europe. In Chapter 29, Wegrich (2011) describes how analysis is not as wedded to issues of political control of agencies in Europe as in the United States. However, there have been calls for greater centralized regulatory oversight in Europe, and the EC has also implemented the Impact Assessment Board described above. These developments will force the EU to grapple with many of the institutional issues described here. Radaelli and Meuwese (2010) argue that these developments have already had the effect of strengthening the Secretariat-General.

The second issue that supporters of cost–benefit analysis have failed to address is the length of time it adds to the rulemaking process. As mentioned above, this was first raised by McGarity (1992) and Mashaw and Harfst (1990). Sunstein recognizes this problem and notes that, if the impact of CBA is to delay beneficial regulations, then CBA itself would fail a cost–benefit test. If, as is shown in the numerous reports to Congress by OIRA, regulations on average have net benefits, then delaying regulations to conduct cost–benefit analysis has a social cost.

Although the question of whether CBA, in its current or future forms, adds sufficient social benefits to regulations to justify these costs is an open one, there is scant evidence to date that rulemaking is decreasing or moving slowly. Coglianese (2009) has cast doubt on Mashaw and Harfst's conclusions about NHTSA. Similarly, Johnson (2008) has cast doubt on the ossification hypothesis at EPA. Informal studies of the numbers of rules and the number of pages annually in the *Federal Register* show no pattern of decline (Crews 2007). Finally, Yackee and Yackee (2010) use the Unified Agenda[18] to examine the factors that affect the time between proposal and finalization of a regulation. They find that rules that are subject to procedural controls, such as cost–benefit analysis, are actually promulgated faster. This implies that the costs of CBA are low.

By contrast, the benefits of CBA, especially if reformed in the ways hoped for by pro-regulation advocates, are likely to be significant. CBA is designed to increase the net benefits of regulation and, if it is correctly and faithfully implemented, it is certainly likely that it will do so in at least some circumstances. This would lead to CBA having potentially large benefits, making any small delays in the promulgation of rules worthwhile.

In the early years of the George W. Bush administration, Sunstein described regulatory policymaking as evolving from "1970s environmentalism" to "the cost–benefit state" (Sunstein 2002b). This conclusion was likely premature. Cost–benefit analysis was still the subject of considerable controversy at that point. Now, however, with Sunstein's own ascension as "regulatory czar" and the publication of works from liberals suggesting reform of cost–benefit analysis rather than repeal, the cost–benefit state may actually be upon us.

Economists inside and outside the government are enhancing the techniques used for CBA. Cost–benefit analysis is being exported to the EU and to the Organisation of Economic Co-operation and Development (OECD) countries rather than having its use restricted to the United States. Reforms to include findings from behavioral economics and to incorporate distributional concerns will likely broaden the support for CBA across the ideological spectrum. If other reforms suggested by Revesz and Livermore (2008) and Harrington et al. (2009) are adopted, this support will only increase.

At this point, the primary remaining concern will be whether CBA as implemented can actually achieve the goals voiced for it by those on both sides of regulatory debate. Examination of CBA will turn to its institutional setting within the regulatory process. Questions about the independence of those conducting the analyses will dominate the debate, and the resolution of these questions may result in institutional structures that further cement cost–benefit analysis as part of the regulatory process.

## NOTES

1. Executive Order 12044 43 Fed. Reg. 12661 (24 March 1978).
2. Exec. Order No. 12291 46 Fed. Reg 13193 (19 February 1981).
3. OIRA had been created the previous year in the Paperwork Reduction Act.
4. Jim Tozzi was the Deputy Administrator of OIRA under Reagan and Bush.
5. Exec. Order No. 12866, 58 Fed Reg. 51735, Admin Mat 45070 (30 September 1993).
6. Blumstein (2001) wrote: "centralized presidential regulatory review has now taken center stage as an institutionalized part of the modern American Presidency."
7. In Chapter 30, Robinson and Hammit (2011) provide a summary of the issues associated with monetized health and mortality risks. See also Viscusi (2009).
8. Elliott had served as General Counsel of EPA.
9. Within government, agencies had also started to accept cost–benefit analysis and attempt to reform it rather than replace it. EPA was at the forefront of this effort, producing its own guidelines on cost–benefit analysis (Revesz and Livermore 2008).
10. http://en.wikipedia.org/wiki/Behavioral_economics

11. Other prominent economists in the Clinton administration such as Alan Blinder and Joseph Stiglitz also voiced cautious support for CBA (Wiener 2006).
12. Farrow notes that all regulatory impact analyses (RIAs) currently assume a constant marginal utility (MU) of income. If, instead of a constant, MU was $y^{-e}$, where e is the elasticity of marginal social welfare with respect to the income of a particular income class, analysis would better incorporate equity concerns.
13. While "impact assessment" is slightly different than CBA, in practice it is likely to be quite similar. CBAs conducted in the United States fall short of economic definitions of CBA (Hahn and Litan 2005), and therefore the impact assessments in Europe will likely resemble the regulatory analyses in the U.S.
14. Oddly the controversy centered on Sunstein's positions on animal rights, not on anything he had written about cost–benefit analysis.
15. On January 21, 2011, President Obama issued Executive Order 13563. E.O. 13563 reaffirmed the importance of cost–benefit analysis and maximizing net benefits in the regulatory process. The E.O. is likely to be the only order issued on this subject by the Obama Administration.
16 OIRA requested comment on a potential new executive order in February 2009.
17. These include regulations issued by independent agencies and regulations with an impact that is less than $100 million/year.
18. The Unified Agenda is issued every six months and lists all regulations planned by all federal agencies.

# BIBLIOGRAPHY

Ackerman, Frank and Lisa Heinzerling (2004), *Priceless: On Knowing the Price of Everything and the Value of Nothing,* New York: New Press.
Adler, Matthew (2006), 'Equity analysis and natural hazards policy', in Ronald Daniels, Howard Kunreuther and Donald Kettl (eds), *On Risk And Disaster: Lessons From Hurricane Katrina,* Philadelphia: University of Pennsylvania Press, pp. 129–52.
Adler, M. and E. Posner (1999), 'Rethinking cost–benefit analysis', *Yale Law Journal,* **109**, 165–230.
Adler, Matthew and Eric Posner (2001), 'Implementing cost–benefit analysis when preferences are distorted', in Matthew Adler and Eric Posner (eds), *Cost–Benefit Analysis: Legal, Economic, and Philosophical Perspectives,* Chicago: University of Chicago Press, pp. 269–312.
Arrow, Kenneth J., Maureen L. Cropper, George C. Eads, Robert W. Hahn, Lester B. Lave, Roger G. Noll, Paul R. Portney, Milton Russell, Richard Schmalensee, V. Kerry Smith and Robert N. Stavins (1996), *Benefit–Cost Analysis in Health and Safety Regulation: A Statement of Principles,* Washington, DC: American Enterprise Institute, Annapolis Center and Resources for the Future.
Blumstein, J. (2001), 'Regulatory review by the Executive Office of the President: an overview and policy analysis of current issues', *Duke Law Journal,* **51**,851–900.
Bressman, L.S. and M. Vandenbergh (2006), 'Inside the administrative state: a critical look at the practice of presidential control', *Michigan Law Review,* **105**, 47–100.
Coglianese, C. (2009), 'Has judicial review caused a rulemaking retreat?', paper presented at the annual meeting of the The Law and Society, J.W. Marriott Resort, Las Vegas, NV, 5 May.
Crews, C. (2007), *Ten Thousand Commandments: An Annual Snapshot of the Regulatory State,* Washington, DC: Competitive Enterprise Institute.
Demuth, C. and D. Ginsburg (1986), 'White House review of agency rulemaking', *Harvard Law Review,* **99**, 1075–1112.
Dreisen, D. (2006), 'Is cost–benefit analysis neutral', *University of Colorado Law Review,* **77**, 335–404.
Elliott, D. (1994), 'TQMing OMB: or why executive review under Executive Order 12291 works poorly and what President Clinton should do about it', *Law and Contemporary Problems,* **57**, 167–84.
Farrow, S. (2009), 'Incorporating equity in regulatory and benefit–cost analysis using risk based preferences', Working paper on file with author.
Friedman, Barry (1995), *Regulation in the Reagan–Bush Era,* Pittsburgh, PA: University of Pittsburgh Press.
Graham, J. (2008), 'Saving lives through *Administrative Law and Economics*', *University of Pennsylvania Law Review,* **157**, 395–540.
Gramm, W. (1986), 'Additional procedures concerning OIRA review under Executive Orders nos. 12291 and 12498 [revised]', reprinted in Appendix III of Regulatory Program of the United States Government, Office of Management and Budget, 1992.
Hahn, R. and R. Litan (2005), 'Counting regulatory benefits and costs: lessons for the US and Europe', *Journal of International Economic Law,* **8**, 473–508.
Harrington, Winston, Lisa Heinzerling and Richard Morgenstern (eds) (2009), *Reforming Regulatory Impact Analysis,* Washington, DC: Resources for the Future Press.

Heinzerling, L. (1997), 'Reductionist regulatory reform', *Fordham Environmental Law Review*, **8**, 459–96.

Heinzerling, L. (1999), 'Discounting life', *Yale Law Journal*, **108**, 1911–16.

Heinzerling, L. (2000), 'The rights of statistical people', *Harvard Environmental Law Review*, **24**, 189–208.

Johnson, S. (2008), 'Ossification's demise: an empirical analysis of EPA rulemaking from 2001–2005', *Environmental Law*, **38**, 767–92.

Kelman, S. (1981), 'Cost–benefit analysis: an ethical critique', *AEI Journal on Government and Society Regulation*, March/April, 33–8.

Mashaw, Jerry and David Harfst (1990), *The Struggle for Auto Safety*, Cambridge: Basic Books.

McGarity, T. (1987), 'Regulatory analysis and regulatory reform', *Texas Law Review*, **65**, 1243–1334.

McGarity, T. (1992), 'Some thoughts on deossifying the rulemaking process', *Duke Law Journal*, **41**, 1385–1462.

Niskanen, W. (2003), 'More lonely numbers', *Regulation*, **26**, 22–7.

Olson, E. (1984), 'The quiet shift of power: Office of Management and Budget supervision of Environmental Protection Agency rulemaking under Executive Order 12291', *Virginia Journal of Natural Resource Law*, **4**, 1–80.

Radaelli, C.M. and A.C.M. Meuwese (2010), 'Hard questions, hard solutions: proceduralisation through impact assessment in the EU', *West European Politics*, **33**, 136–53.

Revesz, Richard and Michael Livermore (2008), *Retaking Rationality: How Cost–Benefit Analysis Can Better Protect the Environment and Our Health*, Oxford: Oxford University Press.

Robinson, Lisa and James Hammitt (2010), 'Valuing Health and Longevity in Regulatory Analysis: Current Issues and Challenges', in David Levi-Faur (ed.), *Handbook on the Politics of Regulation*, Cheltenham: Edward Elgar Publishing.

Shapiro, S. (2005), 'Unequal partners: cost benefit analysis and executive review of regulations', *Environmental Law Reporter*, **35**, 10433–44.

Sinden, A. (2004), 'Cass Sunstein's cost–benefit lite: economics for liberals', *Columbia Journal of Environmental Law*, **29**, 191–242.

Sinden, A., D.A. Kysar and D.M. Driesen (2009), 'Cost–benefit analysis: new foundations on shifting sound', *Regulation & Governance*, **3** (1), 48–71.

Sunstein, Cass (2001a), 'Cognition and cost–benefit analysis', in Matthew Adler and Eric Posner (eds), *Cost–Benefit Analysis: Legal, Economic, and Philosophical Perspectives*, Chicago: University of Chicago Press, pp. 223–68.

Sunstein, C. (2001b), 'Is cost–benefit analysis for everyone?', *Administrative Law Review*, **53**, 299–314.

Sunstein, Cass (2002a), *Risk and Reason*, Cambridge: Cambridge University Press.

Sunstein, Cass (2002b), *The Cost–Benefit State*, Washington, DC: American Bar Association.

Sunstein, Cass (2004), *The Second Bill of Rights: FDR'S Unfinished Revolution and Why We Need It More than Ever*, New York: Basic Books.

Viscusi, W.K. (2009), 'The devaluation of life', *Regulation & Governance*, **3**, 103–27.

Wagner, W. (2009), *The CAIR RIA: Advocacy Dressed Up as Policy Analysis in Reforming Regulatory Impact Analysis*, Washington D.C.: Resources for the Future Press, pp. 56–82.

Wegrich, Kai (2011), 'Regulatory impact assessment: ambition, design and politics', in David Levi-Faur (ed.), *Handbook on the Politics of Regulation*, Cheltenham: Edward Elgar Publishing.

Weidenbaum, M. (1997), 'Regulatory process reform: from Ford to Clinton', *Regulation*, **20** (1).

Wiener, J. (2006), 'Better regulation in Europe', *Current Legal Problems*, **59**, 447–518.

Wiener, J. and A. Alemanno (2010), 'Comparing regulatory oversight bodies across the Atlantic: the Office of Information and Regulatory Affairs in the US and the Impact Assessment Board in the EU', working paper, available at: ssrn.com.

Yackee, J. and S. Yackee (2010), 'Administrative procedures and bureaucratic performance: is federal rule-making ossified?', *Journal of Public Administration Research and Theory*, **20**, 261–82.

# 29 Regulatory impact assessment: ambition, design and politics
## *Kai Wegrich*

When drafting policy proposals, politicians and bureaucrats have to strike a balance between two dimensions of the task. They have to engage with issues of political desirability and feasibility and at the same time develop a 'technically' sound policy proposal. The latter part of the task is increasingly subject to rules and standards that prescribe procedures and analytical methods of drafting regulations. Bureaucrats are required to conduct or commission a cost–benefit analysis or other forms of economic analysis. They are required to take these into account when advocating their preferred regulatory response. This activity is called (regulatory) impact assessment (RIA/IA, also regulatory impact analysis).

In the last three decades, RIA has become a key tool of 'regulatory reform' or 'better regulation' and has been widely diffused internationally. Although its history can be traced back longer, RIA is usually considered to have originated in the US. More specifically, President Reagan's 1981 executive order no. 12291 is seen as the original version of a governmental regulation establishing RIA as a mandatory element in government rulemaking. Since then, RIA has diffused across first Western Europe and then the wider OECD world (OECD 2009: 15). More recently, transition and developing countries have emulated these reforms, with the encouragement of international organisations such as the OECD and the World Bank.

Combined with the unbiased consultation of societal actors, the economic analysis of regulatory options should enhance the quality of government regulation in generally all regulatory domains. In an ideal world, the selection of one regulatory option over others would be based on a comparison of the costs, benefits and potential side effects of various discrete options. However, impact assessment systems are not situated in an ideal world, and the history of RIA is littered with disappointment concerning the effects of RIAs on actual policy choices and contestation concerning the design and operation of RIA regimes. The design and practice of RIA systems vary widely cross-nationally and often deviate from the ideals of methodologically sound cost–benefit analysis. In some cases, the RIA practice does not go beyond symbolic politics (Radaelli 2010).

This chapter argues that variations in RIA practice, as well as disappointment with and contestation around RIA, result from two related characteristics of RIA. First, RIA has developed from different, if not competing, reform traditions, and the purpose of RIA is therefore contested in itself between different advocacy coalitions. Second, RIA systems are a type of meta- or second-order regulation that seeks to establish control structures within government. The establishment of such control structures implies trespassing on the turf of agencies or ministries and therefore often faces resistance from turf-conscious bureaucrats and politicians. In other words, centralising control of RIA practice stirs up opposition from the controlled and undermines the case for RIA. Because of these characteristics, embedding RIA into day-to-day policy-making is a thorny task of institutional reform that is prone to disappointment and contestation.

The following sections will first explore these two characteristics separately and then show how they are shaped by political forces, drawing on different theoretical perspectives that have been explored to understand the political logic of RIA design and application. The chapter argues that RIA design and application will continue to be subject to politics and contestation – a claim that contrasts with the 'textbook image' of RIA as an apolitical tool for rational decision-making.

Empirically, the chapter mainly draws on four governmental contexts: the US, the EU, Britain and Germany. While the US is often regarded as the benchmark case of RIA, the emphasis here is given to the EU's ambitious and comprehensive system of impact assessment. In addition, the German and the British experience of 'better regulation' and different systems of government are contrasted.

## 29.1    REFORM TRADITIONS OF AND RATIONALES FOR RIA

While today regulatory impact assessment is regarded as the flagship tool of the wider better regulation movement that has gained prominence since the late 1990s, it is an offspring of earlier reform developments, in particular those in the 1970s and 1980s. Three reform traditions have been particularly important in shaping the motivation for and design of RIA systems.

The first attempts at establishing impact analysis in the policy-making process have been associated with the movement towards rational policy-making that gained momentum in the mid- to late 1960s. Instruments such as cost–benefit analysis were first established in the process of budget planning (PPBS – Programming, Planning, and Budgeting System), at first in the US, as a reform initiative in the Department of Defense that was later expanded to the other areas of government. In the 1970s, European governments embarked on similar experiments to base budgetary and policy decisions on comprehensive cost–benefit analyses and detailed long-term planning.

The idea of reforming the budgetary process and policy planning using cost–benefit analysis and planning tools was received with strong resistance within government and was also regarded as being insensitive to the real complexities of budget planning and policy-making, and hence soon regarded as a failed reform. However, a range of sector-based initiatives to establish analytical capacities in government was continued (cf., e.g., Wollmann 1989). Today's comprehensive impact assessment systems have been developed on the basis of a variety of sector-specific impact assessments, from environmental impact assessments to business impact tests (cf. Allio 2008: 70ff.). As Table 29.1 shows, the EU Commission's 'integrated' system of RIA – requiring an assessment of all significant economic, social and environmental impacts (the 'three pillars') – was established on the basis of a range of sectoral impact assessments and initiatives (see Table 29.1).

This reform tradition of rational policy-making has shaped the 'textbook approach' to impact assessment promoted by the OECD and the World Bank among others.[1] This textbook model has made strong inroads into European RIA approaches, in particular that of the European Commission and the United Kingdom. RIA is supposed to

*Table 29.1   Major steps in the evolution of the EU Commission's impact assessment system*

| | |
|---|---|
| 1986 | Introduction of the Business Impact Assessment (BIA) as a tool to assess the costs of new legislation on business enterprises. |
| 1993 | DG Environment introduces the Green Star system to ensure that all proposals with a significant environmental impact are subject to an environmental appraisal. |
| 1996 | The President of the European Commission issues Regulatory Policy Guidelines requiring the Explanatory Memoranda, accompanying each legislative proposal, to answer a list of questions related to the likely impacts of a proposal. |
| 1998 | Business test panels (BTPs) established as a complement to BIAs to obtain better information from businesses on significant impacts. |
| 2001 | DG SANCO (Health and Consumers) issues guidelines for the assessment of impacts of policy proposals on consumer interests (to be applied only within DG SANCO). |
| 2002 | Adoption of the integrated IA system to 'integrate, reinforce, streamline and replace' all existing single-sector impact assessments and to establish one approach for all the Commission's services. |
| 2003 | Inter-Institutional Agreement on Better Law-Making: commitment of the European Parliament and the Council to the same IA methodology. |
| 2005 | EC Communication on Better Regulation for Growth and Jobs: stronger focus on economic analysis in impact assessments. |
| 2006 | Introduction of ex ante assessment of administrative costs for business into IA system. |
| 2007 | Introduction of the Impact Assessment Board as a quality control unit. |

*Sources:*   Own compilation based on Renda (2006); Allio (2008); Meuwese (2008); European Commission (2010b).

improve regulatory decision-making by clarifying objectives and identifying the lowest costs to achieve these objectives (cf. Baldwin 2010).[2]

A different, if not competing, reform tradition is associated with eternal complaints about 'too much' governmental regulation and red tape. This reform line is inspired by public choice theories of regulation and its 'regulatory capture' claim that has resulted in deep scepticism towards government regulation being able to act in the public interest (Stigler 1971; cf. Croley 2008). In the regulatory reform debate of this tradition, the critical stance on the government's role as a regulator was picked up (rather than the theory's critical view on the role of industry), and limiting government regulation was regarded as the main purpose of regulatory reform. If regulation is unavoidable, low-intervention forms of regulation are preferred, such as self-regulatory and voluntary schemes.

RIA has been identified as a tool for pursuing these objectives since the mid- to late 1970s. US presidents from Richard Nixon to Ronald Reagan were all concerned about the costs of regulation (on businesses), and their successive efforts to establish mechanisms to review the costs imposed by regulatory agencies have culminated in a comprehensive system of oversight exercised by the Office of Management and Budget (OMB) and the Office of Information and Regulatory Affairs (OIRA) within the OMB (Reagan 1987: 162). The purpose of limiting regulatory activities is manifested in the US system in RIA rules that prescribe that the benefits of new regulation should outweigh or justify the costs.[3] Similarly, in the UK, the idea of impact assessment was put on the agenda in the mid-1980s as an attempt to limit regulatory burden. 'Lifting the burden' was the title of the 1985 white paper seeking to introduce the assessment of compliance costs for business as the core of an impact assessment system. The current UK and the European Commission RIA systems include rules prescribing the active search for alternatives to classic command-and-control regulation and the consideration of the 'do-nothing option' as presumably more market-friendly policy choices.

While these two reform traditions have long dominated regulatory reform debates and the design of RIA systems, a third reform tradition is of relevance. Radaelli and De Francesco (2010) call this tradition 'democratic governance'. Prosser (2010: 214) labels it the 'deliberative type of regulatory reform' (see also Croley 2008: 61–8). All stress the role of RIA in providing societal actors with access to participate in the rule-making process and, in particular, providing equal access to all affected and interested parties. RIA is seen as a tool to institutionalise this access and to provide a forum for debating regulatory issues in an open and transparent way. Administrative procedures are relevant in structuring such debates and organising access to the decision-making process and, in particular, opening up the process for more diffused and poorly organised interests (Croley 2008; Radaelli and De Francesco 2010). The US Administrative Procedure Act from 1946 – requiring the regulatory agency to notify planned regulation in the *Federal Register* and invite comments from the public – is regarded as the original incarnation of such an approach. Today, most RIA systems include regulations regarding the consultation of external stakeholders, although cross-nationally the specificity of these rules varies, as does the practice of handling them.

All three reform traditions play a role in shaping contemporary RIA systems, but their significance varies substantially across countries and over time. In Europe, concerns about too much regulation have made strong inroads into RIA systems since the mid-2000s, shifting the emphasis away from the rational policy-making image of RIA that dominated the agenda in the late 1990s and early 2000s (cf. Radaelli 2007). In the US, recent reforms to the RIA system have focused on strengthening participatory elements and increasing transparency of the rule-making process (Coglianese et al. 2009).

However, real-world RIA systems are shaped not only by these substantial rationales for impact assessment but also by its character as a system of intra-governmental control. Section 29.2 deals with the logic of this specific model of intervention in more detail, before section 29.3 explores how the substantial rationales and the logic of intervention are separately and jointly shaped by the politics of regulation.

## 29.2    THE COMPONENTS OF IMPACT ASSESSMENT SYSTEMS

The essence of impact assessment systems lies in the combination of analytical methods with procedural standards. Process standards include rules concerning the major stages of the rule-making process, for example if and when the public should be consulted, what kind of impact should be assessed (economic, social, environmental), which methods should be applied in the assessment and how the results of the analysis should inform regulatory choice. By defining analytical methods as procedural standards, the use of these methods can be standardised and controlled from the position of an organisation or unit that is separated from the regulatory institution itself. This is needed to avoid patchy and episodic, rather than systematic, usage of the analytical tools prescribed in RIA rules. Establishing such a regulatory (or control) system within government is a challenging task of institutional design, as will become clear when unpacking the different components of such a system.

### 29.2.1 Process Standards

The first component is the set of process standards that regulate both the regulatory decision-making process and the methods of analysis applied in the impact assessment. A key difference across national RIA systems is the scope of these standards. In the US, regulatory agencies of the executive branch are subject to RIA standards and presidential oversight, but not rule-making by independent commissions or the law-making process of Congress. In contrast, ministries that draft the bulk of laws are the main target group of RIA rules in Westminster and continental European systems of government.

Empirical variations also exist concerning how comprehensively the RIA system seeks to regulate the process of regulatory design. However, the 'gold standard', as defined by the OECD (2009) and others (e.g. World Bank 2010), intends to provide for a complete structuring of the whole regulatory process – from the definition of the problem to be addressed to the policy/regulatory choice and the planning of the later ex post evaluation. We can draw on the European Commission's impact assessment system to exemplify this comprehensive logic. Figure 29.1 depicts the IA cycle in its standard form.[4] Prior to the actual impact assessment work, a roadmap providing an estimated timetable for the proposal and setting out how the impact assessment will be taken forward needs to be drafted. Early in the process, an impact assessment steering group (IASG), consisting of the directorates-general whose policies are likely to be affected by or contribute to the objectives of the initiative, is set up in the leading directorate-general. The consultation process is initiated before the impact assessment is drafted in order to generate input on problem definition, formulation of objectives and development of options. This is different from the US, where the 'notice and comment' procedure prescribes the publication of the draft regulation together with the impact analysis.

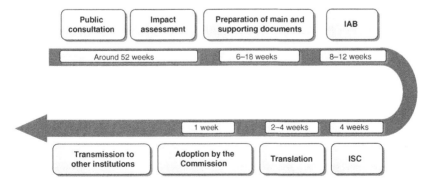

*Source:* Own depiction based on figure in European Commission (2009a, Annex).

*Figure 29.1 European Commission impact assessment system*

The actual impact assessment is carried out on this basis, of which parts are frequently outsourced to research organisations and consultancies. The director-general assumes responsibility for the soundness of the IA by signing off on it before it is presented to the Commission's Impact Assessment Board (IAB, the RIA quality control watchdog in the General Secretariat of the EU Commission), which issues an opinion on the quality of the IA. The board can demand a revision and resubmission of the IA if the quality is considered below standard – which happened in 43 out of 135 cases in 2008. Four of these cases had to be revised and resubmitted one more time (European Court of Auditors 2009: 31). The regulatory proposal, along with the IA material (report, IA board opinion), is submitted first to inter-service consultation (ISC) only on this basis and finally to the College of Commissioners and is published on the EU Commission's website after the Commission has adopted the proposal. The whole process, from the initial proposal to the publication of the proposal on the EU Commission's website, can easily take between one and two years, depending on the complexity of the proposal (cf. TEP 2007: 36).

The impact assessment itself is also regulated in detail. First, unlike in the US, the EU Commission does not make use of a quantifiable threshold for the selection of initiatives that require an IA. Based on a set of predefined criteria, the Secretariat General and the concerned departments decide on a case-by-case basis if an IA is necessary. According to the Commission's IA guidelines, IAs need to be carried out for 'the most important Commission initiatives and those which will have the most far-reaching impacts' (European Commission 2009a: 6).

According to the EU Commission's rules, an impact assessment report should always start with the definition of the problem and the formulation of the objectives of the proposal. Next, the policy options to achieve these objectives should be developed. These options can be very specific and detailed, for example the five different targets for $CO_2$ emissions for new, light-load trucks (European Commission 2009b). However, EU impact assessments frequently compare packages of combined measures that are distinguished according to the type of regulation (regulation, directive, recommendation, open method of coordination). The impact assessment for an action plan on organ donation and transplantation (European Commission 2008), for instance, explores four policy options: 1) the do-nothing option; 2) a non-regulatory approach; 3) a 'flexible' directive; and 4) a 'stringent' directive. These different options are assessed individually and then compared. In terms of the methods to be applied, the EU's system allows for both cost–benefit analysis and other methods of economic analysis to be selected by the leading directorate-general. And, while quantification is demanded whenever possible, the broad policy packages included in regulatory proposals do not always lend themselves easily to strict cost–benefit analysis.[5] More qualitative methods, such as multiple criteria analysis, are applied frequently,[6] although they are only regarded as second-best solutions.

## 29.2.2 Assessment Criteria

Impact assessments play a role in shaping the political debate around policy proposals, for example when findings from impact assessments are used to justify choices or criticise proposals in policy debates. The media increasingly refer to data reported in impact assessments. Data on regulatory costs in particular, but also on economic benefits, are picked up from impact assessments and press releases highlighting these data. For example, new EU standards for home insulation (for purposes of saving energy) are supported by data on jobs created in the building industry (*Financial Times Deutschland*, 22 October 2008). On the other hand, new $CO_2$ emission standards for light trucks have been criticised for increases in the purchase price (*Financial Times Deutschland*, 11 August 2009). Therefore it does matter what kinds of impacts are covered by impact assessments and which are excluded. Political controversies regarding the design of RIA systems often centre around the inclusion and definition of assessment criteria (and linked methods) as a core design element of RIA systems.

The specific problem, if not dilemma, of designing IA systems lies in the trade-off between the depth and breadth of analysis: the more assessment criteria are included, the more complex and burdensome the RIA procedure will be. Considering all assessment criteria in depth, as demanded by today's comprehensive RIA systems, could become an 'impossible job' for policy bureaucracies to carry out or control. With a high number of assessment criteria also comes the problem of weighting them: how should the trade-off between negative environmental impacts and positive economic ones be assessed? In the EU context, economic, social and environmental criteria have equal relevance on paper, but in practice economic impacts – and in particular the impact on business – are frequently the centre of the analysis (cf. European Court of Auditors 2009: 36).

The economic solution to the weighting problem lies in the monetisation of all costs (as practised in the US and also in the insurance business, e.g. the 'value of life'), but these approaches are highly contested in many (European) countries and are loaded with methodological controversies.[7]

### 29.2.3   Control and Enforcement

A final core design component of RIA systems is the control and enforcement of compliance with the process standards. Whole-of-government process standards constitute an intervention from the outside into departmental (or agency) policy-making that usually receives at best a lukewarm reception by 'turf'-conscious executives. In particular, if the impact assessment criteria are not part of the set of criteria usually relevant to a specific unit of government, taking these systematically into account will not be the first priority of the policy bureaucrats in this unit. Thus mechanisms of monitoring and enforcing compliance are needed, but establishing such regulatory relationships is a thorny issue of institutional reform (Lodge and Hood 2010). The unit subject to internal governmental regulation can, in general, refer to similar sources of legitimacy and authority in order to deflect intervention from another governmental organisation. A specific problem of monitoring compliance with RIA rules is the high number of impact assessments annually carried out.[8] Both monitoring of compliance with RIA standards and enforcement activities responding to non-compliance are time-consuming and may come at substantial costs politically. To provide monitoring activity with more clout, some European governments have established independent oversight bodies or commissions that are staffed with retired senior public official, business people and experts.[9]

The difficulty of 'regulation inside government' could be addressed by moving beyond the reliance on hierarchical enforcement as the only alternative to non-enforcement (see Lodge and Hood 2010 on the different modes of control). In practice, many governments have long relied on a combination of hierarchy and cooperative styles of control – usually in the form of combining process standards with a support infrastructure, including so-called 'satellite units' of central better regulation units in departments. One recent shift has been to move to targets as a variation of hierarchical modes of control. Most EU member countries have adopted reduction targets for the administrative burden imposed on businesses by government regulation, usually 25 per cent.[10] The target approach allows for a systematic assessment of progress but also creates incentives to 'game' the numbers. Another trend in control relations is to link quality assurance processes to mechanisms of public naming and shaming. For example, the EU Commission's RIA quality control unit, the Impact Assessment Board, publishes its opinions on the quality of the impact assessments carried out by the Directorates General. Overall, more governments are moving towards smarter forms of quality assurance and RIA control, combining different modes of control, though in many cases, weak internal control mechanisms still exist (Radaelli 2010).

## 29.3 THE POLITICS OF RIA

All components of the RIA system – the procedural standards, the assessment criteria and the modes of control – can be subject to political contestation. It can be seen as one of the paradoxes of RIAs and better regulation policy that such political contestation will increase with the relevance of RIA systems. Only when 'better regulation' policy moves beyond the symbolic adoption of fashionable approaches will the diverse actors in the governmental system – and interest groups – invest political capital in order to shape the system's design. In other words, the increasing relevance of an approach that seeks to depoliticise the regulatory process will lead to increasing politicisation. Such politicisation relates to both the system design and the application practice of RIA. This section discusses the politics of RIA in both respects and draws on two theoretical perspectives for each in order to highlight the underlying causal mechanisms shaping the politics of RIA.

### 29.3.1 The Politics of RIA System Design

Two rather diverse theoretical approaches highlight how the different mechanisms of politics shape the design of RIA systems and better regulation more widely. The first perspective is grounded in rational choice theory and explores RIA systems in the context of principal–agent relations. From that perspective, RIA systems are established as a mechanism of political control of the bureaucracy after delegation. The perspective originated in the US and fits best into this context. In the US, delegated rule-making is of much higher relevance than in the Westminster or continental European parliamentary (and semi-presidential) systems. From a principal–agent perspective, RIAs are one mechanism of dealing with the information asymmetry between political principals and bureaucratic agents that could lead to 'agency slippage'. Two design components are basically regarded as playing a major role in that sense. The first one is the 'notice and comment' procedure prescribing that agencies publish draft regulation for public commenting (already introduced with the Administrative Procedures Act in 1946). Here, the principal draws on third parties ('deck stacking') who exercise control and could potentially alert the political principal ('fire alarm'). The second component is the prescribed cost–benefit analysis according to the standards designed by the Office of Management and Budget in the White House.

It is evident that the US system of government provides both the motivation and the opportunity to utilise RIA for purposes of controlling bureaucracy. This is different in the European context. In some countries, such as the United Kingdom, agency drift has not been a major concern of politicians or top civil servants in ministries, given the vertical integration of public administration. In the German system of cooperative federalism, such vertical integration is almost completely absent, but, within different levels of government, vertical control has not been a concern either (cf. Döhler 2002). However, RIA procedures might be used to exercise horizontal control of departmental policy-making by the core executive. Radaelli and Meuwese (2010) argue that the European Commission's Secretariat General draws on the IA system to increase the grip on directorate-generals' policy development. In inter-institutional relations, IAs are used to defend policy positions against the European Parliament and the Council. Overall, the limited fit of the principal–agent approach beyond the US context does not imply that issues of political control do not matter in other contexts. However, other control relations, for example horizontal or inter-institutional, might be more important than bureaucratic control.

The principal–agent perspective is well suited to explaining the design of the control component of RIA systems. It is less suitable for explaining the criteria of impact used in RIA. For such a purpose, we can draw on grid–group cultural theory and its application to regulatory issues (Hood 1998). The key argument is that institutions are subject to conflicting demands that relate to underlying worldviews of constituencies. In the context of regulation, these worldviews relate to different understandings about the relation between markets, individuals and the state, and are manifested in the different rationales for RIA outlined above. In the design of regulatory institutions, such as impact assessment systems, these different advocacy groups build coalitions and make compromises. The claim of the theoretical perspective is that such compromises plant seeds for later institutional change because what is delivered by the compromise will disappoint each individual worldview.

Lodge and Wegrich (2009) have shown how RIA systems in the European context are shaped by these strategies of coalition building and experiences of disappointment. The history of RIA systems in the UK and in the European Commission has been shaped by contestations between 'technocrats' and 'deregulators'. Since the late 1990s and early 2000s, the 'technocrats' have held the upper hand, successfully advocating comprehensive approaches to cost–benefit analysis of policy packages as the main rationale of RIA. But the rise of the so-called standard cost model (SCM) has changed the balance between these two advocacy groups. This model, developed in the Netherlands, systematically assesses the paperwork costs for business in complying with regulations and was widely perceived as a solution to the long-standing concern of too much 'bureaucratic regulation'. The SCM has quickly diffused across Europe and has provided tailwinds for those who see RIA as a way to limit excessive regulation, if not to reduce it. At the same time, 'technocrats' in countries with weak RIA systems, such as Germany, could live with this 'policy boom', because the SCM method was seen as the first step towards a comprehensive RIA system. However, the SCM has disappointed both advocacy groups. While the reduction of paperwork costs plays too limited a role in the perceived regulatory burden on businesses to satisfy the 'deregulators', the 'technocrats' were disappointed by the crowding out of their concerns by the administrative burden reduction policy boom. At the time of writing (2010), a new cycle of contestation for dominance in the design of RIA systems can be observed in Germany, the UK and the European Commission. From the perspective of grid–group cultural theory, the development of a stable equilibrium in institutional systems such as RIA systems is unlikely to emerge, given the inherent contestation surrounding issues of regulation.

### 29.3.2   The Politics of RIA Practice

Turning to the practice of applying RIA rules and procedures in routine policy-making, we can also draw upon two distinct (though somewhat related) theoretical perspectives. Both perspectives help link frequent observations of unintended consequences of RIA rules and procedures to causal mechanisms of the politics of policy-making. A standard critique of the RIA practice is that compliance with procedural rules has no effect on the process and result of formulating regulations. In developing regulatory options, bureaucrats anticipate political support for some 'solutions' rather than searching for a purely rational response to a given problem. Moreover, they cope with the procedural requirements by engaging in practices of 'formal' or even 'creative compliance', i.e. carrying out individual assessments that are part of the overall IA requirements superficially ('box-ticking exercises') (cf. NAO 2009). While some regard these problems as a matter of RIA system design and strengthening the control of RIA practice, the classic account of the role of analysis in policy-making by Lindblom leads to a more pessimistic view.

As one of the three ingredients of the wider theory of incrementalism, Lindblom captured in the notion of 'incremental analysis' the partial and limited character of (ex ante) policy evaluations (Lindblom 1979). The first core argument of 'incremental analysis' is that the limits of information processing do not allow for complex policy packages to be compared and different combinations of policies to be ranked according to values or preferences. Instead, preference formation is done in relation to specific policy proposals that are accepted or rejected. The second argument is that, in a world of multi-actor constellations, the need to reach compromises is fulfilled by agreement on policy instruments and specific measures, and not on the underlying principles. Policy instruments are not separated from the policy objectives, but are part of a wider package of means and ends. A separation of means and ends – objectives and tools – is hardly feasible and would overload the analytical capacity of bureaucrats. The obvious implication of this classic perspective is that there is a tension – if not a clash – between the rationale of incremental analysis and the desire for better regulation tools to separate tool choice (or assessment) from the political decision stage of policy design. And the political rationale (frequently) prevails when trade-offs have to be made between a 'good analysis' and political feasibility. A recent study on the IA practice in Germany and Sweden provides revealing evidence in that respect: government officials in Germany see hard-nosed measurement exercises in IAs as a substantial hurdle to building up the necessary support for a new policy. Therefore they refrain from measuring all aspects of its impact, for example the costs of implementation (Veit 2010: 261). A case study on an EU impact assessment (supporting a proposal for the liberalisation of the energy market) found that the policy that was finally adopted was not included therein (Torriti 2010). The inter-institutional negotiation process between the Commission, the EU Parliament and member states has simply moved beyond what was initially proposed by the Commission. Again, political feasibility drives out the logic of RIA. This perspective is more relevant for RIA systems applied to law-making and, in particular, in a context where policy-making is shared between different institutions of a governmental system.

The second contribution to the politics of RIA application is more directly related to the impact of procedural rules on better regulation. 'Incrementalism' also features in this account, but more as an unintended effect of better regulation policy than a 'natural' behaviour pattern of policy bureaucrats. The argument made by Robert Baldwin (2010) is that demanding procedural rules, i.e. rules related to conducting a cost–benefit analysis of various policy options in order to select the most cost-efficient one, will probably lead to a more 'incremental', if not overtly cautious, regulatory design process. The starting point of Baldwin's argument is that the 'smart' combination of different policy design aspects (e.g. combining government and self-regulation) makes the policy design process a necessarily complex matter. Procedural requirements prescribing an ever more detailed cost–benefit analysis would be more difficult to conduct the more complex the combination of different regulatory tools is. Thus, when procedural requirements are enforced, policy bureaucrats would limit the design process to relatively simple regulatory options that make the application of a cost–benefit analysis feasible. They also would not seek to depart from the type of tools already in place and hence would limit the number of alternative options considered. So, rather than encouraging a search for the best possible response to a given regulatory problem, RIA procedures would limit the choice of regulatory instruments to those that can be easily accommodated with the requirements imposed by RIA.

## 29.4 CONCLUSION

Regulatory impact assessment systems seek to control all those who regulate and draft regulations and those who demand those regulations. And while the design and application of RIA systems vary widely cross-nationally – reflecting the maturing of the regulatory reform traditions, as much as major differences in the institutional endowment that different government systems provide for RIA procedures – a key common thread in the RIA governance logic is the strengthening of the analytical component vis-à-vis purely political or bureaucratic choices in regulation. However, this chapter has argued that the more stringently RIA systems try to shape regulation, the more these systems will also become the subject of political power battles. On the one hand, the politics of RIA relates to the centralisation of control structures, which comes with 'comprehensive', 'whole-of-government' RIA systems raising opposition from departments and agencies as well as their constituents. On the other hand, the design of RIA systems, in particular what types of impact are assessed and how, is subject to contestation across advocacy coalitions.

Again, such power battles will play out differently in different governmental settings, and it might be that the logic of economic analysis is particularly difficult to reconcile with systems of negotiated policy-making, such as those of the European Union or other consensus democracies.

The politics of RIA will potentially play out against a growing consensus regarding the general need for RIA procedures and centre around presumably apolitical and technical aspects of RIA, i.e. the inclusion or exclusion of assessment criteria and methodological details. But this does not render these issues less political and politically relevant. Concerns arising from this claim relate to issues of transparency and participation: the promise of the 'better regulation' movement towards more transparency and participation in rule-making does not necessarily extend to the design of RIA systems. Even with consultation procedures in place, methodological issues of cost–benefit analysis or the design of an RIA oversight regime are technical themes, which favour insiders and experts. This is not to say that RIA cannot provide tangible improvements of the regulatory process. However, it is less clear what kind of improvements RIAs will deliver. More importantly, RIAs have distinct political consequences. They therefore need to be understood as distinctly political tools. Unfortunately, this is often ignored by some of the more enthusiastic promoters of 'better regulation' and impact assessment.

## ACKNOWLEDGEMENT

I want to thank Andreas Pawelke for his superb research assistance and Corey Barber, Martin Lodge, Jan Tiessen and Sylvia Veit for helpful comments on drafts of the chapter.

## NOTES

1.  See the 2002 report of the OECD on regulatory reform (OECD 2002) and the World Bank (2010) report on regulatory governance in developing countries.
2.  See guidance material on RIA, e.g. European Commission (2009a) and UK Better Regulation Executive (2010).
3.  Under President Reagan's executive order, benefits had to outweigh costs. President Clinton changed that formulation into 'justify'.
4.  See European Commission (2009a).
5.  See Torriti (2010) for the difficulties in applying economic analysis (including macroeconomic impact assessment) to the liberalization of the EU energy market proposal.
6.  A study by the European Court of Auditors (2009: 39) covering all European Commission IAs conducted between 2003 and 2008 shows that 'multi-criteria analysis' was used in 44 per cent of the cases, 'sensitivity analysis' in 12 per cent and 'risk analysis' in 11 per cent.
7.  See the debate in the journal *Regulation & Governance* sparked by Viscusi (2009).
8.  The number of RIAs carried out annually is around 200 in the United Kingdom and approximately 100 in the United States. In Australia, around 80 to 100 RIAs are conducted annually with regard to federal government regulation (OECD 2009: 29). Since 2003, the first year of the implementation of the European Commission's IA system, the number of IAs carried out increased from 21 to 102 in 2007 and 135 in 2008, but dropped again to 79 in 2009 owing to the transition to a new Commission (see European Commission 2010a: 6).
9.  Including Germany, Sweden and the UK, all following (more or less faithfully) the Dutch model of ACTAL – the independent watchdog unit established in 2002 with the task of monitoring departmental measurement of administrative costs for business regulation.

10.  The 25 per cent reduction is measured against a so-called 'baseline', i.e. the administrative costs imposed by all existing government regulations at any given time. Establishing this baseline requires the application of the SCM measurement approach to all pieces of law and secondary legislation.

# REFERENCES

Allio, L. (2008), 'The emergence of better regulation in the European Union', Ph.D. thesis, King's College London.

Baldwin, R. (2010), 'Better regulation: the search and the struggle', in R. Baldwin, M. Cave and M. Lodge (eds), *Oxford Handbook of Regulation*, Oxford: Oxford University Press, pp. 259–78.

Coglianese, C., H. Kilmartin and E. Mendelson (2009), 'Transparency and public participation in the federal rulemaking process: recommendations for the new administration', *George Washington Law Review*, 77, 924–72.

Croley, S.P. (2008), *Regulation and Public Interest: The Possibility of Good Regulatory Government*, Princeton, NJ and Oxford: Princeton University Press.

Döhler, M. (2002), 'Institutional choice and bureaucratic autonomy in Germany', *West European Politics*, 25 (1), 101–24.

European Commission (2008), *Impact Assessment on the Standards of Quality and Safety of Human Organs Intended for Transplantation*, SEC/2008/2956.

European Commission (2009a), *Impact Assessment Guidelines 2009*, SEC/2009/92.

European Commission (2009b), *Impact Assessment on Setting Emission Performance Standards for New Light Commercial Vehicles as Part of the Community's Integrated Approach to Reduce $CO_2$ Emissions from Light-Duty Vehicles*, SEC/2009/1454.

European Commission (2010a), *Impact Assessment Board Report for 2009*, SEC/2009/1728.

European Commission (2010b), *Impact Assessment – Background*, available at: http://ec.europa.eu/ governance/impact/background/background_en.htm (accessed 11 October 2010).

European Court of Auditors (2009), *Impact Assessments in the EU Institutions: Do They Support Decision Making?*, Special Report No. 3/2010.

Hood, C. (1998), *The Art of the State: Culture, Rhetoric and Public Management*, Oxford: Oxford University Press.

Lindblom, C.E. (1979), 'Still muddling, not yet through', *Public Administration Review*, 39, 517–26.

Lodge, M. and K. Wegrich (2009), 'High-quality regulation: its popularity, its tools and its future', *Public Money and Management*, 29 (3), 145–52.

Lodge, M. and C. Hood (2010), 'Regulation inside government: retro-theory vindicated or outdated?', in R. Baldwin, M. Cave and M. Lodge (eds), *The Oxford Handbook of Regulation*, Oxford: Oxford University Press, pp. 590–611.

Meuwese, A.C.M. (2008), *'Impact assessment in EU lawmaking'*, Ph.D. thesis, Universiteit Leiden.

National Audit Office (NAO) (2009), *Delivering High-Quality Impact Assessments*, Report by the Comptroller and Auditor General, HC 128 2008–09, London: Stationary Office.

OECD (2002), *Regulatory Policies in OECD Countries*, Paris: OECD.

OECD (2009), *Regulatory Impact Analysis: A Tool for Policy Coherence*, Paris: OECD.

Prosser, T. (2010), *The Regulatory Enterprise: Government, Regulation, and Legitimacy*, Oxford: Oxford University Press.

Radaelli, C.M. (2007), 'Whither better regulation for the Lisbon Agenda?', *Journal of European Public Policy*, 14 (2), 190–207.

Radaelli, C.M. (2010), 'Regulating rule-making via impact assessment', *Governance*, 23 (1), 89–108.

Radaelli, C.M. and F. De Francesco (2010), 'Regulatory impact assessment', in M. Cave, R. Baldwin and M. Lodge (eds), *Oxford Handbook of Regulation*, Oxford: Oxford University Press, pp. 279–301.

Radaelli, C.M. and A.C.M. Meuwese (2010), 'Hard questions, hard solutions: proceduralisation through impact assessment in the EU', *West European Politics*, 33 (1), 136–53.

Reagan, M.D. (1987), *Regulation: The Policy of Politics*, Boston, MA: Little, Brown.

Renda, A. (2006), *Impact Assessment in the EU: The State of the Art and the Art of the State*, Brussels: Centre for European Policy Studies.

Stigler, G.J. (1971), 'The theory of economic regulation', *Bell Journal of Economics*, 2 (1), 3–21.

The Evaluation Partnership (TEP) (2007), *Evaluation of the Commission's Impact Assessment System*, Richmond: TEP.

Torriti, J. (2010), 'Impact assessment and the liberalization of the EU energy markets: evidence-based policy-making or policy-based evidence-making?', *Journal of Common Market Studies*, 48 (4), 1065–81.

UK Better Regulation Executive (2010), *Impact Assessment Toolkit*, London: UK Department for Business, Innovation and Skills.

Veit, S. (2010), *Bessere Gesetze durch Folgenabschätzung? Deutschland und Schweden im Vergleich*, Wiesbaden: VS Verlag.

Viscusi, W.K. (2009), 'The devaluation of life', *Regulation & Governance*, **3** (2), 103–27.

Wollmann, H. (1989), 'Policy analysis in West Germany's federal government: a case of unfinished governmental and administrative modernization?', *Governance*, **2** (3), 233–66.

World Bank (2010), *Regulatory Governance in Developing Countries*, Washington, DC: Better Regulation for Growth, World Bank Group.

# 30 Valuing health and longevity in regulatory analysis: current issues and challenges
## *Lisa A. Robinson and James K. Hammitt*

Economic valuation of health risks plays a major role in informing decisions about environmental and health and safety regulations, especially as governments around the world increasingly require assessment of regulatory impacts. Regulatory analysis in some form has been mandated in the United States for over 30 years (OMB 1997) and is gradually being implemented in the OECD member countries (OECD 2009). For regulations designed to reduce the risk of illness, injury, or premature mortality, counting the number of cases averted is an important initial step in understanding the impacts of alternative policies. Such counts do not convey the relative severity of each outcome, however, nor can they be meaningfully aggregated across different types of effects. Taking the next step of valuing health outcomes in monetary terms provides additional useful insights.

Valuation is particularly informative when it addresses trade-offs that are similar to those involved in regulatory decisions. Such decisions require choosing whether to devote resources to achieving health risk reductions or whether to allow individuals, firms, or government agencies to use these resources to provide other desirable goods and services. When based on the affected individuals' willingness to pay (WTP) for risk reductions, monetary valuation indicates their preferences for trading income (or wealth) for health improvements. These values can be used to determine whether the benefits of alternative regulatory actions are likely to be commensurate with their costs, and also to identify which action, if any, is most likely to maximize the net benefits to society. In combination with other considerations – such as whether the impacts are distributed equitably, and the implications of nonquantifiable effects and other uncertainties – these findings help support sound decisions.

Individual WTP for risk reductions is likely to differ from the medical costs or productivity losses associated with incurred cases of illness, injury, or premature death. The cost of treating a health condition is not the same as the value of reducing its risk of occurrence. For example, treatment does not necessarily return the individual to his or her original health state. WTP often exceeds medical costs and productivity losses by a significant amount since it reflects the value of averting pain and suffering and other quality-of-life impacts.

Because health risk reductions are not directly bought and sold in the marketplace, economists generally use data on related marketed goods or observed behavior ("revealed preferences") or data from survey research ("stated preferences") to estimate their value. For example, risk is one of many attributes of different housing locations, job choices, and motor vehicle options. Economists often study related decisions, using statistical methods to separate the value of risk differences from the value of other attributes. Alternatively, they may develop a survey that describes the risk of concern and asks respondents to indicate their WTP for reducing it.

Approaches for valuing health risks in regulatory analysis are well established and widely used. Typically, premature mortality and nonfatal illnesses or injuries are valued separately, because only a few empirical studies integrate consideration of both types of effects. Thus this chapter first summarizes the valuation of mortality risks and then discusses nonfatal risks. It focuses primarily on US practices, describing the approaches used as well as key challenges.

## 30.1   VALUING MORTALITY RISKS

As introduced above, health risk reductions are generally valued by estimating individuals' willingness to exchange income for the risk change, based on revealed or stated preference studies. For mortality, this WTP is typically expressed as the "value per statistical life" or VSL.[1]

### 30.1.1   The VSL Concept

Most regulations lead to relatively small changes in health risks at the individual level, often expressed as "statistical cases" for ease of presentation. A statistical case, or statistical life, involves aggregating small risk changes across individuals. For example, a 1 in 10 000 risk reduction affecting 10 000 individuals can be expressed as a statistical case (1/10 000 risk reduction × 10 000 individuals = 1 statistical case), as can a 1 in 100 000 risk reduction affecting 100 000 individuals (1/100 000 risk reduction × 100 000 individuals = 1 statistical case). For most regulations, the specific individuals who would avoid illness or injury, or whose lives would be extended by the policy, cannot be identified in advance. A regulation that is expected to "save" a statistical life is one that is predicted to result in one fewer death in the affected population during a particular time period. "Saving" a statistical life is not the same as saving an identifiable individual from certain death.

The value of these small risk changes, expressed as the VSL, can be calculated by dividing individual WTP for a small risk change by the risk change (see Hammitt 2000). For example, if an individual is willing to pay $600 for a 1 in 10 000 reduction in his or her risk of dying in the current year, the VSL is $6 million ($600 ÷ 1/10 000 = $6 million). Alternatively, individual WTP for small risk reductions can be aggregated across a population. A $6 million VSL also results if each member of a population of 10 000 is willing to pay an average of $600 for a 1 in 10 000 annual risk reduction ($600 × 10 000 = $6 million).

Analysts often estimate the value of mortality risk reductions based on revealed preferences, most frequently using wage-risk studies (also referred to as compensating wage differential or hedonic wage studies).[2] In these studies, researchers compare earnings across workers in different occupations or industries who face varying levels of on-the-job risks, using statistical methods to control for the effects of worker qualifications (such as education and experience) and other factors (such as nonfatal job risks) on this relationship. The objective is to estimate the additional compensation a worker requires to accept a more dangerous job, among the set of jobs for which he is qualified.

In recent years, researchers have completed an increasing number of stated preference studies that estimate these values. Such studies include contingent valuation surveys, which ask respondents to indicate their WTP for risk reductions associated with specific scenarios, and conjoint analyses (or choice experiments), which disaggregate the attributes of the scenarios, asking respondents to make several choices among alternatives to explore their trade-offs. Many of these studies focus on traffic safety or other types of accidents; some consider illnesses associated with air pollution or other contaminants. While revealed preference studies are often viewed as more credible because they are based on actual behavior, they address scenarios that differ from those of concern in many regulatory analyses. Stated preference studies are hypothetical but have the advantage of allowing researchers to tailor the scenario to the risks of concern.

### 30.1.2   Current Practices

Because the scenarios studied in empirical research often differ in significant respects from the risks associated with many regulations, analysts usually apply estimates derived from one scenario (such as job-related accidents) to a somewhat different scenario (such as air pollution, food safety, or homeland security regulations). This "benefit transfer" approach requires carefully considering the quality of the available research (the data and methods used) as well as the suitability of the estimates (the extent to which they consider populations and risks similar to those addressed by the regulation). While in some cases analysts may be able to quantitatively adjust the primary research results to better fit the regulatory scenario, they often must explore the implications of the resulting uncertainties qualitatively owing to the limitations of the research available.

The use of a benefit transfer approach for valuing mortality risks in regulatory analysis is well established. Analysts generally follow a two-step process. First, they develop a best estimate (or range of estimates) of the base VSL from the available research literature. Second, they determine whether to adjust this base estimate quantitatively to reflect differences between the scenarios studied and the regulatory scenario.

Table 30.1 summarizes the base VSL estimates currently used by major US regulatory agencies. The US Office of Management and Budget's (USOMB's) guidance for regulatory analysis (USOMB 2003) notes that the available research suggests that the VSL is generally between roughly $1 million and $10 million (no dollar year reported). While it allows agencies some discretion in determining which VSL estimate best fits their regulations, most use central values somewhat above the middle of this range. Of these agencies, the US Environmental Protection Agency (USEPA) historically has been responsible for the majority of the regulations that include quantified mortality risk reductions, and has devoted considerable attention to the valuation of these risks (Robinson 2007). The US Department of Transportation (USDOT), the US Food and Drug Administration (USFDA), and the US Department of Homeland Security (USDHS) have also promulgated a number of such regulations in recent years. Other agencies generally rely on approaches similar to those followed by these agencies.

These base estimates are derived from selected literature reviews and meta-analyses, which are dominated by wage-risk studies conducted largely in the US and other

*Table 30.1   Base VSL estimates used in US regulatory analyses*

| Agency | Reported VSL estimates (range, dollar year)[a] | Basis |
|---|---|---|
| Office of Management and Budget 2003 guidance | $1 million–$10 million (no dollar year reported) | Available research, allows agency flexibility. |
| Environmental Protection Agency 2010 guidance[b] | $7.4 million (standard deviation: $4.7 million, 2006 dollars) | Viscusi (1992, 1993) literature review. |
| Department of Transportation 2009 guidance | $6.0 million (sensitivity analysis: $3.4 million, $8.6 million, 2008 dollars)[e] | Miller (2000); Mrozek and Taylor (2002); Viscusi and Aldy (2003) meta-analyses; Viscusi (2004) wage-risk study; Kochi et al. (2006). |
| Food and Drug Administration 2010 analysis[c] | $7.9 million (range varies, 2009 dollars) | USEPA guidance |
| Department of Homeland Security 2008 analysis[d] | $6.3 million (95% confidence interval: $4.9 million–$7.9 million, 2007 dollars) | Viscusi (2004) wage-risk study |
| Other agencies | Economically significant rules addressing mortality risks infrequent, approaches generally similar to the above | |

*Notes:*
a.  Estimates reported for the dollar year provided in the guidance or analysis cited. The USDOT and USDHS base estimates include the effects of income growth over time as well as inflation as of the reported year. The USEPA adjusts for income growth separately in each analysis depending on its target year; the value in the table reflects the effects of inflation only.
b.  The USEPA is now updating its guidance.
c.  As reported in USFDA (2010).
d.  Based on Robinson (2008) as reported in US Coast Guard (2008a, 2008b).
e.  Range based on personal communication with Peter Belenky, USDOT, 15 January 2010.

high-income countries.[3] The differences across agencies reflect the particular estimates they choose from these studies, rather than decisions to tailor the values to the particular populations or risks each addresses. The agencies do, however, adjust their base estimates quantitatively for some differences between the underlying studies and the scenarios addressed by their rules. These adjustments reflect changes in real income over time, any significant delays between changes in exposure and changes in mortality incidence (latency or cessation lag), and some external costs (e.g., insured medical costs) not likely to be included in estimates of individual WTP. The agencies differ in how they implement these adjustments, as described in detail in Robinson (2008) and in the references cited in Table 30.1.[4]

Other countries vary in their practices. For example, the European Commission's 2009 *Impact Assessment Guidelines* discuss a number of different approaches to valuation, and suggest that countries use the methodology that is appropriate to the circumstances. The *Guidelines* indicate, however, that the VSL has been estimated at 1–2 million euros in the past (no year indicated), and suggest that this range be used "if no more context specific estimates are available" (European Commission 2009, Annexes, p. 43).

### 30.1.3  Major Issues and Challenges

The VSL has been a controversial issue for many years, largely because of the confusion between placing a monetary value on a particular individual's "life" and reporting the average value that we each place on small reductions in our own mortality risks. The latter is exhibited almost daily as we trade off small risks for convenience (e.g., by driving too fast) or spend money on safety products (e.g., bike helmets) rather than other goods and services. This controversy is reflected in the senior discount debate (discussed below) as well as in several texts that oppose valuation (e.g., Ackerman and Heinzerling 2004) and in recent debates about decreases in values that reflect the results of new research (see Robinson 2009; Viscusi 2009). Cameron (2010) suggests that, to address these problems with semantics, the VSL should instead be referenced as the "willingness to swap alternative goods and services for a microrisk reduction" (p. 163) in a particular type of risk.

In addition to these sorts of communication issues, the summary of current practices above raises concerns related to both the standardization and the differentiation of the VSL estimates used in regulatory analysis. First, the commonalities in practices across US agencies raise the question of whether more standardization is desirable, as long as these agencies are relying on similar approaches. Second, the differences in the risks and populations addressed by these agencies suggest that greater differentiation in the VSL estimates may be desirable, given that preferences for exchanging income for risk reductions may vary depending on these characteristics. At least in the near term, the first issue may be somewhat easier to resolve than the second, because increased tailoring of the estimates is inhibited both by concerns about equity and by limitations of the available research.

### Standardization

As discussed above, US agencies are currently relying on the same general body of literature for their base VSL estimates – primarily wage-risk studies conducted in the US and other high-income countries. However, the estimates vary across agencies because they were developed at different times, based on the individual studies, literature reviews, and meta-analyses then available. Agencies have also made different decisions about which estimates to select from these studies and about how to apply the estimates in their regulatory assessments.

This application of different base estimates despite the commonalities in the approaches suggests than more harmonization may be beneficial, both in reducing the confusion that can result from the application of different values and in increasing the quality and efficiency of the process for developing these values. For example, Viscusi (2009) suggests that a panel of scientific experts should periodically meet to review the evidence and update the VSL estimates used in regulatory analysis. This type of process could be used to determine whether agencies should continue to rely on a common set of studies for their base estimates and, if so, to develop a standard base estimate to be applied across all agencies. To the extent that the agencies are each adjusting these base estimates for some of the same factors (e.g., income growth, cessation lag or latency, and external costs), standardization may also be desirable for these adjustments.

The USEPA already follows an approach for developing its VSL estimates that involves extensive use of independent experts: funding new primary research, periodically evaluating the available evidence, and submitting recommendations to its Science Advisory Board for review (e.g., Stavins et al. 1999, 2000; Cropper et al. 2007). Extending this approach to address the estimates used across agencies would result in more comparable analytic results, allowing decisionmakers and others to more clearly distinguish differences in impacts without the potential confusion caused by the application of different VSLs. It would also reduce duplication of effort across agencies, while providing the additional insights that stem from consultation among experts from different policy areas. The main challenge to implementing this approach is overcoming the institutional and other barriers to cross-agency collaboration, which may be difficult given the longstanding tradition of independently developing VSL estimates.

**Differentiation**

The use of standardized estimates across agencies is a second-best option that results from deficiencies in the research base and other concerns. While increased harmonization may be desirable as long as the agencies continue to rely on similar approaches to estimate the VSL, standardization means that the economic analyses will fall short of the goal of reflecting the preferences of those affected by the regulations. Empirical research suggests that the VSL is likely to vary depending on the characteristics of those affected and of the risks themselves, yet agencies currently tailor their estimates to reflect very few of these differences.

At least in theory, this tailoring could be achieved by moving away from relying primarily on wage-risk studies for base estimates, and instead relying on studies that explicitly address the populations and risks that each agency regulates. Recent reviews, including those cited in Table 30.1, suggest that the research base may be insufficient to support such an approach at this time. An alternative would be to implement additional adjustments to the base estimates to better reflect the differences in the populations or risks addressed, based on research currently available.

The challenges to implementing such adjustments vary somewhat depending on whether the goal is to reflect differences in the individuals affected or differences in the nature of the risks. US agencies generally do not adjust their VSL estimates for differences across population subgroups, despite evidence that individuals' WTP for their own risk reductions varies depending on characteristics such as age and income. This reluctance to make adjustments in part stems from the significant controversy that erupted over the so-called "senior discount": the USEPA's use of lower estimates for older individuals in sensitivity analysis conducted for air pollution rules prior to 2004 (see Robinson 2007). While there is some evidence that the VSL declines at older ages, recent work suggests that this relationship is uncertain (Aldy and Viscusi 2007; Hammitt 2007; Krupnick 2007). As a result, two US expert panels advised against making VSL age adjustments (Cropper et al. 2007; National Academy of Sciences 2008), indicating that more research is needed. US government agencies now use the same VSL for all affected individuals, regardless of age.[5]

In the case of income, the research evidence is more consistent, but adjustment of the VSL to reflect income differences is inhibited by equity concerns. Several studies suggest that, in the US, a 1 percent change in income is likely to lead to about a 0.4 to 0.6 percent change in the VSL (e.g., USEPA 1999; Viscusi and Aldy 2003).[6] While several US agencies use these elasticity estimates to adjust the VSL for changes in real income over time, none of the agencies make adjustments for cross-sectional income differences. Instead, the VSL is based on the average income of the individuals included in the underlying valuation studies, regardless of the income levels of those affected by the regulations.

In the US, the use of estimates based on averages is often viewed as providing more equitable treatment, or equal protection, for different groups in policy decisions. However, whether this approach is in fact equitable depends on how one views the incorporation of individual preferences in these analyses. Some regulations disproportionately affect individuals who differ significantly from the average in terms of age, income, or other characteristics.[7] If these individuals have preferences for spending on their own risk reductions that differ from the population average, an analysis based on the average VSL will not reflect their preferences. In addition, these population averages are anchored in the distribution of health, income, and other characteristics that existed at the time of the underlying studies, and this distribution will change over time.

Adjustments for risk characteristics appear less controversial than adjustments for population characteristics because they avoid these sorts of equity concerns. However, these adjustments are hampered by limitations in the research literature. Agencies generally adjust only for delays between exposure and incidence, by discounting the VSL over the lag period.[8] Some recent studies suggest that illness-related deaths are likely to be valued differently than the injury-related deaths included in the wage-risk studies (e.g., Van Houtven et al. 2008; Cameron and DeShazo 2009), while others (e.g., Hammitt and Haninger 2010) find no difference. Some research also suggests that risks that are viewed as less controllable, voluntary, and familiar may be valued up to twice as highly as other risks (Robinson et al. 2010). However, more research is needed to determine the appropriate adjustment factors.

## 30.2   VALUING NONFATAL RISKS

The approaches used to value nonfatal illnesses and injuries in regulatory analysis are more diverse than those used to value mortality. This occurs largely because estimates of WTP are lacking for many of the nonfatal risks associated with environmental and health and safety regulations. Analysts often use other measures as rough proxies, including monetized estimates of quality-adjusted life years or estimates of averted costs, as discussed below.

### 30.2.1   Conceptual Approach

As introduced earlier, WTP is the maximum amount of income (or wealth) that an individual would willingly exchange for a beneficial outcome, and is the most appropriate measure for use in benefit–cost analysis. However, regulatory agencies often rely on alternative approaches when WTP estimates are not available. One such approach involves monetizing estimates of quality-adjusted life years (QALYs).[9] These measures integrate the effects of health and longevity. They were originally developed as non-monetary measures for use in cost-effectiveness analysis and in comparing health status across populations.

Estimating QALYs is generally a two-step process.[10] First, the impact of a condition on health-related quality of life (HRQL) is represented on a scale anchored at "0" and "1," where "0" represents a state viewed as equivalent to dead and "1" represents a state equal to perfect or full health. Better health states are scored closer to "full health," i.e., closer to a value of 1.0. Second, this estimate is multiplied by the duration of the condition to determine the associated QALYs. For example, a health state that has an HRQL score of 0.9 and lasts for two years is equivalent to 1.8 QALYs (0.9 HRQL × 2.0 years = 1.8 QALYs).

To use these estimates in benefit–cost analysis, they must be assigned a monetary value. Regulatory agencies often estimate the value per statistical life year (VSLY) by dividing an estimate of VSL by the estimated number of (discounted) life years remaining for the average individual studied. They then use this average as the value of a QALY.

This approach only roughly approximates the value of risk reductions for two reasons. First, the studies cited earlier on the relationship between the VSL and age suggest that the VSLY is not a constant; the two expert panels that reviewed this issue recommended against the use of a constant VSLY (Cropper et al. 2007; National Academy of Sciences 2008). Second, QALY estimates reflect different types of trade-offs than WTP estimates (see Hammitt 2002; Haninger and Hammitt 2011). QALYs are based on the trade-off between different health states and their duration, independent of income or wealth. In contrast, WTP estimates are based on the trade-off between spending on health risk reductions and spending on other goods and services. Thus WTP estimates are more consistent with the types of trade-offs involved in regulatory decisions.

A second alternative is to rely on avoided costs as a proxy for WTP, either alone or in combination with monetized QALYs. At minimum, these costs typically include expenditures on medical treatment (i.e., direct costs). In some cases, the value of lost productivity (i.e., indirect costs) is also assessed, based on the effects of injury or illness on paid and often unpaid work time.[11] Other expenditures, such as those related to insurance administration and litigation, may be included as well. These estimates are for incurred cases rather than for *ex ante* risk reductions, addressing an outcome that differs from the effects of potential regulations. Moreover, the costs of treating an illness or injury are not necessarily related to an individual's WTP to avoid the illness or injury: being injured and treated is typically worse than not being injured. In theory, the cost of appropriate treatment may be less than, equal to, or greater than WTP to avoid the illness or injury.

Because estimates of avoided costs exclude the value of avoiding pain and suffering and other quality-of-life impacts, analysts at times add estimates of monetized QALYs to capture these additional effects. Combining these estimates does not, however, address the other limitations of each approach. In contrast, it may be appropriate to add avoided costs when relying on WTP estimates, if the avoided costs would be paid by third parties (such as insurance companies) and hence not incorporated into individual WTP.

### 30.2.2  Current Practices

When valuing nonfatal risks in regulatory analyses, the USOMB recommends that agencies apply estimates of individual WTP, supplemented by estimates of any net changes in economic costs to society (i.e., avoided costs) that are not captured in the WTP values (USOMB 2003). When WTP estimates are not available, the USOMB notes that agencies may apply monetized estimates based on health utility studies (such as QALYs). However, a committee of independent experts (Institute of Medicine 2006) subsequently recommended against this latter approach.

Generally, the USEPA applies WTP estimates to the extent possible and relies on averted cost estimates (including medical costs and lost productivity) only when necessary (e.g., USEPA 2009). In contrast, the USFDA and USDOT routinely use monetized QALYs in their analyses. The USFDA first estimates the QALY gains associated with each regulatory option and then monetizes them using a constant value per QALY, testing the effects of a range of estimates to reflect associated uncertainties (e.g., USFDA 2010). The USDOT follows a somewhat different approach.[12] It first categorizes injuries by severity and then calculates both the economic costs and the monetized QALY losses associated with injuries in each category (e.g., Blincoe et al. 2002). While the USFDA approach is not standardized across analyses, the USDOT applies the same values in all its analyses once they are established for each transportation mode (e.g., trucks, automobiles).

### 30.2.3  Major Issues and Challenges

While reductions in the risks of premature mortality tend to dominate the benefit estimates for many regulatory analyses, regulations also often lead to significant changes in the risks of nonfatal illnesses and injuries. The lack of WTP estimates for many such risks means that the analytic results may not accurately reflect the affected individuals' preferences for reducing these risks. Thus more research on these values is clearly needed.

However, new primary research studies often take several years to complete. In the interim, the methods used to estimate avoided costs and monetized QALYs could be improved based on recent work. In particular, detailed cross-agency guidance on developing avoided cost estimates could encourage greater consistency as well as more accurate estimation. Recent improvements in costing methods for medical care could help inform the development of this guidance (Yabroff et al. 2009). In addition, the approaches used to estimate QALYs could be improved through implementation of the recommendations of a recent expert panel (Institute of Medicine 2006). Finally, it may be possible to use emerging research, such as Haninger and Hammitt (2011), to develop valuation functions for QALYs that move away from reliance on a constant VSLY.

## 30.3  SUMMARY AND CONCLUSIONS

As introduced above, WTP is the maximum amount of income (or wealth) that an individual is willing to exchange for a beneficial outcome, reflecting trade-offs similar to those involved in regulatory decisions. Given constrained resources, regulators must decide whether it is preferable to increase expenditures on risk-reducing policies or to allow the funds to be used for other desired goods and services.

For mortality risks, valuation estimates based on individual WTP are well established. Related controversies stem largely from the confusion caused by referencing the "value of life," indicating the need for clearer communication of the underlying concepts. Other key challenges include promoting greater consistency across agencies when they rely on similar research and analytic approaches, and determining whether and how these esti-mates should be better tailored to the populations and risks that each agency regulates. For nonfatal risks, the key challenge is the need to develop WTP estimates for a greater variety of injuries and illnesses. In the interim, the methods used to develop averted cost and monetized QALY estimates as rough proxies could be improved based on recent research results and expert panel recommendations. Improving the methods for mon-etary valuation will enhance the information available to analysts and decisionmakers when comparing the costs and benefits of alternative policies.

## NOTES

1. Both WTP and willingness to accept compensation (WTA) are consistent with the framework for benefit–cost analysis. However, WTA is used less often in practice owing to difficulties in its measurement. Thus this chapter refers to WTP throughout for simplicity.
2. Viscusi and Aldy (2003) discuss this approach as well as other revealed preference methods in detail, and summarize related studies.
3. The USEPA (2010) values are based on 26 estimates, 21 of which are from wage-risk studies. The Viscusi and Aldy (2003) and Mrozek and Taylor (2002) meta-analyses include only wage-risk studies. Miller's (2000) meta-analysis primarily includes wage-risk studies; stated preference studies are included in some model specifications. The Kochi et al. (2006) estimate used by the USDOT is based on 42 wage-risk studies and 18 stated preference studies.
4. Robinson (2008) has been updated and published in abbreviated form as Robinson et al. (2010).
5. Other countries follow similar practices. For example, the current Canadian guidance for impact assess-ment does not discuss age adjustments (Treasury Board 2007).
6. As discussed in Hammitt and Robinson (2011), these elasticity estimates appear low when transferring VSL estimates across countries in different stages of development. In this context, elasticity estimates greater than 1.0 appear reasonable.
7. For example, the USEPA's air pollution regulations primarily reduce mortality among individuals over age 65 (e.g., USEPA 2006).
8. Recent studies support the use of discounted values for delayed impacts (e.g., Viscusi and Aldy 2003; Hammitt and Liu 2004; Alberini et al. 2006; Van Houtven et al. 2008), although the estimates of the amount (or rate) of the discount vary.
9. US regulatory agencies commonly rely on QALYs; disability-adjusted life years (DALYs) are used in some international studies. Detailed information on the construction and use of DALYs is available on the World Health Organization website: http://www.who.int/.
10. For more information on the use of these measures in regulatory analysis, see Institute of Medicine (2006).
11. The approach used to estimate these indirect costs is often referred to as the "human capital" method.
12. US National Highway Traffic Safety Administration (NHTSA) (2009) provides an example of this approach.

## REFERENCES

Ackerman, F. and L. Heinzerling (2004), *Priceless: On Knowing the Price of Everything and the Value of Nothing*, New York: New Press.
Alberini, A., M. Cropper, A. Krupnick and N. Simon (2006), 'Willingness to pay for mortality risk reductions: does latency matter?', *Journal of Risk and Uncertainty*, **32**, 231–45.
Aldy, J.E. and W.K. Viscusi (2007), 'Age differences in the value of statistical life: revealed preference evi-dence', *Review of Environmental Economics and Policy*, **1** (2), 241–60.
Blincoe, L., A. Seay, E. Zaloshnja, T. Miller, R. Romano, S. Luchter and R. Spicer (2002), *The Economic Impact of Motor Vehicle Crashes, 2000*, DOT HS 809 446, Washington, DC: National Highway Traffic Safety Administration.
Cameron, T.A. (2010), 'Euthanizing the value of a statistical life', *Review of Environmental Economics and Policy*, **4** (2), 161–78.

Cameron, T.A. and J.R. DeShazo (2009), 'Demand for health risk reductions', unpublished manuscript (http://pages.uoregon.edu/cameron/vita/)

Cropper, M. et al. (2007), 'SAB advisory on EPA's issues in valuing mortality risk reduction', memorandum from the Chair, Science Advisory Board, and the Chair, Environmental Economics Advisory Committee, to EPA Administrator Stephen L. Johnson, EPA-SAB-08-001.

European Commission (2009), *Impact Assessment Guidelines*, SEC(2009) 92.

Hammitt, J.K. (2000), 'Valuing mortality risk: theory and practice', *Environmental Science and Technology*, **34**, 1396–1400.

Hammitt, J.K. (2002), 'QALYs versus WTP', *Risk Analysis*, **22** (5), 985–1001.

Hammitt, J.K. (2007), 'Valuing changes in mortality risk: lives saved versus life years saved', *Review of Environmental Economics and Policy*, **1** (2), 228–40.

Hammitt, J.K. and J.-T. Liu (2004), 'Effects of disease type and latency on the value of mortality risk', *Journal of Risk and Uncertainty*, **28** (1), 73–95.

Hammitt, J.K. and K. Haninger (2010), 'Valuing fatal risks to children and adults: effects of disease, latency, and risk aversion', *Journal of Risk and Uncertainty*, **40**, 57–83.

Hammitt, J.K. and L.A. Robinson (2011), 'The income elasticity of the value per statistical life: transferring estimates between high and low income populations', *Journal of Benefit–Cost Analysis*, **2** (1).

Haninger, K. and J.K. Hammitt (2011), 'Diminishing willingness to pay per quality-adjusted life year: valuing acute foodborne illness', Risk Analysis. DOI 10.1111/j.1539-6924.2011.01617.x, published online.

Institute of Medicine (2006), *Valuing Health for Regulatory Cost-Effectiveness Analysis*, ed. W. Miller, L.A. Robinson and R.S. Lawrence, Washington, DC: National Academies Press.

Kochi, I., B. Hubbell and R. Kramer (2006), 'An empirical Bayes approach to combining and comparing estimates of the value of a statistical life for environmental policy analysis', *Environmental and Resource Economics,* **34**, 385–406.

Krupnick, A. (2007), 'Mortality-risk valuation and age: stated preference evidence', *Review of Environmental Economics and Policy*, **1** (2), 261–82.

Miller, T.R. (2000), 'Variations between countries in values of statistical life', *Journal of Transport Economics and Safety*, **34** (2), 169–88.

Mrozek, J.R. and L.O. Taylor (2002), 'What determines the value of life? A meta-analysis', *Journal of Policy Analysis and Management*, **21** (2), 253–70.

National Academy of Sciences, Committee on Estimating Mortality Risk Reduction Benefits from Decreasing Tropospheric Ozone Exposure (2008), *Estimating Mortality Risk Reduction and Economic Benefits from Controlling Ozone Air Pollution*, Washington, DC: National Academies Press.

Organisation for Economic Co-operation and Development (OECD) (2009), *Indicators of Regulatory Management Systems*, Paris: OECD.

Robinson, L.A. (2007), 'How U.S. government agencies value mortality risk reductions,' *Review of Environmental Economics and Policy*, **1** (2), 283–99.

Robinson, L.A. (2008), 'Valuing mortality risk reductions in homeland security regulatory analyses', prepared for US Customs and Border Protection, Department of Homeland Security, under contract to Industrial Economics.

Robinson, L.A. (2009), 'Valuing lives, valuing risks, and respecting preferences in regulatory analysis', *Regulation & Governance*, **3** (3), 298–305.

Robinson, L.A., J.K. Hammitt, J.E. Aldy, A. Krupnick and J. Baxter (2010), 'Valuing the risk of death from terrorist attacks', *Journal of Homeland Security and Emergency Management*, **7** (1), Art. 14.

Stavins, R. et al. (1999), 'An SAB report on the EPA *Guidelines for Preparing Economic Analyses*', memorandum from the Chair, Science Advisory Board, and the Chair, Environmental Economics Advisory Committee, to EPA Administrator Carol M. Browner, EPA-SAB-EEAC-99-020.

Stavins, R. et al. (2000), 'An SAB report on EPA's white paper *Valuing the Benefits of Fatal Cancer Risk Reduction*', memorandum from the Chair, Science Advisory Board, and the Chair, Environmental Economics Advisory Committee, to EPA Administrator Carol M. Browner, EPA-SAB-EEAC-00-013.

Treasury Board of Canada Secretariat (2007), *Canadian Cost–Benefit Analysis Guide: Regulatory Proposals (Interim)*, Ottawa: Treasury Board of Canada Secretariat.

US Coast Guard, US Department of Homeland Security (2008a), *Implementation of the 1995 Amendments to the International Convention on Standards of Training, Certification, and Watchkeeping for Seafarers, 1978, Preliminary Regulatory Analysis and Initial Regulatory Flexibility Analysis*? USCG-2004-17914.

US Coast Guard, US Department of Homeland Security (2008b), *Vessel Requirements for Notices of Arrival and Departure and Automatic Identification System, Regulatory Analysis and Initial Regulatory Flexibility Analysis,* USCG-2005-21869.

US Department of Transportation (2009), 'Treatment of the economic value of a statistical life in departmental analyses, 2009 annual revision', memorandum to secretarial officers and modal administrators from J. Szabat, Deputty Assistant Secretary for Transportation Policy, and L. Knapp, Acting General Counsel.

US Environmental Protection Agency (1999), *The Benefits and Costs of the Clean Air Act, 1990 to 2010*, EPA 410-R-99-001.

US Environmental Protection Agency (USEPA) (2006), *Regulatory Impact Analysis for the National Ambient Air Quality Standards for Particle Pollution*, Washington, DC: USEPA.

US Environmental Protection Agency (USEPA) (2009), *Regulatory Impact Analysis for Proposed National Ambient Air Quality Standard for Sulfur Dioxide*, Washington, DC: USEPA.

US Environmental Protection Agency (USEPA) (2010), *Guidelines for Preparing Economic Analysis*, EPA 240-R-10-001.

US Food and Drug Administration (USFDA) (2010), 'Required warnings for cigarette packages and advertisements', *Federal Register*, **75** (218), 69524–65.

US National Highway Traffic Safety Administration (USNHTSA) (2009), *Final Regulatory Impact Analysis: FMVSS No. 216, Upgrade Roof Crush Resistance*, Washington, DC: NHTSA.

US Office of Management and Budget (OMB) (1997), *Report to Congress on the Costs and Benefits of Federal Regulations*, Washington, DC: OMB.

US Office of Management and Budget (OMB) (2003), *Circular A-4, Regulatory Analysis*, Washington, DC: OMB.

Van Houtven, G., M.B. Sullivan and C. Dockins (2008), 'Cancer premiums and latency effects: a risk tradeoff approach for valuing reductions in fatal cancer risks', *Journal of Risk and Uncertainty*, **36**, 179–99.

Viscusi, W.K. (1992), *Fatal Trade-Offs: Public and Private Responsibilities for Risk*, New York: Oxford University Press.

Viscusi, W.K. (1993), 'The value of risks to life and health', *Journal of Economic Literature*, **31**, 1912–46.

Viscusi, W.K. (2004), 'The value of life: estimates with risks by occupation and industry', *Economic Inquiry*, **42** (1), 29–48.

Viscusi, W.K. (2009), 'The devaluation of life', *Regulation & Governance*, **3**, 103–27.

Viscusi, W.K. and J.E. Aldy (2003), 'The value of a statistical life: a critical review of market estimates throughout the world', *Journal of Risk and Uncertainty*, **27** (1), 5–76.

Yabroff, K.R., M.L. Brown, W.F. Lawrence, P.G. Barnett and J. Lipscomb (eds) (2009), 'Health care costing: data, methods, future directions', *Medical Care*, **47** (7), Supplement 1.

# 31 Process-oriented regulation: conceptualization and assessment
*Sharon Gilad*

The 1980s and 1990s saw an expansion of regulation as a mechanism of governance, including the introduction of independent regulatory agencies, in Europe and beyond and in both economic and social regulatory spheres. Yet alongside this expansion was increased awareness of the limitations and costs of regulation. As discussed in this chapter, detailed rules are an inherently limited tool with which to manage heterogeneous, complex and fast-moving industries. As a result, regulation can pose excessive burdens on regulated firms, while providing consumers with limited benefits. Consequently, regulators were almost bound to attract dual blame for "red tape" and for firms' underperformance.

One response to the criticism and to the apparent failures of prescriptive regulation was the introduction of cost–benefit analysis and thereafter regulatory impact assessment as discussed by Shapiro (2011) and Wegrich (2011). In addition, as discussed in this chapter, regulators in different countries and domains have been experimenting with regulatory strategies that allow firms to adapt regulation to their individual circumstances, while holding them accountable for the adequacy and efficacy of their self-regulation systems. Similar trends have been observed in state regulation of health and safety (e.g. Gunningham 1999, 2007; Hutter 2001; Gunningham and Sinclair 2009), food safety (e.g. Coglianese and Lazer 2003; Fairman and Yapp 2005), financial markets (Black et al. 2007; Power 2007; Black 2008; Ford 2008), environmental protection (e.g. Fiorino 2001; Eisner 2004; Bennear 2006, 2007; Coglianese and Nash 2006), and even airport security (Haines 2009).

Many labels have been coined to categorize the above changes to regulatory form, including: enforced self-regulation, management-based regulation, principles-based regulation, and meta-regulation. To an extent, the diversity of labels reflects real variance in regulatory phenomena. Yet it masks key similarities. To highlight the latter, this chapter proposes that these different regulatory institutions belong to a bigger family of "process-oriented regulation," by which I mean regulation that mandates and monitors firms' self-evaluation, design, and management of their core production (e.g. food processing) and their governance and controls (e.g. internal quality assurance over food processing).

Assessing the efficacy of new forms of process-oriented regulation is particularly pertinent today, in the aftermath of the financial crisis, when any form of firms' self-regulation is regarded with suspicion. Thus this chapter assesses the outcome, and the factors underlying the efficacy of the family of process-oriented regulatory institutions.

The chapter is organized is follows: section 31.1 conceptualizes process-oriented regulation, and distinguishes it from prescriptive and outcome-oriented regulation; section 31.2 builds on existing empirical research to assess the impact of process-oriented regulation on firms' performance; section 31.3 proceeds to analyze the factors underlying the impact of process-oriented regulation on the basis of theoretical and where available empirical literature; and section 31.4 highlights the key findings and their implications.

## 31.1 WHAT IS PROCESS-ORIENTED REGULATION?

To conceptualize process-oriented regulation, it is useful to compare it, as I do in this section, with its two generic alternatives: prescriptive and outcome-oriented regulation. (The analytical distinction between these alternative regulatory families is summarized in Table 31.1, which builds on May 2007).

Regulation often takes the form of prescriptive rules backed up by regulatory monitoring of firms' adherence to prescribed requirements and prohibitions. This traditional form of regulation is appropriate for relatively homogeneous and stable industries, where regulators and legislators are able to devise universal and effective rules. Yet a basic assumption of this chapter is that regulated industries and the tasks that regulators face are more often than not heterogeneous, rapidly changing, and uncertain.

Outcome-oriented regulation, which includes performance-based (e.g. Gunningham 1999; Coglianese et al. 2003; May 2003, 2011; and standards-based regulation (sometimes referred to as principles-based-regulation) (e.g. Kaplow 1992; Braithwaite and Braithwaite 1995; Black 1997), involves regulatory specification of outcomes (e.g. minimize pollution emissions) and goals-oriented duties of care (e.g. treat customers fairly). It requires firms to determine what actions are appropriate in individual cases, and regulators to analyze the congruence between firms' outputs and regulatory objec-

*Table 31.1  Categorization of regulatory institutions*

| Regulatory family | Prescriptive | Outcome-oriented | Process-oriented |
|---|---|---|---|
| Regulatory foci | Prescribed actions. | Outcomes. | System design. |
| Compliance determination | Adherence to prescribed actions. | Achievement of acceptable results. | Acceptable planning (and implementation) of systems and controls. |
| Nature of rules | Detailed specification of required action. | Output specifications. | Design process specifications. |
| Basis for achieving regulatory goals | Adherence to prescriptions assumed to meet goals. | Outputs are closely associated with goals. | Systems are designed to meet goals. |
| Relevant circumstances | Firms are homogeneous and regulators have a good understanding of the association between systems and achievement of regulatory goals. | Firms are heterogeneous and markets are unsubtle, yet regulators and firms nonetheless have reasonable understanding of what good outcomes look like. | Firms are heterogeneous and markets are unstable, yet regulators and firms nonetheless have reasonable understanding of general criteria for good control systems. |

*Source:* Adapted from May (2007).

tives. Outcome-oriented regulation is considered most effective when industries are heterogeneous and/or rapidly changing, yet the outputs that regulators can observe are measurable and closely linked with firms' impacts on regulatory goals (Coglianese and Lazer 2003).

The family of process-oriented regulation (hereafter POR), which is one type of hybrid regulatory constellation (Levi-Faur, Chapter 1), comes in different shades and labels, all of which are united by regulatory monitoring of firms' design and management of internal compliance systems. One analytical construct is what Ayres and Braithwaite (1992) termed "enforced self-regulation," wherein firms devise a set of detailed rules and internal controls in light of regulatory goals. Regulators authorize firms' rulebooks and audit the efficacy of firms' compliance with their internally devised rules. A similar, albeit not identical, concept, management-based-regulation (MBR) (Coglianese and Lazer 2003; Bennear 2006; Coglianese and Nash 2006) or process-based regulation (Gunningham 2007), portrays a regime in which regulators set (and monitor) general criteria to guide firms' analysis of the risks that their operations pose to regulatory objectives, and their design of internal controls to mitigate and monitor these risks. Coglianese and Lazer (2003) propose that MBR is applicable when firms are heterogeneous and/or markets are unstable and it is simultaneously difficult or costly to observe and measure firms' outputs. However, MBR rests on the contested assumption that regulators can make sound judgments about the likely efficacy of firms' proposed systems and controls to yield acceptable outcomes, even if these cannot be readily observed or measured.

The above discussion implies that prescriptive regulation, outcome-oriented regulation (i.e. performance-based, standards-based, and principles-based regulation), and process-oriented regulation (i.e. enforced self-regulation, management-based regulation) are distinct regulatory families. Yet, as elaborated elsewhere (Gilad 2010), POR is likely to involve varied hybrids with prescriptive and outcome-oriented regulation. When combined with prescriptive regulation, POR would require firms to analyze their compliance with existing prescriptive rules, to design additional rules and controls where needed, and to evaluate the effectiveness of their systems in ensuring their compliance. When combined with outcome-oriented specifications, POR entails firms' design, evaluation, and readjustment of rules and controls in pursuit of specific results. Finally, new forms of principles-based regulation (e.g. Black et al. 2007; Black 2008; Ford 2008) combine a requirement that firms systematically analyze, design, manage, and evaluate their performance (i.e. POR) with broad goals-oriented standards. This likely hybrid nature of POR poses a challenge to any review, such as this one, that seeks to draw general predictions and conclusions from current research about its likely operation and impact. In addition, this variance may account for some of the inconsistent findings regarding the impact of POR, as discussed further below.

## 31.2   THE OUTCOME OF PROCESS-ORIENTED REGULATION

A number of studies, employing different labels, assess the impact of a shift to POR on firms' performance. In what follows I go into some detail in describing the empirical examples that these studies focus on, and their methodology and findings. I do not aim to make a nuanced classification of the examples that these studies have looked at, because this would require access to the underlying empirical data. Rather, this section draws tentative conclusions about the efficacy of process-oriented approaches as a family, regardless of their precise configuration.

Coglianese and Lazer's (2003) article illustrates the expected impact of POR by reference to three examples, which they categorize as exemplifying their conceptualization of MBR. One was the American Food and Drug Agency and United States Department of Agriculture implementation of the hazards analysis and critical control points (HACCP) methodology in the domain of food safety. HACCP requires food providers to analyze the risks that their production processes pose to food safety, to set the thresholds at which potential hazards will be maintained, and to design appropriate technologies and controls to ensure that hazards are maintained at these intended levels. The second example regards the Occupational Safety and Health Administration and Environmental Protection Agency's requirements that firms assess and manage the risks to their employees and to the general public as a result of their handling of regulatory-specified hazardous chemical substances. Their third example concerns the Massachusetts Toxic Use Reduction Act (TURA), which requires firms to develop plans that "demonstrate a good faith and reasonable effort to identify and evaluate toxics use reduction options" (Coglianese and Lazer 2003: 713). On the basis of limited data – a general-auditor's report, and government statistics and documentation – the authors tentatively conclude that the new regulatory regimes faced substantial levels of non-compliance, yet their introduction was nonetheless associated with improvement in regulatory outcomes.

A more confident support for POR comes from Bennear's (2006, 2007) statistical analysis of the impact of firms' implementation of what she categorizes as pollution-prevention MBR in 14 American states. She reports substantive positive impact on pollution reduction by states and facilities that were subject to management-based reforms, with facilities' average reduction of approximately 30 percent in toxic chemical releases and their reporting of a wider range of pollution-mitigation activities.

The findings of research in the domain of health and safety are mixed. Hutter's (2001) extensive interview-based study of the implementation of what she categorizes as an enforced self-regulatory regime by British Rail (BR) analyzes the company's response to the regulatory regime's expectation that firms implement appropriate systems to ensure the health and safety of employees "so far as reasonably practicable." She demonstrates that BR has put in place safety policies, a safety rulebook, and institutional safety roles. Yet these institutions had only partial impact on the workforce's behavior. For example, 76 percent of the interviewed workforce reported that they have occasionally breached the firm's internal health and safety regulations (Hutter 2001: 237). Hutter's depiction of trends in injury statistics for the railway industry (2001: 55–7) between 1982 and 1992 shows overall stability in fatal accidents, and an increase in major and minor injuries. (The latter may reflect better reporting systems rather than objectively higher levels of injury.)

Also in the domain of health and safety regulation, Gunningham and Sinclair's (2009) study of what they identify as a management-based occupational health and safety regime in the Australian mining industry points to an overall improvement in safety across the industry. Yet, investigating the implementation of the regulation by two leading companies, the authors reveal substantial variation in performance and in commitment to the regulatory regime across these firms' mining sites.

Gilad's (2011) research concerned the implementation by large insurance firms, retail banks, and building societies in the UK of the Treating Customers Fairly (TCF) initiative. This initiative required firms to analyze their operations against the duty to treat customers fairly, to implement required changes, and to systematically and continuously measure their performance. She shows that alongside the implementation of this initiative almost all firms continued to engage in what from the regulator's perspective was overt customer exploitation.

Finally, Haines (2009) relies on formal documents and interviews to analyze site-level responses to what she classifies as three meta-regulatory reforms in Australia. The first reform applied the "safety case model" (Gunningham 2007) to the regulation of workplace health and safety in major-hazards facilities. The second reform, which was introduced following the 2001 New York and 2002 Bali terrorist attacks, required airports to develop plans for assessment and management of security risks. A third reform regards the auditing of firms' financial reporting, yet the description of this last regime and its consequences receive less focus in the article. Haines finds different levels of attentiveness to risk and risk-mitigation efforts across these industries following the introduction of the new regulatory regimes, with greater commitment in the case of major-hazards facilities regulation.

On the whole, the above studies seem to point to the positive impact of the family of POR on firms' performance. However, they are far from conclusive, and they suggest substantial variance across industries and firms and within firms.

## 31.3    THE SHAPING OF PROCESS-ORIENTED REGULATION

What factors might be shaping the above positive, albeit highly varied, impact of POR? This section builds on theoretical and empirical literature to tentatively answer these questions, comparing prescriptive, outcome-oriented and process-oriented regulation. Table 31.2 summarizes the tentative arguments with the caveat that these regard pure, rather than hybrid, forms of POR.

### 31.3.1    Regulatory Uncertainty, Costs, and Capacity

Regulatory rule making is constrained by regulators' limited knowledge of the risks that firms' operations may pose to regulatory objectives, and of the solutions that could most effectively and efficiently mitigate these risks. More fundamentally, prescriptive regulation is an inherently limited tool for managing complex and dynamic social realities, because detailed rules can never fully match all possible scenarios (Sunstein 1995; Black 1997). In addition, as supervisors and enforcers of firms' adherence to rules, regulators need to be aware of breaches of regulation. The information asymmetries that regulators face in this regard are all too obvious. Moreover, to be effective it is not enough for regulators to detect violations. They need to understand the sources of individual firms' non-compliance and to match their responses accordingly. The alternatives to prescriptive regulation shift some of the costs of regulation to firms, which are presumably better placed to bear them. Yet, as discussed below, shifting the primary responsibility for identifying, monitoring, and managing risks to firms does not liberate regulators of the need

*Table 31.2*   *Ranking process-oriented regulation in comparison with prescriptive and outcome-oriented regulation*

| Ranking criteria | | Prescriptive | Outcome-oriented | Process-oriented |
|---|---|---|---|---|
| Rule adaptation to individual circumstances | | *Low* (rules are uniform and difficult to change). | *High* (outcome specifications, and even more so principles, are malleable to change). | *Medium* (firms translate process specifications into firm-specific rules and controls). |
| Costs incurred by regulators | In setting general standards | *High* (detailed rules require information and unders-tanding of likely impact). | *Low* (broad standards shift the burden of discretion to firms and supervisors). | *Medium* (regulators provide firms with broad process specifications). |
| | In gathering information regarding firms' compliance | *High* (burden of gathering information on supervisors). | *High* (burden of gathering information on supervisors). | *Low* (burden on firms to prove the likely efficacy of their plans to the regulator). |
| | In assessing firms' performance | *Low* (assessment in light of detailed rules is relatively cheap for supervisors). | *High* (broad standards shift ad hoc discretion from legislators to supervisors). | *High* (requires regulators to assess the likely efficacy of firms' variable designs). |
| Micro-mechanisms shaping firms' cooperation and performance | Firms' interpre-tation costs | *Low* (detailed rules entail relatively low interpretation costs). | *High* (broad standards shift interpretation costs to firms). | *Medium* (firms design controls within a regulatory-structured process). |
| | Firms' ability to innovate and extract private gains | *Low* (prescriptive rules leave little room for innovation). | *High* (broad standards allow maximum flexibility to firms). | *Medium* (innovations facilitated within a relatively structured, regulatory-guided framework). |
| | Firms' normative commitment and internali-zation of regulation | *Low* (externally prescribed rules could seem unreasonable and irrelevant). | *Low* (supervisory discretion could seem arbitrary). | *Medium* (internally devised rules more likely to be seen as reasonable and relevant, yet empirical studies suggest limitations in practice). |
| | Firms' self-regulatory capacity | *Low* (no explicit requirement for information systems and controls). | *Low* (no explicit requirement for information systems and controls). | *Medium* (explicit requirement for information systems and controls, yet empirical studies highlight limitations in practice). |

to assess the validity of firms' plans, nor can it eliminate the uncertainty that regulators, and to a lesser extent firms, face.

First, in terms of standard setting, outcome-oriented regulation, at least in its standards-based form, involves the lowest costs for regulators, since broad standards require little *ex ante* information and expertise. Insofar as the outputs that regulators can readily measure and observe are closely associated with the values that regulation seeks to protect or promote, outcome-oriented regulation has the greatest potential for congruence with regulatory goals. In the absence of readily measurable outcomes, POR offers a second-best solution. While it is less flexible and involves firms' delineation of rules and controls that limit their responsiveness to individual circumstances, these rules are tailored to the individual circumstances of each firm. Setting process-oriented regulatory regulations to guide firms' self-evaluation process may require substantial levels of expertise. Yet, in comparison with prescriptive regulation, these costs are nonetheless likely to be low, because the responsibility for identifying firm-specific risks and solutions is shifted to firms, which are expected to have better access to relevant information and expertise.

Second, in terms of information regarding firms' performance, POR capitalizes on firms' better access to information, and requires firms to analyze and to provide regulators with information regarding the risks posed by their operations to regulatory objectives. As Bennear (2006) observes, the obligation on firms to assess and report to regulators on their performance could result in more targeted regulatory supervision, and in better matching of regulatory enforcement styles to firms' compliance profiles. In contrast, outcome-oriented regulation provides regulators with no additional sources of information.

However, for regulators to benefit from the information that firms generate about their performance, they first need to steer firms' robust self-evaluation and thereafter to be able to assess the validity of this information, i.e. does it adequately reflect the reality of firms' operations? The recent financial crisis has alerted us that firms may fail to identify and/or appreciate the risks that they generate and face (Ford 2010). Moreover, even if firms are well placed to understand and control the risks that are associated with their operations, they will not necessarily use their superior information and expertise to identity and manage these risks (Ford 2008). Requiring firms to open their risk management systems to regulatory scrutiny may further discourage them from identifying major sources of risks. Consequently, the success of POR depends on regulators' capacity to independently assess and challenge the validity of the information that firms generate about their performance (Ford 2010).

Third, and most problematic, the assessment of firms' performance under all forms of flexible regulation – i.e. outcome-oriented and process-oriented regulation – may require regulators to make judgment calls on issues regarding which there is little knowledge or consensus. POR, in particular, requires regulators to engage with firms in complex discussions about firm-specific risks, and about the merit of proposed solutions and controls. One danger is that the uncertainty and evaluation costs that regulators and firms face will result in deadlock, wherein firms will await regulatory guidance and assurance that their plans are acceptable, whereas regulators will feel unable to make a judgment. A number of existing studies suggest that this is indeed a common result of POR. Haines's (2009) interviewees claimed that they had wasted considerable resources in developing proposals which were rejected by regulators who lacked a clear picture of what good enough plans might look like. Aalders (2002) similarly narrates that firms' permit applications under the flexible environmental regulatory program in the Netherlands took very long to process and negotiate (seven years in one of their case studies). Eisner (2004) likewise reports that, in the first three years of the Environmental Protection Agency's Project XL, a program that promised firms greater flexibility against superior environmental performance, nearly two-thirds of the proposals "were rejected, formally withdrawn, or became inactive [or] weathered lengthy delays and ongoing demands for information and changes in proposals" (Eisner 2004: 154). These three studies imply that assessing the quality of firms' risk management plans is cognitively complex and time-consuming for regulators, and that this is costly for both regulators and firms and could result in unresolved risks to society.

A second possibility is that the internal control systems that firms design would intentionally, or owing to firms' ignorance, fail to meet regulatory goals and that regulators would not be in a position to identify flaws in firms' programs. May (2003) has shown how the introduction of a performance-based regime to the regulation of building safety in New Zealand ended up with local government regulators and private certifiers' failure to adequately assess the quality of builders' plans, because of their limited experience with new and innovative techniques. The result was inconsistent regulatory licensing and large-scale occurrence of building leakages. Insofar as POR similarly involves regulators' *ex ante* assessment of the likely efficacy of firms' innovative designs of systems and controls, it carries similar risks to those identified by May's research.

A third concern is that high decision-making costs and uncertainty will lead regulators to pursue a de facto "tick-box" approach to assessing firms' compliance with POR, and firms to treat non-binding regulatory or industry guidance and/or consultants' advice as compulsory in an attempt to reduce ambiguity and the risk of enforcement (cf. Schauer 2003; Cunningham 2007; Schwarcz 2008). Under these circumstances, POR could revert to a semi-prescriptive regime, resulting in firms' implementation of extensive and expensive, albeit ineffective, internal compliance programs (Krawiec 2003).

Finally, a direct cost of POR for regulators is that, in comparison with detailed rules, the breach of all forms of flexible regulation is arguably harder to establish, because broad standards are malleable for multiple interpretations. Thus, where POR replaces rather than complements prescriptive regulation, it could weaken regulatory capacity to deter and use enforcement against ill-intentioned firms (Baldwin 1995; Black et al. 2007; Black 2008).

In sum, POR is likely to reduce some regulatory costs by shifting the primary responsibility for identifying risks, setting standards, and monitoring compliance on to firms. Yet empirical research, albeit limited, suggests that regulators often find it difficult to evaluate the quality of firms' risk management programs. The greater the level of uncertainty over the nature of the risks and over what "good" control systems look like, the higher the costs of regulatory evaluation and the higher the risk of incongruence between the implementation of POR and regulatory goals. This is a key challenge for the success of current POR models.

### 31.3.2 The Shaping of Firms' Compliance

A final issue to consider regards the extent to which POR is likely to enlist and enhance firms' self-interest motivations, commitment, and capacity for self-regulation.

**Firms' motivations**

Explanations for firms' responses to regulation reasonably start with a focus on firms' instrumental, profit-seeking motivations. Analyses of outcomes-oriented regulation and POR share an expectation that allowing firms more flexibility will result in the enhanced performance of those firms that can extract private benefits from investing in innovative, cost-effective technologies and/or risk management solutions. The expected gains to firms include reduction in compliance and production costs, improved internal controls, better industrial relations, and improved public image (Coglianese and Lazer 2003; Bennear 2006; Ford 2008).

However, it should be acknowledged that POR does not necessarily remove barriers to innovation, given its likely hybrid form (Gilad 2010). In addition, the identification of risks and the search for cost-effective solutions is itself costly for firms, and therefore providing firms with greater flexibility will not necessarily encourage them to invest in enhanced solutions to regulatory problems. In this regard, POR is likely to be more effective than outcome-oriented regulation alone. Whereas outcome-oriented regulation simply removes barriers to innovation, POR further involves a positive requirement that firms engage in analysis and planning of their operations and report on their efforts to the regulator. The literature on MBR expects that, once mandated to invest in a search for alternative means for achieving regulatory objectives, some firms will find that their gains outweigh their implementation costs (Coglianese and Lazer 2003; Bennear 2006). Coglianese and Lazer (2003) assume that, when this is the case, MBR, and by implication other forms of POR, will be self-executing, and would not require further regulatory monitoring of firms' implementation. Whether or not this is in fact the case is an empirical question; yet empirical research on this point is scarce (but see Bennear 2006, 2007).

Coglianese and Lazer (2003) further stress that in many cases firms would not have an interest in implementing their compliance plans, because the costs are too high or because they have more pressing priorities. Bennear (2006) proposes that even in these cases MBR will enhance firms' motivation to comply owing to its positive impact on regulators' access to information and consequent capacity to target irresponsible firms. Her assumption is that firms' obligation to provide regulators with information increases the reality (and firms' perceptions) of enforcement risk, thereby inducing them to comply. However, as discussed above, firms' reporting duties under all forms of POR, MBR included, do not alleviate regulators' need to validate the information that firms generate. In addition, insofar as POR replaces, rather than complements, prescriptive regulation, it could have a negative impact on regulatory enforcement capacity, in which case firms may perceive a lower risk of enforcement. Ultimately, this is an empirical question, and there is practically no empirical data on how a shift to POR influences firms' perceptions of the threat of enforcement.

Finally, as the previous sections have highlighted, firms' identification of risks and of risk management solutions, be it voluntary or owing to their perception of enforcement risk, may turn out to be misconceived.

In sum, POR is expected to bolster (some) firms' positive motivations for compliance by removing barriers to innovation, as well as via accountability for self-assessment, planning, and implementation of internal controls. Nonetheless, firms' investment in risk assessment, interpretation, and implementation is likely to be costly. As discussed in the previous sections, firms' costs are likely to be exacerbated by their own uncertainty as well as by regulators' prolonged decision making. Driving firms to invest in risk assessments and management necessitates high levels of regulatory monitoring, guidance, and use of enforcement in appropriate cases. The efficacy of these would depend on regulatory capacity and on firms' perceptions of the likelihood of enforcement. As with some other aspects of extant literature, there is very little empirical research regarding the shaping of firms' perceptions of the costs, benefits, and enforcement risks under POR.

**Firms' normative commitment**
Firms' responsiveness to any form of regulation is further shaped by organizational and individual identity (Albert and Whetten 1985; Dutton and Dukerich 1991; Gilad, forthcoming), i.e. the extent to which regulation is perceived as integral to the organizational values and to individuals' tasks. When regulatory requirements are embedded in individuals' professional or group norms this can foster firms' "automatic" compliance (Corneliussen 2005). In contrast, as Kagan and Scholz (1984) highlighted, firms may resist regulation that clashes with their internal definitions of "acceptable" versus "unacceptable" behaviors, and of "reasonable" versus "unreasonable" regulation. In addition, Vaughan (1996) and others (e.g. Hutter 2001; MacLean 2002) have shown how organizational or sub-group norms can constitute systematic non-compliance as normal and rational, resulting in actors' perception of their deviant practices as compliant and legitimate.

The flexibility of outcome-oriented regulation and pure POR, which is intended to allow firms to focus on achieving regulatory goals rather than comply with rigid rules, is expected to ameliorate firms' resistance to regulation. POR is further expected to enhance firms' positive commitment to regulation by requiring them to actively engage in translating broad regulatory goals into internal programs and rules (Ayres and Braithwaite 1992; Coglianese and Lazer 2003; Ford 2008).

Current empirical research, however, does not lend support to the above expectations that POR ameliorates firms' resistance to regulation, boosts their normative commitment, or can challenge systemic deviance. Rather, what this research has shown is that the success of POR, just like prescriptive regulation, is mediated by regulatees' pre-existing organizational, professional, and individual identities, and most prominently by the quality of communication and trust within corporations.

The consequences of organizational and professional identity to the success of POR have been depicted by a number of studies. Haines (2009) has found that site managers' perceptions of the regulatory reforms were shaped by the congruence between regulatory objectives and individuals' professional identity. Managers of major-hazards facilities were generally committed to the success of the new regulations, because they already perceived hazard reduction as "intrinsic to what was considered a good site manager or a good chemical engineer" (Haines 2009: 46). In contrast, the airport industry, particularly small airports, tended to resist the new regime, because a focus on risk management was alien to their professional identity. In larger airports, risk management was the domain of specialized security units that did not experience similar identity conflicts. However, in the latter cases, it was unclear to what extent security was integrated with the airports' business functions.

Fairman and Yapp's (2005) study of British small and medium enterprises (SME) responses to what the authors classify as an enforced self-regulation food-safety regime further demonstrates the role of professional and individual identity. The SMEs' managers did not internalize the new regime's expectation that they proactively and continuously assess the risks posed by their operations and independently devise solutions to mitigate these risks. While these managers aimed to comply with regulation, they perceived themselves as compliant as long as they adhered to whatever was required by (or negotiated with) supervisors in the last inspection. Thus the shift to POR did not alter SMEs' conceptualization of their role vis-à-vis that of regulators.

Equally, Hutter (2001) and Gunningham and Sinclair (2009) demonstrate that one reason for the partial success of POR was managers and employees' perception of safety as secondary to their key responsibility for production. Hutter (2001) shows how both managers and workers perceived certain levels of non-compliance as inevitable and efficient. Consequently, while individuals generally understood the risks involved in their everyday work, they tended to neutralize and normalize them as an inescapable part of their job.

In addition, Hutter (2001) and Gunningham and Sinclair (2009) both point to the quality of firms' internal communications and trust between different corporate levels as a mediating factor of employees' commitment to their firms' internal compliance programs. Many of Hutter's respondents perceived the company's safety policies and detailed rulebook as the board's means of shifting blame to the workforce in the event of accident, rather than a sincere attempt to change organizational practices. They also tended to interpret implicit messages, such as weak enforcement and the non-engaging means by which the corporate policies were communicated, as lack of top-level commitment to health and safety.

Similarly, Gunningham and Sinclair (2009) found that mining sites with poor regulatory performance were those with generally low levels of cooperation and trust between managers and workers. Very much like Hutter's (2001) respondents, the workforce on these sites tended to perceive the companies' health and safety programs as managers' attempt to shift the blame for accidents to them. In contrast, highly performing sites were those with high levels of trust among managers and the workforce, and managerial commitment to health and safety. In the latter sites, cooperation and trust were further nurtured via wide participation and delegation of ownership for health and safety initiatives to workers.

What the above studies suggest is that, for POR to drive transformative change to firms' practices, at least two cultural hurdles need to be surpassed. First, regulatory goals need to be embraced by senior managers. For this to happen, executives' attention has to be drawn to the risks and costs of non-compliance (Parker 2002, Ch. 3). Drawing executives' attention requires a combination of forceful and steady, albeit responsive (Ayres and Braithwaite 1992), regulatory enforcement, buttressed by stakeholder pressure and adverse publicity (Gunningham et al. 2003, 2004).

Second, managers' commitment has to be communicated and internalized beyond the upper echelons of organizations all the way down to front-level employees across the organization. In other words, POR, like – and even more than – prescriptive regulation, relies on the capacity of firms' executives to communicate with their employees and shape their attitudes towards regulatory goals as constituted in firms' internal compliance programs. As Parker (2002) would emphasize, the success of POR ultimately depends on senior managers' capacity to connect regulatory objectives to employees' values and identities via dialogic communication about the content and merit of firms' compliance programs. Yet POR does not necessarily support internal communication, delegation, and participation within firms. Rather, the need to make the evaluation and management of risks easily auditable by regulators could drive firms to centralize and standardize their risk management processes (cf. Power 1997). Allowing different parts of the company to conduct their own analyses of risk and to adopt their own measures, while engendering commitment at lower levels, renders internal analysis of information and external reporting to regulators more difficult. Thus POR runs the risk of exacerbating employees' resistance to internal compliance programs.

### Firms' capacity for self-regulation

Diverse literature suggests that organizational capacity simultaneously enhances firms' compliance and creates greater opportunities for corporate and individual deviance (e.g. Dalton and Kesner 1988; Baucus and Near 1991; McKendall and Wagner 1997). Large firms are more likely to comply, and are better trusted by regulators (e.g. Grabosky and Braithwaite 1986), among other things because they have better resources to meet regulatory requirements. Yet resources create opportunities for firms to pursue risky innovations, and to legally challenge and politically buffer regulatory scrutiny. Moreover, large organizations are structurally complex and suffer internal information asymmetries, which increase the risk for individual or sub-group deviance within organizations. The latter may result in decoupling between the intentions and efforts exerted by senior managers and specialized compliance units and non-compliant business routines.

In contrast with the above mixed findings, the theoretical literature on POR has given surprisingly little attention to the "dark side" of large and complex organizations (but see Ford 2010). The literature tends to perceive large firms as superior sources of expertise and information that regulators need to support and attract for the cooperative fulfillment of regulatory objectives (e.g. Gunningham 1999; Ford 2008). It often recommends that regulators provide non-binding guidance and support to small firms, while giving large firms more freedom to innovate in pursuit of the public good (e.g. Eisner 2004).

The literature's expectation that POR does not suit the limited capabilities of many small firms is confirmed by current research (e.g. Fairman and Yapp 2005). In contrast, Haines (2009) and Hutter (2001) highlight the difficulties that size and complexity pose for firms' implementation of POR by large corporations. Haines (2009) suggests that the implementation of the new regulatory reforms was difficult, because it required "constant monitoring of procedures and the ever-present possibility that site practices will diverge from written procedures" (2009: 55).

Hutter focuses our attention on the role of complexity and internal (mis-)communication in inhibiting the capacity of corporations to control employees and to learn from accidents. First, she found that knowledge and understanding of regulation, including of the company's internal regulations, diminished down the lines of BR's hierarchy. This was partly because the firm's detailed rulebook and other voluminous written communication were daunting and difficult for the workforce to comprehend. Second, upward reporting of accident information was deficient. One of Hutter's respondents estimated that about 50 percent of accidents were not documented (2001: 206). Finally, BR had no centralized mechanism for compiling and learning from accidents and for disseminating knowledge back to staff. Hutter concludes that

> the experience of BR must cause us to ask serious questions about the ability of companies to self-regulate . . . there may be serious difficulties in managing risks in a large and diverse company . . . [including limited] availability of knowledge about how to comply and the ability to implement this. (2001: 313)

The above studies do not necessarily suggest that POR was the *cause* of firms' imperfect self-regulatory capacity. Rather, they indicate that the success of POR, like prescriptive regulation, can be hindered by organizational complexity and generally poor organizational capacity. What current research does not show is whether POR in fact enhances organizational capacity for self-regulation. Nonetheless, as Kagan and Scholz (1984) have argued, it seems plausible that system-based regulation, as they label it, would improve firms' self-regulatory capacity by enhancing organizational awareness to risks, establishing specialized units to handle these risks and providing managers with additional sources of information and control (1984: 83). Hence the question which remains to be answered is whether POR, or an alternative model, can prompt and support managers' efforts to control large and complex organizations.

## 31.4   CONCLUSION AND IMPLICATIONS FOR RESEARCH AND POLICY

Process-oriented regulation (POR), as defined in this chapter, involves regulators' direction and monitoring of firms' self-evaluation, design, and management of their production and internal controls in light of regulatory objectives. This form of regulation comprises a variety of similar, albeit not identical, regulatory arrangements. Whilst recognizing this variance, this chapter aimed to draw general conclusions from current research regarding the impact of POR and the factors that shape it.

Before moving to the findings, it should be stressed that the *empirical* literature on POR is still in its infancy. In particular, limited data is available on regulators' and firms' perceptions of the benefits, costs, and risks of POR.

Extant empirical research, albeit limited, nonetheless indicates that the family of POR tends to have a positive, yet highly varied, impact on firms' performance. The above discussion identifies two key potential drivers of this inconsistent effect: (a) the uncertainty faced by both firms and regulators and its implications for regulatory capacity and for the costs of regulation, and (b) the deficiencies of internal communication, trust, information, and control within large and complex firms.

In contrast with the assumptions of prevalent current research, this chapter stresses that firms do not necessarily have a good appreciation of the risks that their operations pose to regulatory objectives, and of the solutions that would best fit their individual circumstances. Furthermore, even if firms are in a good position to identify and manage the risks that they generate, they may be disinclined to do so, because of the associated costs and lack of sufficient incentives. Moreover, as current research acknowledges, regulators operate under conditions of asymmetric information and expertise. This entails that, whilst POR requires firms to produce and report information regarding their identification and management of risks, regulators may be in a poor position to assess the validity of this information and the likely effectiveness of firms' plans. The combination of regulators' and/or firms' uncertainties could result, depending on the circumstances, in mutual stalemate, firms' design and implementation of internal controls that are incompatible with the risks to be managed, and/or regulators' and firms' co-construction of a de facto standardized interpretation of the systems and controls that firms should introduce.

Hence regulators' information asymmetry and the uncertainty that regulators and firms face pose significant challenges for POR. However, it should be stressed that I am not implying that POR is the *cause* of this uncertainty. Nor am I suggesting that this problem could be overcome if regulatory agencies would only recruit the right, and bright, people from industry. Rather, regulatory uncertainty is inherent to industry heterogeneity, rapid changes to the environments within which firms and regulators operate, limited scientific knowledge, and lack of consensus within regulatory regimes. Prescriptive regulation downplays variance and uncertainty, and thereby provides clear guidance to firms and to their supervisors, at the cost of either over- or under-regulation. The ability to adapt regulation to variability and change, which POR allows, is therefore a move in the right direction. It still, nonetheless, falls short of giving an adequate answer to the problem of uncertainty.

On top of uncertainty, current research reveals that POR is often undermined by internal conflicts and deficiencies of controls within firms. First, empirical studies have revealed two closely linked impediments to organizations' commitment to the implementation of POR: organizational cultures which construct regulatory goals and tasks as tangential to business goals, and lack of trust within corporations. Second, existing empirical research has shown that the theoretical literature on POR tends to be overly optimistic about large and complex organizations' capacity for self-management and for learning from their own experience and failure.

All of the above entails that POR, while associated with overall progress, requires further adaptation. It has to be more sensitive to the problem of regulatory uncertainty (regarding the nature of the risks to society and potential solutions), and both insistent on and supportive of senior managers' efforts to enlist internal commitment and overcome internal asymmetries of information and control. Elsewhere (Gilad 2010) I assess the prospects of an alternative learning-oriented POR model to better deal with these tricky problems.

# REFERENCES

Aalders, Marius (2002), *Drivers and Drawbacks: Regulation and Environmental Risk – Management Systems*, London: ESRC Centre for Analysis of Risk and Regulation, available at: http://www2.lse.ac.uk/research AndExpertise/units/CARR/pdf/DPs/Disspaper10.pdf (accessed 23 December 2010).
Albert, Stuart and David Whetten (1985), 'Organizational identity', *Research in Organizational Behavior*, **7**, 263–95.

Ayres, Ian and John Braithwaite (1992), *Responsive Regulation: Transcending the Deregulation Debate*, New York: Oxford University Press.

Baldwin, Robert (1995), *Rules and Government*, Oxford: Clarendon Press.

Baucus, Mellissa S. and Janet P. Near (1991), 'Can illegal corporate behavior be predicted? An event history analysis', *Academy of Management Journal*, **34** (1), 9–36.

Bennear, L.S. (2006), 'Evaluating management based regulation: a valuable tool in the regulatory toolbox?', in Cary Coglianese and Jennifer Nash (eds), *Leveraging the Private Sector: Management-Based Strategies for Improving Environmental Performance*, Washington, DC: Resources for the Future, pp. 51–86.

Bennear, L.S. (2007), 'Are management-based regulations effective? Evidence from state pollution prevention programs', *Journal of Policy Analysis and Management*, **26** (2), 327–48.

Black, Julia (1997), *Rules and Regulators*, Oxford: Clarendon Press.

Black, Julia (2008), 'Forms and paradoxes of principles-based regulation', *Capital Markets Law Journal*, **3** (4), 425–57.

Black, Julia, Martin Hopper and Christa Band (2007), 'Making a success of principles-based regulation', *Law and Financial Markets Review*, **1** (3), 191–206.

Braithwaite, John and Valerie Braithwaite (1995), 'The politics of legalism: rules versus standards in nursing-home regulation', *Social and Legal Studies*, **4** (3), 307–41.

Coglianese, Cary and David Lazer (2003), 'Management-based regulation: prescribing private management to achieve public goals', *Law and Society Review*, **37** (4), 691–730.

Coglianese, Cary and Jennifer Nash (2006), *Leveraging the Private Sector: Management-Based Strategies for Improving Environmental Performance*, Washington, DC: Resources for the Future.

Coglianese, Cary, Jennifer Nash and Todd Olmstead (2003), 'Performance-based regulation: prospects and limitations in health, safety, and environmental protection', *Administrative Law Review*, **55** (4), 705–28.

Corneliussen, Fillipa (2005), 'The impact of regulations on firms: a case study of the biotech industry', *Law and Policy*, **27** (3), 429–49.

Cunningham, Lawrence A. (2007), 'A prescription to retire the rhetoric of "principles-based systems" in corporate law, securities regulation and accounting', *Vanderbilt Law Review*, **60**, 1409–94.

Dalton, Dan R. and Idalene F. Kesner (1988), 'On the dynamics of corporate size and illegal activity: an empirical assessment', *Journal of Business Ethics*, **7** (11), 861–70.

Dutton, Jane E. and Janet M. Dukerich (1991), 'Keeping an eye on the mirror – image and identity in organizational adaptation', *Academy of Management Journal*, **34** (3), 517–54.

Eisner, Marc A. (2004), 'Corporate environmentalism, regulatory reform, and industry self-regulation: toward genuine regulatory reinvention in the United States', *Governance: An International Journal of Policy and Administration*, **17** (2), 145–67.

Fairman, Robyn and Charlotte Yapp (2005), 'Enforced self regulation, prescription, and conceptions of compliance within small businesses: the impact of enforcement', *Law & Policy*, **27** (4), 491–519.

Fiorino, Daniel J. (2001), 'Environmental policy as learning: a new view of an old landscape', *Public Administration Review*, **61** (3), 322–34.

Ford, Cristie L. (2008), 'New governance, compliance, and principles-based securities regulation', *American Business Law Journal*, **45** (1), 1–60.

Ford, Cristie L. (2010), 'Principles-based securities regulation in the wake of the global financial crisis', *McGill Law Journal*, **55**, 257–310.

Gilad, Sharon (2010), 'It runs in the family: meta regulation and its siblings', *Regulation & Governance*, **4** (4), 485–506.

Gilad, Sharon (2011), 'Institutionalizing fairness in financial markets: mission impossible?', *Regulation & Governance*, **5** (3), 309–332.

Grabosky, Peter N. and John Braithwaite (1986), *Of Manners Gentle: Enforcement Strategies of Australian Business Regulatory Agencies*, Melbourne and New York: Oxford University Press in association with Australian Institute of Criminology.

Gunningham, Neil (1999), 'Integrating management systems and occupational health and safety regulation', *Journal of Law and Society*, **26** (2), 192–214.

Gunningham, Neil (2007), *Mine Safety: Law Regulation Policy*, Sydney: Federation Press.

Gunningham, Neil and Darren Sinclair (2009), 'Organizational trust and the limits of management based regulation', *Law and Society Review*, **43** (4), 865–900.

Gunningham, Neil, Robert A. Kagan and Dorothy Thornton (2003), *Shades of Green: Business, Regulation, and Environment*, Stanford, CA: Stanford University Press.

Gunningham, Neil A., Robert A. Kagan and Dorothy Thornton (2004), 'Social license and environmental protection: why businesses go beyond compliance', *Law and Social Inquiry*, **29** (2), 307–42.

Haines, Fiona (2009), 'Regulatory failures and regulatory solutions: a characteristic analysis of the aftermath of disaster', *Law and Social Inquiry*, **34** (1), 31–60.

Hutter, Bridget M. (2001), *Regulation and Risk: Occupational Health and Safety on the Railways,* Oxford and New York: Oxford University Press.
Kagan, Robert A. and John T. Scholz (1984), 'The criminology of the corporation and regulatory enforcement strategies', in Keith Hawkins and M. John Thomas (eds), *Enforcing Regulation,* Boston, MA: Kluwer-Nijhoff Publishing, pp. 67–97.
Kaplow, Louis (1992), 'Rules versus standards: an economic analysis', *Duke Law Journal,* **42** (3), 557–629.
Krawiec, Kimberly D. (2003), 'Cosmetic compliance and the failure of negotiated governance', *Washington University Law Review,* **81**, 487–544.
Levi-Faur, David (2011), 'Regulation and regulatory governance', in David Levi-Faur (ed.), *Handbook on the Politics of Regulation,* Cheltenham: Edward Elgar.
MacLean, Tammy (2002), 'Reframing organizational misconduct: a study of deceptive sales practices at a major life insurance company', *Business and Society,* **41** (2), 242–50.
May, Peter J. (2003), 'Performance-based regulation and regulatory regimes: the saga of leaky buildings', *Law & Policy,* **25** (4), 381–401.
May, Peter J. (2007), 'Regulatory regimes and accountability', *Regulation & Governance,* **1** (1), 8–26.
May, Peter J. (2011), 'Performance based regulation', in David Levi-Faur (ed.), *Handbook on the Politics of Regulation,* Cheltenham: Edward Elgar.
McKendall, Marie A. and John A. Wagner III (1997), 'Motive, opportunity, choice and corporate illegality', *Organization Science,* **8** (6), 624–47.
Parker, Christine (2002), *The Open Corporation: Effective Self-Regulation and Democracy,* New York: Cambridge University Press.
Power, Michael (1997), *The Audit Society: Rituals of Verification,* Oxford and New York: Oxford University Press.
Power, Michael (2007), *Organized Uncertainty: Designing a World of Risk Management,* Oxford: Oxford University Press.
Schauer, Fredrick (2003), 'The convergence of rules and standards', *New Zealand Law Review,* **2003** (4), 303–28.
Schwarcz, Steven L. (2009), 'The "principles" paradox', *European Business Organization Law Review,* **10**, 175–84.
Shapiro, Martin (2011), 'The evolution of cost-benefit analysis in U.S regulatory decision-making', in David Levi-Faur (ed.), *Handbook on the Politics of Regulation,* Cheltenham: Edward Elgar.
Sunstein, Cass R. (1995), 'Problems with rules', *California Law Review,* **83** (4), 953–1026.
Vaughan, Diane (1996), *The Challenger Launch Decision: Risky Technology, Culture, and Deviance at NASA,* Chicago: University of Chicago Press.
Wegrich, Kai (2011), 'Regulatory impact assessment: ambition, policy model and politics', in David Levi-Faur (ed.), *Handbook on the Politics of Regulation,* Cheltenham: Edward Elgar.

# PART IX

# CIVIL REGULATION

# 32 Certification as a mode of social regulation
## Tim Bartley

Certification of products and companies has long been used as a signal of quality, but its transformation into a mode of social regulation is more recent. Over the past two decades, numerous initiatives have emerged to certify conditions in global supply chains, typically addressing environmental sustainability, labor conditions, human rights, or some combination of these. These include early and influential programs like organic, Fair Trade, and Forest Stewardship Council (FSC) certification, a second wave of programs like the Marine Stewardship Council (MSC) and Social Accountability International (SAI), and a seemingly endless array of newly emerging initiatives, focused on shrimp farming, cocoa production, palm oil, and many others. Such initiatives are typically privately organized and supported by coalitions of NGOs, firms, and foundations, though they are also profoundly shaped by governments. Industry associations have also developed their own certification initiatives, such as the Sustainable Forestry Initiative (SFI) and Worldwide Responsible Apparel Production (WRAP) systems, or have added certification to prior initiatives, like Responsible Care in the chemical industry.

The proliferation of certification and labeling initiatives has led many observers to worry about confusion among consumers and "certification fatigue" among companies. Yet the growth of certification also raises important questions for scholars of regulation and transnational governance. Why has this form emerged across so many industries? Under what conditions can voluntary, privately operated certification initiatives gain governing authority? Does the rise of certification complement or "crowd out" other forms of regulation?

This chapter sheds light on these questions by discussing the character, emergence, evolution, and impacts of certification as a way of addressing the environmental or social conditions of production. It begins with a discussion of certification as a regulatory form, considering its linkages to other modes of "regulation by information," market-based tools, and private governance. It then turns to questions about certification's emergence and evolution. Finally, the chapter considers certification's impacts "on the ground," showing that the relevant mechanisms of influence are varied in type but often limited in consequence. In general, this chapter suggests that certification systems are more intertwined with states and less straightforward in their effects than many previous discussions imply.

## 32.1 CERTIFICATION AS A REGULATORY FORM

While companies make a variety of claims about their environmental or social responsibility, the most credible way to do so is through third-party systems that set standards, require external monitoring, and certify compliance. Most commonly, this occurs through an association that develops standards, accredits auditors, and grants the use of a certification mark or label for consumers. Yet certification is not merely – or even primarily – a marketing device or signal for consumers. It has become a mode of regulation, being put to use by various NGOs, governments, and industry bodies. This is not to suggest that certification carries the authority, coercive power, or legitimacy of state regulation. In most instances, certification is voluntary and administered by private bodies that depend on the support of firms and must compete with other certifiers for credibility and recognition. The authority of certification is certainly patchier than that of states, and the logic of "one dollar, one vote" is ultimately less transformative than the "one person, one vote" logic of democratic citizenship. There are numerous examples of certification systems that are lax in standards or weak in enforcement, as well as evidence that even the most credible programs often fail to significantly improve conditions "on the ground" (Seidman 2007).

Still, calling certification a mode of regulation recognizes that it involves standards that are often precise and prescriptive, plus rationalized procedures for assessing compliance. In addition, certification initiatives' structures for setting standards, enforcing compliance, and adjudicating disputes have evolved to look strikingly similar to state and legal structures (Meidinger 2006). In some countries and supply chains, certification systems have gained substantial, albeit partial, governing authority (Cashore et al. 2004), and at the transnational level they have intertwined with state-based actors to generate hybrid fields of governance (Djelic and Sahlin-Andersson 2006). Furthermore, to make sense of certification, one must consider broader trends in regulatory theory and practice, which have gone beyond the administrative procedures characterized (usually derisively) as "command and control." This includes a number of experiments that use markets, information, deliberation, and "soft law" as regulatory tools (Schneiberg and Bartley 2008). (See Figure 32.1.)

Calls to make regulation "market-based" have motivated a variety of policy proposals, from the strengthening of property rights to "cap and trade." Certification is market-based in that its power to affect behavior derives mainly from market demand. This may come from end consumers practicing "political consumerism" (Micheletti 2003), investors, retailers promoting a particular brand image, or the procurement and licensing policies of large organizations (e.g., governments, universities) (Seidman 2007). In any case, the "price" of non-compliance is set by market forces, not by administrative authority. Certification does not embrace market mechanisms as fully as cap and trade, which uses markets not only to set the price of pollution but also to identify the most efficient ways for firms to improve their performance. Because certification initiatives set particular performance standards, they rely on market forces while also inserting alternative "conventions" (Renard 2003) or "orders of worth" (Boltanski and Thévenot 2006) based in some non-market form of expertise or morality.

Certification also resonates with ideas about "regulation by information." Scholars are increasingly investigating the effects of disclosure, reporting, and public rating, whether related to pollution, financial markets, or universities (Espeland and Sauder 2006; Rona-Tas and Hiss 2010). As Fung et al. (2007) point out, a core feature of information-based initiatives is that the application of rewards and penalties is left to external audiences, which includes not just consumers, but also citizens, workers, and advocacy organiza-

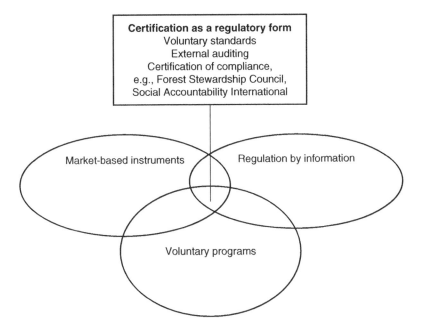

*Figure 32.1    Certification as a regulatory form*

tions. Viewing certification in this light suggests that its enforcement might happen not only within markets but through political and legal mobilization. Yet, unlike programs that disclose relatively "raw" data or grade performance on some scale, certification reveals an aggregated, discrete judgment. In contrast to *mandatory* disclosure initiatives, certification only generates "positive" information on firms that choose to participate and meet the standards. For both of these reasons, certification is a very circumscribed form of regulation by information. If standards or auditing is especially lax, certification may even generate "disinformation" in the form of "greenwash" labeling.

Social and environmental certification initiatives are also types of voluntary programs. As in all voluntary programs, whether publicly or privately run, firms must have some incentive to join, which creates a tension between stringency and participation (Potoski and Prakash 2009). Furthermore, since most certification programs are privately run (with the exception of government-sponsored eco-labels), they face challenges of establishing authority while still garnering support from firms (Cashore et al. 2004). Combined with the fact that participants can easily exit and develop their own standards (discussed later in this chapter), this sets up a complex politics of credibility (Boström 2006). Certification programs can be differentiated from other common forms of voluntary regulation primarily in terms of monitoring and validation. While many codes and principles of good conduct (e.g., industry codes, Global Compact) lack monitoring or rely solely on self-reporting, the certification programs discussed here typically include third-party systems for monitoring performance "on the ground." In contrast to those codes that do require external auditing, certification systems go one step further in using that auditing to award a "seal of approval" of some sort.

Scholars sometimes refer to certification as "soft law." Though certification lacks "hard" enforcement powers, calling it soft law is in many respects misleading. The core idea behind "soft" forms of governance is that behavior can be affected by stimulating informal social pressures, deliberation, and learning within the community of the regulated (Schneiberg and Bartley 2008). Often, this means jettisoning "standards" in favor of guidelines and evolving systems for peer review and benchmarking. In contrast, certification systems tend to embrace standards and develop detailed indicators for auditing. In this sense, they depart from soft law advocates' focus on dialogue among firms, though some certification associations might use collective deliberation to revise their standards over time.

In sum, certification resonates with a range of ideas about how markets and information can be used as regulatory tools, as well as broader shifts toward voluntary programs and private governance. Yet ideas alone did not spawn certification, and its impacts may be far different than what advocates of regulatory innovations suggest.

## 32.2  THE RISE OF SOCIAL AND ENVIRONMENTAL CERTIFICATION

Social and environmental certification is not entirely new. Progressive-era activism over tenement sweatshops in the US led to the National Consumers' League "White Label," which certified garments "made under clean and healthful conditions" from the 1890s to the early 1920s (Sklar 1998). This gave way to the "union label" promoted by American organized labor in the mid-20th century (Frank 1999). Consumer watchdogs that emerged in the 1920s – such as the forerunner to *Consumer Reports* – initially included labor standards in their ratings of products, though this later got sidelined by an "impartial testing" approach focused narrowly on quality (Rao 1998).

For the most part, certification efforts in the 20th century focused on product quality, safety, or technical standards. The Underwriters Laboratories (UL) label signified electrical safety for the American market (Cheit 1990), as did similar certificates in other countries. The International Organization for Standardization (ISO), founded in 1947, promoted certification to a wide range of technical standards to facilitate global trade (Murphy and Yates 2009). In one move toward the expansion of certification into new terrain, the ISO began developing standards for management systems (ISO 9000) in the 1980s and for environmental management systems (ISO 14001) in the 1990s.

The current wave of social and environmental certification purports to go beyond management systems, however, to assess whether practices "on the ground" conform to standards for sustainability or social justice. Much of the inspiration for this wave came from organic agriculture. As a movement of farmers, organics can be traced to the 1930s, but it was in the 1970s that *certification* of organic food began in the US and Europe (Guthman 2004) and standards began to be developed by the International Federation of Organic Agriculture Movements (IFOAM). Government-sponsored eco-labels also began to emerge in the 1970s, starting with Germany's Blue Angel label (Gulbrandsen 2005). Fair Trade-certified coffee and bananas first came on the market in the late 1980s, as a result of partnerships between Northern activists and farmers in Central America, and drawing on an older tradition of alternative trading organizations (Linton et al. 2004; Jaffee 2007).

With organics, Fair Trade, and various government eco-labels as partial models, a major wave of certification arose in the 1990s, with the founding of programs like Rugmark, the Forest Stewardship Council, Social Accountability International, and the Marine Stewardship Council. It is this wave of certification that has most captured the attention of social scientists. Scholars tend to agree that the rise of certification is in some fashion a response to the globalization of production and consumer concerns about exploitation. But, beyond this baseline, attempts to explain the emergence of certification tend to follow two different tracks.

One style of explanation is rooted in theories of self-regulation and private ordering among firms (King et al. 2005; Potoski and Prakash 2009), drawing inspiration from institutional economics and public choice theory. By this account, certification is a solution to information asymmetries and collective action problems, which arise via activist "naming and shaming" of firms as well as consumers' interest in "shopping with a conscience." As activists put companies in the spotlight for exploiting workers or eco-systems, companies begin to make a variety of claims of social or environmental responsibility. Conscientious consumers may be interested in supporting responsible companies but find it difficult to assess the accuracy of their self-serving claims. Given this information problem, the market for responsible production is expected to fail unless credible systems of certification can be created to separate the "wheat from the chaff" (Akerlof 1970; Viscusi 1978). For their part, companies face collective action problems that certification has the potential to solve. In particular, theorists of the "reputation commons problem" (King et al. 2002) and similar accounts (Potoski and Prakash 2009) argue that naming and shaming campaigns leave entire groups of companies "tarred by the same brush." One way to address this problem is to construct external systems of certification. These can distinguish the good apples from the bad, provide "club benefits" to firms that contribute to an improved reputation, exclude free riders, and stabilize competition among leading firms (Spar and Yoffie 2000; Potoski and Prakash 2009).

A second account views certification less as a solution to problems in the market and more as a political settlement and institution-building project (Cashore et al. 2004; Bartley 2007b). Here, following Polanyi (1944), scholars see markets as deeply embedded in social structures and unlikely to self-regulate effectively. The pressures to re-embed markets in social relations that have typically generated state regulation are increasingly giving rise to private certification initiatives (Raynolds 2000; Guthman 2007), as political challenges are mobilized, channeled into particular arenas (i.e., markets), and crystallized into institutional arrangements. As social movements demand standards that can somehow regulate global supply chains, questions arise about the appropriate arena for this. Standards can conceivably be institutionalized in national governmental regulations or in inter-governmental agreements or organizations (e.g., trade agreements, UN, WTO). Yet the strategies of states and NGOs in a context of neoliberalism have tended to channel regulatory politics over international labor and environmental standards to the private sector (Bartley 2007b). Unlike governments, private certification initiatives are relatively immune to WTO restrictions on non-tariff barriers to trade (Bernstein and Cashore 2004). Private efforts have also been perceived by many NGOs as a way to bypass political roadblocks (Cashore et al. 2004; Seidman 2007) and by many powerful governments as consistent with a neoliberal agenda. So, by this account, the rise of certification results largely from a kind of forum-shifting by policy entrepreneurs, congealing into a relatively coherent institution-building project with support from government agencies and philanthropic foundations (Bartley 2007a).

As Bartley (2007b) shows, both theoretical perspectives can help to explain the rise of certification, though neither does so perfectly. The theory of certification as a solution to problems within markets explains the role of firms in the coalitions that created several leading initiatives (like FSC and SAI). This perspective can also help to explain why private regulatory initiatives take different forms (i.e., certification instead of self-regulation without sanctions). But it tends to overstate the causal influence of capitalist collective action and consumer demand. Industry associations have often developed certification systems, but in nearly every case this occurs *after* the development of an NGO-endorsed system in a particular sector. Substantial consumer demand more commonly follows than leads the formation of certification initiatives (Gulbrandsen 2006; McNichol 2006; Conroy 2007), though there is clearly variation between sectors (like coffee) where consumer demand grew rapidly and those (like forest products) where "market-building" campaigns have struggled to stimulate consumers.

Political theories explain why NGO-endorsed programs were the initiators in most sectors and how NGOs, governments, and foundations played major roles in developing them. WWF, for instance, became a key developer of the FSC following disappointments in the UN and other inter-governmental arenas, and then went on to catalyze or cultivate numerous other certification initiatives, including the MSC and the Roundtable on Sustainable Palm Oil. Governments in Europe and North America provided important early funding for most forms of certification and have sometimes turned their procurement policies into key market drivers. On the other hand, this political account has less to say about the precise form that private regulation takes or the conditions under which firms and consumers might expand their participation in certification. Further inquiry can help to clarify the explanatory scope of these theories and consider ways of integrating them.

## 32.3 COMPETITION AND EVOLUTION

The evolution of social and environmental certification has been dynamic and contentious. Many sectors feature multiple, competing initiatives. Competition appears to be an inherent feature of private certification, since firms that are dissatisfied with one initiative can exit for a different program or start their own (Seidman 2007). Not surprisingly, competition between NGO-endorsed programs and those originating with industry associations has been especially intense. Competition between the FSC and industry-based programs like SFI and the Programme for the Endorsement of Forest Certification (PEFC) has led to public relations wars (e.g., the "Don't buy SFI" campaign), strained relationships in the conservation community, and a series of public comparisons of standards. Similar patterns of competition exist among labor standards initiatives (e.g., SAI, the Fair Labor Association, and WRAP) and increasingly in the coffee sector, where multiple initiatives certify fairness and sustainability (including Fair Trade, Rainforest Alliance, Utz Kapeh, and the Common Code for the Coffee Community).

Given the existence of competing programs, it would appear that certification would be plagued by a "race to the bottom," leading to an overall decline in the stringency of standards. Yet at least two other trajectories are also possible: competition might breed a "ratcheting up" of standards, generated by credibility contests, or by learning and benchmarking in the world of certification (Sabel, O'Rourke and Fung 2000); or multiple programs might co-exist (without one undermining another), especially if the markets they target are segmented.

The conditions under which competition breeds laxity, ratcheting up, or market segmentation are not yet clear. However, it is clear that, in at least some circumstances, competition has not undermined relatively strong standards. In forestry, the FSC was able to fend off industry-based challenges in some regions (especially those with export-dependent forest products industries, weak industry associations, and high degrees of public involvement in forest policy) (Cashore 2004). Furthermore, public comparisons led industry-based programs to strengthen their standards over time (Overdevest 2010). While some fear that the FSC's standards were watered down in the process (Rainforest Foundation 2002), it is at least clear from this case that competition need not produce a net decline in standards, though it might facilitate a "race to the middle."

Evidence from other sectors suggests that a "ratcheting up" of standards may not always translate into improvements in implementation. While best practices for labor standards auditing and certification have arguably improved over time – consistent with Sabel et al's (2000) account – initiatives in this sector have also increasingly struggled with audit fraud, falsified records, and recalcitrance (Locke et al. 2009). This reminds one that standards "on paper" and norms in the certification community may be strengthened over time without necessarily generating improvements at the point of production.

Conflicts over credibility in the world of certification have also bred a variety of meta-standardization activities, i.e., standards for the standard-setters and certification of the certifiers. This includes the ISO 65 standard for certification systems themselves and umbrella groups like the International Social and Environmental Accreditation and Labelling (ISEAL) Alliance. Such initiatives appear to be facilitating both greater interconnectedness among certification initiatives and greater homogeneity in their organizational form (Bartley and Smith 2010). This kind of meta-standardization signals the crystallization of certification as a mode of regulation, though it also poses difficulties for implementing certification equitably across diverse local settings (Mutersbaugh 2005).

## 32.4   IMPACTS OF CERTIFICATION

Serious questions remain regarding the consequences of certification initiatives. Are their impacts transformative, marginal, or non-existent? How are standards "on the books" put into practice? Might certification have unintended, perverse consequences? The research literature is too undeveloped to offer full answers to these questions. However, it is clear that the transformative power heralded by many champions of certification and political consumerism is both oversimplified and overstated. Far from transcending socio-economic conflicts, power struggles, and governance failures, even the most credible certification program's operation is deeply influenced by configurations of power and interest at the local, national, and transnational levels. In one striking example, Ponte (2008) shows how MSC certification in South Africa was appropriated by white-owned fishing groups to maintain market control and exclude black-owned companies.

This sort of finding reminds one that certification does not operate in a vacuum and may have a wide range of effects, both intended and unintended.

The difficulties of assessing certification's impacts are partially methodological. Identifying causal impacts poses serious data and research design challenges – including accessing appropriate negative cases for comparison (i.e., uncertified firms) and problems of self-selection (i.e., better-performing firms choosing to get certified) (Hiscox et al. 2009). Furthermore, some impacts of certification may arise over long periods of time (Bernstein and Cashore 2007), raising additional challenges for researchers.

Nevertheless, several findings about impacts have been rigorously established: ISO 14001 certification increases US facilities' compliance with government regulations for air pollution (Prakash and Potoski 2006). Fair Trade certification increases the household nutrition and satisfaction of coffee farmers in Kenya (Becchetti and Costantino 2008). Other analyses have found important differences between certified and conventional producers – as with the prices received by coffee farmers participating in Fair Trade or organic certification (Bacon 2005; Jaffee 2007) – even though questions about causality and countervailing costs remain (Mutersbaugh 2005). In many other instances, however, comparisons of certified and uncertified firms have found differences that are small or ambiguous (Sharma et al. 2000; Agnew et al. 2006; Lima et al. 2009).

The difficulty of assessing certification's impact is also partly theoretical. Scholars have often glossed over or conflated the *variety* of processes through which certification might shape the conditions of production. A closer look at five conceptually distinct but empirically overlapping "mechanisms of influence" can shed further light on the significance and limits of certification.

First, managers may improve particular production practices in order to get (or stay) certified. Studies of forest certification under the FSC, for instance, show that essentially all certified operations have been required by auditors to make some changes (Gullison 2003; Klooster 2006; Newsom et al. 2006). This may mean altering harvesting or conservation practices, though most commonly it means adopting managerial processes that may not necessarily translate into behavioral changes (Nussbaum and Simula 2004). Research on fisheries certification similarly finds that the changes required by auditors are numerous but only occasionally linked directly to discernible "on the water" outcomes (Agnew et al. 2006).

Although much research assumes that spurring managerial improvement is the only way in which certification matters, this ignores several other potentially important processes. Even if it does not cause a *change* in behavior, certification may matter if it provides support for alternative production models (like cooperatives or community-based organizations) or firms that are already "above the bar." Fair Trade certification has boosted the incomes of coffee cooperatives (Bacon 2005; Jaffee 2007), and forest certification has sometimes helped community forestry operations improve access to markets and financing (Nebel et al. 2005; Klooster 2006). Furthermore, this support may generate demonstration effects in which alternative practices spill over from certified to conventional farms – as has happened with some organic farming methods (Jaffee 2007).

Third, certification could conceivably shape dispersed decisions about investment or land use. For instance, supporters of forest certification have often hoped that, by building markets for certified forest products, they could reduce the incentives for large-scale clearing of forests for conversion to agriculture (Johnson and Cabarle 1993). In theory, if certification adds value to socially just or environmentally friendly practices, this could reduce the relative profitability of the most exploitative practices. Yet there is little evidence that this hypothesized influence has actually occurred. Whatever premiums exist for certified products appear far too small to significantly reduce the incentives for exploitative investment and land use. Forest certification has rewarded firms that are already managing forest land for wood and paper production, but the reward has proven far too small to discourage others from converting forests to plantations or cattle pasture (Gullison 2003). Neither does sustainable fisheries certification appear to have altered the fundamental calculus of the industry, as yields and ocean biodiversity have continued to decline (Worm et al. 2006). The ability of certification to alter the logic of resource exploitation throughout a sector appears to be quite limited at the current time.

A fourth mechanism of influence comes through certification's interaction with social movements and transnational activism. Certification may provide a platform for challengers to expose exploitative practices or mobilize global forces to rectify local injustice. Under some conditions, activists may be able to leverage certification to *force* changes that companies would otherwise resist. Labor rights activists have occasionally leveraged transnational standards to gain recognition of insurgent unions, although this strategy has only rarely been successful (Rodríguez-Garavito 2005; Barrientos and Smith 2007). Engagement with certification may also carry dangers of co-optation and de-radicalization (Hughes 2007). More research is needed to assess the conditions under which social movement leveraging of certification can bring about significant changes.

Finally, certification may shape the conditions of production by influencing public authority and government regulation. The direction of this influence is the subject of much debate. Some scholars worry that, even if certification spurs marginal improvements, its net effect may be negative if it crowds out more powerful interventions, like the strengthening of state capacities and citizenship rights. Seidman (2007) argues that Rugmark certification has deflected attention from the Indian state's complicity in child labor and from more promising strategies for reducing it. Vandergeest (2007) suggests that effective local regulation of shrimp aquaculture in Thailand is being crowded out – or at least ignored – by sustainable shrimp certification initiatives. Yet other scholars see certification and government regulation as complementary. Some work suggests that the expansion of private auditing may allow government agencies to focus their limited resources on other parts of the market, thus generating a kind of "uncoordinated complementarity" (Amengual 2010). In other cases, government regulation may explicitly endorse certification or provide regulatory relief to certified operations, as has happened with forestry law in several countries (Nebel et al. 2005; Pattberg 2006). Another account of complementarity suggests that firms that have been certified to high standards may participate in "Baptist–bootlegger" coalitions that lobby for increased regulatory stringency (Vogel 2005; Bernstein and Cashore 2007). Much work remains to be done to understand how certification and governments complement or contradict one another, especially at the point of production in developing countries.

Overall, the ascendance of certification as a mode of regulation – especially for transnational supply chains – has opened up a variety of questions for scholars of regulation. This chapter has sought to guide scholars interested in further developing this literature and citizens and policymakers interested in understanding the character and limits of the certification model. Most importantly, the chapter has shown that what may look like a simple consumer label is a complex set of institutional arrangements, intertwined with states, transnational governance, social movements, and the organization of communities and workers in developing countries. Unpacking the "certification revolution" means taking each of these factors seriously.

# REFERENCES

Agnew, David, Chris Grieve, Pia Orr, Graeme Parkes and Nola Barker (2006), 'Environmental benefits resulting from certification against MSC's Principles and Criteria for Sustainable Fishing', MRAG UK and Marine Stewardship Council, available at: http://www.msc.org/documents/printed-documents/environmental-benefits/MSC_Environmental_Benefits_Report_Phase1_FINAL_4Ma.pdf.

Akerlof, George (1970), 'The market for "lemons": quality uncertainty and the market mechanism', *Quarterly Journal of Economics*, **84**, 488–500.

Amengual, Matthew (2010), 'Complementary labor regulation: the uncoordinated combination of state and private regulators in the Dominican Republic', *World Development*, **38** (3), 405–14.

Bacon, Christopher (2005), 'Confronting the coffee crisis: can fair trade, organic, and specialty coffees reduce small-scale farmer vulnerability in Northern Nicaragua?', *World Development*, **33** (3), 497–511.

Barrientos, Stephanie and Sally Smith (2007), 'Do workers benefit from ethical trade? Assessing codes of labour practice in global production systems', *Third World Quarterly*, **28** (4), 713–29.

Bartley, Tim (2007a), 'How foundations shape social movements: the construction of an organizational field and the rise of forest certification', *Social Problems*, **54** (3), 229–55.

Bartley, Tim (2007b), 'Institutional emergence in an era of globalization: the rise of transnational private regulation of labor and environmental conditions', *American Journal of Sociology*, **113** (2), 297–351.

Bartley, Tim, and Shawna Smith (2010), 'Communities of practice as cause and consequence of transnational governance: the evolution of social and environmental certification', in Marie-Laure Djelic and Sigrid Quack (eds), *Transnational Communities: Shaping Global Economic Governance*, Cambridge: Cambridge University Press, pp. 347–74.

Becchetti, Leonardo and Marco Costantino (2008), 'The effects of Fair Trade on affiliated producers: an impact analysis on Kenyan farmers', *World Development*, **36** (5), 823–42.

Bernstein, Steven and Benjamin Cashore (2004), 'Non-state global governance: Is forest certification a legitimate alternative to a global forest convention?', in John J. Kirton and Michael J. Trebilcock (eds), *Hard Choices, Soft Law: Voluntary Standards in Global Trade, Environment and Social Governance*, Aldershot: Ashgate.

Bernstein, Steven and Benjamin Cashore (2007), 'Can non-state global governance be legitimate? An analytical framework', *Regulation & Governance*, **1** (4), 347–71.

Boltanski, Luc and Laurent Thévenot (2006), *On Justification: Economies of Worth*, Princeton, NJ: Princeton University Press.

Boström, Magnus (2006), 'Regulatory credibility and authority through inclusiveness: standardization organizations in cases of eco-labelling', *Organization*, **13** (3), 345–67.

Cashore, Benjamin, Graeme Auld and Deanna Newsom (2004), *Governing through Markets: Forest Certification and the Emergence of Non-State Authority*, New Haven, CT: Yale University Press.

Cheit, Ross E. (1990), *Setting Safety Standards: Regulation in the Public and Private Sectors*, Berkeley: University of California Press.

Conroy, Michael E. (2007), *Branded! How the Certification Revolution Is Transforming Global Corporations*, Gabriola Island, BC: New Society Publishers.

Djelic, Marie-Laure and Kerstin Sahlin-Andersson (eds) (2006), *Transnational Governance: Institutional Dynamics of Regulation*, New York: Cambridge University Press.

Espeland, Wendy Nelson and Michael Sauder (2006), 'Rankings and reactivity: how public measures recreate social worlds', *American Journal of Sociology*, **113**, 1–40.

Frank, Dana (1999), *Buy American: The Untold Story of Economic Nationalism*, Boston, MA: Beacon Press.

Fung, Archon, Mary Graham and David Weil (2007), *Full Disclosure: The Perils and Promise of Transparency*, New York: Cambridge University Press.

Gulbrandsen, Lars H. (2005), 'Mark of sustainability? Challenges for fishery and forestry eco-labeling', *Environment*, **47** (5), 8–23.

Gulbrandsen, Lars H. (2006), 'Creating markets for eco-labelling: are consumers insignificant?', *International Journal of Consumer Studies*, **30** (5), 477–89.

Gullison, R.E. (2003), 'Does forest certification conserve biodiversity?', *Oryx*, **37** (2), 153–65.

Guthman, Julie (2004), *Agrarian Dreams: The Paradox of Organic Farming in California*, Berkeley: University of California Press.

Guthman, Julie (2007), 'The Polanyian way? Voluntary food labels as neoliberal governance', *Antipode*, **39** (3), 456–78.

Hiscox, Michael J., Claire Schwartz and Michael W. Toffel (2009), 'Evaluating the impact of SA8000 certification', in Deborah Leipziger (ed.), *SA8000: The First Decade: Implementation, Influence, and Impact*, London: Greenleaf Press.

Hughes, Caroline (2007), 'Transnational networks, international organizations and political participation in Cambodia: human rights, labour rights and common rights', *Democratization*, **14** (5), 834–52.

Jaffee, Daniel (2007), *Brewing Justice: Fair Trade Coffee, Sustainability, and Survival*, Berkeley: University of California Press.

Johnson, Nels and Bruce Cabarle (1993), *Surviving the Cut: Natural Forest Management in the Humid Tropics*, Washington, DC: World Resources Institute.

King, Andrew A., Michael J. Lenox and Michael L. Barnett (2002), 'Strategic responses to the reputation commons problem', in Andrew J. Hoffman and Marc J. Ventresca (eds), *Organizations, Policy, and the Natural Environment*, Stanford, CA: Stanford University Press.

King, Andrew A., Michael J. Lenox and Ann Terlaak (2005), 'The strategic use of decentralized institutions: exploring certification with the ISO 14001 management standard', *Academy of Management Journal*, **48** (6), 1091–1106.

Klooster, Dan (2006), 'Environmental certification of forests in Mexico: the political ecology of a nongovernmental market intervention', *Annals of the Association of American Geographers*, **96** (3), 541–65.

Lima, Ana Carolina Barbosa de, A.L.N. Keppe, F.E. Maule, G. Sparovek, M.C. Alves and R.F. Maule (2009), 'Does certification make a difference? Impact assessment study on FSC/SAN certification in Brazil', Piracicaba, SP, Brazil: Imaflora.

Linton, April, Cindy Chiayuan Liou and Kelly Ann Shaw (2004), 'A taste of trade justice: marketing global social responsibility via Fair Trade coffee', *Globalizations*, **1** (2), 223–46.

Locke, Richard, Matthew Amengual and Akshay Mangla (2009), 'Virtue out of necessity? Compliance, commitment and the improvement of labor conditions in global supply chains', *Politics and Society*, **37** (3), 319–51.

McNichol, Jason (2006), 'Transnational NGO certification programs as new regulatory forms: lessons from the forestry sector', in Marie-Laure Djelic and Kerstin Sahlin-Andersson (eds), *Transnational Governance: Institutional Dynamics of Regulation*, New York: Cambridge University Press.

Meidinger, Errol (2006), 'The administrative law of global private–public regulation: the case of forestry', *European Journal of International Law*, **17** (1), 47–87.

Micheletti, Michele (2003), *Political Virtue and Shopping: Individuals, Consumerism, and Collective Action*, New York: Palgrave Macmillan.

Murphy, Craig N. and JoAnne Yates (2009), *The International Organization for Standardization (ISO): Global Governance through Voluntary Consensus*, New York: Routledge.

Mutersbaugh, T. (2005), 'Fighting standards with standards: harmonization, rents, and social accountability in certified agrofood networks', *Environment and Planning A*, **37** (11), 2033–51.

Nebel, Gustav, Lincoln Quevedo, Jette Bredahl Jacobsen and Finn Helles (2005), 'Development and economic significance of forest certification: the case of FSC in Bolivia', *Forest Policy and Economics*, 7, 175–86.

Newsom, Deanna, Volker Bahn and Benjamin Cashore (2006), 'Does forest certification matter? An analysis of operation-level changes required during the SmartWood certification process in the United States', *Forest Policy and Economics*, **9** (3), 197–208.

Nussbaum, Ruth and Markku Simula (2004), 'Forest certification: a review of impacts and assessment frameworks', The Forests Dialogue, Yale University School of Forestry and Environmental Studies, available at: research.yale.edu/gisf/assets/pdf/tfd/TFD%20Certification%20Impacts%20and%20Assessment%20Paper.pdf.

Overdevest, Christine (2010), 'Comparing forest certification schemes: the case of ratcheting standards in the forest sector', *Socio-economic Review*, **8** (1), 47–76.

Pattberg, Philipp (2006), 'The influence of global business regulation: beyond good corporate conduct', *Business and Society Review*, **111** (3), 241–68.

Polanyi, Karl (1944), *The Great Transformation*, Boston, MA: Beacon Press.

Ponte, Stefano (2008), 'Greener than thou: the political economy of fish ecolabeling and its local manifestations in South Africa', *World Development*, **36** (1), 159–75.

Potoski, Matthew and Aseem Prakash (2009), 'A club theory approach to voluntary programs', in Matthew Potoski and Aseem Prakash (eds), *Voluntary Programs: A Club Theory Perspective*, Cambridge, MA: MIT Press.

Prakash, Aseem and Matthew Potoski (2006), *The Voluntary Environmentalists: Green Clubs, ISO 14001, and Voluntary Environmental Regulations*, New York: Cambridge University Press.

Rainforest Foundation (2002), *Trading in Credibility: The Myth and Reality of the Forest Stewardship Council*, London: Rainforest Foundation.

Rao, Hayagreeva (1998), 'Caveat emptor: the construction of nonprofit consumer watchdog organizations', *American Journal of Sociology*, **103**, 912–61.

Raynolds, Laura T. (2000), 'Re-embedding global agriculture: the international organic and Fair Trade movements', *Agriculture and Human Values*, **17**, 297–309.

Renard, Marie-Christine (2003), 'Fair Trade: quality, market and conventions', *Journal of Rural Studies*, **19**, 87–96.

Rodríguez-Garavito, César A. (2005), 'Global governance and labor rights: codes of conduct and anti-sweatshop struggles in global apparel factories in Mexico and Guatemala', *Politics and Society*, **33** (2), 203–33.

Rona-Tas, Akos and Stefanie Hiss (2010), 'The role of ratings in the subprime mortgage crisis: the art of corporate and the science of consumer credit rating', in Michael Lounsbury and Paul M. Hirsch (eds), *Markets on Trial: The Economic Sociology of the U.S. Financial Crisis*, Part A, Research in the Sociology of Organizations, vol. 30, Bingley: Emerald Group Publishing, pp. 115–55.

Sabel, Charles, Dara O'Rourke and Archon Fung (2000), 'Ratcheting labor standards: regulation for continuous improvement in the global workplace', KSG Working Paper No. 00-010, available at: ssrn.com/abstract=253833.

Schneiberg, Marc and Tim Bartley (2008), 'Organizations, regulation, and economic behavior: regulatory dynamics and forms from the 19th to 21st century', *Annual Review of Law and Social Science*, **4**, 31–61.

Seidman, Gay (2007), *Beyond the Boycott: Labor Rights, Human Rights and Transnational Activism*, ASA Rose Series, New York: Russell Sage Foundation.

Sharma, Alakh N., Rajeev Sharma and Nikhil Raj (2000), 'The impact of social labelling on child labour in India's carpet industry', Institute for Human Development, New Delhi.

Sklar, Kathryn Kish (1998), 'The consumers' White Label campaign of the National Consumers' League, 1898–1918', in S. Strasser, C. McGovern and M. Judt (eds), *Getting and Spending: European and American Consumer Societies in the Twentieth Century*, New York: Cambridge University Press.

Spar, Debora L. and David B. Yoffie (2000), 'A race to the bottom or governance from the top?', in Aseem Prakash and Jeffrey A. Hart (eds), *Coping with Globalization*, New York: Routledge.

Vandergeest, Peter (2007), 'Certification and communities: alternatives for regulating the environmental and social impacts of shrimp farming', *World Development*, **35** (7), 1152–71.

Viscusi, W. Kip (1978), 'A note on "lemons" markets with quality certification', *Bell Journal of Economics and Management Science*, **9** (1), 277–9.

Vogel, David (2005), *The Market for Virtue: The Potential and Limits of Corporate Social Responsibility*, New York: Brookings Institution Press.

Worm, Boris et al. (2006), 'Impacts of biodiversity loss on ocean ecosystem services', *Science*, **314** (5800), 787–90.

# 33 Regulation of professions
## Nuno Garoupa

Generally, a profession can be defined as an occupation with the following general characteristics: it requires a specialized skill, partially or fully acquired by intellectual training; it provides a service calling for a high degree of integrity; and it involves direct or fiduciary relations with clients (Ogus, 1994: 216). Certain professions, namely lawyers, notaries, physicians, pharmacists, accountants, architects and engineers, appear to be relatively highly regulated. A trend of more state intervention in the regulation of professions and a decline in self-regulation has been observed in recent times. For many decades formal regulation of professional services was a feature of American legal exceptionalism, whereas Europeans tended to rely more on informal, tacit and consensual mechanisms that were in part conducive to self-regulation. Independent regulatory authorities using new techniques of formal regulation, including more precise rules, paved the way in the 1980s. Quite expectedly, this approach has proliferated into the regulation of professions. Statute law used to play a limited role, whereas self-regulatory rules essentially emerged from professional societies and associations across Europe. Currently, state interventionism, by governments and competition authorities, has reshaped the regulatory framework of the professions throughout Europe. In fact, professional regulatory activities have been included in the current public policy agenda.[1]

The current developments on the regulation of professions can be understood in the larger context of regulation-for-competition (Levi-Faur, 2011). More than an era of deregulation of professional services, we can observe a pattern of reregulation with the explicit goal of promoting more competition and better services after a long period of perceived capture by incumbent professional interests. Unlike other services and industries, the regulation of professions was traditionally not strongly associated with government intervention, but rather with the strong and influential professional associations (which were never perceived as economic regulatory agencies). Such characterization has changed in the last decade or so.

In this chapter, we present a summary of the economic literature on the regulation of professionals, with a special application to legal and medical services. In section 33.1, we discuss the economic theories of the regulation of the professions, in particular the public interest and private interest theories. Besides the economic theories of regulation, political scientists have offered other possible explanations (Yandle, 2011). They are less suggestive in the area of the regulation of the professions because the role of the legislator has been quite limited, although, for example, the self-regulated professions taking moral grounds to pursue particular economic interests is not uncommon. Section 33.2 looks at institutional arrangements, and section 33.3 looks at the different regulatory dimensions. Section 33.4 concludes with some final remarks.

## 33.1    ECONOMIC THEORIES OF THE REGULATION OF PROFESSIONS[2]

The view that regulation pursues public interest in correcting for market failure (Posner 1975; Noll 1989) relies on the inefficiency of the market equilibrium. The main market failure that applies to professional markets is information asymmetry (Stephen and Love 1999). For most clients and consumers, professional services are credence goods (Darby and Karni 1973). The consumer is less informed about the nature and quality of the service, and often relies on the expertise of the professional in order to assess (agency function) and implement the adequate strategy (service function). There is a potentially severe problem encompassing some kind of supplier-induced demand. Under these conditions the market usually fails to produce the socially optimal quantity and quality of the professional service. Some protection for the consumer of professional services is necessary to guarantee quality and mitigate inefficiencies. Protection of consumers frequently takes the form of regulation of the profession and respective market.

Nevertheless we should have in mind that the costs generated by asymmetry of information must be balanced against the benefits of labor specialization. A reduction in information asymmetry might not be efficient if it also implies a substantial loss of benefits from labor specialization. For example, it is important to emphasize that the information asymmetry does not apply to all consumers. Repeat purchasers in the market for professional services are able to acquire experience and knowledge of the market which reduces the asymmetry of information (e.g., corporate clients in the market for legal services). Professionals must also take note of reputational effects which may arise from social networks even when most consumers are not repeat purchasers. Furthermore, when the service function is provided separately from the agency function, there is scope for revelation of information that limits opportunism (e.g., medical diagnosis and treatment by different medical doctors; see Emons 1997).

Besides the moral hazard problem we have so far described, there is of course adverse selection because consumers cannot judge the quality of professionals. The "lemons problem" may arise and thus the need for some kind of licensing or an equivalent mechanism (Leland 1979). Competition among professionals does not solve the problem, since good professionals may be driven out of the market by bad professionals given the inability of the market to pay for quality.

Another information problem may occur in the market for professional services, namely bounded rationality or rational ignorance. Consumers use simplified rules to process information rather than complex rational analysis. They also usually lack the education level, or even the intellectual ability, to be able to understand all available information on services in a correct way. Regulation is justified if the regulatory body has more information and expertise at its disposal than average consumers (Maks and Philipsen 2005).

Legal professionals usually stress the need for self-regulation, arguing that severe losses would occur if poorly trained lawyers were allowed to perform services. This loss is particularly significant in the health sector, where injuries to the body and life represent substantial and eventually under-compensated damages. The consequences of medical maltreatment and legal misrepresentation go beyond the direct customer and generate serious negative externalities for the general public. Good health standards and the quality of the legal system are positively related to the quality of physicians and lawyers (Rubin and Bailey 1994).

Finally, a fifth form of market failure that justifies regulation is the existence of public goods. Information concerning the quality of professional services satisfies the conditions of non-rivalry and non-exclusivity in consumption. Therefore there is the possibility that private provision (by professionals) of information is not efficient. This may well justify mandatory information disclosure with respect to professional quality (Maks and Philipsen 2005).

Regulation of professional services can improve the market equilibrium. Asymmetric information causes moral hazard and adverse selection and eventually negative externalities for the general public, thus precluding an efficient level of health and legal safety from being achieved by the market. The benefits of regulation include a decrease of search costs, improvements in service quality and more adequate supply of information concerning the quality of professional services. Also, and very importantly, a reduction in risk is to be expected. In fact, owing to the asymmetry of information, regulation could be the most adequate substitute for insurance (Zerbe and Urban 1988).

Notice that the case for regulation in a public interest perspective is not controversial among economists; however, it remains unclear which form of regulation should take place. If severe limitations to entry, prohibitions of advertising and regulation of fees are justified under a theory of public interest, it is still much of an open question. What seems clear is that in a market for professional services, where quality is uncertain, confidence and trust in the professionals are important for efficiency. After a couple of visits to a doctor, a patient whose health problems have been solved may start trusting the doctor. An attorney who handles cases with care and arranges affairs with success may create a trust relationship with his or her clients. The problem is of course that most customers are not repeat purchasers and, even if they were, the costs of mistakes in the initial rounds could be very high.

Regulation and legal rules should aim at enhancing the trust relationship by economizing on information costs. There are three reasons why regulation should create a confidence premium (thus rewarding professionals above marginal productivity): (a) the cost of obtaining information is lower for the professional than for the client; (b) the information involved is productive; and (c) the provision of true information must be rewarded in order to avoid strategic behavior or opportunism. At first glance, these reasons explain the need for minimum quality standards and even some regulation of fees, but severe restrictions on entry and on advertising do not seem justified (Van den Bergh 1993).

Regulation of professionals may also pursue other goals of a public nature that does not necessarily include economic efficiency (i.e., correcting for information asymmetries and externalities). These goals may be explained by some kind of patronizing view of the government or of community values, and usually are related to redistribution (Ogus 1994: 218–19).

Confidence, honesty and trust might be values pursued by the government which in turn may actually promote greater social welfare and foster growth. The social willingness to pay for these values may be above its market or economic value, thus justifying the government's intervention. A doctor or a lawyer in a small town may have a socially valuable role or function that goes beyond the professional service he or she provides.

Redistribution in favor of the professional against the consumer is just a form of paying for these social services.

The problem with this explanation is that it can hardly apply to all professionals. If a doctor or a lawyer enjoys local monopolized power in a small town, then we expect her or him to earn extra profits (marginal revenue above marginal cost) that could be in some ways justified by these other social services he or she provides. However, why a lawyer in a big city where he or she surely does not provide such social services should enjoy the same extra profits (owing to regulation of fees) is hardly justified under a theory of public interest. Furthermore, why consumers of professional services should abstain from revealing their willingness to pay for those social services in a competitive market seems odd and could in fact conflict with an adequate welfare analysis.

The last theory of regulation relates to private interest and relies on capture and collusion (Posner 1974). From this perspective the regulation of markets for professional services is seen to arise and be sustained because it is in the interests of the members of the profession. It essentially allows for their cartel-like behavior (Benham and Benham 1975). As a result, the capture theory predicts that professional licensure should decrease the supply of professionals below social optimum, increase the prices charged by professionals, and increase existing professionals' incomes beyond marginal productivity, thus generating rents and quasi-rents (Stigler 1971; McChesney 1987; Olsen 1999; Hadfield 2000; Kleiner and Kudrle 2000).

The most successful groups in obtaining wealth transfers are likely to be small, usually single issue oriented and extremely well organized. On the other side, those who bear the cost of paying rents are large fractions of the population, difficult to organize and with information problems. When these conditions are met, wealth transfers are expected to take place from the public as a whole to the very well-organized interest groups.

The government should protect the public from these interest groups, but incentives to provide public interest legislation can be overcome by pressure by those benefiting from wealth transfers. Moreover, wealth transfers may not be recognized by the public in general, and comparisons with other jobs and occupations can be difficult (Van den Bergh 1993). Just take the case of the confidence premium. Comparing figures about the income situation of professionals and other occupations may provide some evidence about how better paid they are, but we can hardly distinguish the confidence premium from pure rents. Unemployment within the profession below average unemployment could be an indication of rent-seeking but could also just be that the population requires more professional services than other goods and services on average. Less regional variance with respect to payments could help to identify rent-seeking (payments less subject to local market and business conditions indicate some degree of market power), but at the same time it could be that the willingness to pay for health and legal professional services varies less across regions than for other goods and services. Market concentration indices for professional services can be constructed but are of course subject to the appropriate delimitation of the market (e.g., most large law firms are specialized in certain areas of the law) and the distortions of the public sector (e.g., the national health service is the major provider of medical services in many European countries).

The fact that rent-seeking behavior is intrinsically difficult to identify (but not impossible, see Olsen et al. 1991), especially when there are sound public interest arguments for regulation to be made, makes rent-seeking and regulatory capture more likely. Nevertheless, it is possible to develop legal and political instruments to limit it. Promoting competition, in particular by making use of the internal European and US markets (which should promote a free flow of professional services), auditing professional bodies (including comparative institutional analysis) or forcing the separation of the service function from the agency function (e.g., medical diagnosis and treatment by different medical doctors), certainly helps to mitigate the problem.

In contrast to both pure private and public interest theories, the public and the professionals have an impact on the existent forms and contents of professional regulation. Thus professionals will sometimes, but not always, be able to use regulations to limit supply and generate rents. On the other hand, public interest will be pursued sometimes, but not always (Peltzman 1976). In fact, public and private interest theories mirror two distinct historical phases on economic research, emphasizing the corrective and the redistributive roles of regulation. The distinction between these two theories has lost validity even in economic theory owing to game theory and institutional research (Hägg 1997) that combine both.

Different institutional arrangements and regulations are consistent with both theories. In particular, self-regulation is not necessarily a sign of rent-seeking. Professional regulatory bodies are consistent with public interest theory. Identifying rent-seeking requires a more detailed analysis of the legal substance than just the legal form.

## 33.2   INSTITUTIONAL ARRANGEMENTS

Regulation by the government usually includes quality regulation, certification and licensing. The government could subsidize high-quality suppliers to ensure that they remain in the market even if adverse selection persists. Unfortunately it does not guarantee that the higher-quality service will actually be supplied owing to moral hazard. Second, penalties can be imposed on low-quality suppliers, and entry to the market could be restricted to some adequate standard (Dingwall and Fenn 1987). These regulations, however, require a regulatory agency that must avoid capture and be able to do what consumers cannot: assess quality and signal it to potential clients (Stephen and Love 1999). Apart from simple mandatory disclosure measures (e.g., professional specialty, professional education) and prohibiting what seems to be obviously misleading advertising (e.g., professional misrepresentation, that is, saying one is a lawyer or a doctor when one is not), effective quality regulation by the government seems difficult to imagine.

Under certification or licensing, a document (certificate or license) is awarded to an individual who satisfies certain conditions. These conditions may be education or training. The government as well as a private agency may certify or license professionals, and regulate professional education, compulsory periods of training and performance requirements.

The difference between licensing and self-regulation is that, while rules are issued by public authorities in both settings (since the professional body is entrusted with public authority), entry and performance are regulated by the state in the first case (eventually delegated to a private agency independent from the profession) and by the profession in the second case. The consequence is that self-regulation promotes strong professional association (as we know with lawyers and doctors) whereas licensing does not. A profession only becomes a real profession if it has the decisive power to fix remuneration; otherwise it is just a form of licensing (just as with economists and journalists almost everywhere).

The two arguments against licensing and thus making the case for self-regulation are the following: (a) it still does not solve the problem of asymmetric information because neither the government nor a private agency independent from the profession has better knowledge of the quality of the service the profession provides than the profession itself (though it might have better knowledge than the average consumer); (b) it is less flexible (in dynamic markets where innovation is important, agencies should be able to change quickly) and generates costs to be borne by the government rather than by the profession itself (Miller 1985). The second argument nevertheless has serious limitations. First, the profession can regulate fees to cover these costs (hence, they will be borne by taxpayers or consumers in both cases). Second, rents created by the exercise of regulatory powers by the professional body can undermine flexibility. For example, rents may be used to successfully resist competition from other regulatory bodies offering more efficient rules (Curran 1993).

Professional regulators have the necessary information to extract signals in markets for credence goods (the well-known specific knowledge argument by Miller 1985) but can hardly avoid the ultimate form of regulatory capture. Yet these types of bodies persist in most jurisdictions. One view is that there is a social contract between the profession and the community in order to reduce moral hazard. Naturally safeguards are required in order to ensure the profession does not operate a cartel. Also, various watchdogs (e.g., the legal services ombudsman in England and Wales and in Scotland or the medical care independent review program in California and other states) are necessary (Dingwall and Fenn 1987). Another view is that the reduction in costs of extracting information by professionals more than compensates for potential losses due to cartel-like behavior (Ogus 1995). These potential losses can be mitigated if there is more than one professional body in competition with each other (nevertheless in most jurisdictions professional bodies have a national or local monopoly), a large heterogeneous profession (Shaked and Sutton 1982) and adequate legal instruments (e.g., efficient tort law) (Danzon 1985, 1991; Gravelle 1990).

Though self-regulation solves the information problem we have discussed before, it is difficult not to expect that professional bodies use their regulatory powers to restrict competition somehow. Such rent-seeking behavior, alongside other significant costs of administering the regulatory system, causes a significant deadweight loss.

In order to tackle this problem, we should have in mind four specific dilemmas: (a) it will be easier for professionals not to pass their better information and expertise to the users unless of course they have an interest in doing so (this will increase search costs for the consumers since asymmetric information will not be reduced); (b) professionals will induce demand of services that clients, if fully informed, would not require (inefficient allocation of resources); (c) control and enforcement of quality standards will not be very effective owing to collusion (hence we should investigate information concerning sanctions for malpractice); and (d) fees will be set above the confidence premium.

We should note here a recent paper by Ribstein (2004), who provides an alternative rationale for licensing requirements in the legal profession. His argument relies on the observation that lawyer licensing encourages lawyers to participate in lawmaking by capitalizing the benefits of their law-improvement efforts in the value of the law license. State competition gives lawyers an incentive to favor welfare-maximizing state laws that make the state attractive as a location for businesses and as a forum for litigation.

Alternatives to professional regulation have been proposed, most of them never implemented. One solution could be independent rating agencies designed by repeat purchasers to perform the agency function on behalf of infrequent consumers (Stephen and Love 1996). Others suggest deregulation via competition that will generate quality signals with adequate liability rules and removal of informational barriers (Leffler 1978; Klein and Leffler 1981; Carr and Mathewson 1988; Van den Bergh and Faure 1991; Miller and Macey 1995).

There has been a recent trend to relate effective regulation of professional services with litigation. The large scale of litigation in the US allows litigants to use their financial leverage to force changes of a regulatory nature and limit professional opportunism. If appropriate regulation does not exist for professional services, litigation can provide an effective substitute when it generates a transfer of wealth from the profession (the injurers) to the consumers (the injured) (Viscusi 2002). Even so, there are important objections to the use of litigation as a way to stimulate effective regulation: (a) consumers do not have the appropriate information to make a comprehensive analysis as to whether or not negligent behavior, reckless attitudes or professional malpractices were exercised (thus litigation will usually be an inferior substitute for regulation); (b) consumers may be opportunistic when making decisions with respect to filing lawsuits and settling out of court (e.g., nuisance litigation), thus generating too much litigation; (c) litigation may not create adequate incentives for efficient levels of professional services since it usually aims at providing compensation; and (d) litigation may fail in achieving efficient risk-sharing (restoring pre-accident levels of utility may not be possible, specifically in the context of health effects).

In the context of medical malpractice, there is some further controversy concerning the effectiveness of litigation. Kessler and McClellan (1996, 1997, 2002a, 2002c) have shown that malpractice liability provides important incentives for medical care. Doctors in areas with greater malpractice pressure tend to use more defensive medicine; better treatment and medical high productivity seem to be positively related to the willingness of patients to litigate (Olsen 2000). However, once the incentives for hospitals and managed care organizations are explicitly taken into account, the empirical results are less striking. In fact, there is some debate among economists over optimal liability rules for physicians and health organizations, though most agree that tort reform and managed care function are substitutes in achieving incentives for adequate performance (Danzon 1997; Kessler and McClellan 2002b; Agrawal and Hall 2003; Arlen and MacLeod 2003).

## 33.3 REGULATORY DIMENSIONS

### 33.3.1 Entry

Entry restrictions are justified in order to ensure quality of professional services but, on the other hand, they undermine competition by creating professional monopoly rights (Shaked and Sutton 1981; Van den Bergh 1999). These restrictions usually require candidates to have specialized skills acquired by intellectual education at university and by training (for a mandatory period). These requirements of education (a specific diploma) and traineeship may be determined by both the government and the professional body.

Controls over these requirements can be exercised at three levels: (a) by defining the content of intellectual and training requirements; (b) by exercising influence over the organizations that educate and perform training of professionals (Shepherd 2000); and (c) by evaluating candidates after education and training at an exam or other type of screening device (eventually subjecting admission to some kind of *numerus clausus*). From a public interest perspective, we would expect some control over entry requirements but no strong influence over organizations that educate and perform training, as well as a strict examination of candidates. Some level of education and training is indeed positive, as the relationship between human capital and high-quality services is expected to be positive. Moreover, reliance on self-regulation may increase the specificity of human capital investment and individual commitment to the profession (Donabedian 1995).

Entry restrictions can also apply to para-professionals (e.g., para-medicals or other legal professionals) under the argument they supply an inferior-quality service. However, they also do it at lower prices. It turns out that the entry of low-quality para-professionals could be welfare improving (Shaked and Sutton 1981). In other words, restrictions on para-professionals are expected to be undesirable unless the profits of the profession are given a sufficiently high weight in the social welfare (Gehrig and Jost 1995).

From our discussion it is clear that entry restrictions should be more similar to certification rather than a very comprehensive and strict examination of candidates before, during and after education and training take place. Notwithstanding, the absence of severe restrictions on entry does not necessarily imply competition. Professional markets tend to be spatially localized (Stephen and Love 1999). Hence mobility might be seriously undercut and thus promote local monopolies (Pashigian 1979). For example, in many jurisdictions lawyers may only appear before courts in the local area corresponding to the bar into which they have been admitted.

In Europe, many of the entry restrictions are in the process of being removed. The implementation of the Establishment Directive means that it is possible for lawyers and doctors qualified in one member state to become full members of the profession in another member state without further examinations, though, for example, it does not apply to mobility for the legal profession within United Kingdom jurisdictions (Stephen 2003). In the United States, the lack of reciprocity between state bar associations seems to lead to a lower number of practicing lawyers and higher incomes, though not to higher prices of legal services (Lueck et al. 1995).

### 33.3.2   Advertising

Restrictions on advertising can be justified under a public interest perspective inasmuch as they apply to other markets of goods and services. Advertising is a common method to provide information and, from a social welfare perspective, advertising should be allowed when it is productive, that is, it conveys important and relevant information to consumers concerning professional services. There is no reason to suppose that advertising of professional services should be subject to very different regulations than those applied generally to other experience and credence goods and services. This argument conflicts with the claim used by professional bodies that advertising should be prohibited because it threatens the integrity and ethical responsibility of the profession by commercializing it. According to most professional associations, competition would be contrary to the dignity of the profession. However, as we observe in Europe, lawyers seem to be increasingly aware that dignity has a price. When Belgian lawyers seemed to lose business to Dutch and British law firms, the professional association decided to relax constraints on advertising (Faure 1993).

Two kinds of advertising can be distinguished, price advertising being more controversial than quality advertising. When information about price is easier to obtain than information about quality (which is true for experience and credence goods but not for search goods), increasing the availability of price advertising might discourage quality competition and encourage price competition, leading to a degradation of the average quality in the market (Cave 1985). This argument may support some restrictions on price advertising, but not necessarily support banning it.

The general conclusions of empirical evidence seem to be that restrictions on advertising increase the price of professional services and that the more advertising exists the lower the price is. However, there are several articles that contradict these findings (Rizzo and Zeckhauser 1992; Love and Stephen 1996). There is no systematic evidence that distinguishes between the effects of the two forms of advertising (Stephen 2003). Nevertheless, quality advertising is much more common than price advertising (Stephen et al. 1994).

Medical advertising is regulated in most jurisdictions. Competitive pressure and publicity on the internet have led the professional bodies to issue new documents on publicity, clarifying the strictness of the rules justified by the so-called principle of non-commercialization of medical services and alleged protection of consumers. More difficult to understand is why in some countries physicians are not allowed to advertise but managed care organizations can do it. They operate in the same market for professional services, and there is no economic reason to justify why physicians cannot advertise in price and quality but managed care organizations can.

For legal professionals, price advertising is banned in most jurisdictions, except the United States (though regulated by each state bar), under the cover that comparative advertising is strictly prohibited. Quality advertising is usually allowed for partnerships but not for sole practitioners. Competition within the European Union has pushed bars to relax somewhat the constraints.

### 33.3.3 Fees

Restrictions on fees can be seen as a way of ensuring the confidence premium to professionals. Fees can be subject to control by the profession itself, by the courts or by the government by use of mandatory fee schedules. Over time, in most jurisdictions, mandatory scales have been transformed into recommendations. However, in Germany legal fees are still determined by the government. For a long time, in Belgium and the Netherlands, a recommended legal fee schedule was produced by the professional body, and in Belgium there was a recommended minimum, until competition pushed for the abolishment of such rules. Medical fees are set by the government in most public health services (e.g., the NHS in the United Kingdom) or by managed healthcare organizations.

Price fixing is very restrictive and not very common. Moreover, it is unclear if it enforces high-quality production (it seems it would if quality were either high or low and with homogeneous consumer preferences: Maks and Philipsen 2005). Recommended fees suggest a more sophisticated approach to cartel-like behavior. Though we would expect recommended fees to be seen as mandatory by the profession, the evidence provided by Shinnik and Stephen (2000) for conveyancing markets in Scotland and Ireland goes in the opposite direction. The authors nevertheless recognize that these markets satisfy the necessary conditions for successful deviations from collusive agreements. Another possibility is that recommended fees provide a focal point against which professionals discount, thus colluding at a lower level (Stephen 2003).

Limitations on fee contracts (e.g., contingent fee contracts in the market for lawyers are forbidden in Europe) are more difficult to justify on the basis of quality assurance. Moreover, the enforcement of limitations on fee contracts is costly and generates incentives for bargaining on the shadow of the law (e.g., informal contingent fees in Europe). In fact contingent fees for both legal and medical professional services would solve the moral hazard problem. The fundamental argument put against contingent fee contracts in the legal and medical professions is that they conflict with the principle that professionals should not have a vested interest in the cases they take. For example, in the case of lawyers, there could be a conflict of interest between client and lawyer over if and when to settle. The determination of an appropriate fee if settlement takes place would of course solve the problem. Also, we would expect well-informed clients to prefer an hourly fee contract (and avoid conflict over settlement) whereas less experienced litigants would prefer contingent fee contracts.

With respect to legal fees, in most countries prices can be freely negotiated and usually more competent lawyers charge higher fees. Recommended fees existed at some point in Belgium, the Netherlands, Spain and Portugal. Fees are usually based on hours worked, litigation value (except in Belgium) and complexity of the case. Contingent fees are allowed in the United States but generally not in Europe. Usually legal fees take the form of hourly fees or flat fees. A first exception was developed in the United Kingdom (first in Scotland, and in the 1990s in England and Wales) where a lawyer receives an up-rating on the normal fee if the case is won which is not related to the value of damages (conditional fees). Similar arrangements are now being considered in many European countries. As to medical fees, most European countries have a powerful national health service that effectively restrains fee competition. The same does not happen in the United States, where fees can be freely negotiated.

Professional bodies can also manage the subsidies the government supplies to consumers of professional services, usually the national health service for health services and legal aid for legal services. The costs of legal aid and national health services have been growing rapidly. Usually it is caused by the increasing number of cases, rather than by fees paid to lawyers or physicians. Though these fees are usually much lower than normal fees, the profession can use them as a way of attracting consumers. Professionals have no clear incentive to avoid using government subsidies to generate oversupply of services.

### 33.3.4 Organization

Special regulations apply to law and medical firms. Restrictions on organizational forms are difficult to justify by public interest. If some aspects of professional services may favor partnerships rather than incorporation, we should expect the market to solve that, not the professional body.

Common organizational restrictions exclude incorporation (even where incorporation is permitted, usually unlimited liability is maintained and the directors of the firm must be professionals) and multidisciplinary partnerships (i.e., involving members of more than one profession) from possible organizational forms. The usual justification for these restrictions is agency costs. Effort in production and quality are difficult to measure by others outside of the profession, thus making sole practitioners or professional partnerships the most likely form of organization where adequate incentives will be less costly to design (Carr and Mathewson 1990; Matthews 1991). The problem of course is that, by banning other organizational forms, specialization of professionals beyond particular aspects of their service (thus lowering the cost of providing services) and economies of scope (by providing "one-stop shopping" including lawyers, accountants and surveyors or medical doctors, dentists and beauty consultants) are lost. For example, in the European countries where multidisciplinary partnerships are permitted, commercial law is increasingly dominated by the legal branch of the major international accounting firms (Stephen 2002).

A second type of restriction on organizational form concerns the separation between the service function (assess or diagnose the problem) and the agency function (implement the correct solution). This separation limits opportunism and creates incentives for revelation of information (Emons 1997). However, it can be seen as a prohibition on vertical integration between different stages in production, thus generating costs in terms of technology (economies of scale) and agency costs (hold-up problem). The issue then is whether or not the benefits from formally separating the roles outweigh the costs (Stephen 2003).

The structure of legal firms in Europe has been changing rapidly since the 1990s. Sole practitioners or small professional partnerships have been increasingly replaced by large professional partnerships, corporations (where they are allowed) and multidisciplinary organizations. The entry of foreign law firms or partnerships in the market for legal services is not helped by current regulations in some countries where the use of original denomination as well as original organizational form is allowed only under certain limited conditions.

### 33.3.5 Professional Standards

The introduction of professional standards and ethics generates a number of costs, including administrative costs (defining, monitoring and enforcing quality), compliance costs (from fulfilling professional obligations) and opportunity costs (since opportunistic behavior is restricted) (Ogus 1994).

Professionals are expected to pursue an agenda to minimize these costs. They will lobby for their own quality level and standards (Hau and Thum 2000). A standard can be an effective mechanism to protect insiders from competitors by imposing their own quality standard, thus reducing to zero compliance costs. On the other hand, a conflict between the government and the professions with respect to accepting and formally observing conduct rules is not likely, because professionals are usually involved in the actual formation of these rules (Maks and Philipsen 2005).

Administrative costs will depend on how the professional body regulates the conduct of professionals. Many forms of conduct regulation can be found in the professional rules. A code usually describes the tasks and duties of the profession and is often called professional ethics. The professional body also establishes disciplinary procedures in case the restrictions on conduct are violated. These rules usually define under which conditions professionals might be sanctioned and eventually expelled from the profession.

There are two reasons why the enforcement of restrictions on conduct is not expected to be high. First, it is not a problem of controlling entry, but rather of controlling exit. There are clear incentives to avoid conflicts within the profession and making exit too easy. Second, the alternative mechanisms (litigation in court) still rely too much on the profession. By controlling the production of expert witnesses (directly, by providing and managing expert witnesses, and indirectly, by training them), the professional body may block any attempt to force physicians and lawyers to leave the profession for violating professional conduct or gross malpractice. Naturally, in most countries, professionals are subject to contractual and extra-contractual liability; however, it is difficult for judges to make a decision on medical malpractice or negligence in preparing a lawsuit if expert witnesses are not available.

Some limitations to the discretion professional bodies have in dealing with restrictions on conduct have been emerging out of international professional federations (though these are mostly recommendations) and to some extent from EU directives on professional services (not surprisingly usually perceived by professionals as intrusions into national legal and medical culture). However, evidence points out that most disciplinary actions are taken for lack of dignity or improper behavior towards other professionals rather than professional malpractice (Faure 1993; Hellingman 1993).

In the United States, lawsuits for medical negligence are all too frequent nowadays (some people talk about a medical malpractice crisis), but were very infrequent 50 years ago. Physician liability existing prior to the 1960s might actually have been too low, resulting from capture and the consequent use of self-regulation to deny expert witnesses' testimony in malpractice cases. However, after the 1960s, it became much easier to obtain expert witnesses owing to the erosion of local medical societies in disciplining unethical practices and local rules (Olsen 2000). The consequence was an explosion of litigation over medical malpractice and thus the current need for tort reform in medical negligence (Dauer and Marcus 1997; Miller 1997; Sloan and Hall 2002; Fine 2003). Liability for medical malpractice is also of growing importance in European tort litigation. Contrary to the United States experience, the medical malpractice explosion does not seem to have come to a peak yet (Faure and Koziol 2001).

Liability for medical negligence is extremely complex in many European countries. First, it can be contractual (breach of contract in the private sector) or extra-contractual liability (negligence for doctors in the national health system). Whereas for contractual liability the patient has a longer period to sue the physician after the wrongdoing, for extra-contractual liability, the same period is typically much shorter. Such a liability dichotomy exists in England and Wales, but the development of expert witnessing and the structure of the legal system has not produced the chilling effect that is observed in other countries such as Portugal. The problem in some continental European countries is that, whereas for doctors in the private sector law enforcement is exercised by regular courts, doctors in the national health service are under the jurisdiction of administrative courts. Given that many physicians work for the national health service but practice privately part time, conflicts and questions of court jurisdiction usually take place when patients want to sue doctors. Not surprisingly, lawsuits for medical negligence are occasional and unlikely to succeed in such a context.

## 33.4   FINAL REMARKS

In this chapter we have presented a systematized summary of the economic literature on regulation of professionals, with a special application to legal and medical services. We have reviewed the economic theory of the regulation of professional services, the different institutional design (in particular, the choice between self-regulation and regulation by the government) and the different dimensions (entry, advertising, fees, structure and professional standards).

## ACKNOWLEDGMENT

Roya H. Samarghandi has provided excellent research assistance. The usual disclaimers apply.

## NOTES

1. For example, the European Commission, in particular the Directorate-General for Competition, has shown interest in promoting competition in the market for professional services, thus opening a general discussion on the regulatory frameworks (Stocktaking Exercise on Regulation of Professional Services, Overview of Regulation in the EU Member States, 2003).
2. This discussion follows closely Garoupa (2008).

## REFERENCES

Agrawal, G.B. and M.A. Hall (2003), 'What if you could sue your HMO? Managed care liability beyond the ERISA shield', *St. Louis University Law Journal*, **47**, 235–312.
Arlen, J. and B. MacLeod (2003), 'Torts, expertise and authority: liability of physicians and managed care organizations', *New York University Law Review*, **78**, 1929–2006.
Benham, L. and A. Benham (1975), 'Regulating through the professions: a perspective on information control', *Journal of Law and Economics*, **18**, 421–7.
Carr, J. and G.F. Mathewson (1988), 'Unlimited liability as a barrier to entry', *Journal of Political Economy*, **96**, 766–84.
Carr, J. and G.F. Mathewson (1990), 'The economics of law firms: a study in the legal organization of firms', *Journal of Law and Economics*, **33**, 307–30.
Cave, M. (1985), 'Market models and consumer protection', *Journal of Consumer Policy*, **8**, 335–51.

Curran, C. (1993), 'The American experience with self-regulation in the medical and legal professions', in Michael Faure, Jorg Finsinger, Jacques Siegers and Roger Van den Bergh (eds), *Regulation of Professions*, Antwerpen: Maklu.

Danzon, P.M. (1985), 'Liability and liability insurance for medical malpractice', *Journal of Health Economics*, **4**, 309–31.

Danzon, P.M. (1991), 'Liability for medical malpractice', *Journal of Economic Perspectives*, **5**, 51–69.

Danzon, P.M. (1997), 'Tort liability: a minefield for managed care?', *Journal of Legal Studies*, **27**, 491–519.

Darby, M.R. and E. Karni (1973), 'Free competition and the optimal amount of fraud', *Journal of Law and Economics*, **16**, 111–26.

Dauer, E.A. and L.J. Marcus (1997), 'Adapting mediation to link resolution of medical malpractice dispute with health care quality improvement', *Law and Contemporary Problems*, **60**, 185–218.

Dingwall, R. and P.T. Fenn (1987), 'A respectable profession? Sociological and economic perspectives on the regulation of professional services', *International Review of Law and Economics*, **7**, 51–64.

Donabedian, B. (1995), 'Self-regulation and the enforcement of professional codes', *Public Choice*, **85**, 107–18.

Emons, W. (1997), 'Credence goods and fraudulent experts', *RAND Journal of Economics*, **28**, 107–19.

Faure, M. (1993), 'Regulation of attorneys in Belgium', in Michael Faure, Jorg Finsinger, Jacques Siegers and Roger Van den Bergh (eds), *Regulation of Professions*, Antwerpen: Maklu.

Faure, M. and H. Koziol (2001), *Cases on Medical Malpractice in a Comparative Perspective: Tort and Insurance Law*, Vienna: Springer-Verlag.

Fine, D.K. (2003), 'Physician liability and managed care: a philosophical perspective', *Georgia State University Law Review*, **19**, 641–95.

Garoupa, N. (2008), 'Providing a legal framework for the reform of the legal profession: insights from the European experience', *European Business Organization Review*, **9**, 463–95.

Gehrig, T. and P. Jost (1995), 'Quacks, lemons, and self regulation: a welfare analysis', *Journal of Regulatory Economics*, **7**, 309–25.

Gravelle, H. (1990), 'Medical negligence: evaluating alternative regimes', *Geneva Papers on Risk and Insurance*, **15**, 22–6.

Hadfield, G. (2000), 'The price of law: how the market for lawyers distorts the justice system', *Michigan Law Review*, **98**, 953–1006.

Hägg, G.T. (1997), 'Theories on the economics of regulation: a survey of the literature from a European perspective', *European Journal of Law and Economics*, **4**, 337–70.

Hau, H. and M. Thum (2000), 'Lawyers, legislation and social welfare', *European Journal of Law and Economics*, **9**, 231–54.

Hellingman, K. (1993), 'An economic analysis of the regulation of lawyers in the Netherlands', in Michael Faure, Jorg Finsinger, Jacques Siegers and Roger Van den Bergh (eds), *Regulation of Professions*, Antwerpen: Maklu.

Kessler, D. and M. McClellan (1996), 'Do doctors practice defensive medicine?', *Quarterly Journal of Economics*, **111**, 353–90.

Kessler, D. and M. McClellan (1997), 'The effects of malpractice pressure and liability reforms on physicians' perceptions of medical care', *Law and Contemporary Problems*, **60**, 81–106.

Kessler, D. and M. McClellan (2002a), 'Malpractice pressure, managed care, and physician behavior', in W.K. Viscusi (ed.), *Regulation through Litigation*, Washington, DC: AEI–Brookings Joint Center for Regulatory Studies.

Kessler, D. and M. McClellan (2002b), 'How liability law affects medical productivity', *Journal of Health Economics*, **21**, 931–55.

Kessler, D. and M. McClellan (2002c), 'Malpractice law and health care reform: optimal liability policy in an era of managed care', *Journal of Public Economics*, **84**, 175–97.

Klein, B. and K.B. Leffler (1981), 'The role of market forces in assuring contractual performance', *Journal of Political Economy*, **89**, 615–41.

Kleiner, M. and R.T. Kudrle (2000), 'Does regulation affect economic outcomes? The case of dentistry', *Journal of Law and Economics*, **43**, 547–82.

Leffler, K.B. (1978), 'Physician licensure: competition and monopoly in American medicine', *Journal of Law and Economics*, **21**, 165–86.

Leland, H.E. (1979), 'Quacks, lemons, and licensing: a theory of minimum quality standards', *Journal of Political Economy*, **87**, 1325–46.

Levi-Faur, D. (2010), 'Regulation and Regulatory Governance', *Jerusalem Papers in Regulation & Governance*.

Love, J. and F. Stephen (1996), 'Advertising, price and quality in self-regulating professions: a survey', *International Journal of the Economics of Business*, **3**, 227–47.

Lueck, D., R. Olsen and M. Ransom (1995), 'Market and regulatory forces in the pricing of legal services', *Journal of Regulatory Economics*, **7**, 63–83.

Maks, J.A.H. and N.J. Philipsen (2005), 'An economic analysis of the regulation of professions', in E. Crals and L. Vereeck (eds), *The Regulation of Architects in Belgium and the Netherlands: A Law and Economics Approach*, Antwerpen: Intersentia.

Matthews, R. (1991), 'The economics of professional ethics: should the professions be more like businesses?', *Economic Journal*, **101**, 737–50.

McChesney, F. (1987), 'Rent extraction and rent creation in the economic theory of regulation', *Journal of Legal Studies*, **26**, 101–18.

Miller, F.H. (1997), 'Medical discipline in the twenty-first century: are purchasers the answer?', *Law and Contemporary Problems*, **60**, 31–58.

Miller, G. and J.R. Macey (1995), 'Reflections on professional responsibility in a regulatory state', *George Washington Law Review*, **63**, 1105–20.

Miller, J. (1985), 'The FTC and voluntary standards: maximizing the net benefits of self-regulation', *Cato Journal*, **4**, 897–903.

Noll, R. (1989), 'Economic perspectives on the politics of regulation', in R. Schmalensee and R. Willig (eds), *Handbook of Industrial Organization*, vol. 2, Amsterdam: North-Holland, pp. 1253–87.

Ogus, A. (1994), *Regulation: Legal Form and Economic Theory*, Oxford: Oxford University Press.

Ogus, A. (1995), 'Rethinking self-regulation', *Oxford Journal of Legal Studies*, **15**, 97–108.

Olsen, R.N. (1999), 'The regulation of medical professions', in B. Bouckaert and G. de Geest (eds), *Encyclopedia of Law and Economics*, Ghent: University of Ghent, pp. 1018–53.

Olsen, R.N. (2000), 'The efficiency of medical malpractice law: a new appraisal', *Research in Law and Economics*, **19**, 247–73.

Olsen, R.N., D. Lueck and T.E. Plank (1991), 'Why do states regulate admission to the bar? Economic theories and empirical evidence', *George Mason University Law Review*, **14**, 253–86.

Pashigian, B.P. (1979), 'Occupational licensing and the interstate mobility of professionals', *Journal of Law and Economics*, **22**, 1–25.

Peltzman, S. (1976), 'Toward a more general theory of regulation', *Journal of Law and Economics*, **19**, 211–44.

Posner, R.A. (1974), 'Theories of economic regulation', *Bell Journal of Economics and Management Science*, **5**, 335–58.

Posner, R.A. (1975), 'The social costs of monopoly and regulation', *Journal of Political Economy*, **83**, 807–27.

Ribstein, L.E. (2004), 'Lawyers as lawmakers: a theory of lawyer licensing', *Missouri Law Review*, **69**, 299–366.

Rizzo, J.A. and R.J. Zeckhauser (1992), 'Advertising and the price, quantity and quality of primary physician services', *Journal of Human Resources*, **28**, 381–421.

Rubin, P.H. and M.J. Bailey (1994), 'The role of lawyers in changing the law', *Journal of Legal Studies*, **23**, 807–31.

Shaked, A. and J. Sutton (1981), 'The self-regulating profession', *Review of Economic Studies*, **47**, 217–34.

Shaked, A. and J. Sutton (1982), 'Imperfect information, perceived quality, and the formation of professional groups', *Journal of Economic Theory*, **27**, 170–81.

Shepherd, G.B. (2000), 'Cartels and controls in legal training', *Antitrust Bulletin*, **45**, 437–66.

Shinnick, E. and F. Stephen (2000), 'Professional cartels and scale fees: chiseling on the Celtic fringe?', *International Review of Law and Economics*, **20**, 407–23.

Sloan, F.A. and M.A. Hall (2002), 'Market failures and the evolution of state regulation of managed care', *Law and Contemporary Problems*, **65**, 169–208.

Stephen, F. (2002), 'The European single market and the regulation of the legal profession: an economic analysis', *Managerial and Decision Economics*, **23**, 115–25.

Stephen, F. (2003), 'An economic perspective on the regulation of legal service markets', evidence submitted to the Justice 1 Committee's Inquiry into the Regulation of the Legal Profession.

Stephen, F. and J. Love (1996), 'Deregulation of legal services in the UK: evidence from conveyancing', *Hume Papers on Public Policy*, **4**, 53–66.

Stephen, F. and J. Love (1999), 'Regulation of the legal profession', in B. Bouckaert and G. de Geest (eds), *Encyclopedia of Law and Economics*, Ghent: University of Ghent, pp. 987–1017.

Stephen, F., J. Love and A. Peterson (1994), 'Deregulation of conveyancing markets in England and Wales', *Fiscal Studies*, **15**, 102–18.

Stigler, G. (1971), 'The theory of economic regulation', *Bell Journal of Economics and Management Science*, **2**, 3–21.

Van den Bergh, R. (1993), 'Self-regulation in the medical and legal professions and the European internal market in progress', in Michael Faure, Jorg Finsinger, Jacques Siegers and Roger Van den Bergh (eds), *Regulation of Professions*, Antwerpen: Maklu.

Van den Bergh, R. (1999), 'Self-regulation of the medical and legal professions: remaining barriers to competition and EC law', in B. Bortolotti and G. Fiorentini (eds), *Organized Interests and Self-Regulation: An Economic Approach*, Oxford: Oxford University Press.

Van den Bergh, R. and M. Faure (1991), 'Self-regulation of the professions in Belgium', *International Review of Law and Economics*, **11**, 165–82.

Viscusi, W.K. (2002), 'Overview', in W.K. Viscusi (ed.), *Regulation through Litigation*, Washington, DC: AEI–Brookings Joint Center for Regulatory Studies.

Yandle, B. (2011), 'Bootleggers and Baptists in the Theory of Regulation', in David Levi-Faur, *Handbook on the Politics of Regulation*, Cheltenham, Edward Elgar.

Zerbe, R. and N. Urban (1988), 'Including public interest in theories of regulation', *Research in Law and Economics*, **8**, 4–5.

# 34 Varieties of private market regulation: problems and prospects
*Frans van Waarden*

## 34.1 THE CENTRAL PROBLEM: MARKETS NEED SOCIAL ORDER TO FUNCTION

Are markets spontaneous social orders? Mainstream economics has long thought so. Freedom and competition should produce optimal allocation of goods and production factors and thus the greatest prosperity for all. Freedom would *allow* economic actors to pursue their interests, and competition would *stimulate* or even *force* them to do so. By contrast, many political theorists, sociologists and lawyers have started from an opposing assumption. For them, the "natural" societal condition is one of competition, destruction, uncertainty, insecurity and chaos (e.g. Hobbes 1968[1651]: 185). Social order is not a given, but a problem. Indeed, theft, deception, conflict and violence have often been the "natural" condition on unregulated markets. They are of all times and places, as history and anthropology can testify.

Incentives and competition are usually not enough to get economic actors to engage in transactions and to invest. They must also believe in some minimum chance of success. Belief in the possibility and sense of investment and innovation depends on the nature and degree of uncertainties and risks. As these increase, transactions become more of a gamble and less likely. In the "natural" economic disorder, risks and uncertainties may be excessively large. "In such condition, there is no place for Industry; because the fruit thereof is uncertain: and consequently no Culture of the Earth; no Navigation, no commodious Building; and which is worst of all, continuall feare" (Hobbes 1968[1651]: 186).

There are many sources of risk and uncertainty. The threat of getting cheated induces prospective buyers, before entering into transactions, to collect and process information, about what they want, why they may want it, where they can get it, how reliable products and sellers are, and so on. They have to engage in search strategies. Collecting, cognitively processing and evaluating that information involves time, effort, energy and money, i.e. transaction costs.

A specific category of transaction costs is those that emanate from information asymmetries. Usually the seller has more knowledge of the quality than the buyer, and can exploit that, by cheating the buyer. The fiercer the competition, the greater the temptation to do so. Thus, while competition may provide positive incentives, it can also become an incentive for fraud and deception, and increase distrust.

In theory this would eventually destroy the market: consumers would be unwilling to buy anything anymore, and sellers would no longer offer anything for sale. It would be a literal case of "market failure."[1] This depends however on the unrealistic assumption that consumers can wait to engage in a transaction. If it concerns food, shelter, clothing or warmth, buyers cannot always wait. They may have to accept whatever is on offer.

And poor workers cannot wait to sell their labor, even if they receive only a starvation wage. Thus not only do asymmetries in information (1) affect the power relations in potential transactions, but so do asymmetries in the ability to wait (2), as well as in the availability of alternatives (3).

These risks and uncertainties for potential transaction partners provide an answer to the questions of the *what* and *why* of market regulation. Now let's look at *who* could provide and has provided such regulation, and *how* and *why* they may do so.

## 34.2　VARIETIES OF PRIVATE MARKET REGULATION

Though markets may not be spontaneous social orders, they have often provided in the first instance solutions to their own problems. Risks and uncertainties on markets have created a demand for information, reputation, private technical and commercial standards, quality certification, accreditation or insurance. This demand has been met first by *commercial enterprises* trying to earn a living in satisfying this demand. The market has done so in two ways: a) by stimulating producers to care for their commercial reputation and engaging literally in "self-regulation," using their own organization to substantiate a brand image; b) by stimulating other organizations to sell information, certification and other sources of trust. Both are solutions provided by an "invisible hand," in the words of Adam Smith. Where these did not emerge, or did not effectively satisfy the demand, other sources stepped in. The invisible hand was complemented by a "visible hand" (Chandler 1977), i.e. large firm *hierarchies* (Wlliamson 1975), which imposed private standards and codes on suppliers, customers and workers or which integrated market transactions in their organization through mergers with or take-overs of the transaction partner. In the latter case, markets get transformed into hierarchies and the invisible hand becomes visible. One could extend these concepts of Smith and Chandler with two more: the "invisible handshake," i.e. informal merchant *communities* agreeing upon joint informal codes and standards including all kinds of cartelization; and the "visible handshake", i.e. explicit self-regulation by formal *associations* (see on communities and associations Streeck and Schmitter 1985; van Waarden 2002).

All were, in one way or another, private attempts to "regulate" and "regularize" – in the sense of stabilize – commercial, being also social, relations. Different solutions have been tried in different times and places, depending on the specific nature of the good or service to be traded, the state of technology (determining among other things the extent of the market) and the socio-cultural settings in which markets were embedded. History and anthropology provide veritable treasure chests of market-induced ingenuity in finding solutions to the problems of markets. Need for function has produced structure, through agency of course.

Another useful classification of forms of private market regulation is the distinction made by Levi-Faur (2011) between "three major strategies of regulation: first-party regulation, second-party regulation and third-party regulation."[2] First-party regulation would be the invisible hand, the market, forcing intra-organizational self-regulation by the producer or seller through the reputation effect. Second-party regulation can be provided by the visible hand of hierarchy, that is, dominant suppliers or customers imposing standards on their transaction partner. Third-party regulation can be provided by markets (invisible hand), communities (invisible handshake) and associations (visible handshake).

## 34.3 FIRST-PARTY PRIVATE REGULATION: THE INVISIBLE HAND DRIVING THE VISIBLE ONE

First-party regulation is self-regulation by the individual actor, being a person or an organization. Curious as that may sound, such *literal self-regulation* happens everywhere and all the time.

Individuals, such as artisans or traders, develop standards and standard identities for their products or services, and routines or styles regarding production, distribution, and negotiation with customers. They are like artists, developing their own styles to give them recognizable identities. Learning a trade is precisely that: developing and internalizing personal standards and routines.

For organizations, standards, routines and styles pertain to interpersonal relations. Those higher in the hierarchy develop standards and routines, impose them on subordinates and monitor compliance. First-order self-regulation by an organization is done through the principle of "hierarchy."

It may seem strange to refer to such intra-organizational rule-systems in a handbook on regulation; however, they are quite similar in structure, function and problems to inter-organizational ones – this volume's topic. Many organizations encompass smaller organizations. Regulating them by internal authority is a functional equivalent to regulation by an external one. Inter- and intra-organizational regulations are also extensions of each other. External regulation usually gets translated into internal regulation by the regulated organizations.

Why should they do so? Out of self-interest. For one, organizations cannot function without rules. That is what they are: rule-systems regulating the behavior of a group of actors towards a common goal. Rules and standards provide coordination, the necessary complement to differentiation or division of labor. In combination, differentiation and coordination form the competitive strengths of organizations. They make for speediness, efficiency and productivity, but also for standard output. They increase mutual predictability, internally – employees know what to expect from each other – but also externally, in relations with transaction partners. The latter provide the second motive for first-order regulation: *Reputation* is what actors on markets care for, as that makes transactions happen – reputation of reliable quality and supply, which requires the development of standards and routines, including technical and administrative internal quality monitoring systems, e.g. auditing. Markets force such internal private regulation upon transaction partners through the reputation mechanism.

Businesses also frequently try to complement self-regulation with self-certification: developing symbols for their quality, and advertising them among potential customers, i.e. "branding" (Conroy 2007). Once marketing investments have managed to acquire fame and commercial value for a brand image, the corporation has extra incentives to protect that brand reputation by strict maintenance of standards. Brands make businesses more visible and hence more sensitive to blemishes to their reputation, including naming and shaming by external regulators. The saying "A great tree attracts the wind" applies here as well.

These solutions to the problem of risk and uncertainties of market transactions do have their own problems, for buyers as well as sellers, or tend to work only under specific conditions.

First, the buyer must be able to judge the quality of the product, service and/or producer. Such transparency is however often lacking, especially in consumer markets, where buyers tend to be less knowledgeable than in business-to-business markets. Wherever consumers cannot judge quality, they will focus on price, and price competition could exert downward pressure on quality. Bunglers will enter the market with cheaper products of lower quality, a process reinforced by the "lemons" problem – sellers of good quality will withdraw from the market. In the end, the reputation of the whole sector evaporates. First-party regulation cannot prevent this.

Second, the buyer must be able to punish the seller for bad performance, maltreatment or fraud. The standard sanction would be to boycott the seller in a subsequent transaction, but that requires that the buyer is a repeat player. That may be the case in consumer transactions over bread, books or beans, but not over a house, ship or funeral. Furthermore, in order to inflict punishment, buyers must be able to identify the seller, i.e. anonymity – especially of the seller – is detrimental to well-working markets. This goes against mainstream economic teaching, which holds that perfect markets require large numbers of anonymous buyers and sellers, i.e. where parties can "hide" in the masses. Identifying the street-corner baker is easy, but not taxi-drivers or producers of generic goods, like most agricultural products. In such markets, misbehavers cannot be punished easily, increasing the temptation to cheat. And one rotten apple can spoil the whole basket. It is a classical collective action problem: individual rationality produces collective irrationality. For the individual, cheating is rational. He earns more. However, the reputation of the collectivity of taxi-drivers suffers and consumers may avoid the risk of taking taxis. Brands may help, as they identify the seller for the consumer, and expose him to sanctions. That increases the seller's credibility.

Third, a buyer's sanctions should be severe enough to make the seller repent. Often, loss of commercial reputation may also shatter one's social reputation. Humans, being social animals, tend to care for their social reputations. Being at the end of the value chain (retailers) or having a brand name makes one more visible, as pointed out, and hence more vulnerable to collective buyers' sanctions.

Fourth, as self-interest is the motive for first-party private regulation, the "self-regulator" is prone to contradictory incentives. While he shares interests with the buyer in a successful transaction, there is also a conflict of interest. Maximizing profits and minimizing costs, including those of his regulation, might mean externalizing costs. That could go at the expense of the public interest, and reduce his general legitimacy.

Finally, success may breed imitation, which should be prevented. Successful brands attract copycats. The risk is not only and so much that one's reputation gets stolen, but that it might be adulterated. Where buyers cannot distinguish between adulterated and unadulterated brand-name products, the fake, cheaper ones may drive the real but more expensive ones from the market. The problem that haunts generic products – adulteration and the lemons problem – could come to haunt self-certification as well.

Sellers need protection of their property, in this case their intellectual property, by some external authority. Have we reached here the limits of market-based solutions?

If these conditions are not met, the road remains open to fraud and deception. The problems of risk and uncertainty remain unsolved. First-party self-regulation may have advantages for the self-regulator: He remains in full control, and it may be efficient in the sense of involving less bureaucracy. Yet the disadvantages – less credibility with outsiders and the threat of copycats – may outweigh the advantages. Whenever that is the case, external, i.e. second- or third-party, regulation is called for.

## 34.4   SECOND-PARTY PRIVATE REGULATION: VISIBLE HANDS

Second-order private regulation is where one actor involved in the transaction imposes standards upon the other party. He will be able to do so if he has a position of power, thanks to his control over resources the other party desires or even needs: access to a specific market; share in a good reputation; being allowed to use the product of the other, including innovations, patents or copyrights; and political access, such as good relations with politicians, lobbyists, popular lawyers or influential trade union leaders. The regulatory standards are then imposed as part of the transaction, as a condition for it.

The most common case is that of major retailers, like supermarkets (Ahold, Sainsbury, Carrefour), huge department stores (Walmart) or specialty retailers (Ikea, Best Buys), imposing standards on their suppliers. Such retailers "sell" de facto shelf-space, including popular shelf-space (at eye height, in a central place in the store where all consumers pass by, such as near checkouts), to producers and can try to influence or even dictate not only prices but also product composition, quality, looks, packaging or advertising. In principle they could also insist upon the application of environmentally responsible or sustainable production processes or absence of child labor, and so on to such producers. More and more of them do so, either because they care for their reputation among consumers and critical NGOs (van Waarden 2010) or because they may even sincerely believe in "corporate social responsibility" (Vogel 2005).

Their suppliers, e.g. Unilever, Nike or Levi Strauss, may subsequently impose those standards on *their* suppliers, such as clothing sweatshops in India or low-wage producers in China or South Africa. Thus major parties at the end of the product value chain can try to impose standards up the chain. This can be considered the private commercial version of what Vogel (1995) has called the "California effect." Supermarkets imposing their standards on suppliers as a condition of being able to sell at their stores is like California imposing standards on industries for being able to sell within that state.

As retailers have become larger and more powerful, they are better able to impose standards on their suppliers. However, as product value chains are becoming longer, straddle the globe, and involve an ever larger number of different suppliers, suppliers of suppliers, and so on, the monitoring of such standards up the value chains becomes more difficult, although modern ICT does of course facilitate this.

The opposite is also possible, and does happen: suppliers imposing standards on their customers. Intel requires an Intel-label on personal computers; Apple specifies how retailers should exhibit and market its computers; Unilever prescribes the layout of its shelf-space in supermarkets; automobile producers set service programs and procedures for their dealers; bituminous paper producers specify how roofers should apply their products in order for product guarantees to be valid; and so on.

A specific category of suppliers imposing standards upon their customers is insurance companies. They are in the business to insure risks, but also want to limit their own risks. Thus they have provisions to minimize the chances of adverse selection or moral hazard problems. They require a duty of care, and may go into detail: insurance against car theft only if the car is equipped with an alarm, against burglary if the house has security locks, and so on. An early 18th-century collective fire insurance of 40 windmill owners in the Dutch Zaan region specified in detail how many buckets of water and meters of rope had to be present in each windmill (van Waarden 1992).

Where customers or suppliers are individually too weak to impose standards on their transaction partners, they can do so collectively by forming associations and make these put pressures on transaction partners. The classic case is that of trade unions bargaining on behalf of their members, individual employees, with major employers to set standards for wages, working conditions and job and social security, in short the conditions for transacting labor. They may even include strengthening of their own organization as part of the collective labor contract: closed shop or exclusive trade agreements.

There are many more of such second-party private regulations, and they become ever more important as corporations increase in size as well as get more enmeshed in commercial networks along the value chains. However, authors writing about regulation often overlook this major source of regulation of corporate behavior. They could become useful functional alternatives for other forms of regulation, in particular in a world where more and more regulation attempts have of necessity to extend across borders, as markets become more global but states remain "imprisoned" in their territorial jurisdictions.

Such second-party private regulation has major strengths but also some drawbacks. Most of the problems mentioned that are typical of first-party private regulation can be overcome with second-party private regulation. First, commercial customers are usually better able to judge the quality of the products supplied, thanks to their specialized and in-depth knowledge. They have at their disposal techniques and equipment to test quality as well as to monitor the observation of production process standards by their suppliers. Second, they are repeat players in the market, know their sellers well as they often maintain long-standing contractual relations with them, and can make use of severe sanctions: no more shelf-space, boycotts or no more licensing. Furthermore, regulation is done here by an external party. No longer is this a case of the "butcher rating his own meat." That makes for greater objectivity, the more so as the regulator has a personal self-interest in precise observation of the standards. Regulation will also be more efficient and professional, as the regulator is at the same time the enforcer, allowing for experience in enforcement to be fed back into revised and more practical regulations.

Among the drawbacks are that second-party private regulators are motivated by their own self-interest, which may be at odds with that of the final consumer or even the public interest. Actually, the second and first parties may "conspire" against those interests of others, as when they conclude vertical cartel agreements, or as with trade unions and employers externalizing the costs of wage and price increases onto outsiders. A drawback for second-party regulators can be the work and costs involved. That is why they often prefer to outsource such quality regulation to third parties, external to the transaction, who are specialized in it and hence able to both amass expertise and utilize economies of scale.

## 34.5   THIRD-PARTY PRIVATE REGULATION

Given the shortcomings of first- and second-party private regulation in solving the problems of risk and uncertainty in transactions, sooner or later independent third parties, not directly involved in the transaction, were needed in most markets, as information providers, standard setters, regulators, mediators or arbiters.

### 34.5.1   The Invisible Hand Producing Commercial Raters and Certifiers

A first category that has provided solutions to the shortcomings of the market was the market itself, the "invisible hand." Demand produced its supply. A veritable plethora of enterprising entrepreneurs has popped up to fill this expanded market niche for information providers and risk reducers, motivated by commercial self-interest. Commercial information providers, book and magazine publishers, detectives, appraisers, auditors, accountants, certifiers, rating agencies, hallmark producers, accreditors, mediators, real estate agents, art experts, other brokers, dealers, experts and so on have presented themselves. They either themselves provide supposedly more objective third-party information about the quality and reliability of the product and/or the producer or they sell information which confronts buyers and sellers with evidence that the information provided by the supplier has been right or wrong, complete or incomplete. They do so for a great variety of products and services, including raw materials, transport conditions, labor and working conditions. The information turns into regulation when such third parties set standards for good quality and certify first parties only when they satisfy these standards. Often different degrees of quality are distinguished and first parties get rated.

   Product certification is as old as fraud and deception and that has been of all times: smuggling, coining, swindling, embezzlement, gambling with weighted dice, forgery, corruption, tax evasion, and the quacks in the paintings of Bosch. The early Middle Ages knew a lively swindle with relics. Bone pieces of saints were believed to provide protection, both in the political struggle and in economic competition. As long as people believed in that power it was indeed real – following the well-known Thomas theorem ("If men believe something to be real, it is real in its consequences"). It was also believed that objects such as pieces of cloth ("brandea") that had been in contact with relics had acquired the holy power. That led to an extensive fraud with relics, and inflation of their value, which produced a need for certificates of authenticity. The relics that authorized and certified in the name of God the authority of the Carolingian kings themselves needed a certificate from the relic keeper. Little pieces of parchment called "cedula" were with two wax seals of an authoritative person fixed to a piece of bone or cloth and with the text that they were "pars" of one or another saint. The pilgrims who traveled to the relic safekeepings were also in need of a certificate: a pilgrim medal to prove that they had really been there (source: Treasury of Saint Servaas, Maastricht). Church and state needed certificates; so too did ordinary citizens. Thus guilds had their cloth hallmarks, and the witch's stool in the Dutch town of Oudewater certified on request that one was too heavy to be a witch (one could not fly on a broom), a certificate that was valid in the entire Habsburg Empire and could save one's life.

Lately, the number and variety of certifiers and hallmarks have greatly increased. In shops, in newspapers, on the internet and in all kinds of specialized markets, one is greeted by a bewildering array of quality certificates. They scream for attention and pretend to satisfy consumer needs for certainty regarding safety, health or animal or environmental friendliness. We find them in established markets, such as that of financial services, with established raters such as Standard & Poor's, Moody's and Fitch, but also 90 lesser-known ones (Aalbers et al. 2010). We find them also in newly emerging markets, like the emerging market for halal products in non-Muslim societies (van Waarden and van Dalen 2010a, 2010b). Meanwhile there is even a hallmark serving extortionists, albeit unintentionally: a "kidnap and ransom" insurance policy telling potential kidnappers where to find victims who will supply an easy prize (*Volkskrant*, 9 April 2003). Increasingly, certification is also used to certify process rather than product standards, notably social ones such as sustainability, fair labor conditions and human rights (cf. Bartley, Chapter 32, and see Marx 2011 for an overview).

Certification is in principle voluntary. If the use of certificates is imposed upon an entrepreneur, that imposition is done by the transaction partners: customers, investors, workers and even suppliers. Initially it is up to them whether they want this information. However, what started as voluntary tends to become de facto compulsory. At some point one is not a reliable prospective transaction partner without a financial rating, ISO certification, or labels from Fair Trade or the Marine or Forest Stewardship Councils (van Waarden 2010).

Commercial certifiers have to charge a price for their work. Occasionally their customers may be the prospective buyers of the good, for example when the customers buy books and magazines that compare goods, services and producers. However, the customer is often difficult to identify and charge, which is why the producers or sellers are the ones who usually pay for audits, labels and ratings. Some information providers earn their income from advertisements accompanying free information, as with banners and links on websites, comparing products or allowing users to exchange experiences with cameras, hotel services or eBay sellers. eBay has even institutionalized this, and asks buyers to rate the reputations of sellers. It may be that the anonymity of the internet allows for abuse, but so does old-fashioned gossip.

### 34.5.2   The Invisible Handshake: Communities

Transactions are often embedded in webs of socio-economic relations, which over time form groups, communities and cultures, bound together by common activities, tasks, interests and/or interdependencies. These develop shared language, norms, values, identities and bonds, that is, they form cultural communities. Such was the case with medieval merchants, and with current communities of horse traders, farmers or financial dealers.

Transactions can create communities. However, transactions can also be embedded in pre-existing communities, based on habitat, language, ethnicity or religion. They may be locally concentrated or spread out in a diaspora. Such pre-existing communities may have specialized in certain trades. Classic examples are the Italian industrial districts, e.g. textiles in Prato and ceramics in Sassuolo, the Jewish clothing industry in New York, or the Asian diaspora of the trading Chinese.

In both cases, the social structure, shared language, identity, cultural values and informal norms of the community are the institutions that facilitate transactions. They do so first as channels of information. Community gossip spreads, builds, and destroys social reputations. That same gossip is also a sanction. Most people are quite sensitive to what their fellow men hold of them, especially if they meet these fellow men regularly or otherwise cannot escape them. However, communities also have other sanctions, owing to the diffuse and multiplex character of relations in such groups. The members are related in different roles, as family, neighbors, churchgoers, club members, carers, and partners in transactions. These relations offer many channels for social interdependence, social control, and sanctioning. The mutual bonds also facilitate cooperation in fending off joint threats, such as dishonest clients or fly-by-night competitors.

Exchange and monitoring of information and the threat of sanctions facilitate trust. Furthermore, many religions sanction against theft, deceit and dishonesty. Knowing that community members are faithful believers makes it easier for others to trust them.

Trust may be also nurtured by practical norms. Communities may have unwritten rules that prescribe how transactions are to take place, how one should negotiate or how conflicts ought to be settled. They structure mutual expectations between transaction partners. In a Turkish bazaar, both parties expect lengthy bargaining. In a Western department store that is unusual and suspect.

Assets of such informal community rules are cheapness, efficiency, effectiveness, stability, and limited need for explicit enforcement. They may give transaction partners privileged access to resources such as labor, knowledge and capital from within the community. Conversely, liabilities are favoritism, nepotism, insider–outsider discrimination, entry barriers to outsiders, difficulty for outsiders to access reputation information and, for the insiders, limits in resource choice, constraints on freedom and competition, on rational cost accounting and on innovation, and sometimes difficulties in growing beyond the community.

### 34.5.3   The Visible Handshake: Associational Self-Regulation

Third-party solutions have also been offered through "visible handshakes." Producers have formed trade associations to set standards for products, services and processes, and more in general to regulate their markets and thus overcome the problems of first- and second-party regulation, notably the threats posed by copycats, free riders, bunglers and fly-by-nights. Or the associations provided alternatives for first-party regulation. Small businesses and producers of generic goods have formed associations to create and maintain collective brand names. Such associational regulation is often called self-regulation, but it differs from first-party regulation in that it is not individual but collective self-regulation, and to the individual producer such associational regulation may appear as coming from the outside. The association has also an interest in making it appear like that, as it would increase the credibility of self-regulation with potential transaction partners of its members.

We find it in particular in agricultural sectors. Farmers have in many countries formed cooperatives for collective purchasing of feed and machinery, for sharing financial resources through credit unions, and for regulating and standardizing production. They have done so mostly since the late 19th century, when agriculture industrialized. Technological progress made larger-scale operations possible; products could be better preserved and also transported to more distant markets. And, as the distance from farm to fork increased, consumers could no longer rely on personal trust in farmers, butchers or other food-producing craftsmen – meaning that their "face" was no longer first-party certification – so the need for third-party certification increased. French wine and cheese producers formed associations to create collective brand names, often linked to their locality (appellation d'origine contrôlée – AOC), and in order to standardize and protect quality they set detailed standards for the production processes of farming and manufacturing (Colman 2003). In some parts of the US farmers did the same. Thus in 1909 dairy farmers in the Tillamook valley in Oregon created an association, the Tillamook County Creamery Association (TCCA) to standardize and control cheese making and to market their products. It also set detailed regulations regarding, for example, the ventilation of the milking parlor on farms, its required concrete construction, and use of automatic milking equipment (information from the Visitor Center TCCA, Tillamook). Another well-documented US case of associational self-regulation is that in the fire insurance business (Schneiberg 1999; Schneiberg and Bartley 2001; Berk and Schneiberg 2005). Dutch dairy farmers have done the same, starting also around 1900 (van Waarden 1985a). The American and Dutch dairy farmers' associations developed eventually into cooperative hierarchies operating cheese manufacturing themselves, thus turning third- into first-party regulation: the producer certifying its product with a brand name. Also outside of farming, associational self-regulation has become an often-used solution to the problems of first- and second-party regulation, especially after the 1870s. Yet associational self-regulation was certainly not new. It had already been practiced in the Middle Ages by merchants' and craftsmen's guilds.

Trade associations may have done so in their own interest. This interest is however also served by credibility with others, including with a state, which might threaten intervention if the industry itself does not create some order. This is why such associations have also gotten involved in social regulation, for example with the Sustainable Forest Initiative (van Waarden 2010; Marx 2011; Bartley 2011). Therefore this private interest might overlap with the public interest, even in cases of outright cartels (van Waarden 1989; Unger and van Waarden 1999).

Usually, self-regulation has concerned the reputation of the products traded. However, at times, collective self-regulation has also concerned the reputation of producers. Examples are the codes of ethics or corporate governance codes, discussed by Oude Vrielink et al. (2011). They are attempts to establish "moral brand" images of producers. In order to increase their legitimacy, cooperation with other private or public actors may be sought, turning them into hybrid codes.

Associations have also been formed by the other party in the transactions, the buyers. There is quite a variety of them: associations for general consumers; consumers with a specific interest like cars, travel, computers or organic foods; and associations for housewives, sportsmen, the environmentally concerned, students, chronic hospital patients and religious believers. Basically any imaginable social category with specific interests can have associations, foundations or NGOs. These also provide information on products, producers and transaction procedures to their members, among others through comparing and rating producers and sellers. They finance their work from membership dues, grants from private or public supporters, or commercial activities.

### 34.5.4 Strengths and Weaknesses of Third-Party Regulation

Such regulation by third parties has greater credibility with prospective buyers, because these parties are external to the transaction and should have no interest in it. Their judgment carries a higher value, and hence consumers should be willing to pay a price for it. Therefore rating and certification can be an enterprise for which markets may develop.

However, the familiar problems that can haunt marketed products – cutthroat competition, intransparency, copycats, bunglers, information asymmetries, adulteration, fraud, fixation on prices, races to the bottom, the lemons problem, etc. – may also plague their derived products, the quality certificates, and thus decrease credibility. And that is for a product whose only value is its very credibility! Reputation, that is what certifiers sell. It depends largely on their (public image of) independence from those that are rated. The ratees could exert either political or economic influence on the rater.

Political influence is possible where quality standards are set and performance rated by trade associations to which the ratee belongs. Not for nothing is this called "self-regulation." In principle, members could influence the association's decisions regarding standards, strictness of enforcement, and sanctions.

Associational self-regulation suffers also from collective action problems. Free riders easily undercut it: entrepreneurs who profit from collective action to raise the sector's reputation but who improve their own market position by not abiding completely by that action and, for example, adulterate a bit. What can an association do when it finds out? The ultimate sanction of a voluntary association – expulsion – is not easily applied. It might merely mean that the remaining members have a competitor, no longer bound by the regulations. The more that defect, the greater the temptation for others to do so as well. If too many defect, the regulatory goal, maintaining a high collective reputation, will no longer be realized. This has been a main cause for the instability of cartels and trade associations engaging in collective quality certification.

The economic influence of ratees on raters comes through the purse. Not infrequently do the ratees pay for the work of the rater, as when they pay the external auditor who controls their books as third-party in the interest of stockholders. He who pays the piper calls the tune. Financial dependence means that third-party certification turns de facto into first-party regulation. Or it may turn into second-party regulation, where the rater and the ratee have in effect entered into a transaction: the rater sells a certificate to the ratee. As in other instances of second-party regulation, the buyer dictates the terms of the transaction: he pays for a good rating. The rater should only be not too obviously obliging. After all, his rating has value only if it has some minimum reputation. That is also in the ratee's interest. The Enron–Andersen scandal has shown what such a coziness of rater and ratee can do. It was also a blow to the reputation of the whole accountancy industry and another case of collective dependence on individual member performance. This potential threat has motivated collective self-regulation, something the accountancy profession has done widely. The raters, the accountants, have their own regulator, their professional association, but apparently to no avail.

The problems of information asymmetries and fraud that beset the original goods affect their quality certificates as much. Raters have followed similar strategies to protect the reputation of their certificates: advertising, labeling, guarantees, development of a brand name and again third-party verification or accreditation. Thus the chain of certi-fiers of certifiers of certifiers could become endless if suspicions are great enough. We have called this the "homunculus problem of free markets" (van Waarden and van Dalen 2010b). In reality, it cannot be endless of course. All these control levels add to the trans-action costs of the original products. When these become prohibitive, either transactions may not take place or the buyer will have to take some risk. In the end the consumer will have to trust the highest level of certification.

## 34.6   HANDGRASP FROM THE STATE?

Table 34.1 summarizes some strengths and weaknesses of the different modes of private market regulation. The problems of first-, second- and third-party private regulators have eventually led to calls for public support, either from the producers or from the users of private regulation. Such support has been forthcoming over the ages, sometimes at the initiative of public authorities themselves, but more often in response to calls from private actors.

To be sure, the state is itself also a party on markets as producer, buyer or third party, and can hence regulate these markets in the role of first, second and/or third party. Yet it is no ordinary seller, buyer or intermediary. First, it tends to be more neutral, as it is supposed to serve the public interest – and parties, voters and the media will monitor. Therefore it has more legitimacy and trustworthiness. Secondly, it has special powers, derived from its monopolies on the legitimate exercise of force (bestowing legal and political power) and on taxation and the currency, providing economic power. General taxation allows, for example, for funding of certification, avoiding payment by – and possible bias towards – the subjects of certification. These powers are held in check by the rule of law, a constraint adding to the state's legitimacy. Hence state regulation is a special version of the visible hand. Cooperation with first, second or third parties requires a special handshake.

Much state support for first- and second-party regulators started in the form of private law developed bottom up out of custom, practice and court rulings. Transaction partners brought commercial conflicts before public courts. Judges had to decide. They relied on precedents, but also themselves created precedents in a typical path-dependent manner. Based on their decisions over the centuries, private case law developed, which backs first- and second-party private regulation. In continental Europe this was eventu-ally codified. The law sanctions against commercial fraud and cheating, and requires transparency in transactions, for example by honest advertising. Under criminal law the perpetrators are punished. Under tort law they have to compensate their victims. It protects property rights, including brand names. By enforcing commercial contracts the state also backs up second-party private regulation. In return, the law sets minimal conditions for contracts.

To be sure, regulatory initiatives have also come from public authorities. They have long had an interest in the economy. It was the basis of their own prosperity. They could

*Table 34.1 Overview of strengths and weaknesses of different modes of private regulation*

| Mode | Principle | Strengths, assets | Weaknesses, risks |
|---|---|---|---|
| First-party regulation | Invisible hand driving visible: markets driving hierarchies through reputation effect | Seller in control. Knowledgeable regulator. Less bureaucracy. Few enforcement problems. | Bias, low credibility. Info disadvantage of consumer-enforcers. Usually buyers not repeat players. Identifying and sanctioning difficult. Threat of bunglers and copycats. Temptation to cheat. |
| Second-party regulation | Visible hand: hierarchies | Knowledgeable and critical buyers. Buyers repeat players. Powerful enforcement sanctions. Distance makes for objectivity. Self-interest in strict enforcement. Flexibility; easy adjustment to innovations. Useful when long and complex production chains. | Bias through self-interest of hierarchy-enforcers. Abuse of power by powerful suppliers or customers. Collusion by transaction partners at cost of public. Yet problematic monitoring along long supply chains. |
| Third-party regulation | Invisible hand, producing commercial certifiers | Greater credibility of third parties. Usually knowledgeable certifiers. Comparison, making for choice. Raters: new economic activity: jobs and income. | Market problems: fierce competition, amateurs, bunglers, copycats, lack of transparency adulteration, race to bottom, fraud, spoils this derived market. Payment by "to be certified" adds bias. Lack of trustworthiness; homunculus problem. Transaction costs can get high. |

481

*Table 34.1* (continued)

| Mode | Principle | Strengths, assets | Weaknesses, risks |
|---|---|---|---|
| | Invisible handshake: communities | Cheapness, efficiency, effectiveness.<br>Stability.<br>Little need for explicit enforcement.<br>Privileged access to production factors. | Favoritism, nepotism, limits in resource choice.<br>Difficulty to access info for outsiders, bias.<br>Entry barriers to outsiders.<br>Limited freedom, competition, innovation. |
| | Visible handshake: associations | Greater credibility of third parties.<br>Knowledgeable regulators.<br>Some transparency.<br>Informal enforcement possible. | Bias through collective sector-interests.<br>Ratee has political influence in association.<br>Threat of free riders.<br>Limited sanctions.<br>Instability. |
| Fourth-party regulation | Visible hand: the state | Can be first-, second- and third-party regulator.<br>Neutrality, hence high credibility.<br>Powerful enforcement means:<br>– private law sanctions<br>– criminal law sanctions<br>– economic power<br>Rule of law makes for predictability. | Limits to national jurisdiction.<br>Distant from market/producers.<br>Lack of specialized knowledge.<br>Bureaucracy, "state failures."<br>High costs (through taxation). |

collect taxes only if there was something to be taxed. Therefore they helped concentrate transactions in space and time, by encouraging trading in the vicinity and protection of castles and later by granting market privileges to towns. Such concentration increased market transparency, as it facilitated comparison of price and quality of goods, as well as the development of informal social codes of acceptable conduct.

Public authorities intervened also more actively in transactions. Rulers provided standard currencies and municipal ordinances facilitated product comparison by imposing uniform quantitative standards for pricing and, in cooperation with private guilds, also qualitative ones. Thus eventually many standards were created for products, services and production factors, varying from standard weights and measures to standards for advertising mortgage interest rates and diplomas standardizing skills. Weighing was to be done in municipal weighing houses. Early public economic law took the form of, for example, bans on food adulteration. Ancient Greece and Rome had laws against the coloring and flavoring of wine. The British had their impure food laws from 1226 (Coates 1984: 145). The Bavarians had their *Reinheitsgebot* for beer from 1516.

Third-party private regulation also acquired public support once it became more frequent. Associations were aided in solving the free-rider problem by giving them a monopoly on providing assets that were much needed by members, such as certificates of origin required by foreign states. Associations were also supported by imposing compulsory membership on all members of a trade or industry (e.g. the liberal professions and in some countries handicrafts). Private collective contracts – of labor and also sometimes cartels – were publicly "extended", thus elevating them to public law status, binding all actors in the sector. In order to increase the reliability and reputation of private certification, states have verified and accredited certifiers. Only the state with its powers can prevent free riders from undercutting private certification and regulation, accredit private certifiers and enforce private regulations and standards.

Where private regulation and certification could not effectively solve the problems they were meant to, they have been replaced by public regulation. Much state regulation of markets was preceded by private regulation trying to do the same, at least in the Netherlands (van Waarden 1985b). Eventually the state became "the ultimate risk manager" (Moss 2002). However, it has repeatedly sought private support. Over time, hybrids of private and public regulation have developed, different in different times, places and economic sectors.

## 34.7 CONCLUSION

The varieties of private market regulation discussed offer alternative solutions to the problems of markets. They can be considered functional alternatives. Each mode has its own strengths and weaknesses. It may work better in one transaction relation, market, sector and country than in another, depending among other things on: what is traded; the extent of the market (local, global); frequencies of transactions; the number, power and expertise of the transaction partners; the risks and uncertainties involved; and the technical, cultural, political and legal embeddedness. The latter determine, for example, trade customs and the legitimacy and legality of different modes.

Thus associational self-regulation is more distrusted and often illegal in the US, unlike in the Netherlands.

There is a certain logical order among the modes. Economic actors tried solutions to the problems of markets, learned from their problems, and subsequently tried others, involving more parties with more power or more credible reputations. Where people lost trust in first-party self-regulation, like branding, joint regulation by associational self-regulation was tried. Where that too lost legitimacy, third-party commercial certification promised to offer a solution. When that too did not satisfy potential buyers, the state provided verification and accreditation of private certifiers. The rise of one mode has not necessarily meant the disappearance of another. They can also complement each other, as with state accreditation backing private certification.

Is this also a sequential, historical order? Sometimes it has been. State formation led to increased public intervention in the economy, and recently private certification has given rise to public accreditation. Yet it is no linear trend. For that, there is too much historical incidence, and different countries have followed different paths of development. Some forms of public regulation, like customary tort law, are very old, and predate the guilds. At different times, different combinations of modes were tried.

Change seems to have more of a pendulum nature: from guilds in the Middle Ages, to their abolishment by the French revolutionaries and elaboration of contract law in new civil codes of the state, back to a revival of associational self-regulation at the end of the 19th century in many European countries. More recently, neoliberal "deregulation" has fueled booming markets of third-party private certification, but their lack of transparency, information asymmetries, outright fraud and loss of credibility have revived calls for public regulation. Frustration with one mode leads people to try another, until the weaknesses of that mode become apparent again.

New technologies, products, services, markets, transactions, transaction partners, circumstances, ICT and globalization create new challenges and opportunities, including for more effective, efficient, appropriate and legitimate – i.e. "better" – regulation. The various old modes of private regulation, discussed here, offer ingredients for such "better regulation." Global markets, being beyond the jurisdiction of nation-states, exhibit a renewed importance of private market regulation, by first, second and third parties. Supermarket chains set food standards and the Marine Stewardship Council sustainability norms.

## NOTES

1. Strictly speaking one would expect the term "market failure" to mean just that: failure of the market in allocating goods or services, because potential transaction partners refrain from entering into the transaction. Examples would be strikes by workers or consumers. However, economists usually also include among "market failures" all kinds of "collateral damage" of the "free market." In addition to the traditional "externalities" such as exploitation of the environment (pollution) and of (child) labor, one could include here also cheating, distrust, destruction of social capital, class conflict, and exploitation of the less by the more powerful. However, such negative side effects are no failure of real markets, they are real consequences of real markets. What is failing here is at most the idealized perfect market, whereby the costs of such negative externalities are ideally included in the market price.
2. I use this distinction a bit differently from Marx (Chapter 43). While Marx refers to the division of labor in the third-party certification process, I take the original transaction as basis for the distinction.

# REFERENCES

Aalbers, Manuel, Ewald Engelen and Anna Glasmacher (2010), *Securitization in the Netherlands: Shaping and Shaped by Regulation*, The Hague: WRR.

Bartley, Tim (2011), 'Certification as mode of social regulation', in David Levi-Faur (ed.), *Handbook on the Politics of Regulation*, Cheltenham: Edward Elgar.

Berk, Gerald and Marc Schneiberg (2005), 'Varieties in capitalism, varieties of association: collaborative learning in American industry, 1900 to 1925', *Politics and Society*, **1**, 46–87.

Chandler, Alfred D. (1977), *The Visible Hand: The Managerial Revolution in American Business*, Cambridge, MA: Harvard University Press.

Coates, Dudley (1984), 'Food law: Brussels, Whitehall and town hall', in David Lewis and Helen Wallace (eds), *Policies into Practice: Case Studies in Implementation*, London: Heinemann, pp. 144–60.

Colman, Tyler (2003), 'The Politics of Quality: Institutions and Market Stratification in the Wine Sector', Ph.D. thesis, Northwestern University.

Conroy, Michael (2007), *Branded! How the 'Certification Revolution' is Transforming Global Corporations*, Gabriola Island, BC: New Society Publishers.

Hobbes, Thomas (1968[1651]), *Leviathan*, Harmondsworth: Penguin.

Levi-Faur, David (2011), 'Regulation and regulatory governance', in David Levi-Faur (ed.), *Handbook on the Politics of Regulation*, Cheltenham: Edward Elgar.

Marx, Axel (2011), 'Global governance and private regulation of supply chains', in David Levi-Faur (ed.), *Handbook on the Politics of Regulation*, Cheltenham: Edward Elgar.

Moss, David A. (2002), *When All Else Fails: Government as the Ultimate Risk Manager*, Cambridge, MA: Harvard University Press.

Oude Vrielink, Mirjan, Cor van Montfort and Meike Bokhorst (2011), 'Codes as hybrid regulation', in David Levi-Faur (ed.), *Handbook on the Politics of Regulation*, Cheltenham: Edward Elgar.

Schneiberg, Marc (1999), 'Political and institutional conditions for governance by association: private order and price controls in American fire insurance', *Politics and Society*, **27**, 66–102.

Schneiberg, Marc and Tim Bartley (2001), 'Regulating American industries: markets, politics and the institutional determinants of fire insurance regulation', *American Journal of Sociology*, **107**, 101–46.

Streeck, Wolfgang and Philippe Schmitter (1985), 'Community, market, state – and associations?', in W. Streeck and P. Schmitter (eds), *Private Interest Government: Beyond Market and State*, London: Sage.

Unger, Brigitte and Frans van Waarden (1999), 'Interest associations and economic growth', *Review of International Political Economy*, **6** (4), 425–67.

Vogel, David (1995), *Trading Up: Consumer and Environmental Regulation in a Global Economy*, Cambridge, MA: Harvard University Press.

Vogel, David (2005), *The Market for Virtue: The Potential and Limits of Corporate Social Responsibility*, Washington, DC: Brookings Institution Press.

Waarden, Frans van (1985a), 'Varieties of collective self-regulation of business: the example of the Dutch dairy industry', in W. Streeck and P. Schmitter (eds), *Private Interest Government: Beyond Market and State*, London: Sage.

Waarden, Frans van (1985b), 'Regulering en belangenorganisatie van ondernemers', in F.L. van Holthoon (ed.), *De Nederlandse samenleving sinds 1815*, Assen: Van Gorcum.

Waarden, Frans van (1989), *Organisatiemacht van belangenverenigingen*, Amersfoort and Leuven: Acco.

Waarden, Frans van (1992), 'Emergence and development of business interest associations: an example from the Netherlands', *Organization Studies*, **13** (4), 521–61.

Waarden, Frans van (2002), 'Market institutions as communicating vessels', in J. Rogers Hollingsworth, Karl Mueller and Ellen Hollingsworth (eds), *Advancing Socio-economics: An Institutionalist Perspective*, New York: Rowman & Littlefield, 171–212.

Waarden, Frans van (2010), 'Governing global commons: the public–private protection of fish and forests', in J. Swinnen, D. Vogel, A. Marx, H. Riss and J. Wouters (eds), *Handling Global Challenges: Managing Biodiversity/Biosafety in a Global World,* Leuven and Berkeley, CA: Leuven Centre for Global Governance Studies, LICOS Centre for Institutions and Economic Performance and Center on Institutions and Governance, pp. 140–75.

Waarden, Frans van, and Robin van Dalen (2010a), *Hallmarking Halal: A Case Study on Liberal Markets and an Emerging Market for Quality Certificates*, The Hague: WRR.

Waarden, Frans van and Robin van Dalen (2010b), 'Het homunculus probleem van vrije markten', *Beleid en Maatschappij*, **37** (3), 260–79.

Williamson, Oliver (1975), *Markets and Hierarchies*, New York: Free Press.

# 35 Codes as hybrid regulation

*Mirjan Oude Vrielink, Cor van Montfort, and*
*Meike Bokhorst*

## 35.1  INTRODUCTION

Codes may be defined in terms of the function they perform in society, in terms of their core elements, or in terms of what they mean to different actors in daily practice (cf. Black 2002). There is no single definition, but most scholars agree on the observation that codes are written documents that lay down standards which communicate what behaviors are (morally) required (Schwartz 2001; Pater and Van Gils 2003). They are a prevalent regulatory instrument for ethical guidance or social responsibility to be found everywhere from single organizations to professional and trade associations and large multinationals (Wood and Rimmer 2003). Codes still grow in number as governments, associations, and special interest groups increasingly call for the establishment of such codes (Schwartz 2002: 27).[1]

Private organizations like multinationals and banks use codes as a particular instance of civil-to-business and business-to-business regulation. They may have different reasons for doing so, such as the wish to (re)gain the trust of the public, to express their corporate social responsibility, to discourage free riders or to prevent government from imposing too strict legislation. The corporate governance codes of private organizations have inspired several national corporate governance codes. At the international level a harmonization of codes can be observed, for instance through the OECD Principles of Corporate Governance. In a comparative study of corporate governance codes, codes are said to be beneficial in a number of ways:

> Codes stimulate discussion of corporate governance issues, they encourage companies to adopt widely-accepted governance standards, they help explain both governance-related legal requirements and common corporate governance practices to investors, they can be used to benchmark supervisory and management bodies and they may help prepare the ground for changes in securities regulation and company law, where such changes are deemed necessary.[2]

Codes increasingly are applied by civil actors in the non-profit and (semi-)public sectors, where they are adopted to communicate professional or organizational values, to regulate their integrity policy, or for reasons of standardization. A particular instance is professional codes, which are viewed as the most visible and explicit enunciation of norms that embody the collective conscience of a profession (Frankel 1989: 110).[3]

In this chapter we will discuss codes from three different perspectives: an organizational perspective, a governance perspective, and a (public–private) hybrid perspective. The organizational perspective is concerned with codes drawn up by and for a single (private) organization. This type of code is mainly discussed in business ethics literature and refers primarily to internal controls of behavior (codes of ethics and codes of conduct; see Oude Vrielink and Van Montfort 2009) (section 35.3). The governance perspective deals with codes as a regulatory tool to achieve government objectives in the public interest. Governments increasingly stimulate or mandate (legally conditioned) self-regulation to serve public interest issues (section 35.4). In a final step we will argue that arriving at a better understanding of the potential and pitfalls of codes as a new mode of governance requires a closer look at the hybrid nature of both the composition of codes and the coding process. We will distinguish three dimensions to determine to what extent codes can be characterized as either more public or more private. Codes and the coding process are depicted as a "practice between public and private" that varies according to the actual composition of the codes and the actors involved in the coding process. We are of the opinion that the hybrid perspective offers a more refined picture of the chances and risks involved in the use of codes as a new regulatory instrument to protect or advance public objectives. This approach provides a deeper understanding of what components help or hamper the adoption and actual operation of codes. In a final step we will try to work out what strengths and weaknesses are involved in the use of codes.

## 35.2    THE CONCEPT OF CODES

In the most general sense the concept of a code refers to collections of rules and regulations, generally signifying a written set of action prescriptions (Kaptein and Schwartz 2007).[4] Sometimes the sets of rules and regulations are of a similar nature but referred to by different names, such as codes of ethics, codes of conduct, codes of practice, business codes, integrity codes, codes of honor, voluntary agreements, guidelines, and recommendations (Huyse and Parmentier 1990: 255; Petrick and Quinn 1997; Baarsma et al. 2003: 26; Kaptein 2004; Kaptein and Schwartz 2007). Most scholars treat them as synonyms, while others deliberately discern between the different meanings. They use different names to discriminate between more ethical and practical contents or between general and situational applicability, or to express a difference between general ideals and more concrete action prescriptions (e.g. Baarsma et al. 2003: 26; Wood and Rimmer 2003; Anheier and List 2005: 57–8). The common denominator in the various definitions of codes is that they consist of rules and regulations that articulate action prescriptions with the intention of moral guidance. Codes are applied as regulatory tools by public or private actors that – individually or in concerted action – regulate what rules and regulations are to guide individual and collective action. Often codes comprise dispute management rules and provisions to sanction infringements (Huyse and Parmentier 1990; Baarsma et al. 2003). As such, codes among other things deal with an organization's "social license to operate" (Kagan et al. 2003), which might explain why scandals usually invoke a sudden rise in the popularity of codes. Codes are drawn up to visibly express corporate, sector, or professional values in order to (re)gain public trust (cf. Wood and Rimmer 2003). Codes thus assist organizations in their ongoing relationship with society by helping them to balance their pursuit of autonomy and the public's demand for accountability (Frankel 1989; Higgs-Kleyn and Kapelianis 1999).

Codes in principle are autonomous forms of regulation separate from statutory or international law, but since governments have recognized the limited possibilities of law they are looking for alternative forms of regulatory government beyond law (Scott 2009). Governments try to stimulate governance by non-governmental actors. Private standardization, certification (see Bartley, 2011), ranking, voluntary agreements like covenants and also codes are popular tools of self- and co-regulation. The result is a complex mix of hard and soft law arrangements, like legally binding codes in some semi-public sectors. So codes are not necessarily a type of voluntary approach to regulation (VAR) (see Töller, 2011).

But codes do not only offer chances for serving public values, they also bear risks. Most codes have a strong normative profile. It is not always clear how those norms can and will be realized. Some codes do not go beyond the symbolic level. A lack of will, competence, or agreement may be the cause. It is also possible that the code was set up only for the sake of appearances or to prevent government from lawmaking. The attention to the normative site of the code can be so high that the compliance site is a little bit neglected by the participants. In practice many codes face a lack of knowledge about the state of compliance, and if it were to be measured a compliance deficit might be discovered.

Codes have inspired an extensive body of research in various literatures. In business ethics literature, codes predominantly are studied as a device of ethical guidance within single (private) organizations. Topic areas commonly dealt with in business ethics literature are the content of codes and issues related to the effects of codes on behavior. Scholars of governance and of regulation or regulatory reform start from a somewhat different angle. They take an interest in codes as a particular mode or instrument of regulation that is applied in the context of public policy objectives. It is part of a larger debate about new modes of regulation and the role of a government to preserve public interest issues. In past decades, governments of many advanced Western countries encouraged self-regulation as a means to achieve public policy goals. Various terms are in use to label the new regulatory modes.[5] They have in common that private rule-making at least to some extent is conditioned by the state, whereas their variation applies to how and to what extent the state intervenes in the self-regulatory practices.[6] A particular line of inquiry in this debate involves the study of codes as a regulatory tool to regulate the structures and processes of internal governance to serve public interest issues. Literature and research on this type of code can be found in governance literature and mainly involves topics such as oversight, public accountability, or stakeholder dialogues.

## 35.3 CODES FROM AN ORGANIZATIONAL PERSPECTIVE

From an organizational perspective, codes are used to communicate to both insiders and outsiders what norms ought to govern behavior. Modern organizations are regulated by government to prevent them from pursuing their own interest at the cost of the common good. The movement toward increased ethical guidance and government intervention is rooted in what is called the "corporate social contract." In return for legal accountability through organizational management to shareholders and the general public a corporation is given the right to pursue its stated objectives (Brooks 1989: 117). This principle replaces the early industrial belief that "what is good for business is good for the country". In the past few decades unions and governments have awakened to their power to influence or control corporations. Shareholders' rights are no longer looked upon as properly dominating the rights of all other stakeholders. Because of this new operating rationale for corporations in Western, capitalistic societies, companies nowadays face a dual test of legality and moral acceptability (Brooks 1989), which leads them to perform beyond the law (cf. Kagan et al. 2003). Frankel (1989: 109, 110) points to a similar movement toward increased ethical guidance in the context of professions; society's granting of power and privilege to the professions is premised on their willingness and ability to contribute to social well-being and to conduct their affairs in a manner consistent with broader social values. This relationship he refers to as the "society–profession nexus".

In the business ethics literature, conceptual and empirically oriented studies on codes can be divided into two main orientations, that is, content-oriented research (what is or should be in the actual codes) and output-oriented research (what effects on behavior codes have or should have).[7] These lines of inquiry deal with different knowledge interests and bodies of knowledge on codes. Helin and Sandström (2007) reviewed 38 studies on corporate codes with an empirical content, published during the period 1994 to mid-2005. The conclusion of their review is that most of these studies are content-oriented, targeting what is in the actual codes (e.g. Lefebvre and Singh 1996; Preble and Hoffman 1999; Wood 2000; Carasco and Singh 2003; Singh et al. 2005), sometimes with an additional normative view of what they should consist of (e.g. Wood and Rimmer 2003; cf. Boers and van Montfort 2006). They have witnessed a particular focus on mapping the content in terms of country- or non-country-specific characteristics. The overall view that results from content-oriented studies is that, regardless of their geographical origin, codes are similarly designed and basically share the same message of moral behavior. Generally codes contain behavioral rules, rules concerning the endorsement of a code, rules about the sanctioning of infringements, and rules of dispute management. This general pattern can be observed in national as well as cross-national studies, though the latter also reveal some differences. For instance, Australian codes rely less on internal and external watchdogs than American codes do, which is explained by differences in business culture.[8]

The second line of inquiry examines the effectiveness of codes in influencing actions towards "more ethical" behavior and key factors that might explain their effects. Studies dealing with this subject provide divergent and even conflicting conceptual views on the effectiveness of business codes, ranging from largely counterproductive to successful, a mixed view that is mirrored in results of empirical studies conducted in this field (Kaptein and Schwartz 2007). In a similar vein, reviewing 79 empirical studies that examine the effectiveness of business codes, Kaptein and Schwartz (2007: 113) conclude that these studies present a mixed image:

> 35% of the studies have found that codes are effective, 16% have found that the relationship is weak, 33% have found that there is no significant relationship, and 14% have presented mixed results. Only one study has found that business codes could be counterproductive.[9]

To establish the potential of codes in terms of whether they are or could be effective, a different research approach is required; contextual factors inside or outside the corporation should be taken into consideration (Helin and Sandström 2007; Kaptein and Schwartz 2007).

## 35.4   CODES FROM A GOVERNANCE PERSPECTIVE

The various currents in the literature discussed in this section are also engaged in regulating behavior within organizations, but in a different way. The difference with business ethics codes is that organizations or their representatives are invited by the government or entrusted to regulate themselves for the realization of a public interest. A second difference is that, in the governance literature, codes are most often discussed as a certain type of regulation instead of being treated as an independent object of study. In the business ethics literature, codes are frequently an isolated object of study.

In governance literature the growing interest in self-regulation indicates a shift from government to governance. In this literature on governance, codes are dealt with as a particular instance of self-regulatory mechanisms that replace or supplement direct state regulation. Self-regulation describes a horizontal extension of government, as it includes private and societal actors in the regulatory process (Rhodes 1997; Schmitter 2001). State and society share a responsibility for the realization of public policy goals, and consequently self-regulation is perceived as a means to be applied in the public interest. At the vertical level, government is extended by regulatory arrangements at the local, regional, national, supranational and international level. Consequently, the focus is on the interplay between multiple levels of control instead of on the national government (Latzer et al. 2003).

According to Baggott (1989: 435, 436), amongst political scientists at least three perspectives can be identified within the academic debate. Firstly, corporatists tend to see self-regulation as further evidence of a corporate state in which state authority is devolved to private organizations that in turn regulate their members (Schmitter 1985). Secondly, supporters of a minimal state consider self-regulation as a possible means of rolling back the state (Hughes 1985). And thirdly, in a particular strand of public administration literature self-regulation is seen as a particular form of quasi-government, raising questions and problems of accountability and public control (Hood 1978). In addition to this a fourth perspective could be discerned: that of the regulatory state (Majone 1994; Braithwaite 2000; Jordana and Levi-Faur 2004). This line of inquiry deals with the gradual shift from (re)distributive policies to rule-making, taking a special interest in the rise and role of specialized, independent regulatory agencies (Latzer et al. 2003; Christensen and Lægreid 2006). Self-regulation is presented as a particular type of regulatory reform next to deregulation, better regulation, re-regulation and meta-regulation. It represents a further step away from traditional, hierarchic state regulation towards less formalized means of regulation which are carried out by private or semi-private regulatory institutions.

In literature on regulation several scholars have addressed the use of self-regulatory mechanisms to help achieve public interest issues by various names such as "the remix of traditional and alternative regulation" (Latzer et al. 2003: 127), "decentralized regulation" (Black 2002; cf. Scott 2004), "industry self-regulation" (Gunningham and Rees 1997), or "smart regulation" (Gunningam et al. 1998). They start from the premise that government regulation may perform better if it incorporates the benefits of self-regulation. The following potential advantages of self-regulation are perceived: compliance enhancement, flexibility, a quick and informed response, and less public expenditure (Gunningham and Rees 1997; Cutler 2003: 23; Abbott and Snidal 2004: 421, 2009; Trubek and Trubek 2005; Havinga 2006; Trubek et al. 2006).

In sum, in the literature on regulation, regulatory reform and governance codes commonly are treated as a self-regulatory instrument and are discussed in the context of the broader trend to apply new modes of regulation to preserve public interest issues.

## 35.5 CODES FROM A HYBRID PERSPECTIVE

From the organizational perspective the public interest is served in the specific content and output of codes and from the governance perspective the public interest is served in "joining up" the regulatory process or by transferring the regulatory process to private actors. Both perspectives offer however a limited view on risks and chances for serving the public interest by codes. For a better understanding of the strengths and weaknesses involved in the use of codes as a new mode of regulation we need to pay close attention to the question of what the regulation comprises and how the regulation is carried out. In this chapter we therefore argue that a code's potential in serving the public interest can be understood properly only by taking into account (a) its hybrid composition and (b) the hybrid character of the "coding" process.

The content of codes and the process of coding are never purely public or purely private. In civil regulation the shape of codes, both public and private interests, motives, incentives, effects, and behavior always play a role. That is why we above called codes and the coding process a "practice between public and private." Rather than through the state, civil regulation operates beside or around the state; it is based on "soft law" rather than legally binding standards. It is rooted in traditional forms of self-regulation but goes beyond it to include second- and/or third-party regulation.[10] In this hybrid practice the public interest is guaranteed if responsiveness to needs, wishes, and preferences of relevant public and private stakeholders is well served. Therefore in our opinion codes – and with it civil regulation – will serve the public interest better if (1) government, private parties, and stakeholders agree on the norms, (2) the codes are binding, and (3) there are mechanisms to enforce compliance. With regard to the regulatory process ("coding") to arrive at a code, public interest is served best if the relevant public and private stakeholders and interests are involved in this process.

### 35.5.1 The Hybrid Composition of Codes

The hybrid composition of codes appears on three levels:

- The regulatory bodies: who defines the normative content of a code (government, private parties, and/or stakeholders)?
- Legal status: does the code refer to (legal and obligatory) regulation (is it binding from a legislative perspective?) or is it a voluntary non-coercive agreement?
- Compliance mechanism: is there anyone who cares about compliance and, if so, who takes care, who can sanction non-compliance, and do stakeholders have opportunities to complain?

The content (norms) of codes, for example, can be defined by private parties, while they are established in law and are to be enforced by stakeholders. The latter strengthens the public character of the code. In other cases the content of codes might be defined by or at least framed by the government as well (think of norms about integrity or wages).

The typology of codes in terms of hybridity provides us with a means to arrive at a more refined judgment of codes as a device to serve public interest issues. So, to arrive at a better understanding of codes as a regulatory mechanism in the public context, codes should be categorized according to their typical combination of components of public and private regulation. Using components derived from legislation ("public") means that non-compliance is regarded as behavior against the law and can be dealt with accordingly, whereas using components of self-regulation ("private") leaves questions of ethics and discipline to the private organizations or their associations (Brien 1998). Starting from the premise that behavioral effects might occur from the combination of public and private rules identifying and prescribing what behavior is required on the one hand and regulatory provisions to deter or punish non-compliance on the other hand, codes to that effect may comprise components of legislation and self-regulation.

Huyse and Parmentier (1990: 261, 262) point out that all of the arguments for and against the use of codes pertain to situations in which the codes are drafted unilaterally and function indigenously. In cases of other types of codes, such as joint codes or codes administered by a government office, different arguments apply according to the authors. In the latter situation, for example, consumer organizations have more confidence in codes. They feel the code can set higher standards for consumer protection, can guarantee cheap and speedy methods of dispute settlement, and can be (re)negotiated without undue delay. From this observation we learn that the relative dominance of public and private components of a code affects its (perceived) benefits or limitations. This holds true not only for codes, but for other self-regulatory instruments as well. It thus should be possible to surmise what risks and chances the different types of codes involve based on the public–private profiles.

### 35.5.2   Hybridity of the Regulatory Process

It is not only the norms, legal status, or compliance mechanisms that can vary in degree of "publicness" (Bozeman, 2004 [1987]), but also the process of regulation itself.

In recent decades codes increasingly are found in the realm of combined public and private normative orders. They have become prevalent self-regulatory mechanisms applied to help achieve public policy goals. From the early 1980s governments in the United States, Europe, and other advanced Western economies strongly promoted the adoption of such codes. Codes and other instruments of self-regulation were hailed as a more flexible, effective, and efficient alternative for direct state regulation. These new modes of regulation were inspired by various political and economic trends, such as growing protests against the expanding body of government regulation ("juridification"), an emergent awareness of the poor quality and ineffectiveness of state-imposed regulation ("regulatory failure"), and fiscal constraints inspiring a search for cost-effective regulatory controls. Furthermore, the experiments with self-regulation as an alternative or supplement to legislation fitted the turn towards neo-liberal ideology, entailing a trend to employ private sector management practices in the public sector, most typically reflected in new public management (NPM; see Hood 1991). This all has added to a situation in which codes increasingly can be found in the realm of hybrid regulation.

Different strands in socio-legal literatures (e.g. on new governance or the (post-) regulatory state) have shown interest in regulatory hybridization as a strategy to improve rule compliance and social legitimacy of regulation (Ayres and Braithwaite 1992; Sinclair 1997; Gunningham et al. 1998; Scott 2002; Lobel 2004; Trubek et al. 2006).[11] Hybridization in these contexts has three different meanings that overlap both in the empirical world and in scholarly discussion. To quote Halpern (2008: 85) on this subject, regulatory hybridity

> can refer to regulation that combines governmental (public) and non-governmental (private) components. It can refer to oversight arrangements with multiple levels, joining centralized and regional or local features. It can refer to regulatory processes that engage a full range of participants, including professionals, divisions of government, public interest advocates, and representatives of groups being regulated.

Codes produced in the realm of hybrid regulation reveal a great variety in their typical combinations of state and non-state input at different regulatory levels and in the relative dominance of public and private components. We agree on Huyse and Parmentier's (1990: 256) claim that in order to value a code's potential it is important to have a clear understanding of the differences amongst codes. They can be categorized by means of various perspectives, each leading to the identification of certain types of codes. For instance, one way to classify codes applied by Huyse and Parmentier (1990: 257) is by looking at the number of parties involved in adopting a code to distinguish between unilateral, bilateral, and trilateral codes. Another perspective, focusing on means by which codes function once they are established, leads them to the differentiation between indigenous, joint, and administered codes (1990: 258). In this chapter we developed a typology of codes according to what we call their "public–private profile," referring to the relative dominance of public and private regulatory components.

## 35.6   CONCLUSION

The use of codes as an instrument to help achieve public policy objectives is rather new. Traditionally organizations adopt codes to communicate what the organization stands for (e.g. mission statements), to govern individual and organizational conduct in situations of moral ambiguity or conflicts of interests, or to express their social responsibility. Regardless of whether a code is adopted to serve public policy objectives or organizational interests, it almost invariably combines public and private elements. This hybrid nature needs to be taken into account if we want a better understanding of a code's potential as a regulatory tool of civil regulation. The hybridization of codes refers to both the self-regulatory process of standard-setting, implementation, and enforcement and the code as a product of this self-regulatory process. The regulatory bodies involved in this process and the nature of the norms and the compliance mechanisms thus can be public or private.

Codes are an expression of civil regulation, whether we take a look at codes of ethics or governance codes. In most cases this kind of civil regulation is not purely "civil," but a mix of public and private elements. Both the norms, legal status, and compliance mechanisms and the process of regulation show action and influence of the state as well as "bottom-up" initiatives. We argue that the degree of responsiveness to the needs, opinions, and preferences of public and private stakeholders of both the codes and the coding processes (regulation) is crucial for serving the public interest. So the public–private mix that is most responsive on both the codes and the coding processes (regulation) will provide the best guarantee for public interests involved in civil regulation through codes.

To conclude our chapter we will address the issue of the strengths and weaknesses of codes as a regulatory instrument to protect or advance the public interest. Since the codes are promoted as an alternative to direct command-and-control regulation we will describe them in terms of the potential advantages and disadvantages of self-regulation compared to direct regulation.

Codes are stimulated or even mandated by governments to deal with the weaknesses of command-and-control regulation. In Chapter 1, six shortcomings are emphasized: (a) expensive and ineffective regulatory strategies; (b) inflexible regulatory strategies that encourage adversarial enforcement; (c) legal constraints on the subjects, procedures, and scope of regulatory discretion; (d) *regulatees'* resentment, which leads to non-compliance or "creative compliance"; (e) strict regulation that often presents an obstacle to innovation; and (f) regulation that often serves to set a lowest common denominator for regulatees to follow rather than supplying incentives for improved standards.

Codes can have strengths compared to direct regulation, and they can take away the shortcomings of direct regulation, but they have their disadvantages too (see also van Waarden about the strengths and weaknesses of third-party regulation in Chapter 34, Van Waarden, 2011).

According to the governance literature, regulation may perform better if the benefits of both self-regulation and legislation are incorporated into the regulatory system. Then regulation may benefit from the following potential advantages of self-regulation (Selznick 1992; Gunningham and Rees 1997; Teubner 1997; Cutler 2003: 23; Abbott and Snidal 2004: 421, 2009; Trubek and Trubek 2005; Havinga 2006; Trubek et al. 2006; Trubek et al. 2008; Mascini and van Wijk 2009; Dorbeck-Jung et al. 2010):

- Compliance enhancement: self-regulation is said to support the internalization of norms; it is expected that actors usually will accept the rules of conduct they agreed upon and follow them in regulatory practice.
- Responsiveness and flexibility: self-regulation seems to be able to respond to demands for frequent norm changes, diversity, and space for multiple interpretations and experimentation to achieve optimal results according to social and technical development.
- Quick response: self-regulation is set up informally, which seems to speed up regulation.
- Informed response: self-regulation is based on domain expertise, which is said to be essential for effective regulation.
- Efficiency enhancement: if private organizations pay the costs of self-regulation, public expenditures can decrease.

In combinations of self-regulation with legislation, the additional advantages of legislation could be:

- Reliability: legislation is required to be clear, coherent, stable, and predictable. A reliable framework for action is said to be essential for policy goals.
- Sanctions: legislation provides for sanctions; the effectiveness of regulation seems to be supported by credible threats of enforcement.
- Broad interest recognition: legislation is required to pursue public interests and to strike a balance between conflicting interests.

When legislation and self-regulation are combined to achieve public policy goals, however, the result may be to introduce not only the advantages of both regulatory tools, but also their deficiencies. In the case of self-regulation, the potential deficiencies are lack of reliability, transparency, and binding sanctions, as well as biased interest recognition (Levin 1967; Gunningham 1995; Vogel 2009). Theoretically, legislation may be accompanied by the disadvantages of rigidity and lack of tailored control. Furthermore, when legislation and self-regulation are combined, tensions between the interests on which the two regulatory instruments are based (public versus private interests) may be counterproductive in regulatory practice (Gunningham et al. 1998: 28).

## NOTES

1. To illustrate the prevalence of codes we quote Schwartz (2002: 27): "In the U.S., over ninety percent of large corporations have a code of ethics (Center for Business Ethics, 1992), while in Canada eighty-five percent have a code (KPMG, 2000). Of the largest European corporations, fifty-seven percent of U.K. companies have a code (Le Jeune and Webley, 1998), fiftyone percent of German companies have a code (Schlegelmilch and Langlois, 1990), and thirty percent of French companies have a code (Schlegelmilch and Langlois, 1990)." In a comparative study of corporate governance codes from 2002 the Internal Market Directorate General of the European Commission found 35 national corporate governance codes, one-third of them in the United Kingdom.
2. Comparative Study of Corporate Governance Codes Relevant to the European Union and Its Member States on behalf of the European Commission, Internal Market Directorate General, final report and annexes I–III, January 2002, p. 11.
3. They may consist of one or more of three conceptual elements: ideals for which practitioners should strive, norms which can help in dealing with ethical problems, and detailed rules to govern professional conduct and adjudicate grievances (Frankel 1989: 110–11).
4. This focus on explicating behavioral standards on paper links the definition to the Latin origin of the term "code," which indicates wooden boards covered with wax used to write.
5. To name a few examples: coerced self-regulation (Black 1996), mandated self-regulation (Rees 1988), instigated self-regulation (Ukrow 1999), enforced regulation (Brien 1998), co-regulation (Senden 2005), and smart regulation (Gunningham and Grabosky 1998).
6. In the late 1980s, for instance, a trend to more formalized codes and an increasing reliance on statutory or administrative provisions could be observed (Baggott 1989).
7. A third line of inquiry, which is still in its infancy, could be distinguished. It takes an interest in what obstacles organizations have to overcome and the mechanisms they should have in place in order to ensure a code actually comes into practice. Studies adopting this perspective draw attention to issues such as the code's relevance and consistency, and procedures of consultations, communication, education, maintenance, and reinforcement.
8. Taking this perspective a bit further these differences may be explained by legal culture, in particular differences in the degree of legalism and adversarialism. Legalism in this context refers to being formalistic, which "makes for precision, transparency, security and predictability, but at the cost of rigidity, bureaucracy, cumbersomeness and costliness" (van Waarden 2009: 200). Adversarialism refers to antagonistic

relations and reliance on social systems structuring conflict by channeling it formally, for instance in court, in order to be able to control such conflict (van Waarden, 2009: 200). As we will show later on in this chapter, codes may vary on the dimension of legalism, and consequently differ in the risks and chances involved in their use as a means to achieve public objectives.

9.   Kaptein and Schwartz (2007) conceive of a "business code" as a code that is developed by and for a given company. Such codes are one of the layers of a whole range of codes for business, consisting also of professional, industrial, national, and international codes.

10.   Following Levi-Faur (see Chapter 1; see also van Waarden, Chapter 34) we consider first-party regulation to mean forms of self-regulation in which the regulator is also the regulatee. Second-party regulation denotes forms of regulation in which the regulator is independent and distinct from the regulatee. In third-party regulation, the relations between the regulator and the regulatee are mediated by a third party that acts as independent or semi-independent regulatory auditor.

11.   A similar interest could be witnessed among political scientists dealing with issues of self-regulation from a corporatist or quasi-government point of view (Schmitter 1985; Hood 1978).

# REFERENCES

Abbott, K. and D. Snidal (2004), 'Hard and soft law in international governance', *International Organization*, **54**, 421–2.

Abbott, K. and D. Snidal (2009), 'The governance triangle: regulatory standards institutions and the shadow of the state', in W. Mattli and N. Woods (eds), *The Politics of Global Regulation*, Princeton, NJ: Princeton University Press, 44–88.

Anheier, H. and R. List, (2005), *A Dictionary of Civil Society, Philanthropy and the Nonprofit Sector*, vol. 1, pt 4, New York: Routledge.

Ayres, I. and J. Braithwaite (1992), *Responsive Regulation: Transcending the Deregulation Debate*, Oxford: Oxford University Press.

Baarsma, Barbara, Flóra Felsö, Sjoerd van Geffen, José Mulder and André Oostdijk (2003), 'Do it yourself? Stock-taking study of self-regulation instruments', study commissioned by the Ministry of Economic Affairs, Amsterdam.

Baggott, Rob (1989), 'Regulatory reform in Britain: the changing face of self-regulation', *Public Administration*, **67**, 435–54.

Bartley, Tim (2011), 'Certification as a mode of social regulation', in David Levi-Faur *Handbook on the Politics of Regulation*, Cheltenham, Edward Elgar.

Black, J. (1996), 'Constitutionalising self-regulation', *Modern Law Review*, **59** (1), 24–55.

Black, J. (2002), 'Critical reflection on regulation', CARR Discussion Paper Series 4, LSE, London.

Boers, Ineke and Cor van Montfort (2006), 'Goed bestuur in governancecodes: een vergelijking in tien verschillede branches', *Goed Bestuur*, **2** (4), 45–51.

Bozeman, Barry (2004 [1987]), *All Organizations Are Public*, Washington, DC: Beard Books.

Braithwaite, John (2000), 'The new regulatory state and the transformation of criminology', *British Journal of Criminology*, **40**, 222–38.

Brien, Andrew (1998), 'Professional ethics and the culture of trust', *Journal of Business Ethics*, **17** (4), 391–409.

Brooks, Leonard J. (1989), 'Corporate codes of ethics', *Journal of Business Ethics*, 8, 117–29.

Carasco, E.F. and J.B. Singh (2003), 'The content and focus of the codes of ethics of the world's largest transnational corporations', *Business and Society Review*, **108** (1), 71–94.

Christensen, Tom and Per Lægreid (eds) (2006), *Autonomy and Regulation: Coping with Agencies in the Modern State*, Cheltenham, UK and Northampton, MA, USA: Edward Elgar Publishing.

Cutler, A.C. (2003), *Private Power and Global Authority: Transnational Merchant Law in the Global Political Economy*, Cambridge: Cambridge University Press, pp. 23–5.

Dorbeck-Jung, B.R., M.J. Oude Vrielink, J.F. Gosselt, J.J. van Hoof and M.D.T. de Jong (2010), 'Contested hybridization of regulation: failure of the Dutch regulatory system to protect minors from harmful media', *Regulation & Governance*, **4** (2), 154–74.

Frankel, M.S. (1989), 'Professional codes: why, how, and with what impact?', *Journal of Business Ethics*, **8**, 109–15.

Gunningham, N. (1995), 'Environment, self-regulation, and the chemical industry: assessing Responsible Care', *Law and Policy*, **17**, 57–109.

Gunningham, N. and J. Rees (1997), 'Industry self-regulation: an institutional perspective', *Law and Policy*, **19** (4), 363–414.

Gunningham, N. and P. Grabosky (1998), *Smart Regulation: Designing Environmental Policy,* New York: Oxford University Press.

Gunningham, N., P. Grabosky and D. Sinclair (1998), *Smart Regulation: Designing Environmental Policy,* Oxford: Oxford University Press.

Halpern, S (2008), 'Hybrid design, systemic rigidity: institutional dynamics in human research oversight', *Regulation & Governance,* **2,** 85–102.

Havinga, T. (2006), 'Private regulation of food safety by supermarkets', *Law and Policy,* **28** (4), 515–33.

Helin, S. and J. Sandström (2007), 'An inquiry into the study of corporate codes of ethics', *Journal of Business Ethics,* **75,** 253–71.

Higgs-Kleyn, N. and Kapelianis, D. (1999), 'The role of professional codes in regulating ethical conduct', *Journal of Business Ethics,* **19,** 363–74.

Hood, C. (1978), 'Keeping the centre small: explanations of agency type', *Political Studies,* **26** (1), 30–46.

Hood, Christopher (1991), 'A public management for all seasons?', *Public Administration,* **69,** 3–19.

Hughes, M. (1985), 'Debureaucratisation and private interest government: the British state and economic development policy', in W. Streeck and P.C. Schmitter (eds), *Private Interest Government beyond Market and State,* London: Sage, pp. 87–104.

Huyse, L. and S. Parmentier (1990), 'Decoding codes: the dialogue between consumers and suppliers through codes of conduct in the European community', *Journal of Consumer Policy,* **13,** 253–72.

Jordana, Jacint and David Levi-Faur (eds) (2004), *The Politics of Regulation: Institutions and Regulatory Reforms for the Age of Governance,* Cheltenham, UK and Northampton, MA, USA: Edward Elgar Publishing.

Kagan, R.A., N. Gunningham and D. Thornton (2003), 'Explaining corporate environmental performance: how does regulation matter?', *Law and Society Review,* **37** (1), 51–89.

Kaptein, M. (2004), 'Business codes of multinational firms: what do they say?', *Journal of Business Ethics,* **50** (1), 13–33.

Kaptein, M. and M.S. Schwartz (2007), 'The effectiveness of business codes: a critical examination of existing studies and the development of an integrated research model', *Journal of Business Ethics,* **77,** 111–27.

Latzer, Michael, Natascha Just, Florian Saurwein and Peter Slominski (2003), 'Regulation remixed: institutional change through self and co-regulation in the mediamatics sector', Austrian Academy of Sciences, Research Unit for Institutional Change and European Integration (ICE), Vienna.

Lefebvre, M. and J.B. Singh (1996), 'A comparison of the contents and foci of Canadian and American corporate codes of ethics', *International Journal of Management,* **13** (2), 156–70.

Levin, H.J. (1967), 'The limit of self-regulation', *Columbia Law Review,* **67** (4), 603–44.

Lobel, O. (2004), 'The renew deal: the fall of regulation and the rise of governance in contemporary legal thought', *Minnesota Law Review,* **89** (2), 343–470.

Majone, Giandomenico (1994), 'The rise of the regulatory state in Europe', *West European Politics,* **17,** 77–101.

Mascini, P. and E. van Wijk (2009), 'Responsive regulation at the Dutch Food and Consumer Product Safety Authority: an empirical assessment of assumptions underlying the theory', *Regulation & Governance,* **3,** 27–47.

Oude Vrielink, Mirjan and Cor van Montfort (2009), 'Codes of ethics and codes of practice', in H.K. Anheier and S. Toepler (eds), *International Encyclopedia of Civil Society,* New York: Springer, 492–7.

Pater, A. and Van Gils, A. (2003), 'Stimulating ethical decision-making in a business context: effects of ethical and professional codes', *European Management Journal,* **21** (6), 762–72.

Petrick, J.A. and J.F. Quinn (1997), *Management Ethics: Integrity at Work,* Thousand Oaks, CA: Sage.

Preble, J.F. and R.C. Hoffman (1999), 'The nature of ethics codes in franchise associations around the globe', *Journal of Business Ethics,* **18,** 239–53.

Rees, J. (1988), 'Self-regulation: an effective alternative to direct regulation by OSHA?', *Policy Studies Journal,* **3,** 602–14.

Rhodes, R.A.W. (1997), *Understanding Governance: Policy Networks Governance, Reflexivity and Accountability,* Buckingham and Philadelphia, PA: Open University Press.

Schmitter, P.C. (1985), 'Neo-corporatism and the state', in W. Grant, *The Political Economy of Corporatism,* London: Macmillan, pp. 32–62.

Schmitter, P.C. (2001), *What Is There to Legitimise in the European Union . . . and How Might This Be Accomplished?,* Jean Monnet Working Paper No. 6/01, Florence: EUI and New York: University School of Law.

Schwartz, M.S. (2001), 'The nature of the relationship between corporate codes of ethics and behaviour', *Journal of Business Ethics,* **32,** 247–62.

Schwartz, Mark S. (2002), 'A code of ethics for CorporateCode of Ethics', *Journal of Business Ethics,* **41,** 27–43.

Scott, C. (2002), 'Private regulation of the public sector: a neglected facet of contemporary governance', *Journal of Law and Society,* **29,** 56–76.

Scott, Colin (2004), 'Regulation in the age of governance: the rise of the post-regulatory state', in Jacint Jordana and David Levi-Faur (eds), *The Politics of Regulation: Institutions and Regulatory Reforms for the Age of Governance*, Cheltenham, UK and Northampton, MA, USA: Edward Elgar Publishing, pp. 145–74.

Scott, Colin (2009), 'Governing without law or governing without government? New-ish governance and the legitimacy of the EU', *European Law Journal*, **15** (2), 160–73.

Selznick, P. (1992), *The Moral Commonwealth: Social Theory and the Promise of Community*, Berkeley: University of California Press.

Senden, Linda (2005), 'Soft law, self-regulation and co-regulation in European law: where do they meet?', *Electronic Journal of Comparative Law*, **9** (1) , available at http://www.ejcl.org/.

Sinclair, D. (1997), 'Self-regulation versus command and control? Beyond false dichotomies', *Law and Policy*, **19** (4), 529–59.

Singh, J., E. Carasco, G. Svensson, G. Wood and M. Callaghan (2005), 'A comparative study of the contents of corporate codes of ethics in Australia, Canada and Sweden', *Journal of World Business*, **40**, 91–109.

Töller A.E., 'Voluntary approaches to regulation – patterns, causes, and effects', in David Levi-Faur (ed.), *Handbook on the Politics of Regulation*, Cheltenham, Edward Elgar.

Teubner, G. (ed.) (1997), *Global Law without a State*, Aldershot: Dartmouth.

Trubek, D.M. and L.G. Trubek (2005), 'Hard and soft law in the construction of social Europe: the role of the open method of co-ordination', *European Law Journal*, **11** (3), 343–64.

Trubek, D.M., P. Cottrell and M. Nance (2006), 'Soft law, hard law and EU integration', in G. de Burca and J. Scott (eds), *Law and new governance in the EU and the US*, Portland, OR: Hart, pp. 65–94.

Trubek, L.G., J.V. Rees, A.B. Hoflund, M. Farquhar and C.A. Heimer (2008), 'Health care and new governance: the quest for effective regulation', *Regulation & Governance*, **2**, 1–8.

Ukrow, J. (1999), *Self-Regulation in the Media Sector and European Community Law: An Independent Study of European Law*, prepared at the request of the Federal Government Commissioner for Cultural Affairs and the Media, Saarbrücken: Institute of European Media Law.

Van Waarden, F. (2009), 'Power to the legal professionals: is there an Americanization of European law?', *Regulation & Governance*, **3**, 197–216.

Van Waarden F. (2011), 'Problems and prospects of varieties of private market regulation', in David Levi-Faur (ed.), *Handbook on the Politics of Regulation*, Cheltenham: Edward Elgar.

Vogel, D. (2009), 'The private regulation of global corporate conduct', in W. Mattli and N. Woods (eds), *The Politics of Global Regulation*, Princeton, NJ: Princeton University Press, pp. 151–88.

Wood, G. (2000), 'A cross cultural comparison of the contents of codes of ethics: USA, Canada and Australia', *Journal of Business Ethics*, **25** (4), 287–98.

Wood, G. and M. Rimmer (2003), 'Codes of ethics: what are they really and what should they be?', *International Journal of Value-Based Management*, **16**, 181–95.

# 36 Voluntary approaches to regulation – patterns, causes, and effects
## *Annette Elisabeth Töller*

The core idea of a Weberian conception of regulation is that the state adopts collectively binding rules which can be sanctioned by courts and, if necessary, implemented by the use of legitimate force. In the light of this conception, *voluntary* regulation provokes puzzlement. Here there are no binding rules, no role for courts, no forcible implementation by the state, and sometimes no public agency at all (see Kirton and Trebilcock 2004: 9); yet we call it 'regulation'. The rapid 'proliferation' of such forms of 'self-regulation in the shadow of the state' is considered as a core element of the 'new order of regulatory capitalism' (Levi-Faur 2005: 27).

Voluntary regulation can be defined as 'rule structures . . . that seek to persuade firms to incur nontrivial costs of producing positive externalities beyond what the law requires of them' (Potoski and Prakash 2009: ix). The term 'voluntary regulation' is clearly preferable to other terms such as 'civil regulation', 'private regulation', 'cooperative regulation', 'negotiated regulation', 'third-party regulation', 'self-regulation', 'regulated regulation', or 'soft law', for several reasons (see for example Gunningham and Rees 1997; Kirton and Trebilcock 2004; Porter and Ronit 2006: 42; Everett et al. 2008; Levi-Faur, Chapter 1). First, most of these other terms refer to only part of the meaning of voluntary regulation. For example, with 'civic' or 'civil' regulation, civic actors (meaning societal but not business actors) play a role in some cases of voluntary regulation but not in others. With 'cooperative regulation' or 'co-regulation', some of the rules emerge from intense cooperation between private and state actors while others come from a predominantly self-regulatory setting. Again, some are negotiated whereas others emerge from a technocratic procedure. Thus, empirically speaking, 'voluntary regulation' is the lowest common denominator because, irrespective of how and by whom such rules are developed, they are all developed and applied on a voluntary basis.

Second, most of the alternative terms have a normative bias. For instance, 'civil regulation' suggests superior forms of democratic governance (for example, 'regulatory democracy' based on a vibrant civil society; see Levi-Faur, Chapter 1), which might be true in some cases but not in others. In contrast, the term 'voluntary' is neutral.

If all cases of voluntary regulation are equally voluntary in their emergence, their legal nature, and their implementation, much more has to be said about the differences between them. To give an adequate account of voluntary regulation it is necessary not only to address their origin, how participation is organized, or the level of government at which it is situated, but also to study each case in context. This means, first, that we have to study cases in their regulatory environment, focusing especially on how voluntary regulation is related to compulsory regulation. Second, all relevant cases of voluntary approaches to regulation (VAR) in a particular sector should be examined. Third, it is important to consider a time frame of several years, depending on developments in the field. On this conceptual and methodological basis, we should be able to identify patterns of change over time such as the emergence of various forms of voluntary regulation (regulatory diversification), the emergence of competition between VAR (another form of regulatory competition), or the dilution of VAR in new statutory regulation ('legislating away').

The chapter proceeds as follows. In section 36.1 I describe patterns of use of voluntary approaches. In section 36.2 I deal with causality: what explains the emergence of VAR and why are VAR used in preference to statutory regulation? Section 36.3 addresses the effects of VAR, embracing not only the success and failure of VAR but also a wider range of possible effects. Section 36.4 concludes. The issues of the democratic legitimacy of VAR (for example Porter and Ronit 2006: 49) and the forms of VAR that are best suited to handle what types of problem (Gunningham and Rees 1997: 406) lie beyond the scope of this chapter.

## 36.1    PATTERNS

### 36.1.1    VAR in Time and Space

As mentioned above, VAR are by no means a new phenomenon. For example, voluntary agreements have their origin in the late 1960s in France and Germany, strongly focusing on consumer and environmental protection (Töller 2011). In the UK voluntary agreements have been used particularly since the 1970s in such diverse fields as the sale of tobacco products, the handling of pesticides, and the practices of abortion clinics (Baggott 1986: 57). In other countries, including the US, Australia, and Japan, and on the transnational level voluntary agreements were introduced on a larger scale throughout the 1990s (see below). Meanwhile, business codes addressing specific issues like defence procurement fraud, racial inequality, or human rights had already emerged in the 1970s and 1980s in the US and Europe (Rhone et al. 2004: 214). Voluntary approaches have a long history in the field of financial regulation (Coleman 1994), but a more recent history in fields like corporate governance (Töller 2009), pharmaceutical industries' contacts with physicians (Hemphill 2006; Grande 2009), and the shipping industry (DeSombre 2009).

Even though we can observe a growth of VAR since the 1990s in some sectors, there is no overall 'global trend' (Everett et al. 2008: 117) towards VAR and away from traditional 'command and control' strategies (Bartley 2003: 433; Lyon and Maxwell 2004: 149). Generally speaking, similar forms of voluntary regulation are applied in several countries and transnational contexts, yet they differ considerably in form and in practice (see for example Töller 2008).

### 36.1.2    Typology and Examples of Voluntary Regulation

There is a range of ideal types of voluntary regulation, which in practice tend to appear in hybrid forms. Codes are usually designed unilaterally by business players, either individually (on the firm level) or collectively (on the level of associations or in new regulatory arrangements). The term 'agreement' usually denotes that business and government have agreed on rules. Whereas programs are regularly designed unilaterally by government agencies and then offered for participation, with certification schemes the regulation is controlled by non-governmental certification bodies (Bartley 2003: 434). Standards usually differ from other forms of voluntary regulation in that they are developed by standardization organizations (national, transnational, or international), contain relatively elaborate sets of rules, and envisage systematic external verification. We find the largest number of voluntary regulations and the greatest variation in their form in the environmental sector. National voluntary environmental agreements go back to the late 1960s and have been used regularly in many countries since the 1990s (Töller 2008). In the late 1980s, after the Bhopal disaster, the chemical industry initiated Responsible Care, a system of transnational self-regulation. In the early 1990s eco-management systems, applying the idea of quality management to the field of environmental protection of firms and other organizations, were developed on national, European, and international levels (BS 7750, EMAS, and ISO 14001, Nash and Ehrenfield 2001; Delmas and Montiel 2008). On the transnational level the handling of chemicals has for a long time been subject to voluntary regulation developed by transnational branch associations (Schneider and Ronit 1999). Transnational forest certification schemes were also established in the 1990s (Cashore et al. 2003; Bartley 2003, 2009).

### 36.1.3 Involved Actors and Regulatory Structure

If we examine who is involved in the creation of a voluntary regulation, we can distinguish business actors, government actors (usually executive agencies), and NGOs (environmental groups, trade unions, and human rights groups). NGOs can play an indirect role in exposing and publicizing undesirable practices, such as harsh working conditions in the globalized apparel industry or illegally felled timber (Bartley 2003: 442, 2009: 112). Less frequently, they become involved in regulatory schemes themselves, such as WWF in the Forest Stewardship Council (FSC) (Cashore et al. 2003: 227; Bartley 2003: 453).

Governments can be involved by producing a 'shadow of hierarchy' by threatening to introduce statutory regulation; they can design programmes in which firms can participate or they can act as midwife to the birth of voluntary schemes, as the US Clinton administration did in 1996 with the Fair Labor Association (FLA), a non-profit monitoring and certification agency for the apparel industry (Everett et al. 2008: 119; Marx 2008: 254).

Whereas both NGOs and governments may be involved but do not have to be, businesses always play a role. A useful distinction has been made by Flohr et al. (2010), who see business actors either as 'norm consumers', who comply with already existing (voluntary) norms, or as 'norm entrepreneurs', who help develop such norms. Representatives of individual firms or businesses may play a different role from representatives of branch associations or committees in which high-ranking managers represent more general business interests.

In characterizing the regulatory structure of voluntary approaches we can distinguish individual and collective schemes. Individual schemes are developed for use in specific companies and are thus one-level instruments. Most voluntary regulations are collective in nature and are thus two-level instruments: they may be designed by a governmental body (level one) and then offered to companies that may choose to participate (level two). Alternatively, they may be negotiated between government actors and business associations as representatives of their firms (level one); firms are then obliged to participate and associations have to secure compliance (level two).

### 36.1.4   Linking VAR to Compulsory Regulation

On an orthodox reading, voluntary regulation and statutory regulation exclude each other and are thus seen as alternatives. Yet, even if voluntary regulation is chosen, the relationship between them is complex (Kirton and Trebilcock 2004: 11, 24; Levi-Faur, Chapter 1). First, the emergence of voluntary approaches is generally dependent on the existence of either the *shadow of the market* or the *shadow of hierarchy* – the latter meaning a threatened compulsory regulation that would come into force if no voluntary regulation was adopted. Second, particularly in the international context it can be the *failure* to enact international law that makes political players like governments or NGOs choose voluntary approaches as second-best solutions (Bartley 2003; Kirton and Trebilcock 2004: 25).

It is important to examine voluntary approaches in a broader time context, for instance by constructing regulatory courses over time. Such courses rarely start with legal regulation being replaced by voluntary regulation (Baggott 1986: 64; OECD 2003: 118ff.). More often, regulatory courses start with voluntary approaches and eventually end with statutory regulation (Kirton and Trebilcock 2004: 12; Töller 2011). This does not necessarily mean, however, that the voluntary regulation was replaced because it failed, as is often claimed in the literature. Admittedly, there are such cases (Töller 2009: 306; Hey 2010). But there are also cases of highly successful voluntary regulation being replaced by legal regulation, as in the case of voluntary termination of the use of dangerous substances such as asbestos in Germany in the 1980s (Töller 2011). Many voluntary schemes in EU member states have been replaced by statutes because European Union directives required binding laws to be enacted (Baggott 1986: 65; Töller 2011). This is true of, for example, the regulation of chemicals (Schneider and Ronit 1999).

Finally, voluntary and statutory regulations are combined in many ways. The result is hybrid regulation, in several forms. Purely voluntary regulation or self-regulation, in fact, is very uncommon (Gunningham and Rees 1997: 365, 397). One option is conditionality, under which companies (either individually or collectively) can obtain relief from statutory obligations on condition that they voluntarily agree to perform certain duties. This is common in the field of environmental agreements, including in the Netherlands and Japan (Delmas and Terlaak 2002: 17; OECD 2003: 36). Other combinations of voluntary and statutory regulation occur with taxes or charges, for instance in Denmark, the UK, and Australia (OECD 2003: 31ff.).

Another way of combining voluntary and statutory regulation is complementarity. Germany provides a number of examples of this, such as the voluntary agreement on the termination of nuclear energy: whereas the core limitation on the operation of nuclear power plants was regulated on a voluntary basis, the ban on building new plants had to be regulated by law (Töller 2011). In the field of corporate governance in the UK, compliance with the Combined Code is voluntary, but listed companies are legally obliged to make a statement once a year on whether and how far they comply with the code ('comply-or-explain'; see Cadbury 2006). Private rules can also be combined with other private rules. For instance, the London Stock Exchange makes compliance with the aforementioned Combined Code a condition for listing companies at the exchange (Cadbury 2006).

## 36.2  CAUSES

What is striking about the literature on VAR is that contributions tend either to be descriptive or to deal with questions of success or failure while remaining uninterested in *why* VAR are being used. If they are interested, they mostly work with implicit assumptions rather than systematically testing different hypotheses (but see Bartley 2003, 2009; Marx 2008; Töller 2011). But how to explain the use of VAR? I argue that broader institutional approaches are best able to explain why voluntary regulation is used.

### 36.2.1  Power-Centred Explanations

Proceeding from the Olsonian wisdom that specific interests are easier to integrate, organize, and represent than diffuse interests (Olson 1965), one mainstream argument is that globalization has intensified the inequality in power between business and collective interests. Business has become more powerful vis-à-vis the regulatory state because, with globalization, it can credibly threaten to relocate its productive activities elsewhere (Greer and Bruno 1996: 21). 'Whether real or not, the perception of mobility of firms and capital has limited the range of policy instruments used by governments' (Peters 2002: 558f.). From this perspective, voluntary regulation is the result of successful rent-seeking, particularly by transnational corporations. It aims to avert serious statutory regulation and only gives the appearance of regulation, while individual businesses can continue their activities impairing the collective good. Thus voluntary approaches serve business interests by 'greenwashing' their activities, that is, by giving 'an organization the appearance of ethicality and leadership when no such commitment exists' (Laufer 2003: 257) and without seriously having to change their practices (Greer and Bruno 1996: 31; Gunningham and Rees 1997: 370; Beder 2002: 99; OECD 2003: 43).

With a less antagonistic view of the world, the debate on corporate social or environmental responsibility (CSR/CER) addresses voluntary regulation. Coming from the field of management, this approach emphasizes that, with the increasing vulnerability of firms' reputations in times of globalization (Kirton and Trebilcock 2004: 25), business itself takes initiatives, trying to become 'part of the solution rather than part of the problem' (Gunningham 2009: 215). CSR predominantly identifies a change of attitude within corporations: they broaden their focus from profit-maximizing to accommodating the needs and interests of stakeholders other than shareholders, such as employees, the neighbouring community, and the environment. Corporations accept responsibility for the collective good and overcome the alleged conflict between the economy and the environment or other collective goods, for example by acknowledging the innovative potential and thus the competitive advantage that certain forms of regulation can deliver in the long run (Gunningham 2009: 218).

### 36.2.2　The Better-Regulation Explanation

In contrast, the better-regulation hypothesis draws on the entire corpus of criticism with regard to the many deficiencies of traditional regulatory policy instruments. Regulatory law is intrinsically inflexible and simple, and it requires complete information, which the government does not have or which does not (yet) even exist (Black 2001: 107). The law is unable to meet all the specific requirements in regulated firms, is based on an antagonistic relationship between business and government, and is unable to positively motivate its addressees. In addition, society is far too complex and too idiosyncratic to be purposefully influenced by such simple instruments (Black 2001: 106). From this standpoint, it is especially new policy objectives, such as the pursuit of innovation or sustainability, that require new instruments, which can be adopted more quickly, are more flexible, less antagonistic, and less costly, and allow for the use of regulatory knowledge on the part of the regulated or even for collective learning (Gunningham and Rees 1997: 366; de Bruijn and Norberg-Bohm 2005; Hofman and Schrama 2005: 42). In this context, many authors implicitly or explicitly argue in a functionalistic fashion that the advantages of VAR over statutory regulation *explain* their use.[1] Parallel arguments can be found with regard to transnational VAR (Kirton and Trebilcock 2004: 5).

The problem with these approaches is that they all appear plausible in some respects, but they look at the phenomenon from only one side and do not reflect an adequately complex concept of politics. Politics is not about interests automatically producing outcomes or about business players deliberating on how to save the world, nor is it a purely rational process of benevolent government actors solving problems. The better-regulation explanation exaggerates the shortcomings of traditional policy instruments and ignores the fact that these shortcomings do not automatically bring new instruments into being. Rather, multiple path dependencies need to be overcome. The CSR debate disregards differences between countries and cultures. While in the US the debate on CSR may have significantly changed corporate policies, in Europe we witness the opposite development: the corporate responsibility for employees, the environment, and neighbouring communities that has to a certain extent been enshrined in 'Rhenish capitalism' is being replaced by a strong focus on shareholder value (Streeck and Höpner 2003).

### 36.2.3　Institutional Explanations

In line with Kiser and Ostrom (1983), I argue here that three factors above all may have a causal impact on the use of VAR as policy tools: policy problems, actors, and institutions.

Policy problems as such do not produce regulation, nor is regulation a direct response to them, yet we can observe that VAR dealing with specific policy problems are mostly about curtailing the negative externalities of business (see Gunningham and Rees 1997: 365). VAR are partly related to globalization in regulating externalities that have emerged or intensified because of the international division of labour and international trade (Cashore et al. 2003: 236; Everett et al. 2008: 118); the shipping industry provides an example (DeSombre 2009: 133). At the same time globalization raises Western consumers' awareness of the interrelations between the goods they consume and working and environmental conditions in developing countries (Rhone et al. 2004: 210; Levi-Faur 2005: 17). Yet some of the problems that are addressed by VAR are unrelated to globalization. VAR aim at curtailing the external effects of capitalism in the widest sense, for example traditional or new forms of environmental damage, the endangering of children and youth by the media, the damage to health systems perpetrated by the problematic practices of pharmaceutical industries, and so on.

When asking what motivates actors to opt for VAR, we have to keep in mind the aforementioned distinction between business actors, state actors, and NGOs. To consider business actors first, one could claim that it is either the shadow of the market, such as the threat of boycotts (Gunningham and Rees 1997: 391; Kirton and Trebilcock 2004: 25), or the shadow of the state that motivates them to submit to voluntary regulation (see Marx 2008: 257). In this context Stigler, Porter, and others have argued that firms may be interested in being regulated because regulation can protect market shares and so on (Porter 1990). Yet the kinds of regulation we deal with here are costly if they are taken seriously. Thus I would argue that firms accept these costs only if they fear either higher costs arising from legal regulation or the loss of market shares.

At first glance, the shadow of hierarchy can become effective only where there is a state or a similar policymaking entity: 'it is the fear of government regulation that drives the large majority of self-regulatory initiatives' (Gunningham and Rees 1997: 400; Töller 2011). Yet even in the transnational context overall regulatory developments can bring about such a threat, as for example in the case of Responsible Care (Gunningham and Rees 1997: 397). Whether and how much the shadow of the market plays a role depends on the characteristics of firms (for example, whether they are listed on the stock exchange and produce a global 'brand'; see Marx 2008), the market, and the role of NGOs in raising consumer awareness or even organizing consumer boycotts (Marx 2008: 257).

If in national contexts NGOs seem to be sceptical about VAR (Böcher and Töller 2007), in the transnational context the lack or failure of intergovernmental rule-making has made them turn to voluntary regulation.

Even though neo-institutionalism has been emphasizing for more than 20 years the role of institutions not only in organizing what actors can do but also in influencing what they think and want (Hall and Taylor 1996), institutional aspects have so far been the wallflowers among the explanations of VAR – wrongly, since institutions play a major role.

If we want to explain the different use of voluntary approaches on the national level, institutional differences regarding legal traditions or patterns of state–society interaction come to the fore (OECD 1998: 2). If we want to know why VAR have increased in some fields, institutions again play a major explanatory role. International organizations in particular can trigger VAR, both if the regulation succeeds and if it fails. On the one hand, the failure of regulation in the intergovernmental context motivates NGOs and (in part) also governments to curb their aspirations for regulation from international institutions and to consider the option of voluntary regulation. This played a significant role in the field of labour regulation, where the failure to adopt a regulation in the context of the International Labour Organization (ILO) and the GATT in the mid-1990s prompted actors to address the issue in a voluntary context (Bartley 2003; Kirton and Trebilcock 2004: 4). Equally, the protection of forests was one of the most contested issues at the UN Earth Summit in Rio de Janeiro in 1992, and the attempt to adopt a forest convention failed. As Bartley argues, this motivated NGOs in particular to take the private road to regulation.

On the other hand, institutional factors can work in exactly the opposite way. In several instances VAR have been chosen not as second-best solutions but *because* they have no formal legal character (Kirton and Trebilcock 2004: 10). This was the case with governments opting for voluntary forest certification *because* import restrictions would have been in conflict with the WTO's free trade rules (Bartley 2003: 447), with the German government choosing voluntary approaches to environmental regulation *because* VAR were an option to bypass the free trade norms of EC law (Töller 2011), and with the US Environment Protection Agency using voluntary approaches to bypass the institutionalized rights of powerful environmental groups (Lyon and Maxwell 2004: 186).

## 36.3   EFFECTS

The first question usually raised in discussions about VAR is whether they can ever succeed. Two reasons are given for expecting them to fail. First, they lack strong enforcement mechanisms. Second, they produce classic collective action problems: they encourage free riding because the individual firm can benefit from voluntary regulations whether or not it complies with them (Gunningham and Rees 1997: 393–6; Croci 2005: 11). Other observers, however, argue that firms will comply with VAR when they have agreed to do so (see for example Gunningham and Rees 1997: 379). Furthermore, the criteria of the success or failure of VAR are highly contested (Harrington et al. 2004: 4). Yet compliance by participants is one thing; participation rates are another in the case of programmes that companies are free to join or not. For example, in the field of worker protection the overall corporate participation rate in VAR is as low as 18 per cent of the 50 largest US corporations in apparel and footwear (Bartley 2009: 121). Forest certification demonstrates that the question of success is even more complex. The amount of certified forest has increased considerably in recent years. Yet 96 per cent of certified forest is not tropical rainforest (BAFU 2009: 177), and less than 10 per cent of the world's timber is certified (Humphreys 2009: 321). So it seems that regulation did occur, but it missed its objective – success or failure?

The criteria of success are one thing; the factors making for success are another (for example, Gunningham and Rees 1997: 383–9). Whether VAR are successful depends largely on structure. First, have the objectives been defined precisely and transparently enough to make it possible to determine clearly whether they have been attained? Second, is the implementation structure capable of carrying out its task? Firms need management structures that ensure implementation, and branch associations need a membership that is not too heterogeneous and tools with which to discipline their members (for example, naming and shaming or exclusion; Porter and Ronit 2006: 58–61). Third, has an independent monitoring system been put in place? Fourth, what happens if VAR are not complied with? It is far from self-evident that either the market or the hierarchy always reacts and 'punishes' firms that do not participate or that do participate but don't comply with the requirements. In the national context the 'state' may be unable to act. In the international context, the obvious weakness of intergovernmental institutions is both a major reason for the emergence of VAR and a challenge to their implementation. Whether the market responds to non-compliance depends, among other things, on transparency and on public interest in an issue. Thus VAR tend to be more effective if they are combined in one way or another with legal regulation (Gunningham and Rees 1997: 396).

As for effects beyond compliance, one of the benefits firms expect from following voluntary rules is the improvement of their reputation among consumers, investors, business partners, and government officials (Bartley 2009: 107). Unfortunately, this effect tends to materialize independently of whether firms really comply with the rules, which, in turn, nourishes the criticism that VAR have a tendency to 'greenwash' firms and their activities (Bartley 2003: 441). VAR may create transparency and allow for the development of markets for certified products, but they may not (Bartley 2003: 435); much depends here on the behaviour of individual consumers. In addition, the creation of VAR is not without risks. VAR can increase public awareness, as in the case of the FSC, for instance, which substantially raised awareness among the Brazilian population of sustainable forestry practices (Kirton and Trebilcock 2004: 14). They can, however, also have the effect of diverting public awareness from an issue, since after the adoption of a VAR the broader public can assume that the problem is now being taken care of. Moreover, in participating in the schemes NGOs may risk their credibility and lose their natural opposition role.[2] Another possible effect is that VAR can be a vehicle of protectionism: raising standards of workers' protection abroad by voluntary means always has the potential to diminish these countries' comparative advantage (Rhone et al. 2004: 212). Finally, as can be demonstrated in the field of workers' protection, 'having too many codes and too many enforcement regimes . . . at times leads to confused and uncoordinated implementation as well as alienation on the part of factory management and workers' (Everett et al. 2008: 138). VAR can have two more interesting effects. First, not only do voluntary approaches occur in the shadow of hierarchy, but hierarchy stands in the shadow of voluntary approaches. Policy processes that lead to voluntary regulation can have an effect on subsequent policy processes that aim at adopting a non-voluntary measure. For instance, the process of voluntary regulation of corporate governance in Germany strongly influenced the perception of what the problem was and thus influenced the statutory regulations that were adopted later to address issues such as managers' allowances (Töller 2009). Similarly, in the transnational context, the chemical industry's classification of substances and safety data sheets that were developed in a voluntary context were later integrated into EU regulation (Schneider and Ronit 1999). Second, as a number of authors have emphasized, policy instruments are never neutral tools for achieving political objectives (Böcher and Töller 2007; Lascoumes and Le Gales 2007). Rather, instruments may become ends in themselves for ideological or other reasons, as the 'diffusion' of certification schemes for wood products demonstrates.

## 36.4    CONCLUSION

Whereas some authors see VAR primarily as a response to 'regulatory overload' (Gunningham and Rees 1997: 363) and thus as a form of deregulation, examining VAR in their context demonstrates that they in fact form part of an overall development of *increasing*, but stepwise and often hybrid kinds of, regulation.

Yet there is truth in the criticism that VAR tend to affect the system they regulate only on the surface (see for example Bartley 2009: 128). In this vein, an observer recently challenged the entire voluntary approach to regulating the field of consumer protection, asserting that 'there is no right way of consuming in a wrong economic system' (Hartmann 2009). Yet we would not expect *statutory* approaches to regulation to transform the entire capitalist system, would we?

Voluntary approaches are neither mere PR tools to 'greenwash' inherently harmful activities nor silver bullets in dealing with the negative externalities of capitalist production in general and its globalized version in particular. Both their emergence and their implementation are always highly dependent on a shadow either of hierarchy or of the market. They may fulfil an educational function in helping to create or raise public awareness about a problem, but they also run the risk of neutralizing an issue by creating the illusion that something is being done about it. However, empirical studies in a broad range of fields have yielded little evidence that business becomes involved in voluntary approaches with the purely strategic intention of not ultimately complying. Yet compliance is a complex organizational challenge which is easier to meet if the objectives of VAR are not too complicated and are roughly in line with business interests, if the market reacts positively to such regulation, and if monitoring and sanctions can be assured.

## ACKNOWLEDGEMENTS

I would like to thank Renate Reiter, Sandra Schwindenhammer, and David Levi-Faur for their very helpful comments on an earlier version of this chapter.

## NOTES

1. Unsurprisingly these authors tend to see VAR as innovative and positive (de Bruijn and Norberg-Bohm 2005: 380).
2. Certainly, NGOs always have the choice between exit and voice. One case in point is the German environmental group Robin Wood, which in the spring of 2009 left FSC International, protesting against the application of criteria favouring monocultures in developing countries.

## REFERENCES

BAFU (Bundesamt für Umwelt) (2009), *Jahrbuch Wald und Holz 2008,* available at: http://www.bafu.admin. ch/publikationen/publikation/01023/index.html?lang=de (accessed 1 June 2010).
Baggott, Rob (1986), 'By voluntary agreement: the politics of instrument selection', *Public Administration*, **64**, 51–67.
Bartley, Tim (2003), 'Certifying forests and factories: states, social movements, and the rise of private regulation in the apparel and forest products fields', *Politics and Society*, **31** (3), 433–64.
Bartley, Tim (2009), 'Standards for sweatshops: the power and limits of the club approach to voluntary labor standards', in Matthew Potoski and Aseem Prakash (eds), *Voluntary Programs: A Club Theory Perspective*, Cambridge, MA: MIT Press, pp. 107–31.

Beder, Sharon (2002), *Global Spin: The Corporate Assault on Environmentalism*, rev. edn, White River Junction, VT: Chelsea Green Publishing.

Black, Julia (2001), 'Decentring regulation: understanding the role of regulation and self-regulation in a "post-regulatory world"', *Current Legal Problems*, **54**, 103–46.

Böcher, Michael and Annette E. Töller (2007), 'Instrumentenwahl und Instrumentenwandel in der Umweltpolitik: Ein theoretischer Erklärungsrahmen', in Jacob Klaus, Frank Biermann, Per-Olof Busch and Peter H. Feindt (eds), *PVS-Sonderheft Politik und Umwelt*, Wiesbaden: VS Verlag, pp. 299–322.

Cadbury, Adrian (2006), 'The rise of corporate governance', in Marc J. Epstein and Kirk O. Hanson (eds), *The Accountable Corporation, vol. 1 Corporate Governance*, London: Praeger, pp. 15–43.

Cashore, Benjamin, G. Auld and D. Newson (2003), 'Forest certification (eco-labeling) programs and their policy-making authority: explaining divergence among North American and European case studies', *Forest Policy and Economics*, **5**, 225–47.

Coleman, William D. (1994), 'Keeping the shotgun behind the door: governing the securities industry in Canada, the United Kingdom, and the United States', in Joseph Rogers Hollingsworth (ed.), *Governing Capitalist Economies: Performance and Control of Economic Sectors*, New York: Oxford University Press, pp. 244–69.

Croci, Edoardo (2005), 'The economics of environmental voluntary agreements', in Edoardo Croci (ed.), *The Handbook of Environmental Voluntary Agreements: Design, Implementation and Evaluation Issues*, Dordrecht: Springer, pp. 3–30.

De Bruijn, Theo and Vicki Norberg-Bohm (2005), 'Introduction', in Theo de Bruijn and Vicki Norberg-Bohm (eds), *Industrial Transformation: Environmental Policy Innovation in the United States and Europe*, Cambridge and London: MIT Press, pp. 1–35.

Delmas, Magali A. and Ann K. Terlaak (2002), 'Regulatory commitment to negotiated agreements: evidence from the United States, Germany, The Netherlands, and France', *Journal of Comparative Policy Analysis*, **4** (1), 5–29.

Delmas, Magali and Ivan Montiel (2008), 'The diffusion of voluntary international management standards: Responsible Care, ISO 9000, and ISO 14001 in the chemical industry', *Policy Studies Journal*, **36** (1), 65–93.

DeSombre, Elizabeth R. (2009), 'Voluntary agreements in the shipping industry', in Matthew Potoski and Aseem Prakash (eds), *Voluntary Programs: A Club Theory Perspective*, Cambridge, MA: MIT Press, pp. 133–55.

Everett, Jeff S., D. Neu and D. Martinez (2008), 'Multi-stakeholder labour monitoring organizations: egoists, instrumentalists, or moralists?', *Journal of Business Ethics*, **81** (1), 117–42.

Flohr, Annegret, L. Rieth, S. Schwindenhammer and K.D. Wolf (2010), *The Role of Business in Global Governance: Corporations as Norm-Entrepreneurs*, Houndmills: Palgrave Macmillan.

Grande, David (2009), 'Limiting the influence of pharmaceutical industry gifts on physicians: self-regulation or government intervention?', *Journal of General Internal Medicine*, **25** (1), 79–83.

Greer, Jed and Kenny Bruno (1996), *Greenwash: The Reality behind Corporate Environmentalism*, Penang: Apex Press.

Gunningham, Neil (2009), 'Shaping corporate environmental performance: a review', *Environmental Policy and Governance*, **19**, 215–31.

Gunningham, Neil and Joseph Rees (1997), 'Industry self-regulation: an institutional perspective', *Law and Policy*, **19** (4), 363–414.

Hall, Peter A. and Rosemary C.R. Taylor (1996), 'Political science and the three new institutionalisms', *Political Studies*, **44** (5), 936–57.

Harrington, Winston, R.D. Morgenstern, T. Sterner and J.C. (Terry) Davies (2004), 'Lessons from the case studies', in Winston Harrington, R.D. Morgenstern and T. Sterner (eds), *Choosing Environmental Policy: Comparing Instruments and Outcomes in the United States and Europe*, Washington, DC: Resources for the Future, pp. 240–70.

Hartmann, Kathrin (2009), 'Gratisgut. Und beginnt die Veränderung schon beim Einkaufen?', *Süddeutsche Zeitung*, 29 January, p. 11.

Hemphill, Thomas (2006), 'Physicians and the pharmaceutical industry: a reappraisal of marketing codes of conduct', *Business and Society Review*, **111** (3), 323–36.

Hey, Christian (2010), 'The German paradox: climate leader and green car laggard', in Sebastian Oberthür and Marc Pallemaerts (eds), *The Climate Policies of the European Union: Internal Legislation and Climate Diplomacy*, Brussels: VUB University Press, pp. 211–30.

Hofman, Peter S. and Geerten J.I. Schrama (2005), 'Dutch target group policy', in Theo de Bruijn and Vicki Norberg-Bohm (eds), *Industrial Transformation: Environmental Policy Innovation in the United States and Europe*, Cambridge and London: MIT Press, pp. 39–63.

Humphreys, David (2009), 'Discourse as ideology: neoliberalism and the limits of international forest policy', *Forest Policy and Economics*, **11**, 319–25.

Kirton, John J. and Michael J. Trebilcock (2004), 'Introduction: hard choices and soft law in sustainable global governance', in John J. Kirton and Konrad von Moltke (eds), *Hard Choices, Soft Law: Voluntary Standards in Global Trade, Environment and Social Governance*, Burlington, VT: Ashgate Publishing, pp. 3–29.

Kiser, Larry L. and Elinor Ostrom (1983), 'The three worlds of action: a metatheoretical synthesis of institutional approaches', in Elinor Ostrom (ed.), *Strategies of Political Inquiry*, Beverly Hills, CA and London: Sage Publications, pp. 179–222.

Lascoumes, Pierre and Patrick Le Gales (2007), 'Introduction: understanding public policy through its instruments – from the nature of instruments to the sociology of public policy instrumentation', *Governance*, **20** (1), 1–21.

Laufer, William (2003), 'Social accountability and corporate greenwashing', *Journal of Business Ethics*, **43** (3), 253–61.

Levi-Faur, David (2005), 'The global diffusion of regulatory capitalism', *Annals of the American Academy*, **598**, 12–32.

Lyon, Thomas P. and John W. Maxwell (2004), *Corporate Environmentalism and Public Policy*, Cambridge: Cambridge University Press.

Marx, Axel (2008), 'Limits to non-state market regulation: a qualitative comparative analysis of the international sport footwear industry and the Fair Labour Association', *Regulation & Governance*, **2**, 253–73.

Nash, Jennifer and John R. Ehrenfeld (2001), 'Factors that shape EMS outcomes of firms', in Cary Coglianese and Jennifer Nash (eds), *Regulating from the Inside: Can Environmental Management Systems Achieve Policy Goals?*, Washington: RFF Press, pp. 61–81.

OECD (Organisation for Economic Co-operation and Development) (1998), *The Use of Voluntary Agreements in the United States: An Initial Survey*, Paris: OECD.

OECD (2003), *Voluntary Approaches for Environmental Policy: Effectiveness, Efficiency and Usage in Policy Mixes*, Paris: OECD Publication Service.

Olson, Mancur, Jr. (1965), *The Logic of Collective Action: Public Goods and the Theory of Groups*, Cambridge, MA: Harvard University Press.

Peters, Guy B. (2002), 'The politics of tool choice', in Lester M. Salamon (ed.), *The Tools of Government: A Guide to the New Governance*, Oxford: Oxford University Press, pp. 552–64.

Porter, Michael E. (1990), 'The competitive advantage of nations', *Harvard Business Review*, **68** (2), 73–93.

Porter, Tony and Karsten Ronit (2006), 'Self-regulation as policy process: the multiple and criss-crossing stages of private rule-making', *Policy Sciences*, **39**, 41–72.

Potoski, Matthew and Aseem Prakash (eds) (2009), *Voluntary Programs: A Club Theory Perspective*, Cambridge, MA: MIT Press.

Rhone, Gregory, J. Stroud and K. Webb (2004), 'Gap Inc.'s code of conduct for treatment of overseas workers', in Kernaghan Webb (ed.), *Voluntary Codes: Private Governance, the Public Interest and Innovation*, Ottawa: Carleton Research Unit for Innovation, Science and Environment, pp. 209–26.

Schneider, Volker and Karsten Ronit (1999), 'Global governance through private organizations', *Governance*, **12** (3), 243–66.

Streeck, Wolfgang and Martin Höpner (2003), 'Einleitung: Alle Macht dem Markt?', in Wolfgang Streeck and Martin Höpner (eds), *Alle Macht dem Markt? Fallstudien zur Abwicklung des Deutschland AG*, Frankfurt am Main: Campus Verlag, pp. 11–59.

Töller, Annette Elisabeth (2008), 'Kooperation als Trend? Verwendungsmuster und Ursachen kooperativer Politikformen in den Niederlanden, Deutschland und den USA', *Zeitschrift für Vergleichende Politikwissenschaft*, **2**, 315–46.

Töller, Annette Elisabeth (2009), 'Freiwillige Regulierung zwischen Staat und Markt: Der Deutsche Corporate Governance-Kodex (DCGK)', *Der Moderne Staat*, **2** (2), 293–313.

Töller, Annette Elisabeth (2011), *Warum kooperiert der Staat? Kooperative Umweltpolitik im Schatten der Hierarchie*, Baden-Baden: Nomos.

# PART X

# REGULATORY GOVERNANCE IN THE EUROPEAN UNION

# 37 European regulatory governance
*Sandra Eckert*

## 37.1 INTRODUCTION

Regulatory governance within the European Union (EU) has become a topical issue ever since Majone first introduced the notion of a 'regulatory state' (Majone 1994) in the mid-1990s. It points to a specific situation at EU level where a restrictive budget forecloses comprehensive measures of (re)distribution. Instead, there has been a significant expansion of supranational rule-making over time (Majone 1994; Thatcher 2001: 304; Kohler-Koch et al. 2004). The scope of centralized, supranational rule-making capacity however remains limited in the multi-level governance system of the EU, where supranational and national public actors as well as private actors engage in the formulation and implementation of rules.

This chapter analyses regulation within the EU, combining concepts of a rather EU-centred literature on governance and broader discussions in political science research on regulation. The declared objective will be to capture the structure and actor constellations characterizing European regulatory governance rather than assessing its policy impact. Regulation is understood as being distinct from both legislation and judicial rule-making. To account for the fact that regulation takes place at different territorial levels of governance and involves a variety of actors, I will distinguish between three modes of regulatory governance for both levels and actors: centralized regulation, multi-level regulation and national regulation on the one hand; and public regulation, co-regulation and self-regulation on the other hand. Section 37.2 defines and discusses these concepts and develops a framework for analysis. Section 37.3 looks at regulatory governance in policy areas where the EU has developed considerable rule-making capacity. In so doing the chapter tackles the following questions: Which modes of regulation are predominant? How do they evolve over time and how are they interrelated?

## 37.2 CONCEPTUALIZING REGULATORY GOVERNANCE

This conceptual part defines key notions and develops a framework for analysis. I will first provide a definition of 'regulation' which deviates from a generic use of the term in most of the literature on European regulatory governance. Then I go on to set out six modes of regulation which allow for an analytical distinction between both different levels of regulation and different actor constellations. Finally, I will formulate expectations about how different modes of regulation may combine and evolve over time.

### 37.2.1 Defining Regulation

*Regulation* is a multi-faceted notion which has been defined in a myriad of ways. For the purposes of this chapter the definition suggested by David Levi-Faur (Levi-Faur 2011: 6) is most suitable: regulation is about prescriptive rules and encompasses several phases of the policy cycle, such as formulation, implementation and enforcement; it excludes those rules which are formulated directly by the legislature or the judiciary. Regulation is thus the product of rule-making by non-elected bodies, setting aside the special case of courts, and private actors. Administrative and bureaucratic actors engaging in regulation have public authority in a concise area of regulatory activity, although they are not directly elected by the people or managed by elected officials. Such delegated governance materializes in different forms, varying in terms of the public–private distinction and the level of organizational autonomy (Flinders 2008: 5). Alongside public institutions, semi-private and private actors may be endowed with regulatory tasks. Thus the chosen definition of regulation shifts the focus of analysis away from state actors and towards non-state and private actors. This is why in comparison to the notion of a 'regulatory state' the one of a 'regulatory capitalism' (Levi-Faur 2005) appears more adequate to capture the full governance continuum.

Paradoxically, the 'regulatory state' hypothesis (Majone 1994), which has been of central importance in describing the emerging European order (as critically discussed by Finger 2011), relies on a wider rather than a narrower understanding of regulation. In line with the typology established by Lowi (1964) the notion of the regulatory state has been used to describe all types of rule-setting by all types of actors which do not involve a (re) distribution of resources (Héritier 1987: 39). Such an encompassing use of the term has allowed scholars to capture the multiple aspects of regulatory expansion at the European level and across levels. At the same time the lack of a concise definition has made it difficult to confine the boundaries of research on EU regulatory governance (Lodge 2008: 269). Narrowing down the notion of regulation does not mean that the rule-making capacity of the legislature and the judiciary, which indeed has significantly contributed to regulatory expansion in the EU, will as such be excluded from analysis. Rather, the definition should help in focusing on the empirical core of regulatory governance which derives from rule-making by EU and national officials, agency staff and private actors.

### 37.2.2 Modes of Regulation

In order to take into account variation in levels of regulation as well as in actor constellations, it is useful to differentiate three modes of regulation each time. These modes are analytically distinct, but in reality may often overlap or combine. Focusing on the allocation of competencies across levels, I will distinguish centralized regulation, where supranational actors hold direct rule-setting capacity, from multi-level regulation, where public authority is spread across levels of governance (Levi-Faur 2011: 11) and national regulation, where rule-making capacity resides exclusively at member state level. In areas where centralization is strongly developed, supranational actors are in a position to directly devise and enforce rules. Here the predominant mode of action is hierarchy (Börzel 2010: 198–200). Given that EU legislation can be formulated only as a result of successfully conducted negotiation, it most of the time introduces multi-level regulatory

*Figure 37.1   Regulation – at which level?*

*Figure 37.2   Regulation – by whom?*

frameworks where the formulation of more detailed rules and/or their implementation is delegated to lower levels of governance. Also, areas which are of vital national interest may be completely left within the realm of national regulation.

Focusing on the allocation of competencies between public and private actors, a basic distinction can be made between public regulation, where solely public actors are involved in rule-making, co-regulation, where public and private actors share rule-making capacity, and self-regulation, where solely private actors engage in rule-setting.[1] Public regulation outside the legislature and judiciary is produced by administrative and bureaucratic bodies such as ministerial departments, executive agencies, non-ministerial departments, non-departmental bodies or central banks. Scholars and practitioners interested in their role and activity have been very creative in denominating them (Chester 1979), using terms such as 'non-majoritarian institutions' (e.g. Thatcher and Stone Sweet 2002), 'para-statal bodies', 'extra-governmental organisations' or 'quangos' (Barker 1982). Co-regulation constitutes a middle course where rules or policy objectives are being defined by a public authority, but are being complemented with regulatory detail, and also implemented by private actors. Such arrangements, which are thus characterized by joint decision-making with public actors, have also been coined 'regulated self-regulation', 'delegated self-regulation' (Ronit and Schneider 2000: 23) or 'negotiated agreements' (OECD 1999: 18). While a co-regulatory arrangement is characterized by shared responsibility, self-regulatory arrangements are instances of 'first-party regulation' or 'meta-regulation' where regulator and regulatee coincide (Levi-Faur 2011: 8, 11). Under pure self-regulation, private organizations devise and manage their own rules without outside interference. Alternative terms which have been used to describe such arrangements are for instance 'autonomous and voluntary regulation' (Ronit and Schneider 2000: 23) or 'unilateral commitment' (OECD 1999: 16). Since it is often difficult to draw the borderline between co- and self-regulation in dynamic governance arrangements, some authors have suggested adding an intermediate category such as for example 'enforced self-regulation' (Levi-Faur 2011: 10).

### 37.2.3   Governance Mix and Evolution

Different modes of regulation will not exist in isolation, but most of the time will combine as a governance mix with manifold effects of interaction. Owing to the high

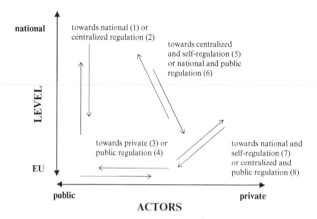

*Figure 37.3    Regulation – how does it evolve?*

capacity requirements for hierarchical steering, the scope of centralized regulation will necessarily be limited and notably will not embrace all phases of the policy cycle. Multi-level regulation is thus very likely to combine with centralized regulation in many instances, notably where implementation tasks are being delegated to lower levels of territorial governance. Regulatory powers and implementation tasks may further also be delegated to the regulatees. Thus co- or self-regulatory arrangements may combine with centralized regulation, especially in sectors where regulatory design and/or enforcement involve a high level of complexity or uncertainty. Even where there is no obvious or formal link between modes of regulation, these do not merely coexist. Rather, important effects of interaction can be expected. The possibility of centralized rule-making arrangements casting a 'shadow of hierarchy' (Scharpf 1993: 67) on less centralized modes has been widely discussed in the literature on EU governance (e.g. Héritier and Lehmkuhl 2008; Börzel 2010). The underlying assumption is that the mere possibility of hierarchical intervention will significantly alter actor behaviour. Thus a credible threat to engage in centralized regulation may change the way in which multi-level regulation and national regulation, as well as co-regulation and self-regulation, are being executed.

Over time different patterns of interaction and evolution can be expected: there may be tendencies towards either centralization or decentralization, or hybrid solutions resulting in complex governance structures; actor-wise there may be empowerment of private or public actors, respectively, with trends such as agencification, emergence of network governance or the promotion of voluntary approaches. Thus the evolution of regulatory modes may go in all possible directions. Combining levels of regulation and actor constellations, eight different trends of evolution may be discerned, as indicated in Figure 37.3.

## 37.3  REGULATORY GOVERNANCE IN THE EU

Analysing regulatory governance in the EU, I will first address the spread of regulation across levels of governance, and then go on to examine relevant actor constellations.

Finally, I will discuss dynamics over time and pose the question of whether there is a general trend of evolution. Within the scope of this chapter the empirical examples will only allow the drawing of a general picture, which by necessity will remain incomplete. Since it will not be possible to address all fields of policy-making in the EU, the focus is on areas where regulatory governance plays a particularly prominent role.[2]

### 37.3.1 European Regulation – at Which Level?

This question touches upon the key challenge to reconcile regulatory expansion at the supranational level with opposition and reservations to a further loss in policy-making capacity at the national level. The degree of centralization varies substantially. The EU has exclusive competence in the field of customs union, competition rules in the internal market, monetary policy, specific areas of fishery and the common commercial policy, as specified in article 3 of the Treaty on the Functioning of the European Union (TFEU). Shared competence applies to a number of policy fields such as for example the internal market, energy policy, environment, or justice and home affairs (article 4 TFEU). In the realm of economic and employment policies there is merely coordination (article 5 TFEU), while in other areas the EU may support or complement national policies such as in culture or tourism (article 6 TFEU).

The regulatory landscape reflects this uneven allocation of powers. Centralized regulation by supranational bureaucratic bodies is most developed in the area of the Economic and Monetary Union (EMU), in European competition policy where the Commission acts as a regulator (Groenleer 2011) and in specific policy areas through EU-level agencies. Monetary rule-setting has been delegated to the European Central Bank (ECB). The ECB enjoys a degree of statutory independence which stands out in comparison to national central banks elsewhere. The bank is an EU institution (article 13 TFEU) with a legal personality in its own right. Its statutes form part of the treaties and may thus only be revised following member state agreement and the usual process of ratification. The ECB is subject to fewer checks and balances than the Commission, and the European Parliament's role in monetary policy is minor in comparison to other areas (Hodson 2010: 168). The European Commission's Directorate General (DG) Competition has direct rule-setting capacity in its role as the European competition authority (for an overview see Cini and McGowan 1998; Wilks 2010). DG Competition can conduct investigations, impose sanctions and take legal recourse to the European Court of Justice when suspecting distortions of competition caused by cartelization (article 101 TFEU), abuse of a dominant position (article 102 TFEU) or state aid (articles 107, 108 TFEU). In the case of public undertakings the Commission is even mandated (article 106.3 TFEU) to single-handedly adopt directives or decisions where national policies are considered to constitute a significant impediment to the realization of the internal market. The European competition law regime exhibits key features of what Majone has described as the regulatory state (Wilks 2005: 134–5): treaty-based competencies are specified through regulations and decisions supplemented by a whole array of soft law, and compliance costs are completely borne by courts, national legal systems and firms so that they do not affect the Community budget. EU-level agencies have centralized regulatory capacity in a few specific areas and sectors (see also Cardwell 2011; Groenleer 2011). However, in view of strong member state opposition these have not been entrusted with general rule-setting capacity, but at their best can formulate decisions on individual cases (Dehousse 2008: 799). Currently there are 29 EU agencies, out of which 23 are first-pillar agencies, and 11 of these engage in regulatory tasks (for an overview see Wonka and Rittberger 2010: 15). Statutory independence is most developed in the case of the four regulatory agencies engaging in economic regulation, while the independence of agencies with tasks in social regulation varies (Wonka and Rittberger 2010: 16–17). Even where a regulatory agency exhibits a rather low degree of statutory independence, it may develop significant rule-setting capacity. This is illustrated by the example of the European Medicines Agency (EMEA), which was introduced in 2004.[3] The authorization of pharmaceuticals in practice has been agency-driven to the extent that the Commission in its proposals for the ensuing comitology procedure simply rubberstamped EMEA recommendations (Gehring et al. 2007: 240). The most recent innovation in the EU's agency landscape has been the creation of the European Chemicals Agency (ECHA), which has been operative since 1 June 2007. In the coming years at least three new agencies will start to operate in the area of energy, telecoms and securities regulation, namely the European Agency for the Cooperation of Energy Regulators (ACER, established by EC no. 713/2009), the Body of European Regulators of Electronic Communications (BEREC, established by EC no. 1221/2009) and the European Securities and Market Authority (ESMA, proposed by COM 2009 503).

Capturing variants of multi-level regulation is a more challenging endeavour. Even in those policy fields which are characterized by centralized regulation, rule-setting at lower levels of governance continues to play an important role. The European Central Bank, for instance, relies on a relatively decentralized decision-making structure which heavily involves the governors of national central banks (Hodson 2010: 168). Similarly, the enforcement of EU competition policy increasingly relies on national competition authorities (Wilks 2005: 131–4; Lehmkuhl 2008; Töller 2008: 133–6). They cooperate within the European Network of Competition Authorities (ECN), operating since 2004, which builds a bridge between central rule-setting and decentralized enforcement. Network governance involving national authorities is also a characteristic feature of the functioning of EU agencies. The scientific opinions provided by EMEA, for instance, are in fact elaborated by a network of experts from national regulators (Gehring and Krapohl 2007: 215). In some areas regulatory networks have functioned as a substitute for more centralized modes of regulation. This was the case in securities (Committee of European Securities Regulation, CESR, established in 2001), telecoms (European Regulators Group, ERG, established in 2002) and energy (European Regulators Group for Electricity and Gas, ERGEG, established in 2002), i.e. in those three sectors where the creation of supranational agencies is under way. Such multi-level arrangements will be even more relevant in areas which exhibit a weaker degree of regulatory centralization.

Finally, national regulation is a natural component of multi-level regulation where important regulatory powers remain in the realm of national authority. European legislation, especially in the form of directives, merely sets a broad regulatory framework which allows for the emergence of very different regulatory regimes across member states and sectors (e.g. Héritier and Coen 2005). The establishment and functioning of national regulatory authorities is only one element which clearly illustrates this situation: member states may seek to resist delegation to sector regulation, which was the case for Germany in energy (Eberlein 2001) and France in postal services (Eckert 2010); once introduced, national agencies vary significantly in terms of their formal and de facto independence (Gilardi 2005; Maggetti 2007; Gilardi and Maggetti 2011); post-delegation they function in very different ways and generate differential policy outcomes (Levi-Faur 1999; Thatcher 2007; Maggetti 2009; Eckert 2010).

### 37.3.2 European Regulation – by Whom?

So far the focus has been on levels of territorial governance and thus on regulation by public actors. The allocation of regulatory powers across levels however goes hand in hand with the involvement of a wider array of actors and includes private actors. As stated earlier, public regulation requires close cooperation between regulator and regulatees. The European and national central banks, DG Competition and national competition agencies, and EU and national regulatory agencies all engage in intense working relations with the firms they regulate. The question is at which stage it is adequate to speak about co-regulation. In competition policy, regulated firms normally need to comply with relevant decisions and bear possible sanctions or, if cases are settled informally, need to implement suggested remedies so as to accommodate competition law concerns. Thus here rule-setting is clearly in the hands of the competition authority. The same holds where regulatees are required to implement the rules formulated by regulatory authorities.

Co-regulation has emerged in highly complex areas of ex ante regulation, where there is a growing need to address international and cross-border issues, but where it is difficult to build up centralized capacity. Co-regulatory arrangements have played a prominent role in European environmental policy. Early examples are the European Eco-Management and Audit Scheme (EMAS), introduced in 1993 (Jordan and Wurzel 2005: 488; van Gestel 2005: 2), and the Auto Oil Programme initiated in the mid-1990s. Here industry fulfilled an expert role in the policy formulation process, to the extent that academic commentators found evidence for regulatory capture (van Calster and Deketelaere 2001: 232–3; Lenschow and Rottmann 2010: 73, 75). A more recent example is the EU's Integrated Product Policy (European Commission 2003), which materializes in sector-specific measures such as the Ecodesign Framework Directive for Energy-related products (2009/125/EC). Under this directive self-regulation may replace implementing measures if a set of criteria stipulated in the directive are fulfilled. Similarly, the new regulatory framework governing the registration, evaluation, authorization and restriction of chemicals (REACH, EC no. 1907/2006) has been described as an instance of 'regulated self-regulation' (Hey et al. 2008: 436), since it is the task of industry actors to evaluate and, in case of concern, by themselves signal risks to the public authorities. In the energy sector co-regulation has been used to bridge the gap between an increasing need to manage cross-border energy flows and the lack of centralized regulatory capacity. The third energy package therefore introduced a co-regulatory arrangement where private actors (transmission system operators) engage in detailed rule-making, in accordance with broader guidelines set out by the national regulators and under the supervision of the European Commission (EC no. 714/2009).

Self-regulation does not easily emerge at European level, since it is highly demanding in terms of the required organizational capacity of private actors and their associations. When engaging in EU-wide self-regulation, they have to bear considerable costs involved in coordinating the implementation of and compliance with voluntary rules. Nevertheless, a number of voluntary agreements have been concluded at the European level to address environmental issues (for an overview see Schnabl 2005). The European Automobile Manufacturers' Association (ACEA) agreement to reduce $CO_2$ emissions is probably the most prominent example, which has been widely discussed in the literature (van Calster and Deketelaere 2001: 228–32; Volpi and Singer 2001; Lenschow and Rottmann 2010: 76–81). Despite considerable pressure exercised by the European Commission and the ACEA hierarchy on its members, the targets set were not achieved (Lenschow and Rottmann 2010: 80). This is why self-regulation has ultimately been replaced by mandatory legislation (EC no. 2009/44). In the area of waste management, cross-sectoral comparison of EU-level industry self-regulation to implement recycling targets has illustrated that compliance may to a considerable extent be driven by positive economic incentives, while a regulatory threat may be conducive to the emergence of self-regulation, but over time may become too weak to incentivize private actors to abide by their goals (Héritier and Eckert 2008, 2009).

### 37.3.3    Trends in European Regulation

It is difficult to identify an overall trend of evolution in a governance system which is characterized by polycentricity and a dilution of powers (Dehousse 2008: 803–04). Inferring from declared political objectives, one might expect a move towards more decentralized and private regulation. The EU's strategy on 'better regulation', which was launched in the mid-1990s,[4] aims at formulating transversal strategies and setting broad regulatory frameworks rather than introducing sector- or product-specific harmonization rules. Also, co- and self-regulation have been promoted in this context, particularly in the White Paper on Governance (COM 2001 428 final), as 'better' modes of governance based on the superior expertise of private actors shaping the policy measures, and being immediate in their application, with the possibility for speedy change if need arises (European Commission 2002). As a result, one would expect that detailed regulation is increasingly being delegated, for example to standard-setting bodies, regulatory agencies or business. REACH is a prime example in this respect. Besides a 'traditional regulatory core' this new regime includes mechanisms of public risk communication, mandatory self-regulation and cooperative, decentralized procedures (Hey et al. 2008: 435–6).

Looking at actual developments in those policy fields which have been discussed throughout the chapter, the picture appears to be less clear. Today's situation within the EMU illustrates that the discrepancy between centralized regulation in some areas and multi-level and national regulation in other areas may pose difficulties. Whether the current crisis will be conducive to more centralized regulation is yet to be seen (Enderlein and Verdun 2009). In the realm of competition policy we have witnessed a trend towards decentralized implementation and soft modes (Wilks 2005: 131–4; Lehmkuhl 2008; Töller 2008: 133–6). In substance, however, these changes have been found to deepen the Europeanization of national competition law regimes (Lehmkuhl 2008: 157; Töller 2008: 134). It is probably uncontroversial that European governance has witnessed an intense process of agencification (see also Cardwell 2011; Finger 2011; Groenleer 2011). The tricky question is whether this process has been one of centralization or decentralization. The introduction of EU agencies in the early 1990s has been interpreted as a strategic move of the Commission to strengthen centralized regulation in a situation where it lacked the capacity to embrace a wider range of tasks while member states were not willing to give more powers to the supranational executive (Dehousse 1997; Kelemen 2002: 99–102). The emergence of regulatory networks has been explained in functional terms as equivalents for more centralized steering where regulatory gaps persisted (Eberlein and Grande 2005). These initially informal mechanisms have been endorsed by the Commission, resulting in a clear tendency towards formalization and centralization with the creation of a number of European regulatory networks that have a formal mandate (Thatcher and Coen 2008). New regulatory approaches such as co- and self-regulation have most widely been used in environmental policy (Lenschow 2002). Yet even there the bulk of European rules continues to originate in legislation (Jordan and Wurzel 2005: 489–90; Holzinger et al. 2006: 412). Overall the emergence of co- and self-regulatory arrangements has certainly affected the public–private relationship in EU governance, yet changes should not be overstated (Holzinger et al. 2006). Rather than replacing more centralized, hierarchical modes, these decentralized and non-hierarchical modes coexist, and are often being 'solidified' by public authority (Porter and Ronit 2006).

## 37.4   CONCLUSIONS

In order to analyse regulatory governance within the multi-level context of the EU, I have first defined regulation as being distinct from both legislation and judicial rule-making. Then I went on to conceptualize regulatory modes according to levels of governance and actor constellations: distinguishing centralized regulation, multi-level regulation and national regulation on the one hand; and public regulation, co-regulation and self-regulation on the other hand. Finally, I have discussed how different modes may combine and how they may evolve over time.

Overall European governance has an important regulatory component, i.e. non-elected as well as private actors play a key role. Yet the allocation of regulatory competence across levels varies substantially. The example of competition policy has illustrated that a rather centralized mode may witness reforms in the direction of decentralization and broader actor participation, whereas monetary policy is likely to develop towards more centralized modes. European regulatory agencies are for the most part formalized networks of national authorities rather than truly centralized, single regulators. Networks between national regulators, on the contrary, have experienced a double process of formalization and centralization so that step-by-step supranational regulatory capacity has been strengthened. Incidents of co- and self-regulation constitute another example of decentralized steering, this time with or by private actors. Here empirical research points to the fact that such arrangements mostly emerge and function in the shadow of hierarchy, i.e. they presuppose a certain degree of centralized steering.

Generally speaking the importance of centralized regulation is increasing, sustained by EU-level legislation and jurisdiction. However, the bulk of rule-making capacity lies in the realm of multi-level and co-regulation. This situation can easily be explained by the member states' concern about a vertical power shift towards the supranational level. Thanks to the 'governance turn' in EU studies (Kohler-Koch and Rittberger 2006), the scope of our analysis has been widened so as to capture the full variety of levels and actors which are at play simultaneously. There is not a single trend of evolution over time, so that different modes coexist and develop incrementally. Thus the multi-layered and polycentral structure of European regulatory governance is here to stay.

## NOTES

1. This basic distinction between three modes of actor involvement is rather generic, and a more sophisticated categorization is possible within all three modes; see for example David Levi-Faur (Chapter 1) on different variants of co- and self-regulation.
2. These are policies which traditionally formed part of the EC's first pillar, i.e. I will address neither EU activities in justice and home affairs, nor those in foreign and security issues. This is not to deny that regulation plays a role in these policy areas, which particularly holds for EU regulatory expansion in justice and home affairs (part of which has been integrated into the first pillar with the Treaty of Amsterdam).
3. The independence score of EMEA is 0.33 (going from 0.00 for zero to 1.00 for full formal independence), which places the agency on rank 9 out of a total of 29 agencies, i.e. EMEA is amongst the less independent agencies. See Wonka and Rittberger (2010: 15).
4. See the Commission's 'better regulation' agenda at: http://ec.europa.eu/governance/better_regulation (accessed 14 June 2010).

## REFERENCES

Barker, A. (1982), *Quangos in Britain*, London: Macmillan.
Börzel, T.A. (2010), 'European governance – negotiation and competition in the shadow of hierarchy', *Journal of Common Market Studies*, **48** (2), 191–219.
Cardwell, J. (2011), 'The changing nature of European regulatory governance', in D. Levi-Faur (ed.), *Handbook on the Politics of Regulation*, Cheltenham: Edward Elgar, pp. 536–47.
Chester, D.N. (1979), 'Fringe bodies, quangos and all that', *Public Administration*, **57**, (51–4).
Cini, M. and L. McGowan (1998), *Competition Policy in the European Union*, Basingstoke: Palgrave Macmillan.
Dehousse, R. (1997), 'Regulation by networks in the European Community: the role of European agencies', *Journal of European Public Policy*, **4** (2).
Dehousse, R. (2008), 'Delegation of powers in the European Union: the need for a multi-principals model', *West European Politics*, **31** (4), 789–805.
Eberlein, B. (2001), 'To regulate or not to regulate electricity: explaining the German Sonderweg in the EU context', *Journal of Network Industries*, **2**, 353–84.
Eberlein, B. and E. Grande (2005), 'Beyond delegation: transnational regulatory regimes and the EU regulatory state', *Journal of European Public Policy*, **12** (1), 89–112.
Eckert, S. (2010), 'Between commitment and control: varieties of delegation in the European postal sector', *Journal of European Public Policy*, **17** (8).
Enderlein, H. and A. Verdun (2009), 'EMU's teenage challenge: what have we learned and can we predict from political science?', *Journal of European Public Policy*, **16** (4), 490–507.
European Commission (2002), *Communication from the Commission to the European Parliament, the Council, the Economic and Social Committee and the Committee of the Regions. Environmental Agreements at Community Level. Within the Framework of the Action Plan on the Simplification and Improvement of the Regulatory Environment*, Luxembourg: Office for Official Publications of the European Communities.
European Commission (2003), *Communication from the Commission to the Council and the European Parliament. Integrated Product Policy. Building on Environmental Life-Cycle Thinking*, COM (2003) 302 final, Luxembourg: Office for Official Publications of the European Communities.
Finger, M. (2011), 'Towards a European model of regulatory governance?' in D. Levi-Faur (ed.), *Handbook on the Politics of Regulation*, Cheltenham: Edward Elgar, pp. 525–35.
Flinders, M. (2008), *Delegated Governance and the British State: Walking without Order*, Oxford: Oxford University Press.
Gehring, T. and S. Krapohl (2007), 'Supranational regulatory agencies between independence and control:

the EMEA and the authorization of pharmaceuticals in the European Single Market', *Journal of European Public Policy,* **14** (2), 208–26.

Gehring, T., A.K. Michael and S. Krapohl (2007), 'Risikoregulierung im europäischen Binnenmarkt. Regulierungsagenturen, Normungsinstrumente und Komitologie-Ausschüsse', in I. Tömmel (ed.), *Die Europäische Union: Governance und Policy-Making. Politische Vierteljahresschrift. Sonderheft 40,* Wiesbaden: Verlag für Sozialwissenschaften, pp. 231–52.

Gilardi, F. (2005), 'The institutional foundations of regulatory capitalism: the diffusion of independent regulatory agencies in Western Europe', *Annals of the American Academy of Political and Social Science,* **598,** March, 84–101.

Gilardi, F. and Maggetti, M. (2011), 'Formal and informal aspects of regulatory independence', in D. Levi-Faur (ed.), *Handbook on the Politics of Regulation,* Cheltenham: Edward Elgar, pp. 201–14.

Groenleer, M. (2011), 'Regulatory governance in the European Union: the role of committees, agencies and networks', in D. Levi-Faur (ed.), *Handbook on the Politics of Regulation,* Cheltenham: Edward Elgar, pp. 548–60.

Héritier, A. (1987), *Policy Analyse – Eine Einführung,* Frankfurt am Main and New York: Campus Verlag.

Héritier, A. and D. Coen (2005), *Refining Regulatory Regimes: Utilities in Europe,* Cheltenham, UK and Northampton, MA, USA: Edward Elgar Publishing.

Héritier, A. and S. Eckert (2008), 'New modes of governance in the shadow of hierarchy: self-regulation by industry in Europe', *Journal of Public Policy,* **28** (1), 113–38.

Héritier, A. and D. Lehmkuhl (2008), 'New modes of governance and the shadow of hierarchy: sectoral governance and territorially bound democratic government', *Journal of Public Policy,* **28** (1), special issue, 1–17.

Héritier, A. and S. Eckert (2009), 'Self-regulation by associations: a collective action problem in environmental regulation', *Business and Politics,* **11** (1).

Hey, C., K. Jacob and A. Volkery (2008), 'REACH als Beispiel für hybride Formen von Steuerung und Governance', in G.F. Schuppert and M. Zürn (eds), *Governance in einer sich wandelnden Welt. Politische Vierteljahresschrift, Sonderheft 41,* Wiesbaden: VS Verlag Sozialwissenschaften.

Hodson, D. (2010), 'Economic and monetary union', in H. Wallace, M.A. Pollack and A.R. Young (eds), *Policy-Making in the European Union,* Oxford: Oxford University Press.

Holzinger, K., C. Knill and A. Schäfer (2006), 'Rhetoric or reality? "New governance" in EU environmental policy', *European Law Journal,* **12** (3), 403–20.

Jordan, A. and R.K.W. Wurzel (2005), 'The rise of "New" policy instruments in comparative perspective: has governance eclipsed government?', *Political Studies,* **53,** 477–96.

Kelemen, D.R. (2002), 'The politics of "Eurocratic" structure and the new European agencies', *West European Politics,* **25** (4), 93–118.

Kohler-Koch, B. and B. Rittberger (2006), 'Review article: the "governance turn" in EU studies', *Journal of Common Market Studies,* **44** (1), 27–49.

Kohler-Koch, B., T. Conzelmann and M. Knodt (2004), 'Der Aufstieg der regulativen Politik', in B. Kohler-Koch, T. Conzelmann and M. Knodt (eds), *Europäische Integration – europäisches Regieren,* Wiesbaden: VS Verlag für Sozialwissenschaften, pp. 151–63.

Lehmkuhl, D. (2008), 'On Government, governance and judicial review: the shadow of European courts and the development of EC competition policy', *Journal of Public Policy,* **28** (1), 139–59.

Lenschow, A. (2002), 'New regulatory approaches in "Greening" EU policies', *European Law Journal,* **8** (1), 19–37.

Lenschow, A. and K. Rottmann (2010), 'The evolving role of industry in European Union environmental governance', in A. O'Connor (ed.), *Managing Economies, Trade and International Business,* Basingstoke: Palgrave Macmillan, pp. 67–85.

Levi-Faur, D. (1999), 'Governing the Dutch telecommunications reform: state–business interactions in the transformation of national policy regimes to (European) embedded policy regimes', *Journal of European Public Policy,* **6** (1), 102–22.

Levi-Faur, D. (2005), 'The global diffusion of regulatory capitalism ', *Annals of the American Academy of Political and Social Science,* **598** (1), 12–32.

Levi-Faur, D. (2011), 'Regulation and regulatory governance', in D. Levi-Faur (ed.), *Handbook on the Politics of Regulation,* Cheltenham: Edward Elgar, pp. 3–21.

Lodge, M. (2008), 'Regulation, the regulatory state and European politics', *West European Politics,* **31** (1), 280–301.

Lowi, T. (1964), 'American business, public policy, case-studies, and political theory', *World Politics,* **16** (4), 677–715.

Maggetti, M. (2007), 'De facto independence after delegation: a fuzzy-set analysis', *Regulation & Governance,* **1,** 271–94.

Maggetti, M. (2009), 'The role of independent regulatory agencies in policy-making: a comparative analysis', *Journal of European Public Policy,* **16** (3), 450–70.

Majone, G. (1994), 'The rise of the regulatory state in Europe', *West European Politics,* **17** (3), 77–101.

OECD (1999), *Voluntary Approaches for Environmental Policy: An Assessment,* Paris: Organisation for Economic Co-operation and Development.

Porter, T. and K. Ronit (2006), 'Self-regulation as policy process: the multiple and criss-crossing stages of private rule-making', *Policy Sciences,* **39**, 41–72.

Ronit, K. and V. Schneider (2000), *Private Organizations in Global Politics,* London and New York: Routledge.

Scharpf, F.W. (1993), *Games in Hierarchies and Networks: Analytical and Empirical Approaches to the Study of Governance Institutions,* Frankfurt am Main: Campus Verlag.

Schnabl, G. (2005), 'The evolution of environmental agreements at the level of the European Union', in E. Croci (ed.), *The Handbook of Environmental Voluntary Agreements: Design, Implementation and Evaluation Issues,* Berlin, Heidelberg and New York: Springer, pp. 93–106.

Thatcher, M. (2001), 'European regulation', in J. Richardson (ed.), *European Union: Power and Policy-Making,* London: Routledge, pp. 303–20.

Thatcher, M. (2007), 'Regulatory agencies, the state and markets: a Franco-British comparison', *Journal of European Public Policy,* **14** (7), 1028–47.

Thatcher, M. and A. Stone Sweet (2002), 'Theory and practice of delegation to non-majoritarian institutions', *West European Politics,* **25** (1), 1–22.

Thatcher, M. and D. Coen (2008), 'Reshaping European regulatory space: an evolutionary analysis', *West European Politics,* **4**, 806–36.

Töller, A.E. (2008), 'Wettbewerbspolitik', in H. Heinelt and M. Knodt (eds), *Politikfelder im EU-Mehrebenensystem,* Baden-Baden: Nomos, pp. 115–39.

van Calster, G. and K. Deketelaere (2001), 'The use of voluntary agreements in the European Community's environmental policy', in E.W. Orts and K. Deketelaere (eds), *Environmental Contracts: Comparative Approaches to Regulatory Innovation in the United States and Europe,* London, The Hague and Boston, MA: Kluwer International, pp. 199–246.

van Gestel, R. (2005), 'Self-regulation and environmental law', *Electronic Journal of Comparative Law,* **9** (1).

Volpi, G. and S. Singer (2001), 'EU-level agreements: a successful tool? Lessons from the agreement with the automotive industry', in P. ten Brink (ed.), *Voluntary Environmental Agreements: Process, Practice and Future Use,* Sheffield: Greenleaf Publishing, pp. 142–54.

Wilks, S. (2005), 'Competition policy: challenge and reform', in H. Wallace, W. Wallace and M.A. Pollack (eds), *Policy-Making in the European Union,* Oxford: Oxford University Press, pp. 113–39.

Wilks, S. (2010), 'Competition policy', in H. Wallace, W. Wallace and M. Pollack (eds), *Policy-Making in the European Union,* Oxford: Oxford University Press.

Wonka, A. and B. Rittberger (2010), 'Paths to independence: determinants of institutional independence of twenty-nine EU agencies', *West European Politics,* **33** (4).

# 38 Towards a European model of regulatory governance?
## Matthias Finger

The chapter is in three sections. Section 38.1 offers a critical analysis of the literature on the emergence of the European Regulatory State and calls for a distinction between its global and its particularly European causes and features. Section 38.2 therefore places the emergence of the European Regulatory State within a worldwide context, especially where it is relevant to the global economic effects wrought by network industries. It thus crystallizes the broad causes and features of this prominent entity. Section 38.3 shows how the European Regulatory State – even though sharing some of these broad features – is nevertheless unique, owing to Europe's need to position itself competitively within the global economy, which in turn explains the particularly complex and ongoing interplay between national politics, independent national regulatory authorities, transnational corporations, and European regulatory operators.

Overall, this chapter argues that the complex institutional dynamics in Europe – at least in the case of the network industries – is unique and unprecedented because Europe itself is using liberalization and especially regulation as a means to position itself competitively within the global economy. In order to understand the particular features of this model of regulatory governance, one must therefore separate out the European characteristics from the broader global trends, starting with a critical analysis of the existing literature on regulatory governance and the Regulatory State.

## 38.1  TOWARDS A REGULATORY STATE

Historically, the argument about the emergence of a Regulatory State remains linked to the development of the European Union in general and the European Commission in particular. This is, in my opinion, because the authors who wrote early on about the phenomenon (e.g., Majone 1996) observed the emergence of the Regulatory State in Europe. However, from an intellectual point of view, it is important to disentangle the phenomenon of the rise from its particular European features. My main argument is that it is not the Regulatory State that is a European phenomenon; rather, there is a European specificity to the Regulatory State, which in turn stems from the fact that Europe – at least in the case of network industries – uses deregulation and more especially re-regulation as a means to increase its global competitiveness.

There is indeed an emerging idea of a Regulatory State, especially in the political science literature (Majone 1994, 1997). One has to distinguish, on the one hand, between the literature concerned with the general characteristics of such a Regulatory State or regulatory capitalism for that matter, namely in regard to democratic participation (e.g., Majone 1999; Levi-Faur 2005; also Eckert 2011) and the literature that identifies characteristics of the Regulatory State, in particular the emergence of independent regulatory authorities and their diffusion, on the other (Gilardi 2005; Gilardi et al. 2007).

### 38.1.1   General Characteristics of a Regulatory State

Many political scientists have highlighted the fact that the modern nation-state has undergone substantial transformation since the 1980s, that is, since the era of globalization. For Majone (1996) and many others, these transformations can be summarized as being (1) privatization and (2) the crisis of the Keynesian welfare state, a phenomenon which, they say, mainly affects Europe. Both, individually and combined, lead to the fact that the State increasingly plays a role in regulating markets, rather than in distributive politics. In other words, the rise of regulation results from a broader change in the economy, characterized by the growing importance of markets and market solutions. In my view this is, in turn, directly the result of globalization, to which I will return later.

Lodge has written the history of the Regulatory State[1] by tracing it back to Majone's article "The rise of the regulatory state in Europe" (1994), which identified (1) the trend to "use legal authority or regulation over other tools of stabilization and redistribution," as well as (2) the "European Commission's expansionist role through the use of influence over policy content in the absence of other, especially budgetary tools" (Lodge 2008: 280). For Majone, the rise of the Regulatory State results from a combination of privatization, Europeanization, and governance by proxy. Lodge, in turn, identifies a series of characteristics of the so-called Regulatory State, namely (p. 282): (1) the privatization of activities formerly undertaken as part of state ownership, (2) the emergence of quasi-autonomous agencies with quasi-legislative powers responsible for the regulation of private or privatized activities, and (3) the formalization and contractualization of relationships within the regulated domain. Let me state that the latter is, in my opinion, not a phenomenon of the Regulatory State, but rather an outgrowth from public sector reform in general and new public management philosophy in particular. It is most widely spread in the UK. Also, privatization as a cause of the emerging Regulatory State is a typically British and thus somewhat limited phenomenon. There remain thus only the independent regulatory authorities or agencies (IRAs) as a general characteristic of the rise of the Regulatory State. According to Lodge, these three phenomena are caused by (a) the "exhaustion of the 'positive' welfare state and the subsequent move towards the use of authority rather than the 'cheque book' as the preferred policy tool at the national level," and (b) the "attempts by the European Commission to maximize its influence over policy content given the absence of other substantial discretionary resources" (p. 282).

It is important to note and criticize the fact that this idea of a Regulatory State so far confuses generic global and specific European causes and features. I suggest it is necessary to distinguish between global causes and features of the Regulatory State on the one hand (section 38.2) and the particular European causes and features on the other (section 38.3), because Europe, being a subset of the global economy, has to position itself competitively within it.

### 38.1.2  Particular Characteristics of the Regulatory State

Political scientists have mainly focused on one, albeit important, characteristic of the Regulatory State, namely the emergence of the IRAs and this at the nation-state level (see Gilardi 2005, 2008). Without considering the broad context of the above transformation of the State, these authors show that the rise of the IRAs is a global and statistically significant phenomenon (see Gilardi et al. 2007). IRAs seem to be mainly concentrated in economic areas where markets are already globalized (e.g., finance, pharmaceuticals) or where they are emerging (e.g., telecommunications, energy, transport).

The reasons given to explain this emergence seem to me quite narrow, lacking the broader context and picture: IRAs are said to be created for three main reasons, namely the need for credibility of political commitment (e.g., investment security), the need to limit the discretionary power of future policy makers, and to limit the power of veto players (Gilardi 2008: 4–5). If taken at the level of political strategy, for example tying the hands of future policy makers and reducing the power of veto players, the explanation of the rise of IRAs seems to me to be quite short-sighted, though not wrong. However, if put into the larger context, all three explanations perfectly fit into a broader argument which will be developed in more detail below: indeed, all three reasons given by political scientists for the emergence of IRAs pertain to the fact that the nation-state, in the age of globalization, needs to offer more credibility to global investors (e.g., legal security) in order to remain competitive: technocratic IRAs provide more legal security than increasingly volatile policy makers. In this sense, the emergence of IRAs is a perfect illustration of the changing nature of the State in the age of globalization, albeit a quite simplistic one. Often, the explanations as to whether IRAs emerge do not take into account the profound nature of the phenomenon in question (e.g., globalization) and the deep and long-lasting implications for the nation-state. Indeed, most likely the emergence of the IRAs is only a passing phenomenon, as the transformation of the nation-state is much more profound. Perhaps they are only a temporary answer to the problem, at least when it comes to the national level, as we shall see in the case of Europe.

To summarize, the dominant literature on the Regulatory State sometimes places its emergence within the context of globalization, sometimes within the particular context of Europe, and sometimes simply within everyday political behavior and strategy. It is in my opinion important first, to disentangle these causes by isolating the causes and features as they relate to economic globalization and, second, to place the emergence of the European Regulatory State within this global economic context. As I will argue in section 38.2, the Regulatory State and its regulatory bodies are above all a reaction, and perhaps a response, to globalization at the national level, helping nation-states to become more competitive in the context of economic globalization. Whether the Regulatory State is a stable model capable of withstanding the dynamics of globalization remains to be seen and is not the point of this chapter. In the specific case of Europe, as I will show in section 38.3, regulation appears to be used as a supra-national response to economic globalization, which gives the European Regulatory State its particular dynamics and features.

## 38.2   GLOBAL CAUSES AND FEATURES OF THE REGULATORY STATE

Thatcher, among others, explicitly places the Regulatory State within the broader framework of how the nation-state reacts and adapts to globalization (Thatcher 2002b): regulation and the Regulatory State, as opposed to the positive state, are emerging because of growing competition, including competition among nation-states. Regulation is needed as a new means of dealing at the nation-state level with such competition. Subsequently, the Regulatory State is characterized by lawyers, experts, and regulators. Authors here seem to be mainly concerned by the fact that, in the Regulatory State, decision-making power is taken away from the democratic process and delegated to regulators, who are basically technocrats.

The analysis of why this is so is unfortunately not very much developed. Such delegation is simply said to be caused by the predominance of markets, deregulation, and privatization. Thatcher and others also generally observe a wide variation in such delegation, especially when it comes to the emergence of independent regulatory agencies (Thatcher 2002a).

> The "regulatory state" hypothesis suggests that, since the 1980s, the main functions of the regulatory state have become the correction of market failures through rule-making. Its characteristics are independent bodies, parliamentary committees and courts, replacing legislatures, departments and nationalized industries. Political conflict centers on rule-making, and the central actors are single issue movements, regulators, experts and judges, instead of political parties, civil servants and corporate groups. Regulatory politics combines a rule-bound legalistic policy style, a pluralist political culture and indirect political accountability. (Thatcher 2002b: 867)

In short, current literature links the rise of a Regulatory State to liberalization, privatization, the dominance of markets, and more generally the expansion of market-like approaches to public affairs. This reading sees the State as adapting to this new situation (1) by removing entire areas from democratic policy making, (2) by focusing on markets or quasi-markets, and (3) by handing over the regulation of these to independent regulatory authorities. However, these authors observe a big variety among Regulatory States, a variety which, in their view, is due to path dependency and institutionalism more generally. While the newly emerging Regulatory State is in my opinion well identified, characterized, and critiqued, the very reasons for its emergence often remain obscure. In particular, it is not clear why such a Regulatory State is emerging, except that liberalization and ultimately ideological choices are part of the process. The case of the network industries may demonstrate the dynamics that lead to the Regulatory State in the context of economic globalization.

### 38.2.1   The Globalization of the Network Industries and the Subsequent Need for Regulation

I concur with the authors discussed above that the deepest underlying driver of the need for regulatory governance is without doubt economic globalization. The network industries perfectly illustrate this process, starting with the area of telecommunications, which by now has become a truly global industry. But similar processes can also be found in the areas of transportation like air and sea as well as in energy, particularly in oil and gas.

Along with this process goes the pressure to deregulate and privatize state monopolies, followed by the emergence of transnational corporations (TNCs). Their creation and the growing need to regulate them, as well as their ability to shape such regulation, are by now well-known phenomena. Liberalization accompanying economic globalization has led to the emergence of transnational infrastructure corporations, some of which may still be publicly owned, but which behave like TNCs once they operate outside of their national borders.

Especially in the network industries – but actually anywhere market concentration takes place – liberalization is in principle accompanied by a need to regulate. Indeed, this need stems from the fact that markets in these infrastructures and beyond are necessarily imperfect, that liberalization leads to the need to coordinate the different market parameters (e.g., technical standards), and that public policy objectives persist in most of the liberalized network industries (e.g., security of supply in energy, public service needs to be satisfied, for example in transportation, water, or telecommunications, but also in health), as markets fail to provide non-lucrative public services. The need to regulate, as will be argued in section 38.3, is rooted in this very failure of globalizing and liberalized markets, at least in the case of the infrastructures, but certainly also in the case of health care, finance, pharmaceuticals, chemicals, and agro-food.

The answer to this need to regulate imperfect markets in a global and liberalizing economy inevitably leads to complex institutional dynamics between national governments which are sometimes still the partial owners of globally operating TNCs, national regulators that are expected to impede market distortions in inherently imperfect markets, and supra-national regulatory bodies which have become necessary because of the need to coordinate markets and market players. TNCs, though not overtly part of this dynamic, do play an instrumental role. Again, the network industries perfectly illustrate these complex institutional dynamics.

Overall, globalization means that decisions are increasingly made by TNCs, which results in complaints about the loss of democratic control. It also means that state ownership is privatized or otherwise exposed to competition and thus no longer manageable via ownership, and that therefore the only power left to the nation-state is the regulation of imperfect markets. In this sense, the loss of democratic control, though simultaneous with the emergence of regulation, does not mean they are causally related. This happens as a consequence of economic globalization, as with regulation. This analysis also shows that the emergence of the Regulatory State, which now can be defined much more precisely as the reduction of the role of the State since it gives up policy making and service delivery, is by definition a global phenomenon. This phenomenon of course also takes place in Europe, as Europe as a whole and all individual European nation-states are exposed to the same process of economic globalization.

### 38.2.2 European Dynamics within Global Dynamics

One therefore needs to distinguish between the emergence of the Regulatory State, which is a global phenomenon, and the European situation, which is an integral part

530  *Handbook on the politics of regulation*

of this global process. The fact that this emergence was attributed in the literature to a European phenomenon, in the context of the European Union, has led to a confusion which it is important to disentangle: we have failed to distinguish between what is truly global and what is uniquely European. Focusing on the dynamics between national regulatory authorities and national governments on the one hand and the European regulators and the European Commission on the other has not helped either. Rather, it has reinforced the belief that the regulatory phenomenon must be a result of purely EU-specific dynamics.

Let me therefore develop the following argument: if the emergence of the Regulatory State is explained as a reaction to globalization because regulating markets promotes competitiveness, then Regulatory Europe can be seen as being the result of the same reaction vis-à-vis globalization at a supra-national level. The delegation of regulatory powers to Europe and the subsequent creation of European regulatory authorities through the will to create an integrated European market and corresponding institutions can thus be seen as an attempt to cope with globalization, because each European nation-state alone is not capable of facing up to globalization and taking advantage of it on its own. The creation of a Regulatory Europe can thus be interpreted as Europe's institutional answer to globalization. And, as Majone (1996) has rightly pointed out, the interaction between regulation at both the national and the European levels is very much at the core of these complex institutional dynamics.

The driver of these dynamics is the strategic behavior of the key players within the context of globalization, consisting of the European Commission, the national governments, the independent national regulatory authorities, European agencies, and, generally neglected in the literature about Regulatory Europe, the TNCs, which see a regulated European market as a business opportunity. From a theoretical perspective, this process of integration of regulation must be understood in institutional economic terms (e.g., Williamson 1996): indeed institutional economics sees institutions competing in a global market, where only the most efficient institutions or institutional arrangements will ultimately survive. In the global economy, Europe, and especially Regulatory Europe, precisely emerges as such an institutional answer. What we thus currently observe is the dynamics of the process by which both member states and Europe adapt to globalization through regulation. There is gradual integration because the states pursue identical objectives, use the same means, learn from each other, build on each other, and are driven by the same TNCs.

At the beginning these regulatory dynamics were sector specific, and they still are predominantly; thus we see the creation of sector-specific European regulatory bodies (e.g., European Railway Agency – ERA; European Aviation Safety Agency – EASA; Body of European Regulators for Electronic Communications – BEREC; Agency for the Cooperation of Energy Regulators – ACER). However, we can now see dynamics that go beyond the separate sectors. In this sense, the process of regulatory integration in Europe is not yet finished and is actually likely to continue in parallel with the pursuit of globalization. It is therefore too early to identify a European model of regulatory governance other than to observe that national and European regulatory dynamics gradually integrate, driven as they are simultaneously by globalization pressures and the strategic behavior of all the operators, not least the TNCs.

## 38.3   REGULATORY STATE

Having located the emergence of the Regulatory State within the broader context of the nation-state's transformation and its adaptation to globalization, let me now turn to the question of Europe. I will proceed in two steps. First, I will recall what the literature says about the complex relationship between Europe and regulation. Second, I will try to link this discussion to the considerations made above, which will allow me to formulate more precisely the idea of a European model of regulatory governance.

### 38.3.1   Regulatory Europe

Rarely is the question of the rise of Europe, and especially of Regulatory Europe, placed within the context of a reaction of the nation-state to globalization. Rather the formation of the Regulatory State is usually seen as a phenomenon which results from the rise of Europe (e.g., Cardwell 2011; Groenleer 2011). In this sense, and up to today, the growing literature on this subject reflects the three topical areas that Majone had already identified in 1996 (Majone 1996: 265–7), namely: the question of the relationship between national and European regulation and between the Commission and nation-states more generally; the question of regulatory independence, including the independence of the European Commission from the nation-states; and the question of networks of national regulators and their relationship with the European Commission. When we talk about a European model of regulatory governance this is generally still done within the context of the evolving relationship between the European nation-states and the European Commission. As I will show, we shall have to go beyond this relationship and look at its context if we want to understand the European model.

Political scientists, in particular, focus on this relationship between Europe and nation-states, which they characterize as a two-way relationship: on the one hand the European Commission impacts upon nation-states, while on the other hand nation-states also press their interests onto the European Commission, thus using the Commission to promote their own interests or to disguise national objectives as European ones so as to have them accepted in their own countries (Coen and Héritier 2005). This gives rise to a policy and an institutional dimension. Much has been written about the impact of European policies on the various nation-states and the mitigation processes by which nation-states adopt or twist European policies (e.g., Peterson 1995). There is less but still a significant amount of literature that pertains to the way nation-states influence and even shape European policies (Beyers and Trondal 2004). In both cases, it is interesting to examine the mediating factors such as ideologies, institutions and power relationships. In addition, there is a whole area of research to be developed in order to understand the role TNCs play in this two-way policy relationship.

However, I will concentrate here not so much on the policies as on the institutions: the interesting phenomenon is indeed the emergence of European institutions in selected policy areas, as well as their relationship with the corresponding or otherwise institutions at the national level. Fleischer (2005), for example, has offered a case study of this complex relationship for pharmaceuticals and food safety. The analysis focuses on the attributes, mandate, competencies, attributes, and operations of the national and EU agencies in these two policy areas to conclude that the relationship is characterized by contradiction: the EU agencies do indeed create new regulations and seek to enhance their power by self-defining their roles in a dynamic approach. National agencies, in return, create alliances to protect themselves from these European agencies, but also to take advantage at national levels of the opportunities EU regulation creates for them. Again, it would be interesting to enlarge the case study to include the roles pharmaceutical and food TNCs play in such regulatory dynamics. At this point, we unfortunately have only anecdotal evidence of this, but it is obvious that such an interesting dynamic between EU and national agencies, mediated by TNCs, is at the core of the European model of regulatory governance.

In section 38.1, I have already discussed the phenomenon of the emergence of independent regulatory authorities at the nation-state level. Indeed, a second debate pertains to the question of how much independence there really is, as well as about the factors that might lead to independence. At the European level, however, the enigma is quite different: while one may question the independence of the Commission from the Parliament or the Council of Ministers, the more important concern here is about the independence of the Commission vis-à-vis nation-states. What policy instruments and subsequent institutional arrangements can the Commission use to increase its powers over nation-states? One may mention here the directives, comitology (committee procedures), EU agencies, or meta-regulation (e.g., networks of regulators, see below). From an institutional perspective, EU agencies and meta-regulation are certainly the most interesting instruments, allowing the Commission some independence from the nation-states or the national regulators.

Coen and Thatcher, in their 2008 article, highlight the phenomenon of emerging networks of European regulators in the telecommunications and the securities sectors, but also mention electricity (Florence Forum) and gas (Madrid Forum).[2] They show how the emergence of these networks is the result of what they call a "double delegation," that is, the nation-states delegating regulatory powers to independent regulatory agencies at the national level and delegating regulatory powers to the European Commission on the international level. As a result of this double-delegation process, the Commission is now organizing the coordination of independent national regulators in order to stem the "uneven development by coordinating implementation of regulation by member states" (p. 50). Coen and Thatcher try to get at this phenomenon by way of principal–agent theory but come to the conclusion that an explanation by way of power relationships and corresponding compromises is more appropriate. As a matter of fact, they clearly state that what the Commission ultimately wants is a fully fledged European sector-specific regulator, but, lacking the support from the member states, the Commission settles for European regulators' networks (ERNs). In my view, Coen and Thatcher perfectly capture a step in the overall process and thus of the model; they also capture the drivers behind it, namely power rather than efficiency. However, ERNs are, in my view, only an intermediate step and by no means a stable model, especially if one considers the role played by TNCs, which Coen and Thatcher unfortunately do not. Nevertheless, their contribution is extremely helpful when developing a model of European regulatory governance.

Eberlein and Grande (2005) precede Coen and Thatcher's arguments: they use the concept of "transnational regulatory regimes" to characterize the unique European approach to regulation and examine it against the Europeanization of regulation on the one hand and the nationalization of regulation on the other. The idea of defining the unique European model of regulatory governance as being one of transnational regulatory regimes is an attractive one. However, upon critical examination of their argument, the key feature remains the networks of regulators, perhaps somewhat enriched by complex up- and downward relationships with EU institutions and national bodies. In my view, the concept of transnational regulatory regimes would only develop its full power if one also included TNCs as playing an active role in creating, developing, and maintaining such regimes. A reference to the regime theory literature, which includes TNCs as being active partners in such regimes, would be useful in this context (e.g., Young 1982).

### 38.3.2   Towards a European Model of Regulatory Governance?

What is then the specificity of a European model of regulatory governance, other than the fact that national bodies interact in a highly complex fashion, by way of procedures, directives, rules, and so on with EU bodies, with networks of regulators playing the mediating role? In short, this model is above all characterized by the institutional dynamics between all these elements. The literature considers the networks of regulators as being pivotal to these dynamics, which it certainly is. In this case, however, at least three other dimensions must be highlighted.

There are first the dimensions of the dynamics between directives, some of which directly create national IRAs, as with the network industries, the networks of national regulatory authorities, and the European agencies. More precisely, it will be interesting to know how they are related, whether there is a logical sequence leading from one to the other, particularly in the case of networks of regulators to EU agencies, and whether there will be a converging outcome.

There is secondly the dimension of the dynamics between the regulatory institutions such as EU agencies, networks of regulators, and national regulatory authorities on the one hand and the political institutions like the EU Parliament, Council of Ministers and Commission and national politics on the other. Of particular interest here is the role the Commission and the various director generals play in the different sectors, because it is the Commission that can choose between the different institutional options. The Commission also constantly navigates between political policy and the regulatory realm.

Thirdly there is the role TNCs play in the overall dynamics: TNCs are interested in the creation of a single European market and especially in regulatory conditions for such a market that favors them over competitors. They thus lobby all the institutions, for example national governments, especially if they are still or partly state-owned, national regulators, European regulatory bodies, the European Commission, and so on, but they also play these different constituents against each other to get their way. Conversely, the European Commission and some governments actively help or even need these TNCs to further market integration and overall competitiveness of Europe in the global economy. More research on the role of the TNCs in promoting and shaping Regulatory Europe is certainly needed.

In short, the question whether there is a model of regulatory governance in Europe is in my view above all the question of the institutional dynamics between national regulators, some of which will have been mandated by Commission directives, at least in the case of the network industries, European bodies, such as the Commission and European agencies where they exist, intermediaries, such as networks of regulators, and TNCs. It is easy to understand that there is not yet a stable model, nor is the exact outcome clear. All one can say at this point is that it is this dynamic which already constitutes an unprecedented and unique European model of regulatory governance.

## ACKNOWLEDGEMENTS

I would like to thank David Levi-Faur for his helpful comments on earlier versions of this chapter.

## NOTES

1. However, the phenomenon of a Regulatory State goes back further and is linked to a new, regulatory type of intervention of the American government in its economy in the 1930s (e.g., Moran 2002).
2. Both networks have in the meantime been institutionalized in the form of the Agency for the Cooperation of Energy Regulators (ACER), based in Slovenia.

## REFERENCES

Beyers, J. and J. Trondal (2004), 'How nation states "hit" Europe: ambiguity and representation in the European Union', *West European Politics*, **27** (5), 919–42.
Cardwell, J. (2011), 'The changing nature of European regulatory governance', in D. Levi-Faur (ed.), *Handbook on the Politics of Regulation*, Cheltenham: Edward Elgar.
Coen, D. and A. Héritier (eds) (2005), *Refining Regulatory Regimes: Utilities in Europe*, Cheltenham, UK and Northampton, MA, USA: Edward Elgar Publishing.
Coen, D. and M. Thatcher (2008), 'Network governance and multi-level delegation: European networks of regulatory agencies', *Journal of Public Policy*, **28** (1), 49–71.
Eberlein, B. and E. Grande (2005), 'Beyond delegation: transnational regulatory regimes and the European regulatory state', *Journal of European Public Policy*, **12** (1), 89–112.
Eckert, S. (2011), 'European regulatory governance', in D. Levi-Faur (ed.), *Handbook on the Politics of Regulation*, Cheltenham: Edward Elgar.
Fleischer, J. (2005), 'European agencies as engines of regulation? On different architectural strategies of the regulatory state', paper presented at the 3rd ECPR Conference, 8–10 September, Budapest.
Gilardi, F. (2005), 'The institutional foundations of regulatory capitalism: the diffusion of independent regulatory agencies in Western Europe', *Annals of the American Academy of Political and Social Science*, **598** (1), 84–101.
Gilardi, F. (2008), *Delegation in the Regulatory State: Independent Regulatory Agencies in Western Europe*, Cheltenham, UK and Northampton, MA, USA: Edward Elgar Publishing.
Gilardi, F., J. Jordana and D. Levi-Faur (2007), 'Regulation in the age of globalization: the diffusion of regulatory agencies across Europe and Latin America', in A.G. Hodge (ed.), *Privatization and Market Development*, Cheltenham, UK and Northampton, MA, USA: Edward Elgar Publishing, pp. 127–47.
Groenleer, M. (2011), 'Regulatory governance in the European Union: the role of committees, agencies and networks', in D. Levi-Faur (ed.), *Handbook on the Politics of Regulation*, Cheltenham: Edward Elgar.
Levi-Faur, D. (2005), 'The global diffusion of regulatory capitalism', *Annals of the American Academy of Political and Social Science*, **598** (1), 12–32.
Lodge, M. (2008), 'Regulation, the regulatory state and European politics', *West European Politics*, **31** (1–2), 280–301.
Majone, G. (1994), 'The rise of the regulatory state in Europe', *West European Politics*, **17** (3), 77–101.
Majone, G. (1996), *Regulating Europe*, London: Routledge.

Majone, G. (1997), 'From the positive to the regulatory state: causes and consequences in the mode of governance', *Journal of Public Policy*, **17**, 139–67.

Majone, G. (1999), 'The regulatory state and its legitimacy problems', *West European Politics*, **22** (1), 1–24.

Moran, M. (2002), 'Review article: understanding the regulatory state', *British Journal of Political Science*, **32**, 391–413.

Peterson, J. (1995), 'Decision-making in the European Union: towards a framework for analysis', *Journal of European Public Policy*, **2** (1), 69–93.

Thatcher, M. (2002a), 'Regulation after delegation: independent regulatory agencies in Europe', *Journal of European Public Policy*, **9** (6), 954–72.

Thatcher, M. (2002b), 'Analysing regulatory reform in Europe', *Journal of European Public Policy*, **9** (6), 859–72.

Williamson, O. (1996), *The Mechanisms of Governance*, Oxford: Oxford University Press.

Young, O. (1982), *Resource Regimes: Natural Resources and Social Institutions*, Berkeley: University of California Press.

# 39 The changing nature of European regulatory governance
## *Paul James Cardwell*

Membership of the European Union (EU) has had a profound impact on the political and legal systems of the member states. No other system of regional integration has been as successful in producing a system of regulatory governance with the aim of legislative and policy harmonization across national boundaries. The growth of the EU from six states in 1957 to 27, with more waiting in the wings, is a testament to the EU's success but also brings new challenges as integration adapts to the 21st century. Governance through regulation, which has always been at the very heart of the means of pursuing the European integration project, is facing increasing challenges and political choices brought about by both internal and external circumstances. As noted in Chapter 1, regulation is a contested concept – and EU regulation is no exception, since it forms the basis of a supranational political project to forge 'an ever closer Union among the peoples of Europe'.[1] EU regulatory governance is faced with (some of) the competing interests which exist at nation state level too, including over the nature of administrative agency and the effect of 'soft' as well as 'hard' legal methods.

The purpose of this chapter is to trace the development of the EU regulatory framework, to explore the changing nature of regulatory governance and to explain the emergence of new features and actors on the EU's regulatory horizon. Regulatory governance at the EU level has traditionally been understood to focus on regulations and directives: legally binding, enforceable instruments in the member states. These instruments emerge from a complex institutional framework and policy process which is only partly recognizable from the original institutional framework from 1957.

Regulations and directives are not the only manifestations of the EU's system of regulatory governance since the advent of new modes of governance which have markedly different characteristics. Similarly, the scope of the EU institutions involved in the creation of regulatory instruments is no longer limited to the 'traditional' actors (Commission, Council and European Parliament) but now includes other EU bodies which have begun to play an increasingly important role in EU regulatory governance. Both of these developments have occurred in a more extensive manner since the 1990s as additions to the regulatory horizon and, as such, merit further exploration. Thus the conceptualization of regulatory governance is wide and focuses on 'hard' legal measures as well as emphasizing 'softer' measures and institutional (agency) forms which have a bearing on social norms.[2]

The chapter proceeds as follows. Section 39.1 outlines the advantages and limitations of traditional instruments of regulatory governance as the EU has moved towards a more advanced stage of integration. This is followed in section 39.2 by an examination of the emergence of new institutional actors within the policy- and decision-making processes, including the specialized EU agencies, which have markedly different roles depending on the policy area in question. Finally, section 39.3 discusses the new modes of governance, including the open method of coordination (OMC), which have begun to take an increasingly important place alongside the traditional regulatory instruments in the governance of the EU. The analysis of the new modes places them in the political context of the recent development of the EU. The chapter concludes that, as the enlarged EU of the 21st century will continue to face challenges in terms of legitimacy, future direction and *raison d'être*, it will be obliged to continue to seek innovative approaches in regulatory governance to exist alongside more established methods and processes.

## 39.1   TRADITIONAL INSTRUMENTS OF REGULATORY GOVERNANCE AT THE EU LEVEL

The most widely recognizable regulatory regime at the EU level is set out in the Treaty on the Functioning of the European Union (TFEU), formerly the European Community (EC) Treaty. Article 288 TFEU lays down the general characteristics of regulations and directives. Both have general application across the member states and have become the hallmarks of the system of EU regulatory governance. They are legally binding, although directives leave the 'choice of form and methods' to member states, which are obliged to transpose them into their national systems as they see fit. The Commission enjoys the role of 'guardian' of the Treaties and as such has the power to issue reasoned opinions to member states that it believes are not fulfilling their obligations under the Treaty.[3] This can also lead to the member state(s) in question being brought before the European Court of Justice if they fail in their duties under the Treaty.[4] In a seminal series of decisions, the Court has clearly stated that the regulatory instruments have direct effect in the member states and enjoy supremacy over national law, including constitutional law.[5] The importance of the instruments cannot therefore be overstated.

The extent to which regulatory instruments have been used over the course of the European integration project from 1957 until the present day is exemplified by the enlargement process. Any prospective member state must incorporate into its system the entirety of EU law and policy in force, which extends to 17 455 acts in total.[6] Some instruments are extremely lengthy; for example, the 2006 regulation on chemical substances (REACH) has 849 pages.[7] Regulatory governance at the EU level is extensive, detailed and extremely diverse.

The process of creating regulations and directives has evolved over time. The Commission enjoys a monopoly on the power to propose measures in the areas of competence contained in the Treaty. Most regulatory measures must be passed according to the 'ordinary legislative procedure', i.e. the Council (composed of ministers of the 27 member states) and European Parliament (directly elected by all EU citizens every five years) must both vote favourably on the text for it to enter into force.[8] One constant theme which has emerged from every major Treaty revision is the increase in powers of the European Parliament in the regulatory regime. To combat the assertion that the increasing volume and binding qualities of regulatory instruments emerge from a structure which does not live up to the democratic standards employed in the member states, the majority of instruments must now be agreed upon by the European Parliament (directly elected by the citizens of the EU every five years) as well as the Council. The exact procedure depends upon the Treaty basis upon which the measure is being proposed. One consequence of the detail involved in EU regulatory governance is the need for further implementation measures, which bring in actors and political processes not mentioned in the Treaty. This point is the focus of section 39.2.

The core place of regulatory instruments within the EU's system of governance cannot be overestimated. It is unlikely that the Union would have moved so far along the path of integration had the political choice to create binding, enforceable measures not been made. However, these instruments were created for an entity of six members. The expansion in members, with more set to join in coming years, has been accompanied by a gradual expansion in the competences allowing the EU to regulate in more diverse policy areas. Questions have been raised about the appropriateness of an EU regulatory model which, at its core, was conceived for the harmonization of six member states: accountability and the limits of the institutions to act have become pressing issues (Majone 2009: 175). There has also been the view amongst several member states that the volume of binding legislation has become overly burdensome, and there is a need for a reduction in the number of regulations and directives in force. 'Better regulation' and cutting 'unnecessary red-tape' were stated objectives of the Barroso Commission upon taking office (Barroso 2004). Again in the context of EU enlargement, the nature of 'one-size-fits-all' legislative measures applicable to a much more diverse EU has been raised. The issue of ensuring that the differences, for example in economic and social terms, are respected in the integration process is an apt one:

> growing heterogeneity in the enlarged Union will contribute to the obsolescence of harmonization even more than will the member states' distrust of the supranational institutions. Significant inter-country differences in socio-economic conditions are necessarily mirrored in a diversity of national priorities and policy preferences, and this implies that welfare-enhancing regulations have to be different rather than harmonized. (Majone 2009: 186)

Within the context of the global economic crisis occurring at the end of the 2000s, whether EU member states old and new can or should respond to economic challenges in the same way is inherently linked to the regulatory framework of the EU polity and its effectiveness, legitimacy and accountability – all of which have come increasingly under the spotlight.

## 39.2 THE EMERGENCE AND PROLIFERATION OF NEW INSTITUTIONAL ACTORS IN EU REGULATORY GOVERNANCE

Deidre Curtin has recently noted that the executive power of the EU has become increasingly fragmented and plural (Curtin 2009: 53). Certainly, the EU regulatory system of governance is only partly recognizable from the beginning of the integration process in 1957 and the founding Treaty. The number of new actors, in the form of specialized agencies, has greatly increased and reflects trends in many economically developed states. However, the constitutional foundations of the EU do not fully account for all the bodies which have an input into the regulatory process or the 'governance mix' (Eckert, Chapter 37). A wider scope of analysis is needed to account for the totality of the regulatory regime at the EU level. This section focuses on two institutional dimensions: the 'comitology' regime relating to the implementation of regulatory instruments and the emergence of EU specialized agencies. A further example of regulatory organization in the EU is the existence of regulatory networks which coordinate national regulators in a more or less formal way. These networks have been a visible feature of the European regulatory horizon, though agencification now seems to be more prevalent as a regulatory solution (Levi-Faur 2010: 9; Groenleer, Chapter 40), which explains the emphasis placed on the creation and role of agencies here.

### 39.2.1   Comitology

Implementation of regulatory instruments typically falls to the executive in a national context. This is problematic when considering that the EU, as a supranational polity, does not embody traditional separation of powers principles. Of particular concern in the EU context is the interface between the member states and the EU institutions insofar as the implementation of legislation is concerned. Directives, which are binding 'as to the result to be achieved' but 'leave to the national authorities the choice of form and methods', require close surveillance by the Commission in order to ensure that the integration process functions correctly. Needless to say, the potentially different ways in which 27 member states transpose directives are numerous: the risk associated with their continued use is that they become worthless if changes do not occur on the ground.

Debate on whether the task of implementation falls to the Commission or the Council resulted in the emergence of the compromise system of 'comitology'. Member states are responsible for implementing regulatory instruments, but the Commission is empowered to take implementing measures if uniform implementing conditions are required. The Commission may do so only under the supervision of a committee composed of national representatives relevant to the sector in which the measure is being taken. There are approximately 300 such committees, which makes their use extremely widespread and particularly important since the committee may play a decisive role in the eventual legal and policy effects of the regulation (Verhoeven, 2005: 164). Comitology is more than a technical process for the implementation of regulatory instruments but a political issue which goes to the heart of the Union's institutional balance. Since 1999,[9] three types of committee are visible: advisory, management and regulatory. In cases of the latter, the Commission can adopt implementing measures only if it obtains the approval by qualified majority[10] of the member states meeting within the committee. Although not universally criticized,[11] the comitology regime as a feature of regulatory governance is often viewed as being problematic in terms both of institutional balances and of legitimacy, as the processes are obscure, highly complex and lacking in accountability (Vos 2005: 108). Others have noted that the regime is lacking in the expected features of a system of good governance despite its advantages of promoting consensus and effectiveness at the interface between the EU institutions and the member states (de Búrca 1999: 73).

Reforms to comitology were achieved in 1999 and 2006,[12] which in particular strengthened the hand of the European Parliament, which had long feared that its increased role in the legislative process would be undermined if implementation measures were then effectively changed within a committee structure made up of national representatives and in which it had no role. The reform of 2006 represented the success of the European Parliament in gaining the power to block the adoption of draft implementing measures and therefore 'the possibility of exercising its role of holding certain comitology committees to account for decisions that they are intending to pass and to block their adoption' (Curtin 2009: 273).

The basis for the comitology regime, Article 202 EC, was removed by the Treaty of Lisbon. The Treaty now states that, 'Where uniform conditions for implementing legally binding Union acts are needed, those acts shall confer implementing powers on the Commission' (Article 291(2) TFEU) but only once the Parliament and Council have laid down the 'rules and general principles concerning mechanisms for control by member states of the Commission's exercise of implementing powers' (Article 291(3) TFEU). Measures will now be known as 'implementing acts' (Article 291(4) TFEU). Further reforms are thus required by the Treaty in order for this procedure to operate. With the European Parliament being wary of any moves which undermine its status, there is a distinct possibility that it will be some time before the arrangements on the role of the institutions (and member states) involved are satisfactorily resolved.

### 39.2.2    Agencies

In the narrow sense of regulatory governance, that is to say the creation of regulatory instruments as outlined in section 39.1, there is little formal role for EU-level bodies beyond the core institutions of Commission, Parliament and Council. Aside from the comitology procedures, the only institutions which are specifically mentioned in the Treaty are the Economic and Social Committee and the Committee of the Regions. These bodies give their opinions on proposals for regulatory instruments as advisory bodies, though they have no separate power of initiation and no delegated functions (Articles 300–307 TFEU).

Specialized agencies and organs have been created incrementally and, in the words of the Commission, are 'typified by their diversity' (Commission 2005: 2). The first agencies (the European Centre for the Development of Vocational Training (CEDEFOP) and the European Foundation for the Improvement of Living and Working Conditions (EUROFOUND)) emerged in the 1970s. However, the moves towards completion of the Single Market in the 1990s and towards the closer integration of Europe in a more diverse range of fields necessitated the creation of specialized agencies. The extent to which agencies have become increasingly commonplace across the policy fields in which the EU acts, or is beginning to act, led one commentator to state that

> one could even get the impression that for each and every new threat that the European Union is faced with (fraud; bio terrorism; unsafe food; planes falling from the sky; chemical attacks; unsafe trains; diseases; illegal fishing; violations of human rights; etc.) the first reaction is to set up another Agency. (van Ooik 2005: 126)

In a general sense, 'agency' does not have a single definition, and 'regulatory agency' is a term applied to the EU agencies with some difficulty. The growth of agencies in Europe (at both nation state and EU levels) has been commented upon as a possible influence of the US system (Kagan 2007: 103), though most EU agencies do not fall fully within the criteria common to their US counterparts (Shapiro and Stone Sweet 2002: 373; Majone 2006: 191). The explanation for this is that many of the agencies *assist* the Commission in the performance of its executive tasks, rather than having full regulatory powers of their own.

The growth of EU agencies can be explained by reference to both general characteristics of agencies in nation states, that is to say the need for specialized, technical assistance and implementation of key tasks, and perceived advantages which are rather more EU-specific. These include the ability to locate agencies outside Brussels, making the EU institutional machinery appear less centralized and (physically) closer to the populations of member states. Agencies enable the Commission to outsource some of the more specialized or technical tasks it is responsible for and concentrate on core tasks, such as enforcement. Furthermore, because most areas of EU competence are shared with the member states, agencies can have an important networking role between counterpart national organs. This networking function is reflected in some of the names of the agencies.[13]

Agencies themselves do not appear in the Treaty, save for the provisions on actions for annulment of EU bodies (Article 267 TFEU). There have been no overarching rules on the creation of agencies. Since 2002, a legal basis for the creation of agencies has been provided by Regulation 58/2003, a statute under which agencies may be entrusted with the management of programmes and tasks. The Regulation only concerns 'executive' agencies, which may be given tasks required to implement an EU programme but not 'tasks requiring discretionary powers in translating political choices into action'.[14] They cannot adopt general regulatory measures. Examples of the five agencies created under this Regulation since 2002 are the Education, Audiovisual and Culture Executive Agency (EACEA) and the Executive Agency for Competitiveness and Innovation (EACI).

Other agencies have been created under Article 352 TFEU, a general power to take measures to attain the objectives of the Treaty, or under a Treaty provision relevant to the sector in which the agency operates.[15] Some of these agencies come closer to being correctly termed as regulatory agencies, though they are not officially designated as such. In particular, several agencies are empowered to take individual decisions which have legally binding effects on third parties, which is understood to be the main reason why terming them 'regulatory' agencies is appropriate. These agencies include the Office for the Harmonization in the Internal Market (OHIM), the Community Plant Variety Office (CPVO), the European Aviation Safety Agency (EASA) and the European Chemicals Agency (ECHA).

One might expect that the growth of agencies challenges the Commission's position of responsibility as the closest institution the EU has to an executive. The 2002 Agencies Regulation makes clear that the Commission enjoys direct control over the agencies and can 'outsource' management tasks to them, the political aims of which have already been decided upon (Lenaerts and Van Nuffel 2005: 619). This goes some way in explaining why the Commission has been supportive of the creation of certain types of agencies (Commission 2001: 24). As Everson (1999: 286) has noted, agencies are thus largely shielded from explicitly *political* processes. Clearly, however, the 'regulatory' agencies which enjoy the largest amounts of power fall outside the scope of the 2002 Regulation, and the Commission has encouraged the setting up of a framework for how these agencies exercise their powers and how they can be reviewed. A Commission proposal for an interinstitutional agreement on the operating framework for European regulatory agencies[16] was dropped after the Council expressed doubts on the use of an interinstitutional agreement for such a purpose. In its most recent communication, 'European agencies – the way forward', the Commission expresses its desire for a relaunch of debate on the role and place of agencies in regulatory governance (Commission 2008). The Commission is clearly nervous about its central regulatory role being gradually usurped. However, against the backdrop of lengthy institutional reforms achieved in the Treaty of Lisbon, it is unlikely the Council in particular will have any appetite for debate on institutional reform and competences in the near future.

## 39.3  'NEW' MODES OF GOVERNANCE AT THE EU LEVEL

In recent years, 'new governance' has been increasingly discussed in relation to the EU. 'New governance' does not have a settled meaning, and its use is not restricted to the EU. Its use is indicative of a broad move towards something 'new' in EU governance which, in general terms, can be seen as differing from the ways and means of 'old' governance. The point of reference for 'old governance' in the EU is represented by the regulatory regime outlined earlier. 'New governance' suggests a move with the process of integration away from the traditional regulatory model towards incorporation of more participatory, inclusive and 'soft' measures. The language of new governance points towards these qualities in terms which are generally seen as positive in that they emphasize a closer relationship between citizens and institutions. The use of specialist agencies and networks is often understood to be part of this process.

More specific *modes* of governance have emerged within the European integration process, which forms the subject of this section. Though the 'newness' of these modes can be contested by tracing their (albeit less explicit) existence far back in the EU's history, it is only since the 1990s that their use has dramatically increased to the extent of a 'phenomenon' (Scott and Trubek 2002: 1). New modes of governance do not require the same level of express Treaty competence as for traditional regulatory measures, which makes their use as much a political issue as a legal one.

The clearest example of a new mode of governance in operation in the EU is the open method of coordination. The OMC was explicitly recognized as a mode of governance at the Lisbon European Council Summit in 2000, though its roots in EC/EU policy stretch as far back as 1958 (Hodson and Maher 2001: 720). The OMC is composed of four elements: fixing short-, medium- and long-term goals and guidelines for the Union; benchmarking and using quantitative and qualitative indicators as a means of comparing best practice; translating the guidelines and goals into national and regional policies through specific targets; and using monitoring, evaluation and peer review as mutual learning processes (European Council 2000: 37). These characteristics therefore move the EU away from its traditional regulatory approach. Using OMC does not necessarily seek to establish a single common framework, but instead places the member states on a path towards achieving common objectives while respecting different underlying values and arrangements. The OMC has appeared in a number of policy areas, which can be characterized as those in which there has been limited regulation. These include the information society, research and development, education, employment and social exclusion (de la Porte 2002: 39–40).

The EU's competences have expanded into new areas where binding legislative measures might not appear the most appropriate, or in areas sensitive for member states because of closeness to state sovereignty. Whilst traditional measures may be theoretically possible, their use faces resistance from (some of) the member states. Employment policy is one such example. Considerations of sovereignty in terms of member states would suggest that they have much to benefit from alternative modes of governance if their main characteristic is the lack of legal enforceability. Since the new modes of governance would not appear to involve formal competences on the part of the EU institutions, they do not need to be grounded in a Treaty article – which may involve complex, lengthy intergovernmental conference negotiations if the Treaty is to be reformed. Further, the lack of enforcement provisions suggests that the new modes of governance do not involve the pooling of sovereignty and resist 'competence creep'. In addition, a public which may be sceptical of European integration generally or in certain areas can be assured that cooperation remains strictly at the intergovernmental cooperation level.

It is interesting to note, however, that, amongst the diverse origins of the inspiration for the OMC, Hodson and Maher (2001: 727) identify the monetary coordination procedure used in the Economic and Monetary Union (EMU) process as the model. In this situation, member states wishing to enter EMU agreed to adhere to certain benchmarks and policy guidelines: in the event of non-compliance, a non-binding recommendation could be made by the Council against a member state. However, although this served as a model for the OMC, the situations in which the OMC have been applied, as noted above, have not operated within a comparable situation, since the benchmarks in EMU revolved around a hegemonic force (i.e. the German economy), which is not the case for social and employment policy (Hodson and Maher 2001: 729).

One of the distinctive features of the OMC which allows member states to fulfil these common objectives is the importance and role of a range of actors, and in particular 'social partners' and 'civil society'. This is also a common feature of other new modes of governance, such as mainstreaming and benchmarking, and suits the discourse emerging from the institutions about the need to connect with citizens to a much greater extent:

> [new modes of governance] build on the participation of private actors in policy formation, relying on broad consultation and substantive input. Policy-making follows a procedural logic in which there is joint target-setting and peer assessment of national performances under broad and unsanctioned European guidance. (Eberlein and Kerwer 2004: 123)

The engagement of non-governmental actors in policy processes is one of the strongest characterizations of new governance. The inclusion of 'social partners' and 'civil society' also points to why talking about *new* governance can have ideological and normative connotations, since they are invariably associated with the connotations of what a modern system of governance *should* be.

The Commission issued a White Paper on governance in 2001. It did not discuss the use of new modes of governance in specific areas, but took a wider view as to the place of new governance within European integration. The Commission noted that, despite the achievements of European integration, which has 'delivered fifty years of stability, peace and economic prosperity' (Commission 2001: 7), there is without a doubt the problem that Europeans do not feel involved in decision-making at the European level. Questions about the relationship between the EU and national policy-making processes become highly apt (Commission 2001).

The White Paper identified areas for action on the part of the institutions and member states, with the general aim of rendering decision-making clearer to the citizen, who should also be more involved (individually or as a group) in law and policy-making. This is especially true since the areas in which the EU institutions, particularly the Commission, had a clear mandate to pursue integration (especially the Single Market) have largely been achieved (Caporaso and Wittenbrinck 2006: 473). These action points are underpinned by five principles of good governance: openness, participation, accountability, effectiveness and coherence, therefore making the link with the normative connotations of 'new' governance (Commission 2001: 10). New governance approaches may offer enough flexibility so that the institutions are not faced with gridlock or an impossible task of ensuring implementation of directives and so on.

It must also be recalled, however, that the Commission has a self-interest in presenting new modes of governance as a variation on the traditional regulatory method (where it enjoys a monopoly on the initiation of legislative measures), rather than a more radical departure. It is not in the Commission's interest to portray the new modes as a reinforcement of the role and sovereignty of the member states at its expense. The White Paper was therefore notable for the importance placed on the continued need for traditional regulatory instruments. Nevertheless, Eberlein and Kerwer warn against being overly sceptical about the Commission's motives:

> one should not rush to dismiss new modes of governance as nothing but a smokescreen for the Commission as it attempts to pursue revitalised but old-style regulation. Most importantly, documents such as the White Paper cannot be viewed as authoritative guides to the 'real' policy approach of key actors such as the Commission. They are notoriously political, ambiguous, and thus difficult to decipher. And they are not reliable guides to a complex 'policy reality'. (Eberlein and Kerwer 2004: 124)

It may be that fewer regulations and directives are made in the future, especially when compared to the period prior to the completion of the Single Market, but it should not be taken to mean that methods of new governance such as the OMC will always be appropriate as alternatives. Similarly, it should not be argued that one form of governance is necessarily superior: the binding nature of rules and the voluntarism of new modes of governance both have their place within the integration process depending on the aims and context. In this respect, discussion of 'old' governance (meaning the traditional regulatory regime) and 'new' governance (including the OMC) can be misleading. The important point to draw out is that the system of regulatory governance in the Union is more complex than the Treaty provisions would suggest. Neither is it suggested that the 'new' will replace the 'old'. Even a narrow view of the new modes of governance as limited to very specific instruments, such as the OMC, shows that understanding the EU's regulatory regime must take account of a greater variety of actors involved in the processes and the effects of measures which may not have explicitly stated binding characteristics. The level of citizenship participation thus varies as to what measures are pursued, whether within the new modes of governance or more traditional measures. However, the extent of citizen participation in the new modes of governance is unclear, given their lack of definition.

## 39.6   CONCLUSION

The 21st century has been a time of great change for the EU, including for its regulatory regime. Key achievements, notably enlargements, have brought significant challenges which go to the heart of the integration project. In particular, as the EU has attempted to undertake comprehensive reforms through the Constitutional Treaty and the compromise Treaty of Lisbon, it has been beset by sets of political questions which challenge the way in which the EU has operated throughout its history. In particular, the traditional means of pursuing integration and harmonization through regulations and directives has been increasingly questioned as to its appropriateness for a larger Union. The reticence amongst some member states for the same kind of Union envisaged in past decades has been reflected in the shocks to the system from sections of the European population (for example, the French, Dutch and Irish) who were previously amongst the most enthusiastic supporters of European integration but who have responded negatively in referenda on EU reforms. Nevertheless, there is no evidence to suggest that the traditional regulatory regime is obsolete. Rather, the emergence of new actors, including specialist agencies and new modes of governance, reflects developments in many European and non-European states and can be taken as a sign of the growing maturity of the EU's system of governance. As the EU develops internally, it must continue to seek innovative approaches to regulatory governance to exist alongside more established methods and processes. The key task is to ensure that its system of regulatory governance confronts ongoing issues of legitimacy, accountability and effectiveness in the eyes of the citizens of Europe.

## NOTES

1. Article 1 TEU. References to treaty articles in this chapter are to the consolidated versions of the new treaties from 1 December 2009, upon the entry into force of the Treaty of Lisbon. Previous EC Treaty article numbers are given where appropriate.
2. See Levi-Faur (Chapter 1: 000).
3. Article 258 TFEU (formerly Article 226 EC).
4. Ibid.
5. Case 6/64 *Costa v ENEL* [1964] ECR 585; Case 11/70 *Internationale Handelsgesellschaft* [1970] ECR 1125; Case 106/77 *Simmenthal* [1978] ECR 629.
6. Source: EUR-Lex Directory, http://eur-lex.europa.eu/en/legis/20091101/index.htm (accessed 18 December 2009).
7. Regulation (EC) No. 1907/2006, as published in OJ L396/1.
8. Article 289(1) TFEU: 'The ordinary legislative procedure shall consist in the joint adoption by the European Parliament and the Council of a regulation, directive or decision on a proposal from the Commission.' According to Article 289(2) TFEU, there are some exceptions where the 'special legislative procedure' applies as defined in the Treaty. The difference between the ordinary and special legislative procedures is the more limited role of the Parliament in the latter in favour of the Council.
9. Council Decision 99/468/EC on the Procedure for the exercise of implementing powers conferred on the Commission (1999).

10. Qualified majority voting is a system used in the Council whereby the number of votes held by each member state is proportionate to its population. The current number of votes allocated to each member state is found in Protocol No. 36 attached to the Treaties, Article 3.
11. Joerges (2002) in particular praised the comitology regime as 'deliberative supra-nationalism'.
12. Council Decision 99/468/EC on the Procedure for the exercise of implementing powers conferred on the Commission (1999) and Council Decision 2006/512/EC amending Decision 1999/468/EC laying down the procedures for the exercise of implementing powers conferred on the Commission (2006).
13. For example, the European Network and Information Security Agency (ENISA) and the Trans-European Transport Network Executive Agency (TEN-TEA).
14. Council Regulation (EC) No. 58/2003 of 19 December 2002 laying down the statute for executive agencies to be entrusted with certain tasks in the management of Community programmes, Article 6(1).
15. For example, the European Environment Agency was created by Regulation (EEC) 1210/90 in 1990 on the basis of the provisions relating to environmental protection (now Articles 191–193 TFEU).
16. COM (2005) 59 final.

# BIBLIOGRAPHY

Barroso, José Manuel (2004), 'Strategic objectives', address to the European Parliament, Strasbourg, Speech 04/539, 14 December.
Caporaso, James A. and Joerg Wittenbrinck (2006), 'The new modes of governance and political authority in Europe', *Journal of European Public Policy*, **13** (4), 471–80.
Commission of the European Communities (2001), 'European governance: a White Paper', COM (2001) 428 final.
Commission (EC) (2005) 'Draft interinstitutional agreement on the operating framework for the European regulatory agencies', COM (2005) 59 final.
Commission (EC) (2008) 'Communication from the Commission to the European Parliament and the Council: European agencies – the way forward', COM (2008) 135 final.
Curtin, Deirdre (2009), *Executive Power of the European Union: Law, Practices, and the Living Constitution*, Oxford: Oxford University Press.
de Búrca, Gráinne (1999), 'Institutional development of the EU', in Paul Craig and Gráinne de Búrca (eds), *The Evolution of EU Law*, Oxford: Oxford University Press, pp. 55–81.
de la Porte, Caroline (2002), 'Is the open method of coordination appropriate for organising activities at European level in sensitive policy areas?', *European Law Journal*, **8** (1), 38–58.
Eberlein, Burkhard and Dieter Kerwer (2004), 'New governance in the European Union: a theoretical perspective', *Journal of Common Market Studies*, **42** (1), 121–42.
European Council (2000), 'Presidency conclusion of the Lisbon European Council' (Lisbon Strategy), 23–24 March.
Everson, Michelle (1999), 'The constitutionalisation of European administrative law: legal oversight of a stateless internal market', in Christian Joerges and Ellen Vos (eds), *EU Committees: Social Regulation, Law and Politics*, Oxford: Hart, pp. 281–309.
Hodson, Dermot and Imelda Maher (2001), 'The open method as a new mode of governance: the case of soft economic policy coordination', *Journal of Common Market Studies*, **39** (4), 719–46.
Joerges, Christian (2002), 'Deliberative supranationalism – two defences', *European Law Journal*, **8** (1), 133–51.
Kagan, Robert (2007), Globalization and legal change: the "Americanization" of European law?', *Regulation & Governance*, **1** (2), 99–120.
Lenaerts, Koen and Piet Van Nuffel (2005), *Constitutional Law of the European Union*, London: Sweet & Maxwell.
Levi-Faur, David (2010), 'Europeanization and regulatory agencification: towards a single European regulatory space', paper presented at a workshop on 'Agency Governance in the EU and its Consequences' (RECON/MZES), University of Mannheim, 16–17 September.
Majone, Giandomenico (2006), 'Managing Europeanization: the European agencies', in John Peterson and Michael Shackleton (eds), *The Institutions of the European Union*, 2nd edn, Oxford: Oxford University Press, pp. 190–209.
Majone, Giandomenico (2009), *Europe as the Would-Be World Power*, Cambridge: Cambridge University Press.
Scott, Joanne and David Trubek (2002), 'Mind the gap: law and new approaches to governance in the European Union', *European Law Journal*, **8** (1), 1–18.

Shapiro, Martin and Alec Stone Sweet (2002), *On Law, Politics and Judicialization*, Oxford: Oxford University Press.

van Ooik, Ronald (2005), 'The growing importance of agencies in the EU: shifting governance and the institutional balance', in Deirdre Curtin and Ramses A. Wessel (eds), *Good Governance and the European Union: Reflections on Concepts, Institutions and Substance*, Antwerp: Intersentia, pp. 125–52.

Verhoeven, Amaryllis (2005), 'Democratic life in the European Union, according to its constitution', in Deirdre Curtin and Ramses A. Wessel (eds), *Good Governance and the European Union: Reflections on Concepts, Institutions and Substance*, Antwerp: Intersentia, pp. 153–72.

Vos, Ellen (2005), 'The role of comitology in European governance', in Deirdre Curtin and Ramses A. Wessel (eds), *Good Governance and the European Union: Reflections on Concepts, Institutions and Substance*, Antwerp: Intersentia, pp. 107–24.

# 40 Regulatory governance in the European Union: the political struggle over committees, agencies and networks

*Martijn Groenleer*

Until recently, little attention has been paid to bureaucratic and administrative actors at the European Union (EU) level and the way these actors are involved in the actual implementation of policy and legislation. At the same time, "*non-legislation* has moved much more to the centre stage in terms of the actual overall output of the EU" (Curtin 2009: 3).

The promulgation of EU rules, for instance those aimed at preventing misconduct by businesses and addressing risks following from economic activity, has increased significantly in the past decades. Today, a considerable number of rules applied in the EU, including those on food and drug safety, occupational health risks, aviation and maritime safety and environmental pollution, have been produced through *executive* rather than legislative action. In recent years, in reaction to the threat of international terrorism and shortages in energy supply and in response to the global financial crisis, the capacity available at the EU level to enforce European legislation in such diverse areas as justice and home affairs, energy and, notably, financial services has grown substantially.

This chapter concentrates on regulatory governance in the European Union and the increasingly important role played by bureaucratic and administrative actors at the EU level. It argues that EU regulatory governance entails the strategic interaction of a wide variety of actors across multiple levels. The existing literature usually considers EU regulatory governance as a purely "legalistic" process, with key roles for the European Commission and the European Court of Justice, or as a process that is fully in the hands of the EU member states and their regulatory agencies and courts. This chapter focuses instead on three forms of EU-level regulatory capacity – comitology committees, specialized EU-level agencies and European regulatory networks – whose evolution is highly related and indicative of the institutionalization of the EU's regulatory space.

The chapter is structured as follows. Section 40.1 examines the characteristics of the multi-actor and multi-level setting in which EU regulatory governance takes place. The focus in section 40.2 is on the role of the Commission and on governance through committees. The shift towards EU agencies and European regulatory networks is discussed in sections 40.3 and 40.4 respectively, and the chapter ends with section 40.5 on the EU's evolving regulatory space.

## 40.1 THE DEVELOPMENT OF REGULATORY GOVERNANCE IN THE EU

EU regulatory governance has long been about legislative processes. With the development of the Single European Market, removing barriers between the national economies of the member states, a European approach to the (re-)regulation of these often liberalized markets emerged. This approach is characterized by the large-scale production of EU law, a combination of harmonization and mutual recognition of standards and the legal enforcement of the application of EU rules (McGowan and Wallace 1996; Wallace et al. 2005). It entails the involvement of a wide variety of actors, ranging from the European institutions, notably the European Commission and the European Court of Justice, to national governments and courts, and to stakeholders such as private companies and consumer groups.

While proposals for new EU laws come from the European Commission, the Council of Ministers and the European Parliament subsequently decide on their adoption. Whereas the Commission is often depicted as the EU executive, the member states are responsible for adopting the necessary legislative and regulatory measures to implement EU laws as well as applying and enforcing them in their respective territories. This usually means that member states first have to transpose EU laws into their national legislation (Kaeding 2008). When member states do not comply with EU law, either failing to take the necessary legislative or regulatory measures, or taking measures that render EU legislation ineffective, the Commission, as the "guardian of the treaties," can initiate infringement proceedings at the Court.

### 40.1.1   Beyond Legislative Processes

Implementation is much broader than mere transposition, however. Member states are also responsible for the creation of policy instruments and tools, the establishment of independent agencies, and monitoring and inspection through national regulators (Dimitrakopoulos and Richardson 2001). In spite of its role as guardian of the treaties, the Commission thus heavily relies on the member states and national bodies involved in the implementation of EU policy and legislation. As member states often lack the executive capacity or the political willingness to implement, even laws may be unevenly implemented across the EU (Börzel 2001; Falkner et al. 2005; Berglund et al. 2006; Versluis 2007; Kaeding 2008).

When studying European regulatory governance one therefore has to move beyond mere legislative processes to bureaucratic or administrative processes. Such processes are, according to Peters (1992: 76), characterized by "a gradual accretion of common policies and standards through the European bureaucracy (and its masters within the Commission) and through its contacts with national bureaucracies and national and transnational interest groups." Egeberg (2006) and Egeberg and Curtin (2008) argue that this gradual accretion is leading to the transformation of executive politics in Europe and resulting in the development of a genuine Union administration, bringing together various actors and spanning different levels of governance (see also Curtin 2009; Eckert, Chapter 37).

As part of this multi-actor and multi-level administration, forms of regulatory capacity have emerged in which the Commission and the member states cooperate to put EU laws into practice. One such form that developed quite soon after the EU's inception is the system of committee governance or "comitology," which is discussed in the following section.

## 40.2 THE COMMISSION, RULE-MAKING AND THE COMITOLOGY SYSTEM

The implementation of EU laws by EU member states takes place under the authority of the Council. When the amount of legislation increased, the Council's workload increased concomitantly. Implementation thus demanded administrative functions that could be performed only by a large-scale bureaucratic organization at the EU level, and it became necessary for the Council to delegate some of its implementation powers to the Commission.

In a few areas, notably competition, the Commission is directly involved in implementation (see also Eckert, Chapter 37). The Commission has a wide range of powers to ensure that rules on, for instance, mergers and cartels are enforced in the EU member states. To that end, it can investigate businesses (think of the Microsoft case), hold hearings and grant exemptions, amongst other activities. Yet, even in the area of competition, the Commission has found its executive role restricted as a result of limited staff to carry out its functions. In 2004, the Commission therefore relegated some of its enforcement functions to the member states, allowing national competition authorities and courts to apply and enforce certain rules.

Even when not directly involved in implementation, the Commission still has an influence on member states' implementation activities, devoting a significant part of its resources to its rule-making function, laying down rules that member states and national agencies have to follow when implementing EU laws.[1] Often this rule-making function is restricted to "day-to-day management decisions" that require "little or no exercise of discretion" (Pedler and Bradley 2006: 238). Sometimes, such as in the electronic communications sector, the Commission can, for instance, supervise the independent national regulatory agencies created to execute EU rules by formulating rules and guidelines *ex ante* as well as vetoing national decisions *ex post* (Hancher and Lavrijssen-Heijmans 2007).

### 40.2.1 The Comitology System

To avoid member states losing too much control to the Commission in the case of decisions requiring an exercise of discretion, committees made up of national civil servants and Commission officials were created to fill in the details of legislation. The first committees involving member state representatives were created in the 1960s to take decisions on the implementation of common agricultural policies. Today, committee governance or comitology has become a characteristic feature of the EU regulatory process, with well over 200 committees responsible for implementation in a wide variety of policy domains (Bergström 2005; Blom-Hansen 2008).

Committees operate according to a range of different procedures, which vary with regard to the way the Council and increasingly the European Parliament supervise the Commission; nevertheless, they have several characteristics in common.[2] While the members of the committee are representatives of the member states, the committee is chaired by the Commission, which also sets the agenda and puts forward a draft upon which the member state representatives vote (Pedler and Bradley 2006; Blom-Hansen and Brandsma 2009). Committees make it possible to discuss the implementation of measures before they are adopted so as to ensure that these measures are applicable to the situation in the member states (e.g. Christiansen and Larsson 2007; Christiansen et al. 2009).

There are different images of regulatory governance through committees, reflecting the difference between rational choice and sociological constructivist theories. According to some scholars, comitology can be seen as an effort by the member states to control the Commission when it comes to the implementation of EU legislation through the creation of detailed rules (e.g. Ballman et al. 2002; Pollack 2003). Intergovernmental bargaining is thus considered the main mechanism underlying committee governance. Other scholars consider the most important mechanism driving governance by committee to be supranational deliberation (e.g. Joerges and Neyer 1997a, 1997b; Wessels 1998; Dehousse 2003), with members meeting to discuss common problems based on substantive arguments and attempting to achieve consensus. Blom-Hansen and Brandsma (2009; see also Egeberg et al. 2003) argue that both images may be true, depending on factors such as the technical complexity of the cases handled and the length of time members have participated in the committee.

Hence, rather than one actor structurally dominating the other, ensuring implementation through comitology entails a process of interaction between the Commission and the member states. While the Commission plays a central role in comitology, it can play this role only because the member states have the opportunity to adapt EU laws through detailed rules formulated at the implementation stage (Curtin 2009). Granting the Commission full executive powers to draft and implement detailed rules without taking into account member states' particular concerns would almost certainly come at the expense of the efficiency and legitimacy of the legislative decision-making process (Pedler and Bradley 2006).

### 40.2.2 A Regulatory Governance Dilemma

By the end of the 1980s, the shortcomings of "a purely legislative approach to market integration" became increasingly clear (Majone 2002: 329). While problems with economic integration in the EU persisted, new problems emerged that could not effectively be dealt with by using existing institutional solutions such as comitology committees. The adoption of the Single European Act in 1986 led to a significant increase in workload for the Commission, with it not only having to solve economic problems but also having to deal with environmental issues, health and safety in the workplace and even security issues. The negotiation of the Maastricht Treaty in 1992 also gave a boost to the responsibilities of the EU in a vast number of areas, such as public health, consumer protection and social policy.

The rapid increase of the EU's responsibilities with regard to the implementation of legislation and the execution of policies placed growing demands on the Commission as an executive actor. Even though it had grown in size over the years and was bigger than most international organizations, the Commission still had a limited number of staff and a restricted budget compared to the member states, owing to restrictions imposed by the Parliament and the Council (Kelemen 2002). Furthermore, taking on these new responsibilities would mean that the Commission, traditionally oriented towards the initiation of new policies, would increasingly have to play a regulatory role. As the European

Commission is more a political decision-maker than a neutral administrator (at least in some fields), this would mean that the implementation of legislation or the execution of policies could become even more entangled with political issues.

Faced with demands for action to solve persistent problems, the EU was thus confronted with a dilemma. Whereas the member states were responsible for the actual implementation of laws drafted at the EU level, they did not always meet their responsibilities in this regard. At the same time, the EU usually did not have the competence or the capacity to enforce rules on the ground, the rise of comitology further straining the Commission's resources. The idea of investing the Commission with the competence to directly oversee the application of Community legislation in more policy areas or increasing its capacity to regulate in a more indirect way has been found unacceptable by most member states. It has also generally been seen as unfeasible from the EU's perspective, given that supranational EU institutions will probably never be able to obtain the knowledge required to regulate specific national circumstances.

As a result, however, regulatory practices could still diverge across the different member states, which could lead to the competitive advantage of some companies over others or to some citizens being exposed to a higher risk than others. Given the functional need for regulatory capacity and the political difficulty in obtaining this in another way, the delegation of tasks to functionally decentralized bodies became an attractive option for the Commission. These bodies, also referred to as agencies of the European Union, are examined in the next section.

## 40.3   RESORTING TO INDEPENDENT AGENCIES AT THE EU LEVEL[3]

A second and increasingly used form of regulatory capacity concerns the delegation of tasks to independent agencies at the EU level (Groenleer 2009; see also Eckert, Chapter 37; Cardwell, Chapter 39).[4] Agencies are bodies governed by European public law which are distinct from the Community institutions and which have their own legal personality. They are usually set up by an act of secondary legislation.[5]

Agencies have proliferated in different policy domains, especially since the 1990s. To date, there are over 30 agencies of the EU. They have a wide variety of tasks, including regulatory ones, such as the management of the EU's chemical policy and the authorization of medicinal products, and thus potentially fulfill an important role in implementing EU legislation and in regulating European policy sectors. To fulfill this role, they spend over one billion euros per year and have more than 4000 employees. Unlike the main EU institutions, they are not located in Brussels or in Luxembourg, but are geographically dispersed throughout the EU.

### 40.3.1   Reasons for Agency Creation

From a Principal-Agent perspective, the delegation of powers to agencies can be explained in terms of the functional advantages. EU agencies are, for instance, supposed to organize independent expertise at the EU level, increase the transparency and visibility of EU policymaking, offer cost savings to industry and business, and reduce transaction costs for national governments, thereby increasing bureaucratic efficiency (e.g. Majone 1996, 1997; Kelemen 2002, 2005; Vos 2003).

In particular, the creation of agencies is supposed to contribute to the efficient and flexible implementation of Community policies, mostly in areas requiring frequent decisions based on technical or scientific considerations and where uncertainty is great, such as food or chemicals policy (Majone 1997). Besides improving the EU's capacity to monitor policy implementation, the creation of agencies is also meant to encourage the harmonization of regulatory practices in the member states. By creating and coordinating networks of national regulatory agencies, EU agencies can diffuse regulatory practices and styles across Europe (Dehousse 1997; Chiti 2000). Another frequently cited reason for agency creation is to remedy the perceived shortcomings of the committee framework (Everson et al. 1999), which before recent reforms was seen as "among the least transparent policy-making processes in the democratic world" (Shapiro 1997: 291). The BSE crisis in 1996 clearly demonstrated the downside of this process, when anonymous experts were propelled into decision-making positions. In contrast to the opaque comitology system, the agency option seems to be more transparent.

Agencies are established not only for functional reasons, as political motives also play a role. Agencies are created to show the willingness of EU and national politicians to solve novel, pervasive and urgent problems, particularly in the wake of crises. Consider the example of the European Maritime Safety Agency (EMSA), advising the Commission on draft legislation and enforcing EU rules on maritime safety, which was created after the accident with the 25-year-old single-hull tanker *Erika* in 1999. The creation of agencies should further be seen as resulting from the inter-institutional politics between the Commission, the Parliament and the Council (Kelemen 2002, 2005; Dehousse 2008). In the early 1990s, agency creation was not only a welcome solution to pressing problems with regard to implementation; it was also politically acceptable from the viewpoint of the Commission, the Council and the Parliament, because they all felt they could somehow gain through the process of agencification.

While functional and political explanations largely account for the creation of EU agencies, these explanations do not sufficiently allow for the influence of institutional factors on the agencification process occurring at the EU level. The decision to use the agency option, and to use it increasingly frequently since the early 1990s, has also been the result of a process of transnational policy diffusion. When it comes to the creation of EU agencies, EU institutions have been influenced by the spread of, most notably, New Public Management (NPM) norms in the member states. When it comes to the design of individual agencies, however, there has been some borrowing and comparing between already existing EU agencies and newly created ones, but "detailed rules and structures differ because they reflect the norms and practices that constitute sector-specific regulatory regimes" (Demortain 2008: 3).

### 40.3.2   EU Agencies' Inclusive Design

Most agencies have a limited mandate. They have an advisory function and are generally not invested with broad regulatory powers. The European Environment Agency (EEA), for instance, provides information on the environment at the European level to support the Community and the member states. It does not monitor the member states' implementation of environmental legislation, as such a task could in fact hamper the agency's ability to obtain information from the member states (Groenleer 2009). Nevertheless, by gathering information, the EEA, and other agencies alike, may shape decisions taken by the Commission and the member states. Rather than by formal authority, they can thus "regulate by information" (Majone 1997).

Some EU agencies have a regulatory function. They are invested with a variety of tasks related – either directly or indirectly – to implementation. These tasks can be grouped into four categories (Groenleer et al. 2010): decision-making, inspection, training and research, of which decision-making and inspection tasks are assumed to have the most significant effect on implementation and harmonization.

Thus far, only a few agencies have been granted decision-making tasks, which allow them to act on behalf of the Commission or the member states in individual cases: the Office for Harmonization in the Internal Market (OHIM) registers Community trademarks and designs, the Community Plant Variety Office (CPVO) grants Community plant variety rights, and the European Aviation Safety Agency (EASA) issues certificates for aeronautical products. Although these agencies are not empowered to adopt legislative measures of general application, Schout (2008) gives the example of an airplane of a particular type being grounded by EASA. Since such a decision would in practice also affect other airplanes of that type it would thus be "general" despite being rendered in an individual case.

Several other agencies, including the European Medicines Agency (EMA), the European Food Safety Authority (EFSA) and the European Chemicals Agency (ECHA), do not have decision-making power, but the Commission must take the opinions issued by these agencies into account when considering whether or not to grant authorization for medicines, food products or chemical substances. The case of the EMA shows that even if agencies only render opinions these can in fact turn out to be very influential, as the Commission usually "rubberstamps" them without discussion, lacking the scientific expertise required to determine whether the advice is scientifically sound and realizing that any questioning of such advice could decrease the legitimacy of the regulatory system (Gehring and Krapohl 2007; Groenleer 2009).

An increasing number of agencies have inspection tasks. Consider again the example of EASA, which conducts investigations of regulated companies and inspections of member states' inspection agencies. Up until now, the investigations have mainly concerned companies that have designed, produced or maintained products, parts or appliances approved or certified by the agency. Member states were not keen on completely transferring the investigative task, not only because some have considerable capacity of their own which would otherwise become redundant, but also because they consider the monitoring of aviation safety – even though done in collaboration with EU and international bodies – a national responsibility, for which they are held accountable by their publics (Groenleer et al. 2010).

The opposition of member states, seeing the creation of EU agencies as a threat to existing national authorities and as a centralization of competences at the EU level, is usually smothered by the inclusive design of EU agencies. While they include representatives of the Commission, and sometimes also experts designated by the Parliament, agency management boards generally consist of member state representatives, usually the heads of national agencies. Furthermore, much of the actual work of agencies is done by technical or scientific committees of experts from the member states. Thus, even if regulatory competences are transferred to EU agencies, member states are still able to exert significant control over regulation through the agency make-up (Kelemen 2002; Groenleer 2009).

### 40.3.3   Restrictions to EU Agencies' Added Value

Groenleer et al. (2010) mention some restrictions to the added value of EU agencies in enforcing EU rules at the street level. This added value depends on at least two factors. First is the willingness of member state authorities to actually transfer implementation powers to the EU level. Thus far, the member states have not done this in all sectors, or have done so in various ways. Second, added value depends on the willingness of the European Commission to involve the agency in ensuring actual implementation. To date, the Commission has not always followed up on agencies' activities, or has done so in an inconsistent way. It can therefore be argued, as has been done by Schout (2008, 2012) in the case of EASA, that creating EU (semi-)regulatory agencies does not in fact add to the competence invested in and capacity already available to the Commission.

Moreover, EU agencies usually do not build up significant autonomous capacities, do not centralize executive tasks at the EU level and certainly do not completely take over national government tasks (Groenleer 2009; see also Busuioc et al. 2012; Eckert, Chapter 37). Through their design, most agencies are closely linked to the Commission and are heavily influenced by the member states. Given the power of pre-existing national agencies, often endowed with a relatively high level of formal autonomy, EU agencies have usually been designed as network agencies, and most have evolved such that they complement national bureaucracies rather than replace them (Kelemen 2005).

Through their networks, EU agencies encourage the involvement of stakeholders and the exchange of information and best practices (Groenleer et al. 2010). Indeed, EU agencies potentially add most value when they stimulate mutual learning processes among national regulatory authorities and when they serve as platforms for discussion and debate among European and national stakeholders. In that sense, the agencies' contribution to EU regulatory governance does not seem that different from European networks of national regulators, to which we now turn.

## 40.4   EUROPEAN NETWORKS OF NATIONAL REGULATORY AGENCIES

The creation of EU agencies is closely related to a third form of regulatory capacity at the EU level: European networks of national regulators (Coen and Thatcher 2008; Thatcher and Coen 2008). In some policy areas, such as aviation safety, networks of national regulators have been formalized into EU-level agencies (Pierre and Peters 2009); in others, such as food safety, EU agencies bring national authorities together in newly created networks. In yet others, such as telecom and energy, which until recently were dominated by state monopolies and are still subject to considerable regulation by national executives, European networks have served as an alternative to a single EU regulator, which was unacceptable to the member states (Kelemen 2002; Geradin and Petit 2004; Coen and Thatcher 2008).

European networks have often emerged as a result of and sometimes in parallel with member states creating more or less independent agencies at the national level. Once established, these national agencies often realized they were part of a transnational regulatory structure comprising both national and EU institutions. They therefore engaged in informal means of cooperation at the EU level, "softly" harmonizing member states' regulatory activities (Eberlein and Grande 2005: 100). Consider in this respect the example of the European Union Network for the Implementation and Enforcement of Environmental Law (IMPEL), which, for instance, formulates technical guidelines for environmental authorities and organizes exchange programs for inspectors (Martens 2006).

As a result of a simultaneous process of delegation to national agencies and to the European level (Eberlein and Newman 2008), national agencies increasingly fulfil a dual or "double-hatted" role (Egeberg 2006). They are part both of national administrations, as "agents" of national ministries, and of the European administration, where they cooperate with agencies of other member states, EU agencies and, as pointed out below, the European Commission. Indeed, as they often directly interact with their European counterparts, bypassing ministerial departments, national regulatory agencies may gain power vis-à-vis their "principals" at the national level. Networking at the EU level thus allows national agencies to increase their autonomy vis-à-vis ministerial departments, which may also explain why in some cases (notably telecom) EU agencies have either not been created at all or only take a networked form.

### 40.4.1   European Networks and the European Commission

In addition to loosely organized networks, the past decade has seen the creation of more formal European regulatory networks. Often this creation merely meant a formalization of existing practices at the EU level. A distinctive feature as compared to informal networks, however, is the position of the European Commission. Not only do national regulatory agencies work together through these networks; they also assist and advise the European Commission in implementing EU rules. An example is the field of competition policy, where the Commission, invested with broad executive powers, cooperates with national regulators via the European Competition Network (ECN).

Such formal networks may serve several functions, including coordinated implementation, regulatory convergence and supervisory convergence (Hancher and Lavrijssen-Heijmans, 2007). National authorities can coordinate implementation when they have the competence to, for example, transpose certain European measures into national measures and/or advise the legislator when transposing EU law. Regulatory convergence is attained through adopting common positions on the implementation of EU law, formulating best practices and conducting peer reviews. Networks of national regulators, finally, may enhance cooperation with regard to enforcement and supervision in cases of mutual interest, for example through information sharing and coordination of national procedures.

### 40.4.2   The Limitations of European Networks

As national authorities still have considerable discretion in regulating certain market sectors, this also means that cooperation through European networks in the past has not necessarily led to the level of harmonization required to create a level or fair playing field (Coen and Thatcher 2008; Kelemen and Tarrant 2011). National regulators are usually not compelled to follow the advice and opinions rendered by European networks. In addition, common positions and peer reviews generally remain without binding effect, as a result of which member states may still implement EU rules in various manners. The European Regulators Group (ERG) for instance, a network in the area of telecom, has in the past been criticized particularly by the Commission for being overly oriented towards consensus. It was therefore transformed, taking a more agency-like structure and being renamed the Body of European Regulators for Electronic Communications, albeit after fierce opposition from national politicians and regulators, as well as the European Parliament (see also Levi-Faur 2011).

Moreover, networks are vulnerable to "re-politicization." As member states often have divergent interests and their national agencies may lack the level of mutual trust required to cooperate in an effective manner, regulatory measures may still be blocked and the functioning of the internal market may be hampered (Eberlein and Grande 2005; Coen and Thatcher 2008). Cooperation is further hindered by the different competences of national regulators as well as their varying levels of independence from politics. It is at least partly for these two reasons that the European Regulators Group for Electricity and Gas (ERGEG), a network in the area of energy, was recently converted into the EU Agency for the Cooperation of Energy Regulators (ACER). This transformation was not only pushed for by the Commission but also generally supported by national politicians and regulators as well as the energy industry.

The perceived regulatory gap at the transnational level has thus spurred the transformation of both informal and formal networks into agencies or agency-like entities. This development is particularly clear in the area of financial services. After the financial crisis in 2008, three rather unique networks of experts (officially referred to as "Lamfalussy committees"), in banking, in insurance and occupational pensions and in securities, were upgraded to European authorities. While being invested with the power to directly supervise banks and other financial actors under exceptional circumstances only, these authorities do have significant powers to coordinate national regulators and may well see their powers grow in the future.

## 40.5   THE INSTITUTIONALIZATION OF THE EU'S REGULATORY SPACE

This chapter focused on the institutions of European regulatory governance, going beyond regulation through legislative instruments. It showed that, rather than merely being driven by functional interests or by hierarchical authority, regulation in the EU is a complex political process in which multiple actors interact across different levels of governance. Such interaction has led to the gradual build-up of regulatory capacity via committees, agencies and networks, and the institutionalization of the EU's regulatory space.

The chapter also demonstrated that European regulatory governance is the product of strategic interaction, actors expecting that they can somehow benefit from further developing the EU's regulatory capacity. Whereas new forms of regulatory capacity *on paper* play an increasingly important role in implementing EU legislation on the ground, the development of such capacity *in practice* often means that EU policy processes remain more or less intact, with the Commission, the member states or their national authorities exerting control over comitology committees, EU agencies and European regulatory networks (cf. Kelemen and Tarrant 2011; Schout 2008, 2012).

Thus the gradual development from committees and networks to EU agencies, as also observed by Thatcher and Coen (2008), does not necessarily signify the increased centralization of EU regulation. External factors, such as transboundary crises, may spur intensified cooperation at the EU level between the Commission, the member states and their national regulatory authorities, as the recent process of agencification in the financial services sector has shown. However, novel forms of regulatory capacity are likely to build on pre-existing institutional arrangements and power distributions. That is, the creation as well as the design of committees, networks and agencies should be seen as resulting from the political struggle between these actors (Groenleer 2009).

What is apparent is that committees, agencies and networks exist alongside traditional governmental organizations and established EU institutions, resulting in a multilayered system of governance (Egeberg and Curtin 2008; Curtin 2009; see also Eckert, Chapter 37). They serve as alternatives to both national sovereignty – which is increasingly inadequate in view of transnational problems – and centralization at the EU level, which is often unacceptable from the perspective of national interests and will probably never be possible in view of the difficulty of obtaining sufficient resources (Everson et al. 1999; Metcalfe 2000; Eberlein and Grande 2005). Thus the growth of regulatory capacity, especially the shift towards agencies, is not merely quantitative. Albeit gradually, it alters EU governance and testifies to the institutional changes to which the Union continues to be subject.

## NOTES

1. The Lisbon Treaty distinguishes between two types of non-legislative measures used to implement legislation: delegated acts (a new type) and implementing acts. Whereas the former work out the details of legislation, the latter adopt the necessary rules to apply legally binding acts in a uniform way.
2. Under the Lisbon Treaty, the Parliament and the Council have extensive supervisory powers in the case of delegated acts, while implementing acts remain subject to the supervision of member state representatives in comitology committees.
3. This section draws on Groenleer (2009).
4. See the EU's website for a complete list of all agencies: http://europa.eu/agencies/index_en.htm.
5. Even though agencies are mentioned, the Treaty of Lisbon does not provide much clarity on their creation and design.

## REFERENCES

Ballman, A., D. Epstein and S. O'Halloran (2002), 'Delegation, comitology and the separation of powers in the European Union', *International Organization*, **56** (3), 551–74.

Berglund, S., I. Gange and F. van Waarden (2006), 'Mass production of law. Routinization in the transposition of European directives: a sociological-institutionalist account', *Journal of European Public Policy*, **13** (5), 692–716.

Bergström, C.F. (2005), *Comitology: Delegation of Powers in the European Union and the Committee System*, Oxford: Oxford University Press.

Blom-Hansen, J. (2008), 'The origins of the EU comitology system: a case of informal agenda-setting by the Commission', *Journal of European Public Policy*, **15** (2), 208–26.

Blom-Hansen, J. and G.J. Brandsma (2009), 'The EU comitology system: intergovernmental bargaining *and* deliberative supranationalism?', *Journal of Common Market Studies*, **47** (4), 719–40.

Börzel, T.A. (2001), 'Non-compliance in the European Union: pathology or statistical artifact?', *Journal of European Public Policy*, **8** (5), 803–24.

Busuioc, M., M. Groenleer and J. Trondal (eds) (2012), *The Agency Phenomenon in the European Union: Emergence, Institutionalisation and Everyday Decision-Making*, Manchester: Manchester University Press.

Chiti, E. (2000), 'The emergence of a Community administration: the case of European agencies', *Common Market Law Review*, **37** (2), 309–43.

Christiansen, T. and T. Larsson (2007), *The Role of Committees in the EU Policy-Process*, Cheltenham, UK and Northampton, MA, USA: Edward Elgar Publishing.

Christiansen, T., J. Oettel and B. Vaccari (2009), *21st Century Comitology: Implementing Committees in the Enlarged European Union*, Maastricht: EIPA.

Coen, D. and M. Thatcher (2008), 'Network governance and multi-level delegation: European networks of regulatory agencies', *Journal of Public Policy*, **28** (1), 49–71.

Curtin, D. (2009), *Executive Power of the European Union: Law, Practices and the Living Constitution*, Oxford: Oxford University Press.

Dehousse, R. (1997), 'Regulation by networks in the European Community: the role of European agencies', *Journal of European Public Policy*, **4** (2), 246–61.

Dehousse, R. (2003), 'Comitology: who watches the watchmen?', *Journal of European Public Policy*, **10** (5), 798–813.

Dehousse, R. (2008), 'Delegation of powers in the European Union: the need for multi-principals models', *West European Politics*, **31** (4), 789–805.

Demortain, D. (2008), *Institutional Isomorphism: The Designing of the European Food Safety Authority with Regard to the European Medicines Authority*, Discussion Paper No. 50, London: CARR/LSE.

Dimitrakopoulos, D. and J. Richardson (2001), 'Implementing EU public policy', in J. Richardson (ed.), *European Union: Power and Policy-Making*, London and New York: Routledge, pp. 335–56.

Eberlein, B. and E. Grande (2005), 'Beyond delegation: transnational regulatory regimes and the EU regulatory state', *Journal of European Public Policy*, **12** (1), 89–112.

Eberlein, B. and A. Newman (2008), 'Escaping the international governance dilemma? Incorporated transgovernmental networks in the European Union', *Governance*, **21** (1), 25–52.

Egeberg, M. (ed.) (2006), *Multilevel Administration: The Transformation of Executive Politics in Europe*, Basingstoke: Palgrave Macmillan.

Egeberg, M. and D. Curtin (2008), 'Tradition and innovation: Europe's accumulated executive order', *West European Politics*, **31** (4), 639–61.

Egeberg, M., G.F. Schaefer and J. Trondal (2003), 'The many faces of committee governance', *West European Politics*, **26** (3), 19–40.

Everson, M., G. Majone, L. Metcalfe and A. Schout (1999), 'The role of specialised agencies in decentralising EU governance', report presented to the Commission.

Falkner, G., O. Treib, M. Hartlapp and S. Leiber (2005), *Complying with Europe? The Impact of EU Minimum Harmonisation and Soft Law in the Member States*, Cambridge: Cambridge University Press.

Gehring, T. and S. Krapohl (2007), 'Supranational regulatory agencies between independence and control: the EMEA and the authorization of pharmaceuticals in the European Single Market', *Journal of European Public Policy*, **14** (2), 208–26.

Geradin, D. and N. Petit (2004), 'The development of agencies at EU and national levels: conceptual analysis and proposals for reform', Jean Monnet Working Paper No. 01/04.

Groenleer, M. (2009), *The Autonomy of European Union Agencies: A Comparative Study of Institutional Development*, Delft: Eburon.

Groenleer, M., M. Kaeding and E. Versluis (2010), 'Regulatory governance through EU agencies? The role of the European agencies for maritime and aviation safety in the implementation of European transport legislation', *Journal of European Public Policy*, **17** (8), 1210–28.

Hancher, L. and S. Lavrijssen-Heijmans (2007), 'Europese regulators in de netwerksectoren: revolutie of evolutie?', *Sociaal-Economische Wetgeving*, **11**, 447–63.

Joerges, C. and J. Neyer (1997a), 'From intergovernmental bargaining to deliberative political processes: the constitutionalisation of comitology', *European Law Journal*, **3** (3), 272–99.

Joerges, C. and J. Neyer (1997b), 'Transforming strategic interaction into deliberative problem-solving: European comitology in the foodstuffs sector', *Journal of European Public Policy,* **4** (4), 609–25.

Kaeding, M. (2008), 'Lost in translation or full steam ahead: the transposition of EU transport directives across member states', *European Union Politics,* **9** (1), 115–43.

Kelemen, R.D. (2002), 'The politics of Eurocratic structure and the new European agencies', *West European Politics,* **25** (4), 93–118.

Kelemen, R.D. (2005), 'The politics of Eurocracy: building a new European state?', in N. Jabko and C. Parsons (eds), *With US or against US? European Trends in American Perspective,* vol. 7, Oxford: Oxford University Press, pp. 173–89.

Keleman, R.D. and A. Tarrant (2011), 'The political foundations of the Eurocracy', *West European Politics,* **34** (5), 922–47.

Levi-Faur, D. (2011), 'Regulatory networks and regulatory agencification: toward a single European regulatory space', *Journal of European Public Policy,* **15** (6), 810–29.

Majone, G. (1996), *Regulating Europe,* London: Routledge.

Majone, G. (1997), 'The new European agencies: regulation by information', *Journal of European Public Policy,* **4** (2), 262–75.

Majone, G. (2002), 'Delegation of regulatory powers in a mixed polity', *European Law Journal,* **8** (4), 319–39.

Martens, M. (2006), 'National regulators between union and governments: a study of the EU's environmental policy network IMPEL', in M. Egeberg (ed.), *Multilevel Union Administration: The Transformation of Executive Politics in Europe,* Basingstoke: Palgrave Macmillan, pp. 124–42.

McGowan, F. and H. Wallace (1996), 'Towards a European regulatory state', *Journal of European Public Policy,* **3** (4), 560–76.

Metcalfe, L. (2000), 'Linking levels of government: European integration and globalization', *International Review of Administrative Sciences,* **66** (1), 119–42.

Pedler, R.H. and K.S.C. Bradley (2006), 'The Commission, policy management and comitology', in D. Spence (ed.), *The European Commission,* London: John Harper Publishing, pp. 235–62.

Peters, B.G. (1992), 'Bureaucratic politics and the institutions of the European Community', in A. Sbragia (ed.), *Euro-Politics,* Washington, DC: Brookings Institution, pp. 75–122.

Pierre, J. and B.G. Peters (2009), 'From a club to a bureaucracy: JAA, EASA, and European aviation regulation', *Journal of European Public Policy,* **16** (3) 337–55.

Pollack, M. (2003), 'Control mechanism or deliberative democracy? Two images of comitology', *Comparative Political Studies,* **36** (1–2), 125–55.

Schout, A. (2008), 'Agencies and inspection powers – the case of EASA as new or more of the same?', in E. Vos (ed.), *European Risk Governance: Its Science, Its Inclusiveness and Its Effectiveness,* Connex Book Series, Mannheim: Mannheim University Press, pp. 257–94.

Schout, A. (2011), 'Changing the EU's institutional landscape? The added value of an agency', in M. Busuioc, M. Groenleer and J. Trondal (eds), *The Agency Phenomenon in the European Union: Emergence, Institutionalisation and Everyday Decision-Making,* Manchester: Manchester University Press.

Shapiro, M. (1997), 'The problems of independent agencies in the United States and the European Union', *Journal of European Public Policy,* **4** (2), 276–91.

Thatcher, M. and D. Coen (2008), 'Reshaping European regulatory space: an evolutionary analysis', *West European Politics,* **31** (4), 806–36.

Versluis, E. (2007), 'Even rules, uneven practices: opening the "black box" of EU law in action', *West European Politics,* **30** (1), 50–67.

Vos, E. (2003), 'Agencies and the European Union', in L. Verhey and T. Zwart (eds), *Agencies in European and Comparative Law,* Maastricht: Intersentia, pp. 113–47.

Wallace, H., W. Wallace and M. Pollack (eds) (2005), *Policy-Making in the European Union,* 5th edn, Oxford: Oxford University Press.

Wessels, W. (1998), 'Comitology: fusion in action. Politico-administrative trends in the EU system', *Journal of European Public Policy,* **5** (2), 209–34.

# PART XI

# GLOBAL REGULATION

# 41 Regulating in global regimes
## Colin Scott

## 41.1 INTRODUCTION

An increased emphasis on global regulation is a response to the recognition of economic, social and cultural interdependence between the world's nations and peoples. Policy problems as diverse as reckless behaviour by financial institutions, exploitation of sweatshop labour in emerging economies, and the threat of climate change present collective action problems which cannot be resolved through the deployment of the state's authority, capacity and legitimacy alone (Cerny 1995: 597). In common with others, I suggest it is helpful to think in terms of regulatory regimes rather than regulators, where regime is understood to constitute the range of policies, institutions and actors which shape outcomes within a policy domain (Eisner 2000; Eberlein and Grande 2005; Scott 2006). Even at domestic level few regulatory regimes operate in classic style, as regulatory power is more typically fragmented not only amongst state bodies, but also between state and non-state organisations. Given the even more fragmented quality of supranational governance structures we should not expect global regulation frequently to be characterised by the emergence of powerful public agencies to make and enforce rules. Rather regimes with global reach frequently involve a high degree of fragmentation in which many actors are involved in the key activities which together may constitute a more or less effective regime.

The fragmented character of many global regimes involves both a variety of organisations in exercising the various requirements of a viable regulatory regime and a diffuse range of instruments or mechanisms through which the norms of the regime are created and made effective. A regimes approach to global regulation recognises that global regulatory practices date back to antiquity but highlights the proliferation of regulatory norms with global reach, particularly since the 1970s, and the fragmented governance structures through which such norms are made, monitored and enforced (Braithwaite and Drahos 2000: 3). Such a conception of regulation in global regimes is not inconsistent with analysis of contemporary global governance generally, which emphasises the displacement of state-centred and hierarchical models, by the emergence and/or recognition of the centrality of networked forms of governing which engage a wide range of actors including state organisations and actors beyond the state (Slaughter 2004; Lazer 2005).

Global regulation, in this regimes sense, elides two significant trends which deviate significantly from classical conceptions of state regulation. First, there is a trend towards supranational regulatory governance, and in particular the setting of rules and standards by inter-governmental organisations (Braithwaite and Drahos 2000). Second, there is a trend towards the establishment of regulatory regimes by non-governmental actors, which has been particularly marked at the supranational level – engaging both NGOs and firms (Haufler 2001; Abbott and Snidal 2009). Much discussion on the evolution of global regulation focuses on the distinction between regulatory regimes which are fundamentally governmental in character, established by states or more typically associations of states or inter-governmental organisations, on the one hand, and regimes which are predominantly non-state in their origins and character, involving NGOs and firms or associations of firms (Ronit and Schneider 1999; Brunsson and Jacobsson 2000). The bifurcation of inter-governmental and non-governmental regulatory regimes underpins a widespread assumption, particularly within policy circles, that governmental regulation may be both more effective and more legitimate.

These trends have raised concerns about the increasing significance of non-governmental regulation and its effects on coherence, effectiveness and legitimacy. I suggest in this chapter that this distinction between inter-governmental and non-governmental regulation is increasingly unimportant. First, concerns about lack of coherence in global regulation are of equal, and perhaps more, relevance to governmental as to non-governmental regimes. Few global regulatory regimes resemble classical national regulatory models in the sense of combining all the regulatory functions – setting, monitoring and enforcing norms – in a single powerful agency. Indeed many national regulatory models lack this coherence – this was a major criticism levelled at the US regime for regulation of financial services in the post-mortem on the global financial crisis of 2007–09. Fragmentation occurs in part because of the interdependence between governmental and non-governmental actors in establishing the capacity for effective action in particular domains. Paradoxically, non-state regimes are more likely to engage all the characteristics of a viable regulatory regime in a single organisation with global reach than is true of inter-governmental organisations, in which typically the capacity to monitor and enforce is not co-located with the capacity and authority to set norms.

Second, there is a concern that weaknesses in instruments and in particular their lack of bindingness may undermine the claims to normative effectiveness of non-governmental regimes. Again this argument obscures the potential that non-governmental regimes have to invoke legal rules, for example through contracts, and other normative pressures, for example through markets and community. Indeed many legal regimes which operate inter-governmentally appear to lack legal reach to those actors whose behaviour is to be shaped. With both governmental and non-governmental regimes there are plenty of examples of non-binding instruments taking on substantive effects through a variety of extra-legal processes.

The third concern relates to the diminished legitimacy of non-governmental activity. Legitimacy is of importance to both inter-governmental and non-governmental actors because, with limited sovereignty and authority, coercive capacity is limited and support for initiatives is required (Abbott and Snidal 2009: 48). Here there is an important debate as to whether the procedures for enrolling stakeholders in the making of norms and their implementation create a basis for both legitimate and effective action that may at least equal that of inter-governmental actors. These debates are of particular importance during a period of tensions surrounding regulatory objectives and effects because of a reaction to a financial crisis which tends to blame, and seek to reduce, the role of self-regulation and other non-governmental regimes, whilst playing up and perhaps overstating the potential for effectiveness of governmental and inter-governmental activity.

Taken together these observations call for a reconceptualisation of global regulatory regimes which embraces and works with their inevitably fragmented character.

Arguably, political science has been more effective in understanding the role of diffuse actors within policy-making processes than in implementation and enforcement. Indeed, Mattli and Woods suggest that NGOs have strong incentives to focus on agenda-setting, as it offers high visibility for their activities with a lesser commitment of resources than is required to attend to the detail of implementation (Mattli and Woods 2009: 29). It has been argued that political science has been less able than some other disciplines, notably sociology, to take full account of non-state activity in such implementation processes (Rosenau 2000: 167–8). This is not to ignore the capacity and role of states in global regulation. Important empirical studies have concluded that governments are central to both the initiation and the implementation of much transnational regulatory activity (Braithwaite and Drahos 2000), but governmental activity is far from being the only show in town. Effective regimes are also to be found, for example, amongst the 'green clubs' of businesses which seek to enhance market reputation through devising norms and appropriate monitoring and enforcement mechanisms to deliver on those commitments (Prakash and Potoski 2006). The trend for institutionalising regulatory capacity within non-governmental regimes so as to bolster their legitimacy is also targeted at extending their reach and effectiveness. In the remainder of this chapter I address how patterns of emergence of regulatory regimes tend towards a fragmented quality, examine the implications of this fragmentation for the range and effectiveness of regulatory instruments available and then follow this with an evaluation of the legitimacy challenges associated with both implicit and explicit delegation upwards to intergovernmental bodies and towards non-governmental actors such as companies, trade associations and other civil society organisations.

## 41.2   EMERGENCE OF GLOBAL REGULATORY REGIMES

Processes of emergence of regulatory regimes provide part of the key to their fragmented quality. One aspect of the rise of global regulation involves changes in the way that problems are perceived, and in particular a sense that problems which might once have been conceived of as national or regional now have a broader transnational character. Financial markets are only the most prominent examples of vigorous international markets which simultaneously address problems for market actors (such as limited national demand) whilst generating new problems (such a creating stress on traditional trust within markets). Other key examples include the perceptions of unacceptable degrees of variation in terms and conditions arising from the growth in international labour markets in areas as diffuse as merchant shipping, call centres and garment production. In the environmental domain, we may think of the externalities which flow across borders as a result of production and/or international trade, not limited to $CO_2$ emissions, but including also marine pollution and threatening stability to sustainable forestry. Other externalities generated by international markets include the costs associated with product defects which, because of transactions costs in pursuing them, are not attributed to the producer responsible for them. The costs associated with international trade facilitated by the internet include the difficulties of attributing responsibility to originators of products ordered and/or delivered via the medium of the world wide web. More generally, though it is not the only source of such problems, a good deal of concern about human rights violations arises as a consequence of the effects of international trade.

Policy problems do not achieve the status of requiring responses on their own, of course. Rather they are the subject matter of discourse and often campaigning involving not only national governments but also interest groups such as businesses, civil society organisations and others. A key question is what are the variations in conditions that produce regimes which appear to protect employees, consumers or other large and diffuse groups (such as the mass of people adversely affected by environmental degradation), on the one hand, as compared with the significant number of regimes which appear to entrench dominant producer interests, on the other (Mattli and Woods 2009: 8–11). As with domestic regulation, there may be a tendency towards the regime benefiting narrow and powerful interests where the demand for the regime is narrowly based among such interests. Whilst the nature and extent of procedures for enrolling the various actors affected by policy choices make some difference to outcomes, the most important difference between regimes captured by dominant producer interests and those which serve some broader conception of the public interest is the extent to which there is a broader and sustained level of activity by coalitional groups seeking a better public interest outcome (Mattli and Woods 2009: 16). Political contestation over appropriate norms and processes of implementation is emergent across a wide range of sectors engaging market and community actors, and within which traditional electoral politics may have a limited role (Bartley 2007). The presence and activity of 'policy entrepreneurs' both in developing ideas and in providing leadership has been significant in some domains, such as environmental protection (Canan and Reichman 2002).

In those policy domains which are characterised by broad participation of stakeholders beyond governmental and industry interests, non-governmental organisations have emerged at transnational level both as demanding change and as bearers of change through their activities, for example in developing regimes for engaging in one or more of the core regulatory functions of setting, monitoring or enforcing compliance with norms (Mattli and Woods 2009: 28–9). Firms are also amongst key civil society actors that play a role in agenda-setting, though their roles are varied in different policy domains (Mattli and Woods 2009: 32–6). For example, the global reforms of telecommunications regulation were substantially driven by the interests of large multinational enterprises seeking the benefits of liberalisation on the provision of services and pricing to them as *consumers* of those services (Sandholtz 1998). Other actors instrumental in liberalisation processes were those firms that sought to challenge dominant incumbents, either from a position of diversifying into telecommunications services from a related industry or presenting themselves as new entrants in many countries when they remained a dominant incumbent in one country. In other instances firms initiate or support regulation to protect their viability, for example by maintaining confidence in markets or products. Where such demands are met there may be close alignment between public and producer interest, as with the emergence of self-regulation in the US nuclear power industry following the Three Mile Island accident in 1979 (Rees 1994). Another class of corporate entrepreneurship involves firms subject to tight domestic regulation seeking to export those higher standards in order to level the playing field for their products (Mattli and Woods 2009: 35–6).

Whilst it is possible to identify organisations involved with global regulation that are primarily inter-governmental in character (for example the OECD), significant numbers of global regulatory regimes predominantly involve NGOs or firms, and a growing number engage both, with or without governmental involvement as well (Abbott and Snidal 2009). So, for example, in the domain that addresses workers' rights in developing countries, NGOs leading on rule making include Amnesty International (Human Rights Guidelines for Companies, established 1997), the Clean Clothes Campaign (Code of Labour Practices for Apparel, 1998) and the Worker Rights Consortium (2000). There are also individual businesses and associations of businesses involved in regulating in the same policy area. These include the GAP individual labour rights scheme (1992) and the Worldwide Responsible Accredited Production Apparel Certification Program (2000) (Abbott and Snidal 2009: 50–51). A number of organisations active in this policy domain combine governmental, NGO and business involvement. These include the tripartite International Labour Organization (ILO, established in 1919) and the Apparel Industry Partnership (AIP, 1996) (Abbott and Snidal 2009: 50–51). These regimes have emerged in the face of concerns about weaknesses in state capacity to regulate employment rights in developing countries and out of market processes in which multinational businesses have suffered reputational damage (risking reductions in market share) because of revelations about the conditions under which products are made in sweatshop conditions (O'Rourke 2003: 4). A key driver of these regimes is a recognition that some consumers in the industrialised countries are exhibiting a 'preferences for processes' such that the price/quality ratio of a product is less important than confidence that it was produced ethically (Kysar 2004). Governance within this policy domain is characterised as diffuse, heterarchical and networked in character (O'Rourke 2003: 6). Indeed, in the absence of strong governmental capacity, it is argued that the success of such regimes is likely to be dependent on their ability to invoke the capacity of the diverse network participants to engage in monitoring and enforcement (Braithwaite 2006: 890–91). The issues of variety in modes of regulating are addressed in the next section of this chapter.

## 41.3 INSTRUMENTS OF GLOBAL REGULATION

Regulation has traditionally been characterised as the policy instrument which places central emphasis on law as steering the behaviour of its target. This characterisation is in turn linked to ideas about not only the effects of law, but also the sovereignty of states in making and enforcing law. Trends in global regulation do not require a rejection of the idea of the centrality of law to regulation, but rather a re-evaluation of the nature and effects of law in regulatory settings. There has been, it is argued, a 'blurring of the distinctions between normative forms', involving both the growth of soft law and the blurring of a simple public–private divide in the promulgation and enforcement of law' (Picciotto 2006: 11). The fragmented institutional picture, noted in the previous section, is mirrored by diffusion in the instruments through which norms, standards and rules are set down (Busch et al. 2005).

The classic supranational legal instrument is the treaty created by agreements between governments in which norms, standards or rules are set down which apply to the signatory governments themselves. A key example of such a treaty is the Kyoto Protocol ratified by a majority of states and setting down targets and mechanisms for reducing emissions of greenhouse gases. It is striking that the contest over the Kyoto Protocol has continued since its adoption in 1997 and that the Treaty has been very uneven in its implementation by the states which adopted it. Notwithstanding the setting down of obligations within a legal instrument it must be questioned whether the Kyoto Protocol establishes a regulatory regime or not. In particular there are weaknesses in arrangements for monitoring and enforcement, creating a degree of fragmentation that causes some to think that it would be more effective to displace legal instruments with more explicit processes of bargaining and cooperation (Asselt et al. 2008). The question of reach of international treaties can be addressed through changing the mechanisms and processes through which they are implemented (Mitchell 1994). The limited reach of treaties, which are generally addressed to states and are typically restricted in their monitoring and enforcement mechanisms, creates a gap in global governance which has been filled by a variety of other instruments.

At the other end of the scale from treaties, in terms of legal bindingness, are technical standards set by bodies such as the International Organization for Standardization (the ISO) and numerous international and national standard-setting bodies, the majority of which are non-governmental. The globalisation of markets has increased the demand for standardisation in the absence of more complete global regulatory regimes (Brunsson 2000: 38). Standard-setting regimes typically do not carry with them mechanisms for monitoring and enforcement (although such standards are sometimes incorporated into enforceable legal instruments such as legislation and contracts) but are substantially dependent upon the market for standards in determining their take-up and effectiveness. It is these market requirements that have driven a high degree of institutionalisation in the enrolment of expertise in the development of technical standards (Hallström 2004). Whilst the relative bindingness of instruments which express regulatory norms is significant, the issue of bindingness is frequently deployed as a proxy for effectiveness (Kerwer 2005: 612). The more important question is not whether the rules are enforced or capable of being enforced, but rather whether they are followed. The nature and provenance of regulatory norms is, arguably, as important to understanding the extent to which they are likely to be followed as their potential for formal enforcement. Concerning the issue of fragmented capacity, the variety of stakeholders affected by a particular policy domain may be seen as a virtue of global regulation in the sense that stakeholders who are enrolled in determining, for example, the broad objectives and norms of a regime are, other things being equal, likely both to better understand and to commit to the applicable norms (Black 2003).

Indeed, in his assessment of the effectiveness of a range of non-state regulatory regimes, David Vogel identified the core problem not as being about the following of the norms by the participants in the regime, but rather as being limited enrolment of industry actors to regimes in such issue areas as fairly traded coffee and sustainable forestry (Vogel 2009). Accordingly a key question concerns the factors which pull and push businesses towards engagement with legally voluntary regimes – a central push factor being pressure from NGOs and a threat to reputation of leading brands (Marx 2008). Vogel suggests that the engagement of a variety of active stakeholders enhances the credibility of regimes and thus their value to those who buy into them as regulatees (Vogel 2009: 183). This credibility issue is centrally linked to the market reputation and market access of regulatees. So, for example, many homewares stores in the United States and the UK find it advantageous within their markets to sell only wood products certified under the Forest Stewardship Council regime, whilst suppliers of wood products find it difficult to access those markets without such certification (Meidinger 2003). There is a social dimension also to the development of and compliance with norms. Analyses of the relationship between firms within extractive industries and their neighbours have been extended to develop the idea that there is a 'social licence to operate' which invokes implicit expectations on businesses as to how they affect the communities within which they operate (Gunningham 2002: 160–62). Without community support businesses are unable to operate effectively, and serious breaches of implicit social licences may result in business disruption through both boycotts and direct action.

A central question of much research is what distinguishes the effective from the ineffective regimes (Gunningham and Sinclair 2002). The conclusion of a major study of 'green clubs' which engage in voluntary environmental regulation is that the nature and quality of institutionalisation and the market environment are key factors in their effectiveness (Prakash and Potoski 2006: 17). The key variables in institutionalisation concern the rules and their enforcement. In their analysis the institutionalisation of effective monitoring and enforcement is central to effectiveness (Prakash and Potoski 2006). The stringency of the norms is less important, they argue, though it may affect the attractiveness of the regimes for members – regimes with a reputation for stringency are likely to better enhance the market reputation of members (Prakash and Potoski 2006: 55).

Key mechanisms of applying and enforcing new codes include supply chain contracts, for example in the clothing industry (O'Rourke 2003: 6) and in respect of environmental protection (Vandenbergh 2007). Thus, though codes of conduct are frequently presented as voluntary, compliance with them can be converted into a compulsory condition of market participation through the imposition of contract terms by purchasers. Many multinational enterprises have substantial groups within their firms involved in monitoring and enforcing contract terms over suppliers, frequently engaging third-party monitors also, such as accounting and consultancy firms (O'Rourke 2003: 7). The credibility of such contractually enforced regimes frequently depends on a sense of independence in the monitoring function (O'Rourke 2006).

The issues of soft law, voluntariness and privateness are frequently conflated in both policy and academic discussion of regulatory norms, so it is necessary to set out some terminological classifications here. Within the term 'soft law', soft refers to a lack of legal bindingness and law refers, somewhat inaccurately, to the official provenance of the applicable norms (Mörth 2004: 7). Attempts to equate soft law with self-regulation or non-state voluntary or associational initiatives are apt to be misleading (see for example Kirton and Trebilcock 2004: 9). Equally, a more expansive conception of softening to take in not only obligation but also softening of precision and delegation in legal instruments (Abbott and Snidal 2000: 422) may be conceptually unhelpful (Mörth 2004: 5–6). Soft law instruments consist of the normative measures deriving from governmental and inter-governmental sources which are intended to change behaviour, but which are not legally binding (Snyder 1993: 198). Such instruments derive their authority and effectiveness from their governmental or inter-governmental provenance. Key examples of global soft law include the various codes issued by the OECD relating to such matters as electronic commerce and the conduct of transnational corporations. Such codes provide the basis for behavioural change both by national governments and by firms, and may involve the establishment of monitoring mechanisms, but not of legal enforcement.

Self-regulatory regimes, established, for example, by trade associations, typically engage rules which are binding on the members of the association. An example is Responsible Care, the regime of the global chemical industry, established following the Bhopal disaster in 1984 (Rees 1997). From the industry perspective the regime was established voluntarily, but, from the perspective of the firms that are members of trade associations involved, compliance with the rules of the regime is compulsory as a condition of membership. Membership of trade associations is important to firms in the chemical industry for market access and credibility.

The diffusion of mechanisms for setting down norms is an uncoordinated response to the absence of anything resembling a global legal system and is sometimes characterised in terms of global legal pluralism (Perez 2004). Actors involved in developing regimes have routinely engaged in processes which generate norms in a form that offer some degree of workability in the particular context. Those that are subject to these diffuse norms may comply variously because they are incorporated with national law and mechanisms from monitoring and enforcing, because members of a community (whether formalised within an association or less formally) expect it, because a buyer requires it as a condition of contracting, or because market access or market reputation is enhanced through such compliance. Such mechanisms are likely to be reinforcing of each other to some degree (Lehmkuhl 2008).

## 41.4   RECONCEPTUALISING LEGITIMACY IN GLOBAL REGULATORY REGIMES AND PROCESSES

Whatever the mix of actors and outcomes emerging from global regulatory regimes, the effects of a regime by themselves do not necessarily determine the extent of its legitimacy. Legitimacy is concerned with the nature and extent of acceptance that institutional arrangements and normative choices, from among the possible configurations, are more or less right for the time being. Sufficiency may be assessed by reference to 'compliance with government policies even if these violate the actor's own interests or normative preferences, and even if official sanctions could be avoided at low cost' (Scharpf 2003). Global regulatory activity presents particular challenges to legitimacy because of a widespread sense that it is far removed from well-understood principles and processes associated with domestic democratic politics. The mature institutional structures of the European Union, for example, even though they engage both an elected European Parliament and an important and direct role for the governments of the member states through the Council of Ministers, are, nevertheless, perpetually on the defensive against claims of a glaring 'democratic deficit' (Follesdal and Hix 2006). Resort to a technocratic or outputs-based legitimacy for democratically weak EU regulatory decision-making processes has increasingly been challenged. It has been suggested that the EU experience 'may not be *sui generis*, but rather reflective of the democratic legitimation problems of supra-state governing generally' (Skogstad 2003: 335).

Solutions to the legitimacy problems associated with global regulation need to adapt to the diffuse and networked character of contemporary governance rather than to seek to impose a traditional model of state accountability on the emergent structures (Ladeur 2004: 5–7, 10–12). A recognition of the normative force of nominally non-binding norms accentuates the need for legitimacy structures to attach to standard-setting regimes which fall outside traditional public governance (Kerwer 2005: 620–28). In other ways the effectiveness of regimes based on diffuse norms of uncertain effects is likely to be premised on the legitimacy of the key actors engaging in promulgating or implementing the norms (Black 2008: 148).

The kinds of broad networks that generate some of the legitimacy concerns arising from increasingly fragmented regulatory governance do themselves offer an answer to the accountability deficit through the kind of mutual interdependence which is generated within such regimes (Kerwer 2005: 625–6). Within the context of eco-labelling regimes it has been suggested that an equilibrium based on the institutionalised interdependence of the various stakeholders enhances both the credibility and the authority of the regime (Boström 2006). This is an example of the kind of extended accountability which I have previously argued creates a functional equivalent to more traditional hierarchical accountability regimes (Scott 2000). Julia Black goes further in arguing that the actors within a regulatory regime can take responsibility for constructing their own legitimacy with other stakeholders. This may be done on a pragmatic basis (the activities suit the interests of others), a normative basis ( the 'right thing to do') or a cognitive basis (nothing else is imaginable) (Black 2008: 147).

Pragmatic legitimacy is frequently likely to be based on outcomes for the actors involved – suggesting the weakness that it may not sustain a regime through decisions that may be normatively justifiable but against the interests of key stakeholders. Indeed psychological research on compliance with the law suggests that a sense of procedural fairness in the promulgation of rules may be more important than fear of the consequences for breach (Tyler 2006). An important strand of thinking about the construction of normative legitimacy focuses on the development of procedures for inclusiveness and engagement with key stakeholders in transnational governance regimes through the development of a set of procedural norms. Dubbed a 'global administrative law', such proceduralisation trends may go some way towards tackling the normative legitimacy issue. Key features of these arrangements include much-enhanced transparency and widespread engagement in key processes such as rule making and the development of reasoned decision-making and review processes (Kingsbury et al. 2005: 37–41), and might be extended to address also other concerns such as the protection of human rights (Harlow 2006). This proceduralisation is often restricted to rule making, and does not extend to monitoring and enforcement procedures. Where there is a concentrated organisational focus to a regime, transparency may be both feasible and attractive. But the disinfective properties of sunlight reach less into more diffuse structures such as networks of national regulators, which are often characterised by a degree of opacity (Maher 2002; Eberlein and Grande 2005; Mattli and Woods 2009: 19–20). A further limit to the global administrative law is that, while it addresses private regulatory organisations (Kingsbury et al. 2005: 20), it has little to say about firms which use their contracting power to regulate others, such as their suppliers.

Arguments for stronger proceduralisation as a guard against capture of regimes by powerful producer interests might be strengthened by extending the concept of capture beyond a mutual identification of interests, to recognise that regulators, even where they reject any direct attempts at capture by producers, nevertheless experience a form of epistemic dependence on those powerful stakeholders (Hardwig 1985). To the extent that regulators experience such dependence, what is thinkable and doable is substantially shaped by the producers, in the absence of transparent mechanisms for testing those assumptions through exposure to a broader cohort of stakeholders (Power 2003). For this reason authority is incompletely defined and is effectively shared within the regime. The whole appeal of proceduralisation is not simply the inclusion of broader interests within key decision-making processes, but the inclusion and perhaps creation of a broader community shaping and re-shaping what counts as knowledge in the particular policy domain. Both accountability and authority are diffused within such procedural-ised regimes (Bohman 2004: 332). The epistemic dependence of key actors within regulatory regimes bears not only on the normative legitimacy of a regime, but also on the cognitive legitimacy which flows from a sense that roles, issues, processes and outcomes could not be other than they are. More inclusive and reflexive processes may be positive both from the perspective of learning and also because they engage participants with opportunities for self-determination (Lenoble and Maesschalck 2010).

## 41.5   CONCLUSIONS: WHERE NEXT FOR THE POLITICS OF GLOBAL REGULATION?

The financial crisis of 2007–09, together with other pressing concerns such as climate change, has resulted in increasing clamour for more stringent, coordinated and central-ised global regulation. Without wholly precluding the possibility of such regimes, experience suggests that global regulatory regimes tend to emerge in a fragmented manner, with aspects of their origins and implementation diffused between different levels of government and between state and non-state actors. In policy domains such as human rights and the environment, key regulators and principal targets of regulation are found in both public and private sectors, and this kind of mixed and fragmented model appears more typical.

Consistent with this analysis future investigations might focus on understanding better the relations between state and non-state actors within global regimes, moving beyond analysis of policy making and norm setting to examine processes of implementation more thoroughly. Such examination would include questions as to who monitors behaviour and why, and what are the processes through which regulatory norms (whatever their provenance or legal status) become more or less effective. Such an approach must consider the significance of contractual mechanisms for setting and enforcing regulatory norms, alongside more traditional public law and soft law instruments. Whilst it has significant potential, regulation by contract raises particular issues concerning both the concentration of power and the relative opacity of the relationships involved. Accordingly a role for governmental and inter-governmental organisations engaged in observing such processes might be to establish ground rules for the acknowledgement of regulation by contract within governmental regimes.

The effects and effectiveness of global regulatory regimes are not simply technocratic matters. Inter-governmental and non-state organisations which operate with a degree of global reach typically have in common a degree of distance from the democratic processes which characterise and legitimate domestic government. Examples of regimes which structure the engagement of affected participants so as to promote not only understanding but also mutual learning about the objectives and mechanisms which lie behind regulation provide an indication of how more reflexive governance at global level might also engage revised forms of democratic decision making, characterised by better participation and communication between those affected. The emergence of such processes is resulting in part from the active attempts by NGOs to manage the legitimacy of the regulatory regimes in which they participate. A broad concept of proceduralisation might extend beyond the processes for setting norms, which show significant evidence of proceduralisation, to address also monitoring and enforcement, each of which provides opportunities both for wider participation and for learning about the regime through feedback about its operation. Broad proceduralisation provides a set of mechanisms for reconciling an understanding of the strong presence of non-governmental actors in a manner which effectively reconceptualises global regulation as a phenomenon which is inevitably both hybrid and fragmented.

# REFERENCES

Abbott, Kenneth W. and Duncan Snidal (2000), 'Hard and soft law in international governance', *International Organization*, **54**, 421–56.

Abbott, Kenneth and Duncan Snidal (2009), 'The governance triangle: regulatory standards institutions and the shadow of the state', in Walter Mattli and Ngaire Woods (eds), *The Politics of Global Regulation*, Princeton, NJ: Princeton University Press, pp. 44–88.

Asselt, Harro van, Francesco Sindico and Michael A. Mehling (2008), 'Global climate change and the fragmentation of international law', *Law and Policy*, **30**, 423–49.

Bartley, Tim (2007), 'Institutional emergence in an era of globalization: the rise of transnational private regulation of labor and environmental conditions', *American Journal of Sociology*, **113**, 297–351.

Black, Julia (2003), 'Enrolling actors in regulatory systems: examples from UK financial services regulation', *Public Law*, **2003**, 63–91.

Black, Julia (2008), 'Constructing and contesting legitimacy and accountability in polycentric regulatory regimes', *Regulation & Governance*, **2** (2), 137–64.

Bohman, James (2004), 'Constitution making and democratic innovation', *European Journal of Political Theory*, **3**, 315–37.

Boström, Magnus (2006), 'Regulatory credibility and authority through inclusiveness: standardization organizations in cases of eco-labelling', *Organization Studies*, **13**, 345–67.

Braithwaite, John (2006), 'Responsive regulation and developing economies', *World Development*, **34**, 884–98.

Braithwaite, John and Peter Drahos (2000), *Global Business Regulation*, Cambridge: Cambridge University Press.

Brunsson, Nils (2000), 'Organizations, markets and standardization', in Nils Brunsson, Bengt Jacobsson and Associates (eds), *A World of Standards*, Oxford: Oxford University Press, pp. 21–40.

Brunsson, Nils and Bengt Jacobsson (2000), 'The contemporary expansion of standardization', in Nils Brunsson, Bengt Jacobsson and Associates (eds), *A World of Standards*, Oxford: Oxford University Press, pp. 1–17.

Busch, Per-Olof, Helge Jörgens and Kerstin Tews (2005), 'The global diffusion of regulatory instruments: the making of a new international environmental regime', *Annals of the American Academy of Political and Social Science*, **598**, 146–67.

Canan, Penelope and Nancy Reichman (2002), *Ozone Connections: Expert Networks in Global Environmental Governance*, Sheffield: Greenleaf.

Cerny, Philip G. (1995), 'Globalization and the changing logic of collective action', *International Organization*, **49**, 595–625.

Eberlein, Burkard and Edgar Grande (2005), 'Beyond delegation: transnational regulatory regimes and the EU regulatory state', *Journal of European Public Policy*, **12**, 89–112.

574    *Handbook on the politics of regulation*

Eisner, Marc Allen (2000), *Regulatory Politics in Transition*, 2nd edn, Baltimore: Johns Hopkins University Press.
Follesdal, Andreas and Simon Hix (2006), 'Why there is a democratic deficit in the EU: a response to Majone and Moravcsik', *Journal of Common Market Studies*, **44**, 533–62.
Gunningham, Neil (2002), 'Voluntary approaches to environmental protection: lessons from mining and forestry sectors', in OECD (ed.), *Foreign Direct Investment and the Environment*, Paris: OECD.
Gunningham, Neil and Darren Sinclair (2002), *Leaders and Laggards: Next-Generation Environmental Regulation*, Sheffield: Greenleaf Publishing.
Hallström, Kristina Tamm (2004), *Organizing International Standardization: ISO and the IASC in Quest of Authority*, Cheltenham, UK and Northampton, MA, USA: Edward Elgar Publishing.
Hardwig, John (1985), 'Epistemic dependence', *Journal of Philosophy*, **82**, 335–49.
Harlow, Carol (2006), 'Global administrative law: the quest for principles and values', *European Journal of International Law*, **17**, 187–214.
Haufler, Virginia (2001), *A Public Role for the Private Sector*, Washington, DC: Carnegie Endowment for International Peace.
Kerwer, Dieter (2005), 'Rules that many use: standards and global regulation', *Governance*, **18**, 611–32.
Kingsbury, Benedict, Nico Krisch and Richard B. Stewart (2005), 'The emergence of global administrative law', *Law and Contemporary Problems*, **68**, 15–61.
Kirton, John J. and Michael J. Trebilcock (2004), 'Introduction: hard choices and soft law in sustainable global governance', in J.J. Kirton and M.J. Trebilcock (eds), *Hard Choices, Soft Law*, Aldershot: Ashgate, pp. 3–29.
Kysar, Douglas A. (2004), 'Preferences for processes', *Harvard Law Review*, **118**, 525–642.
Ladeur, Karl-Heinz (2004), 'Globalization and public governance – a contradiction?', in K.-H. Ladeur (ed.), *Public Governance in the Age of Globalization*, Aldershot: Ashgate, pp. 1–22.
Lazer, David (2005), 'Regulatory capitalism as a networked order: the international system as an informational network', *Annals of the American Academy of Political and Social Science*, **598**, 52–66.
Lehmkuhl, Dirk (2008), 'Control modes in the age of transnational governance', *Law and Policy*, **30**, 336–63.
Lenoble, Jacques and Marc Maesschalck (2010), 'Renewing the theory of public interest: the quest for a reflexive and a learning-based approach to governance', in Olivier de Schutter and Jacques Lenoble (eds), *Reflexive Governance: Redefining the Public Interest in a Pluralistic World*, Oxford: Hart Publishing, pp. 3–22.
Maher, Imelda (2002), 'Competition law in the international domain: networks as a new form of governance', *Journal of Law and Society*, **29**, 111–37.
Marx, Axel (2008), 'Limits to non-state market regulation: a qualitative comparative analysis of the international sports footwear industry and the Fair Labor Association', *Regulation & Governance*, **2**, 253–73.
Mattli, Walter and Ngaire Woods (2009), 'In whose benefit? Explaining regulatory change in global politics', in W. Mattli and N. Woods (eds), *The Politics of Global Regulation*, Princeton, NJ: Princeton University Press, pp. 1–43.
Meidinger, Errol (2003), 'Forest certification as a global civil society regulatory institution', in Errol Meidinger, Chris Elliott and Gerhard Oesten (eds), *Social and Political Dimensions of Forest Certification*, Remagen–Oberwinter: Forstbuch, pp. 265–89.
Mitchell, Ronald B. (1994), *Intentional Oil Pollution at Sea*, Cambridge, MA: MIT Press.
Mörth, Ulrika (2004), 'Introduction', in U. Mörth (ed.), *Soft Law and Governance in Regulation: An Interdisciplinary Analysis*, Cheltenham, UK and Northampton, MA, USA: Edward Elgar Publishing, pp. 1–10.
O'Rourke, Dara (2003), 'Outsourcing regulation: analyzing non-governmental systems of labor standards and monitoring', *Policy Studies Journal*, **49**, 1–29.
O'Rourke, Dara (2006), 'Multi-stakeholder regulation: privatizing or socializing global labor standards?', *World Development*, **34**, 899–918.
Perez, Oren (2004), *Ecological Sensitivity and Global Legal Pluralism*, Oxford: Oxford University Press.
Picciotto, Sol (2006), 'Regulatory networks and global governance', paper presented at the W.G. Hart Legal Workshop, 27–29 June, London.
Power, Michael (2003), 'Evaluating the audit explosion', *Law and Policy*, **25**, 185–205.
Prakash, Aseem and Matthew Potoski (2006), *The Voluntary Environmentalists: Green Clubs, ISO 14001, and Voluntary Environmental Regulations*, Cambridge: Cambridge University Press.
Rees, Joseph (1994), *Hostages of Each Other: The Transformation of Nuclear Safety since Three Mile Island*, Chicago: University of Chicago Press.
Rees, Joseph (1997), 'The development of communitarian regulation in the chemical Industry', *Law and Policy*, **19**, 477–528.
Ronit, Karsten and Volker Schneider (1999), 'Global governance through private organisations', *Governance*, **12** (3), 243–66.

Rosenau, James N. (2000), 'Change, complexity and governance in globalising space', in Jon Pierre (ed.), *Debating Governance*, Oxford: Oxford University Press.

Sandholtz, Wayne (1998), 'The emergence of a supranational telecommunications regime', in Wayne Sandholtz and Alec Stone Sweet (eds), *European Integration and Supranational Governance*, Oxford: Oxford University Press.

Scharpf, Fritz W. (2003), *Problem-Solving Effectiveness and Democratic Accountability in the EU*, Köln: Max Planck Institute for the Study of Societies.

Scott, Colin (2000), 'Accountability in the regulatory state', *Journal of Law and Society*, **27**, 38–60.

Scott, Colin (2006), 'Privatization and regulatory regimes', in Michael Moran, Martin Rein and Robert E. Goodin (ed.), *Oxford Handbook of Public Policy*, Oxford: Oxford University Press.

Skogstad, Grace (2003), 'Legitimacy and/or policy effectiveness? Network governance and GMO regulation in the European Union', *Journal of European Public Policy*, **10**, 321–38.

Slaughter, Anne-Marie (2004), *A New World Order*, Princeton, NJ: Princeton University Press.

Snyder, Francis (1993), 'The effectiveness of European Community law: institutions, processes, tools and techniques', *Modern Law Review*, **56**, 19–54.

Tyler, Tom (2006), *Why People Obey the Law*, Princeton, NJ: Princeton University Press.

Vandenbergh, Michael (2007), 'The new Wal-Mart effect: the role of private contracting in global governance', *UCLA Law Review*, **54**, 913–70.

Vogel, David (2009), 'The private regulation of global conduct', in Walter Mattli and Ngaire Woods (eds), *The Politics of Global Regulation*, Princeton, NJ: Princeton University Press.

# 42 The geography of regulation
## Michael W. Dowdle

## 42.1 INTRODUCTION: REGULATION IN THE PERIPHERY

Present-day developmental and regulatory thinking presume that a state's capacity to implement new regulatory options is limited only by its "political will." There is good reason to question this presumption, however, particularly insofar as developing countries are concerned. A country's regulatory capacities are significantly affected by its socio-economic structuring, and advances in economic geography suggest that such structurings are in turn shaped to a considerable extent by transnational, economic-geographical dynamics. All this can cause developing countries to experience economic and regulatory structurings that are not only divergent from those that operate in the industrialized North Atlantic states – those states that serve as our principal regulatory models – but also innately divergent for reasons that operate outside of political control.

This chapter explores how economic geography affects regulatory capacity, particularly in the world's less developed regions. In section 42.2, we examine how different regulatory strategies can be more or less effective depending on a country's larger socio-economic organization. In particular, we look at the degree to which contemporary Weberian models of "rule of law" regulation are presumed to be and are dependent upon a prior industrialization for their effectiveness. Section 42.3 investigates how a country's socio-economic organization is itself often strongly shaped by geographic forces that lie outside the reach of that country's regulatory or political institutions. Section 42.4 then looks at how this geographical structuring can generate distinctive "regulatory logics" in developing countries, and in section 42.5 we use the case of business licensing as a way of further demonstrating these distinct logics. We conclude by arguing that understanding the distinctive regulatory logics of more peripheral economies suggests that many of the distinctive regulatory features of these environments are not ersatz regulatory practices, as is too often assumed. At least some of them can be functional responses to the particular dynamics unique to more peripheral socio-economic environments.

## 42.2 ON THE SYMBIOSIS OF REGULATORY CAPACITY ON SOCIO-ECONOMIC STRUCTURING

A country's regulatory capacities are often symbiotically related to details in its larger socio-economic environment. Consider, along these lines, the Weberian regulatory model that scholars and organizations working in the area of legal and economic development use to evaluate the regulatory effectiveness of developing countries. This model, which is often captured in the rubric of "rule of law," sees regulation largely in terms of stable, rationalized, predictable and codified rules that are technocratically enforced by neutral and independent third-party agents (see Weingast 1997; Carothers 1998).

This notion of rule of law is often presented as if it were eternal (e.g., North 2005), but it is actually only a recent invention. It emerges as a regulatory model in response to the onset of Fordist industrialization, or what Alfred Chandler (1984) has termed "managerial capitalism," in the United States in the late 19th century (see also Chandler 1977), and its effectiveness as a regulatory model was vitally dependent on larger evolutions in the social and economic structure of American society that this new form of capitalism worked to catalyze. These included: the stabilization and unification of national socio-economic space, which allowed regulatory rules to have predictable and uniform effect throughout the nation; the concentration of capital into nation-sized entities, which facilitated the monitoring and enforcement of these rules; and the development of a professionalized, managerial class (e.g., lawyers, accountants, financiers) with the skills and training necessary to coherently administer very large-scale organizations (Piore and Sabel 1984: 49–54; Dowdle 2006).

Rule of law regulation continues to rely on advanced Fordism for its effectiveness. This has been recently demonstrated by international efforts to help Thailand provide social welfare protection to rural populations made vulnerable by the 1997 Asian financial crisis (see generally Pasuk and Baker 2000: 35–82, 97–104). Many in the international development community had attributed that crisis at least in part to a failure on the part of the affected Asian countries to adopt effective regulatory institutions. This, they argued, had allowed corruption and "cronyism" to corrode the efficiency of these countries' economies and markets. For this reason, initial efforts by the Asian Development Bank (ADB) and the World Bank to assist Thailand in implementing a social safety net for persons left vulnerable by this crisis were framed in rigorously Weberian, rule of law terms – terms that provide detailed, rationalized, rule-bound standards for eligibility, project structure and fiscal monitoring. Such rigorous regulatory framing, it was believed, was necessary to prevent the cronyism and corruption that had allegedly caused that crisis from corrupting the effectiveness of these projects.

The resulting aid program – the World Bank's Social Investment Fund (SIF) – was a failure. Inaugurated in August of 1998, by June of 1999 the SIF had only been able to disburse 5 percent of its available capital, and one month later the World Bank suspended the project.

The failure of the SIF program was due to the fact that, for the most part, Thailand does not sport the modernized, industrialized form of social organization presumed by the SIF's rule of law regulatory strategies. Thailand's economy is dominated by small enterprises and agriculture, rather than large enterprises and manufacturing. Because businesses are small and relational, accounting practices are not especially developed, particularly in the rural areas where almost 70 percent of the population lives. Industrial labor is primarily migrant and seasonal, rather than permanent. (See also Deyo 2000; Pasuk and Baker 2000: 82.) The result is a highly fragmented, dynamic, diverse and opaque socio-economic environment. Such an environment is simply not conducive to the remote (i.e., centralized), standardized, rule-based processes the SIF used to identify, reach and monitor appropriate targets for funding (Pasuk and Baker 2000: 80–81; cf. Sabel 1994; Scott 1998).

On the other hand, another international social welfare assistance program that had eschewed the classical regulatory organization, and simply dispersed funds directly and in a pro forma manner to rural leaders, actually proved much more effective in reaching Thailand's rural populations. This was the Miyazawa Scheme that Japan set up in late 1998. In stark contrast to the SIF, the Miyazawa Scheme "abandoned all pretence of careful targeting [and] elaborate bureaucratic procedures" and "disbursed funds through local government bodies" (Pasuk and Baker 2000: 81.) By eschewing reliance on a rationalized and centralized regulatory structure, the Miyazawa Scheme actually proved quite effective in identifying and reaching vulnerable populations. Like the SIF program, the Miyazawa Scheme was given an annual budget of around 10 billion baht, but, whereas the SIF was able to disburse only some 5 percent of its funds in the nine months of its operation, the Miyazawa Scheme successfully disbursed almost all of its funds within the same time frame (Pasuk and Baker 2000: 81). Follow-up studies found that rurally located Miyazawa-funded projects had been quite effective and efficient at getting assistance to vulnerable populations. Corruption in the administration of these rural programs, or in the disbursement or use of funds, was minimal (United Nations Economic and Social Commission for Asia and the Pacific 2001: 57–108).

In sum, in eschewing traditional rural of law regulatory strategies – something for which it was initially criticized by the World Bank and other "Western" transnational economic development actors – the Miyazawa Scheme was able to free itself from the often overlooked regulatory dependencies of rule of law regulation, dependencies that simply were not viable given the structuring of Thailand's social-economic environment. Ultimately, the World Bank would come around to the Miyazawa Scheme's way of thinking, redesigning its successor to the SIF to make it much more in line with that scheme's non-Weberian philosophy. All this argues that rule of law regulation remains as dependent on Fordism today as it was when it first emerged in the newly industrializing America of the late 19th century.

## 42.3   ECONOMIC GEOGRAPHY AND CORE–PERIPHERAL ORDERINGS

All in all, in order to be effective, Weberian rule of law regulation presumes the existence of a stable and relatively wealthy socio-economic environment. Orthodox models of development, such as those associated with new institutional economics, also claim that effective rule of law institutions can at the same time generate such environments, effectively bootstrapping their way to development (Rodrik et al. 2004; North 2005; see also World Bank 2008).

But this claim is highly suspect. Numerous studies are showing that socio-economic structuring and performance are often to a significant degree hardwired into the geography (both human and physical) of a region (see generally Schwartz 2007; cf. Arrighi et al. 2003). This being the case, then simply "getting the institutions right" cannot by itself bring about the stability and wealth of advanced Fordism. Contrary to the claims of orthodox theories on legal and economic development, "rule of law" regulatory institutions cannot by themselves self-generate a regulatory environment that is conducive to "rule of law" regulation.

The symbiotic effect of geography on Fordist socio-economic structuring is well evinced in the core–periphery patterns of global economic ordering that dominate the world's economic geography (Krugman 1991; Schwartz 2007). Simply put, Fordist economic development tends to clump, with highly developed countries generally being located in close proximity to one another, for example North America, Western Europe and Northeast Asia. (A similar developmental pattern has been found to exist within countries as well.) These core economies are characterized by high quantities of wealth, as evinced in high standards of living, high consumer and property prices, higher wages and higher levels of public revenue and resources, and by pronounced economic stability, as evinced by more diverse economies, more ready access to capital markets, and greater emphasis on product competition rather than price-based competition. (See also Braudel 1992 [1979]: 35–44.) These are also the regions in which Weberian, rule of law styles of regulation are more pronounced and most effective (cf. Peerenboom 2004), and they are the regions whose regulatory practices and experiences provide the regulatory models for the legal and economic development of less developed regions.

As one moves farther away from this core, these conditions deteriorate. Standards of living, consumer and property prices, wages, and levels of public revenue and public resources decrease. Economic volatility, in the form of boom–bust economic cycles, increases. Economies become less diverse and increasingly dominated by price-based competition rather than product competition. We are moving into what is often called "the periphery" – although it is important to emphasize that this core–periphery terminology describes a gradient and not a dichotomy. (See generally Braudel 1992 [1979]: 35–44; Schwartz 2007; cf. Meade 1961; Clarke 2007.)

The pervasiveness of this core–periphery geographical patterning of economic development argues strongly that the wealth and stability that are preconditions for effective rule of law regulation are not simply matters of possessing sufficient political will for "getting the institutions right" – obviously, geography operates independently of political institutions or political intentionality. (See, e.g., Sachs 2003.) This core–peripheral ordering is the product of a number of geographical dynamics. These include transportation costs, agglomeration effects (also known as external economies) and the dynamics of transnational capital flows. Core–peripheral differentiations can be further aggravated by the growing disaggregation of production chains associated with the growing global emphasis on flexible production and, to a lesser extent, the ecological disadvantages suffered by tropical or landlocked countries. (See generally Braudel 1992 [1979]; Sachs 2003; Schwartz 2007.)

### 42.3.1 Transportation Costs

One of the principal causes of core–peripheral patterning is simple transportation costs. Indeed, econometric studies have shown how distance-sensitive transportation costs can by themselves produce core–peripheral patterns of the kind described above. Peripheral economies work primarily to feed inputs into the core economy. The farther away one is from that core economy, the more one must spend (in both money and effort) to get one's goods or services to that core. This has a number of consequences for the peripheral economy. First, it reduces wealth generation, since in peripheral economies a proportionally greater amount of wealth must be fed into transportation. It also decreases land prices, since people prefer to live closer to core economies to better enjoy the higher standards of living these economies provide. This further diminishes the overall wealth residing in the local economy. This, in turn, limits the resources that can be devoted to education and reproduction of the labor force. This pushes local industries into price-based rather than product competition (product competition generally requires a more educated workforce) (Thünen 1966 [1826]; Braudel 1992 [1979]; Krugman and Venables 1995; Schwartz 2007).

Because price-based competition suppresses producer profits, this further limits the wealth-generating capacities of local industries. Moreover, the benefits of price-based competition accrue to consumers, who insofar as peripheral economies are concerned are more likely to be located outside those economies (remember that economic activity in peripheral economies is directed primarily to providing inputs for the core economy) (see also Jessop and Sum 2006: 161–85). Finally, price-based competition also reduces the region's economic diversity, since the farther one is from the core, the more one's profits depend on producing only those kinds of goods that travel well and whose markets are less time-sensitive (Thünen 1966 [1826]; Schwartz 2007). This lessening of economic diversity, in turn, makes the peripheral economy more vulnerable to economic shock.

### 42.3.2   Agglomeration Effects (External Economies)

Further catalyzing the comparative economic advantages of core economies in high-wealth-generating activities is a geographical phenomenon known as "agglomeration effects" (also known as "external economies") (see Storper 1997; Sonn and Storper 2008). As noted above, product competition tends to capture more wealth than price competition. Product competition is design based, and design-based production tends to involve close interaction among a variety of industries. These complementary industries tend to clump together in a particular locale in order to take better advantage of economies of scope. Such clumping allows participants to develop and exploit horizontal linkages among themselves to generate detailed local knowledge about relevant markets and production processes. This results in what Michael Storper (1997: 5, 28) has famously referred to as "untraded interdependencies," and, according to him, these work to give the supporting region an absolute (as opposed to merely comparative) advantage in the industries involved.

Agglomeration effects are much less likely to occur in more peripheral economies. As noted above, peripheral economies are likely to have difficulty supporting the diversity of economic activity and skilled economic actors necessary to trigger such effects. This is confirmed in a recent study by Borello et al. (2008) examining for agglomeration effects in the automotive and steel sectors in Buenos Aires, one of the few studies to look at agglomeration in peripheral economies. That study found that:

> From the perspective of production networks, one of the main traits of the firms studied in this survey is their poor interaction with agents and institutions. Isolation and vertical integration are a widespread characteristic of the firms studied, even in these relatively complex and mature networks such as the automotive and the iron and steel industry. The geographic reflection of that isolation and that vertical integration is the existence of geographic proximity with inter-actional distance. That is, firms in similar or related industries can be geographically close but may not have relations amongst themselves. Thus, firms do not realize the external economies which may be emanating from a close location.

Lack of capacity for agglomeration further encourages peripheral economies to engage in low-wealth price competition.

### 42.3.3   Capital Flows, or "Money Flows like Mercury"

Economic-geographical distinctions between core and periphery are further accentuated by the dynamics of global capital flows. Simply put, "capital likes to stay at home" – meaning that, everything else being equal, international investors will prefer investment opportunities that are located in social and cultural environments which they find familiar (Clark 2005; Saxenian and Sabel 2008). Since core economies are the principal repositories of wealth, this means that the closer a particular region's culture is to that of a core economy, the more appealing it is for global capital. And, since cultural proximity often correlates roughly to geographical proximity, patterns of investment appeal will roughly track core–peripheral distinctions.

   This imparts a distinctive volatility to peripheral economies. First, because international investors feel less secure in a peripheral economic environment, transnational capital tends to evince herding behavior the farther it enters into the periphery. Gordon Clark (2005: 105) has referred to this phenomenon as one in which "money flows like mercury" – meaning that transnational capital flows in the periphery tend to "(1) run together at speed, (2) form in pools, (3) re-form in [new] pools if disturbed, [and] (4) follow the rivulets and channels of any surface however smooth it may appear to be." In addition, transnational capital's greater skittishness in unfamiliar cultures means that enterprises in peripheral economies have to offer higher returns in order to attract transnational investment. Higher returns correlate with higher risk, and greater engagement in higher risk means more volatility for the economy. Finally, transnational capital further accentuates economic volatility in peripheral environments by demanding that global financial transactions be denominated in American dollars, which in turn forces the peripheral borrower rather than the core lender to bear the disruptions caused by fluctuations in global currency markets (McKinnon 2000).

### 42.3.4   Production Chains and the Disaggregation of Production

Core–peripheral economic variation can also be further catalyzed by the increasing disaggregation production associated with a growing global emphasis on productive flexibility and responsiveness. These are the transnational (or trans-regional) "production chains" that are particularly prominent in East and Southeast Asia, but are increasingly being found emerging from North Atlantic economies as well.[1] A "production chain" describes a production relationship in which a downstream firm controls the designing and final assembly of a product, while contracting out the production of component parts to upstream manufacturers, often located in other countries where the cost of unskilled and semi-skilled labor is less. Such production chains are able to increase a product's dynamic responsiveness to changes in market demand (also known as productive "flexibility"), and many argue that, as demand in global product markets becomes ever more volatile in the wake of advances in information technology and globalization, such flexibility is increasingly the principal determinant of a firm's economic success (Sabel 1994).

Because of these production chains, market fluctuations have a particularly destabilizing social affect in peripheral economies. Production chains tend to flow along core–peripheral economic gradients. The downstream ends of product chains tend to engage in product competition (flexibility of design being the source of their competitiveness) and thus are more conducive to the socio-economic conditions found in core economic regions, namely agglomeration effects. Upstream production, which focuses on more standardized component products that are not in need of design flexibility (and hence whose production is contracted out by core downstream firms), is more engaged in price competition and thus tends to favor more peripheral economies where labor and land costs are less (Storper 2000; Deyo et al. 2001).

As noted above, the function of these production chains is to make production more flexible and more responsive to fluctuations in market demand. At the downstream side, this is done by increasing the diversity of skills possessed by the workforce, thus allowing rapid evolutions in both design and assembly processes – what is sometimes called "qualitative flex" or "flexible specialization." Upstream, however, design flexibility is not as much a factor in competitiveness. There, flexibility and market responsiveness focus more on flexibility in the hiring and firing of limited-skill, and hence lower-cost, workers – what is sometimes called "numerical flex." Numerical flex thus causes fluctuations in global market demand to be reflected in peripheral economies in greater employment instability. (By contrast, because qualitative flex increases the value to the firm of the individual worker, core firms are less likely to respond to market fluctuations by hiring and firing workers.) Such employment instabilities, in turn, reduce the stability of the periphery's larger socio-economic environment (Deyo et al. 2001).

### 42.3.5  Ecological Factors

Recent studies by Jeffrey Sachs, conducted with a variety of co-authors, suggest "that levels of per capita income, economic growth, and other economic and demographic dimensions are strongly correlated with key geographical and ecological variables, such as climate zone, disease ecology, and distance from the coast" (Sachs 2003). This is due to a number of factors. First, as famously argued by Jared Diamond (1997), industrial and societal innovation has been shaped primarily by needs and resources particular to temperate latitudes. More tropical geographies, by contrast, tend to suffer from "higher disease burdens and limitations on agricultural productivity." In addition, countries that lack access to navigable rivers or to the ocean suffer from innately higher trade and transportation costs, which as we saw above would also limit their economic-developmental potential (Sachs 2003). All of this would work to impose additional, innate, structural constraints on the developmental capacities of the many peripheral economies located in tropical and landlocked geographies.

## 42.4  IDENTIFYING THE "REGULATORY LOGIC" OF THE PERIPHERY

Orthodox regulatory theory develops its regulatory paradigms and understandings virtually exclusively from the practices of advanced industrial economies, overwhelmingly those of the North Atlantic. This limited focus made sense given the ubiquitous presumption that both economic development and effective regulation are simply a product of getting the institutions right, i.e., of political will. But recognizing the significant possibility that (1) the shape of a country's regulatory capacity is sometimes tied to the structurings of its socio-economic environment, and (2) some of these structurings are likely to operate outside of human intentionality, at least insofar as more peripheral economies are concerned, demands that we expand the scope of our regulatory awareness. It demands that we also recognize that the seemingly ersatz regulatory practices commonly found in developing countries are not necessary ersatz at all – that some of them could represent functional regulatory responses to the distinctive socio-economic conditions that are innate to more peripheral economies.

In this section, we will explore the regulatory implications of the distinctive socio-economic patternings that economic geography tends to impose on more peripheral economies. Recall that the orthodox, Weberian rule of law regulatory model that informs our evaluations of a region's economic and legal development "will" presumes access to significant levels of wealth and significant environmental stability. But these presumptions are actually ill suited to more peripheral economies. This means that peripheral economies are likely to have their own regulatory logics, logics that take into account a relative poverty and relative instability that can never be completely escaped.

Below we will briefly explore some of the distinctive regulatory logics that might be more present in more peripheral regulatory socio-economic environments. These include the administrative costs, dynamic efficiencies, and ambiguation. As we shall see, regulatory practices associated with each of these logics have been frequently identified with more peripheral regulatory environments, but for the most part they have been identified as ersatz or dysfunctional forms of regulation. Recognizing that peripheral environments have their own regulatory logics, on the other hand, suggests that these practices are not necessarily dysfunctional or ersatz, but can represent affirmative, positive responses to the distinct regulatory conditions and capacities of the periphery.

### 42.4.1 Administrative Cost Effects

The fact that the regulatory ambitions of peripheral regulators are often likely to be constrained by cost concerns that are not such a factor in more economically developed regulatory environments would seem to be so obvious as to require no elucidation, so it is particularly interesting to note that the cost of maintaining a particular regulatory regime is virtually never discussed in the law and development literature. (For a rare exception, see Braithwaite 2006.) To the extent this is considered at all, the overwhelming presumption seems to be that more sophisticated economic-regulatory systems will pay for themselves through the economic growth they will promote (cf. Rodrik et al. 2004).

But our investigation into the dynamics of economic geography argues that the presumption may often be unjustifiable (see also Glaeser et al. 2004). As we explored above, peripheral capacity for endogenous economic growth is often limited by a number of exogenous factors that simply operate beyond the reach of that environment's regulatory institutions. This suggests that, in at least some scenarios, the adoption of more expensive, but more economically beneficial, regulatory strategies will not pay for themselves. Along these lines, studies by Randall Peerenboom (2004) suggest that growth-effective regulatory reforms seem to become much more difficult to implement in intermediate-peripherally developing countries such as China and India when they reach mid-range levels of economic development. Peerenboom attributes this primarily to a failure of political will, but it is difficult to see why it should fail here and not earlier in the developmental process.

An alternative hypothesis is that, at lower levels of economic development, developing countries are able to "develop" by exploiting unexplored economic possibilities that are internal to their environment. At some point, these opportunities are exhausted, and their growth capacity is increasingly limited by external factors. Unable to pay for themselves by promoting further economic growth, more expensive, more advanced regulatory reforms might simply be becoming increasingly unsustainable. Peerenboom's "middle-income blues" might not evince a country "trapped in transition": it might evince a country reaching the end of its particular transition – reaching the particular equilibrium point as delimited by its location in a core–peripheral economic-geographical gradient.

### 42.4.2   Focus on Dynamic Efficiency (Resilience)

Another distinctive characteristic of more peripheral regulatory environments is their relative lack of stability. As we explored above, the periphery's lesser economic diversity, together with the dynamics of transnational capital and transnational supply chains, works to impart a distinct volatility in peripheral economies. Contemporary visions of regulation, by contrast, are invariably modeled off the regulatory experiences of much more stable, core economies. As famously shown by Joseph Schumpeter (1976 [1943]: 78–9), institutional features that are functional within the context of a stable environment can often become dysfunctional in a non-stable environment, and vice versa. We will explore some of these below.

One of the common ways in which institutions respond to environmental volatility is by founding cooperation and coordination on longer-term relationships (such as "relational contracting") rather than on shared generalized expectations. In the realm of private firms, this tendency is sometimes referred to as "relational governance" (Carson et al. 2006). But the institutional effects of volatility are no less pronounced on the public sector. In more volatile, more peripheral environments, the institutional logic of relationalism is therefore very likely to be manifest there as well.

Of course, relational public governance has often been recognized as a distinctive feature of many peripheral governments (and even some non-peripheral governments, such as those of Japan and corporatist Europe in the early part of the 20th century; see Sabel 1994). However, it has invariably been conceptualized in terms of an economic-developmental strategy rather than those of an evolutionary logic. And the debate ("relational capitalism" versus "crony capitalism") has therefore revolved exclusively about how such a strategy does or does not contribute to economic growth and development. My argument here is different: I am suggesting that the better explanation for the prevalence of relational governance in peripheral economies might have little to do with conscious regulatory strategizing. Instead, it might simply be a spontaneous product of an innately volatile regulatory structure whose survival depends on its capacity to weather volatility rather than on its capacity to facilitate growth or corruption (cf. Williamson 1985).

### 42.4.3  Public–Private Ambiguation

One of the cornerstones of contemporary developmental thinking is that regulatory regimes should maintain a sharp distinction between the public and the private, particularly insofar as economies are concerned. There are two reasons for this, both of which relate to issues of economic growth. The first is that public–private distinctions promote economic growth directly, by allowing the private economy to focus solely on promoting aggregate social welfare, which is its absolute regulatory advantage. More specifically, it is argued that the comparative regulatory advantage of the private economy lies in its capacity to promote aggregate wealth. For this reason, regulatory environments should have private economies focus solely on wealth generation, while leaving issues of wealth distribution to distinct, public law regimes. (See, e.g., Kaplow and Shavell 2002.) The second of these reasons is that public–private distinctions also promote economic growth indirectly, by allowing the visibilization of corruption, which in turn prevents economic growth (Offe 2004).

Both these arguments rely upon two related presumptions, however. The first is that economic growth is not being constrained by factors external to the regulatory environment. But this, as we have discussed above, is in some cases likely to be false – if for no other reason than the dynamics of economic geography. Where this is the case, then the growth benefits of public–private segregation will obviously be compromised. This leads us to the second presumption of the relationship between a public–private distinction and economic growth, that which implies that the cost of maintaining a public–private regulatory distinction is insignificant insofar as regulatory strategy is concerned.

In fact, maintaining a strict distinction between public and private can involve considerable costs that are likely to be especially relevant to peripheral economies in particular. These include both administrative costs and costs to dynamic efficiency.

Moving money is not itself free. There are significant administrative costs associated with transferring wealth, including transferring wealth from the private to the public sectors. These administrative costs increase the less industrialized or modernized the economy. Factors such as private wealth concentration, credit-based versus cash-based economies (see Dorotinsky and Pradhan 2007: 272) and uniformity of accounting practices are all critical in facilitating efficient wealth transfers from the private to the public sector. (See also Bird and Smart 2001.) These factors are generally associated with industrialization, and with managerial capitalism in particular (Chandler 1977). Since peripheral economies are significantly less likely to be industrialized in this manner, costs of wealth transfers are likely to be much more significant. In fact, the failure of the World Bank's SIF program in Thailand, discussed above, is a very good example of this.

The other cost associated with maintaining a stark distinction between public and private involves its effect on dynamic efficiency – responsiveness to larger environmental change. Simply put, the division of wealth and other resources into distinctly public and private pools effectively converts these resources into what we might call regulatory fixed assets, in that it makes each resource available only for a particular kind of use. Fixed assets are problematic dynamically changing environments; when the environment shifts to demanding a good or service to which a fixed asset does not contribute, that asset becomes deadweight, thus impeding productive efficiency (Piore and Sabel 1984). The more dynamic the environment, the more that environment will favor asset flexibility.

And, as we saw above, peripheral environments are likely to be particularly dynamic, in the sense of being volatile.

One of the principal manifestations of this logic of ambiguities is giving private enterprises public responsibilities. A particularly well-studied example of this is the township and village enterprises (TVEs) that emerged throughout rural China during the earlier stages of China's transition to a free market economy. (See generally Taube 2002.) These TVEs serve a variety of purposes, some private, such as private wealth generation in a free market environment, and some public, such as providing social welfare for the village and serving as residual sources of village governmental resources. Many argue that this dual role allowed these firms to help buffer rural China from the socially dislocating effects of economic transition that were experienced by other transitioning economies. (See also Stiglitz 2002.) A similar ambiguation of the role played by ostensibly "private" firms has been found throughout Southeast Asia (Deyo 2004; see also Deyo 2000), in transitional Hungary (Stark 2001), and in South Africa (Barchiesi 2011; cf. Alexander 2006).

## 42.5   A DEMONSTRATION: THE CASE OF BUSINESS LICENSING

The issue of business licensing gives us a good window into understanding the different regulatory logics of the periphery and can help us make better sense of regulatory practices there. As analyzed by the World Bank (2006) in its annual *Doing Business* reports, peripheral economies tended to impose more onerous application requirements for business-related licenses than do more economically advanced economies. This, in turn, is widely thought to limit economic diversity, capacity for innovation and hence economic growth in these regions. These reports have thus consistently urged that peripheral countries streamline business licensing procedures and focus business regulation on ex post monitoring of on-going business activity rather than ex ante evaluations of suitability for entry. In doing so, they effectively dismiss the periphery's existing regulatory focus on ex ante evaluations as simply representing a kind of regulatory negative – as representing the absence of effective regulation, rather than as possibly representing an alternative regulatory logic with its own distinct, affirmative dimensions of social utility. (See, e.g., World Bank 2006: 15–20.)

But is the report really justified in simply dismissing peripheral licensing practices in this way? In fact, studies suggest that ex post monitoring regimes can be quite expensive to maintain relative to alterative regimes that focus on ex ante evaluations (Ogus and Zhang 2005: 131). And, as we noted, one of the distinctive regulatory logics of the periphery is that administrative costs matter in a way they don't matter for more developed economies. Viewed from this perspective, a focus on ex ante evaluation would be more understandable than the report suggests. The report's authors might respond by arguing such cost differentials are irrelevant, because the economic growth facilitated by a regulatory shift to ex post monitoring would increase public wealth and thus more than pay for the greater expense of the ex post regime. But, as we have explored throughout this chapter, the dynamics of economic geography renders this presumption questionable: the capacity of more peripheral economies to grow economically, and beyond that to capture and convert private wealth into increased public resources, is innately constrained by factors that lie far beyond the reach of regulatory structure. Simply reducing business start-up costs would neither reduce transportation costs nor contribute to agglomeration effects. It would not soothe the jitters of foreign capital.

Regime focus on ex ante licensing may also bring to peripheral economies other important regulatory benefits, benefits that would be lost in a shift to ex post monitoring. Recall that peripheral economies are much more susceptible to social disruption due to economic fluctuation than are core economies. Such fluctuations carry their own regulatory and economic costs: they threaten regulatory coherence; they increase costs associated with regulatory and economic planning; and they impose considerable burdens on local civil society. The regulation of this flux thus brings proportionally greater benefits to such regions. And there is good reason to suspect that a regulatory focus on ex ante licensing is better suited to this task.

But, by increasing up-front business costs, ex ante licensing is actually consistent with the distinctly "relational" logic of more peripheral regulatory environments. It causes those who do choose to enter the regulatory environment to more likely be committed to longer-term timelines, since they will need to stay in that environment longer in order to recoup the higher costs of entry. This, in turn, will help ensure that there is more stability and permanence among those that do choose to enter, which would in turn impart greater stability to otherwise more volatile peripheral societal and economic environments.

## NOTE

1. Dicken et al. (2001) have correctly pointed out that such "chains" are perhaps better thought of as "networks." The added insight contributed by the "network" metaphor is not particularly relevant to my analysis, however, whereas the "chain" metaphor does help me highlight the point-to-point relationships that feature in this argument.

## REFERENCES

Alexander, Gregory S. (2006), *The Global Debate over Constitutional Property: Lessons for American Takings Jurisprudence*, Chicago: University of Chicago Press.
Arrighi, G., B. Silver and B. Brewer (2003), 'Industrial convergence, globalization, and the persistence of the North–South divide', *Studies in Comparative International Development*, **38** (1), 3–31.
Barchiesi, Franco (2011), *Precarious Liberation: Workers, the State, and Contested Social Citizenship in Postapartheid South Africa*, Albany: State University of New York Press.
Bird, Richard M. and Michael Smart (2001), 'Intergovernmental fiscal transfers: some lessons from international experience', Tokyo, Hitotsubashi University Symposium on Intergovernmental Transfers in Asian Countries: Issues and Practices, Asian Tax and Public Policy Program.
Borello, J., H. Morhorlang and D.S. Failde (2008), 'Agglomeration economies in semi-industrialized countries: some evidence from Argentina and some general inferences about research and policy in similar countries', Association of American Geographers 2008 Annual Meeting, Boston, MA.
Braithwaite, J. (2006), 'Responsive regulation and developing economies', *World Development*, **34** (5), 884–98.
Braudel, Fernand (1992 [1979]), *Civilization and Capitalism, 15th–18th Century*, vol. 3: *The Perspective of the World*, Berkeley: University of California Press.
Carothers, T. (1998), 'The rule of law revival', *Foreign Affairs*, **77** (2), 95–106.
Carson, S., A. Madhok and T. Wu (2006), 'Uncertainty, opportunism, and governance: the effects of volatility and ambiguity on formal and relational contracting', *Academy of Management Journal*, **49** (5), 1058–77.

Chandler, Alfred D., Jr. (1977), *The Visible Hand: The Managerial Revolution in American Business*, Cambridge, MA: Harvard University Press.
Chandler, A. (1984), 'The emergence of managerial capitalism', *Business History Review*, **58** (4), 473–503.
Clark, Gordon L. (2005), 'Money flows like mercury: the geography of global finance', *Geografiska Annaler: Series B, Human Geography*, **87** (2), 99–112.
Clarke, Gregory (2007), *A Farewell to Alms: A Brief Economic History of the World*, Princeton, NJ: Princeton University Press.
Deyo, F. (2000), 'Reform, globalization and crisis: reconstructing Thai labor', *Journal of Industrial Relations*, **42** (4), 258–74.
Deyo, F. (2004), 'Reforming labor, belaboring reform: structural adjustment in Thailand and East Asia', in Yoichiro Sato (ed.), *Growth and Governance in Asia*, Honolulu, HI: Asia-Pacific Center for Security Studies, pp. 97–114.
Deyo, Frederic C., Richard F. Doner and Eric Hershberg (eds) (2001), *Economic Governance and the Challenge of Flexibility in East Asia*, Lanham, MD: Rowman & Littlefield.
Diamond, Jared (1997), *Guns, Germs and Steel*, New York: W.W. Norton.
Dorotinsky, W. and S. Pradhan (2007), 'Exploring corruption in public financial management', in J. Edgardo Campos and Sanjay Pradhan (eds), *The Many Faces of Corruption: Tracking Vulnerability at the Sector Level*, Washington, DC: World Bank, pp. 267–94.
Dowdle, Michael W. (2006), 'Public accountability in alien terrain: exploring for constitutional accountability in the People's Republic of China', in Michael W. Dowdle (ed.), *Public Accountability: Designs, Dilemmas and Experiences*, Cambridge and New York: Cambridge University Press, pp. 329–57.
Glaeser, E., R. La Porta, F. Lopez-de-Silanes and A. Shleifer (2004), 'Do institutions cause growth?', *Journal of Economic Growth*, **9** (3), 271–303.
Jessop, Bob and Ngai-Ling Sum (2006), *Beyond the Regulation Approach: Putting Capitalist Economies in Their Place*, Cheltenham, UK and Northampton, MA, USA: Edward Elgar Publishing.
Kaplow, Louis and Steven Shavell (2002), *Fairness versus Welfare*, Cambridge, MA: Harvard University Press.
Krugman, P. (1991), 'Increasing returns and economic geography', *Journal of Political Economy*, **99** (3), 483–99.
Krugman, P. and A. Venables (1995), 'Globalization and the inequality of nations', *Quarterly Journal of Economics*, **110** (4), 857–80.
McKinnon, R. (2000), 'On the periphery of the international dollar standard: Canada, Latin America, and East Asia', *North American Journal of Economics and Finance*, **11** (2), 105–21.
Meade, J. (1961), 'Mauritius: a case study in Malthusian economics', *Economic Journal*, **71** (283), 521–34.
North, Douglass C. (2005), *Understanding the Process of Institutional Change*, Princeton, NJ: Princeton University Press.
Offe, Clause (2004), 'Political corruption: conceptual and practical issues', in János Kornai and Susan Rose-Ackerman (eds), *Building a Trustworthy State in Post-Socialist Transition*, New York: Palgrave, pp. 77–99.
Ogus, Anthony and Qing Zhang (2005), 'Licensing regimes East and West', *International Review of Law and Economics*, **25** (1), 124–42.
Pasuk Phongpaichit and Chris Baker (2000), *Thailand's Crisis*, Chiang Mai: Silkworm Books.
Peerenboom, R. (2004), 'Show me the money: the dominance of wealth in determining rights performance in Asia', *Duke Journal of Comparative and International Law*, **15** (1), 75–150.
Piore, Michael J. and Charles F. Sabel (1984), *The Second Industrial Divide: Possibilities for Prosperity*, New York: Basic Books.
Rodrik, D., A. Subramanian and F. Trebbi (2004), 'Institutions rule: the primacy of institutions over geography and integration in economic development', *Journal of Economic Growth*, **9** (2), 131–65.
Sabel, Charles F. (1994), 'Learning by monitoring: the institutions of economic development', in Neil Smelser and Richard Swedberg (eds), *The Handbook of Economic Sociology*, Princeton, NJ: Princeton University Press and Russell Sage Foundation, pp. 137–65.
Sachs, J. (2003), 'Institutions don't rule: direct effects of geography on per capita income', Working Paper 9490, National Bureau of Economic Research, Washington, DC.
Saxenian, A. and C. Sabel (2008), 'Venture capital in the "periphery": the new Argonauts, global search, and local institution building', *Economic Geography*, **84** (4), 379–94.
Schumpeter, Joseph (1976 [1943]), *Capitalism, Socialism and Democracy*, London: George Allen & Unwin.
Schwartz, H. (2007), 'Dependency or institutions? Economic geography, causal mechanisms, and logic in the understanding of development', *Studies in Comparative International Development*, **42** (1–2), 115–35.
Scott, James C. (1998), *Seeing like a State: How Certain Schemes to Improve the Human Condition Have Failed*, New Haven, CT: Yale University Press.
Sonn, J. and M. Storper (2008), 'The increasing importance of geographical proximity in knowledge production: an analysis of US patent citations, 1975–1997', *Environment and Planning A*, **40** (5), 1020–39.
Stark, David (2001), 'Ambiguous assets for uncertain environments: heterarchy in postsocialist firms', in

Paul DiMaggio (ed.), *The Twenty-First-Century Firm: Changing Economic Organization in International Perspective*, Princeton, NJ: Princeton University Press, pp. 69–104.

Stiglitz, Joseph E. (2002), *Globalization and Its Discontents*, New York: W.W. Norton.

Storper, Michael (1997), *The Regional World: Territorial Development in a Global Economy*, New York: Guilford Press.

Storper, Michael (2000), 'Globalization, localization and trade', in Gordon L. Clark, Meric S. Gertler and Maryann P. Feldman (eds), *The Oxford Handbook of Economic Geography*, Oxford: Oxford University Press, pp. 146–65.

Taube, M. (2002), 'Stability in instability: China's TVEs and the evolution of property rights', *ASIEN*, **84**, July, 59–66.

Thünen, Johann Heinrich von (1966 [1826]), *Von Thunen's Isolated State: An English Edition of Der Isolierte Staat*, ed. Peter Hall, trans. Carla M. Wartenberg, Oxford: Pergamon Press.

United Nations Economic and Social Commission for Asia and the Pacific (2001), 'Social safety nets in Thailand: analysis and prospects', in *Strengthening Policies and Programmes on Social Safety Nets: Issues, Recommendations and Selected Studies*, Social Policy Paper No. 8, ST/ESCAP/2163, New York: United Nations, pp. 57–108.

Weingast, B. (1997), 'The political foundations of democracy and the rule of law', *American Political Science Review*, **91** (2), 245–63.

Williamson, Oliver E. (1985), *The Economic Institutions of Capitalism: Firms, Markets, Relational Contracting*, New York: Free Press.

World Bank (2006), 'Dealing with licenses: who is reforming? What to reform? Why reform?', in *Doing Business in 2006: Creating Jobs*, Washington, DC: World Bank and International Finance Corporation, pp. 15–20.

World Bank (2008), *Doing Business Report 2009*, Washington, DC: World Bank and International Finance Corporation.

# 43 Global governance and the certification revolution: types, trends and challenges
*Axel Marx*

Products are increasingly being manufactured, assembled and traded on an international scale. Multinational companies manage production chains that are organised on transnational lines and sometimes consist of thousands of suppliers. Many of these suppliers are established in countries or specific geographical zones within countries where there are few if any social regulations in the field of the environment, labour and human rights. In global terms, there are fears that production will move to countries with no social or environmental standards. Over the past two decades this has led to various protest actions by non-governmental organisations (NGOs). Some of these actions have been directed at 'the system' as such (the anti-globalisation movement), while others have targeted specific multinational companies. Multinationals such as Home Depot, Nike, Adidas and Toys R Us have been confronted with various types of actions ranging from boycotts and street protests to the systematic monitoring of companies' actions in areas such as the environment and human rights (the various 'watch' websites) and the exposure of malpractices in the media.

At the same time, global private regulatory initiatives have emerged, aimed at imposing voluntary obligations on producers concerning environmental protection, labour conditions or product safety. These private regulatory initiatives develop specific social and/or ecological standards. When producers meet these standards, they receive a certificate or a label that is used in external communication intended for consumers and other companies. The past few years have seen a significant increase in such initiatives. The literature includes references to the rise of civil regulation (Vogel 2008; Levi-Faur, Chapter 1) or to the 'certification revolution' (Conroy 2007). These initiatives attempt to give international trade an ethical and/or sustainable dimension. In other words, certification initiatives link the 'North' to the 'South' by managing production chains and giving a specific interpretation to the concept of development cooperation by enabling companies and consumers to take part in it.

This chapter outlines this phenomenon and discusses the main trends and challenges.

## 43.1 PRIVATE FORMS OF SOCIAL REGULATION: A TYPOLOGY

The past two decades have witnessed a proliferation of private forms of social regulation.[1] The emergence of private standard or certification initiatives has been sparked by many interrelated factors which have caused private standards to become institutionalised in current governance regimes. Bartley (Chapter 32) discusses two possible theoretical explanations for the emergence of certification systems.

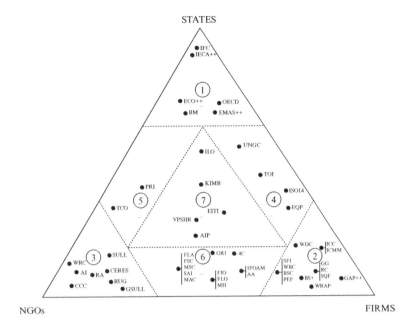

STATES

NGOs

FIRMS

*Source:*   Abbott and Snidal (2009).

*Figure 43.1    The governance triangle*

Various initiatives have been developed with a view to implementing voluntary product or production standards on a transnational basis. The various initiatives differ from one another. Most initiatives, however, are characterised by the fact that an organisation defines social and ecological standards and that there is a procedure to check that products or production processes conform to these standards (i.e. conformity assessment). When products or production processes comply with the defined standards, a certificate is awarded which may or may not be used for external communication (label).

Abbott and Snidal (2009) have recently developed a means of classifying these systems. They subdivide the new initiatives on the basis of the actors involved in defining the standards. They distinguish between three major actors, the state, companies and non-governmental organisations, which develop the rules and standards, either separately or together, that govern the global production chains. These three actors form the 'governance triangle' (see Figure 43.1). Within this triangle, Abbott and Snidal distinguish seven zones, depending on how many parties are involved in defining standards. They place new regulatory initiatives in each of these zones. Three zones contain initiatives in which one actor develops the standards, three zones contain initiatives in which two actors develop standards, and one zone contains standard-setting initiatives which are developed by the three parties.

A typical example of zone 1 initiatives is the OECD Guidelines for Multinational Enterprises, adopted in 1976. These are recommendations, accepted by governments, made to multinational companies regarding socially responsible business operations. The Guidelines define voluntary principles and standards for responsible behaviour among companies, relating to matters such as the environment, fighting corruption, labour relations and competition. Zone 2 is characterised by company-driven or industrial sector-driven initiatives such as Responsible Care in the chemical sector or the charter of employment rights of the clothing giant GAP. Zone 3 comprises NGO-driven initiatives, such as the Clean Clothes Campaign, which strives to achieve better terms of employment in textile production plants in developing countries. Zone 4 covers forms of cooperation between NGOs and the state, including the UN Principles for Responsible Investment. Zone 5 contains cooperation initiatives between (international) authorities and companies, such as the UN Global Compact. Zone 6 contains initiatives that result from cooperation between companies and NGOs, such as the Forest Stewardship Council. Finally, Zone 7 comprises initiatives in which the three parties are involved, such as the 1977 declaration of the International Labour Organization on multinational companies or the Kimberley process relating to conflict diamonds that was started in 2003.

The Abbott and Snidal classification outlines the diversity of various forms of public–private and private transnational regulation. However, the classification covers only part of the complex tangle of private regulatory initiatives, because it is based mainly on the dimension of who develops standards but pays little attention to how the actual implementation or enforcement of the standards is achieved. Defining and developing standards is only one part of the regulatory process. Implementing and monitoring the implementation of standards is another element, and this can be done in various ways.

Labour, human rights and/or environmental standards can be enforced by companies, a sector organisation or an independent organisation. The literature refers in this context to first-party, second-party and third-party certification, in essence referring to the number of parties involved in the standard-setting and standard-enforcement process (Gereffi et al. 2001; Levi-Faur, Chapter 1; van Waarden, Chapter 34). This process, also referred to as the certification process, consists of defining standards, accrediting an organisation that examines conformity with the standards, applying for a certificate, carrying out a conformity assessment (testing whether organisations, systems and products satisfy the proposed standards) and awarding a certificate.

First-party certification is characterised by the fact that a company or an organisation checks compliance with standards which are defined by the company or organisation itself. With second-party certification, the enforcement of standards is done by an entity that is legally separate from the organisation applying for a certificate but not truly independent, since they often share similar interests. In this case, the standards are often defined and enforced by an organisation representing the companies that are applying for a certificate, such as industrial sector organisations. The best-known example of second-party certification is the initial Responsible Care programme developed by the chemical sector. There are also a number of sector-specific certification programmes in the wood and paper-processing industry, such as the Standard Forestry Initiative. With third-party certification, the standards are developed by an independent organisation, often a multi-stakeholder body, which also accredits organisations to carry out conformity assessments. Accreditation guarantees that the organisation that carries out the conformity assessment is competent to do this and operates independently. These accredited organisations are autonomous bodies that carry out conformity assessments at companies that apply for a certificate. In most cases a conformity assessment involves an unannounced audit of production sites. In this case, three parties are involved, which

*Table 43.1   Private and public–private social standards matrix*

| Actors | | Implementation of standards | | |
|---|---|---|---|---|
| | | First party | Second party | Third party |
| Standard setting | Company | 1 | 2 | 3 |
| | Civil society | 4 | 5 | 6 |
| | Company–state | 7 | 8 | 9 |
| | Civil Society–state | 10 | 11 | 12 |
| | Company–civil society | 13 | 14 | 15 |
| | Company–civil society–state | 16 | 17 | 18 |

are independent of one another. These parties are a company applying for a certificate, a body setting the standards and an accredited party assessing conformity with standards.

In other words, types of private social regulation vary in two dimensions. The first dimension, the governance triangle, describes who defines the rules or standards. The second dimension describes how the standards are enforced. On the basis of these two dimensions, a private standards matrix can be developed in which the various initiatives can be situated (see Table 43.1). The matrix includes only private and public–private standards systems.

The matrix demonstrates that there are a great many different types of private governance. A detailed analysis of the various systems to place them in the different cells goes beyond the scope of this chapter. The matrix refines the seven-fold typology of Abbott and Snidal to create an 18-fold typology, the main difference being the attention paid to the enforcement of standards. The latter is important because there may be significant differences in terms of the impact of these systems depending on how they are enforced. A code of conduct driven by a company or a business sector (cells 1 to 3), which is implemented by the company or the business sector itself (such as the Shell Code of Conduct or the Responsible Care initiative in the chemical sector), is probably less effective in achieving defined targets than a company-driven initiative that uses third-party enforcement such as GLOBALGAP. Multi-stakeholder initiatives can also differ as regards the means of enforcement. The Fair Wear Foundation is a multi-stakeholder initiative that leaves enforcement of the standards it develops to the companies themselves and only carries out additional checks itself. It does not use accredited independent organisations in the enforcement process. From an analytical point of view, developing a matrix has the additional advantage that this approach is more suited for analysing the dynamics in the field of private standard-setting, since private standard-setting initiatives might evolve from one type into another type in two dimensions.

Not all types are equally relevant in the context of private regulation. The academic literature has focused most on private standard-setting initiatives in cell 15, as 'one of the most innovative and startling institutional designs of the past 50 years' (Cashore et al. 2004: 4). Some of the most prominent and representative examples of these private regulatory initiatives are the Fairtrade Labelling Organization, the Forest Stewardship Council and Social Accountability International. The Fairtrade Labelling Organization (FLO), established in 1997, was founded to enable producers and workers in developing countries to evolve from a position of vulnerability to a position of economic security and self-sufficiency. The core of the system focuses on the concept of a fair price. The Forest Stewardship Council (FSC), set up in 1993, is an international, multi-stakeholder, consensus-based sustainable forestry initiative. FSC provides a guarantee that a wood or paper product has been made using material from a sustainably managed forest. Social Accountability International (SAI) is a non-governmental, international, multi-stakeholder and non-profit organisation whose mission is to promote the rights of workers worldwide and to improve working conditions by applying socially responsible standards. The SAI standards are based on internationally recognised guidelines, including various International Labour Organization (ILO) conventions, the UN Convention on the Rights of the Child and the Universal Declaration of Human Rights.

## 43.2   MAJOR TRENDS: STRONG GROWTH AND INTEGRATION IN NEW POLICY ARRANGEMENTS

The development of private forms of social regulation has recently been characterised by two major trends, namely a sharp increase in the use of the systems on the one hand and increasing recognition from (international) public authorities and policymakers on the other hand, so that they are beginning to be part of new forms of public policy arrangements. This has led to increased professionalisation of private standard-setting schemes. These trends are discussed in greater detail.

First of all, the use of private regulatory standards is proliferating (for a different perspective see Töller, Chapter 36). This is reflected in the increase in the sale of certified products, the number of firms that have their products certified and the growth of the certification sector itself. Take a few examples. In 2007, sales of FLO-certified products worldwide amounted to over 2.3 billion euros. This is a rise of 47 per cent compared with 2006. There are an increasing number of distributors offering consumers FLO-certified products. These products are mainly distributed via supermarkets. In 2008, over 113 million hectares of forest across the globe were FSC-certified, which corresponds to 5 per cent of commercially exploited forests worldwide. There are also more than 14000 companies throughout the world that have an FSC chain-of-custody (COC) certificate for products that they offer. This certificate guarantees that products have been made using wood from sustainably managed forests. The global market for products certified by the Marine Stewardship Council (MSC) grew by almost 100 per cent in 2008 to reach a total sales value of 1 billion US dollars. Mass distributors such as Wal-Mart are increasingly demanding MSC certification from the fish-producing industry and are striving to broaden substantially their range of certified fish products. Marks & Spencer, updating its Plan A in 2010, has committed 'to become the world's most sustainable major retailer by 2015' (Marks & Spencer 2010: 3). This strategy, by 2020, will include building in environmental and social principles in *all* 2.7 billion individual products. In most cases this will be done by using recognised external environmental or social certificates (Marks & Spencer 2010: 14). Moreover, strong growth can also be seen in the market for accredited certification organisations. As mentioned above, compliance with standards is checked by means of a conformity assessment carried out by an independent, accredited organisation. Accredited organisations may be international consultancy firms such as SGS and Bureau Veritas, NGOs or local organisations. Blair et al. (2008)

identify various new major players on the certification market and describe the growth of the sector as exponential.

This increase may be attributed to a number of factors. With the increasing growth in international trade and outsourcing on the one hand and the rising demand for quality guarantees in various areas among product customers (consumers and companies) on the other, the need for business management instruments that enable global business management is growing. Consequently certification systems are increasingly becoming risk and reputation management instruments that are part of regular business management. Concerning risk management, more and more companies are making use of certification to monitor suppliers and the quality (in terms of various parameters) of the products they are offering. In the food-processing industry, in particular, with the increasing liability borne by companies, certification is used as a risk management tool (Henson and Humphrey 2008). Several of these certificates include standards relating to the environment and labour conditions. In this context, certificates are business-to-business tools and are used relatively little for the purpose of external communication. Certification as a means of reputation management, on the other hand, is used mainly by companies that supply directly to consumers and are (very) sensitive to negative publicity, as this can impact on both sales and share value. For instance, a number of prominent clothing brands (Adidas, Nike and others), which wish to avoid 'sweatshop' claims, work with certification organisations to monitor the employment conditions in their supply facilities (Marx 2008).

Secondly, private standards enable companies to differentiate between products. Whereas certified products once tended to be niche products offered by small-scale organisations, they are now increasingly becoming a permanent component of the range offered by multinational companies supplying products via large distributors. Consumer demand for certified products has grown in recent years, and this has resulted in giants such as Unilever and IKEA offering various certified products. Traditional niche products such as the Max Havelaar (FLO-certified products) range are also increasingly available in supermarkets. As a result, the market for specialised, certified products is establishing a place for itself among the 'mainstream' brands. Some supermarkets specialise in certified products.

Another major trend is that these certification systems are increasingly gaining recognition from public authorities and multilateral organisations, with the result that they are beginning to be part of innovative policy arrangements. Public authorities use private certification initiatives in their day-to-day work and they outsource certain tasks such as implementing sustainability initiatives. A distinction can be made between three ways in which certification systems are used by public authorities: (1) by applying for certificates themselves for their own assets or operations; (2) by including certification as a mandatory requirement in legislation; and (3) through their purchasing policy (i.e. public procurement). These three applications are briefly presented.

First of all, authorities use certificates to manage their own assets or operations by applying for a certificate themselves. This is seen mainly in modern-day forestry management, in which certification is sought for forests under the management of the government. The Forest Stewardship Council is increasingly being used to help give form to national or regional forest management. An analysis of countries with the highest density of FSC-certified forests, including Croatia, Poland, Latvia, Lithuania, Estonia, the United Kingdom and the Netherlands, reveals that, in these countries, the main applicants for FSC certification are national or regional authorities (Marx and Cuypers 2010). In addition, outside the field of forestry management, authorities use certification initiatives in the field of labour inspection. SAI cooperates with authorities to carry out labour inspections or to train labour inspectors who work for the government (Carey 2008a).

Secondly, the use of certification systems is anchored in law or existing standards, developed in the context of private standard-setting certification systems, which are used as input for legislation. It may, for example, be observed that private forest owners or concession holders are sometimes obliged by law to obtain certificates. This requirement is included, among others, in Bolivia's New Forest Law 1700 (Carey and Guttenstein 2008: 15). Outside the field of forest management it may be seen, for instance, that Israel stipulates in its legislation on the trade in and import of live aquatic fauna that imported animals must be certified by the Marine Aquarium Council (Carey 2008b).

Thirdly, authorities are increasingly using their purchasing policy to achieve certain social and ecological objectives. For instance, national and regional authorities stipulate that wood-based products that are purchased must bear a sustainability label. This is the case in countries such as Denmark, Japan, New Zealand, the United Kingdom, the Netherlands, France and Germany. Requiring certificates in purchasing policy is not confined to forest-based products. Fair trade certification is also increasingly required for the purchase of agricultural products (Groningen, Sweden) or Fair Wear certification for the purchase of clothing products (the Netherlands) (Carey and Guttenstein 2008: 12–13).

## 43.3   CHALLENGES: SCALE, LEGITIMACY, COORDINATION AND EQUITY

The world of private social standards is growing exponentially, and changes are following one another at an ever faster pace. Consequently, the various initiatives are confronted with a number of challenges. These challenges relate to issues of scope and scale, legitimacy, coordination and competition, and equity.

The first challenge concerns the scope and scale of private social governance regimes. The number of products and production processes that are certified remains limited (see also Scott, Chapter 41). This limitation may be observed at three levels: at sector level, within the sector at product level and within the product level at producer level. Table 43.2 provides an overview of the main systems and the sectors in which they are applied. It shows that there are various sectors, such as the food producing and processing industry, the textile sector, the wood and paper sector and the tourism sector, where a number of initiatives are operational. In other major sectors, such as the metal sector, the chemical sector and the mining exploitation sector, to name a few, there are few if any certification initiatives. It is worth pointing out that, in some sectors, exploratory initiatives are being undertaken to examine whether a certification system can be developed, but it remains the case that the current certification systems are limited to a number of sectors.

In sectors where several certification initiatives are in operation, it should also be pointed out that usually only some of the products are certified. For instance, FLO has

*Table 43.2*   *Overview of main private standards certification initiatives ranked by sector*

| Certification initiative | Sector |
| --- | --- |
| IFAT/World Fair Trade Organization | Craft products |
| Rugmark International | Carpet industry |
| Responsible Care | Chemicals |
| Flower Label Program | Cut flowers |
| Kimberley Process | Diamonds |
| Roundtable on Sustainable Biofuels | Energy |
| Coalition for Environmentally Responsible Economies | Finance |
| Equator Principles | Finance |
| UN Principles for Responsible Investing | Finance |
| Better Sugarcane Initiative | Food |
| BRC/IOP Global Standard | Food |
| Common Code for the Coffee Community Association (4C) | Food |
| Efico Foundation | Food |
| EUREPGAP | Food |
| Fairtrade Labelling Organizations International | Food |
| GLOBALGAP | Food |
| HACCP | Food |
| International Food Standard | Food |
| International Cocoa Initiative | Food |
| Marine Stewardship Council | Food |
| Soil Association Organic Standard | Food |
| UK Banana Industry Code of Best Practice | Food |
| UTZ Certified | Food |
| WWF Aquaculture Dialogues | Food |
| Rainforest Alliance | Food |
| Belgian Social Label | General |
| Eco-Management and Audit Scheme | General |
| Ethical Trading Initiative | General |
| Global Footprint Network | General |
| Global Reporting Initiative | General |
| Global Sullivan Principles of CSR | General |
| ICC Business Charter for Sustainable Development | General |
| ISO standards 26000/22000/9000/14001 | General |
| UN Global Compact | General |
| AA1000 Assurance Standards | Reporting |
| Center for Resource Solutions | Energy consumption |
| Alliance for Water Stewardship | Water consumption |
| International Council on Metals Sustainable Development Charter | Metal |
| Initiative for Responsible Mining Assurance | Mining exploitation |
| European Petroleum Industry Association Standard | Petroleum |
| Clean Clothes Campaign/Schone Kleren Campagne | Textiles |
| Fair Wear Foundation | Textiles |
| Fair Labor Association | Textiles |
| Made by | Textiles |
| Made in Dignity/Kutim | Textiles |
| Oko-Tex Standard 100 | Textiles |

*Table 43.2*    (continued)

| Certification initiative | Sector |
| --- | --- |
| Social Accountability International | Textiles |
| Worker Rights Consortium | Textiles |
| World Federation of the Sporting Goods Industry | Textiles |
| World Responsible Apparel Production | Textiles |
| Certification for Sustainable Tourism | Tourism |
| ECOTEL | Tourism |
| Green Globe 21 | Tourism |
| International Ecotourism Standard | Tourism |
| National Ecotourism Accreditation Programme | Tourism |
| World Tourism Organization Global Code | Tourism |
| International Council of Toy Industries Code | Toys |
| Toy Industries of Europe | Toys |
| American Tree Farm System | Wood and paper |
| Canadian Standards Association's Sustainable Forest Management System | Wood and paper |
| Forest Stewardship Council | Wood and paper |
| International Tropical Timber Organization | Wood and paper |
| Sustainable Forestry Initiative | Wood and paper |
| Pan-European Forest Certification | Wood and paper |

developed product standards for only 17 agricultural food products, including bananas, cocoa and coffee.

Finally, the level of penetration within specific product markets is also limited. Research in the sports footwear market, for instance, shows that it is mainly sports shoe manufacturers listed on the stock market that are sensitive to negative media campaigns by NGOs, such as the well-known sports shoe brands Nike and Adidas, that join systems that certify employment conditions, such as the Fair Labor Association (Marx 2008). Other companies, which, for instance, produce goods for the discount markets and are not brands in themselves, are far less inclined to take part in certification initiatives. This means that it cannot be said that all companies within a given product market are certified.

A second challenge concerns the legitimacy of these systems. Legitimate systems in this context are systems which have elaborate rules and procedures with regard to input and output legitimacy (Scharpf 1999; van Kersbergen and van Waarden 2001). Input legitimacy refers to the degree of inclusiveness and transparency of the internal decision-making process with regard to setting standards. Output legitimacy refers to the effectiveness of the standard-setting initiatives and focuses on the enforcement mechanisms. Some authors have focused on the issue of the legitimacy of certification initiatives and concluded that these systems can be considered legitimate measured by certain criteria such as transparency and collaborative decision-making (Dingwerth 2007). However, studies so far have two limitations. One is that they focus on specific systems such as the Forest Stewardship Council. This focus on specific cases does not tell us much about the several hundred other systems which have emerged or are emerging. As discussed above, several types of systems can be distinguished, which differ in several dimensions relevant to both input legitimacy (who is involved in setting standards) and output legitimacy (how standards are implemented). Secondly, little research attention has been paid to output legitimacy. Relatively little empirical evidence is available to assess the impact of certification systems on ecosystems, workers or producers. Measuring the impact and demonstrating empirically that such systems contribute towards managing biodiversity, improving employment conditions and/or reducing poverty, on both the micro- and the macro-level, present a key challenge. Only verified empirical results concerning the socio-economic and ecological impact will help ensure the lasting output legitimacy of the systems.

The main policy implication with regard to the legitimacy challenge concerns the need to distinguish legitimate from non-legitimate systems. There is an increasing need for the independent certification of the 'certifiers' by a multilateral organisation or by a private organisation. A number of authors argue in favour of multilateral organisations taking on a pro-active role in this field (Sabel et al. 2000; van Waarden 2009). To date, however, no initiatives have been launched at the multilateral level with a view to achieving this objective. Within the private standards sector itself, initiatives are being developed with a view to distinguishing effective third-party certification systems from other certification systems. The best known of these initiatives is the International Social and Environmental Accreditation and Labelling (ISEAL) Alliance. It was established in 2000 by eight existing certification organisations, including FLO, FSC and SAI. It is an umbrella members' organisation that codifies best practices in the design and implementation of certification initiatives. ISEAL has drawn up a Code of Good Practice for Setting Social and Environmental Standards, i.e. a standard for organisations that set standards, against which existing initiatives can be tested. Membership of the ISEAL Alliance implies that the certification system fulfils certain criteria for independent certification. However, the membership structure implies that the ISEAL Alliance is not an independent certification or accreditation organisation but rather a 'sector organisation' that aims mainly to organise the dissemination of knowledge among its members as a network organisation. Hence the ISEAL Alliance's potential to act as an independent body that screens certification organisations may be limited.

A third challenge revolves around coordination and competition in the field of certification initiatives. Various organisations that basically have the same social objectives are currently operating alongside one another. Initiatives are being developed within the various fields to achieve greater cooperation, but the results of these efforts remain insufficient. For instance, in 2005 an initiative was launched in relation to labour conditions and workers' rights with a view to organising cooperation between the Clean Clothes Campaign, the Ethical Trading Initiative, the Fair Labor Association, the Fair Wear Foundation, Social Accountability International and the Worker Rights Consortium in a pilot project in Turkey. The 'Jo-In' pilot project (Joint Initiative) aimed to promote closer cooperation between the various initiatives so as to increase the impact of the systems. This pilot project did not lead to closer cooperation, and the various systems continue to operate separately. In addition, there is still strong competition between the various certification organisations with regard to various agricultural projects, such as in the cut flowers sector (Riisgaard 2009a, 2009b) or the coffee sector. Even in sectors where international convergence of standards has been achieved up to a certain level, such as with the certification of organic agricultural projects, this has not yet led to full convergence or integrated global standards (Winickoff and Klein 2009).

This internal competition hampers attempts to achieve convergence among standards at international level and makes it difficult to generate benefits related to economies of scale, which can affect the efficiency of the systems. In the context of increasing demand, this fragmentation can result in capacity problems in areas such as the development of standards for new products or new geographical areas. Certification organisations tend to be small, fast-growing organisations that have to deal with the same challenges as other small enterprises and organisations. Developing one's own organisation with a clear strategic plan as regards capacity development is a major challenge. One component that may be important in this context is cooperation with other, similar organisations.

A final challenge has to do with equity in an increasingly international trading regime. The costs of gaining certification can be high. For many small producers or concession holders it is difficult to enter the system. This creates an exclusionary mechanism that can have negative social and economic consequences. In the context of food quality standards, this has already resulted in protests by countries within the SPS committee of the World Trade Organization. The Saint Vincent and the Grenadines island group maintain that the costs of certification to fulfil the GLOBALGAP private standards, which are more stringent than the (public) Codex Alimentarius standards, are too high for their producers, which means that they cannot obtain certification and are excluded from access to certain prominent Western supermarket outlets (Wouters et al. 2009). With regard to fulfilling standards determined by the FSC, as well, it may be observed that forest managers in the least developed countries do not apply for certificates, and this is probably connected to the high costs involved in obtaining certificates (Marx and Cuypers 2010). Hence the question whether private standards hinder trade is becoming increasingly relevant. Private standards could be regarded as new, non-tariff barriers to international trade and hence as denying certain producers and countries export opportunities. More research in this area is required.

## 43.4   CONCLUSION

Products are increasingly produced and traded globally. Developing and newly industrialised countries, often with weak or non-existent environmental, health and safety regulatory frameworks, are becoming major producers of agricultural and industrial products. This rise in production capacity is affecting the global environment and the safe handling and production of products. As a result, regulatory gaps are occurring. Many critics have argued that existing multilateral and governmentally driven initiatives are incapable of addressing global environmental and social challenges which result from trade liberalisation and increased globalisation. At the same time, one can observe the emergence of new private regulatory certification initiatives which aim to fill these regulatory gaps. These initiatives aim to govern supply chains across the globe according to a set of standards.

With the rise of new private regulatory initiatives imposing social and environmental standards on multinational companies on a global scale, a new trend appears to have started in the field of transnational regulation and global governance. This chapter outlined different types of private governance initiatives, analysed the major trends with regard to private governance and discussed the main challenges. The chapter stressed that there are many different types of initiatives emerging, ranging from self-regulatory systems developed by companies or economic sectors to independently operating third-party systems in which the implementation of private standards is controlled by accredited and independent specialised organisations. In addition, it was argued that a typology framework should enable researchers to capture the dynamics in the field of private governance. For this purpose a governance matrix was developed in two dimensions: who sets the standards and how they are implemented. The chapter also identified two major trends, namely a sharp increase in the use of the certification systems and increasing recognition from (international) public authorities and policymakers. The latter is resulting in the increasing integration of private governance regimes in new forms of public policy arrangements. Finally, the chapter discussed the four main challenges with which these systems are confronted in order to fulfil their potential. First, the initiatives have to scale up their impact. So far, a limited number of products in a limited number of economic sectors in a limited number of countries are being certified. Secondly, there is an increasing need to distinguish legitimate from non-legitimate certification initiatives, especially with regard to their output legitimacy, i.e. effectiveness. Thirdly, in order to achieve economies of scale, several of these initiatives should cooperate more. This requires an ability to compromise. So far this has proved to be difficult. In the long run, however, it is necessary to scale up the impact. Finally, and paradoxically, several of these initiatives were developed to address social and environmental issues in developing countries. However, many developing countries are excluded from the 'certification game' owing to the high costs involved. This creates unequal access to markets in developed countries. This new form of exclusion and inequality should be analysed.

## ACKNOWLEDGEMENTS

The author thanks the editor, David Levi-Faur, for comments on a previous version of the chapter and *Vanderbilt Journal of Transnational Law* and Ken Abbott for permission to use Figure 43.1.

## NOTE

1. In the context of this chapter, reference is made to private social regulation, as distinct from private regulation in the field of technical standards. This latter form of private regulation is more widespread and has existed for a longer period of time. For instance, Harm Schepel (2005: 145) estimates that in the United States alone there are more than 49 000 private technical standards that have been developed in over 600 industry associations. For some key discussions on private social regulation see Bartley (2003) on the emergence of the FSC and the Fair Labor Association, Blair et al. (2008) on the proliferation of the certification sector, Cashore et al. (2004) on the emergence and development of forest certification in different countries, Gereffi et al. (2001) on the rise of multi-stakeholder certification and the importance of NGOs attacking brands, Mattli and Woods (2009) on different forms of global regulation including private regulation, O'Rourke (2003) and Sabel et al. (2000) on the emergence and development of labour conditions

certification in different countries, Brown and Woods (2007) on the effectiveness of private regulation, Swinnen (2007) on private regulation in the food industry and Vogel (2005, 2008) for a general assessment of private social regulation and the link with corporate social responsibility.

# REFERENCES

Abbott, K. and D. Snidal (2009), 'Strengthening international regulation through transnational new governance: overcoming the orchestration deficit', *Vanderbilt Journal of Transnational Law*, **42** (2), 501–78.
Bartley, T. (2003), 'Certifying forests and factories: states, social movements, and the rise of private regulation in the apparel and forest products fields', *Politics and Society*, **31** (3), 433–64.
Blair, M., C. Williams and L. Lin (2008), 'The new role for assurance services in global commerce', *Journal of Corporation Law*, **33** (2), 325–60.
Brown, D. and N. Woods (2007), *Making Global Self-Regulation Effective in Developing Countries*, Oxford: Oxford University Press.
Carey, C. (2008a), *Governmental Use of Voluntary Standards Case Study 10: Tuscany Region (Italy) and the SA8000 Standard for Social Accountability*, London: ISEAL Alliance.
Carey, C. (2008b), *Governmental Use of Voluntary Standards Case Study 5: Israel and Marine Aquarium Council Standards*, London: ISEAL Alliance.
Carey, C. and E. Guttenstein (2008), *Governmental Use of Voluntary Standards: Innovation in Sustainability Governance*, London: ISEAL Alliance.
Cashore, B., G. Auld and D. Newsom (2004), *Governing through Markets: Forest Certification and the Emergence of Non-State Authority*, New Haven, CT and London: Yale University Press.
Conroy, M. (2007), *Branded! How the Certification Revolution Is Transforming Global Corporations*, Gabriola Island, BC: New Society Publishers.
Dingwerth, K. (2007), *The New Transnationalism: Private Transnational Governance and Its Democratic Legitimacy*, Basingstoke: Palgrave Macmillan.
Gereffi, G., R. Garcia-Johnson and E. Sasser (2001), 'The NGO–industrial complex', *Foreign Policy*, **125**, July–August, 56–65.
Henson, S. and J. Humphrey, (2008), 'Understanding the complexities of private standards in global agri-food chains', paper presented at International Workshop on Globalization, Global Governance and Private Standards, Leuven Centre for Global Governance Studies, Leuven.
Marks & Spencer (2010), *Our Plan A Commitments 2010–2015*, London: Marks & Spencer.
Marx, A. (2008), 'Limits to non-state market regulation: a qualitative comparative analysis of the international sport footwear industry and the Fair Labor Association', *Regulation & Governance*, **2** (2), 253–73.
Marx, A. and D. Cuypers (2010), 'Forest certification as a global environmental governance tool: what is the impact of the Forest Stewardship Council?', *Regulation & Governance*, **4** (4), 408–34.
Mattli, W. and N. Woods (eds) (2009), *The Politics of Global Regulation*, Princeton, NJ: Princeton University Press.
O'Rourke, D. (2003), 'Outsourcing regulation: analyzing nongovernmental systems of labor standards and monitoring', *Policy Studies Journal*, **31** (1), 1–29.
Riisgaard, L. (2009a), 'Global value chains, labor organization and private social standards: lessons from East African cut flower industries', *World Development*, **37** (2), 326–40.
Riisgaard, L. (2009b), 'How the market for standards shapes competition in the market for goods: sustainability standards in the cut flower industry', DIIS Working Paper no. 2009/07.
Sabel, C., A. Fung and D. O'Rourke (2000), *Ratcheting Labor Standards: Regulation for Continuous Improvement in the Global Workplace*, Washington, DC: World Bank.
Scharpf, F. (1999), *Governing in Europe: Effective and Democratic*, Oxford: Oxford University Press.
Schepel, H. (2005), *The Constitution of Private Governance: Product Standards in the Regulation of Integrating Markets*, Oxford and Portland, OR: Hart Publishing.
Swinnen, J. (2007), *Global Supply Chains, Standards and the Poor: How the Globalization of Food Systems and Standards Affects Rural Development and Poverty*, Oxford and Cambridge: CAB International.
van Kersbergen, Kees and Frans van Waarden (2001), *Shifts in Governance: Problems of Legitimacy and Accountability*, Den Haag: NOW.
van Waarden, F. (2009), 'Governing global commons: public–private-protection of fish and forests', in J. Swinnen, D. Vogel, A. Marx, H. Riss and J. Wouters (eds), *Handling Global Challenges,* Leuven: Leuven Centre for Global Governance Studies, pp. 140–75.
Vogel D. (2005), *The Market for Virtue: The Potential and Limits of Corporate Social Responsibility*, Washington, DC: Brookings Institution.

Vogel, D. (2008), 'Private global business regulation', *Annual Review of Political Science*, **11**, 261–82.

Winickoff, D. and K. Klein (2009), 'Food labels and the environment: development and harmonization of organic regulation in the EU and US', in J. Swinnen, D. Vogel, A. Marx, H. Riss and J. Wouters (eds), *Handling Global Challenges*, Leuven: Leuven Centre for Global Governance Studies, pp. 200–223.

Wouters, J., A. Marx and N. Hachez (2009), 'Private standards, global governance and transatlantic cooperation: the case of global food safety governance', in J. Swinnen, D. Vogel, A. Marx, H. Riss and J. Wouters (eds), *Handling Global Challenges*, Leuven: Leuven Centre for Global Governance Studies, pp. 176–99.

# 44 Global regulation through a diversity of norms: comparing hard and soft law
## *Sylvia I. Karlsson-Vinkhuyzen*

International legal scholars tend to see the rule of law as the fundamental tool in creating order and facilitating cooperation in the international system, while many international relations scholars have made governance the central analytical concept in their study of the same system. This has created a false dichotomy between law and governance. In unpacking both approaches, the role of a whole range of different kinds of norms, including but going beyond legal norms, comes to the fore. This chapter focuses on the diversity of norms that are used as tools in global governance and poses the question: what is the difference between governing through legal norms (law) and governing through non-legal norms?

There is a plethora of terms for formalized 'standards of behaviour' in global governance and law literature that are used differently or interchangeably or that sometimes even overlap. This handbook uses 'rules' as the central component of the regulatory process, as does much of the regulation literature. However, this chapter follows Shelton (2000: 5) and others who consider that '[n]orms includes all rules of conduct' and opts for 'norms'. The notion of norms covers both hard and soft law, the central concepts of which are discussed below. At the same time the meaning of the concept of 'institutions' in political science ranges from multilateral treaties to informal social codes of conduct. However, the term 'institutions' often specifies not only norms, but also organizations (e.g. Keohane 1988), while others make a clear distinction between institutions as rules and organizations as bodies with agency of their own (e.g. Young 1999). Legal scholars refer to international 'law' when norms have fulfilled certain criteria, while Franck (1990) for one refers to international law as rules rather than law because he considers them to be so fundamentally different in character from law in a national context.

In this chapter the analytical focus is on comparing the character and political function of the diversity of norms along the continuum from 'hard law' to 'soft law'. First the concept of legalization is described, and various definitions of hard and soft law are given. Then the actors who are involved in the development and application of these diverse norms are discussed, and the relationship between hard and soft law over time and governance levels is explored. The chapter concludes with a review of the reported strengths and weaknesses of hard and soft law, first by assessing a whole plethora of criteria and then by more systematically comparing their effectiveness and legitimacy.

## 44.1 THE DIVERSITY OF NORMS IN GLOBAL GOVERNANCE

The disciplinary boundaries between legal scholarship and political science, international law and international relations create what appears to be a significant divide between law and governance. One concept that has been used to bridge this divide at the international level is 'legalization', which refers to regulation through a diversity of norms with particular characteristics (see below) along the continuum 'from hard law through varied forms of soft law' (Abbott et al. 2000: 41) that fills the space of global governance.[1] The legalization literature distinguishes between hard and soft law, terms that are being used increasingly in both international law and international relations literature. There is, not surprisingly, considerable diversity in how these terms are defined, and the boundaries are blurred. Although some authors ignore soft law as they consider it irrelevant, the major argument of the legalization approach is that norms matter because they have some influence regardless of where they sit on the whole continuum between hard and soft.

### 44.1.1   Hard Law

Hard law includes all forms of international law. Its sources and its implications on states (*pacta sunt servanda*) are reasonably well defined and commonly accepted. The two major categories of international law are those based on treaties and those based on custom (state practice over time), as listed in Article 38 of the Statute of the International Court of Justice (ICJ). Nonetheless, there are still ambiguous cases where it is less clear which norms belong to hard law. For example, either certain provisions in a treaty are of a soft character, being weak and 'obscurely worded', or the very formulations are in the form of principles, such that it becomes unclear 'whether any real obligations are created' (Boyle and Chinkin 2007: 220). The *instrumentum* is hard, but its obligation is softened because its developers have decided to cast its content, its *negotium*, in non-normative terms (d'Aspremont 2008).

The designation of an international law as 'hard law' is thus not sufficient to capture the variation in 'hardness' that it can exhibit in the language of legalization. Abbott and Snidal (2000) apply the three criteria which define the legalization concept (see Abbott et al. 2000) to determine how hard an international norm is. They base hardness on the degree to which a norm provides binding *obligation,* is *precisely* worded, and provides for some type of *delegation* to third parties in the interpretation and implementation of the law, including the resolution of disputes and possibly even the authority to make further rules. Obligation varies from binding rule to expressly non-legal norm. The degree of obligation a norm carries can be reduced in a number of ways, such as making it contingent on the fulfilment of certain conditions or by using escape clauses. The second criterion is precision, which can vary from precise, highly elaborated rule to vague principle (Abbott et al. 2000). Precision and elaboration are particularly strong hallmarks of legalization at the international level since norms here are created through direct consent by all states and they are then interpreted by those same states (Abbott et al. 2000). The degree of delegation can vary from international court, organization or domestic application with mediation, arbitration or even adjudication to diplomacy with pure political decision-making (Abbott et al. 2000).

It is not only in legalization literature that variation is recognized in the degree of obligation that international law can possess. In national legal systems it is commonly accepted that there is a hierarchy of norms depending on their source and form: from constitutional law and legislation to administrative rules and even unwritten law

(Shelton 2006). Yet, in the international system, making distinctions between different types of law is more controversial. This applies both to the possibility of some types of hard law having higher normativity than others and to considering hard and soft law in the same analysis (Shelton 2006). In the former case the debate is focused on the concept of *jus cogens*, a term applied to norms that are claimed to be 'peremptory' to other types of international hard law and that would thus override law derived from both treaty and custom and bind all states (Shelton 2006).[2] However, even without this concept it has been argued that, for example, human rights law should have priority over other types of international law, such as trade law (Shelton 2006). Some legal scholars, such as Weil (1983), have strongly criticized this tendency towards a fragmentation of normativity in international law because of the uncertainties it creates.

### 44.1.2 Soft Law

There is no clear definition of soft law (Charney 2000), except that these norms are not legally binding by themselves (Shelton 2000). Soft law constitutes norms that govern international relations yet do not originate from the sources of law referred to in Article 38 of the Statute of the ICJ (Thürer 2000). For many legal scholars who insist on the clear distinction between law and non-law (see below), the term 'soft law', if accepted at all, does not need more definition or categories than this. In contrast, other scholars see the concept as covering a considerable diversity of international non-legally binding instruments (Boyle and Chinkin 2007), which implies that further categorization would be valuable.

Chinkin (2000) distinguishes two major categories of soft law: 'legal soft law' (imprecise hard law) and 'non-legal soft law' (e.g. resolutions, declarations, codes of conduct and guidelines formulated by international or regional organizations). In this latter category she includes the outcomes of intergovernmental conferences and summits. Chinkin further notes that different kinds of non-legal soft law can vary extensively in specificity and even be inconsistent with each other. She has an additional category of soft law that encompasses those principles, codes of conduct and so on that are developed without the involvement of states (see next section).

Abbott and Snidal (2000) apply the term 'soft law' when a norm is weakened along one or more of the dimensions of obligation, precision and delegation. Their definition also highlights that the borderline between hard and soft law is not sharp. A significant part of international hard law is indeed quite soft, as was discussed above. Some argue that the distinction between hard and soft law does not necessarily follow the line between treaties and other instruments (Boyle and Chinkin 2007). Furthermore, the development of soft law shares many similarities with the development of hard law; it is 'carefully negotiated, often carefully drafted statements', and in some cases soft law instruments 'serve much the same law-making purposes' as multilateral treaties (Boyle and Chinkin 2007: 214). In some cases supervisory organs have been established to monitor compliance with soft law, and in other cases states are invited to send in reports on their implementation in a way that is similar to that used for treaties (Shelton 2006).

While generally formulated principles can form a part of treaties, they are even more frequently found in soft law that is used by both national and international decision-makers and courts in interpreting treaties and deciding cases. This practice can be best understood if such principles are considered as general principles of law, because as such they can 'set limits, or provide guidance, or determine how conflicts between other rules or principles will be resolved' (Boyle and Chinkin 2007: 224).

Many legal scholars reject the very idea of terming soft law instruments 'law'. They prefer to keep the integrity of the law/non-law distinction, arguing that a norm is either legally binding or not, with nothing in between (Thürer 2000). By the use of the term 'international soft law', the currency of law may be depreciated (Bilder 2000). On the other hand, all legal systems have the problem of the transition from non-law to law, particularly underframed in the debate on how to distinguish between moral and legal obligation (Weil 1983: 415). Those who negotiate soft norms emphasize that they are not legally binding and thus not law (Thürer 2000), another reason to keep the distinction and avoid the term.

### 44.1.3 Law by Whom, for Whom?

The question of who develops norms and for whom they are intended is a fundamental one. In a national context, law is adopted by parliaments but can apply to a wide range of actors. International hard law is predominantly developed and adopted by states. It has been claimed that a distinct feature of hard law is that its only formal subjects are states (Chinkin 2000) and that governance through hard law relies primarily on the authority and power of the state (Kirton and Trebilcock 2004). However, this reflects only a partial understanding of the social and political systems of global governance. On the one hand, there are international treaties whose subjects include, for example, intergovernmental organizations (IGOs).[3] There are also treaties that explicitly use private actors in their mechanisms of monitoring and enforcement. The whole field of international criminal law that applies to individuals has been developing rapidly since the 1990s, signifying a considerable change in the outreach of hard law. Non-state actors such as non-governmental organizations (NGOs) have had a significant influence in the development of several international treaties, such as the Landmines Convention and the establishment of the International Criminal Court (Boyle and Chinkin 2007).

Non-state actors may well influence the development of hard law, but they do not have any formal role in decision-making, which is still the exclusive remit of states. States also play the primary role in developing several types of soft law, such as UN General Assembly resolutions and the outcomes of UN conferences and summits. However, there is a whole category of soft law in which non-state actors have a larger or even central role, both as norm developers and as norm subjects; indeed in some cases states may be entirely absent. This category of soft law goes under several names. Reinicke and Witte (2000) refer to these norms as non-binding international legal agreements (NBILAs), while Bernstein and Cashore (2007) refer to non-state market-driven governance systems (NSMDs) for such efforts of regulation. Levi-Faur (2010) discusses the global expansion of rule-based governance as consisting of a large number of micro-regimes at the global level that are neither entirely private nor entirely public regimes but hybrids. The wide range of constellations of actors who are involved in the development of this type of soft law can be illustrated by cases in the field of international standards.

Abbott and Snidal (2009) identify five constellations of actors engaged in developing this type of norm: states or coalitions of states through an IGO developing standards for businesses; business and industry self-regulatory schemes; NGOs and NGO coalitions; actors from two categories (states and NGOs, NGOs and businesses or states and businesses) working together as the major partners in standard development; and, finally, where all three major groups of actors (states, NGOs and businesses) are engaged. A growing body of literature on international standards and other types of business regulation reveals how much global regulation is taking place beyond the realm of intergovernmental settings (Braithwaite and Drahos 2000; Bernstein and Cashore 2007; Mattli and Woods 2009).

### 44.1.4   Dynamics between Hard and Soft Law

Hard and soft law do not live separate lives; there is significant interdependency between them. The dynamics work in different directions. Softer law can generate harder law over time, and harder law can generate softer law. The progression from soft to hard law can occur in various ways, not only through the direct negotiation of a treaty based on a previously existing soft instrument or through the negotiation of a hard framework convention into an even harder protocol. Soft law has a 'complex and potentially large impact in the development of international law' (Shelton 2000: 1). In particular it can contribute to the creation of customary law by generating widespread and consistent state practice and/or provide evidence of *opinio juris* (Boyle and Chinkin 2007: 215). Soft law is also used in making authoritative interpretations or amplifications of the terms of hard law (treaties) (Boyle and Chinkin 2007). Soft laws can have immediate legal effect through the principle of good faith, which implies that 'relevant actors are not allowed to contradict their own conduct' (Thürer 2000: 457). In the other direction, hard law such as conventions can generate 'secondary' or 'delegated' soft law, for example statements and practice that are developed to supplement or correct a treaty text (Chinkin 2000). There are also many examples where hard law indirectly makes soft law 'harder', where treaties by implied reference refer to soft law (Boyle and Chinkin 2007). Examples are seen in the references in the World Trade Organization (WTO) agreements to various international standards (such as the Codex Alimentarius food standards) that had previously been entirely voluntary, but have made these indirectly legally binding upon WTO members (Karlsson 2000).

International soft law can become hard law at lower levels of governance even if it remains a soft international instrument. One example of this is the development of the regional United Nations Economic Commission for Europe Convention on Access to Information, Public Participation in Decision-Making and Access to Justice in Environmental Matters that stemmed from Principle 10 in the global soft Rio Declaration (Wates 2005). Another example is a country not signing an international treaty, such as the USA and the Kyoto Protocol, yet sub-national governments developing legally binding instruments towards fulfilling its objectives. In a more general sense soft law can inspire or provide components of new municipal (i.e. domestic) law (Thürer 2000). In the other direction, international hard law can still vary considerably in how hard or soft it becomes through and after the ratification process in a national context depending on the constitution and political will.

## 44.2 CHOOSING THE BEST – HARD OR SOFT LAW?

There have been some efforts to compare hard and soft law. However, these tend to suffer from several weaknesses. Comparisons cover a diversity of qualities that are difficult to cluster. Evaluative statements are often made without more narrowly identifying where the norm is located on the legalization continuum from hard to soft law; how 'hard' (in terms of obligation, precision and delegation) is the hard law they are considering and indeed how 'soft' is the soft law instrument they are judging? Moreover, considering the large diversity of soft law in terms of actors involved (only states, only non-state actors, etc.) and the type and universality of negotiation processes, assessments can look very different for various categories of soft law, yet this diversity is seldom taken into account in the literature. Judgements are occasionally based on how hard and soft law perform independently; in other cases performance between hard and soft law is compared. In yet other cases, the analysis is focused on the reasons states prefer hard or soft law.[4] These weaknesses have to be borne in mind when considering the following review of reported qualities of hard and soft law, which is summarized in Table 44.1.

### 44.2.1 What is Good about Hard Law and What is Not?

There are often explicit or implicit assumptions that hard law elicits more compliance. This assumption is surely tied to drawing parallels with what happens at the national level, where law is expected to influence behaviour quite significantly. International hard law can be expected to have more influence than soft law partly because it has to be ratified and become part of national law and partly because the mere act of signing on to it indicates a stronger commitment (Boyle and Chinkin 2007). The mechanisms through which international hard law can elicit compliance are, however, rather different from those operating at a national level. Sanctions are rarely tied to treaties, and compliance

*Table 44.1 Summarizing strengths and weaknesses of hard and soft law*

|  | Hard law | Soft law |
| --- | --- | --- |
| Influence (e.g. through ratification) | Higher | Lower |
| Surveillance and enforcement | Higher | Lower |
| Resources for implementation | Guaranteed | Uncertain |
| Speed of development | Slower | Faster |
| Speed of implementation | Slower | Faster |
| Ability to deal with change (flexibility) | Smaller | Greater |
| Ability to deal with uncertainty | Smaller | Greater |
| Ability to deal with diversity | Smaller | Greater |
| Sovereignty costs | Higher | Lower |
| Transaction costs | Higher | Lower |
| Ability to set international agendas | Lower | Higher |
| Ability to facilitate cooperation and compromise | Lower | Higher |
| Ability to produce innovative principles and norms | Lower | Higher |
| Legitimacy (e.g. from its legality) | Higher | Lower |
| Participation of non-state actors | Absent | Possible |

may be more a result of reputational sanctions, learning over time, capacity building and so on (Chayes and Chayes 1995). Some authors expect that hard law has strong surveillance and enforcement and guaranteed resources for implementation (Kirton and Trebilcock 2004). However, the possibility of enforcement varies significantly among treaties and is usually quite weak, with some exceptions, for example in EU and WTO law. Hard law is still assumed, in relative terms, to have stronger enforcement mechanisms than soft law. For example, hard law elicits compliance through its legitimacy (see discussion below); actors comply with norms simply according to how legitimate they perceive them to be (Franck 1990).[5] When breach of a law leads to injury, hard law carries with it the obligation to make reparation through restitution, monetary indemnity and so on (Abbott et al. 2000).

Reported negative aspects of hard law include that it is slow and costly to develop, inflexible, less able to deal with challenges from globalization, developed in processes that are not very open, and slow to implement owing to the ratification process (Reinicke and Witte 2000). Hard law has been seen in a negative light in EU governance both because it treats all subjects the same way, even though there is a need for diversity, and because it is difficult to change and thus not good at handling uncertainty (Trubek et al. 2005).

### 44.2.2    What is Good about Soft Law and What is Not?

Positive aspects that have been raised for soft law include that:[6] it is good at dealing with uncertainty (Abbott and Snidal 2000; Shelton 2000); it is more flexible (Boyle and Chinkin 2007), which enables it to deal with a changing and technology-driven environment (Reinicke and Witte 2000); and it has lower sovereignty cost (Reinicke and Witte 2000; Trubek et al. 2005). Furthermore, it is claimed to facilitate cooperation (Chinkin 2000) and compromise over time (Abbott and Snidal 2000), as well as learning, norm diffusion and changing interests (Abbott and Snidal 2000; Reinicke and Witte 2000; Trubek et al. 2005). Soft law is supposedly easier to achieve (Cloghesy 2004), has lower transaction costs (Reinicke and Witte 2000; Trubek et al. 2005) and provides room for states with varying degrees of readiness for legalization (Abbott and Snidal 2000). It thus allows stakeholders to go further (Kirton and Trebilcock 2004) and provides a tool for setting international agendas (Chinkin 2000). It is good at coping with diversity, is simple and quick, sets the stage for hard law (Trubek et al. 2005), avoids the waiting typical of slow ratification processes (Boyle and Chinkin 2007) and produces innovative principles and norms (Kirton and Trebilcock 2004). In addition, it can allow participation of non-state stakeholders in its development (Reinicke and Witte 2000; Kirton and Trebilcock 2004).[7]

Among the reported negative aspects of soft law are that it lacks the legitimacy, strong surveillance and enforcement offered by hard law (Kirton and Trebilcock 2004), elicits less compliance (Brown Weiss 2000; Shelton 2000) and elicits less condemnation (a reputational rather than legal sanction) when violated than hard law does (Thürer 2000). Other aspects are that courts cannot influence actors' behaviour through soft law (Brown Weiss 2000) and that it is unsuitable for use in adjudication (Chinkin 1989). Furthermore, soft law can lead to uncertainty when there are competing soft laws (Kirton and Trebilcock 2004); it lacks clarity and precision and bypasses normal systems of accountability (Trubek et al. 2005); it is costly and complex to implement for weak stakeholder groups (Rezende de Azevedo 2004); it compromises democratic participation when certain stakeholders are left out (Kirton and Trebilcock 2004) and it raises legitimacy concerns, particularly in practical applications (Bernstein and Cashore 2004; Cragg 2004; Trebilcock 2004).

## 44.3   COMPARING THE EFFECTIVENESS AND LEGITIMACY OF HARD AND SOFT LAW

Much remains to be done in terms of systematic comparison of the qualities of harder and softer law, in terms both of using comparable criteria and of being more specific regarding where on the soft–hard continuum the norms in question are located. However, it is also important to bring into the comparison a coherent analytical framework that can be linked to understanding the politics of choosing norms in global regulation. One such framework clusters qualities for hard or soft law into the overarching criteria of effectiveness and legitimacy (Karlsson-Vinkhuyzen and Vihma 2009). Effectiveness refers to how well norms exert influence and contribute to solving the problem for which they were created, and legitimacy refers to how norms are accepted as justified limitations of authority. These two criteria are frequently used in the evaluation of governance, and clustering the qualities assigned to hard and soft law into these categories can tell a more coherent story of meaningful differences between these different types of norms.

Looking first at effectiveness, evaluative judgements between hard and soft law are usually tied to assumptions about compliance. As discussed above, the prevailing hypothesis is that the 'harder' a law is, the higher the degree of compliance. This hypothesis is primarily linked to looking at what drives the behaviour of actors, particularly states, within a logic of consequences. The underlying assumption here is that mechanisms that promote compliance – hard and soft sanctions and systems of rewards – are stronger on the hard law end of the continuum. However, the examples of very hard sanctions (military, economic, etc.) with enforcement and delegation are few in international law, and these have little relevance for variations along the rest of the continuum. It is still reasonable for there to be a gradation of weaker soft sanctions along the hard–soft continuum, partly because the less precise a law is, the less clear it becomes whether violations can be claimed, and partly because reputational sanctions are likely to be weaker with soft law. Rewards for compliance in the form of material resource flows are also mostly associated with hard law.

In contrast to this reasoning, those who assign more importance to motivations for behaviour within the logic of appropriateness often see soft law as having more influence. This is based on the assumption that it is better at facilitating learning, diffusing norms and changing interests. However, as noted above, it is obvious that a large amount of learning is taking place in hard law regimes owing to intensive interactions and institutional building over a long period. It is also clear that the resources available for capacity building in relation to implementation are far more abundant for hard law regimes, such as international environmental treaties or the various WTO agreements. Such resources can even be included as part of the negotiated regime package and as being explicit or implicit prerequisites binding certain groups of countries to comply. In contrast, the types of resources available for the implementation of soft law action plans in such cases as the large conferences of the 1990s consist of more indirect, meagre and ad hoc flows through bilateral and multilateral aid. Flexibility is another quality that could strengthen a norm's effectiveness, at least in certain circumstances. Soft law, with its acclaimed higher flexibility, would thus score higher here, particularly if it is able to target its design towards the changing character or understanding of a problem.

When legitimacy is used as the evaluative criterion, it is often linked to the logic of appropriateness. The perceived legitimacy of the norm becomes an important pull of compliance, and the question is then to identify the various sources for the legitimacy of international norms. These sources can, for example, be clustered into input and output legitimacy (Scharpf 1999). Depending on the emphasis put on these two sources of legitimacy and various subcomponents that contribute to each of them, expectations differ as to whether hard or soft law will score better. Furthermore, such expectations depend on who is evaluating legitimacy. Hard law and soft law developed by governments only are most commonly negotiated in a multilateral arena, such as the UN, which tend to score high on legitimacy for most states. This high score can be linked to input legitimacy derived partly from the decision-making procedures applied in those arenas, which are usually consensus-based and considered fair for all governments, and partly from the assumption that it is easier to hold states more accountable using hard law, with its more precise obligations. Soft law, on the other hand, lacks clarity and precision and can bypass normal systems of accountability, particularly as it is not submitted to parliaments for ratification and integration into domestic law. Lastly, when a norm is packaged as 'law' this can in itself lead to a higher score for legitimacy. For multiple reasons hard law is supposed to exert an independent pull towards compliance (Charney 2000). Legal obligations are claimed to be 'different from obligations resulting from coercion, comity or morality alone' (Abbott et al. 2000: 408), and there is a social norm of 'obedience to law' (Abbott and Snidal 2000: 425).[8] However, this line of reasoning has the caveat that, for those actors who fundamentally disagree with the content of the law and thus refuse to consent with it, its 'hardness' is unlikely to increase its legitimacy in their eyes, but quite the opposite.

The comparison of hard and soft law results in a different outcome if the emphasis is placed on the value of broader participation of non-state actors in the process of norm development as a way to compensate for the acclaimed democratic deficit in global governance. It is often asserted that soft law allows more non-state participation than does hard law. However, with the exception of soft law developed by multi-stakeholder coalitions or private actors that allow them to be part of decision-making, it is difficult to see any clear differences in the ability to participate that are linked to the hard–soft gradient.[9] Access varies more between regimes. For example, in the environmental field there are more or less similar access rules for civil society observers at summits that generate soft law or at negotiations that generate hard law. The WTO, on the other hand, has far less access for civil society participation.

There is a great need to address the common challenges of humankind through norms, a greater need than currently can be filled with hard law alone. There are many areas where 'international law knows no norm at all, but a lacuna' (Weil 1983: 414). Norms along the whole hard–soft law continuum can fill this lacuna, but, in choosing the best instrument for each specific governance problem, actors could benefit from more research-based and systematic knowledge on the advantages and disadvantages of hard and soft law.

This summary of some of the reported strengths and weaknesses of international hard and soft law is significantly constrained by the limitations of the literature discussed in the text. Statements that one type of law (hard or soft) is performing particularly well on one particular characteristic have here been used as inferring that the other type of law is performing more poorly even if this is not always explicitly stated in the sources.

## NOTES

1. The focus here is on formal norms, i.e. norms which have been explicitly negotiated and agreed to in written form. International customary law is a special case, as it may not be written but is still binding in international law.
2. Peremptory, *jus cogens*, norms have been attributed to sources such as 'state consent, natural law, necessity, international public order, and the development of constitutional principles' (Shelton 2006: 302).
3. Soft law can also have a binding effect on IGOs, such as in the case of the Universal Declaration of Human Rights' norms against discrimination of women, which is binding in the UN system (Thürer 2000).
4. For a more detailed discussion on the weaknesses of the existing literature, see Karlsson-Vinkhuyzen and Vihma (2009).
5. For an overview of how international norms can exert influence on actors in general, see Karlsson-Vinkhuyzen and Vihma (2009).
6. Most of the assessments of soft law in this section focus on the most common definition of soft law as being non-legal instruments, and thus exclude legal soft law as in Chinkin's hierarchy.
7. Some of these statements are also valid for hard law, such as the involvement of non-state actors.
8. It is another question whether it could also be applied to international soft law. Using the term 'soft law' itself 'seems to contain a normative element leading to expectations of compliance' (Shelton 2000: 2).
9. It is also important to note that the mere possibility of participation is not sufficient to ensure fairness of the voices heard. The resources needed to participate in a meaningful way are not evenly distributed across the stakeholders who are affected (Mattli and Woods 2009). Furthermore, there are many non-state regulatory forums that 'are and remain exclusive and secretive, serving as effective vehicles for capture' (Mattli and Woods 2009: 20).

## REFERENCES

Abbott, K.W. and D. Snidal (2000), 'Hard and soft law in international governance', *International Organization*, **54** (3), 421–56.
Abbott, K.W. and Snidal, D. (2009), 'The governance triangle: regulatory standards institutions and the shadow of the state', in W. Mattli and N. Woods (eds), *The Politics of Global Regulation*, Princeton, NJ: Princeton University Press, pp. 44–88.
Abbott, K.W., R.O. Keohane, A. Moravcsik, A.-M. Slaughter and D. Snidal (2000), 'The concept of legalization', *International Organization*, **54** (3), 401–419.
Bernstein, S. and B. Cashore (2004), 'Non-state global governance: is forest certification a legitimate alternative to a global forest convention?', in J.J. Kirton and M.J. Trebilcock (eds), *Hard Choices, Soft Law: Voluntary Standards in Global Trade, Environment and Social Governance*, Bodmin, Cornwall: Ashgate, pp. 33–63.
Bernstein, S. and B. Cashore (2007), 'Can non-state global governance be legitimate? An analytical framework', *Regulation & Governance*, **1**, 347–71.
Bilder, R.B. (2000), 'Beyond compliance: helping nations cooperate', in D. Shelton (ed.), *Commitment and Compliance: The Role of Non-Binding Norms in the International Legal System*, Oxford: Oxford University Press, pp. 65–73.
Boyle, A. and C. Chinkin (2007), *The Making of International Law*, Oxford: Oxford University Press.
Braithwaite, J. and P. Drahos (2000), *Global Business Regulation*, Cambridge: Cambridge University Press.
Brown Weiss, E. (2000), 'Conclusions: understanding compliance with soft law', in D. Shelton (ed.), *Commitment and Compliance: The Role of Non-Binding Norms in the International Legal System*, Oxford: Oxford University Press, pp. 535–53.
Charney, J.L. (2000), 'Commentary: compliance with international soft law', in D. Shelton (ed.), *Commitment*

*and Compliance: The Role of Non-Binding Norms in the International Legal System*, Oxford: Oxford University Press, pp. 115–18.

Chayes, A. and A.H. Chayes (1995), *The New Sovereignty: Compliance with International Regulatory Agreements*, London: Harvard University Press.

Chinkin, C.M. (1989), 'The challenge of soft law: development and change in international law', *International and Comparative Law Quarterly*, **38**, 850–66.

Chinkin, C. (2000), 'Normative development in the international legal system', in D. Shelton (ed.), *Commitment and Compliance: The Role of Non-Binding Norms in the International Legal System*, Oxford: Oxford University Press, pp. 21–42.

Cloghesy, M.E. (2004), 'A corporate perspective on globalisation, sustainable development, and soft law', in J.J. Kirton and M.J. Trebilcock (eds), *Hard Choices, Soft Law: Voluntary Standards in Global Trade, Environment and Social Governance*, Bodmin, Cornwall: Ashgate, pp. 323–8.

Cragg, W. (2004), 'Multinational corporations, globalisation, and the challenge of self-regulation', in J.J. Kirton and M.J. Trebilcock (eds), *Hard Choices, Soft Law: Voluntary Standards in Global Trade, Environment and Social Governance*, Bodmin, Cornwall: Ashgate, pp. 213–227.

d'Aspremont, J. (2008), 'Softness in international law: a self-serving quest for new legal materials', *European Journal of International Law*, **19** (5), 1075–93.

Franck, T.M. (1990), *The Power of Legitimacy among Nations*, Oxford: Oxford University Press.

Karlsson, S. (2000), *Multilayered Governance: Pesticides in the South – Environmental Concerns in a Globalised World*, Linköping: Linköping University.

Karlsson-Vinkhuyzen, S.I. and A. Vihma (2009), 'Comparing the legitimacy and effectiveness of global hard and soft law: an analytical framework', *Regulation & Governance*, **3** (4), 400–420.

Keohane, R.O. (1988), 'International institutions: two approaches', *International Studies Quarterly*, **32**, 379–96.

Kirton, J.J. and M.J. Trebilcock (2004), 'Introduction: hard choices and soft law in sustainable global governance', in J.J. Kirton, and M.J. Trebilcock (eds), *Hard Choices, Soft Law: Voluntary Standards in Global Trade, Environment and Social Governance*, Bodmin, Cornwall: Ashgate, pp. 3–29.

Levi-Faur, D. (2010), 'Regulatory architectures for a global democracy: on democratic varieties of regulatory capitalism', in T. Porter and K. Ronit (eds), *The Challenges of Global Business Authority: Democratic Renewal, Stalemate, or Decay?*, New York: SUNY Press, pp. 205–26.

Mattli, W. and N. Woods (eds) (2009), *The Politics of Global Regulation*, Princeton, NJ: Princeton University Press.

Reinicke, W.H. and J.M. Witte (2000), 'Interdependence, globalization, and sovereignty: the role of nonbinding international legal accords', in D. Shelton (ed.), *Commitment and Compliance: The Role of Non-Binding Norms in the International Legal System*, Oxford: Oxford University Press, pp. 75–100.

Rezende de Azevedo, T. (2004), 'The Forest Stewardship Council: a developing country perspective', in J.J. Kirton and M.J. Trebilcock (eds), *Hard Choices, Soft Law: Voluntary Standards in Global Trade, Environment and Social Governance*, Bodmin, Cornwall: Ashgate, pp. 64–92.

Scharpf, F.W. (1999), *Governing in Europe: Effective and Democratic?*, New York: Oxford University Press.

Shelton, D. (2000), 'Introduction: law, non-law and the problem of "soft law"', in D. Shelton (ed.), *Commitment and Compliance: The Role of Non-Binding Norms in the International Legal System*, Oxford: Oxford University Press, pp. 1–18.

Shelton, D. (2006), 'Normative hierarchy in international law', *American Journal of International Law*, **100** (2), 291–323.

Thürer, D. (2000), 'Soft law', in R. Bernhardt (ed.), *Encyclopedia of Public International Law*, vol. 4, Amsterdam: Elsevier, pp. 452–60.

Trebilcock, M.J. (2004), 'Trade policy and labour standards: objectives, instruments and institutions', in J.J. Kirton and M.J. Trebilcock (eds), *Hard Choices, Soft Law: Voluntary Standards in Global Trade, Environment and Social Governance*, Bodmin, Cornwall: Ashgate, pp. 170–85.

Trubek, D.M., P. Cottrell and M. Nance (2005), '"Soft law", "hard law" and European integration', in G. de Búrca and J. Scott (eds), *Law and New Governance in the EU and the US*, Oxford: Hart, pp. 65–94.

Wates, J. (2005), 'The Aarhus Convention: a driving force for environmental democracy', *Journal for European and Environmental Planning Law*, **1**, 2–11.

Weil, P. (1983), 'Towards relative normativity in international law?', *American Journal of International Law*, 77 (3), 413–42.

Young, O.R. (1999), *Institutional Dimensions of Global Environmental Change Science Plan*, Bonn: International Human Dimensions Programme on Global Environmental Change.

# 45 Money laundering regulation: from Al Capone to Al Qaeda
## *Brigitte Unger*

Money laundering – bringing illicit proceeds from drugs, fraud and other crime back into the legal economy – owes its name to Al Capone. He literally used launderettes for disguising illegal alcohol revenues during prohibition in the US. Launderettes, a flourishing cash-intensive business in the 1930s, when almost no household had a washing machine, were an ideal location to slip the money from illegal alcohol sales into the cash register. Disguising the origin of such money is, however, even older than Al Capone's "washing of money." One of the oldest techniques to circumvent government scrutiny was to use international trade to move money, undetected, from one country to another, by means of fake invoicing or falsely declared merchandise (Zdanowicz 2009).

Though money laundering is an old way of trying to hide the illicit proceeds from crime, it became an issue of international concern only in the last 20 years; and it is only since 9/11 that it figures as a prominent issue of national and international safety on the agenda of international organizations. How was it possible that a problem which existed for centuries was suddenly considered a topic of major international concern which had to be regulated? And how was it possible that its scope expanded from Al Capone's whiskey business to protecting national security and fighting Al Qaeda?

I will discuss the characteristics of the problems to be regulated in section 45.1 and what they mean for the private support and public interest in regulating laundering in section 45.2. Section 45.3 shows the regulatory responses and section 45.4 the problems of the effectiveness, enforcement and legitimacy of anti-money regulation. The conclusions in section 45.5 on regulating global issues focus mainly on the role of the EU.

## 45.1   THE CHARACTERISTICS OF THE PROBLEM TO BE REGULATED

After criminalization of drug abuse in 1922 in the US, there followed almost a century of hopeless efforts to reduce drug trafficking, which led to the need for combating money laundering to be put on the international agenda. If one could not get at drug dealers and eventually other criminals directly, then at least they should be discouraged by the realization that they could not reap the monetary benefits of their acts. The following characteristics make money laundering a particular regulatory challenge.

### 45.1.1   Victimless Crime

While money laundering makes crime pay because the launderer can safely disguise his illicit proceeds, it does not have direct victims. No one suffers from the fact that the

Colombian drugs mafia sends 10 billion dollars from one country to another. There are, hence, no victims who would complain, no liability claims that would be raised, and no tort law that could be applied. No direct harm comes from this.

The question heavily debated in legal literature is whether crime without victims should be punished at all and whether punishment is a deterrent (for a survey see Polinsky and Shavell 1997). Should the government leave people their free will and not forcibly prevent them from engaging in crime that does not harm others (Mill 1999[1869]: 21) or would society be damaged by this maleficent behavior and fall into decadence? 'Public order crime' is now the preferred term for "victimless" crime, based on the idea that there are always secondary victims such as family, friends, acquaintances and society at large. (For further reading see Siegel 2006; Siegel and Senna 2008.)

### 45.1.2    No Direct Effects of Laundering

The harm of money laundering is only very indirect. Unger (2007) lists 25 negative and positive effects that money laundering can have. It can deter honest business activities, if criminals invest their money in particular sectors like the transport industry, restaurants and housing; it can lead to changes in relative prices, savings, output, employment and growth, or it can affect the liquidity, reputation, integrity and stability of the financial sector. The public sector can suffer from unpaid taxes, and criminals might buy up public enterprises during privatization efforts.

There are also social and political effects like increased corruption and bribery. Professionals, like lawyers, notaries public, real estate agents and accountants, can become contaminated, since laundering needs facilitators. Criminals might undermine political institutions. That none of these effects can be directly observed poses problems for regulation.

### 45.1.3    Ambiguous Relation Between Money Laundering and Terrorism Financing

Money laundering can also increase terrorist activity if the proceeds of crime are used to finance it. Here laundering serves two purposes: concealing both the illegal origin of the money and the illegal destination of the funds (Masciandaro 2007). Most experts agree that the sale and trade of drugs seem to be a sizable financial contributor to terrorist organizations. The Taliban, for example, profited from the trafficking of opium and taxing the drug trade in areas under its control, and these funds were subsequently used to support terrorist organizations like Al Qaeda (Schneider 2004).

However, very often terrorism is financed with clean money by abusing donations and foreign aid. This involves a process completely different from money laundering: "money dirtying," which is the reverse of money laundering. Regulating terrorism together with money laundering therefore poses an additional challenge.

### 45.1.4    Unknown Size of the Problem

The regulator has a difficult business to do: there are no victims, the link between money laundering and crime is only a very vague one, and between money laundering and terrorist financing this link is even more doubtful. The regulator also does not know how big the problem is that he regulates. Estimates on global money laundering are still in their infancy, first because the underlying crime is unknown and second because the proceeds of this unknown crime can only be estimated. As Reuter and Greenfield (2001: 171) observe, "knowing the value of drug exports from Mexico to the US is $1–3 billion rather than $10–20 billion may be very important for purposes of allocating resources for money laundering investigations or even passing money laundering regulations in Mexico." Global estimates for money laundering range from between $45 million and $280 million (Reuter and Greenfield 2001), and $1.5 trillion in the IMF and Human Development Report 1999 (see TNI 2003) to $2.85 trillion (Walker 1995, 2002; Walker and Unger 2009).

### 45.1.5 A Global Phenomenon

Money laundering is a global phenomenon, and regulation of it increased with the deregulation of financial markets, which has made countries more vulnerable. Today, money can be pumped around the world within a second through the push of a computer button. The fact that financial capital can move freely between countries has created new ways for organized crime to disguise the origin of illegal proceeds. Instruments like bearer shares, over-the-counter derivatives outside the control of national banks, techniques like bank-to-bank loans, and international mortgages created room for maneuver also for criminals. Innovations which benefit legal transfers open doors for illegal moves. The international dimension also implies that regulating money laundering in one country will depend heavily on simultaneous action in other countries. The winners and losers of regulation might differ: some countries might profit from the additional money, while others might suffer from increased crime. Loopholes in the anti-money laundering regime will be used by launderers; therefore some sorts of international instruments and cooperation are needed.

## 45.2 THE POLITICAL ECONOMY OF MONEY LAUNDERING

Yandle (2011) distinguishes five theories of regulation: public interest theory, which assumes that regulators serve a broad public interest; capture theory, which recognizes that politicians are captured by rent-seeking groups; special interest theory, which specifies which party will be most influential in this process; the money-for-nothing theory, which focuses on the financial support politicians can gain by threatening industry with regulation; and the bootleggers and Baptists theory, which shows regulation as the outcome of odd alliances which share common interests for quite different reasons. This chapter focuses on the first three theories.

### 45.2.1 Lack of Private Interest for Regulating Money Laundering

According to the economic theory of regulation (see Becker 1968; Stigler 1971), special interest groups and other political participants will use the regulatory and coercive powers of government to shape laws and regulations in a way that is beneficial to them. But such a "capture" by the most influential group evidently does not take place with money laundering, because it is a victimless crime. The lack of victims means that there are also no private groups involved that would specially lobby for regulating money laundering.

Given the lack of private interest in lobbying for money laundering regulation, not much support of the private sector in law implementation and enforcement can be expected. The private sector can quietly ignore the rule, or can actively counteract it, but are very unlikely to be supportive, nor to contribute voluntarily to the costs of enforcing a government rule which does not have any advantage for them. Economists stress the information problem inherent in such a situation, where the regulator will act as the principal and the private sector as an agent in a "principal–agent setting" (see Rees 1985a, 1985b; Rosen 1986; Stiglitz 1987; Sappington 1991). Political scientists would add problems of political and bureaucratic power of the agent (Moe 2006), which can frustrate and even counteract the enforcement of rules.

### 45.2.2  Public Interest Theory of Regulation and US Interests

Seen from a public interest theoretical point of view, the reason for regulating money laundering was a very pragmatic one. After years of losing the war on drugs, exemplified by the constant or ever increasing amounts of drugs produced and consumed (see UNODC drug reports, e.g. UNODC 2006), a new strategy has evolved. Now it is a case of "following the money instead of having to chase the criminal," of hitting international crime the most by getting at its money and "making crime less profitable." The grounds for this process are shaky and lobbied for only by the United States, which eventually got international organizations and some governments to truly, voluntarily comply.

With money laundering, it is the government, and more specifically the US government, and not the private sector which has an interest in regulation. The government claims it has to protect the public good where the nation's health is threatened by drugs and national security is threatened by terrorism. Those in favor of public choice see this as a problem. Their aim is to protect individual free will, and so they are very critical of governmental regulatory intervention which purports to protect public goods (Huntington 1952; Bernstein 1955; Levine and Forrence 1990; Laffont and Tirole 1991).

Money laundering was not considered much of a problem until the 1980s, when the US started criminalizing money laundering in the context of its "war on drugs." In 1986, it became the first country to make money laundering a crime (Title 18, US Code Sec. 1956), with penalties of up to 20 years in prison and $500000 in fines. In addition, the law permits civil penalty lawsuits by the government for the value of the funds or property involved in the transaction (Takats 2007).

From a legal point of view, the Achilles' heel in defining money laundering relates to the so-called "predicate offences" which generate the proceeds that make laundering necessary. Hiding or disguising the source of certain proceeds will, of course, not amount to money laundering *unless* these proceeds were obtained from a criminal activity (Busuioc 2007). The United States has developed a list of over 130 predicate crimes for money laundering. Originally mainly crimes with regard to drugs were on the list; eventually fraud, counterfeiting, fencing, illegal work and so on were added and, after 9/11, terrorist financing. The developments in the US explain why money laundering came so late on the international agenda and why it became an issue in fighting Al Qaeda.

With regard to law enforcement, the Banking Secrecy Act (1970) can be seen as an early starting point. It in fact curbed banking secrecy to fight money laundering, and was followed by a series of laws to further strengthen enforcement: the Money Laundering Control Act (1986), the Annunzio–Wylie Money Laundering Act (1992), the Money Laundering Suppression Act (1994), the Money Laundering and Financial Crimes Strategy Act (1998) and finally the USA Patriot Act (2001) (Takats 2007, fn. 1).

It is not surprising that the US, with the largest number of money launderers in the world, has been the first country and the strictest when it comes to money laundering regulations. Half of the globally laundered funds are probably transferred through American banks (Walker 1999; Unger 2007).

## 45.3   THE REGULATORY RESPONSES

### 45.3.1   The Reporting System and Problems with it

Originally, the regulations were rule-based. Money laundering enforcement relied on the private sector reporting to public law enforcement agencies. In the US, banks had to file a rule-based currency transaction report (CTR) for cash transactions exceeding $10 000. Rule-based regulation was less risky for both the private sector and the government. As there were explicit criteria for reporting, it was a standard disclosure process. Bank reports were ex post verifiable.

The precision of rule-based regulation however also had disadvantages. Not only banks but also money launderers were aware of the criteria for suspected money laundering and could circumvent them. Thus they could "smurf," that is, divide up large cash deposits to keep them under the reporting threshold of $10 000 (Takats 2007: 8).

The weaknesses of rule-based reports led the US in 1996 to introduce a discretionary report, the suspicious activity report (SAR). The definition of "suspicious" was left vague to keep both money launderers and banks in uncertainty (Takats 2007: 8).

A rule-based approach provides precise rules and hence legal certainty, but it also encourages, apart from smurfing, formalistic over-reporting. This is why not only the US but also Europe switched from a rule-based to a risk-based approach. The change to a risk-based approach also happened at a time when governments everywhere introduced supposedly less bureaucratic, more subject-friendly, more responsive regulations (Ayres and Braithwaite 1992; Hutter 2005, 2006).

Yet the risk-based approach had the opposite effect and encouraged even more relatively useless over-reporting, also called the "crying wolf problem" (Takats 2007; Dalla Pellegrina and Masciandaro 2009). The regulation gave private actors more discretion about what to report and instructed them to report transactions that *they* considered suspicious. It gave them vaguer criteria as to which transactions to report. This meant not only that private actors had to estimate the risks of a transaction being suspect, but also that they themselves ran the risk of getting accused of false reporting or more generally of being held responsible for whether they did a good job or not. The liability might induce businesses with a reporting duty to play it safe, by reporting as many cases as possible. Reporting units, according to Takats, might behave strategically and on purpose dilute information, by behaving like the little boy in the fairy tale and "crying wolf" so often that, when there was real money laundering, no one would take the cry seriously.

Unger and van Waarden (2009) showed that countries' reactions depended heavily on the legal system within which the private sector had to report. In the US, the fierceness of the legal conflict, the often severe sanctions, and the uncertainty of outcomes induced people to be formalistic and choose to "go by the book" (Bardach and Kagan 1982). Here the risk-based approach indeed led to an increase of reports and a decline in convictions, indicating a crying wolf problem. In the Netherlands, however, with a consensual legal system, where the regulator worked out the new rules in cooperation with the private sector, and where fines were extremely low, reporting went down drastically and the number of convictions increased (Unger and van Waarden 2009).

### 45.3.2  Seeking for Alliances and Expanding Regulation: From the War on Drugs to the War on Terror

Aware of the problem's international dimension, the US needed alliances with its anti-money laundering policy. It put pressure on international organizations to fight drugs. Similarly, international legislation of money laundering began with the criminalization of the proceeds of drug-related offences, as provided by the 1988 UN Convention against the Illicit Traffic in Narcotic Drugs and Psychotropic Substances (the Vienna Drug Convention). Since money laundering was mainly a problem for rich countries, which provide financial expertise, low corruption and high stability for placing illicit funds, the US pressured its G-7 partners to create an organization that would coordinate their efforts; thus the Financial Action Task Force (FATF) emerged in 1989 (Huelsse 2009). Officially only a task force, the FATF is an intergovernmental organization with a small secretariat based within the OECD building in Paris. Membership of the FATF was initially very exclusive – restricted to the G-7 countries plus other OECD members.

The organization's club-like character (Drezner 2007: 122, 142) enabled FATF members to agree quickly on a set of common standards, the Forty Recommendations, which were intended as a benchmark for national anti-money laundering legislation. As recommendations, they are not binding rules but standards of behavior that states can adopt voluntarily (Huelsse 2009).

Over the years, these recommendations have been revised with one important addition: Following the 9/11 attacks, FATF published "Eight Special Recommendations on Terrorist Finance" (later extended to nine). Though money laundering and the finance of terrorism are two rather distinct activities, linking them has given an enormous boost to combating money laundering. The FATF was now engaged in the "war on terror" (Winer and Roule 2002).

By 2009 the FATF included 34 members plus five associate members, who represented regions (see www.fatf.org). There are also a number of international organizations especially involved in combating money laundering, like the Egmont Group, which started in 1995 with 14 members and now consists of 116 members. It is a network designed to improve interaction among financial intelligence units in the areas of communications, information sharing and training coordination.

### 45.3.3 Setting an International Standard for Money Laundering: The Forty plus Nine Recommendations

By now the FATF's 40 recommendations for money laundering and nine on terrorist financing have become the international standard. FATF member states have to adopt these recommendations, and compliance is checked through mutual assessments of FATF member countries.

The recommendations include issues regarding the legal system and law enforcement, that is to say, the criminalization of money laundering on the basis of the UN Vienna Convention, the application of the law to corporations, penalties, the possibility of confiscation, the absence of bank secrecy, customer due diligence, the know-your-customer rule applied by financial institutions, the prosecution of politically exposed persons (PEPs), reporting requirements to financial intelligence units and other reporting units, training, auditing, sanctions for not reporting and non-compliance, establishment of a financial intelligence unit, existence of supervision, and the establishment of one central database.

Similarly, regarding the financing of terrorism the requirements are the criminalization of terrorism, the implementation of the UN instruments on terrorism contained in the 1999 United Nations International Convention for the Suppression of the Financing of Terrorism, the United Nations Security Council Resolution 1373, and others. Countries must have measures in place to detect the physical cross-border transportation of currency and bearer negotiable instruments. There are also recommendations concerning the confiscation of assets (see www.fatf.org).

## 45.4 ENFORCEMENT, EFFECTIVENESS AND LEGITIMACY PROBLEMS

### 45.4.1 Instruments to Achieve Countries' Compliance

In the absence of any legal instruments to make non-members follow its rules, FATF relied on soft instruments like "seminar diplomacy" and peer review (Sharman 2008). The cooperation of countries was not always "voluntary" in the proper sense, since the relationship between FATF members and non-members is hardly symmetrical (Tranøy 2002). On the one side we have the world's richest countries led by the global hegemony of the US (Simmons 2000, 2001; Williams 2001; Naylor 2002), and on the other side there is a heterogeneous group of states, ranging from developing countries to offshore centers, with none of them being anywhere near equal in power to the FATF members. Though non-members are legally free to ignore the FATF rules, it may not be very wise for them to do so. Hence there surely exists a shadow of hierarchy, which explains why non-member countries comply even in the absence of explicit threats and coercive measures. "To call this voluntary compliance hardly seems the correct label for such rule following behavior" (Huelsse 2009).

In addition, the FATF uses direct hierarchical means to enforce non-members' compliance with its rules. In 1995 the government of the Seychelles, an island state of some 80 000 people in the Indian Ocean, passed the Economic Development Act (EDA) through which the islands invited internationals to invest a minimum of US$10 million and in return the Seychelles government would grant immunity from prosecution. The US Department of the Treasury issued an advisory to banks and financial institutions urging them to exercise strict caution in their financial dealings with the Seychelles. The Republic Bank of New York stopped all payments to and from the Seychelles. The FATF issued its first ever public condemnation of an individual country. One year later, the Seychelles also introduced an Anti-Money Laundering Act (Simmons 2000: 258–9; Sharman and Rawlings 2006; Unger and Rawlings 2008: 333).

By intervening, FATF was paving the way for its later strategy of blacklisting countries considered to be tolerant of money laundering (Unger and Rawlings 2008). The blacklist contains 25 "negative" criteria, such as banking secrecy and some loopholes of law and financial regulation (for the complete list see FATF 2000). Countries that succumb to some of these are listed by the FATF as non-cooperative countries and/ or territories (NCCTs). Between its first appearance in 2000 and 2006 this blacklist has become shorter and shorter. In October 2006, Myanmar, the only country left on the list, was finally also removed (Unger and Ferwerda 2008).

The blacklist of the FATF suffered from severe problems. First, the list contained only 23 subjectively selected countries and no large country. Second, countries could show compliance with the FATF recommendations by filling in written statements. Thirdly, only when a certain not precisely defined threshold of declared compliance was not reached were they put on the list. Overall, the blacklist, therefore, did not sufficiently fulfill the transparency criteria for being a successful instrument of naming and shaming (Braithwaite 1989; Erp 2007). The list was judged discriminatory towards small islands and countries (Unger and Ferwerda 2008). Rawlings (2007) showed that blacklisting might have had reverse effects. Some states have experienced loss of business, but other offshore centers have prospered. Examples of these are the Cayman Islands, Bermuda, Jersey, Guernsey and the Isle of Man. Since all the countries have been removed, the list can be viewed as having failed to identify countries with a lax anti-money laundering policy.

For fairness it has to be mentioned that there are some positive effects. The fact that no country is left on the blacklist suggests that all countries have adjusted and improved their regulatory framework to combat money laundering, perhaps because of FATF (FATF 2006). The fragile legitimacy of FATF was definitely not improved with blacklisting. It had been looking repeatedly for cooperation with the IMF and the World Bank, which originally did not consider money laundering as their mandate (interview with Richard Gordon, May 2008). But since 9/11 cooperation has started, in particular with writing a common methodology. The IMF and World Bank – their own legitimacy problems notwithstanding (Barnett and Finnemore 2004) – are universal organizations, which gives them an advantage over the exclusive FATF (see Reuter and Truman 2004; Huelsse 2009). One condition for this cooperation set by them was that the FATF give up blacklisting (interview with Richard Gordon, May 2008).

The disappointing experience of blacklisting non-cooperative countries by the FATF confirms earlier findings on ratings under globalization: blacklisting and ratings by international organizations are less powerful than when done by private companies, because the former stand under the influence and pressure of large states which shape and finance them (see Graz and Noelke 2008; van Waarden 2008: 84–98). Van Waarden (2011) mentions as examples the judgments of rating agencies such as Standard & Poor's, Moody's and Fitch, which receive much broader acceptance than rankings of international organizations. Since 2009 the FATF has started a more differentiated grey list.

### 45.4.2  Some Regulatory Weaknesses

The Achilles' heel of the anti-money laundering and combating terrorist financing (AML/CFT) regime is the veritable patchwork of national lists of predicate offences. Some countries like China and Italy exclude home country laundering from their money laundering definition. In these countries, a drug dealer who is caught when laundering his own proceeds of crime cannot be prosecuted for money laundering but only for the drug crime itself. Austria only included home country laundering in 2010, under the pressure of criticism from FATF. To find a common denominator of predicate crimes for money laundering that includes the most serious crimes like drugs, weapons, human trafficking and all crimes committed by organized gangs seems a necessary and important step towards legislation that does not create opportunities for avoidance by launderers. Also, whether corporations can be prosecuted as opposed to individuals differs in the laws. Whether PEPs can be prosecuted for money laundering or are under immunity is also differently regulated. This can make it difficult to prosecute corrupt officials for money laundering. Especially in many Asian and African countries PEPs cannot be prosecuted. Counterfeiting and product piracy is a predicate crime in the US, but it often does not fit into European penal law, since it is considered private law there. This gives rise to irritations with negative FATF evaluations. Often tax evasion is related to money laundering, but in most countries tax evasion is not a predicate crime for laundering (see Unger 2007).

### 45.4.3  Effectiveness

What started as soft law became hard law in Europe. In Europe, the EU has transposed the FATF recommendations by establishing three directives which have to be integrated into national law by its member states. The first EU directive, 91/308/EEG, for the prevention of the use of the financial system for the purpose of money laundering foresaw a need for financial institutions to identify and report any suspicious financial transactions. The second directive, 2001/97/EG, for the prevention of the use of the financial system for the purpose of money laundering extended the remit of the first recommendation to other groups. Since 2001 car dealers and sellers of ships, art and antiques, gold, silver and jewelry and, since June 2003, also lawyers, notaries public, tax consultants, accountants and real estate agents have been under-reporting duty.

The third and most recent directive, 2005/60/EG, on the prevention of the use of the financial system for the purpose of money laundering and terrorism financing broadened the definition of money laundering, by including financing terrorism. It replaced the first EU directive.

With regard to cash, the EU regulation no. 1889/2005 on cash entering or leaving the EU says that any individual entering or leaving the Community and carrying cash of a value of 10 000 euros or more shall declare that sum to the competent authorities of the member state.

As with the US, enforcement problems occurred in Europe. Reporting systems are under heavy criticism. With regard to suspicious transactions, reporting outputs rather than outcomes are evaluated: what countries do with suspicious transaction report data remains in its infancy (Levi and Reuter 2006). Reuter and Truman (2004) showed that only 7.5 percent of the suspicious reports are used for further investigation in the US. A similar criticism of low performance holds true for the Dutch system of reporting unusual transactions. In a recent report, the Dutch Court of Audit criticized, among others, the inefficient way of handling reporting data (Algemene Rekenkamer 2008).

The fact that by now the IMF and World Bank also are busy with combating money laundering has increased in particular the collection and development of data that allow assessment of anti-money-laundering policy. An IMF working group is busy developing a methodology to assess the attractiveness of countries and their vulnerability to money laundering. A task force at Eurostat has started to collect statistical indicators for assessing the effectiveness of the anti-money-laundering policy.

### 45.4.4   Legitimacy Problems

Anti-money-laundering policy runs the risk of contravening human rights. Vervaele (2005) criticized the paradigm change in law that followed from the incorporation of financing terrorism. Making laundering an issue of national security means that the enforcement authorities can enter people's houses without notification and can secretly tape phone calls or establish cameras. Today, a person suspected of laundering is treated as a potential terrorist. This can mean a severe violation of people's privacy.

Lawyers in several countries object to their reporting duty. They claim that they are bound to professional privacy protection on behalf of their clients.

The anti-money-laundering policy will have to prove some success very soon; otherwise it will face serious problems of legitimacy. Police in the Netherlands claim that the money laundering law helps them to catch drug dealers, because, when suspected of money laundering, the criminal has to provide proof of the origin of his funds, while, when there is suspicion of drug dealing, the police must prove the crime, so there seem to be some benefits. But overall the policy has to be able to prevent additional laundering or to reduce existing amounts of laundering, or to prevent or reduce predicate crimes. These benefits of the policy will have to outweigh its costs and are yet to be shown.

## 45.5   CONCLUSIONS

With money laundering, the EU basically implements US policy rather than exports its own policy to other countries. However, the regulatory powers of the EU provide it with the means increasingly to shape international standards (Schimmelfenning forthcoming). While money laundering legislation is only and can only be soft law at the global regulatory level in the Financial Action Task Force, the EU can and does use hard law and imposes it through directives on its member states. This development of international soft law becoming hard law at lower levels of governance can also be found in other areas like environmental regulation (see Karlsson-Vinkuyzen 2011).

So far, money laundering, though a global problem, continues to be handled by cooperation between nation-states and by entities like the EU which are still public in character, unlike multi-level governance entities like the WTO (see Zürn forthcoming). The norms imposed on individual nation-states tend to be mostly subjects of discussion at international levels, like that of EU working groups and G-20 meetings, where a broad democratic discourse is missing. In money laundering policy, the FATF becomes increasingly important through its evaluation system. Though nation-states influence, through their national legal institutions, implementation and enforcement, international organizations exert a dominant influence on standard setting as well as on monitoring and evaluation. The instruments used so far by the FATF, like blacklisting, have because of their lack of transparency and of fair treatment of all member states lacked legitimacy. Since monitoring and verification of international rules are increasingly carried out by actors that are not directly under the control of nation-states (Zürn forthcoming), money laundering issues face more and more problems typical of global regimes. As Coleman (forthcoming) stresses, in a global policy-making context, the term public "policy does" not refer to state actors anymore. The distinction between private and public organizations also becomes blurred (Scott 2011).Typical examples of this development are private organizations like Transparency International, which rates predicate crimes such as corruption, or private firms that establish risk-based reporting mechanisms for banks. What Marx (2011) finds for business regulation might also eventually hold for money laundering regulation through an increase in private standards. With the switch from rule-based to risk-based money laundering standards, more room is left for private organizations to define these standards and implement them, for example bank warning systems. However, the standards which form the bases for their evaluation are set by the FATF and display a strong touch of Americanism and lack of knowledge of European legal traditions and institutions.

Thus money laundering regulation displays features as well as deficiencies of global regulation. Scott (2011) argues that the enforcement of global regulations can imply that actors do not feel bound by these norms and can create problems of compliance and fragmentation. First impressions of the effectiveness of anti-money-laundering policy support this view: "crying wolf" by over-reporting and copying and pasting of FATF regulations by new member states, in the hope that nobody will monitor the execution of the policy, are examples of this. The FATF seems to define itself as the central coordinator by giving other international institutions some directions, and the EU seems to accept these directions willingly. However, it might face problems of legitimacy and lack of compliance with a policy that seems to attract neither business nor citizens but is only a public interest perceived by international organizations and governments.

# BIBLIOGRAPHY

Algemene Rekenkamer (2008), 'Bestrÿden witwassen en terrorismefinanciering', report of the Dutch Court of Audit (Algemene Rekenkamer), 3 June, available at: www.rekenkamer.nl.
Ayres, I. and J. Braithwaite (1992), *Responsive Regulation: Transcending the Deregulation Debate*, New York: Oxford University Press.
Bardach, E. and R.A. Kagan (1982), *Going by the Book: The Problem of Regulatory Unreasonableness*, Philadelphia, PA: Temple University Press.

Barnett, M. and M. Finnemore (2004), *Rules for the World: International Organizations in Global Politics*, Ithaca, NY: Cornell University Press.

Becker, Gary (1968), 'Crime and punishment: an economic approach', *Journal of Political Economy*, **76**, 169–217.

Bernstein, M. (1955), *Regulating Business by Independent Commission*, Princeton, NJ: Princeton University Press.

Braithwaite, J. (1989), *Crime, Shame and Reintegration*, New York: Cambridge University Press.

Busuioc, E.M. (2007), 'Defining money laundering', in B. Unger, *The Scale and Impacts of Money Laundering*, Cheltenham, UK and Northampton, MA, USA: Edward Elgar Publishing.

Coleman, William D. (forthcoming), 'Governance and global public policy', in David Levi-Faur (ed.), *Oxford Handbook of Governance*, Oxford: Oxford University Press.

Dalla Pellegrina, L. and D. Masciandaro (2009), 'The risk based approach in the new European anti money laundering legislation: a law and economics view', *Review of Law and Economics,* December.

Drezner, D.W. (2007), *All Politics Is Global: Explaining International Regulatory Regimes*, Princeton, NJ: Princeton University Press.

FATF (Financial Action Task Force against Money Laundering) (2000), 'Report on non-cooperative countries and territories', available at: http://www.fatf-gafi.org/dataoecd/57/22/33921735.pdf.

FATF (Financial Action Task Force against Money Laundering) (2006), *Annual Report 2005–2006*, 23 June, Paris: FATF.

Graz, J.C. and A. Noelke (eds) (2008), *Transnational Private Governance and Its Limits*, ECPR Studies in European Political Science, London and New York: Routledge.

Huelsse, Rainer (2009), 'Even clubs can't do without legitimacy: why the anti-money laundering blacklist was suspended', *Regulation & Governance*, **2** (4), 459–79.

Huntington, S. (1952), 'The marasmus of the ICC: the Commission, the railroads, and the public interest', *Yale Law Journal*, **614**, 467–509.

Hutter, Bridget M. (2005), 'Afterword', in J. Castillo et al. (eds), *Governance and NGOs of the Future*, London: European Policy Forum, pp. 73–5.

Hutter, Bridget M. (2006), 'The role of non-state actors in regulation', in G.F. Schuppert (ed.), *Global Governance and the Role of Non-State Actors*, Berlin: Nomos, pp. 63–79.

Karlsson-Vinkhuyzen, Sylvia I. (2011), 'Bridging governance and law: global regulation through a diversity of norms', in David Levi-Faur (ed.), *Handbook of the Politics of Regulation*, Cheltenham: Edward Elgar.

Laffont, J.J. and J. Tirole (1991), 'The politics of government decision making: a theory of regulatory capture', *Quarterly Journal of Economics*, **106** (4), 1089–1127.

Levi, M. and P. Reuter (2006), 'Money laundering: a review of current controls and their consequences', in M. Tonry (ed.), *Crime and Justice: An Annual Review of Research*, vol. 34, Chicago: Chicago University Press.

Levine, M.E. and J.L. Forrence (1990), 'Regulatory capture, public interest, and the public agenda: toward a synthesis', *Journal of Law, Economics, and Organization*, **6**, 167–98.

Marx, Axel (2011), 'Global governance and private regulation of supply chains. types, trends and challenges', in David Levi-Faur (ed.), *Handbook on the Politics of Regulation*, Cheltenham: Edward Elgar.

Masciandaro, D. (1999), 'Money laundering: the economics of regulation', *European Journal of Law and Economics*, **7**, 225–40.

Masciandaro, D. (2007), 'Microeconomics of money laundering', in D. Masciandaro, E. Takats and B. Unger (eds), *Black Finance: The Economics of Money Laundering*, Cheltenham, UK and Northampton, MA, USA: Edward Elgar Publishing.

Masciandaro, D., E. Takats and B. Unger (2007), *Black Finance: The Economics of Money Laundering*, Cheltenham, UK and Northampton, MA, USA: Edward Elgar Publishing.

Mill, J.S. (1999 [1869]), *On Liberty*, Bartleby.com.

Moe, Terry (2006), 'Political control and the power of the agent', *Journal of Law, Economics, and Organization*, **22** (1), Spring, 1–29.

Naylor, R.T. (2002), *Wages of Crime: Black Markets, Illegal Finance, and the Underworld Economy*, Ithaca, NY: Cornell University Press.

Polinsky, A. Mitchell (1980), 'Private versus public enforcement of fines', *Journal of Legal Studies*, **IX** (1), 105–27.

Polinsky, A. Mitchell and Steven Shavell (1997), 'On the disutility and discounting of imprisonment and the theory of deterrence', NBER Working Papers 6259, National Bureau of Economic Research.

Rawlings, G. (2007), 'Taxes and transnational treaties: responsive regulation and the reassertion of offshore sovereignty', *Law and Policy*, **29** (1), 51–66.

Rees, R. (1985a), 'The theory of principal and agent – part I', *Bulletin of Economic Research*, **37** (1), 3–26.

Rees, R. (1985b), 'The theory of principal and agent – part II', *Bulletin of Economic Research*, **37** (2), 75–97.

Reuter, P. and V. Greenfield (2001), 'Measuring global drug markets: how good are the numbers and why should we care about them?', *World Economics*, **2** (4), October–December.

Reuter, P. and E.M. Truman (2004), *Chasing Dirty Money: Progress on Anti-Money Laundering*, Washington, DC: Institute for International Economics.

Rosen, S. (1986), 'Prizes and incentives in elimination tournaments', *American Economic Review*, **76** (4), 701–15.

Sappington, David E.M. (1991), 'Incentives in principal–agent relationships', *Journal of Economic Perspectives*, **5** (2), Spring, 45–66.

Schimmelfenning, Frank (forthcoming), 'EU external governance and Europeanization beyond the EU', in David Levi-Faur (ed.), *Oxford Handbook of Governance*, Oxford: Oxford University Press.

Schneider, Friedrich (2004), 'Macroeconomics: the financial flows of Islamic terrorism', in Donato Masciandaro (ed.), *Global Financial Crime: Terrorism, Money Laundering and Offshore Centres*, Farnham: Ashgate.

Schur, E.M. (1965), *Crimes without Victims: Deviant Behavior and Public Policy: Abortion, Homosexuality, Drug Addiction*, Englewood Cliffs, NJ: Prentice Hall.

Scott, Colin (2011), 'Regulating in global regimes', in David Levi-Faur (ed.), *Handbook on the Politics of Regulation*, Cheltenham: Edward Elgar.

Sharman, J.C. (2008), 'Power and discourse in policy diffusion: anti-money laundering in developing states', *International Studies Quarterly*, **52**, 635–56.

Sharman, J. and G. Rawlings (2006), 'National tax blacklists: a comparative analysis', *Journal of International Taxation*, **17** (9), 38–47, 64.

Siegel, Larry J. (2006), *Criminology: Theories, Patterns, and Typologies*, 9th edn, Belmont, CA: Wadsworth Publishing.

Siegel, L.J. and J.J. Senna (2008), *Introduction to Criminal Justice*, Belmont, CA: Thomson Wadsworth.

Simmons, B.A. (2000), 'International efforts against money laundering', in D. Shelton (ed.), *Commitment and Compliance: The Role of Non-Binding Norms in the International Legal System*, Oxford: Oxford University Press, pp. 244–63.

Simmons, B.A. (2001), 'The international politics of harmonization: the case of capital market regulation', *International Organization*, **55**, 589–620.

Stigler, G. (1971), 'The theory of economic regulation', *Bell Journal of Economics*, **2**, 3–21.

Stiglitz, Joseph E. (1987), 'Principal and agent', J. Eatwell, M. Milgate and P. Newman (eds), *The New Palgrave: A Dictionary of Economics*, vol. 3, Houndmills: Palgrave Macmillan, pp. 966–71.

Takats, Elod (2007), 'A theory of "crying wolf": the economics of money laundering enforcement', IMF Working Paper No. 07/81, April, available at: http://ssrn.com/abstract=979035.

TNI (Transnational Institute) (2003), 'Crime and Globalisation: The Economic Impact of the Illicit Drug Industry', seminar, The Netherlands, December, available at: http://www.tni.org/crime-docs/impact.pdf.

Tranøy, B.S. (2002), *Offshore Finance and Money Laundering: The Politics of Combating Parasitic State Strategies*, Oslo: Norwegian Ministry of Foreign Affairs.

Unger, B. (2007), *The Scale and Impacts of Money Laundering*, Cheltenham, UK and Northampton, MA, USA: Edward Elgar Publishing.

Unger, B. (2008), *Illicit Financial Flows in the Context of Afghanistan's Opium Economy*, study prepared for the Paris Pact Expert Round Table on the financial flows to and from Afghanistan linked to the illicit production of and trafficking in opiates, October/November, Vienna: UNODC.

Unger, B. and J. Ferwerda (2008), 'Regulating money laundering and tax havens: the role of blacklisting', paper prepared for the ECPR conference, June, also published as a Tjallings Koopmans Institute working paper at Utrecht University, 2008.

Unger, B. and G. Rawlings (2008), 'Competing for criminal money', *Global Business and Economics Review*, **10** (3), 331–52.

Unger, B. and F. van Waarden (2009), 'Attempts to dodge drowning in data: rule- and risk-based anti money laundering policies compared', *Review of Law and Economics*, December.

United Nations (UN) (1988), *UN Convention against the Illicit Traffic in Narcotic Drugs and Psychotropic Substances*, Vienna: UN.

United Nations (1998), 'Social and economic costs of illicit drugs', *United Nations Chronicle*, online edn, **35** (2).

United Nations (1998), 'Report on financial havens, banking secrecy and money laundering', available at: http://www.imolin.org/imolin/finhaeng.html.

United Nations Development Programme (1996), *Human Development Report 1996*, New York and Oxford: Oxford University Press.

United Nations Office on Drugs and Crime (UNODC) (2006), World Drug Report 2006, 2 vols, available at: http://www.unodc.org/pdf/WDR_2006/wdr2006_volume1.pdf.

van Erp, J.G. (2007), *Informatie en communicatie in het handhavingsbeleid, inzichten uit wetenschappelijk onderzoek*, The Hague: Boom Juridische Uitgevers.

van Waarden, Frans (2008), 'Where to find a "demos" for controlling global risk regulators? From private to public regulations and back', in J.C. Graz and A. Noelke (eds), *Transnational Private Governance and Its Limits*, London and New York: Routledge, pp. 84–97.

van Waarden, Frans (2011), 'Varieties of private market regulation: problems and prospects', in David Levi-Faur (ed.), *Handbook on the Politics of Regulation*, Cheltenham: Eward Elgar.

Vervaele, J.A.E. (2005), 'The anti-terrorist legislation in the US: inter arma silent leges?', *European Journal of Crime, Criminal Law and Criminal Justice*, **13** (2), 201–54.

Walker, J. (1995), 'Estimates of the extent of money laundering in and through Australia', paper prepared for the Australian Transaction Reports and Analysis Centre by John Walker Consulting Services, Queanbeyan, NSW, September.

Walker, J. (1999), 'How big is global money laundering?', *Journal of Money Laundering Control*, **3** (1).

Walker, J. (2002), *Just How Big Is Global Money Laundering?*, Sydney: Australian Institute of Criminology Seminar.

Walker, J. and B. Unger (2009), 'Estimating money laundering: the Walker gravity model', *Review of Law and Economics*, December.

Williams, P. (2001), 'Crime, illicit markets, and money laundering', in P.J. Simmons and C. de Jonge Oudrat (eds), *Managing Global Issues: Lessons Learned*, Washington, DC: Brookings Institution Press, pp. 106–50.

Winer, J.M. and T.J. Roule (2002), 'Fighting terrorist finance', *Survival*, **44**, 87–104.

Yandle, Bruce (2011), 'Bootleggers and Baptists in the theory of regulation', in David Levi-Faur (ed.), *Handbook on the Politics of Regulation*, Cheltenham: Edward Elgar.

Zdanowicz, John (2009), 'Trade-based money laundering and terrorist financing', *Review of Law and Economics*, December.

Zürn, Michael (forthcoming), 'Global multi level governance', in David Levi-Faur (ed.), *Oxford Handbook of Governance*, Oxford: Oxford University Press.

# 46 Regulatory approaches to climate change mitigation
## *Ian Bartle*

The challenge posed by climate change encapsulates a number of the key themes in modern regulatory governance. One important theme is how to interpret climate science and respond to risk and uncertainty. Despite the consensus among climate scientists about global warming, a difficult policy issue is the balance between a strategy of mitigation (limiting the greenhouse effect by reducing emissions) and a strategy of adaptation (reducing the negative effects of climate change). Modern 'risk-based' regulation, which involves attempts to inject objectivity into regulation with a more measured and calculative approach to risk (Hutter 2005), might suggest one approach. Precise assessments of climate change risk could inform decisions about how to respond; in particular, cost–benefit analysis could be undertaken on how to apportion money between mitigation and adaptation (Tol 2005). However, uncertainty pervades scientific knowledge of climate change, including the timing of temperature rises, what is 'dangerous' climate change, and whether and when a 'tipping point' will be reached after which catastrophic effects will ensue (Pachauri 2006; Schneider and Lane 2006: 7–23). Uncertainty suggests that a calculation to determine the balance between mitigation and adaptation cannot be undertaken in any meaningful way and points towards the importance of a strategy of mitigation.

This leads to a second and central theme in regulatory governance: the regulatory approach to be adopted to reduce carbon emissions in order to mitigate climate change. As in the wider debates on regulatory governance, there is no consensus on the best approach to reduce emissions. Reflecting this, a wide range of regulatory instruments have been proposed and deployed, and four broad types can be distinguished. First is a 'command and control' or interventionist approach in which the state is the leading actor in setting and enforcing regulations. Second is a market-based approach focusing on economic incentives and a carbon price. The carbon price is set in the market, which itself is shaped by a carbon cap or tax set by the government. Third is a voluntary approach, including self-regulatory agreements and the encouragement of voluntary behavioural and attitudinal change by information and education. A fourth and more variegated hybrid approach can also be distinguished which combines elements of the other three.

A third theme in regulatory governance is the state institutions set up to govern regulation. Independent state regulatory agencies which set and enforce regulation are a distinct feature of modern regulatory governance and might have a role to play in climate change. For many years the management of policies and regulations to reduce greenhouse gases has been undertaken by a range of environment and energy ministries and regulatory agencies. However, with the increasing concerns about climate change and its higher political profile, greater policy focus could be provided with specialist institutions. An idea from regulatory governance is that independent agencies detached from the vagaries of politics are necessary to ensure commitment to policy objectives. In this vein it has been proposed to establish independent agencies to manage carbon reductions at national and possibly international levels.

The chapter firstly considers the interpretation of risk and uncertainty in climate change and the debate on the balance between strategies of mitigation and adaptation. This is followed by a discussion of the different regulatory approaches instruments deployed. After that the argument for independent regulatory agencies in climate change is considered.

## 46.1   RISK AND UNCERTAINTY IN CLIMATE CHANGE: MITIGATION OR ADAPTATION?

Conventional wisdom suggests that the two main policy responses to risk and uncertainty in climate change – mitigation and adaptation – are separate and cannot be traded off or substituted. The level of mitigation is determined by the predictions of climate science, the need to avoid dangerous climate change, and the quantity of greenhouse gas emissions to be avoided. Adaptation occurs separately in reaction to and anticipation of the damage caused by the temperature rises to which we are committed and is determined by the best way of minimising the effects in particular locations.

### 46.1.1   A Trade-Off between Mitigation and Adaptation?

Ideas connected to risk-based regulation however suggest that strategies of mitigation and adaptation should be more closely connected. A central aim of risk-based regulation is to increase objectivity and transparency in the regulatory process with a move from qualitative approaches to risk towards the use of more scientific, measured and calculative methods and a 'cost benefit analysis culture' (Hutter 2005: 3–4). In this vein a viewpoint put forward by some economists suggests that mitigation and adaptation should be more closely linked, the balance between them being determined primarily by cost–benefit analysis.[1] This view is well summarised by Richard Tol, a climate change economist and advocate of this position:

> Adaptation to climate change and mitigation of climate change are policy substitutes, as both reduce the impacts of climate change. Adaptation and mitigation should therefore be analysed together, as they indeed are, in a rudimentary way, in cost–benefit analyses of emission abatement. (Tol 2005: 572)

Cost–benefit tests could determine the best combination of mitigation and adaptation to pursue.

Proponents of this approach argue that conventional mitigation strategies rest on an overly rigid interpretation of climate science, particularly the idea of dangerous climate change. It is argued that the science does not point unequivocally to a single temperature rise such as 2 °C (the EU's target) above which catastrophe will occur (Tol 2007). Connecting emissions reductions targets to such a temperature rise implies that the target must be met irrespective of costs and benefits when adaptation and mitigation are compared (Tol 2007: 430). The 2 °C target is not justified on the basis of credible science, and tying policy to such a target 'should therefore be replaced by focused efforts to calibrate the costs and benefits of climate policy' (Tol and Yohe 2006: 296).

If decisions on the balance of mitigation and adaptation are not based on credible cost–benefit analysis, the argument runs, not only will some economic welfare be sacrificed, but also the impact of climate change could increase. This is particularly the case for some developing countries in which there is a 'potential for overly ambitious mitigation to increase vulnerability to climate change by slowing economic growth' and thus reducing their capacity to effectively adapt to climate change (Tol and Yohe 2006: 297). However, they note that 'policy makers have decided to ignore' the literature on the cost–benefit analysis on greenhouse gas abatement (Tol 2007: 430).

### 46.1.2 Uncertainty and the Problems of a Mitigation–Adaptation Trade-Off

There are however some significant drawbacks of this argument, particularly in relation to uncertainty. There is a contradiction on the one hand between drawing on the uncertainty of the science on dangerous climate change while on the other hand having confidence in the certainty of quantitative models used to assess the effects of mitigation and adaptation and to undertake the cost–benefit analyses. While advocates of cost–benefit analysis accept some uncertainty in their analyses, they often assume that the uncertainties can be overcome by the use of techniques such as quantified error bands (Tol 2005: 152–66; Tol and Yohe 2006: 296). However, it has been argued that there are more fundamental problems with cost–benefit analysis, in particular the considerable uncertainties in the cause–effect assumptions made in econometric models (van den Bergh 2004). In addition, there are significant variations in the certainty of the effects of mitigation or adaptation strategies. While many 'projected effects, on both global and regional scales . . . carry high confidence estimates', many other impacts have only 'low confidence ratings and others that have not yet been postulated – ie, "surprises" and irreversible impacts' (Schneider and Lane 2006: 14).

Drawing on this critique, a view stresses the catastrophic potential and the need to take a precautionary approach. In this view the principal uncertainty is the degree of climate change and the timing of its impacts. While it is undoubtedly difficult to ascribe a precise temperature threshold to dangerous climate change, there is a broad consensus among scientists that there will be increasingly severe impacts between 1 °C and 3 °C above pre-industrial levels, and non-linear biological and geophysical transitions with possible irreversibilities will become increasingly likely (Schneider and Lane 2006; IPCC 2007). Although the need for some adaptation is recognised, this view stresses that irrespective of the amount of adaptation a specific and significant level of mitigation is required to avoid catastrophe (Drake 2000: 210; Stehr and von Storch 2005: 537–40).

The policy implication of this is that, irrespective of whatever adaptation can be undertaken, significant mitigation is necessary. This also reflects the approach of governments in Europe; for example, in the British government's climate change programme mitigation predominates and is driven by the broadly accepted figure of a 2 °C limit to temperature rise (Defra 2006). Adaptation is recognised to be necessary but primarily to adapt to climate change that is unavoidable.

This position can be justified by the 'precautionary principle' which is often deployed to translate scientific uncertainty into policy and regulatory certainty. It is a key EU principle of sustainable development, but it is controversial – many see it constraining scientific and technological development – and practice falls short of the principle. The principle 'states that if an action or policy might cause severe or irreversible harm to the public, in the absence of a scientific consensus that harm would not ensue, the burden of proof falls on those who would advocate taking the action'.[2] The principle is particularly pertinent in complex systems such as the environment, climate system and human health where the consequences of actions are often unpredictable. In the case of climate change the principle implies that the burden of proof falls on those advocating the continuing high emissions of greenhouse gases and large increases of $CO_2$ in the atmosphere. Yet on the basis of the scientific consensus proof seems to point to the opposite – that severe and irreversible harm will ensue if the action continues.

In practice the policy approach by many governments reflects this position. Irrespective of whether it might be better use of money to adapt to significant temperature increases, politicians and policy makers, notably in the EU, have set a maximum temperature rise target, and targets have been set within international agreements for specific reductions of greenhouse gas emissions, though the failure of the international negotiations in 2009 in Copenhagen and the poor record of many countries indicate the difficulty of realising this. There is therefore a need to focus on regulatory approaches to mitigation.

## 46.2   REGULATORY APPROACHES TO CLIMATE CHANGE MITIGATION

The many regulatory instruments deployed in climate change mitigation can be categorised into three classical approaches: (i) command and control, (ii) market methods and (iii) civil and voluntary. A fourth 'hybrid' approach can also be identified which involves combinations of elements of all three approaches. The different approaches can be distinguished in many ways. Four important elements considered here are: (i) the role of law, in particular 'hard' and 'soft' law; (ii) the main actors – state, market and civil society; (iii) efficiency and effectiveness; and (iv) how legitimacy is established. Table 46.1 provides a summary of the three main approaches.

### 46.2.1   Command and Control

Command and control policies and regulations are set by government and have the backing of 'hard law'. Regulations are legally binding and can be expected to be enforced by agents with state authority. The classic command and control instrument is the statutory regulation, whose objective is to prohibit or control certain activities or actions. Government initiatives which depend on policies other than statutory regulations, such as financial support provided for infrastructure or technological development, can also be considered as a form of command and control. The principal actors are the state as regulator (central or local government department or regulatory agency) and the regulated body. Other parties, such as those in civil society, may have an involvement such as in monitoring and ensuring compliance. The chief advantage of the command and

*Table 46.1   Summary of main regulatory approaches to climate change mitigation*

|  | Command and control | Market | Civil/voluntary |
|---|---|---|---|
| Law | 'Hard' law. | 'Hard' law (specifying tax or cap). | 'Soft' law. |
| Actors | Primary: state, regulated parties.<br>Secondary: consumers, civil society actors. | Primary: market actors (producers and consumers), state.<br>Secondary: civil society actors. | Primary: regulated parties, civil society actors.<br>Secondary: state. |
| Efficiency and effectiveness | Effectiveness in meeting objectives with the backing of hard law. | Efficiency derived from market mechanisms. | Efficiency from responsiveness to changing circumstances, and space for innovation. |
| Legitimacy | Formal democratic and administrative processes. | Choices made voluntarily within market. | Attuned with social and economic norms. |
| Instruments | Statutory regulations to prohibit or constrain carbon emissions.<br>Infrastructure/technology policies. | Carbon tax.<br>Cap and trade schemes. | Self-regulatory agreements.<br>Information and education to encourage low-carbon behaviour. |

control approach is that clarity and legally backed processes of enforcement can ensure the effectiveness in meeting regulatory objectives. A high degree of legitimacy can be expected with the formal democratic and administrative processes involved in the formation of regulations.

In climate change, command and control instruments operate by imposing or mandating behavioural change to achieve carbon reductions. Important statutory regulations include product standards such as in the manufacture of consumer goods (e.g. car emissions standards) or the construction of buildings (e.g. the requirement for energy-efficient buildings). Regulations also include those which prohibit the sale and use of certain goods (e.g., inefficient incandescent light bulbs) or those which prohibit or control the emission of certain greenhouse gases (e.g., CFCs and methane).

Government-backed science, technology and innovation policies can make low-carbon technology available at lower costs. These can involve direct support, for example in the form of subsidies or favourable tax policies for research and development in public organisations and the encouragement of research and development in private companies. Government-led infrastructure policies can impact on the level of greenhouse gas emissions from transport and energy networks and the built environment. The availability of networks which facilitate lower carbon emissions, for example railway lines for freight to be transported by rail rather than road, can reduce emissions. Governments have a crucial role, which can vary from financing and building infrastructure to planning rules and granting permission for private proposals.

### 46.2.2 The Market-Based Approach

The control mechanism of the market-based approach is price. In climate change the price of carbon-emitting products is modified by a tax on carbon emissions or a permit-based system with a carbon cap in order to reduce consumption of high-carbon products. Hard law plays an important role. The level of the carbon tax or cap is set by law, and some elements of trading schemes might also be prescribed by hard law. Two parties are predominantly involved: the government in setting taxes or caps, and the market actors, producers and consumers, who are subject to the price changes. Other actors, such as industry and consumer organisations, are also involved in assisting and advising market actors. Price-based mechanisms have been widely stressed as the best way to achieve emissions reductions; for example, in his Nobel prize acceptance speech in 2007 Al Gore noted: 'and most important of all, we need to put a price on carbon' (Gore 2007). They are seen as more efficient and effective, as actors make decisions within a market and react to specific circumstances rather than in the prescriptive way of command and control. Consumers will be faced with higher prices for carbon-intensive goods and services and thus incentivised to shift to low-carbon products. Producers similarly are induced to produce goods and services with lower-carbon contents and to develop technological innovations. Legitimacy is achieved by effectiveness and efficiency and leaving producers to make their own choices within the carbon constraint.

The principal market-based instruments in climate change are carbon tax, and cap and trade systems. In taxation systems a tax is charged on each carbon unit of carbon emitted, normally from the burning of fossil fuels. An economic incentive to reduce carbon emissions is thus created. In cap and trade systems an aggregate cap on carbon emissions is set up within a system of tradable permits. The carbon price is set in the market for the permits and is connected to the cap and the costs of reducing carbon emissions. A significant example of a carbon tax is the tax applied to the fuel for road transport, which has been applied in Europe for many years. Examples of cap and trade include a renewables obligation (a system of tradable permits in the electricity sector) and the EU emissions trading scheme, which encompasses several industrial sectors and about 50 per cent of emissions.

### 46.2.3 The Voluntary/Civil Approach

In the voluntary approach behavioural change is sought without compulsion, often by increasing awareness, encouraging reorientation in thinking and changing attitudes. The voluntary approach includes traditional industry self-regulation in which rules are set and enforced by industry. There are no legally binding rules or 'hard law', but 'soft law' prevails, which includes the voluntarily agreed rules of self-regulation and the social norms, principles and codes of conduct which govern actors' behaviour. The state's role varies from background observation to encouraging and cajoling industry to agree regulations which meet governmental objectives. In traditional self-regulatory schemes, the principal actors are the regulated parties, with state actors taking a secondary role. Voluntary regulatory schemes often have the involvement of civil society actors, including in 'soft' forms of compliance such as assessing, monitoring, publicising and certification. They may also be involved in assisting processes of increasing awareness and encouraging reorientation of thinking and changing behaviour.

Voluntary regulatory schemes can be more efficient than command and control by enabling regulations to be responsive to changing circumstances, allowing the regulated parties to innovate while complying with regulations. There are numerous problems with command and control which voluntary schemes might overcome. Command and control regulations can become inappropriate and burdensome, governments can be slow to respond to changing circumstances, the good will of regulated parties may be lost, the scope for discretion is reduced and enforcement processes may be adversarial. Information and education can increase awareness and bring about attitudinal and value change, creating a more deeply embedded means of effective behavioural change which is automatic and spontaneous, rather than being contingent on law or financial incentives as in the other two approaches. Legitimacy can be enhanced by a range of social norms, such as trust, which are not imposed by government diktat or rule of law, and nor do they result from financial incentives.

In climate change, governments have sought to facilitate voluntary self-regulatory agreements, particularly in major industries. For example, for many years European governments and the European Commission have sought to get car manufacturers to agree to introduce more stringent new car emission standards (Defra 2006: 65–6). Industries are often incentivised to adopt a self-regulatory approach to avoid more direct interventionist measures.

Other voluntary approaches in climate change are information and education campaigns by government aimed at informing consumers and industry on ways to lower their carbon emissions such as by introducing energy-efficiency measures. Information and education campaigns are normally led by central or local government but often have significant third-party civil society involvement. Environmental and charity groups often work closely with government and government-backed charities (such as the UK's Energy Saving Trust and the Carbon Trust) to better inform individuals, organisations and companies on how to reduce their carbon emissions.

### 46.2.4 The Hybrid Approach

The hybrid approach involves a variety of actors and institutions pursuing different strategies and interacting in complex ways. The identification of a hybrid approach is partly a recognition that in practice regulatory instruments involve a combination of different elements of the above approaches. For example, market-based approaches have a significant element of command and control in them: the tax level or the overall cap on carbon emissions is set by government or EU institutions. Also elements of different regulatory approaches can complement each other. For example, increased consumer knowledge of alternative lower-carbon options can reduce the demand for high-carbon goods and services, overcoming 'information asymmetry' in markets, enabling them to operate more effectively. There is also a significant element of civil regulation in market-based approaches. Civil society groups, notably the major environmental groups, have played a major role, for example in monitoring and assessing the development of the EU carbon trading scheme, and have lobbied strongly for changes.

The hybrid approach is also a recognition that many regulatory regimes have become more complex and are not adequately captured by one of the above categories. For example, many self-regulatory schemes have an evolved complexity such that it is not accurate to describe them as purely voluntary. In particular, the state has developed a significant role in many schemes to the extent that some can be described as 'mandated' forms of self-regulation (Bartle and Vass 2007). Even in non-mandated forms of self-regulation the state has a significant role in facilitating, tacitly supporting or constraining voluntary action, in particular with the threat of stronger statutory regulation. In climate change regulation, an important example is car emissions standards in the EU. For many years a non-mandated strategy was pursued with self-regulatory industry agreements. However, these were monitored closely by governments, the European Commission and environmental groups and were shown to be not fully successful. This eventually led to the introduction, in 2009, of a set of mandated standards at EU level.[3]

## 46.3    ASSESSING REGULATORY APPROACHES TO CLIMATE CHANGE MITIGATION

In any assessment of regulatory approaches in climate change the well-rehearsed debates between command and control and voluntary approaches and the parallel debates between hard and soft law are pertinent. Command and control instruments have the advantage of clarity and the legal backing of hard law. There is little uncertainty about regulatory objectives amongst the regulated entities and other interested parties. With legally backed processes of enforcement, compliance can be expected to be better than for voluntary schemes, and the formal and democratic processes involved in the formation of command and control regulations can lead to greater legitimacy. However, regulations can become inappropriate, burdensome and inefficient, and poor compliance may mean regulatory objectives are not achieved. The voluntary approach in contrast can be more in tune with social and economic norms and more responsive to changing circumstances, and can allow more space for the regulated to innovate while complying with self-regulatory rules. However, a crucial problem is that a high-consumption society is a deeply embedded social norm and is counter to many of the initiatives to reduce carbon emissions. Unfortunately, there is no easy resolution to this debate.

In many ways climate change regulation reflects this unresolved debate. On the one hand voluntary approaches have not been particularly successful, a notable example being the voluntary agreement on new car emissions standards. Emissions from road transport remain stubbornly high, and attempts by governments to persuade people to move towards lower-carbon forms of transport have met with limited success. There is also some evidence of a move towards more 'hierarchical' forms of regulation in climate change, for example car emissions standards and the mandatory cap element of trading schemes (Hey 2008). The high importance of combating climate change appears not only to demand strong regulation but also to require the more formal legitimising processes involved in making command and control regulations. On the other hand recent experience (notably the failure to reach a strong international agreement at Copenhagen in 2009 and Cancun in 2010) shows that governments are reluctant to introduce the strong regulations required to meet the emissions reductions demanded by many climate scientists because of the huge costs and changes required to society and industry. Legitimacy is needed not only from democratic administrative procedures but also from a broader change in social norms towards acceptance of the changes required, which seem easier with the use of voluntary approaches and soft law.

To what extent can a market-based approach overcome the tensions between command and control and the voluntary approach? Market-based approaches with their combination of certainty (government tax or cap) and flexibility (choices made within a market) have distinct appeal. However, there are drawbacks of market-based approaches. There are for example doubts about the fairness and legitimacy of emissions trading schemes (Baldwin 2008). In theory it is possible to embed fairness in trading schemes by democratically made decisions on the distribution of emissions allocations, while efficiency is achieved by the trading mechanism. However, in practice this separation is difficult to achieve, and the market mechanism often dominates and exaggerates inequalities by favouring the well informed and well resourced (Baldwin 2008: 203–04). This is particularly the case in the EU scheme, in which the emissions of large polluters are controlled. Allocations, which are a possible means of promoting equity, are made between large polluters, not between consumers or citizens.

More fundamentally the market approach defines people in terms of their economic interests. It is founded on a single form of human behaviour: the rational economic actor – 'homo economicus' – who responds only in a self-interested way to price signals.

There is a significant body of sociocultural research which suggests that the ways in which individuals and organisations think and act are more variable. It suggests four contrasting sociocultural frames which condition people's thoughts and actions: egalitarianism, hierarchy, individualism and fatalism (Thompson et al. 1990: 5–11), and these have a particular relevance to climate change (Verweij et al. 2006). In climate change, egalitarians emphasise the damage caused by the profligate patterns of production and consumption and note that more equitable relationships are required between humans and between humanity and nature. Egalitarians prefer a regulatory approach which fosters deep-rooted attitudinal change, which could include a combination of voluntary and command and control approaches. Hierarchicalists stress that better national and global governance and planning are required to ensure the natural world and its resources are better managed. The primary approach would be command and control. Individualists are sceptical about planned collective change and stress that human beings are resourceful and innovative and will respond with technical developments driven primarily by market forces. A market-based regulatory approach would be preferred. Finally, fatalists see no reason in nature and little possibility of effecting change.

This sociocultural variety reinforces the lack of resolution between the different regulatory approaches and that multiple or hybrid rather than single-policy and regulatory approaches should be adopted. In this vein Verweij et al. advocate 'clumsy' policies and institutions to ensure the effectiveness and legitimacy of attempts to tackle major problems (2006: 840).

> Clumsy solutions are creative, flexible mixes of four ways of organising, perceiving and justifying that satisfy the adherents to some ways of life more than other courses of actions, while leaving no actor worse off. As such, they alleviate social ills better than other courses of actions do.

They maintain that 'clumsy' solutions offer a happy medium between the 'monologue' process of 'single-metric rationality' and the other extreme of the 'incoherence of complete relativism'.

## 46.4    INDEPENDENT AGENCIES FOR CREDIBLE COMMITMENT?

Two regulatory approaches to climate change, command and control and the market approach, involve the state in a significant way, and this raises questions about state institutions. A key theme of modern regulatory governance is the establishment of independent and specialised state agencies for the setting and enforcement of regulation. At the global level there are UN institutions dedicated to climate change, but at national and EU levels there have been few dedicated institutions; the issues have normally been handled by environmental departments or directorates. Some nascent governing institutions have begun to appear; for example, in the UK the Office of Climate Change has been set up in the environment department, and an independent Committee on Climate Change has been established to advise on carbon reductions.

An argument has been put forward for the adoption of independent agencies (a 'carbon authority') for credible commitment to defined reductions of carbon emissions over decades. Credibility is a common problem, and the notion of 'credible commitment' is a key feature of regulatory governance and appears crucial for successful long-term carbon reduction (Helm et al. 2005). A central feature of this is functional specialisation by an independent regulatory authority – in utility regulation it has become entrenched in many countries (OECD 2002: 95). One of the key reasons for delegating powers is the commitment problem which occurs when there is a 'time inconsistency'. This is when 'a government's optimal long-run policy differs from its preferred short-run policy so that government in the short run has an incentive to renege on its long term commitment' (Majone 2001: 103–22). Delegating powers to an independent agent is a means of ensuring policy makers remain committed to their long-run policy preference (OECD 2002: 95).

Credibility and commitment achieved by an independent agency are important features of modern monetary policy and might provide lessons for climate change policy (Helm et al. 2005). Credibility is assured by independent central banks being delegated the task of controlling inflation with the instrument of interest rates. Current carbon policy in many countries lacks this kind of credibility. In Britain, for example, responsibility for carbon reduction is diffused across several government departments and agencies (Helm et al. 2005: 308). An independent carbon agency, analogous to an independent central bank, could be delegated the task of ensuring carbon reduction targets are met and empowered to operate the necessary policy levers, for example setting a carbon tax or an emissions cap in a trading system (Helm et al. 2005: 317).

Care, however, is required in directly reading across an institutional framework, notably an independent carbon authority, from monetary policy. Helm et al. (2005: 316) note some differences between monetary policy and carbon policy, particularly between the short and long term. In monetary policy the trade-offs between inflation and output/ employment generally occur in the short and medium term not the long term, while trade-offs between energy prices and emissions are often long-term. Also in monetary policy key expectations (in price and wage setting) have a period of about one to two years, while expectations in carbon policy can affect investments which last several decades.

Another important difference is that monetary policy in developed countries, particularly that conducted by independent central banks, has been built up over many decades. Over this time, within certain bounds and in generally favourable economic and political contexts, it has proved to be workable and legitimate (Berman and McNamara 1999; McNamara 2002). Legitimacy is important: key stakeholders accept and understand the monetary policy regime, in particular the costs imposed on individuals and the economy when interest rates are increased. Also, in many developing countries where political and economic contexts are less favourable and orthodox monetary regimes have less legitimacy, the introduction of independent central banks has proved less successful (Berman and McNamara 1999; McNamara 2002). In contrast to monetary policy, carbon reduction policy run by an independent agency remains untried. We do not know how workable it would be nor the costs it would impose on individuals and society and, crucially, the level of acceptance when those costs rise.

All of this suggests that establishing an independent institution, while arguably necessary for credibility, is not sufficient. A workable and legitimate whole policy regime is required which would include at least a set of complementary policies and regulations to ensure workability and a clear policy discourse and political communication to spread understanding and increase legitimacy.

## 46.5 CONCLUSION

Climate change regulation is suffused with many of the key themes and debates of modern regulatory governance. One key theme is the regulation of risk. Differing perspectives on risk and uncertainty are reflected in the balance to strike between mitigation and adaptation and the extent to which trade-offs are possible between the two. Modern risk-based regulation stresses the importance of formalised, quantitative approaches to risk and can reinforce an argument that the appropriate balance can be assessed using cost–benefit analysis. Critics of this emphasise, however, that much of the uncertainty in the science and the economics of climate change cannot be reduced to statistical probabilities. Qualitative judgements are required about the interpretation of the science, about the risks involved in disturbing complex systems and about pursuing a precautionary strategy. In this view, while cost–benefit analysis and risk-based techniques could contribute to deciding between specific regulations, a defined and significant level of mitigation should be pursued as determined by climate science and irrespective of any economics-based cost–benefit calculations. This reflects the position of many governments, particularly in Europe, which are striving towards significant carbon reductions.

A central theme of regulatory governance is the regulatory approaches to be deployed. Many different approaches and instruments have been deployed in climate change, which has been suggested to lead to policy confusion and complexity. Rather than a consistent and integrated set of policies focused on the main policy objective, policies appear to be proliferating in an apparently ad hoc fashion (Helm 2005: 27–9). A simpler policy approach based on fewer policy instruments has allure. One such approach could be a market-based approach such as cap and trade, which has become the central plank of climate policy in the EU. Simple and clear instruments, such as this, have the advantage of consistency across economy policies and of clearly connecting regulatory instruments to the overall policy objective.

There is a seductive allure of this approach, but it does not readily overcome some of the age-old debates between different regulatory approaches. In particular, climate change regulation is a good illustration of the lack of a clear resolution between command and control, voluntary approaches and the various gradations in between. Despite the advantages of clarity and simplicity of a cross-sectoral market-based approach, it rests on one particular form of human behaviour – that of the rational, self-interested economic man. Sociocultural plurality suggests that people respond in different ways to different policy approaches, and relying on one form of behaviour might not be socially viable or politically legitimate. In an area such as climate change, a more viable strategy might be one which draws on this plurality. This tends to suggest that a hybrid regulatory approach is more appropriate, drawing on multiple regulatory instruments.

A third key theme of regulatory governance is the adoption of independent agencies to offer focus, expertise and credible commitment to policy objectives. However, to be successful independent agencies tend to require a favourable context and an established and legitimate broader policy regime. In climate change this favourable context appears distant given the big changes needed to modern industrial society and the manifest difficulty of achieving an international agreement on emissions reductions. Independent agencies might have a partial contribution to make, but given the need to draw on a hybrid regulatory approach and multiple instruments they are unlikely to play a central role as in monetary policy.

## NOTES

1. An extensive debate on mitigation, adaptation and the economics of climate change took place in the journal *World Economics* in 2006–07 (see for example Byatt et al. 2006; Carter et al. 2006, 2007; Dietz et al. 2007; Simmonds and Steffen 2007).
2. http://en.wikipedia.org/wiki/Precautionary_principle.
3. http://ec.europa.eu/clima/policies/vehicules/cars_en.htm.

## REFERENCES

Baldwin, R. (2008), 'Regulation lite: the rise of emissions trading', *Regulation & Governance*, **2**, 193–215.
Bartle, I. and P. Vass (2007), 'Self-regulation within the regulatory state: towards a new regulatory paradigm?', *Public Administration*, **85** (4), 885–905.
Berman, S. and K.R. McNamara (1999), 'Bank on democracy: why central banks need public oversight', *Foreign Affairs*, **78** (2), 2–8.
Byatt, I., I. Castles, I.M. Goklany, D. Henderson, N. Lawson, R. McKitrick, J. Morris, A. Peacock, C. Robinson and R. Skidelsky (2006), 'Part II: economic aspects', *World Economics*, **7** (4), 199–230.
Carter, R.M., C.R. de Freitas, I.M. Goklany, D. Holland and R.S. Lindzen (2006), 'The Stern Review: a dual critique, part I: the science', *World Economics*, **7** (4), 165–98.
Carter, R.M., C.R. de Freitas, I.M. Goklany, D. Holland and R.S. Lindzen (2007), 'Climate science and the Stern Review', *World Economics*, **8** (2).

Defra (2006), *Climate Change: The UK Programme 2006*, Cm6764, March, London: Department for Environment, Food and Rural Affairs.
Dietz, S., D. Anderson, N. Stern, C. Taylor and D. Zenghelis (2007), 'Right for the right reasons: a final rejoinder on the Stern Review', *World Economics*, **8** (2), 229–58.
Drake, F. (2000), *Global Warming: The Science of Climate Change*, London: Arnold.
Gore, A. (2007), 'Nobel lecture, Oslo, Norway', available at: http://nobelprize.org/nobel_prizes/peace/laureates/2007/gore-lecture_en.html (accessed 8 April 2009).
Helm, D. (2005), 'Climate change policy: a survey', in D. Helm (ed.), *Climate Change Policy*, Oxford: Oxford University Press, pp. 11–29.
Helm, D., C. Hepburn and R. Mash (2005), 'Credible carbon policy', in D. Helm (ed.), *Climate Change Policy*, Oxford: Oxford University Press, pp. 305–21.
Hey, C. (2008), 'Rediscovery of hierarchy: the new EU climate policies', paper at Conference on EU Environmental Policy and Governance, European University Institute, Florence, 20–21 June.
Hutter, B.M. (2005), 'The attractions of risk-based regulation: accounting for the emergence of risk ideas in regulation', Discussion Paper 33, ESRC Centre for the Analysis of Risk and Regulation, LSE, London, March.
IPCC (2007), *Climate Change 2007: The Physical Science Basis. Summary for Policymakers*, Geneva: Intergovernmental Panel on Climate Change, Secretariat.
Majone, G. (2001), 'Two logics of delegation, agency and fiduciary relations in EU governance', *European Union Politics*, **2** (1), 103–22.
McNamara, K.R. (2002), 'Rational fictions: central bank independence and the social logic of delegation', *West European Politics*, **25** (1), 47–76.
OECD (2002), *Regulatory Policies in OECD Countries: From Interventionism to Regulatory Governance*, Paris: OECD.
Pachauri, R. (2006), 'Avoiding dangerous climate change', in H.J. Schellnhuber (ed.), *Avoiding Dangerous Climate Change*, Cambridge: Cambridge University Press, pp. 3–6.
Schneider, S.H. and J. Lane (2006), 'An overview of dangerous climate change', in H.J. Schellnhuber (ed.), *Avoiding Dangerous Climate Change*, Cambridge: Cambridge University Press, pp. 7–23.
Simmonds, I. and W. Steffen (2007), 'Response to "The Stern Review: a dual critique, part I: the science"', *World Economics*, **8** (2).
Stehr, N. and H. von Storch (2005), 'Introduction to papers on mitigation and adaptation strategies for climate change: protecting nature from society or protecting society from nature?', *Environmental Science and Policy*, **8**, 537–40.
Thompson, M., R. Ellis and A. Wildavsky (1990), *Cultural Theory*, Boulder, CO and Oxford: Westview Press.
Tol, R.S.J. (2005), 'Adaptation and mitigation: trade-offs in substance and methods', *Environmental Science and Policy*, **8**, 572–8.
Tol, R.S.J. (2007), 'Europe's long term climate target: a critical evaluation', *Energy Policy*, **35**, 424–32.
Tol, R.S.J. and G.W. Yohe (2006), 'Of dangerous climate change and dangerous emission reduction', in H.J. Schellnhuber (ed.), *Avoiding Dangerous Climate Change*, Cambridge: Cambridge University Press, pp. 291–8.
van den Bergh, J.C.J.M. (2004), 'Optimal climate policy is a utopia: from quantitative to qualitative cost–benefit analysis', *Ecological Economics*, **48**, 385–93.
Verweij, M., M. Douglas, R. Ellis, C. Engel, F. Hendricks, S. Lohmann, S. Ney, S. Rayner and M. Thompson (2006), 'Clumsy solutions for a complex world: the case of climate change', *Public Administration*, **84** (4), 817–43.

# 47 After the fall: regulatory lessons from the global financial crisis
*John W. Cioffi*

## 47.1 INTRODUCTION

The global financial crisis of 2007–09 was the most devastating economic collapse since the Great Depression. The bursting of the American real estate bubble and a rising tide of defaults on subprime mortgages underlying complex debt securities triggered the rapid collapse of major American banks, a global run on the shadow banking system, and international market crashes and banking crises. The contagion of financial panic spread from the American financial sector through the international financial system and into the "real" economy with breathtaking speed. Only unprecedented governmental and central bank interventions around the world bailed out major financial institutions and averted an imminent second Great Depression. But the crisis crippled the international financial system and left the global economy mired in the Great Recession.

Pervasive regulatory failures created the pre-conditions for the crisis and fueled its catastrophic depth and scope.[1] The abject and multi-faceted failure of the American regulatory state was a product of the neoliberal turn in American economic and regulatory policy embraced by both the Republican and Democratic parties. During the past 25 years, political and financial elites increasingly embraced theories of regulatory pathologies and idealized self-regulating markets that denigrated government and law and lauded the market and private sector. This ideational dimension of neoliberalism eventually led erstwhile regulators to favor the policy preferences of large, internationalized financial institutions in pursuing policies of deregulation and self-regulation.[2] The neoliberal policy trajectory frequently constrained, impaired, and eroded financial regulation, even as it privileged, enriched, and empowered the financial sector.

Theories of agency capture, bureaucratic inefficiency, and regulatory rent-seeking provided critical intellectual support for anti-regulation and pro-market policy agendas. Preoccupation with government failure, however, favored deregulation, "light-touch" regulation, and self-regulation that ultimately made state failure a self-fulfilling prophecy and serious market failures inevitable. Compounding this irony, the global financial crisis, made possible by political attacks and limits on financial regulation, supplied abundant evidence to support theories criticizing the regulatory state as ineffective, captured, or corrupt.

In short, the crisis was not a random, extreme "black swan" market event.[3] The structural causes of the crisis originated in policy decisions that reflected both the growing political influence of large financial institutions and a widespread faith in the self-regulating capacity of financial markets and the financial sector. This merger of power and faith produced a toxic combination of pro-financier politics, neoliberal ideology, weak regulation, unrestrained opportunism, and market failures that inexorably drove the financial system toward collapse.

Not only was the American financial system and neoliberal approach to financial regulation the proximate origin of the crisis, but it also influenced financial system and regulatory reforms in other countries, which facilitated global contagion. Neoliberal economic and policy ideas also influenced many Western European policy and regulatory reforms designed, in part, to promote a pan-European market-based financial system, but national regulatory capacity lagged the growth of financial markets and the development of new instruments. American and European regulators failed to recognize or respond to the growing risks created by the explosive growth of securitized debt and derivatives markets, and unbridled financial globalization that produced a largely unregulated and opaque global shadow banking system.[4] These risks multiplied amid institutionalized blindness and denial as a global debt bubble of historic proportions inflated and burst to unleash a cascade of collapsing financial markets and institutions.

## 47.2   THEORIES REGULATION AND REGULATORY FAILURE

Most prominent theories of regulation (and regulatory failure) recognize the import of principal–agent conflicts, collective action problems, market failures, and negative externalities drawn from economic theory.[5] "Public interest" and "private interest" theories, however, differ fundamentally in their accounts of the purposes and interests served by regulation, and therefore in their assessment of the regulatory state. Public interest theories argue that regulation plays a necessary and beneficial role in addressing problems of collective action, transaction costs, negative externalities, public goods, and other forms of market failure (Breyer 1982; Sunstein 1990, chap. 2). Such arguments proceed from the observation that the world bears little similarity to the one described by the austere but unrealistic assumptions and perfectly functioning markets of neoclassical economics. The abstract universe of neoclassical economic theory is defined and governed by clear preferences, complete information, perfectly rational calculation of utility and efficiency maximization, and zero transaction costs. In a world defined by these assumptions, regulation is unnecessary and optimal social and economic outcomes are achieved through private bargaining and market transactions (with a critical legal role reserved for property and contract rights).

The real world, however, is one of ambiguous and multivalent preferences, conflicts of interest, imperfect (or asymmetrical) information, cognitive limitations and biases, bounded rationality, and ubiquitous – and often steep – transaction costs. The inherent costs, limitations, and deficiencies of private bargaining help explain the consequent prevalence and destructive effects of market failures. These less than ideal conditions justify regulatory institutions and constraints on individual and collective behavior as the necessary and inevitable price of a modern market economy – necessary not only to curb inefficient and welfare destroying behavior, but also to enable and sustain productive economic activities and efficient markets. To achieve these ends, regulatory institutions also must have sufficient capacity, in terms of authority, expertise, structure, and autonomy, for effective rulemaking and enforcement, and to continually adapt and respond to evolving efforts to circumvent their strictures or compromise their functional integrity.

Since the 1970s, private interest theories critical of regulation and favoring private bargaining and market transactions largely unfettered by legal rules have been increasingly influential in policy debates, particularly with respect to financial regulation. Theoretical critiques of regulation contend that regulatory intervention generally detracts from the superior efficiency of private ordering through markets and contracting, and that regulatory capture by powerful interest groups poses greater threats to aggregate welfare than (and may cause) market failure. Theories of regulatory capture and government failure extend the logic of rent-seeking, conflicts of interest, and market failure to the state. Following Stigler's (1971) seminal work on the subject, the economic, or special interest, theory of regulation has focused on how wealthy, well-organized groups secure favorable laws and regulatory policies and rules – and frustrate democratic accountability, market competition, and public interest theories of regulation.[6] The self-interested behavior of elected politicians, state bureaucrats, and interest groups inevitably leads to the appropriation of state power by private interests to achieve their particularistic ends at public expense. Public power is subject to, and constituted by, the same failures and pathologies that pervade private transactions and markets. The difference is that regulatory capture poses far greater social costs and political dangers by simultaneously warping state power for predatory and extractive rent-seeking, rendering it less democratically accountable, and thereby entrenching the power and privileged status of private interests by insulating them from effective legal constraints and often from market competition. The centralization and expansion of governmental power embodied in the regulatory state intensifies these risks of rent-seeking by making influence over law and policy more valuable.

Both views capture critically important functions and effects of economic regulation, yet each poses inescapable dilemmas of policy and institutional design. Public interest theories are quite correct that the rise of the regulatory state reflects the requisite institutional and legal underpinnings of a developed market economy. But, by expanding the reach and power of the state, development of modern regulation magnifies the risks identified by private interest theories that it will fail to supply or actively erode the foundations of functional markets. If public interest theories may display excessive optimism about the performance of regulatory rules and institutions, private interest theories tend to unduly denigrate their necessity and have legitimated neoliberal political agendas of deregulation and regulatory erosion that furthered the capture and corruption they decry. The global financial crisis, and its origins in the United States in particular, provides stark evidence of these paradoxes.

## 47.3    FINANCIAL SYSTEM FRAGILITY AND REGULATORY RESPONSES

Financial systems can be as threatening as they are essential to the functioning of a modern market economy. The financial system performs the vital functions of aggregating savings, creating credit, and allocating investment capital on which the rest of the economy relies. Yet the structural characteristics of modern financial systems drive them to become dangerously unstable and destructively extractive. The mechanisms of private ordering – contract, market incentives, and informal norms – either generate or fail to ameliorate the principal–agent and collective action problems that riddle the financial system: conflicts of interest, asymmetric and incomplete information, cognitive limitations and biases of individuals, irrational herd behavior, and the potentially huge negative externalities of financial crises.

Conflicts of interest coupled with imperfect and asymmetric information plague modern finance. They reinforce and exacerbate each other to magnify the risks of governance and market failures in the financial sector. Conflicts of interest within financial institutions, markets, and transactions increase the risks of opportunistic rent-seeking and misappropriation by strategically located insiders.[7] Information asymmetries that flow from the complexity and frequent opacity of modern finance further increase agency and transaction costs, uncertainty, and risk at the transactional, corporate, and systemic levels.[8] Banking poses particularly acute risks of panics and contagion because of its defining characteristics of high leverage and the financing of long-term liabilities with short-term assets (i.e., large loan portfolios backed by a smaller base of demand deposits, leading to problems of time inconsistency). This capital structure magnified uncertainty over the solvency of banks and created perverse incentives among individual depositors that triggered the classic collective action problem of bank runs that turned fears of insolvency and the loss of savings into a self-fulfilling prophecy at the first hint of real or imagined financial trouble (Diamond and Dybvig 1983).

Securities markets, often viewed as alternatives to traditional bank lending, also display high levels of volatility and instability. Depending on their structure, asset composition, transparency, or liquidity, these markets can spread risk or amplify it. Leaving aside complications introduced by illiquid markets, computerized trading, and systematic manipulation of material information, these markets have been recurrently buffeted by unpredictable and unsustainable feedback loops of irrational exuberance and panic as the mass psychology of collective hubris, greed, and fear overtakes economic fundamentals as determinants of market prices. The interconnectedness of financial institutions and securities markets poses dangers of contagion that not only amplify firm-level risks of financial institution failures, but also transform them into categorically more serious systemic and macroeconomic risks.

Absent effective regulation and state guarantees, the ever-present risks of severe governance and market failures render financial systems highly susceptible to manipulation, rent-seeking, speculative booms and bubbles, panics and crashes, and bank runs (Diamond and Dybvig 1983; Reinhart and Rogoff 2009). Therefore state policies in support of financial system stability, including deposit insurance, guarantees of financial assets, and central bank lender of last resort facilities, have become nearly universal underpinnings for modern financial systems. Securities regulation, encompassing financial disclosure, accounting, and market transparency rules, has become increasingly important world-wide as a means of protecting investors and stabilizing securities markets by addressing informational market failures. Private ratings agencies like Moody's and Standard & Poor's came to play major (and deeply problematic) informational and gatekeeper roles, often mandated by law, particularly in debt markets.

Yet the unintended consequences of financial regulation pose additional serious policy dilemmas. No government can allow the domestic financial system to collapse and thus court broader economic devastation; yet state intervention to preserve systemic trust and stability creates problems of moral hazard that can exacerbate its self-destructive tendencies. Insuring deposits or other obligations of financial institutions via explicit or implicit public guarantees magnifies systemic risk incentivizing greater risk-taking among bankers and financiers. Similarly, securities regulation deliberately induces increased investor confidence and market development, but also may increase risk tolerance and speculation to dangerous levels. Accordingly, state intervention to enhance trust, confidence, and stability may beget further intervention through prudential regulation and oversight of financial institutions (e.g., bank capital, leverage ratios, risk management, and auditing rules/standards), along with more stringent, prescriptive, and expansive forms of securities, financial market, and corporate governance regulation to contain these firm-level and systemic moral hazards.

Post-New Deal financial regulation in the United States stabilized the financial system by containing the kind of systemic market and governance failures that precipitated financial collapse and produced the Great Depression. The creation of the Federal Deposit Insurance Corporation (FDIC) to insure bank deposits prevented bank runs, while prudential banking regulation reduced risks of bank failures. The Glass–Steagall Act's separation of depository banking from securities-related business lines insulated the traditional core of the financial system from speculative excesses, while limiting moral hazards and the residual risks borne by the public. Securities regulation and corporate governance law improved financial disclosure, market transparency, and investor protection. Most Western European countries during the post-war era eschewed both deposit insurance and financial market segmentation, and instead adopted a mix of prudential banking regulation, industrial policies and other forms of state control over finance, and weak securities market regulation. These divergent approaches produced different kinds of financial institutions and systems. The American regime fostered an increasingly innovative and dynamic market-driven financial system within the constraints of the regulatory state. Glass–Steagall's prohibition of universal banking promoted market-oriented functional specialization and innovations in services and products by financial institutions within market segments. In contrast, the general European approach to financial system regulation and economic governance tended to entrench bank-based financial systems and dampen the development of financial markets. It fostered universal banking across market segments and favored cautious relational lending practices over market-driven financial services and proprietary trading.

During the last quarter-century, dramatic changes in the American and European financial systems and regulatory regimes undermined their hard-won systemic stability and functionality. Since the 1980s, the prevailing dynamics of American interest group and partisan politics, informed by an ascendant neoliberal ideology, systematically weakened the post-New Deal regulatory regime and strengthened the political and economic position of the financial sector. During the same period, British regulatory and economic policies spurred financial sector development as London came to rival Wall Street as an international financial hub. During the 1990s and continuing into the mid-2000s, many Western European countries began to implement more market-friendly forms of financial regulation in pursuit of higher growth.[9] Facing intensifying demands from shareholders and competition from the American and British financial institutions, many large European banks adopted more market-oriented and international business models in search of higher returns. Notwithstanding cross-national variations in regulatory reforms, the diffusion of pro-finance and pro-market regulatory agendas during the

1990s valorized the financial sector and the development of securities markets as the key to economic dynamism and growth (see Tiberghien 2007; Cioffi 2010). However, these policy agendas also reflected skepticism towards regulation and an idealization of private ordering through contract and self-regulating markets that allowed the systemic risks inherent in banking and finance to proliferate and intensify.

## 47.4 THE AMERICAN BUBBLE MACHINE AND THE POLITICS OF REGULATORY FAILURE

### 47.4.1 The Debt Securitization Cycle and Regulatory Arbitrage

The global financial crisis revealed egregious failures of financial sector regulation in most industrialized countries, but those in the United States were by far the most important. Since the 1980s, deep and enduring dynamics of American political economic development fostered the financialization of the American economy and an increasing reliance on soaring levels of private debt to fuel consumption and investment growth (Cioffi 2010). This transformation of the American political economy and the global financial crisis it spawned were enabled by and inseparable from politically driven deregulation and corrosive regulatory dysfunction. The global financial crisis emanated from the unregulated and least regulated parts of the American financial system: sub-prime mortgage lending; credit rating agencies; leverage ratios and capital requirements; and the "shadow" banking system's investment banks, their off-balance sheet "special purpose vehicles" (SPVs), hedge funds, securitized debt instruments, and derivatives. At each point, regulation failed and private opportunism flourished.

Mortgage securitization required a constant circulation of capital through a cycle in which brokers made home loans and sold the mortgages to investment banks for repackaging into debt securities, and the banks marketed the securities to investors. The proceeds from this chain of transactions helped finance the next round of lending and securitization, while the profits attracted more capital and participants. By examining how each component of this cycle functioned as part of the whole, and then how the cycle was embedded in the wider web of financial relationships and markets, one can see more clearly how securitization mutated into a recursive process that massively inflated asset prices and amplified systemic risk. Viewing securitization as the product of multiple mutually dependent parts also reveals how comprehensively regulation failed. Effective regulation at any point in the securitization cycle could have prevented, or at least curtailed, its pathogenic development and the incalculable damage it wrought.

During the early 2000s, American financial institutions began a widespread adoption of an "originate and distribute" mortgage lending and securitization business model (see Fender and Mitchell 2009). The strategy exploited – and required – lax federal financial regulation and the Federal Reserve's prolonged low interest rate policies. In response to a series of foreign and domestic financial crises from 1994 through 2002, the Fed under Alan Greenspan repeatedly slashed interest rates to historically low levels to increase market liquidity and reinflate the economy. However, unlike a direct Keynesian stimulus of consumer demand or business investment, the strategy stimulated demand indirectly by increasing private debt and inflating asset bubbles. As private lending inflated the

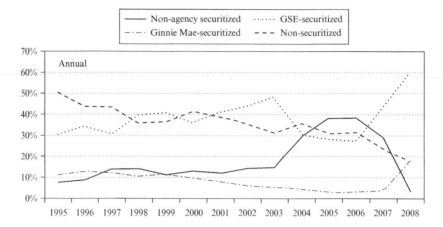

*Source:*   Financial Crisis Inquiry Commission (2010).

*Figure 47.1    Share of residential mortgage originations and securitization, 1995–2008*

subprime mortgage bubble after 2003 (see Figure 47.1), the Fed refused to use its regulatory powers to curb predatory or excessively risky mortgage lending or deploy prudential regulatory oversight to ensure adequate bank capital levels and contain systemic risk. It would not even acknowledge the *existence* of an asset bubble.

Beyond the Fed, the fragmentation of banking and financial market regulation left gaps in the law and allowed financial institutions to pursue "regulatory arbitrage" by strategically organizing their corporate structures and financial products to evade regulation or to choose the most lenient regulator possible.[10] For example, AIG and Countrywide maneuvered themselves into oversight by the notoriously lax Office of Thrift Supervision. Much of the shadow banking system and the complex securities it created arose from strategies to avoid regulation and oversight. The boom in derivatives in part reflected the fact that they were unregulated, despite being designed in many cases to mimic or replicate regulated securities or insurance policies. The rapidly growing and immensely lucrative hedge fund segment of the shadow banking system was left almost entirely unregulated – a status its principals and political allies fought fiercely to preserve (with the aid of court rulings by an increasingly conservative federal judiciary). This structure also incentivized a perverse "race to the bottom" by regulators eager to protect turf and, in the case of the Office of Thrift Supervision and Office of the Comptroller of the Currency, maximize fees paid by regulated entities. Interest group politics and the interests of congressional committees in retaining oversight jurisdiction (and thus campaign contributions) insulated these ineffective overseers from abolition or consolidation.

### 47.4.2    Shell Games: The Mechanics of Securitization, the Leverage, and the Failure of Disclosure

The Fed's rejection of regulation and continued low interest rates fostered mutually reinforcing real estate and securitization bubbles. Figures 47.2 and 47.3 sketch the basic steps

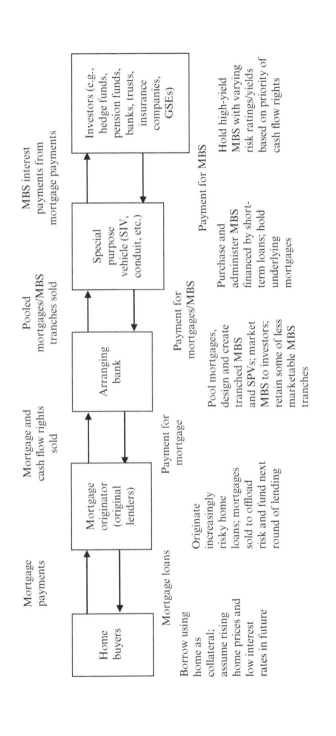

*Figure 47.2   Securitization and distribution of subprime mortgage-backed securities (MBS)*

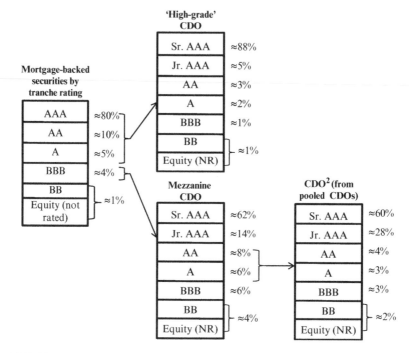

*Source:*   IMF (2008: 60).

*Figure 47.3    Stylized CDO formation and structure*

and relationships in mortgage securitizations. Mortgage lenders (originators) immediately sold the loans they issued to an investment bank (the arranger), which pooled and securitized them by slicing the cash flow rights into "tranches" of mortgage-backed securities (MBSs) (Figure 47.2). The priority of cash flow rights to the underlying mortgage payments defines these tranches, with the lower tranches posing higher risks of default rated lower and paying higher interest rates.[11] Lower tranche MBSs (e.g., rated less than AAA, and often at "junk" status – less than BBB– or Baa3) were then pooled and their cash flows sliced once again into tranches of collateralized debt obligations (CDOs) with senior tranches once again rated AAA.[12]

Arranging banks moved the MBSs and CDOs off their books by creating highly leveraged SPVs called "structured investment vehicles" (SIVs) and "conduits" (shell corporations or trusts ostensibly legally separate from the arranging bank) to purchase them and then sell the tranched securities to investors. They also engaged in second-order securitizations by bundling lower tranches of multiple CDOs into *another* SPV and marketed them as an even more complex, opaque, and highly leveraged "CDO squared."[13] In each stage of securitization, the "senior" tranche, often over 80 or even 90 percent of securities created, were rated AAA by the ratings agencies, suggesting that they were as safe as government bonds.

SIVs and conduits financed purchases of the arranging banks' long-term CDO assets by heavy short-term borrowing. By offsetting long-term assets (unsold or retained MBSs or CDOs) with short-term liabilities (typically commercial paper financing), these SPVs took on the crisis-prone characteristics of banks, but without the effective prudential regulation and deposit insurance that had prevented bank runs since the Great Depression. Yet SIVs and conduits often remained tethered to the banks that created them by guaranteed credit lines that, in a crisis, could push their huge debts back onto bank balance sheets with potentially devastating results.

The banks designed the structure of the securitization process and the new financial instruments to circumvent the disclosure regime imposed by securities law by exploiting loopholes in accounting rules and prudential banking regulation. They used SIVs and derivatives to scrub residual MBS and CDO risks from their balance sheets and game the calculation of risk-based capital requirements under the Basel Accords. Theoretically, provisions of the Sarbanes–Oxley Act of 2002 (SOx) and regulatory reforms adopted by the SEC and Public Company Accounting Oversight Board (PCAOB) prohibited the use of off-balance sheet vehicles to hide liabilities and financial risks after similar subterfuges played a role in Enron's notorious accounting frauds and bankruptcy. Critics had attacked SOx and the PCAOB relentlessly for burdening business, but the compliance costs of those reforms paled beside the price of their ineffectiveness in preventing a recurrence of accounting abuses.

The steady erosion and repeal of the Glass–Steagall Act's separation of commercial and investment banking worsened the increasing concentration of risk in the banking sector. Large numbers of Democrats also joined Republicans in accepting, and at times championing, the deregulation of banking and securities business. The Clinton administration and a large majority of Democrats in Congress supported the final repeal of Glass–Steagall by the Gramm–Leach–Bliley Act of 1999. However, the increase in systemic risks had been largely enabled prior to Glass–Steagall's formal repeal by its long and deliberate erosion spearheaded by the Federal Reserve, albeit with the support from the Treasury and other banking regulators under both Republican and Democratic administrations. The consequent emergence of an American variant of universal banking allowed traditional banks to become far more involved in the creation, marketing, and purchase of exotic debt securities than would have been permitted under the New Deal regulatory regime.

The prevalence of deregulation and "light touch" regulatory approaches also reflected a widely held belief in the self-regulating capacities of markets and firms that eroded disclosure and accounting standards over time. A critical and disastrous example of what economist Willem Buiter (2008) has called "cognitive capture" was policy decisions that allowed financial institutions to increase leverage, the amount of debt relative to equity, which magnifies returns per share but also magnifies losses and risk of default. The Federal Reserve had allowed banks to use derivatives hedging to reduce capital requirements since 1996, inviting "balance sheet arbitrage," and permitted them to use bubble-inflated mark-to-market values as well as valuation models that routinely overstated the value of illiquid debt securities (mark-to-make believe).[14]

In 2004, the SEC took the lead in relaxing leverage limitations on investment banks (Buiter 2008). Striking a political deal to avert stricter EU regulation of American investment banks, the banks agreed to voluntarily submit to limited SEC monitoring in exchange for the ability to use their own quantitative risk models to calculate capital requirements and thus increase leverage levels – a form of self-regulation without the check or balance of formal enforcement power (Labaton 2008). In an indication of how influential the neoliberal vision of markets and financial firms had become, the vote was unanimous and uncontroversial, garnering the support of commissioners known as zealous regulators (Labaton 2008). Afterward, average leverage ratios among major American investment banks and hedge funds nearly tripled from under 10:1 to approximately 27:1 at the height of the real estate and CDO bubble – meaning that a 4 percent decline in asset value would wipe out the equity, and the solvency, of the average institution (see Tett 2009: 134).

At the same time, traditional securities regulation by the SEC, once a jewel of the post-New Deal regulatory state, eroded by neglect and design. Under chairman Christopher Cox, SEC enforcement actions declined at an accelerating rate from 2005 to 2008 as lengthy, burdensome, and contentious authorization and review processes discouraged investigations of large financial institutions (Scannell and Craig 2008; Adler 2009; see generally GAO 2009). The dollar value of SEC penalties fell 39 percent in 2006, 48 percent in 2007, and 49 percent in 2008 (Farrell 2009). The number of enforcement attorneys declined over 11 percent during this period (Farrell 2009; GAO 2009). The agency's monitoring of investment banks was hopelessly understaffed and lax. As financial institutions enhanced bubble-driven profits through leverage, the post-New Deal regime of prudential and disclosure regulation gave way to a new opaque financial system increasingly prone to crisis and collapse.

### 47.4.3   The Ratings Game

The financial alchemy of securitization depended on the assistance of ratings agencies to make the "senior" tranches marketable. Since the mid-1970s, the three dominant ratings agencies, Standard & Poor's, Moody's, and Fitch, have been recognized by the Securities and Exchange Commission as "nationally recognized statistical rating organizations" (NRSROs). Since the 1970s, federal regulators empowered NRSROs as market gatekeepers, and created a de facto regulatory cartel, whose ratings determined the capital requirements of broker-dealers and the eligibility of securities for purchase by savings and loans associations, credit unions, and federally regulated pension funds. The NRSROs remained almost entirely unregulated, even after their egregious ratings failures during the stock market bubble of the 1990s.[15]

Ratings were indispensable to the creation and marketing of complex debt securities that were difficult if not impossible for purchasers to value independently. They transmuted high-risk mortgages into nominally risk-free high-yield investments. This financial alchemy, however, was the product of flawed risk models and glaring conflicts of interest created by the issuer banks' selection of the NRSRO and of its fees. Payment of fees up front left the NRSROs with no residual risk to discourage unduly high ratings; payments calculated on the volume of rated securities sold encouraged them. Beholden to the banks, the NRSROs routinely underestimated default risks and gave AAA ratings to the vast majority of MBS and CDO issues. Miraculously, these AAA securities were rated as far safer than the mortgage debt underlying them, yet were protected from default by ever-thinner layers of higher-risk equity and lower tranche securities (see Nadauld and Sherlund 2009). With this seal of approval, regulated financial institutions and pension funds could buy the securities, opening up huge markets for arranging banks and sowing the global financial system with undisclosed and underpriced risk.

### 47.4.4   Derivatives Unbound and the Explosion of Credit Default Swaps

Credit default swaps (CDSs) provided the final essential ingredient of the CDO boom and the financial crisis that followed. These derivatives served as a form of unregulated insurance on securitized debt instruments, including CDOs. In exchange for regular cash payments, the seller of the CDS protection compensated the buyer for the loss of the CDO's value in the event of default or other contractually specified conditions.

Derivatives, including CDSs, had been *preemptively deregulated* under American law – and with the complicity of Democrats in the Clinton White House and Congress. Republicans had long championed financial deregulation, but the Democratic Party embraced much of the cause during the early 1990s. During the Clinton administration, Greenspan, Treasury Secretary Robert Rubin, and then-Assistant Treasury Secretary Lawrence Summers thwarted an attempt to regulate derivatives by Brooksley Born, then chair of the Commodities Futures Trading Commission (Faiola et al. 2008). Countering warnings that the unregulated marketing and trading of derivatives posed enormous potential systemic risks, they argued that regulation would hamper beneficial financial innovations, and that the self-interest of sophisticated parties along with the efficiency of global markets would provide adequate self-regulation (Faiola et al 2008; see, e.g., Greenspan 2002). Phil Gramm, then the powerful Republican chairman of the Senate Banking Committee and a fierce anti-regulation ideologue, drafted the Commodity Futures Modernization Act of 2000, which foreclosed virtually all future regulation of derivatives and passed with barely a murmur of dissent from the Clinton administration and congressional Democrats (Lipton 2008; Lipton and Labaton 2008). In less than a decade, unregulated derivatives would become a multi-*trillion* dollar market.

As "over the counter" (OTC) securities not traded on any regulated exchange with transparent pricing, CDSs and the CDOs underlying them were far removed from regulatory oversight, disclosure rules, or prudential regulation. They were intrinsically difficult to value, and no one knew with confidence who held them and in what amounts. These characteristics made the CDS business immensely profitable – and dangerous. The London-based financial products unit of AIG, the world's largest insurance company, became the world's largest CDS issuer in the CDO market.[16] AIG's CDS "coverage" of debt securities enabled big banks to avoid booking additional capital reserves against this growing share of their balance sheets, giving them another means to increase leverage (Nocera 2009). Freed from regulation, CDS issuers like AIG were not required to set aside reserves to cover potential claims or collateral calls in the event of defaults, price declines, or ratings downgrades. In the regulatory netherworld of derivatives, investors could place immense and highly leveraged bets on the CDO market through "naked CDS" issues (protection bought by a party that did not own the "insured" assets) and "synthetic CDOs" consisting solely of derivatives designed to mimic the CDO cash flow payments to investors coupled with naked CDSs held by parties betting that CDOs would default.[17] (See Figure 47.3.)

CDSs unleashed a massive increase in financial speculation as parties on either side of CDS trades placed, in the aggregate, trillions of dollars' worth of undisclosed and often unhedged bets on the future value of CDOs. Absent disclosure regulation, the opacity of these CDS positions markets both obscured and magnified systemic risk by creating impenetrable uncertainty over the size and location of potential liabilities. By the end of the boom, the nominal (face) value of CDS issues exceeded the value of CDOs by an esti-mated ratio of 10:1. The mutation of CDSs into synthetic CDOs kept the securitization bubble growing by allowing banks (most notoriously Goldman Sachs) to collude with hedge funds in creating securities designed to default and trigger huge payouts to funds shorting the precarious MBS and CDO markets.

### 47.4.5  The Securitization Cycle and the Web of Conflicts

Each of the components discussed above fit together to create a lending–securitization cycle (represented by the cash flow arrows in Figure 47.2) that inflated the real estate bubble and drove the massive expansion of credit and leverage within the shadow banking system. The cycle was self-perpetuating so long as surging investor demand and a global financial system awash in cheap credit provided the capital to channel back into mortgage lending. Figure 47.4 illustrates part of the broader web of relationships in which the securitization cycle was situated. None of the parties linked in the securitiza-tion web acknowledged, and many never understood, the dangers posed by an increas-ingly obvious real estate bubble. The securitization cycle depended on, and the "value at risk" models used by the banks and ratings agencies assumed, continually rising real estate prices that kept mortgage default rates low. Many parties maintained an illusory sense of security based on blind faith in the financial alchemy of securitization, flawed risk management models, erroneous debt ratings, and the risk-spreading properties of derivatives. Others within the securitization cycle opportunistically exploited the con-flicts of interest and information asymmetries within the complex tangle of counterparty relationships.

The ubiquity of severe conflicts of interest was a striking characteristic of the secu-ritization web, as was the absence of transparency characterizing so many of these relationships. The product of spontaneous private ordering (no central party designed and assembled all these pieces), this elaborate financial subsystem appears designed for market failure and collapse. Mortgage lenders had an incentive to debase lending stand-ards for loans they sold off immediately. The arranging banks externalized part of their risk by selling off MBSs and CDOs as quickly as possible with the aid of inflated debt ratings, courtesy of compromised rating agencies. They obscured the location and size of their growing residual exposure to these securities through SIVs or CDS hedging, and often marketed securities around the world through off-shore subsidiaries that further insulated them from regulatory oversight.

The securitization cycle also subsumed and destabilized the traditional banking sector. Bankers and fund managers took advantage of cheap credit and relied on implausi-bly high debt ratings in buying MBSs and CDOs for high yields and to boost returns through increased leverage, deliberately or unwittingly exposing their investors, deposi-tors, beneficiaries, and the public to immense risks. The end of the legal separation of commercial and investment banking in the US allowed large commercial banks with investment banking units to join in the securitization boom, but the costs of this moral hazard could and would be externalized onto taxpayers. European universal banks, turning away from traditional relational banking, sought higher returns and profits in the new financial marketplace, but many had insufficient expertise to discern and manage the risks that entailed.

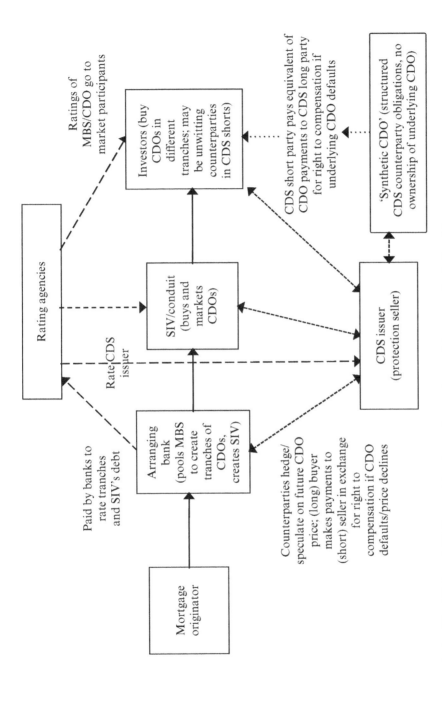

Figure 47.4  *The CDO and CDS securitization web – main participants and relationships*

Ratings of MBS/CDO go to market participants

Investors (buy CDOs in different tranches; may be unwitting counterparties in CDS shorts)

CDS short party pays equivalent of CDO payments to CDS long party for right to compensation if underlying CDO defaults

'Synthetic CDO' (structured CDS counterparty obligations, no ownership of underlying CDO)

Rating agencies

SIV/conduit (buys and markets CDOs)

CDS issuer (protection seller)

Rate CDS issuer

Arranging bank (pools MBS to create tranches of CDOs, creates SIV)

Paid by banks to rate tranches and SIV's debt

Counterparties hedge/speculate on future CDO price; (long) buyer makes payments to (short) seller in exchange for right to compensation if CDO defaults/price declines

Mortgage originator

655

Regulation could have curtailed or broken the securitization cycle by addressing the opacity, misrepresentations, conflicts of interest, and predatory behavior pervading the shadow banking system, thereby reducing the capital flows and weakening the forces that inflated the real estate and credit bubbles. And, at every point, regulation failed. Even with effective regulation there may have been a housing boom, but the regulatory failures that enabled leverage, speculation, and systemic risks to soar turned the inevitable bust into a global financial catastrophe.

## 47.5 ARCHITECTURE OF COLLAPSE: A BRIEF SUMMARY OF THE FINANCIAL CRISIS OF 2007–09

The financial crisis that culminated in the panic of September–October 2008 had been looming since early 2007. Subprime mortgage lending stalled in 2006. After mortgage defaults started to rise in late 2006 the MBS and CDO markets began to implode in the summer of 2007. Soaring subprime default rates during 2007 and 2008 triggered a worsening credit crunch that, in turn, produced an intensifying liquidity crisis in the subprime mortgage and securitized debt markets. Without the continual recycling and growth of credit and debt that drove the lending–securitization cycle, the grossly inflated prices and markets for real estate, subprime mortgages, MBSs, and CDOs collapsed. In March 2008, Bear Stearns' heavy losses on and exposure to CDOs precipitated a panic that left it insolvent within days.[18] Fearing systemic contagion, the Federal Reserve Bank of New York arranged Bear's purchase by JPMorgan Chase by guaranteeing $30 billion of the failed firm's toxic assets.

Lehman Brothers, one of the world's largest and most globally interconnected investment banks, had suffered vast – and largely undisclosed – losses on MBSs and related derivatives. Fatally misjudging the market and political realities, its senior managers, along with many of the bank's counterparties and other market participants, hoped for a merger with another bank or a government bailout. Senior officials of the US Treasury and Federal Reserve were deeply troubled by the moral hazards of a second bailout and chastened by the breadth and intensity of public hostility towards the Bear Stearns bailout (see Solomon et al. 2008). Their faith in rational self-interest and efficient markets led them to bet that major banks, counterparties, and investors had unwound or hedged their exposure to a potential Lehman bankruptcy. They withheld government intervention and let Lehman Brothers fail (see Reddy and Hilsenrath 2008; Solomon et al. 2008).

Lehman Brothers' collapse in mid-September 2008 set off a global financial panic and a cascade of financial catastrophes. Market participants knew enormous bad debts and risk exposures lurked throughout the global financial system, but had no idea where they were located or which institutions would be next to fall. Large, interconnected, and overleveraged financial institutions and investment funds suffered immense losses on accumulated securities holdings; they could find no buyers at precisely the moment they most desperately needed to sell assets to rebuild capital cushions and loss reserves. Mark-to-market accounting rules helped inflate the asset bubble on the way up; they now accelerated the crash by forcing financial institutions to book huge losses as investors and institutions hoarded cash and liquid assets. Panic and mistrust seized the core of the banking system, accompanied by a global chain reaction of deleveraging as liquidity disappeared, counterparty risks soared, and credit contracted. The credit crunch froze short-term interbank lending and rendered otherwise solvent institutions incapable of financing continuing operations. The evaporation of short-term finance accelerated the systemic collapse by forcing the liabilities of highly levered SIVs and conduits back onto arranging bank balance sheets.

The massive wave of MBS and CDO defaults triggered billions in CDS and bond insurance claims. Bond default claims brought the major bond insurers to the verge of bankruptcy. CDS claims magnified the scale of the losses and threatened AIG and some of the world's largest financial institutions with insolvency. The reckless CDS speculation exemplified by AIG had concentrated, amplified, and globalized systemic risk (see Nocera 2009; Tett 2009).[19] AIG had retained nearly three trillion dollars of CDS exposure – one trillion of it to a dozen of the world's largest financial institutions. Some 300 billion dollars of exposure was to European banks that had hedged their own risks and used CDSs to reduce their "regulatory capital" (i.e., increase their leverage even more than US banks) and likely could not have survived a collapse of AIG. Not willing to risk another round of panic and contagion, the Treasury and Federal Reserve nationalized AIG, along with Fannie Mae and Freddie Mac.

Within weeks, the global financial panic transformed the American and European political economies. Bank of America bought Merrill Lynch at a distress price in a government-brokered deal. The Treasury and Federal Reserve nationalized AIG, Fannie Mae, and Freddie Mac, and bailed out Citigroup and Bank of America. Goldman Sachs and Morgan Stanley were unable to continue as investment banks and became bankholding companies to qualify for government bailout funds. As the November presidential election loomed, the Bush administration relied primarily on Democratic support to pass the controversial $700 billion Troubled Asset Relief Program (TARP). Even more controversially, the government paid off CDS claims against AIG at 100 cents on the dollar – without transparency or accountability – to provide an additional unrecoverable $80 billion "backdoor bailout" to some of the world's major financial institutions (Walsh 2009).[20]

These were merely the most visible forms of government intervention on an extraordinary scale (Montgomery and Kane 2008). Unprecedented and controversial federal lending and asset guarantees, much of it by the Federal Reserve, propped up the entire shattered financial system by supporting the very institutions that had caused the collapse. As of September 2009, the American government's support for the financial sector totaled $545.3 billion in expenditures (of which $72.9 billion had been repaid) and another $23.7 *trillion* in asset guarantees (representing nominal asset value, not the likely real costs) (SIGTARP 2009a: 137–8, Table 3.4, 2009b: 31; IMF 2009).[21] European governments, beginning with the Irish, moved to halt a run on their banking systems and extended deposit insurance for the first time, and exposed government budgets to potentially huge liabilities. They were forced to grant asset guarantees and bailouts to many of their banks, and nationalized a score of others (a step the US refused to take). The European Central Bank and Bank of England also engaged in vast lending and liquidity operations to prop up European banks. In addition to the immediate economic carnage, the crisis was a nightmare of moral hazard. "Too big to fail" was now an officially confirmed reality.

## 47.6   THE POST-CRISIS POLITICS OF REFORM

In the immediate aftermath of the global financial crisis and the collapse of Wall Street, there was a near universal expectation that a revival of the regulatory state would rapidly transform financial sectors and markets around the world. It is now far from clear that the American or European political systems are capable of undertaking such fundamental structural and regulatory reforms. The Obama administration refused to seriously consider nationalizing major financial institutions, and it was noticeably reluctant to endorse far-reaching financial system reforms.[22] Hampered by the fragmented structure of the EU and the severity of the Eurozone sovereign debt crisis, the pace of European reforms is even slower, with major reforms still in planning.

Congress finally passed a financial reform bill, the Dodd–Frank Act, in July 2010. Some of the most important proposals were blocked or enfeebled during the legislative process: the regulatory reduction in excessive leverage and the size of too-big-to-fail banks, a ban on proprietary trading by banks, derivatives regulation, regulatory oversight and control of systemic risk, resolution authority to process the bankruptcies of large systemically sensitive financial institutions, and the creation of a strong independent consumer financial protection agency. Consolidation and rationalization of federal regulatory authority was jettisoned in favor of strengthening the role of the Federal Reserve in financial regulation. The regulatory politics of finance capitalism during the past 25 years created the conditions for this crisis. Yet, in the absence of structural reform of the financial system, the financial sector, and the regulatory state, the reforms emerging from the post-crisis political environment rely on the competence, integrity, and functional capacity of regulators.

To some extent, the sluggish pace and meandering path of reform reflect a political paradox of the financial crisis: the financial sector's *economic* weakness shielded it at precisely the moment when it was *politically* weakest. The magnitude of the crisis made the financial sector's rescue more pressing than its fundamental reform. But the sluggish pace and compromised character of financial system reform also reflected the dysfunctional state of American politics in an era of increasingly bitter partisan conflict, corporate political influence, and a crisis of confidence, if not legitimacy, in government integrity and competence. Even under conditions of popular outrage against the financial sector, government's capacity to act in response to an extraordinary crisis has, to date, proved inadequate to achieve fundamental reform of a financial system that had fundamentally failed.

Saved by vast infusions of public funds and assets guarantees, the bailout expanded the size and political power of the largest financial institutions, and they have fought to shape regulatory reform when they could not kill it. Even in a weakened state, the financial sector remains a powerful force in American politics, and its interests are most intense when fighting reforms threatening the most profitable business activities of surviving financial institutions that have grown larger through public subsidies. In 2009, the six largest American banks held assets worth over 60 percent of GDP (up from less than 20 percent in 1995) and two-thirds of all deposits (Faiola et al. 2008; Cho 2009; Johnson and Kwak 2010: 203, fig. 7-1). Explicit or implicit federal recognition of these institutions as too-big-to-fail lowered their costs of capital, setting the stage for further sectoral concentration.[23]

Neoliberal finance capitalism has mutated into an inversion of the liberal market ideal. American finance capitalism now embodies a fusion of public and private power corrosive to democratic governance and posing a demonstrable threat to economic stability (see generally Johnson and Kwak 2010; Smith 2010). In Europe, the crisis of the shadow banking system became a solvency crisis in the traditional banking system, and the bad debts of large private banks have shifted implicitly, if not explicitly, onto the state. In Europe this banking crisis is at the core of the ongoing sovereign debt crisis that threatens the future of the euro and perhaps the EU. The corrosive perception of state capture by the financial sector is a portent of an intensifying legitimacy crisis afflicting American and European politics across the political spectrum. Financial collapse exposed massive regulatory failures and revealed the intellectual, ideological, and economic bankruptcy of the neoliberal variant of finance capitalism. Should the reform of financial regulation prove inadequate to prevent another serious crisis, the next catastrophic bankruptcy may be that of political economic order.

## ACKNOWLEDGEMENTS

An early version of this chapter was published in *Policy Matters*, the public policy paper series of the University of California, Riverside.

## NOTES

1.  The argument here is that regulatory failures were a necessary, not a sufficient, condition for the crisis. Monetary and macroeconomic policies, trade and balance of payments imbalances, and intensifying income and wealth inequality also played critically important roles, but are beyond the scope of this chapter.
2.  I am not arguing that the financial elite sought a pure laissez-faire economic order. They often favor regulation that serves their economic interests (e.g., rules designed to enhance depositor and investor confidence and otherwise promote the growth of financial services, securities markets, and financial returns) (Cioffi 2010).
3.  Taleb (2008) argues that widespread underestimation of the frequency of financial crises may increase their likelihood by encouraging herding or clustering of behaviors that increase systemic vulnerability and risk.
4.  Notably, Japan and other East Asian banking systems, having been chastened by their financial crises during the 1990s, were less exposed to the securitized debt and derivatives markets that precipitated the financial crisis.
5.  This discussion is largely restricted to economic theories of regulation, but even those that advance non-economic goals and justifications for regulation (e.g., Sunstein 1990) resort to economic concepts and theoretical argumentation.
6.  For an overview of private interest and public choice theories, see Sunstein (1990, chap. 2); Croley (1998).
7.  Framing these problems as conflicts of interest rather than principal–agent problems avoids the normative and empirical difficulties of determining who is a principal and who is an agent.
8.  These levels encompass the most important relationships within the financial system: borrowers and lenders, shareholders and managers, managers and employees engaged in complex transactions involving vast sums of money, and among investors and financial intermediaries (e.g., investment bankers and other advisors, fund managers, brokers, or traders).
9.  The EU's single market agenda also generated political pressures for reform, but EU policy is constrained by member state preferences, and regulatory reforms at the national level often anticipated or exceeded liberalizing EU financial market directives.
10. Financial institutions could be regulated, in whole or in part, by the Federal Reserve, the Office of Thrift Supervision, the Office of the Comptroller of the Currency, the Federal Deposit Insurance Corporation,

the Securities and Exchange Commission, the Commodity Futures Trading Commission, and state law (which was often preempted by more permissive federal regulation).
11.  For the development of this securitization model, see generally Tett (2009); Smith (2010).
12.  This discussion necessarily simplifies the extraordinarily complex and diverse structural features of securitization and "structured finance." It also glosses over terminological inconsistencies common in practice.
13.  Moreover, CDOs encompass a much wider array of securitized debt instruments, ranging from private equity loans to credit card debt. The crash in mortgage-backed CDOs also undermined the markets for these instruments, intensifying and broadening the credit crunch.
14.  These asset classification and valuation standards were codified in FASB's Federal Accounting Standard 157, revised and renamed as FASB Topic 820 in January 2010.
15.  NRSROs were also insulated from regulation by court opinions ruling that debt ratings are protected opinions under the First Amendment, shielding them from liability even if grossly negligent.
16.  For an analysis of AIG's CDS business, see generally Dennis and O'Harrow 2008; O'Harrow and Dennis 2008a, 2008b; Sjostrom (2009).
17.  Incredible as it seems in hindsight, "synthetic" CDOs were first developed to satisfy excess investor demand for CDOs limited by the supply of subprime mortgages.
18.  In August 2007, monetary interventions by the Fed and the European Central Bank contained a prior panic triggered by large subprime-related losses suffered by Bear Stearns and BNP Paribas hedge funds.
19.  Advocates of deregulated derivatives markets had claimed that they spread risk efficiently among sophisticated parties according to their ability and inclination to bear it, thus contributing to financial system stability. A long line of critics had countered that derivatives were too complex to be understood by even sophisticated financiers and fostered dangerous levels of systemic opacity and potential volatility. The events of late 2008 proved the critics correct.
20.  A partial list of AIG bailout recipients includes (in billions): Goldman Sachs ($12.9), Société Générale ($12), Deutsche Bank ($12), Barclays ($8.5), Merrill Lynch ($6.8), Bank of America ($5.2), UBS ($5), Citigroup ($2.3) and Wachovia ($1.5) (Walsh, 2009).
21.  The IMF's (2009) estimate of the ultimate costs was still $3.68 trillion ($1.85 trillion in asset purchase commitments; $1.83 trillion in guarantee commitments).
22.  AIG and the public–private hybrid mortgage guarantor agencies Fannie Mae and Freddie Mac were notable exceptions to the non-nationalization policy, for reasons that are still hotly debated.
23.  In 2007, large American banks (in excess of $100 billion in assets) paid 0.08 percent less interest in borrowing costs than smaller rivals; by late 2009 that advantage had quadrupled to 0.34 percent (Cho 2009, using FDIC figures).

# REFERENCES

Adler, Joe (2009), 'In reports on failures, regulators also fail', *American Banker*, 15 April.
Breyer, Stephen (1982), *Regulation and Its Reform*, Cambridge, MA: Harvard University Press.
Buiter, Willem H. (2008), 'Lessons from the North Atlantic financial crisis', paper presented at the conference The Role of Money Markets, Columbia Business School and the Federal Reserve Bank of New York, 29–30 May.
Cho, David (2009), 'Banks "too big to fail" have grown even bigger', *Washington Post*, 28 August.
Cioffi, John W. (2010), *Public Law and Private Power: Corporate Governance Reform in the Age of Finance Capitalism*, Ithaca, NY: Cornell University Press.
Croley, Steven P. (1998), 'Theories of regulation: incorporating the administrative process', *Columbia Law Review*, **98** (1), 1–106.
Dennis, Brady and Robert O'Harrow, Jr. (2008), 'A Crack in the System', *Washington Post*, 30 December.
Diamond, Douglas W. and Philip H. Dybvig (1983), 'Bank runs, deposit insurance, and liquidity', *Journal of Political Economy*, **91**, 401–19.
Faiola, Anthony, Ellen Nakashima and Jill Drew (2008), 'What Went Wrong', *Washington Post*, 15 October.
Farrell, Greg (2009), 'Cox regime at SEC under fire', *Financial Times*, 7 May.
Fender, Ingo and Janet Mitchell (2009), 'The future of securitisation: how to align incentives?', *BIS Quarterly Review*, September, 27–43.
Financial Crisis Inquiry Commission (2010), 'Preliminary staff report: securitization and the mortgage crisis', 7 April, available at: http://fcic.gov/reports/ (accessed 8 April 2010).
GAO (United States Government Accountability Office) (2009), 'Securities and Exchange Commission: greater attention needed to enhance communication and utilization of resources in the division of enforcement', report to congressional requesters, GAO-09-358, March.

Greenspan, Alan (2002), Remarks before the Society of Business Economists, London, 25 September.

IMF (International Monetary Fund) (2008), *Global Financial Stability Report: Containing Systemic Risks and Restoring Financial Soundness*, April, available at: http://www.imf.org/External/Pubs/FT/GFSR/2008/01/ index.htm (accessed 25 October 2010).

IMF (International Monetary Fund) (2009), *Global Financial Stability Report: Responding to the Financial Crisis and Measuring Systemic Risks*, April, available at: http://www.imf.org/external/pubs/ft/gfsr/2009/01/ index.htm (accessed 12 April 2010).

Johnson, Simon and James Kwak (2010), *13 Bankers: The Wall Street Takeover and the Next Financial Meltdown,* New York: Random House.

Labaton, Stephen (2008), 'Agency's '04 rule lets banks pile up new debt', *New York Times*, 3 October.

Lipton, Eric (2008), 'Gramm and the "Enron Loophole"', *New York Times*, 17 November.

Lipton, Eric and Stephen Labaton (2008), 'Deregulator looks back, unswayed', *New York Times*, 17 November.

Montgomery, Lori and Paul Kane (2008), 'Lawmakers reach accord on huge financial rescue', *Washington Post*, 28 September.

Nadauld, Taylor D. and Shane M. Sherlund (2009), 'The role of the securitization process in the expansion of subprime credit', Finance and Economics Discussion Paper 2009-28, Federal Reserve Board, Divisions of Research and Statistics and Monetary Affairs, Washington, DC.

Nocera, Joe (2009), 'Propping up a house of cards', *New York Times*, 28 February.

O'Harrow, Robert, Jr. and Brady Dennis (2008a), 'The beautiful machine', *Washington Post*, 29 December.

O'Harrow, Robert, Jr. and Brady Dennis (2008b), 'Downgrades and downfall', *Washington Post*, 31 December.

Reddy, Sudeep and Jon Hilsenrath (2008), 'The government stood firm: was it the right call?', *Wall Street Journal*, 15 September.

Reinhart, Carmen M. and Kenneth S. Rogoff (2009), *This Time Is Different: Eight Centuries of Financial Folly,* Princeton, NJ: Princeton University Press.

Scannell, Kara and Susanne Craig (2008), 'SEC chief under fire as Fed seeks bigger Wall Street role', *Wall Street Journal*, 23 June.

SIGTARP (Special Inspector General, Troubled Asset Relief Program) (2009a), Quarterly Report to Congress, 21 July.

SIGTARP (Special Inspector General, Troubled Asset Relief Program (2009b), Quarterly Report to Congress, 1 October.

Sjostrom, William K., Jr. (2009), 'The AIG bailout', *Washington and Lee Law Review*, **66**, 943–91.

Smith, Yves (2010), *ECONned: How Unenlightened Self Interest Undermined Democracy and Corrupted Capitalism*, New York: Palgrave Macmillan.

Solomon, Deborah, Dennis K. Berman, Susanne Craig and Carrick Mollenkamp (2008), 'Ultimatum by Paulson sparked frantic end', *Wall Street Journal*, 15 September.

Stigler, George J. (1971), 'The theory of economic regulation', *Bell Journal of Economics and Management Science*, **3**, 3–18.

Sunstein, Cass R. (1990), *After the Rights Revolution: Reconceiving the Regulatory State,* Cambridge, MA: Harvard University Press.

Taleb, Nassim Nicholas (2008), *The Black Swan: The Impact of the Highly Improbable*, New York: Random House.

Tett, Gillian (2009), *Fool's Gold: How the Bold Dream of a Small Tribe at J.P. Morgan Was Corrupted by Wall Street Greed and Unleashed a Catastrophe*, New York: Simon & Schuster.

Tiberghien, Yves (2007), *Entrepreneurial States: Reforming Corporate Governance in France, Japan, and Korea*, Ithaca, NY: Cornell University Press.

Walsh, Mary Williams (2009), 'A.I.G. lists firms it paid with taxpayer money', *New York Times*, 16 March.

# 48 The regulatory state and regulatory capitalism: an institutional perspective
## David Levi-Faur

This chapter discusses the concepts of the regulatory state and regulatory capitalism in an effort to draw an institutional perspective on the politics of regulation. While the notion of the regulatory state allows us to capture the extent, scope and direction in which regulation shapes national-level institutions, that of regulatory capitalism allows us to explore the relations of the state and other political actors to the capitalist order itself. Regulatory capitalism draws attention to the political economy of regulation and it does so without necessarily privileging a state-centered perspective. This may allow us to embed the two notions in the international and comparative political economy literatures and to assess how the regulatory state and the concept of regulatory capitalism stand in comparison with other forms of states (e.g. the positive state, the developmental state, the competitive state and the welfare state) and the global political economy (e.g. laissez-faire, crony capitalism and transnational elites). At the same time, in the spirit of the governance perspective, I move the discussion beyond the state, not because the state is not important or even the most important actor, but because state-centered analysis is limited and should be augmented by society-centered analysis not only at the national but also at the global level.

## 48.1   THE REGULATORY STATE

The notion of the regulatory state seems to capture the imagination of many scholars around the world (Majone 1994; Loughlin and Scott 1997; Moran 2002). Like many other key notions, it means different things to different scholars. Only a few efforts have been made so far to clarify the subject and identify its various applications. Against this background, not surprisingly, the notion of the regulatory state itself has become a focus for criticism. Michael Moran, who is among the main culprits in the popularization of the notion of the regulatory state, raises the question of the extent to which it is "a sort of intellectual brazier around which [scholars of regulation] can all gather, to warm our hands and speak to each other, in a world of increasingly fragmented academic professionalism" (Moran 2002: 411–12). Yet, asks Moran, who cares about the shape of the brazier or the fuel used in it, as long as it helps moderate the crisis of communication in the social sciences? I concur but at the same time strive to suggest a more ambitious understanding of the notion, starting with an analysis of the origins of the concept of the regulatory state in order to identify its various meanings.

    While Giandomenico Majone was probably the first to employ and develop the notion of the regulatory state in a systematic and comprehensive manner, the idea itself originates from the title of a book written by James Anderson: *The Emergence of the Modern*

*Regulatory State* (1962). This book aimed at capturing the peculiar use of regulation via independent agencies that specialized in it as a mode of administrative governance in the United States. Anderson did not make an effort to conceptualize the term or to employ it in a comparative or theoretical manner. His main effort was towards understanding the development and expansion of the administrative state at the federal level. The term caught on only slowly in the US, and its uses were confined to scholars who studied American political development, American administrative law and American public administration.

The notion of the regulatory state that was born in the US never captured the imagination of American scholars in the way it has European ones since the mid-1990s. Most of the research efforts were focused on the benefits and costs of administrative forms of regulation, the characteristics and the pitfalls of agencies and the relations between the agencies and other branches of the government (Mitnick 1980; Wilson 1980). It might well be that the preferences towards notions such as the "regulatory system" as applied by Barry Mitnick in his seminal book reflect the "statelessness" of the US polity (see Nettl 1968; King and Lieberman 2009). Still, maybe as part of the effort to bring the state "back in" (Skocpol 1985) the notion of the regulatory state has gained some visibility in US law and society and law and economics circles since the late 1980s with the works of Sunstein (1989, 1990) and Rose-Ackerman (1992). Most notably, however, it appears as the subtitle of the fourth edition of the late Harold Seidman's *Politics, Position, and Power: From the Positive to the Regulatory State* (Seidman and Gilmour 1986). With it came a new understanding of the regulatory state. Like his predecessor, Seidman does not define the regulatory state, but there is something new in his understanding of the notion. Let me explain it by contrasting it with that of James Anderson. For Anderson it was a command and control or hierarchical state which was born – at least at the federal level – at the end of the 19th century and as a result of political struggle of popular movements against big business. For Seidman, on the other hand, the notion of the regulatory state is used in order to capture steering or "government by proxy," less hierarchy, more governance. The context is no longer the working of popular movements but that of a general dissatisfaction with the administrative state, which was followed by the outsourcing of administrative functions by the federal government. Unlike Anderson, who equated the regulatory state with the independent regulatory agencies at the federal level that were established in three waves from the end of the 19th century onwards, for Seidman the rise of the regulatory state has happened since the mid-1970s. In other words, Seidman and Anderson understand the regulatory state in different ways, depending on different periods and different characteristics.

Still, the notion of the regulatory state was not central to Seidman's work, and he did not develop it further. In the fifth edition of the book that came out ten years later, he dropped the subtitle with its reference to the regulatory state (instead he opted for *The Dynamics of Federal Organization*). Still, the title and the notion of the regulatory state had captured the interest of Giandomenico Majone, who applied it to the EU system of governance in two important papers (Majone 1994, 1997). In the latter he explicitly adopted Seidman's subtitle and transformed it into a title: 'From the positive to the regulatory state' (Majone 1997). Majone's conceptualization is similar to Seidman's: government by proxy – a state that puts administrative and economic efficiency first. Majone does not define the notion of the regulatory state but instead does an excellent job of characterizing the politics of regulation and of the regulatory space (building to some extent on Lowi 1964 and Wilson 1980). Majone's level of analysis is at the EU level of seeing the growth of the European regulatory state in the context of the severe limits on taxation and spending imposed by Brussels. Regulatory agencies at the EU level are not part of Majone's conceptualization, partly because the EU at the time concentrated regulatory powers in the Commission rather than agencies (radical change occurred only in 2000) and partly because the EU member states were only beginning frantically to establish and reform regulatory agencies across various sectors.

A somewhat different perspective or approach to the regulatory state was evident in the study of "regulation within government" by Hood and his colleagues (1999). They observed that regulation is expanding not only at the EU level but also at the national level. Thus they wrote that in its most straightforward form the term "regulatory state" "suggests [that] modern states are placing more emphasis on the use of authority, rules and standard-setting, partially displacing an earlier emphasis on public ownership, public subsidies, and directly provided services" (Hood et al. 1999: 3). What Hood and his colleagues did was to expand the notion of the regulatory state from the federal or EU level and apply it to the national level, as it referred to both the government regulation of its own employees and organizations and the regulation of civil and economic life.

Outside the political science literature, but with a broad social sciences perspective, John Braithwaite coined in 2000 the notion of a "new regulatory state" (see also Scott 2004). In a manner similar to Seidman and Majone, he also pointed to the rise of the (new) regulatory state in the context of public administration reforms. His regulatory state is doing more steering than rowing, and is contrasted with the night-watchman state on the one hand and the old regulatory state. The new regulatory state differs from the old in its reliance on self-regulatory organizations, enforced self-regulation, compliance systems, codes of practice and other responsive techniques that substitute for direct command and control. The new regulatory state therefore is about the decentering of the state, responsive regulation, "rule at a distance," ranking and shaming and other forms of soft regulation (Braithwaite 2000). Braithwaite's distinction between the new and the old regulatory state allows for a better understanding of the relations between the original notions of Anderson's administrative state that was born at the end of 19th century and the regulatory state at the end of the 20th century. While both the old and the new relied on regulation, they employed different strategies, with the old more hierarchical than the new. Note that the change in administrative strategies of the state is understood by some of the authors also as the decline of the positive state, the welfare state and Keynesianism more generally. The preference for steering rather than rowing is said or at least hinted to reflect similarly the retreat from high modernism, that is, the retreat from commitment to rapid social and economic change that is led by the political and administrative machine of the state.

Braithwaite's distinction between old and new regulatory states is useful in order to capture the reforms in the US administrative apparatus and to distinguish between the regulatory strategies and approaches that dominated the periods before and after the 1980s. In both periods regulation was a dominant, visible and strategic instrument of the federal government despite the growth in taxing and spending before the 1980s and the effort to deregulate after the 1980s. Still, the notion of "old" and "new" regulatory state did not capture two important political economy aspects. First, it failed to capture the exceptionalism of the US regulatory state. If the US had an old regulatory state, the rest of the world embedded regulation in centralized decision making and a wide public program of ownership that for most of the twentieth century did not allow regulatory governance to evolve as a distinct mode of governance. The independent regulatory agencies, after the American style of the Federal Trade Commission, the Securities and Exchange Commission and the Federal Communications Commission (possibly with the exception of the Central Bank), did not exist in the same manner and with the same arm's-length relations with politicians as in the United States. The notion of the "old regulatory state" is highly ambiguous in the context of the centralization of authority and growth of the administrative state outside the US. It is not that regulation was not employed outside the United States, or that it was not employed before the 20th century, but that the regulatory functions and institutions were not developed distinctively in this period. In addition, the growth of taxing and spending (or the tax state) obscured the expansion of regulation.

Second, the most impressive transformation is not necessarily the one that was observed in the US by Seidman, namely, in the style of governing. Instead it is the rapid growth of the regulatory state outside the United States – as captured by the proxy of the growth of independent agencies. My own work with Jordana, Fernandez and Gilardi demonstrated the growth in the number of agencies since the mid-1980s across different sectors and countries (Levi-Faur 2003; Gilardi et al. 2006; Jordana et al. forthcoming). What we found is that the regulatory state is not necessarily European and that major regulatory capacities were developed at the national level in the so-called era of "deregulation." This work extended and confirmed expectations of an interventionist mode of regulation that was characterized as regulation-*for*-competition (Levi-Faur 1998). The ambition to regulate-for-competition placed the regulatory state not as a mere re-regulator but as possessing an ambitious modernist agenda (Levi-Faur 1998).

A similar conceptualization of a rather interventionist regulatory state appears in Moran's book *The British Regulatory State* (2003). Moran's notion of the regulatory state emphasizes the destruction of an anachronistic governance system that was based on trust and tacit agreements between business and governmental elites and its replacement by a modern system of arm's-length regulation. For the first two-thirds of the 20th century, Britain, according to Moran, was the most stable and least innovative country in the capitalist world. Once a byword for stagnation, since the 1980s Britain has been a pioneer of institutional and policy change resulting in a system of governance of "increasing institutional formality and hierarchy, where the authority of public institutions has been reinforced . . . by substantial fresh investment in bureaucratic resources to ensure compliance" (pp. 20–22). This new hierarchical system is at the same time made more transparent and open "by the provision of systematic information accessible both to insiders and outsiders, and by reporting and control mechanisms that offer the chance of public control" (p. 7), which allows and encourages higher levels of politicization. Thus, in contrast to images of withdrawal and hollowing-out of the state, with a transfer of power to international agencies and domestic actors that is emphasized by other concepts (or shall we say images or characterizations) of the regulatory state, the change described by Moran is of a vigorous regulatory state whose central ambitions have not diminished. On the contrary, it uses command and control regulation to colonize new areas, develop new agencies and reform old ones (pp. 20–21). The tools it applies to achieve these ambitions are entirely congruent with "high modernism", that is, standardization, central control, and synoptic legibility to the center (pp. 6, 8).

The various conceptualizations and applications of the notion of the regulatory state allow us to offer six major characteristics of the regulatory state (cf. Levi-Faur and Gilad 2004; Levi-Faur 2005). First, bureaucratic functions of regulation are being separated from service delivery. With the withdrawal of the state from direct provision of services (i.e. via privatization of existing services and the nurturing of private provision of value-added services), regulatory functions are becoming increasingly salient and are the new frontiers where the state redefines itself. The visible element of this division of labor is the rise of the regulatory agency; less salient but no less important is the role of "regulatory auditors," mainly lawyers and accountants, who are dispersed in various government ministries and are involved with various forms of contracting out (Power 1997). They are responsible for (a) the formation, monitoring and enforcement of contracts with a multitude of for-profit and voluntary organizations that provide public services; and (b) the auditing of government action itself. The estimated growth of total staffing in public sector regulatory bodies is 90 percent for the period between 1976 and 1995 (Hood et al. 1999: 29–31). Hood et al. (1999: 42) estimate that, if the patterns of regulatory growth and civil service downsizing had continued at the 1975–95 rate indefinitely, late in the present decade the civil service would have had more than two regulators for every "doer" and over ten regulatory organizations for every major government department. These new auditors, the *regulatory auditors,* are not as visible as their fellow regulocrats who chair and run agencies, yet their role is increasingly important in the formation and implementation of public policy.

Second, the regulatory functions of government are being separated from policy-making functions and, thus, the regulators are being placed at arm's length from their political masters; the autonomy of regulators and regulatory agencies is institutionalized, which further extends the sphere of "apolitical" policy making. Regulatory agencies become the citadels which fortify the autonomous and influential role of the regulocrats in the policy process. We are witnessing the strengthening of the regulators at the expense of politicians on the one hand and of the managerial elite on the other.

Third, and as a result of the first two elements, regulation and rule making emerge as a separate stage in the policy-making process. Accordingly, regulation is emerging as a distinct professional and administrative identity. The Weberian bureaucratic model is being augmented or even replaced by a new regulatory model: regulocracy, not only bureaucracy.

Fourth, a degree of arm's-length and rule-based relations replaces the club-style, intimate and informal relations that characterized older styles of decision making. The relations among regulators and between regulators and other players are based on formal rules and contracts rather than discretion.

Fifth, there is a proliferation of new technologies of regulation and an extensive search for better instruments of governance. "Smart regulation," as Gunningham and Grabosky (1998) call it, is defined by the use of a mixture of instruments, by the mobilization of new actors and third parties, and by harnessing the enlightened self-interest of individuals and corporations. One of the most interesting indications of the rise of regulatory capitalism is, therefore, the rise of new instruments: from eco-labeling and league tables to auctioning, and from "gatekeepers" and "awards" to RPI minus X.[1] Some of these instruments such as price control (even in its RPI minus X form) are compulsory, while others, such as eco-labeling, are voluntary. Some are promoted and enforced by non-governmental international organizations; others are enforced by governments and intergovernmental organizations.

Sixth, the regulatory state is a multilevel and international player. It has capacities to shape global and regional rules in a way that at least partly serves its interests and modes of governance. The new servants of the states, the regulocrats, are part of a new transnational order where regional and global networks of experts become a major source of innovations, world views, accountability and legitimacy.

Beyond these six characteristics the literature on this topic makes one implicit assumption about the possibility of state autonomy. If we adopt Nordlinger's concept of autonomy (1987), that regulators can adopt and promote their own preferences, then they enjoy both preferences and policy capabilities. The possibility of autonomy might seem natural to my readers, but it stands in contrast to Stigler's dictum: "as a rule, *regulation is acquired by the industry and is designed and operated primarily for its benefit*" (1971). Given the dominance of this approach in theoretical discussions about regulation, the very idea of the regulatory state as an autonomous institution that may govern with the public interest in mind seems brave. The idea of regulatory capture is still there as one of the first concepts that we take to public discussions or teach our students, but scholars of the regulatory state, of all kinds, just ignore the "dictum" and treat capture as a theoretical and empirical challenge (rather than assumption) when they think about the regulatory state (Croley, 2011; Christensen, 2011).

More obvious and less implicit in the writing on the issue of the regulatory state is the divergence of views on its "orientation" and "political colors." The notion that the regulatory state represents a neoliberal alternative to the positive state (e.g. Majone's interpretation) seems to come from a neo-Marxist perspective. Thus, for example, Kanishka Jayasuriya (2001) suggests that the emerging regulatory state is best understood in terms of the notion of negative coordination as opposed to the positive coordination of economic management within social corporatist and developmental state structures. Nicola Phillips's critical reading of the notion of the regulatory state is similar. For Phillips (2006) the regulatory state is an alternative to the welfare and developmental states and not another face of the state. There are two related issues here. One is the interaction between different institutional features of the state: the developmental, the redistributive and the regulatory. The other is the orientation or color of the state. What we need to do is think of the regulatory state not as an alternative to the welfare and the development state but as a new dimension of an ever expanding state. This will allow us to identify different varieties of regulatory state and to contextualize (rather than generalize) their neoliberal features.

In my interpretation, the regulatory state is not necessarily replacing the developmental state or the welfare state (see Haber 2011; Mabbett, 2011). It is also not necessarily the by-product of privatization or globalization. The regulatory state represent efforts to define better the role of politicians, and to exert control over administrative discretion and more generally the problem and challenges of trust and distrust in post-modern societies (Jordana and Levi-Faur 2004). The logic of regulation as a separate and distinct institution to govern the policy process and mediate between service and planning is strong even under public ownership and not necessarily only as a credible commitment to private investors. The understanding of the regulatory state as a neoliberal alternative to the positive state is also being challenged by the prevalence of efforts to regulate-*for*-competition (that is, to enforce competition in an ambitious manner and with the help of sector-specific agencies in addition to competition agencies; see Levi-Faur 1998), the high modernism of Moran's British regulatory state and by evidence on the relative stability of the welfare state in the North. The welfare state is not expanding anymore, but no expansion does not mean decline. Can it be that the so-called transformation from one type of state to another is only a change of balance between two modes of governance? If this is indeed the case, the rise of the regulatory state does not necessarily mean the decline of the welfare state and the developmental state. The ability to employ regulation as an ambitious, highly modern instrument for social and economic engineering may suggest that the rise of the regulatory state does not necessarily mean a transformation towards a neoliberal form of capitalism (Levi-Faur 1998; Moran 2003; Zedner 2006).

## 48.2 REGULATORY CAPITALISM: BEYOND THE STATE

This chapter now moves beyond the regulatory state to explore the notion of regulatory capitalism. Why regulatory capitalism? What is wrong with the notion of the regulatory state? As should now be clear there is nothing wrong with it – old or new – but the notion of regulatory capitalism offers a broader and more challenging concept. What is regulatory is not only the state but the organization of capitalist society and economy. Regulation expands in the organization of society, politics and economics and governs the interaction of all three. Thus the term "regulatory capitalism" denotes the importance of regulation in defining and shaping the capitalist systems of governance in a way that the regulatory state does not. It points to (a) the intertwining of society, economy and politics via regulatory instruments and institutions; (b) the growth in scope, importance and impact of regulation at the national and global levels; (c) the growing investments of political, economic and social actors in regulation in general and regulatory strategies in particular; and (d) the emergence, extension and consolidation of hybrid forms of regulation which shape diverse and more complex forms of regulatory regimes. These forms can sometimes work even without the state (Scott 2009; Börzel and Risse 2010).

The notion of regulatory capitalism suggests that regulation and rule making are the major instruments in the expansion of global governance. In doing so it takes regulation theory and regulatory analysis beyond national boundaries (hence also beyond the nation-state) and beyond formal state-centered rule making (therefore toward civil and business regulation and decentered analysis of regulatory systems; see Levi-Faur, 2011). It also denotes a world where regulation is increasingly a hybrid of different systems of control, where statist regulation co-evolves with civil regulation, national regulation expands with international and global regulation, private regulation co-evolves and expands with public regulation, business regulation co-evolves with social regulation, voluntary regulations expand with coercive ones, and the market itself is used or mobilized as a regulatory mechanism.

From the point of view of regulatory capitalism, the growth of regulation is manifested not solely in the growth of the regulatory state but also in the growth in the number of civil and business actors who "invest" in regulation, and accordingly also in the growth of civil and business-to-business regulatory institutions and instruments. At the same time there are indications of the transformation of the politics of interest groups and non-governmental organizations. Civil actors are often associated with advocacy (e.g. lobbying) and service provision (e.g. replacing the state in the provision of welfare), but in our areas of study they also produce, monitor and enforce regulation. The concept of civil regulation aims to capture this evolving feature of civil politics (Beer et al. forthcoming). The term "civil regulation" refers to the institutionalization of voluntary global and national forms of regulation through the creation of private (non-state) forms of regulation intended to govern markets and firms (Vogel 2005, 2009). It attempts to embed international markets and firms in a normative order that prescribes responsible business conduct. "What distinguishes the legitimacy, governance and implementation of civil regulation," Vogel tells us, "is that it is not rooted in public [i.e. state] authority. Operating beside or around the state rather than through it, civil regulations are based on "soft law" rather than legally binding standards: violators are subject often to market rather than legal penalties" (Vogel 2009). A distinction between "voluntary regulation" and "civil regulation" might be useful. While the two are close, civil regulation, unlike voluntary, may, at least in principle, possess coercive aspects.[2] Civil regulation tends to rest on old and traditional forms of self-regulation but goes beyond them to include regulatory techniques such as third-party accreditation and certification (Gunningham and Grabosky 1998), gatekeeping strategies (Kraakman 1986), meta-regulation (Parker 2002; Braithwaite 2003; Morgan 2003), enforced self-regulation (Ayres and Braithwaite 1992; Héritier and Lehmkuhl 2008), self-regulation (Ogus 1995; Gunningham and Rees 1997) and leagues tables (Sauder and Espeland 2006).

Regulatory capitalism concerns regulation as a defining feature of the capitalist mode of production. It is also about the globalization of regulation via state and civil and business actors, and at the same time it encompasses civil and business forms of regulation rather than only state regulation. Yet it captures something more than these features. It suggests that in order to understand regulation and regulatory governance we need to understand the interaction of the regulatory state with social and business actors. In this sense the regulatory state is not necessarily a technocratic project but a political one. The state can be in conflict or partnership with business and social forces. In order to see how political and society-led the regulatory state can be, one needs to look at the history of the United States. There, from the second half of the 19th century until the mid-1970s, the regulatory state was the result of popular demand: not the so-called credible commitment for foreign investors, or institutional organizations with reformative zeal, but a product of domestic popular conflicts with local heroes, prophets and real or imagined enemies in the form of big business. This is not the only example where state-like regulatory institutions were created as part of a sustained effort by a domestic constituency – effort that had a broader vision of a reformed polity beyond the peculiarities of one or another crisis or urgent problem. Social reformers with a relatively wide understanding of the regulatory demands of modern urban life led the popular and urban movements towards the improvement of public safety and the business environment in liberal polities. In authoritarian countries where the rulers were in fear of their subjects, regulation came from above. This was the case in 19th century authoritarian Berlin, where the regulator that took care of fire regulation, water quality, business licensing, town planning, gambling and public health was the head of the police (Read and Fisher 1994). The origins of regulations and the institutions that enforced them in Berlin were strikingly different from those in more liberal and bourgeois cities such as London.

Distinguishing between the institutional arrangements that allow for strong states, societies and economies (as opposed to weak ones) necessitates in turn a study of the regulatory responses of the countries that adopt regulatory institutions and characterizing the strength of the state, civil society and business in each of the cases (Migdal and Schlichte 2005). Regulatory failures, resistance or capture should be assessed against the strength of the business community, the civil society and the state. This might allow us a better understanding of the relations between democratic systems of governance and the regulatory institutions that govern our societies, economies and polities. In short, the notions of regulatory state and regulatory capitalism allow us to extend the research agenda on regulation from the fields of public administration, compliance and administrative law to the fields of comparative politics, global governance, international political economy and political sociology. As demonstrated by the various chapters that are offered in this handbook this can be a fruitful and exciting enterprise.

## NOTES

1.  RPI minus X is a method of price regulation whereby tariffs of monopolies are regulated according to the Retail Price Index (RPI) minus some measure of efficiency (X). It was first applied to British Telecom in 1984, and then extended to other British utilities as they were privatized. It is now widely used across different sectors and countries.
2.  The term "voluntary regulation" captures some of the sources of compliance that are often associated with civil regulation. It includes a broad category of social and human behavior in which regulatory compliance is not imposed on the individual or the organization but is partly or wholly based on the choice and the institutional design of the *regulatees*. The motivations for voluntary regulation may differ, and so do the results, yet there is one constant feature that characterizes it and that serves as an umbrella for a broad range of regulatory strategies. This feature is the consistent commitment, which is not required by law, to control behavior in such a way as to minimize the *regulatee's* freedom of action.

## BIBLIOGRAPHY

Anderson, E. James (1962), *The Emergence of the Modern Regulatory State*, Washington, DC: Public Affairs Press.
Ayres, I. and J. Braithwaite (1992), *Responsive Regulation: Transcending the Deregulation Debate*, Oxford: Oxford University Press.
Beer, Christopher T., Tim Bartley and Wade T. Roberts forthcoming, 'NGOs: between advocacy, service provision, and regulation', in David Levi-Faur (ed.), *Oxford Handbook of Governance*, Oxford: Oxford University Press.
Börzel, T.A. and T. Risse (2010), 'Governance without a state: can it work?', *Regulation & Governance*, **4**, 113–34.
Braithwaite, J. (2000), 'The new regulatory state and the transformation of criminology', *British Journal of Criminology*, **40**, 222–38.
Braithwaite, J. (2003), 'Meta regulation for access to justice', paper presented at the General Aspects of Law (GALA) Seminar Series, University of California, Berkeley, 13 November.
Christensen J. (2011), 'Competing theories of regulatory governance: reconsidering public interest theory of regulation', in David Levi-Faur (ed.), *Handbook of the Politics of Regulation*, Cheltenham: Edward Elgar.
Croley, Steven (2011), 'Beyond capture: towards a new theory of regulation', in David Levi-Faur (ed.), *Handbook of the Politics of Regulation*, Cheltenham: Edward Elgar.
Gilardi, Fabrizio, Jacint Jordana and D. Levi-Faur (2006), 'Regulation in the age of governance: the diffusion of regulatory agencies across Europe and Latin America', in A. Graeme Hodge (ed.), *Privatization*

*and Market Development*, Cheltenham, UK and Northampton, MA, USA: Edward Elgar Publishing, pp. 127–47.

Gunningham, N. and J. Rees (1997), 'Industry self regulation: an institutional perspective', *Law and Policy*, **19**, 363–414.

Gunningham, N. and P.N. Grabosky (1998), *Smart Regulation: Designing Environmental Policy*, Oxford: Clarendon.

Haber, H. (2011), 'Regulating-*for*-welfare: a comparative study of "regulatory welfare regimes" in the Israeli, British, and Swedish electricity sectors', *Law and Policy*, **33**, 116–48.

Héritier, Adrienne and Dirk Lehmkuhl (2008), 'The shadow of hierarchy and new modes of governance: sectoral governance and democratic government', *Journal of Public Policy*, **28**, 1–17.

Hood, C., C. Scott, O. James, G. Jones and T. Travers (1999), *Regulation inside Government*, Oxford: Oxford University Press.

Hutter, B. (2001), *Regulation and Risk: Occupational Health and Safety on the Railways*, Oxford: Oxford University Press.

Jayasuriya, K. (2001), 'Globalization and the changing architecture of the state: regulatory state and the politics of negative coordination', *Journal of European Public Policy*, **8** (1), 101–23.

Jordana, J. and D. Levi-Faur (2004), 'The politics of regulation in the age of governance', in J. Jordana and D. Levi-Faur (eds), *The Politics of Regulation*, Cheltenham, UK and Northampton, MA, USA: Edward Elgar Publishing, pp. 1–28.

Jordana, J., D. Levi-Faur and X. Fernandez i Marin forthcoming, 'The global diffusion of regulatory agencies: institutional emulation and the restructuring of modern bureaucracy'.

King, Desmond and R.C. Lieberman (2009), 'Ironies of the American state', *World Politics*, **61**, 547–88.

Kraakman, R. (1986), 'Gatekeepers: the anatomy of a third-party enforcement strategy', *Journal of Law, Economics and Organization*, **2**, 53–104.

Levi-Faur, D. (1998), 'The competition state as a neomercantilist state: restructuring global telecommunications', *Journal of Socio-Economics* 27, 665–85.

Levi-Faur, D. (2003), 'The politics of liberalization: privatization and regulation-for-competition in Europe's and Latin America's telecoms and electricity industries', *European Journal of Political Research*, **42** (5), 705–40.

Levi-Faur, D. (2005), 'The global diffusion of regulatory capitalism', *Annals of the American Academy of Political and Social Sciences*, **598**, 12–32.

Levi-Faur, D. (2011), 'Regulation and regulatory governance', in David Levi-Faur (ed.), *Handbook on the Politics of Regulation*, Cheltenham: Edward Elgar.

Levi-Faur, D. and S. Gilad (2004), 'The rise of the British regulatory state: transcending the privatization debate', *Comparative Politics*, **37** (1), 105–24.

Loughlin, M. and C. Scott (1997), 'The regulatory state', in P. Dunleavy, I. Holliday, A. Gamble and G. Peele (eds), *Developments in British Politics*, vol. 5, Basingstoke: Macmillan.

Lowi, T.J. (1964), 'American business, public policy, case studies, and political theory', *World Politics*, **16**, 677–715.

Mabbett, D. (2011), 'The regulatory rescue of the Welfare State?', in David Levi-Faur (ed.), *Handbook on the Politics of Regulation*, Cheltenham: Edward Elgar.

Majone, G. (1994), 'The rise of the regulatory state in Europe', *West European Politics*, **17**, 77–101.

Majone, G. (1997), 'From the positive to the regulatory state', *Journal of Public Policy*, **17**, 139–67.

Migdal, J.S. and K. Schlichte (2005), 'Rethinking the state', in K. Schlichte (ed.), *The Dynamics of State*, Ashgate: Aldershot.

Mitnick, B. (1980), *The Political Economy of Regulation*, New York: Columbia University Press.

Moran, M. (2002), 'Review article: understanding the regulatory state', *British Journal of Political Science*, **32**, 391–413.

Moran, M. (2003), *The British Regulatory State: High Modernism and Hyper-Innovation*, Oxford: Oxford University Press.

Morgan, B. (2003), *Social Citizenship in the Shadow of Competition: The Bureaucratic Politics of Regulatory Justification*, Aldershot: Ashgate.

Nettl, J.P. (1968), 'The state as a conceptual variable', *World Politics*, **20** (4), 559–92.

Nordlinger, Eric (1987), 'Taking the state seriously', in M. Weiner and P.S. Huntington (eds), *Understanding Political Development*, Boston, MA: Little, Brown, pp. 353–90.

Ogus, A. (1995), 'Rethinking self-regulation', *Oxford Journal of Legal Studies*, **15**, 97–108.

Parker, C. (2002), *The Open Corporation: Effective Self-Regulation and Democracy*, New York: Cambridge University Press.

Phillips, N. (2006), 'States and modes of regulation in the global political economy', in Martin Minogue and Ledivina Carino (eds), *Regulatory Governance in Developing Countries*, Cheltenham, UK and Northampton, MA, USA: Edward Elgar Publishing, pp. 7–38.

Polanyi, K. (1944), *The Great Transformation*, New York: Rinehart.

Power, M. (1997), *The Audit Society: Rituals of Verification*, Oxford: Oxford University Press.

Read, A. and D. Fisher (1994), *Berlin: The Biography of a City*, London: Pimlico.

Rose-Ackerman, Susan (1992), *Rethinking the Progressive Agenda: The Reform of the American Regulatory State*, New York: Free Press.

Sauder, M. and W. Espeland (2006), 'Strength in numbers? A comparison of law and business school rankings', *Indiana Law Journal*, **81**, 205–27.

Scott, C. (2004), 'Regulation in the age of governance: the rise of the post-regulatory state', in J. Jordana and D. Levi-Faur (eds), *The Politics of Regulation in the Age of Governance*, Cheltenham, UK and Northampton, MA, USA: Edward Elgar Publishing, pp. 145–74.

Scott, J. (2009), *The Art of Not Being Governed*, New Haven, CT: Yale University Press.

Seidman, H. and R.S. Gilmour (1986), *Politics, Position, and Power: From the Positive to the Regulatory State*, Oxford: Oxford University Press.

Skocpol, T. (1985), 'Bringing the state back in: strategies of analysis in current research', in P. Evans, D. Rueschemeyer and T. Skocpol (eds), *Bringing the State Back In*, Cambridge: Cambridge University Press, pp. 3–43.

Stigler, G.J. (1971), 'The theory of economic regulation', *Bell Journal of Economics*, **2**, pp. 3–21.

Sunstein, C.R. (1989), 'Interpreting statutes in the regulatory state', *Harvard Law Review*, **103**, 405–505.

Sunstein, C.R., (1990), *After the Rights Revolution*, Cambridge, MA: Harvard University Press.

Vogel, D. (2005), *The Market for Virtue: The Potential and Limits of Corporate Social Responsibility*, Washington, DC: Brookings Institution.

Vogel, D. (2009), 'The private regulation of global corporate conduct', in Walter Mattli and Ngaire Woods (eds), *The Politics of Global Regulation*, Princeton, NJ, Princeton University Press, pp. 151–88.

Wilson, J.Q. (1980), *The Politics of Regulation*, New York: Basic Books.

Zedner, L. (2006), 'Liquid security: managing the market for crime control', *Criminology and Criminal Justice*, **6**, 267–88.

# Name index

Levi-Faur, D. 470, 514, 607
Levy, J. 224
Li Keqiang 150
Libecap, G.D. 120
Lindblom, C.E. 406
Lipsky, M. 323
Litan, R. 388
Litman, J. 255
Livermore, M. 385, 391, 392, 394
Lobel, O. 187
Lodge, M. 405, 526
Lowi, T. 514
Luhmann, N. 275

McAdams, R.H. 337
McChesney, F.S. 30
McClellan, M. 459
McConnell, G. 38
MacCoun, R. 336
McCubbins, M.D. 107, 178–9
McGarity, T. 385, 386–7, 393
McQuail, D. 261–2
Madison, J./administration 115
Magat, W. 63
Maggetti, M. 207
Maher, I. 543
Majone, G. 201, 215, 223, 289, 513, 517, 526, 530, 531, 538, 662–4
Makkai, T. 41
Marks, M.S. 124
Marsden, C.T. 262
Marvel, H.P. 32
Marx, A. 625
Mashaw, J. 299, 387, 393
Mattli, W. 565
May, P.J. 149, 379, 381, 430
Mayhew, D. 180
Meacham, B. 376, 382
Mead, M. 227
Mendeloff, J.M. 298
Meuwese, A.C.M. 393, 405
Meyer, J.M. 221
Mitnick, B. 96, 663
Moran, M. 221, 662, 665, 668
Morgan, B. 11
Morgenstern, R. 391
Murray, A.D. 262

Napoli, P.M. 248
Negroponte, N. 268
Nelson, J.P. 256
Niskanen, W.A. 97, 99
Nixon, D. 63
Nixon, R./administration 386, 399
Noll, R. 59–60

Nonet, P. 186
Nordlinger, E. 667
Novak, W.J. 113, 116

Obama, B./administration 385, 388, 391, 392, 658
Olson, E. 386, 393
Olson, M. 27
Olson, M. Jr 503
Orleans, S. 340
Ostrom, E. 504
Oude Vrielink, M. 478

Packard, V. 256
Parker, C. 11, 434
Parmentier, S. 492–3
Paternoster, R. 340
Peerenboom, R. 583–4
Peltzman, S. 29, 42
Pennock, P.E. 257
Peters, B.G. 549
Phillips, N. 667
Pires, R. 331
Polanyi, K. 445
Pollay, R.W. 258
Pollitt, C. 363
Pomeranz, J.L. 381–2
Ponte, S. 447–8
Posner, E. 337, 389
Post, D.G. 270–71, 274–5
Potoski, M. 352
Potter, D. 258
Powell, Justice 299
Prakash, A. 352
Pressman, J.L. 323
Prosser, T. 400

Quijano, R. 289

Raab, C.D. 232
Radaelli, C.M. 393, 400, 405
Reagan, R./administration 129–30, 301, 385, 386, 387, 397, 399
Reichert, T. 259
Reidenberg, J. 271–2, 274
Reinicke, W.H. 607
Reuter, P. 336, 617, 624
Revesz, R. 385, 391, 392, 394
Ribstein, L.E. 458–9
Robinson, L.A. 414
Roosevelt, T./administration 121
Rose, N. 219, 224
Rose-Ackerman, S. 663
Rotfeld, H.J. 254, 256
Rubin, R. 653

# Subject index

forestry sector regulation 446–7, 448–9, 501, 505–506, 507, 569
formalization 521
fourth-party regulation 482
fragmented governance 74, 563–4, 568, 571, 606
France 192, 204, 243, 250, 304, 518, 545
fraud 480
Freddie Mac (Federal Home Loan Mortgage Corporation) 138, 657
freedom of expression 248
Freedom of Information Act 62
French Regulation School 3
FTSE4Good Index Series 349–50, 352, 354
fuel-economy standards 31
functionalist definition 5
FUNDACENTRO 328
fuzzy practices 193–5, 197

GAQSIQ 150
gas sector regulation 532
gatekeepers 7
genetically modified organisms (GMO) sector regulation 290
geography of regulation 576–87
   administrative cost effects 583–4
   agglomeration effects (external economies) 580–81
   business licensing 586–7
   capital flows 581
   core–peripheral orderings 579, 581
   dynamic efficiency (resilience) 584
   ecological factors 582
   production chains and disaggregation of production 581–2
   public–private ambiguation 585–6
   regulatory capacity and socio-economic structuring 576–8
   transportation costs 579–80
Germany 204, 222, 236, 302, 405–406, 461, 518, 669–70
   Air Pollution Control Act (1974) 286
   AQUMED 220
   BAFIN (finance regulator) 207
   Basic Law 246
   Institute for Norms (DIN) 176
   risk regulation 306
   voluntary regulation 506, 507
Glass–Steagall Banking Act (1933) 137, 646, 651
global best practice 145
global convergence 349
global governance and certification 590–602
   competition 599–600
   coordination 599–600

   equity 600
   growth and integration 594–6
   private forms of social regulation 590–94
   private standard-setting 596
   producer level 596
   product level 596
   scale, legitimacy, coordination and equity 596–600
   sector level 596
global regulation 13, 563–73
   emergence 565–7
   instruments 567–70
   legitimacy reconceptualization 570–72
   standards 607–608
global regulation and norm diversity: hard and soft law comparison 604–13
   advantages 609–11
   disadvantages 609, 610–11
   dynamics 608
   effectivness and legitimacy 611–13
   'hard' law 605–606, 607
   'soft' law 606–607
Global Reporting Initiative (GRI) 348–9, 354, 355
GLOBALGAP 600
globalization 15, 503, 504–505, 526, 527
   of network industries 528–9
Go Global Strategy 146
Goldman Sachs 657
GoNGOs (state actors as regulators) 7–9
good faith principle 86, 608
governance:
   of regulatory regimes 14–16
   triangle 591, 593
Government Accountability Office 76–7
Gramm–Leach–Bliley Financial Services Modernization Act (1999) (GLBA) 137, 651
Greece 258
green clubs 352, 565, 569
green labels 351
'greenwash' 94, 350–54, 503, 507, 508
grid-group cultural theory 405–406
growth hormones in cattle raising 303
Guidelines International Network (GIN) 220

hallmarks 476
'hammers' 74
'hard' law 6
   climate change regulation 632, 633, 634, 636
   codes 488
   European Union 536
   legal rules and regulation 187
   *see also* global regulation and norm diversity
harmonization 261, 304, 552

Public Health Ministry 160
rise of regulation 160–63
social regulation 161–2
*superintendencias* 157–8, 160, 162–3, 165
utilities regulation 161–2
law-as-coercion 187
least feasible risk 297–8, 300, 301
legal rules and regulation 185–97, 232, 272,
    276
  content 185
  domestic rules 188, 190–91
  fuzzy practices 193–5, 197
  legality, illegality and the role of law 193–5
  role and form of regulation 185–8
  transnational rules 189, 191–2
legalization 605
legislative dominance 51
legislative motivation 53
legitimacy 338–40
  climate change regulation 639
  cognitive 572
  diminished 564
  input 598–9, 612
  normative 572
  output 598–9, 612
  pragmatic 571–2
  'soft' law 610–11
  value-oriented 340
Lehman Brothers 656
'lemons' problem 123, 454, 472
*Lex Mercatoria* 271
licensing 457–8
life cycle model 34, 54
'light touch' regulatory approach 651
limitation rider 75
litigation 459
Low Pay Commission 218

Magna Carta (1225) 32
majoritarian democracy 215, 223
Malaysia 247
management committees 539
management-based regulation (MBR) 14–15,
    425, 426, 431
managerial capitalism 577
MaNGOs (market actors as regulators) 7, 9, 10
Marine Stewardship Council (MSC) 594
maritime safety regulation 552
market coordination 215
market failure 217–18
market transparency rules 645–6
market-based regulation 442, 629, 633, 634,
    637, 638, 640
markets (modality of regulation) 272, 276
Marks & Spencer Plan A 594

Massachusetts Board of Railroad
    Commissioners 117
Massachusetts Toxic Use Reduction Act 426
means-oriented approach 324
Meat Inspection Act (1891) 119
meat inspection regulation 119–21
meat and poultry safety 378
media coverage 210–11
media regulation 243–51
  as cultural paternalism 247–8
  as economic regulation 244–5
  as promoter of democracy 248–50
  as technological challenge 245–7
Merrill Lynch 657
meta-regulation 11
meta-standardization 447
Mexico 159, 164, 290, 332
minority voice and representation 249–50
Money Laundering Control Act (1986) 619
Money Laundering and Financial Crimes
    Strategy Act (1998) 619
money laundering regulation 615–25
  alliances and expansion of regulation 620
  difficulty in estimating scale of problem
      616–17
  effectiveness 623–4
  as a global phenomenon 617
  instruments to achieve compliance 621–3
  international standard setting 621
  legitimacy problems 624
  negative and positive effects 616
  private interest, lack of 617–18
  public interest theory 618–19
  regulatory weaknesses 623
  reporting system 619–20
  and terrorism financing 616, 623
  victimless crime 615–16
Money Laundering Suppression Act (1994)
    619
money-for-nothing theory 617
monism 192
monitoring 565, 569
  external 90
moral hazard 92, 454–5, 457–8, 657
moral-oriented individual 338, 339
morality 340, 343, 487
Morgan Stanley 657
mortgage-backed securities (MBSs) 650–51,
    652, 654, 656–7
motivation 314, 340–41, 431–2
Motor Carriers Act (1935) 29, 135
muckraking journalism 122
multi-level regulation 11, 514, 516, 518, 521
multi-stakeholder initiatives 593
Myanmar 622

Printed and bound by CPI Group (UK) Ltd, Croydon, CR0 4YY

16/04/2025

14658387-0004